ALMANAC OF BUSINESS AND INDUSTRIAL FINANCIAL RATIOS

2007 EDITION

LEO TROY, Ph.D.

CCH
a Wolters Kluwer business

Editorial Staff

Production..Christopher Zwirek
Design .... Craig Arritola

This publication is designed to provide accurate and authoritative information in regard to the subject matter covered. It is sold with the understanding that the publisher is not engaged in rendering legal, accounting, or other professional service and that the author is not offering such advice in this publication. If legal advice or other professional assistance is required, the services of a competent professional person should be sought.

ISBN 13: 978-0-8080-1568-0
ISBN 10: 0-8080-1568-0

© 2006, CCH. All Rights Reserved.
4025 W. Peterson Avenue
Chicago, IL 60646-6085
1 800 248 3248
www.CCHGroup.com

No claim is made to original government works; however, within this Product or Publication, the following are subject to CCH's copyright: (1) the gathering, compilation, and arrangement of such government materials; (2) the magnetic translation and digital conversion of data, if applicable; (3) the historical, statutory and other notes and references; and (4) the commentary and other materials.

Printed in the United States of America

Dedicated

**To Alexander, Suzannah, Dale, Ariel Sarah Troy, Abigayle Hannah Troy,
and Rachel Ilana Troy**

Preface

Now in its 38th Edition, the *Almanac of Business and Industrial Financial Ratios* provides a precise benchmark for evaluating an individual company's financial performance. The performance data is derived from the latest available IRS figures on U.S. and international companies, and tracks 50 operating and financial factors in nearly 200 industries. The *Almanac* provides competitive norms in actual dollar amounts for revenue and capital factors, as well as important average operating costs in percent of net sales. It also provides other critical financial factors in percentage, including debt ratio, return on assets, return on equity, profit margin, and more. Beyond its reliable insights into corporate behavior, the *Almanac* can be used by other countries looking to model their economies on American performance.

Also included with the text, in a special pocket provided in the inside cover of the book, is a CD-ROM that contains all the materials found in the book including the explanatory discussion, the data tables, and the supporting index. Also included on the CD, but not in the book itself, is a special template that allows the reader to add individual company data of interest to compare and contrast with data from the book.

2007 Edition Highlights

The 2007 Edition of the *Almanac of Business and Industrial Financial Ratios* has been updated to include the following:

- **Broad scope:** *2007 Almanac* features the North American Industry Classification System (NAICS), so you can benchmark or analyze results consistently with corporations in the United States, Canada, and Mexico.

- **Most industry types:** *2007 Almanac* highlights most industry types, including industries with advanced technologies and newly emerging industries such as paging and wireless communications.

- **A truer picture** of corporate financial performance, since the data isn't based on a mixed bag of averages that might include partnerships or sole proprietors. *2007 Almanac* features a homogeneous universe of American corporate financial performance.

- **Many classifications:** *2007 Almanac* analyzes 197 industries with 50 financial performance items.

- **Benchmarks:** *2007 Almanac* provides 13 benchmarks, including such critical measures as Receipts to Cash Flow, Debt to Total Assets, and Return on Equity both before and after taxes.

- **Analytical tables:** *Table I, Corporations with and without Net Income (All Corporations), and Table II, Corporations with Net Income.*

- **Easier apples-to-apples comparisons:** Each table is divided into 13 asset sizes.

- **More comprehensive:** Total receipts of all corporations covered by *2007 Almanac* is $20.7 trillion, making the *Almanac* the Anatomy of American Corporate Capitalism.

Leo Troy, Ph. D.

November 2006

About the Author

Dr. Leo Troy is Professor of Economics at Rutgers University. He has been a faculty member of Rutgers for 50 years. In addition to authoring the widely praised *Almanac*, he has written many other books and articles published in leading journals. Professor Troy has been the recipient of numerous awards including two from the National Science Foundation, and two Fulbright grants. In addition, he has received numerous awards from private foundations. Dr. Troy received his Ph.D. from Columbia University and is a member of Phi Beta Kappa. He is a veteran of World War II with three battle stars and the combat infantry badge. He is the father of two children and is also a grandfather of three girls, including twins.

Acknowledgments

I wish to acknowledge the contributions of five people in particular for the development of the 38th Edition of the *Almanac*: Phil Wilson, Alan Kovar of Brighton Best, Lawrence R. Chodor, CPA, CVA, Wiss & Company, Marvin Sunshine, and Karen Kane.

Philip is responsible for the programming, which dealt with a very large amount of data, covering both the current and trend information. Alan, drawing upon his knowledge and experience as a CPA and Partner of Wiss and Company of Livingston, N.J., contributed significantly to the new content of the book. To Marvin Sunshine, Esq, my appreciation for actions and support that helped make the *Almanac* a continuing publication. Karen Kane is acknowledged for her contributions to the graphics of this issue.

Special acknowledgement is due my late friend and colleague, Stan Katz, CPA, and to Professor Emeritus of Accounting, Rutgers University, John Gilmour. I thank, too, Professor David Zaumeyer, Ph.D., CPA, and Director of Accounting at Rutgers, for recommending several ratios that continue to be included in the *Almanac*. I thank Mr. Ka-Neng Au, Business Librarian, Rutgers University, for significant contributions to the *Almanac*.

I wish to recognize, too, the cooperation of members of the Statistics of Income Division of the Internal Revenue Service—in particular, Ken Szeflinksi, Martha A. Harris, and Phyllis J. Whiles of the Corporation Returns Analysis Section. Without their data and its reliability, the Almanac would not be possible. Responsibility for the use of their facts and figures is, of course, solely my own. In this regard, I recall the valuable assistance I received from Barry Rosenstein, MBA, CPA, in checking procedures, in earlier editions, and which have continued into the current one. Finally, I wish to recognize the help of Suzannah B. Troy in bringing about the 38th annual edition of the *Almanac*. I anticipate continuation of her valuable assistance in subsequent editions.

INTRODUCTION

QUESTIONS, ANSWERS AND COMMENTS ON THE ALMANAC

Some users have requested further information on the use of the Almanac's ratios and statistics. This Q & A addition to the Almanac is in response to that demand.

1. What are the general purposes of the Almanac?

The goal of the Almanac is to provide users with a reliable and comprehensive source of standard financial ratios and financial statistics on all corporations, public and private, including those filing 1120S returns in the United States. Excluded are all individual proprietorships and partnerships. The Almanac makes available key business and financial statistics, which are consistent and neutral (unbiased by any commercial publisher or trade association).

2. What is the source and reliability of the Almanac's results?

The Almanac's results are computed from the Department of the Treasury, Internal Revenue Service's statistical sampling of the tax returns of all corporations. Dividends received from foreign corporations are included in total receipts of those corporations affected. The statistics apply to the company rather than the establishment.

3. Are international comparisons available?

Yes. Because of the adoption of a common system of industrial classification by the U.S., Canada and Mexico, known as the North American Industrial Classification System of industries (NAICS), under the North American Free Trade Agreement, users in Canada and Mexico can compare and contrast their results with those corporations in the United States.

4. What about comparisons within the U.S?

These are the most important applications of the Almanac. Results are available for each and every corporation within the U.S., whether public or private, and include small business corporations, those which file the 1120S tax return. Therefore, users can compare their corporate performance with that of their industry and asset size group of corporate enterprise in the United States.

5. How many corporations are covered in the Almanac?

The Almanac's results are derived from more than 5.4 million corporation tax returns. Furthermore, the user can easily determine the number of enterprises for the total of each industry and by each of the 12 asset size groups. This makes for a total of 13 asset size comparisons.

6. What about differences in the size of corporations?

In addition to the results for each industry, the Almanac displays 12 columns of performance by the size of assets. Again, this makes for a total of 13 asset size comparisons.

7. Does the Almanac distinguish between the profitability of corporations?

In a word, yes. Each industry is divided between two tables: Table I reports the results of all corporations in an industry, that is, those with and without net income. It is followed by a second table for the same industry, Table II, which reports only those corporations with net income.

8. How many items of information are there for each industry?

There are 50 indicators of corporate performance in each table and each industry and for all asset size groups, except where the IRS' data sample is too small, or it does not supply the necessary information.

9. Who are the users of the Almanac?

Accountants, corporate managers, business consultants, investors evaluating a corporate takeover, entrepreneurs considering new businesses, lawyers, and students of accounting, business, and management.

10. What accounting time period is covered?

The Internal Revenue Service provides the most recent statistics publicly available for the Almanac. For the 2007 Almanac, these statistics apply to the accounting period from July 2003 through June 2004.

WHAT'S NEW IN THIS EDITION

Beginning with the year 2002, the *Almanac of Business and Industrial Financial Ratios* began using the North American Industry Classification System (NAICS). NAICS replaces the Internal Revenue Service's own system, which it had used for many years, an adaptation of Standard Industrial Classification (SIC); all previous *Almanacs* had used that adaptation.

The new industrial classification system is the product of the North American Free Trade Agreement (NAFTA), and it replaces the existing classification systems not only of the United States but also of Canada and Mexico. Hence, the new system applies uniformly to the three countries, and users of the *Almanac 2007*, utilizing the new international industrial classification system, can now compare their results with corporations in all three nations.

In the United States, the new manual was created by the Office of Management and Budget (OMB). The NAICS system gives special attention to industries producing and furnishing advanced technologies, new and emerging industries, as well as service industries in general. NAICS divides the economy into 21 sectors, five in the predominantly goods-producing area, and 16 in the service producing area.

INDUSTRY SECTORS

Particularly noteworthy is NAICS's introduction of an Information sector. This sector assembles the industries from Newspaper Publishers (511110) to Internet Service Providers, Web Portals, and Data Processing Services (518115). Within this span, NAICS and therefore the *Almanac* include such important industries as software publishing, database and directory publishing, satellite telecommunications, paging and cellular, and other wireless communications. NAICS and the *Almanac* also provide a category of industries on Professional, Scientific, and Technical Services, industries in which human capital is the major input. The sector includes Legal Services (541115) and Scientific Research and Development Services (541700), as well as Management, Scientific, and Technical Services (541600) and Computer Systems Design and Related Services (541515).

Other important sectors are the Arts, Entertainment, and Recreation including Amusement, Gambling, and Recreation (713105), and the Health Care and Social Assistance including

Offices of Physicians (621115), Hospitals, Nursing, and Residential Care Facilities (622005). Within Manufacturing, the key goods sector industry, there is now a category embracing Computer and Electronic Product Manufacturing. It spans industries such as Computer and Peripheral Equipment (334110) to Navigational, Measuring, Electromedical, and Control Instruments (334500).

The source of the IRS's data are the tax returns of all *active* public and private corporations. Because the *Almanac's* data are derived only from corporate tax returns, there is a mixture of corporate with the financial performance of partnerships and individual proprietorships; the *Almanac's* information constitutes a **homogeneous universe**. The tax returns are classified by the IRS on the basis of the business activity which accounts for a corporation's largest percentage of total receipts. Large corporations with dissimilar business activities are included in only one industry, despite operations that are unrelated to the industry in which they are grouped.

The data developed by the IRS are derived from a stratified probability sample of corporation income tax returns. Where the sample data from the sample are small and should those numbers be used in a denominator, the result is reported as a hyphen (-) in the *Almanac*. Returns of the largest corporations are generally in the sample from year to year, but comparability can be affected by consolidations and mergers, changes in the law and the tax forms, and changes in the industrial classification system used over the years.

REPRESENTATIVE INDUSTRIES

The *Almanac* reports on nearly 200 industries. Minor industries are denoted by a six-digit code; major industries are designated by a three-digit industry code; industrial sectors by a two-digit code; and industrial divisions by a two-digit code. When the data are the same for minor, major, sector, and industrial division, the IRS reports only the industrial division, and similarly for other identities applicable to the major and sectoral industries; the *Almanac* follows this procedure.

Almanac 2007 continues the previous coverage of reporting information: for all industries, **Table I, Corporations with and without Net Income** (that is, the entire universe of active reporting corporations), and **Table II, Corporations with Net Income**, a subset of the universe. In the *Almanac 2007*, Table I covers over 5.4 million enterprises (corporations), and Table II covers 2.9 million corporations with net income. This implies that 2.5 million corporations reported deficits. The IRS defines net income (or deficit) as the companies' net profit or loss from taxable sources of income reduced by allowable deductions. Total receipts of the 5.4 million corporations reported in *Almanac 2007* was $20.7 trillion, up by $1 trillion.

The *Almanac* continues to report performance results not only by the total for each industry, but by 12 other asset size groups (a total of 13 asset size groups), providing 50 items of data and/or ratios on corporate performance:

Total

Zero
$1 to $500,000
$500,001 to $1,000,000
$1,000,001 to $5,000,000
$5,000,001 to $10,000,000
$10,000,001 to $25,000,000
$25,000,001 to $50,000,000
$50,000,001 to $100,000,000
$100,000,001 to $250,000,000
$250,000,001 to $500,000,000
$500,000,001 to $2,500,000,000
$2,500,000,001 or more

All data in Tables I and II cover an accounting period identified on all tables and are the most recent information available from the IRS. For the *Almanac 2007*, the accounting period is July 2003 through June 2004. The dating of the data is counterbalanced by the most extensive industrial coverage available in any report on financial performance, the number of items of corporate performance, and their availability in thirteen asset size groups. Moreover, the timing of the data are also counterbalanced by the stability of the *Almanac's* values as past trends have indicated. Therefore, the *Almanac's* financial results are reliable in assessing current corporate performance.

Beyond its reliable insights into corporate behavior on a micro basis, its comprehensive and detailed coverage make the *Almanac* the **Anatomy of American Corporate Capitalism**. In this macro sense, it constitutes **the** example to those countries desirous of modeling their economies on the American performance.

How to Use the Almanac

On the micro level, the *Almanac* multiplies manyfold the power of financial analysis to evaluate an individual company's financial performance: In contrast to many standard reports, the *Almanac* gives management, and analysts independent of any company, more of the fundamental analytical tools needed to compare their company with companies in the same industry and of the same asset size. The *Almanac* can enhance the value of any company's annual report because it affords the analyst and the stockholder detailed background of financial information for comparison.

All items and ratios are listed in Both Table I and Table II. No figures are reported in the *Almanac* when the IRS has either suppressed the underlying data, or the sample size, or other reasons affecting a calculated result, and where the ratio/item was not applicable to an industry. The 50 tax-based items that provide that financial analysis are as follows:

1. Number of Enterprises

These are the count of corporate tax returns filed by active corporations on one of the Form 1120-series returns.

Special Note: Net Sales is used to compute the percentage of items 3 to 7 to Net Sales for all industries, except Finance, Insurance, and Real Estate (FIRE). For the FIRE industries, Total Receipts are used to compute the percentage of items 3 to 7.

Revenues ($ in thousands), Items 2 to 9

2. Operating Income (Net Sales)

This is the IRS item Business Receipts, the gross operating receipts reduced by the cost of returned goods and allowances.

3. Interest

Taxable interest includes interest on U.S. Government obligations, loans, notes, mortgages, arbitrage bonds, nonexempt private activity bonds, corporate bonds, bank deposits, and tax refunds; interest received from tax-exempt state or local municipal bonds and ESOP loans are not included in this item.

4. Rents

These are the gross amounts received from the use or occupancy of property by corporations whose principal activities did not involve operating rental properties.

5. Royalties

These are gross payments received for the use of property rights before taking deductions.

6. Other Portfolio Income

These consist of cash, notes, and accounts receivable, less allowance for bad debts and inventories.

7. Other Receipts

These receipts include such items as income from minor operations, cash discounts, claims, license rights, judgments, and joint ventures.

8. Total Receipts

Total receipts are the sum of ten items: 1. Business receipts; 2. Interest; 3. Interest on government obligations: state and local; 4. Rents; 5. Royalties; 6. Net capital gains (excluding long-term gains from regulated investment companies); 7. Net gain, noncapital assets; 8. Dividends received from domestic corporations; 9. Dividends received from foreign corporations; 10. Other receipts.

9. Average Total Receipts

Total receipts divided by the number of enterprises.

OPERATING COSTS/OPERATING INCOME, ITEMS 10 TO 22

10. Cost of Operations

This is the IRS's Costs of Goods Sold; it consists of the costs incurred in producing the goods or furnishing the services that generated the corporations' business receipts.

11. Salaries and Wages

These include the amount of salaries and wages paid as well as bonuses and director's fees, but no contributions to pension plans (see item 16) nor compensation of officers (see item 20).

12. Taxes Paid

Excludes Federal Income Taxes; they are the amounts paid for ordinary state and local taxes, social security, payroll taxes, unemployment insurance taxes, excise taxes, import and tariff duties, and business license and privilege taxes.

13. Interest Paid

These amounts consist of interest paid on all business indebtedness.

14. Depreciation

The charges allowed are governed principally by the IRS rules in effect in 1997, basically enacted in 1986, but also include other modifications. Hence, depreciation could represent amounts computed by different sets of rules.

15. Amortization and Depletion

Most amortization is calculated on a straight-line basis. Depletion is allowed for the exhaustion of natural deposits and timber.

16. Pensions, Profit-Sharing, Stock Bonus, and Annuity Plans

These are amounts deducted during the current year for qualified pension, profit-sharing, or other funded deferred compensation plans.

17. Employee Benefits

These are employer contributions to death benefit, insurance, health, accident, and sickness, and other welfare plans.

18. Advertising

Amounts include promotion and publicity expenses.

19. Other Expenses

These include expenses for repairs, bad debts, rent paid on business property, contributions and gifts, and expenses not allocable to specific deductible items.

20. Officers' Compensation

Salaries, wages, stock bonuses, bonds, and other forms of compensation are included in this item.

21. Operating Margin

This is the net income after all operating costs have been deducted.

22. Operating Margin Before Officers' Compensation

This measure takes into account the effect of Officers' Compensation on the operating margin.

SELECTED AVERAGE BALANCE SHEET ITEMS ($ IN THOUSANDS) ITEMS 23 TO 29

23. Average Net Receivables

The total of Notes and Accounts Receivable, less Allowance for Bad Debts, divided by the number of enterprises. Notes and Accounts Receivable are the gross amounts arising from business sales or services to customers on credit in the course of ordinary trade or business. This includes commercial paper, charge accounts, current intercompany receivables, property investment loans, and trade acceptances.

24. *Average Inventories*

Total inventories are divided by the number of enterprises. Inventories include finished goods, partially finished goods, new materials and supplies acquired for sale, merchandise on hand or in transit, and growing crops reported as assets by agricultural enterprises.

25. *Average Net Property, Plant and Equipment*

This includes depreciable assets less accumulated depreciation, depletable assets less accumulated depletion, and land; the sum is divided by the number of enterprises. Depreciable assets consist of end-of-year balance sheet tangible property, such as buildings and equipment used in trade or business, or held for the production of income, and that has a useful life of one year or more. The amount of accumulated depreciation represents the portion written off in the current year, as well as in prior years. Depletable assets represent the end-of-year value of mineral property, oil and gas wells, and other natural resources; standing timber; intangible development and drilling costs capitalized; and leases and leaseholds, subject to depletion. Accumulated depletion represents the cumulative adjustment of these assets.

26. *Average Total Assets*

Total Assets (and Total Liabilities) are amounts reported in the end-of-year balance sheet. Total Assets are net amounts after reduction from accumulated depreciation, accumulated amortization, accumulated depletion, and the reserve for bad debts. Total Liabilities include the claims of creditors and stockholders' equity, and were net after reduction by the cost of treasury stock. The average of total assets was obtained by dividing it by the number of enterprises.

27. *Average of Notes and Loans Payable, and Mortgages*

These liabilities were separated on the balance sheet according to the time to maturity of the obligations. Time to maturity was based on the date of the balance sheet, rather than the date of issue of the obligations. The total was divided by the number of enterprises.

28. *Average of All Other Liabilities*

These included accounts payable, and other liabilities including other current liabilities. The total was divided by the number of enterprises.

29. *Average Net Worth*

Net Worth represents the stockholders' equity in the corporation (total assets minus the claims of creditors). It consists of Capital Stock, Paid-In Capital Surplus, Retained Earnings Appropriated, Retained Earnings Unappropriated, less cost of treasury stock.

SELECTED FINANCIAL RATIOS, NUMBER OF TIMES TO ONE, RATIOS 30 TO 44

30. *Current Ratio*

The items that used Current Assets for this ratio are Cash; Notes and Accounts Receivable, Less: Allowance for Bad Debts; Inventories; Government Obligations; Tax-Exempt Securities; and Other Current Assets. For Current Liabilities, the following items were included: Accounts Payable; Mortgages and Notes Maturing in Less than 1 Year; and Other Current Liabilities.

This ratio, rated highest by CPAs as a measure of liquidity, gauges the ability of a company to meet its short-term financial obligations should it be compelled to liquidate its assets.

However, it is not an absolute measure of the company's ability to meet its obligations. It is obtained by dividing current assets by current liabilities. The standard guideline has been a ratio of 2 to 1; however, some companies have found that in their experience, a ratio less than 2 to 1 is adequate, while others consider a larger one to be necessary. The ratio is affected by the method of valuation of inventory (LIFO or FIFO) and by inflation. The Almanac provides measures that can be treated as standards by size of asset.

31. Quick Ratio

This ratio is also known as the "Acid Test Ratio" because it is often used to estimate a company's general liquidity. There is some disagreement about the inclusion of inventory in the numerator because it may be slow moving, obsolete, or pledged to specific creditors, and, therefore, not be readily convertible into cash. The *Almanac* adopts a conservative approach and does not include the item in calculating the ratio. Excluding inventories and other current assets, the numerator is the same as that used in determining current assets. The denominator, current liabilities, is unchanged. The ratio of 1 to 1 has been considered a reasonable standard, but it is jeopardized because accounts and notes receivable may not be convertible into cash at face value and at short notice. The *Almanac* provides measures that can be treated as standards by size of asset.

32. Net Sales to Working Capital

This is an efficiency, or turnover, ratio that measures the rate at which current assets less current liabilities (Working Capital) is used in making sales. (In industries in Finance, Insurance, and Real Estate, total receipts rather than net sales is used.) A low ratio indicates a less efficient (profitable) use of working capital in making sales. The *Almanac* provides measures that can be treated as standards by size of asset. Working Capital is the difference between current assets and current liabilities.

33. Coverage Ratio

This ratio measures the number of times all interest paid by the company is covered by earnings before interest charges and taxes (EBIT). For that reason, the ratio is also known as the "times interest earned ratio." The ratio indicates the company's ability to service its debt based on its income.

34. Total Asset Turnover

The ratio is an efficiency ratio because it indicates the effectiveness of the company's use of its total assets in generating sales. It is measured by dividing net sales by total assets.

35. Inventory Turnover

Inventory turnover measures the liquidity of the inventory. It is computed by dividing the cost of goods sold by the average inventory. The result shows the number of times that the average inventory can be converted into receivables or cash. The ratio reflects both on the quality of the inventory and the efficiency of management. Typically, the higher the turnover rate, the more likely profits will be higher.

SPECIAL NOTE: Inventory turnover is not computed for industries in Finance, Insurance, and Real Estate.

36. Receivables Turnover

This ratio measures the liquidity of accounts receivable. It indicates the average collection period throughout the year. It is obtained by dividing sales average by net receivables. It is not computed in the Finance, Insurance, and Real Estate industries (although it is calculated for all other industries even though conventional analysis typically omits it) for many of the industries in the *Almanac*.

37. Total Liabilities to Net Worth

This ratio indicates the extent to which the company's funds are supplied by short- and long-term creditors compared to its owners. It is an indicator of the company's long-term debt paying ability. The ratio is one of the most important bearing on the company's capital structure. Net worth is defined in ratio 29.

38. Current Assets to Working Capital

The dependence of Working Capital in part on current assets is important to understanding this part of the source of Working Capital. Current Assets are defined in ratio 30 and Working Capital is defined in ratio 32.

39. Current Liabilities to Working Capital

The dependence of Working Capital in part on current liabilities is important to understanding this part of the source of Working Capital. Current Liabilities are defined in ratio 30 and Working Capital is defined in ratio 32.

40. Working Capital to Net Sales or Total Receipts

The purpose of this ratio is to determine the working capital needed in relation to projected sales or receipts. Working Capital is defined in ratio 32.

41. Inventory to Working Capital

This ratio, by showing the proportion of Working Capital invested in Inventory, indicates the part of Current Assets that are least liquid. Inventories which exceed working capital indicate that current liabilities exceed liquid current assets. Working Capital is defined in ratio 32.

42. Total Receipts to Cash Flow

Cash Flow is the difference between cash receipts and cash disbursements. The ratio of total receipts to cash flow could suggest steps which management might take to improve the company's cash position.

43. Cost of Goods to Cash Flow

This ratio can be the basis for projections of cash requirements needed to fund projected costs of production. Cash flow is defined in ratio 42.

44. Cash Flow to Total Debt

This ratio indicates the extent to which a company could service its total debt from cash flow. It is analogous to the coverage ratio; refer to ratio 33. Cash flow is defined in ratio 42.

SELECTED FINANCIAL FACTORS (IN PERCENTAGES), ITEMS 45 TO 50

45. Debt Ratio (Total Liabilities to Total Assets)

This ratio indicates the company's ability to pay all its debts. It measures the creditors' and owners' of the company's ability to withstand losses. It is an indicator of the long-run solvency of the firm.

46. Return on Total Assets

The ratio combines the turnover and profit ratios (Sales/Total Assets x [times] Profit/Sales) and yields the return on investment (Total Assets). The result is the end product of the DuPont System of financial analysis. The system takes into account both operating income and operating assets. In Table I of each industry, the Return on Investment (ROI) is net income less deficit before income taxes divided by total assets. In Table II of each industry, the ROI is net income before income taxes divided by Total Assets. Total Assets are used because management has discretion in the investment of the resources provided by both the creditors and owners.

47. Return on Equity Before Income Taxes

This ratio measures the profitability of the company's operations to owners, before income taxes. For Table I this is net income, less deficit before income taxes and before credits. For Table II this is net income minus income tax before credits.

48. Return on Equity After Income Taxes

This ratio measures the profitability of the company's operations to owners, after income taxes. For Table I this is net income, less deficit and minus income tax before credits. For Table II this is net income minus income tax and before credits.

49. Profit Margin (Before Income Tax)

This is net income before income tax divided by net sales (or total receipts) and indicates the contribution of sales to the profitability of the company. Competition, capital structure, and operating characteristics cause the margin to vary within and among industries. For Table I, net income less deficit and before income taxes is the numerator; for Table II it is net income before tax.

50. Profit Margin (After Income Tax)

This ratio is the same as ratio 49 except that income taxes are taken into account.

Table of Contents

Page references to tables for industries with net income are in italic

PRINCIPAL BUSINESS ACTIVITY (BASED ON NAICS)

ALMANAC
of Business and Industrial FINANCIAL RATIOS

38th ANNUAL EDITION
2007

Table I
Corporations with and without Net Income

AGRICULTURAL PRODUCTION

MONEY AMOUNTS AND SIZE OF ASSETS IN THOUSANDS OF DOLLARS

Item Description for Accounting Period 7/03 Through 6/04	Total	Zero Assets	Under 500	500 to 1,000	1,000 to 5,000	5,000 to 10,000	10,000 to 25,000	25,000 to 50,000	50,000 to 100,000	100,000 to 250,000	250,000 to 500,000	500,000 to 2,500,000	2,500,000 and over
Number of Enterprises 1	100571	•	64079	13981	12727	912	431	118	76	41	10	7	•
Revenues ($ in Thousands)													
Net Sales 2	81530986	835228	11932661	8300837	17205366	6158636	8110084	4971853	6156856	7701131	3010086	7148247	•
Interest 3	302500	4898	51938	45707	72600	15483	20530	14010	9816	18508	4446	44565	•
Rents 4	659993	2925	138937	151448	226467	35764	26702	16930	29426	14964	3527	12906	•
Royalties 5	115262	2325	6267	29940	16686	5400	6028	690	10633	9718	988	26587	•
Other Portfolio Income 6	1224090	103158	308411	108589	326211	62967	67274	18622	78372	54372	21433	74681	•
Other Receipts 7	7832724	161062	2579199	1527929	1996077	347167	303522	171722	131922	137996	164661	311462	•
Total Receipts 8	91665555	1109596	15017413	10164450	19843407	6625417	8534140	5193827	6417025	7936689	3205141	7618448	•
Average Total Receipts 9	911	136	234	727	1559	7265	19801	44015	84435	193578	320514	1088350	•
Operating Costs/Operating Income (%)													
Cost of Operations 10	51.5	44.4	18.1	41.9	41.8	51.6	62.0	63.5	68.5	77.4	77.1	69.3	•
Salaries and Wages 11	8.9	9.1	12.8	9.6	11.2	9.8	6.9	6.8	5.2	4.7	2.2	8.9	•
Taxes Paid 12	2.5	4.7	3.4	3.6	3.4	2.1	1.6	1.6	1.4	1.7	1.7	1.0	•
Interest Paid 13	2.7	3.4	3.3	2.8	3.4	2.8	1.7	1.9	1.4	1.5	1.4	4.0	•
Depreciation 14	6.6	8.6	10.0	8.3	8.8	6.6	4.3	4.6	4.1	4.1	3.9	2.9	•
Amortization and Depletion 15	0.2	0.8	0.0	0.2	0.1	0.2	0.1	0.5	0.2	0.7	0.1	0.5	•
Pensions and Other Deferred Comp. 16	0.3	0.2	0.1	0.5	0.2	0.5	0.2	0.2	0.1	0.1	0.3	0.4	•
Employee Benefits 17	1.3	1.2	1.3	1.3	1.4	1.1	0.7	0.8	1.2	0.7	1.3	2.8	•
Advertising 18	0.4	0.5	0.5	0.2	0.5	0.3	0.3	0.3	0.2	0.2	0.2	0.5	•
Other Expenses 19	35.3	53.2	72.7	48.3	41.9	33.7	26.5	21.1	19.6	8.3	8.6	15.0	•
Officers' Compensation 20	2.2	3.7	3.9	4.4	3.4	1.4	1.1	1.1	0.7	0.7	0.7	0.5	•
Operating Margin 21	•	•	•	•	•	•	•	•	•	•	2.5	•	•
Operating Margin Before Officers' Comp. 22	•	•	•	•	•	•	•	•	•	0.5	3.1	•	•

Selected Average Balance Sheet ($ in Thousands)

Item	1	2	3	4	5	6	7	8	9	10	11	12	
Net Receivables 23	69	0	4	27	81	328	1687	5235	9514	19371	22411	278922	•
Inventories 24	84	0	10	39	171	750	1971	4718	11396	17680	43893	136794	•
Net Property, Plant and Equipment 25	411	0	89	427	1115	3538	6683	14987	29036	57461	128852	252438	•
Total Assets 26	869	0	166	710	1912	6606	15121	35455	69484	150533	315570	1600499	•
Notes and Loans Payable 27	467	0	163	348	1077	4411	7383	16111	28724	53143	85226	515505	•
All Other Liabilities 28	122	0	10	52	147	951	2258	5903	14269	28376	83811	489593	•
Net Worth 29	281	0	-7	309	688	1244	5480	13442	26491	69014	146534	595401	•

Selected Financial Ratios (Times to 1)

Item	1	2	3	4	5	6	7	8	9	10	11	12	
Current Ratio 30	1.3	•	1.3	1.3	1.3	1.0	1.3	1.3	1.5	1.6	2.2	1.3	•
Quick Ratio 31	0.7	•	0.8	0.7	0.7	0.5	0.6	0.7	0.7	0.8	0.8	0.7	•
Net Sales to Working Capital 32	12.5	•	20.4	18.3	10.8	639.0	15.4	13.5	8.1	8.9	5.2	9.4	•
Coverage Ratio 33	1.3	1.9	0.9	1.5	0.7	0.1	0.8	2.0	1.8	2.8	7.5	1.6	•
Total Asset Turnover 34	0.9	•	1.1	0.8	0.7	1.0	1.2	1.2	1.2	1.0	1.0	0.6	•
Inventory Turnover 35	5.0	•	3.4	6.4	3.3	4.6	5.9	5.7	4.9	8.2	5.3	5.2	•
Receivables Turnover 36	11.8	•	50.1	24.7	16.4	18.7	11.3	8.0	9.3	8.8	17.3	3.7	•
Total Liabilities to Net Worth 37	2.1	•	•	1.3	1.8	4.3	1.8	1.6	1.6	1.2	1.2	1.7	•
Current Assets to Working Capital 38	4.0	•	4.7	4.4	4.0	164.8	4.7	4.5	3.0	2.7	1.9	4.9	•
Current Liabilities to Working Capital 39	3.0	•	3.7	3.4	3.0	163.8	3.7	3.5	2.0	1.7	0.9	3.9	•
Working Capital to Net Sales 40	0.1	•	0.0	0.1	0.1	0.0	0.1	0.1	0.1	0.1	0.2	0.1	•
Inventory to Working Capital 41	1.3	•	1.1	0.9	1.4	50.4	1.8	1.6	1.2	0.9	0.9	1.3	•
Total Receipts to Cash Flow 42	3.8	3.2	2.7	2.1	3.4	4.6	4.6	4.9	5.9	11.4	6.8	7.8	•
Cost of Goods to Cash Flow 43	2.0	1.4	1.2	0.4	1.4	2.4	2.9	3.1	4.0	8.8	5.2	5.4	•
Cash Flow to Total Debt 44	0.4	•	0.5	0.5	0.3	0.3	0.4	0.4	0.3	0.2	0.3	0.1	•

Selected Financial Factors (in Percentages)

Item	1	2	3	4	5	6	7	8	9	10	11	12	
Debt Ratio 45	67.7	•	104.0	56.4	64.0	81.2	63.8	62.1	61.9	54.2	53.6	62.8	•
Return on Total Assets 46	3.2	•	3.4	3.5	1.8	0.2	1.7	4.7	3.0	5.4	9.9	4.0	•
Return on Equity Before Income Taxes 47	2.1	•	5.9	2.5	•	•	•	6.3	3.4	7.5	18.4	3.9	•
Return on Equity After Income Taxes 48	0.3	•	14.4	2.0	•	•	•	4.6	1.8	5.2	12.5	1.7	•
Profit Margin (Before Income Tax) 49	0.7	3.0	1.3	•	•	•	•	2.0	1.1	2.8	9.0	2.3	•
Profit Margin (After Income Tax) 50	0.1	•	1.0	•	•	•	•	1.5	0.6	1.9	6.1	1.0	•

1

Table II
Corporations with Net Income

AGRICULTURAL PRODUCTION

MONEY AMOUNTS AND SIZE OF ASSETS IN THOUSANDS OF DOLLARS

Item Description for Accounting Period 7/03 Through 6/04	Total	Zero Assets	Under 500	500 to 1000	251 to 500	501 to 1,000	1,001 to 5,000	5,001 to 10,000	10,001 to 25,000	25,001 to 50,000	50,001 to 100,000	100,001 to 250,000	250,001 and over
Number of Enterprises **1**	54228	3987	33011	8911	7491	457	221	74	38	23	•	•	•
Revenues ($ in Thousands)													
Net Sales **2**	55145545	553527	8178502	6350619	12103847	3479456	5178706	3559832	3217552	4728827	•	•	•
Interest **3**	176136	3994	24174	29050	54982	12296	15718	9373	4605	10032	•	•	•
Rents **4**	441352	2675	77918	77133	184187	28115	15320	10111	21723	12636	•	•	•
Royalties **5**	96777	2325	6267	25771	13594	2551	5414	649	6657	9244	•	•	•
Other Portfolio Income **6**	920725	88977	229980	87763	246026	49398	49785	11467	24983	40469	•	•	•
Other Receipts **7**	5286986	132581	1609104	1200383	1272473	238630	168234	111439	113245	104526	•	•	•
Total Receipts **8**	62067521	784079	10125945	7770719	13875109	3810446	5433177	3702871	3388765	4905734	•	•	•
Average Total Receipts **9**	1145	197	307	872	1852	8338	24585	50039	89178	213293	•	•	•
Operating Costs/Operating Income (%)													
Cost of Operations **10**	52.7	36.6	18.3	47.5	39.9	63.0	64.0	70.4	71.0	76.6	•	•	•
Salaries and Wages **11**	7.6	7.0	9.9	7.7	9.7	6.4	5.2	5.8	4.9	4.5	•	•	•
Taxes Paid **12**	2.3	5.0	2.8	3.3	3.1	2.0	1.4	1.6	1.3	1.8	•	•	•
Interest Paid **13**	1.9	3.1	2.2	2.1	2.6	1.9	1.1	1.4	1.2	1.0	•	•	•
Depreciation **14**	5.4	4.2	7.7	5.6	7.8	4.5	3.3	3.8	3.4	3.9	•	•	•
Amortization and Depletion **15**	0.2	0.6	0.0	0.1	0.2	0.2	0.1	0.3	0.2	0.6	•	•	•
Pensions and Other Deferred Comp. **16**	0.2	0.3	0.1	0.6	0.3	0.1	0.2	0.3	0.2	0.2	•	•	•
Employee Benefits **17**	1.1	0.9	0.9	1.2	1.2	0.7	0.6	0.7	0.8	1.0	•	•	•
Advertising **18**	0.3	0.1	0.3	0.2	0.2	0.3	0.3	0.3	0.3	0.2	•	•	•
Other Expenses **19**	30.4	43.8	64.0	42.1	38.6	22.3	22.7	11.5	14.2	7.3	•	•	•
Officers' Compensation **20**	2.3	5.4	3.6	4.4	3.5	1.6	1.1	1.1	0.6	0.7	•	•	•
Operating Margin **21**	•	•	•	•	•	•	0.0	2.8	2.0	2.4	•	•	•
Operating Margin Before Officers' Comp. **22**	•	•	•	•	•	1.1	1.1	3.9	2.6	3.1	•	•	•

Selected Average Balance Sheet ($ in Thousands)

Item										
Net Receivables 23	67	0	4	34	72	454	2008	5025	11761	25184
Inventories 24	94	0	7	45	187	605	2163	5051	12189	20752
Net Property, Plant and Equipment 25	409	0	88	381	1011	3030	5535	13896	21320	58702
Total Assets 26	904	0	177	702	1871	6650	15261	35754	70820	145530
Notes and Loans Payable 27	373	0	95	236	857	3683	6276	13669	25854	45727
All Other Liabilities 28	114	0	7	65	115	593	2299	5379	15472	29009
Net Worth 29	417	0	75	401	899	2374	6687	16707	29495	70794

Selected Financial Ratios (Times to 1)

Item										
Current Ratio 30	1.5	•	1.2	1.6	1.4	1.2	1.5	1.5	2.0	1.7
Quick Ratio 31	0.8	•	0.9	1.0	0.7	0.5	0.7	0.8	1.0	0.8
Net Sales to Working Capital 32	9.6	•	30.6	11.0	9.8	23.1	10.1	9.3	4.8	7.6
Coverage Ratio 33	5.4	12.3	7.2	4.5	3.9	4.5	5.5	5.8	7.2	7.2
Total Asset Turnover 34	1.1	•	1.4	1.0	0.9	1.1	1.5	1.3	1.2	1.4
Inventory Turnover 35	5.7	•	6.9	7.5	3.5	7.9	6.9	6.7	4.9	7.6
Receivables Turnover 36	16.4	•	65.3	24.4	23.7	22.0	12.7	9.0	7.4	7.6
Total Liabilities to Net Worth 37	1.2	•	1.4	0.8	1.1	1.8	1.3	1.1	1.4	1.1
Current Assets to Working Capital 38	2.9	•	6.2	2.8	3.3	5.9	3.0	2.9	2.0	2.4
Current Liabilities to Working Capital 39	1.9	•	5.2	1.8	2.3	4.9	2.0	1.9	1.0	1.4
Working Capital to Net Sales 40	0.1	•	0.0	0.1	0.1	0.0	0.1	0.1	0.2	0.1
Inventory to Working Capital 41	1.1	•	1.1	0.6	1.4	1.9	1.2	1.1	0.8	0.9
Total Receipts to Cash Flow 42	3.4	1.9	1.8	2.6	2.9	4.3	4.2	6.4	5.3	9.3
Cost of Goods to Cash Flow 43	1.8	0.7	0.3	1.2	1.2	2.7	2.7	4.5	3.8	7.1
Cash Flow to Total Debt 44	0.6	•	1.4	0.9	0.6	0.4	0.6	0.4	0.4	0.3

Selected Financial Factors (in Percentages)

Item										
Debt Ratio 45	53.9	•	57.8	42.9	51.9	64.3	56.2	53.3	58.4	51.4
Return on Total Assets 46	11.3	•	22.7	9.7	8.8	9.7	9.2	11.1	10.1	9.9
Return on Equity Before Income Taxes 47	20.0	•	46.3	13.2	13.6	21.2	17.2	19.7	20.9	17.5
Return on Equity After Income Taxes 48	17.7	•	44.8	12.5	12.6	19.0	15.5	17.4	18.0	13.4
Profit Margin (Before Income Tax) 49	8.2	34.6	13.9	7.4	7.6	6.6	4.9	6.8	7.3	6.0
Profit Margin (After Income Tax) 50	7.2	26.9	13.5	7.0	7.0	5.9	4.4	6.1	6.3	4.6

FORESTRY AND LOGGING

Table I

Corporations with and without Net Income

MONEY AMOUNTS AND SIZE OF ASSETS IN THOUSANDS OF DOLLARS

Item Description for Accounting Period 7/03 Through 6/04	Total	Zero Assets	Under 500	500 to 1,000	1,000 to 5,000	5,000 to 10,000	10,000 to 25,000	25,000 to 50,000	50,000 to 100,000	100,000 to 250,000	250,000 to 500,000	500,000 to 2,500,000	2,500,000 and over
Number of Enterprises 1	10765	869	8099	690	958	47	63	24	5	5	•	•	4
Revenues ($ in Thousands)													
Net Sales 2	10889627	331047	2504179	849891	3277042	25939	987589	394461	255884	1354518	•	•	909076
Interest 3	35853	571	3075	345	6217	691	1252	2384	467	2797	•	•	18054
Rents 4	47909	759	5601	461	6327	0	2485	8249	231	1143	•	•	22653
Royalties 5	3552	1158	0	2115	6	0	75	0	56	0	•	•	142
Other Portfolio Income 6	283394	30406	4710	41139	31716	5276	13640	22081	22320	33932	•	•	78174
Other Receipts 7	267139	10130	48227	6683	91324	-9212	10370	31291	778	16604	•	•	60945
Total Receipts 8	11527474	374071	2565792	900634	3412632	22694	1015411	458466	279736	1408994	•	•	1089044
Average Total Receipts 9	1071	430	317	1305	3562	483	16118	19103	55947	281799	•	•	272261
Operating Costs/Operating Income (%)													
Cost of Operations 10	66.6	96.9	46.2	36.1	69.7	50.1	78.1	96.2	82.4	83.1	•	•	75.7
Salaries and Wages 11	7.0	1.0	9.1	13.1	8.9	14.8	4.2	5.4	4.3	2.3	•	•	2.2
Taxes Paid 12	2.3	0.4	2.2	3.0	2.9	7.1	2.0	4.4	1.6	1.3	•	•	1.7
Interest Paid 13	3.0	0.5	1.9	2.3	1.2	2.9	1.7	2.4	1.3	3.1	•	•	15.6
Depreciation 14	8.1	0.5	11.9	19.2	7.9	5.8	4.4	5.4	2.5	4.1	•	•	3.2
Amortization and Depletion 15	0.9	0.2	0.0	0.1	0.0	0.1	1.0	0.7	0.0	5.4	•	•	1.3
Pensions and Other Deferred Comp. 16	0.3	0.0	•	0.0	0.6	1.5	0.3	0.2	0.1	0.3	•	•	0.0
Employee Benefits 17	1.0	0.3	1.7	3.0	0.8	2.6	1.1	1.3	0.5	0.1	•	•	0.0
Advertising 18	0.1	0.0	0.1	0.1	0.0	0.1	0.1	0.1	0.1	0.1	•	•	0.2
Other Expenses 19	13.5	4.4	22.9	24.7	9.3	85.0	9.1	14.2	4.6	4.4	•	•	14.1
Officers' Compensation 20	2.9	0.5	6.0	3.8	2.9	8.6	1.6	1.7	0.6	0.5	•	•	0.4
Operating Margin 21	•	•	•	•	•	•	•	•	2.0	•	•	•	•
Operating Margin Before Officers' Comp. 22	•	4.1	•	•	•	•	•	•	2.6	•	•	•	•

Selected Average Balance Sheet ($ in Thousands)

Net Receivables 23	56	0	7	34	96	155	1069	1838	2218	23831	46164
Inventories 24	84	0	4	8	165	144	1618	1134	5839	12803	119455
Net Property, Plant and Equipment 25	485	0	87	495	1032	340	7453	18519	28872	119815	378512
Total Assets 26	1081	0	125	721	2165	6514	15050	34701	67121	238497	1108177
Notes and Loans Payable 27	500	0	100	593	1234	1002	5062	11722	18734	80397	458877
All Other Liabilities 28	142	0	5	11	227	449	1815	5670	5457	46751	183038
Net Worth 29	438	0	20	118	705	5062	8173	17308	42930	111349	466262

Selected Financial Ratios (Times to 1)

Current Ratio 30	1.5	•	1.0	0.9	1.0	2.8	1.8	1.1	2.3	1.9	2.2
Quick Ratio 31	0.6	•	0.8	0.7	0.6	0.4	0.7	0.7	0.6	0.8	0.4
Net Sales to Working Capital 32	9.8	•	18.2	•	•	0.6	7.4	36.9	5.2	7.3	1.3
Coverage Ratio 33	1.1	•	1.4	1.2	0.8	0.6	•	9.4	0.8	•	1.4
Total Asset Turnover 34	0.9	•	2.5	1.7	1.6	0.1	1.0	0.5	0.8	1.1	0.2
Inventory Turnover 35	8.0	•	36.2	56.4	14.4	1.9	7.6	14.0	7.2	17.6	1.4
Receivables Turnover 36	19.4	•	53.5	25.5	34.5	4.7	14.1	9.8	12.6	18.0	5.2
Total Liabilities to Net Worth 37	1.5	•	5.4	5.1	2.1	0.3	0.8	1.0	0.6	1.1	1.4
Current Assets to Working Capital 38	3.0	•	•	•	•	1.6	2.3	14.1	1.8	2.1	1.8
Current Liabilities to Working Capital 39	2.0	•	•	•	0.6	1.3	13.1	0.8	1.1	•	0.8
Working Capital to Net Sales 40	0.1	•	•	•	1.7	0.1	0.0	0.2	0.1	•	0.8
Inventory to Working Capital 41	1.2	•	•	•	0.0	0.9	0.9	0.7	0.5	•	1.3
Total Receipts to Cash Flow 42	12.0	29.4	5.7	6.2	18.5	•	17.5	•	14.8	36.3	9.3
Cost of Goods to Cash Flow 43	8.0	28.5	2.6	2.2	12.9	•	13.7	•	12.2	30.2	7.1
Cash Flow to Total Debt 44	0.1	•	0.5	0.3	0.1	•	0.1	•	0.1	0.1	0.0

Selected Financial Factors (in Percentages)

Debt Ratio 45	59.4	•	84.3	83.7	67.5	22.3	45.7	50.1	36.0	53.3	57.9
Return on Total Assets 46	2.9	•	6.2	4.6	1.6	1.0	•	•	9.6	2.9	4.3
Return on Equity Before Income Taxes 47	0.4	•	10.2	4.6	•	•	•	•	13.4	•	2.7
Return on Equity After Income Taxes 48	•	•	10.0	3.6	•	•	•	•	12.2	•	0.4
Profit Margin (Before Income Tax) 49	0.2	8.2	0.6	0.4	•	•	•	•	11.3	•	5.5
Profit Margin (After Income Tax) 50	•	6.7	0.6	0.3	•	•	•	•	10.2	•	0.9

3

Table II

Corporations with Net Income

FORESTRY AND LOGGING

MONEY AMOUNTS AND SIZE OF ASSETS IN THOUSANDS OF DOLLARS

Item Description for Accounting Period 7/03 Through 6/04	Total	Zero Assets	Under 500	500 to 1,000	1,000 to 5,000	5,000 to 10,000	10,000 to 25,000	25,000 to 50,000	50,000 to 100,000	100,000 to 250,000	250,000 to 500,000	500,000 to 2,500,000	2,500,000 and over
Number of Enterprises 1	5682	331	4426	480	396	4	28	•	•	•	3	•	•
Revenues ($ in Thousands)													
Net Sales 2	7124045	3639	1757253	530533	2083096	25939	735244	•	•	•	1360260	•	•
Interest 3	16190	571	2610	122	1979	450	851	•	•	•	8370	•	•
Rents 4	15747	759	0	461	2179	0	2262	•	•	•	3601	•	•
Royalties 5	3527	1158	2115	•	0	0	75	•	•	•	123	•	•
Other Portfolio Income 6	168733	30406	4564	31817	11457	5034	8463	•	•	•	354	•	•
Other Receipts 7	130269	10130	45631	6478	1678	933	6667	•	•	•	31187	•	•
Total Receipts 8	7458511	46663	1810058	571526	2100389	32356	753562	•	•	•	1403895	•	•
Average Total Receipts 9	1313	141	409	1191	5304	8089	26913	•	•	•	467965	•	•
Operating Costs/Operating Income (%)													
Cost of Operations 10	64.9	15.6	52.3	23.9	70.0	50.1	78.3	•	•	•	73.4	•	•
Salaries and Wages 11	5.3	73.4	6.7	16.1	4.6	14.6	3.4	•	•	•	1.7	•	•
Taxes Paid 12	2.1	28.7	1.5	3.3	3.1	6.4	1.5	•	•	•	1.6	•	•
Interest Paid 13	2.3	37.7	1.8	1.9	1.2	2.9	0.9	•	•	•	4.3	•	•
Depreciation 14	6.8	39.0	8.5	22.8	6.7	5.5	3.1	•	•	•	2.4	•	•
Amortization and Depletion 15	0.4	18.9	0.0	0.1	0.0	0.1	0.1	•	•	•	1.4	•	•
Pensions and Other Deferred Comp. 16	0.4	0.8	•	0.0	0.9	1.5	0.3	•	•	•	0.2	•	•
Employee Benefits 17	0.6	2.0	0.1	3.3	0.7	2.5	0.8	•	•	•	•	•	•
Advertising 18	0.1	0.1	0.1	0.2	0.1	0.1	0.0	•	•	•	0.0	•	•
Other Expenses 19	11.3	166.7	19.3	29.5	5.6	15.5	8.4	•	•	•	6.9	•	•
Officers' Compensation 20	2.7	•	4.4	3.2	4.0	8.2	1.2	•	•	•	0.1	•	•
Operating Margin 21	3.1	•	5.3	•	3.2	•	2.0	•	•	•	7.8	•	•
Operating Margin Before Officers' Comp. 22	5.8	•	9.7	•	7.2	1.0	3.2	•	•	•	7.9	•	•

Selected Average Balance Sheet ($ in Thousands)

Net Receivables 23	44	0	10	24	120	1799	1390	•	23878
Inventories 24	134	0	6	10	347	1354	2684	•	312839
Net Property, Plant and Equipment 25	378	0	75	576	911	3271	6154	•	168567
Total Assets 26	1159	0	120	783	2391	7982	15634	•	1140025
Notes and Loans Payable 27	383	0	106	569	854	2980	4757	•	207755
All Other Liabilities 28	162	0	7	8	259	655	3015	•	212312
Net Worth 29	614	0	8	206	1278	4347	7862	•	719958

Selected Financial Ratios (Times to 1)

Current Ratio 30	2.8	•	1.1	2.6	1.6	2.0	1.9	7.6
Quick Ratio 31	0.9	•	0.9	2.3	0.8	1.6	0.7	0.5
Net Sales to Working Capital 32	5.3	•	122.7	11.1	14.3	4.4	8.2	1.5
Coverage Ratio 33	4.4	24.3	5.7	2.8	4.4	7.1	6.2	3.5
Total Asset Turnover 34	1.1	•	3.3	1.4	2.2	0.8	1.7	0.4
Inventory Turnover 35	6.1	•	33.5	27.3	10.6	2.4	7.7	1.1
Receivables Turnover 36	32.8	•	48.6	20.1	42.9	5.5	18.1	38.0
Total Liabilities to Net Worth 37	0.9	•	14.2	2.8	0.9	0.8	1.0	0.6
Current Assets to Working Capital 38	1.5	•	10.0	1.6	2.7	2.0	2.2	1.2
Current Liabilities to Working Capital 39	0.5	•	9.0	0.6	1.7	1.0	1.2	0.2
Working Capital to Net Sales 40	0.2	•	0.0	0.1	0.1	0.2	0.1	0.7
Inventory to Working Capital 41	0.9	•	1.4	0.1	1.0	0.2	1.0	1.0
Total Receipts to Cash Flow 42	6.6	0.4	4.5	4.4	12.6	8.8	9.7	5.7
Cost of Goods to Cash Flow 43	4.3	0.1	2.4	1.0	8.8	4.4	7.6	4.2
Cash Flow to Total Debt 44	0.3	•	0.8	0.4	0.4	0.2	0.3	0.2

Selected Financial Factors (in Percentages)

Debt Ratio 45	47.0	•	93.4	73.7	46.5	45.5	49.7	36.8
Return on Total Assets 46	10.9	•	33.2	7.4	11.5	16.6	9.0	6.1
Return on Equity Before Income Taxes 47	15.8	•	415.9	17.9	16.6	26.2	15.0	6.9
Return on Equity After Income Taxes 48	13.8	•	415.1	17.1	16.4	17.3	13.3	4.6
Profit Margin (Before Income Tax) 49	7.7	880.5	8.3	3.3	4.0	17.5	4.5	11.0
Profit Margin (After Income Tax) 50	6.7	752.3	8.3	3.2	4.0	11.6	4.0	7.3

4

AGRICULTURE, FORESTRY, FISHING AND HUNTING

SUPPORT ACTIVITIES AND FISHING, HUNTING AND TRAPPING

Table I

Corporations with and without Net Income

MONEY AMOUNTS AND SIZE OF ASSETS IN THOUSANDS OF DOLLARS

Item Description for Accounting Period 7/03 Through 6/04	Total	Zero Assets	Under 500	500 to 1,000	1,000 to 5,000	5,000 to 10,000	10,000 to 25,000	25,000 to 50,000	50,000 to 100,000	100,000 to 250,000	250,000 to 500,000	500,000 to 2,500,000	2,500,000 and over
Number of Enterprises **1**	31683	4581	23510	1674	1461	334	88	26	5	3	•	•	•
Revenues ($ in Thousands)													
Net Sales **2**	21407769	383856	7427262	2404286	3721247	3609612	1828074	865639	406366	761427	•	•	•
Interest **3**	30618	1335	3607	4830	8686	1562	5422	3363	1128	687	•	•	•
Rents **4**	25867	0	666	7760	4053	7573	5496	308	12	0	•	•	•
Royalties **5**	541	0	0	0	0	103	60	0	377	0	•	•	•
Other Portfolio Income **6**	163364	9438	69351	5396	19821	19589	4298	17435	17963	74	•	•	•
Other Receipts **7**	920263	16110	379063	226643	117716	64362	47457	36959	12287	19663	•	•	•
Total Receipts **8**	22548422	410739	7879949	2648915	3871523	3702801	1890807	923704	438133	781851	•	•	•
Average Total Receipts **9**	712	90	335	1582	2650	11086	21486	35527	87627	260617	•	•	•
Operating Costs/Operating Income (%)													
Cost of Operations **10**	59.6	12.0	53.1	56.4	55.5	68.5	76.7	80.0	62.5	70.4	•	•	•
Salaries and Wages **11**	8.6	12.8	7.0	10.4	11.4	10.0	5.1	6.1	14.5	4.5	•	•	•
Taxes Paid **12**	2.3	3.3	2.2	1.9	3.0	2.1	1.3	1.4	2.3	3.6	•	•	•
Interest Paid **13**	1.1	0.5	1.2	0.5	1.8	0.5	1.1	1.7	0.9	2.2	•	•	•
Depreciation **14**	4.2	2.7	3.7	6.2	5.5	3.3	3.1	4.1	3.3	5.7	•	•	•
Amortization and Depletion **15**	0.2	1.0	0.1	0.0	0.4	0.0	0.1	0.2	0.9	0.1	•	•	•
Pensions and Other Deferred Comp. **16**	0.2	•	0.1	0.5	0.1	0.6	0.2	0.1	0.3	0.1	•	•	•
Employee Benefits **17**	0.6	0.0	0.6	0.6	0.7	0.7	0.7	0.8	1.7	0.4	•	•	•
Advertising **18**	0.4	0.0	0.6	0.1	0.2	0.4	0.2	0.3	1.6	0.2	•	•	•
Other Expenses **19**	21.3	64.7	26.2	25.2	24.5	11.5	10.8	10.8	10.7	11.5	•	•	•
Officers' Compensation **20**	3.4	2.6	5.8	2.2	2.2	3.2	1.2	0.7	1.6	0.3	•	•	•
Operating Margin **21**	•	0.4	•	•	•	•	•	•	•	1.1	•	•	•
Operating Margin Before Officers' Comp. **22**	1.4	3.0	5.2	•	•	2.5	0.6	•	1.3	1.4	•	•	•

Selected Average Balance Sheet ($ in Thousands)

Net Receivables 23	54	0	11	34	289	1209	3265	5329	9303	27757
Inventories 24	38	0	5	43	158	479	1978	6714	4913	88615
Net Property, Plant and Equipment 25	147	0	36	327	858	2970	5190	9599	10719	85132
Total Assets 26	387	0	105	695	1918	7640	15125	33494	67113	246509
Notes and Loans Payable 27	178	0	98	258	837	1403	5383	14602	11281	100725
All Other Liabilities 28	75	0	18	96	265	1886	3796	7382	14751	61009
Net Worth 29	134	0	-11	341	816	4351	5946	11510	41081	84776

Selected Financial Ratios (Times to 1)

Current Ratio 30	1.5	•	1.5	1.3	1.7	1.5	1.2	1.2	1.6	1.9
Quick Ratio 31	1.0	•	1.3	0.8	1.2	1.1	0.8	0.6	1.1	0.7
Net Sales to Working Capital 32	11.9	•	21.2	31.8	9.0	8.2	10.3	10.4	8.2	3.6
Coverage Ratio 33	3.9	15.1	5.4	12.4	0.3	4.8	3.5	1.3	9.6	2.7
Total Asset Turnover 34	1.7	•	3.0	2.1	1.3	1.4	1.4	1.0	1.2	1.0
Inventory Turnover 35	10.6	•	36.9	18.8	8.9	15.4	8.1	4.0	10.3	2.0
Receivables Turnover 36	12.9	•	29.5	22.1	9.3	10.4	6.4	6.5	7.9	9.9
Total Liabilities to Net Worth 37	1.9	•	1.0	1.3	0.8	1.5	1.9	0.6		1.9
Current Assets to Working Capital 38	2.9	•	2.9	4.8	2.4	2.9	3.6	5.1	2.6	2.2
Current Liabilities to Working Capital 39	1.9	•	1.9	3.8	1.4	1.9	2.6	4.1	1.6	1.2
Working Capital to Net Sales 40	0.1	•	0.0	0.0	0.1	0.1	0.1	0.1	0.1	0.3
Inventory to Working Capital 41	0.6	•	0.3	0.2	0.5	0.4	1.1	2.1	0.5	1.3
Total Receipts to Cash Flow 42	5.2	1.8	4.1	4.2	5.1	9.4	9.0	11.8	7.6	7.9
Cost of Goods to Cash Flow 43	3.1	0.2	2.2	2.4	2.8	6.4	6.9	9.4	4.8	5.6
Cash Flow to Total Debt 44	0.5	•	0.7	1.0	0.5	0.3	0.3	0.1	0.4	0.2

Selected Financial Factors (in Percentages)

Debt Ratio 45	65.5	•	110.7	50.9	57.4	43.0	60.7	65.6	38.8	65.6
Return on Total Assets 46	7.9	•	20.2	13.9	0.7	3.2	5.4	2.2	10.2	6.2
Return on Equity Before Income Taxes 47	16.9	•	•	26.0	•	4.4	9.9	1.5	14.9	11.4
Return on Equity After Income Taxes 48	15.8	•	•	25.0	•	4.0	8.9	•	10.1	10.2
Profit Margin (Before Income Tax) 49	3.4	7.4	5.5	6.2	•	1.8	2.8	0.5	7.5	3.8
Profit Margin (After Income Tax) 50	3.1	6.4	5.4	5.9	•	1.6	2.5	•	5.1	3.4

Table II
Corporations with Net Income

SUPPORT ACTIVITIES AND FISHING, HUNTING AND TRAPPING

MONEY AMOUNTS AND SIZE OF ASSETS IN THOUSANDS OF DOLLARS

Item Description for Accounting Period 7/03 Through 6/04	Total	Zero Assets	Under 500	500 to 1,000	1,000 to 5,000	5,000 to 10,000	10,000 to 25,000	25,000 to 50,000	50,000 to 100,000	100,000 to 250,000	250,000 to 500,000	500,000 to 2,500,000	2,500,000 and over
Number of Enterprises **1**	17371	2682	12573	1056	756	227	57	•	•	•	•	•	•
Revenues ($ in Thousands)													
Net Sales **2**	15394554	370932	5348386	1904270	2451468	2475180	1411335	•	•	•	•	•	•
Interest **3**	20348	1113	2173	2082	5971	1044	4783	•	•	•	•	•	•
Rents **4**	19778	0	76	6197	3764	5467	3965	•	•	•	•	•	•
Royalties **5**	104	0	0	0	0	103	0						
Other Portfolio Income **6**	143191	9426	61179	2669	12082	19334	3730	•	•	•	•	•	•
Other Receipts **7**	694551	16977	306799	186944	40629	77231	25635	•	•	•	•	•	•
Total Receipts **8**	16272526	398448	5718613	2102162	2513914	2578359	1449448	•	•	•	•	•	•
Average Total Receipts **9**	937	149	455	1991	3325	11358	25429	•	•	•	•	•	•
Operating Costs/Operating Income (%)													
Cost of Operations **10**	58.7	12.3	55.6	62.5	47.8	63.0	76.3	•	•	•	•	•	•
Salaries and Wages **11**	8.7	13.2	5.3	9.6	14.5	12.1	5.0	•	•	•	•	•	•
Taxes Paid **12**	2.0	3.3	2.1	1.2	2.8	1.8	1.1	•	•	•	•	•	•
Interest Paid **13**	0.8	0.3	0.6	0.3	1.5	0.5	0.8	•	•	•	•	•	•
Depreciation **14**	3.2	1.7	2.0	3.6	5.4	3.4	2.4	•	•	•	•	•	•
Amortization and Depletion **15**	0.1	0.0	0.0	0.0	0.6	0.0	0.0	•	•	•	•	•	•
Pensions and Other Deferred Comp. **16**	0.3	•	0.1	0.6	0.1	0.8	0.3	•	•	•	•	•	•
Employee Benefits **17**	0.7	0.0	0.5	0.7	0.7	0.9	0.6	•	•	•	•	•	•
Advertising **18**	0.4	0.0	0.6	0.1	0.3	0.6	0.3	•	•	•	•	•	•
Other Expenses **19**	19.0	63.6	22.1	19.7	23.0	12.4	9.2	•	•	•	•	•	•
Officers' Compensation **20**	3.4	2.7	5.3	2.3	2.5	3.8	1.2	•	•	•	•	•	•
Operating Margin **21**	2.6	2.9	5.8	•	0.9	0.8	2.8	•	•	•	•	•	•
Operating Margin Before Officers' Comp. **22**	6.0	5.6	11.1	1.7	3.4	4.5	4.0	•	•	•	•	•	•

Selected Average Balance Sheet ($ in Thousands)

Net Receivables 23	58	0	9	46	225	1189	3914
Inventories 24	52	0	6	19	195	547	2481
Net Property, Plant and Equipment 25	138	0	29	158	865	2589	4231
Total Assets 26	432	0	110	624	2001	7661	15417
Notes and Loans Payable 27	145	0	43	197	821	1891	4237
All Other Liabilities 28	80	0	16	75	297	1248	4368
Net Worth 29	207	0	51	352	882	4522	6813

Selected Financial Ratios (Times to 1)

Current Ratio 30	1.8	•	2.0	1.8	1.6	2.0	1.5
Quick Ratio 31	1.2	•	1.7	1.2	1.2	1.7	0.9
Net Sales to Working Capital 32	9.8	•	15.4	13.3	14.0	5.4	9.0
Coverage Ratio 33	11.6	32.9	22.1	30.7	3.3	11.4	7.6
Total Asset Turnover 34	2.1	•	3.9	2.9	1.6	1.4	1.6
Inventory Turnover 35	10.0	•	41.9	59.6	7.9	12.6	7.6
Receivables Turnover 36	13.8	•	36.3	22.8	9.8	11.1	6.3
Total Liabilities to Net Worth 37	1.1	•	1.2	0.8	1.3	0.7	1.3
Current Assets to Working Capital 38	2.3	•	2.0	2.3	2.6	2.0	3.1
Current Liabilities to Working Capital 39	1.3	•	1.0	1.3	1.6	1.0	2.1
Working Capital to Net Sales 40	0.1	•	0.1	0.1	0.1	0.2	0.1
Inventory to Working Capital 41	0.5	•	0.1	0.1	0.5	0.3	0.9
Total Receipts to Cash Flow 42	4.3	1.8	3.4	3.7	4.4	6.9	8.0
Cost of Goods to Cash Flow 43	2.5	0.2	1.9	2.3	2.1	4.4	6.1
Cash Flow to Total Debt 44	0.9	•	2.1	1.8	0.7	0.5	0.4

Selected Financial Factors (in Percentages)

Debt Ratio 45	52.1	•	53.5	43.6	55.9	41.0	55.8
Return on Total Assets 46	18.6	•	51.3	29.1	7.9	7.5	10.1
Return on Equity Before Income Taxes 47	35.4	•	105.3	49.8	12.5	11.6	19.9
Return on Equity After Income Taxes 48	34.0	•	104.4	48.3	12.0	11.0	18.5
Profit Margin (Before Income Tax) 49	8.3	10.3	12.7	9.7	3.4	4.8	5.5
Profit Margin (After Income Tax) 50	7.9	9.3	12.6	9.4	3.3	4.6	5.1

Table I

Corporations with and without Net Income

OIL AND GAS EXTRACTION

MONEY AMOUNTS AND SIZE OF ASSETS IN THOUSANDS OF DOLLARS

Item Description for Accounting Period 7/03 Through 6/04	Total	Zero Assets	Under 500	500 to 1,000	1,000 to 5,000	5,000 to 10,000	10,000 to 25,000	25,000 to 50,000	50,000 to 100,000	100,000 to 250,000	250,000 to 500,000	500,000 to 2,500,000	2,500,000 and over
Number of Enterprises 1	16040	2737	9361	1501	1465	359	266	128	73	63	31	41	14
Revenues ($ in Thousands)													
Net Sales 2	88431957	1402680	1872027	846453	3595947	1675075	1932031	2392407	2084380	3770498	3391103	22600215	42869142
Interest 3	2015864	10714	1625	2431	12948	7820	15678	10120	14580	33863	55791	116315	1733980
Rents 4	115256	778	4	1066	12605	1938	7928	14239	1619	11527	2929	17977	42647
Royalties 5	486166	742	41368	423	31236	15305	42596	46188	41189	48841	12404	92576	113297
Other Portfolio Income 6	2790311	125286	33008	47165	214128	34275	77698	31087	143730	195459	749646	495569	643261
Other Receipts 7	5227100	-23242	126826	23308	282679	80000	231273	229343	448233	356059	284062	603190	2585364
Total Receipts 8	99066654	1516958	2074858	920846	4149543	1814413	2307204	2723384	2733731	4416247	4495935	23925842	47987691
Average Total Receipts 9	6176	554	222	613	2832	5054	8674	21276	37448	70099	145030	583557	3427692
Operating Costs/Operating Income (%)													
Cost of Operations 10	49.9	15.9	12.9	3.3	51.4	44.3	33.7	39.7	27.3	24.6	33.5	54.5	57.1
Salaries and Wages 11	4.5	9.7	7.2	10.1	6.2	6.3	8.7	5.7	10.8	6.6	6.4	2.8	3.9
Taxes Paid 12	2.7	3.4	4.6	6.1	3.3	4.0	4.7	3.6	4.8	3.9	4.1	2.1	2.3
Interest Paid 13	5.9	6.1	1.3	1.6	1.8	0.8	2.0	2.7	3.8	4.8	3.1	3.1	8.6
Depreciation 14	5.6	10.7	5.6	3.7	3.9	5.5	7.7	7.6	8.4	8.2	7.8	5.2	5.0
Amortization and Depletion 15	5.4	9.8	2.1	3.3	3.7	3.3	6.4	6.7	6.9	9.5	11.0	5.6	4.7
Pensions and Other Deferred Comp. 16	0.3	0.1	1.2	0.4	0.8	0.3	0.5	0.3	0.7	0.3	0.2	0.3	0.3
Employee Benefits 17	0.8	0.5	1.0	2.3	0.2	2.3	0.9	0.6	0.8	1.1	0.5	0.5	1.0
Advertising 18	0.0	0.0	0.2	0.1	0.1	0.1	0.1	0.1	0.0	0.1	0.0	0.0	0.0
Other Expenses 19	23.1	48.3	42.6	60.1	23.3	25.7	30.1	27.2	37.4	33.4	30.8	21.4	18.8
Officers' Compensation 20	1.4	0.6	10.1	5.0	4.5	2.8	3.3	2.1	3.3	1.7	2.6	0.6	0.8
Operating Margin 21	0.2	•	11.2	4.0	0.9	4.5	1.7	3.6	•	6.0	•	4.0	•
Operating Margin Before Officers' Comp. 22	1.6	•	21.2	9.0	5.4	7.3	5.0	5.7	•	7.7	•	4.6	•

Selected Average Balance Sheet ($ in Thousands)

Net Receivables 23	1372	0	23	144	396	625	1952	4155	6087	18337	32269	82771	981008
Inventories 24	102	0	0	3	16	34	155	440	599	882	3849	5676	74605
Net Property, Plant and Equipment 25	5401	0	49	80	777	2651	5250	15231	29508	78149	195950	614048	3020560
Total Assets 26	12437	0	130	601	2444	7317	15194	36068	70037	154079	350370	1037312	8163983
Notes and Loans Payable 27	4551	0	52	412	854	1490	3659	9865	18358	43709	110553	237791	3614538
All Other Liabilities 28	2728	0	58	277	616	1674	3500	7373	12774	33921	66389	226171	1786590
Net Worth 29	5158	0	20	-88	974	4153	8036	18830	38906	76449	173428	573350	2762856

Selected Financial Ratios (Times to 1)

Current Ratio 30	1.4	•	0.9	0.6	1.6	1.2	1.5	1.6	1.7	1.8	1.5	1.4	1.4
Quick Ratio 31	1.2	•	0.8	0.6	1.3	1.0	1.2	1.3	1.4	1.3	1.4	0.9	1.2
Net Sales to Working Capital 32	7.6	•	•	•	6.3	11.2	3.6	4.3	3.3	2.9	5.2	11.2	7.8
Coverage Ratio 33	3.1	1.5	17.8	9.2	9.8	16.0	11.7	7.5	8.1	5.9	4.9	4.2	2.1
Total Asset Turnover 34	0.4	•	1.5	0.9	1.0	0.6	0.5	0.5	0.4	0.4	0.3	0.5	0.4
Inventory Turnover 35	27.0	•	96.8	7.1	78.7	60.9	15.8	16.9	13.0	16.7	9.5	52.9	23.4
Receivables Turnover 36	4.4	•	7.8	5.8	6.4	5.0	4.4	4.6	4.6	3.2	3.6	7.6	3.5
Total Liabilities to Net Worth 37	1.4	•	5.6	•	1.5	0.8	0.9	0.9	0.8	1.0	1.0	0.8	2.0
Current Assets to Working Capital 38	3.4	•	•	•	2.8	6.8	3.0	2.7	2.4	2.3	3.1	3.4	3.4
Current Liabilities to Working Capital 39	2.4	•	•	•	1.8	5.8	2.0	1.7	1.4	1.3	2.1	2.4	2.4
Working Capital to Net Sales 40	0.1	•	•	•	0.2	0.1	0.3	0.2	0.3	0.3	0.2	0.1	0.1
Inventory to Working Capital 41	0.2	•	•	•	0.0	0.1	0.1	0.1	0.1	0.0	0.1	0.2	0.2
Total Receipts to Cash Flow 42	3.3	2.3	1.7	1.5	3.0	3.0	2.3	2.5	1.8	2.0	2.6	3.5	4.2
Cost of Goods to Cash Flow 43	1.6	0.4	0.2	0.1	1.5	1.3	0.8	1.0	0.5	0.5	0.9	1.9	2.4
Cash Flow to Total Debt 44	0.2	•	1.0	0.5	0.6	0.5	0.4	0.4	0.5	0.4	0.2	0.3	0.1

Selected Financial Factors (in Percentages)

Debt Ratio 45	58.5	•	84.9	114.7	60.2	43.2	47.1	47.8	44.5	50.4	50.5	44.7	66.2
Return on Total Assets 46	8.1	•	35.8	13.4	17.9	8.6	11.1	10.4	12.6	11.0	11.7	7.0	6.8
Return on Equity Before Income Taxes 47	13.3	•	223.4	•	40.4	14.1	19.2	17.3	19.9	18.3	18.9	9.6	10.6
Return on Equity After Income Taxes 48	10.2	•	217.2	•	38.7	13.3	17.9	15.4	17.1	14.4	12.6	7.2	7.5
Profit Margin (Before Income Tax) 49	12.4	3.0	22.0	12.8	16.0	12.6	21.2	17.4	27.1	23.4	29.9	10.0	9.5
Profit Margin (After Income Tax) 50	9.6	0.8	21.4	12.2	15.3	11.9	19.8	15.5	23.3	18.4	19.9	7.5	6.8

Table II
Corporations with Net Income

OIL AND GAS EXTRACTION

MONEY AMOUNTS AND SIZE OF ASSETS IN THOUSANDS OF DOLLARS

Item Description for Accounting Period 7/03 Through 6/04		Total	Zero Assets	Under 500	500 to 1,000	1,000 to 5,000	5,000 to 10,000	10,000 to 25,000	25,000 to 50,000	50,000 to 100,000	100,000 to 250,000	250,000 to 500,000	500,000 to 2,500,000	2,500,000 and over
Number of Enterprises	1	10350	1128	6421	967	1164	258	173	82	55	40	22	•	•
Revenues ($ in Thousands)														
Net Sales	2	74706709	958221	1614484	766332	3277727	1618640	1591203	1899571	1829895	3044600	2833171	•	•
Interest	3	1759023	8303	1317	2099	8007	3579	9682	6859	13270	22901	47038	•	•
Rents	4	90467	63	4	1066	12605	1936	5597	9681	1501	11042	2750	•	•
Royalties	5	418527	459	37608	336	29050	15300	41593	43355	36797	47964	3677	•	•
Other Portfolio Income	6	2640284	113352	32999	47161	205686	33992	56349	22778	141627	186358	734581	•	•
Other Receipts	7	4734745	-12900	111464	21120	271874	54382	188853	207563	412892	306039	224755	•	•
Total Receipts	8	84349755	1067498	1797876	838114	3804949	1727829	1893277	2189807	2435982	3618904	3845972	•	•
Average Total Receipts	9	8150	946	280	867	3269	6697	10944	26705	44291	90473	174817	•	•
Operating Costs/Operating Income (%)														
Cost of Operations	10	49.7	21.8	7.0	3.7	52.3	45.4	31.1	35.3	25.9	25.2	38.2	•	•
Salaries and Wages	11	4.2	5.4	7.9	7.7	4.7	4.2	6.8	4.9	11.0	6.3	6.1	•	•
Taxes Paid	12	2.7	1.9	4.9	5.8	3.2	3.7	4.8	3.7	4.7	3.9	3.7	•	•
Interest Paid	13	5.6	6.4	1.1	0.7	1.4	0.7	1.4	1.9	3.3	2.0	6.1	•	•
Depreciation	14	5.2	8.3	5.6	4.1	3.5	5.1	7.0	6.3	7.4	7.8	7.3	•	•
Amortization and Depletion	15	5.0	10.5	2.2	3.6	2.8	3.2	5.3	6.7	5.1	6.7	8.6	•	•
Pensions and Other Deferred Comp.	16	0.3	0.0	1.4	0.4	0.9	0.3	0.5	0.3	0.8	0.2	0.2	•	•
Employee Benefits	17	0.8	0.3	1.0	2.3	0.2	2.0	0.7	0.6	0.6	1.0	0.4	•	•
Advertising	18	0.0	0.0	0.2	0.0	0.1	0.1	0.1	0.1	0.0	0.1	0.0	•	•
Other Expenses	19	20.6	32.9	34.5	45.0	21.5	20.9	23.6	24.0	33.7	25.7	22.9	•	•
Officers' Compensation	20	1.4	0.6	10.5	3.8	4.6	2.5	2.6	1.8	3.3	1.7	2.4	•	•
Operating Margin	21	4.3	11.9	23.7	22.8	5.0	11.9	16.0	14.5	4.2	19.5	4.1	•	•
Operating Margin Before Officers' Comp.	22	5.8	12.5	34.3	26.6	9.5	14.4	18.7	16.3	7.5	21.1	6.5	•	•

Selected Average Balance Sheet ($ in Thousands)

Net Receivables 23	1869	0	33	90	418	495	1816	4836	7043	20002	40269	•
Inventories 24	112	0	0	4	13	44	123	385	739	1016	3125	•
Net Property, Plant and Equipment 25	6171	0	58	101	702	1941	5161	14006	26884	73584	160281	•
Total Assets 26	15404	0	157	621	2505	7104	15290	35887	72162	154897	347420	•
Notes and Loans Payable 27	5639	0	36	66	737	870	3215	8081	18266	32122	96263	•
All Other Liabilities 28	3045	0	64	236	568	1002	2988	7550	13906	33992	70891	•
Net Worth 29	6720	0	57	320	1200	5231	9088	20255	39989	88783	180266	•

Selected Financial Ratios (Times to 1)

Current Ratio 30	1.7	•	1.3	1.3	1.8	2.2	1.9	1.8	1.8	2.1	1.7	•
Quick Ratio 31	1.4	•	1.1	1.2	1.5	1.7	1.6	1.5	1.4	1.7	1.6	•
Net Sales to Working Capital 32	5.6	•	13.9	10.1	5.2	4.0	3.2	3.8	3.2	2.9	4.0	•
Coverage Ratio 33	4.1	4.6	34.1	46.1	16.1	28.8	25.8	16.7	12.4	19.9	7.9	•
Total Asset Turnover 34	0.5	•	1.6	1.3	1.1	0.9	0.6	0.6	0.5	0.5	0.4	•
Inventory Turnover 35	32.0	•	110.8	7.4	113.7	65.4	23.2	21.3	11.7	18.9	15.7	•
Receivables Turnover 36	4.5	•	7.3	15.3	7.7	6.3	6.1	5.1	5.6	4.5	4.1	•
Total Liabilities to Net Worth 37	1.3	•	1.7	0.9	1.1	0.4	0.7	0.8	0.8	0.7	0.9	•
Current Assets to Working Capital 38	2.5	•	4.8	4.2	2.2	1.8	2.1	2.3	2.2	1.9	2.4	•
Current Liabilities to Working Capital 39	1.5	•	3.8	3.2	1.2	0.8	1.1	1.3	1.2	0.9	1.4	•
Working Capital to Net Sales 40	0.2	•	0.1	0.1	0.2	0.2	0.3	0.3	0.3	0.3	0.3	•
Inventory to Working Capital 41	0.1	•	0.0	0.1	0.0	0.0	0.0	0.0	0.1	0.1	0.1	•
Total Receipts to Cash Flow 42	3.0	2.0	1.6	1.4	2.7	2.8	1.9	2.0	1.6	1.7	2.5	•
Cost of Goods to Cash Flow 43	1.5	0.4	0.1	0.1	1.4	1.3	0.6	0.7	0.4	0.4	1.0	•
Cash Flow to Total Debt 44	0.3	•	1.6	1.8	0.8	1.2	0.8	0.8	0.7	0.7	0.3	•

Selected Financial Factors (in Percentages)

Debt Ratio 45	56.4	•	63.4	48.5	52.1	26.4	40.6	43.6	44.6	42.7	48.1	•
Return on Total Assets 46	10.8	•	58.0	41.9	25.0	16.9	22.0	20.4	18.7	20.0	17.9	•
Return on Equity Before Income Taxes 47	18.8	•	153.6	79.7	48.9	22.1	35.5	34.0	31.0	33.2	30.2	•
Return on Equity After Income Taxes 48	15.2	•	150.5	78.2	47.1	21.2	33.7	31.4	27.5	27.9	21.6	•
Profit Margin (Before Income Tax) 49	17.5	23.3	35.1	32.2	20.8	18.4	35.1	29.7	37.3	38.7	42.2	•
Profit Margin (After Income Tax) 50	14.1	20.0	34.4	31.6	20.1	17.7	33.3	27.4	33.0	32.5	30.2	•

Table I

Corporations with and without Net Income

COAL MINING

MONEY AMOUNTS AND SIZE OF ASSETS IN THOUSANDS OF DOLLARS

Item Description for Accounting Period 7/03 Through 6/04	Total	Zero Assets	Under 500	500 to 1,000	1,000 to 5,000	5,000 to 10,000	10,000 to 25,000	25,000 to 50,000	50,000 to 100,000	100,000 to 250,000	250,000 to 500,000	500,000 to 2,500,000	2,500,000 and over
Number of Enterprises 1	1213	3	788	78	207	58	39	16	11	4	•	5	4
Revenues ($ in Thousands)													
Net Sales 2	14117244	36096	591166	58698	298904	332607	976950	604732	1041353	661820	•	3496891	6018028
Interest 3	164923	0	0	197	399	38	2236	144	3262	7373	•	24609	126666
Rents 4	17723	0	0	28	827	505	1626	680	1353	3989	•	4497	4217
Royalties 5	119285	0	0	5615	1683	15845	2623	459	1473	11540	•	27184	52862
Other Portfolio Income 6	292231	2819	0	4404	16632	1705	3507	2833	17165	8106	•	75834	159229
Other Receipts 7	602885	-1860	-2956	-4548	10644	25514	6635	18860	22022	49447	•	228797	250326
Total Receipts 8	15314291	37055	588210	64394	329089	376214	993577	627708	1086628	742275	•	3857812	6611328
Average Total Receipts 9	12625	12352	746	826	1590	6486	25476	39232	98784	185569	•	771562	1652832
Operating Costs/Operating Income (%)													
Cost of Operations 10	68.2	90.1	82.2	96.6	61.9	76.6	70.8	47.5	75.5	75.3	•	70.2	64.7
Salaries and Wages 11	3.6	2.4	2.3	6.5	3.9	1.0	4.8	7.4	3.0	2.2	•	2.1	4.3
Taxes Paid 12	7.9	8.5	4.4	25.1	3.8	6.8	4.8	5.5	4.0	7.1	•	7.6	10.0
Interest Paid 13	5.0	2.7	0.6	0.3	7.3	1.6	1.5	1.7	1.4	4.4	•	9.1	4.8
Depreciation 14	7.2	1.1	6.6	0.5	13.5	8.7	7.0	9.9	6.3	4.5	•	5.9	8.0
Amortization and Depletion 15	4.5	0.5	0.7	•	2.1	0.3	1.8	2.1	3.0	4.5	•	4.4	6.3
Pensions and Other Deferred Comp. 16	1.2	0.0	•	•	0.0	0.2	0.3	0.2	0.5	2.8	•	3.0	0.7
Employee Benefits 17	4.2	0.3	0.0	•	7.5	1.1	3.7	3.2	1.9	1.7	•	6.2	4.4
Advertising 18	0.1	•	0.1	0.0	0.1	0.0	0.0	0.0	0.0	0.0	•	0.1	0.1
Other Expenses 19	12.4	10.0	6.2	27.2	29.8	29.9	36.1	27.2	10.4	6.3	•	7.0	9.9
Officers' Compensation 20	0.6	1.2	2.7	0.1	3.7	0.2	0.8	0.9	0.5	0.4	•	0.5	0.3
Operating Margin 21	•	•	•	•	•	•	•	•	•	•	•	•	•
Operating Margin Before Officers' Comp. 22	•	•	•	•	•	•	•	•	•	•	•	•	•

Selected Average Balance Sheet ($ in Thousands)

Net Receivables 23	4048	0	69	175	296	2187	3726	6412	22908	•	77014	1039469
Inventories 24	764	0	0	112	147	523	954	2790	10779	•	50408	133509
Net Property, Plant and Equipment 25	10384	0	102	1022	1655	5344	15539	26530	145537	•	514610	2074247
Total Assets 26	25853	0	240	2049	6926	15468	32262	69515	276671	•	1140085	5403109
Notes and Loans Payable 27	7249	0	88	2183	1377	10676	13094	23726	131136	•	468381	1106546
All Other Liabilities 28	13390	0	32	583	1126	10280	6414	25015	169942	•	683629	2779203
Net Worth 29	5215	0	119	-717	4423	-5488	12753	20774	-24408	•	-11925	1517360

Selected Financial Ratios (Times to 1)

Current Ratio 30	1.0	•	3.1	0.6	1.6	0.4	1.2	0.7	1.2	•	0.7	1.2
Quick Ratio 31	0.8	•	2.8	0.2	1.3	0.3	0.9	0.5	0.8	•	0.5	1.0
Net Sales to Working Capital 32	•	•	10.0	•	10.1	29.7	•	•	16.1	•	•	6.4
Coverage Ratio 33	•	•	•	•	•	•	1.7	•	1.7	•	0.4	0.3
Total Asset Turnover 34	0.5	•	3.1	0.7	0.8	1.6	1.2	1.4	0.6	•	0.6	0.3
Inventory Turnover 35	10.4	•	745.8	8.0	29.9	33.9	18.8	25.6	11.6	•	9.7	7.3
Receivables Turnover 36	3.2	•	1194.3	9.3	7.9	10.7	10.4	16.3	7.0	•	6.9	1.7
Total Liabilities to Net Worth 37	4.0	•	1.0	•	0.6	•	1.5	2.3	•	•	•	2.6
Current Assets to Working Capital 38	•	•	1.5	•	2.7	•	6.8	•	5.9	•	•	6.1
Current Liabilities to Working Capital 39	•	•	0.5	•	1.7	•	5.8	•	4.9	•	•	5.1
Working Capital to Net Sales 40	•	•	0.1	0.0	0.1	•	0.0	•	0.1	•	0.4	0.2
Inventory to Working Capital 41	•	•	•	•	0.1	•	0.9	•	0.9	•	•	0.7
Total Receipts to Cash Flow 42	•	•	•	•	•	•	6.1	27.1	13.2	•	•	188.3
Cost of Goods to Cash Flow 43	•	•	•	•	•	•	2.9	20.4	10.0	•	•	121.8
Cash Flow to Total Debt 44	•	•	•	•	•	•	0.3	0.1	0.0	•	•	0.0

Selected Financial Factors (in Percentages)

Debt Ratio 45	79.8	•	50.3	116.5	135.0	36.1	135.5	60.5	70.1	108.8	101.0	71.9
Return on Total Assets 46	•	•	•	•	47.6	•	4.5	•	•	•	2.0	0.4
Return on Equity Before Income Taxes 47	•	•	391.4	•	•	136.6	•	•	•	•	344.3	•
Return on Equity After Income Taxes 48	•	•	409.8	48.9	•	136.9	•	•	•	•	353.0	•
Profit Margin (Before Income Tax) 49	•	•	•	•	•	•	•	3.1	•	•	•	•
Profit Margin (After Income Tax) 50	•	•	•	•	•	•	•	1.4	•	•	•	•

Table II
Corporations with Net Income

COAL MINING

MONEY AMOUNTS AND SIZE OF ASSETS IN THOUSANDS OF DOLLARS

Item Description for Accounting Period 7/03 Through 6/04	Total	Zero Assets	Under 500	500 to 1,000	1,000 to 5,000	5,000 to 10,000	10,000 to 25,000	25,000 to 50,000	50,000 to 100,000	100,000 to 250,000	250,000 to 500,000	500,000 to 2,500,000	2,500,000 and over
Number of Enterprises 1	563	•	•	58	19	12	15	6	6	•	•	•	•
Revenues ($ in Thousands)													
Net Sales 2	3174105	•	•	0	39681	26059	427726	320458	418484	•	•	•	•
Interest 3	22667	•	•	182	169	34	1116	72	2926	•	•	•	•
Rents 4	5331	•	•	23	0	505	979	0	2596	•	•	•	•
Royalties 5	38916	•	•	5615	0	15845	1994	0	12623	•	•	•	•
Other Portfolio Income 6	142576	•	•	4286	4462	579	1837	177	15829	•	•	•	•
Other Receipts 7	249553	•	•	805	3210	9784	2731	13362	39486	•	•	•	•
Total Receipts 8	3633148	•	•	10911	47522	52806	436383	334069	491944	•	•	•	•
Average Total Receipts 9	6453	•	•	188	2501	4400	29092	55678	81991	•	•	•	•
Operating Costs/Operating Income (%)													
Cost of Operations 10	60.9	•	•	•	20.5	141.3	75.7	46.8	66.8	•	•	•	•
Salaries and Wages 11	8.2	•	•	•	6.4	0.3	3.3	7.8	2.0	•	•	•	•
Taxes Paid 12	6.6	•	•	•	4.7	15.6	2.9	4.7	6.2	•	•	•	•
Interest Paid 13	2.9	•	•	•	1.3	3.5	0.3	0.5	1.2	•	•	•	•
Depreciation 14	6.7	•	•	•	10.8	9.5	4.5	5.7	7.2	•	•	•	•
Amortization and Depletion 15	4.4	•	•	•	3.9	2.1	2.6	2.6	7.2	•	•	•	•
Pensions and Other Deferred Comp. 16	1.3	•	•	•	0.1	•	0.3	0.3	1.2	•	•	•	•
Employee Benefits 17	4.2	•	•	•	•	1.2	1.4	4.0	3.1	•	•	•	•
Advertising 18	0.0	•	•	•	•	•	0.0	0.0	0.0	•	•	•	•
Other Expenses 19	8.5	•	•	•	38.3	14.2	6.3	27.5	7.0	•	•	•	•
Officers' Compensation 20	1.0	•	•	•	2.4	0.8	1.1	0.8	0.9	•	•	•	•
Operating Margin 21	•	•	•	•	11.7	•	1.6	•	•	•	•	•	•
Operating Margin Before Officers' Comp. 22	•	•	•	•	14.1	•	2.6	0.0	•	•	•	•	•

Selected Average Balance Sheet ($ in Thousands)

	All						
Net Receivables 23	5205	1	601	1146	1871	5356	12944
Inventories 24	394	0	492	35	552	1338	2303
Net Property, Plant and Equipment 25	2842	67	725	1200	6517	9428	58518
Total Assets 26	19313	523	2613	5400	16191	34118	118731
Notes and Loans Payable 27	1437	0	1141	2908	2242	9414	40343
All Other Liabilities 28	6847	5	190	1190	3453	8290	67466
Net Worth 29	11028	518	1282	1302	10496	16414	10922

Selected Financial Ratios (Times to 1)

Current Ratio 30	1.5	97.0	10.2	1.8	1.8	1.6	1.6
Quick Ratio 31	1.3	96.0	7.5	1.7	1.4	1.3	1.3
Net Sales to Working Capital 32	2.6		1.3	3.9	10.5	11.7	5.7
Coverage Ratio 33	4.4	1307.0	26.1	5.1	11.7	7.6	13.7
Total Asset Turnover 34	0.3		0.8	0.4	1.8	1.6	0.6
Inventory Turnover 35	8.7		0.9	86.6	39.1	18.7	20.2
Receivables Turnover 36	1.1		1.6	3.8	9.9	8.2	10.8
Total Liabilities to Net Worth 37	0.8	0.0	1.0	3.1	0.5	1.1	9.9
Current Assets to Working Capital 38	3.1	1.0	1.1	2.3	2.3	2.6	2.7
Current Liabilities to Working Capital 39	2.1	0.0	0.1	1.3	1.3	1.6	1.7
Working Capital to Net Sales 40	0.4		0.7	0.3	0.1	0.2	0.2
Inventory to Working Capital 41	0.1		0.2	0.1	0.2	0.2	0.2
Total Receipts to Cash Flow 42	8.2		1.9	6.3	12.9	4.1	5.1
Cost of Goods to Cash Flow 43	5.0		0.4	8.8	9.8	1.9	3.4
Cash Flow to Total Debt 44	0.1	10.2	0.8	0.1	0.4	0.7	0.1

Selected Financial Factors (in Percentages)

Debt Ratio 45	42.9	0.9	50.9	75.9	35.2	51.9	90.8
Return on Total Assets 46	3.7	12.9	26.1	7.1	6.9	6.3	9.3
Return on Equity Before Income Taxes 47	5.0	13.0	51.2	23.7	9.7	11.3	94.1
Return on Equity After Income Taxes 48	4.6	8.8	43.2	22.0	9.3	11.2	77.3
Profit Margin (Before Income Tax) 49	9.7	31.5	14.2	3.6	11.2	3.5	14.7
Profit Margin (After Income Tax) 50	9.0	26.5	13.2	3.4	3.6	3.4	12.1

Table I

Corporations with and without Net Income

METAL ORE MINING

MONEY AMOUNTS AND SIZE OF ASSETS IN THOUSANDS OF DOLLARS

Item Description for Accounting Period 7/03 Through 6/04	Total	Zero Assets	Under 500	500 to 1,000	1,000 to 5,000	5,000 to 10,000	10,000 to 25,000	25,000 to 50,000	50,000 to 100,000	100,000 to 250,000	250,000 to 500,000	500,000 to 2,500,000	2,500,000 and over
Number of Enterprises **1**	1975	23	1751	59	52	21	23	16	7	4	7	6	7
Revenues ($ in Thousands)													
Net Sales **2**	16228920	374658	27846	6770	85	0	5011	195814	106860	481064	1107806	2556539	11366466
Interest **3**	374024	4442	203	5	1703	1417	907	2686	2174	995	12312	40419	306762
Rents **4**	24720	0	4305	0	55	0	411	835	0	0	190	1146	17779
Royalties **5**	132734	0	0	0	0	0	0	262	20148	5	3234	30632	78453
Other Portfolio Income **6**	226046	3278	521	0	0	0	392	6262	2589	128	21743	31931	159201
Other Receipts **7**	398930	-12438	10580	680	190	0	47	1636	3080	15343	16218	91423	272171
Total Receipts **8**	17385374	369940	43455	7455	2033	1417	6768	207495	134851	497535	1161503	2752090	12200832
Average Total Receipts **9**	8803	16084	25	126	39	67	294	12968	19264	124384	165929	458682	1742976
Operating Costs/Operating Income (%)													
Cost of Operations **10**	58.1	39.1	24.0	13.0	•	•	0.1	73.9	58.3	75.6	61.9	88.4	50.7
Salaries and Wages **11**	3.8	14.9	28.4	20.3	21700.0	•	42.5	6.7	1.8	2.1	1.8	0.7	4.1
Taxes Paid **12**	2.2	2.5	8.1	2.3	1456.5	•	12.1	1.3	3.4	0.8	1.4	1.6	2.4
Interest Paid **13**	5.5	6.2	6.2	0.5	5121.2	•	74.6	1.6	6.0	0.5	1.7	3.6	6.5
Depreciation **14**	9.8	16.7	33.9	4.9	814.1	•	19.7	13.8	7.0	7.1	7.2	5.3	10.8
Amortization and Depletion **15**	10.2	9.1	10.8	0.1	1947.1	•	87.2	6.0	22.7	7.6	10.6	3.4	11.7
Pensions and Other Deferred Comp. **16**	0.7	0.6	•	1.8	4.7	•	0.3	0.0	0.3	0.0	0.2	1.0	0.7
Employee Benefits **17**	1.6	0.2	5.7	2.6	6803.5	•	5.5	0.7	0.9	0.0	0.6	0.7	2.0
Advertising **18**	0.0	0.0	0.0	•	116.5	•	0.2	0.0	0.0	•	0.0	0.0	0.1
Other Expenses **19**	13.0	20.2	256.9	87.5	•	•	326.7	38.5	25.4	18.4	18.9	6.8	11.9
Officers' Compensation **20**	0.7	•	22.4	9.5	350.6	•	14.1	4.0	3.7	0.9	1.1	0.4	0.6
Operating Margin **21**	•	•	•	•	•	•	•	•	•	•	•	•	•
Operating Margin Before Officers' Comp. **22**	•	•	•	•	•	•	•	•	•	•	•	•	•

Selected Average Balance Sheet ($ in Thousands)

Line Item													
Net Receivables 23	2752	0	0	7	19	1679	4001	1430	17274	8252	171807	594858
Inventories 24	1161	0	0	4	1326	1727	1628	19167	26171	104002	191275	
Net Property, Plant and Equipment 25	8874	0	7	497	1122	3508	13663	3744	37807	48751	115731	413106	1899928
Total Assets 26	34986	0	90	638	2119	15701	32427	84983	157943	299834	1050238	8302049
Notes and Loans Payable 27	5868	0	18	51	188	7589	12969	22188	11669	76837	167352	1307054
All Other Liabilities 28	8002	0	77	42	349	5699	15710	11583	98499	109685	451931	1614935
Net Worth 29	21116	0	-6	546	1583	2413	3748	51213	47775	113312	430954	5380060

Selected Financial Ratios (Times to 1)

Line Item													
Current Ratio 30	1.7	•	0.9	0.3	2.2	1.6	2.1	3.2	0.5	1.4	1.4	1.5	1.9
Quick Ratio 31	1.2	•	0.9	0.2	1.8	1.1	1.2	2.6	0.2	0.7	0.7	1.0	1.4
Net Sales to Working Capital 32	3.3	•	•	•	0.0	0.1	1.6	1.2	•	6.5	3.8	2.7
Coverage Ratio 33	1.5	•	•	•	•	0.4	•	1.1	•	•	2.2
Total Asset Turnover 34	0.2	•	0.2	0.2	0.0	0.4	0.2	0.2	0.8	0.5	0.4	0.2
Inventory Turnover 35	4.1	•	•	7.1	•	5.2	5.5	•	4.7	3.7	3.6	4.3
Receivables Turnover 36	3.1	•	663.0	4.6	0.1	0.1	3.0	14.1	6.9	25.2	2.4	2.9
Total Liabilities to Net Worth 37	0.7	•	•	0.2	0.3	5.5	7.7	0.7	2.3	1.6	1.4	0.5
Current Assets to Working Capital 38	2.5	•	•	•	1.9	2.7	1.9	1.4	•	3.6	3.0	2.1
Current Liabilities to Working Capital 39	1.5	•	•	•	0.9	1.7	0.9	0.4	•	2.6	2.0	1.1
Working Capital to Net Sales 40	0.3	•	•	186.5	8.8	0.6	0.9	•	0.2	0.3	0.4
Inventory to Working Capital 41	0.5	•	•	0.0	0.6	0.3	0.1	•	1.2	0.9	0.3
Total Receipts to Cash Flow 42	10.8	18.9	2.1	•	•	5.7	•	6.2	83.5	8.6
Cost of Goods to Cash Flow 43	6.3	7.4	0.3	•	•	3.3	•	3.9	73.8	4.3
Cash Flow to Total Debt 44	0.1	•	0.6	0.0	0.0	0.1	•	0.1	0.0	0.1

Selected Financial Factors (in Percentages)

Line Item													
Debt Ratio 45	39.6	•	106.1	14.4	25.3	161.5	84.6	88.4	39.7	69.8	62.2	59.0	35.2
Return on Total Assets 46	2.0	•	•	•	•	•	•	•	0.5	•	1.0	•	2.8
Return on Equity Before Income Taxes 47	1.1	•	698.2	•	13.1	•	•	•	•	•	0.3	•	2.3
Return on Equity After Income Taxes 48	0.0	•	698.2	•	13.1	•	•	•	•	•	•	•	1.2
Profit Margin (Before Income Tax) 49	2.9	•	•	•	•	•	•	•	•	•	0.2	•	7.8
Profit Margin (After Income Tax) 50	0.1	•	•	•	•	•	•	•	•	•	•	•	3.8

Table II

Corporations with Net Income

METAL ORE MINING

MONEY AMOUNTS AND SIZE OF ASSETS IN THOUSANDS OF DOLLARS

Item Description for Accounting Period 7/03 Through 6/04	Total	Zero Assets	Under 500	500 to 1,000	1,000 to 5,000	5,000 to 10,000	10,000 to 25,000	25,000 to 50,000	50,000 to 100,000	100,000 to 250,000	250,000 to 500,000	500,000 to 2,500,000	2,500,000 and over
Number of Enterprises **1**	47	·	·	·	31	·	3	·	3	·	3	·	·
Revenues ($ in Thousands)													
Net Sales **2**	6119610	·	·	·	0	·	4962	·	318565	·	634149	·	·
Interest **3**	167135	·	·	·	1625	·	59	·	434	·	28463	·	·
Rents **4**	4788	·	·	·	0	·	0	·	0	·	193	·	·
Royalties **5**	78285	·	·	·	0	·	0	·	20129	·	11326	·	·
Other Portfolio Income **6**	103281	·	·	·	0	·	0	·	19	·	1898	·	·
Other Receipts **7**	113875	·	·	·	0	·	1908	·	670	·	10033	·	·
Total Receipts **8**	6586974	·	·	·	1625	·	6929	·	339817	·	686062	·	·
Average Total Receipts **9**	140148	·	·	·	52	·	2310	·	113272	·	228687	·	·
Operating Costs/Operating Income (%)													
Cost of Operations **10**	36.6	·	·	·	·	·	·	·	87.4	·	42.6	·	·
Salaries and Wages **11**	5.0	·	·	·	·	·	1.8	·	0.7	·	2.0	·	·
Taxes Paid **12**	0.7	·	·	·	·	·	0.1	·	0.8	·	1.7	·	·
Interest Paid **13**	5.0	·	·	·	·	·	0.0	·	0.9	·	1.5	·	·
Depreciation **14**	9.9	·	·	·	·	·	0.5	·	1.7	·	9.7	·	·
Amortization and Depletion **15**	16.5	·	·	·	·	·	22.0	·	3.6	·	17.0	·	·
Pensions and Other Deferred Comp. **16**	0.4	·	·	·	·	·	0.0	·	0.0	·	0.0	·	·
Employee Benefits **17**	0.1	·	·	·	·	·	0.1	·	·	·	0.2	·	·
Advertising **18**	0.1	·	·	·	·	·	·	·	·	·	·	·	·
Other Expenses **19**	13.3	·	·	·	·	·	54.6	·	6.3	·	17.8	·	·
Officers' Compensation **20**	0.7	·	·	·	·	·	·	·	0.5	·	0.1	·	·
Operating Margin **21**	11.6	·	·	·	·	·	20.9	·	·	·	7.4	·	·
Operating Margin Before Officers' Comp. **22**	12.3	·	·	·	·	·	20.9	·	·	·	7.5	·	·

Selected Average Balance Sheet ($ in Thousands)

Net Receivables 23	60560	0	6708	17465	7291
Inventories 24	11527	0	2625	6729	12104
Net Property, Plant and Equipment 25	132375	0	4924	46339	237368
Total Assets 26	702361	1021	20286	108499	387059
Notes and Loans Payable 27	78604	0	10757	19287	96478
All Other Liabilities 28	141686	9	-1373	100977	98049
Net Worth 29	482071	1012	10902	-11765	192533

Selected Financial Ratios (Times to 1)

Current Ratio 30	1.9	28.9	7.4	0.6	1.5
Quick Ratio 31	1.5	27.9	7.3	0.5	1.2
Net Sales to Working Capital 32	2.3		0.2		6.7
Coverage Ratio 33	5.5	1502.5	6.7	6.7	11.7
Total Asset Turnover 34	0.2	0.1	0.1	1.0	0.5
Inventory Turnover 35	4.1			13.8	7.4
Receivables Turnover 36	2.4		0.3	12.2	58.0
Total Liabilities to Net Worth 37	0.5	0.0	0.9		1.0
Current Assets to Working Capital 38	2.2	1.0	1.2		2.9
Current Liabilities to Working Capital 39	1.2	0.0	0.2		1.9
Working Capital to Net Sales 40	0.4		5.4		0.1
Inventory to Working Capital 41	0.2				0.4
Total Receipts to Cash Flow 42	4.0		0.9	9.1	3.3
Cost of Goods to Cash Flow 43	1.5			8.0	1.4
Cash Flow to Total Debt 44	0.1	5.2	0.2	0.1	0.3

Selected Financial Factors (in Percentages)

Debt Ratio 45	31.4	0.9	46.3	110.8	50.3
Return on Total Assets 46	5.1	3.2	4.9	5.6	9.3
Return on Equity Before Income Taxes 47	6.1	3.2	9.2		17.1
Return on Equity After Income Taxes 48	4.1	2.7	7.1		15.8
Profit Margin (Before Income Tax) 49	22.5		60.5	4.8	15.6
Profit Margin (After Income Tax) 50	15.1		46.6	4.7	14.4

Table I
Corporations with and without Net Income

NONMETALLIC MINERAL MINING AND QUARRYING

MONEY AMOUNTS AND SIZE OF ASSETS IN THOUSANDS OF DOLLARS

Item Description for Accounting Period 7/03 Through 6/04	Total	Zero Assets	Under 500	500 to 1,000	1,000 to 5,000	5,000 to 10,000	10,000 to 25,000	25,000 to 50,000	50,000 to 100,000	100,000 to 250,000	250,000 to 500,000	500,000 to 2,500,000	2,500,000 and over
Number of Enterprises 1	4883	1259	2368	454	476	82	143	48	23	17	5	9	·
Revenues ($ in Thousands)													
Net Sales 2	20353566	294201	229334	333441	1268426	753638	1903222	1180609	1474035	1884767	1430485	9601407	·
Interest 3	101811	325	84	1010	730	390	3836	2573	6989	8972	2521	74381	·
Rents 4	48757	0	0	520	327	568	2994	7494	7267	6702	519	22366	·
Royalties 5	35816	0	0	0	0	9927	33	240	0	1651	196	23768	·
Other Portfolio Income 6	372651	924	1142	302	947	1443	18252	13600	21717	62078	1795	250453	·
Other Receipts 7	338064	862	11567	7200	5518	18101	21566	19585	22760	23301	43644	163960	·
Total Receipts 8	21250665	296312	242127	342473	1275948	784067	1949903	1224101	1532768	1987471	1479160	10136335	·
Average Total Receipts 9	4352	235	102	754	2681	9562	13636	25502	66642	116910	295832	1126259	·
Operating Costs/Operating Income (%)													
Cost of Operations 10	61.6	10.3	30.3	55.1	54.5	65.0	62.0	66.5	70.0	64.9	61.0	62.3	·
Salaries and Wages 11	4.6	22.4	6.3	7.0	2.1	3.6	4.6	4.1	5.2	4.5	4.1	4.4	·
Taxes Paid 12	3.0	7.0	3.9	5.2	4.1	2.8	2.9	3.0	2.3	2.0	4.1	2.9	·
Interest Paid 13	3.2	1.4	5.0	1.6	2.5	1.9	1.6	1.3	1.3	2.7	3.5	4.3	·
Depreciation 14	8.3	2.0	17.7	3.1	7.1	8.0	8.8	10.0	7.7	8.8	7.1	8.5	·
Amortization and Depletion 15	3.0	6.6	0.3	1.7	1.2	1.2	2.2	2.5	2.2	3.2	3.6	3.6	·
Pensions and Other Deferred Comp. 16	1.3	0.2	0.0	0.3	1.1	0.2	0.6	0.7	0.9	1.1	0.8	2.0	·
Employee Benefits 17	2.3	0.0	1.1	1.7	1.7	2.6	1.6	1.1	3.0	3.4	3.9	2.2	·
Advertising 18	0.2	0.3	0.4	0.4	0.1	0.2	0.3	0.1	0.3	0.2	0.1	0.1	·
Other Expenses 19	13.1	55.1	23.2	12.7	20.6	12.9	10.8	8.9	11.3	8.9	13.6	12.7	·
Officers' Compensation 20	1.3	5.6	0.9	2.7	2.8	2.4	2.5	2.5	1.3	2.1	0.9	0.3	·
Operating Margin 21	·	·	10.9	8.5	2.3	·	2.0	·	·	·	·	·	·
Operating Margin Before Officers' Comp. 22	·	·	11.8	11.2	5.1	1.5	4.5	1.8	·	·	·	0.3	·

Selected Average Balance Sheet ($ in Thousands)

Net Receivables 23	515	0	2	100	306	1473	2038	3322	10530	17041	35034	115492 •
Inventories 24	405	0	11	106	94	534	1454	2592	5652	13569	29429	108505 •
Net Property, Plant and Equipment 25	2392	0	34	350	1233	3424	6234	15210	34726	68060	167571	683969 •
Total Assets 26	8030	0	70	697	2169	7902	15008	33089	72165	154348	374026	3017835 •
Notes and Loans Payable 27	1740	0	54	218	956	3903	4379	6527	27898	35035	170185	496483 •
All Other Liabilities 28	1147	0	11	200	340	1226	2003	4788	19223	39126	57839	367697 •
Net Worth 29	5143	0	5	279	873	2774	8627	21773	25044	80187	146003	2153654 •

Selected Financial Ratios (Times to 1)

Current Ratio 30	2.0	•	1.1	1.1	1.9	2.4	2.4	2.1	1.4	2.1	1.3	2.1 •
Quick Ratio 31	1.1	•	0.5	1.0	1.6	1.4	1.6	1.5	0.9	1.0	0.6	1.1 •
Net Sales to Working Capital 32	4.9	•	44.7	40.4	6.2	4.3	3.5	4.0	8.1	4.0	16.4	4.5 •
Coverage Ratio 33	1.8	•	4.3	8.1	2.1	2.7	3.7	3.2	•	2.3	1.2	1.6 •
Total Asset Turnover 34	0.5	•	1.4	1.1	1.2	1.2	0.9	0.7	0.9	0.7	0.8	0.4 •
Inventory Turnover 35	6.3	•	2.6	3.8	15.5	11.2	5.7	6.3	7.9	5.3	5.9	6.1 •
Receivables Turnover 36	7.7	•	13.8	5.6	7.4	6.2	6.9	6.7	8.2	6.8	8.0	8.2 •
Total Liabilities to Net Worth 37	0.6	•	14.5	1.5	1.5	1.8	0.7	0.5	1.9	0.9	1.6	0.4 •
Current Assets to Working Capital 38	2.0	•	9.7	12.4	2.1	1.7	1.7	1.9	3.3	1.9	4.9	1.9 •
Current Liabilities to Working Capital 39	1.0	•	8.7	11.4	1.1	0.7	0.7	0.9	2.3	0.9	3.9	0.9 •
Working Capital to Net Sales 40	0.2	•	0.0	0.0	0.2	0.2	0.3	0.3	0.1	0.2	0.1	0.2 •
Inventory to Working Capital 41	0.5	•	3.8	1.1	0.3	0.2	0.4	0.4	1.0	0.5	1.6	0.4 •
Total Receipts to Cash Flow 42	10.7	5.1	3.9	4.9	7.1	10.4	9.4	11.1	21.8	12.2	10.4	11.9 •
Cost of Goods to Cash Flow 43	6.6	0.5	1.2	2.7	3.9	6.8	5.9	7.3	15.3	7.9	6.4	7.4 •
Cash Flow to Total Debt 44	0.1	•	0.4	0.4	0.3	0.2	0.2	0.2	0.1	0.1	0.1	0.1 •

Selected Financial Factors (in Percentages)

Debt Ratio 45	36.0	•	93.5	59.8	59.9	64.9	42.5	34.2	65.3	48.0	61.0	28.6 •
Return on Total Assets 46	3.0	•	29.8	13.4	6.6	6.0	5.4	3.2	•	4.5	3.2	2.4 •
Return on Equity Before Income Taxes 47	2.1	•	353.8	29.4	8.7	10.6	6.8	3.3	8.1	5.0	1.3	1.3 •
Return on Equity After Income Taxes 48	1.4	•	352.2	29.4	8.7	8.8	6.2	2.3	•	2.8	0.9	0.7 •
Profit Margin (Before Income Tax) 49	2.6	•	16.5	11.2	2.9	3.2	2.9	2.9	•	3.6	0.7	2.5 •
Profit Margin (After Income Tax) 50	1.8	•	16.4	11.2	2.8	2.7	2.0	2.0	•	2.0	0.5	1.5 •

MINING
212315

Table II
Corporations with Net Income

NONMETALLIC MINERAL MINING AND QUARRYING

MONEY AMOUNTS AND SIZE OF ASSETS IN THOUSANDS OF DOLLARS

Item Description for Accounting Period 7/03 Through 6/04	Total	Zero Assets	Under 500	500 to 1,000	1,000 to 5,000	5,000 to 10,000	10,000 to 25,000	25,000 to 50,000	50,000 to 100,000	100,000 to 250,000	250,000 to 500,000	500,000 to 2,500,000	2,500,000 and over
Number of Enterprises **1**	2924	•	1593	•	388	38	97	31	12	13	•	6	•
Revenues ($ in Thousands)													
Net Sales **2**	14370030	•	184280	•	1154857	291726	1317789	841523	723387	1441277	•	7172277	•
Interest **3**	87682	•	81	•	210	188	2522	1946	4804	7825	•	67391	•
Rents **4**	27117	•	0	•	327	315	2226	3514	4420	5574	•	10557	•
Royalties **5**	23134	•	0	•	0	9927	5	230	0	1252	•	11530	•
Other Portfolio Income **6**	341863	•	0	•	54	1230	15394	10181	14779	56007	•	242134	•
Other Receipts **7**	193105	•	11539	•	4788	11508	21432	10406	11258	17795	•	75174	•
Total Receipts **8**	15042931	•	195900	•	1160236	314894	1359368	867800	758648	1529730	•	7579063	•
Average Total Receipts **9**	5145	•	123	•	2990	8287	14014	27994	63221	117672	•	1263177	•
Operating Costs/Operating Income (%)													
Cost of Operations **10**	58.8	•	27.4	•	52.9	57.5	58.6	63.7	61.3	62.0	•	58.5	•
Salaries and Wages **11**	4.5	•	4.1	•	2.1	3.2	4.4	4.1	6.2	4.4	•	5.0	•
Taxes Paid **12**	3.0	•	3.1	•	4.0	2.8	3.1	2.8	2.2	2.2	•	3.1	•
Interest Paid **13**	3.0	•	4.7	•	2.5	1.3	1.3	0.6	1.6	1.5	•	4.3	•
Depreciation **14**	8.1	•	18.7	•	6.9	8.2	8.5	8.7	5.9	9.4	•	8.4	•
Amortization and Depletion **15**	2.8	•	•	•	1.3	2.1	2.5	2.8	2.9	2.9	•	3.3	•
Pensions and Other Deferred Comp. **16**	1.7	•	0.0	•	1.2	0.3	0.8	0.7	0.8	1.4	•	2.5	•
Employee Benefits **17**	2.0	•	0.8	•	1.7	4.4	1.7	1.0	2.5	2.8	•	1.7	•
Advertising **18**	0.2	•	0.3	•	0.1	0.1	0.2	0.1	0.3	0.2	•	0.1	•
Other Expenses **19**	13.1	•	18.5	•	20.9	13.2	9.6	6.6	13.7	8.3	•	14.3	•
Officers' Compensation **20**	1.2	•	0.1	•	2.8	2.4	2.8	2.9	1.4	2.3	•	0.3	•
Operating Margin **21**	1.5	•	22.5	•	3.6	4.4	6.5	6.0	1.1	2.7	•	•	•
Operating Margin Before Officers' Comp. **22**	2.8	•	22.6	•	6.4	6.9	9.3	8.9	2.5	4.9	•	•	•

Selected Average Balance Sheet ($ in Thousands)

Net Receivables 23	535	2	312	1242	2151	3518	9277	16267	97888
Inventories 24	470	17	94	634	1430	2613	5514	13823	104190
Net Property, Plant and Equipment 25	2776	31	1444	3632	6001	13773	36444	69195	736060
Total Assets 26	10434	68	2368	8799	14736	32124	70538	155893	3750692
Notes and Loans Payable 27	1666	45	1001	4191	3041	4123	20765	30124	443063
All Other Liabilities 28	1256	15	382	1200	1906	4809	16771	26813	388711
Net Worth 29	7511	9	986	3407	9789	23193	33002	98957	2918918

Selected Financial Ratios (Times to 1)

Current Ratio 30	2.2	1.5	1.6	2.8	2.9	1.6	2.5	2.2
Quick Ratio 31	1.2	0.6	1.4	2.0	2.0	1.0	1.2	1.1
Net Sales to Working Capital 32	4.3	13.0	8.6	3.1	3.3	6.3	3.3	4.2
Coverage Ratio 33	3.1	7.2	2.6	8.5	15.3	4.6	6.8	2.1
Total Asset Turnover 34	0.5	1.7	1.3	0.9	0.8	0.9	0.7	0.3
Inventory Turnover 35	6.1	1.9	16.7	5.6	6.6	6.7	5.0	6.7
Receivables Turnover 36	8.0	11.1	9.9	7.2	7.4	8.4	13.6	24.4
Total Liabilities to Net Worth 37	0.4	6.8	1.4	0.5	0.4	1.1	0.6	0.3
Current Assets to Working Capital 38	1.9	3.1	2.6	1.5	1.5	2.7	1.7	1.8
Current Liabilities to Working Capital 39	0.9	2.1	1.6	0.5	0.5	1.7	0.7	0.8
Working Capital to Net Sales 40	0.2	0.1	0.1	0.3	0.3	0.2	0.3	0.2
Inventory to Working Capital 41	0.4	1.4	0.3	0.3	0.3	0.7	0.4	0.4
Total Receipts to Cash Flow 42	7.9	2.8	6.5	6.8	7.4	7.2	8.4	9.2
Cost of Goods to Cash Flow 43	4.7	0.8	3.4	4.0	4.7	4.4	5.2	5.4
Cash Flow to Total Debt 44	0.2	0.7	0.3	0.4	0.4	0.2	0.2	0.2

Selected Financial Factors (in Percentages)

Debt Ratio 45	28.0	87.2	58.4	61.3	33.6	27.8	53.2	36.5	22.2
Return on Total Assets 46	4.4	56.9	8.3	11.9	10.0	8.2	6.5	7.3	2.8
Return on Equity Before Income Taxes 47	4.1	380.9	12.3	27.9	13.3	10.7	10.9	9.8	1.9
Return on Equity After Income Taxes 48	3.4	379.7	12.3	24.9	12.5	9.2	8.9	7.5	1.3
Profit Margin (Before Income Tax) 49	6.3	28.8	4.1	12.4	9.6	9.1	6.0	8.7	4.6
Profit Margin (After Income Tax) 50	5.2	28.7	4.1	11.1	9.0	7.9	4.9	6.7	3.1

Table I

Corporations with and without Net Income

SUPPORT ACTIVITIES FOR MINING

MONEY AMOUNTS AND SIZE OF ASSETS IN THOUSANDS OF DOLLARS

Item Description for Accounting Period 7/03 Through 6/04	Total	Zero Assets	Under 500	500 to 1,000	1,000 to 5,000	5,000 to 10,000	10,000 to 25,000	25,000 to 50,000	50,000 to 100,000	100,000 to 250,000	250,000 to 500,000	500,000 to 2,500,000	2,500,000 and over
Number of Enterprises 1	6141	438	4183	761	618	29	47	18	7	6	8	19	7
Revenues ($ in Thousands)													
Net Sales 2	39187535	328888	2092635	1398893	1824478	157431	857351	650436	337426	834429	1617426	9810874	19277266
Interest 3	517473	487	988	159	3378	1922	820	2116	1126	2824	38399	101321	363933
Rents 4	142036	0	0	0	304	0	1847	1687	1206	11962	5307	113458	6266
Royalties 5	113576	0	0	4390	3372	30	1	125	0	59	4	32435	73160
Other Portfolio Income 6	504549	235	6239	1683	6521	9255	10658	2801	1631	3185	37673	85147	339523
Other Receipts 7	708101	-42	5215	3772	136506	1047	13083	7445	4446	4375	21275	158505	352473
Total Receipts 8	41173270	329568	2105077	1408897	1974559	169685	883760	664610	345835	856834	1720084	10301740	20412621
Average Total Receipts 9	6705	752	503	1851	3195	5851	18803	36923	49405	142806	215010	542197	2916089
Operating Costs/Operating Income (%)													
Cost of Operations 10	57.3	31.7	23.4	41.7	17.7	49.6	48.5	53.5	51.5	72.7	58.3	50.0	70.0
Salaries and Wages 11	12.3	10.0	15.0	18.3	23.2	10.6	13.4	12.3	17.0	7.3	7.0	12.4	11.1
Taxes Paid 12	2.1	1.9	3.6	3.7	3.8	2.8	2.6	3.9	2.2	2.0	3.4	2.0	1.5
Interest Paid 13	4.5	3.6	0.4	1.0	2.0	1.3	1.2	2.1	2.2	2.1	3.2	5.6	5.4
Depreciation 14	10.4	24.2	3.0	7.7	9.4	6.4	6.1	11.0	9.4	8.9	10.2	16.1	8.6
Amortization and Depletion 15	0.6	0.1	0.0	0.1	0.5	0.4	0.2	0.4	0.3	0.7	1.1	1.3	0.4
Pensions and Other Deferred Comp. 16	0.7	2.2	0.3	0.1	0.2	0.3	0.2	0.4	0.2	0.1	0.7	0.3	1.0
Employee Benefits 17	2.2	5.7	1.4	2.3	1.9	1.3	1.2	1.3	0.7	1.0	3.2	2.7	2.0
Advertising 18	0.2	0.1	0.3	0.2	0.3	0.4	0.2	0.2	0.1	0.1	0.1	0.2	0.1
Other Expenses 19	15.3	29.9	40.7	20.2	42.3	19.6	21.8	12.7	21.6	8.5	16.1	20.3	6.8
Officers' Compensation 20	1.3	3.6	6.6	7.1	2.9	3.9	2.2	1.3	0.3	1.0	0.5	0.7	0.4
Operating Margin 21	•	•	5.2	•	•	3.6	2.5	1.0	•	•	•	•	•
Operating Margin Before Officers' Comp. 22	•	•	11.8	4.8	7.4	7.4	4.7	2.2	•	•	•	•	•

Selected Average Balance Sheet ($ in Thousands)

Net Receivables 23	1368	0	16	104	456	1851	4096	8453	21473	30856	71888	131807	593852
Inventories 24	309	0	0	10	100	76	583	1222	4710	6960	13638	36064	129794
Net Property, Plant and Equipment 25	3911	0	53	316	991	1765	3830	16524	19771	69788	105702	615786	1330441
Total Assets 26	13372	0	120	657	2154	6480	15145	35517	89840	150111	331709	1203221	7314078
Notes and Loans Payable 27	4218	0	45	406	1310	1361	3973	14064	30362	57376	95202	411687	2139354
All Other Liabilities 28	2516	0	30	86	248	1296	4205	9730	37801	29280	67709	188006	1448569
Net Worth 29	6638	0	45	165	595	3823	6967	11722	21677	63455	168799	603528	3726156

Selected Financial Ratios (Times to 1)

Current Ratio 30	2.6	•	1.9	1.0	2.8	1.9	1.7	1.2	1.1	1.6	3.8	1.9	3.6
Quick Ratio 31	1.8	•	1.7	0.9	2.3	1.8	1.3	1.0	0.9	1.3	3.0	1.2	2.5
Net Sales to Working Capital 32	3.1	•	23.2	211.6	5.2	3.4	5.3	13.8	20.5	7.7	2.6	3.7	2.3
Coverage Ratio 33	0.8	•	14.4	•	3.0	9.8	5.7	2.4	•	2.2	2.2	•	1.0
Total Asset Turnover 34	0.5	•	4.2	2.8	1.4	0.8	1.2	1.0	0.5	0.9	0.6	0.4	0.4
Inventory Turnover 35	11.8	•	301.7	74.9	5.2	35.5	15.2	15.8	5.3	14.5	8.6	7.2	14.9
Receivables Turnover 36	4.9	•	33.1	18.8	6.9	2.5	4.8	5.2	2.8	5.3	2.8	4.0	5.0
Total Liabilities to Net Worth 37	1.0	•	1.7	3.0	2.6	0.7	1.2	2.0	3.1	1.4	1.0	1.0	1.0
Current Assets to Working Capital 38	1.6	•	2.2	28.0	1.5	2.1	2.4	5.9	12.3	2.6	1.4	2.1	1.4
Current Liabilities to Working Capital 39	0.6	•	1.2	27.0	0.5	1.1	1.4	4.9	11.3	1.6	0.4	1.1	0.4
Working Capital to Net Sales 40	0.3	•	0.0	0.0	0.2	0.3	0.2	0.1	0.0	0.1	0.4	0.3	0.4
Inventory to Working Capital 41	0.2	•	0.0	1.9	0.0	0.0	0.2	0.4	1.5	0.3	0.2	0.3	0.1
Total Receipts to Cash Flow 42	12.2	8.4	2.3	7.3	2.8	4.0	4.7	7.9	6.4	33.1	7.6	13.5	169.8
Cost of Goods to Cash Flow 43	7.0	2.7	0.5	3.0	0.5	2.0	2.3	4.2	3.3	24.0	4.4	6.7	118.9
Cash Flow to Total Debt 44	0.1	•	2.8	0.5	0.7	0.5	0.2	0.2	0.1	0.0	0.2	0.1	0.0

Selected Financial Factors (in Percentages)

Debt Ratio 45	50.4	•	62.8	74.9	72.4	41.0	54.0	67.0	75.9	57.7	49.1	49.8	49.1
Return on Total Assets 46	1.7	•	25.8	•	8.4	10.6	8.0	5.3	•	0.3	4.2	•	2.0
Return on Equity Before Income Taxes 47	•	•	64.7	•	20.1	16.2	14.4	9.5	•	•	4.4	•	•
Return on Equity After Income Taxes 48	•	•	64.4	•	14.0	14.6	12.0	6.8	•	•	2.3	•	•
Profit Margin (Before Income Tax) 49	•	•	5.8	•	4.1	11.4	5.5	3.1	•	•	•	•	•
Profit Margin (After Income Tax) 50	•	•	5.7	•	2.8	10.3	4.6	2.2	•	•	•	•	•

Table II

Corporations with Net Income

SUPPORT ACTIVITIES FOR MINING

MONEY AMOUNTS AND SIZE OF ASSETS IN THOUSANDS OF DOLLARS

Item Description for Accounting Period 7/03 Through 6/04	Total	Zero Assets	Under 500	500 to 1,000	1,000 to 5,000	5,000 to 10,000	10,000 to 25,000	25,000 to 50,000	50,000 to 100,000	100,000 to 250,000	250,000 to 500,000	500,000 to 2,500,000	2,500,000 and over
Number of Enterprises **1**	3267	415	2071	•	352	16	31	12	4	•	•	8	•
Revenues ($ in Thousands)													
Net Sales **2**	2329091	113633	1310905	•	1150755	86386	505275	453255	573190	•	•	17759449	•
Interest **3**	374673	64	584	•	2660	1894	347	1632	3204	•	•	325937	•
Rents **4**	31396	0	0	•	77	0	1756	795	12501	•	•	10964	•
Royalties **5**	106141	0	0	•	3372	30	1	125	59	•	•	98164	•
Other Portfolio Income **6**	395597	0	150	•	5858	8670	9227	2025	4036	•	•	327698	•
Other Receipts **7**	362498	0	1004	•	127119	850	12724	6142	2607	•	•	188226	•
Total Receipts **8**	24563396	113697	1312643	•	1289841	97830	529330	463974	595597	•	•	18710438	•
Average Total Receipts **9**	7519	274	634	•	3664	6114	17075	38664	148899	•	•	2338805	•
Operating Costs/Operating Income (%)													
Cost of Operations **10**	62.3	•	2.3	•	18.7	48.7	46.6	56.2	57.2	•	•	72.5	•
Salaries and Wages **11**	11.3	26.3	18.2	•	23.9	5.2	13.7	9.3	11.4	•	•	9.9	•
Taxes Paid **12**	1.9	3.2	4.1	•	3.7	1.1	3.1	4.1	2.4	•	•	1.4	•
Interest Paid **13**	2.7	2.8	0.3	•	0.9	0.4	1.0	1.0	2.2	•	•	3.1	•
Depreciation **14**	5.9	3.5	1.4	•	6.9	4.1	4.8	8.8	7.1	•	•	5.8	•
Amortization and Depletion **15**	0.2	•	0.0	•	0.2	0.1	0.1	0.2	0.2	•	•	0.2	•
Pensions and Other Deferred Comp. **16**	0.3	6.2	0.4	•	0.2	0.3	0.2	0.5	0.2	•	•	0.3	•
Employee Benefits **17**	1.5	15.3	0.1	•	1.1	0.4	1.3	1.3	0.0	•	•	1.5	•
Advertising **18**	0.2	•	0.2	•	0.3	0.1	0.2	0.2	0.1	•	•	0.1	•
Other Expenses **19**	12.4	15.5	52.5	•	41.0	14.4	17.6	10.9	16.5	•	•	6.5	•
Officers' Compensation **20**	1.2	10.2	4.9	•	2.7	2.9	2.7	1.3	1.0	•	•	0.5	•
Operating Margin **21**	0.2	16.9	15.6	•	0.4	22.3	8.6	6.0	1.7	•	•	•	•
Operating Margin Before Officers' Comp. **22**	1.4	27.1	20.4	•	3.1	25.2	11.3	7.3	2.7	•	•	•	•

Selected Average Balance Sheet ($ in Thousands)

Net Receivables 23	1443	0	13	668	657	3493	9952	35162	440484
Inventories 24	402	0	0	150	115	618	1064	5615	134720
Net Property, Plant and Equipment 25	2211	0	64	498	1879	3666	14717	37318	729244
Total Assets 26	11796	0	159	1730	7131	14009	34930	135578	4228042
Notes and Loans Payable 27	2305	0	61	466	1370	3310	8552	57219	765748
All Other Liabilities 28	2406	0	37	246	619	3487	9709	19426	913644
Net Worth 29	7085	0	61	1018	5141	7213	16669	58934	2548650

Selected Financial Ratios (Times to 1)

Current Ratio 30	4.2	•	1.6	3.4	4.4	2.3	1.7	2.5	4.6
Quick Ratio 31	2.8	•	1.5	2.8	3.9	1.8	1.4	1.9	2.9
Net Sales to Working Capital 32	2.6	•	28.5	4.1	2.2	3.8	5.3	4.6	2.3
Coverage Ratio 33	3.6	7.0	52.6	14.6	83.5	14.0	9.7	3.6	2.6
Total Asset Turnover 34	0.6	•	4.0	1.9	0.8	1.2	1.1	1.1	0.5
Inventory Turnover 35	11.1	•	1014.0	4.1	22.9	12.3	20.0	14.6	11.9
Receivables Turnover 36	4.8	•	31.6	6.4	2.9	4.4	4.8	8.2	4.8
Total Liabilities to Net Worth 37	0.7	•	1.6	0.7	0.4	0.9	1.1	1.3	0.7
Current Assets to Working Capital 38	1.3	•	2.7	1.4	1.3	1.8	2.5	1.7	1.3
Current Liabilities to Working Capital 39	0.3	•	1.7	0.4	0.3	0.8	1.5	0.7	0.3
Working Capital to Net Sales 40	0.4	•	0.0	0.2	0.4	0.3	0.2	0.2	0.4
Inventory to Working Capital 41	0.1	•	0.0	0.2	0.0	0.2	0.1	0.2	0.1
Total Receipts to Cash Flow 42	7.2	3.6	1.5	2.2	2.3	4.2	5.9	5.7	16.0
Cost of Goods to Cash Flow 43	4.5	•	0.0	0.4	1.1	1.9	3.3	3.3	11.6
Cash Flow to Total Debt 44	0.2	•	4.2	2.1	1.2	0.6	0.4	0.3	0.1

Selected Financial Factors (in Percentages)

Debt Ratio 45	39.9	•	61.4	41.2	27.9	48.5	52.3	56.5	39.7
Return on Total Assets 46	5.8	•	63.8	25.4	27.4	16.6	10.1	8.2	4.3
Return on Equity Before Income Taxes 47	6.9	•	162.4	40.2	37.5	30.0	19.0	13.6	4.5
Return on Equity After Income Taxes 48	5.3	•	161.8	33.9	35.4	26.5	16.2	9.1	3.0
Profit Margin (Before Income Tax) 49	6.9	16.9	15.7	12.5	35.7	13.3	8.4	5.6	5.1
Profit Margin (After Income Tax) 50	5.2	12.5	15.6	10.5	33.7	11.7	7.2	3.7	3.5

Table I

Corporations with and without Net Income

ELECTRIC POWER GENERATION, TRANSMISSION AND DISTRIBUTION

MONEY AMOUNTS AND SIZE OF ASSETS IN THOUSANDS OF DOLLARS

Item Description for Accounting Period 7/03 Through 6/04	Total	Zero Assets	Under 500	500 to 1,000	1,000 to 5,000	5,000 to 10,000	10,000 to 25,000	25,000 to 50,000	50,000 to 100,000	100,000 to 250,000	250,000 to 500,000	500,000 to 2,500,000	2,500,000 and over
Number of Enterprises 1	895	259	341	•	77	41	36	29	14	25	12	30	31
Revenues ($ in Thousands)													
Net Sales 2	246160039	5008772	192517	•	42389	411209	663019	709590	1576189	1575380	1302402	17367241	217311331
Interest 3	4474949	131294	178	•	7949	1824	9730	5554	6267	22366	106256	505169	3678362
Rents 4	2178709	0	0	•	270	1687	556	1212	460	613	7139	29099	2137672
Royalties 5	73719	0	0	•	0	0	0	107	82	0	0	20939	52591
Other Portfolio Income 6	2001974	108922	0	•	4153	3967	9804	19233	123	15900	18206	288089	1533579
Other Receipts 7	9695042	170999	16	•	14006	2697	26281	39585	17148	44673	34137	618396	8727103
Total Receipts 8	264584432	5419987	192711	•	68767	421384	709390	775281	1600269	1658932	1468140	18828933	233440638
Average Total Receipts 9	295625	20927	565	•	893	10278	19705	26734	114305	66357	122345	627631	7530343
Operating Costs/Operating Income (%)													
Cost of Operations 10	65.1	2.0	9.6	•	29.0	33.1	72.2	67.0	88.4	49.0	49.9	66.5	66.6
Salaries and Wages 11	4.2	0.4	16.5	•	19.2	19.6	10.3	6.7	1.9	3.1	4.7	3.5	4.3
Taxes Paid 12	3.4	0.1	9.7	•	9.1	1.1	1.8	2.3	0.9	2.6	2.7	2.2	3.6
Interest Paid 13	6.7	2.7	0.8	•	0.4	0.7	2.3	3.3	1.8	6.5	17.7	6.4	6.8
Depreciation 14	8.4	0.4	0.2	•	10.1	2.9	2.5	3.9	2.5	7.2	12.3	8.6	8.6
Amortization and Depletion 15	0.9	0.0	•	•	0.0	0.1	0.7	1.0	0.2	0.2	0.4	3.3	0.8
Pensions and Other Deferred Comp. 16	0.8	•	•	•	0.4	0.1	0.5	0.2	0.1	0.2	1.1	0.4	0.9
Employee Benefits 17	1.0	0.1	0.0	•	2.4	0.4	0.9	0.7	0.3	1.3	0.4	0.7	1.0
Advertising 18	0.1	•	0.1	•	0.0	0.0	0.2	0.5	0.3	0.1	0.4	0.1	0.1
Other Expenses 19	18.1	111.4	42.9	•	74.6	39.4	14.5	19.2	8.1	29.7	27.2	17.8	15.9
Officers' Compensation 20	0.3	0.2	0.1	•	0.2	1.5	1.7	1.4	0.2	0.7	0.9	0.3	0.3
Operating Margin 21	•	•	20.0	•	•	1.1	•	•	•	•	•	•	•
Operating Margin Before Officers' Comp. 22	•	•	20.1	•	•	2.6	•	•	•	0.2	•	•	•

Selected Average Balance Sheet ($ in Thousands)

Item												
Net Receivables 23	46411	0	0	52	226	2954	6144	9151	12392	33374	94413	1211910
Inventories 24	8690	0	0	12	490	176	368	812	1102	3773	18941	228617
Net Property, Plant and Equipment 25	320479	0	3	963	4427	4070	14413	24288	57113	162898	640223	8486400
Total Assets 26	652916	·	380	2533	7099	16082	33975	65721	152028	347792	1226796	17305851
Notes and Loans Payable 27	274978	0	55	502	4587	90155	12555	38144	75016	220611	662582	7010185
All Other Liabilities 28	217343	0	338	724	1164	4065	18813	18751	49993	120012	302919	5857140
Net Worth 29	160594	0	-14	1308	1348	-78137	2606	8826	27019	7169	261295	4438525

Selected Financial Ratios (Times to 1)

Item												
Current Ratio 30	0.9	1.0	·	2.9	2.1	1.3	1.1	0.8	1.5	0.8	1.3	0.9
Quick Ratio 31	0.5	1.0	·	2.5	0.8	1.0	0.9	0.7	1.2	0.6	0.9	0.5
Net Sales to Working Capital 32	·	·	·	0.8	8.2	14.2	32.1	·	5.8	·	12.8	·
Coverage Ratio 33	0.8	·	27.2	41.8	6.0	0.7	2.0	1.7	1.7	0.7	0.8	0.8
Total Asset Turnover 34	0.4	1.5	·	0.2	1.4	1.1	0.7	1.7	0.4	0.3	0.5	0.4
Inventory Turnover 35	20.6	·	·	13.3	6.8	75.5	44.5	122.5	28.0	14.4	20.3	20.4
Receivables Turnover 36	6.0	·	3105.1	11.0	39.7	7.6	4.9	11.7	5.0	4.6	6.9	5.8
Total Liabilities to Net Worth 37	3.1	·	·	0.9	4.3	·	12.0	6.4	4.6	47.5	3.7	2.9
Current Assets to Working Capital 38	·	·	·	1.5	1.9	5.0	13.5	·	3.0	·	4.1	·
Current Liabilities to Working Capital 39	·	·	·	0.5	0.9	4.0	12.5	·	2.0	·	3.1	·
Working Capital to Net Sales 40	·	·	·	1.2	0.1	0.0	0.0	·	0.2	·	0.1	·
Inventory to Working Capital 41	·	·	·	0.0	0.2	0.5	0.5	·	0.1	·	0.4	·
Total Receipts to Cash Flow 42	8.5	2.1	·	1.5	2.3	9.0	7.9	52.8	3.2	6.1	8.9	10.5
Cost of Goods to Cash Flow 43	5.6	0.0	0.2	0.4	0.8	6.5	5.3	46.7	1.6	3.1	5.9	7.0
Cash Flow to Total Debt 44	0.1	·	0.7	0.3	0.0	0.1	0.0	0.0	0.2	0.1	0.1	0.1

Selected Financial Factors (in Percentages)

Item												
Debt Ratio 45	75.4	103.7	·	48.4	81.0	585.9	92.3	86.6	82.2	97.9	78.7	74.4
Return on Total Assets 46	2.2	·	31.1	3.7	6.1	2.0	4.6	·	4.6	4.0	2.4	2.2
Return on Equity Before Income Taxes 47	7.1	·	·	7.1	26.6	0.1	29.5	·	10.7	·	·	·
Return on Equity After Income Taxes 48	3.9	·	·	3.9	14.1	0.3	14.5	·	6.1	·	·	·
Profit Margin (Before Income Tax) 49	16.8	·	20.1	3.6	·	3.1	·	·	4.6	·	·	·
Profit Margin (After Income Tax) 50	9.3	·	20.1	1.9	·	1.5	·	·	2.6	·	·	·

Table II
Corporations with Net Income

ELECTRIC POWER GENERATION, TRANSMISSION AND DISTRIBUTION

MONEY AMOUNTS AND SIZE OF ASSETS IN THOUSANDS OF DOLLARS

Item Description for Accounting Period 7/03 Through 6/04	Total	Zero Assets	Under 500	500 to 1,000	1,000 to 5,000	5,000 to 10,000	10,000 to 25,000	25,000 to 50,000	50,000 to 100,000	100,000 to 250,000	250,000 to 500,000	500,000 to 2,500,000	2,500,000 and over
Number of Enterprises 1	486	3	337	•	22	24	21	20	5	17	3	13	20
Revenues ($ in Thousands)													
Net Sales 2	150531618	31291	173599	•	42007	257030	545032	454904	1001655	1180361	448150	9117391	137280198
Interest 3	2315427	1094	0	•	2071	1283	7191	3446	2597	5420	7667	187376	2097281
Rents 4	1502821	0	0	•	270	0	293	819	131	602	6938	14341	1479427
Royalties 5	66467	0	0	•	0	0	0	107	0	0	0	20915	45445
Other Portfolio Income 6	1767953	95893	0	•	3842	0	8025	12502	29	14005	2827	190834	1439996
Other Receipts 7	6323641	39935	0	•	14104	1748	21058	21760	127	20156	16626	243498	5944629
Total Receipts 8	162507927	168213	173599	•	62294	260061	581599	493538	1004539	1220544	482208	9774355	148286976
Average Total Receipts 9	334378	56071	515	•	2832	10836	27695	24677	200908	71797	160736	751873	7414349
Operating Costs/Operating Income (%)													
Cost of Operations 10	63.8	11.3	•	•	19.6	0.6	68.5	55.7	94.2	52.7	71.2	67.4	63.6
Salaries and Wages 11	4.3	0.0	17.9	•	13.0	30.8	11.1	9.6	0.4	3.3	1.4	2.2	4.4
Taxes Paid 12	3.5	•	10.7	•	9.0	0.8	1.7	3.0	0.1	2.6	2.5	2.0	3.6
Interest Paid 13	6.2	63.5	0.7	•	0.4	0.0	1.5	2.6	0.7	3.7	5.5	5.1	6.3
Depreciation 14	7.8	10.8	0.3	•	10.0	0.6	1.4	5.0	0.5	6.9	8.0	6.6	8.0
Amortization and Depletion 15	1.0	2.7	•	•	•	0.0	0.6	1.4	0.1	0.3	0.5	5.7	0.7
Pensions and Other Deferred Comp. 16	1.0	•	•	•	0.3	0.0	0.5	0.2	0.0	0.2	0.6	0.5	1.1
Employee Benefits 17	0.8	•	•	•	1.2	0.0	1.1	1.1	0.1	1.2	0.1	0.5	0.8
Advertising 18	0.1	•	0.1	•	•	•	0.1	0.7	•	0.1	1.1	0.1	0.1
Other Expenses 19	14.8	147.2	43.6	•	58.2	56.5	11.4	17.9	2.1	22.5	11.9	12.9	14.8
Officers' Compensation 20	0.3	•	•	•	•	2.3	1.0	1.8	0.0	0.6	1.8	0.2	0.3
Operating Margin 21	•	•	26.7	•	•	8.5	1.2	1.0	1.7	6.0	•	•	•
Operating Margin Before Officers' Comp. 22	•	•	26.7	•	•	10.8	2.2	2.8	1.7	6.6	•	•	•

Selected Average Balance Sheet ($ in Thousands)

Item	1	2	3	4	5	6	7	8	9	10	11	12
Net Receivables 23	37758	0	0	66	170	4316	4568	9557	8516	18919	108870	824916
Inventories 24	11123	0	0	42	782	219	349	1359	1227	4338	13461	257966
Net Property, Plant and Equipment 25	344902	0	2	1840	4967	3001	15373	24984	64701	140439	599260	7882751
Total Assets 26	690972	0	381	3410	8234	16654	34929	63455	151113	351666	1259570	15702377
Notes and Loans Payable 27	265874	0	0	10	5435	4321	10310	17420	52742	136771	669106	5934748
All Other Liabilities 28	226793	0	0	677	1158	4551	24108	12595	53691	93371	361334	5178981
Net Worth 29	198305	0	179	2724	1642	7782	512	33440	44680	121524	229129	4588648

Selected Financial Ratios (Times to 1)

Item	1	2	3	4	5	6	7	8	9	10	11	12
Current Ratio 30	0.8	1.9	•	2.0	2.9	1.5	1.1	1.5	1.4	1.7	1.3	0.8
Quick Ratio 31	0.4	1.9	•	1.4	1.0	1.3	0.9	1.0	1.1	0.8	0.9	0.4
Net Sales to Working Capital 32	•	2.9	•	4.1	4.8	9.6	35.6	31.1	7.7	6.8	14.4	•
Coverage Ratio 33	1.7	37.6	5.8	92.5	276.5	6.3	4.6	3.7	3.5	1.5	1.8	1.7
Total Asset Turnover 34	0.4	1.4	•	0.6	1.3	1.6	0.7	3.2	0.5	0.4	0.6	0.4
Inventory Turnover 35	17.8	•	•	8.9	0.1	81.0	36.3	138.9	29.8	24.5	35.1	16.9
Receivables Turnover 36	6.2	•	•	16.6	61.0	7.9	7.5	15.6	10.0	6.7	10.1	6.0
Total Liabilities to Net Worth 37	2.5	1.1	•	0.3	4.0	1.1	67.3	0.9	2.4	1.9	4.5	2.4
Current Assets to Working Capital 38	•	2.1	•	2.0	1.5	3.0	14.3	3.1	3.3	2.4	3.9	•
Current Liabilities to Working Capital 39	•	1.1	•	1.0	0.5	2.0	13.3	2.1	2.3	1.4	2.9	•
Working Capital to Net Sales 40	•	0.3	•	0.2	0.2	0.1	0.0	0.0	0.1	0.1	0.1	•
Inventory to Working Capital 41	•	•	•	0.1	0.7	0.1	0.4	0.3	0.2	0.1	0.3	•
Total Receipts to Cash Flow 42	7.0	1.8	0.7	1.3	1.5	6.0	5.1	24.7	3.4	8.6	7.7	7.1
Cost of Goods to Cash Flow 43	4.5	•	0.1	0.3	0.0	4.1	2.8	23.2	1.8	6.1	5.2	4.5
Cash Flow to Total Debt 44	0.1	1.4	•	2.1	1.1	0.5	0.1	0.3	0.2	0.1	0.1	0.1

Selected Financial Factors (in Percentages)

Item	1	2	3	4	5	6	7	8	9	10	11	12
Debt Ratio 45	71.3	53.1	•	20.1	80.1	53.3	98.5	47.3	70.4	65.4	81.8	70.8
Return on Total Assets 46	4.7	•	•	20.7	12.6	14.6	7.9	8.5	5.9	3.6	5.1	4.6
Return on Equity Before Income Taxes 47	6.8	77.0	•	25.7	62.9	26.3	421.8	11.9	14.3	3.7	12.3	6.3
Return on Equity After Income Taxes 48	4.7	77.0	•	20.3	45.3	22.7	310.9	10.9	10.3	3.2	10.0	4.2
Profit Margin (Before Income Tax) 49	4.4	302.1	26.7	36.6	9.6	7.9	9.5	2.0	9.2	3.0	4.0	4.2
Profit Margin (After Income Tax) 50	3.0	297.9	26.7	29.0	6.9	6.8	7.0	1.8	6.6	2.6	3.3	2.8

Table I

Corporations with and without Net Income

NATURAL GAS DISTRIBUTION

MONEY AMOUNTS AND SIZE OF ASSETS IN THOUSANDS OF DOLLARS

Item Description for Accounting Period 7/03 Through 6/04

Item	Total	Zero Assets	Under 500	500 to 1,000	1,000 to 5,000	5,000 to 10,000	10,000 to 25,000	25,000 to 50,000	50,000 to 100,000	100,000 to 250,000	250,000 to 500,000	500,000 to 2,500,000	2,500,000 and over
Number of Enterprises 1	1182	303	554	•	221	24	•	•	10	10	3	10	16
Revenues ($ in Thousands)													
Net Sales 2	9244718	555378	14371	•	405242	99419	•	•	2163313	2132861	1180296	14823426	69198915
Interest 3	2230962	10011	0	•	145	338	•	•	1274	1323	756	13179	2202558
Rents 4	86978	0	0	•	0	0	•	•	2093	467	106	5844	76657
Royalties 5	37048	0	0	•	0	0	•	•	19	298	0	51	36681
Other Portfolio Income 6	1154067	25585	0	•	10387	1220	•	•	1162	14292	44	11665	1082210
Other Receipts 7	3903859	60765	0	•	1827	3606	•	•	11763	20182	11186	68260	3718989
Total Receipts 8	99661632	651739	14371	•	417601	104583	•	•	2179624	2169423	1192388	14922425	76316010
Average Total Receipts 9	84316	2151	26	•	1890	4358	•	•	217962	216942	397463	1492242	4769751
Operating Costs/Operating Income (%)													
Cost of Operations 10	77.7	40.3	77.9	•	57.8	38.7	•	•	93.9	85.6	75.3	81.2	76.4
Salaries and Wages 11	3.3	0.9	1.8	•	11.3	7.9	•	•	1.0	1.4	2.3	1.4	3.9
Taxes Paid 12	2.1	11.0	0.1	•	2.0	3.4	•	•	0.4	1.3	2.6	2.1	2.1
Interest Paid 13	6.2	22.6	•	•	1.2	0.4	•	•	0.3	1.4	1.5	2.3	7.4
Depreciation 14	6.2	42.0	17.1	•	6.3	8.6	•	•	1.2	3.6	4.4	5.0	6.5
Amortization and Depletion 15	0.8	2.4	•	•	0.0	0.2	•	•	0.0	0.2	0.3	1.3	0.8
Pensions and Other Deferred Comp. 16	0.2	0.0	•	•	0.1	1.4	•	•	0.1	0.2	0.2	0.3	0.2
Employee Benefits 17	1.1	0.0	•	•	1.5	1.7	•	•	0.3	0.4	0.7	0.7	1.2
Advertising 18	0.0	•	0.1	•	0.4	0.3	•	•	0.0	0.0	0.1	0.1	0.0
Other Expenses 19	9.9	2.7	37.7	•	17.7	16.7	•	•	1.9	3.5	9.3	4.8	11.7
Officers' Compensation 20	0.3	•	•	•	1.0	2.6	•	•	0.2	0.3	0.5	0.2	0.3
Operating Margin 21	•	•	•	•	0.8	18.1	•	•	0.5	2.2	2.7	0.5	•
Operating Margin Before Officers' Comp. 22	•	•	•	•	1.8	20.6	•	•	0.7	2.4	3.2	0.7	•

Selected Average Balance Sheet ($ in Thousands)

Net Receivables 23	52972	0	1	136	472	•	16013	19109	47080	112783	3799433
Inventories 24	3214	0	0	57	6	•	4213	9386	32004	77444	172425
Net Property, Plant and Equipment 25	64046	0	0	714	3449	•	23664	85910	185418	953419	4002506
Total Assets 26	218281	0	14	1714	6634	•	67585	145164	321115	1482634	14933465
Notes and Loans Payable 27	92619	0	0	414	375	•	9094	49963	124969	537888	6425569
All Other Liabilities 28	105964	0	0	375	996	•	26018	49555	87423	447440	7465640
Net Worth 29	19698	0	13	924	5263	•	32473	45646	108723	497306	1042256

Selected Financial Ratios (Times to 1)

Current Ratio 30	0.9	32.0	2.0	3.6	•	1.2	1.2	1.1	0.8	0.9
Quick Ratio 31	0.7	32.0	0.5	2.5	•	0.9	0.8	0.6	0.4	0.7
Net Sales to Working Capital 32	•	1.9	3.7	4.5	•	47.7	37.0	28.5	•	•
Coverage Ratio 33	1.1	•	4.4	54.2	0.8	4.8	3.8	3.4	1.5	1.0
Total Asset Turnover 34	0.4	1.9	1.1	0.6	•	3.2	1.5	1.2	1.0	0.3
Inventory Turnover 35	18.9	•	18.7	278.7	•	48.2	19.5	9.3	15.5	19.2
Receivables Turnover 36	1.6	31.0	17.0	17.6	•	12.8	9.2	13.0	11.3	1.2
Total Liabilities to Net Worth 37	10.1	0.0	0.9	0.3	•	1.1	2.2	2.0	2.0	13.3
Current Assets to Working Capital 38	•	1.0	2.0	1.4	•	6.6	7.1	8.6	•	•
Current Liabilities to Working Capital 39	•	0.0	1.0	0.4	•	5.6	6.1	7.6	•	•
Working Capital to Net Sales 40	•	0.5	0.3	0.2	•	0.0	0.0	0.0	•	•
Inventory to Working Capital 41	•	•	0.2	0.0	•	1.1	0.9	4.2	•	•
Total Receipts to Cash Flow 42	13.3	39.1	6.6	2.8	•	34.2	15.4	7.9	22.9	11.8
Cost of Goods to Cash Flow 43	10.3	30.4	3.8	1.1	•	32.1	13.2	6.0	18.6	9.0
Cash Flow to Total Debt 44	0.0	1.5	0.4	1.1	•	0.2	0.1	0.2	0.1	0.0

Selected Financial Factors (in Percentages)

Debt Ratio 45	91.0	3.1	46.1	20.7	•	52.0	68.6	66.1	66.5	93.0
Return on Total Assets 46	2.3	•	5.4	14.3	•	5.1	7.8	6.5	3.4	2.2
Return on Equity Before Income Taxes 47	1.6	•	7.7	17.7	•	8.4	18.2	13.6	3.5	0.1
Return on Equity After Income Taxes 48	•	•	7.7	16.7	•	7.4	12.9	12.6	1.8	•
Profit Margin (Before Income Tax) 49	0.4	•	3.9	22.4	•	1.3	3.9	3.8	1.2	0.0
Profit Margin (After Income Tax) 50	•	•	3.9	21.2	•	1.1	2.8	3.5	0.6	•

19

Table II

Corporations with Net Income

NATURAL GAS DISTRIBUTION

MONEY AMOUNTS AND SIZE OF ASSETS IN THOUSANDS OF DOLLARS

Item Description for Accounting Period 7/03 Through 6/04		Total	Zero Assets	Under 500	500 to 1,000	1,000 to 5,000	5,000 to 10,000	10,000 to 25,000	25,000 to 50,000	50,000 to 100,000	100,000 to 250,000	250,000 to 500,000	500,000 to 2,500,000	2,500,000 and over
Number of Enterprises	1	526	•	260	•	172	24	18	4	•	10	•	•	12
Revenues ($ in Thousands)														
Net Sales	2	74446743	•	7583	•	300096	99419	1083452	454903	•	2980567	•	•	53804962
Interest	3	1711045	•	0	•	125	338	859	284	•	1300	•	•	1694608
Rents	4	58173	•	0	•	0	0	782	1029	•	489	•	•	48895
Royalties	5	36870	•	0	•	0	0	0	0	•	298	•	•	36522
Other Portfolio Income	6	1027060	•	0	•	10387	1220	3343	4031	•	14321	•	•	985393
Other Receipts	7	1685292	•	0	•	1826	3606	4256	2763	•	21028	•	•	1589821
Total Receipts	8	78965183	•	7583	•	312434	104583	1092692	463010	•	3018003	•	•	58160201
Average Total Receipts	9	150124	•	29	•	1816	4358	60705	115752	•	301800	•	•	4846683
Operating Costs/Operating Income (%)														
Cost of Operations	10	76.0	•	63.0	•	62.0	38.7	92.9	94.9	•	83.4	•	•	73.0
Salaries and Wages	11	3.4	•	•	•	11.2	7.9	1.4	0.4	•	1.2	•	•	4.1
Taxes Paid	12	2.0	•	•	•	2.0	3.4	0.5	0.6	•	1.7	•	•	2.1
Interest Paid	13	5.0	•	•	•	0.5	0.4	0.3	0.2	•	1.2	•	•	6.4
Depreciation	14	5.6	•	•	•	3.6	8.6	0.9	1.2	•	2.9	•	•	6.2
Amortization and Depletion	15	0.7	•	•	•	0.0	0.2	0.1	0.0	•	0.1	•	•	0.6
Pensions and Other Deferred Comp.	16	0.2	•	•	•	0.1	1.4	0.1	0.1	•	0.1	•	•	0.2
Employee Benefits	17	1.1	•	•	•	1.7	1.7	0.2	0.1	•	0.3	•	•	1.3
Advertising	18	0.0	•	•	•	0.1	0.3	0.0	0.0	•	0.0	•	•	0.0
Other Expenses	19	8.9	•	2.7	•	14.4	16.7	2.1	1.4	•	5.6	•	•	10.8
Officers' Compensation	20	0.3	•	•	•	0.8	2.6	0.6	0.2	•	0.3	•	•	0.3
Operating Margin	21	•	•	34.2	•	3.6	18.1	0.8	0.9	•	3.3	•	•	3.3
Operating Margin Before Officers' Comp.	22	•	•	34.2	•	4.4	20.6	1.4	1.1	•	3.6	•	•	3.6

Selected Average Balance Sheet ($ in Thousands)

Net Receivables 23	35818	0	113	472	3965	14212	30928	1434034
Inventories 24	5042	0	41	5	430	1535	20810	144692
Net Property, Plant and Equipment 25	114634	0	377	3449	4904	10381	99898	4213756
Total Assets 26	212042	27	1521	6634	15363	31836	185744	7942851
Notes and Loans Payable 27	95888	0	178	375	4680	6306	66404	3776413
All Other Liabilities 28	74409	0	255	996	5063	14379	63261	2817903
Net Worth 29	41745	27	1088	5263	5620	11150	56078	1348535

Selected Financial Ratios (Times to 1)

Current Ratio 30	1.0		2.9	3.6	1.3	1.3	1.2	1.0
Quick Ratio 31	0.6		0.6	2.5	1.1	1.1	0.7	0.6
Net Sales to Working Capital 32		1.1	2.3	4.5	37.1	21.8	25.7	665.1
Coverage Ratio 33	1.6		16.2	54.2	6.1	16.4	4.9	1.5
Total Asset Turnover 34	0.7	1.1	1.1	0.6	3.9	3.6	1.6	0.6
Inventory Turnover 35	21.3		26.3	304.0	130.1	70.3	11.9	22.6
Receivables Turnover 36	6.1		23.7	13.2	13.7	11.5	19.3	5.1
Total Liabilities to Net Worth 37	4.1		0.4	0.3	1.7	1.9	2.3	4.9
Current Assets to Working Capital 38		1.0	1.5	1.4	4.2	3.9	6.1	391.2
Current Liabilities to Working Capital 39			0.5	0.4	3.2	2.9	5.1	390.2
Working Capital to Net Sales 40	0.9		0.4	0.2	0.0	0.0	0.0	0.0
Inventory to Working Capital 41			0.1	0.0	0.3	0.5	1.8	31.6
Total Receipts to Cash Flow 42	9.8	2.7	5.0	2.8	32.8	35.7	10.6	8.3
Cost of Goods to Cash Flow 43	7.5	1.7	3.1	1.1	30.5	33.9	8.9	6.1
Cash Flow to Total Debt 44	0.1		0.8	1.1	0.2	0.2	0.2	0.1

Selected Financial Factors (in Percentages)

Debt Ratio 45	80.3		28.5	20.7	63.4	65.0	69.8	83.0
Return on Total Assets 46	5.4	37.4	9.5	14.3	7.8	10.2	9.2	5.4
Return on Equity Before Income Taxes 47	10.1	37.4	12.4	17.7	17.8	27.2	24.3	10.5
Return on Equity After Income Taxes 48	7.2	32.3	12.4	16.7	14.9	25.9	19.5	7.3
Profit Margin (Before Income Tax) 49	3.0	34.2	7.7	22.4	1.7	2.7	4.6	3.1
Profit Margin (After Income Tax) 50	2.1	29.6	7.7	21.2	1.4	2.5	3.7	2.2

Table I

Corporations with and without Net Income

WATER, SEWAGE AND OTHER SYSTEMS

MONEY AMOUNTS AND SIZE OF ASSETS IN THOUSANDS OF DOLLARS

Item Description for Accounting Period 7/03 Through 6/04	Total	Zero Assets	Under 500	500 to 1,000	1,000 to 5,000	5,000 to 10,000	10,000 to 25,000	25,000 to 50,000	50,000 to 100,000	100,000 to 250,000	250,000 to 500,000	500,000 to 2,500,000	2,500,000 and over
Number of Enterprises 1	6390	103	5205	441	518	39	40	21	6	7	4	7	•
Revenues ($ in Thousands)													
Net Sales 2	6173890	43416	896104	189436	536232	123087	289364	182231	81044	191002	394527	3247448	•
Interest 3	127725	1001	1970	697	1136	370	509	3208	229	2300	1932	114373	•
Rents 4	15726	8	433	0	0	769	876	1045	66	2026	1869	8634	•
Royalties 5	776	0	0	0	7	0	767	0	0	0	0	3	•
Other Portfolio Income 6	141494	1375	12542	1361	29888	0	6714	1191	8	588	856	86971	•
Other Receipts 7	105389	338	2497	4257	13076	4130	1754	17127	1117	6932	3765	50394	•
Total Receipts 8	6565000	46138	913546	195751	580339	128356	299984	204802	82464	202848	402949	3507823	•
Average Total Receipts 9	1027	448	176	444	1120	3291	7500	9752	13744	28978	100737	501118	•
Operating Costs/Operating Income (%)													
Cost of Operations 10	30.4	18.1	24.0	33.0	50.1	26.2	39.7	42.2	37.0	28.4	39.5	26.4	•
Salaries and Wages 11	7.3	13.1	8.9	7.0	9.0	14.3	18.8	9.2	3.3	9.5	7.5	5.0	•
Taxes Paid 12	7.3	4.3	4.6	4.8	6.7	7.9	4.1	8.7	7.4	8.7	7.1	8.5	•
Interest Paid 13	10.3	5.8	1.2	4.2	4.6	3.9	6.1	6.2	10.5	12.1	5.4	15.5	•
Depreciation 14	16.5	19.2	7.5	7.1	12.1	14.3	10.4	11.7	23.5	23.7	13.7	20.9	•
Amortization and Depletion 15	4.8	0.5	0.0	2.6	0.5	0.0	0.3	5.6	0.9	0.2	0.2	8.4	•
Pensions and Other Deferred Comp. 16	1.0	2.1	0.7	0.6	0.2	0.1	0.3	0.5	1.2	1.6	0.5	1.3	•
Employee Benefits 17	2.6	5.5	1.2	•	0.7	1.3	6.1	2.6	4.2	3.1	4.2	2.9	•
Advertising 18	0.5	0.0	2.0	0.4	0.6	0.1	0.1	0.1	0.1	1.0	0.1	0.1	•
Other Expenses 19	24.0	43.1	39.5	36.4	36.7	32.0	14.7	25.7	14.1	17.1	14.7	18.9	•
Officers' Compensation 20	2.5	•	6.8	6.6	3.1	3.7	2.1	2.8	1.8	4.2	1.4	0.9	•
Operating Margin 21	•	•	3.5	•	•	•	•	•	•	•	5.6	•	•
Operating Margin Before Officers' Comp. 22	•	•	10.3	3.9	•	•	•	•	•	•	7.0	•	•

Selected Average Balance Sheet ($ in Thousands)

Net Receivables 23	107	0	12	52	129	510	708	1363	1471	2905	11168	53910
Inventories 24	31	0	3	32	7	17	90	75	374	20072	1350	1548
Net Property, Plant and Equipment 25	2723	0	73	341	1664	4682	10695	22479	58816	101218	264473	1829551
Total Assets 26	4522	0	119	662	2376	5707	16245	33278	76783	168081	319075	3181370
Notes and Loans Payable 27	1975	0	57	347	1472	2943	6952	7964	31403	81386	80924	1395327
All Other Liabilities 28	1015	0	26	72	615	1621	4915	11280	22435	39603	133094	651572
Net Worth 29	1532	0	36	242	289	1143	4378	14034	22945	47092	105056	1134471

Selected Financial Ratios (Times to 1)

Current Ratio 30	0.6	•	1.5	3.0	1.1	0.6	1.2	2.8	1.2	4.3	0.8	0.3
Quick Ratio 31	0.4	•	1.4	1.7	1.0	0.5	0.8	2.4	0.9	1.4	0.7	0.2
Net Sales to Working Capital 32	•	•	13.9	4.4	47.6	•	16.5	1.4	12.9	0.9	•	•
Coverage Ratio 33	0.9	0.3	5.5	1.2	1.1	1.1	1.1	0.5	0.8	0.7	2.4	0.9
Total Asset Turnover 34	0.2	•	1.4	0.6	0.4	0.6	0.4	0.3	0.2	0.2	0.3	0.1
Inventory Turnover 35	9.6	•	16.4	4.5	71.1	48.5	31.9	48.6	13.4	0.4	28.9	79.3
Receivables Turnover 36	8.4	•	14.5	12.8	6.6	11.1	6.5	6.9	11.2	7.1	7.7	7.9
Total Liabilities to Net Worth 37	2.0	•	2.3	1.7	7.2	4.0	2.7	1.4	2.3	2.6	2.0	1.8
Current Assets to Working Capital 38	•	•	3.1	1.5	18.8	•	5.5	1.5	5.0	1.3	•	•
Current Liabilities to Working Capital 39	•	•	2.1	0.5	17.8	•	4.5	0.5	4.0	0.3	•	•
Working Capital to Net Sales 40	•	•	0.1	0.2	0.0	0.1	0.1	0.7	0.1	1.1	•	•
Inventory to Working Capital 41	•	•	•	0.6	0.5	•	0.1	0.0	0.4	0.7	•	•
Total Receipts to Cash Flow 42	5.4	3.3	2.8	3.1	9.1	4.0	7.9	5.4	11.8	9.3	5.0	6.8
Cost of Goods to Cash Flow 43	1.6	0.6	0.7	1.0	4.6	1.1	3.1	2.3	4.4	2.6	2.0	1.8
Cash Flow to Total Debt 44	0.1	•	0.7	0.3	0.1	0.2	0.1	0.1	0.0	0.0	0.1	0.0

Selected Financial Factors (in Percentages)

Debt Ratio 45	66.1	•	69.6	63.4	87.8	80.0	73.0	57.8	70.1	72.0	67.1	64.3
Return on Total Assets 46	2.0	•	9.7	3.1	•	2.4	3.1	0.8	1.5	1.4	4.1	2.1
Return on Equity Before Income Taxes 47	•	•	26.0	1.1	•	1.1	1.3	•	•	•	7.2	•
Return on Equity After Income Taxes 48	•	•	25.2	1.0	•	•	0.0	•	•	•	4.8	•
Profit Margin (Before Income Tax) 49	•	•	5.5	0.6	•	0.4	0.8	•	•	•	7.7	•
Profit Margin (After Income Tax) 50	•	•	5.3	0.6	•	•	0.0	•	•	•	5.1	•

Table II

Corporations with Net Income

WATER, SEWAGE AND OTHER SYSTEMS

MONEY AMOUNTS AND SIZE OF ASSETS IN THOUSANDS OF DOLLARS

Item Description for Accounting Period 7/03 Through 6/04	Total	Zero Assets	Under 500	500 to 1,000	1,000 to 5,000	5,000 to 10,000	10,000 to 25,000	25,000 to 50,000	50,000 to 100,000	100,000 to 250,000	250,000 to 500,000	500,000 to 2,500,000	2,500,000 and over
Number of Enterprises 1	3393	•	2662	379	186	13	23	15	•	3	4	•	•
Revenues ($ in Thousands)													
Net Sales 2	2675741	•	424898	151165	308324	45981	185050	133344	•	82574	394527	•	•
Interest 3	9135	•	1725	316	345	8	118	472	•	1038	1932	•	•
Rents 4	6598	•	0	0	0	81	577	918	•	824	1869	•	•
Royalties 5	26	•	0	0	7	0	19	0	•	0	0	•	•
Other Portfolio Income 6	108005	•	5609	1361	28826	0	4747	215	•	346	856	•	•
Other Receipts 7	32742	•	456	3907	1851	4055	-91	652	•	4989	3765	•	•
Total Receipts 8	2832247	•	432688	156749	339353	50125	190420	135601	•	89771	402949	•	•
Average Total Receipts 9	835	•	163	414	1824	3856	8279	9040	•	29924	100737	•	•
Operating Costs/Operating Income (%)													
Cost of Operations 10	31.8	•	7.0	41.3	36.0	45.2	53.1	41.9	•	26.0	39.5	•	•
Salaries and Wages 11	7.4	•	11.3	8.8	8.2	2.0	7.5	4.2	•	6.3	7.5	•	•
Taxes Paid 12	7.2	•	6.1	2.7	7.0	9.8	3.5	8.5	•	8.8	7.1	•	•
Interest Paid 13	5.9	•	0.7	5.0	2.7	6.6	3.7	4.0	•	8.8	5.4	•	•
Depreciation 14	13.8	•	8.3	6.2	6.2	10.6	8.7	11.8	•	22.6	13.7	•	•
Amortization and Depletion 15	0.4	•	0.0	3.3	0.1	0.0	0.2	0.2	•	0.2	0.2	•	•
Pensions and Other Deferred Comp. 16	0.7	•	0.6	0.1	0.2	0.0	0.2	0.6	•	1.7	0.5	•	•
Employee Benefits 17	2.0	•	0.9	•	1.1	0.2	1.4	2.0	•	1.3	4.2	•	•
Advertising 18	0.4	•	1.9	0.5	0.6	0.0	0.1	0.0	•	0.0	0.1	•	•
Other Expenses 19	21.4	•	38.4	25.9	37.5	20.0	11.8	20.9	•	13.0	14.7	•	•
Officers' Compensation 20	2.5	•	7.7	8.3	1.6	0.6	1.6	1.1	•	2.8	1.4	•	•
Operating Margin 21	6.4	•	17.1	•	•	5.0	8.2	5.1	•	8.4	5.6	•	•
Operating Margin Before Officers' Comp. 22	9.0	•	24.8	6.2	0.3	5.6	9.8	6.1	•	11.2	7.0	•	•

Selected Average Balance Sheet ($ in Thousands)

Net Receivables 23	114	16	61	238	260	944	1447	3368	11168
Inventories 24	11	0	37	5	7	49	75	549	1350
Net Property, Plant and Equipment 25	1877	40	299	1915	4965	10258	25004	112338	264473
Total Assets 26	2513	105	644	2720	5762	15136	32453	135836	319075
Notes and Loans Payable 27	831	18	380	1019	3581	5325	7705	35129	80924
All Other Liabilities 28	773	23	69	409	1352	4829	11243	42721	133094
Net Worth 29	909	65	194	1293	829	4981	13506	57986	105056

Selected Financial Ratios (Times to 1)

Current Ratio 30	1.1	3.0	2.8	0.7	0.4	0.8	2.0	1.4	0.8
Quick Ratio 31	0.8	2.9	1.5	0.6	0.3	0.7	1.6	1.3	0.7
Net Sales to Working Capital 32	23.5	4.3	3.9	•	•	•	3.5	7.5	•
Coverage Ratio 33	3.1	28.3	1.3	4.3	3.1	4.0	2.7	2.9	2.4
Total Asset Turnover 34	0.3	1.5	0.6	0.6	0.6	0.5	0.3	0.2	0.3
Inventory Turnover 35	23.2	44.8	4.5	113.8	223.7	86.3	49.3	13.0	28.9
Receivables Turnover 36	5.1	9.8	11.0	5.6	27.2	17.0	9.3	16.3	7.7
Total Liabilities to Net Worth 37	1.8	0.6	2.3	1.1	6.0	2.0	1.4	1.3	2.0
Current Assets to Working Capital 38	8.7	1.5	1.6	•	•	•	2.0	3.5	•
Current Liabilities to Working Capital 39	7.7	0.5	0.6	•	•	•	1.0	2.5	•
Working Capital to Net Sales 40	0.0	0.2	0.3	•	•	•	0.3	0.1	•
Inventory to Working Capital 41	0.4	•	0.7	•	•	•	0.0	0.2	•
Total Receipts to Cash Flow 42	3.6	2.1	4.3	3.0	3.5	4.8	3.9	3.6	5.0
Cost of Goods to Cash Flow 43	1.1	0.1	1.8	1.1	1.6	2.5	1.6	0.9	2.0
Cash Flow to Total Debt 44	0.1	1.9	0.2	0.4	0.2	0.2	0.1	0.1	0.1

Selected Financial Factors (in Percentages)

Debt Ratio 45	63.8	38.4	69.8	52.5	85.6	67.1	58.4	57.3	67.1
Return on Total Assets 46	5.7	29.8	4.1	7.0	12.6	7.9	2.9	5.2	4.1
Return on Equity Before Income Taxes 47	10.6	46.7	3.2	11.3	59.7	17.9	4.4	8.0	7.2
Return on Equity After Income Taxes 48	8.8	45.8	3.1	7.9	44.1	16.0	3.8	5.3	4.8
Profit Margin (Before Income Tax) 49	12.3	19.0	1.6	8.8	14.0	11.1	6.7	16.8	7.7
Profit Margin (After Income Tax) 50	10.1	18.6	1.5	6.2	10.3	9.9	5.8	11.1	5.1

Table I

Corporations with and without Net Income

COMBINATION GAS AND ELECTRIC

MONEY AMOUNTS AND SIZE OF ASSETS IN THOUSANDS OF DOLLARS

Item Description for Accounting Period 7/03 Through 6/04		Total	Zero Assets	Under 500	500 to 1,000	1,000 to 5,000	5,000 to 10,000	10,000 to 25,000	25,000 to 50,000	50,000 to 100,000	100,000 to 250,000	250,000 to 500,000	500,000 to 2,500,000	2,500,000 and over
Number of Enterprises	1	37	•	•	•	•	•	•	•	•	•	•	3	30
Revenues ($ in Thousands)														
Net Sales	2	177302280	•	•	•	•	•	•	•	•	•	•	2943300	173628806
Interest	3	3658766	•	•	•	•	•	•	•	•	•	•	10085	3646134
Rents	4	1237126	•	•	•	•	•	•	•	•	•	•	8590	1226661
Royalties	5	23576	•	•	•	•	•	•	•	•	•	•	0	23540
Other Portfolio Income	6	2190489	•	•	•	•	•	•	•	•	•	•	9015	2181140
Other Receipts	7	5633765	•	•	•	•	•	•	•	•	•	•	11278	5617077
Total Receipts	8	190046002	•	•	•	•	•	•	•	•	•	•	2982268	186323358
Average Total Receipts	9	5136378	•	•	•	•	•	•	•	•	•	•	994089	6210779
Operating Costs/Operating Income (%)														
Cost of Operations	10	50.9	•	•	•	•	•	•	•	•	•	•	63.4	50.6
Salaries and Wages	11	5.5	•	•	•	•	•	•	•	•	•	•	8.0	5.5
Taxes Paid	12	4.6	•	•	•	•	•	•	•	•	•	•	4.3	4.6
Interest Paid	13	9.0	•	•	•	•	•	•	•	•	•	•	6.9	9.1
Depreciation	14	10.3	•	•	•	•	•	•	•	•	•	•	6.2	10.4
Amortization and Depletion	15	0.8	•	•	•	•	•	•	•	•	•	•	1.3	0.8
Pensions and Other Deferred Comp.	16	1.0	•	•	•	•	•	•	•	•	•	•	1.1	1.0
Employee Benefits	17	1.4	•	•	•	•	•	•	•	•	•	•	2.8	1.4
Advertising	18	0.1	•	•	•	•	•	•	•	•	•	•	0.4	0.1
Other Expenses	19	24.1	•	•	•	•	•	•	•	•	•	•	32.0	24.0
Officers' Compensation	20	0.2	•	•	•	•	•	•	•	•	•	•	0.5	0.2
Operating Margin	21	•	•	•	•	•	•	•	•	•	•	•	•	•
Operating Margin Before Officers' Comp.	22	•	•	•	•	•	•	•	•	•	•	•	•	•

Selected Average Balance Sheet ($ in Thousands)

Net Receivables 23	1906764	71522	2342610
Inventories 24	247961	17122	304314
Net Property, Plant and Equipment 25	6275917	738020	7655887
Total Assets 26	15767921	1310512	19292462
Notes and Loans Payable 27	5676910	814546	6913539
All Other Liabilities 28	5020100	391406	6140959
Net Worth 29	5070911	104559	6237965

Selected Financial Ratios (Times to 1)

Current Ratio 30	1.0	1.5	1.0
Quick Ratio 31	0.7	0.5	0.7
Net Sales to Working Capital 32	9.3	9.3	•
Coverage Ratio 33	0.9	•	1.0
Total Asset Turnover 34	0.3	0.7	0.3
Inventory Turnover 35	9.8	36.3	9.6
Receivables Turnover 36	2.5	27.4	2.4
Total Liabilities to Net Worth 37	2.1	11.5	2.1
Current Assets to Working Capital 38	•	2.8	•
Current Liabilities to Working Capital 39	•	1.8	•
Working Capital to Net Sales 40	•	0.1	•
Inventory to Working Capital 41	•	0.2	•
Total Receipts to Cash Flow 42	5.2	•	5.1
Cost of Goods to Cash Flow 43	2.7	•	2.6
Cash Flow to Total Debt 44	0.1	•	0.1

Selected Financial Factors (in Percentages)

Debt Ratio 45	67.8	92.0	67.7
Return on Total Assets 46	2.5	•	2.6
Return on Equity Before Income Taxes 47	•	•	•
Return on Equity After Income Taxes 48	•	•	•
Profit Margin (Before Income Tax) 49	•	•	•
Profit Margin (After Income Tax) 50	•	•	•

23

Table II

Corporations with Net Income

COMBINATION GAS AND ELECTRIC

MONEY AMOUNTS AND SIZE OF ASSETS IN THOUSANDS OF DOLLARS

Item Description for Accounting Period 7/03 Through 6/04	Total	Zero Assets	Under 500	500 to 1,000	1,000 to 5,000	5,000 to 10,000	10,000 to 25,000	25,000 to 50,000	50,000 to 100,000	100,000 to 250,000	250,000 to 500,000	500,000 to 2,500,000	2,500,000 and over
Number of Enterprises **1**	21	•	•	•	•	•	•	3	•	•	•	•	18
Revenues ($ in Thousands)													
Net Sales **2**	106395815	•	•	•	•	•	•	1087841	•	•	•	•	105307974
Interest **3**	981416	•	•	•	•	•	•	3436	•	•	•	•	977980
Rents **4**	324837	•	•	•	•	•	•	1419	•	•	•	•	323418
Royalties **5**	10020	•	•	•	•	•	•	36	•	•	•	•	9984
Other Portfolio Income **6**	975616	•	•	•	•	•	•	8864	•	•	•	•	966753
Other Receipts **7**	3036022	•	•	•	•	•	•	23053	•	•	•	•	3012968
Total Receipts **8**	111723726	•	•	•	•	•	•	1124649	•	•	•	•	110599077
Average Total Receipts **9**	5320177	•	•	•	•	•	•	374883	•	•	•	•	6144393
Operating Costs/Operating Income (%)													
Cost of Operations **10**	41.7	•	•	•	•	•	•	72.6	•	•	•	•	41.4
Salaries and Wages **11**	6.4	•	•	•	•	•	•	0.8	•	•	•	•	6.4
Taxes Paid **12**	5.2	•	•	•	•	•	•	3.0	•	•	•	•	5.2
Interest Paid **13**	6.3	•	•	•	•	•	•	2.0	•	•	•	•	6.4
Depreciation **14**	10.1	•	•	•	•	•	•	5.6	•	•	•	•	10.1
Amortization and Depletion **15**	0.5	•	•	•	•	•	•	0.5	•	•	•	•	0.5
Pensions and Other Deferred Comp. **16**	0.8	•	•	•	•	•	•	1.2	•	•	•	•	0.8
Employee Benefits **17**	1.4	•	•	•	•	•	•	0.3	•	•	•	•	1.4
Advertising **18**	0.2	•	•	•	•	•	•	0.1	•	•	•	•	0.2
Other Expenses **19**	27.3	•	•	•	•	•	•	12.5	•	•	•	•	27.4
Officers' Compensation **20**	0.2	•	•	•	•	•	•	0.4	•	•	•	•	0.2
Operating Margin **21**	•	•	•	•	•	•	•	0.9	•	•	•	•	•
Operating Margin Before Officers' Comp. **22**	0.2	•	•	•	•	•	•	1.3	•	•	•	•	0.2

Selected Average Balance Sheet ($ in Thousands)

Net Receivables **23**	916943	50148	1061409
Inventories **24**	254057	11499	294844
Net Property, Plant and Equipment **25**	6511307	274369	7550797
Total Assets **26**	12761957	511047	14803776
Notes and Loans Payable **27**	4476634	221311	5185855
All Other Liabilities **28**	4496977	103798	5229173
Net Worth **29**	3788346	185938	4388748

Selected Financial Ratios (Times to 1)

Current Ratio **30**	1.0	0.8	1.0
Quick Ratio **31**	0.6	0.6	0.6
Net Sales to Working Capital **32**			
Coverage Ratio **33**	1.8	3.1	1.8
Total Asset Turnover **34**	0.4	0.7	0.4
Inventory Turnover **35**	8.3	22.9	8.2
Receivables Turnover **36**	2.6		2.6
Total Liabilities to Net Worth **37**	2.4	1.7	2.4
Current Assets to Working Capital **38**			
Current Liabilities to Working Capital **39**			
Working Capital to Net Sales **40**			
Inventory to Working Capital **41**			
Total Receipts to Cash Flow **42**	3.5	7.5	3.4
Cost of Goods to Cash Flow **43**	1.4	5.5	1.4
Cash Flow to Total Debt **44**	0.2	0.1	0.2

Selected Financial Factors (in Percentages)

Debt Ratio **45**	70.3	63.6	70.4
Return on Total Assets **46**	4.5	4.5	4.5
Return on Equity Before Income Taxes **47**	6.7	8.4	6.7
Return on Equity After Income Taxes **48**	4.4	6.1	4.4
Profit Margin (Before Income Tax) **49**	5.0	4.3	5.0
Profit Margin (After Income Tax) **50**	3.3	3.1	3.3

Table I

Corporations with and without Net Income

CONSTRUCTION OF BUILDINGS

MONEY AMOUNTS AND SIZE OF ASSETS IN THOUSANDS OF DOLLARS

Item Description for Accounting Period 7/03 Through 6/04	Total	Zero Assets	Under 500	500 to 1,000	1,000 to 5,000	5,000 to 10,000	10,000 to 25,000	25,000 to 50,000	50,000 to 100,000	100,000 to 250,000	250,000 to 500,000	500,000 to 2,500,000	2,500,000 and over
Number of Enterprises 1	193545	19077	129317	18203	21859	2658	1666	427	190	76	33	32	7
Revenues ($ in Thousands)													
Net Sales 2	472052006	3265211	67831024	30985558	90647154	39281207	50182319	28579646	25288098	20318683	18835263	53180204	43657640
Interest 3	1011810	7474	23810	24579	64088	22362	32736	20426	19528	14871	45641	333029	403266
Rents 4	562000	10305	32576	22589	86121	30326	50367	25618	63587	47305	94042	67120	32046
Royalties 5	206375	0	0	0	1	7	0	2	134	292	10383	178421	17135
Other Portfolio Income 6	1022074	54000	88454	37259	132840	55599	78850	33506	30373	143383	61169	87277	219364
Other Receipts 7	5775027	173203	656621	134603	693534	345761	364738	251858	219131	307470	257385	776181	1594538
Total Receipts 8	480629292	3510193	68632485	31204588	91623738	39735262	50709010	28911056	25620851	20832004	19303883	54622232	45923989
Average Total Receipts 9	2483	184	531	1714	4192	14949	30438	67707	134847	274105	584966	1706945	6560570
Operating Costs/Operating Income (%)													
Cost of Operations 10	81.2	70.7	70.0	82.1	85.1	88.3	88.3	88.9	89.3	87.6	85.8	83.9	58.3
Salaries and Wages 11	3.7	4.5	5.3	3.4	3.3	2.4	2.5	2.4	2.8	3.3	3.7	4.2	5.9
Taxes Paid 12	1.1	1.2	1.8	1.3	1.0	0.8	0.9	0.6	0.6	0.7	1.0	0.8	1.5
Interest Paid 13	0.7	1.4	0.5	0.6	0.6	0.3	0.4	0.4	0.4	0.4	0.8	1.2	1.4
Depreciation 14	0.8	1.2	1.3	0.9	0.9	0.7	0.6	0.5	0.6	0.6	1.1	0.5	0.4
Amortization and Depletion 15	0.1	0.0	0.0	0.0	0.0	0.0	0.0	0.0	0.1	0.0	0.1	0.4	0.2
Pensions and Other Deferred Comp. 16	0.2	0.1	0.3	0.3	0.3	0.2	0.2	0.2	0.2	0.2	0.5	0.2	0.1
Employee Benefits 17	0.5	0.4	0.9	0.8	0.4	0.5	0.6	0.4	0.4	0.3	0.4	0.5	0.3
Advertising 18	0.3	0.3	0.3	0.4	0.2	0.2	0.2	0.2	0.2	0.3	0.5	0.5	0.7
Other Expenses 19	7.4	21.9	13.6	5.5	4.8	3.1	3.1	2.9	2.8	2.8	4.9	4.0	25.4
Officers' Compensation 20	2.1	2.5	4.6	3.6	2.6	1.9	1.6	1.3	1.0	0.9	0.8	0.9	0.4
Operating Margin 21	1.9	•	1.3	1.0	0.8	1.5	1.7	2.1	1.5	2.8	0.4	2.9	5.5
Operating Margin Before Officers' Comp. 22	4.0	•	5.9	4.6	3.4	3.5	3.3	3.5	2.5	3.7	1.1	3.8	5.9

Selected Average Balance Sheet ($ in Thousands)

Item													
Net Receivables 23	253	0	15	83	394	1700	4173	9855	21944	35018	94373	191657	721168
Inventories 24	313	0	18	172	536	1759	3025	6600	11516	45886	51536	286269	2042051
Net Property, Plant and Equipment 25	138	0	25	111	244	679	1481	2978	7405	17050	69109	131070	187842
Total Assets 26	1310	0	105	695	2165	6966	14881	33857	67059	155419	350990	1129988	7129243
Notes and Loans Payable 27	504	0	67	345	956	2324	4366	9881	18956	40152	105053	309116	3444911
All Other Liabilities 28	465	0	27	242	781	3018	6906	15747	32531	63259	143103	435586	1310482
Net Worth 29	340	0	11	108	427	1624	3589	8228	15572	52009	102833	385285	2373850

Selected Financial Ratios (Times to 1)

Item													
Current Ratio 30	1.5	•	1.6	1.3	1.4	1.5	1.3	1.4	1.4	1.6	1.5	1.8	2.0
Quick Ratio 31	0.7	•	0.9	0.5	0.5	0.7	0.7	0.8	0.8	0.7	0.9	0.7	0.6
Net Sales to Working Capital 32	7.8	•	21.7	14.0	8.1	8.2	10.0	8.7	9.7	6.4	8.2	5.0	3.5
Coverage Ratio 33	6.4	3.1	5.7	3.9	4.1	9.2	8.6	9.3	7.9	11.7	4.4	5.6	8.8
Total Asset Turnover 34	1.9	•	5.0	2.5	1.9	2.1	2.0	2.0	2.0	1.7	1.6	1.5	0.9
Inventory Turnover 35	6.3	•	20.1	8.1	6.6	7.4	8.8	9.0	10.3	5.1	9.5	4.9	1.8
Receivables Turnover 36	9.7	•	34.6	19.1	10.7	7.5	7.2	6.8	6.4	8.0	5.8	8.6	10.3
Total Liabilities to Net Worth 37	2.9	•	8.2	5.4	4.1	3.3	3.1	3.1	3.3	2.0	2.4	1.9	2.0
Current Assets to Working Capital 38	2.9	•	2.8	4.1	3.4	3.1	3.9	3.5	3.8	2.8	3.1	2.2	2.0
Current Liabilities to Working Capital 39	1.9	•	1.8	3.1	2.4	2.1	2.9	2.5	2.8	1.8	2.1	1.2	1.0
Working Capital to Net Sales 40	0.1	•	0.0	0.1	0.1	0.1	0.1	0.1	0.1	0.2	0.1	0.2	0.3
Inventory to Working Capital 41	1.1	•	0.8	1.6	1.1	1.0	1.0	0.9	0.8	1.3	0.7	0.9	1.3
Total Receipts to Cash Flow 42	10.0	4.6	7.0	17.0	17.6	19.9	20.3	18.4	20.4	13.6	15.2	11.5	2.9
Cost of Goods to Cash Flow 43	8.1	3.2	4.9	13.9	14.9	17.5	17.9	16.3	18.2	11.9	13.1	9.7	1.7
Cash Flow to Total Debt 44	0.3	•	0.8	0.2	0.1	0.1	0.1	0.1	0.1	0.2	0.2	0.2	0.5

Selected Financial Factors (in Percentages)

Item													
Debt Ratio 45	74.0	•	89.2	84.5	80.3	76.7	75.8	75.7	76.8	66.5	70.7	65.9	66.7
Return on Total Assets 46	8.1	•	15.0	5.8	4.7	6.4	6.3	7.3	6.4	8.9	6.0	10.1	10.5
Return on Equity Before Income Taxes 47	26.2	•	114.4	27.5	18.1	24.4	23.0	26.7	23.9	24.3	15.9	24.3	28.1
Return on Equity After Income Taxes 48	21.7	•	112.3	25.9	16.5	23.4	21.6	25.2	22.7	23.2	12.5	17.3	18.7
Profit Margin (Before Income Tax) 49	3.7	3.1	2.5	1.7	1.9	2.7	2.7	3.3	2.8	4.7	2.9	5.6	10.7
Profit Margin (After Income Tax) 50	3.0	3.0	2.4	1.6	1.7	2.6	2.6	3.1	2.7	4.5	2.3	4.0	7.1

Table II
Corporations with Net Income

CONSTRUCTION OF BUILDINGS

MONEY AMOUNTS AND SIZE OF ASSETS IN THOUSANDS OF DOLLARS

Item Description for Accounting Period 7/03 Through 6/04	Total	Zero Assets	Under 500	500 to 1,000	1,000 to 5,000	5,000 to 10,000	10,000 to 25,000	25,000 to 50,000	50,000 to 100,000	100,000 to 250,000	250,000 to 500,000	500,000 to 2,500,000	2,500,000 and over
Number of Enterprises 1	115666	10022	77277	10679	13803	1989	1284	338	150	61	27	29	7
Revenues ($ in Thousands)													
Net Sales 2	380506176	2095672	44922642	22530419	63161414	32638927	42152315	24311542	21543066	17550008	16042764	49899767	43657640
Interest 3	906969	2116	12802	16543	41727	14996	25833	14291	18224	11198	30090	315885	403266
Rents 4	408111	0	13386	16803	52826	25076	34150	15577	45981	31685	73461	67120	32046
Royalties 5	206072	0	0	0	1	7	0	2	134	0	10373	178421	17135
Other Portfolio Income 6	690059	51361	64348	19529	92619	30592	64860	28477	17906	16216	22147	62640	219364
Other Receipts 7	5188322	162829	571867	138390	518773	298212	300057	235308	180285	319944	195539	672579	1594538
Total Receipts 8	387905709	2311978	45585045	22721684	63867360	33007810	42577215	24605197	21805596	17929051	16374374	51196412	45923989
Average Total Receipts 9	3354	231	590	2128	4627	16595	33160	72796	145371	293919	606458	1765394	6560570
Operating Costs/Operating Income (%)													
Cost of Operations 10	80.0	65.2	66.4	80.1	83.7	87.8	87.7	88.4	89.0	86.8	85.5	83.4	58.3
Salaries and Wages 11	3.5	2.8	5.0	3.1	2.9	2.3	2.4	2.3	2.5	3.2	3.3	4.2	5.9
Taxes Paid 12	1.0	1.1	1.8	1.2	0.9	0.8	0.8	0.6	0.6	0.7	1.0	0.8	1.5
Interest Paid 13	0.7	1.0	0.6	0.6	0.5	0.3	0.3	0.3	0.4	0.4	0.7	1.2	1.4
Depreciation 14	0.6	0.8	1.2	0.7	0.8	0.4	0.5	0.4	0.4	0.5	1.1	0.5	0.4
Amortization and Depletion 15	0.1	0.0	0.0	0.0	0.0	0.0	0.0	0.0	0.1	0.0	0.1	0.1	0.2
Pensions and Other Deferred Comp. 16	0.2	0.1	0.3	0.4	0.3	0.2	0.2	0.1	0.2	0.2	0.3	0.2	0.1
Employee Benefits 17	0.4	0.4	0.7	0.7	0.4	0.5	0.5	0.4	0.4	0.2	0.4	0.5	0.3
Advertising 18	0.3	0.3	0.2	0.4	0.2	0.2	0.2	0.2	0.2	0.4	0.5	0.6	0.7
Other Expenses 19	7.3	20.5	14.0	4.7	4.3	2.7	2.9	2.6	2.6	2.8	4.0	3.7	25.4
Officers' Compensation 20	1.9	2.8	4.5	3.5	2.4	2.0	1.6	1.4	1.0	0.9	0.7	1.0	0.4
Operating Margin 21	3.9	5.1	5.3	4.5	3.6	3.0	2.8	3.2	2.7	3.9	2.6	4.0	5.5
Operating Margin Before Officers' Comp. 22	5.8	7.9	9.8	8.0	6.0	5.0	4.4	4.6	3.7	4.8	3.3	5.0	5.9

Selected Average Balance Sheet ($ in Thousands)

Net Receivables 23	327	0	14	103	353	1680	4330	10199	21735	34828	94871	189856	721168
Inventories 24	451	0	19	185	630	1892	3241	7378	12763	51931	60297	298225	2276563
Net Property, Plant and Equipment 25	155	0	21	96	215	606	1321	2388	6089	15224	66508	125748	187842
Total Assets 26	1740	0	105	691	2232	7047	14862	33939	67336	155821	355010	1077362	7129243
Notes and Loans Payable 27	630	0	60	267	960	2113	4080	9175	17224	41166	96910	267025	3444911
All Other Liabilities 28	602	0	21	239	793	3180	6735	15751	32930	61041	145242	428719	1310482
Net Worth 29	508	0	24	185	479	1754	4046	9013	17181	53614	112858	381617	2373850

Selected Financial Ratios (Times to 1)

Current Ratio 30	1.6	•	1.9	1.5	1.5	1.5	1.4	1.4	1.4	1.6	1.5	1.8	2.0
Quick Ratio 31	0.7	•	1.1	0.7	0.5	0.7	0.7	0.8	0.8	0.7	0.9	0.7	0.6
Net Sales to Working Capital 32	7.3	•	17.1	11.9	7.9	8.6	9.9	8.6	10.1	6.0	7.8	5.4	3.5
Coverage Ratio 33	10.0	16.5	13.2	10.7	9.9	16.4	13.2	14.7	11.6	16.5	8.1	6.5	8.8
Total Asset Turnover 34	1.9	•	5.5	3.1	2.1	2.3	2.2	2.1	2.1	1.8	1.7	1.6	0.9
Inventory Turnover 35	5.8	•	20.7	9.1	6.1	7.6	8.9	8.6	10.0	4.8	8.4	4.8	1.6
Receivables Turnover 36	10.2	•	41.7	22.4	12.0	19.5	7.6	7.1	6.7	8.5	6.2	9.8	17.3
Total Liabilities to Net Worth 37	2.4	•	3.3	2.7	3.7	3.0	2.7	2.8	2.9	1.9	2.1	1.8	2.0
Current Assets to Working Capital 38	2.7	•	2.1	3.0	3.1	3.0	3.7	3.3	3.9	2.6	3.0	2.3	2.0
Current Liabilities to Working Capital 39	1.7	•	1.1	2.0	2.1	2.0	2.7	2.3	2.9	1.6	2.0	1.3	1.0
Working Capital to Net Sales 40	0.1	•	0.1	0.1	0.1	0.1	0.1	0.1	0.1	0.2	0.1	0.2	0.3
Inventory to Working Capital 41	1.1	•	0.6	1.1	1.1	1.0	1.0	1.0	0.9	1.3	0.8	1.0	1.3
Total Receipts to Cash Flow 42	8.2	3.0	5.2	11.4	12.3	16.2	17.2	15.8	17.0	12.2	13.0	10.6	2.9
Cost of Goods to Cash Flow 43	6.6	2.0	3.5	9.1	10.3	14.3	15.0	14.0	15.2	10.6	11.1	8.8	1.7
Cash Flow to Total Debt 44	0.3	•	1.4	0.4	0.2	0.2	0.2	0.2	0.2	0.2	0.2	0.2	0.5

Selected Financial Factors (in Percentages)

Debt Ratio 45	70.8	•	76.9	73.3	78.5	75.1	72.8	73.4	74.5	65.6	68.2	64.6	66.7
Return on Total Assets 46	12.2	•	40.6	18.1	10.7	10.1	9.2	10.0	9.2	11.9	8.8	12.5	10.5
Return on Equity Before Income Taxes 47	37.7	•	162.1	61.2	44.8	38.3	31.2	35.0	32.8	32.4	24.3	29.8	28.1
Return on Equity After Income Taxes 48	32.6	•	160.4	59.7	42.6	37.1	29.6	33.2	31.4	31.1	20.6	22.0	18.7
Profit Margin (Before Income Tax) 49	5.8	15.3	6.8	5.4	4.7	4.1	3.8	4.4	3.9	6.0	4.6	6.6	10.7
Profit Margin (After Income Tax) 50	5.0	15.2	6.7	5.2	4.5	4.0	3.6	4.2	3.8	5.8	3.9	4.9	7.1

Table I

Corporations with and without Net Income

HEAVY AND CIVIL ENGINEERING CONSTRUCTION

MONEY AMOUNTS AND SIZE OF ASSETS IN THOUSANDS OF DOLLARS

Item Description for Accounting Period 7/03 Through 6/04	Total	Zero Assets	Under 500	500 to 1,000	1,000 to 5,000	5,000 to 10,000	10,000 to 25,000	25,000 to 50,000	50,000 to 100,000	100,000 to 250,000	250,000 to 500,000	500,000 to 2,500,000	2,500,000 and over
Number of Enterprises 1	26687	1133	13957	3531	5721	1229	751	195	102	40	10	13	5
Revenues ($ in Thousands)													
Net Sales 2	161049126	681805	10056535	5781262	31312936	16449390	22775758	11325705	11213563	8588916	5676622	15382139	21804495
Interest 3	934150	2173	8038	6743	19034	11934	19949	10806	10182	11215	16309	73067	744700
Rents 4	173869	315	14733	6838	16972	3280	33106	13815	8851	580	8346	38802	28229
Royalties 5	57826	0	0	0	36	0	2633	500	349	3319	0	8135	42854
Other Portfolio Income 6	638553	6520	33710	21772	122750	77735	74012	85315	55911	29928	11761	102596	16540
Other Receipts 7	1694647	3489	70264	78310	159194	127709	109936	79738	92536	98025	30540	73273	771639
Total Receipts 8	164548171	694302	10183280	5894925	31630922	16670048	23015394	11515879	11381392	8731983	5743578	15678012	23408457
Average Total Receipts 9	6166	613	730	1669	5529	13564	30646	59056	111582	218300	574358	1206001	4681691
Operating Costs/Operating Income (%)													
Cost of Operations 10	74.7	69.4	43.4	55.0	64.6	75.5	80.8	82.8	80.2	82.4	90.5	83.0	82.2
Salaries and Wages 11	4.5	2.1	11.0	11.1	5.2	4.0	2.9	2.7	3.2	3.3	2.6	4.1	4.0
Taxes Paid 12	1.9	1.5	3.2	2.9	2.5	2.0	1.7	1.6	1.6	1.2	3.1	1.6	0.8
Interest Paid 13	1.5	0.4	0.9	1.3	0.7	0.6	0.6	0.6	0.6	0.7	1.1	1.3	6.5
Depreciation 14	4.1	6.6	5.0	6.9	4.8	4.4	4.0	4.1	4.1	4.4	2.6	2.2	3.1
Amortization and Depletion 15	0.3	0.0	0.0	0.0	0.0	0.0	0.1	0.1	0.2	0.4	0.2	0.7	1.4
Pensions and Other Deferred Comp. 16	0.5	0.0	0.3	0.7	0.9	0.3	0.4	0.5	0.3	0.4	0.1	0.2	0.7
Employee Benefits 17	1.2	0.3	1.7	1.0	1.0	2.6	1.2	1.1	1.1	1.0	1.5	0.8	0.9
Advertising 18	0.1	0.3	0.5	0.5	0.1	0.1	0.1	0.1	0.1	0.1	0.0	0.1	0.0
Other Expenses 19	10.7	20.6	23.6	14.4	17.2	9.2	6.1	5.6	7.0	5.8	4.4	6.9	10.8
Officers' Compensation 20	2.3	4.8	9.0	6.1	3.6	2.0	1.8	1.5	1.1	1.0	0.8	0.6	0.5
Operating Margin 21	•	•	1.3	•	•	•	0.3	•	0.6	•	•	•	•
Operating Margin Before Officers' Comp. 22	0.4	•	10.3	6.1	2.9	1.2	2.1	0.9	1.6	0.5	•	•	•

Selected Average Balance Sheet ($ in Thousands)

	1	2	3	4	5	6	7	8	9	10	11	12	13
Net Receivables 23	956	0	23	130	697	2415	5261	10984	19231	37844	120589	250475	749487
Inventories 24	113	0	5	6	87	406	439	825	2216	5619	5142	13685	151069
Net Property, Plant and Equipment 25	922	0	80	282	747	1934	4195	8461	18715	40707	82635	146588	954192
Total Assets 26	3513	0	173	630	2230	7113	15253	33279	67125	139138	317612	782607	4781838
Notes and Loans Payable 27	841	0	112	273	703	2191	3551	7886	14080	41612	124168	178951	468967
All Other Liabilities 28	1578	0	36	103	715	2436	5541	12475	21537	46237	161270	333141	3514174
Net Worth 29	1094	0	25	254	812	2486	6160	12918	31508	51290	32173	270515	798697

Selected Financial Ratios (Times to 1)

	1	2	3	4	5	6	7	8	9	10	11	12	13
Current Ratio 30	1.3	•	1.2	2.0	1.5	1.7	1.5	1.5	1.7	1.3	1.1	1.3	1.0
Quick Ratio 31	1.0	•	1.1	1.8	1.3	1.3	1.2	1.2	1.3	1.0	1.0	0.9	0.7
Net Sales to Working Capital 32	12.8	•	52.6	11.1	12.5	7.3	9.3	8.1	7.1	13.2	24.9	12.8	•
Coverage Ratio 33	1.1	•	4.0	2.4	1.5	1.9	3.4	2.9	4.4	2.5	•	1.3	0.5
Total Asset Turnover 34	1.7	•	4.2	2.6	2.5	1.9	2.0	1.7	1.6	1.5	1.8	1.5	0.9
Inventory Turnover 35	40.0	•	67.3	148.3	40.7	24.9	55.9	58.3	39.8	31.5	99.9	71.7	23.7
Receivables Turnover 36	6.5	•	30.8	14.0	8.9	5.8	6.1	5.3	5.9	5.5	5.0	5.0	5.6
Total Liabilities to Net Worth 37	2.2	•	5.9	1.5	1.7	1.9	1.5	1.6	1.1	1.7	8.9	1.9	5.0
Current Assets to Working Capital 38	3.9	•	5.4	2.0	2.9	2.5	3.0	2.9	2.5	4.4	8.0	4.8	•
Current Liabilities to Working Capital 39	2.9	•	4.4	1.0	1.9	1.5	2.0	1.9	1.5	3.4	7.0	3.8	•
Working Capital to Net Sales 40	0.1	•	0.0	0.1	0.1	0.1	0.1	0.1	0.1	0.1	0.0	0.1	•
Inventory to Working Capital 41	0.3	•	0.4	0.1	0.2	0.3	0.1	0.1	0.2	0.3	0.3	0.1	•
Total Receipts to Cash Flow 42	14.3	8.3	5.1	8.7	8.3	25.5	23.2	33.4	17.0	23.2	•	21.8	17.6
Cost of Goods to Cash Flow 43	10.7	5.8	2.2	4.8	5.4	19.3	18.7	27.7	13.6	19.1	•	18.1	14.5
Cash Flow to Total Debt 44	0.2	•	0.5	0.5	0.1	0.1	0.1	0.1	0.2	0.1	•	0.1	0.1

Selected Financial Factors (in Percentages)

	1	2	3	4	5	6	7	8	9	10	11	12	13
Debt Ratio 45	68.9	•	85.6	59.7	63.6	65.0	59.6	61.2	53.1	63.1	89.9	65.4	83.3
Return on Total Assets 46	2.9	•	14.5	8.5	2.6	2.2	3.8	2.7	4.2	2.7	•	2.5	2.8
Return on Equity Before Income Taxes 47	0.9	•	75.4	12.4	2.5	2.9	6.7	4.6	7.0	4.4	•	1.6	•
Return on Equity After Income Taxes 48	•	•	73.2	11.4	1.9	1.8	5.8	3.6	6.4	3.6	•	•	•
Profit Margin (Before Income Tax) 49	0.2	•	2.6	1.9	0.4	0.5	1.4	1.0	2.0	1.0	0.1	0.4	•
Profit Margin (After Income Tax) 50	•	•	2.5	1.8	0.3	0.3	1.2	0.8	1.8	0.9	•	•	•

Table II

Corporations with Net Income

HEAVY AND CIVIL ENGINEERING CONSTRUCTION

MONEY AMOUNTS AND SIZE OF ASSETS IN THOUSANDS OF DOLLARS

Item Description for Accounting Period 7/03 Through 6/04	Total	Zero Assets	Under 500	500 to 1,000	1,000 to 5,000	5,000 to 10,000	10,000 to 25,000	25,000 to 50,000	50,000 to 100,000	100,000 to 250,000	250,000 to 500,000	500,000 to 2,500,000	2,500,000 and over
Number of Enterprises **1**	15543	706	7636	2083	3800	590	504	115	66	27	4	•	•
Revenues ($ in Thousands)													
Net Sales **2**	107415210	583486	6832621	3254577	23373183	7825959	15806212	6759972	7595035	6891604	2824796	•	•
Interest **3**	183580	1685	5889	3912	12524	8915	13297	7179	8222	4215	6307	•	•
Rents **4**	123792	193	10001	1673	14773	1914	13184	7927	7012	323	2746	•	•
Royalties **5**	48705	0	0	0	36	0	1602	487	301	174	0	•	•
Other Portfolio Income **6**	395018	4264	26432	19129	57450	46958	37543	42934	39645	20846	4281	•	•
Other Receipts **7**	1451628	1206	27001	56858	184996	74539	92680	45249	89751	93665	27941	•	•
Total Receipts **8**	109617933	590834	6901944	3336149	23642962	7958285	15964518	6863748	7739966	7010827	2886071	•	•
Average Total Receipts **9**	7053	837	904	1602	6222	13489	31676	59685	117272	259660	716518	•	•
Operating Costs/Operating Income (%)													
Cost of Operations **10**	73.2	73.6	39.0	50.6	61.0	75.2	79.3	79.8	80.0	82.5	89.2	•	•
Salaries and Wages **11**	4.5	2.0	11.3	9.6	5.1	4.8	2.8	2.9	3.1	2.9	1.7	•	•
Taxes Paid **12**	1.8	1.2	3.3	3.0	2.5	1.6	1.7	1.8	1.4	1.1	1.1	•	•
Interest Paid **13**	0.7	0.3	0.7	0.9	0.6	0.5	0.4	0.5	0.5	0.5	0.8	•	•
Depreciation **14**	3.5	6.5	4.3	7.2	4.2	3.9	3.7	4.0	3.6	4.0	1.6	•	•
Amortization and Depletion **15**	0.2	0.0	0.0	0.0	0.0	0.0	0.0	0.1	0.1	0.3	0.1	•	•
Pensions and Other Deferred Comp. **16**	0.6	0.0	0.4	0.9	1.2	0.2	0.4	0.5	0.3	0.4	0.0	•	•
Employee Benefits **17**	0.9	0.2	1.4	1.1	1.0	1.2	1.1	1.0	0.8	1.0	0.7	•	•
Advertising **18**	0.1	0.0	0.4	0.4	0.2	0.1	0.1	0.1	0.1	0.1	0.0	•	•
Other Expenses **19**	9.9	12.1	21.9	14.1	18.5	7.1	5.8	5.4	6.6	4.3	2.3	•	•
Officers' Compensation **20**	2.6	0.4	10.6	7.9	3.9	2.4	1.9	1.6	1.0	1.0	0.7	•	•
Operating Margin **21**	2.0	3.6	6.7	4.5	1.9	3.0	2.8	2.3	2.7	2.0	1.7	•	•
Operating Margin Before Officers' Comp. **22**	4.6	4.1	17.3	12.3	5.8	5.4	4.7	4.0	3.7	3.0	2.4	•	•

Selected Average Balance Sheet ($ in Thousands)

Line Item											
Net Receivables 23	1033	0	17	92	713	2454	5283	10437	20344	38508	156450
Inventories 24	80	0	2	5	44	169	432	838	2257	7437	6961
Net Property, Plant and Equipment 25	914	0	88	256	692	1823	3831	8196	16958	41932	77042
Total Assets 26	3656	0	197	604	2177	7056	15176	33066	67674	139617	334240
Notes and Loans Payable 27	749	0	79	246	593	1709	2861	5737	11347	30120	68746
All Other Liabilities 28	1360	0	20	82	704	2368	5453	12055	21733	38880	157221
Net Worth 29	1547	0	99	276	880	2978	6862	15275	34595	70617	108273

Selected Financial Ratios (Times to 1)

Line Item											
Current Ratio 30	1.5	.	2.0	2.5	1.6	1.8	1.6	1.6	1.8	1.8	1.6
Quick Ratio 31	1.2	.	1.8	2.2	1.4	1.5	1.3	1.3	1.4	1.3	1.5
Net Sales to Working Capital 32	10.9	.	20.2	9.2	12.8	6.1	8.1	7.4	6.5	7.9	8.5
Coverage Ratio 33	6.7	18.8	12.2	8.9	5.9	10.6	9.9	9.6	11.0	8.5	4.9
Total Asset Turnover 34	1.9	.	4.5	2.6	2.8	1.9	2.1	1.8	1.7	1.8	2.1
Inventory Turnover 35	63.0	.	150.1	152.9	85.2	59.1	57.6	56.0	40.8	28.3	90.5
Receivables Turnover 36	6.9	.	36.4	30.5	9.9	10.8	6.0	5.0	5.9	5.7	5.5
Total Liabilities to Net Worth 37	1.4	.	1.0	1.2	1.5	1.4	1.2	1.2	1.0	1.0	2.1
Current Assets to Working Capital 38	3.2	.	2.0	1.7	2.7	2.2	2.6	2.6	2.2	2.3	2.8
Current Liabilities to Working Capital 39	2.2	.	1.0	0.7	1.7	1.2	1.6	1.6	1.2	1.3	1.8
Working Capital to Net Sales 40	0.1	.	0.0	0.1	0.1	0.2	0.1	0.1	0.2	0.1	0.1
Inventory to Working Capital 41	0.1	.	0.1	0.0	0.1	0.1	0.1	0.1	0.2	0.2	0.1
Total Receipts to Cash Flow 42	9.6	6.8	4.3	6.3	11.8	15.3	17.2	11.6	16.9		21.6
Cost of Goods to Cash Flow 43	7.0	5.0	1.7	3.2	8.9	12.1	13.7	9.3	14.0		19.3
Cash Flow to Total Debt 44	0.3	.	2.1	0.8	0.8	0.3	0.2	0.2	0.3	0.2	0.1

Selected Financial Factors (in Percentages)

Line Item											
Debt Ratio 45	57.7	.	49.9	54.3	59.6	57.8	54.8	53.8	48.9	49.4	67.6
Return on Total Assets 46	8.8	.	38.0	20.3	10.4	9.7	8.7	7.7	8.5	7.6	8.2
Return on Equity Before Income Taxes 47	17.8	.	69.6	39.5	21.3	20.9	17.2	14.8	15.1	13.2	20.1
Return on Equity After Income Taxes 48	16.1	.	68.6	37.9	20.4	19.1	16.0	13.5	14.3	12.4	14.5
Profit Margin (Before Income Tax) 49	4.0	4.9	7.7	7.0	3.1	4.7	3.8	3.9	4.5	3.7	3.1
Profit Margin (After Income Tax) 50	3.6	4.5	7.6	6.7	2.9	4.3	3.5	3.5	4.3	3.4	2.2

Table I

Corporations with and without Net Income

LAND SUBDIVISION

Money Amounts and Size of Assets in Thousands of Dollars

Item Description for Accounting Period 7/03 Through 6/04	Total	Zero Assets	Under 500	500 to 1,000	1,000 to 5,000	5,000 to 10,000	10,000 to 25,000	25,000 to 50,000	50,000 to 100,000	100,000 to 250,000	250,000 to 500,000	500,000 to 2,500,000	2,500,000 and over
Number of Enterprises **1**	50408	3094	31322	5174	8705	1245	566	167	71	42	12	9	•
Revenues ($ in Thousands)													
Net Sales **2**	35238726	421594	3393633	1323966	8756384	4582024	4514524	2631384	1668878	2637447	1680246	3628644	•
Interest **3**	358797	6587	10349	5456	54325	17240	25108	27390	22090	66827	36772	86652	•
Rents **4**	470163	9763	27777	8597	48902	16754	43976	20690	47466	68583	71460	106196	•
Royalties **5**	16114	7643	0	0	652	5597	768	1422	0	32	0	0	•
Other Portfolio Income **6**	503147	87165	99392	17681	28142	24525	38503	23574	11887	27222	35449	109607	•
Other Receipts **7**	2360655	152002	272530	2860	601908	120540	249694	132851	250107	73063	136933	368169	•
Total Receipts **8**	38947602	684754	3803681	1358560	9490313	4766680	4872573	2837311	2000428	2873174	1960860	4299268	•
Average Total Receipts **9**	773	221	121	263	1090	3829	8609	16990	28175	68409	163405	477696	•
Operating Costs/Operating Income (%)													
Cost of Operations **10**	67.4	29.3	48.3	52.5	70.3	73.1	74.7	74.7	65.9	70.0	62.6	67.4	•
Salaries and Wages **11**	6.2	14.4	13.3	4.8	3.3	4.5	5.3	5.3	6.5	9.3	10.3	5.5	•
Taxes Paid **12**	2.3	2.8	4.0	2.9	2.0	1.6	1.6	1.6	2.3	1.8	5.7	2.5	•
Interest Paid **13**	3.9	3.7	3.5	3.3	4.1	3.0	2.7	3.8	5.7	3.7	8.7	3.8	•
Depreciation **14**	2.1	2.5	3.6	1.8	1.2	2.0	1.8	1.9	2.1	2.7	2.7	2.6	•
Amortization and Depletion **15**	0.1	1.8	0.0	0.0	0.0	0.1	0.1	0.1	0.2	0.2	0.4	0.1	•
Pensions and Other Deferred Comp. **16**	0.7	0.1	3.6	0.3	1.0	0.1	0.2	0.1	0.1	0.5	0.2	0.1	•
Employee Benefits **17**	0.6	0.2	1.8	0.3	0.2	0.3	0.4	0.4	0.4	0.7	1.4	0.9	•
Advertising **18**	0.8	0.7	0.5	0.1	0.5	1.3	0.9	0.9	0.8	0.6	1.3	0.8	•
Other Expenses **19**	15.9	75.6	28.6	32.2	15.1	12.2	8.6	8.5	20.7	15.8	15.6	10.3	•
Officers' Compensation **20**	2.5	7.4	6.0	4.0	2.7	1.4	2.4	2.3	2.3	2.0	1.1	0.3	•
Operating Margin **21**	•	•	•	•	•	0.2	1.2	0.5	•	•	•	5.7	•
Operating Margin Before Officers' Comp. **22**	0.0	•	1.8	2.2	1.6	2.2	3.7	2.8	•	•	•	6.1	•

Selected Average Balance Sheet ($ in Thousands)

Net Receivables 23	117	0	11	19	185	218	1292	2499	5201	17397	19163	124982	•
Inventories 24	327	0	21	150	549	1860	3295	9125	13360	19824	81760	199119	•
Net Property, Plant and Equipment 25	387	0	39	240	526	2069	4099	8030	13166	41671	124251	227119	•
Total Assets 26	1478	0	126	704	2037	7063	15303	34452	70019	151864	364041	1139117	•
Notes and Loans Payable 27	881	0	154	412	1306	4852	8919	22717	33808	59193	211397	418149	•
All Other Liabilities 28	289	0	62	101	336	1191	2759	5778	12590	38720	63325	211552	•
Net Worth 29	308	0	-90	191	395	1020	3625	5958	23621	53951	89318	509416	•

Selected Financial Ratios (Times to 1)

Current Ratio 30	1.9	•	1.1	2.5	2.0	2.0	1.9	2.0	2.7	1.7	1.6	1.5	•
Quick Ratio 31	0.5	•	0.4	0.8	0.6	0.3	0.6	0.5	0.8	0.7	0.4	0.6	•
Net Sales to Working Capital 32	2.2	•	27.8	1.2	1.8	2.0	2.1	1.7	1.2	2.6	3.4	2.9	•
Coverage Ratio 33	3.1	7.5	0.7	1.1	2.9	2.4	4.4	3.2	3.2	1.5	1.8	7.3	•
Total Asset Turnover 34	0.5	•	0.9	0.4	0.5	0.5	0.5	0.5	0.3	0.4	0.4	0.4	•
Inventory Turnover 35	1.4	•	2.5	0.9	1.3	1.4	1.8	1.3	1.2	2.2	1.1	1.4	•
Receivables Turnover 36	6.4	•	13.6	5.0	6.5	14.9	6.8	6.3	3.9	4.9	6.6	3.5	•
Total Liabilities to Net Worth 37	3.8	•	2.7	4.2	5.9	3.2	4.8	2.0	1.8	3.1	1.2		•
Current Assets to Working Capital 38	2.2	•	15.6	1.7	2.0	2.1	2.0	2.0	1.6	2.4	2.6	2.9	•
Current Liabilities to Working Capital 39	1.2	•	14.6	0.7	1.0	1.0	1.1	1.0	0.6	1.4	1.6	1.9	•
Working Capital to Net Sales 40	0.5	•	0.0	0.8	0.6	0.5	0.5	0.6	0.8	0.4	0.3	0.3	•
Inventory to Working Capital 41	1.1	•	7.0	0.6	1.0	1.2	0.9	1.0	0.8	0.9	1.5	1.7	•
Total Receipts to Cash Flow 42	4.9	1.5	5.0	3.4	4.6	7.6	6.4	6.7	3.3	7.2	5.3	3.5	•
Cost of Goods to Cash Flow 43	3.3	0.4	2.4	1.8	3.3	5.6	4.8	5.0	2.2	5.0	3.3	2.4	•
Cash Flow to Total Debt 44	0.1	•	0.1	0.1	0.1	0.1	0.1	0.1	0.2	0.1	0.1	0.2	•

Selected Financial Factors (in Percentages)

Debt Ratio 45	79.2	•	171.8	72.9	80.6	85.6	76.3	82.7	66.3	64.5	75.5	55.3	•
Return on Total Assets 46	5.7	•	2.0	1.4	5.9	3.8	6.2	5.6	6.2	2.2	5.9	9.9	•
Return on Equity Before Income Taxes 47	18.3	•	1.4	0.6	20.1	15.3	20.1	22.3	12.7	2.1	10.5	19.1	•
Return on Equity After Income Taxes 48	14.7	•	1.5	0.2	19.4	12.7	19.2	20.0	11.0	0.9	6.5	12.0	•
Profit Margin (Before Income Tax) 49	8.0	23.8	•	0.4	7.9	4.2	9.1	8.4	12.7	1.8	6.7	24.2	•
Profit Margin (After Income Tax) 50	6.5	19.6	•	0.2	7.6	3.5	8.7	7.6	11.1	0.8	4.1	15.2	•

Table II

Corporations with Net Income

LAND SUBDIVISION

MONEY AMOUNTS AND SIZE OF ASSETS IN THOUSANDS OF DOLLARS

Item Description for Accounting Period 7/03 Through 6/04	Total	Zero Assets	Under 500	500 to 1,000	1,000 to 5,000	5,000 to 10,000	10,000 to 25,000	25,000 to 50,000	50,000 to 100,000	100,000 to 250,000	250,000 to 500,000	500,000 to 2,500,000	2,500,000 and over
Number of Enterprises **1**	20005	1094	10813	2319	4587	684	331	•	43	19	•	•	•
Revenues ($ in Thousands)													
Net Sales **2**	25313580	108610	1501292	979061	5982412	2928281	3574464	•	1415091	1916594	•	•	•
Interest **3**	221981	1397	8646	5184	33105	12360	18731	•	17254	38919	•	•	•
Rents **4**	275598	2247	26801	8176	34576	15136	30570	•	18254	38393	•	•	•
Royalties **5**	2250	0	0	0	7	54	767	•	0	0	•	•	•
Other Portfolio Income **6**	447619	82485	96289	17681	25493	22259	32864	•	8211	7605	•	•	•
Other Receipts **7**	1844582	253433	151983	-646	325957	107343	190550	•	160655	72736	•	•	•
Total Receipts **8**	28105610	448172	1785011	1009456	6401550	3085433	3847946	•	1619465	2074247	•	•	•
Average Total Receipts **9**	1405	410	165	435	1396	4511	11625	•	37662	109171	•	•	•
Operating Costs/Operating Income (%)													
Cost of Operations **10**	67.8	59.6	49.2	46.6	64.1	71.8	73.9	•	68.4	73.5	•	•	•
Salaries and Wages **11**	4.2	2.3	7.6	0.3	2.8	1.9	4.5	•	5.1	7.3	•	•	•
Taxes Paid **12**	1.7	7.4	2.4	2.6	1.6	1.5	1.3	•	1.9	1.2	•	•	•
Interest Paid **13**	2.6	5.0	4.1	1.7	3.2	2.2	1.9	•	2.9	2.4	•	•	•
Depreciation **14**	1.3	1.6	1.3	1.8	1.1	1.2	1.2	•	1.3	1.8	•	•	•
Amortization and Depletion **15**	0.1	0.1	0.0	0.0	0.0	0.1	0.0	•	0.2	0.1	•	•	•
Pensions and Other Deferred Comp. **16**	0.2	0.2	0.4	0.4	0.4	0.1	0.2	•	0.1	0.4	•	•	•
Employee Benefits **17**	0.4	0.2	1.2	0.2	0.2	0.2	0.3	•	0.3	0.1	•	•	•
Advertising **18**	0.7	0.1	0.6	0.1	0.7	0.9	0.8	•	0.6	0.4	•	•	•
Other Expenses **19**	10.3	81.5	19.2	29.7	10.0	9.0	6.2	•	9.7	9.1	•	•	•
Officers' Compensation **20**	2.1	0.4	6.0	5.2	2.9	1.4	1.8	•	2.2	1.3	•	•	•
Operating Margin **21**	8.6	•	7.9	11.4	13.1	9.7	7.9	•	7.3	2.5	•	•	•
Operating Margin Before Officers' Comp. **22**	10.7	•	13.9	16.7	16.0	11.1	9.7	•	9.4	3.8	•	•	•

Selected Average Balance Sheet ($ in Thousands)

Net Receivables 23	190	0	4	43	201	269	1410	2934	25343
Inventories 24	530	0	23	133	592	2013	3794	16696	32637
Net Property, Plant and Equipment 25	461	0	30	312	443	1730	3320	12786	33547
Total Assets 26	2162	0	126	700	2102	7225	15284	69808	152312
Notes and Loans Payable 27	1051	0	83	377	1123	4470	7837	28267	55827
All Other Liabilities 28	435	0	107	74	370	1041	2493	10971	37701
Net Worth 29	677	0	-64	249	609	1714	4953	30571	58783

Selected Financial Ratios (Times to 1)

Current Ratio 30	2.1	•	2.7	2.1	2.1	2.0	2.1	2.8	1.9
Quick Ratio 31	0.6	•	1.1	0.6	0.5	0.9	0.6	0.8	0.9
Net Sales to Working Capital 32	2.2	•	4.0	2.3	2.0	3.0	2.0	1.6	2.7
Coverage Ratio 33	8.4	52.0	7.5	9.3	8.0	9.4	7.3	8.5	5.5
Total Asset Turnover 34	0.6	•	1.1	0.7	0.6	0.6	0.6	0.5	0.7
Inventory Turnover 35	1.6	•	3.0	2.1	1.5	1.5	1.4	1.3	2.3
Receivables Turnover 36	7.1	•	31.6	8.7	31.8	6.5	7.2	6.7	5.3
Total Liabilities to Net Worth 37	2.2	•	•	2.1	3.2	1.8	2.5	1.3	1.6
Current Assets to Working Capital 38	1.9	•	1.6	1.9	1.9	2.0	1.9	1.5	2.1
Current Liabilities to Working Capital 39	0.9	•	0.6	0.9	0.9	1.0	0.9	0.5	1.1
Working Capital to Net Sales 40	0.5	•	0.3	0.4	0.5	0.3	0.5	0.6	0.4
Inventory to Working Capital 41	1.0	•	0.8	0.9	0.9	0.6	1.1	0.8	1.0
Total Receipts to Cash Flow 42	3.7	0.4	2.7	5.0	4.5	2.4	3.5	3.3	5.8
Cost of Goods to Cash Flow 43	2.5	0.2	1.3	3.7	3.3	1.1	2.2	2.3	4.2
Cash Flow to Total Debt 44	0.2	•	0.3	0.2	0.2	0.4	0.3	0.3	0.2

Selected Financial Factors (in Percentages)

Debt Ratio 45	68.7	•	150.9	67.6	76.3	64.4	71.0	56.2	61.4
Return on Total Assets 46	13.0	•	34.1	12.3	10.2	9.8	14.4	11.6	8.6
Return on Equity Before Income Taxes 47	36.6	•	•	33.8	37.6	24.6	42.8	23.3	18.3
Return on Equity After Income Taxes 48	32.6	•	24.0	32.7	34.8	24.0	41.9	21.2	16.0
Profit Margin (Before Income Tax) 49	19.6	253.9	26.8	15.5	15.1	14.5	20.0	21.7	10.7
Profit Margin (After Income Tax) 50	17.4	237.4	26.5	15.0	13.9	14.2	19.6	19.7	9.3

30

Table I

Corporations with and without Net Income

ELECTRICAL CONTRACTORS

MONEY AMOUNTS AND SIZE OF ASSETS IN THOUSANDS OF DOLLARS

Item Description for Accounting Period 7/03 Through 6/04	Total	Zero Assets	Under 500	500 to 1,000	1,000 to 5,000	5,000 to 10,000	10,000 to 25,000	25,000 to 50,000	50,000 to 100,000	100,000 to 250,000	250,000 to 500,000	500,000 to 2,500,000	2,500,000 and over
Number of Enterprises 1	45496	4472	34652	2855	2645	606	212	35	13	6	•	•	•
Revenues ($ in Thousands)													
Net Sales 2	61001563	753990	13972092	5656346	14832760	9815176	7475642	2648711	2077417	3769428	•	•	•
Interest 3	58156	508	4520	1868	17868	3796	2220	301	1384	25690	•	•	•
Rents 4	16616	0	7338	524	4355	1796	1301	166	422	714	•	•	•
Royalties 5	848	0	0	0	0	848	0	0	0	0	•	•	•
Other Portfolio Income 6	88077	36234	8306	3623	15009	7917	7649	2450	5924	965	•	•	•
Other Receipts 7	219193	8069	10211	-65565	85489	40432	36038	34993	13755	55772	•	•	•
Total Receipts 8	61384453	798801	14002467	5596796	14955481	9869965	7522850	2686621	2098902	3852569	•	•	•
Average Total Receipts 9	1349	179	404	1960	5654	16287	35485	76761	161454	642095	•	•	•
Operating Costs/Operating Income (%)													
Cost of Operations 10	70.3	58.0	49.5	67.1	77.9	76.3	77.6	78.8	81.8	81.6	•	•	•
Salaries and Wages 11	6.5	11.1	11.3	6.6	4.0	4.8	5.6	5.6	4.4	5.8	•	•	•
Taxes Paid 12	2.8	3.3	3.7	2.9	2.8	2.5	2.5	3.2	2.0	1.3	•	•	•
Interest Paid 13	0.7	1.4	0.8	0.6	0.4	0.4	0.3	0.3	0.2	2.8	•	•	•
Depreciation 14	1.7	3.3	2.4	1.7	1.4	1.4	1.0	1.0	1.0	3.0	•	•	•
Amortization and Depletion 15	0.1	0.5	0.0	0.0	0.0	0.0	0.0	0.1	0.1	1.6	•	•	•
Pensions and Other Deferred Comp. 16	0.6	2.7	0.4	0.4	0.4	1.2	0.6	0.5	0.3	0.1	•	•	•
Employee Benefits 17	2.9	0.8	2.2	1.7	2.8	4.3	3.7	3.0	4.6	1.1	•	•	•
Advertising 18	0.2	1.1	0.4	0.3	0.1	0.1	0.1	0.2	0.1	0.1	•	•	•
Other Expenses 19	8.9	17.2	16.9	12.2	6.2	5.3	4.4	4.3	4.9	7.3	•	•	•
Officers' Compensation 20	4.5	7.1	8.7	5.7	3.9	2.7	2.4	1.9	2.0	0.7	•	•	•
Operating Margin 21	0.8	•	3.6	0.8	0.2	0.8	1.6	1.1	•	•	•	•	•
Operating Margin Before Officers' Comp. 22	5.3	0.5	12.3	6.4	4.1	3.5	4.0	3.0	0.7	0.7	•	•	•

Selected Average Balance Sheet ($ in Thousands)

Item										
Net Receivables 23	213	0	20	302	936	3566	8051	15855	37289	121984
Inventories 24	25	0	8	45	131	336	498	765	534	4643
Net Property, Plant and Equipment 25	75	0	30	99	253	762	1360	2991	5129	81078
Total Assets 26	518	0	101	716	2197	6911	15027	34454	71758	453308
Notes and Loans Payable 27	138	0	62	163	349	1704	2497	6249	4074	149234
All Other Liabilities 28	197	0	21	238	930	2993	6874	15938	40495	122408
Net Worth 29	183	0	17	315	917	2215	5656	12268	27189	181665

Selected Financial Ratios (Times to 1)

Item										
Current Ratio 30	1.7	•	1.6	2.0	1.6	1.4	1.6	1.6	1.5	2.5
Quick Ratio 31	1.3	•	1.2	1.6	1.2	1.1	1.3	1.2	1.2	1.8
Net Sales to Working Capital 32	8.9	•	20.5	6.9	8.4	9.1	7.2	7.1	8.3	4.5
Coverage Ratio 33	3.2	0.6	5.6	0.5	3.8	4.0	7.5	9.1	•	•
Total Asset Turnover 34	2.6	•	4.0	2.8	2.6	2.3	2.3	2.2	2.2	1.4
Inventory Turnover 35	37.0	•	24.5	29.5	33.4	36.8	55.0	77.9	244.6	110.4
Receivables Turnover 36	6.2	•	21.8	7.5	5.6	5.2	4.7	4.1	4.5	7.7
Total Liabilities to Net Worth 37	1.8	•	4.8	1.3	1.4	2.1	1.7	1.8	1.6	1.5
Current Assets to Working Capital 38	2.5	•	2.8	2.0	2.6	3.2	2.6	2.7	3.0	1.6
Current Liabilities to Working Capital 39	1.5	•	1.8	1.0	1.6	2.2	1.6	1.7	2.0	0.6
Working Capital to Net Sales 40	0.1	•	0.0	0.1	0.1	0.1	0.1	0.1	0.1	0.2
Inventory to Working Capital 41	0.2	•	0.4	0.2	0.2	0.2	0.1	0.1	0.0	0.1
Total Receipts to Cash Flow 42	12.4	7.7	5.7	13.1	17.6	20.9	19.5	18.2	37.1	51.8
Cost of Goods to Cash Flow 43	8.7	4.5	2.8	8.8	13.7	15.9	15.1	14.4	30.3	42.2
Cash Flow to Total Debt 44	0.3	•	0.8	0.4	0.2	0.2	0.2	0.2	0.1	0.0

Selected Financial Factors (in Percentages)

Item									
Debt Ratio 45	64.6	82.7	56.1	58.3	68.0	62.4	64.4	62.1	59.9
Return on Total Assets 46	5.5	18.5	0.9	3.5	4.2	6.0	6.3	•	•
Return on Equity Before Income Taxes 47	10.8	87.7	•	6.2	9.8	13.8	15.8	•	•
Return on Equity After Income Taxes 48	9.4	86.0	•	4.3	8.2	12.2	14.6	•	•
Profit Margin (Before Income Tax) 49	1.5	3.8	•	1.0	1.3	2.2	2.6	•	•
Profit Margin (After Income Tax) 50	1.3	3.7	•	0.7	1.1	2.0	2.4	•	•

31

Table II

Corporations with Net Income

ELECTRICAL CONTRACTORS

MONEY AMOUNTS AND SIZE OF ASSETS IN THOUSANDS OF DOLLARS

Item Description for Accounting Period 7/03 Through 6/04		Total	Zero Assets	Under 500	500 to 1,000	1,000 to 5,000	5,000 to 10,000	10,000 to 25,000	25,000 to 50,000	50,000 to 100,000	100,000 to 250,000	250,000 to 500,000	500,000 to 2,500,000	2,500,000 and over
Number of Enterprises	1	26340	1727	21229	1308	1407	466	166	26	8	3	•	•	•
Revenues ($ in Thousands)														
Net Sales	2	40403426	515375	9606656	2380997	10106275	7652003	5923826	2200399	1328776	689120	•	•	•
Interest	3	20730	498	2192	962	12900	2063	1736	184	189	7	•	•	•
Rents	4	6373	0	1406	524	2674	957	564	125	123	0	•	•	•
Royalties	5	848	0	0	0	0	848	0	0	0	0			
Other Portfolio Income	6	62979	36221	1956	1715	13225	3861	2109	967	1962	965	•	•	•
Other Receipts	7	185931	21	1938	2217	57929	33190	32750	35564	9204	13113			
Total Receipts	8	40680287	552115	9614148	2386415	10193003	7692922	5960985	2237239	1340254	703205	•	•	•
Average Total Receipts	9	1544	320	453	1824	7244	16508	35910	86048	167532	234402			
Operating Costs/Operating Income (%)														
Cost of Operations	10	68.3	60.2	45.3	56.2	78.6	75.1	77.3	79.0	79.1	76.1	•	•	•
Salaries and Wages	11	6.7	9.9	12.4	9.0	3.4	4.8	5.0	5.9	4.4	7.9	•	•	•
Taxes Paid	12	2.8	3.6	3.5	3.1	2.6	2.5	2.4	3.0	2.0	1.7	•	•	•
Interest Paid	13	0.4	0.7	0.8	0.2	0.2	0.3	0.3	0.2	0.2	1.4	•	•	•
Depreciation	14	1.5	2.5	2.1	1.8	1.4	1.3	0.9	0.9	1.2	3.8	•	•	•
Amortization and Depletion	15	0.0	0.0	0.0	0.0	0.0	0.0	0.0	0.0	0.0	0.8			
Pensions and Other Deferred Comp.	16	0.6	4.0	0.2	0.3	0.4	1.1	0.8	0.6	0.5	0.2	•	•	•
Employee Benefits	17	2.4	0.4	1.7	1.4	1.6	4.1	3.3	2.0	1.1	3.6	•	•	•
Advertising	18	0.2	0.7	0.3	0.3	0.1	0.1	0.1	0.1	0.1	0.1	•	•	•
Other Expenses	19	8.2	13.0	16.6	13.5	5.3	5.2	4.3	4.0	5.1	1.9	•	•	•
Officers' Compensation	20	4.5	6.0	8.4	6.9	3.8	2.8	2.5	2.0	2.5	1.2	•	•	•
Operating Margin	21	4.4	•	8.7	7.2	2.5	2.8	3.1	2.4	3.8	1.4	•	•	•
Operating Margin Before Officers' Comp.	22	8.9	5.2	17.0	14.1	6.3	5.5	5.6	4.3	6.3	2.6	•	•	•

Selected Average Balance Sheet ($ in Thousands)

Net Receivables 23	230	0	23	191	1079	3389	8049	17255	38454	47966
Inventories 24	23	0	6	58	98	233	460	776	800	1698
Net Property, Plant and Equipment 25	72	0	33	88	278	650	1075	2872	6148	30873
Total Assets 26	526	0	105	674	2337	6590	14812	35402	73640	136305
Notes and Loans Payable 27	104	0	49	87	311	1294	2016	3986	4043	31553
All Other Liabilities 28	206	0	20	101	1026	2867	6931	16108	40260	64843
Net Worth 29	215	0	36	486	999	2429	5865	15308	29336	39910

Selected Financial Ratios (Times to 1)

Current Ratio 30	1.7	•	1.5	5.2	1.7	1.5	1.7	1.7	1.7	1.4
Quick Ratio 31	1.4	•	1.2	4.5	1.4	1.2	1.3	1.3	1.4	1.2
Net Sales to Working Capital 32	9.3	•	26.0	4.1	8.9	8.9	7.0	7.1	6.4	12.1
Coverage Ratio 33	13.1	10.7	11.4	38.2	15.4	13.0	13.6	18.8	31.3	3.5
Total Asset Turnover 34	2.9	•	4.3	2.7	3.1	2.5	2.4	2.4	2.3	1.7
Inventory Turnover 35	45.4	•	36.4	17.8	57.6	52.9	59.9	86.1	164.3	103.0
Receivables Turnover 36	6.0	•	23.5	6.7	5.6	9.7	4.7	4.1	4.3	9.6
Total Liabilities to Net Worth 37	1.4	•	1.9	0.4	1.3	1.7	1.5	1.3	1.5	2.4
Current Assets to Working Capital 38	2.4	•	3.0	1.2	2.4	3.0	2.5	2.5	2.4	3.4
Current Liabilities to Working Capital 39	1.4	•	2.0	0.2	1.4	2.0	1.5	1.5	1.4	2.4
Working Capital to Net Sales 40	0.1	•	0.0	0.2	0.1	0.1	0.1	0.1	0.2	0.1
Inventory to Working Capital 41	0.1	•	0.3	0.1	0.1	0.1	0.1	0.1	0.0	0.1
Total Receipts to Cash Flow 42	8.9	6.3	4.5	5.3	13.9	15.2	15.3	15.0	12.9	24.5
Cost of Goods to Cash Flow 43	6.1	3.8	2.0	3.0	11.0	11.4	11.8	11.8	10.2	18.6
Cash Flow to Total Debt 44	0.6	•	1.4	1.8	0.4	0.3	0.3	0.3	0.3	0.1

Selected Financial Factors (in Percentages)

Debt Ratio 45	59.1	•	65.8	27.9	57.2	63.1	60.4	56.8	60.2	70.7
Return on Total Assets 46	15.9	•	41.3	20.5	11.1	8.9	9.7	10.2	10.7	8.1
Return on Equity Before Income Taxes 47	35.9	•	110.2	27.7	24.2	22.3	22.6	22.2	26.0	19.8
Return on Equity After Income Taxes 48	33.9	•	108.8	27.1	20.9	20.4	20.6	20.9	22.5	19.7
Profit Margin (Before Income Tax) 49	5.0	6.3	8.7	7.4	3.4	3.3	3.7	4.0	4.6	3.4
Profit Margin (After Income Tax) 50	4.7	6.3	8.6	7.2	2.9	3.0	3.4	3.8	4.0	3.4

Table I

Corporations with and without Net Income

PLUMBING, HEATING, AND AIR-CONDITIONING CONTRACTORS

MONEY AMOUNTS AND SIZE OF ASSETS IN THOUSANDS OF DOLLARS

Item Description for Accounting Period 7/03 Through 6/04	Total	Zero Assets	Under 500	500 to 1,000	1,000 to 5,000	5,000 to 10,000	10,000 to 25,000	25,000 to 50,000	50,000 to 100,000	100,000 to 250,000	250,000 to 500,000	500,000 to 2,500,000	2,500,000 and over
Number of Enterprises **1**	67289	7591	51119	4372	3390	583	189	33	8	4	•	•	•
Revenues ($ in Thousands)													
Net Sales **2**	92818305	1128249	31127737	9957398	22812256	11269314	6817486	3420653	1465589	4819621	•	•	•
Interest **3**	35143	8	6814	4244	10797	4138	2321	1901	63	4858	•	•	•
Rents **4**	28255	0	2738	4986	13086	2474	3518	631	710	112	•	•	•
Royalties **5**	6627	0	0	0	0	65	0	57	0	6506	•	•	•
Other Portfolio Income **6**	163928	4127	60741	29447	33077	3574	5021	2383	149	25409	•	•	•
Other Receipts **7**	278478	38467	38900	23227	71313	22302	37764	38732	523	7250	•	•	•
Total Receipts **8**	93330736	1170851	31236930	10019302	22940529	11301867	6866110	3464357	1467034	4863756	•	•	•
Average Total Receipts **9**	1387	154	611	2292	6767	19386	36329	104981	183379	1215939	•	•	•
Operating Costs/Operating Income (%)													
Cost of Operations **10**	67.9	53.7	55.8	64.1	72.7	77.0	80.1	83.7	76.1	82.6	•	•	•
Salaries and Wages **11**	7.9	13.4	11.0	8.3	6.4	5.1	4.9	5.8	8.0	5.1	•	•	•
Taxes Paid **12**	2.7	1.9	3.2	3.0	2.6	2.3	2.1	1.4	1.8	2.7	•	•	•
Interest Paid **13**	0.5	0.7	0.6	0.4	0.4	0.3	0.3	0.7	0.5	0.4	•	•	•
Depreciation **14**	1.6	2.3	2.1	1.8	1.5	1.3	0.9	0.7	0.7	0.7	•	•	•
Amortization and Depletion **15**	0.1	0.0	0.0	0.0	0.0	0.0	0.2	0.1	0.1	0.5	•	•	•
Pensions and Other Deferred Comp. **16**	0.5	0.7	0.3	0.7	0.5	0.9	0.5	0.3	0.1	0.1	•	•	•
Employee Benefits **17**	1.9	0.6	1.4	2.9	2.1	2.6	2.5	1.1	2.1	1.7	•	•	•
Advertising **18**	0.6	0.9	1.1	0.8	0.4	0.2	0.2	0.1	0.2	0.1	•	•	•
Other Expenses **19**	10.0	26.8	13.8	10.2	8.4	5.6	5.2	4.5	8.8	9.4	•	•	•
Officers' Compensation **20**	5.0	4.6	7.7	6.2	4.2	2.8	2.3	1.1	1.1	1.6	•	•	•
Operating Margin **21**	1.4	•	2.9	1.6	0.9	1.9	0.7	0.5	0.6	•	•	•	•
Operating Margin Before Officers' Comp. **22**	6.3	•	10.6	7.8	5.1	4.7	2.9	1.6	1.7	•	•	•	•

Selected Average Balance Sheet ($ in Thousands)

Net Receivables 23	178	0	25	255	1016	4052	7910	21178	39781	316988
Inventories 24	22	0	8	53	137	256	493	2425	2714	5299
Net Property, Plant and Equipment 25	61	0	29	139	321	767	1158	4272	5978	29230
Total Assets 26	398	0	108	674	2122	7353	14174	34435	77201	603989
Notes and Loans Payable 27	100	0	52	175	466	1227	2021	9981	15648	36316
All Other Liabilities 28	186	0	29	215	981	3693	7544	21204	43123	538075
Net Worth 29	112	0	26	285	676	2433	4610	3250	18430	29598

Selected Financial Ratios (Times to 1)

Current Ratio 30	1.5	•	1.6	1.9	1.5	1.5	1.4	1.7	1.3	
Quick Ratio 31	1.2	•	1.3	1.6	1.2	1.2	1.2	1.4	1.1	
Net Sales to Working Capital 32	13.2	•	24.8	9.9	12.0	9.4	9.6	10.6	7.1	10.7
Coverage Ratio 33	5.1	•	6.4	6.6	4.8	7.9	5.2	3.4	2.4	•
Total Asset Turnover 34	3.5	•	5.7	3.4	3.2	2.6	2.5	3.0	2.4	2.0
Inventory Turnover 35	43.1	•	43.5	27.7	35.6	58.2	58.7	35.8	51.4	187.8
Receivables Turnover 36	8.2	•	26.9	9.2	6.6	5.6	4.9	5.4	3.5	7.6
Total Liabilities to Net Worth 37	2.5	•	3.1	1.4	2.1	2.0	2.1	9.6	3.2	19.4
Current Assets to Working Capital 38	2.9	•	2.6	2.1	3.0	2.9	3.2	3.3	2.5	4.1
Current Liabilities to Working Capital 39	1.9	•	1.6	1.1	2.0	1.9	2.2	2.3	1.5	3.1
Working Capital to Net Sales 40	0.1	•	0.0	0.1	0.1	0.1	0.1	0.1	0.1	0.1
Inventory to Working Capital 41	0.2	•	0.3	0.2	0.2	0.1	0.1	0.3	0.1	0.0
Total Receipts to Cash Flow 42	10.7	6.2	7.0	9.9	13.6	15.8	21.1	20.3	12.4	172.4
Cost of Goods to Cash Flow 43	7.3	3.3	3.9	6.4	9.9	12.2	16.9	17.0	9.4	142.4
Cash Flow to Total Debt 44	0.4	•	1.1	0.6	0.3	0.2	0.2	0.2	0.3	0.0

Selected Financial Factors (in Percentages)

Debt Ratio 45	71.8	•	75.5	57.8	68.2	66.9	67.5	90.6	76.1	95.1
Return on Total Assets 46	8.2	•	22.0	8.8	5.8	6.5	4.3	7.6	2.9	
Return on Equity Before Income Taxes 47	23.4	•	75.6	17.7	14.4	17.2	10.8	56.6	7.1	
Return on Equity After Income Taxes 48	22.1	•	74.5	17.5	12.7	16.1	9.1	52.6	5.1	
Profit Margin (Before Income Tax) 49	1.9	•	3.3	2.2	1.5	2.2	1.4	1.8	0.7	
Profit Margin (After Income Tax) 50	1.8	•	3.2	2.2	1.3	2.0	1.2	1.6	0.5	

Table II

Corporations with Net Income

PLUMBING, HEATING, AND AIR-CONDITIONING CONTRACTORS

MONEY AMOUNTS AND SIZE OF ASSETS IN THOUSANDS OF DOLLARS

Item Description for Accounting Period 7/03 Through 6/04	Total	Zero Assets	Under 500	500 to 1,000	1,000 to 5,000	5,000 to 10,000	10,000 to 25,000	25,000 to 50,000	50,000 to 100,000	100,000 to 250,000	250,000 to 500,000	500,000 to 2,500,000	2,500,000 and over
Number of Enterprises **1**	41392	3273	32271	2943	2287	425	159	•	•	•	•	•	•
Revenues ($ in Thousands)													
Net Sales **2**	68102872	556708	21929622	7071446	17632595	7842573	5809801	•	•	•	•	•	•
Interest **3**	18193	8	3377	3176	6101	2839	1975	•	•	•	•	•	•
Rents **4**	14237	0	1830	3940	4586	2345	1351	•	•	•	•	•	•
Royalties **5**	65	0	0	0	0	65	0						
Other Portfolio Income **6**	93085	4127	48074	22497	11127	2727	2868	•	•	•	•	•	•
Other Receipts **7**	187034	38465	16584	17649	50977	17048	26914	•	•	•	•	•	•
Total Receipts **8**	68415486	599308	21999487	7118708	17705386	7867597	5842909	•	•	•	•	•	•
Average Total Receipts **9**	1653	183	682	2419	7742	18512	36748						
Operating Costs/Operating Income (%)													
Cost of Operations **10**	67.2	51.9	53.3	62.4	71.3	77.5	79.3	•	•	•	•	•	•
Salaries and Wages **11**	7.5	7.7	10.9	8.7	6.4	4.1	4.6	•	•	•	•	•	•
Taxes Paid **12**	2.6	1.6	3.1	3.0	2.5	2.0	2.2	•	•	•	•	•	•
Interest Paid **13**	0.3	0.4	0.4	0.3	0.3	0.2	0.2	•	•	•	•	•	•
Depreciation **14**	1.5	3.8	1.8	1.8	1.5	1.1	0.8	•	•	•	•	•	•
Amortization and Depletion **15**	0.0	0.0	0.0	0.0	0.0	0.0	0.0	•	•	•	•	•	•
Pensions and Other Deferred Comp. **16**	0.6	1.4	0.4	0.8	0.5	1.1	0.6	•	•	•	•	•	•
Employee Benefits **17**	1.8	0.9	1.1	3.2	1.9	2.2	2.6	•	•	•	•	•	•
Advertising **18**	0.5	0.6	0.9	0.7	0.4	0.2	0.2	•	•	•	•	•	•
Other Expenses **19**	8.8	22.1	13.2	9.4	8.3	4.6	4.5	•	•	•	•	•	•
Officers' Compensation **20**	5.1	4.9	8.1	5.9	4.2	3.2	2.4	•	•	•	•	•	•
Operating Margin **21**	4.1	4.7	6.7	3.8	2.6	3.7	2.8	•	•	•	•	•	•
Operating Margin Before Officers' Comp. **22**	9.2	9.6	14.8	9.8	6.8	6.9	5.1	•	•	•	•	•	•

Selected Average Balance Sheet ($ in Thousands)

Net Receivables 23	208	0	26	263	1025	3688	8134
Inventories 24	23	0	7	53	127	212	378
Net Property, Plant and Equipment 25	68	0	28	139	355	674	1025
Total Assets 26	469	0	116	680	2230	7118	14152
Notes and Loans Payable 27	89	0	39	133	442	1058	1598
All Other Liabilities 28	205	0	29	214	1014	3422	7572
Net Worth 29	175	0	49	334	774	2638	4981

Selected Financial Ratios (Times to 1)

Current Ratio 30	1.6	•	2.1	2.0	1.5	1.6	1.5
Quick Ratio 31	1.3	•	1.7	1.8	1.2	1.3	1.3
Net Sales to Working Capital 32	12.0	•	17.5	9.5	12.6	8.0	8.7
Coverage Ratio 33	15.0	32.5	18.1	17.6	10.2	17.3	16.6
Total Asset Turnover 34	3.5	•	5.8	3.5	3.5	2.6	2.6
Inventory Turnover 35	49.0	•	49.8	28.3	43.3	67.3	76.7
Receivables Turnover 36	8.7	•	32.8	8.9	7.6	10.0	4.9
Total Liabilities to Net Worth 37	1.7	•	1.4	1.0	1.9	1.7	1.8
Current Assets to Working Capital 38	2.6	•	1.9	2.0	2.9	2.5	2.9
Current Liabilities to Working Capital 39	1.6	•	0.9	1.0	1.9	1.5	1.9
Working Capital to Net Sales 40	0.1	•	0.1	0.1	0.1	0.1	0.1
Inventory to Working Capital 41	0.2	•	0.2	0.2	0.2	0.1	0.1
Total Receipts to Cash Flow 42	8.9	3.5	5.7	8.5	11.2	13.2	16.4
Cost of Goods to Cash Flow 43	6.0	1.8	3.0	5.3	8.0	10.2	13.0
Cash Flow to Total Debt 44	0.6	•	1.8	0.8	0.5	0.3	0.2

Selected Financial Factors (in Percentages)

Debt Ratio 45	62.7	•	58.0	50.9	65.3	62.9	64.8
Return on Total Assets 46	17.0	•	43.3	16.9	11.5	11.1	9.1
Return on Equity Before Income Taxes 47	42.6	•	97.3	32.4	29.9	28.2	24.4
Return on Equity After Income Taxes 48	41.2	•	96.4	32.2	27.7	26.8	22.6
Profit Margin (Before Income Tax) 49	4.5	12.3	7.0	4.5	3.0	4.0	3.3
Profit Margin (After Income Tax) 50	4.4	12.2	6.9	4.5	2.8	3.8	3.1

34

Table I

Corporations with and without Net Income

OTHER SPECIALTY TRADE CONTRACTORS

MONEY AMOUNTS AND SIZE OF ASSETS IN THOUSANDS OF DOLLARS

Item Description for Accounting Period 7/03 Through 6/04	Total	Zero Assets	Under 500	500 to 1,000	1,000 to 5,000	5,000 to 10,000	10,000 to 25,000	25,000 to 50,000	50,000 to 100,000	100,000 to 250,000	250,000 to 500,000	500,000 to 2,500,000	2,500,000 and over
Number of Enterprises 1	292694	29291	231401	16038	13508	1500	710	147	64	27	7	·	·
Revenues ($ in Thousands)													
Net Sales 2	306674727	5586440	116891927	38148037	74578970	20521730	23635938	10386547	8291364	6441900	2191874	·	·
Interest 3	167578	3761	17697	18193	34862	11360	11769	9487	8368	24202	27879	·	·
Rents 4	266350	4914	30827	14222	56453	4148	14967	27631	1185	37332	74670	·	·
Royalties 5	18506	0	14487	0	42	76	1632	1904	327	18	21	·	·
Other Portfolio Income 6	539886	60064	187817	64304	73151	41955	37924	20830	25622	23049	5171	·	·
Other Receipts 7	1120338	15452	342790	55371	277839	144746	158862	71324	33132	12155	8665	·	·
Total Receipts 8	308787385	5670631	117485545	38300127	75021317	20724015	23861092	10517723	8359998	6538656	2308280	·	·
Average Total Receipts 9	1055	194	508	2388	5554	13816	33607	71549	130625	242172	329754	·	·
Operating Costs/Operating Income (%)													
Cost of Operations 10	64.8	58.0	54.5	61.9	70.0	76.6	79.0	79.2	80.1	79.3	69.7	·	·
Salaries and Wages 11	8.2	10.5	10.9	9.6	6.7	3.9	4.3	4.8	4.9	5.6	8.8	·	·
Taxes Paid 12	2.5	1.8	2.8	2.6	2.6	2.0	2.0	1.4	1.7	1.1	0.9	·	·
Interest Paid 13	0.6	0.7	0.5	0.7	0.6	0.5	0.5	0.5	0.9	1.6	4.7	·	·
Depreciation 14	2.6	2.6	2.6	2.6	2.8	2.6	2.1	1.9	2.2	2.9	2.6	·	·
Amortization and Depletion 15	0.1	0.1	0.0	0.0	0.0	0.0	0.1	0.2	0.2	0.7	1.5	·	·
Pensions and Other Deferred Comp. 16	0.4	0.1	0.2	0.5	0.4	0.4	0.5	0.3	0.4	0.4	0.2	·	·
Employee Benefits 17	1.5	1.0	1.1	1.8	1.8	1.6	1.7	1.4	1.3	0.7	1.0	·	·
Advertising 18	0.5	0.5	0.6	0.8	0.4	0.1	0.3	0.2	0.3	0.1	0.2	·	·
Other Expenses 19	13.0	18.6	17.9	12.9	10.0	8.3	6.3	7.9	6.1	11.7	18.5	·	·
Officers' Compensation 20	4.5	5.1	6.6	5.1	3.6	2.9	1.9	1.6	1.3	0.7	1.0	·	·
Operating Margin 21	1.4	0.9	2.3	1.4	1.0	1.1	1.3	0.7	0.7	·	·	·	·
Operating Margin Before Officers' Comp. 22	5.9	6.0	8.9	6.5	4.6	4.0	3.2	2.3	2.0	·	·	·	·

Selected Average Balance Sheet ($ in Thousands)

Net Receivables 23	113	0	14	236	837	2560	6757	14308	28024	52951	86167	•
Inventories 24	15	0	4	35	105	349	594	1496	2100	3517	10400	•
Net Property, Plant and Equipment 25	78	0	31	184	483	1170	2455	5148	11281	32148	43344	•
Total Assets 26	322	0	80	722	2071	6764	14718	32651	65851	146371	369420	•
Notes and Loans Payable 27	111	0	46	267	629	1731	3332	6322	16478	38756	175881	•
All Other Liabilities 28	114	0	19	198	727	3041	6468	16130	31319	53664	122806	•
Net Worth 29	97	0	15	257	715	1991	4917	10199	18054	53950	70734	•

Selected Financial Ratios (Times to 1)

Current Ratio 30	1.5	•	1.4	1.7	1.5	1.3	1.5	1.5	1.4	1.5	1.3
Quick Ratio 31	1.1	•	1.2	1.4	1.2	0.9	1.1	1.1	1.1	1.1	0.8
Net Sales to Working Capital 32	15.5	•	42.3	12.5	11.3	10.8	9.6	9.6	10.6	7.9	6.9
Coverage Ratio 33	4.4	4.5	6.9	3.7	3.5	5.2	5.4	5.2	2.7	•	0.2
Total Asset Turnover 34	3.3	•	6.3	3.3	2.7	2.0	2.3	2.2	2.0	1.6	0.8
Inventory Turnover 35	46.3	•	77.0	42.6	36.7	30.0	44.3	37.4	49.4	53.8	21.0
Receivables Turnover 36	9.4	•	33.7	11.2	6.8	5.0	5.0	5.2	5.3	5.3	3.0
Total Liabilities to Net Worth 37	2.3	•	4.2	1.8	1.9	2.4	2.0	2.2	2.6	1.7	4.2
Current Assets to Working Capital 38	3.1	•	3.3	2.5	2.9	3.9	3.2	3.2	3.6	2.9	4.0
Current Liabilities to Working Capital 39	2.1	•	2.3	1.5	1.9	2.9	2.2	2.2	2.6	1.9	3.0
Working Capital to Net Sales 40	0.1	•	0.0	0.1	0.1	0.1	0.1	0.1	0.1	0.1	0.1
Inventory to Working Capital 41	0.2	•	0.3	0.2	0.2	0.3	0.2	0.2	0.2	0.1	0.2
Total Receipts to Cash Flow 42	8.5	6.0	5.8	8.9	12.4	13.8	16.8	13.3	20.1	16.5	9.1
Cost of Goods to Cash Flow 43	5.5	3.5	3.2	5.5	8.7	10.6	13.2	10.5	16.1	13.1	6.4
Cash Flow to Total Debt 44	0.5	•	1.3	0.6	0.3	0.2	0.2	0.2	0.1	0.2	0.1

Selected Financial Factors (in Percentages)

Debt Ratio 45	69.8	•	80.8	64.4	65.5	70.6	66.6	68.8	72.6	63.1	80.9
Return on Total Assets 46	8.7	•	20.9	8.1	5.9	5.2	6.2	5.2	4.7	•	0.8
Return on Equity Before Income Taxes 47	22.3	•	93.2	16.7	12.2	14.2	15.3	13.5	10.9	•	•
Return on Equity After Income Taxes 48	20.8	•	91.2	15.9	11.1	12.0	14.0	11.7	9.4	•	•
Profit Margin (Before Income Tax) 49	2.1	2.4	2.8	1.8	1.6	2.1	2.3	1.9	1.5	•	•
Profit Margin (After Income Tax) 50	1.9	2.1	2.8	1.7	1.4	1.7	2.1	1.7	1.3	•	•

Table II
Corporations with Net Income

OTHER SPECIALTY TRADE CONTRACTORS

MONEY AMOUNTS AND SIZE OF ASSETS IN THOUSANDS OF DOLLARS

Item Description for Accounting Period 7/03 Through 6/04	Total	Zero Assets	Under 500	500 to 1,000	1,000 to 5,000	5,000 to 10,000	10,000 to 25,000	25,000 to 50,000	50,000 to 100,000	100,000 to 250,000	250,000 to 500,000	500,000 to 2,500,000	2,500,000 and over
Number of Enterprises **1**	182775	15283	145983	10281	9472	1067	521	101	•	19	•	•	•
Revenues ($ in Thousands)													
Net Sales **2**	224836005	3410909	85005954	26352633	56243777	14800940	18302011	7588055	•	5410974	•	•	•
Interest **3**	105971	2751	8595	9174	21020	6837	8554	7268	•	6634	•	•	•
Rents **4**	182980	0	12320	9392	46052	1236	13948	18327	•	5854	•	•	•
Royalties **5**	15270	0	14487	0	25	76	554	0	•	18	•	•	•
Other Portfolio Income **6**	349383	45409	105593	44317	47571	24280	26890	16923	•	23012	•	•	•
Other Receipts **7**	1030639	3942	327295	86402	242916	139931	128465	48035	•	19183	•	•	•
Total Receipts **8**	226520248	3463011	85474244	26501918	56601361	14973300	18480422	7678608	•	5465675	•	•	•
Average Total Receipts **9**	1239	227	586	2578	5976	14033	35471	76026	•	287667	•	•	•
Operating Costs/Operating Income (%)													
Cost of Operations **10**	64.3	58.4	54.0	61.3	68.8	75.8	78.4	77.5	•	79.9	•	•	•
Salaries and Wages **11**	7.8	7.4	10.4	8.6	6.7	3.8	4.2	4.4	•	5.5	•	•	•
Taxes Paid **12**	2.3	1.3	2.5	2.5	2.4	1.9	2.0	1.5	•	0.7	•	•	•
Interest Paid **13**	0.5	0.4	0.4	0.5	0.5	0.3	0.4	0.4	•	1.1	•	•	•
Depreciation **14**	2.2	1.1	2.1	2.3	2.4	2.4	1.8	1.7	•	2.3	•	•	•
Amortization and Depletion **15**	0.1	0.1	0.1	0.0	0.0	0.0	0.0	0.0	•	0.5	•	•	•
Pensions and Other Deferred Comp. **16**	0.3	0.1	0.2	0.5	0.4	0.4	0.6	0.2	•	0.4	•	•	•
Employee Benefits **17**	1.4	1.1	1.0	1.8	1.6	1.6	1.6	1.6	•	0.5	•	•	•
Advertising **18**	0.4	0.4	0.5	0.5	0.5	0.1	0.2	0.2	•	0.1	•	•	•
Other Expenses **19**	12.0	14.1	16.8	12.6	9.7	7.1	5.7	8.0	•	5.3	•	•	•
Officers' Compensation **20**	4.4	5.1	6.1	5.3	3.6	3.2	2.0	1.6	•	0.7	•	•	•
Operating Margin **21**	4.4	10.7	5.9	4.1	3.5	3.3	3.1	2.8	•	2.8	•	•	•
Operating Margin Before Officers' Comp. **22**	8.8	15.8	12.0	9.4	7.0	6.5	5.1	4.5	•	3.5	•	•	•

Selected Average Balance Sheet ($ in Thousands)

Net Receivables 23	127	0	15	253	847	2369	7052	15248	•	56703
Inventories 24	16	0	4	35	109	342	566	1373	•	3642
Net Property, Plant and Equipment 25	78	0	30	167	425	1231	2167	4511	•	28014
Total Assets 26	355	0	87	732	2051	6454	14626	33213	•	141667
Notes and Loans Payable 27	98	0	38	222	476	1343	2794	5111	•	38715
All Other Liabilities 28	121	0	20	165	721	2855	6260	15096	•	51637
Net Worth 29	136	0	29	345	854	2256	5573	13005	•	51315

Selected Financial Ratios (Times to 1)

Current Ratio 30	1.6	•	1.7	2.1	1.7	1.5	1.6	1.5	•	1.5
Quick Ratio 31	1.3	•	1.4	1.7	1.4	1.0	1.3	1.2	•	1.2
Net Sales to Working Capital 32	13.3	•	32.8	9.5	10.0	10.0	8.4	9.1	•	9.9
Coverage Ratio 33	11.8	29.9	17.1	10.0	9.5	13.9	11.3	11.8	•	4.7
Total Asset Turnover 34	3.5	•	6.7	3.5	2.9	2.1	2.4	2.3	•	2.0
Inventory Turnover 35	48.1	•	76.8	44.8	37.3	30.7	48.7	42.4	•	62.5
Receivables Turnover 36	9.9	•	39.7	11.6	7.0	5.2	5.1	5.1	•	6.3
Total Liabilities to Net Worth 37	1.6	•	2.0	1.1	1.4	1.9	1.6	1.6	•	1.8
Current Assets to Working Capital 38	2.6	•	2.5	1.9	2.5	3.2	2.7	3.0	•	2.9
Current Liabilities to Working Capital 39	1.6	•	1.5	0.9	1.5	2.2	1.7	2.0	•	1.9
Working Capital to Net Sales 40	0.1	•	0.0	0.1	0.1	0.1	0.1	0.1	•	0.1
Inventory to Working Capital 41	0.2	•	0.2	0.1	0.2	0.3	0.1	0.1	•	0.1
Total Receipts to Cash Flow 42	7.0	4.4	4.9	7.0	9.4	11.4	13.4	10.3	•	15.1
Cost of Goods to Cash Flow 43	4.5	2.6	2.7	4.3	6.5	8.6	10.5	8.0	•	12.1
Cash Flow to Total Debt 44	0.8	•	2.1	0.9	0.5	0.3	0.3	0.4	•	0.2

Selected Financial Factors (in Percentages)

Debt Ratio 45	61.6	•	66.2	52.9	58.4	65.0	61.9	60.8	•	63.8
Return on Total Assets 46	19.5	•	45.9	18.1	13.3	10.3	10.7	10.0	•	10.2
Return on Equity Before Income Taxes 47	46.6	•	127.9	34.6	28.7	27.4	25.6	23.3	•	22.1
Return on Equity After Income Taxes 48	44.9	•	126.2	33.7	27.3	24.7	24.1	21.2	•	19.0
Profit Margin (Before Income Tax) 49	5.2	12.2	6.4	4.7	4.1	4.5	4.1	4.0	•	4.0
Profit Margin (After Income Tax) 50	5.0	11.6	6.3	4.5	3.9	4.0	3.8	3.7	•	3.4

Table I

Corporations with and without Net Income

ANIMAL FOOD AND GRAIN AND OILSEED MILLING

MONEY AMOUNTS AND SIZE OF ASSETS IN THOUSANDS OF DOLLARS

Item Description for Accounting Period 7/03 Through 6/04	Total	Zero Assets	Under 500	500 to 1,000	1,000 to 5,000	5,000 to 10,000	10,000 to 25,000	25,000 to 50,000	50,000 to 100,000	100,000 to 250,000	250,000 to 500,000	500,000 to 2,500,000	2,500,000 and over
Number of Enterprises **1**	1748	11	953	133	371	129	80	23	20	14	6	4	4
Revenues ($ in Thousands)													
Net Sales **2**	72048930	238848	1022130	373070	2054061	2411989	2676920	1882692	2533156	2933901	2103161	3519153	50299848
Interest **3**	236181	20	222	872	728	261	5733	1740	1714	3035	12807	17983	191066
Rents **4**	165421	247	277	0	36	148	2053	291	1026	227	404	366	160346
Royalties **5**	541442	0	0	0	0	0	333	0	577	0	6527	31629	502375
Other Portfolio Income **6**	191513	0	0	2782	459	2527	10157	1092	7148	2033	25378	41517	98418
Other Receipts **7**	1806392	902	4437	42	24868	24288	50334	26355	26755	21684	2529	66694	1557508
Total Receipts **8**	74989879	240017	1027066	376766	2080152	2439213	2745530	1912170	2570376	2960880	2150806	3677342	52809561
Average Total Receipts **9**	42900	21820	1078	2833	5607	18909	34319	83138	128519	211491	358468	919336	13202390
Operating Costs/Operating Income (%)													
Cost of Operations **10**	76.2	73.8	67.7	82.6	80.6	73.9	75.9	79.3	78.2	79.1	64.6	85.2	75.8
Salaries and Wages **11**	3.4	5.4	10.0	2.1	2.7	8.7	5.4	4.5	3.9	3.7	5.0	2.7	2.9
Taxes Paid **12**	0.9	0.5	3.3	0.9	1.1	1.3	1.3	1.0	0.8	1.1	1.6	1.0	0.8
Interest Paid **13**	2.5	0.2	0.1	0.2	0.7	1.2	0.7	0.6	0.9	1.0	3.2	2.7	3.0
Depreciation **14**	2.5	3.0	0.4	1.1	2.5	4.1	3.1	2.5	2.5	3.6	5.9	3.8	2.1
Amortization and Depletion **15**	0.2	0.4	0.5	•	0.0	0.1	0.1	0.1	0.2	0.9	1.3	0.7	0.1
Pensions and Other Deferred Comp. **16**	0.5	0.2	•	1.2	0.4	0.2	0.3	0.5	0.3	0.2	2.0	0.6	0.6
Employee Benefits **17**	1.0	0.7	0.7	1.3	0.3	0.6	0.8	0.8	0.4	1.2	0.9	1.2	1.1
Advertising **18**	6.1	9.4	0.0	0.0	0.3	0.4	0.7	0.8	2.2	1.0	3.1	0.1	8.3
Other Expenses **19**	8.1	9.6	15.2	3.1	5.8	8.3	8.2	9.2	7.1	4.9	11.6	5.4	8.2
Officers' Compensation **20**	0.6	0.1	6.1	6.5	2.9	0.5	1.2	1.0	0.7	1.0	0.7	0.5	0.2
Operating Margin **21**	•	•	•	0.9	2.8	0.6	2.3	•	2.9	2.2	0.3	•	•
Operating Margin Before Officers' Comp. **22**	•	•	2.0	7.4	5.7	1.1	3.5	0.8	3.6	3.2	0.9	•	•

Selected Average Balance Sheet ($ in Thousands)

Net Receivables 23	2562	0	64	129	444	1234	3081	8085	13453	21694	74874	102330	553070
Inventories 24	3357	0	83	236	672	786	3023	6394	11110	18996	31496	93813	1001227
Net Property, Plant and Equipment 25	7432	0	24	249	539	5163	5652	10400	23130	50706	126365	267030	2094870
Total Assets 26	36802	0	265	856	1829	7938	15893	33077	72437	146092	339028	896038	12779112
Notes and Loans Payable 27	16268	0	38	91	689	5454	4619	8919	19837	49147	101850	350844	5938709
All Other Liabilities 28	9874	0	78	86	648	1435	3759	11820	15162	38264	86589	273987	3430464
Net Worth 29	10661	0	150	680	493	1049	7515	12338	37438	58682	150588	271206	3409940

Selected Financial Ratios (Times to 1)

Current Ratio 30	1.1	•	3.0	4.9	1.6	0.9	1.7	1.5	1.9	1.6	1.5	1.3	0.9
Quick Ratio 31	0.4	•	1.7	4.6	0.7	0.6	1.0	0.9	1.0	0.8	1.0	0.7	0.3
Net Sales to Working Capital 32	68.2	•	6.7	5.8	12.5	•	9.9	12.2	7.3	10.5	8.4	12.3	•
Coverage Ratio 33	1.9	•	•	6.0	6.9	2.4	8.1	3.1	6.1	4.1	1.8	1.4	1.7
Total Asset Turnover 34	1.1	•	4.0	3.3	3.0	2.4	2.1	2.5	1.7	1.4	1.0	1.0	1.0
Inventory Turnover 35	9.4	•	8.7	9.8	6.6	17.6	8.4	10.2	8.9	8.7	7.2	8.0	9.5
Receivables Turnover 36	16.9	•	32.5	11.1	8.7	16.4	10.4	11.2	7.6	10.3	6.8	10.0	23.8
Total Liabilities to Net Worth 37	2.5	•	0.8	0.3	2.7	6.6	1.1	1.7	0.9	1.5	1.3	2.3	2.7
Current Assets to Working Capital 38	14.9	•	1.5	1.3	2.7	•	2.5	2.8	2.1	2.7	2.9	4.1	•
Current Liabilities to Working Capital 39	13.9	•	0.5	0.3	1.7	•	1.5	1.8	1.1	1.7	1.9	3.1	•
Working Capital to Net Sales 40	0.0	•	0.1	0.2	0.1	•	0.1	0.1	0.1	0.1	0.1	0.1	•
Inventory to Working Capital 41	5.8	•	0.5	0.1	1.4	•	0.9	1.0	0.7	1.0	0.8	1.3	•
Total Receipts to Cash Flow 42	12.3	17.6	12.7	21.7	12.1	13.4	8.7	12.3	9.9	14.4	8.8	24.5	12.3
Cost of Goods to Cash Flow 43	9.4	13.0	8.6	18.0	9.8	9.9	6.6	9.7	7.8	11.4	5.7	20.9	9.3
Cash Flow to Total Debt 44	0.1	•	0.7	0.7	0.3	0.2	0.5	0.3	0.4	0.2	0.2	0.1	0.1

Selected Financial Factors (in Percentages)

Debt Ratio 45	71.0	•	43.5	20.6	73.1	86.8	52.7	62.7	48.3	59.8	55.6	69.7	73.3
Return on Total Assets 46	5.2	•	4.4	4.4	14.3	7.0	11.6	4.9	9.1	5.9	6.0	3.6	5.0
Return on Equity Before Income Taxes 47	8.5	•	•	4.6	45.5	31.1	8.9	21.5	14.7	11.1	6.2	3.1	7.7
Return on Equity After Income Taxes 48	6.0	•	•	4.4	44.1	26.8	19.9	13.3	8.2	7.3	4.0	0.3	5.0
Profit Margin (Before Income Tax) 49	2.2	•	1.1	4.0	1.7	4.8	1.3	4.3	3.1	2.7	1.0	1.0	2.1
Profit Margin (After Income Tax) 50	1.5	•	1.1	3.9	1.5	4.5	1.1	3.9	2.3	1.7	1.0	0.1	1.4

Table II

Corporations with Net Income

ANIMAL FOOD AND GRAIN AND OILSEED MILLING

MONEY AMOUNTS AND SIZE OF ASSETS IN THOUSANDS OF DOLLARS

Item Description for Accounting Period 7/03 Through 6/04	Total	Zero Assets	Under 500	500 to 1,000	1,000 to 5,000	5,000 to 10,000	10,000 to 25,000	25,000 to 50,000	50,000 to 100,000	100,000 to 250,000	250,000 to 500,000	500,000 to 2,500,000	2,500,000 and over
Number of Enterprises **1**	581	•	•	133	120	126	61	15	13	•	•	•	4

Revenues ($ in Thousands)

Item	Total	Zero Assets	Under 500	500 to 1,000	1,000 to 5,000	5,000 to 10,000	10,000 to 25,000	25,000 to 50,000	50,000 to 100,000	100,000 to 250,000	250,000 to 500,000	500,000 to 2,500,000	2,500,000 and over
Net Sales **2**	65173421	•	•	373070	868369	2285157	2281625	1238458	2063659	•	•	•	50299848
Interest **3**	230452	•	•	872	262	191	5079	652	1023	•	•	•	191066
Rents **4**	164129	•	•	0	13	0	1894	93	840	•	•	•	160346
Royalties **5**	534538	•	•	0	0	0	0	0	23	•	•	•	502375
Other Portfolio Income **6**	190684	•	•	2782	383	2513	10129	773	7137	•	•	•	98418
Other Receipts **7**	1752154	•	•	42	16574	24617	41198	21463	26049	•	•	•	1557508
Total Receipts **8**	68045378	•	•	376766	885601	2312478	2339925	1261439	2098731	•	•	•	52809561
Average Total Receipts **9**	117118	•	•	2833	7380	18353	38359	84096	161441	•	•	•	13202390

Operating Costs/Operating Income (%)

Item	Total	Zero Assets	Under 500	500 to 1,000	1,000 to 5,000	5,000 to 10,000	10,000 to 25,000	25,000 to 50,000	50,000 to 100,000	100,000 to 250,000	250,000 to 500,000	500,000 to 2,500,000	2,500,000 and over
Cost of Operations **10**	75.7	•	•	82.6	75.8	72.6	74.7	77.7	77.1	•	•	•	75.8
Salaries and Wages **11**	3.3	•	•	2.1	2.7	9.1	5.5	5.0	4.1	•	•	•	2.9
Taxes Paid **12**	0.9	•	•	0.9	1.2	1.4	1.3	1.0	0.8	•	•	•	0.8
Interest Paid **13**	2.6	•	•	0.2	0.2	1.3	0.5	0.4	0.4	•	•	•	3.0
Depreciation **14**	2.4	•	•	1.1	2.6	4.3	2.6	2.6	2.2	•	•	•	2.1
Amortization and Depletion **15**	0.2	•	•	•	0.0	0.1	0.1	0.1	0.1	•	•	•	0.1
Pensions and Other Deferred Comp. **16**	0.6	•	•	1.2	0.7	0.2	0.3	0.6	0.3	•	•	•	0.6
Employee Benefits **17**	1.1	•	•	1.3	0.2	0.6	0.8	0.7	0.4	•	•	•	1.1
Advertising **18**	6.7	•	•	0.0	0.3	0.4	0.8	1.0	2.5	•	•	•	8.3
Other Expenses **19**	7.9	•	•	3.1	3.8	8.7	7.6	8.1	7.2	•	•	•	8.2
Officers' Compensation **20**	0.4	•	•	6.5	2.4	0.5	1.2	0.9	0.7	•	•	•	0.2
Operating Margin **21**	•	•	•	0.9	10.1	1.0	4.5	2.0	4.2	•	•	•	•
Operating Margin Before Officers' Comp. **22**	•	•	•	7.4	12.5	1.5	5.7	2.9	4.9	•	•	•	•

Selected Average Balance Sheet ($ in Thousands)

Net Receivables 23	6355	129	552	1213	3343	7670	17091	553070
Inventories 24	8851	141	1069	657	2924	6622	13400	1001227
Net Property, Plant and Equipment 25	20312	249	534	5182	5375	11061	19442	2094870
Total Assets 26	103648	856	2014	7923	15929	32410	73228	12779112
Notes and Loans Payable 27	45575	91	196	5436	3673	7420	17038	5938709
All Other Liabilities 28	27496	86	448	1403	3752	8198	18945	3430464
Net Worth 29	30578	680	1370	1084	8504	16792	37246	3409940

Selected Financial Ratios (Times to 1)

Current Ratio 30	1.1	4.9	2.9	0.9	1.9	1.8	2.1	0.9
Quick Ratio 31	0.4	4.6	1.3	0.6	1.1	1.1	1.2	0.3
Net Sales to Working Capital 32	94.9	5.8	7.5	•	9.0	10.4	6.4	•
Coverage Ratio 33	2.1	6.0	62.1	2.8	14.1	11.5	15.5	1.7
Total Asset Turnover 34	1.1	3.3	3.6	2.3	2.3	2.5	2.2	1.0
Inventory Turnover 35	9.6	16.4	5.1	20.0	9.6	9.7	9.1	9.5
Receivables Turnover 36	18.5	14.7	6.8	19.3	11.6	10.7	9.1	23.8
Total Liabilities to Net Worth 37	2.4	0.3	0.5	6.3	0.9	0.9	1.0	2.7
Current Assets to Working Capital 38	20.3	1.3	1.5	•	2.2	2.3	1.9	•
Current Liabilities to Working Capital 39	19.3	0.3	0.5	•	1.2	1.3	0.9	•
Working Capital to Net Sales 40	0.0	0.2	0.1	•	0.1	0.1	0.2	•
Inventory to Working Capital 41	7.8	0.1	0.8	•	0.7	0.8	0.6	•
Total Receipts to Cash Flow 42	11.6	21.7	6.7	12.3	7.6	9.6	8.6	12.3
Cost of Goods to Cash Flow 43	8.8	18.0	5.1	8.9	5.7	7.4	6.7	9.3
Cash Flow to Total Debt 44	0.1	0.7	1.7	0.2	0.7	0.6	0.5	0.1

Selected Financial Factors (in Percentages)

Debt Ratio 45	70.5	20.6	32.0	86.3	46.6	48.2	49.1	73.3
Return on Total Assets 46	5.8	4.4	44.1	7.9	17.7	10.6	13.7	5.0
Return on Equity Before Income Taxes 47	10.2	4.6	63.8	36.7	30.8	18.7	25.1	7.7
Return on Equity After Income Taxes 48	7.6	4.4	62.4	32.4	28.9	17.0	22.9	5.0
Profit Margin (Before Income Tax) 49	2.8	1.1	12.1	2.2	7.0	3.8	5.9	2.1
Profit Margin (After Income Tax) 50	2.1	1.1	11.8	1.9	6.6	3.4	5.4	1.4

Table I

Corporations with and without Net Income

SUGAR AND CONFECTIONERY PRODUCT

MONEY AMOUNTS AND SIZE OF ASSETS IN THOUSANDS OF DOLLARS

Item Description for Accounting Period 7/03 Through 6/04	Total	Zero Assets	Under 500	500 to 1,000	1,000 to 5,000	5,000 to 10,000	10,000 to 25,000	25,000 to 50,000	50,000 to 100,000	100,000 to 250,000	250,000 to 500,000	500,000 to 2,500,000	2,500,000 and over
Number of Enterprises 1	1229	28	•	120	116	•	30	12	14	6	3	6	3
Revenues ($ in Thousands)													
Net Sales 2	34605680	173396	•	246207	374182	•	1103550	555333	1609675	1650505	911603	3703782	23006017
Interest 3	129944	1827	•	0	235	•	513	300	780	548	6864	40150	78342
Rents 4	60430	0	•	0	0	•	276	2555	1473	337	4	44404	11068
Royalties 5	122465	1158	•	0	0	•	115	279	5	1418	0	95227	24263
Other Portfolio Income 6	362027	4124	•	0	3	•	597	177	364	22988	119	260242	73329
Other Receipts 7	269881	59	•	1565	668	•	5664	4103	2165	1124	6947	56134	190758
Total Receipts 8	35550427	180564	•	247772	375088	•	1110715	562747	1614462	1676920	925537	4199939	23383777
Average Total Receipts 9	28926	6449	•	2065	3234	•	37024	46896	115319	279487	308512	699990	7794592
Operating Costs/Operating Income (%)													
Cost of Operations 10	52.2	62.2	•	72.2	55.0	•	74.0	75.1	68.4	79.7	54.9	57.2	45.5
Salaries and Wages 11	6.6	7.1	•	7.1	9.0	•	4.2	5.7	6.2	4.4	7.3	6.6	6.8
Taxes Paid 12	1.3	1.1	•	1.2	3.3	•	1.3	1.7	1.6	0.7	1.7	1.6	1.1
Interest Paid 13	2.7	5.1	•	0.4	1.8	•	0.8	1.2	0.7	2.4	9.6	1.7	3.0
Depreciation 14	3.0	4.4	•	0.5	5.3	•	3.0	4.5	3.1	4.0	4.1	4.0	2.7
Amortization and Depletion 15	0.9	1.0	•	0.1	1.5	•	0.5	0.1	0.1	0.3	2.6	0.8	1.0
Pensions and Other Deferred Comp. 16	2.3	0.2	•	3.6	1.1	•	0.3	0.5	0.7	0.3	0.3	1.4	3.0
Employee Benefits 17	1.8	4.5	•	1.3	1.0	•	1.0	1.0	2.0	1.1	1.2	2.1	2.0
Advertising 18	5.9	7.9	•	0.0	2.0	•	1.5	0.9	3.8	1.5	3.0	5.5	7.2
Other Expenses 19	20.8	25.8	•	10.0	14.4	•	7.9	9.1	9.8	7.2	11.6	18.0	24.8
Officers' Compensation 20	0.9	0.3	•	5.4	7.9	•	3.3	1.0	1.3	0.6	0.9	0.7	0.6
Operating Margin 21	1.6	•	•	•	•	•	2.1	•	2.3	•	2.9	0.2	2.2
Operating Margin Before Officers' Comp. 22	2.5	•	•	3.7	5.6	•	5.4	0.3	3.6	•	3.8	0.9	2.8

Selected Average Balance Sheet ($ in Thousands)

Net Receivables 23	3811	0	•	540	289	•	3081	5206	11349	25482	74916	111600	1039924
Inventories 24	2758	0	•	143	671	•	3755	11063	17721	41946	32982	98295	600822
Net Property, Plant and Equipment 25	6405	0	•	14	625	•	5828	12621	21072	71322	86136	275912	1572049
Total Assets 26	35612	0	•	761	1880	•	17212	33217	66297	172354	466044	1137694	10667581
Notes and Loans Payable 27	17065	0	•	294	1131	•	4589	12799	16842	73471	360497	111896	5992884
All Other Liabilities 28	8023	0	•	204	599	•	3510	7512	13080	50219	82920	213234	2480519
Net Worth 29	10524	0	•	263	149	•	9113	12906	36374	48664	22627	812564	2194178

Selected Financial Ratios (Times to 1)

Current Ratio 30	0.9	•	•	2.0	1.1	•	1.6	1.9	2.1	2.1	2.6	1.9	0.7
Quick Ratio 31	0.5	•	•	1.5	0.7	•	0.8	0.7	0.9	0.7	1.9	0.8	0.4
Net Sales to Working Capital 32	•	•	•	5.7	36.8	•	11.4	5.3	5.9	6.4	3.5	3.4	•
Coverage Ratio 33	3.4	•	•	•	•	•	4.6	1.6	5.1	0.8	1.5	10.7	3.2
Total Asset Turnover 34	0.8	•	•	2.7	1.7	•	2.1	1.4	1.7	1.6	0.7	0.5	0.7
Inventory Turnover 35	5.3	•	•	10.4	2.6	•	7.2	3.1	4.4	5.2	5.1	3.6	5.8
Receivables Turnover 36	8.4	•	•	4.3	9.0	•	12.5	8.7	11.1	11.8	5.1	7.3	8.2
Total Liabilities to Net Worth 37	2.4	•	•	1.9	11.6	•	0.9	1.6	0.8	2.5	19.6	0.4	3.9
Current Assets to Working Capital 38	•	•	•	2.0	11.3	•	2.7	2.1	1.9	1.9	1.6	2.1	•
Current Liabilities to Working Capital 39	•	•	•	1.0	10.3	•	1.7	1.1	0.9	0.9	0.6	1.1	•
Working Capital to Net Sales 40	•	•	•	0.2	0.0	•	0.1	0.2	0.2	0.2	0.3	0.3	•
Inventory to Working Capital 41	•	•	•	0.5	3.8	•	1.1	1.2	1.0	1.1	0.3	0.6	•
Total Receipts to Cash Flow 42	4.3	12.7	•	16.9	12.0	•	10.5	13.1	8.9	25.5	6.8	3.4	3.7
Cost of Goods to Cash Flow 43	2.2	7.9	•	12.2	6.6	•	7.8	9.8	6.1	20.3	3.7	1.9	1.7
Cash Flow to Total Debt 44	0.3	•	•	0.2	0.2	•	0.4	0.2	0.4	0.1	0.6	0.6	0.2

Selected Financial Factors (in Percentages)

Debt Ratio 45	70.4	•	•	65.4	92.1	•	47.1	61.1	45.1	71.8	95.1	28.6	79.4
Return on Total Assets 46	7.3	•	•	•	•	•	7.5	2.6	6.1	3.2	9.3	9.9	6.9
Return on Equity Before Income Taxes 47	17.4	•	•	•	•	•	11.0	2.4	8.9	•	62.2	12.5	23.2
Return on Equity After Income Taxes 48	11.4	•	•	•	•	•	9.7	2.4	6.6	•	47.9	7.9	15.2
Profit Margin (Before Income Tax) 49	6.5	•	•	•	•	•	2.7	0.7	2.8	•	4.6	16.5	6.6
Profit Margin (After Income Tax) 50	4.3	•	•	•	•	•	2.4	0.7	2.1	•	3.6	10.4	4.4

Table II

Corporations with Net Income

SUGAR AND CONFECTIONERY PRODUCT

MONEY AMOUNTS AND SIZE OF ASSETS IN THOUSANDS OF DOLLARS

Item Description for Accounting Period 7/03 Through 6/04	Total	Zero Assets	Under 500	500 to 1,000	1,000 to 5,000	5,000 to 10,000	10,000 to 25,000	25,000 to 50,000	50,000 to 100,000	100,000 to 250,000	250,000 to 500,000	500,000 to 2,500,000	2,500,000 and over
Number of Enterprises 1	1097	•	864	53	104	•	20	8	11	•	•	•	3
Revenues ($ in Thousands)													
Net Sales 2	31252002	•	785142	140897	352885	•	676199	394895	1269166	•	•	•	23006017
Interest 3	110847	•	0	0	222	•	330	279	687	•	•	•	78342
Rents 4	56716	•	0	0	0	•	83	551	9	•	•	•	11068
Royalties 5	112796	•	0	0	0	•	1	0	5	•	•	•	24263
Other Portfolio Income 6	349542	•	0	0	3	•	418	34	238	•	•	•	73329
Other Receipts 7	254695	•	416	1415	667	•	3923	3263	1448	•	•	•	190758
Total Receipts 8	32136598	•	785558	142312	353777	•	680954	399022	1271553	•	•	•	23383777
Average Total Receipts 9	29295	•	909	2685	3402	•	34048	49878	115596	•	•	•	7794592
Operating Costs/Operating Income (%)													
Cost of Operations 10	49.7	•	61.3	61.5	53.9	•	67.7	72.2	66.0	•	•	•	45.5
Salaries and Wages 11	6.7	•	7.4	12.3	7.8	•	5.2	6.0	6.9	•	•	•	6.8
Taxes Paid 12	1.4	•	4.7	1.6	3.3	•	1.5	1.7	1.7	•	•	•	1.1
Interest Paid 13	2.6	•	•	0.6	1.7	•	0.5	1.0	0.6	•	•	•	3.0
Depreciation 14	2.9	•	2.0	0.7	4.8	•	3.1	4.7	2.7	•	•	•	2.7
Amortization and Depletion 15	0.9	•	0.0	0.2	1.6	•	0.2	0.1	0.1	•	•	•	1.0
Pensions and Other Deferred Comp. 16	2.4	•	•	0.2	1.2	•	0.3	0.6	0.8	•	•	•	3.0
Employee Benefits 17	1.9	•	•	2.2	1.1	•	1.2	0.9	2.5	•	•	•	2.0
Advertising 18	6.2	•	2.6	0.0	1.4	•	1.9	1.0	2.7	•	•	•	7.2
Other Expenses 19	22.0	•	17.4	16.1	11.6	•	8.4	8.0	10.9	•	•	•	24.8
Officers' Compensation 20	0.9	•	0.9	4.8	7.8	•	4.8	1.1	1.5	•	•	•	0.6
Operating Margin 21	2.5	•	3.7	•	3.7	•	5.2	2.7	3.8	•	•	•	2.2
Operating Margin Before Officers' Comp. 22	3.4	•	4.6	4.7	11.5	•	9.9	3.8	5.2	•	•	•	2.8

Selected Average Balance Sheet ($ in Thousands)

Net Receivables 23	3640	70	417	297	3187	6844	11820	1039924
Inventories 24	2632	24	221	426	3636	11308	20196	609021
Net Property, Plant and Equipment 25	6524	35	31	636	5590	11782	18695	1572049
Total Assets 26	36222	166	711	1905	17276	34624	65514	10667581
Notes and Loans Payable 27	18021	8	255	1001	3316	13487	12542	5992884
All Other Liabilities 28	8332	66	284	507	3327	6986	12725	2480519
Net Worth 29	9869	92	171	397	10633	14150	40247	2194178

Selected Financial Ratios (Times to 1)

Current Ratio 30	0.9	2.0	1.2	1.5	2.0	2.5	2.4	0.7
Quick Ratio 31	0.5	1.6	0.8	0.9	1.1	1.0	1.1	0.4
Net Sales to Working Capital 32	•	14.0	23.3	10.4	7.5	3.9	5.1	•
Coverage Ratio 33	4.0	•	2.4	3.2	12.4	4.7	8.6	3.2
Total Asset Turnover 34	0.8	5.5	3.7	1.8	2.0	1.4	1.8	0.7
Inventory Turnover 35	5.4	23.4	7.4	4.3	6.3	3.2	3.8	5.7
Receivables Turnover 36	8.6	15.1	12.8	10.9	11.3	8.5	9.7	14.7
Total Liabilities to Net Worth 37	2.7	0.8	3.1	3.8	0.6	1.4	0.6	3.9
Current Assets to Working Capital 38	•	2.0	5.7	3.2	2.0	1.7	1.7	•
Current Liabilities to Working Capital 39	•	1.0	4.7	2.2	1.0	0.7	0.7	•
Working Capital to Net Sales 40	•	0.1	0.0	0.1	0.1	0.3	0.2	•
Inventory to Working Capital 41	•	0.4	1.9	1.0	0.7	0.9	0.9	•
Total Receipts to Cash Flow 42	3.9	8.0	7.6	8.5	7.7	10.7	7.5	3.7
Cost of Goods to Cash Flow 43	1.9	4.9	4.7	4.6	5.2	7.7	4.9	1.7
Cash Flow to Total Debt 44	0.3	1.5	0.6	0.3	0.7	0.2	0.6	0.2

Selected Financial Factors (in Percentages)

Debt Ratio 45	72.8	44.7	75.9	79.1	38.5	59.1	38.6	79.4
Return on Total Assets 46	8.1	20.7	5.7	10.1	12.5	6.7	8.3	6.9
Return on Equity Before Income Taxes 47	22.3	37.5	13.7	33.5	18.6	13.0	11.9	23.2
Return on Equity After Income Taxes 48	15.1	37.5	11.6	27.7	17.0	12.9	9.3	15.2
Profit Margin (Before Income Tax) 49	7.7	3.8	0.9	3.9	5.9	3.7	4.2	6.6
Profit Margin (After Income Tax) 50	5.2	3.8	0.7	3.2	5.3	3.7	3.3	4.4

Table I

Corporations with and without Net Income

FRUIT AND VEGETABLE PRESERVING AND SPECIALTY FOOD

MONEY AMOUNTS AND SIZE OF ASSETS IN THOUSANDS OF DOLLARS

Item Description for Accounting Period 7/03 Through 6/04	Total	Zero Assets	Under 500	500 to 1,000	1,000 to 5,000	5,000 to 10,000	10,000 to 25,000	25,000 to 50,000	50,000 to 100,000	100,000 to 250,000	250,000 to 500,000	500,000 to 2,500,000	2,500,000 and over
Number of Enterprises **1**	478	4	•	3	232	•	75	31	28	19	•	7	3
Revenues ($ in Thousands)													
Net Sales **2**	37392773	55029	•	649	1119807	•	1923327	1701087	3124876	4459744	•	8635432	14983020
Interest **3**	474072	78	•	23	644	•	1271	1918	1345	6232	•	45630	416830
Rents **4**	23293	1455	•	0	202	•	890	1336	2277	5117	•	6031	5974
Royalties **5**	398792	0	•	0	0	•	0	1703	0	365	•	308742	87981
Other Portfolio Income **6**	493057	1547	•	3619	13	•	17709	661	5306	29887	•	92258	342009
Other Receipts **7**	711021	7873	•	1689	7420	•	20626	18829	37857	79889	•	486531	47853
Total Receipts **8**	39493008	65982	•	5980	1128086	•	1963823	1725534	3171661	4581234	•	9574624	15883667
Average Total Receipts **9**	82621	16496	•	1993	4862	•	26184	55662	113274	241118	•	1367803	5294556
Operating Costs/Operating Income (%)													
Cost of Operations **10**	68.8	66.4	•	148.4	78.1	•	76.5	74.9	75.1	72.1	•	59.4	69.5
Salaries and Wages **11**	5.1	18.4	•	284.1	1.5	•	4.4	4.0	3.6	4.9	•	11.7	2.2
Taxes Paid **12**	1.3	1.2	•	9.2	2.0	•	1.6	1.4	1.2	1.5	•	1.7	1.0
Interest Paid **13**	3.1	0.5	•	37.3	1.2	•	1.2	2.1	1.3	1.4	•	2.5	5.1
Depreciation **14**	2.8	4.8	•	43.1	2.6	•	3.5	3.4	3.0	3.9	•	3.6	2.0
Amortization and Depletion **15**	0.9	0.0	•	18.3	1.2	•	0.2	0.3	0.3	0.3	•	0.9	1.3
Pensions and Other Deferred Comp. **16**	0.6	0.0	•	•	0.4	•	0.2	0.3	0.3	0.3	•	1.2	0.6
Employee Benefits **17**	1.4	0.4	•	•	2.2	•	0.8	1.1	1.4	0.8	•	2.7	1.0
Advertising **18**	3.2	0.9	•	0.5	0.5	•	1.4	1.3	1.4	2.8	•	4.6	3.7
Other Expenses **19**	13.8	4.7	•	990.3	5.7	•	9.1	10.2	9.8	10.2	•	18.2	14.2
Officers' Compensation **20**	0.7	1.4	•	•	4.1	•	1.8	0.9	0.9	0.8	•	0.7	0.1
Operating Margin **21**	•	1.2	•	•	0.6	•	•	0.1	1.7	1.0	•	•	•
Operating Margin Before Officers' Comp. **22**	•	2.6	•	•	4.6	•	1.1	1.0	2.5	1.8	•	•	•

Selected Average Balance Sheet ($ in Thousands)

Net Receivables 23	17929	0		359	2867	5795	10321	18887	56708	2318410
Inventories 24	10090	0	102	733	4857	12135	22886	47402	206800	447205
Net Property, Plant and Equipment 25	13782	0		481	5392	11498	18974	63674	278992	637785
Total Assets 26	83608	0	724	1978	16715	36234	67031	183305	1168248	7651023
Notes and Loans Payable 27	37151	0	2057	749	6866	13681	25696	55592	563694	3533207
All Other Liabilities 28	11990	0	2860	391	3972	9334	17755	45539	7444	1163798
Net Worth 29	34467	0	-4193	839	5878	13218	23580	82174	597110	2954018

Selected Financial Ratios (Times to 1)

Current Ratio 30	1.3	•	0.0	1.9	1.5	1.8	1.4	1.7	2.4	1.1
Quick Ratio 31	0.8	•	0.0	0.9	0.6	0.6	0.4	0.6	0.9	0.9
Net Sales to Working Capital 32	10.0	•	•	9.9	8.3	6.5	9.4	6.0	5.9	25.1
Coverage Ratio 33	2.6	42.1	•	2.1	2.2	1.7	3.4	3.7	4.0	2.2
Total Asset Turnover 34	0.9	•	0.3	2.4	1.5	1.5	1.7	1.3	1.1	0.7
Inventory Turnover 35	5.3	•	3.1	5.1	4.0	3.4	3.7	3.6	3.5	7.8
Receivables Turnover 36	4.4	•	0.3	11.9	9.2	8.3	12.1	14.4	2.3	4.3
Total Liabilities to Net Worth 37	1.4	•	•	1.4	1.8	1.7	1.8	1.2	1.0	1.6
Current Assets to Working Capital 38	4.3	•	•	2.1	3.0	2.3	3.4	2.3	1.7	14.7
Current Liabilities to Working Capital 39	3.3	•	•	1.1	2.0	1.3	2.4	1.3	0.7	13.7
Working Capital to Net Sales 40	0.1	•	•	0.1	0.1	0.2	0.1	0.2	0.2	0.0
Inventory to Working Capital 41	1.4	•	•	1.1	1.7	1.3	2.1	1.4	0.7	2.2
Total Receipts to Cash Flow 42	6.6	4.6	•	21.0	11.1	10.1	8.9	8.6	5.4	5.9
Cost of Goods to Cash Flow 43	4.5	3.1	•	16.4	8.5	7.6	6.7	6.2	3.2	4.1
Cash Flow to Total Debt 44	0.2	•	•	0.2	0.2	0.2	0.3	0.3	0.4	0.2

Selected Financial Factors (in Percentages)

Debt Ratio 45	58.8	•	679.4	57.6	64.8	63.5	64.8	55.2	48.9	61.4
Return on Total Assets 46	7.6	•	•	6.0	4.1	5.5	7.4	6.5	10.3	7.3
Return on Equity Before Income Taxes 47	11.4	•	31.5	7.4	6.2	6.2	14.9	10.6	15.1	10.4
Return on Equity After Income Taxes 48	7.6	•	31.5	6.6	5.4	4.2	12.1	7.1	9.7	6.9
Profit Margin (Before Income Tax) 49	5.0	21.1	•	1.3	1.4	1.5	3.1	3.7	7.3	6.2
Profit Margin (After Income Tax) 50	3.4	18.8	•	1.2	1.2	1.0	2.6	2.5	4.7	4.1

41

Table II

Corporations with Net Income

FRUIT AND VEGETABLE PRESERVING AND SPECIALTY FOOD

MONEY AMOUNTS AND SIZE OF ASSETS IN THOUSANDS OF DOLLARS

Item Description for Accounting Period 7/03 Through 6/04	Total	Zero Assets	Under 500	500 to 1,000	1,000 to 5,000	5,000 to 10,000	10,000 to 25,000	25,000 to 50,000	50,000 to 100,000	100,000 to 250,000	250,000 to 500,000	500,000 to 2,500,000	2,500,000 and over
Number of Enterprises **1**	328	4	•	•	202	13	43	20	21	13	•	•	3
Revenues ($ in Thousands)													
Net Sales **2**	32061518	55029	•	•	914352	199921	1110854	1106313	2579447	3337030	•	•	14983020
Interest **3**	458107	78	•	•	621	102	335	943	1320	3965	•	•	416830
Rents **4**	21179	1455	•	•	0	13	462	337	2001	4907	•	•	5974
Royalties **5**	360368	0	•	•	0	0	0	1703	0	0	•	•	87981
Other Portfolio Income **6**	491932	1547	•	•	13	6	17489	181	5257	29623	•	•	342009
Other Receipts **7**	687281	7873	•	•	6479	490	15885	10775	34607	76753	•	•	47853
Total Receipts **8**	34080385	65982	•	•	921465	200532	1145025	1120252	2622632	3452278	•	•	15883667
Average Total Receipts **9**	103904	16496	•	•	4562	15426	26628	56013	124887	265560	•	•	5294556
Operating Costs/Operating Income (%)													
Cost of Operations **10**	68.0	66.4	•	•	77.9	84.2	74.5	76.0	74.5	70.9	•	•	69.5
Salaries and Wages **11**	5.3	18.4	•	•	1.3	2.8	4.3	3.2	3.5	5.2	•	•	2.2
Taxes Paid **12**	1.3	1.2	•	•	1.8	1.2	1.5	1.3	1.3	1.8	•	•	1.0
Interest Paid **13**	3.2	0.5	•	•	1.3	0.1	1.0	1.5	1.0	1.1	•	•	5.1
Depreciation **14**	2.7	4.8	•	•	2.4	1.4	3.0	3.2	3.0	3.6	•	•	2.0
Amortization and Depletion **15**	0.9	0.0	•	•	1.4	0.1	0.1	0.2	0.1	0.2	•	•	1.3
Pensions and Other Deferred Comp. **16**	0.7	0.0	•	•	0.0	0.1	0.3	0.3	0.4	0.3	•	•	0.6
Employee Benefits **17**	1.4	0.4	•	•	1.2	0.8	0.8	1.0	1.3	0.8	•	•	1.0
Advertising **18**	3.3	0.9	•	•	0.6	1.1	1.0	0.9	1.6	2.1	•	•	3.7
Other Expenses **19**	13.9	4.7	•	•	7.4	4.9	8.2	8.0	9.5	10.5	•	•	14.2
Officers' Compensation **20**	0.6	1.4	•	•	3.6	1.9	1.6	0.9	1.0	0.8	•	•	0.1
Operating Margin **21**	•	1.2	•	•	1.2	1.4	3.7	3.4	2.8	2.5	•	•	•
Operating Margin Before Officers' Comp. **22**	•	2.6	•	•	4.8	3.3	5.4	4.2	3.8	3.3	•	•	•

Selected Average Balance Sheet ($ in Thousands)

Net Receivables 23	24853	0	•	•	396	1438	3004	6234	11325	20779	•	2318410
Inventories 24	11421	0	•	•	686	5071	5749	13709	26877	43369	•	447205
Net Property, Plant and Equipment 25	16606	0	•	•	490	2917	4670	10124	19839	62940	•	637785
Total Assets 26	109901	0	•	•	1957	6773	16315	36498	69022	178603	•	7651023
Notes and Loans Payable 27	48688	0	•	•	853	202	4750	12424	21699	49929	•	3553207
All Other Liabilities 28	14393	0	•	•	426	1165	3902	7837	16623	47707	•	1163798
Net Worth 29	46820	0	•	•	678	5407	7664	16237	30700	80967	•	2954018

Selected Financial Ratios (Times to 1)

Current Ratio 30	1.3	•	•	•	1.6	3.3	1.7	1.9	1.6	1.5	•	1.1
Quick Ratio 31	0.8	•	•	•	0.8	2.1	0.6	0.6	0.5	0.5	•	0.9
Net Sales to Working Capital 32	10.5	42.1	•	•	12.9	6.1	6.3	5.6	7.4	8.9	•	25.1
Coverage Ratio 33	3.0	•	•	•	2.5	19.3	8.1	4.0	5.5	6.6	•	2.2
Total Asset Turnover 34	0.9	•	•	•	2.3	2.3	1.6	1.5	1.8	1.4	•	0.7
Inventory Turnover 35	5.8	•	•	•	5.1	2.6	3.3	3.1	3.4	4.2	•	7.8
Receivables Turnover 36	4.1	•	•	•	10.1	4.5	7.9	8.1	11.1	17.7	•	4.3
Total Liabilities to Net Worth 37	1.3	•	•	•	1.9	0.3	1.1	1.2	1.2	1.2	•	1.6
Current Assets to Working Capital 38	4.6	•	•	•	2.7	1.4	2.4	2.2	2.5	3.1	•	14.7
Current Liabilities to Working Capital 39	3.6	•	•	•	1.7	0.4	1.4	1.2	1.5	2.1	•	13.7
Working Capital to Net Sales 40	0.1	•	•	•	0.1	0.2	0.2	0.2	0.1	0.1	•	0.0
Inventory to Working Capital 41	1.3	•	•	•	1.3	0.4	1.4	1.3	1.6	1.9	•	2.2
Total Receipts to Cash Flow 42	6.1	4.6	•	•	14.1	16.2	7.3	9.3	8.0	7.2	•	5.9
Cost of Goods to Cash Flow 43	4.2	3.1	•	•	11.0	13.6	5.4	7.1	6.0	5.1	•	4.1
Cash Flow to Total Debt 44	0.3	•	•	•	0.3	0.7	0.4	0.3	0.4	0.4	•	0.2

Selected Financial Factors (in Percentages)

Debt Ratio 45	57.4	•	•	•	65.4	20.2	53.0	55.5	55.5	54.7	•	61.4
Return on Total Assets 46	8.5	•	•	•	7.6	4.1	12.3	9.4	9.7	10.1	•	7.3
Return on Equity Before Income Taxes 47	13.4	•	•	•	13.3	4.8	22.9	15.8	17.9	18.9	•	10.4
Return on Equity After Income Taxes 48	9.3	•	•	•	12.2	3.3	21.9	13.3	15.1	13.8	•	6.9
Profit Margin (Before Income Tax) 49	6.4	21.1	•	•	2.0	1.7	6.8	4.6	4.5	6.0	•	6.2
Profit Margin (After Income Tax) 50	4.5	18.8	•	•	1.8	1.2	6.5	3.9	3.8	4.4	•	4.1

Table I

Corporations with and without Net Income

DAIRY PRODUCT

MONEY AMOUNTS AND SIZE OF ASSETS IN THOUSANDS OF DOLLARS

Item Description for Accounting Period 7/03 Through 6/04	Total	Zero Assets	Under 500	500 to 1,000	1,000 to 5,000	5,000 to 10,000	10,000 to 25,000	25,000 to 50,000	50,000 to 100,000	100,000 to 250,000	250,000 to 500,000	500,000 to 2,500,000	2,500,000 and over
Number of Enterprises **1**	496	5	105	53	153	59	55	31	16	9	4	6	•
Revenues ($ in Thousands)													
Net Sales **2**	31511991	864659	69063	165173	1359312	1570901	2698344	2602894	2271140	3131552	2850087	13928865	
Interest **3**	197756	99	403	230	1808	1021	1349	2984	1449	3539	2440	182434	
Rents **4**	52517	183	0	0	287	1718	2576	1608	2505	385	291	42963	
Royalties **5**	86566	26	0	0	0	0	0	2267	0	19	0	84253	
Other Portfolio Income **6**	105908	6178	400	0	9391	2088	12616	1774	922	296	2013	70230	
Other Receipts **7**	283848	1470	248	3416	1534	2971	14114	11296	2443	25376	13028	207954	
Total Receipts **8**	32238586	872615	70114	168819	1372332	1578699	2728999	2622823	2278459	3161167	2867859	14516699	
Average Total Receipts **9**	64997	174523	668	3185	8969	26758	49618	84607	142404	351241	716965	2419450	
Operating Costs/Operating Income (%)													
Cost of Operations **10**	76.4	76.7	33.7	84.3	78.0	76.4	79.8	76.3	77.2	83.5	76.0	74.0	
Salaries and Wages **11**	5.7	1.9	19.2	2.5	5.1	6.8	5.4	7.2	5.0	2.2	3.7	7.0	
Taxes Paid **12**	1.1	1.6	5.0	2.3	2.0	1.5	1.2	1.2	1.1	0.7	1.1	1.0	
Interest Paid **13**	1.8	0.7	0.1	0.2	0.6	0.4	0.6	0.6	0.5	1.9	0.8	3.0	
Depreciation **14**	3.5	3.7	0.7	1.9	2.2	1.9	2.5	3.2	3.2	3.0	3.6	4.2	
Amortization and Depletion **15**	0.8	0.3	•	•	0.0	0.1	0.1	0.1	0.1	0.6	0.7	1.5	
Pensions and Other Deferred Comp. **16**	0.4	0.1	2.5	•	0.9	0.4	0.3	0.6	0.5	0.3	0.5	0.3	
Employee Benefits **17**	1.2	3.2	1.9	3.4	1.9	0.6	1.0	1.4	1.0	0.8	2.0	1.1	
Advertising **18**	1.6	4.0	1.5	•	0.4	0.8	0.9	0.7	1.8	1.5	3.7	1.6	
Other Expenses **19**	8.3	7.9	27.8	9.6	7.9	7.8	6.4	6.0	6.2	3.9	7.4	10.5	
Officers' Compensation **20**	0.7	0.5	9.1	4.8	1.9	2.6	1.1	1.0	0.6	0.3	0.2	0.3	
Operating Margin **21**	•	•	•	•	•	0.7	0.7	1.8	2.9	1.3	0.3	•	
Operating Margin Before Officers' Comp. **22**	•	0.0	7.7	•	1.0	3.4	1.8	2.8	3.4	1.6	0.5	•	

Selected Average Balance Sheet ($ in Thousands)

Net Receivables 23	5117	0	15	127	527	2378	4147	7599	12540	22912	41960	211735	•
Inventories 24	3910	0	10	57	542	1720	2654	5577	12304	21239	41419	146349	•
Net Property, Plant and Equipment 25	12214	0	20	170	1281	2476	6312	14523	27909	62675	182243	527987	•
Total Assets 26	45053	0	220	511	2882	6706	16764	35977	69706	165099	392961	2541513	•
Notes and Loans Payable 27	12744	0	13	92	861	1498	5138	9742	14022	73075	173053	656018	•
All Other Liabilities 28	14195	0	100	167	609	2518	4650	9204	17724	38394	95169	871472	•
Net Worth 29	18113	0	107	252	1412	2689	6976	17031	37961	53631	124739	1014022	•

Selected Financial Ratios (Times to 1)

Current Ratio 30	0.9	•	2.0	1.3	1.7	1.7	1.4	1.7	1.6	1.8	1.1	0.6	•
Quick Ratio 31	0.5	•	1.9	1.1	1.0	1.1	0.9	1.0	0.8	1.1	0.5	0.3	•
Net Sales to Working Capital 32	•	•	6.8	43.0	15.6	15.5	18.4	11.6	11.0	10.4	103.5	•	•
Coverage Ratio 33	1.5	1.6	3.5	•	1.1	4.5	4.1	5.6	7.0	2.2	2.2	0.9	•
Total Asset Turnover 34	1.4	•	3.0	6.1	3.1	4.0	2.9	2.3	2.0	2.1	1.8	0.9	•
Inventory Turnover 35	12.4	•	22.4	45.9	12.8	11.8	14.8	11.5	8.9	13.7	13.1	11.7	•
Receivables Turnover 36	12.7	•	85.1	21.4	14.1	9.4	12.4	11.3	12.9	14.9	17.0	11.5	•
Total Liabilities to Net Worth 37	1.5	•	1.1	1.0	1.0	1.5	1.4	1.1	0.8	2.1	2.2	1.5	•
Current Assets to Working Capital 38	•	•	2.0	4.0	2.5	2.4	3.3	2.5	2.6	2.3	13.6	•	•
Current Liabilities to Working Capital 39	•	•	1.0	3.0	1.5	1.4	2.3	1.5	1.6	1.3	12.6	•	•
Working Capital to Net Sales 40	•	•	0.1	0.0	0.1	0.1	0.1	0.1	0.1	0.1	0.0	•	•
Inventory to Working Capital 41	•	•	0.1	0.7	0.9	0.6	1.0	0.7	1.1	0.7	6.1	•	•
Total Receipts to Cash Flow 42	13.8	15.0	4.3	•	17.4	14.5	16.0	14.5	12.2	18.7	15.5	12.3	•
Cost of Goods to Cash Flow 43	10.6	11.5	1.4	•	13.6	11.1	12.8	11.0	9.4	15.6	11.8	9.1	•
Cash Flow to Total Debt 44	0.2	•	1.4	•	0.3	0.5	0.3	0.3	0.4	0.2	0.2	0.1	•

Selected Financial Factors (in Percentages)

Debt Ratio 45	59.8	•	51.2	50.7	51.0	59.9	58.4	52.7	45.5	67.5	68.3	60.1	•
Return on Total Assets 46	3.7	•	0.6	•	2.0	6.3	7.0	7.2	7.5	8.6	3.1	2.5	•
Return on Equity Before Income Taxes 47	2.9	•	0.8	•	0.5	12.2	12.6	12.5	11.8	14.5	5.3	•	•
Return on Equity After Income Taxes 48	1.7	•	0.8	•	•	9.0	10.6	11.3	9.1	13.4	5.3	•	•
Profit Margin (Before Income Tax) 49	0.8	0.4	0.1	•	0.1	1.2	1.8	2.5	3.2	2.2	0.9	•	•
Profit Margin (After Income Tax) 50	0.5	0.4	0.1	•	•	0.9	1.5	2.3	2.4	2.1	0.9	•	•

Table II

Corporations with Net Income

DAIRY PRODUCT

MONEY AMOUNTS AND SIZE OF ASSETS IN THOUSANDS OF DOLLARS

Item Description for Accounting Period 7/03 Through 6/04	Total	Zero Assets	Under 500	500 to 1,000	1,000 to 5,000	5,000 to 10,000	10,000 to 25,000	25,000 to 50,000	50,000 to 100,000	100,000 to 250,000	250,000 to 500,000	500,000 to 2,500,000	2,500,000 and over
Number of Enterprises 1	302	•	105	•	60	46	39	24	13	•	•	•	•
Revenues ($ in Thousands)													
Net Sales 2	23140991	•	69063	•	849604	1110123	2028957	1975949	1802081	•	•	•	•
Interest 3	189702	•	403	•	534	232	1054	1261	1019	•	•	•	•
Rents 4	6541	•	0	•	287	322	2558	778	189	•	•	•	•
Royalties 5	85672	•	0	•	0	0	0	2267	0	•	•	•	•
Other Portfolio Income 6	99916	•	400	•	7477	544	12320	1572	903	•	•	•	•
Other Receipts 7	211595	•	248	•	719	919	1288	7662	1174	•	•	•	•
Total Receipts 8	23734417	•	70114	•	858621	1112140	2046177	1989489	1805366	•	•	•	•
Average Total Receipts 9	78591	•	668	•	14310	24177	52466	82895	138874	•	•	•	•
Operating Costs/Operating Income (%)													
Cost of Operations 10	77.1	•	33.7	•	79.9	68.0	78.7	77.9	78.3	•	•	•	•
Salaries and Wages 11	4.8	•	19.2	•	5.4	9.5	5.5	6.1	4.0	•	•	•	•
Taxes Paid 12	1.0	•	5.0	•	1.2	1.8	1.2	1.1	1.0	•	•	•	•
Interest Paid 13	1.8	•	0.1	•	0.4	0.3	0.5	0.5	0.4	•	•	•	•
Depreciation 14	3.4	•	0.7	•	2.0	2.2	2.3	3.3	3.0	•	•	•	•
Amortization and Depletion 15	0.7	•	•	•	•	0.1	0.1	0.1	0.1	•	•	•	•
Pensions and Other Deferred Comp. 16	0.3	•	2.5	•	0.5	0.5	0.3	0.5	0.4	•	•	•	•
Employee Benefits 17	1.0	•	1.9	•	2.2	0.5	0.8	1.3	0.7	•	•	•	•
Advertising 18	1.0	•	1.5	•	0.5	1.1	0.8	0.6	2.1	•	•	•	•
Other Expenses 19	7.6	•	27.8	•	6.2	10.5	6.0	4.8	5.4	•	•	•	•
Officers' Compensation 20	0.6	•	9.1	•	0.6	3.7	1.1	0.9	0.5	•	•	•	•
Operating Margin 21	0.6	•	•	•	1.2	1.8	2.7	2.9	4.0	•	•	•	•
Operating Margin Before Officers' Comp. 22	1.2	•	7.7	•	1.7	5.5	3.9	3.8	4.6	•	•	•	•

Selected Average Balance Sheet ($ in Thousands)

Net Receivables 23	6455	15	805	2184	4413	7484	11712
Inventories 24	4859	10	855	1902	2801	5558	12143
Net Property, Plant and Equipment 25	14065	20	1083	2586	5764	14560	25536
Total Assets 26	49116	220	3149	6882	16537	35281	69023
Notes and Loans Payable 27	13469	13	1040	1520	4607	8784	10791
All Other Liabilities 28	18069	100	937	2485	4644	8354	17379
Net Worth 29	17578	107	1172	2876	7286	18142	40853

Selected Financial Ratios (Times to 1)

Current Ratio 30	0.9	2.0	1.6	1.8	1.7	1.8	1.9
Quick Ratio 31	0.5	1.9	1.0	1.1	1.1	1.1	0.9
Net Sales to Working Capital 32	•	6.8	19.5	13.3	13.7	10.7	8.3
Coverage Ratio 33	2.7	3.5	6.3	7.7	8.3	8.1	11.1
Total Asset Turnover 34	1.6	3.0	4.5	3.5	3.1	2.3	2.0
Inventory Turnover 35	12.2	22.4	13.2	8.6	14.6	11.5	8.9
Receivables Turnover 36	12.0	85.1	12.8	8.0	11.5	11.6	15.0
Total Liabilities to Net Worth 37	1.8	1.1	1.7	1.4	1.3	0.9	0.7
Current Assets to Working Capital 38	•	2.0	2.8	2.3	2.4	2.3	2.1
Current Liabilities to Working Capital 39	•	1.0	1.8	1.3	1.4	1.3	1.1
Working Capital to Net Sales 40	•	0.1	0.1	0.1	0.1	0.1	0.1
Inventory to Working Capital 41	•	0.1	1.0	0.6	0.7	0.7	0.9
Total Receipts to Cash Flow 42	11.3	4.3	16.3	10.4	13.0	14.6	11.7
Cost of Goods to Cash Flow 43	8.7	1.4	13.1	7.0	10.2	11.3	9.1
Cash Flow to Total Debt 44	0.2	1.4	0.4	0.6	0.4	0.3	0.4

Selected Financial Factors (in Percentages)

Debt Ratio 45	64.2	51.2	62.8	58.2	55.9	48.6	40.8
Return on Total Assets 46	7.7	0.6	11.9	8.0	12.8	9.4	9.3
Return on Equity Before Income Taxes 47	13.7	0.8	27.0	16.7	25.5	16.0	14.3
Return on Equity After Income Taxes 48	11.6	0.8	20.2	12.9	22.7	14.6	11.1
Profit Margin (Before Income Tax) 49	3.1	0.1	2.2	2.0	3.6	3.5	4.2
Profit Margin (After Income Tax) 50	2.7	0.1	1.7	1.5	3.2	3.2	3.3

Table I

Corporations with and without Net Income

MEAT AND SEAFOOD PROCESSING

MONEY AMOUNTS AND SIZE OF ASSETS IN THOUSANDS OF DOLLARS

Item Description for Accounting Period 7/03 Through 6/04	Total	Zero Assets	Under 500	500 to 1,000	1,000 to 5,000	5,000 to 10,000	10,000 to 25,000	25,000 to 50,000	50,000 to 100,000	100,000 to 250,000	250,000 to 500,000	500,000 to 2,500,000	2,500,000 and over
Number of Enterprises **1**	2093	26	1178	266	202	175	117	50	33	30	5	5	5
Revenues ($ in Thousands)													
Net Sales **2**	123909659	358624	510733	296848	1476405	2885176	5753999	4721391	7095316	10747723	2190312	9002522	78870611
Interest **3**	239074	657	28	2710	830	2917	2332	1430	2464	6153	792	24658	194101
Rents **4**	27411	214	1	313	2318	3653	3229	673	299	2973	29	2257	11452
Royalties **5**	238810	0	0	0	0	63	0	171	0	0	0	21424	217151
Other Portfolio Income **6**	227141	690	0	976	4679	18158	3188	3625	3549	3069	0	28449	160753
Other Receipts **7**	852615	3418	302	1723	3419	32450	37874	33890	39686	61018	43686	98298	496858
Total Receipts **8**	125494710	363603	511064	302570	1487651	2942417	5800622	4761180	7141314	10820936	2234819	9177608	79950926
Average Total Receipts **9**	59959	13985	434	1137	7365	16814	49578	95224	216403	360698	446964	1835522	15990185
Operating Costs/Operating Income (%)													
Cost of Operations **10**	81.7	83.2	71.9	63.5	80.1	79.2	80.9	82.5	80.9	85.3	75.3	76.0	82.3
Salaries and Wages **11**	4.2	5.3	4.4	5.7	4.6	4.4	4.6	3.1	3.4	2.6	2.5	7.4	4.2
Taxes Paid **12**	0.8	1.0	2.8	2.9	1.8	1.5	1.2	1.2	0.8	0.9	1.6	1.4	0.6
Interest Paid **13**	1.2	1.3	0.2	0.0	0.7	0.8	0.6	0.9	0.7	0.7	1.9	1.2	1.4
Depreciation **14**	1.9	1.7	1.5	1.3	1.9	2.5	1.9	2.1	2.1	2.0	3.3	3.7	1.6
Amortization and Depletion **15**	0.2	0.7	0.1	•	0.0	0.0	0.1	0.2	0.2	0.2	0.6	0.1	0.2
Pensions and Other Deferred Comp. **16**	0.1	0.1	0.0	0.1	0.1	0.2	0.2	0.2	0.2	0.1	0.4	0.2	0.1
Employee Benefits **17**	1.5	1.3	2.1	1.2	0.4	0.8	1.0	0.9	0.9	0.9	1.1	1.9	1.7
Advertising **18**	0.8	0.5	0.5	1.5	0.5	0.2	0.7	0.9	2.1	0.8	0.9	0.6	0.8
Other Expenses **19**	6.5	1.5	11.9	21.9	8.1	8.1	5.9	5.7	5.8	4.8	9.8	8.1	6.5
Officers' Compensation **20**	0.4	0.7	5.5	7.4	3.4	2.3	1.3	1.0	0.5	0.5	0.3	0.2	0.1
Operating Margin **21**	0.7	2.6	•	•	•	•	1.6	1.3	2.5	1.4	2.3	•	0.6
Operating Margin Before Officers' Comp. **22**	1.1	3.4	4.5	1.9	2.0	2.3	3.0	2.3	3.1	1.9	2.6	•	0.7

Selected Average Balance Sheet ($ in Thousands)

Net Receivables 23	4828	0	2	232	647	1482	3364	6714	12980	31013	47735	115527	1349377
Inventories 24	5036	0	1	66	330	1121	3280	7357	15695	30756	64820	326588	1253998
Net Property, Plant and Equipment 25	7554	0	30	72	1021	2491	5851	12008	25033	49787	87784	407723	1806003
Total Assets 26	31160	0	44	633	2279	6197	16239	35795	68829	150642	283074	1317061	8994442
Notes and Loans Payable 27	10879	0	6	13	969	5057	5433	13839	20801	52102	142181	228007	3250180
All Other Liabilities 28	10705	0	13	30	442	1472	3685	9022	16487	38332	58472	521460	3311696
Net Worth 29	9577	0	25	590	868	-332	7121	12934	31541	60208	82421	567594	2432566

Selected Financial Ratios (Times to 1)

Current Ratio 30	1.4	•	1.8	9.0	1.6	1.8	1.7	1.3	1.6	1.4	1.9	1.1	1.4
Quick Ratio 31	0.5	•	1.5	7.7	1.2	1.2	0.9	0.7	0.8	0.8	0.8	0.3	0.4
Net Sales to Working Capital 32	14.5	•	72.3	3.6	21.0	13.8	14.4	23.2	16.6	15.5	7.5	44.5	13.2
Coverage Ratio 33	2.9	4.0	•	•	0.0	3.3	5.3	3.4	5.9	4.0	3.3	2.1	2.8
Total Asset Turnover 34	1.9	•	9.8	1.8	3.2	2.7	3.0	2.6	3.1	2.4	1.5	1.4	1.8
Inventory Turnover 35	9.6	•	222.2	10.7	17.7	11.6	12.1	10.6	11.1	9.9	5.1	4.2	10.4
Receivables Turnover 36	11.3	•	24.8	5.6	10.2	10.7	15.1	14.0	16.0	13.6	18.4	8.4	10.7
Total Liabilities to Net Worth 37	2.3	•	0.7	0.1	1.6	•	1.3	1.8	1.2	1.5	2.4	1.3	2.7
Current Assets to Working Capital 38	3.8	•	2.3	1.1	2.8	2.3	2.5	4.5	2.6	3.3	2.1	13.5	3.9
Current Liabilities to Working Capital 39	2.8	•	1.3	0.1	1.8	1.3	1.5	3.5	1.6	2.3	1.1	12.5	2.9
Working Capital to Net Sales 40	0.1	•	0.0	0.3	0.0	0.1	0.1	0.0	0.1	0.1	0.1	0.0	0.1
Inventory to Working Capital 41	1.3	•	0.3	0.1	0.5	0.5	1.0	1.7	1.2	1.3	1.1	7.2	1.1
Total Receipts to Cash Flow 42	13.7	38.0	12.8	6.9	17.6	12.6	14.2	14.6	12.5	17.1	7.7	14.4	13.5
Cost of Goods to Cash Flow 43	11.1	31.6	9.2	4.4	14.1	10.0	11.5	12.0	10.1	14.6	5.8	10.9	11.1
Cash Flow to Total Debt 44	0.2	1.8	3.8	0.3	0.2	0.4	0.3	0.3	0.5	0.2	0.3	0.2	0.2

Selected Financial Factors (in Percentages)

Debt Ratio 45	69.3	•	42.7	6.8	61.9	105.4	56.1	63.9	54.2	60.0	70.9	56.9	73.0
Return on Total Assets 46	6.7	•	•	•	0.0	7.4	9.1	8.1	12.0	6.5	9.7	3.4	6.7
Return on Equity Before Income Taxes 47	14.3	•	•	•	•	•	16.8	15.9	21.6	12.2	23.1	4.0	15.8
Return on Equity After Income Taxes 48	10.2	•	•	•	•	•	15.3	14.7	18.8	10.6	15.2	2.7	10.4
Profit Margin (Before Income Tax) 49	2.3	4.0	•	•	1.9	2.2	2.4	2.2	3.2	2.1	4.3	1.3	2.4
Profit Margin (After Income Tax) 50	1.7	3.7	•	•	1.8	2.0	2.2	2.0	2.8	1.8	2.9	0.9	1.6

Table II

Corporations with Net Income

MEAT AND SEAFOOD PROCESSING

MONEY AMOUNTS AND SIZE OF ASSETS IN THOUSANDS OF DOLLARS

Item Description for Accounting Period 7/03 Through 6/04	Total	Zero Assets	Under 500	500 to 1,000	1,000 to 5,000	5,000 to 10,000	10,000 to 25,000	25,000 to 50,000	50,000 to 100,000	100,000 to 250,000	250,000 to 500,000	500,000 to 2,500,000	2,500,000 and over
Number of Enterprises 1	782	15	300	67	127	·	85	38	26	21	·	·	5
Revenues ($ in Thousands)													
Net Sales 2	110666606	252630	315193	6906	1149571	·	4438124	3485185	5709269	7552101	·	·	78870611
Interest 3	229029	316	28	1320	260	·	1180	1168	2398	5579	·	·	194101
Rents 4	21022	0	0	0	1514	·	1895	191	299	2875	·	·	11452
Royalties 5	238639	0	0	0	0	·	0	0	0	0	·	·	217151
Other Portfolio Income 6	196599	647	0	0	4264	·	2582	1608	1205	3047	·	·	160753
Other Receipts 7	747000	2787	56	0	382	·	35065	29869	32604	45909	·	·	496858
Total Receipts 8	112098895	256380	315277	8226	1155991	·	447846	3518021	5745775	7609511	·	·	79950926
Average Total Receipts 9	143349	17092	1051	123	9102	·	52692	92580	220991	362358	·	·	15590185
Operating Costs/Operating Income (%)													
Cost of Operations 10	81.2	83.3	65.2	57.0	78.8	·	79.4	81.4	80.1	82.5	·	·	82.3
Salaries and Wages 11	4.4	4.7	0.0	1.5	5.4	·	4.9	3.2	3.1	3.1	·	·	4.2
Taxes Paid 12	0.7	1.0	3.8	0.6	1.5	·	1.2	1.1	0.8	0.8	·	·	0.6
Interest Paid 13	1.2	0.7	0.0	1.2	0.5	·	0.5	0.5	0.4	0.7	·	·	1.4
Depreciation 14	1.8	1.8	1.0	1.1	1.1	·	1.8	2.0	2.0	1.9	·	·	1.6
Amortization and Depletion 15	0.2	0.0	·	·	0.0	·	0.1	0.1	0.1	0.2	·	·	0.2
Pensions and Other Deferred Comp. 16	0.1	0.0	·	·	0.1	·	0.2	0.3	0.2	0.1	·	·	0.1
Employee Benefits 17	1.5	1.4	3.5	·	0.1	·	1.0	0.9	0.9	0.8	·	·	1.7
Advertising 18	0.9	0.6	0.6	·	0.4	·	0.7	1.0	2.4	0.7	·	·	0.8
Other Expenses 19	6.5	·	13.2	14.8	8.1	·	5.6	5.2	5.6	5.3	·	·	6.5
Officers' Compensation 20	0.4	1.0	8.9	2.4	3.5	·	1.4	1.0	0.6	0.6	·	·	0.1
Operating Margin 21	1.2	6.3	3.7	21.4	0.5	·	3.0	3.2	3.8	3.1	·	·	0.6
Operating Margin Before Officers' Comp. 22	1.6	7.2	12.6	23.8	4.0	·	4.4	4.2	4.4	3.7	·	·	0.7

Selected Average Balance Sheet ($ in Thousands)

Net Receivables 23	11399	0	9	425	887	•	3506	7099	13473	27835	•	1349377
Inventories 24	10792	0	1	119	293	•	3323	7674	15507	31092	•	1360327
Net Property, Plant and Equipment 25	16383	0	101	57	708	•	5637	11668	24912	45859	•	1806003
Total Assets 26	73354	0	147	540	1949	•	16094	35586	71231	141993	•	8994442
Notes and Loans Payable 27	25400	0	4	32	742	•	4968	9775	16654	49467	•	3250180
All Other Liabilities 28	24983	0	30	4	434	•	3479	8914	17102	32613	•	3311696
Net Worth 29	22972	0	113	505	774	•	7646	16897	37475	59913	•	2432566

Selected Financial Ratios (Times to 1)

Current Ratio 30	1.4	•	1.5	14.4	2.7	•	1.8	1.7	1.8	1.7	•	1.4
Quick Ratio 31	0.5	•	1.5	14.4	2.1	•	0.9	0.9	0.9	0.8	•	0.4
Net Sales to Working Capital 32	12.5	•	65.2	0.2	11.9	•	13.0	11.7	13.7	11.7	•	13.2
Coverage Ratio 33	3.4	12.6	111.8	34.7	2.9	•	9.4	8.7	11.2	6.5	•	2.8
Total Asset Turnover 34	1.9	•	7.2	0.2	4.6	•	3.2	2.6	3.1	2.5	•	1.8
Inventory Turnover 35	10.6	•	1284.9	0.5	24.3	•	12.5	9.7	11.3	9.5	•	9.5
Receivables Turnover 36	12.0	•	232.3	0.4	10.1	•	15.7	12.5	15.9	14.3	•	23.4
Total Liabilities to Net Worth 37	2.2	•	0.3	0.1	1.5	•	1.1	1.1	0.9	1.4	•	2.7
Current Assets to Working Capital 38	3.3	•	2.8	1.1	1.6	•	2.3	2.4	2.2	2.5	•	3.9
Current Liabilities to Working Capital 39	2.3	•	1.8	0.1	0.6	•	1.3	1.4	1.2	1.5	•	2.9
Working Capital to Net Sales 40	0.1	•	0.0	4.4	0.1	•	0.1	0.1	0.1	0.1	•	0.1
Inventory to Working Capital 41	1.1	•	0.0	0.0	0.3	•	0.9	0.9	1.0	1.1	•	1.1
Total Receipts to Cash Flow 42	12.8	25.6	7.4	2.1	13.3	•	12.1	11.6	11.0	12.3	•	13.5
Cost of Goods to Cash Flow 43	10.4	21.3	4.8	1.2	10.5	•	9.6	9.4	8.8	10.2	•	11.1
Cash Flow to Total Debt 44	0.2	•	4.2	1.4	0.6	•	0.5	0.4	0.6	0.4	•	0.2

Selected Financial Factors (in Percentages)

Debt Ratio 45	68.7	•	23.0	6.5	60.3	•	52.5	52.5	47.4	57.8	•	73.0
Return on Total Assets 46	7.8	•	26.7	8.0	7.5	•	14.2	12.3	15.0	11.6	•	6.7
Return on Equity Before Income Taxes 47	17.6	•	34.4	8.3	12.4	•	26.7	23.0	26.0	23.3	•	15.8
Return on Equity After Income Taxes 48	13.1	•	29.2	8.3	10.1	•	24.8	21.7	23.0	21.0	•	10.4
Profit Margin (Before Income Tax) 49	2.9	7.8	3.7	40.5	1.1	•	3.9	4.2	4.4	3.9	•	2.4
Profit Margin (After Income Tax) 50	2.1	7.3	3.1	40.5	0.9	•	3.6	4.0	3.9	3.5	•	1.6

Table I

Corporations with and without Net Income

BAKERIES AND TORTILLA

MONEY AMOUNTS AND SIZE OF ASSETS IN THOUSANDS OF DOLLARS

Item Description for Accounting Period 7/03 Through 6/04	Total	Zero Assets	Under 500	500 to 1,000	1,000 to 5,000	5,000 to 10,000	10,000 to 25,000	25,000 to 50,000	50,000 to 100,000	100,000 to 250,000	250,000 to 500,000	500,000 to 2,500,000	2,500,000 and over
Number of Enterprises 1	5137	97	4189	337	180	193	68	29	21	9	4	11	•
Revenues ($ in Thousands)													
Net Sales 2	86554580	8167	1696981	262959	1115526	2427800	2056354	2286364	2693573	1878972	1999446	70128438	•
Interest 3	1496605	0	6	1	364	828	741	1423	3145	6430	188	1483478	•
Rents 4	2257111	5	0	99	2687	423	376	3201	10750	107	717	223746	•
Royalties 5	2183468	0	0	0	0	0	73	355	0	37156	16228	2129657	•
Other Portfolio Income 6	770121	0	4085	302	1793	1380	764	1337	1681	711	427	757642	•
Other Receipts 7	2461718	526	16898	16461	1011	30656	6984	6104	11400	56950	11058	2303669	•
Total Receipts 8	95723603	8698	1717970	279822	1121381	2461087	2065292	2298784	2720549	1980326	2028064	79041630	•
Average Total Receipts 9	18634	90	410	830	6230	12752	30372	79268	129550	220036	507016	7185603	•
Operating Costs/Operating Income (%)													
Cost of Operations 10	51.1	39.4	36.1	66.0	69.1	62.2	63.4	68.3	60.1	57.3	68.6	48.9	•
Salaries and Wages 11	7.4	3.0	22.7	6.8	7.6	8.0	7.7	8.9	12.1	15.7	11.2	6.5	•
Taxes Paid 12	6.6	2.3	4.0	1.9	2.4	2.7	2.1	1.8	2.0	2.2	2.6	7.5	•
Interest Paid 13	4.9	0.5	0.5	2.6	0.3	0.8	0.8	0.8	1.3	1.6	1.8	5.8	•
Depreciation 14	4.5	1.3	3.1	8.5	4.0	6.7	3.8	4.5	4.3	5.8	2.8	4.5	•
Amortization and Depletion 15	0.6	0.1	0.4	0.4	0.2	0.1	0.2	0.1	0.2	2.1	0.6	0.7	•
Pensions and Other Deferred Comp. 16	1.8	•	0.1	0.1	0.2	0.6	0.4	1.0	1.6	0.3	1.8	2.0	•
Employee Benefits 17	2.9	•	0.2	1.3	2.5	2.3	2.6	2.5	3.9	2.2	2.2	3.0	•
Advertising 18	2.1	0.4	1.1	0.1	0.2	0.5	1.2	0.9	1.3	2.0	0.4	2.3	•
Other Expenses 19	21.0	181.3	24.8	14.5	11.3	11.6	12.3	10.3	12.4	17.1	6.9	22.8	•
Officers' Compensation 20	0.7	0.4	10.9	3.5	1.8	3.1	2.6	1.0	1.2	0.4	0.3	0.3	•
Operating Margin 21	•	•	•	•	0.4	1.2	2.8	•	•	•	0.9	•	•
Operating Margin Before Officers' Comp. 22	•	•	7.6	2.2	2.2	4.4	5.5	0.9	0.8	•	1.3	•	•

Selected Average Balance Sheet ($ in Thousands)

Net Receivables 23	1539	0	26	85	618	934	2888	5716	10232	16678	50278	595361
Inventories 24	745	0	9	41	506	414	1340	3452	5910	18147	37351	270708
Net Property, Plant and Equipment 25	2198	0	23	374	1117	2784	6414	18177	32667	73477	79297	700175
Total Assets 26	25724	0	79	637	3204	6475	15165	35333	73794	184617	319402	11202490
Notes and Loans Payable 27	5666	0	52	537	310	1802	4330	11788	22364	33797	106106	2406228
All Other Liabilities 28	8928	0	19	168	516	1344	3069	10537	20028	60126	80689	3961343
Net Worth 29	11130	0	8	-69	2378	3330	7766	13008	31402	90693	132607	4834919

Selected Financial Ratios (Times to 1)

Current Ratio 30	0.6	•	2.5	1.3	3.4	2.3	1.9	1.2	1.0	1.1	1.1	0.5
Quick Ratio 31	0.3	•	1.9	0.9	2.0	1.5	1.3	0.7	0.6	0.7	0.6	0.3
Net Sales to Working Capital 32	•	•	13.9	20.1	4.6	7.9	9.9	36.7	•	45.6	64.7	•
Coverage Ratio 33	3.4	•	•	1.3	3.9	4.2	5.2	1.6	1.4	0.1	2.3	3.4
Total Asset Turnover 34	0.7	•	5.2	1.2	1.9	1.9	2.0	2.2	1.7	1.1	1.6	0.6
Inventory Turnover 35	11.6	•	16.0	12.7	8.5	18.9	14.3	15.6	13.0	6.6	9.2	11.5
Receivables Turnover 36	15.5	•	22.3	13.3	7.6	15.4	10.7	14.4	12.2	8.6	11.2	16.7
Total Liabilities to Net Worth 37	1.3	•	-8.9	•	0.3	0.9	1.0	1.7	1.3	1.0	1.4	1.3
Current Assets to Working Capital 38	•	•	1.7	4.2	1.4	1.8	2.2	6.0	•	8.6	13.2	•
Current Liabilities to Working Capital 39	•	•	0.7	3.2	0.4	0.8	1.2	5.0	•	7.6	12.2	•
Working Capital to Net Sales 40	•	•	0.1	0.0	0.2	0.1	0.1	0.0	•	0.0	0.0	•
Inventory to Working Capital 41	•	•	0.4	1.0	0.4	0.4	0.5	1.6	•	2.8	4.3	•
Total Receipts to Cash Flow 42	3.9	•	6.8	8.6	9.8	9.8	7.5	12.3	11.1	7.8	13.7	3.4
Cost of Goods to Cash Flow 43	2.0	•	2.5	5.7	6.8	6.1	4.8	8.4	6.7	4.5	9.4	1.7
Cash Flow to Total Debt 44	0.3	•	0.8	0.1	0.8	0.4	0.5	0.3	0.3	0.3	0.2	0.3

Selected Financial Factors (in Percentages)

Debt Ratio 45	56.7	•	89.9	110.8	25.8	48.6	48.8	63.2	57.4	50.9	58.5	56.8
Return on Total Assets 46	10.8	•	•	4.1	2.3	6.7	8.0	2.8	3.2	0.2	6.4	11.4
Return on Equity Before Income Taxes 47	17.6	•	•	•	2.3	9.9	12.6	2.8	2.1	•	8.8	18.7
Return on Equity After Income Taxes 48	11.4	•	•	•	2.3	7.3	10.7	1.4	1.4	•	7.0	12.1
Profit Margin (Before Income Tax) 49	11.6	•	0.8	•	0.9	2.6	3.2	0.5	0.5	•	2.3	14.2
Profit Margin (After Income Tax) 50	7.5	•	0.7	0.7	0.9	1.9	2.7	0.2	0.4	•	1.8	9.1

Table II
Corporations with Net Income

BAKERIES AND TORTILLA

MONEY AMOUNTS AND SIZE OF ASSETS IN THOUSANDS OF DOLLARS

Item Description for Accounting Period 7/03 Through 6/04

	Total	Zero Assets	Under 500	500 to 1,000	1,000 to 5,000	5,000 to 10,000	10,000 to 25,000	25,000 to 50,000	50,000 to 100,000	100,000 to 250,000	250,000 to 500,000	500,000 to 2,500,000	2,500,000 and over
Number of Enterprises **1**	2018	9	1348	271	158	146	47	15	12	5	•	7	•

Revenues ($ in Thousands)

	Total	Zero Assets	Under 500	500 to 1,000	1,000 to 5,000	5,000 to 10,000	10,000 to 25,000	25,000 to 50,000	50,000 to 100,000	100,000 to 250,000	250,000 to 500,000	500,000 to 2,500,000	2,500,000 and over
Net Sales **2**	73356693	3042	1007680	148844	1047848	1768326	1481165	999442	1526446	1923974	•	63661926	•
Interest **3**	1429294	0	6	1	337	322	518	630	276	781	•	1426423	•
Rents **4**	2245658	5	0	99	2385	0	376	3130	1372	252	•	2238038	•
Royalties **5**	2118916	0	0	0	0	0	73	0	0	35467	•	2083376	•
Other Portfolio Income **6**	752274	0	0	302	2	1252	440	572	1448	459	•	747802	•
Other Receipts **7**	2402726	10	16116	16324	957	11889	5302	3136	7963	46208	•	2294817	•
Total Receipts **8**	82517561	3057	1023802	165570	1051529	1781789	1487874	1006910	1537505	2007141	•	72452382	•
Average Total Receipts **9**	40891	340	759	611	6655	12204	31657	67127	128125	401428	•	10350340	•

Operating Costs/Operating Income (%)

	Total	Zero Assets	Under 500	500 to 1,000	1,000 to 5,000	5,000 to 10,000	10,000 to 25,000	25,000 to 50,000	50,000 to 100,000	100,000 to 250,000	250,000 to 500,000	500,000 to 2,500,000	2,500,000 and over
Cost of Operations **10**	49.7	68.5	29.7	71.8	69.5	59.0	62.1	59.6	63.1	56.1	•	48.4	•
Salaries and Wages **11**	6.3	8.2	29.5	12.0	7.3	8.3	7.5	10.1	8.6	17.0	•	5.4	•
Taxes Paid **12**	7.2	2.5	4.3	1.5	2.2	2.8	2.0	2.2	1.6	2.4	•	7.9	•
Interest Paid **13**	5.4	1.1	0.2	3.4	0.2	0.8	0.7	0.7	0.7	1.1	•	6.1	•
Depreciation **14**	4.5	3.5	2.4	3.8	3.8	6.7	3.7	4.4	4.0	5.0	•	4.5	•
Amortization and Depletion **15**	0.5	0.4	•	0.7	0.1	0.1	0.2	0.1	0.1	0.9	•	0.6	•
Pensions and Other Deferred Comp. **16**	1.5	•	•	0.2	0.3	0.6	0.5	1.4	0.5	0.2	•	1.7	•
Employee Benefits **17**	2.7	•	0.0	2.2	2.5	2.7	1.9	2.9	3.3	1.9	•	2.8	•
Advertising **18**	2.2	1.0	0.1	0.2	0.1	0.5	1.5	0.8	1.2	0.9	•	2.4	•
Other Expenses **19**	22.7	10.4	21.4	13.6	10.9	11.1	11.1	12.9	12.6	12.9	•	24.2	•
Officers' Compensation **20**	0.6	1.1	12.9	0.6	1.2	3.0	3.1	1.2	1.5	0.3	•	0.2	•
Operating Margin **21**	•	3.5	•	2.0	4.4	5.7	3.6	•	2.6	1.4	•	•	•
Operating Margin Before Officers' Comp. **22**	•	4.5	12.5	3.2	7.4	8.9	4.8	•	4.1	1.7	•	•	•

Selected Average Balance Sheet ($ in Thousands)

Net Receivables 23	3428	0	59	57	679	861	2747	5259	11271	30237	•	870707
Inventories 24	1675	0	12	9	525	424	1359	4040	5281	24947	•	405550
Net Property, Plant and Equipment 25	4021	0	33	390	1125	2483	6467	15991	32102	95951	•	859226
Total Assets 26	61377	0	116	622	3347	6042	15762	33941	74584	254110	•	1695301
Notes and Loans Payable 27	12929	0	30	542	271	1422	3853	10449	16494	41544	•	3558328
All Other Liabilities 28	21400	0	30	179	568	937	2954	7187	18186	63100	•	6012664
Net Worth 29	27049	0	55	-99	2508	3683	8956	16305	39904	149466	•	7387309

Selected Financial Ratios (Times to 1)

Current Ratio 30	0.6	•	2.5	0.9	3.4	2.4	2.1	1.5	1.4	1.3	•	0.5
Quick Ratio 31	0.3	•	2.1	0.7	2.0	1.4	1.5	0.9	1.0	0.8	•	0.3
Net Sales to Working Capital 32	•	•	15.8	•	4.6	8.0	8.5	15.0	17.3	25.3	•	•
Coverage Ratio 33	3.7	4.6	7.0	1.4	11.3	7.2	9.8	6.9	5.7	6.0	•	3.6
Total Asset Turnover 34	0.6	•	6.5	0.9	2.0	2.0	2.0	2.0	1.7	1.5	•	0.5
Inventory Turnover 35	10.8	•	18.6	42.5	8.8	16.8	14.4	9.8	15.2	8.7	•	10.9
Receivables Turnover 36	15.9	•	25.3	•	7.7	15.8	11.1	11.5	12.0	10.9	•	17.0
Total Liabilities to Net Worth 37	1.3	•	1.1	•	0.3	0.6	0.8	1.1	0.9	0.7	•	1.3
Current Assets to Working Capital 38	•	•	1.7	•	1.4	1.7	1.9	2.9	3.5	4.6	•	•
Current Liabilities to Working Capital 39	•	•	0.7	•	0.4	0.7	0.9	1.9	2.5	3.6	•	•
Working Capital to Net Sales 40	•	•	0.1	•	0.2	0.1	0.1	0.1	0.1	0.0	•	•
Inventory to Working Capital 41	•	•	0.3	•	0.4	0.4	0.4	0.8	0.8	1.3	•	•
Total Receipts to Cash Flow 42	3.4	8.8	6.1	7.4	8.9	8.0	6.6	7.1	9.2	6.2	•	3.1
Cost of Goods to Cash Flow 43	1.7	6.0	1.8	5.3	6.2	4.7	4.1	4.2	5.8	3.5	•	1.5
Cash Flow to Total Debt 44	0.3	•	2.0	0.1	0.9	0.6	0.7	0.5	0.4	0.6	•	0.3

Selected Financial Factors (in Percentages)

Debt Ratio 45	55.9	•	52.3	115.8	25.1	39.0	43.2	52.0	46.5	41.2	•	56.4
Return on Total Assets 46	11.8	•	8.8	4.2	5.0	11.9	13.7	10.0	6.9	10.4	•	11.8
Return on Equity Before Income Taxes 47	19.4	•	15.8	•	6.1	16.8	21.7	17.7	10.6	14.7	•	19.6
Return on Equity After Income Taxes 48	12.8	•	15.6	•	6.1	13.7	19.2	15.6	9.7	11.9	•	12.8
Profit Margin (Before Income Tax) 49	14.4	4.0	1.2	1.4	2.3	5.1	6.2	4.3	3.3	5.7	•	16.0
Profit Margin (After Income Tax) 50	9.5	3.6	1.2	1.2	2.3	4.2	5.5	3.8	3.0	4.6	•	10.4

Table I

Corporations with and without Net Income

OTHER FOOD

MONEY AMOUNTS AND SIZE OF ASSETS IN THOUSANDS OF DOLLARS

Item Description for Accounting Period 7/03 Through 6/04	Total	Zero Assets	Under 500	500 to 1,000	1,000 to 5,000	5,000 to 10,000	10,000 to 25,000	25,000 to 50,000	50,000 to 100,000	100,000 to 250,000	250,000 to 500,000	500,000 to 2,500,000	2,500,000 and over
Number of Enterprises **1**	3959	119	2588	452	328	182	142	74	34	24	6	10	•
Revenues ($ in Thousands)													
Net Sales **2**	69583358	1585377	164366	550357	1950886	3646616	4643503	4415221	4083904	6307662	1828376	40407090	•
Interest **3**	2047408	8108	2	31	396	1489	2130	3851	8931	9981	39880	1972609	•
Rents **4**	133132	77	0	73	485	1770	1822	566	1209	1494	8298	117338	•
Royalties **5**	952446	46	0	0	0	400	1471	2554	17404	7064	907	922601	•
Other Portfolio Income **6**	191446	0	58446	30	556	2948	4720	16292	9106	10461	11955	76932	•
Other Receipts **7**	1560389	-1930	1	448	6188	48904	27943	13277	30494	44909	9896	1380257	•
Total Receipts **8**	74468179	1591678	222815	550939	1958511	3702127	4681589	4451761	4151048	6381571	1899312	44876827	•
Average Total Receipts **9**	18810	13375	86	1219	5971	20341	32969	60159	122090	265899	316552	4487683	•
Operating Costs/Operating Income (%)													
Cost of Operations **10**	66.0	70.4	48.5	54.2	63.3	67.1	72.7	69.1	67.0	69.4	63.6	64.5	•
Salaries and Wages **11**	5.8	4.2	14.4	9.3	7.9	15.1	5.7	7.0	8.3	6.2	6.8	4.4	•
Taxes Paid **12**	1.3	1.1	2.5	3.4	1.7	1.4	1.3	1.6	1.5	1.4	1.5	1.2	•
Interest Paid **13**	4.9	7.5	2.1	2.4	0.5	0.3	0.8	1.4	1.5	1.0	3.5	7.3	•
Depreciation **14**	2.8	2.8	14.1	5.9	3.1	1.6	2.6	3.1	3.7	3.5	3.9	2.6	•
Amortization and Depletion **15**	0.6	3.1	0.3	0.0	0.1	0.1	0.2	0.8	0.7	0.4	1.4	0.6	•
Pensions and Other Deferred Comp. **16**	1.2	0.2	•	0.0	0.3	0.3	0.2	0.5	0.4	0.3	0.8	1.8	•
Employee Benefits **17**	0.9	1.7	•	0.2	0.6	0.8	0.9	1.7	1.7	1.3	1.2	0.8	•
Advertising **18**	5.5	2.1	2.9	1.7	1.6	0.5	1.8	2.3	2.4	3.3	0.4	7.9	•
Other Expenses **19**	14.1	16.3	67.2	17.5	15.3	10.0	10.5	12.2	10.4	9.7	14.3	15.6	•
Officers' Compensation **20**	0.8	0.2	3.9	6.6	3.9	1.6	1.8	1.3	1.4	0.8	0.8	0.2	•
Operating Margin **21**	•	•	•	•	1.8	1.3	1.6	•	1.1	2.8	1.9	•	•
Operating Margin Before Officers' Comp. **22**	•	•	•	5.3	5.7	2.9	3.3	0.2	2.5	3.6	2.7	•	•

Selected Average Balance Sheet ($ in Thousands)

Net Receivables 23	26485	0	7	47	455	1650	3135	5607	10349	22381	34315	10240951	•
Inventories 24	1176	0	6	32	588	1505	3442	7146	14098	30531	34968	172147	•
Net Property, Plant and Equipment 25	2830	0	16	306	556	1642	5013	10125	24419	54275	81609	645777	•
Total Assets 26	50914	0	48	833	1992	6981	15492	33530	71469	153562	347670	18626148	•
Notes and Loans Payable 27	5051	0	39	420	380	2151	5479	11476	21771	33459	87050	1549519	•
All Other Liabilities 28	32923	0	2	60	562	2207	4625	8271	21191	34691	46170	12662741	•
Net Worth 29	12940	0	8	353	1050	2623	5388	13783	28507	85412	214450	4413888	•

Selected Financial Ratios (Times to 1)

Current Ratio 30	0.9	•	1.1	3.3	1.8	1.3	1.6	1.5	2.1	5.0	0.9	•	•
Quick Ratio 31	0.8	•	0.3	3.0	0.9	0.7	0.8	0.7	1.1	2.2	0.8	•	•
Net Sales to Working Capital 32	•	•	24.0	5.2	10.8	15.7	8.8	11.4	7.9	2.2	•	•	•
Coverage Ratio 33	1.7	•	•	0.5	5.7	4.0	0.9	2.8	5.1	2.6	1.6	•	•
Total Asset Turnover 34	0.3	•	1.3	1.5	3.0	2.1	1.8	1.7	1.7	0.9	0.2	•	•
Inventory Turnover 35	9.9	•	5.1	20.5	6.4	6.9	5.8	5.7	6.0	5.5	15.1	•	•
Receivables Turnover 36	1.3	•	10.7	42.1	10.9	11.0	10.4	10.8	10.5	7.9	0.8	•	•
Total Liabilities to Net Worth 37	2.9	•	5.3	1.4	0.9	1.9	1.4	1.5	0.8	0.6	3.2	•	•
Current Assets to Working Capital 38	•	•	11.0	1.4	2.3	4.2	2.6	3.1	1.9	1.3	•	•	•
Current Liabilities to Working Capital 39	•	•	10.0	0.4	1.3	3.2	1.6	2.1	0.9	0.3	•	•	•
Working Capital to Net Sales 40	•	•	0.0	0.2	0.1	0.1	0.1	0.1	0.1	0.5	•	•	•
Inventory to Working Capital 41	•	•	2.2	0.1	0.8	1.7	1.0	1.3	0.8	0.3	•	•	•
Total Receipts to Cash Flow 42	6.6	16.6	4.0	10.1	6.7	9.6	9.1	13.1	9.0	8.2	5.6	5.5	•
Cost of Goods to Cash Flow 43	4.3	11.7	1.9	5.5	4.2	6.5	6.6	9.1	6.0	5.7	3.5	3.6	•
Cash Flow to Total Debt 44	0.1	•	0.4	0.3	0.9	0.5	0.4	0.2	0.3	0.5	0.4	0.1	•

Selected Financial Factors (in Percentages)

Debt Ratio 45	74.6	•	84.1	57.7	47.3	62.4	65.2	58.9	60.1	44.4	38.3	76.3	•
Return on Total Assets 46	2.9	•	•	1.6	7.9	8.8	6.7	2.2	7.3	8.6	8.1	2.6	•
Return on Equity Before Income Taxes 47	4.7	•	•	•	12.3	21.6	14.5	•	11.7	12.4	8.1	4.2	•
Return on Equity After Income Taxes 48	2.9	•	•	•	8.7	16.6	11.9	•	8.4	9.9	6.0	2.7	•
Profit Margin (Before Income Tax) 49	3.4	•	•	•	2.2	2.8	2.4	•	2.8	4.0	5.7	4.6	•
Profit Margin (After Income Tax) 50	2.2	•	•	•	1.5	2.2	2.0	•	2.0	3.2	4.2	2.9	•

49

Table II
Corporations with Net Income

OTHER FOOD

MONEY AMOUNTS AND SIZE OF ASSETS IN THOUSANDS OF DOLLARS

Item Description for Accounting Period 7/03 Through 6/04	Total	Zero Assets	Under 500	500 to 1,000	1,000 to 5,000	5,000 to 10,000	10,000 to 25,000	25,000 to 50,000	50,000 to 100,000	100,000 to 250,000	250,000 to 500,000	500,000 to 2,500,000	2,500,000 and over
Number of Enterprises 1	1606	9	768	237	271	125	92	50	22	19	6	7	•
Revenues ($ in Thousands)													
Net Sales 2	58338261	58120	150134	226038	1748818	1868061	3104783	3270240	2765632	5652099	1828376	37665961	•
Interest 3	2025815	4	2	31	392	1375	1726	2720	3674	9711	39880	1966299	•
Rents 4	131154	0	0	73	485	1713	876	544	592	1235	8298	117338	•
Royalties 5	939978	0	0	0	0	346	11	2474	6612	7043	907	922585	•
Other Portfolio Income 6	183518	0	58446	30	556	2122	4256	15090	4636	9494	11955	76932	•
Other Receipts 7	1456075	0	1	438	4808	28319	17393	10348	8821	32432	9896	1343620	•
Total Receipts 8	63074801	58124	208583	226610	1755059	1901936	3129045	3301416	2789967	5712014	1899312	42092735	•
Average Total Receipts 9	39274	6458	272	956	6476	15215	34011	66028	126817	300632	316552	6013248	•
Operating Costs/Operating Income (%)													
Cost of Operations 10	65.6	91.6	51.5	42.5	62.9	67.6	71.4	69.5	64.7	69.7	63.6	64.5	•
Salaries and Wages 11	5.1	0.6	9.6	5.7	7.9	7.0	5.6	5.8	8.0	5.6	6.8	4.4	•
Taxes Paid 12	1.3	0.2	1.9	3.9	1.6	1.9	1.3	1.5	1.3	1.3	1.5	1.2	•
Interest Paid 13	5.1	0.1	2.4	0.2	0.3	0.4	0.6	1.2	1.2	0.8	3.5	7.3	•
Depreciation 14	2.7	0.9	7.0	6.7	3.2	1.9	2.2	2.5	3.5	3.2	3.9	2.5	•
Amortization and Depletion 15	0.4	•	0.0	0.0	0.1	0.0	0.1	0.6	0.5	0.4	1.4	0.3	•
Pensions and Other Deferred Comp. 16	1.4	•	•	0.0	0.3	0.5	0.3	0.6	0.5	0.3	0.8	1.9	•
Employee Benefits 17	0.8	•	•	0.5	0.4	1.1	0.9	1.7	1.3	1.1	1.2	0.7	•
Advertising 18	6.2	0.1	1.9	3.5	1.6	0.7	1.4	1.8	2.5	3.5	0.4	8.4	•
Other Expenses 19	13.8	5.8	55.8	21.3	15.1	11.0	8.7	8.6	9.7	9.3	14.3	15.4	•
Officers' Compensation 20	0.8	•	4.3	7.6	3.9	2.9	2.1	1.2	1.7	0.8	0.8	0.2	•
Operating Margin 21	•	0.6	•	8.0	2.6	5.0	5.5	5.0	5.1	3.9	1.9	•	•
Operating Margin Before Officers' Comp. 22	•	0.6	•	15.6	6.6	7.8	7.5	6.2	6.8	4.7	2.7	•	•

Selected Average Balance Sheet ($ in Thousands)

Item													
Net Receivables 23	64800	0	22	1	511	1605	3087	6267	11579	25885	34315	14594749	•
Inventories 24	2383	0	2	12	606	1638	3719	8134	15377	33589	39058	293238	•
Net Property, Plant and Equipment 25	5662	0	39	228	561	1755	4381	9597	21369	54717	81609	822117	•
Total Assets 26	120659	0	126	718	2015	6747	15302	34225	69040	161964	347670	2605926	•
Notes and Loans Payable 27	9758	0	120	72	291	2045	4216	9159	17866	29750	87050	1843130	•
All Other Liabilities 28	79922	0	4	5	536	1401	4007	8159	19546	36776	46170	17978148	•
Net Worth 29	30980	0	2	641	1187	3301	7079	16907	31628	95438	214450	6224647	•

Selected Financial Ratios (Times to 1)

Item													
Current Ratio 30	0.9	•	0.9	11.9	2.0	1.8	1.6	2.0	1.6	2.3	5.0	0.9	•
Quick Ratio 31	0.8	•	0.3	11.5	1.1	1.0	0.9	1.0	0.7	1.2	2.2	0.8	•
Net Sales to Working Capital 32	•	•	•	2.2	10.3	8.4	9.8	6.8	9.9	7.2	2.2	•	•
Coverage Ratio 33	2.1	8.4	2.9	44.0	11.7	16.3	12.3	6.2	6.1	7.0	2.6	1.7	•
Total Asset Turnover 34	0.3	•	1.6	1.3	3.2	2.2	2.2	1.9	1.8	1.8	0.9	0.2	•
Inventory Turnover 35	10.0	•	51.4	34.9	6.7	6.2	6.5	5.6	5.3	6.2	5.0	11.8	•
Receivables Turnover 36	1.1	•	17.7	1794.0	11.0	8.2	10.5	10.5	9.5	11.0	17.8	0.7	•
Total Liabilities to Net Worth 37	2.9	•	51.2	0.1	0.7	1.0	1.2	1.0	1.2	0.7	0.6	3.2	•
Current Assets to Working Capital 38	•	•	•	1.1	2.0	2.2	2.6	2.0	2.8	1.8	1.3	•	•
Current Liabilities to Working Capital 39	•	•	•	0.1	1.0	1.2	1.6	1.0	1.8	0.8	0.3	•	•
Working Capital to Net Sales 40	•	•	•	0.5	0.1	0.1	0.1	0.1	0.1	0.1	0.5	•	•
Inventory to Working Capital 41	•	•	•	0.0	0.7	0.9	1.0	0.8	1.3	0.8	0.3	•	•
Total Receipts to Cash Flow 42	5.9	17.7	2.7	4.8	6.4	6.3	7.5	7.9	7.4	7.8	5.6	5.4	•
Cost of Goods to Cash Flow 43	3.9	16.2	1.4	2.0	4.0	4.3	5.4	5.5	4.8	5.4	3.5	3.5	•
Cash Flow to Total Debt 44	0.1	•	0.6	2.6	1.2	0.7	0.5	0.5	0.5	0.6	0.4	0.1	•

Selected Financial Factors (in Percentages)

Item													
Debt Ratio 45	74.3	•	98.1	10.7	41.1	51.1	53.7	50.6	54.2	41.1	38.3	76.1	•
Return on Total Assets 46	3.1	•	10.8	11.2	10.5	16.0	15.0	13.8	13.0	10.7	8.1	2.6	•
Return on Equity Before Income Taxes 47	6.3	•	371.4	12.2	16.3	30.7	29.7	23.5	23.6	15.6	8.1	4.5	•
Return on Equity After Income Taxes 48	4.5	•	366.0	12.2	12.4	25.0	26.6	20.0	19.1	12.7	6.0	3.0	•
Profit Margin (Before Income Tax) 49	5.4	0.6	4.6	8.2	3.0	6.8	6.2	6.1	5.9	5.0	5.7	5.3	•
Profit Margin (After Income Tax) 50	3.9	0.4	4.5	8.2	2.3	5.5	5.6	5.2	4.8	4.1	4.2	3.4	•

Table I

Corporations with and without Net Income

SOFT DRINK AND ICE

MONEY AMOUNTS AND SIZE OF ASSETS IN THOUSANDS OF DOLLARS

Item Description for Accounting Period 7/03 Through 6/04	Total	Zero Assets	Under 500	500 to 1,000	1,000 to 5,000	5,000 to 10,000	10,000 to 25,000	25,000 to 50,000	50,000 to 100,000	100,000 to 250,000	250,000 to 500,000	500,000 to 2,500,000	2,500,000 and over
Number of Enterprises 1	536	•	•	132	201	11	54	28	8	16	5	7	6
Revenues ($ in Thousands)													
Net Sales 2	49868136	•	•	69230	899900	234012	1969996	2165461	942979	3603600	1776718	7853127	30200596
Interest 3	679010	•	•	8	261	99	520	1138	504	20293	1877	73418	580893
Rents 4	89051	•	•	0	3537	0	4443	1210	723	677	3018	3009	72435
Royalties 5	978288	•	•	0	0	0	220	0	0	0	0	80978	897090
Other Portfolio Income 6	816533	•	•	243	7783	253	10299	4322	3192	8392	447	2822	778778
Other Receipts 7	1927416	•	•	703	527	9422	11672	30758	22936	55653	14558	134746	1645635
Total Receipts 8	54358434	•	•	70184	912008	243786	1997150	2202889	970334	3688615	1796618	8148100	34175427
Average Total Receipts 9	101415	•	•	532	4537	22162	36984	78675	121292	230538	359324	1164014	5695904
Operating Costs/Operating Income (%)													
Cost of Operations 10	50.9	•	•	10.8	68.5	73.6	69.0	70.1	70.4	66.1	59.7	45.8	46.1
Salaries and Wages 11	12.6	•	•	25.4	11.6	5.5	8.0	10.9	9.4	10.2	12.2	12.2	13.7
Taxes Paid 12	1.9	•	•	4.3	2.0	1.4	1.6	1.8	2.1	1.6	2.5	1.8	1.9
Interest Paid 13	3.8	•	•	7.7	0.5	0.9	0.4	0.6	1.4	1.2	3.5	3.0	5.0
Depreciation 14	4.7	•	•	12.2	3.2	3.9	3.7	3.5	4.5	4.4	7.1	5.4	4.6
Amortization and Depletion 15	0.9	•	•	•	0.0	0.1	0.1	0.2	0.2	0.5	0.8	0.9	1.1
Pensions and Other Deferred Comp. 16	0.3	•	•	0.5	0.5	0.2	0.4	0.6	0.4	0.3	0.6	0.2	0.3
Employee Benefits 17	3.0	•	•	1.1	2.0	0.7	1.7	1.6	2.0	2.9	0.2	2.8	3.4
Advertising 18	2.9	•	•	0.2	1.4	1.1	3.6	2.3	1.0	2.0	1.6	0.6	3.9
Other Expenses 19	18.4	•	•	32.8	4.8	12.0	8.1	7.3	9.8	8.4	8.8	21.8	21.4
Officers' Compensation 20	0.5	•	•	7.4	4.6	1.4	1.4	1.0	0.5	0.5	0.6	0.5	0.3
Operating Margin 21	0.5	•	•	0.9	0.9	•	2.0	0.2	•	1.8	2.3	5.0	•
Operating Margin Before Officers' Comp. 22	0.5	•	•	5.5	5.5	0.7	3.4	1.2	•	2.4	2.9	5.5	•

Selected Average Balance Sheet ($ in Thousands)

Net Receivables 23	14156	78	610	1412	2525	6299	9941	18919	61253	149583	897460
Inventories 24	5092	22	160	1383	1856	3957	5354	10206	17769	40204	314347
Net Property, Plant and Equipment 25	24279	536	847	3009	5744	12425	25574	43041	131605	322945	1377349
Total Assets 26	143136	653	2082	8361	15647	36185	71111	140851	339657	1255641	10154106
Notes and Loans Payable 27	53762	623	820	2795	3739	8614	28037	25942	177290	562002	3770538
All Other Liabilities 28	32334	8	350	1622	3835	8796	14200	29634	72140	260579	2335329
Net Worth 29	57040	22	912	3944	8072	18776	28875	85275	90226	433060	4048239

Selected Financial Ratios (Times to 1)

Current Ratio 30	1.2	5.2	1.0	1.3	1.6	1.7	1.7	1.8	1.5	1.3	1.1
Quick Ratio 31	0.7	4.1	0.8	0.7	1.1	1.0	1.3	1.2	1.1	0.9	0.6
Net Sales to Working Capital 32	22.1	5.5	105.0	28.6	12.9	12.3	10.4	10.9	11.2	20.9	32.6
Coverage Ratio 33	4.2	0.9	5.2	4.8	9.3	4.2	1.7	4.4	2.0	3.9	4.4
Total Asset Turnover 34	0.6	0.8	2.2	2.5	2.3	2.1	1.7	1.6	1.0	0.9	0.5
Inventory Turnover 35	9.3	2.5	19.2	11.3	13.6	13.7	15.5	14.6	11.9	12.8	7.4
Receivables Turnover 36	1.1	6.0	14.7	6.5	14.3	12.2	11.6	11.8	6.6	8.3	0.7
Total Liabilities to Net Worth 37	1.5	28.3	1.3	1.1	0.9	0.9	1.5	0.7	2.8	1.9	1.5
Current Assets to Working Capital 38	6.6	1.2	22.3	4.5	2.7	2.5	2.4	2.3	3.1	5.0	11.3
Current Liabilities to Working Capital 39	5.6	0.2	21.3	3.5	1.7	1.5	1.4	1.3	2.1	4.0	10.3
Working Capital to Net Sales 40	0.0	0.2	0.0	0.0	0.1	0.1	0.1	0.1	0.1	0.0	0.0
Inventory to Working Capital 41	1.0	0.2	3.8	1.5	0.6	0.6	0.4	0.5	0.7	0.8	1.4
Total Receipts to Cash Flow 42	3.9	4.1	18.0	7.7	10.6	14.0	11.4	9.0	12.2	3.6	3.2
Cost of Goods to Cash Flow 43	2.0	0.4	12.3	5.7	7.3	9.8	8.1	6.0	7.3	1.6	1.5
Cash Flow to Total Debt 44	0.3	0.2	0.2	0.6	0.5	0.3	0.2	0.4	0.1	0.4	0.3

Selected Financial Factors (in Percentages)

Debt Ratio 45	60.1	96.6	56.2	52.8	48.4	48.1	59.4	39.5	73.4	65.5	60.1
Return on Total Assets 46	10.4	5.7	6.1	11.0	8.7	5.4	3.8	8.6	7.2	10.6	10.7
Return on Equity Before Income Taxes 47	19.8		11.2	18.5	15.0	7.9	3.9	10.9	13.4	22.7	20.7
Return on Equity After Income Taxes 48	13.3		9.2	18.4	11.4	6.7	3.2	8.7	8.2	14.9	13.8
Profit Margin (Before Income Tax) 49	12.2		2.3	3.4	3.3	1.9	0.9	4.1	3.4	8.8	16.6
Profit Margin (After Income Tax) 50	8.2		1.9	3.4	2.5	1.6	0.8	3.3	2.1	5.8	11.1

Table II

Corporations with Net Income

SOFT DRINK AND ICE

MONEY AMOUNTS AND SIZE OF ASSETS IN THOUSANDS OF DOLLARS

Item Description for Accounting Period 7/03 Through 6/04	Total	Zero Assets	Under 500	500 to 1000	251 to 500	501 to 1,000	1,001 to 5,000	5,001 to 10,000	10,001 to 25,000	25,001 to 50,000	50,001 to 100,000	100,001 to 250,000	250,001 and over
Number of Enterprises 1	402	•	66	66	168	7	42	19	•	•	•	•	6
Revenues ($ in Thousands)													
Net Sales 2	46651145	•	126490	40517	850499	138542	1498688	1324232	•	•	•	•	30200596
Interest 3	675717	•	0	1	217	90	484	743	•	•	•	•	580893
Rents 4	77984	•	0	0	654	0	2018	420	•	•	•	•	72435
Royalties 5	978288	•	0	0	0	0	220	0	•	•	•	•	897090
Other Portfolio Income 6	809406	•	0	243	7783	226	6455	2399	•	•	•	•	778778
Other Receipts 7	1891692	•	0	702	503	8419	9613	24781	•	•	•	•	1645635
Total Receipts 8	51084232	•	126490	41463	859656	147277	1517478	1352575	•	•	•	•	34175427
Average Total Receipts 9	127075	•	1917	628	5117	21040	36130	71188	•	•	•	•	5695904
Operating Costs/Operating Income (%)													
Cost of Operations 10	49.5	•	58.1	13.8	69.4	63.8	66.0	66.8	•	•	•	•	46.1
Salaries and Wages 11	12.9	•	0.5	27.0	12.2	8.0	8.6	10.7	•	•	•	•	13.7
Taxes Paid 12	1.9	•	2.5	5.0	2.0	1.6	1.5	1.7	•	•	•	•	1.9
Interest Paid 13	3.9	•	1.0	2.7	0.3	1.1	0.3	0.5	•	•	•	•	5.0
Depreciation 14	4.7	•	5.0	8.5	1.6	3.6	3.5	3.8	•	•	•	•	4.6
Amortization and Depletion 15	0.9	•	0.7	•	0.0	0.1	0.1	0.1	•	•	•	•	1.1
Pensions and Other Deferred Comp. 16	0.4	•	2.7	•	0.5	0.2	0.4	0.7	•	•	•	•	0.3
Employee Benefits 17	3.1	•	0.3	1.9	2.1	0.6	1.9	1.6	•	•	•	•	3.4
Advertising 18	3.1	•	1.5	0.1	1.5	1.4	4.4	3.3	•	•	•	•	3.9
Other Expenses 19	18.9	•	21.3	25.2	3.6	10.4	7.6	7.5	•	•	•	•	21.4
Officers' Compensation 20	0.5	•	3.8	12.0	4.8	1.7	1.3	1.2	•	•	•	•	0.3
Operating Margin 21	0.3	•	2.6	3.7	2.1	7.5	4.3	2.1	•	•	•	•	•
Operating Margin Before Officers' Comp. 22	0.8	•	6.4	15.7	6.9	9.2	5.6	3.3	•	•	•	•	•

Selected Average Balance Sheet ($ in Thousands)

Net Receivables 23	18134	97	17	686	1596	2406	5378	897460
Inventories 24	5751	154	28	146	692	1855	3716	220796
Net Property, Plant and Equipment 25	29602	86	568	435	1867	5488	10924	1377349
Total Assets 26	184008	475	638	1851	8138	15428	35461	10154106
Notes and Loans Payable 27	67845	189	520	455	3014	2702	6836	3770538
All Other Liabilities 28	41882	60	1	378	1130	3470	6779	2335329
Net Worth 29	74281	226	117	1018	3994	9256	21846	4048239

Selected Financial Ratios (Times to 1)

Current Ratio 30	1.2	4.9	2.3	1.3	1.7	1.8	2.2	1.1
Quick Ratio 31	0.7	2.2	0.7	1.0	1.2	1.3	1.5	0.6
Net Sales to Working Capital 32	21.9	8.2	15.8	20.6	14.6	10.9	8.5	32.6
Coverage Ratio 33	4.4	3.6	3.2	11.0	13.7	16.9	9.1	4.4
Total Asset Turnover 34	0.6	4.0	1.0	2.7	2.4	2.3	2.0	0.5
Inventory Turnover 35	10.0	7.2	3.1	24.1	18.3	12.7	12.5	10.5
Receivables Turnover 36	1.0	39.7	6.1	9.8	24.8	14.1	11.2	11.2
Total Liabilities to Net Worth 37	1.5	1.1	4.4	0.8	1.0	0.7	0.6	1.5
Current Assets to Working Capital 38	6.7	1.3	1.8	4.3	2.4	2.2	1.9	11.3
Current Liabilities to Working Capital 39	5.7	0.3	0.8	3.3	1.4	1.2	0.9	10.3
Working Capital to Net Sales 40	0.0	0.1	0.1	0.0	0.1	0.1	0.1	0.0
Inventory to Working Capital 41	0.9	0.7	1.1	0.7	0.5	0.4	0.4	1.4
Total Receipts to Cash Flow 42	3.7	6.1	3.8	17.3	4.7	8.8	10.0	3.2
Cost of Goods to Cash Flow 43	1.8	3.5	0.5	12.0	3.0	5.8	6.7	1.5
Cash Flow to Total Debt 44	0.3	1.3	0.3	0.4	1.0	0.7	0.5	0.3

Selected Financial Factors (in Percentages)

Debt Ratio 45	59.6	52.5	81.6	45.0	50.9	40.0	38.4	60.1
Return on Total Assets 46	10.8	14.5	8.5	9.6	36.2	13.5	9.2	10.7
Return on Equity Before Income Taxes 47	20.6	22.0	31.9	15.9	68.4	21.2	13.4	20.7
Return on Equity After Income Taxes 48	14.0	18.7	31.9	13.7	68.3	19.4	11.8	13.8
Profit Margin (Before Income Tax) 49	13.2	2.6	6.1	3.2	13.8	5.5	4.2	16.6
Profit Margin (After Income Tax) 50	9.0	2.2	6.1	2.8	13.8	5.0	3.7	11.1

Table I

Corporations with and without Net Income

BREWERIES

MONEY AMOUNTS AND SIZE OF ASSETS IN THOUSANDS OF DOLLARS

Item Description for Accounting Period 7/03 Through 6/04	Total	Zero Assets	Under 500	500 to 1,000	1,000 to 5,000	5,000 to 10,000	10,000 to 25,000	25,000 to 50,000	50,000 to 100,000	100,000 to 250,000	250,000 to 500,000	500,000 to 2,500,000	2,500,000 and over
Number of Enterprises 1	560	•	•	•	36	4	8	7	4	•	•	•	3

Revenues ($ in Thousands)

Net Sales 2	23616168	•	•	•	270676	35038	240892	267051	300100	•	•	•	22349298
Interest 3	26727	•	•	•	0	517	184	202	43	•	•	•	25769
Rents 4	21871	•	•	•	0	0	0	0	1	•	•	•	21870
Royalties 5	304892	•	•	•	0	0	0	163	0	•	•	•	304729
Other Portfolio Income 6	204653	•	•	•	0	5128	0	6	457	•	•	•	199014
Other Receipts 7	228877	•	•	•	0	311	1422	1077	1320	•	•	•	224745
Total Receipts 8	24403188	•	•	•	270676	40994	242498	268499	301921	•	•	•	23125425
Average Total Receipts 9	43577	•	•	•	7519	10248	30312	38357	75480	•	•	•	7708475

Operating Costs/Operating Income (%)

Cost of Operations 10	41.7	•	•	•	90.8	65.4	71.0	63.2	58.1	•	•	•	40.2
Salaries and Wages 11	8.6	•	•	•	3.4	7.5	2.5	4.8	3.6	•	•	•	8.8
Taxes Paid 12	13.7	•	•	•	•	6.5	6.1	3.9	6.7	•	•	•	14.2
Interest Paid 13	2.3	•	•	•	0.0	0.9	1.2	1.4	0.1	•	•	•	2.4
Depreciation 14	5.7	•	•	•	•	4.1	3.0	10.6	3.6	•	•	•	5.8
Amortization and Depletion 15	0.2	•	•	•	0.0	1.6	0.3	0.2	0.0	•	•	•	0.2
Pensions and Other Deferred Comp. 16	2.1	•	•	•	•	0.2	0.9	0.7	0.5	•	•	•	2.2
Employee Benefits 17	1.1	•	•	•	•	0.4	0.6	1.2	0.7	•	•	•	1.2
Advertising 18	8.0	•	•	•	0.9	1.1	3.6	2.1	1.4	•	•	•	8.4
Other Expenses 19	8.2	•	•	•	2.6	21.4	6.5	11.5	7.2	•	•	•	8.1
Officers' Compensation 20	0.5	•	•	•	•	3.1	0.7	0.8	0.8	•	•	•	0.5
Operating Margin 21	7.7	•	•	•	2.3	•	3.7	•	17.5	•	•	•	8.0
Operating Margin Before Officers' Comp. 22	8.2	•	•	•	2.3	•	4.4	0.4	18.3	•	•	•	8.5

Selected Average Balance Sheet ($ in Thousands)

Net Receivables 23	2086	•	279	846	1470	5872	3207	•	354680
Inventories 24	1694	•	333	347	2677	2289	3757	•	292507
Net Property, Plant and Equipment 25	18694	•	0	1909	6929	23906	39414	•	3337437
Total Assets 26	53513	•	1733	7866	16142	36294	86119	•	9668515
Notes and Loans Payable 27	23710	•	0	1998	4502	19260	1559	•	4364115
All Other Liabilities 28	11734	•	1514	2179	5616	3751	5408	•	2129400
Net Worth 29	18069	•	219	3688	6023	13282	79152	•	3175000

Selected Financial Ratios (Times to 1)

Current Ratio 30	0.7	•	0.6	2.4	1.0	2.3	3.6	•	0.7
Quick Ratio 31	0.4	•	0.3	1.9	0.6	1.6	2.9	•	0.4
Net Sales to Working Capital 32	•	•	2.9	116.8	7.1	5.4	•	•	•
Coverage Ratio 33	5.8	•	238.8	6.3	4.7	1.1	144.5	•	5.8
Total Asset Turnover 34	0.8	•	4.3	1.1	1.9	1.1	0.9	•	0.8
Inventory Turnover 35	10.4	•	20.5	16.5	8.0	10.5	11.6	•	10.2
Receivables Turnover 36	17.7	•	53.9	20.7	18.1	7.1	14.1	•	18.2
Total Liabilities to Net Worth 37	2.0	•	6.9	1.1	1.7	1.7	0.1	•	2.0
Current Assets to Working Capital 38	•	•	1.7	24.8	1.8	1.4	•	•	•
Current Liabilities to Working Capital 39	•	•	0.7	23.8	0.8	0.4	•	•	•
Working Capital to Net Sales 40	•	•	0.3	0.0	0.1	0.2	•	•	•
Inventory to Working Capital 41	•	•	0.1	9.3	0.5	0.2	•	•	•
Total Receipts to Cash Flow 42	5.8	•	20.5	13.9	11.1	10.0	4.1	•	5.7
Cost of Goods to Cash Flow 43	2.4	•	18.6	9.1	7.9	6.3	2.4	•	2.3
Cash Flow to Total Debt 44	0.2	•	0.2	0.2	0.3	0.2	2.6	•	0.2

Selected Financial Factors (in Percentages)

Debt Ratio 45	66.2	•	87.3	53.1	62.7	63.4	8.1	•	67.2
Return on Total Assets 46	10.8	•	9.9	6.4	10.4	1.7	15.9	•	11.0
Return on Equity Before Income Taxes 47	26.5	•	78.3	11.5	21.8	0.5	17.1	•	27.6
Return on Equity After Income Taxes 48	17.3	•	55.4	10.9	18.9	•	17.1	•	18.0
Profit Margin (Before Income Tax) 49	11.3	•	2.3	4.8	4.4	0.2	18.1	•	11.8
Profit Margin (After Income Tax) 50	7.4	•	1.6	4.6	3.8	•	18.1	•	7.7

Table II

Corporations with Net Income

BREWERIES

MONEY AMOUNTS AND SIZE OF ASSETS IN THOUSANDS OF DOLLARS

Item Description for Accounting Period 7/03 Through 6/04	Total	Zero Assets	Under 500	500 to 1,000	1,000 to 5,000	5,000 to 10,000	10,000 to 25,000	25,000 to 50,000	50,000 to 100,000	100,000 to 250,000	250,000 to 500,000	500,000 to 2,500,000	2,500,000 and over
Number of Enterprises **1**	160	·	105	·	·	·	·	3	·	·	·	·	·
Revenues ($ in Thousands)													
Net Sales **2**	23381226	·	124137	·	·	·	·	121065	·	·	·	·	·
Interest **3**	26117	·	12	·	·	·	·	145	·	·	·	·	·
Rents **4**	21871	·	0	·	·	·	·	0	·	·	·	·	·
Royalties **5**	304892	·	0	·	·	·	·	163	·	·	·	·	·
Other Portfolio Income **6**	204225	·	0	·	·	·	·	0	·	·	·	·	·
Other Receipts **7**	227273	·	0	·	·	·	·	9	·	·	·	·	·
Total Receipts **8**	24165604	·	124149	·	·	·	·	121382	·	·	·	·	·
Average Total Receipts **9**	151035	·	1182	·	·	·	·	40461	·	·	·	·	·
Operating Costs/Operating Income (%)													
Cost of Operations **10**	41.6	·	63.5	·	·	·	·	71.7	·	·	·	·	·
Salaries and Wages **11**	8.6	·	·	·	·	·	·	4.3	·	·	·	·	·
Taxes Paid **12**	13.8	·	6.6	·	·	·	·	1.6	·	·	·	·	·
Interest Paid **13**	2.4	·	·	·	·	·	·	0.8	·	·	·	·	·
Depreciation **14**	5.6	·	·	·	·	·	·	3.7	·	·	·	·	·
Amortization and Depletion **15**	0.2	·	·	·	·	·	·	0.1	·	·	·	·	·
Pensions and Other Deferred Comp. **16**	2.1	·	·	·	·	·	·	0.3	·	·	·	·	·
Employee Benefits **17**	1.1	·	·	·	·	·	·	0.8	·	·	·	·	·
Advertising **18**	8.1	·	·	·	·	·	·	3.1	·	·	·	·	·
Other Expenses **19**	8.0	·	18.5	·	·	·	·	9.3	·	·	·	·	·
Officers' Compensation **20**	0.5	·	·	·	·	·	·	0.6	·	·	·	·	·
Operating Margin **21**	8.0	·	11.3	·	·	·	·	3.5	·	·	·	·	·
Operating Margin Before Officers' Comp. **22**	8.5	·	11.3	·	·	·	·	4.2	·	·	·	·	·

Selected Average Balance Sheet ($ in Thousands)

Net Receivables 23	7203	202	11095
Inventories 24	5797	0	4135
Net Property, Plant and Equipment 25	63799	0	15386
Total Assets 26	185231	489	37492
Notes and Loans Payable 27	82410	0	19024
All Other Liabilities 28	40869	244	3366
Net Worth 29	61951	245	15103

Selected Financial Ratios (Times to 1)

Current Ratio 30	0.7	2.0	6.0
Quick Ratio 31	0.4	2.0	4.5
Net Sales to Working Capital 32		4.8	3.1
Coverage Ratio 33	6.0		5.5
Total Asset Turnover 34	0.8	2.4	1.1
Inventory Turnover 35	10.5		7.0
Receivables Turnover 36	17.7	11.7	3.6
Total Liabilities to Net Worth 37	2.0	1.0	1.5
Current Assets to Working Capital 38		2.0	1.2
Current Liabilities to Working Capital 39		1.0	0.2
Working Capital to Net Sales 40	0.2	0.2	0.3
Inventory to Working Capital 41			0.3
Total Receipts to Cash Flow 42	5.8	8.9	8.0
Cost of Goods to Cash Flow 43	2.4	5.6	5.8
Cash Flow to Total Debt 44	0.2	0.5	0.2

Selected Financial Factors (in Percentages)

Debt Ratio 45	66.6	49.9	59.7
Return on Total Assets 46	11.1	27.3	5.0
Return on Equity Before Income Taxes 47	27.5	54.5	10.2
Return on Equity After Income Taxes 48	18.2	40.1	7.8
Profit Margin (Before Income Tax) 49	11.7	11.3	3.8
Profit Margin (After Income Tax) 50	7.7	8.3	2.9

Table I

Corporations with and without Net Income

WINERIES AND DISTILLERIES

MONEY AMOUNTS AND SIZE OF ASSETS IN THOUSANDS OF DOLLARS

Item Description for Accounting Period 7/03 Through 6/04	Total	Zero Assets	Under 500	500 to 1,000	1,000 to 5,000	5,000 to 10,000	10,000 to 25,000	25,000 to 50,000	50,000 to 100,000	100,000 to 250,000	250,000 to 500,000	500,000 to 2,500,000	2,500,000 and over
Number of Enterprises **1**	807	•	•	336	150	97	58	25	18	8	3	3	4
Revenues ($ in Thousands)													
Net Sales **2**	18090987	•	•	222627	188393	336311	523569	674126	813037	847314	1020117	3232119	10187329
Interest **3**	185757	•	•	143	644	550	628	1013	1429	2084	2574	6401	170280
Rents **4**	9610	•	•	0	0	0	791	183	169	1563	16	6350	509
Royalties **5**	251624	•	•	0	1487	0	0	0	0	0	0	224	249913
Other Portfolio Income **6**	170886	•	•	0	2473	184	2923	2864	10515	9745	69	2021	134607
Other Receipts **7**	485160	•	•	2866	17884	10152	33202	15990	9042	1319	10374	254333	129256
Total Receipts **8**	19194024	•	•	225636	210881	347197	561113	694176	834192	862025	1033150	3501448	10871894
Average Total Receipts **9**	23784	•	•	672	1406	3579	9674	27767	46344	107753	344383	1167149	2717974
Operating Costs/Operating Income (%)													
Cost of Operations **10**	50.1	•	•	37.4	46.6	45.0	51.7	60.5	61.5	71.7	47.8	56.9	45.2
Salaries and Wages **11**	7.0	•	•	3.3	13.2	16.5	10.6	7.5	6.1	4.7	4.2	8.9	6.4
Taxes Paid **12**	12.9	•	•	4.9	4.2	4.1	9.6	7.0	7.5	1.9	23.2	11.4	14.9
Interest Paid **13**	5.3	•	•	5.1	4.5	3.0	4.1	1.1	2.6	4.1	1.5	1.8	7.6
Depreciation **14**	3.9	•	•	5.5	8.9	9.7	8.0	6.0	5.9	4.4	2.3	6.8	2.2
Amortization and Depletion **15**	1.6	•	•	0.2	0.3	0.1	0.5	0.5	1.5	0.7	1.1	0.3	2.4
Pensions and Other Deferred Comp. **16**	0.3	•	•	0.1	1.7	0.2	0.2	0.4	0.5	0.3	0.4	0.6	0.1
Employee Benefits **17**	1.3	•	•	1.5	2.1	1.8	1.2	1.1	0.8	1.2	0.9	1.7	1.3
Advertising **18**	6.8	•	•	3.3	1.6	1.0	1.8	1.6	2.6	1.4	5.2	3.7	9.7
Other Expenses **19**	12.1	•	•	14.1	26.4	14.7	14.5	10.4	8.5	7.5	5.3	14.0	12.3
Officers' Compensation **20**	1.1	•	•	14.0	5.5	2.8	2.6	2.0	1.6	0.9	0.4	0.6	0.6
Operating Margin **21**	•	•	•	10.6	•	1.2	•	1.9	0.8	1.2	7.6	•	•
Operating Margin Before Officers' Comp. **22**	•	•	•	24.6	•	3.9	•	3.9	2.4	2.1	8.1	•	•

Selected Average Balance Sheet ($ in Thousands)

Net Receivables 23	10103	•	•	7	568	317	1254	3938	7221	21792	54051	133908	1748861
Inventories 24	7487	•	•	366	1063	2438	5726	9287	21162	55867	127977	830256	605741
Net Property, Plant and Equipment 25	6795	•	•	211	751	3085	6516	14263	24590	42526	65397	391967	526573
Total Assets 26	40194	•	•	678	2329	6546	16315	34929	67619	155354	334257	1194975	577699
Notes and Loans Payable 27	14257	•	•	491	717	4347	7027	7929	25131	65164	83313	361907	1954130
All Other Liabilities 28	8052	•	•	24	232	308	2630	4907	11374	37906	57095	187853	1225207
Net Worth 29	17885	•	•	163	1380	1890	6659	22094	31114	52284	193848	645215	2398362

Selected Financial Ratios (Times to 1)

Current Ratio 30	2.3	•	•	6.3	4.8	5.6	1.6	2.7	1.7	1.8	2.9	3.2	2.2
Quick Ratio 31	1.3	•	•	0.7	2.3	0.9	0.4	0.9	0.4	0.5	0.8	0.7	1.5
Net Sales to Working Capital 32	2.0	•	•	1.7	1.1	1.3	2.9	2.4	3.1	3.1	2.6	2.4	1.8
Coverage Ratio 33	1.7	•	•	3.3	0.3	2.5	1.6	5.4	2.3	1.7	7.1	1.9	1.6
Total Asset Turnover 34	0.6	•	•	1.0	0.5	0.5	0.6	0.8	0.7	0.7	1.0	0.9	0.5
Inventory Turnover 35	1.5	•	•	0.7	0.6	0.6	0.8	1.8	1.3	1.4	1.3	0.7	1.9
Receivables Turnover 36	3.5	•	•	87.4	2.4	11.7	7.0	7.7	6.5	4.5	6.1	3.8	2.9
Total Liabilities to Net Worth 37	1.2	•	•	3.2	0.7	2.5	1.5	0.6	1.2	2.0	0.7	0.9	1.3
Current Assets to Working Capital 38	1.7	•	•	1.2	1.3	1.2	2.6	1.6	2.4	2.3	1.5	1.5	1.8
Current Liabilities to Working Capital 39	0.7	•	•	0.2	0.3	0.2	1.6	0.6	1.4	1.3	0.5	0.5	0.8
Working Capital to Net Sales 40	0.5	•	•	0.6	0.9	0.8	0.3	0.4	0.3	0.3	0.4	0.4	0.6
Inventory to Working Capital 41	0.7	•	•	1.1	0.7	1.0	1.9	0.9	1.6	1.5	1.0	0.9	0.4
Total Receipts to Cash Flow 42	7.2	•	•	4.7	7.0	6.2	7.8	7.7	10.2	10.9	7.4	7.7	6.8
Cost of Goods to Cash Flow 43	3.6	•	•	1.8	3.2	2.8	4.1	4.7	6.3	7.8	3.5	4.4	3.1
Cash Flow to Total Debt 44	0.1	•	•	0.3	0.2	0.1	0.1	0.3	0.1	0.1	0.3	0.3	0.1

Selected Financial Factors (in Percentages)

Debt Ratio 45	55.5	•	•	76.0	40.7	71.1	59.2	36.7	54.0	66.3	42.0	46.0	57.0
Return on Total Assets 46	5.2	•	•	16.7	0.8	3.9	3.6	4.5	4.0	4.8	10.6	3.2	5.4
Return on Equity Before Income Taxes 47	4.9	•	•	48.5	•	8.1	3.3	5.8	4.9	6.1	15.7	2.9	4.6
Return on Equity After Income Taxes 48	3.1	•	•	48.1	•	7.0	2.5	4.5	3.0	4.1	10.6	1.6	2.8
Profit Margin (Before Income Tax) 49	3.9	•	•	11.9	•	4.4	2.4	4.8	3.4	3.0	8.9	1.7	4.4
Profit Margin (After Income Tax) 50	2.5	•	•	11.8	•	3.8	1.8	3.7	2.0	2.0	6.0	1.0	2.6

Table II

Corporations with Net Income

WINERIES AND DISTILLERIES

MONEY AMOUNTS AND SIZE OF ASSETS IN THOUSANDS OF DOLLARS

Item Description for Accounting Period 7/03 Through 6/04	Total	Zero Assets	Under 500	500 to 1,000	1,000 to 5,000	5,000 to 10,000	10,000 to 25,000	25,000 to 50,000	50,000 to 100,000	100,000 to 250,000	250,000 to 500,000	500,000 to 2,500,000	2,500,000 and over
Number of Enterprises 1	564	•	•	336	•	84	27	16	12	•	•	•	•
Revenues ($ in Thousands)													
Net Sales 2	16305041	•	•	222627	•	317174	316139	601562	659029	•	•	•	•
Interest 3	181813	•	•	143	•	550	429	453	353	•	•	•	•
Rents 4	8070	•	•	0	•	0	68	159	0	•	•	•	•
Royalties 5	251624	•	•	0	•	0	0	0	0	•	•	•	•
Other Portfolio Income 6	155481	•	•	0	•	167	243	821	7815	•	•	•	•
Other Receipts 7	426842	•	•	2866	•	9043	28993	14271	4051	•	•	•	•
Total Receipts 8	17328871	•	•	225636	•	326934	345872	617266	671248	•	•	•	•
Average Total Receipts 9	30725	•	•	672	•	3892	12810	38579	55937				
Operating Costs/Operating Income (%)													
Cost of Operations 10	48.6	•	•	37.4	•	45.3	46.0	58.5	56.7	•	•	•	•
Salaries and Wages 11	6.8	•	•	3.3	•	14.8	9.2	6.7	6.0	•	•	•	•
Taxes Paid 12	13.8	•	•	4.9	•	3.8	11.4	7.2	8.6	•	•	•	•
Interest Paid 13	5.3	•	•	5.1	•	2.7	2.6	0.7	2.2	•	•	•	•
Depreciation 14	3.2	•	•	5.5	•	8.5	7.1	4.4	5.0	•	•	•	•
Amortization and Depletion 15	1.6	•	•	0.2	•	0.1	0.2	0.2	1.6	•	•	•	•
Pensions and Other Deferred Comp. 16	0.3	•	•	0.1	•	0.2	0.3	0.4	0.4	•	•	•	•
Employee Benefits 17	1.3	•	•	1.5	•	1.6	1.0	1.1	0.7	•	•	•	•
Advertising 18	7.3	•	•	3.3	•	1.0	1.8	1.7	2.8	•	•	•	•
Other Expenses 19	11.5	•	•	14.1	•	16.7	9.8	9.2	7.5	•	•	•	•
Officers' Compensation 20	1.0	•	•	14.0	•	2.8	2.5	1.8	1.6	•	•	•	•
Operating Margin 21	•	•	•	10.6	•	2.5	8.2	8.0	6.9	•	•	•	•
Operating Margin Before Officers' Comp. 22	0.3	•	•	24.6	•	5.3	10.8	9.9	8.5	•	•	•	•

Selected Average Balance Sheet ($ in Thousands)

Item						
Net Receivables 23	10310	7	343	1704	5380	7947
Inventories 24	8583	366	2542	5928	10876	22850
Net Property, Plant and Equipment 25	6791	211	2772	6235	11698	21796
Total Assets 26	44242	678	6275	17737	36675	67422
Notes and Loans Payable 27	15300	491	4513	6011	7295	21556
All Other Liabilities 28	8010	24	327	3091	5301	12162
Net Worth 29	20931	163	1435	8635	24079	33704

Selected Financial Ratios (Times to 1)

Item						
Current Ratio 30	2.6	6.3	5.5	1.9	3.1	1.6
Quick Ratio 31	1.3	0.7	0.9	0.5	1.2	0.4
Net Sales to Working Capital 32	2.3	1.7	1.4	2.8	2.7	4.3
Coverage Ratio 33	2.1	3.3	3.1	7.8	15.9	4.9
Total Asset Turnover 34	0.7	1.0	0.6	0.7	1.0	0.8
Inventory Turnover 35	1.6	0.7	0.7	0.9	2.0	1.4
Receivables Turnover 36	4.3	87.4	22.0	7.4	7.9	6.9
Total Liabilities to Net Worth 37	1.1	3.2	3.4	1.1	0.5	1.0
Current Assets to Working Capital 38	1.6	1.2	1.2	2.1	1.5	2.8
Current Liabilities to Working Capital 39	0.6	0.2	0.2	1.1	0.5	1.8
Working Capital to Net Sales 40	0.4	0.6	0.7	0.4	0.4	0.2
Inventory to Working Capital 41	0.7	1.1	0.9	1.4	0.8	1.9
Total Receipts to Cash Flow 42	6.5	4.7	5.1	4.0	5.5	7.1
Cost of Goods to Cash Flow 43	3.2	1.8	2.3	1.8	3.2	4.0
Cash Flow to Total Debt 44	0.2	0.3	0.2	0.3	0.5	0.2

Selected Financial Factors (in Percentages)

Item						
Debt Ratio 45	52.7	76.0	77.1	51.3	34.3	50.0
Return on Total Assets 46	7.2	16.7	5.0	13.4	11.6	8.9
Return on Equity Before Income Taxes 47	7.9	48.5	14.7	23.9	16.5	14.2
Return on Equity After Income Taxes 48	5.7	48.1	13.1	22.6	14.6	11.5
Profit Margin (Before Income Tax) 49	5.7	11.9	5.6	17.7	10.6	8.7
Profit Margin (After Income Tax) 50	4.1	11.8	5.0	16.7	9.3	7.1

Table I

Corporations with and without Net Income

TOBACCO MANUFACTURING

MONEY AMOUNTS AND SIZE OF ASSETS IN THOUSANDS OF DOLLARS

Item Description for Accounting Period 7/03 Through 6/04	Total	Zero Assets	Under 500	500 to 1,000	1,000 to 5,000	5,000 to 10,000	10,000 to 25,000	25,000 to 50,000	50,000 to 100,000	100,000 to 250,000	250,000 to 500,000	500,000 to 2,500,000	2,500,000 and over
Number of Enterprises 1	18	•	•	•	•	•	6	•	3	•	3	3	3
Revenues ($ in Thousands)													
Net Sales 2	17609550	•	•	•	•	•	325139	•	383404	•	608114	1527141	14765751
Interest 3	157538	•	•	•	•	•	32	•	206	•	16425	61510	79366
Rents 4	31339	•	•	•	•	•	0	•	0	•	682	1076	29581
Royalties 5	92213	•	•	•	•	•	0	•	14	•	3767	9046	79386
Other Portfolio Income 6	26764	•	•	•	•	•	44	•	103	•	2703	712	23199
Other Receipts 7	572571	•	•	•	•	•	1427	•	-6148	•	11148	3398	562749
Total Receipts 8	18489975	•	•	•	•	•	326642	•	377579	•	642839	1602883	15540032
Average Total Receipts 9	1027221	•	•	•	•	•	54440	•	125860	•	214280	534294	5180011
Operating Costs/Operating Income (%)													
Cost of Operations 10	51.2	•	•	•	•	•	52.7	•	29.0	•	74.2	40.4	51.9
Salaries and Wages 11	4.2	•	•	•	•	•	3.3	•	3.1	•	3.9	6.4	4.0
Taxes Paid 12	12.2	•	•	•	•	•	27.8	•	21.4	•	0.8	17.1	11.6
Interest Paid 13	2.7	•	•	•	•	•	0.3	•	0.7	•	3.5	7.4	2.2
Depreciation 14	1.4	•	•	•	•	•	1.9	•	3.4	•	2.6	2.9	1.1
Amortization and Depletion 15	0.2	•	•	•	•	•	0.0	•	0.1	•	0.6	1.7	0.0
Pensions and Other Deferred Comp. 16	0.9	•	•	•	•	•	0.4	•	1.4	•	0.3	0.4	0.9
Employee Benefits 17	1.4	•	•	•	•	•	0.1	•	1.0	•	2.9	1.9	1.3
Advertising 18	7.5	•	•	•	•	•	0.9	•	0.5	•	0.7	2.2	8.7
Other Expenses 19	11.5	•	•	•	•	•	4.3	•	13.2	•	14.9	12.4	11.4
Officers' Compensation 20	0.6	•	•	•	•	•	0.9	•	2.3	•	0.6	1.5	0.4
Operating Margin 21	6.3	•	•	•	•	•	7.3	•	23.9	•	•	5.7	6.4
Operating Margin Before Officers' Comp. 22	6.9	•	•	•	•	•	8.3	•	26.2	•	•	7.2	6.8

Selected Average Balance Sheet ($ in Thousands)

Net Receivables 23	95346	2294	6287	68093	24512	468595
Inventories 24	164133	5446	18888	82877	90711	816463
Net Property, Plant and Equipment 25	120881	4247	30961	27842	78524	579467
Total Assets 26	1238146	22830	97898	326166	822077	6137077
Notes and Loans Payable 27	473436	7141	22672	44668	261164	2497831
All Other Liabilities 28	516807	6992	9624	74314	238465	2764452
Net Worth 29	247904	8697	65603	207183	322448	874794

Selected Financial Ratios (Times to 1)

Current Ratio 30	1.2	1.9	2.6	3.1	1.9	1.0
Quick Ratio 31	0.6	0.8	1.8	1.3	0.7	0.6
Net Sales to Working Capital 32	18.3	7.9	4.1	1.6	5.5	83.1
Coverage Ratio 33	5.3	26.8	31.1	1.7	2.5	6.3
Total Asset Turnover 34	0.8	2.4	1.3	0.6	0.6	0.8
Inventory Turnover 35	3.1	5.2	2.0	1.8	2.3	3.1
Receivables Turnover 36	6.2	24.3	4.0	1.3	41.5	6.7
Total Liabilities to Net Worth 37	4.0	1.6	0.5	0.6	1.5	6.0
Current Assets to Working Capital 38	7.3	2.1	1.6	1.5	2.2	31.6
Current Liabilities to Working Capital 39	6.3	1.1	0.6	0.5	1.2	30.6
Working Capital to Net Sales 40	0.1	0.1	0.2	0.6	0.2	0.0
Inventory to Working Capital 41	1.9	0.8	0.5	0.4	1.0	7.7
Total Receipts to Cash Flow 42	4.6	9.1	2.9	7.0	4.8	4.6
Cost of Goods to Cash Flow 43	2.4	4.8	0.8	5.2	1.9	2.4
Cash Flow to Total Debt 44	0.2	0.4	1.4	0.2	0.2	0.2

Selected Financial Factors (in Percentages)

Debt Ratio 45	80.0	61.9	33.0	36.5	60.8	85.7
Return on Total Assets 46	11.2	19.2	30.2	3.6	11.5	11.2
Return on Equity Before Income Taxes 47	45.5	48.6	43.6	2.3	17.6	66.1
Return on Equity After Income Taxes 48	31.1	46.0	43.5	1.0	14.2	43.3
Profit Margin (Before Income Tax) 49	11.5	7.8	22.4	2.3	11.1	11.8
Profit Margin (After Income Tax) 50	7.9	7.4	22.3	1.0	9.0	7.7

Table II

Corporations with Net Income

TOBACCO MANUFACTURING

MONEY AMOUNTS AND SIZE OF ASSETS IN THOUSANDS OF DOLLARS

Item Description for Accounting Period 7/03 Through 6/04	Total	Zero Assets	Under 500	500 to 1,000	1,000 to 5,000	5,000 to 10,000	10,000 to 25,000	25,000 to 50,000	50,000 to 100,000	100,000 to 250,000	250,000 to 500,000	500,000 to 2,500,000	2,500,000 and over
Number of Enterprises **1**	13	•	•	•	•	•	•	3	•	•	•	•	3
Revenues ($ in Thousands)													
Net Sales **2**	16522201	•	•	•	•	•	•	408947	•	•	•	•	14765751
Interest **3**	80645	•	•	•	•	•	•	0	•	•	•	•	79366
Rents **4**	29581	•	•	•	•	•	•	0	•	•	•	•	29581
Royalties **5**	79426	•	•	•	•	•	•	0	•	•	•	•	79386
Other Portfolio Income **6**	24056	•	•	•	•	•	•	103	•	•	•	•	23199
Other Receipts **7**	558594	•	•	•	•	•	•	-6252	•	•	•	•	562749
Total Receipts **8**	17294503	•	•	•	•	•	•	402798	•	•	•	•	15540032
Average Total Receipts **9**	1330346	•	•	•	•	•	•	134266	•	•	•	•	5180011
Operating Costs/Operating Income (%)													
Cost of Operations **10**	51.6	•	•	•	•	•	•	38.4	•	•	•	•	51.9
Salaries and Wages **11**	4.0	•	•	•	•	•	•	3.2	•	•	•	•	4.0
Taxes Paid **12**	11.4	•	•	•	•	•	•	11.1	•	•	•	•	11.6
Interest Paid **13**	2.2	•	•	•	•	•	•	0.4	•	•	•	•	2.2
Depreciation **14**	1.2	•	•	•	•	•	•	3.1	•	•	•	•	1.1
Amortization and Depletion **15**	0.1	•	•	•	•	•	•	0.1	•	•	•	•	0.0
Pensions and Other Deferred Comp. **16**	0.9	•	•	•	•	•	•	1.2	•	•	•	•	0.9
Employee Benefits **17**	1.4	•	•	•	•	•	•	0.8	•	•	•	•	1.3
Advertising **18**	7.9	•	•	•	•	•	•	0.7	•	•	•	•	8.7
Other Expenses **19**	11.1	•	•	•	•	•	•	7.9	•	•	•	•	11.4
Officers' Compensation **20**	0.5	•	•	•	•	•	•	1.9	•	•	•	•	0.4
Operating Margin **21**	7.8	•	•	•	•	•	•	31.2	•	•	•	•	6.4
Operating Margin Before Officers' Comp. **22**	8.3	•	•	•	•	•	•	33.1	•	•	•	•	6.8

Selected Average Balance Sheet ($ in Thousands)

Net Receivables 23	115514	5048	468595
Inventories 24	211753	20701	816463
Net Property, Plant and Equipment 25	153302	27113	579467
Total Assets 26	1611947	91700	6137077
Notes and Loans Payable 27	619610	11365	2497831
All Other Liabilities 28	674086	8623	2764452
Net Worth 29	318251	71713	874794

Selected Financial Ratios (Times to 1)

Current Ratio 30	1.1	3.6	1.0
Quick Ratio 31	0.6	2.4	0.6
Net Sales to Working Capital 32	22.1	3.4	83.1
Coverage Ratio 33	6.8	70.6	6.3
Total Asset Turnover 34	0.8	1.5	0.8
Inventory Turnover 35	3.1	2.5	3.1
Receivables Turnover 36	6.1	4.5	6.7
Total Liabilities to Net Worth 37	4.1	0.3	6.0
Current Assets to Working Capital 38	8.6	1.4	31.6
Current Liabilities to Working Capital 39	7.6	0.4	30.6
Working Capital to Net Sales 40	0.0	0.3	0.0
Inventory to Working Capital 41	2.2	0.4	7.7
Total Receipts to Cash Flow 42	4.4	2.7	4.6
Cost of Goods to Cash Flow 43	2.3	1.0	2.4
Cash Flow to Total Debt 44	0.2	2.5	0.2

Selected Financial Factors (in Percentages)

Debt Ratio 45	80.3	21.8	85.7
Return on Total Assets 46	11.7	44.8	11.2
Return on Equity Before Income Taxes 47	50.4	56.4	66.1
Return on Equity After Income Taxes 48	34.8	56.4	43.3
Profit Margin (Before Income Tax) 49	12.6	29.7	11.8
Profit Margin (After Income Tax) 50	8.7	29.7	7.7

Table I

Corporations with and without Net Income

TEXTILE MILLS

MONEY AMOUNTS AND SIZE OF ASSETS IN THOUSANDS OF DOLLARS

Item Description for Accounting Period 7/03 Through 6/04	Total	Zero Assets	Under 500	500 to 1,000	1,000 to 5,000	5,000 to 10,000	10,000 to 25,000	25,000 to 50,000	50,000 to 100,000	100,000 to 250,000	250,000 to 500,000	500,000 to 2,500,000	2,500,000 and over
Number of Enterprises 1	1207	468	180	124	238	38	90	22	18	13	10	6	•
Revenues ($ in Thousands)													
Net Sales 2	16245374	34187	133371	232346	782597	369578	2252639	1044637	1747250	2374471	2936079	4338219	•
Interest 3	172717	0	2	55	3367	639	1645	737	7284	5788	17135	136065	•
Rents 4	10165	0	0	0	1203	1000	1419	326	336	1658	3010	1212	•
Royalties 5	89744	0	0	0	0	0	0	0	0	224	13225	76295	•
Other Portfolio Income 6	462568	0	129	84	137	956	10822	2075	3652	81854	5701	357156	•
Other Receipts 7	669443	130	10037	36	4815	6228	11064	-1643	37309	49042	43520	508909	•
Total Receipts 8	17650011	34317	143539	232521	792119	378401	2277589	1046132	1795831	2513037	3018670	5417856	•
Average Total Receipts 9	14623	73	797	1875	3328	9958	25307	47551	99768	193311	301867	902976	•
Operating Costs/Operating Income (%)													
Cost of Operations 10	74.8	19.8	88.2	69.2	76.1	72.4	79.7	78.9	77.9	72.7	71.7	73.7	•
Salaries and Wages 11	6.8	4.3	3.1	3.3	4.5	5.3	5.5	4.6	5.4	6.9	6.6	9.4	•
Taxes Paid 12	2.1	0.4	1.4	3.3	2.0	2.5	2.0	2.1	2.1	1.8	1.6	2.6	•
Interest Paid 13	2.4	1.1	2.7	0.3	1.1	0.7	1.0	1.1	2.1	2.1	3.1	3.8	•
Depreciation 14	4.3	4.3	0.7	1.0	2.2	4.8	3.2	5.4	3.7	4.0	6.2	4.2	•
Amortization and Depletion 15	0.4	0.8	0.4	0.0	0.1	0.4	0.1	0.5	0.3	0.3	0.2	0.8	•
Pensions and Other Deferred Comp. 16	0.8	0.2	0.2	0.1	0.1	0.3	0.2	0.4	0.7	0.5	0.8	1.6	•
Employee Benefits 17	1.3	0.4	0.3	0.1	1.4	1.9	1.4	0.9	1.3	2.2	1.1	0.9	•
Advertising 18	0.7	0.0	0.1	0.2	0.1	0.2	0.2	0.3	1.0	0.5	0.3	1.6	•
Other Expenses 19	10.6	55.9	26.3	14.2	15.9	10.9	7.4	6.5	8.3	11.1	12.4	10.5	•
Officers' Compensation 20	1.5	1.1	6.3	8.0	4.2	2.6	2.3	1.1	0.9	0.9	1.1	0.8	•
Operating Margin 21	•	11.6	•	0.3	•	•	•	•	•	•	•	•	•
Operating Margin Before Officers' Comp. 22	•	12.7	•	8.3	•	0.5	•	•	•	•	•	•	•

Selected Average Balance Sheet ($ in Thousands)

Net Receivables **23**	1896	0	84	145	643	1223	2723	6912	10450	26290	47597	108782 •
Inventories **24**	1995	0	50	148	722	2222	3827	7853	16232	27121	42234	90090 •
Net Property, Plant and Equipment **25**	3811	0	19	217	320	1993	4580	14583	25462	49468	107453	251378 •
Total Assets **26**	15816	0	182	757	2251	6020	15550	36813	72578	161297	342476	1526971 •
Notes and Loans Payable **27**	5502	0	805	104	1659	2048	5002	16215	22782	41439	124827	501154 •
All Other Liabilities **28**	3484	0	229	262	482	1673	3140	8563	14148	51531	100873	258168 •
Net Worth **29**	6830	0	-851	391	110	2300	7408	12035	35648	68327	116776	767649 •

Selected Financial Ratios (Times to 1)

Current Ratio **30**	1.8	•	0.5	1.0	1.5	1.9	1.4	2.8	1.8	1.3	2.7	•
Quick Ratio **31**	1.1	•	0.3	0.5	0.7	0.9	0.8	1.4	0.9	0.7	1.9	•
Net Sales to Working Capital **32**	5.0	12.0	•	306.1	9.6	5.9	9.1	4.1	5.7	12.8	2.5	•
Coverage Ratio **33**	2.3	•	•	2.2	1.4	•	•	0.4	2.3	0.3	5.1	•
Total Asset Turnover **34**	0.9	•	4.1	2.5	1.6	1.6	1.3	1.3	1.1	0.9	0.5	•
Inventory Turnover **35**	5.0	•	13.1	8.8	3.2	5.2	4.8	4.7	4.9	5.0	5.9	•
Receivables Turnover **36**	6.5	•	2.9	7.5	4.4	8.6	6.2	8.5	6.9	6.9	6.0	•
Total Liabilities to Net Worth **37**	1.3	•	•	0.9	1.6	1.1	2.1	1.0	1.4	1.9	1.0	•
Current Assets to Working Capital **38**	2.2	•	•	50.5	3.1	2.2	3.5	1.5	2.2	4.6	1.6	•
Current Liabilities to Working Capital **39**	1.2	•	•	49.5	2.1	1.2	2.5	0.5	1.2	3.6	0.6	•
Working Capital to Net Sales **40**	0.2	•	•	0.0	0.1	0.2	0.1	0.2	0.2	0.1	0.4	•
Inventory to Working Capital **41**	0.7	•	23.7	•	1.0	0.9	1.4	0.6	0.9	1.9	0.3	•
Total Receipts to Cash Flow **42**	10.9	1.5	10.7	76.3	13.1	28.1	29.5	19.0	10.3	16.7	5.4	•
Cost of Goods to Cash Flow **43**	8.2	0.3	7.4	58.1	9.5	22.4	23.3	14.8	7.5	12.0	4.0	•
Cash Flow to Total Debt **44**	0.1	•	0.5	0.0	0.2	0.1	0.1	0.1	0.2	0.1	0.2	•

Selected Financial Factors (in Percentages)

Debt Ratio **45**	56.8	•	567.0	48.3	95.1	61.8	52.4	67.3	50.9	57.6	65.9	49.7 •
Return on Total Assets **46**	4.7	•	•	1.7	•	1.6	•	•	1.2	5.6	0.8	9.0 •
Return on Equity Before Income Taxes **47**	6.1	•	19.2	1.8	•	1.2	•	•	7.6	•	14.3 •
Return on Equity After Income Taxes **48**	2.6	•	19.2	1.2	•	•	•	5.3	9.2 •
Profit Margin (Before Income Tax) **49**	3.1	12.0	•	0.4	0.3	•	•	2.8	15.2 •
Profit Margin (After Income Tax) **50**	1.3	12.0	•	0.3	0.2	•	•	2.0	9.8 •

59

Table II
Corporations with Net Income

TEXTILE MILLS

MONEY AMOUNTS AND SIZE OF ASSETS IN THOUSANDS OF DOLLARS

Item Description for Accounting Period 7/03 Through 6/04	Total	Zero Assets	Under 500	500 to 1,000	1,000 to 5,000	5,000 to 10,000	10,000 to 25,000	25,000 to 50,000	50,000 to 100,000	100,000 to 250,000	250,000 to 500,000	500,000 to 2,500,000	2,500,000 and over
Number of Enterprises 1	775	•	•	•	146	17	50	11	10	8	•	•	3
Revenues ($ in Thousands)													
Net Sales 2	9550916	•	•	•	379190	226999	1288307	470378	977159	1875115	•	•	2849196
Interest 3	151134	•	•	•	3344	0	1100	211	6503	3512	•	•	134727
Rents 4	5360	•	•	•	0	0	724	12	42	1044	•	•	1191
Royalties 5	73480	•	•	•	0	0	0	0	0	58	•	•	70125
Other Portfolio Income 6	432170	•	•	•	77	19	3281	481	3428	67661	•	•	352788
Other Receipts 7	590358	•	•	•	2140	2790	5834	1177	5142	42532	•	•	491086
Total Receipts 8	10803418	•	•	•	384751	229808	1299246	472259	992274	1989922	•	•	3899113
Average Total Receipts 9	13940	•	•	•	2635	13518	25985	42933	99227	248740	•	•	1299704
Operating Costs/Operating Income (%)													
Cost of Operations 10	70.3	•	•	•	73.2	68.7	74.6	70.3	75.9	70.2	•	•	68.8
Salaries and Wages 11	7.8	•	•	•	2.6	5.2	5.7	5.5	6.8	6.9	•	•	11.9
Taxes Paid 12	2.3	•	•	•	2.2	2.0	2.3	1.9	2.3	1.8	•	•	2.9
Interest Paid 13	2.5	•	•	•	0.6	0.3	0.9	1.2	0.8	2.2	•	•	4.9
Depreciation 14	3.9	•	•	•	1.1	1.7	2.5	4.2	2.4	4.2	•	•	3.7
Amortization and Depletion 15	0.4	•	•	•	0.0	0.6	0.0	0.3	0.0	0.3	•	•	0.8
Pensions and Other Deferred Comp. 16	1.0	•	•	•	0.2	0.5	0.2	0.2	0.5	0.5	•	•	2.3
Employee Benefits 17	1.3	•	•	•	1.9	1.0	1.3	1.0	0.7	2.3	•	•	0.9
Advertising 18	1.0	•	•	•	0.1	0.3	0.4	0.4	0.8	0.6	•	•	2.2
Other Expenses 19	10.4	•	•	•	12.5	8.8	7.0	8.7	5.3	10.8	•	•	13.0
Officers' Compensation 20	1.5	•	•	•	3.6	0.7	2.7	1.5	1.1	0.8	•	•	0.6
Operating Margin 21	•	•	•	•	2.0	10.2	2.4	4.9	3.2	•	•	•	•
Operating Margin Before Officers' Comp. 22	•	•	•	•	5.6	10.9	5.1	6.4	4.3	0.2	•	•	•

Selected Average Balance Sheet ($ in Thousands)

Net Receivables 23	1381	486	1717	2637	7252	10648	25610	75770
Inventories 24	1702	640	4278	3817	8093	19403	27784	78871
Net Property, Plant and Equipment 25	3055	205	1008	3954	10765	16309	58198	280479
Total Assets 26	14684	2028	6009	14519	32227	69075	157708	2070317
Notes and Loans Payable 27	3833	228	747	3040	9703	10122	29286	591299
All Other Liabilities 28	2140	252	789	3033	6368	12697	51960	179848
Net Worth 29	8712	1547	4472	8446	16156	46256	76463	1299171

Selected Financial Ratios (Times to 1)

Current Ratio 30	2.4	6.1	3.8	2.4	2.1	2.8	1.7	3.2
Quick Ratio 31	1.5	3.9	2.3	1.2	1.2	1.3	0.8	2.4
Net Sales to Working Capital 32	3.8	2.5	4.8	4.7	4.9	3.8	8.7	2.2
Coverage Ratio 33	5.4	7.2	42.5	4.6	5.5	6.5	3.5	6.1
Total Asset Turnover 34	0.8	1.3	2.2	1.8	1.3	1.4	1.5	0.5
Inventory Turnover 35	5.1	3.0	2.1	5.0	3.7	3.8	5.9	8.3
Receivables Turnover 36	7.4	3.0	3.1	9.1	5.6	7.6	7.9	25.1
Total Liabilities to Net Worth 37	0.7	0.3	0.3	0.7	1.0	0.5	1.1	0.6
Current Assets to Working Capital 38	1.7	1.2	1.4	1.7	1.9	1.6	2.5	1.5
Current Liabilities to Working Capital 39	0.7	0.2	0.4	0.7	0.9	0.6	1.5	0.5
Working Capital to Net Sales 40	0.3	0.4	0.2	0.2	0.2	0.3	0.1	0.5
Inventory to Working Capital 41	0.5	0.4	0.4	0.7	0.8	0.6	1.1	0.2
Total Receipts to Cash Flow 42	6.1	7.9	6.0	11.8	8.2	12.4	8.4	3.6
Cost of Goods to Cash Flow 43	4.3	5.8	4.1	8.8	5.8	9.4	5.9	2.5
Cash Flow to Total Debt 44	0.3	0.7	1.5	0.4	0.3	0.3	0.3	0.3

Selected Financial Factors (in Percentages)

Debt Ratio 45	40.7	23.7	25.6	41.8	49.9	33.0	51.5	37.2
Return on Total Assets 46	11.4	5.1	26.0	7.2	8.6	7.8	11.4	13.8
Return on Equity Before Income Taxes 47	15.6	5.8	34.1	9.7	14.0	9.9	16.9	18.4
Return on Equity After Income Taxes 48	11.3	5.4	29.8	8.7	10.5	8.5	13.6	12.3
Profit Margin (Before Income Tax) 49	11.1	3.5	11.4	3.2	5.3	4.7	5.5	25.1
Profit Margin (After Income Tax) 50	8.0	3.2	10.0	2.8	4.0	4.0	4.4	16.8

Table I

Corporations with and without Net Income

TEXTILE PRODUCT MILLS

MONEY AMOUNTS AND SIZE OF ASSETS IN THOUSANDS OF DOLLARS

Item Description for Accounting Period 7/03 Through 6/04		Total	Zero Assets	Under 500	500 to 1,000	1,000 to 5,000	5,000 to 10,000	10,000 to 25,000	25,000 to 50,000	50,000 to 100,000	100,000 to 250,000	250,000 to 500,000	500,000 to 2,500,000	2,500,000 and over
Number of Enterprises	1	2256	109	1123	286	530	34	93	38	18	13	5	5	3
Revenues ($ in Thousands)														
Net Sales	2	69506898	50522	562666	677016	2612401	504771	2596396	1916620	1725026	2577910	1909683	5900034	48473853
Interest	3	3516561	1426	7	7	461	127	1676	627	1855	5171	2364	8444	3494396
Rents	4	701457	30	89	0	294	0	512	585	643	2856	725	2388	693336
Royalties	5	171566	0	0	0	0	0	0	1164	216	961	516	45880	122829
Other Portfolio Income	6	4090607	155	2640	59	361	1	2855	3727	3474	94819	982	11494	3970044
Other Receipts	7	11104692	49	13	0	11911	2278	7380	13536	16334	342735	34169	24646	10651636
Total Receipts	8	89091781	52182	565415	677082	2625428	507177	2608819	1936259	1747548	3024452	1948439	5992886	67406094
Average Total Receipts	9	39491	479	503	2367	4954	14917	28052	50954	97086	232650	389688	1198577	22468698
Operating Costs/Operating Income (%)														
Cost of Operations	10	77.3	85.0	62.7	70.2	72.4	65.9	74.9	71.5	77.4	70.6	64.8	69.8	80.1
Salaries and Wages	11	8.3	4.7	3.1	6.5	6.2	9.8	6.1	6.9	4.8	7.3	10.3	9.8	8.5
Taxes Paid	12	2.0	1.4	4.2	2.1	2.1	2.2	1.7	2.3	1.9	1.7	2.3	2.4	1.9
Interest Paid	13	2.1	6.1	0.7	0.5	1.1	1.7	0.9	1.2	1.1	1.6	4.4	3.7	2.1
Depreciation	14	2.9	3.5	0.6	0.8	2.0	4.2	2.4	3.6	4.0	2.1	5.6	4.1	2.7
Amortization and Depletion	15	0.4	1.1	•	•	0.0	0.3	0.2	0.3	0.2	0.3	1.2	0.3	0.4
Pensions and Other Deferred Comp.	16	0.6	0.2	•	•	0.7	1.1	0.2	0.4	0.4	0.3	0.5	1.2	0.5
Employee Benefits	17	1.7	2.5	0.1	1.3	1.3	3.1	1.3	1.7	2.3	3.3	3.4	3.0	1.5
Advertising	18	0.7	0.2	0.0	0.4	0.3	0.3	0.7	0.5	0.7	1.2	1.9	1.0	0.6
Other Expenses	19	16.9	137.8	12.5	11.3	11.4	8.4	7.6	8.6	7.9	55.9	10.3	8.9	17.6
Officers' Compensation	20	0.8	1.1	10.7	3.9	4.6	3.5	2.3	2.0	0.7	1.0	1.0	0.9	0.3
Operating Margin	21	•	•	5.3	3.0	•	•	1.7	0.9	•	•	•	•	•
Operating Margin Before Officers' Comp.	22	•	•	16.0	6.9	2.5	3.0	4.0	2.9	•	•	•	•	•

Selected Average Balance Sheet ($ in Thousands)

Item													
Net Receivables 23	5254	0	54	250	473	2151	3727	6698	13652	29129	55278	250527	2880574
Inventories 24	2617	0	31	240	519	2331	4348	10114	16054	34808	68284	353106	1319843
Net Property, Plant and Equipment 25	5524	0	26	30	346	2774	3581	10382	22790	25842	134520	309286	2818338
Total Assets 26	133141	148	618	1964	7854	15982	35312	70282	139316	402529	1186025		94956426
Notes and Loans Payable 27	13007	0	277	859	1748	4584	12069	19873	34075	232839	762301		7281230
All Other Liabilities 28	34969	0	18	247	486	3644	8043	16944	51253	61668	408452		24815332
Net Worth 29	85165	0	-89	93	619	2333	7753	15199	33465	53987	108022	15272	62859865

Selected Financial Ratios (Times to 1)

Item													
Current Ratio 30	1.0	•	0.8	1.7	1.6	1.0	2.1	1.7	1.7	1.4	1.3	1.2	0.9
Quick Ratio 31	0.5	•	0.7	0.9	0.7	0.5	1.0	0.8	0.8	0.7	0.5	0.7	0.5
Net Sales to Working Capital 32	•	•	•	10.1	8.4	88.2	5.2	6.1	6.6	9.7	11.4	11.4	•
Coverage Ratio 33	7.6	•	9.0	6.4	•	1.0	3.5	2.6	0.9	•	0.2	0.1	11.5
Total Asset Turnover 34	0.2	•	3.4	3.8	2.5	1.9	1.7	1.4	1.4	1.4	0.9	1.0	0.2
Inventory Turnover 35	9.1	•	10.3	6.9	6.9	4.2	4.8	3.6	4.6	4.0	3.6	2.3	9.8
Receivables Turnover 36	8.9	•	6.1	9.6	12.6	5.6	8.0	6.9	7.1	6.8	13.8	3.5	11.2
Total Liabilities to Net Worth 37	0.6	•	•	5.6	2.2	2.4	1.1	1.3	1.1	1.6	2.7	76.7	0.5
Current Assets to Working Capital 38	•	•	•	2.4	2.7	28.8	1.9	2.4	2.5	3.7	4.5	5.2	•
Current Liabilities to Working Capital 39	•	•	•	1.4	1.7	27.8	0.9	1.4	1.5	2.7	3.5	4.2	•
Working Capital to Net Sales 40	•	•	0.1	0.1	0.1	0.0	0.2	0.2	0.2	0.1	0.1	0.1	•
Inventory to Working Capital 41	•	•	•	1.1	0.9	11.7	0.9	1.1	1.1	1.6	2.0	2.3	•
Total Receipts to Cash Flow 42	3.9	•	5.9	9.9	14.7	14.4	12.9	11.9	15.7	5.3	21.2	35.3	3.0
Cost of Goods to Cash Flow 43	3.1	•	3.7	6.9	10.7	9.5	9.7	8.5	12.2	3.7	13.8	24.6	2.4
Cash Flow to Total Debt 44	0.2	•	0.4	0.5	0.2	0.2	0.3	0.2	0.2	0.4	0.1	0.0	0.2

Selected Financial Factors (in Percentages)

Item													
Debt Ratio 45	36.0	•	160.4	84.9	68.5	70.3	51.5	57.0	52.4	61.2	73.2	98.7	33.8
Return on Total Assets 46	3.8	•	21.9	13.5	•	3.0	5.3	4.4	1.4	•	0.8	0.2	4.2
Return on Equity Before Income Taxes 47	5.1	•	•	75.5	•	•	7.8	6.3	•	•	•	•	5.8
Return on Equity After Income Taxes 48	3.3	•	•	74.0	•	•	6.5	4.7	•	•	•	•	3.8
Profit Margin (Before Income Tax) 49	14.2	•	5.7	3.0	•	•	2.2	1.9	•	•	•	•	22.4
Profit Margin (After Income Tax) 50	9.0	•	5.7	2.9	•	•	1.8	1.4	•	•	•	•	14.9

Table II
Corporations with Net Income

TEXTILE PRODUCT MILLS

MONEY AMOUNTS AND SIZE OF ASSETS IN THOUSANDS OF DOLLARS

Item Description for Accounting Period 7/03 Through 6/04	Total	Zero Assets	Under 500	500 to 1,000	1,000 to 5,000	5,000 to 10,000	10,000 to 25,000	25,000 to 50,000	50,000 to 100,000	100,000 to 250,000	250,000 to 500,000	500,000 to 2,500,000	2,500,000 and over
Number of Enterprises **1**	1062	•	•	•	264	7	62	25	11	8	•	•	3
Revenues ($ in Thousands)													
Net Sales **2**	58714550	•	•	•	1828684	187692	1833161	1358304	1040806	1719517	•	•	48473853
Interest **3**	3503809	•	•	•	457	15	764	414	537	2410	•	•	3494396
Rents **4**	697884	•	•	•	90	0	238	585	632	1756	•	•	693336
Royalties **5**	139652	•	•	•	0	0	0	0	3	0	•	•	122829
Other Portfolio Income **6**	3984741	•	•	•	361	1	1285	1249	2413	4984	•	•	3970044
Other Receipts **7**	10751483	•	•	•	11160	1792	4206	5370	14502	21168	•	•	10651636
Total Receipts **8**	77792119	•	•	•	1840752	189500	1839654	1365922	1058893	1749835	•	•	67406094
Average Total Receipts **9**	73251	•	•	•	6973	27071	29672	54637	96263	218729	•	•	22468698
Operating Costs/Operating Income (%)													
Cost of Operations **10**	78.1	•	•	•	69.9	58.8	73.9	69.0	74.7	70.9	•	•	80.1
Salaries and Wages **11**	8.2	•	•	•	5.3	11.2	5.9	7.1	5.2	5.6	•	•	8.5
Taxes Paid **12**	1.9	•	•	•	1.9	2.2	1.5	2.3	1.9	1.5	•	•	1.9
Interest Paid **13**	1.9	•	•	•	0.6	0.2	0.6	0.8	1.1	1.0	•	•	2.1
Depreciation **14**	2.7	•	•	•	1.9	1.8	2.0	2.3	4.0	2.4	•	•	2.7
Amortization and Depletion **15**	0.4	•	•	•	0.0	0.0	0.1	0.3	0.2	0.1	•	•	0.4
Pensions and Other Deferred Comp. **16**	0.5	•	•	•	1.0	0.6	0.2	0.5	0.4	0.4	•	•	0.5
Employee Benefits **17**	1.6	•	•	•	1.1	1.0	1.2	2.0	2.4	1.8	•	•	1.5
Advertising **18**	0.7	•	•	•	0.2	0.5	0.8	0.5	0.5	1.4	•	•	0.6
Other Expenses **19**	16.1	•	•	•	9.2	5.3	6.9	7.5	5.4	9.7	•	•	17.6
Officers' Compensation **20**	0.7	•	•	•	5.6	5.0	2.5	2.4	0.7	1.1	•	•	0.3
Operating Margin **21**	•	•	•	•	3.4	13.5	4.4	5.3	3.6	4.1	•	•	•
Operating Margin Before Officers' Comp. **22**	•	•	•	•	9.0	18.5	6.9	7.7	4.3	5.2	•	•	•

Selected Average Balance Sheet ($ in Thousands)

Net Receivables 23	9368	•	723	2255	3704	6840	12703	32892	•	2880574
Inventories 24	3979	•	717	5269	4882	10583	14389	43552	•	1319843
Net Property, Plant and Equipment 25	9232	•	460	1479	3206	7464	23051	29458	•	2818338
Total Assets 26	274149	•	2175	8045	15794	33890	70287	148118	•	94956426
Notes and Loans Payable 27	22284	•	595	474	3396	7656	18905	31754	•	7281230
All Other Liabilities 28	71437	•	488	1993	3534	6915	14820	41455	•	2481532
Net Worth 29	180428	•	1093	5578	8864	19319	36563	74910	•	62859865

Selected Financial Ratios (Times to 1)

Current Ratio 30	1.0	•	2.8	3.1	2.6	2.7	1.7	1.6	•	0.9
Quick Ratio 31	0.5	•	1.7	1.7	1.2	1.3	0.8	0.7	•	0.5
Net Sales to Working Capital 32	•	•	6.5	6.3	4.5	4.0	7.1	6.6	•	•
Coverage Ratio 33	11.0	•	7.6	80.9	9.3	8.5	5.7	6.9	•	11.5
Total Asset Turnover 34	0.2	•	3.2	3.3	1.9	1.6	1.3	1.5	•	0.2
Inventory Turnover 35	10.9	•	6.8	3.0	4.5	3.5	4.9	3.5	•	9.8
Receivables Turnover 36	9.6	•	11.1	4.3	7.8	7.5	7.2	13.1	•	11.2
Total Liabilities to Net Worth 37	0.5	•	1.0	0.4	0.8	0.8	0.9	1.0	•	0.5
Current Assets to Working Capital 38	•	•	1.6	1.5	1.6	1.6	2.5	2.6	•	•
Current Liabilities to Working Capital 39	•	•	0.6	0.5	0.6	0.6	1.5	1.6	•	•
Working Capital to Net Sales 40	•	•	0.2	0.2	0.2	0.2	0.1	0.2	•	•
Inventory to Working Capital 41	•	•	0.6	0.5	0.7	0.7	1.1	1.3	•	•
Total Receipts to Cash Flow 42	3.4	•	8.7	5.6	9.8	8.6	10.6	7.3	•	3.0
Cost of Goods to Cash Flow 43	2.7	•	6.1	3.3	7.3	5.9	7.9	5.2	•	2.4
Cash Flow to Total Debt 44	0.2	•	0.7	1.9	0.4	0.4	0.3	0.4	•	0.2

Selected Financial Factors (in Percentages)

Debt Ratio 45	34.2	•	49.8	30.7	43.9	43.0	48.0	49.4	•	33.8
Return on Total Assets 46	4.3	•	14.9	48.7	10.1	10.6	8.7	9.9	•	4.2
Return on Equity Before Income Taxes 47	5.9	•	25.8	69.3	16.0	16.4	13.8	16.7	•	5.8
Return on Equity After Income Taxes 48	4.0	•	24.8	66.2	14.3	14.4	12.8	15.6	•	3.8
Profit Margin (Before Income Tax) 49	19.3	•	4.1	14.4	4.8	5.8	5.4	5.8	•	22.4
Profit Margin (After Income Tax) 50	13.2	•	3.9	13.8	4.3	5.1	4.9	5.4	•	14.9

Table I

Corporations with and without Net Income

APPAREL KNITTING MILLS

MONEY AMOUNTS AND SIZE OF ASSETS IN THOUSANDS OF DOLLARS

Item Description for Accounting Period 7/03 Through 6/04	Total	Zero Assets	Under 500	500 to 1,000	1,000 to 5,000	5,000 to 10,000	10,000 to 25,000	25,000 to 50,000	50,000 to 100,000	100,000 to 250,000	250,000 to 500,000	500,000 to 2,500,000	2,500,000 and over
Number of Enterprises **1**	169	•	•	•	106	13	35	6	4	5	•	•	•
Revenues ($ in Thousands)													
Net Sales **2**	3537360	•	•	•	525580	174518	1141322	461676	263558	970706	•	•	•
Interest **3**	2069	•	•	•	614	471	363	297	5	319	•	•	•
Rents **4**	348	•	•	•	0	0	1	40	5	302	•	•	•
Royalties **5**	18671	•	•	•	0	0	0	0	5708	12963	•	•	•
Other Portfolio Income **6**	2766	•	•	•	1	0	678	124	1914	49	•	•	•
Other Receipts **7**	24289	•	•	•	2460	39	8225	1062	408	12095	•	•	•
Total Receipts **8**	3585503	•	•	•	528655	175028	1150589	463199	271598	996434	•	•	•
Average Total Receipts **9**	21216	•	•	•	4987	13464	32874	77200	67900	199287	•	•	•
Operating Costs/Operating Income (%)													
Cost of Operations **10**	73.3	•	•	•	72.4	72.6	74.3	81.1	76.5	68.1	•	•	•
Salaries and Wages **11**	5.5	•	•	•	5.3	6.6	5.1	3.7	6.6	6.2	•	•	•
Taxes Paid **12**	2.4	•	•	•	4.3	3.6	1.9	2.0	1.4	2.1	•	•	•
Interest Paid **13**	1.5	•	•	•	1.4	1.1	0.9	0.6	0.6	3.1	•	•	•
Depreciation **14**	2.8	•	•	•	2.9	3.0	2.2	3.5	2.4	3.0	•	•	•
Amortization and Depletion **15**	0.4	•	•	•	0.1	0.1	0.2	0.1	0.1	1.2	•	•	•
Pensions and Other Deferred Comp. **16**	0.2	•	•	•	0.0	•	0.2	0.3	0.0	0.4	•	•	•
Employee Benefits **17**	1.1	•	•	•	1.3	2.4	1.6	0.9	0.4	0.4	•	•	•
Advertising **18**	1.9	•	•	•	1.1	0.2	1.3	0.0	1.7	4.1	•	•	•
Other Expenses **19**	7.8	•	•	•	9.8	11.5	8.0	2.7	9.4	8.0	•	•	•
Officers' Compensation **20**	2.0	•	•	•	3.4	1.8	2.3	1.6	1.4	1.1	•	•	•
Operating Margin **21**	1.2	•	•	•	•	•	1.9	3.6	•	2.3	•	•	•
Operating Margin Before Officers' Comp. **22**	3.2	•	•	•	1.4	•	4.1	5.2	0.9	3.4	•	•	•

Selected Average Balance Sheet ($ in Thousands)

Net Receivables 23	2520	•	468	128	3748	10485	10721	27540
Inventories 24	4563	•	580	4919	4432	14005	13823	67058
Net Property, Plant and Equipment 25	2919	•	737	1741	3710	8184	11044	33896
Total Assets 26	13098	•	2498	6438	16497	36697	71320	156435
Notes and Loans Payable 27	4900	•	1082	1173	4520	9074	9762	89313
All Other Liabilities 28	2857	•	797	1281	3272	8003	9010	36643
Net Worth 29	5340	•	620	3984	8705	19620	52548	30479

Selected Financial Ratios (Times to 1)

Current Ratio 30	2.2	•	1.5	2.2	2.3	2.2	4.0	2.1
Quick Ratio 31	1.1	•	0.8	0.1	1.1	1.2	2.4	1.0
Net Sales to Working Capital 32	4.7	•	11.3	5.9	5.6	5.4	2.2	3.5
Coverage Ratio 33	2.7	•	0.0	•	3.9	7.8	5.6	2.6
Total Asset Turnover 34	1.6	•	2.0	2.1	2.0	2.1	0.9	1.2
Inventory Turnover 35	3.4	•	6.2	2.0	5.5	4.5	3.6	2.0
Receivables Turnover 36	6.2	•	21.2	3.9	9.7	5.6	6.4	4.6
Total Liabilities to Net Worth 37	1.5	•	3.0	0.6	0.9	0.9	0.4	4.1
Current Assets to Working Capital 38	1.9	•	3.2	1.9	1.8	1.8	1.3	1.9
Current Liabilities to Working Capital 39	0.9	•	2.2	0.9	0.8	0.8	0.3	0.9
Working Capital to Net Sales 40	0.2	•	0.1	0.2	0.2	0.2	0.5	0.3
Inventory to Working Capital 41	0.8	•	1.3	1.4	0.8	0.7	0.5	0.9
Total Receipts to Cash Flow 42	11.5	•	14.6	19.0	11.0	19.1	10.5	8.8
Cost of Goods to Cash Flow 43	8.4	•	10.5	13.8	8.2	15.5	8.1	6.0
Cash Flow to Total Debt 44	0.2	•	0.2	0.3	0.4	0.2	0.3	0.2

Selected Financial Factors (in Percentages)

Debt Ratio 45	59.2	•	75.2	38.1	47.2	46.5	26.3	80.5
Return on Total Assets 46	6.6	•	0.1	•	7.1	9.4	2.9	10.1
Return on Equity Before Income Taxes 47	10.2	•	•	•	10.1	15.3	3.2	32.1
Return on Equity After Income Taxes 48	6.7	•	•	•	7.9	12.9	2.7	20.1
Profit Margin (Before Income Tax) 49	2.6	•	•	•	2.7	3.9	2.5	5.0
Profit Margin (After Income Tax) 50	1.7	•	•	•	2.1	3.3	2.2	3.2

Table II
Corporations with Net Income

APPAREL KNITTING MILLS

MONEY AMOUNTS AND SIZE OF ASSETS IN THOUSANDS OF DOLLARS

Item Description for Accounting Period 7/03 Through 6/04	Total	Zero Assets	Under 500	500 to 1,000	1,000 to 5,000	5,000 to 10,000	10,000 to 25,000	25,000 to 50,000	50,000 to 100,000	100,000 to 250,000	250,000 to 500,000	500,000 to 2,500,000	2,500,000 and over
Number of Enterprises 1	86	•	•	•	38	•	25	•	4	•	•	•	•
Revenues ($ in Thousands)													
Net Sales 2	2379232	•	•	•	107995	•	920964	•	263558	•	•	•	•
Interest 3	1336	•	•	•	594	•	292	•	5	•	•	•	•
Rents 4	46	•	•	•	0	•	1	•	5	•	•	•	•
Royalties 5	5708	•	•	•	0	•	0	•	5708	•	•	•	•
Other Portfolio Income 6	2366	•	•	•	0	•	313	•	1914	•	•	•	•
Other Receipts 7	7417	•	•	•	168	•	5297	•	408	•	•	•	•
Total Receipts 8	2396105	•	•	•	108757	•	926867	•	271598	•	•	•	•
Average Total Receipts 9	27862	•	•	•	2862	•	37075	•	67900	•	•	•	•
Operating Costs/Operating Income (%)													
Cost of Operations 10	74.5	•	•	•	64.3	•	72.5	•	76.5	•	•	•	•
Salaries and Wages 11	4.4	•	•	•	3.7	•	4.6	•	6.6	•	•	•	•
Taxes Paid 12	2.2	•	•	•	5.0	•	1.9	•	1.4	•	•	•	•
Interest Paid 13	0.8	•	•	•	0.4	•	0.8	•	0.6	•	•	•	•
Depreciation 14	2.6	•	•	•	2.3	•	1.8	•	2.4	•	•	•	•
Amortization and Depletion 15	0.1	•	•	•	0.0	•	0.2	•	0.1	•	•	•	•
Pensions and Other Deferred Comp. 16	0.2	•	•	•	•	•	0.3	•	0.0	•	•	•	•
Employee Benefits 17	1.1	•	•	•	•	•	1.6	•	0.4	•	•	•	•
Advertising 18	1.1	•	•	•	3.7	•	1.6	•	1.7	•	•	•	•
Other Expenses 19	6.4	•	•	•	9.1	•	8.1	•	9.4	•	•	•	•
Officers' Compensation 20	1.5	•	•	•	1.7	•	2.1	•	1.4	•	•	•	•
Operating Margin 21	5.0	•	•	•	9.8	•	4.4	•	0.9	•	•	•	•
Operating Margin Before Officers' Comp. 22	6.5	•	•	•	11.4	•	6.5	•	0.9	•	•	•	•

Selected Average Balance Sheet ($ in Thousands)

Net Receivables 23	3173	256	3936	10721
Inventories 24	4836	228	4969	13826
Net Property, Plant and Equipment 25	3530	214	3744	11044
Total Assets 26	17324	1655	16518	71320
Notes and Loans Payable 27	3452	0	3977	9762
All Other Liabilities 28	3526	517	3224	9010
Net Worth 29	10346	1138	9316	52548

Selected Financial Ratios (Times to 1)

Current Ratio 30	3.0	1.6	2.5	4.0
Quick Ratio 31	1.5	1.3	1.1	2.4
Net Sales to Working Capital 32	3.6	9.8	5.9	2.2
Coverage Ratio 33	8.2	25.5	7.5	5.6
Total Asset Turnover 34	1.6	1.7	2.2	0.9
Inventory Turnover 35	4.3	8.0	5.4	3.6
Receivables Turnover 36	6.8	11.6	9.6	12.3
Total Liabilities to Net Worth 37	0.7	0.5	0.8	0.4
Current Assets to Working Capital 38	1.5	2.7	1.7	1.3
Current Liabilities to Working Capital 39	0.5	1.7	0.7	0.3
Working Capital to Net Sales 40	0.3	0.1	0.2	0.5
Inventory to Working Capital 41	0.7	0.4	0.8	0.5
Total Receipts to Cash Flow 42	9.7	6.1	8.4	10.5
Cost of Goods to Cash Flow 43	7.2	3.9	6.1	8.1
Cash Flow to Total Debt 44	0.4	0.9	0.6	0.3

Selected Financial Factors (in Percentages)

Debt Ratio 45	40.3	31.3	43.6	26.3
Return on Total Assets 46	10.4	18.7	13.0	2.9
Return on Equity Before Income Taxes 47	15.3	26.1	20.0	3.2
Return on Equity After Income Taxes 48	11.7	17.9	17.2	2.7
Profit Margin (Before Income Tax) 49	5.7	10.5	5.1	2.5
Profit Margin (After Income Tax) 50	4.4	7.2	4.3	2.2

Table I

Corporations with and without Net Income

CUT AND SEW APPAREL CONTRACTORS AND MFRS.

MONEY AMOUNTS AND SIZE OF ASSETS IN THOUSANDS OF DOLLARS

Item Description for Accounting Period 7/03 Through 6/04	Total	Zero Assets	Under 500	500 to 1,000	1,000 to 5,000	5,000 to 10,000	10,000 to 25,000	25,000 to 50,000	50,000 to 100,000	100,000 to 250,000	250,000 to 500,000	500,000 to 2,500,000	2,500,000 and over
Number of Enterprises **1**	7371	1209	4707	746	416	95	119	33	16	17	5	5	4
Revenues ($ in Thousands)													
Net Sales **2**	42524711	159267	2055004	1702730	3691807	1529260	5270527	2347876	1833355	3315832	2371483	3862669	14384901
Interest **3**	199076	110	37	153	391	289	1217	2017	526	4779	883	101756	86917
Rents **4**	22766	52	52	0	67	0	321	1200	0	1073	0	66	19936
Royalties **5**	758737	0	5	0	96	0	1493	4572	0	21419	55240	229812	446101
Other Portfolio Income **6**	88157	662	1436	507	249	223	1680	1525	3550	6567	419	39322	32019
Other Receipts **7**	596318	3098	3807	70280	11740	24859	73487	5776	14563	12713	50974	84647	240372
Total Receipts **8**	44189765	163189	2060341	1773670	3704350	1554631	5348725	2362966	1851994	3362383	2478999	4318272	15210246
Average Total Receipts **9**	5995	135	438	2378	8905	16365	44947	71605	115750	197787	495800	863654	3802562
Operating Costs/Operating Income (%)													
Cost of Operations **10**	65.3	43.2	32.6	75.4	67.6	60.4	72.9	67.9	76.2	69.2	59.4	68.3	63.6
Salaries and Wages **11**	10.4	14.4	29.8	4.8	12.0	15.3	8.4	6.9	7.6	11.4	10.2	9.3	9.1
Taxes Paid **12**	2.1	2.7	4.5	1.0	2.0	3.9	2.1	2.2	1.7	2.1	1.9	2.9	1.5
Interest Paid **13**	2.2	0.4	0.4	0.5	0.9	1.3	0.8	1.3	0.9	3.1	0.9	4.6	3.3
Depreciation **14**	1.2	1.3	1.3	0.4	0.3	0.6	0.8	0.8	1.7	2.3	2.2	2.2	0.9
Amortization and Depletion **15**	0.6	1.6	0.0	0.0	0.1	0.1	0.1	0.2	0.4	0.5	0.3	1.3	1.0
Pensions and Other Deferred Comp. **16**	0.5	0.2	0.2	0.0	0.2	0.1	0.1	0.2	0.3	0.4	1.1	0.6	0.8
Employee Benefits **17**	1.1	2.5	0.9	0.1	0.5	1.0	0.6	0.8	1.4	1.6	2.1	0.8	1.5
Advertising **18**	2.5	1.1	0.8	0.3	1.4	1.2	0.8	1.2	1.4	1.5	4.0	3.7	4.0
Other Expenses **19**	13.0	46.4	28.1	14.7	10.5	13.3	8.7	9.8	4.7	6.2	14.9	17.9	14.0
Officers' Compensation **20**	2.2	3.5	6.5	4.1	3.0	3.8	3.0	2.9	1.4	2.4	1.2	0.7	1.2
Operating Margin **21**	•	•	•	•	1.4	•	1.7	5.8	2.3	•	1.7	•	•
Operating Margin Before Officers' Comp. **22**	1.1	•	1.3	2.9	4.5	2.9	4.7	8.7	3.7	1.7	2.9	•	0.3

Selected Average Balance Sheet ($ in Thousands)

Net Receivables 23	733	0	15	285	863	1577	3551	8356	14534	30148	94212	142498	496052
Inventories 24	877	0	33	78	979	4424	5607	15757	31255	26493	117011	140379	499424
Net Property, Plant and Equipment 25	424	0	11	92	379	425	1678	2811	8056	21328	50604	95695	321522
Total Assets 26	4259	0	94	677	2731	6456	15676	35171	71261	154418	336541	773418	4089022
Notes and Loans Payable 27	1165	0	52	165	1005	1562	4266	11252	12957	67739	41542	145623	1119987
All Other Liabilities 28	1262	0	28	459	790	1571	4835	11099	10198	28048	100783	178465	1342580
Net Worth 29	1832	0	14	53	936	3323	6575	12819	48106	58631	194215	449330	1628456

Selected Financial Ratios (Times to 1)

Current Ratio 30	2.0	•	2.1	1.0	2.5	1.9	1.8	1.9	3.7	2.1	2.7	3.2	1.7
Quick Ratio 31	1.0	•	0.9	0.6	1.4	0.7	0.7	0.8	1.6	1.1	1.4	1.8	0.8
Net Sales to Working Capital 32	5.5	•	13.4	•	6.8	6.4	7.9	5.7	3.5	4.7	3.3	2.4	6.4
Coverage Ratio 33	2.4	•	•	7.5	2.9	1.6	5.0	6.1	4.5	1.3	8.2	0.9	2.7
Total Asset Turnover 34	1.4	•	4.7	3.4	3.3	2.5	2.8	2.0	1.6	1.3	1.4	1.0	0.9
Inventory Turnover 35	4.3	•	4.3	22.2	6.1	2.2	5.8	3.1	2.8	5.1	2.4	3.8	4.6
Receivables Turnover 36	7.4	•	24.1	11.0	10.6	6.0	12.3	8.3	5.7	7.8	3.0	6.8	6.9
Total Liabilities to Net Worth 37	1.3	•	5.9	11.8	1.9	0.9	1.4	1.7	0.5	1.6	0.7	0.7	1.5
Current Assets to Working Capital 38	2.0	•	1.9	•	1.7	2.1	2.2	2.2	1.4	1.9	1.6	1.5	2.4
Current Liabilities to Working Capital 39	1.0	•	0.9	•	0.7	1.1	1.2	1.2	0.4	0.9	0.6	0.5	1.4
Working Capital to Net Sales 40	0.2	•	0.1	•	0.1	0.2	0.1	0.2	0.3	0.2	0.6	0.4	0.2
Inventory to Working Capital 41	0.8	•	1.0	•	0.6	0.9	1.1	1.1	0.7	0.7	0.6	0.5	0.9
Total Receipts to Cash Flow 42	7.8	13.8	6.8	•	9.9	8.7	9.9	6.8	15.8	25.1	6.0	7.0	6.3
Cost of Goods to Cash Flow 43	5.1	6.0	2.3	5.1	6.7	5.2	7.2	4.6	12.1	17.4	3.5	4.8	4.0
Cash Flow to Total Debt 44	0.3	0.8	0.5	0.5	0.5	0.6	0.5	0.5	0.3	0.1	0.6	0.3	0.2

Selected Financial Factors (in Percentages)

Debt Ratio 45	57.0	85.5	92.2	65.7	48.5	58.1	63.6	32.5	62.0	42.3	41.9	60.2	
Return on Total Assets 46	7.2	•	11.6	8.8	5.1	11.3	15.7	6.8	5.0	10.0	4.0	7.8	
Return on Equity Before Income Taxes 47	9.9	•	128.3	17.0	3.7	21.5	36.0	7.9	2.8	15.2	•	12.3	
Return on Equity After Income Taxes 48	6.2	•	122.8	16.6	1.4	20.3	33.0	6.3	0.7	14.8	•	6.5	
Profit Margin (Before Income Tax) 49	3.1	•	3.0	1.8	0.8	3.2	6.5	3.3	0.8	6.2	•	5.6	
Profit Margin (After Income Tax) 50	2.0	•	2.9	1.7	0.3	3.0	6.0	2.7	0.2	6.0	•	2.9	

65

Table II
Corporations with Net Income

CUT AND SEW APPAREL CONTRACTORS AND MFRS.

MONEY AMOUNTS AND SIZE OF ASSETS IN THOUSANDS OF DOLLARS

Item Description for Accounting Period 7/03 Through 6/04	Total	Zero Assets	Under 500	500 to 1,000	1,000 to 5,000	5,000 to 10,000	10,000 to 25,000	25,000 to 50,000	50,000 to 100,000	100,000 to 250,000	250,000 to 500,000	500,000 to 2,500,000	2,500,000 and over
Number of Enterprises 1	4316	265	2714	746	370	79	81	29	11	•	5	•	•
Revenues ($ in Thousands)													
Net Sales 2	33997706	59037	1524842	1702730	3174882	1062430	4260448	2176630	1272553	•	2371483	•	•
Interest 3	106451	0	24	153	272	186	920	1275	504	•	883	•	•
Rents 4	21868	0	52	0	5	0	229	1200	0	•	0	•	•
Royalties 5	524147	0	0	0	0	0	260	95	0	•	55240	•	•
Other Portfolio Income 6	26972	624	1406	507	7	132	570	1410	3550	•	419	•	•
Other Receipts 7	532097	0	1410	70280	1672	23005	39388	3521	13432	•	50974	•	•
Total Receipts 8	35209241	59661	1527734	1773670	3176838	1085753	4301815	2184131	1290039	•	2478999	•	•
Average Total Receipts 9	8158	225	563	2378	8586	13744	53109	75315	117276	•	495800	•	•
Operating Costs/Operating Income (%)													
Cost of Operations 10	63.9	66.3	21.6	75.4	66.8	53.4	72.1	67.5	77.0	•	59.4	•	•
Salaries and Wages 11	10.4	3.4	34.4	4.8	11.7	17.8	7.8	6.5	6.7	•	10.2	•	•
Taxes Paid 12	2.1	1.4	5.2	1.0	2.1	2.0	2.1	2.1	1.7	•	1.9	•	•
Interest Paid 13	1.2	0.4	0.3	0.5	0.8	1.1	0.7	1.1	0.3	•	0.9	•	•
Depreciation 14	1.1	0.1	1.4	0.4	0.2	0.5	0.7	0.8	1.0	•	2.2	•	•
Amortization and Depletion 15	0.5	0.0	0.0	0.0	0.1	0.1	0.0	0.3	0.1	•	0.3	•	•
Pensions and Other Deferred Comp. 16	0.5	0.1	•	0.0	0.2	0.1	0.1	0.2	0.3	•	1.1	•	•
Employee Benefits 17	1.0	0.2	0.9	0.1	0.4	1.2	0.6	0.7	0.9	•	2.1	•	•
Advertising 18	2.3	0.3	0.2	0.3	1.5	1.6	0.6	1.0	1.2	•	4.0	•	•
Other Expenses 19	12.1	8.6	27.9	14.7	9.4	13.4	7.7	9.7	4.4	•	14.9	•	•
Officers' Compensation 20	2.2	4.1	6.3	4.1	3.0	4.4	3.0	3.0	1.3	•	1.2	•	•
Operating Margin 21	2.8	15.2	1.8	•	3.7	4.3	4.6	7.3	5.1	•	1.7	•	•
Operating Margin Before Officers' Comp. 22	5.0	19.3	8.0	2.9	6.8	8.7	7.6	10.3	6.4	•	2.9	•	•

Selected Average Balance Sheet ($ in Thousands)

Net Receivables 23	1026	0	21	285	878	1550	3437	9028	14414	94212
Inventories 24	1179	0	15	90	899	5005	6342	15809	33203	90372
Net Property, Plant and Equipment 25	550	0	14	92	378	342	1731	2796	6200	50604
Total Assets 26	5122	0	106	677	2773	6382	16095	34915	70647	336541
Notes and Loans Payable 27	1075	0	40	165	888	1372	3612	8157	6407	41542
All Other Liabilities 28	1327	0	23	459	733	1346	5055	10901	9968	100783
Net Worth 29	2720	0	42	53	1152	3664	7429	15857	54271	194215

Selected Financial Ratios (Times to 1)

Current Ratio 30	2.3	•	2.3	1.0	2.7	2.0	1.9	2.0	3.8	2.7
Quick Ratio 31	1.1	•	1.3	0.6	1.6	0.6	0.7	0.9	1.6	1.4
Net Sales to Working Capital 32	5.0	•	15.6	•	6.1	5.4	8.3	5.2	3.5	3.3
Coverage Ratio 33	6.3	41.2	8.0	7.5	5.6	6.7	9.3	8.0	21.4	8.2
Total Asset Turnover 34	1.5	•	5.3	3.4	3.1	2.1	3.3	2.1	1.6	1.4
Inventory Turnover 35	4.3	•	8.3	19.1	6.4	1.4	6.0	3.2	2.7	3.1
Receivables Turnover 36	7.2	•	33.6	16.0	10.4	4.5	13.8	9.0	5.2	10.1
Total Liabilities to Net Worth 37	0.9	•	1.5	11.8	1.4	0.7	1.2	1.2	0.3	0.7
Current Assets to Working Capital 38	1.8	•	1.8	•	1.6	2.0	2.1	2.0	1.4	1.6
Current Liabilities to Working Capital 39	0.8	•	0.8	•	0.6	1.0	1.1	1.0	0.4	0.6
Working Capital to Net Sales 40	0.2	•	0.1	•	0.2	0.2	0.1	0.2	0.3	0.3
Inventory to Working Capital 41	0.7	•	0.6	•	0.6	0.9	1.1	1.0	0.7	0.6
Total Receipts to Cash Flow 42	6.4	4.6	4.3	6.8	9.0	5.8	8.6	6.3	10.8	6.0
Cost of Goods to Cash Flow 43	4.1	3.1	0.9	5.1	6.0	3.1	6.2	4.2	8.3	3.5
Cash Flow to Total Debt 44	0.5	•	2.0	0.5	0.6	0.8	0.7	0.6	0.7	0.6

Selected Financial Factors (in Percentages)

Debt Ratio 45	46.9	•	60.3	92.2	58.5	42.6	53.8	54.6	23.2	42.3
Return on Total Assets 46	12.2	•	11.8	11.6	14.3	16.1	20.4	18.9	11.1	10.0
Return on Equity Before Income Taxes 47	19.3	•	26.0	128.3	28.3	23.9	39.3	36.4	13.7	15.2
Return on Equity After Income Taxes 48	15.1	•	22.0	122.8	28.0	21.4	37.7	33.7	11.7	14.8
Profit Margin (Before Income Tax) 49	6.7	16.3	1.9	3.0	3.8	6.5	5.6	7.7	6.4	6.2
Profit Margin (After Income Tax) 50	5.2	14.0	1.6	2.9	3.8	5.8	5.3	7.1	5.5	6.0

Table I

Corporations with and without Net Income

APPAREL ACCESSORIES AND OTHER APPAREL

MONEY AMOUNTS AND SIZE OF ASSETS IN THOUSANDS OF DOLLARS

Item Description for Accounting Period 7/03 Through 6/04		Total	Zero Assets	Under 500	500 to 1,000	1,000 to 5,000	5,000 to 10,000	10,000 to 25,000	25,000 to 50,000	50,000 to 100,000	100,000 to 250,000	250,000 to 500,000	500,000 to 2,500,000	2,500,000 and over
Number of Enterprises	1	3928	3	2945	439	418	47	38	22	12	4	·	·	·
Revenues ($ in Thousands)														
Net Sales	2	10939211	10202	2500653	684853	2186150	608411	1148683	1333511	1751886	714861	·	·	·
Interest	3	14804	0	15	685	1633	1473	225	486	1964	8323	·	·	·
Rents	4	1520	0	0	0	0	49	60	386	120	904	·	·	·
Royalties	5	669	0	0	0	0	0	416	155	0	98	·	·	·
Other Portfolio Income	6	8923	0	0	33	4370	29	3592	700	185	15	·	·	·
Other Receipts	7	109821	0	7427	6683	39943	2361	33931	4081	9567	5830	·	·	·
Total Receipts	8	11074948	10202	2508095	692254	2232096	612323	1186907	1339319	1763722	730031	·	·	·
Average Total Receipts	9	2819	3401	852	1577	5340	13028	31234	60878	146977	182508	·	·	·
Operating Costs/Operating Income (%)														
Cost of Operations	10	64.6	33.9	59.3	60.4	60.9	73.8	65.9	74.3	68.3	62.2	·	·	·
Salaries and Wages	11	8.5	59.6	10.2	5.8	9.4	6.6	10.0	5.6	6.8	10.1	·	·	·
Taxes Paid	12	2.4	27.6	2.1	2.7	2.2	1.6	2.7	2.4	2.8	2.7	·	·	·
Interest Paid	13	1.1	16.8	0.5	1.3	0.7	1.4	1.0	1.3	1.1	3.2	·	·	·
Depreciation	14	1.8	8.5	1.1	1.8	2.9	2.2	1.3	2.4	1.1	1.2	·	·	·
Amortization and Depletion	15	0.2	2.3	0.0	0.0	0.0	0.3	0.2	0.2	0.1	0.8	·	·	·
Pensions and Other Deferred Comp.	16	0.2	0.2	0.4	0.2	0.1	0.3	0.3	0.1	0.2	0.2	·	·	·
Employee Benefits	17	1.2	1.8	0.5	3.7	1.5	1.0	1.0	1.3	0.9	1.3	·	·	·
Advertising	18	1.5	0.4	1.0	1.0	2.1	0.7	1.1	0.9	2.2	2.0	·	·	·
Other Expenses	19	13.5	120.4	17.2	21.2	14.6	11.0	11.8	7.3	10.0	13.3	·	·	·
Officers' Compensation	20	3.2	1.7	3.6	4.6	4.5	1.9	3.6	1.8	2.1	1.5	·	·	·
Operating Margin	21	1.9	·	4.0	1.0	1.0	·	1.0	2.3	4.3	1.5	·	·	·
Operating Margin Before Officers' Comp.	22	5.1	·	7.7	1.8	5.5	1.2	4.6	4.1	6.4	3.0	·	·	·

Selected Average Balance Sheet ($ in Thousands)

	1	2	3	4	5	6	7	8	9	10
Net Receivables 23	284	0	77	98	438	1973	5212	7822	14216	7985
Inventories 24	434	0	62	374	748	2871	6175	9845	29038	36274
Net Property, Plant and Equipment 25	178	0	37	63	351	1092	1927	5821	8729	14244
Total Assets 26	1263	0	241	744	1979	7881	16537	34947	69017	125671
Notes and Loans Payable 27	1051	0	98	5809	434	3164	4601	11869	25829	53292
All Other Liabilities 28	460	0	71	1156	776	2485	3747	6729	16167	40698
Net Worth 29	-248	0	71	-6220	768	2232	8190	16349	27020	31682

Selected Financial Ratios (Times to 1)

	1	2	3	4	5	6	7	8	9	10
Current Ratio 30	1.9	•	1.7	3.1	2.0	1.7	2.3	2.0	1.8	1.7
Quick Ratio 31	0.8	•	1.1	1.3	0.9	0.6	1.2	0.8	0.6	0.5
Net Sales to Working Capital 32	6.0	•	10.3	3.4	7.3	5.2	4.0	5.2	6.2	5.3
Coverage Ratio 33	4.0	•	9.6	•	5.3	1.0	5.3	3.1	5.9	2.2
Total Asset Turnover 34	2.2	•	3.5	2.1	2.6	1.6	1.8	1.7	2.1	1.4
Inventory Turnover 35	4.2	•	8.1	2.5	4.3	3.3	3.2	4.6	3.4	3.1
Receivables Turnover 36	9.5	•	15.0	9.7	23.9	4.6	4.8	9.1	9.2	13.8
Total Liabilities to Net Worth 37	•	•	2.4	•	1.6	2.5	1.0	1.1	1.6	3.0
Current Assets to Working Capital 38	2.1	•	2.5	1.5	2.0	2.4	1.8	2.0	2.2	2.4
Current Liabilities to Working Capital 39	1.1	•	1.5	0.5	1.0	1.4	0.8	1.0	1.2	1.4
Working Capital to Net Sales 40	0.2	•	0.1	0.3	0.1	0.2	0.3	0.2	0.2	0.2
Inventory to Working Capital 41	1.0	•	0.8	0.8	1.0	1.2	0.7	1.0	1.2	1.2
Total Receipts to Cash Flow 42	7.5	•	5.5	7.3	8.1	10.6	6.9	11.9	7.7	8.3
Cost of Goods to Cash Flow 43	4.8	•	3.3	4.4	4.9	7.8	4.6	8.8	5.3	5.1
Cash Flow to Total Debt 44	0.2	•	0.9	0.0	0.5	0.2	0.5	0.3	0.5	0.2

Selected Financial Factors (in Percentages)

	1	2	3	4	5	6	7	8	9	10
Debt Ratio 45	119.6	•	70.6	935.7	61.2	71.7	50.5	53.2	60.9	74.8
Return on Total Assets 46	9.5	•	17.1	•	10.1	2.2	9.8	6.9	13.8	9.7
Return on Equity Before Income Taxes 47	•	•	52.1	0.4	21.0	•	16.0	10.0	29.2	20.6
Return on Equity After Income Taxes 48	•	•	52.1	0.5	19.7	•	14.7	9.0	24.1	17.3
Profit Margin (Before Income Tax) 49	3.2	•	4.3	3.1	3.1	•	4.3	2.7	5.4	3.7
Profit Margin (After Income Tax) 50	2.9	•	4.3	2.9	2.9	•	4.0	2.4	4.5	3.1

Manufacturing

Table II
Corporations with Net Income

APPAREL ACCESSORIES AND OTHER APPAREL

MONEY AMOUNTS AND SIZE OF ASSETS IN THOUSANDS OF DOLLARS

Item Description for Accounting Period 7/03 Through 6/04	Total	Zero Assets	Under 500	500 to 1,000	1,000 to 5,000	5,000 to 10,000	10,000 to 25,000	25,000 to 50,000	50,000 to 100,000	100,000 to 250,000	250,000 to 500,000	500,000 to 2,500,000	2,500,000 and over
Number of Enterprises 1	2954	•	2144	337	397	•	25	•	12	•	•	•	•
Revenues ($ in Thousands)													
Net Sales 2	9390367	•	2357677	611858	2033238	•	901717	•	1960905	•	•	•	•
Interest 3	4199	•	15	126	1391	•	138	•	2189	•	•	•	•
Rents 4	1337	•	0	0	0	•	8	•	1024	•	•	•	•
Royalties 5	62	•	0	0	0	•	53	•	0	•	•	•	•
Other Portfolio Income 6	4737	•	0	33	2529	•	1314	•	196	•	•	•	•
Other Receipts 7	98234	•	7413	6683	39946	•	29016	•	9267	•	•	•	•
Total Receipts 8	9498936	•	2365105	618700	2077104	•	932246	•	1973581	•	•	•	•
Average Total Receipts 9	3216	•	1103	1836	5232	•	37290	•	164465	•	•	•	•
Operating Costs/Operating Income (%)													
Cost of Operations 10	64.0	•	60.5	61.0	60.2	•	65.5	•	64.9	•	•	•	•
Salaries and Wages 11	8.4	•	9.9	5.0	10.0	•	9.1	•	7.9	•	•	•	•
Taxes Paid 12	2.4	•	2.0	2.5	2.4	•	2.4	•	2.9	•	•	•	•
Interest Paid 13	0.7	•	0.3	0.1	0.8	•	0.9	•	1.2	•	•	•	•
Depreciation 14	1.3	•	0.7	0.4	2.2	•	0.9	•	1.1	•	•	•	•
Amortization and Depletion 15	0.1	•	0.0	0.0	0.0	•	0.2	•	0.2	•	•	•	•
Pensions and Other Deferred Comp. 16	0.2	•	0.4	0.3	0.1	•	0.2	•	0.1	•	•	•	•
Employee Benefits 17	1.0	•	0.3	4.1	0.9	•	1.1	•	1.0	•	•	•	•
Advertising 18	1.4	•	0.9	1.1	2.2	•	1.0	•	2.1	•	•	•	•
Other Expenses 19	13.0	•	16.2	18.9	15.0	•	10.6	•	10.6	•	•	•	•
Officers' Compensation 20	3.5	•	3.8	5.2	4.8	•	4.0	•	2.3	•	•	•	•
Operating Margin 21	3.9	•	5.1	1.6	1.5	•	4.1	•	5.6	•	•	•	•
Operating Margin Before Officers' Comp. 22	7.4	•	8.9	6.8	6.3	•	8.1	•	7.9	•	•	•	•

315990

Selected Average Balance Sheet ($ in Thousands)

Net Receivables 23	298	82	94	460	5755	12811
Inventories 24	460	61	458	625	6915	30549
Net Property, Plant and Equipment 25	132	14	23	205	1447	8904
Total Assets 26	1241	262	748	1873	16866	76978
Notes and Loans Payable 27	301	58	10	353	4713	26679
All Other Liabilities 28	378	77	255	758	4286	22593
Net Worth 29	561	127	482	761	7867	27706

Selected Financial Ratios (Times to 1)

Current Ratio 30	2.0	1.9	2.8	2.1	2.3	1.8
Quick Ratio 31	0.9	1.2	1.0	1.0	1.2	0.6
Net Sales to Working Capital 32	6.1	9.3	3.9	6.6	4.4	6.2
Coverage Ratio 33	8.3	18.8	54.6	5.9	9.1	6.5
Total Asset Turnover 34	2.6	4.2	2.4	2.7	2.1	2.1
Inventory Turnover 35	4.4	10.8	2.4	4.9	3.4	3.5
Receivables Turnover 36	10.5	20.3	38.6	14.4	5.5	25.5
Total Liabilities to Net Worth 37	1.2	1.1	0.6	1.5	1.1	1.8
Current Assets to Working Capital 38	2.0	2.1	1.6	1.9	1.8	2.3
Current Liabilities to Working Capital 39	1.0	1.1	0.6	0.9	0.8	1.3
Working Capital to Net Sales 40	0.2	0.1	0.3	0.2	0.2	0.2
Inventory to Working Capital 41	0.9	0.8	1.0	1.0	0.7	1.2
Total Receipts to Cash Flow 42	6.7	5.4	6.1	7.4	6.1	7.1
Cost of Goods to Cash Flow 43	4.3	3.3	3.7	4.5	4.0	4.6
Cash Flow to Total Debt 44	0.7	1.5	1.1	0.6	0.7	0.5

Selected Financial Factors (in Percentages)

Debt Ratio 45	54.8	51.5	35.5	59.4	53.4	64.0
Return on Total Assets 46	15.1	24.0	6.8	12.0	18.0	16.6
Return on Equity Before Income Taxes 47	29.4	46.9	10.3	24.6	34.4	39.2
Return on Equity After Income Taxes 48	27.0	46.8	8.4	23.2	32.3	32.9
Profit Margin (Before Income Tax) 49	5.2	5.4	2.7	3.7	7.5	6.6
Profit Margin (After Income Tax) 50	4.8	5.4	2.2	3.4	7.0	5.6

Manufacturing 316115

Table I

Corporations with and without Net Income

Leather and Allied Product Manufacturing

Money Amounts and Size of Assets in Thousands of Dollars

Item Description for Accounting Period 7/03 Through 6/04	Total	Zero Assets	Under 500	500 to 1,000	1,000 to 5,000	5,000 to 10,000	10,000 to 25,000	25,000 to 50,000	50,000 to 100,000	100,000 to 250,000	250,000 to 500,000	500,000 to 2,500,000	2,500,000 and over
Number of Enterprises **1**	1987	958	598	181	181	4	29	12	10	6	5	3	•
Revenues ($ in Thousands)													
Net Sales **2**	9340602	58653	125826	239889	570418	122784	805918	876825	1263797	1055576	2239453	1981463	•
Interest **3**	26652	0	0	45	91	0	1717	778	3320	1288	12010	7404	•
Rents **4**	8549	7	0	2416	1453	0	611	378	1814	0	1649	221	•
Royalties **5**	76240	0	0	0	0	0	102	812	359	13080	39374	22513	•
Other Portfolio Income **6**	29819	10334	0	0	1159	0	1004	1372	1321	0	14386	243	•
Other Receipts **7**	85068	104	31	51	58	61	3636	6157	7602	22512	19314	25541	•
Total Receipts **8**	9566930	69098	125857	242401	573179	122845	812988	886322	1278213	1092456	2326186	2037385	•
Average Total Receipts **9**	4815	72	210	1339	3167	30711	28034	73860	127821	182076	465237	679128	•
Operating Costs/Operating Income (%)													
Cost of Operations **10**	63.2	67.9	45.1	25.9	67.7	69.9	69.8	67.8	62.9	62.8	64.7	60.8	•
Salaries and Wages **11**	9.6	3.9	11.4	18.9	7.6	8.6	7.8	8.6	9.3	11.8	9.8	9.3	•
Taxes Paid **12**	1.7	1.4	1.9	2.3	3.0	1.3	1.7	1.7	1.8	1.7	1.6	1.3	•
Interest Paid **13**	1.7	1.3	•	0.4	0.1	1.1	1.0	0.8	1.7	2.0	3.2	1.4	•
Depreciation **14**	1.8	1.3	0.9	4.6	1.3	1.0	1.5	1.2	1.5	1.8	2.3	2.0	•
Amortization and Depletion **15**	0.3	0.0	•	0.4	0.0	0.0	0.2	0.1	0.3	0.6	0.1	0.6	•
Pensions and Other Deferred Comp. **16**	0.5	0.0	•	0.6	0.0	0.2	0.3	0.2	0.5	0.3	0.7	0.6	•
Employee Benefits **17**	1.2	0.5	•	0.4	0.4	1.6	1.4	1.3	1.0	1.6	0.9	1.4	•
Advertising **18**	2.6	1.2	0.4	1.7	1.2	0.9	1.4	3.1	2.1	2.7	2.2	4.3	•
Other Expenses **19**	13.8	39.7	32.9	18.4	17.9	9.2	8.9	11.2	15.3	14.5	15.5	10.3	•
Officers' Compensation **20**	1.9	3.0	7.4	5.0	3.8	2.2	2.5	1.8	3.1	1.0	1.1	1.1	•
Operating Margin **21**	1.7	•	•	21.5	•	4.0	3.6	2.2	0.5	•	•	6.6	•
Operating Margin Before Officers' Comp. **22**	3.6	•	7.4	26.6	0.1	6.2	6.1	4.0	3.6	0.2	•	7.8	•

Selected Average Balance Sheet ($ in Thousands)

Net Receivables 23	778	0	28	128	172	2208	4117	11331	21948	55598	42703	148217	•
Inventories 24	823	0	69	122	587	25837	5376	10579	21298	30802	98056	127489	•
Net Property, Plant and Equipment 25	448	0	2	232	246	696	1944	4218	8383	14466	61225	72111	•
Total Assets 26	3417	0	149	770	1752	7081	15677	35191	65883	137432	350451	701001	•
Notes and Loans Payable 27	830	0	9	1046	145	5354	4880	9896	16834	22783	116148	86736	•
All Other Liabilities 28	1035	0	1	74	722	4246	3437	7739	22722	31238	176031	135738	•
Net Worth 29	1552	0	139	-350	885	-2518	7360	17556	26327	83411	58272	478528	•

Selected Financial Ratios (Times to 1)

Current Ratio 30	2.1	•	165.2	12.5	1.5	1.0	2.1	1.9	2.2	3.8	1.3	3.1	•
Quick Ratio 31	1.0	•	66.7	7.3	0.4	0.5	0.9	1.1	1.0	2.6	0.4	1.8	•
Net Sales to Working Capital 32	4.2	•	1.4	3.0	7.6	152.5	4.5	5.7	4.6	2.4	11.1	2.7	•
Coverage Ratio 33	3.5	•	•	63.9	•	4.7	5.5	5.1	2.0	2.4	1.8	7.5	•
Total Asset Turnover 34	1.4	•	1.4	1.7	1.8	4.3	1.8	2.1	1.9	1.3	1.3	0.9	•
Inventory Turnover 35	3.6	•	1.4	2.8	3.6	0.8	3.6	4.7	3.7	3.6	3.0	3.2	•
Receivables Turnover 36	6.0	•	9.1	17.0	12.7	1.9	5.7	6.7	6.3	3.2	5.6	8.9	•
Total Liabilities to Net Worth 37	1.2	•	0.1	•	1.0	•	1.1	1.0	1.5	0.6	5.0	0.5	•
Current Assets to Working Capital 38	1.9	•	1.0	1.1	2.9	27.7	1.9	2.1	1.8	1.4	5.0	1.5	•
Current Liabilities to Working Capital 39	0.9	•	0.0	0.1	1.9	26.7	0.9	1.1	0.8	0.4	4.0	0.5	•
Working Capital to Net Sales 40	0.2	•	0.7	0.3	0.1	0.0	0.2	0.2	0.2	0.4	0.1	0.4	•
Inventory to Working Capital 41	0.7	•	0.6	0.4	1.2	13.5	0.8	0.8	0.9	0.4	1.6	0.5	•
Total Receipts to Cash Flow 42	7.0	8.1	4.2	2.8	8.7	8.5	8.4	8.0	6.9	7.6	9.4	5.5	•
Cost of Goods to Cash Flow 43	4.4	5.5	1.9	0.7	5.9	5.9	5.8	5.4	4.3	4.8	6.1	3.3	•
Cash Flow to Total Debt 44	0.4	4.9	0.4	0.4	0.4	0.4	0.4	0.5	0.5	0.4	0.2	0.5	•

Selected Financial Factors (in Percentages)

Debt Ratio 45	54.6	•	6.8	145.4	49.5	135.6	53.1	50.1	60.0	39.3	83.4	31.7	•
Return on Total Assets 46	8.2	•	0.0	39.5	•	22.4	9.8	8.5	6.3	6.2	7.2	10.3	•
Return on Equity Before Income Taxes 47	12.9	•	0.0	•	•	•	17.1	13.7	7.8	6.0	18.7	13.1	•
Return on Equity After Income Taxes 48	10.7	•	•	•	•	•	15.5	13.2	6.7	3.2	9.6	11.7	•
Profit Margin (Before Income Tax) 49	4.2	•	0.0	22.6	•	4.1	4.5	3.3	1.6	2.8	2.4	9.5	•
Profit Margin (After Income Tax) 50	3.5	•	•	22.6	•	4.1	4.1	3.2	1.4	1.5	1.3	8.5	•

Table II

Corporations with Net Income

LEATHER AND ALLIED PRODUCT MANUFACTURING

Money Amounts and Size of Assets in Thousands of Dollars

Item Description for Accounting Period 7/03 Through 6/04	Total	Zero Assets	Under 500	500 to 1,000	1,000 to 5,000	5,000 to 10,000	10,000 to 25,000	25,000 to 50,000	50,000 to 100,000	100,000 to 250,000	250,000 to 500,000	500,000 to 2,500,000	2,500,000 and over
Number of Enterprises **1**	1074	483	299	·	126	·	22	8	7	·	5	·	·
Revenues ($ in Thousands)													
Net Sales **2**	7140367	40661	98786	·	243405	·	663530	601228	859269	·	3483556	·	·
Interest **3**	7752	0	0	·	25	·	930	84	788	·	4888	·	·
Rents **4**	5967	0	0	·	0	·	611	378	1814	·	748	·	·
Royalties **5**	26892	0	0	·	0	·	43	764	32	·	26053	·	·
Other Portfolio Income **6**	22187	10334	0	·	1156	·	923	1355	1221	·	7198	·	·
Other Receipts **7**	65452	0	0	·	32	·	2871	5996	6689	·	28650	·	·
Total Receipts **8**	7268617	50995	98786	·	244618	·	668908	609805	869813	·	3551093	·	·
Average Total Receipts **9**	6768	106	330	·	1941	·	30405	76226	124259	·	710219	·	·
Operating Costs/Operating Income (%)													
Cost of Operations **10**	61.6	58.8	49.1	·	44.1	·	69.9	67.3	59.4	·	62.5	·	·
Salaries and Wages **11**	9.5	2.7	13.7	·	9.3	·	7.3	8.6	9.1	·	9.3	·	·
Taxes Paid **12**	1.7	0.4	2.1	·	4.0	·	1.6	2.0	1.9	·	1.4	·	·
Interest Paid **13**	1.1	1.6	·	·	0.1	·	0.7	0.7	0.9	·	1.2	·	·
Depreciation **14**	1.8	1.7	1.1	·	1.2	·	1.5	1.5	1.5	·	2.2	·	·
Amortization and Depletion **15**	0.2	0.0	·	·	0.0	·	0.1	0.1	0.2	·	0.3	·	·
Pensions and Other Deferred Comp. **16**	0.5	·	·	·	0.0	·	0.3	0.2	0.6	·	0.6	·	·
Employee Benefits **17**	1.1	·	·	·	0.2	·	1.4	1.5	0.9	·	1.0	·	·
Advertising **18**	2.4	1.6	0.3	·	1.1	·	1.4	1.9	2.2	·	3.2	·	·
Other Expenses **19**	12.2	52.2	21.0	·	33.9	·	7.1	9.9	14.3	·	11.1	·	·
Officers' Compensation **20**	2.0	0.4	9.4	·	5.1	·	2.6	1.7	4.3	·	1.0	·	·
Operating Margin **21**	6.0	·	3.2	·	0.9	·	6.0	4.6	4.7	·	6.2	·	·
Operating Margin Before Officers' Comp. **22**	8.0	12.7	·	·	6.0	·	8.6	6.4	9.0	·	7.2	·	·

Selected Average Balance Sheet ($ in Thousands)

Item								
Net Receivables 23	1199	0	56	93	4616	11151	25222	108570
Inventories 24	1136	0	18	405	5194	10369	18858	118107
Net Property, Plant and Equipment 25	618	0	3	193	2125	4707	8020	84464
Total Assets 26	4063	0	155	1608	16041	34592	66952	452389
Notes and Loans Payable 27	606	0	0	141	4185	7978	8282	56729
All Other Liabilities 28	1033	0	1	787	3464	7886	24372	109485
Net Worth 29	2425	0	154	680	8391	18728	34298	286175

Selected Financial Ratios (Times to 1)

Item								
Current Ratio 30	2.6	108.6	1.2	2.6	1.8	2.0		2.8
Quick Ratio 31	1.4	81.9	0.3	1.2	1.0	1.0		1.5
Net Sales to Working Capital 32	3.9	2.2	10.6	4.2	6.5	4.5		3.9
Coverage Ratio 33	8.0	4.8		10.3	10.1	7.9		8.0
Total Asset Turnover 34	1.6	2.1	1.2	1.9	2.2	1.8		1.5
Inventory Turnover 35	3.6	9.0	2.1	4.1	4.9	3.9		3.7
Receivables Turnover 36	5.5	7.2	9.8	6.4	7.6	5.9		12.8
Total Liabilities to Net Worth 37	0.7	0.0	1.4	0.9	0.8	1.0		0.6
Current Assets to Working Capital 38	1.6	1.0	5.7	1.6	2.2	2.0		1.6
Current Liabilities to Working Capital 39	0.6	0.0	4.7	0.6	1.2	1.0		0.6
Working Capital to Net Sales 40	0.3	0.5	0.1	0.2	0.2	0.2		0.3
Inventory to Working Capital 41	0.6	0.2	1.4	0.7	0.9	0.9		0.7
Total Receipts to Cash Flow 42	6.0	4.3	4.1	3.4	7.9	7.1	5.3	6.7
Cost of Goods to Cash Flow 43	3.7	2.6	1.5	5.5	4.8	3.1		4.2
Cash Flow to Total Debt 44	0.7	57.1	0.6	0.5	0.7	0.7		0.6

Selected Financial Factors (in Percentages)

Item								
Debt Ratio 45	40.3	0.9	57.7	47.7	45.9	48.8		36.7
Return on Total Assets 46	14.7	6.9	1.3	14.3	14.6	12.5		14.4
Return on Equity Before Income Taxes 47	21.5	6.9	2.9	24.8	24.3	21.3		19.9
Return on Equity After Income Taxes 48	18.9	6.6	2.3	22.9	23.5	20.1		16.6
Profit Margin (Before Income Tax) 49	7.8	6.0	3.2	1.0	6.9	6.1	6.0	8.2
Profit Margin (After Income Tax) 50	6.9	6.0	3.1	0.8	6.4	5.9	6.0	6.8

Table I

Corporations with and without Net Income

WOOD PRODUCT MANUFACTURING

MONEY AMOUNTS AND SIZE OF ASSETS IN THOUSANDS OF DOLLARS

Item Description for Accounting Period 7/03 Through 6/04		Total	Zero Assets	Under 500	500 to 1,000	1,000 to 5,000	5,000 to 10,000	10,000 to 25,000	25,000 to 50,000	50,000 to 100,000	100,000 to 250,000	250,000 to 500,000	500,000 to 2,500,000	2,500,000 and over
Number of Enterprises	1	14775	1216	9543	1111	2025	395	279	107	54	22	8	12	3
Revenues ($ in Thousands)														
Net Sales	2	86138254	1070218	6293856	2226474	10618834	6690843	8453151	6287163	5699428	4026985	3239076	11757219	19775008
Interest	3	682712	895	815	1210	5829	7959	3971	5847	10099	13857	7244	52829	572155
Rents	4	39025	3265	2126	117	4314	4822	6573	839	3152	1125	306	1916	10470
Royalties	5	57846	2612	0	392	0	7	27	419	170	4292	0	15154	34773
Other Portfolio Income	6	427806	20297	101126	3479	25090	3763	39203	98207	7100	14422	4160	22415	88544
Other Receipts	7	805456	91611	3942	2908	38286	29658	39067	61058	55682	44951	52420	144371	241503
Total Receipts	8	88151099	1188898	6401865	2234580	10692353	6737052	8541992	6453533	5775631	4105632	3303206	11993904	20722453
Average Total Receipts	9	5966	978	671	2011	5280	17056	30616	60313	106956	186620	412901	999492	6907484
Operating Costs/Operating Income (%)														
Cost of Operations	10	73.8	68.1	58.5	62.7	72.4	77.3	79.8	78.6	80.1	74.3	78.8	71.3	74.2
Salaries and Wages	11	5.9	8.5	12.1	9.0	7.4	5.1	4.1	4.5	4.5	5.6	5.2	6.7	4.1
Taxes Paid	12	1.6	1.9	2.8	2.5	2.1	2.1	1.7	1.5	1.6	1.5	1.2	1.5	0.8
Interest Paid	13	2.9	1.8	0.9	0.6	0.9	0.6	0.9	1.2	1.4	1.8	1.5	2.3	8.3
Depreciation	14	3.5	2.8	2.2	3.2	2.5	2.7	3.0	3.0	2.6	4.0	2.8	3.4	5.3
Amortization and Depletion	15	0.6	0.2	0.1	0.0	0.0	0.0	0.2	0.3	0.5	0.2	0.6	0.9	1.5
Pensions and Other Deferred Comp.	16	0.6	0.8	0.4	0.1	0.2	1.1	0.3	0.3	0.2	0.5	0.3	1.0	0.9
Employee Benefits	17	1.1	0.6	1.4	1.2	1.4	1.1	1.3	1.1	1.1	1.1	1.3	2.1	0.3
Advertising	18	0.7	3.2	0.9	0.2	0.3	0.4	0.4	0.5	0.5	1.6	0.6	1.0	1.0
Other Expenses	19	7.8	10.5	13.7	13.2	8.3	7.0	5.2	7.1	5.8	8.3	8.4	8.3	6.6
Officers' Compensation	20	1.6	3.9	6.3	2.9	2.9	2.1	1.4	1.2	0.8	0.7	0.9	0.4	0.3
Operating Margin	21	•	•	0.7	4.4	1.6	0.5	1.7	0.6	0.9	0.3	•	1.1	•
Operating Margin Before Officers' Comp.	22	1.5	1.7	7.0	7.3	4.5	2.6	3.1	1.7	1.7	1.0	•	1.4	•

Selected Average Balance Sheet ($ in Thousands)

Net Receivables 23	1520	0	38	218	378	1761	2542	5696	8591	18668	30816	119048	5506298
Inventories 24	617	0	18	160	571	2070	4246	8048	13091	23603	38178	86200	726097
Net Property, Plant and Equipment 25	1425	0	56	182	663	1650	5202	10883	21987	59349	88912	334654	2831769
Total Assets 26	6606	0	172	761	2055	6707	15339	34623	68556	149381	338422	718909	20667218
Notes and Loans Payable 27	1653	0	88	331	881	1974	5948	10822	24870	51368	67392	233980	4004922
All Other Liabilities 28	2338	0	31	120	431	1409	2657	6594	10932	26625	73915	209836	8982079
Net Worth 29	2615	0	52	310	743	3324	6734	17207	32753	71389	197115	275092	7680217

Selected Financial Ratios (Times to 1)

Current Ratio 30	1.1	•	2.6	2.2	1.7	2.0	1.9	1.8	1.9	2.5	1.1	1.4	0.8
Quick Ratio 31	0.8	•	1.9	1.3	0.9	1.1	0.8	0.7	0.9	1.2	0.5	0.8	0.7
Net Sales to Working Capital 32	26.5	•	11.4	7.1	11.3	7.3	7.3	7.1	6.9	4.6	47.5	12.5	•
Coverage Ratio 33	1.9	5.9	2.9	8.7	3.5	3.1	3.9	3.6	2.6	2.3	1.3	2.3	1.3
Total Asset Turnover 34	0.9	•	3.8	2.6	2.6	2.5	2.0	1.7	1.5	1.2	1.2	1.4	0.3
Inventory Turnover 35	7.0	•	21.3	7.9	6.6	6.3	5.7	5.7	6.5	5.8	8.4	8.1	6.7
Receivables Turnover 36	5.6	•	20.9	9.9	11.5	8.9	12.8	12.0	12.4	10.1	13.2	10.5	2.0
Total Liabilities to Net Worth 37	1.5	•	2.3	1.5	1.8	1.0	1.3	1.0	1.1	1.1	0.7	1.6	1.7
Current Assets to Working Capital 38	11.6	•	1.6	1.8	2.5	2.0	2.1	2.3	2.1	1.7	11.0	3.2	•
Current Liabilities to Working Capital 39	10.6	•	0.6	0.8	1.5	1.0	1.1	1.3	1.1	0.7	10.0	2.2	•
Working Capital to Net Sales 40	0.0	•	0.1	0.1	0.1	0.1	0.1	0.1	0.1	0.2	0.0	0.1	•
Inventory to Working Capital 41	2.8	•	0.4	0.6	1.0	0.8	1.0	1.0	0.9	0.6	4.0	1.2	•
Total Receipts to Cash Flow 42	12.4	6.5	8.5	7.9	12.3	16.7	15.2	12.0	14.7	11.1	13.2	10.2	15.5
Cost of Goods to Cash Flow 43	9.1	4.4	5.0	5.0	8.9	12.9	12.1	9.5	11.8	8.2	10.4	7.2	11.5
Cash Flow to Total Debt 44	0.1	•	0.6	0.6	0.3	0.3	0.2	0.3	0.2	0.2	0.2	0.2	0.0

Selected Financial Factors (in Percentages)

Debt Ratio 45	60.4	•	69.6	59.3	63.8	50.4	56.1	50.3	52.2	52.2	41.8	61.7	62.8
Return on Total Assets 46	4.8	•	10.3	14.2	8.3	4.5	7.3	7.5	5.6	4.9	2.3	7.3	3.4
Return on Equity Before Income Taxes 47	5.5	•	22.3	30.9	16.4	6.1	12.3	10.9	7.2	5.8	0.9	10.9	2.1
Return on Equity After Income Taxes 48	4.5	•	21.5	29.1	15.4	5.0	10.9	9.1	6.0	3.4	0.9	8.2	1.5
Profit Margin (Before Income Tax) 49	2.5	8.8	1.8	4.8	2.3	1.2	2.7	3.2	2.2	2.2	0.4	3.1	2.4
Profit Margin (After Income Tax) 50	2.0	8.0	1.7	4.5	2.2	1.0	2.4	2.7	1.9	1.3	0.4	2.3	1.8

71

Table II

Corporations with Net Income

WOOD PRODUCT MANUFACTURING

MONEY AMOUNTS AND SIZE OF ASSETS IN THOUSANDS OF DOLLARS

Item Description for Accounting Period 7/03 Through 6/04	Total	Zero Assets	Under 500	500 to 1,000	1,000 to 5,000	5,000 to 10,000	10,000 to 25,000	25,000 to 50,000	50,000 to 100,000	100,000 to 250,000	250,000 to 500,000	500,000 to 2,500,000	2,500,000 and over
Number of Enterprises 1	8230	673	4842	704	1453	230	192	69	37	14	4	12	•
Revenues ($ in Thousands)													
Net Sales 2	67443375	935998	4388258	1810190	7739675	4015756	6390598	4364901	3454857	2763491	2270697	29308954	•
Interest 3	607488	894	71	906	1867	6718	2992	4400	3760	3276	56	582547	•
Rents 4	24175	3265	0	108	2082	4312	3403	709	211	395	252	9439	•
Royalties 5	48001	2612	0	0	0	7	27	410	25	587	0	44332	•
Other Portfolio Income 6	333007	19429	32365	1310	18591	2906	35548	93135	4204	13351	3780	108389	•
Other Receipts 7	589445	90084	2356	2684	11009	18827	30354	21656	47418	32584	14392	318081	•
Total Receipts 8	69045491	1052282	4423050	1815198	7773224	4048526	6462922	4485211	3510475	2813684	2289177	30071742	•
Average Total Receipts 9	8389	1564	913	2578	5350	17602	33661	65003	94878	200977	572294	2530978	•
Operating Costs/Operating Income (%)													
Cost of Operations 10	72.6	66.1	57.6	61.7	69.1	76.1	79.0	77.0	78.0	70.9	82.6	73.0	•
Salaries and Wages 11	5.7	7.7	11.3	9.5	7.9	4.3	3.8	4.3	4.4	6.6	3.4	4.9	•
Taxes Paid 12	1.5	1.7	2.9	2.5	2.0	1.6	1.7	1.4	1.5	1.7	0.9	1.1	•
Interest Paid 13	3.1	1.1	0.4	0.4	0.8	0.3	0.7	1.0	1.2	1.1	1.2	6.2	•
Depreciation 14	3.5	2.6	1.4	2.6	2.6	2.1	2.5	2.8	3.0	3.9	2.6	4.7	•
Amortization and Depletion 15	0.7	0.2	0.1	0.0	0.0	0.0	0.1	0.2	0.5	0.2	0.0	1.4	•
Pensions and Other Deferred Comp. 16	0.7	0.8	0.2	0.1	0.3	1.7	0.3	0.4	0.3	0.6	0.2	1.0	•
Employee Benefits 17	1.1	0.3	1.6	0.9	1.2	1.2	1.3	1.0	1.1	1.3	0.9	0.9	•
Advertising 18	0.7	3.6	0.3	0.1	0.3	0.4	0.4	0.7	0.6	1.5	0.7	1.0	•
Other Expenses 19	7.0	9.1	11.6	12.9	8.0	5.5	4.7	6.1	5.2	8.0	5.8	6.6	•
Officers' Compensation 20	1.5	4.3	6.7	3.0	3.1	2.3	1.4	1.2	1.0	0.6	0.5	0.3	•
Operating Margin 21	1.9	2.5	5.9	6.4	4.7	4.5	4.2	3.9	3.3	3.7	1.2	•	•
Operating Margin Before Officers' Comp. 22	3.4	6.9	12.6	9.3	7.8	6.8	5.6	5.1	4.3	4.3	1.7	•	•

Selected Average Balance Sheet ($ in Thousands)

Net Receivables 23	2351	0	51	290	395	1907	2575	5667	7835	18792	40713	1357278	•
Inventories 24	679	0	23	151	568	1675	4281	7797	12343	23199	55039	232412	•
Net Property, Plant and Equipment 25	2055	0	37	163	573	1529	4658	10667	21282	55266	128740	977135	•
Total Assets 26	10057	0	194	799	1963	6553	15264	34267	65312	156420	327812	5474660	•
Notes and Loans Payable 27	2225	0	47	310	719	881	4537	8644	21131	43878	83978	1118213	•
All Other Liabilities 28	3729	0	37	134	303	1463	2663	6019	9960	28311	87743	2299601	•
Net Worth 29	4104	0	111	355	940	4209	8065	19603	34220	84231	156090	2056845	•

Selected Financial Ratios (Times to 1)

Current Ratio 30	1.0	•	3.7	2.1	2.4	2.6	2.2	2.1	2.3	2.7	1.3	0.8	•
Quick Ratio 31	0.7	•	2.7	1.3	1.4	1.6	1.0	0.9	1.1	1.4	0.6	0.7	•
Net Sales to Working Capital 32	764.8	•	9.4	8.4	7.4	6.1	6.6	6.4	5.3	4.3	19.4	•	•
Coverage Ratio 33	2.5	15.0	17.5	17.9	7.7	19.4	8.5	7.4	5.1	6.1	2.7	1.5	•
Total Asset Turnover 34	0.8	•	4.7	3.2	2.7	2.7	2.2	1.8	1.4	1.3	1.7	0.4	•
Inventory Turnover 35	8.8	•	23.1	10.5	6.5	7.9	6.1	6.2	5.9	6.0	8.5	7.7	•
Receivables Turnover 36	5.5	•	23.9	17.7	11.8	9.3	13.7	12.7	12.8	9.8	12.7	3.6	•
Total Liabilities to Net Worth 37	1.5	•	0.8	1.2	1.1	0.6	0.9	0.7	0.9	0.9	1.1	1.7	•
Current Assets to Working Capital 38	338.4	•	1.4	1.9	1.7	1.6	1.8	1.9	1.8	1.6	4.1	•	•
Current Liabilities to Working Capital 39	337.4	•	0.4	0.9	0.7	0.6	0.8	0.9	0.8	0.6	3.1	•	•
Working Capital to Net Sales 40	0.0	•	0.1	0.1	0.1	0.2	0.2	0.2	0.2	0.2	0.1	•	•
Inventory to Working Capital 41	73.9	•	0.3	0.5	0.7	0.5	0.9	0.8	0.8	0.5	1.4	•	•
Total Receipts to Cash Flow 42	10.7	4.8	7.1	7.1	9.5	11.4	11.4	9.2	11.2	8.5	13.8	13.1	•
Cost of Goods to Cash Flow 43	7.8	3.2	4.1	4.4	6.6	8.6	9.0	7.1	8.7	6.0	11.4	9.5	•
Cash Flow to Total Debt 44	0.1	•	1.5	0.8	0.5	0.7	0.4	0.5	0.3	0.3	0.2	0.1	•

Selected Financial Factors (in Percentages)

Debt Ratio 45	59.2	•	43.1	55.5	52.1	35.8	47.2	42.8	47.6	46.2	52.4	62.4	•
Return on Total Assets 46	6.3	•	32.9	22.6	16.1	15.0	13.2	14.2	8.6	8.3	5.5	4.2	•
Return on Equity Before Income Taxes 47	9.2	•	54.4	48.1	29.3	22.1	22.0	21.5	13.2	12.9	7.3	3.8	•
Return on Equity After Income Taxes 48	8.0	•	53.7	45.6	28.1	20.5	20.3	19.0	11.5	9.8	7.2	2.9	•
Profit Margin (Before Income Tax) 49	4.6	14.8	6.6	6.6	5.2	5.3	5.3	6.7	4.8	5.5	2.0	3.2	•
Profit Margin (After Income Tax) 50	4.0	13.9	6.6	6.3	5.0	4.9	4.9	5.9	4.2	4.2	2.0	2.5	•

Table I

Corporations with and without Net Income

PULP, PAPER, AND PAPERBOARD MILLS

MONEY AMOUNTS AND SIZE OF ASSETS IN THOUSANDS OF DOLLARS

Item Description for Accounting Period 7/03 Through 6/04	Total	Zero Assets	Under 500	500 to 1,000	1,000 to 5,000	5,000 to 10,000	10,000 to 25,000	25,000 to 50,000	50,000 to 100,000	100,000 to 250,000	250,000 to 500,000	500,000 to 2,500,000	2,500,000 and over
Number of Enterprises 1	229	•	•	•	89	37	21	22	8	13	5	21	9

Revenues ($ in Thousands)

Item Description for Accounting Period 7/03 Through 6/04	Total	Zero Assets	Under 500	500 to 1,000	1,000 to 5,000	5,000 to 10,000	10,000 to 25,000	25,000 to 50,000	50,000 to 100,000	100,000 to 250,000	250,000 to 500,000	500,000 to 2,500,000	2,500,000 and over
Net Sales 2	96094687	•	•	•	930032	220621	694645	1278904	646457	1979519	1153634	18504604	70583881
Interest 3	528426	•	•	•	1	0	1531	457	337	14867	1715	113998	395518
Rents 4	45361	•	•	•	0	0	304	234	21	305	2382	6442	35673
Royalties 5	212112	•	•	•	0	0	0	0	0	0	12	56580	155508
Other Portfolio Income 6	810061	•	•	•	0	2077	1956	3001	11	1577	11079	138701	649655
Other Receipts 7	1191880	•	•	•	900	1122	6880	3097	2171	4615	6173	144844	1020908
Total Receipts 8	98882527	•	•	•	930933	223820	705316	1285693	648997	2000883	1174995	18965169	72841143
Average Total Receipts 9	431801	•	•	•	10460	6049	33586	58441	81125	153914	234999	903103	8093460

Operating Costs/Operating Income (%)

Item Description for Accounting Period 7/03 Through 6/04	Total	Zero Assets	Under 500	500 to 1,000	1,000 to 5,000	5,000 to 10,000	10,000 to 25,000	25,000 to 50,000	50,000 to 100,000	100,000 to 250,000	250,000 to 500,000	500,000 to 2,500,000	2,500,000 and over
Cost of Operations 10	78.3	•	•	•	94.1	69.7	83.5	85.3	81.9	76.2	78.3	79.3	77.7
Salaries and Wages 11	4.8	•	•	•	1.6	6.3	3.8	4.4	4.1	5.1	6.0	4.7	4.9
Taxes Paid 12	1.3	•	•	•	0.6	1.6	1.4	1.3	1.0	1.5	1.7	1.2	1.3
Interest Paid 13	4.2	•	•	•	0.6	0.1	2.0	1.0	2.4	6.3	2.2	3.7	4.5
Depreciation 14	5.7	•	•	•	1.2	1.3	4.0	4.3	4.9	6.7	13.9	7.1	5.3
Amortization and Depletion 15	0.3	•	•	•	•	0.0	0.2	0.3	0.4	0.4	0.6	0.5	0.2
Pensions and Other Deferred Comp. 16	0.6	•	•	•	0.0	1.2	0.3	0.7	0.5	1.4	1.7	1.0	0.4
Employee Benefits 17	1.7	•	•	•	1.3	1.4	1.8	1.6	2.0	2.7	3.6	1.2	1.7
Advertising 18	0.3	•	•	•	0.0	0.2	0.2	0.2	0.7	0.1	0.2	0.3	0.4
Other Expenses 19	8.3	•	•	•	9.4	10.3	6.1	7.8	3.9	7.6	7.7	7.8	8.5
Officers' Compensation 20	0.3	•	•	•	2.9	1.4	1.4	0.9	1.4	0.6	0.4	0.6	0.2
Operating Margin 21	•	•	•	•	•	6.5	•	•	•	•	•	•	•
Operating Margin Before Officers' Comp. 22	•	•	•	•	•	7.9	•	•	•	•	•	•	•

Selected Average Balance Sheet ($ in Thousands)

Line Item										
Net Receivables **23**	51036	409	436	3164	7011	9028	15554	21521	139559	900112
Inventories **24**	42918	95	444	2419	5787	11230	15301	43203	95905	787618
Net Property, Plant and Equipment **25**	256617	1771	359	7924	15727	32004	82875	203201	557556	4899180
Total Assets **26**	688623	2194	6326	16860	36255	63425	188548	305414	1071083	14348233
Notes and Loans Payable **27**	286224	2995	132	10076	14408	23529	123796	109041	333818	6154047
All Other Liabilities **28**	171446	181	241	6912	11805	18055	24404	81658	357978	3382549
Net Worth **29**	230953	-982	5953	-129	10042	21841	40347	114715	379286	4811638

Selected Financial Ratios (Times to 1)

Line Item										
Current Ratio **30**	0.9	2.4	6.7	0.9	1.2	1.5	1.7	1.9	1.6	0.8
Quick Ratio **31**	0.5	2.4	3.8	0.5	0.6	0.8	0.7	0.8	0.9	0.4
Net Sales to Working Capital **32**	43.6	•	4.1	18.2	8.9	7.1	7.4	8.7	•	•
Coverage Ratio **33**	0.3	67.0	•	•	•	•	•	•	•	0.6
Total Asset Turnover **34**	0.6	4.8	0.9	2.0	1.6	1.3	0.8	0.8	0.8	0.5
Inventory Turnover **35**	7.7	103.4	9.4	11.4	8.6	5.9	7.6	4.2	7.3	7.7
Receivables Turnover **36**	7.8	35.0	27.4	8.9	10.0	6.5	10.0	4.7	5.5	8.6
Total Liabilities to Net Worth **37**	2.0	•	0.1	•	2.6	1.9	3.7	1.7	1.8	2.0
Current Assets to Working Capital **38**	•	1.7	1.2	5.3	2.8	2.4	2.1	2.8	•	•
Current Liabilities to Working Capital **39**	0.7	•	0.2	4.3	1.8	1.4	1.1	1.8	•	•
Working Capital to Net Sales **40**	0.0	•	0.2	0.1	0.1	0.1	0.1	0.1	•	•
Inventory to Working Capital **41**	•	0.3	•	2.1	0.9	0.7	1.1	0.8	•	•
Total Receipts to Cash Flow **42**	38.8	7.1	61.7	•	•	738.0	•	•	279.3	27.7
Cost of Goods to Cash Flow **43**	30.4	4.9	51.5	•	604.0	•	•	•	221.6	21.5
Cash Flow to Total Debt **44**	0.0	2.3	0.0	•	0.0	•	•	•	0.0	0.0

Selected Financial Factors (in Percentages)

Line Item										
Debt Ratio **45**	66.5	144.8	5.9	100.8	72.3	65.6	78.6	62.4	64.6	66.5
Return on Total Assets **46**	0.9	•	7.1	•	•	•	•	•	•	1.5
Return on Equity Before Income Taxes **47**	124.4	•	7.5	808.0	•	•	•	•	•	•
Return on Equity After Income Taxes **48**	124.4	7.2	897.6	•	•	•	•	•	•	•
Profit Margin (Before Income Tax) **49**	7.4	7.4	•	•	•	•	•	•	•	•
Profit Margin (After Income Tax) **50**	7.2	7.2	•	•	•	•	•	•	•	•

Table II

Corporations with Net Income

PULP, PAPER, AND PAPERBOARD MILLS

MONEY AMOUNTS AND SIZE OF ASSETS IN THOUSANDS OF DOLLARS

Item Description for Accounting Period 7/03 Through 6/04	Total	Zero Assets	Under 500	500 to 1,000	1,000 to 5,000	5,000 to 10,000	10,000 to 25,000	25,000 to 50,000	50,000 to 100,000	100,000 to 250,000	250,000 to 500,000	500,000 to 2,500,000	2,500,000 and over
Number of Enterprises 1	67	•	•	•	•	•	10	6	•	•	•	6	6
Revenues ($ in Thousands)													
Net Sales 2	29583580	•	•	•	•	•	322382	461022	•	•	•	5117751	•
Interest 3	160365	•	•	•	•	•	288	101	•	•	•	22583	•
Rents 4	16682	•	•	•	•	•	304	83	•	•	•	3927	•
Royalties 5	51181	•	•	•	•	•	0	0	•	•	•	4614	•
Other Portfolio Income 6	231771	•	•	•	•	•	14	171	•	•	•	50879	•
Other Receipts 7	431663	•	•	•	•	•	3428	217	•	•	•	10989	•
Total Receipts 8	30475242	•	•	•	•	•	326416	461594	•	•	•	5210743	•
Average Total Receipts 9	454854	•	•	•	•	•	32642	76932	•	•	•	868457	•
Operating Costs/Operating Income (%)													
Cost of Operations 10	78.6	•	•	•	•	•	78.3	82.8	•	•	•	77.3	•
Salaries and Wages 11	4.4	•	•	•	•	•	4.5	3.5	•	•	•	5.0	•
Taxes Paid 12	0.9	•	•	•	•	•	1.2	1.0	•	•	•	0.9	•
Interest Paid 13	4.0	•	•	•	•	•	1.0	0.8	•	•	•	2.2	•
Depreciation 14	5.4	•	•	•	•	•	2.3	2.3	•	•	•	4.3	•
Amortization and Depletion 15	0.3	•	•	•	•	•	0.2	0.6	•	•	•	0.6	•
Pensions and Other Deferred Comp. 16	0.4	•	•	•	•	•	0.3	0.7	•	•	•	1.2	•
Employee Benefits 17	0.5	•	•	•	•	•	1.1	0.9	•	•	•	1.0	•
Advertising 18	0.3	•	•	•	•	•	0.4	0.2	•	•	•	0.3	•
Other Expenses 19	5.4	•	•	•	•	•	6.7	4.9	•	•	•	7.1	•
Officers' Compensation 20	0.2	•	•	•	•	•	1.8	1.1	•	•	•	0.3	•
Operating Margin 21	•	•	•	•	•	•	2.2	1.2	•	•	•	•	•
Operating Margin Before Officers' Comp. 22	•	•	•	•	•	•	4.0	2.3	•	•	•	0.2	•

Selected Average Balance Sheet ($ in Thousands)

Net Receivables 23	59650	3777	11026	100404
Inventories 24	44625	3154	9103	88593
Net Property, Plant and Equipment 25	291865	6355	10711	436564
Total Assets 26	672195	16723	39000	894266
Notes and Loans Payable 27	287192	4915	15516	295566
All Other Liabilities 28	166948	5010	11406	240893
Net Worth 29	218056	6798	12078	357807

Selected Financial Ratios (Times to 1)

Current Ratio 30	1.5	1.4	1.5
Quick Ratio 31	0.9	0.8	0.7
Net Sales to Working Capital 32	11.6	13.9	10.3
Coverage Ratio 33	1.6	4.5	2.0
Total Asset Turnover 34	0.7	1.9	1.0
Inventory Turnover 35	7.8	8.0	7.4
Receivables Turnover 36	7.2	6.9	8.9
Total Liabilities to Net Worth 37	2.1	1.5	1.5
Current Assets to Working Capital 38	3.0	3.4	3.0
Current Liabilities to Working Capital 39	2.0	2.4	2.0
Working Capital to Net Sales 40	0.1	0.1	0.1
Inventory to Working Capital 41	1.0	1.1	1.2
Total Receipts to Cash Flow 42	17.2	11.6	16.7
Cost of Goods to Cash Flow 43	13.5	9.1	12.9
Cash Flow to Total Debt 44	0.1	0.3	0.1

Selected Financial Factors (in Percentages)

Debt Ratio 45	67.6	59.4	69.0
Return on Total Assets 46	4.4	8.6	4.1
Return on Equity Before Income Taxes 47	5.3	16.5	8.3
Return on Equity After Income Taxes 48	3.8	13.0	7.1
Profit Margin (Before Income Tax) 49	2.6	3.5	1.3
Profit Margin (After Income Tax) 50	1.9	2.7	1.1

Table I

Corporations with and without Net Income

CONVERTED PAPER PRODUCT

MONEY AMOUNTS AND SIZE OF ASSETS IN THOUSANDS OF DOLLARS

Item Description for Accounting Period 7/03 Through 6/04	Total	Zero Assets	Under 500	500 to 1,000	1,000 to 5,000	5,000 to 10,000	10,000 to 25,000	25,000 to 50,000	50,000 to 100,000	100,000 to 250,000	250,000 to 500,000	500,000 to 2,500,000	2,500,000 and over
Number of Enterprises 1	3171	•	•	455	997	242	163	65	30	21	5	7	4
Revenues ($ in Thousands)													
Net Sales 2	76582374	•	•	930076	5666209	3803926	4849550	3490445	2914508	5035497	2251152	7562731	37762508
Interest 3	1538076	•	•	329	1402	1315	5286	3520	2287	6218	6201	73492	1437460
Rents 4	94576	•	•	0	1178	2362	651	2220	179	2595	1357	2177	81698
Royalties 5	965365	•	•	0	0	1261	147	3127	15	1092	614	40742	917147
Other Portfolio Income 6	905786	•	•	0	913	1587	7646	7217	10545	8077	3806	52146	812629
Other Receipts 7	2341705	•	•	2463	-6571	32689	16651	12215	54767	33806	3327	140922	2043584
Total Receipts 8	82427882	•	•	932868	5663131	3843140	4879931	3518744	2982301	5087285	2266457	7872210	43055026
Average Total Receipts 9	25994	•	•	2050	5680	15881	29938	54135	99410	242252	453291	1124601	10763756
Operating Costs/Operating Income (%)													
Cost of Operations 10	72.5	•	•	80.1	63.2	74.3	72.2	71.1	72.0	75.0	69.0	75.0	73.0
Salaries and Wages 11	8.1	•	•	4.8	9.1	6.4	6.3	7.1	7.8	5.5	8.5	6.5	9.4
Taxes Paid 12	1.4	•	•	1.3	2.2	1.9	1.9	2.0	1.8	1.6	1.8	1.4	0.9
Interest Paid 13	2.7	•	•	0.9	1.4	1.4	1.1	1.4	1.3	1.5	1.6	3.5	3.6
Depreciation 14	4.2	•	•	2.2	3.4	3.3	4.1	3.8	4.1	4.3	4.0	5.3	4.4
Amortization and Depletion 15	0.6	•	•	0.2	0.0	0.1	0.2	0.4	0.2	0.3	0.7	0.7	0.8
Pensions and Other Deferred Comp. 16	1.4	•	•	0.3	0.3	0.2	0.5	0.5	0.7	0.4	0.5	1.2	2.4
Employee Benefits 17	2.3	•	•	1.1	1.8	1.6	1.3	1.9	1.6	1.7	1.2	2.6	2.8
Advertising 18	0.7	•	•	0.2	0.1	0.3	0.2	0.2	0.4	0.5	0.8	0.2	1.1
Other Expenses 19	8.6	•	•	3.1	10.9	9.4	8.2	8.6	7.8	7.5	10.5	7.0	8.8
Officers' Compensation 20	1.2	•	•	8.9	4.5	1.9	2.4	1.7	1.1	0.7	0.9	0.3	0.3
Operating Margin 21	•	•	•	•	2.9	•	1.5	1.3	1.2	1.1	0.5	•	•
Operating Margin Before Officers' Comp. 22	•	•	•	5.9	7.4	1.1	3.9	3.0	2.3	1.8	1.4	•	•

Selected Average Balance Sheet ($ in Thousands)

Item													
Net Receivables 23	2562	•	•	289	585	1500	3518	7012	12663	27500	45351	97352	1012584
Inventories 24	1710	•	•	81	314	1281	3004	5794	12956	24276	57492	97074	520258
Net Property, Plant and Equipment 25	6634	•	•	171	812	2715	5997	12029	25190	62631	122915	467438	2933056
Total Assets 26	34630	•	•	640	2254	6783	15706	34920	67574	164411	364352	1096580	21397240
Notes and Loans Payable 27	8388	•	•	386	941	3217	7512	11549	21213	52600	88223	483953	4194030
All Other Liabilities 28	18043	•	•	218	630	1860	4119	7233	15127	46853	126967	255343	12743737
Net Worth 29	8200	•	•	36	682	1706	4075	16137	31235	64958	149162	357284	4459472

Selected Financial Ratios (Times to 1)

Item													
Current Ratio 30	0.7	•	•	1.3	1.6	1.3	1.2	1.9	2.0	1.7	1.4	1.7	0.6
Quick Ratio 31	0.2	•	•	1.0	1.2	0.6	0.7	1.1	1.2	0.9	0.6	0.8	0.1
Net Sales to Working Capital 32	•	•	•	23.4	11.9	19.9	20.3	7.1	6.0	8.3	10.5	10.0	•
Coverage Ratio 33	2.7	•	•	•	3.0	1.1	3.0	2.5	3.6	2.5	1.9	1.2	3.2
Total Asset Turnover 34	0.7	•	•	3.2	2.5	2.3	1.9	1.5	1.4	1.5	1.2	1.0	0.4
Inventory Turnover 35	10.2	•	•	20.3	11.5	9.1	7.1	6.6	5.4	7.4	5.4	8.3	13.3
Receivables Turnover 36	9.5	•	•	6.2	10.2	21.0	8.3	7.7	7.7	8.8	8.8	10.2	9.5
Total Liabilities to Net Worth 37	3.2	•	•	16.8	2.3	3.0	2.9	1.2	1.2	1.5	1.4	2.1	3.8
Current Assets to Working Capital 38	•	•	•	4.8	2.6	4.6	5.4	2.2	2.0	2.3	3.6	2.4	•
Current Liabilities to Working Capital 39	•	•	•	3.8	1.6	3.6	4.4	1.2	1.0	1.3	2.6	1.4	•
Working Capital to Net Sales 40	•	•	•	0.0	0.1	0.1	0.0	0.1	0.2	0.1	0.1	0.1	•
Inventory to Working Capital 41	•	•	•	0.7	0.6	1.6	2.0	0.8	0.7	0.8	1.3	0.9	•
Total Receipts to Cash Flow 42	9.6	•	•	•	9.8	17.0	12.8	12.5	10.8	12.8	10.0	17.3	7.3
Cost of Goods to Cash Flow 43	6.9	•	•	•	6.2	12.6	9.2	8.9	7.8	9.6	6.9	13.0	5.3
Cash Flow to Total Debt 44	0.1	•	•	•	0.4	0.2	0.2	0.2	0.2	0.2	0.2	0.1	0.1

Selected Financial Factors (in Percentages)

Item													
Debt Ratio 45	76.3	•	•	94.4	69.7	74.8	74.1	53.8	53.8	60.5	59.1	67.4	79.2
Return on Total Assets 46	5.0	•	•	•	10.6	3.4	6.1	5.4	6.7	5.6	3.7	4.1	5.0
Return on Equity Before Income Taxes 47	13.4	•	•	•	23.3	0.6	15.7	6.9	10.5	8.6	4.3	1.9	16.3
Return on Equity After Income Taxes 48	8.8	•	•	•	22.2	•	13.2	5.5	9.1	6.4	2.6	•	10.5
Profit Margin (Before Income Tax) 49	4.5	•	•	•	2.8	0.1	2.2	2.1	3.4	2.3	1.4	0.6	7.7
Profit Margin (After Income Tax) 50	3.0	•	•	•	2.7	•	1.8	1.7	2.9	1.7	0.9	0.1	5.0

75

Table II

Corporations with Net Income

CONVERTED PAPER PRODUCT

Money Amounts and Size of Assets in Thousands of Dollars

Item Description for Accounting Period 7/03 Through 6/04	Total	Zero Assets	Under 500	500 to 1,000	1,000 to 5,000	5,000 to 10,000	10,000 to 25,000	25,000 to 50,000	50,000 to 100,000	100,000 to 250,000	250,000 to 500,000	500,000 to 2,500,000	2,500,000 and over
Number of Enterprises **1**	1707	·	712	102	561	·	105	45	·	13	·	3	·
Revenues ($ in Thousands)													
Net Sales **2**	46689263	·	1092201	295782	3977153	·	3290571	2382420	·	3186595	·	4320249	·
Interest **3**	775717	·	0	329	1400	·	4154	2000	·	2748	·	5240	·
Rents **4**	9091	·	0	0	692	·	587	726	·	2219	·	311	·
Royalties **5**	919072	·	0	0	0	·	147	3127	·	605	·	8560	·
Other Portfolio Income **6**	743202	·	0	0	540	·	3618	4880	·	6993	·	23759	·
Other Receipts **7**	1846823	·	0	6	8211	·	10905	6568	·	25578	·	9597	·
Total Receipts **8**	51163168	·	1092201	296117	3987996	·	3309982	2399721	·	3224738	·	4367716	·
Average Total Receipts **9**	29973	·	1534	2903	7109	·	31524	53327	·	248057	·	1455905	·
Operating Costs/Operating Income (%)													
Cost of Operations **10**	63.9	·	72.5	66.1	64.0	·	70.8	68.6	·	73.3	·	69.0	·
Salaries and Wages **11**	10.2	·	1.5	5.6	9.6	·	6.3	6.5	·	5.0	·	6.3	·
Taxes Paid **12**	1.6	·	2.1	1.0	2.6	·	1.8	2.0	·	1.5	·	1.7	·
Interest Paid **13**	2.5	·	0.2	0.1	0.5	·	0.9	1.2	·	0.8	·	2.3	·
Depreciation **14**	4.7	·	0.1	0.1	3.6	·	3.7	3.8	·	3.9	·	5.7	·
Amortization and Depletion **15**	0.7	·	·	0.0	0.0	·	0.1	0.3	·	0.3	·	0.8	·
Pensions and Other Deferred Comp. **16**	2.2	·	·	0.9	0.4	·	0.5	0.6	·	0.4	·	1.7	·
Employee Benefits **17**	3.1	·	1.0	0.2	2.0	·	1.2	1.8	·	1.5	·	2.6	·
Advertising **18**	1.0	·	0.4	0.4	0.1	·	0.2	0.2	·	0.7	·	0.2	·
Other Expenses **19**	10.1	·	9.2	4.6	7.8	·	7.7	8.5	·	8.4	·	6.7	·
Officers' Compensation **20**	1.3	·	7.3	21.0	3.3	·	2.6	2.0	·	0.9	·	0.4	·
Operating Margin **21**	5.8	·	5.8	·	6.1	·	4.2	4.5	·	3.3	·	2.6	·
Operating Margin Before Officers' Comp. **22**	0.0	·	13.1	21.0	9.3	·	6.8	6.5	·	4.2	·	3.0	·

Selected Average Balance Sheet ($ in Thousands)

Net Receivables 23	3636	103	459	692	3684	6862	26973	136755
Inventories 24	2378	22	99	373	2963	5515	28515	144898
Net Property, Plant and Equipment 25	8342	14	10	997	5855	11672	54794	572645
Total Assets 26	46372	224	699	2578	15820	34352	162873	1437249
Notes and Loans Payable 27	11919	49	236	706	7833	9640	34073	665698
All Other Liabilities 28	21613	55	332	457	4358	6734	49227	285886
Net Worth 29	12840	120	131	1415	3628	17978	79573	485665

Selected Financial Ratios (Times to 1)

Current Ratio 30	1.0	2.2	2.0	2.3	1.1	2.2	1.7	1.7
Quick Ratio 31	0.2	1.8	1.9	1.8	0.7	1.3	1.0	0.6
Net Sales to Working Capital 32	173.8	13.2	8.5	8.4	30.4	6.0	8.3	9.3
Coverage Ratio 33	4.6	36.8	1.8	13.3	6.3	5.3	7.0	2.8
Total Asset Turnover 34	0.6	6.9	4.2	2.8	2.0	1.5	1.5	1.0
Inventory Turnover 35	7.4	49.5	19.4	12.2	7.5	6.6	6.3	6.9
Receivables Turnover 36	7.5	28.3	3.9	10.0	8.2	8.0	8.1	21.1
Total Liabilities to Net Worth 37	2.6	0.9	4.3	0.8	3.4	0.9	1.0	2.0
Current Assets to Working Capital 38	120.2	1.8	2.0	1.8	7.8	1.9	2.4	2.4
Current Liabilities to Working Capital 39	119.2	0.8	1.0	0.8	6.8	0.9	1.4	1.4
Working Capital to Net Sales 40	0.0	0.1	0.1	0.1	0.0	0.2	0.1	0.1
Inventory to Working Capital 41	15.0	0.4	0.1	0.4	2.7	0.6	0.9	0.9
Total Receipts to Cash Flow 42	6.3	10.9	22.8	9.2	10.0	9.0	9.2	11.0
Cost of Goods to Cash Flow 43	4.1	7.9	15.0	5.9	7.0	6.2	6.8	7.6
Cash Flow to Total Debt 44	0.1	1.3	0.2	0.7	0.3	0.4	0.3	0.1

Selected Financial Factors (in Percentages)

Debt Ratio 45	72.3	46.5	81.2	45.1	77.1	47.7	51.1	66.2
Return on Total Assets 46	6.7	40.6	0.9	18.9	11.4	9.9	8.5	6.2
Return on Equity Before Income Taxes 47	18.9	73.8	2.1	31.8	41.8	15.3	14.9	11.7
Return on Equity After Income Taxes 48	13.5	73.8	2.1	30.8	37.4	13.5	12.0	8.4
Profit Margin (Before Income Tax) 49	8.8	5.8	0.1	6.3	4.8	5.2	4.8	4.0
Profit Margin (After Income Tax) 50	6.3	5.8	0.1	6.2	4.3	4.6	3.9	2.8

Table I

Corporations with and without Net Income

PRINTING AND RELATED SUPPORT ACTIVITIES

MONEY AMOUNTS AND SIZE OF ASSETS IN THOUSANDS OF DOLLARS

Item Description for Accounting Period 7/03 Through 6/04	Total	Zero Assets	Under 500	500 to 1,000	1,000 to 5,000	5,000 to 10,000	10,000 to 25,000	25,000 to 50,000	50,000 to 100,000	100,000 to 250,000	250,000 to 500,000	500,000 to 2,500,000	2,500,000 and over
Number of Enterprises **1**	32676	2678	22746	3045	3175	534	313	103	38	17	7	15	3
Revenues ($ in Thousands)													
Net Sales **2**	83783734	774531	8237545	5791284	13285078	7001401	8279903	5589595	3569456	2774935	3221073	14604569	10654364
Interest **3**	247410	636	2440	2476	6896	7035	4688	3050	2511	15185	36369	77579	88544
Rents **4**	49414	0	92	4450	4594	7058	1795	675	63	1975	2583	22315	3815
Royalties **5**	516520	0	8	0	0	4457	11987	2570	72	639	12725	308189	175873
Other Portfolio Income **6**	244669	757	7759	14360	19662	9436	17298	17671	4066	1366	5634	146659	1
Other Receipts **7**	1365522	22756	36579	52806	147942	48901	77972	38269	18168	36451	2642	548257	334778
Total Receipts **8**	86207269	798680	8284423	5865376	13464172	7078288	8393643	5651830	3594336	2830551	3281026	15707568	11257375
Average Total Receipts **9**	2638	298	364	1926	4241	13255	26817	54872	94588	166503	468718	1047171	3752458
Operating Costs/Operating Income (%)													
Cost of Operations **10**	60.3	55.0	45.9	49.6	59.5	66.2	66.7	65.4	67.6	57.1	60.4	55.2	72.4
Salaries and Wages **11**	10.3	12.5	11.5	14.5	10.5	8.0	9.2	10.3	7.7	8.5	13.2	12.5	6.7
Taxes Paid **12**	2.6	1.9	3.3	2.6	3.1	2.6	2.4	2.3	2.1	2.2	1.9	2.3	2.6
Interest Paid **13**	2.1	2.6	1.1	0.8	1.5	1.5	1.2	1.5	1.2	4.2	5.0	2.4	4.1
Depreciation **14**	5.0	2.7	4.6	3.7	5.1	5.2	5.0	4.9	4.4	4.5	3.1	5.8	5.9
Amortization and Depletion **15**	0.4	0.5	0.2	0.0	0.3	0.1	0.2	0.3	0.5	1.0	1.1	0.4	0.7
Pensions and Other Deferred Comp. **16**	0.6	0.3	0.1	0.6	0.4	0.3	0.4	0.6	0.5	0.8	0.5	1.0	0.7
Employee Benefits **17**	2.2	1.9	1.2	1.2	1.6	1.2	1.6	2.3	1.6	2.7	4.1	3.7	3.0
Advertising **18**	0.9	0.4	1.3	0.5	0.4	0.5	0.7	1.5	1.9	1.4	1.2	1.3	0.0
Other Expenses **19**	13.0	20.0	24.6	17.4	11.1	10.5	8.8	8.0	9.4	12.5	10.3	16.3	8.7
Officers' Compensation **20**	3.2	4.4	8.3	7.9	5.5	3.5	2.5	2.0	1.5	1.7	0.9	0.5	0.5
Operating Margin **21**	•	•	•	1.3	1.0	0.3	1.3	0.9	1.6	3.4	•	•	•
Operating Margin Before Officers' Comp. **22**	2.7	2.3	6.1	9.1	6.5	3.8	3.8	2.9	3.1	5.1	•	•	•

Selected Average Balance Sheet ($ in Thousands)

Net Receivables 23	338	0	20	215	463	1759	3969	7977	11951	21944	59404	220601	304981
Inventories 24	127	0	5	41	162	935	1690	4137	7881	12671	29011	63938	175748
Net Property, Plant and Equipment 25	561	0	46	220	899	2985	5729	12670	21365	40041	72733	256285	1073141
Total Assets 26	1870	0	103	707	2043	7404	14945	34059	69578	158034	317966	979145	5244217
Notes and Loans Payable 27	680	0	85	279	952	3089	5392	13207	19103	83633	159492	300076	1321314
All Other Liabilities 28	600	0	35	184	387	1903	3912	8803	18756	38691	112639	320080	2303879
Net Worth 29	590	-17	0	243	704	2412	5641	12049	31719	35709	45834	358989	1619024

Selected Financial Ratios (Times to 1)

Current Ratio 30	1.3	•	1.1	1.8	1.6	1.4	1.4	1.5	1.5	1.4	1.0	1.3	0.9
Quick Ratio 31	0.9	•	0.9	1.5	1.2	0.9	1.0	1.0	1.0	0.9	0.6	0.9	0.3
Net Sales to Working Capital 32	16.3	•	139.9	9.8	12.4	13.6	11.3	10.1	8.5	12.3	•	11.4	•
Coverage Ratio 33	2.1	1.4	•	4.1	2.6	1.9	3.2	2.3	2.8	2.3	1.1	3.6	1.0
Total Asset Turnover 34	1.4	•	3.5	2.7	2.0	1.8	1.8	1.6	1.4	1.0	1.4	1.0	0.7
Inventory Turnover 35	12.1	•	30.9	22.8	15.3	9.3	10.4	8.6	8.1	7.4	9.6	8.4	14.6
Receivables Turnover 36	7.5	•	15.4	10.9	8.3	7.1	6.8	6.6	7.9	7.1	6.3	4.0	23.3
Total Liabilities to Net Worth 37	2.2	•	•	1.9	1.9	2.1	1.6	1.8	1.2	3.4	5.9	1.7	2.2
Current Assets to Working Capital 38	4.3	•	17.4	2.3	2.8	3.7	3.2	3.0	2.9	3.5	•	4.3	•
Current Liabilities to Working Capital 39	3.3	•	16.4	1.3	1.8	2.7	2.2	2.0	1.9	2.5	•	3.3	•
Working Capital to Net Sales 40	0.1	•	0.0	0.1	0.1	0.1	0.1	0.1	0.1	0.1	•	0.1	•
Inventory to Working Capital 41	0.8	•	1.5	0.2	0.5	1.0	0.7	0.8	0.8	0.9	•	0.5	•
Total Receipts to Cash Flow 42	8.7	5.6	7.0	7.7	10.3	12.9	11.5	13.3	10.5	6.7	12.9	5.2	13.7
Cost of Goods to Cash Flow 43	5.3	3.1	3.2	3.8	6.1	8.5	7.7	8.7	7.1	3.8	7.8	2.9	9.9
Cash Flow to Total Debt 44	0.2	•	0.4	0.5	0.3	0.2	0.2	0.2	0.2	0.2	0.1	0.3	0.1

Selected Financial Factors (in Percentages)

Debt Ratio 45	68.5	116.1	•	65.6	65.5	67.4	62.3	64.6	54.4	77.4	85.6	63.3	69.1
Return on Total Assets 46	6.1	•	•	9.0	7.8	5.1	6.8	5.6	4.8	9.9	7.6	8.7	2.9
Return on Equity Before Income Taxes 47	10.1	34.2	•	19.9	13.7	7.6	12.4	9.0	6.8	24.9	3.0	17.1	0.4
Return on Equity After Income Taxes 48	7.6	35.4	•	19.3	12.3	6.1	11.1	8.0	5.9	19.7	•	11.6	•
Profit Margin (Before Income Tax) 49	2.3	1.0	•	2.5	2.3	1.4	2.6	2.0	2.3	5.5	0.3	6.3	0.2
Profit Margin (After Income Tax) 50	1.7	0.6	•	2.5	2.1	1.1	2.4	1.8	2.0	4.3	•	4.3	•

77

Table II

Corporations with Net Income

PRINTING AND RELATED SUPPORT ACTIVITIES

MONEY AMOUNTS AND SIZE OF ASSETS IN THOUSANDS OF DOLLARS

Item Description for Accounting Period 7/03 Through 6/04		Total	Zero Assets	Under 500	500 to 1,000	1,000 to 5,000	5,000 to 10,000	10,000 to 25,000	25,000 to 50,000	50,000 to 100,000	100,000 to 250,000	250,000 to 500,000	500,000 to 2,500,000	2,500,000 and over
Number of Enterprises	1	14941	1651	9026	1605	2023	•	210	64	25	11	•	•	•
Revenues ($ in Thousands)														
Net Sales	2	54628812	539063	3555364	3361316	8889629	•	5803801	3599847	2539329	1962484	•	•	•
Interest	3	128086	88	790	1077	4552	•	3301	1900	1619	14828	•	•	•
Rents	4	32992	0	92	783	2463	•	1456	667	63	1975	•	•	•
Royalties	5	300389	0	8	0	0	•	11977	92	72	585	•	•	•
Other Portfolio Income	6	193109	575	5267	3481	13721	•	8191	13701	2899	752	•	•	•
Other Receipts	7	901157	20111	33485	30016	137785	•	60440	26974	17223	16818	•	•	•
Total Receipts	8	56184545	559837	3595006	3396673	9048150	•	5889166	3643181	2561205	1997442	•	•	•
Average Total Receipts	9	3760	339	398	2116	4473	•	28044	56925	102448	181586	•	•	•
Operating Costs/Operating Income (%)														
Cost of Operations	10	58.7	47.3	41.7	44.9	58.8	•	65.3	61.4	65.7	53.6	•	•	•
Salaries and Wages	11	10.3	14.7	9.3	14.6	10.4	•	9.2	10.9	7.3	8.7	•	•	•
Taxes Paid	12	2.4	1.8	3.2	1.9	2.9	•	2.3	2.1	2.2	2.1	•	•	•
Interest Paid	13	1.7	3.1	0.8	0.6	1.2	•	1.0	1.0	1.0	4.0	•	•	•
Depreciation	14	4.8	2.7	5.1	3.1	4.0	•	4.3	4.6	4.0	4.2	•	•	•
Amortization and Depletion	15	0.4	0.6	0.1	0.1	0.4	•	0.2	0.3	0.4	0.7	•	•	•
Pensions and Other Deferred Comp.	16	0.5	0.2	0.3	0.9	0.3	•	0.5	0.6	0.6	1.1	•	•	•
Employee Benefits	17	2.1	1.8	0.7	0.6	1.3	•	1.6	2.2	1.6	2.5	•	•	•
Advertising	18	1.0	0.5	0.6	0.4	0.5	•	0.8	2.2	2.5	1.8	•	•	•
Other Expenses	19	11.7	20.3	23.6	17.6	10.1	•	8.3	8.2	8.9	12.4	•	•	•
Officers' Compensation	20	3.1	3.8	7.7	8.6	5.9	•	2.6	2.1	1.8	1.8	•	•	•
Operating Margin	21	3.3	3.2	6.7	6.6	4.2	•	3.9	4.5	4.0	7.0	•	•	•
Operating Margin Before Officers' Comp.	22	6.4	7.0	14.4	15.2	10.0	•	6.5	6.5	5.8	8.8	•	•	•

Selected Average Balance Sheet ($ in Thousands)

Net Receivables 23	460	0	23	223	475	·	3874	8493	12575	21414
Inventories 24	181	0	8	26	169	·	1811	4487	9405	13001
Net Property, Plant and Equipment 25	760	0	53	222	771	·	5375	11664	21771	42167
Total Assets 26	2455	0	129	717	2029	·	14793	34057	68917	166387
Notes and Loans Payable 27	868	0	68	245	771	·	4542	9904	15588	89005
All Other Liabilities 28	742	0	31	165	385	·	3550	8693	18652	41996
Net Worth 29	844	0	30	307	873	·	6701	15461	34676	35386

Selected Financial Ratios (Times to 1)

Current Ratio 30	1.4	·	1.6	2.1	1.6	·	1.6	1.7	1.6	1.6
Quick Ratio 31	0.9	·	1.4	2.0	1.2	·	1.1	1.2	1.1	1.0
Net Sales to Working Capital 32	13.4	·	17.7	9.2	11.9	·	9.2	8.0	7.6	9.9
Coverage Ratio 33	4.7	3.3	10.7	13.4	5.9	·	6.6	6.9	5.8	3.2
Total Asset Turnover 34	1.5	·	3.1	2.9	2.2	·	1.9	1.7	1.5	1.1
Inventory Turnover 35	11.9	·	20.8	35.9	15.3	·	10.0	7.7	7.1	7.4
Receivables Turnover 36	7.7	·	14.6	9.9	8.6	·	7.3	6.3	8.4	8.8
Total Liabilities to Net Worth 37	1.9	·	3.3	1.3	1.3	·	1.2	1.2	1.0	3.7
Current Assets to Working Capital 38	3.6	·	2.7	1.9	2.6	·	2.6	2.5	2.5	2.7
Current Liabilities to Working Capital 39	2.6	·	1.7	0.9	1.6	·	1.6	1.5	1.5	1.7
Working Capital to Net Sales 40	0.1	·	0.1	0.1	0.1	·	0.1	0.1	0.1	0.1
Inventory to Working Capital 41	0.7	·	0.2	0.0	0.5	·	0.6	0.6	0.8	0.8
Total Receipts to Cash Flow 42	7.0	4.2	4.4	5.4	7.8	·	8.9	8.9	8.7	5.4
Cost of Goods to Cash Flow 43	4.1	2.0	1.8	2.4	4.6	·	5.8	5.4	5.7	2.9
Cash Flow to Total Debt 44	0.3	·	0.9	0.9	0.5	·	0.4	0.3	0.3	0.3

Selected Financial Factors (in Percentages)

Debt Ratio 45	65.6	·	76.6	57.2	57.0	·	54.7	54.6	49.7	78.7
Return on Total Assets 46	11.7	·	26.4	24.0	15.5	·	11.8	10.9	8.6	13.7
Return on Equity Before Income Taxes 47	26.7	·	102.5	52.0	29.9	·	22.2	20.6	14.2	44.3
Return on Equity After Income Taxes 48	22.8	·	100.7	51.1	28.2	·	20.6	19.3	13.0	36.2
Profit Margin (Before Income Tax) 49	6.2	7.0	7.8	7.6	5.9	·	5.4	5.7	4.8	8.8
Profit Margin (After Income Tax) 50	5.3	6.5	7.7	7.5	5.6	·	5.0	5.3	4.4	7.2

Table I

Corporations with and without Net Income

PETROLEUM REFINERIES (INCLUDING INTEGRATED)

MONEY AMOUNTS AND SIZE OF ASSETS IN THOUSANDS OF DOLLARS

Item Description for Accounting Period 7/03 Through 6/04	Total	Zero Assets	Under 500	500 to 1,000	1,000 to 5,000	5,000 to 10,000	10,000 to 25,000	25,000 to 50,000	50,000 to 100,000	100,000 to 250,000	250,000 to 500,000	500,000 to 2,500,000	2,500,000 and over
Number of Enterprises 1	321	3	265	•	•	•	6	5	6	6	6	6	18
Revenues ($ in Thousands)													
Net Sales 2	834905614	3466685	0	•	•	•	229406	403156	726661	2076980	6768432	9390960	811843334
Interest 3	9410334	1729	0	•	•	•	348	180	340	2220	9671	13617	9382226
Rents 4	2064142	56	0	•	•	•	158	7	751	5225	8311	12023	2037611
Royalties 5	816712	344	0	•	•	•	0	0	0	10809	32	982	804544
Other Portfolio Income 6	11579211	11809	4517	•	•	•	176	865	0	201130	29785	17724	11313204
Other Receipts 7	19393471	65262	1250	•	•	•	385	2108	12291	16275	4550	57194	19234162
Total Receipts 8	878169484	3545885	5767	•	•	•	230473	406316	740043	2312639	6820781	9492500	854615081
Average Total Receipts 9	2735730	1181962	22	•	•	•	38412	81263	123340	385440	1136797	1582083	47478616
Operating Costs/Operating Income (%)													
Cost of Operations 10	84.2	95.4	•	•	•	•	86.8	86.2	90.3	89.2	92.5	86.5	84.0
Salaries and Wages 11	1.6	0.6	•	•	•	•	2.3	1.5	2.3	1.6	1.7	2.5	1.6
Taxes Paid 12	2.9	0.3	•	•	•	•	0.5	1.0	0.5	0.7	0.7	2.4	3.0
Interest Paid 13	1.7	0.0	•	•	•	•	1.5	0.9	0.8	1.0	2.9	1.3	1.7
Depreciation 14	1.9	0.8	•	•	•	•	1.2	2.7	1.5	1.9	2.6	2.1	1.9
Amortization and Depletion 15	0.6	0.0	•	•	•	•	1.0	1.2	0.0	0.2	0.2	0.2	0.6
Pensions and Other Deferred Comp. 16	0.5	0.2	•	•	•	•	0.1	0.1	0.0	0.1	0.0	0.3	0.5
Employee Benefits 17	0.4	0.1	•	•	•	•	0.0	0.3	0.2	0.2	0.5	0.2	0.4
Advertising 18	0.1	0.0	•	•	•	•	0.0	0.5	0.2	0.0	0.0	0.0	0.1
Other Expenses 19	6.0	2.7	•	•	•	•	8.7	5.8	2.8	3.8	15.7	4.3	6.0
Officers' Compensation 20	0.1	0.1	•	•	•	•	0.9	0.8	0.3	0.7	0.1	0.4	0.0
Operating Margin 21	•	•	•	•	•	•	•	•	0.9	0.4	•	•	0.1
Operating Margin Before Officers' Comp. 22	0.0	•	•	•	•	•	•	•	1.2	1.1	0.1	•	0.2

Selected Average Balance Sheet ($ in Thousands)

	1	2	3	4	5	6	7	8	9	10	11
Net Receivables 23	244929	0	0	•	4727	10395	11833	24167	40188	98990	4305040
Inventories 24	65207	0	0	•	1249	6662	9647	13270	41006	142804	1091647
Net Property, Plant and Equipment 25	527426	0	0	•	3957	17535	21982	38535	126059	247216	9254983
Total Assets 26	3841357	0	87	•	16794	38873	57213	179241	349201	623700	68083395
Notes and Loans Payable 27	666644	0	87	•	11294	13001	10006	7206	270979	216084	11711730
All Other Liabilities 28	1369184	0	2	•	4220	9452	27471	76094	138772	182797	24271330
Net Worth 29	1805529	0	-2	•	1282	16421	19737	95941	-60550	224818	32100335

Selected Financial Ratios (Times to 1)

	1	2	3	4	5	6	7	8	9	10	11
Current Ratio 30	0.4	•	0.8	•	2.2	1.8	0.9	1.5	0.6	1.5	0.4
Quick Ratio 31	0.2	•	0.8	•	1.5	1.3	0.5	1.2	0.3	0.8	0.2
Net Sales to Working Capital 32	•	•	•	•	7.1	10.5	•	9.3	•	18.5	•
Coverage Ratio 33	4.7	45.3	5.0	•	0.9	2.1	4.3	12.4	•	1.6	5.1
Total Asset Turnover 34	0.7	•	•	•	2.3	2.1	2.1	1.9	3.2	2.5	0.7
Inventory Turnover 35	33.6	•	•	•	26.6	10.4	11.3	23.3	25.5	9.5	34.7
Receivables Turnover 36	10.6	•	•	•	8.0	7.3	6.7	16.8	32.1	9.6	10.5
Total Liabilities to Net Worth 37	1.1	•	•	•	12.1	1.4	1.9	0.9	•	1.8	1.1
Current Assets to Working Capital 38	•	•	•	•	1.8	2.3	•	2.9	•	3.1	•
Current Liabilities to Working Capital 39	•	•	•	•	0.8	1.3	•	1.9	•	2.1	•
Working Capital to Net Sales 40	•	•	•	•	0.1	0.1	•	0.1	•	0.1	•
Inventory to Working Capital 41	•	•	•	•	0.2	0.5	•	0.3	•	1.3	•
Total Receipts to Cash Flow 42	9.9	22.8	•	•	17.0	21.4	22.2	10.2	•	24.6	9.6
Cost of Goods to Cash Flow 43	8.3	21.7	•	•	14.7	18.4	20.0	9.1	•	21.3	8.0
Cash Flow to Total Debt 44	0.1	0.2	•	•	0.1	0.2	0.1	0.4	•	0.2	0.1

Selected Financial Factors (in Percentages)

	1	2	3	4	5	6	7	8	9	10	11
Debt Ratio 45	53.0	102.4	•	•	92.4	57.8	65.5	46.5	117.3	64.0	52.9
Return on Total Assets 46	5.8	24.1	•	•	•	1.7	7.5	24.7	•	5.3	5.9
Return on Equity Before Income Taxes 47	9.8	•	•	•	•	16.8	16.8	42.4	304.1	5.7	10.0
Return on Equity After Income Taxes 48	6.3	•	•	•	•	13.8	13.8	29.3	305.6	3.8	6.5
Profit Margin (Before Income Tax) 49	6.8	2.0	•	•	•	2.7	2.7	11.8	•	0.8	7.1
Profit Margin (After Income Tax) 50	4.4	1.9	•	•	•	2.3	2.3	8.1	•	0.5	4.6

Table II

Corporations with Net Income

PETROLEUM REFINERIES (INCLUDING INTEGRATED)

MONEY AMOUNTS AND SIZE OF ASSETS IN THOUSANDS OF DOLLARS

Item Description for Accounting Period 7/03 Through 6/04	Total	Zero Assets	Under 500	500 to 1,000	1,000 to 5,000	5,000 to 10,000	10,000 to 25,000	25,000 to 50,000	50,000 to 100,000	100,000 to 250,000	250,000 to 500,000	500,000 to 2,500,000	2,500,000 and over
Number of Enterprises 1	33	•	•	•	•	•	•	•	•	•	3	3	12

Revenues ($ in Thousands)

Net Sales 2	721269983	•	•	•	•	•	•	•	•	•	2186833	4003128	710002192
Interest 3	9039748	•	•	•	•	•	•	•	•	•	9499	3232	9022634
Rents 4	1955563	•	•	•	•	•	•	•	•	•	585	2230	1951337
Royalties 5	816224	•	•	•	•	•	•	•	•	•	32	982	804400
Other Portfolio Income 6	10625895	•	•	•	•	•	•	•	•	•	11883	14974	10380742
Other Receipts 7	18725217	•	•	•	•	•	•	•	•	•	3410	40899	18606366
Total Receipts 8	762432630	•	•	•	•	•	•	•	•	•	2212242	4065445	750767671
Average Total Receipts 9	23104019	•	•	•	•	•	•	•	•	•	737414	1355148	62563973

Operating Costs/Operating Income (%)

Cost of Operations 10	83.1	•	•	•	•	•	•	•	•	•	88.0	86.7	83.0
Salaries and Wages 11	1.7	•	•	•	•	•	•	•	•	•	1.9	2.5	1.7
Taxes Paid 12	3.3	•	•	•	•	•	•	•	•	•	0.6	1.0	3.3
Interest Paid 13	1.6	•	•	•	•	•	•	•	•	•	1.2	0.3	1.6
Depreciation 14	1.8	•	•	•	•	•	•	•	•	•	2.5	2.0	1.9
Amortization and Depletion 15	0.6	•	•	•	•	•	•	•	•	•	0.4	0.1	0.6
Pensions and Other Deferred Comp. 16	0.5	•	•	•	•	•	•	•	•	•	0.0	0.4	0.5
Employee Benefits 17	0.4	•	•	•	•	•	•	•	•	•	0.4	0.2	0.4
Advertising 18	0.1	•	•	•	•	•	•	•	•	•	0.1	0.0	0.1
Other Expenses 19	6.2	•	•	•	•	•	•	•	•	•	3.4	5.3	6.2
Officers' Compensation 20	0.0	•	•	•	•	•	•	•	•	•	0.2	0.5	0.0
Operating Margin 21	0.6	•	•	•	•	•	•	•	•	•	1.4	1.0	0.6
Operating Margin Before Officers' Comp. 22	0.7	•	•	•	•	•	•	•	•	•	1.6	1.5	0.6

Selected Average Balance Sheet ($ in Thousands)

Net Receivables 23	2084698	44093	126519	5674733
Inventories 24	489889	52226	81212	1305250
Net Property, Plant and Equipment 25	424856	148359	162788	1576188
Total Assets 26	35046337	347536	622412	9045582
Notes and Loans Payable 27	5429832	75521	134384	14870652
All Other Liabilities 28	12689266	105050	174187	34800597
Net Worth 29	16927238	166965	313841	46374334

Selected Financial Ratios (Times to 1)

Current Ratio 30	0.4	1.5	1.6	0.4
Quick Ratio 31	0.2	1.0	0.9	0.2
Net Sales to Working Capital 32	•	12.5	12.7	•
Coverage Ratio 33	6.1	3.2	8.8	6.1
Total Asset Turnover 34	0.6	2.1	2.1	0.6
Inventory Turnover 35	37.1	12.3	14.3	37.6
Receivables Turnover 36	10.5	33.1	10.9	10.4
Total Liabilities to Net Worth 37	1.1	1.1	1.0	1.1
Current Assets to Working Capital 38	•	3.0	2.8	•
Current Liabilities to Working Capital 39	•	2.0	1.8	•
Working Capital to Net Sales 40	•	0.1	0.1	•
Inventory to Working Capital 41	•	0.9	1.0	•
Total Receipts to Cash Flow 42	8.6	19.8	15.2	8.6
Cost of Goods to Cash Flow 43	7.2	17.4	13.2	7.1
Cash Flow to Total Debt 44	0.1	0.2	0.3	0.1

Selected Financial Factors (in Percentages)

Debt Ratio 45	51.7	52.0	49.6	51.7
Return on Total Assets 46	6.1	7.8	6.1	6.1
Return on Equity Before Income Taxes 47	10.7	11.2	10.8	10.6
Return on Equity After Income Taxes 48	7.0	10.2	8.0	7.0
Profit Margin (Before Income Tax) 49	8.2	2.6	2.5	8.3
Profit Margin (After Income Tax) 50	5.4	2.3	1.9	5.4

Table I

Corporations with and without Net Income

ASPHALT PAVING, ROOFING, OTHER PETROLEUM AND COAL PRODUCTS

MONEY AMOUNTS AND SIZE OF ASSETS IN THOUSANDS OF DOLLARS

Item Description for Accounting Period 7/03 Through 6/04	Total	Zero Assets	Under 500	500 to 1,000	1,000 to 5,000	5,000 to 10,000	10,000 to 25,000	25,000 to 50,000	50,000 to 100,000	100,000 to 250,000	250,000 to 500,000	500,000 to 2,500,000	2,500,000 and over
Number of Enterprises 1	1278	11	725	251	122	72	59	14	12	6	6	•	•
Revenues ($ in Thousands)													
Net Sales 2	12481300	38719	439753	461734	593755	694668	1744680	760427	1638565	975160	5133840	•	•
Interest 3	21452	5	0	80	1070	123	785	520	716	5156	12998	•	•
Rents 4	7045	686	0	0	450	212	3506	139	35	0	2016	•	•
Royalties 5	30250	0	0	0	0	5	9	0	205	2103	27928	•	•
Other Portfolio Income 6	107950	0	2830	5	15	696	2263	5968	10133	2349	83690	•	•
Other Receipts 7	89089	7766	-68264	278	741	78	14001	10327	13001	31983	79178	•	•
Total Receipts 8	12737086	47176	374319	462097	596031	695782	1765244	777381	1662655	1016751	5339650	•	•
Average Total Receipts 9	9966	4289	516	1841	4886	9664	29919	55527	138555	169458	889942	•	•
Operating Costs/Operating Income (%)													
Cost of Operations 10	71.5	56.1	8.9	30.3	66.9	79.2	74.4	71.5	83.1	76.9	74.4	•	•
Salaries and Wages 11	6.6	16.8	24.2	25.1	9.0	4.7	5.6	5.1	3.4	6.2	5.1	•	•
Taxes Paid 12	1.3	2.0	3.1	3.3	1.6	1.4	1.4	2.0	0.7	1.3	0.9	•	•
Interest Paid 13	1.8	2.4	0.0	2.6	3.0	2.1	0.7	0.9	0.8	1.2	2.7	•	•
Depreciation 14	3.8	1.4	2.8	5.2	3.2	6.5	3.9	5.2	2.5	3.2	3.7	•	•
Amortization and Depletion 15	0.2	0.4	0.0	•	•	0.3	0.1	0.3	0.4	0.8	0.1	•	•
Pensions and Other Deferred Comp. 16	0.4	0.4	•	0.2	0.8	0.9	0.3	0.4	0.2	0.2	0.4	•	•
Employee Benefits 17	0.9	0.3	•	0.8	0.5	0.9	0.8	0.7	0.9	0.8	1.2	•	•
Advertising 18	0.5	0.5	0.0	0.3	0.0	2.4	0.4	0.7	0.1	0.1	0.5	•	•
Other Expenses 19	10.8	36.3	52.0	27.2	11.4	•	8.0	7.6	4.7	13.1	10.3	•	•
Officers' Compensation 20	1.7	9.9	5.6	4.5	6.3	4.5	1.9	1.4	1.1	1.0	0.5	•	•
Operating Margin 21	0.5	•	3.3	0.6	•	0.1	2.4	4.1	2.0	•	0.2	•	•
Operating Margin Before Officers' Comp. 22	2.2	•	8.9	5.1	3.6	4.6	4.3	5.5	3.1	•	0.7	•	•

Selected Average Balance Sheet ($ in Thousands)

Net Receivables 23	1214	0	0	130	805	1086	4193	7692	17930	25944	102683
Inventories 24	628	0	3	0	105	691	2066	4634	8479	14476	60299
Net Property, Plant and Equipment 25	2195	0	18	467	1964	3662	5191	11316	18324	40205	207689
Total Assets 26	6131	0	42	703	3406	7135	15767	33922	67718	158983	588080
Notes and Loans Payable 27	2371	0	39	142	4829	3478	4005	9942	14111	35184	228458
All Other Liabilities 28	1803	0	242	502	1233	1448	3924	7149	19280	44781	152748
Net Worth 29	1957	0	-240	59	-2655	2209	7838	16830	34327	79018	206873

Selected Financial Ratios (Times to 1)

Current Ratio 30	1.5	•	21.3	1.3	0.7	0.9	2.0	2.2	2.2	1.2	1.7
Quick Ratio 31	1.0	•	21.3	1.3	0.7	0.7	1.4	1.3	1.5	0.6	1.0
Net Sales to Working Capital 32	11.1	•	27.4	34.0	•	•	6.8	5.7	6.6	18.5	10.7
Coverage Ratio 33	2.4	•	•	1.3	0.2	1.1	5.8	8.1	5.3	0.4	2.7
Total Asset Turnover 34	1.6	•	14.6	2.6	1.4	1.4	1.9	1.6	2.0	1.0	1.5
Inventory Turnover 35	11.1	•	16.4	•	30.9	11.0	10.6	8.4	13.4	8.6	10.6
Receivables Turnover 36	8.5	•	36.9	28.2	6.0	5.8	7.4	6.9	8.3	7.7	9.7
Total Liabilities to Net Worth 37	2.1	•	•	10.9	•	2.2	1.0	1.0	1.0	1.0	1.8
Current Assets to Working Capital 38	2.8	•	1.0	4.0	•	•	2.0	1.9	1.9	7.5	2.3
Current Liabilities to Working Capital 39	1.8	•	0.0	3.0	•	•	1.0	0.9	0.9	6.5	1.3
Working Capital to Net Sales 40	0.1	•	0.0	0.0	•	•	0.1	0.2	0.1	0.1	0.1
Inventory to Working Capital 41	0.7	•	•	•	•	•	0.5	0.5	0.4	1.9	0.8
Total Receipts to Cash Flow 42	9.2	3.5	2.7	4.1	35.0	•	10.6	9.1	13.4	10.9	8.5
Cost of Goods to Cash Flow 43	6.6	1.9	0.2	1.2	23.4	•	7.9	6.5	11.1	8.4	6.3
Cash Flow to Total Debt 44	0.3	•	0.8	0.7	0.0	•	0.4	0.3	0.3	0.2	0.3

Selected Financial Factors (in Percentages)

Debt Ratio 45	68.1	•	676.7	91.6	177.9	69.0	50.3	50.4	49.3	50.3	64.8
Return on Total Assets 46	7.1	•	•	8.4	1.0	3.1	8.1	11.6	8.6	0.6	10.5
Return on Equity Before Income Taxes 47	13.2	•	29.3	20.4	4.2	0.7	13.6	20.4	13.7		18.6
Return on Equity After Income Taxes 48	10.3	•	29.3	17.3	4.6	0.5	12.7	15.8	11.0		16.1
Profit Margin (Before Income Tax) 49	2.6	•	•	0.7	•	0.2	3.6	6.3	3.5		4.5
Profit Margin (After Income Tax) 50	2.1	•	•	0.6	•	0.1	3.4	4.9	2.8		3.9

Table II

Corporations with Net Income

ASPHALT PAVING, ROOFING, OTHER PETROLEUM AND COAL PRODUCTS

MONEY AMOUNTS AND SIZE OF ASSETS IN THOUSANDS OF DOLLARS

Item Description for Accounting Period 7/03 Through 6/04	Total	Zero Assets	Under 500	500 to 1,000	1,000 to 5,000	5,000 to 10,000	10,000 to 25,000	25,000 to 50,000	50,000 to 100,000	100,000 to 250,000	250,000 to 500,000	500,000 to 2,500,000	2,500,000 and over
Number of Enterprises **1**	759	·	536	62	54	33	·	·	·	·	6	·	·
Revenues ($ in Thousands)													
Net Sales **2**	10481268	·	426245	196687	281964	323475	·	·	·	·	5133840	·	·
Interest **3**	19356	·	0	80	1070	115	·	·	·	·	12998	·	·
Rents **4**	5059	·	0	0	450	212	·	·	·	·	2016	·	·
Royalties **5**	29215	·	0	0	0	0	·	·	·	·	27928	·	·
Other Portfolio Income **6**	106583	·	2830	5	15	690	·	·	·	·	83690	·	·
Other Receipts **7**	131273	·	2533	39	741	40	·	·	·	·	79178	·	·
Total Receipts **8**	10772754	·	431608	196811	284240	324532	·	·	·	·	5339650	·	·
Average Total Receipts **9**	14193	·	805	3174	5264	9834	·	·	·	·	889942	·	·
Operating Costs/Operating Income (%)													
Cost of Operations **10**	72.1	·	9.2	68.1	70.5	63.3	·	·	·	·	74.4	·	·
Salaries and Wages **11**	6.0	·	25.0	6.8	5.7	9.2	·	·	·	·	5.1	·	·
Taxes Paid **12**	1.2	·	3.2	1.4	1.9	1.9	·	·	·	·	0.9	·	·
Interest Paid **13**	1.6	·	0.0	0.0	0.0	0.4	·	·	·	·	2.7	·	·
Depreciation **14**	3.4	·	2.9	3.4	1.8	1.5	·	·	·	·	3.7	·	·
Amortization and Depletion **15**	0.2	·	0.0	·	·	0.0	·	·	·	·	0.1	·	·
Pensions and Other Deferred Comp. **16**	0.4	·	·	0.0	1.6	1.8	·	·	·	·	0.4	·	·
Employee Benefits **17**	0.9	·	·	0.2	0.4	0.8	·	·	·	·	1.2	·	·
Advertising **18**	0.5	·	0.0	0.1	0.1	0.5	·	·	·	·	0.5	·	·
Other Expenses **19**	10.0	·	50.4	8.0	7.1	5.1	·	·	·	·	10.3	·	·
Officers' Compensation **20**	1.6	·	5.8	10.5	7.3	6.8	·	·	·	·	0.5	·	·
Operating Margin **21**	2.1	·	3.4	1.5	3.6	3.9	·	·	·	·	0.2	·	·
Operating Margin Before Officers' Comp. **22**	3.7	·	9.2	12.0	10.9	10.7	·	·	·	·	0.7	·	·

Selected Average Balance Sheet ($ in Thousands)

Net Receivables 23	1651	0	309	621	587	102683
Inventories 24	876	0	0	235	678	64106
Net Property, Plant and Equipment 25	2727	25	208	527	2094	207689
Total Assets 26	8312	55	756	2272	5984	588080
Notes and Loans Payable 27	2572	1	55	6	749	228458
All Other Liabilities 28	2082	0	456	828	1853	152748
Net Worth 29	3658	54	245	1438	3383	206873

Selected Financial Ratios (Times to 1)

Current Ratio 30	1.9	20.4	1.2	2.1	1.8	1.7
Quick Ratio 31	1.2	20.4	1.2	2.0	1.3	1.0
Net Sales to Working Capital 32	8.3	27.8	38.2	6.1	7.3	10.7
Coverage Ratio 33	4.0	1238.4	32.0	169.5	10.7	2.7
Total Asset Turnover 34	1.7	14.5	4.2	2.3	1.6	1.5
Inventory Turnover 35	11.4	.	.	15.7	9.2	9.9
Receivables Turnover 36	8.9	120.8	20.5	4.9	5.3	16.7
Total Liabilities to Net Worth 37	1.3	0.0	2.1	0.6	0.8	1.8
Current Assets to Working Capital 38	2.1	1.1	6.6	1.9	2.3	2.3
Current Liabilities to Working Capital 39	1.1	0.1	5.6	0.9	1.3	1.3
Working Capital to Net Sales 40	0.1	0.0	0.0	0.2	0.1	0.1
Inventory to Working Capital 41	0.6	.	.	0.0	0.6	0.8
Total Receipts to Cash Flow 42	7.8	1.9	12.9	10.3	11.7	8.5
Cost of Goods to Cash Flow 43	5.6	0.2	8.8	7.3	7.4	6.3
Cash Flow to Total Debt 44	0.4	281.7	0.5	0.6	0.3	0.3

Selected Financial Factors (in Percentages)

Debt Ratio 45	56.0	2.7	67.6	36.7	43.5	64.8
Return on Total Assets 46	11.0	67.2	6.6	10.2	7.2	10.5
Return on Equity Before Income Taxes 47	18.8	69.0	19.8	16.1	11.6	18.6
Return on Equity After Income Taxes 48	16.3	69.0	16.8	14.3	11.3	16.1
Profit Margin (Before Income Tax) 49	5.0	4.6	1.5	4.4	4.0	4.5
Profit Margin (After Income Tax) 50	4.3	4.6	1.3	3.9	3.9	3.9

Table I

Corporations with and without Net Income

BASIC CHEMICAL

MONEY AMOUNTS AND SIZE OF ASSETS IN THOUSANDS OF DOLLARS

Item Description for Accounting Period 7/03 Through 6/04	Total	Zero Assets	Under 500	500 to 1,000	1,000 to 5,000	5,000 to 10,000	10,000 to 25,000	25,000 to 50,000	50,000 to 100,000	100,000 to 250,000	250,000 to 500,000	500,000 to 2,500,000	2,500,000 and over
Number of Enterprises 1	896	24	99	311	140	115	77	33	22	16	13	26	19
Revenues ($ in Thousands)													
Net Sales 2	101170959	1001748	94220	393007	588646	835063	1536820	1423510	1573482	2948143	3379012	22237351	65159956
Interest 3	2287935	2578	0	0	2141	1059	4285	1528	9249	8084	21607	136931	2100472
Rents 4	280795	34	0	0	0	860	1736	1118	847	25289	3750	8996	238166
Royalties 5	3448787	0	0	29301	601	0	141	2883	4875	6341	15341	260413	3128892
Other Portfolio Income 6	1384396	481	0	5745	4047	247	3126	3214	1048	29317	19379	474068	843720
Other Receipts 7	3002400	-7080	1455	5733	1381	2324	13556	9743	18248	19396	51843	483911	2401894
Total Receipts 8	111575272	997761	95675	433786	596816	839553	1559664	1441996	1607749	3036570	3490932	23601670	73873100
Average Total Receipts 9	124526	41573	966	1395	4263	7300	20255	43697	73080	189786	268533	907757	3888058
Operating Costs/Operating Income (%)													
Cost of Operations 10	73.2	65.1	69.4	50.1	60.4	69.6	69.5	62.6	73.6	73.4	69.2	69.1	75.6
Salaries and Wages 11	6.3	5.7	3.0	10.3	9.0	5.8	8.2	8.5	6.2	7.2	6.1	7.3	5.8
Taxes Paid 12	1.5	2.6	2.8	4.3	3.0	2.5	1.8	2.0	1.6	1.2	1.5	1.4	1.5
Interest Paid 13	5.6	2.3	0.3	1.1	0.7	2.2	0.9	1.6	1.8	1.7	3.6	3.4	7.1
Depreciation 14	5.5	11.3	1.2	2.2	2.0	3.5	4.4	5.9	8.1	4.3	6.4	5.4	5.5
Amortization and Depletion 15	0.8	1.1	2.2	•	0.0	0.8	0.3	0.4	0.9	0.6	1.4	1.2	0.7
Pensions and Other Deferred Comp. 16	0.7	0.2	0.0	1.1	0.1	0.4	0.6	0.6	0.4	0.4	0.9	1.0	0.7
Employee Benefits 17	2.5	1.7	2.4	2.5	0.7	1.4	1.4	1.7	1.6	1.2	1.6	2.4	2.7
Advertising 18	0.7	0.1	•	0.1	0.6	0.3	0.3	0.3	0.3	0.1	0.2	2.1	0.3
Other Expenses 19	10.4	7.9	8.4	13.3	20.6	8.5	10.2	11.7	11.4	10.0	10.9	12.2	9.8
Officers' Compensation 20	0.6	0.2	11.6	11.9	6.4	3.3	2.1	1.6	1.4	0.6	0.7	0.5	0.4
Operating Margin 21	•	1.8	•	3.2	•	1.7	0.2	3.0	•	•	•	•	•
Operating Margin Before Officers' Comp. 22	•	2.0	10.4	15.0	2.8	5.0	2.2	4.6	•	•	•	•	•

Selected Average Balance Sheet ($ in Thousands)

Line Item												
Net Receivables 23	65064	167	255	724	1099	3165	6950	14007	22479	45182	119546	2796694
Inventories 24	13284	148	146	425	1184	2383	4659	13509	17847	37971	134344	355385
Net Property, Plant and Equipment 25	47921	14	107	521	2133	5174	14754	25371	48067	109689	351880	1568262
Total Assets 26	293765	403	670	2476	6555	15286	35098	74587	150298	343915	1162428	11620494
Notes and Loans Payable 27	116270	20	503	730	2258	4658	12108	26376	55547	88366	423224	4698837
All Other Liabilities 28	83714	62	187	486	1664	3302	7799	21744	33327	81596	404425	3241307
Net Worth 29	93781	322	-21	1260	2633	7325	15191	26467	61424	173954	334779	3680349

Selected Financial Ratios (Times to 1)

Line Item												
Current Ratio 30	1.0	3.8	0.9	2.2	2.0	1.8	1.7	1.4	1.2	2.0	1.5	0.9
Quick Ratio 31	0.8	2.4	0.7	1.8	1.0	1.1	1.0	0.8	0.6	1.1	0.7	0.7
Net Sales to Working Capital 32	•	4.2	•	5.4	4.2	5.6	6.7	7.1	23.6	4.6	7.3	•
Coverage Ratio 33	1.6	1.9	13.3	•	2.0	2.8	3.6	•	2.3	1.3	1.2	1.7
Total Asset Turnover 34	0.4	2.4	1.9	1.7	1.1	1.3	1.2	1.0	1.2	0.8	0.7	0.3
Inventory Turnover 35	6.2	4.5	4.3	6.0	4.3	5.8	5.8	3.9	7.6	4.7	4.4	7.3
Receivables Turnover 36	1.8	1.9	9.9	4.4	5.1	6.7	6.9	4.9	7.6	5.7	6.4	1.3
Total Liabilities to Net Worth 37	2.1	0.3	•	1.0	1.5	1.1	1.3	1.8	1.4	1.0	2.5	2.2
Current Assets to Working Capital 38	•	1.4	•	1.8	2.0	2.2	2.4	3.3	7.4	2.0	2.9	•
Current Liabilities to Working Capital 39	•	0.4	•	0.8	1.0	1.2	1.4	2.3	6.4	1.0	1.9	•
Working Capital to Net Sales 40	•	0.2	•	0.2	0.2	0.2	0.1	0.1	0.0	0.2	0.1	•
Inventory to Working Capital 41	•	0.5	•	0.3	0.6	0.7	0.8	1.2	2.3	0.7	1.1	•
Total Receipts to Cash Flow 42	10.4	17.8	4.4	9.2	10.9	9.9	7.3	31.9	9.5	10.4	12.3	9.9
Cost of Goods to Cash Flow 43	7.6	12.3	2.2	5.6	7.6	6.9	4.6	23.5	7.0	7.2	8.5	7.5
Cash Flow to Total Debt 44	0.1	0.7	0.4	0.4	0.2	0.3	0.3	0.0	0.2	0.1	0.1	0.0

Selected Financial Factors (in Percentages)

Line Item												
Debt Ratio 45	68.1	20.3	103.1	49.1	59.8	52.1	56.7	64.5	59.1	49.4	71.2	68.3
Return on Total Assets 46	3.5	1.6	27.6	•	4.9	3.4	7.2	•	4.9	3.6	3.0	3.5
Return on Equity Before Income Taxes 47	4.1	0.9	•	6.2	6.2	4.5	12.1	•	6.8	1.7	1.7	4.4
Return on Equity After Income Taxes 48	2.5	0.8	•	3.0	3.0	2.7	9.4	•	4.7	•	0.1	2.8
Profit Margin (Before Income Tax) 49	3.4	0.3	13.6	2.3	2.3	1.6	4.2	•	2.3	1.2	0.7	4.8
Profit Margin (After Income Tax) 50	2.0	0.7	13.4	1.1	1.1	1.0	3.3	•	1.6	•	0.0	3.0

Table II

Corporations with Net Income

BASIC CHEMICAL

Money Amounts and Size of Assets in Thousands of Dollars

Item Description for Accounting Period 7/03 Through 6/04	Total	Zero Assets	Under 500	500 to 1,000	1,000 to 5,000	5,000 to 10,000	10,000 to 25,000	25,000 to 50,000	50,000 to 100,000	100,000 to 250,000	250,000 to 500,000	500,000 to 2,500,000	2,500,000 and over
Number of Enterprises 1	649	18	99	258	74	80	49	18	7	12	9	14	11
Revenues ($ in Thousands)													
Net Sales 2	68612631	420326	94220	280825	458273	659533	1170485	885792	762705	2401376	2179154	14805204	44494738
Interest 3	1820086	2140	0	0	2116	990	3840	1338	314	4605	21082	85400	1698260
Rents 4	220059	34	0	0	0	855	291	1113	321	25236	3499	5407	183303
Royalties 5	2850160	0	0	29301	601	0	100	2846	3193	6341	15341	93968	2698469
Other Portfolio Income 6	1118162	481	0	0	4032	197	2887	981	246	28029	12428	465307	603575
Other Receipts 7	2327279	12986	1455	5732	976	729	9567	8310	5241	17764	42300	380408	1841810
Total Receipts 8	76948377	435967	95675	315858	465998	662304	1187170	900380	772020	2483351	2273804	15635694	51520155
Average Total Receipts 9	118565	24220	966	1224	6297	8279	24228	50021	110289	206946	252645	1131121	4683650
Operating Costs/Operating Income (%)													
Cost of Operations 10	71.6	39.4	69.4	54.0	56.6	65.1	68.5	56.1	73.5	73.3	63.5	67.7	74.3
Salaries and Wages 11	6.2	12.7	3.0	6.6	8.7	5.3	8.3	10.1	5.7	7.5	8.3	7.0	5.6
Taxes Paid 12	1.5	5.3	2.8	4.7	2.8	2.6	1.8	2.1	1.7	1.3	1.6	1.3	1.4
Interest Paid 13	5.4	2.8	0.3	0.8	0.6	0.7	0.7	0.8	1.4	1.1	2.3	3.2	6.9
Depreciation 14	5.3	10.9	1.2	1.3	1.2	3.1	3.5	4.3	3.1	4.2	5.9	4.0	5.9
Amortization and Depletion 15	0.6	2.0	2.2	•	•	0.7	0.2	0.3	0.5	0.3	1.2	1.1	0.5
Pensions and Other Deferred Comp. 16	0.8	0.4	0.0	0.5	0.2	0.5	0.7	0.6	0.5	0.2	0.9	1.0	0.8
Employee Benefits 17	2.4	3.3	2.4	1.5	0.9	1.6	1.3	1.7	1.5	0.7	1.7	2.7	2.4
Advertising 18	0.8	0.1	•	0.0	0.6	0.3	0.3	0.3	0.3	0.1	0.2	3.0	0.2
Other Expenses 19	10.1	14.6	8.4	10.3	21.1	7.0	8.0	10.9	6.9	9.9	13.0	11.4	9.4
Officers' Compensation 20	0.6	•	11.6	12.7	6.6	3.6	2.0	2.0	1.7	0.5	0.7	0.5	0.3
Operating Margin 21	•	8.4	•	7.5	0.6	9.3	4.7	10.8	3.1	0.8	0.7	•	•
Operating Margin Before Officers' Comp. 22	•	8.4	10.4	20.2	12.9	7.2	6.8	12.8	4.8	1.4	1.4	•	•

Selected Average Balance Sheet ($ in Thousands)

Net Receivables 23	80126	0	167	221	1129	1203	3786	7399	17139	22483	44789	120672	4449761
Inventories 24	9223	0	140	112	486	1109	2676	3641	18805	15616	42188	130247	281787
Net Property, Plant and Equipment 25	43041	0	14	74	342	2350	4538	13534	20658	47682	109673	386516	1829003
Total Assets 26	307737	0	403	621	2840	6245	15685	35009	74787	151597	334032	1436565	15631968
Notes and Loans Payable 27	115279	0	20	471	553	1083	3703	6862	16721	38491	50111	438713	6098889
All Other Liabilities 28	85887	0	62	152	470	553	2982	9182	21867	35423	66685	505974	4276628
Net Worth 29	106571	0	322	-3	1817	4609	9000	18964	36199	77683	217236	491878	5256452

Selected Financial Ratios (Times to 1)

Current Ratio 30	1.0	•	3.8	0.9	3.1	4.9	2.4	2.1	1.5	1.3	2.0	1.9	0.9
Quick Ratio 31	0.8	•	2.4	0.6	2.7	2.5	1.5	1.3	0.9	0.6	1.1	0.9	0.8
Net Sales to Working Capital 32	•	•	4.2	•	4.2	2.9	4.6	5.6	9.0	13.9	4.1	5.6	•
Coverage Ratio 33	2.5	5.3	1.9	25.8	4.7	14.4	9.4	17.0	4.1	5.0	3.5	2.4	2.4
Total Asset Turnover 34	0.3	•	2.4	1.8	2.2	1.3	1.5	1.4	1.5	1.3	0.7	0.7	0.3
Inventory Turnover 35	8.2	•	4.7	5.3	7.2	4.8	6.1	7.6	4.3	9.4	3.6	5.5	10.7
Receivables Turnover 36	1.8	•	4.8	6.7	5.0	6.1	6.7	7.8	4.8	8.5	5.5	9.2	1.2
Total Liabilities to Net Worth 37	1.9	•	0.3	•	0.6	0.4	0.7	0.8	1.1	1.0	0.5	1.9	2.0
Current Assets to Working Capital 38	•	•	1.4	•	1.5	1.3	1.7	1.9	2.8	4.2	2.0	2.1	•
Current Liabilities to Working Capital 39	•	•	0.4	•	0.5	0.3	0.7	0.9	1.8	3.2	1.0	1.1	•
Working Capital to Net Sales 40	•	•	0.2	•	0.2	0.4	0.2	0.2	0.1	0.1	0.2	0.2	•
Inventory to Working Capital 41	•	•	0.5	•	0.2	0.3	0.5	0.6	1.0	1.2	0.7	0.9	•
Total Receipts to Cash Flow 42	7.1	4.1	17.8	3.4	6.6	6.4	8.0	4.7	10.3	8.0	6.1	8.7	6.7
Cost of Goods to Cash Flow 43	5.1	1.6	12.3	1.9	3.8	4.2	5.4	2.6	7.6	5.9	3.9	5.9	5.0
Cash Flow to Total Debt 44	0.1	•	0.7	0.5	0.9	0.8	0.4	0.6	0.3	0.3	0.3	0.1	0.1

Selected Financial Factors (in Percentages)

Debt Ratio 45	65.4	•	20.3	100.5	36.0	26.2	42.6	45.8	51.6	48.8	35.0	65.8	66.4
Return on Total Assets 46	4.6	•	1.6	36.5	6.3	13.8	10.5	18.6	8.4	7.2	5.7	5.7	4.3
Return on Equity Before Income Taxes 47	8.0	•	0.9	•	7.8	17.4	16.3	32.3	13.1	11.2	6.3	9.8	7.3
Return on Equity After Income Taxes 48	6.0	•	0.8	•	6.0	14.7	14.0	28.4	10.9	9.0	4.2	7.7	5.4
Profit Margin (Before Income Tax) 49	8.1	12.1	0.3	20.0	2.3	9.7	6.1	12.5	4.4	4.3	5.7	4.6	9.5
Profit Margin (After Income Tax) 50	6.1	10.5	0.3	19.8	1.8	8.2	5.3	10.9	3.6	3.5	3.8	3.6	7.0

84

Table I

Corporations with and without Net Income

RESIN, SYNTHETIC RUBBER AND FIBERS AND FILAMENTS

MONEY AMOUNTS AND SIZE OF ASSETS IN THOUSANDS OF DOLLARS

Item Description for Accounting Period 7/03 Through 6/04	Total	Zero Assets	Under 500	500 to 1,000	1,000 to 5,000	5,000 to 10,000	10,000 to 25,000	25,000 to 50,000	50,000 to 100,000	100,000 to 250,000	250,000 to 500,000	500,000 to 2,500,000	2,500,000 and over
Number of Enterprises 1	397	11	250	•	41	24	24	17	10	5	7	5	3
Revenues ($ in Thousands)													
Net Sales 2	34055287	0	0	•	161284	130536	576510	782747	973425	566777	1705132	6368528	22790347
Interest 3	1774639	723	0	•	3	695	585	1173	919	9187	16467	30053	1714833
Rents 4	71483	0	0	•	0	0	6	449	418	1278	555	4322	64454
Royalties 5	680928	0	0	•	0	2691	0	0	270	0	1411	13270	663287
Other Portfolio Income 6	230082	0	0	•	0	50	98	8170	5855	4564	29046	5449	176849
Other Receipts 7	1057403	3139	0	•	37	1825	4541	2800	4259	2054	15676	137265	885809
Total Receipts 8	37869822	3862	0	•	161324	135797	581740	795339	985146	583860	1768287	6558887	26295579
Average Total Receipts 9	95390	351	0	•	3935	5658	24239	46785	98515	116772	252612	1311777	8765193
Operating Costs/Operating Income (%)													
Cost of Operations 10	70.0	•	•	•	44.8	66.3	71.7	70.6	80.8	79.8	83.6	82.4	64.9
Salaries and Wages 11	2.6	•	•	•	2.0	8.4	6.4	6.3	3.6	5.3	3.9	5.2	1.5
Taxes Paid 12	0.8	•	•	•	1.4	0.9	1.6	1.3	1.2	1.3	1.1	0.7	0.7
Interest Paid 13	6.8	•	•	•	0.1	2.6	1.1	1.3	1.4	5.2	2.1	2.3	9.1
Depreciation 14	4.3	•	•	•	3.1	2.8	3.5	4.5	4.2	8.0	4.5	3.5	4.4
Amortization and Depletion 15	0.3	•	•	•	0.0	1.1	0.2	0.4	0.6	2.3	0.3	0.6	0.1
Pensions and Other Deferred Comp. 16	0.2	•	•	•	0.0	0.1	0.3	0.9	0.1	0.1	0.5	0.3	0.2
Employee Benefits 17	3.0	•	•	•	1.2	4.1	1.2	1.9	2.1	1.2	2.0	0.9	3.9
Advertising 18	0.3	•	•	•	0.1	0.5	0.6	0.2	0.2	0.1	0.1	0.0	0.4
Other Expenses 19	22.6	•	•	•	8.6	16.5	11.0	8.7	4.0	8.7	7.2	6.2	30.4
Officers' Compensation 20	0.2	•	•	•	1.2	0.9	2.0	1.8	1.0	1.2	0.7	0.2	0.1
Operating Margin 21	•	•	•	•	37.6	•	0.5	2.1	0.6	•	•	•	•
Operating Margin Before Officers' Comp. 22	•	•	•	•	38.8	•	2.5	4.0	1.6	•	•	•	•

Selected Average Balance Sheet ($ in Thousands)

Net Receivables 23	15953	0	0	329	1464	3078	7202	11261	18524	25509	162731	1630294
Inventories 24	10668	0	0	1334	828	3278	4561	11655	12422	25761	114653	1024037
Net Property, Plant and Equipment 25	37339	0	0	269	1744	5317	12255	26223	57944	107637	484869	3568383
Total Assets 26	261316	0	0	1764	6206	15007	33281	72349	162023	320031	1429726	30557600
Notes and Loans Payable 27	54915	0	0	257	2158	5265	11293	17481	61212	123696	509588	5842034
All Other Liabilities 28	93266	0	0	68	2045	4681	9763	24532	23608	41764	382874	11375481
Net Worth 29	113134	0	0	1440	2003	5061	12226	30336	77204	154571	537264	13340086

Selected Financial Ratios (Times to 1)

Current Ratio 30	1.0	•	•	4.6	1.3	1.4	1.6	1.1	1.1	1.5	2.6	0.8
Quick Ratio 31	0.6	•	•	3.2	0.7	0.8	1.0	0.6	0.6	0.8	2.0	0.5
Net Sales to Working Capital 32	•	•	•	3.4	6.6	10.1	7.2	28.0	32.8	8.3	3.7	•
Coverage Ratio 33	1.3	•	•	312.3	0.9	2.3	3.9	2.3	•	0.1	1.3	1.3
Total Asset Turnover 34	0.3	•	•	2.2	0.9	1.6	1.4	1.3	0.7	0.8	0.9	0.2
Inventory Turnover 35	5.6	•	•	1.3	4.4	5.3	7.1	6.7	7.3	7.9	9.2	4.8
Receivables Turnover 36	5.9	•	•	2.7	4.7	7.1	6.4	9.4	4.4	9.2	8.0	5.4
Total Liabilities to Net Worth 37	1.3	•	•	0.2	2.1	2.0	1.7	1.4	1.1	1.1	1.7	1.3
Current Assets to Working Capital 38	•	•	•	1.3	4.5	3.4	2.6	10.1	3.1	3.1	1.6	•
Current Liabilities to Working Capital 39	•	•	•	0.3	3.5	2.4	1.6	9.1	10.0	2.1	0.6	•
Working Capital to Net Sales 40	•	•	•	0.3	0.2	0.1	0.1	0.0	0.0	0.1	0.3	•
Inventory to Working Capital 41	•	•	•	0.4	1.2	1.3	0.7	3.7	3.2	1.0	0.3	•
Total Receipts to Cash Flow 42	5.1	•	•	2.3	7.0	9.2	9.2	22.0	•	25.2	17.1	3.8
Cost of Goods to Cash Flow 43	3.5	•	•	1.0	4.7	6.6	6.5	17.8	21.1	21.1	14.1	2.5
Cash Flow to Total Debt 44	0.1	•	•	5.4	0.2	0.3	0.2	0.1	0.1	0.1	0.1	0.1

Selected Financial Factors (in Percentages)

Debt Ratio 45	56.7	•	•	18.4	67.7	66.3	63.3	58.1	52.4	51.7	62.4	56.3
Return on Total Assets 46	3.0	•	•	84.2	2.2	4.0	6.8	4.4	•	0.2	2.7	3.0
Return on Equity Before Income Taxes 47	1.7	•	•	102.8	•	6.7	13.8	5.9	•	•	1.8	1.7
Return on Equity After Income Taxes 48	0.8	•	•	102.8	•	3.8	13.0	4.4	•	•	•	0.9
Profit Margin (Before Income Tax) 49	2.2	•	•	37.6	•	1.4	3.7	1.8	•	•	0.8	2.9
Profit Margin (After Income Tax) 50	1.0	•	•	37.6	•	0.8	3.5	1.4	•	•	•	1.6

Table II
Corporations with Net Income

RESIN, SYNTHETIC RUBBER AND FIBERS AND FILAMENTS

MONEY AMOUNTS AND SIZE OF ASSETS IN THOUSANDS OF DOLLARS

Item Description for Accounting Period 7/03 Through 6/04	Total	Zero Assets	Under 500	500 to 1,000	1,000 to 5,000	5,000 to 10,000	10,000 to 25,000	25,000 to 50,000	50,000 to 100,000	100,000 to 250,000	250,000 to 500,000	500,000 to 2,500,000	2,500,000 and over
Number of Enterprises 1	110	11	•	•	•	•	13	12	5	•	3	•	•
Revenues ($ in Thousands)													
Net Sales 2	25014615	0	•	•	•	•	354474	598962	527698	•	1099430	•	•
Interest 3	1731991	723	•	•	•	•	416	278	587	•	6720	•	•
Rents 4	24893	0	•	•	•	•	6	219	126	•	527	•	•
Royalties 5	667528	0	•	•	•	•	0	0	139	•	1411	•	•
Other Portfolio Income 6	213442	0	•	•	•	•	79	582	5065	•	27808	•	•
Other Receipts 7	910883	3139	•	•	•	•	3045	2430	4072	•	12086	•	•
Total Receipts 8	28563352	3862	•	•	•	•	358020	602471	537687	•	1147982	•	•
Average Total Receipts 9	259667	351	•	•	•	•	27540	50206	107537	•	382661	•	•
Operating Costs/Operating Income (%)													
Cost of Operations 10	63.5	•	•	•	•	•	64.5	67.6	80.1	•	86.3	•	•
Salaries and Wages 11	1.8	•	•	•	•	•	7.4	7.4	4.4	•	3.3	•	•
Taxes Paid 12	0.8	•	•	•	•	•	2.0	1.3	1.3	•	1.3	•	•
Interest Paid 13	8.1	•	•	•	•	•	0.9	1.1	0.4	•	0.7	•	•
Depreciation 14	4.5	•	•	•	•	•	3.0	3.9	3.8	•	1.6	•	•
Amortization and Depletion 15	0.1	•	•	•	•	•	0.2	0.4	0.0	•	0.0	•	•
Pensions and Other Deferred Comp. 16	0.2	•	•	•	•	•	0.2	0.5	0.2	•	0.6	•	•
Employee Benefits 17	3.8	•	•	•	•	•	0.9	1.7	1.6	•	2.0	•	•
Advertising 18	0.4	•	•	•	•	•	0.7	0.3	0.4	•	0.1	•	•
Other Expenses 19	28.4	•	•	•	•	•	14.1	7.7	2.3	•	6.2	•	•
Officers' Compensation 20	0.2	•	•	•	•	•	2.3	1.8	0.7	•	0.7	•	•
Operating Margin 21	•	•	•	•	•	•	3.8	6.3	4.9	•	•	•	•
Operating Margin Before Officers' Comp. 22	•	•	•	•	•	•	6.2	8.1	5.6	•	•	•	•

Selected Average Balance Sheet ($ in Thousands)

Net Receivables 23	49348	0	3181	7121	13176	40533
Inventories 24	27917	0	3622	4330	10796	39717
Net Property, Plant and Equipment 25	89841	0	4386	10938	23916	118595
Total Assets 26	844531	0	13863	33801	69511	341107
Notes and Loans Payable 27	148117	0	4357	9627	8525	89457
All Other Liabilities 28	312448	0	3285	7723	20621	40339
Net Worth 29	383965	0	6221	16451	40365	211309

Selected Financial Ratios (Times to 1)

Current Ratio 30	1.0		1.7	1.9	1.9	2.9
Quick Ratio 31	0.7		1.0	1.1	1.2	2.0
Net Sales to Working Capital 32	1132.1		8.1	6.0	5.7	4.0
Coverage Ratio 33	1.7		6.3	7.5	17.7	4.5
Total Asset Turnover 34	0.3		2.0	1.5	1.5	1.1
Inventory Turnover 35	5.2		4.9	7.8	7.8	8.0
Receivables Turnover 36	5.2		6.9	7.7	4.7	18.1
Total Liabilities to Net Worth 37	1.2		1.2	1.1	0.7	0.6
Current Assets to Working Capital 38	499.1		2.4	2.1	2.1	1.5
Current Liabilities to Working Capital 39	498.1		1.4	1.1	1.1	0.5
Working Capital to Net Sales 40	0.0		0.1	0.2	0.2	0.2
Inventory to Working Capital 41	139.2		0.9	0.6	0.6	0.4
Total Receipts to Cash Flow 42	3.7		5.8	7.8	14.1	13.8
Cost of Goods to Cash Flow 43	2.3		3.8	5.2	11.3	11.9
Cash Flow to Total Debt 44	0.1		0.6	0.4	0.3	0.2

Selected Financial Factors (in Percentages)

Debt Ratio 45	54.5		55.1	51.3	41.9	38.1
Return on Total Assets 46	3.6		11.3	11.6	10.9	3.4
Return on Equity Before Income Taxes 47	3.1		21.2	20.7	17.7	4.3
Return on Equity After Income Taxes 48	2.2		16.8	19.8	15.4	3.2
Profit Margin (Before Income Tax) 49	5.3		4.8	6.8	6.8	2.5
Profit Margin (After Income Tax) 50	3.7		3.8	6.5	5.9	1.8

Table I
Corporations with and without Net Income

PHARMACEUTICAL AND MEDICINE

MONEY AMOUNTS AND SIZE OF ASSETS IN THOUSANDS OF DOLLARS

Item Description for Accounting Period 7/03 Through 6/04	Total	Zero Assets	Under 500	500 to 1,000	1,000 to 5,000	5,000 to 10,000	10,000 to 25,000	25,000 to 50,000	50,000 to 100,000	100,000 to 250,000	250,000 to 500,000	500,000 to 2,500,000	2,500,000 and over
Number of Enterprises 1	1120	34	330	67	257	125	85	56	48	47	13	33	24

Revenues ($ in Thousands)

Net Sales 2	273870756	23523	49963	222050	1142207	1078688	1485350	1785215	2257181	5212465	3028995	25977957	231607163
Interest 3	4973248	39280	186	140	1715	2751	5461	9920	21646	35866	15300	238775	4602208
Rents 4	250659	2052	0	0	1988	235	993	116	691	2558	98	9959	231969
Royalties 5	18066448	32448	0	0	1287	543	583	4169	23224	43514	4452	829663	17124765
Other Portfolio Income 6	12286386	8635	0	0	5205	32302	2401	24689	81941	23821	572	340690	11766128
Other Receipts 7	15728002	456178	0	51	26278	7808	37311	55527	90864	195058	169261	673670	14015997
Total Receipts 8	325173699	562116	50149	222241	1178680	1122327	1532099	1879636	2475547	5513282	3218678	28070714	279334230
Average Total Receipts 9	290334	16533	152	3317	4586	8979	18025	33565	51574	117304	247591	850628	11639510

Operating Costs/Operating Income (%)

Cost of Operations 10	53.7	42.5	5.3	63.6	64.8	61.3	62.6	49.7	53.9	38.7	30.1	44.0	55.4
Salaries and Wages 11	13.5	52.3	40.1	10.5	9.6	8.9	13.2	14.4	13.7	13.1	10.4	11.2	13.8
Taxes Paid 12	1.6	69.2	3.0	3.2	2.9	3.3	2.6	2.2	2.5	2.2	2.3	1.7	1.5
Interest Paid 13	3.5	3.8	0.6	0.8	0.7	1.8	1.3	1.5	2.2	1.7	2.6	2.3	3.8
Depreciation 14	3.0	23.6	2.6	1.7	4.1	5.2	4.1	4.8	4.8	3.4	2.4	2.3	3.1
Amortization and Depletion 15	1.1	2.1	8.4	0.0	0.7	0.5	1.7	2.0	1.5	1.4	2.3	1.2	1.0
Pensions and Other Deferred Comp. 16	1.5	0.6	•	•	0.3	0.1	0.2	0.6	0.6	0.6	0.1	0.7	1.7
Employee Benefits 17	1.8	6.1	0.3	1.9	2.3	1.2	1.7	2.1	2.6	2.2	1.7	1.9	1.8
Advertising 18	4.1	2.7	0.1	0.1	0.2	0.5	1.7	3.9	2.3	2.4	1.1	3.4	4.3
Other Expenses 19	23.5	1859.2	65.1	20.3	18.2	21.7	24.5	27.0	29.7	31.5	29.5	23.3	23.0
Officers' Compensation 20	0.5	18.8	•	3.1	8.3	3.7	4.1	3.6	3.3	2.1	2.7	1.0	0.3
Operating Margin 21	•	•	•	•	•	•	•	•	•	0.7	14.7	7.1	•
Operating Margin Before Officers' Comp. 22	•	•	•	•	•	•	•	•	•	2.8	17.5	8.0	•

Selected Average Balance Sheet ($ in Thousands)

Net Receivables 23	120228	0	1	192	394	1427	2470	5646	9540	19592	35628	157766	5282866
Inventories 24	27464	0	10	260	618	798	2446	4833	8203	13996	42581	111823	1029411
Net Property, Plant and Equipment 25	58737	0	15	87	1213	1819	3945	8208	14732	26266	35038	145688	2384826
Total Assets 26	604168	0	131	711	2695	6623	16559	36734	75128	166041	332182	1153140	25742119
Notes and Loans Payable 27	244120	0	110	237	825	6058	4120	8817	19186	36876	54664	280842	10788190
All Other Liabilities 28	158350	0	25	289	489	1594	5886	11262	12226	30416	83977	243093	6864083
Net Worth 29	201699	0	-5	186	1381	-1030	6553	16655	43716	98749	193541	629205	8089846

Selected Financial Ratios (Times to 1)

Current Ratio 30	0.9	•	3.3	2.3	2.1	2.4	1.7	2.2	2.3	2.7	2.7	2.4	0.9
Quick Ratio 31	0.7	•	1.9	1.4	1.2	1.5	1.1	1.5	1.6	1.6	1.4	1.3	0.6
Net Sales to Working Capital 32	•	•	2.1	9.5	5.8	3.8	4.1	2.6	2.0	2.0	1.8	2.6	•
Coverage Ratio 33	5.1	81.6	•	•	•	•	•	•	•	4.9	9.2	7.8	5.0
Total Asset Turnover 34	0.4	•	1.2	4.7	1.6	1.3	1.1	0.9	0.6	0.7	0.7	0.7	0.4
Inventory Turnover 35	4.8	•	0.8	8.1	4.7	6.6	4.5	3.3	3.1	3.1	1.6	3.1	5.2
Receivables Turnover 36	2.4	•	52.3	19.4	7.4	7.2	7.0	5.5	4.6	5.5	4.5	5.6	2.2
Total Liabilities to Net Worth 37	2.0	•	•	2.8	1.0	•	1.5	1.2	0.7	0.7	0.7	0.8	2.2
Current Assets to Working Capital 38	•	•	1.4	1.8	1.9	1.7	2.4	1.9	1.7	1.6	1.6	1.7	•
Current Liabilities to Working Capital 39	•	•	0.4	0.8	0.9	0.7	1.4	0.9	0.7	0.6	0.6	0.7	•
Working Capital to Net Sales 40	•	•	0.5	0.1	0.2	0.3	0.2	0.4	0.5	0.5	0.6	0.4	•
Inventory to Working Capital 41	•	•	0.1	0.6	0.7	0.5	0.6	0.4	0.3	0.3	0.2	0.4	•
Total Receipts to Cash Flow 42	3.3	•	3.0	11.9	17.0	8.3	17.4	6.0	8.4	2.8	2.1	2.8	3.3
Cost of Goods to Cash Flow 43	1.8	•	0.2	7.6	11.0	5.1	10.9	3.0	4.5	1.1	0.6	1.2	1.8
Cash Flow to Total Debt 44	0.2	•	0.4	0.5	0.2	0.1	0.1	0.3	0.2	0.6	0.8	0.5	0.2

Selected Financial Factors (in Percentages)

Debt Ratio 45	66.6	•	103.6	73.9	48.8	115.6	60.4	54.7	41.8	40.5	41.7	45.4	68.6
Return on Total Assets 46	7.2	•	•	•	•	•	•	•	•	5.5	16.8	12.1	7.0
Return on Equity Before Income Taxes 47	17.3	•	806.8	•	•	34.6	•	•	7.4	7.4	25.8	19.3	17.9
Return on Equity After Income Taxes 48	11.1	•	806.8	•	•	39.8	•	•	0.5	0.5	16.2	11.8	11.8
Profit Margin (Before Income Tax) 49	14.3	308.9	•	•	•	•	•	•	6.6	6.6	21.4	15.4	15.0
Profit Margin (After Income Tax) 50	9.2	15.0	•	•	•	•	•	•	0.5	0.5	13.4	9.4	9.9

Table II
Corporations with Net Income

PHARMACEUTICAL AND MEDICINE

MONEY AMOUNTS AND SIZE OF ASSETS IN THOUSANDS OF DOLLARS

Item Description for Accounting Period 7/03 Through 6/04	Total	Zero Assets	Under 500	500 to 1,000	1,000 to 5,000	5,000 to 10,000	10,000 to 25,000	25,000 to 50,000	50,000 to 100,000	100,000 to 250,000	250,000 to 500,000	500,000 to 2,500,000	2,500,000 and over
Number of Enterprises 1	553	11	61	55	170	87	42	26	23	27	8	22	21
Revenues ($ in Thousands)													
Net Sales 2	248004084	0	44329	221944	1038266	792707	1096306	1245591	1687560	4324857	2740694	23277388	211534442
Interest 3	4557264	38518	161	0	259	2017	1327	3597	7709	8839	4706	150660	4339471
Rents 4	182816	2052	0	0	1988	228	150	116	414	28	98	9164	168578
Royalties 5	17053048	32353	0	0	0	0	570	1024	15914	14884	4319	551843	16432142
Other Portfolio Income 6	12092803	0	0	0	12	32123	1521	2074	53591	22446	69	268072	11712892
Other Receipts 7	14002951	456137	1	0	24755	4557	16457	44275	57004	147899	2832	489023	12760014
Total Receipts 8	295892966	529060	44491	221944	1065280	831632	1116331	1296677	1822192	4518953	2752718	24746150	256947539
Average Total Receipts 9	535069	48096	729	4035	6266	9559	26579	49872	79226	167369	344090	1124825	12235597
Operating Costs/Operating Income (%)													
Cost of Operations 10	53.4	•	•	63.6	64.1	57.8	62.5	46.3	42.3	36.0	29.6	44.5	55.1
Salaries and Wages 11	13.0	•	20.1	8.1	6.1	7.4	6.8	12.3	9.9	8.2	7.0	9.7	13.7
Taxes Paid 12	1.5	•	1.2	2.9	2.4	3.3	1.6	2.1	2.2	1.8	1.9	1.5	1.5
Interest Paid 13	3.4	•	•	0.7	0.4	0.6	0.8	1.0	1.5	0.9	2.2	1.5	3.7
Depreciation 14	2.8	•	•	1.2	3.2	3.5	2.6	3.9	3.5	2.2	1.9	1.9	2.9
Amortization and Depletion 15	0.9	•	•	•	0.1	0.0	0.3	0.3	0.8	0.8	1.6	0.6	1.0
Pensions and Other Deferred Comp. 16	1.6	•	•	•	0.3	0.1	0.2	0.7	0.6	0.6	0.1	0.7	1.8
Employee Benefits 17	1.8	•	0.3	1.9	1.9	1.0	1.1	1.5	1.9	1.7	1.3	1.8	1.8
Advertising 18	4.1	•	•	0.1	0.1	0.5	0.6	4.9	2.7	2.1	1.0	3.5	4.3
Other Expenses 19	21.8	•	30.4	13.7	11.4	15.9	11.9	15.6	21.3	24.4	23.8	19.2	22.0
Officers' Compensation 20	0.4	•	•	1.7	7.3	2.9	2.9	2.5	2.2	1.2	1.6	0.9	0.3
Operating Margin 21	•	•	48.0	6.1	2.6	6.7	8.8	8.8	11.0	19.9	28.1	14.2	•
Operating Margin Before Officers' Comp. 22	•	•	48.0	7.9	10.0	9.7	11.7	11.3	13.2	21.1	29.7	15.1	•

Selected Average Balance Sheet ($ in Thousands)

	1	2	3	4	5	6	7	8	9	10	11	12
Net Receivables 23	228855	0	234	528	1620	3047	7311	10479	25042	38314	177743	5755286
Inventories 24	48396	0	317	639	1244	3146	7361	11436	19781	52158	159933	1023687
Net Property, Plant and Equipment 25	101009	0	55	1425	1466	3669	9103	17657	21737	30297	167505	2389236
Total Assets 26	1120333	454	694	2941	6583	15535	36410	75014	159738	326252	1200449	27702299
Notes and Loans Payable 27	443506	0	287	893	6953	4433	7766	11966	32396	34834	129092	11420458
All Other Liabilities 28	292648	0	291	434	1184	3960	8989	13817	31280	103130	282615	7287464
Net Worth 29	384178	454	116	1614	-1554	7143	19655	49231	96062	188288	788741	8994377

Selected Financial Ratios (Times to 1)

	1	2	3	4	5	6	7	8	9	10	11	12
Current Ratio 30	0.9	•	2.2	3.1	1.8	2.2	2.9	2.2	1.9	2.2	0.8	
Quick Ratio 31	0.6	•	1.1	2.0	1.0	1.4	1.7	1.2	1.2	1.1	0.6	
Net Sales to Working Capital 32	•	1.8	11.6	6.0	3.1	3.7	2.8	3.5	4.1	3.3	•	
Coverage Ratio 33	6.4	560.9	9.9	12.8	20.2	14.6	13.9	13.5	27.1	14.4	14.8	5.7
Total Asset Turnover 34	0.4	1.6	5.8	2.1	1.7	1.3	1.0	1.0	0.9	1.1	0.4	
Inventory Turnover 35	5.0	•	8.1	6.1	4.2	5.2	2.7	2.9	2.9	1.9	5.4	
Receivables Turnover 36	2.3	•	19.4	10.6	11.2	8.4	6.3	5.6	5.8	5.0	5.9	2.1
Total Liabilities to Net Worth 37	1.9	•	5.0	0.8	1.2	0.9	0.5	0.7	0.7	0.5	2.1	
Current Assets to Working Capital 38	•	1.0	1.8	1.5	2.3	1.8	1.5	1.8	2.2	1.8	2.1	
Current Liabilities to Working Capital 39	•	•	0.8	0.5	1.3	0.8	0.5	0.8	1.2	0.8	•	
Working Capital to Net Sales 40	•	0.5	0.1	0.2	0.2	0.3	0.4	0.3	0.2	0.3	•	
Inventory to Working Capital 41	•	•	0.8	0.7	0.7	0.6	0.4	0.5	0.5	0.6	•	
Total Receipts to Cash Flow 42	3.1	•	7.3	6.8	4.4	5.0	3.7	2.9	2.1	1.9	2.7	3.2
Cost of Goods to Cash Flow 43	1.6	•	4.6	4.4	2.5	3.1	1.7	1.2	0.8	0.6	1.2	1.8
Cash Flow to Total Debt 44	0.2	•	1.0	0.7	0.3	0.6	0.8	1.0	1.2	1.3	1.0	0.2

Selected Financial Factors (in Percentages)

	1	2	3	4	5	6	7	8	9	10	11	12
Debt Ratio 45	65.7	•	83.3	45.1	123.6	54.0	46.0	34.4	39.9	42.3	34.3	67.5
Return on Total Assets 46	8.6	77.5	39.7	11.8	16.9	18.2	20.3	25.5	32.7	19.8	7.8	
Return on Equity Before Income Taxes 47	21.2	77.5	213.3	19.9	•	31.3	28.6	40.9	52.7	28.0	19.7	
Return on Equity After Income Taxes 48	14.5	77.5	213.3	19.0	•	35.2	26.6	22.6	28.7	36.7	19.0	13.5
Profit Margin (Before Income Tax) 49	18.1	48.4	6.1	5.2	11.6	10.7	12.8	19.2	24.5	29.0	20.9	17.6
Profit Margin (After Income Tax) 50	12.4	48.4	6.1	5.0	10.7	9.6	10.9	15.1	17.2	20.1	14.2	12.1

Table I

Corporations with and without Net Income

PAINT, COATING, AND ADHESIVE

MONEY AMOUNTS AND SIZE OF ASSETS IN THOUSANDS OF DOLLARS

Item Description for Accounting Period 7/03 Through 6/04		Total	Zero Assets	Under 500	500 to 1,000	1,000 to 5,000	5,000 to 10,000	10,000 to 25,000	25,000 to 50,000	50,000 to 100,000	100,000 to 250,000	250,000 to 500,000	500,000 to 2,500,000	2,500,000 and over
Number of Enterprises	1	1692	191	363	345	531	136	60	32	13	6	6	6	3
Revenues ($ in Thousands)														
Net Sales	2	34268327	102296	83740	534738	1863772	2429888	1902431	1606118	1288210	1249545	1983610	6356265	14867713
Interest	3	174432	41	0	29	1420	966	1587	992	1110	10621	4228	36571	116866
Rents	4	9133	0	0	0	26	145	1182	746	105	62	2793	760	3314
Royalties	5	382836	0	0	0	0	293	6	1232	595	0	31357	103652	245701
Other Portfolio Income	6	441511	95	0	0	6294	742	1740	1047	1977	1830	9051	51659	367078
Other Receipts	7	257828	116	5637	45	35965	3900	14046	7263	4692	6724	14959	38615	125867
Total Receipts	8	35534067	102548	89377	534812	1907477	2435934	1920992	1617398	1296689	1268782	2045998	6587522	15726539
Average Total Receipts	9	21001	537	246	1550	3592	17911	32017	50544	99745	211464	341000	1097920	5242180
Operating Costs/Operating Income (%)														
Cost of Operations	10	58.5	61.8	54.4	64.7	56.0	63.3	65.5	59.9	70.9	59.8	60.7	64.3	52.7
Salaries and Wages	11	11.1	20.8	11.4	5.1	10.8	5.6	10.6	9.8	7.9	12.4	12.5	8.5	13.4
Taxes Paid	12	2.1	2.7	2.7	2.0	2.4	3.1	1.7	1.7	1.9	1.7	2.0	1.6	2.4
Interest Paid	13	2.3	0.3	3.4	0.6	0.8	0.8	0.8	0.6	0.8	2.5	3.9	3.5	2.7
Depreciation	14	2.9	0.8	0.9	3.7	1.7	2.2	2.1	2.6	3.4	2.3	3.5	2.9	3.1
Amortization and Depletion	15	0.7	0.2	•	0.0	0.1	0.1	0.2	0.3	0.2	0.9	1.5	1.0	0.7
Pensions and Other Deferred Comp.	16	1.6	•	•	0.9	0.2	0.5	0.5	0.5	1.0	3.0	0.6	1.8	2.2
Employee Benefits	17	2.2	0.3	4.5	0.6	2.0	2.1	1.1	1.7	1.5	1.7	1.7	1.5	3.1
Advertising	18	1.6	0.5	0.1	0.3	1.2	2.0	1.0	1.2	0.7	0.7	1.3	1.0	2.3
Other Expenses	19	15.0	16.8	26.0	18.4	16.2	11.4	12.5	15.3	9.2	11.5	13.9	14.4	16.8
Officers' Compensation	20	1.5	1.6	4.0	10.5	7.0	5.1	2.1	2.2	1.3	1.2	1.1	0.4	0.3
Operating Margin	21	0.5	•	•	•	1.6	3.9	1.9	4.1	1.4	2.4	•	•	•
Operating Margin Before Officers' Comp.	22	2.0	•	•	3.9	8.6	9.1	4.0	6.3	2.7	3.6	•	•	0.7

Selected Average Balance Sheet ($ in Thousands)

Net Receivables 23	3036	0	26	165	483	2233	4090	7830	14301	28477	39779	209300	720760
Inventories 24	1883	0	31	166	378	957	4327	5513	10247	24903	34422	87418	445498
Net Property, Plant and Equipment 25	3831	0	10	123	329	1932	3650	8361	23088	29227	63700	240458	1070448
Total Assets 26	19256	0	71	668	1728	6642	15614	33788	73730	149532	346618	1480166	5223224
Notes and Loans Payable 27	4672	0	34	320	620	2271	4175	7388	18763	22594	115740	569500	722213
All Other Liabilities 28	7876	0	38	130	623	2159	3956	8420	18891	50208	73931	453795	2807630
Net Worth 29	6708	0	-1	218	485	2212	7484	17980	36076	76730	156946	456872	1693381

Selected Financial Ratios (Times to 1)

Current Ratio 30	1.4	•	1.6	1.5	1.4	1.1	2.0	2.2	1.7	1.8	2.3	1.0	1.4
Quick Ratio 31	0.7	•	0.8	0.8	0.9	0.7	1.1	1.4	1.0	0.8	1.1	0.6	0.7
Net Sales to Working Capital 32	11.0	•	10.2	13.6	9.6	55.5	6.1	5.1	6.9	6.1	5.9	71.1	10.6
Coverage Ratio 33	3.0	•	0.8	•	5.6	6.3	4.6	9.0	3.5	2.6	1.2	2.0	3.6
Total Asset Turnover 34	1.1	•	3.2	2.3	2.0	2.7	2.0	1.5	1.3	1.4	1.0	0.7	0.9
Inventory Turnover 35	6.3	•	4.0	6.0	5.2	11.8	4.8	5.5	6.9	5.0	5.8	7.8	5.9
Receivables Turnover 36	6.4	•	8.1	9.0	7.2	10.0	7.9	6.8	7.7	5.8	9.2	4.6	6.3
Total Liabilities to Net Worth 37	1.9	•	•	2.1	2.6	2.0	1.1	0.9	1.0	0.9	1.2	2.2	2.1
Current Assets to Working Capital 38	3.6	•	2.7	3.1	3.3	12.0	2.0	1.8	2.5	2.3	1.8	25.9	3.5
Current Liabilities to Working Capital 39	2.6	•	1.7	2.1	2.3	11.0	1.0	0.8	1.5	1.3	0.8	24.9	2.5
Working Capital to Net Sales 40	0.1	•	0.1	0.1	0.1	0.0	0.2	0.2	0.1	0.2	0.2	0.0	0.1
Inventory to Working Capital 41	1.0	•	1.3	1.2	1.0	3.2	0.8	0.6	0.9	0.6	0.7	5.9	1.0
Total Receipts to Cash Flow 42	6.8	9.8	4.1	12.5	6.0	9.6	7.9	5.4	9.9	8.5	8.5	6.5	6.3
Cost of Goods to Cash Flow 43	4.0	6.1	2.2	8.1	3.3	6.1	5.2	3.3	7.0	5.1	5.2	4.2	3.3
Cash Flow to Total Debt 44	0.2	•	0.8	0.3	0.5	0.4	0.5	0.6	0.3	0.2	0.2	0.2	0.2

Selected Financial Factors (in Percentages)

Debt Ratio 45	65.2	•	101.2	67.3	71.9	66.7	52.1	46.8	51.1	48.7	54.7	69.1	67.6
Return on Total Assets 46	7.3	•	8.4	•	9.5	13.4	7.6	8.2	3.8	9.0	4.4	4.9	9.0
Return on Equity Before Income Taxes 47	14.0	•	222.0	•	27.9	33.8	12.4	13.7	5.5	10.8	1.4	7.8	20.1
Return on Equity After Income Taxes 48	10.2	•	222.0	•	24.4	30.9	9.8	10.9	3.7	10.7	0.0	4.5	14.7
Profit Margin (Before Income Tax) 49	4.6	•	•	•	3.9	4.2	2.9	4.9	2.0	4.0	0.7	3.4	6.9
Profit Margin (After Income Tax) 50	3.4	•	•	•	3.4	3.8	2.3	3.9	1.3	3.9	0.0	1.9	5.0

Table II

Corporations with Net Income

PAINT, COATING, AND ADHESIVE

MONEY AMOUNTS AND SIZE OF ASSETS IN THOUSANDS OF DOLLARS

Item Description for Accounting Period 7/03 Through 6/04	Total	Zero Assets	Under 500	500 to 1,000	1,000 to 5,000	5,000 to 10,000	10,000 to 25,000	25,000 to 50,000	50,000 to 100,000	100,000 to 250,000	250,000 to 500,000	500,000 to 2,500,000	2,500,000 and over
Number of Enterprises **1**	808	•	98	122	•	•	41	24	•	•	•	•	•
Revenues ($ in Thousands)													
Net Sales **2**	29182841	•	62512	423038	•	•	1361682	1293178	•	•	•	•	•
Interest **3**	151711	•	0	29	•	•	1024	797	•	•	•	•	•
Rents **4**	7899	•	0	0	•	•	124	684	•	•	•	•	•
Royalties **5**	345751	•	0	0	•	•	0	1119	•	•	•	•	•
Other Portfolio Income **6**	434044	•	0	0	•	•	1382	491	•	•	•	•	•
Other Receipts **7**	238417	•	5637	1	•	•	9152	6931	•	•	•	•	•
Total Receipts **8**	30360663	•	68149	423068	•	•	1373364	1303200	•	•	•	•	•
Average Total Receipts **9**	37575	•	695	3468	•	•	33497	54300	•	•	•	•	•
Operating Costs/Operating Income (%)													
Cost of Operations **10**	56.9	•	66.0	66.1	•	•	63.6	56.9	•	•	•	•	•
Salaries and Wages **11**	11.4	•	11.6	4.0	•	•	9.9	9.5	•	•	•	•	•
Taxes Paid **12**	2.1	•	1.6	1.9	•	•	1.6	1.7	•	•	•	•	•
Interest Paid **13**	2.1	•	0.2	0.2	•	•	0.7	0.3	•	•	•	•	•
Depreciation **14**	2.8	•	1.3	0.6	•	•	2.2	2.2	•	•	•	•	•
Amortization and Depletion **15**	0.6	•	•	0.0	•	•	0.1	0.1	•	•	•	•	•
Pensions and Other Deferred Comp. **16**	1.7	•	•	1.2	•	•	0.6	0.5	•	•	•	•	•
Employee Benefits **17**	2.3	•	3.6	0.7	•	•	0.9	1.6	•	•	•	•	•
Advertising **18**	1.8	•	•	0.2	•	•	0.9	1.5	•	•	•	•	•
Other Expenses **19**	15.0	•	18.2	13.4	•	•	12.5	16.0	•	•	•	•	•
Officers' Compensation **20**	1.4	•	5.4	11.7	•	•	2.3	2.4	•	•	•	•	•
Operating Margin **21**	1.8	•	•	0.1	•	•	4.9	7.3	•	•	•	•	•
Operating Margin Before Officers' Comp. **22**	3.2	•	•	11.8	•	•	7.2	9.7	•	•	•	•	•

Selected Average Balance Sheet ($ in Thousands)

Net Receivables 23	5491	•	94	328	•	•	4223	7901
Inventories 24	3197	•	105	312	•	•	4600	5327
Net Property, Plant and Equipment 25	6820	•	37	61	•	•	3548	8222
Total Assets 26	34706	•	240	727	•	•	15548	33576
Notes and Loans Payable 27	7022	•	0	166	•	•	3798	4398
All Other Liabilities 28	14502	•	140	283	•	•	3719	6983
Net Worth 29	13182	•	100	278	•	•	8030	22196

Selected Financial Ratios (Times to 1)

Current Ratio 30	1.4	•	1.4	1.9	•	•	2.3	2.7
Quick Ratio 31	0.8	•	0.7	1.2	•	•	1.3	1.7
Net Sales to Working Capital 32	9.9	•	10.5	11.2	•	•	5.4	4.5
Coverage Ratio 33	3.9	•	5.5	1.6	•	•	9.8	26.6
Total Asset Turnover 34	1.0	•	2.7	4.8	•	•	2.1	1.6
Inventory Turnover 35	6.4	•	4.0	7.4	•	•	4.6	5.8
Receivables Turnover 36	6.4	•	13.5	10.2	•	•	7.4	7.5
Total Liabilities to Net Worth 37	1.6	•	1.4	1.6	•	•	0.9	0.5
Current Assets to Working Capital 38	3.3	•	3.3	2.1	•	•	1.7	1.6
Current Liabilities to Working Capital 39	2.3	•	2.3	1.1	•	•	0.7	0.6
Working Capital to Net Sales 40	0.1	•	0.1	0.1	•	•	0.2	0.2
Inventory to Working Capital 41	0.9	•	1.7	0.6	•	•	0.7	0.5
Total Receipts to Cash Flow 42	6.1	•	5.2	8.2	•	•	6.3	4.5
Cost of Goods to Cash Flow 43	3.5	•	3.4	5.4	•	•	4.0	2.6
Cash Flow to Total Debt 44	0.3	•	0.9	0.9	•	•	0.7	1.1

Selected Financial Factors (in Percentages)

Debt Ratio 45	62.0	•	58.2	61.8	•	•	48.4	33.9
Return on Total Assets 46	8.8	•	3.1	1.6	•	•	13.8	13.6
Return on Equity Before Income Taxes 47	17.2	•	6.0	1.5	•	•	24.0	19.7
Return on Equity After Income Taxes 48	13.1	•	6.0	1.4	•	•	20.4	16.6
Profit Margin (Before Income Tax) 49	6.3	•	0.9	0.1	•	•	5.8	8.1
Profit Margin (After Income Tax) 50	4.8	•	0.9	0.1	•	•	4.9	6.9

Table I

Corporations with and without Net Income

SOAP, CLEANING COMPOUND, AND TOILET PREPARATION

MONEY AMOUNTS AND SIZE OF ASSETS IN THOUSANDS OF DOLLARS

Item Description for Accounting Period 7/03 Through 6/04		Total	Zero Assets	Under 500	500 to 1,000	1,000 to 5,000	5,000 to 10,000	10,000 to 25,000	25,000 to 50,000	50,000 to 100,000	100,000 to 250,000	250,000 to 500,000	500,000 to 2,500,000	2,500,000 and over
Number of Enterprises	1	2228	279	1161	348	288	31	50	26	12	9	7	8	9
Revenues ($ in Thousands)														
Net Sales	2	106226443	62376	669200	518919	2670347	430360	1489030	1703558	1181568	1480041	2954725	9961915	83104404
Interest	3	934297	5090	85	185	400	2270	3545	1784	1380	3269	1513	91578	823199
Rents	4	95362	0	0	28	2204	110	470	565	61	134	1954	49681	40155
Royalties	5	2464279	3	0	0	3910	419	1275	465	135	143	25120	301070	2131740
Other Portfolio Income	6	2972431	291680	6	172	7110	204	7482	1682	2569	20667	12380	511593	2116884
Other Receipts	7	1353389	6565	14621	787	5591	1168	3282	1572	38066	-1383	4813	182466	1095841
Total Receipts	8	114046201	365714	683912	520091	2689562	434531	1505084	1709626	1223779	1502871	3000505	11098303	89312223
Average Total Receipts	9	51188	1311	589	1495	9339	14017	30102	65755	101982	166986	428644	1387288	9923580
Operating Costs/Operating Income (%)														
Cost of Operations	10	61.4	40.4	53.9	56.1	54.3	62.8	61.2	59.8	62.4	45.5	56.7	43.0	64.4
Salaries and Wages	11	6.9	2.5	13.3	11.0	12.1	8.6	9.4	8.6	7.4	7.4	10.0	14.2	5.5
Taxes Paid	12	1.0	3.3	1.8	3.0	1.1	2.0	1.7	1.7	1.6	1.0	1.4	1.9	0.9
Interest Paid	13	2.7	•	3.5	0.7	0.4	1.0	1.2	0.9	1.8	1.4	1.7	2.7	2.9
Depreciation	14	2.3	2.8	1.7	1.8	1.0	2.4	2.4	1.9	2.5	3.0	3.7	2.1	2.4
Amortization and Depletion	15	1.2	2.2	0.0	0.0	0.0	0.2	0.4	0.3	0.8	0.6	0.9	1.5	1.3
Pensions and Other Deferred Comp.	16	1.3	•	0.1	2.4	1.0	0.3	0.5	0.2	0.5	0.5	0.6	2.3	1.3
Employee Benefits	17	1.4	1.5	1.2	3.1	0.8	1.0	1.5	1.4	1.2	1.1	1.2	2.7	1.3
Advertising	18	5.5	21.0	0.3	0.2	8.2	1.1	2.2	4.7	3.6	15.5	5.3	5.1	5.4
Other Expenses	19	14.3	20.9	22.8	12.7	11.5	18.1	15.2	13.0	11.5	14.0	16.3	24.0	13.1
Officers' Compensation	20	0.9	•	5.6	10.7	3.5	2.7	2.1	3.1	1.5	1.3	0.8	1.5	0.6
Operating Margin	21	1.1	5.2	•	•	6.1	•	2.1	4.3	5.4	8.8	1.5	•	1.0
Operating Margin Before Officers' Comp.	22	2.0	5.2	1.4	8.9	9.6	2.7	4.2	7.3	6.9	10.0	2.3	0.4	1.6

Selected Average Balance Sheet ($ in Thousands)

Net Receivables 23	10043	0	68	165	1344	1592	4132	9660	13682	18834	54961	162754	2147155
Inventories 24	3068	0	70	115	549	4649	3606	7254	14613	17060	43918	167897	451597
Net Property, Plant and Equipment 25	6783	0	23	85	413	988	4166	8321	11960	35222	80738	156864	1355636
Total Assets 26	65750	0	227	638	3210	7171	16596	37614	69596	154739	333834	1457889	14091498
Notes and Loans Payable 27	23940	0	364	122	539	1637	5205	11780	22648	58092	109278	504642	5167195
All Other Liabilities 28	15535	0	84	81	977	2270	4666	9835	17614	33376	78160	434952	3234189
Net Worth 29	26275	0	-221	435	1693	3264	6726	15998	29335	63271	146396	518296	5690114

Selected Financial Ratios (Times to 1)

Current Ratio 30	1.0	•	2.1	5.5	2.3	2.3	1.7	1.7	2.2	1.1	1.6	1.5	0.9
Quick Ratio 31	0.7	•	1.2	2.3	1.4	1.1	0.9	0.9	1.3	0.5	0.7	0.6	0.7
Net Sales to Working Capital 32	87.4	•	5.4	3.4	6.6	4.8	7.5	6.8	4.5	31.6	8.7	7.0	•
Coverage Ratio 33	4.9	•	0.4	•	18.5	1.9	3.7	6.4	6.0	8.4	3.0	6.0	4.6
Total Asset Turnover 34	0.7	•	2.5	2.3	2.9	1.9	1.8	1.7	1.4	1.1	1.3	0.9	0.7
Inventory Turnover 35	9.5	•	4.5	7.3	9.2	1.9	5.1	5.4	4.2	4.4	5.5	3.2	13.2
Receivables Turnover 36	5.1	•	9.5	8.5	8.6	3.2	6.8	8.5	5.1	9.4	8.4	9.0	4.6
Total Liabilities to Net Worth 37	1.5	•	•	0.5	0.9	1.2	1.5	1.4	1.4	1.4	1.3	1.8	1.5
Current Assets to Working Capital 38	30.1	•	1.9	1.2	1.8	1.8	2.4	2.4	1.9	10.3	2.8	3.1	•
Current Liabilities to Working Capital 39	29.1	•	0.9	0.2	0.8	0.8	1.4	1.4	0.9	9.3	1.8	2.1	•
Working Capital to Net Sales 40	0.0	•	0.2	0.3	0.2	0.2	0.1	0.1	0.2	0.0	0.1	0.1	•
Inventory to Working Capital 41	5.4	•	0.7	0.2	0.4	0.8	0.9	0.9	0.6	3.8	1.0	0.9	•
Total Receipts to Cash Flow 42	4.9	0.2	6.5	11.6	6.4	6.1	6.6	6.3	5.4	4.5	5.6	3.5	5.1
Cost of Goods to Cash Flow 43	3.0	0.1	3.5	6.5	3.4	3.8	4.1	3.8	3.4	2.0	3.2	1.5	3.3
Cash Flow to Total Debt 44	0.2	•	0.2	0.6	1.0	0.6	0.5	0.5	0.5	0.4	0.4	0.4	0.2

Selected Financial Factors (in Percentages)

Debt Ratio 45	60.0	•	197.1	31.8	47.2	54.5	59.5	57.5	57.8	59.1	56.1	64.4	59.6
Return on Total Assets 46	9.5	3.7	•	20.4	3.8	7.8	9.6	15.2	12.4	6.2	13.8	8.8	
Return on Equity Before Income Taxes 47	18.9	•	5.2	36.6	4.1	14.2	19.0	29.9	26.7	9.4	32.3	17.0	
Return on Equity After Income Taxes 48	12.4	•	5.2	35.4	2.1	11.3	15.3	18.8	25.9	5.7	21.9	11.0	
Profit Margin (Before Income Tax) 49	10.4	587.5	•	6.7	1.0	3.2	4.6	8.9	10.3	3.3	13.4	10.5	
Profit Margin (After Income Tax) 50	6.9	380.1	•	6.5	0.5	2.6	3.7	7.7	7.2	2.0	9.1	6.8	

Table II

Corporations with Net Income

SOAP, CLEANING COMPOUND, AND TOILET PREPARATION

MONEY AMOUNTS AND SIZE OF ASSETS IN THOUSANDS OF DOLLARS

Item Description for Accounting Period 7/03 Through 6/04		Total	Zero Assets	Under 500	500 to 1,000	1,000 to 5,000	5,000 to 10,000	10,000 to 25,000	25,000 to 50,000	50,000 to 100,000	100,000 to 250,000	250,000 to 500,000	500,000 to 2,500,000	2,500,000 and over
Number of Enterprises	1	875	•	339	183	235	26	29	23	•	•	•	•	•
Revenues ($ in Thousands)														
Net Sales	2	101737334	•	294118	348876	2355478	378045	908442	1522992	•	•	•	•	•
Interest	3	771773	•	0	185	263	2186	2598	1735	•	•	•	•	•
Rents	4	87172	•	0	28	1186	110	262	565	•	•	•	•	•
Royalties	5	2381844	•	0	0	3910	0	879	383	•	•	•	•	•
Other Portfolio Income	6	2715153	•	0	172	6753	146	7154	752	•	•	•	•	•
Other Receipts	7	1267819	•	0	787	5234	833	4361	1048	•	•	•	•	•
Total Receipts	8	108961095	•	294118	350048	2372824	381320	923696	1527475	•	•	•	•	•
Average Total Receipts	9	124527	•	868	1913	10097	14666	31852	66412	•	•	•	•	•
Operating Costs/Operating Income (%)														
Cost of Operations	10	61.5	•	54.3	52.2	51.3	61.3	55.5	60.2	•	•	•	•	•
Salaries and Wages	11	6.7	•	14.4	13.7	12.8	7.4	10.4	8.1	•	•	•	•	•
Taxes Paid	12	1.0	•	2.1	2.7	0.9	1.8	1.9	1.7	•	•	•	•	•
Interest Paid	13	2.3	•	0.0	1.1	0.2	1.1	0.8	0.8	•	•	•	•	•
Depreciation	14	2.3	•	0.0	2.1	1.0	2.3	2.1	1.6	•	•	•	•	•
Amortization and Depletion	15	1.2	•	0.0	0.0	0.0	0.0	0.3	0.4	•	•	•	•	•
Pensions and Other Deferred Comp.	16	1.3	•	•	0.6	1.0	0.0	0.5	0.3	•	•	•	•	•
Employee Benefits	17	1.3	•	0.2	2.9	0.6	0.2	1.2	1.6	•	•	•	•	•
Advertising	18	5.5	•	0.1	0.0	9.2	0.7	2.2	4.6	•	•	•	•	•
Other Expenses	19	13.9	•	16.3	14.3	12.3	17.3	15.5	12.0	•	•	•	•	•
Officers' Compensation	20	0.8	•	8.9	9.7	3.2	2.6	2.1	3.3	•	•	•	•	•
Operating Margin	21	2.1	•	3.7	0.8	7.3	4.4	7.5	5.6	•	•	•	•	•
Operating Margin Before Officers' Comp.	22	2.8	•	12.6	10.5	10.6	7.0	9.6	8.9	•	•	•	•	•

Selected Average Balance Sheet ($ in Thousands)

Net Receivables 23	23492	75	228	1504	1547	4096	10062
Inventories 24	7168	156	98	487	2668	3935	7215
Net Property, Plant and Equipment 25	16352	0	117	441	1012	4164	7304
Total Assets 26	155517	263	681	3386	7150	16396	38045
Notes and Loans Payable 27	53647	20	232	352	1168	4311	10124
All Other Liabilities 28	35930	23	134	1095	2119	4111	10231
Net Worth 29	65941	220	316	1940	3863	7973	17690

Selected Financial Ratios (Times to 1)

Current Ratio 30	1.0	6.1	3.2	2.7	2.3	2.2	1.9
Quick Ratio 31	0.7	2.5	1.8	1.7	1.0	1.2	1.0
Net Sales to Working Capital 32	235.3	3.9	5.2	5.8	5.0	5.7	5.9
Coverage Ratio 33	5.8	3677.0	2.1	36.7	5.7	11.8	8.6
Total Asset Turnover 34	0.7	3.3	2.8	3.0	2.0	1.9	1.7
Inventory Turnover 35	10.0	3.0	10.2	10.5	3.3	4.4	5.5
Receivables Turnover 36	5.2	7.2	10.5	8.6	18.8	6.2	8.6
Total Liabilities to Net Worth 37	1.4	0.2	1.2	0.7	0.9	1.1	1.2
Current Assets to Working Capital 38	77.0	1.2	1.5	1.6	1.8	1.9	2.1
Current Liabilities to Working Capital 39	76.0	0.2	0.5	0.6	0.8	0.9	1.1
Working Capital to Net Sales 40	0.0	0.3	0.2	0.2	0.2	0.2	0.2
Inventory to Working Capital 41	14.0	0.7	0.3	0.3	0.9	0.7	0.8
Total Receipts to Cash Flow 42	4.8	5.8	8.4	5.5	5.0	4.7	6.2
Cost of Goods to Cash Flow 43	2.9	3.1	4.4	2.8	3.1	2.6	3.7
Cash Flow to Total Debt 44	0.3	3.5	0.6	1.3	0.9	0.8	0.5

Selected Financial Factors (in Percentages)

Debt Ratio 45	57.6	16.4	53.6	42.7	46.0	51.4	53.5
Return on Total Assets 46	10.1	12.4	6.2	24.2	13.0	19.1	11.6
Return on Equity Before Income Taxes 47	19.6	14.8	6.9	41.0	19.9	35.9	22.1
Return on Equity After Income Taxes 48	13.1	14.8	6.1	39.7	17.9	31.8	18.3
Profit Margin (Before Income Tax) 49	11.1	3.7	1.1	7.9	5.3	9.2	5.9
Profit Margin (After Income Tax) 50	7.4	3.7	1.0	7.7	4.8	8.1	4.9

Table I

Corporations with and without Net Income

CHEMICAL PRODUCT AND PREPARATION

MONEY AMOUNTS AND SIZE OF ASSETS IN THOUSANDS OF DOLLARS

Item Description for Accounting Period 7/03 Through 6/04		Total	Zero Assets	Under 500	500 to 1,000	1,000 to 5,000	5,000 to 10,000	10,000 to 25,000	25,000 to 50,000	50,000 to 100,000	100,000 to 250,000	250,000 to 500,000	500,000 to 2,500,000	2,500,000 and over
Number of Enterprises	1	3700	31	2513	227	513	139	126	52	37	26	15	18	3
Revenues ($ in Thousands)														
Net Sales	2	51832063	522938	1114316	394187	1922835	1628205	3081178	2637015	2973229	4918413	5152857	15289606	12197282
Interest	3	332927	4057	17	66	5579	1583	3810	3093	10562	28145	12069	231093	32854
Rents	4	28925	390	0	831	1	3303	1893	130	1041	389	3901	15620	1426
Royalties	5	491212	0	0	142	39304	83	3581	8928	6328	25393	46153	199981	161319
Other Portfolio Income	6	878883	97	1	0	2153	1437	5149	6363	8095	41051	69107	361128	384305
Other Receipts	7	920502	20055	5342	5907	13127	67134	37725	37198	44408	62209	96616	470053	60727
Total Receipts	8	54448512	547537	1119676	401133	1982999	1701745	3133336	2692727	3043663	5075600	5380703	16567481	12837913
Average Total Receipts	9	14726	17662	446	1767	3865	12243	24868	51783	82261	195215	358714	920416	4279304
Operating Costs/Operating Income (%)														
Cost of Operations	10	69.2	75.9	50.3	66.2	51.6	61.2	69.9	67.2	63.8	65.6	73.4	65.5	80.6
Salaries and Wages	11	7.9	8.0	8.2	8.4	8.6	11.9	7.5	8.9	9.8	9.9	6.5	8.9	5.3
Taxes Paid	12	1.5	1.2	3.0	4.0	2.6	1.7	1.7	1.5	2.2	1.8	1.2	1.5	0.6
Interest Paid	13	2.7	1.3	1.5	1.4	0.6	2.1	1.3	0.8	1.6	2.0	2.8	5.1	1.7
Depreciation	14	3.8	2.3	3.3	1.6	2.3	3.5	3.5	2.9	3.8	3.7	4.7	5.0	2.8
Amortization and Depletion	15	0.9	0.6	0.0	0.0	0.1	0.4	0.2	0.7	0.4	1.0	2.0	1.0	0.8
Pensions and Other Deferred Comp.	16	0.9	0.5	0.1	0.5	0.6	0.3	0.5	0.6	0.8	0.5	0.6	1.0	1.4
Employee Benefits	17	1.5	1.0	0.8	0.9	1.6	1.3	1.4	1.6	2.1	1.7	1.9	2.0	0.5
Advertising	18	1.2	0.2	1.2	0.2	0.6	0.9	0.6	0.5	0.7	1.4	0.9	2.3	0.6
Other Expenses	19	13.9	12.7	21.5	12.2	20.1	15.2	11.1	12.0	13.2	11.8	10.9	18.0	10.5
Officers' Compensation	20	1.2	1.0	7.0	7.5	6.2	3.4	2.1	2.0	1.3	0.7	0.7	0.5	0.2
Operating Margin	21	•	•	3.1	•	5.2	1.6	0.2	1.3	0.1	0.0	•	•	•
Operating Margin Before Officers' Comp.	22	•	•	10.1	4.7	11.4	2.3	3.3	1.4	0.7	0.7	•	•	•

Selected Average Balance Sheet ($ in Thousands)

Net Receivables 23	2070	0	62	179	454	1753	3889	7211	12255	28074	50401	143651	532080
Inventories 24	1860	0	28	212	288	1521	2918	6405	11528	25635	35609	105972	723421
Net Property, Plant and Equipment 25	3290	0	59	96	343	2334	4794	8383	20219	40898	119845	285042	574090
Total Assets 26	13817	0	179	640	1752	7243	15785	36379	72915	164602	377130	1265534	3108927
Notes and Loans Payable 27	5056	0	156	289	429	2780	5689	9658	22833	43717	124292	559760	833696
All Other Liabilities 28	4833	0	38	184	400	1822	4115	9022	20120	43736	139849	406862	1665444
Net Worth 29	3928	0	-16	168	923	2641	5981	17699	29962	77150	112989	298912	609786

Selected Financial Ratios (Times to 1)

Current Ratio 30	1.2	•	1.3	1.7	2.2	1.3	1.8	1.8	1.4	1.7	1.4	1.2	0.9
Quick Ratio 31	0.7	•	0.9	0.8	1.4	0.8	1.0	0.9	0.7	0.9	0.7	0.6	0.4
Net Sales to Working Capital 32	14.2	•	21.8	8.4	6.1	13.5	5.9	5.8	9.0	6.6	8.8	14.7	•
Coverage Ratio 33	1.3	1.1	3.3	0.2	15.0	2.3	2.5	5.1	2.6	2.7	0.9	0.7	1.2
Total Asset Turnover 34	1.0	•	2.5	2.7	2.1	1.6	1.5	1.4	1.1	1.1	0.9	0.7	1.3
Inventory Turnover 35	5.2	•	8.1	5.4	6.7	4.7	5.9	5.3	4.4	4.8	7.1	5.3	4.5
Receivables Turnover 36	4.9	•	8.2	9.7	10.1	5.3	7.0	7.6	7.1	5.7	7.7	6.8	2.5
Total Liabilities to Net Worth 37	2.5	•	•	2.8	0.9	1.7	1.6	1.1	1.4	1.1	2.3	3.2	4.1
Current Assets to Working Capital 38	5.1	•	4.9	2.3	1.9	4.6	2.2	2.3	3.7	2.4	3.2	6.4	•
Current Liabilities to Working Capital 39	4.1	•	3.9	1.3	0.9	3.6	1.2	1.3	2.7	1.4	2.2	5.4	•
Working Capital to Net Sales 40	0.1	•	0.0	0.1	0.2	0.1	0.2	0.2	0.1	0.2	0.1	0.1	•
Inventory to Working Capital 41	1.6	•	1.4	1.1	0.5	1.4	0.7	0.8	1.4	0.9	1.0	2.0	•
Total Receipts to Cash Flow 42	8.9	9.7	4.7	19.3	4.0	6.4	9.2	7.2	7.2	7.8	16.8	8.0	14.9
Cost of Goods to Cash Flow 43	6.1	7.4	2.4	12.7	2.0	3.9	6.4	4.8	4.6	5.1	12.3	5.2	12.0
Cash Flow to Total Debt 44	0.2	•	0.5	0.2	1.1	0.4	0.3	0.4	0.3	0.1	0.1	0.1	0.1

Selected Financial Factors (in Percentages)

Debt Ratio 45	71.6	•	108.7	73.8	47.3	63.5	62.1	51.3	58.9	53.1	70.0	76.4	80.4
Return on Total Assets 46	3.7	•	12.8	0.7	19.2	7.7	5.1	5.9	4.4	6.2	2.3	2.5	2.8
Return on Equity Before Income Taxes 47	3.2	•	•	•	34.0	11.8	8.0	9.8	6.6	8.5	•	•	2.9
Return on Equity After Income Taxes 48	0.8	•	•	•	31.1	5.7	5.6	6.6	3.9	5.6	•	•	0.7
Profit Margin (Before Income Tax) 49	0.9	0.1	3.6	•	8.4	2.7	2.0	3.4	2.4	3.4	•	•	0.4
Profit Margin (After Income Tax) 50	0.2	•	3.6	•	7.7	1.3	1.4	2.3	1.5	2.3	•	•	0.1

Table II
Corporations with Net Income

CHEMICAL PRODUCT AND PREPARATION

MONEY AMOUNTS AND SIZE OF ASSETS IN THOUSANDS OF DOLLARS

Item Description for Accounting Period 7/03 Through 6/04	Total	Zero Assets	Under 500	500 to 1,000	1,000 to 5,000	5,000 to 10,000	10,000 to 25,000	25,000 to 50,000	50,000 to 100,000	100,000 to 250,000	250,000 to 500,000	500,000 to 2,500,000	2,500,000 and over
Number of Enterprises 1	2557	5	1634	165	475	93	86	37	25	18	7	11	•
Revenues ($ in Thousands)													
Net Sales 2	34442358	437942	1015742	237808	1660040	1180372	2339416	2083641	2176062	3439519	2922944	16948872	•
Interest 3	154804	4015	1	17	5457	929	1735	2408	9779	16468	6076	107920	•
Rents 4	17101	390	0	831	1	2938	1669	104	1016	84	3723	6347	•
Royalties 5	326494	0	0	142	38708	83	972	8806	6133	23634	11817	236198	•
Other Portfolio Income 6	484253	97	0	0	1983	309	1633	4705	8063	41006	68597	357861	•
Other Receipts 7	545611	19936	5342	285	13070	59392	30701	25968	32054	19120	31990	307750	•
Total Receipts 8	35970621	462380	1021085	239083	1719259	1244023	2376126	2125632	2233107	3539831	3045147	17964948	•
Average Total Receipts 9	14068	92476	625	1449	3619	13377	27629	57450	89324	196657	435021	1633177	•
Operating Costs/Operating Income (%)													
Cost of Operations 10	70.3	76.1	52.4	63.2	47.4	57.0	68.8	65.3	58.1	62.2	76.0	77.5	•
Salaries and Wages 11	6.8	7.2	6.0	6.0	8.7	12.2	6.7	8.7	11.0	9.4	5.4	5.2	•
Taxes Paid 12	1.4	1.3	2.8	3.2	2.6	1.6	1.6	1.5	2.7	1.9	1.0	1.0	•
Interest Paid 13	1.6	1.6	1.6	1.0	0.6	1.1	0.8	0.6	1.4	1.5	1.3	2.0	•
Depreciation 14	3.3	2.4	3.4	1.3	2.0	2.6	2.7	2.5	3.7	3.7	4.5	3.3	•
Amortization and Depletion 15	0.7	0.7	•	0.0	0.1	0.4	0.2	0.7	0.4	0.8	0.7	0.9	•
Pensions and Other Deferred Comp. 16	0.5	0.5	0.2	0.8	0.7	0.2	0.4	0.7	1.1	0.5	0.9	0.4	•
Employee Benefits 17	1.4	1.1	0.9	0.5	1.7	1.5	1.1	1.4	2.5	1.7	1.7	1.2	•
Advertising 18	0.9	0.0	1.2	0.3	0.6	1.1	0.6	0.4	0.5	1.8	0.2	0.9	•
Other Expenses 19	12.4	10.8	18.2	8.9	21.5	16.4	10.2	11.9	14.6	12.0	7.8	11.9	•
Officers' Compensation 20	1.3	0.4	7.6	10.8	6.6	3.0	2.0	2.1	1.4	0.7	0.6	0.3	•
Operating Margin 21	•	5.7	•	4.0	7.4	2.9	4.8	4.1	2.6	3.8	•	•	•
Operating Margin Before Officers' Comp. 22	0.8	•	13.3	14.8	14.1	5.9	6.9	6.2	4.1	4.5	0.5	•	•

Selected Average Balance Sheet ($ in Thousands)

Item												
Net Receivables 23	1921	0	87	165	448	1974	3755	7793	13848	31662	54807	221337
Inventories 24	1599	0	23	91	291	1556	3143	5810	10250	20901	30208	113529
Net Property, Plant and Equipment 25	2378	0	86	117	280	1699	4283	8086	21055	39878	113825	265541
Total Assets 26	10454	0	256	580	1670	7105	15531	36441	71909	164530	378831	1333482
Notes and Loans Payable 27	2795	0	211	250	404	1885	3866	6741	17443	38981	93413	365487
All Other Liabilities 28	3352	0	34	121	391	1748	3663	9485	17739	40089	131956	490343
Net Worth 29	4307	0	11	209	875	3472	8002	20215	36726	85460	153462	477652

Selected Financial Ratios (Times to 1)

Item												
Current Ratio 30	1.7	•	1.6	1.5	2.2	2.1	1.9	2.0	1.7	1.8		1.5
Quick Ratio 31	1.0	•	1.1	0.8	1.4	1.2	1.1	1.2	1.0	0.9		0.9
Net Sales to Working Capital 32	7.9	•	11.4	11.8	5.7	5.6	5.6	5.1	6.7	6.6		10.4
Coverage Ratio 33	3.9	3.1	4.9	5.6	9.2	8.5	10.8	4.8	5.2	2.3		
Total Asset Turnover 34	1.3	•	2.4	2.5	2.1	1.8	1.8	1.5	1.2	1.1		1.2
Inventory Turnover 35	5.9	•	14.1	10.0	5.7	4.6	4.6	6.3	4.9	5.7		10.5
Receivables Turnover 36	4.6	•	10.9	8.5	9.4	5.4	7.6	8.2	7.0	5.6	9.8	13.9
Total Liabilities to Net Worth 37	1.4	•	21.4	1.8	0.9	1.0	0.9	0.8	1.0	1.5		1.8
Current Assets to Working Capital 38	2.5	•	2.6	3.0	1.9	2.1	1.9	2.1	2.0	2.2	2.4	3.1
Current Liabilities to Working Capital 39	1.5	•	1.6	2.0	0.9	1.1	0.9	1.1	1.0	1.2	1.4	2.1
Working Capital to Net Sales 40	0.1	•	0.1	0.1	0.2	0.2	0.2	0.2	0.2	0.2	0.1	0.1
Inventory to Working Capital 41	0.7	•	0.7	1.3	0.5	0.6	0.7	0.6	0.6	0.6	0.8	0.8
Total Receipts to Cash Flow 42	7.1	8.7	4.9	8.1	3.4	4.4	6.8	6.1	5.6	5.9	11.0	8.9
Cost of Goods to Cash Flow 43	5.0	6.6	2.5	5.1	1.6	2.5	4.7	4.0	3.2	3.7	8.3	6.9
Cash Flow to Total Debt 44	0.3	•	0.5	0.5	1.3	0.8	0.5	0.6	0.2	0.1	0.2	0.2

Selected Financial Factors (in Percentages)

Item												
Debt Ratio 45	58.8	•	95.5	64.0	47.6	51.1	48.5	44.5	48.9	48.1	59.5	64.2
Return on Total Assets 46	8.0	•	18.9	13.9	24.2	16.7	12.6	10.5	8.0	9.9	7.4	5.3
Return on Equity Before Income Taxes 47	14.4	•	336.6	31.6	43.9	30.2	21.9	17.2	12.5	15.7	14.8	8.2
Return on Equity After Income Taxes 48	11.2	•	333.1	28.5	40.7	23.2	19.3	13.2	9.3	12.0	10.9	5.5
Profit Margin (Before Income Tax) 49	4.6	3.4	6.2	4.6	11.0	8.3	6.4	6.2	5.3	7.0	5.4	2.5
Profit Margin (After Income Tax) 50	3.6	2.5	6.1	4.1	10.2	6.4	5.7	4.7	3.9	5.3	4.0	1.7

Table I

Corporations with and without Net Income

PLASTICS PRODUCT

MONEY AMOUNTS AND SIZE OF ASSETS IN THOUSANDS OF DOLLARS

Item Description for Accounting Period 7/03 Through 6/04	Total	Zero Assets	Under 500	500 to 1,000	1,000 to 5,000	5,000 to 10,000	10,000 to 25,000	25,000 to 50,000	50,000 to 100,000	100,000 to 250,000	250,000 to 500,000	500,000 to 2,500,000	2,500,000 and over
Number of Enterprises **1**	10233	1039	4413	1384	2234	355	428	155	110	71	18	22	3
Revenues ($ in Thousands)													
Net Sales **2**	91213706	1093324	2530867	1929008	8816165	3816367	11565893	7826418	11053536	13609493	5308313	16950364	6713960
Interest **3**	299444	4658	24040	1633	2758	2819	8563	6152	25598	47403	31332	83317	61171
Rents **4**	36184	34	0	378	1572	471	3133	1538	4576	6109	11352	5665	1358
Royalties **5**	212383	12076	19348	0	0	308	1290	3976	5757	41501	21952	32644	73533
Other Portfolio Income **6**	315961	46987	16393	2856	11117	25687	22043	12660	28536	52899	25028	57537	14215
Other Receipts **7**	1126415	3460	89842	5024	62996	30046	55069	84481	97613	113594	42670	120383	421234
Total Receipts **8**	93204093	1160539	2680490	1938899	8894608	3875698	11655991	7935225	11215616	13870999	5440647	17249910	7285471
Average Total Receipts **9**	9108	1117	607	1401	3981	10917	27234	51195	101960	195366	302258	784087	2428490
Operating Costs/Operating Income (%)													
Cost of Operations **10**	70.3	68.0	68.4	61.3	66.0	65.7	72.1	70.8	72.4	71.9	68.9	73.7	64.9
Salaries and Wages **11**	6.2	6.5	4.7	9.9	7.5	8.7	6.2	6.6	5.1	5.6	6.0	5.9	6.2
Taxes Paid **12**	1.9	2.1	2.7	3.5	2.9	2.3	2.0	2.1	1.8	1.7	1.6	1.5	1.5
Interest Paid **13**	2.6	4.6	6.1	0.9	1.0	0.9	1.1	1.6	1.5	2.2	3.4	4.0	7.1
Depreciation **14**	4.4	4.0	1.5	2.6	3.5	5.3	4.4	5.2	5.1	4.2	5.3	4.9	3.1
Amortization and Depletion **15**	0.5	0.7	0.2	0.2	0.1	0.3	0.2	0.3	0.5	0.9	0.8	0.9	0.4
Pensions and Other Deferred Comp. **16**	0.5	0.9	0.1	0.2	0.4	0.2	0.4	0.5	0.4	0.4	0.5	0.5	1.2
Employee Benefits **17**	1.8	2.7	1.1	1.6	1.9	1.6	1.7	1.7	1.7	2.2	2.1	1.6	2.1
Advertising **18**	0.6	0.8	0.3	0.5	0.5	2.3	0.5	0.3	0.7	0.6	0.3	0.2	1.3
Other Expenses **19**	10.2	14.2	16.2	18.0	10.5	9.9	7.9	8.0	9.2	9.5	11.1	8.1	18.9
Officers' Compensation **20**	1.7	3.0	8.0	6.3	4.6	2.1	1.9	1.6	1.0	0.7	1.1	0.4	0.4
Operating Margin **21**	•	•	•	•	1.1	0.6	1.8	1.4	0.3	0.0	•	•	•
Operating Margin Before Officers' Comp. **22**	0.9	•	•	1.4	5.8	2.7	3.7	3.0	1.3	0.8	•	•	•

Selected Average Balance Sheet ($ in Thousands)

Net Receivables 23	1381	0	50	175	503	1275	3846	7384	14332	25813	45593	144935	626253
Inventories 24	935	0	23	145	467	1253	3055	5867	11042	20441	35400	70480	221604
Net Property, Plant and Equipment 25	2123	0	26	178	554	2586	5426	12653	25272	43002	118648	244629	524056
Total Assets 26	7930	0	134	675	2029	6661	15741	35582	71700	149440	371847	977605	4589947
Notes and Loans Payable 27	3253	0	131	295	610	2244	5804	12969	26315	50645	174803	491865	1729841
All Other Liabilities 28	2306	0	51	172	505	1632	3948	8822	18367	36496	70186	238110	2417962
Net Worth 29	2371	0	-48	208	914	2785	5989	13790	27018	62299	126858	247630	442143

Selected Financial Ratios (Times to 1)

Current Ratio 30	1.4	•	1.6	1.6	2.1	1.4	1.6	1.5	1.4	1.6	1.8	1.1	1.1
Quick Ratio 31	0.8	•	1.2	1.0	1.3	0.8	0.9	0.8	0.7	0.9	1.0	0.6	0.7
Net Sales to Working Capital 32	10.4	•	15.6	8.5	6.0	12.7	8.6	9.1	11.0	8.4	5.6	55.2	13.1
Coverage Ratio 33	1.6	0.7	0.5	•	3.0	3.3	3.2	2.7	2.2	1.9	1.4	1.2	1.2
Total Asset Turnover 34	1.1	•	4.3	2.1	1.9	1.6	1.7	1.4	1.4	1.3	0.8	0.8	0.5
Inventory Turnover 35	6.7	•	17.0	5.9	5.6	5.6	6.4	6.1	6.6	6.7	5.7	8.1	6.6
Receivables Turnover 36	6.5	•	22.8	16.0	7.3	7.0	7.1	7.0	7.2	7.6	5.5	5.9	3.4
Total Liabilities to Net Worth 37	2.3	•	•	2.3	1.2	1.4	1.6	1.6	1.7	1.4	1.9	2.9	9.4
Current Assets to Working Capital 38	3.6	•	2.7	2.7	1.9	3.7	2.8	3.1	3.5	2.6	2.3	20.9	8.1
Current Liabilities to Working Capital 39	2.6	•	1.7	1.7	0.9	2.7	1.8	2.1	2.5	1.6	1.3	19.9	7.1
Working Capital to Net Sales 40	0.1	•	0.1	0.1	0.2	0.1	0.1	0.1	0.1	0.1	0.2	0.0	0.1
Inventory to Working Capital 41	1.1	•	0.6	0.9	0.7	1.2	1.0	1.1	1.3	0.9	0.7	5.4	1.3
Total Receipts to Cash Flow 42	10.9	10.4	14.4	12.5	10.8	11.4	11.8	11.4	11.1	10.8	9.8	17.0	5.2
Cost of Goods to Cash Flow 43	7.7	7.1	9.8	7.6	7.1	7.5	8.5	8.1	8.0	7.8	6.8	12.5	3.3
Cash Flow to Total Debt 44	0.1	•	0.2	0.2	0.3	0.2	0.2	0.2	0.2	0.2	0.1	0.1	0.1

Selected Financial Factors (in Percentages)

Debt Ratio 45	70.1	135.7	69.2	55.0	58.2	62.0	61.2	62.3	58.3	65.9	74.7	90.4
Return on Total Assets 46	4.7	•	12.4	5.9	5.0	6.3	6.2	4.7	5.4	3.9	3.8	4.3
Return on Equity Before Income Taxes 47	5.7	•	38.4	8.7	8.2	11.4	10.1	6.8	6.3	3.5	2.6	8.2
Return on Equity After Income Taxes 48	3.7	•	39.0	8.0	6.2	9.9	7.9	4.6	4.7	2.2	0.5	0.9
Profit Margin (Before Income Tax) 49	1.5	•	•	2.0	2.1	2.5	2.8	1.8	2.0	1.5	0.8	1.6
Profit Margin (After Income Tax) 50	1.0	•	•	1.8	1.6	2.2	2.2	1.2	1.5	1.0	0.2	0.2

Table II
Corporations with Net Income

PLASTICS PRODUCT

MONEY AMOUNTS AND SIZE OF ASSETS IN THOUSANDS OF DOLLARS

Item Description for Accounting Period 7/03 Through 6/04	Total	Zero Assets	Under 500	500 to 1,000	1,000 to 5,000	5,000 to 10,000	10,000 to 25,000	25,000 to 50,000	50,000 to 100,000	100,000 to 250,000	250,000 to 500,000	500,000 to 2,500,000	2,500,000 and over
Number of Enterprises **1**	4375	22	•	552	1528	165	284	105	70	•	12	13	•
Revenues ($ in Thousands)													
Net Sales **2**	58518408	634034	•	830347	6698512	2042890	8155623	5669630	7897645	•	3767723	12725006	•
Interest **3**	147323	648	•	894	2107	1004	6953	4432	9256	•	15086	79075	•
Rents **4**	17719	34	•	378	226	132	1035	1145	3439	•	6435	1888	•
Royalties **5**	141567	0	•	0	0	0	67	2356	5701	•	20329	58730	•
Other Portfolio Income **6**	239222	46465	•	2417	9230	17160	10857	7408	19324	•	23008	49836	•
Other Receipts **7**	537388	6207	•	3867	53326	23578	53491	74646	68860	•	31614	127595	•
Total Receipts **8**	59601627	687388	•	837903	6763401	2084764	8228026	5759617	8004225	•	3864195	13042130	•
Average Total Receipts **9**	13623	31245	•	1518	4426	12635	28972	54853	114346	•	322016	1003241	•
Operating Costs/Operating Income (%)													
Cost of Operations **10**	68.9	70.4	•	58.1	66.6	63.5	70.6	69.5	71.0	•	68.6	69.0	•
Salaries and Wages **11**	6.1	4.5	•	4.3	6.9	8.3	6.0	6.2	4.7	•	5.8	6.6	•
Taxes Paid **12**	2.0	2.4	•	3.5	2.8	1.9	1.9	2.1	1.8	•	1.8	1.7	•
Interest Paid **13**	1.7	3.5	•	0.6	0.6	0.6	0.9	1.2	1.1	•	2.4	3.1	•
Depreciation **14**	4.1	3.3	•	3.5	2.8	3.3	3.9	4.7	5.1	•	4.7	4.1	•
Amortization and Depletion **15**	0.4	0.3	•	0.2	0.1	0.3	0.2	0.2	0.2	•	0.5	0.8	•
Pensions and Other Deferred Comp. **16**	0.5	0.2	•	0.3	0.5	0.2	0.4	0.6	0.5	•	0.5	0.8	•
Employee Benefits **17**	1.8	2.8	•	1.5	1.8	0.9	1.6	1.5	1.7	•	1.9	2.0	•
Advertising **18**	0.6	0.1	•	0.7	0.4	2.3	0.5	0.3	0.7	•	0.2	0.8	•
Other Expenses **19**	8.8	8.9	•	17.3	8.7	9.2	7.4	7.5	8.8	•	10.4	8.5	•
Officers' Compensation **20**	1.7	0.8	•	8.2	5.1	2.3	2.0	1.7	1.0	•	0.9	0.4	•
Operating Margin **21**	3.4	2.8	•	1.8	3.8	7.0	4.7	4.5	3.4	•	2.4	2.1	•
Operating Margin Before Officers' Comp. **22**	5.1	3.6	•	10.1	8.8	9.3	6.7	6.2	4.4	•	3.3	2.5	•

Selected Average Balance Sheet ($ in Thousands)

Net Receivables 23	2023	0	•	195	552	1635	3990	7924	14722	•	47394	217280	•
Inventories 24	1403	0	•	139	467	1500	3269	5904	12626	•	31542	96451	•
Net Property, Plant and Equipment 25	2928	0	•	166	479	2107	4978	12234	26768	•	106489	285114	•
Total Assets 26	11452	0	•	687	2125	6796	15713	36131	72629	•	353200	1594393	•
Notes and Loans Payable 27	4315	0	•	110	389	1324	4636	10591	20674	•	145279	776494	•
All Other Liabilities 28	2633	0	•	182	514	1680	3558	7606	17592	•	63923	373822	•
Net Worth 29	4505	0	•	395	1222	3792	7520	17934	34363	•	143999	444076	•

Selected Financial Ratios (Times to 1)

Current Ratio 30	1.5	•	2.4	2.5	2.1	1.9	1.8	1.6	•	1.7	1.1	•
Quick Ratio 31	0.9	•	1.6	1.6	1.2	1.1	1.0	0.9	•	0.9	0.7	•
Net Sales to Working Capital 32	8.3	•	5.3	5.4	6.2	6.5	7.0	8.4	•	6.5	31.9	•
Coverage Ratio 33	4.3	4.2	5.8	8.4	15.8	7.4	6.3	5.2	•	3.2	2.9	•
Total Asset Turnover 34	1.2	•	2.2	2.1	1.8	1.8	1.5	1.6	•	0.9	0.6	•
Inventory Turnover 35	6.6	•	6.3	6.2	5.2	6.2	6.4	6.3	•	6.8	7.0	•
Receivables Turnover 36	6.5	•	15.4	7.5	6.0	7.1	7.3	7.4	•	7.2	9.0	•
Total Liabilities to Net Worth 37	1.5	•	0.7	0.7	0.8	1.1	1.0	1.1	•	1.5	2.6	•
Current Assets to Working Capital 38	2.9	•	1.7	1.7	1.9	2.1	2.3	2.6	•	2.4	14.8	•
Current Liabilities to Working Capital 39	1.9	•	0.7	0.7	0.9	1.1	1.3	1.6	•	1.4	13.8	•
Working Capital to Net Sales 40	0.1	•	0.2	0.2	0.2	0.2	0.1	0.1	•	0.2	0.0	•
Inventory to Working Capital 41	0.8	•	0.5	0.5	0.6	0.7	0.8	0.9	•	0.7	3.1	•
Total Receipts to Cash Flow 42	8.4	6.0	8.6	9.2	6.6	8.9	8.5	8.6	•	7.7	8.8	•
Cost of Goods to Cash Flow 43	5.8	4.2	5.0	6.1	4.2	6.3	5.9	6.1	•	5.3	6.1	•
Cash Flow to Total Debt 44	0.2	•	0.6	0.5	0.6	0.4	0.3	0.3	•	0.2	0.1	•

Selected Financial Factors (in Percentages)

Debt Ratio 45	60.7	•	42.5	42.5	44.2	52.1	50.4	52.7	•	59.2	72.1	•
Return on Total Assets 46	8.4	•	7.3	11.0	17.6	11.8	10.9	9.2	•	6.7	5.4	•
Return on Equity Before Income Taxes 47	16.3	•	10.5	16.9	29.5	21.3	18.4	15.7	•	11.3	12.7	•
Return on Equity After Income Taxes 48	13.8	•	9.7	16.1	26.2	19.5	16.0	12.9	•	9.6	9.0	•
Profit Margin (Before Income Tax) 49	5.5	11.2	2.8	4.7	9.1	5.6	6.1	4.8	•	5.2	5.7	•
Profit Margin (After Income Tax) 50	4.6	9.9	2.5	4.5	8.0	5.1	5.3	3.9	•	4.4	4.1	•

Table I

Corporations with and without Net Income

RUBBER PRODUCT

MONEY AMOUNTS AND SIZE OF ASSETS IN THOUSANDS OF DOLLARS

Item Description for Accounting Period 7/03 Through 6/04	Total	Zero Assets	Under 500	500 to 1,000	1,000 to 5,000	5,000 to 10,000	10,000 to 25,000	25,000 to 50,000	50,000 to 100,000	100,000 to 250,000	250,000 to 500,000	500,000 to 2,500,000	2,500,000 and over
Number of Enterprises 1	1034	224	79	50	480	60	74	23	22	4	7	7	3
Revenues ($ in Thousands)													
Net Sales 2	45630600	0	106491	93872	4041105	685322	2256596	1149165	2120650	420565	2579223	10545313	21632296
Interest 3	280939	0	7	6	394	175	1715	464	4745	3088	17837	70603	181906
Rents 4	28300	0	0	40	0	0	337	2103	105	1369	1304	4185	18856
Royalties 5	534748	0	0	0	0	184	2	82	2598	3373	1502	165597	361410
Other Portfolio Income 6	377812	0	2451	0	1353	5217	1660	3144	27136	294	19067	99316	218179
Other Receipts 7	286519	28167	1098	453	30727	27078	10797	9913	1233	7604	40506	70390	58551
Total Receipts 8	47138918	28167	110047	94371	4073579	717976	2271107	1164871	2156467	436293	2659439	10955404	22471198
Average Total Receipts 9	45589	126	1393	1887	8487	11966	30691	50647	98021	109073	379920	1565058	7490399
Operating Costs/Operating Income (%)													
Cost of Operations 10	68.7	•	33.6	80.3	68.5	68.2	71.3	71.7	75.0	60.6	69.4	73.6	65.5
Salaries and Wages 11	7.6	•	25.4	5.5	8.1	10.4	7.0	5.6	4.8	12.2	5.8	5.6	8.8
Taxes Paid 12	1.5	•	7.0	1.5	2.0	1.8	2.5	2.9	1.9	2.0	1.6	1.3	1.2
Interest Paid 13	1.7	•	1.2	0.5	0.8	0.5	1.4	1.5	2.9	2.0	2.9	2.4	1.4
Depreciation 14	3.5	•	1.9	1.5	2.3	3.7	3.5	3.9	4.0	3.6	2.6	4.1	3.5
Amortization and Depletion 15	0.4	•	•	•	0.0	0.0	0.5	0.4	0.7	2.1	1.3	0.6	0.2
Pensions and Other Deferred Comp. 16	1.0	•	•	•	0.7	0.7	0.6	0.3	0.6	1.3	1.2	0.8	1.2
Employee Benefits 17	3.5	•	4.9	•	0.9	1.8	2.0	2.1	2.6	3.9	2.3	4.1	4.1
Advertising 18	1.2	•	0.0	•	0.9	0.1	0.3	0.4	0.5	0.8	0.8	0.8	1.8
Other Expenses 19	13.5	•	11.3	8.0	7.9	5.6	7.6	9.1	8.7	16.1	13.0	9.6	18.1
Officers' Compensation 20	0.9	•	19.4	3.2	4.7	4.8	1.9	1.5	0.9	0.9	0.6	0.3	0.1
Operating Margin 21	•	•	•	•	2.9	2.3	1.6	0.4	•	•	•	•	•
Operating Margin Before Officers' Comp. 22	•	•	14.7	2.7	7.7	7.1	3.5	1.9	•	•	•	•	•

Selected Average Balance Sheet ($ in Thousands)

Net Receivables 23	6823	0	135	266	957	1156	3899	7979	13229	11567	43254	181788	1372557
Inventories 24	5779	0	86	295	695	1240	3445	6977	9118	33832	52225	148122	1127740
Net Property, Plant and Equipment 25	10112	0	44	89	725	2722	5920	10052	21239	17573	74991	400490	1800518
Total Assets 26	38593	0	267	693	2995	6467	16712	31652	69923	129855	332250	1429113	7223864
Notes and Loans Payable 27	12452	0	423	201	561	1032	6425	13794	35759	61892	139865	388415	2325287
All Other Liabilities 28	16579	0	111	180	647	1366	2953	8329	20898	28088	97237	486041	3888977
Net Worth 29	9562	0	-267	311	1787	4069	7333	9529	13267	39875	95148	554657	1009600

Selected Financial Ratios (Times to 1)

Current Ratio 30	1.5	•	2.0	1.8	2.1	1.9	1.6	1.3	1.4	2.0	1.0	1.4	1.5
Quick Ratio 31	0.8	•	1.2	0.8	1.3	1.4	0.9	0.7	0.9	0.9	0.5	0.6	0.9
Net Sales to Working Capital 32	8.9	•	12.1	7.1	7.9	7.5	8.9	12.0	10.5	3.9	•	11.8	7.2
Coverage Ratio 33	1.3	•	•	1.0	5.7	14.4	2.6	2.2	0.6	0.1	1.7	1.5	0.6
Total Asset Turnover 34	1.1	•	5.1	2.7	2.8	1.8	1.8	1.6	1.4	0.8	1.1	1.1	1.0
Inventory Turnover 35	5.2	•	5.3	5.1	8.3	6.3	6.3	5.1	7.9	1.9	4.9	7.5	4.2
Receivables Turnover 36	6.9	•	20.0	14.1	10.0	7.0	7.9	6.2	8.2	6.7	8.3	9.3	5.6
Total Liabilities to Net Worth 37	3.0	•	•	1.2	0.7	0.6	1.3	2.3	4.3	2.3	2.5	1.6	6.2
Current Assets to Working Capital 38	3.0	•	2.0	2.2	1.9	2.1	2.7	4.1	3.3	2.0	•	3.6	2.8
Current Liabilities to Working Capital 39	2.0	•	1.0	1.2	0.9	1.1	1.7	3.1	2.3	1.0	•	2.6	1.8
Working Capital to Net Sales 40	0.1	•	0.1	0.1	0.1	0.1	0.1	0.1	0.1	0.3	•	0.1	0.1
Inventory to Working Capital 41	1.2	•	0.8	1.1	0.7	0.5	1.0	1.6	1.1	1.0	•	1.3	1.1
Total Receipts to Cash Flow 42	9.5	•	13.0	47.8	10.1	9.1	12.9	11.3	20.3	9.9	7.7	11.2	8.2
Cost of Goods to Cash Flow 43	6.5	•	4.4	38.4	6.9	6.2	9.2	8.1	15.2	6.0	5.3	8.2	5.4
Cash Flow to Total Debt 44	0.2	•	0.2	0.1	0.7	0.5	0.3	0.2	0.1	0.1	0.2	0.2	0.1

Selected Financial Factors (in Percentages)

Debt Ratio 45	75.2	•	200.1	55.1	40.3	37.1	56.1	69.9	81.0	69.3	71.4	61.2	86.0
Return on Total Assets 46	2.7	•	•	1.5	12.6	13.4	6.5	5.2	2.6	0.1	5.5	3.7	0.8
Return on Equity Before Income Taxes 47	2.8	6.8	•	•	17.5	19.9	9.1	9.3	•	•	8.1	3.1	•
Return on Equity After Income Taxes 48	1.3	6.8	•	•	17.2	17.6	7.2	7.3	•	•	5.8	0.6	•
Profit Margin (Before Income Tax) 49	0.6	•	•	•	3.7	7.1	2.2	1.8	•	•	2.1	1.1	•
Profit Margin (After Income Tax) 50	0.3	•	•	•	3.7	6.3	1.7	1.4	•	•	1.5	0.2	•

Table II

Corporations with Net Income

RUBBER PRODUCT

MONEY AMOUNTS AND SIZE OF ASSETS IN THOUSANDS OF DOLLARS

Item Description for Accounting Period 7/03 Through 6/04	Total	Zero Assets	Under 500	500 to 1,000	1,000 to 5,000	5,000 to 10,000	10,000 to 25,000	25,000 to 50,000	50,000 to 100,000	100,000 to 250,000	250,000 to 500,000	500,000 to 2,500,000	2,500,000 and over
Number of Enterprises 1	489	•	•	•	357	49	45	15	12	•	•	7	•
Revenues ($ in Thousands)													
Net Sales 2	23585208	•	•	•	3138002	599134	1591793	792367	1435434	•	•	1541056	•
Interest 3	70089	•	•	•	313	171	966	340	3531	•	•	64400	•
Rents 4	16932	•	•	•	0	0	288	2064	79	•	•	13714	•
Royalties 5	168836	•	•	•	0	0	2	40	1051	•	•	166765	•
Other Portfolio Income 6	152100	•	•	•	1078	4806	1004	2834	23318	•	•	99285	•
Other Receipts 7	142162	•	•	•	30330	1813	5087	1764	1401	•	•	83910	•
Total Receipts 8	24135327	•	•	•	3169723	605924	1599140	799409	1464814	•	•	15769130	•
Average Total Receipts 9	49356	•	•	•	8879	12366	35536	53294	122068	•	•	2252733	•
Operating Costs/Operating Income (%)													
Cost of Operations 10	69.5	•	•	•	67.3	66.7	69.0	69.5	76.3	•	•	69.8	•
Salaries and Wages 11	5.7	•	•	•	7.6	10.0	7.9	6.6	4.0	•	•	5.0	•
Taxes Paid 12	1.4	•	•	•	1.8	1.5	2.5	2.0	2.0	•	•	1.1	•
Interest Paid 13	1.1	•	•	•	0.8	0.4	1.0	1.0	2.0	•	•	1.2	•
Depreciation 14	3.3	•	•	•	2.4	1.9	2.8	3.4	3.3	•	•	3.7	•
Amortization and Depletion 15	0.5	•	•	•	0.0	0.0	0.5	0.3	0.5	•	•	0.5	•
Pensions and Other Deferred Comp. 16	1.2	•	•	•	0.8	0.8	0.5	0.4	0.7	•	•	1.5	•
Employee Benefits 17	3.9	•	•	•	0.6	0.4	2.0	2.6	2.2	•	•	5.2	•
Advertising 18	1.0	•	•	•	1.1	0.1	0.3	0.5	0.5	•	•	1.1	•
Other Expenses 19	9.9	•	•	•	7.3	3.4	6.7	7.5	6.5	•	•	11.2	•
Officers' Compensation 20	1.1	•	•	•	4.3	5.3	1.8	1.4	0.9	•	•	0.3	•
Operating Margin 21	1.4	•	•	•	5.9	9.4	5.0	4.8	1.2	•	•	•	•
Operating Margin Before Officers' Comp. 22	2.5	•	•	•	10.3	14.8	6.8	6.2	2.1	•	•	•	•

Selected Average Balance Sheet ($ in Thousands)

Net Receivables 23	7664	941	1201	4453	8817	16415	393463
Inventories 24	5174	655	1365	4075	8152	9407	253049
Net Property, Plant and Equipment 25	10594	720	2760	5508	10116	23245	578501
Total Assets 26	37509	3195	6427	17100	31469	68347	2000685
Notes and Loans Payable 27	10415	410	1048	5246	12287	29289	565664
All Other Liabilities 28	13526	558	1038	1949	8380	23744	817753
Net Worth 29	13569	2227	4342	9904	10802	15314	617268

Selected Financial Ratios (Times to 1)

Current Ratio 30	1.4	3.0	2.3	1.8	1.5	1.5	1.3
Quick Ratio 31	0.8	1.8	1.7	1.0	0.9	1.0	0.7
Net Sales to Working Capital 32	10.1	6.2	6.5	7.3	8.1	9.9	12.5
Coverage Ratio 33	4.5	9.4	26.0	6.3	6.8	2.6	3.2
Total Asset Turnover 34	1.3	2.8	1.9	2.1	1.7	1.8	1.1
Inventory Turnover 35	6.5	9.0	6.0	6.0	4.5	6.0	6.0
Receivables Turnover 36	6.7	11.3	7.2	7.6	5.7	10.0	11.1
Total Liabilities to Net Worth 37	1.8	0.4	0.5	0.7	1.9	3.5	2.2
Current Assets to Working Capital 38	-3.3	1.5	1.8	2.3	2.9	2.9	4.4
Current Liabilities to Working Capital 39	2.3	0.5	0.8	1.3	1.9	1.9	3.4
Working Capital to Net Sales 40	0.1	0.2	0.2	0.1	0.1	0.1	0.1
Inventory to Working Capital 41	1.1	0.6	0.4	0.9	1.1	0.9	1.4
Total Receipts to Cash Flow 42	8.3	7.9	7.7	10.0	8.6	14.3	8.4
Cost of Goods to Cash Flow 43	5.8	5.3	5.2	6.9	6.0	10.9	5.9
Cash Flow to Total Debt 44	0.2	1.2	0.8	0.5	0.3	0.2	0.2

Selected Financial Factors (in Percentages)

Debt Ratio 45	63.8	30.3	32.4	42.1	65.7	77.6	69.1
Return on Total Assets 46	6.5	21.4	20.9	13.3	11.2	9.2	4.0
Return on Equity Before Income Taxes 47	14.0	27.4	29.7	19.3	27.9	25.1	8.9
Return on Equity After Income Taxes 48	11.8	27.1	27.1	17.1	25.3	20.7	6.6
Profit Margin (Before Income Tax) 49	3.9	7.0	10.6	5.4	5.7	3.2	2.5
Profit Margin (After Income Tax) 50	3.3	6.9	9.6	4.8	5.2	2.7	1.9

Table I

Corporations with and without Net Income

CLAY, REFRACTORY AND OTHER NONMETALLIC MINERAL PRODUCT

MONEY AMOUNTS AND SIZE OF ASSETS IN THOUSANDS OF DOLLARS

Item Description for Accounting Period 7/03 Through 6/04	Total	Zero Assets	Under 500	500 to 1,000	1,000 to 5,000	5,000 to 10,000	10,000 to 25,000	25,000 to 50,000	50,000 to 100,000	100,000 to 250,000	250,000 to 500,000	500,000 to 2,500,000	2,500,000 and over
Number of Enterprises **1**	2729	•	1630	•	604	81	68	26	14	11	•	5	•
Revenues ($ in Thousands)													
Net Sales **2**	15806028	•	347077	•	2085734	1071552	1314720	1029612	1047160	1335286	•	6999331	•
Interest **3**	201106	•	422	•	349	210	538	816	2775	3292	•	186921	•
Rents **4**	25522	•	0	•	0	102	536	133	2184	639	•	21927	•
Royalties **5**	251204	•	0	•	6748	0	228	292	1100	1288	•	241548	•
Other Portfolio Income **6**	58560	•	33	•	3256	1148	9036	2196	769	6199	•	29657	•
Other Receipts **7**	198468	•	-2243	•	5157	17175	-107	4722	38029	15962	•	118760	•
Total Receipts **8**	16540888	•	345289	•	2101244	1090187	1324951	1037771	1092017	1362666	•	7598144	•
Average Total Receipts **9**	6061	•	212	•	3479	13459	19485	39914	78001	123879	•	1519629	•
Operating Costs/Operating Income (%)													
Cost of Operations **10**	68.3	•	50.3	•	63.3	71.0	70.2	65.2	75.0	61.7	•	70.9	•
Salaries and Wages **11**	7.8	•	17.1	•	6.4	5.5	7.4	7.7	6.8	8.8	•	8.1	•
Taxes Paid **12**	2.0	•	3.2	•	2.7	2.1	2.7	2.1	1.6	2.5	•	1.4	•
Interest Paid **13**	2.2	•	0.7	•	1.2	0.9	1.3	1.2	1.3	1.3	•	3.4	•
Depreciation **14**	4.9	•	5.3	•	3.6	3.8	4.5	6.4	5.9	7.7	•	4.5	•
Amortization and Depletion **15**	0.6	•	0.0	•	0.3	0.1	0.3	0.2	0.5	0.4	•	1.0	•
Pensions and Other Deferred Comp. **16**	1.6	•	0.3	•	0.4	0.3	0.7	0.7	0.5	1.0	•	2.9	•
Employee Benefits **17**	2.1	•	1.7	•	1.8	1.2	2.3	2.6	1.1	2.9	•	2.4	•
Advertising **18**	0.6	•	0.2	•	0.5	0.5	0.5	0.7	0.4	0.7	•	0.8	•
Other Expenses **19**	12.8	•	16.9	•	13.0	9.0	8.6	8.1	6.1	11.4	•	16.1	•
Officers' Compensation **20**	1.8	•	3.9	•	5.9	3.2	2.3	1.6	1.4	1.4	•	0.4	•
Operating Margin **21**	•	•	0.4	•	0.9	2.3	•	3.4	1.4	0.0	•	0.4	•
Operating Margin Before Officers' Comp. **22**	•	•	4.2	•	6.8	5.6	1.5	5.0	0.9	1.4	•	1.4	•

Selected Average Balance Sheet ($ in Thousands)

Net Receivables 23	2916	14	348	1385	3107	5382	9305	30951	1347025
Inventories 24	704	13	355	2060	3665	6835	11648	22038	131962
Net Property, Plant and Equipment 25	1656	21	651	2864	5239	15004	27457	53069	421831
Total Assets 26	11833	66	1944	7943	16031	36220	66305	163586	5086678
Notes and Loans Payable 27	3981	80	766	1985	4623	11826	19119	28443	1744387
All Other Liabilities 28	4681	5	399	1451	3816	5552	10593	40860	2274130
Net Worth 29	3170	-19	780	4508	7593	18841	36593	94283	1068161

Selected Financial Ratios (Times to 1)

Current Ratio 30	1.4	9.2	1.8	2.5	1.8	2.0	2.1	1.9	1.3
Quick Ratio 31	0.8	4.4	0.9	0.9	1.0	1.0	1.0	1.2	0.8
Net Sales to Working Capital 32	4.0	5.3	7.8	4.6	5.1	4.3	4.9	3.6	3.0
Coverage Ratio 33	1.0	0.8	2.4	5.4	1.2	4.4	4.0	2.7	0.2
Total Asset Turnover 34	0.5	3.2	1.8	1.7	1.2	1.1	1.1	0.7	0.3
Inventory Turnover 35	5.6	8.4	6.2	4.6	3.7	3.8	4.8	3.4	7.5
Receivables Turnover 36	2.1	13.0	12.7	10.5	6.0	7.7	8.4	4.3	1.1
Total Liabilities to Net Worth 37	2.7	•	1.5	0.8	1.1	0.9	0.8	0.7	3.8
Current Assets to Working Capital 38	3.7	1.1	2.2	1.7	2.3	2.0	1.9	2.1	4.9
Current Liabilities to Working Capital 39	2.7	0.1	1.2	0.7	1.3	1.0	0.9	1.1	3.9
Working Capital to Net Sales 40	0.3	0.2	0.1	0.2	0.2	0.2	0.2	0.3	0.3
Inventory to Working Capital 41	0.5	0.3	1.0	0.9	0.9	0.8	0.8	0.7	0.2
Total Receipts to Cash Flow 42	12.6	6.9	11.8	8.9	14.7	9.4	12.0	9.6	16.1
Cost of Goods to Cash Flow 43	8.6	3.5	7.5	6.3	10.3	6.1	9.0	5.9	11.4
Cash Flow to Total Debt 44	0.1	0.4	0.3	0.4	0.2	0.2	0.2	0.2	0.0

Selected Financial Factors (in Percentages)

Debt Ratio 45	73.2	129.0	59.9	43.2	52.6	48.0	44.8	42.4	79.0
Return on Total Assets 46	1.1	1.9	5.1	8.3	1.8	5.8	5.7	2.6	0.2
Return on Equity Before Income Taxes 47	•	1.8	7.4	12.0	0.5	8.6	7.7	2.9	•
Return on Equity After Income Taxes 48	•	3.1	6.6	10.2	•	6.1	5.9	•	•
Profit Margin (Before Income Tax) 49	•	•	1.7	4.1	0.2	4.1	3.8	•	•
Profit Margin (After Income Tax) 50	•	•	1.5	3.5	•	2.9	2.9	•	•

CLAY, REFRACTORY AND OTHER NONMETALLIC MINERAL PRODUCT

Table II
Corporations with Net Income

MONEY AMOUNTS AND SIZE OF ASSETS IN THOUSANDS OF DOLLARS

Item Description for Accounting Period 7/03 Through 6/04	Total	Zero Assets	Under 500	500 to 1,000	1,000 to 5,000	5,000 to 10,000	10,000 to 25,000	25,000 to 50,000	50,000 to 100,000	100,000 to 250,000	250,000 to 500,000	500,000 to 2,500,000	2,500,000 and over
Number of Enterprises **1**	1410	10	864	129	262	75	37	17	10	7	•	•	•
Revenues ($ in Thousands)													
Net Sales **2**	6635163	326891	228252	222135	1193802	988670	862647	759121	814870	1238775	•	•	•
Interest **3**	16993	5021	2	763	267	79	354	536	2434	7539	•	•	•
Rents **4**	3554	0	0	0	0	60	360	130	2184	819	•	•	•
Royalties **5**	8628	0	0	0	6748	0	141	283	1100	357	•	•	•
Other Portfolio Income **6**	17528	6266	0	0	706	67	2693	2127	769	4898	•	•	•
Other Receipts **7**	105090	948	109	66	3968	17233	4167	3770	34893	39937	•	•	•
Total Receipts **8**	6786956	339126	228363	222964	1205491	1006109	870362	765967	856250	1292325	•	•	•
Average Total Receipts **9**	4813	33913	264	1728	4601	13415	23523	45057	85625	184618	•	•	•
Operating Costs/Operating Income (%)													
Cost of Operations **10**	64.6	69.6	50.3	53.0	60.5	70.2	66.2	65.4	71.7	61.4	•	•	•
Salaries and Wages **11**	6.8	3.9	12.3	15.2	5.4	5.4	7.4	6.7	6.9	7.2	•	•	•
Taxes Paid **12**	2.4	3.0	1.9	3.9	2.9	2.1	2.5	2.1	1.7	2.3	•	•	•
Interest Paid **13**	1.3	2.4	0.6	0.5	1.4	0.8	0.9	0.9	1.1	2.2	•	•	•
Depreciation **14**	5.0	11.6	7.1	2.6	2.4	3.8	3.7	4.3	5.4	8.0	•	•	•
Amortization and Depletion **15**	0.4	•	•	0.1	0.1	0.0	0.4	0.3	0.5	1.2	•	•	•
Pensions and Other Deferred Comp. **16**	0.6	1.4	•	1.0	0.5	0.3	0.6	0.7	0.7	0.6	•	•	•
Employee Benefits **17**	1.4	0.1	0.0	3.1	1.2	1.2	2.4	1.2	1.1	1.5	•	•	•
Advertising **18**	0.6	0.8	0.1	0.0	0.4	0.6	0.4	0.7	0.4	0.9	•	•	•
Other Expenses **19**	9.6	5.8	16.9	15.6	13.4	8.7	7.9	7.8	6.9	9.1	•	•	•
Officers' Compensation **20**	3.1	0.8	3.6	3.9	7.4	3.3	2.5	2.0	1.7	1.1	•	•	•
Operating Margin **21**	4.3	0.4	7.2	1.2	4.4	3.6	5.0	7.9	1.9	4.6	•	•	•
Operating Margin Before Officers' Comp. **22**	7.3	1.2	10.8	5.1	11.8	6.9	7.5	9.9	3.6	5.6	•	•	•

Selected Average Balance Sheet ($ in Thousands)

Net Receivables 23	641	0	13	208	539	1328	3306	6084	9227	43872
Inventories 24	663	0	10	55	464	1986	4116	6957	12721	25645
Net Property, Plant and Equipment 25	1169	0	23	206	426	2909	4939	12349	26320	87963
Total Assets 26	3716	0	51	664	1892	7873	16123	35969	66576	307136
Notes and Loans Payable 27	948	0	27	208	752	1822	3517	10036	15080	71669
All Other Liabilities 28	679	0	0	217	687	1381	3159	4996	11735	46515
Net Worth 29	2089	0	24	238	453	4670	9448	20937	39761	188953

Selected Financial Ratios (Times to 1)

Current Ratio 30	2.2	•	74.6	1.6	1.3	2.5	2.2	2.3	2.1	2.8
Quick Ratio 31	1.2	•	70.1	1.4	0.7	0.9	1.2	1.2	1.0	1.8
Net Sales to Working Capital 32	5.2	•	9.5	12.5	15.3	4.5	4.6	4.0	5.1	3.1
Coverage Ratio 33	6.1	2.7	13.9	4.2	4.9	7.6	7.8	10.9	7.2	5.0
Total Asset Turnover 34	1.3	•	5.1	2.6	2.4	1.7	1.4	1.2	1.2	0.6
Inventory Turnover 35	4.6	•	13.2	16.6	5.9	4.7	3.8	4.2	4.6	4.2
Receivables Turnover 36	6.8	•	12.5	8.4	10.9	10.9	6.6	8.5	17.7	8.1
Total Liabilities to Net Worth 37	0.8	•	1.2	1.8	3.2	0.7	0.7	0.7	0.7	0.6
Current Assets to Working Capital 38	1.8	•	1.0	2.8	3.9	1.7	1.9	1.7	1.9	1.6
Current Liabilities to Working Capital 39	0.8	•	0.0	1.8	2.9	0.7	0.9	0.7	0.9	0.6
Working Capital to Net Sales 40	0.2	•	0.1	0.1	0.1	0.2	0.2	0.3	0.2	0.3
Inventory to Working Capital 41	0.7	•	0.1	0.3	1.7	0.9	0.7	0.7	0.8	0.4
Total Receipts to Cash Flow 42	7.2	14.1	4.7	7.9	6.5	8.1	8.2	6.6	7.9	6.3
Cost of Goods to Cash Flow 43	4.6	9.8	2.4	4.2	3.9	5.7	5.5	4.3	5.7	3.9
Cash Flow to Total Debt 44	0.4	2.0	0.5	0.5	0.5	0.4	0.4	0.4	0.4	0.2

Selected Financial Factors (in Percentages)

Debt Ratio 45	43.8	•	53.9	64.1	76.1	40.7	41.4	41.8	40.3	38.5
Return on Total Assets 46	10.0	•	40.0	5.3	16.2	10.4	10.3	12.0	9.9	6.4
Return on Equity Before Income Taxes 47	14.8	•	80.5	11.2	53.7	15.1	15.3	18.7	14.3	8.3
Return on Equity After Income Taxes 48	12.1	•	78.5	9.9	50.6	13.3	13.5	15.2	11.9	5.5
Profit Margin (Before Income Tax) 49	6.6	4.1	7.2	1.5	5.3	5.4	6.2	8.8	7.0	8.9
Profit Margin (After Income Tax) 50	5.4	2.9	7.0	1.4	5.0	4.7	5.5	7.1	5.8	5.9

Table I

Corporations with and without Net Income

GLASS AND GLASS PRODUCT

MONEY AMOUNTS AND SIZE OF ASSETS IN THOUSANDS OF DOLLARS

Item Description for Accounting Period 7/03 Through 6/04	Total	Zero Assets	Under 500	500 to 1,000	1,000 to 5,000	5,000 to 10,000	10,000 to 25,000	25,000 to 50,000	50,000 to 100,000	100,000 to 250,000	250,000 to 500,000	500,000 to 2,500,000	2,500,000 and over
Number of Enterprises 1	2199	•	1541	•	390	93	34	11	8	6	4	8	•
Revenues ($ in Thousands)													
Net Sales 2	22681415	•	1161592	•	1348052	1054500	898007	453556	746403	1521285	1445913	13812941	•
Interest 3	81517	•	701	•	817	75	1450	480	19	9209	8570	60193	•
Rents 4	16732	•	0	•	11	0	714	462	0	2328	646	12572	•
Royalties 5	96379	•	0	•	0	0	2	171	0	0	2125	91286	•
Other Portfolio Income 6	138774	•	718	•	3503	485	12065	558	1108	573	18796	100968	•
Other Receipts 7	158409	•	3996	•	-1416	5659	9170	2056	1920	43868	14168	78562	•
Total Receipts 8	23173226	•	1167007	•	1350967	1060719	921408	457283	749450	1577263	1490218	14156522	•
Average Total Receipts 9	10538	•	757	•	3464	11406	27100	41571	93681	262877	372554	1769565	•
Operating Costs/Operating Income (%)													
Cost of Operations 10	65.9	•	43.6	•	61.4	75.2	72.3	69.5	70.2	60.6	65.0	67.5	•
Salaries and Wages 11	6.3	•	16.6	•	7.0	4.8	6.2	7.7	4.1	12.3	9.0	4.6	•
Taxes Paid 12	2.4	•	2.6	•	2.5	1.3	2.0	3.1	2.5	2.2	2.6	2.5	•
Interest Paid 13	3.3	•	0.4	•	0.8	1.5	1.3	2.4	1.0	1.6	1.6	4.5	•
Depreciation 14	4.9	•	1.4	•	3.2	4.0	3.4	3.9	3.6	3.9	4.3	5.9	•
Amortization and Depletion 15	0.5	•	0.0	•	0.1	0.3	0.2	0.6	0.3	0.4	0.3	0.6	•
Pensions and Other Deferred Comp. 16	1.2	•	•	•	0.1	0.1	0.4	0.4	0.6	0.7	0.9	1.7	•
Employee Benefits 17	3.2	•	0.1	•	1.4	0.5	1.9	2.0	3.6	3.1	5.1	3.9	•
Advertising 18	0.6	•	2.0	•	0.3	0.3	0.3	0.5	0.1	2.2	0.7	0.3	•
Other Expenses 19	12.4	•	22.0	•	13.5	11.0	11.9	9.2	5.7	15.0	12.5	11.7	•
Officers' Compensation 20	1.4	•	6.5	•	9.9	1.3	1.5	1.6	0.8	0.7	0.5	0.3	•
Operating Margin 21	•	•	4.6	•	•	•	•	•	7.5	•	•	•	•
Operating Margin Before Officers' Comp. 22	•	•	11.2	•	9.7	1.1	0.1	0.8	8.3	•	•	•	•

Selected Average Balance Sheet ($ in Thousands)

Net Receivables 23	1282	54	592	1341	2838	5952	13829	22428	70146	208843
Inventories 24	1421	54	364	1062	3017	4922	10560	27230	56045	268738
Net Property, Plant and Equipment 25	3500	34	526	3402	5314	9612	25429	54586	76351	748336
Total Assets 26	12769	228	1739	7118	14712	33542	68860	159426	352117	2817456
Notes and Loans Payable 27	5163	137	664	3981	6215	14386	23375	24645	97745	1175904
All Other Liabilities 28	3299	39	290	1689	3420	7819	17995	72664	85495	719134
Net Worth 29	4307	52	784	1448	5077	11337	27491	62116	168877	922418

Selected Financial Ratios (Times to 1)

Current Ratio 30	1.3	4.0	3.0	1.5	1.3	1.4	1.3	2.2	2.9	1.1
Quick Ratio 31	0.6	2.3	1.7	0.7	0.7	0.8	0.6	1.1	1.6	0.5
Net Sales to Working Capital 32	12.5	6.4	4.5	10.7	15.3	10.2	12.1	5.7	3.2	39.6
Coverage Ratio 33	1.1	13.2	1.0	1.3	1.9	1.0	9.2	1.7	1.4	0.8
Total Asset Turnover 34	0.8	3.3	2.0	1.6	1.8	1.2	1.4	1.6	1.0	0.6
Inventory Turnover 35	4.8	6.1	5.8	8.0	6.3	5.8	6.2	5.6	4.2	4.3
Receivables Turnover 36	8.0	11.8	7.1	11.3	9.7	7.6	8.5	9.9	5.4	7.9
Total Liabilities to Net Worth 37	2.0	3.4	1.2	3.9	1.9	2.0	1.5	1.6	1.1	2.1
Current Assets to Working Capital 38	4.3	1.3	1.5	3.1	4.3	3.5	4.1	1.9	1.5	14.0
Current Liabilities to Working Capital 39	3.3	0.3	0.5	2.1	3.3	2.5	3.1	0.9	0.5	13.0
Working Capital to Net Sales 40	0.1	0.2	0.2	0.1	0.1	0.1	0.1	0.2	0.3	0.0
Inventory to Working Capital 41	1.7	0.5	0.5	1.4	1.7	1.3	1.8	0.7	0.4	5.9
Total Receipts to Cash Flow 42	11.8	4.7	11.9	12.1	9.6	14.9	8.4	8.0	10.8	15.2
Cost of Goods to Cash Flow 43	7.8	2.0	7.3	9.1	6.9	10.4	5.9	4.9	7.0	10.3
Cash Flow to Total Debt 44	0.1	0.9	0.3	0.2	0.3	0.1	0.3	0.3	0.2	0.1

Selected Financial Factors (in Percentages)

Debt Ratio 45	66.3	77.1	54.9	79.7	65.5	66.2	60.1	61.0	52.0	67.3
Return on Total Assets 46	2.8	18.2	1.6	3.0	4.3	3.0	12.1	4.2	2.3	2.3
Return on Equity Before Income Taxes 47	0.5	73.4	•	3.0	5.8	•	27.0	4.3	1.4	•
Return on Equity After Income Taxes 48	•	73.4	•	1.6	3.9	•	20.3	0.7	0.5	•
Profit Margin (Before Income Tax) 49	0.2	5.1	•	0.4	1.1	•	7.9	1.1	0.6	•
Profit Margin (After Income Tax) 50	•	5.1	•	0.2	0.7	•	6.0	0.2	0.3	•

Table II
Corporations with Net Income

GLASS AND GLASS PRODUCT

MONEY AMOUNTS AND SIZE OF ASSETS IN THOUSANDS OF DOLLARS

Item Description for Accounting Period 7/03 Through 6/04	Total	Zero Assets	Under 500	500 to 1000	251 to 500	501 to 1,000	1,001 to 5,000	5,001 to 10,000	10,001 to 25,000	25,001 to 50,000	50,001 to 100,000	100,001 to 250,000	250,001 and over
Number of Enterprises 1	1303	•	863	•	298	56	18	4	5	•	•	4	•
Revenues ($ in Thousands)													
Net Sales 2	14303453	•	943583	•	1331078	675100	599670	123023	474120	•	•	8805930	•
Interest 3	46205	•	701	•	728	20	1139	436	16	•	•	38950	•
Rents 4	3079	•	0	•	11	0	152	462	0	•	•	2179	•
Royalties 5	27069	•	0	•	0	0	2	0	0	•	•	22769	•
Other Portfolio Income 6	103990	•	718	•	3357	18	11982	334	1106	•	•	69771	•
Other Receipts 7	54586	•	3930	•	-2648	919	7737	1118	859	•	•	27147	•
Total Receipts 8	14538382	•	948932	•	1332526	676057	620682	125373	476101	•	•	8966746	•
Average Total Receipts 9	11158	•	1100	•	4472	12072	34482	31343	95220	•	•	2241686	•
Operating Costs/Operating Income (%)													
Cost of Operations 10	63.3	•	39.7	•	61.7	77.9	72.2	59.8	71.1	•	•	64.5	•
Salaries and Wages 11	6.3	•	16.6	•	6.2	4.8	5.6	6.2	2.0	•	•	5.3	•
Taxes Paid 12	2.4	•	2.7	•	2.3	1.0	1.8	3.6	2.0	•	•	2.5	•
Interest Paid 13	1.7	•	0.4	•	0.8	0.5	1.1	3.1	0.6	•	•	2.2	•
Depreciation 14	4.8	•	1.4	•	2.9	2.0	2.4	5.9	4.9	•	•	5.9	•
Amortization and Depletion 15	0.5	•	0.0	•	0.0	0.0	0.1	0.3	0.2	•	•	0.7	•
Pensions and Other Deferred Comp. 16	1.5	•	•	•	0.1	0.1	0.1	0.6	0.4	•	•	2.3	•
Employee Benefits 17	3.0	•	0.1	•	1.4	0.6	1.9	2.1	2.5	•	•	3.7	•
Advertising 18	0.6	•	2.0	•	0.3	0.4	0.2	1.6	0.0	•	•	0.5	•
Other Expenses 19	11.0	•	19.7	•	12.3	7.3	11.5	11.4	2.8	•	•	10.2	•
Officers' Compensation 20	1.8	•	7.5	•	10.1	0.7	1.5	1.0	0.5	•	•	0.2	•
Operating Margin 21	2.9	•	9.9	•	1.9	4.5	1.5	4.3	13.0	•	•	1.9	•
Operating Margin Before Officers' Comp. 22	4.7	•	17.4	•	11.9	5.2	3.1	5.4	13.5	•	•	2.2	•

Selected Average Balance Sheet ($ in Thousands)

Net Receivables 23	1358	75	591	1747	3356	3926	14896	261217
Inventories 24	1380	46	325	1014	2836	5875	12484	307568
Net Property, Plant and Equipment 25	3332	22	447	1893	4808	8018	30491	876094
Total Assets 26	11429	254	1803	6053	14493	35976	70694	2978588
Notes and Loans Payable 27	3664	100	842	1876	5867	10046	14939	930648
All Other Liabilities 28	3003	33	351	1215	4039	6441	18052	797312
Net Worth 29	4763	120	610	2962	4586	19488	37704	1250628

Selected Financial Ratios (Times to 1)

Current Ratio 30	1.2	6.5	2.7	2.7	1.3	1.9	1.2	1.0
Quick Ratio 31	0.6	4.7	1.4	1.6	0.7	1.0	0.6	0.5
Net Sales to Working Capital 32	15.5	6.6	5.4	5.2	19.5	4.8	19.8	*
Coverage Ratio 33	3.7	27.7	3.5	10.0	5.4	3.0	22.0	2.7
Total Asset Turnover 34	1.0	4.3	2.5	2.0	2.3	0.9	1.3	0.7
Inventory Turnover 35	5.0	9.5	8.5	9.3	8.5	3.1	5.4	4.6
Receivables Turnover 36	8.2	11.8	10.0	8.9	10.7	5.6	12.7	8.2
Total Liabilities to Net Worth 37	1.4	1.1	2.0	1.0	2.2	0.8	0.9	1.4
Current Assets to Working Capital 38	5.1	1.2	1.6	1.6	4.9	2.1	6.4	*
Current Liabilities to Working Capital 39	4.1	0.2	0.6	0.6	3.9	1.1	5.4	*
Working Capital to Net Sales 40	0.1	0.2	0.2	0.2	0.1	0.2	0.1	*
Inventory to Working Capital 41	2.1	0.3	0.6	0.6	1.8	0.9	2.6	*
Total Receipts to Cash Flow 42	8.5	4.2	10.7	8.5	7.3	6.6	6.5	9.9
Cost of Goods to Cash Flow 43	5.4	1.6	6.6	6.7	5.3	4.0	4.6	6.4
Cash Flow to Total Debt 44	0.2	2.0	0.4	0.5	0.5	0.3	0.4	0.1

Selected Financial Factors (in Percentages)

Debt Ratio 45	58.3	52.8	66.2	51.1	68.4	45.8	46.7	58.0
Return on Total Assets 46	6.1	46.8	6.9	10.3	14.2	7.8	19.0	4.5
Return on Equity Before Income Taxes 47	10.6	95.6	14.5	19.0	36.5	9.6	34.0	6.7
Return on Equity After Income Taxes 48	8.7	95.6	11.7	17.8	32.5	7.2	26.2	5.3
Profit Margin (Before Income Tax) 49	4.6	10.5	2.0	4.7	5.0	6.1	13.5	3.8
Profit Margin (After Income Tax) 50	3.8	10.5	1.6	4.4	4.5	4.6	10.4	3.0

Table I

Corporations with and without Net Income

CEMENT, CONCRETE, LIME AND GYPSUM PRODUCT

MONEY AMOUNTS AND SIZE OF ASSETS IN THOUSANDS OF DOLLARS

Item Description for Accounting Period 7/03 Through 6/04		Total	Zero Assets	Under 500	500 to 1,000	1,000 to 5,000	5,000 to 10,000	10,000 to 25,000	25,000 to 50,000	50,000 to 100,000	100,000 to 250,000	250,000 to 500,000	500,000 to 2,500,000	2,500,000 and over
Number of Enterprises	1	5085	218	2543	688	1163	193	159	55	20	18	8	15	6
Revenues ($ in Thousands)														
Net Sales	2	53591965	711314	1111678	1338093	5738021	2171056	3884114	2663069	2085578	3195097	2438583	10989428	17265934
Interest	3	637583	851	245	937	6959	4110	4114	2434	1962	17462	44293	289759	264456
Rents	4	67232	747	5	2785	5565	1645	3966	1476	1206	3206	2670	27740	16220
Royalties	5	35644	285	0	0	0	159	522	130	63	2175	9350	10003	12957
Other Portfolio Income	6	295479	12844	24	181	8251	10311	19341	5727	7139	3086	13807	20519	194249
Other Receipts	7	821201	1618	8773	14528	93289	10561	65269	9171	11380	51315	19039	147814	388445
Total Receipts	8	55449104	727659	1120725	1356524	5852085	2197842	3977326	2682007	2107328	3272341	2527742	11485263	18142261
Average Total Receipts	9	10904	3338	441	1972	5032	11388	25015	48764	105366	181797	315968	765684	3023710
Operating Costs/Operating Income (%)														
Cost of Operations	10	65.8	71.2	48.8	57.7	64.1	64.9	70.3	67.4	69.5	70.0	63.5	66.1	65.6
Salaries and Wages	11	6.2	4.2	16.4	9.4	6.3	6.8	6.1	7.1	4.4	4.6	6.9	4.3	6.8
Taxes Paid	12	2.3	1.8	4.9	2.1	3.1	2.5	2.4	2.3	2.0	2.4	2.3	2.1	1.9
Interest Paid	13	3.6	1.9	1.0	1.1	1.0	1.7	0.8	0.9	1.1	1.6	4.8	5.8	5.5
Depreciation	14	6.1	7.9	3.5	6.1	5.5	5.3	4.9	5.9	6.0	6.1	6.6	7.8	5.7
Amortization and Depletion	15	1.0	1.1	0.1	0.1	0.0	0.1	0.2	0.4	0.5	0.9	2.1	1.4	1.6
Pensions and Other Deferred Comp.	16	0.7	0.0	•	0.7	0.4	0.6	0.5	0.7	0.6	0.8	0.7	0.8	1.0
Employee Benefits	17	2.4	3.1	0.6	1.4	1.9	1.4	1.6	2.1	2.6	1.6	2.1	2.5	3.3
Advertising	18	0.4	0.4	0.9	0.6	0.4	0.4	0.4	0.4	0.6	0.8	0.2	0.1	0.4
Other Expenses	19	10.6	8.4	21.7	17.3	13.0	11.0	9.7	7.6	8.3	7.6	10.6	8.7	11.4
Officers' Compensation	20	1.1	0.4	2.5	3.0	3.3	2.6	1.9	1.9	1.0	0.8	0.9	0.4	0.3
Operating Margin	21	•	•	•	0.6	1.0	2.6	1.2	3.3	3.3	2.8	•	0.1	•
Operating Margin Before Officers' Comp.	22	0.8	•	2.1	3.6	4.3	5.1	3.1	5.2	4.4	3.6	0.2	0.5	•

Selected Average Balance Sheet ($ in Thousands)

Net Receivables 23	1480	0	34	190	675	1530	3845	7477	16214	24115	41240	100940	433942
Inventories 24	813	0	11	67	227	851	1611	3697	6766	11628	27516	74636	247925
Net Property, Plant and Equipment 25	5381	0	88	253	1018	3049	5574	15197	33822	66677	186038	677997	1655645
Total Assets 26	12342	0	165	683	2469	7116	15117	34237	74517	160639	396447	1340504	4279164
Notes and Loans Payable 27	4061	0	79	304	951	2985	3953	9726	16541	38065	133342	429620	1478014
All Other Liabilities 28	3480	0	36	130	370	1681	3121	6752	15674	35025	87460	383556	1416149
Net Worth 29	4800	0	50	249	1148	2450	8043	17759	42302	87550	175644	527328	1385001

Selected Financial Ratios (Times to 1)

Current Ratio 30	1.4	•	1.4	2.5	2.3	1.5	2.0	1.9	1.8	1.9	2.0	1.3	1.0
Quick Ratio 31	0.9	•	1.1	2.0	1.8	1.1	1.4	1.2	1.2	1.2	1.2	0.8	0.6
Net Sales to Working Capital 32	11.8	•	23.8	8.7	6.5	9.6	5.9	6.6	7.4	6.8	6.0	13.4	89.3
Coverage Ratio 33	1.9	2.0	1.3	2.8	4.0	3.2	5.4	5.5	5.1	4.3	1.7	1.8	1.3
Total Asset Turnover 34	0.9	•	2.6	2.8	2.0	1.6	1.6	1.4	1.4	1.1	0.8	0.5	0.7
Inventory Turnover 35	8.5	•	19.0	16.8	13.9	8.6	10.7	8.8	10.7	10.7	7.0	6.5	7.6
Receivables Turnover 36	6.2	•	15.3	11.8	8.2	6.6	6.8	7.0	7.0	7.9	7.0	7.4	4.4
Total Liabilities to Net Worth 37	1.6	•	2.3	1.7	1.2	1.9	0.9	0.9	0.8	0.8	1.3	1.5	2.1
Current Assets to Working Capital 38	3.8	•	3.4	1.7	1.7	2.8	2.0	2.1	2.2	2.2	2.0	4.5	33.4
Current Liabilities to Working Capital 39	2.8	•	2.4	0.7	0.7	1.8	1.0	1.1	1.2	1.2	1.0	3.5	32.4
Working Capital to Net Sales 40	0.1	•	0.0	0.1	0.2	0.1	0.2	0.2	0.1	0.1	0.2	0.1	0.0
Inventory to Working Capital 41	0.9	•	0.7	0.3	0.3	0.7	0.4	0.5	0.5	0.5	0.6	1.2	7.8
Total Receipts to Cash Flow 42	9.4	12.4	5.9	7.0	8.7	8.7	10.1	11.1	9.6	9.6	8.9	9.2	10.0
Cost of Goods to Cash Flow 43	6.2	8.8	2.9	4.0	5.6	5.7	7.1	7.4	6.6	6.7	5.7	6.1	6.5
Cash Flow to Total Debt 44	0.1	•	0.6	0.6	0.4	0.3	0.3	0.3	0.3	0.3	0.2	0.1	0.1

Selected Financial Factors (in Percentages)

Debt Ratio 45	61.1	•	69.8	63.5	53.5	65.6	46.8	48.1	43.2	45.5	55.7	60.7	67.6
Return on Total Assets 46	5.8	•	3.6	8.8	7.9	8.7	7.1	6.9	7.6	7.5	6.1	5.7	4.8
Return on Equity Before Income Taxes 47	6.9	•	2.9	15.5	12.8	17.5	10.9	10.9	10.8	10.6	5.5	6.5	3.6
Return on Equity After Income Taxes 48	4.6	•	1.5	15.2	12.2	14.2	9.9	9.2	9.3	6.8	3.4	3.9	1.0
Profit Margin (Before Income Tax) 49	3.2	1.8	0.3	2.0	3.0	3.8	3.6	4.0	4.4	5.2	3.2	4.7	1.7
Profit Margin (After Income Tax) 50	2.1	1.5	0.2	1.9	2.8	3.1	3.3	3.4	3.8	3.4	1.9	2.8	0.5

Table II

Corporations with Net Income

CEMENT, CONCRETE, LIME AND GYPSUM PRODUCT

MONEY AMOUNTS AND SIZE OF ASSETS IN THOUSANDS OF DOLLARS

Item Description for Accounting Period 7/03 Through 6/04	Total	Zero Assets	Under 500	500 to 1,000	1,000 to 5,000	5,000 to 10,000	10,000 to 25,000	25,000 to 50,000	50,000 to 100,000	100,000 to 250,000	250,000 to 500,000	500,000 to 2,500,000	2,500,000 and over
Number of Enterprises 1	2959	•	1051	•	629	171	113	44	16	12	5	10	•
Revenues ($ in Thousands)													
Net Sales 2	40967814	•	829355	•	3631357	1957226	2743896	2191448	1721236	2240306	1502595	7633049	•
Interest 3	401492	•	236	•	3597	2513	3282	2175	1608	9282	9917	112213	•
Rents 4	58160	•	5	•	1881	1645	3134	1357	811	3045	1900	26208	•
Royalties 5	34465	•	0	•	0	63	18	130	63	2175	9350	9908	•
Other Portfolio Income 6	226988	•	24	•	6069	7878	15900	4235	3402	2837	10641	19509	•
Other Receipts 7	670498	•	8728	•	35938	10431	59382	5024	10575	55565	12598	108419	•
Total Receipts 8	42359417	•	838348	•	3678842	1979756	2825612	2204369	1737695	2313210	1547001	7909306	•
Average Total Receipts 9	14315	•	798	•	5849	11578	25005	50099	108606	192768	309400	790931	•
Operating Costs/Operating Income (%)													
Cost of Operations 10	65.3	•	40.1	•	58.0	62.9	68.3	66.0	67.9	68.1	66.9	66.2	•
Salaries and Wages 11	6.4	•	20.2	•	7.1	6.8	6.4	6.9	4.3	4.7	3.7	3.7	•
Taxes Paid 12	2.2	•	5.7	•	3.1	2.7	2.3	2.3	2.0	2.4	2.0	2.2	•
Interest Paid 13	3.0	•	1.0	•	0.8	1.5	0.7	0.9	0.9	1.1	2.8	3.7	•
Depreciation 14	5.5	•	4.0	•	4.5	5.2	5.0	5.5	6.0	5.3	6.7	6.5	•
Amortization and Depletion 15	1.0	•	0.1	•	0.0	0.1	0.2	0.3	0.4	0.6	2.2	1.7	•
Pensions and Other Deferred Comp. 16	0.8	•	•	•	0.4	0.7	0.6	0.7	0.7	0.6	0.5	0.8	•
Employee Benefits 17	2.4	•	0.1	•	2.0	1.4	1.6	2.0	2.3	1.6	2.0	2.8	•
Advertising 18	0.4	•	0.3	•	0.4	0.4	0.3	0.4	0.6	1.1	0.2	0.1	•
Other Expenses 19	9.3	•	21.8	•	14.5	11.4	8.6	7.4	8.4	6.9	9.3	7.9	•
Officers' Compensation 20	1.1	•	1.7	•	3.2	2.7	2.2	2.0	1.0	0.7	1.2	0.4	•
Operating Margin 21	2.6	•	5.0	•	6.1	4.2	3.8	5.5	5.3	6.9	2.7	4.1	•
Operating Margin Before Officers' Comp. 22	3.7	•	6.8	•	9.2	7.0	6.0	7.5	6.3	7.6	3.8	4.5	•

Selected Average Balance Sheet ($ in Thousands)

Net Receivables **23**	2041	42	754	1575	3714	7383	16773	24886	45929	100043
Inventories **24**	985	7	221	805	1665	3963	7700	12198	29397	66864
Net Property, Plant and Equipment **25**	6568	194	817	3007	5411	13930	33899	59516	184806	692028
Total Assets **26**	15099	296	2384	7190	15221	34420	77155	159233	377692	1415063
Notes and Loans Payable **27**	4846	128	588	2831	3465	8922	15751	40092	103727	431518
All Other Liabilities **28**	3951	21	425	1635	2638	6663	15368	29770	93244	347242
Net Worth **29**	6301	147	1371	2724	9118	18836	46036	89371	180721	636303

Selected Financial Ratios (Times to 1)

Current Ratio **30**	1.5	1.9	2.5	1.6	2.4	2.1	1.8	1.9	2.3	1.3
Quick Ratio **31**	1.0	1.8	2.0	1.1	1.7	1.3	1.2	1.3	1.4	0.8
Net Sales to Working Capital **32**	9.0	23.4	6.7	9.2	5.0	5.7	7.5	6.6	4.6	12.8
Coverage Ratio **33**	3.0	7.0	10.3	4.5	10.3	8.1	7.8	10.1	3.1	3.1
Total Asset Turnover **34**	0.9	2.7	2.4	1.6	1.6	1.4	1.4	1.2	0.8	0.5
Inventory Turnover **35**	9.2	46.0	15.2	8.9	10.0	8.3	9.5	10.4	6.8	7.6
Receivables Turnover **36**	5.8	19.2	8.8	7.2	6.7	7.2	12.8	7.9	13.1	7.5
Total Liabilities to Net Worth **37**	1.4	1.0	0.7	1.6	0.7	0.8	0.7	0.8	1.1	1.2
Current Assets to Working Capital **38**	3.0	2.1	1.7	2.7	1.7	1.9	2.3	2.1	1.8	4.5
Current Liabilities to Working Capital **39**	2.0	1.1	0.7	1.7	0.7	0.9	1.3	1.1	0.8	3.5
Working Capital to Net Sales **40**	0.1	0.0	0.2	0.1	0.2	0.2	0.1	0.2	0.2	0.1
Inventory to Working Capital **41**	0.7	0.1	0.2	0.7	0.3	0.5	0.5	0.4	0.5	1.2
Total Receipts to Cash Flow **42**	8.3	4.5	5.9	7.5	8.1	9.1	8.2	7.0	7.5	7.8
Cost of Goods to Cash Flow **43**	5.4	1.8	3.4	4.7	5.5	6.0	5.5	4.8	5.0	5.2
Cash Flow to Total Debt **44**	0.2	1.2	1.0	0.3	0.5	0.3	0.4	0.4	0.2	0.1

Selected Financial Factors (in Percentages)

Debt Ratio **45**	58.3	50.5	42.5	62.1	40.1	45.3	40.3	43.9	52.2	55.0
Return on Total Assets **46**	8.3	19.0	19.8	11.0	12.0	10.1	10.1	13.3	7.0	6.3
Return on Equity Before Income Taxes **47**	13.3	32.9	31.0	22.6	18.0	16.1	14.7	21.3	9.9	9.5
Return on Equity After Income Taxes **48**	10.1	31.7	30.0	19.3	16.8	14.1	13.0	15.8	6.7	6.3
Profit Margin (Before Income Tax) **49**	6.0	6.1	7.4	5.4	6.8	6.1	6.3	10.2	6.0	7.9
Profit Margin (After Income Tax) **50**	4.6	5.9	7.1	4.6	6.3	5.3	5.5	7.6	4.0	5.2

Table I

Corporations with and without Net Income

IRON, STEEL MILLS AND STEEL PRODUCT

MONEY AMOUNTS AND SIZE OF ASSETS IN THOUSANDS OF DOLLARS

Item Description for Accounting Period 7/03 Through 6/04		Total	Zero Assets	Under 500	500 to 1,000	1,000 to 5,000	5,000 to 10,000	10,000 to 25,000	25,000 to 50,000	50,000 to 100,000	100,000 to 250,000	250,000 to 500,000	500,000 to 2,500,000	2,500,000 and over
Number of Enterprises	1	3776	19	2676	323	376	122	110	44	38	34	8	20	5
Revenues ($ in Thousands)														
Net Sales	2	73681224	2767338	1523295	436877	2836544	2014083	2914751	2250813	3568928	6625887	3730293	21285446	23726970
Interest	3	421592	16847	0	114	595	1945	1722	1636	11186	32398	39740	167551	147859
Rents	4	50962	6344	0	0	52	34	304	2700	698	4533	1013	11802	23483
Royalties	5	329245	883	0	0	0	26	89	0	2403	2159	13488	179790	130406
Other Portfolio Income	6	365574	45490	8576	566	1994	14063	2447	829	1605	8575	42648	52836	185944
Other Receipts	7	1889136	989881	1704	928	30261	51845	8604	11838	24866	37905	51713	497246	182345
Total Receipts	8	76737733	3826783	1533575	438485	2869446	2081996	2927917	2267816	3609686	6711457	3878895	22194671	24397007
Average Total Receipts	9	20322	201410	573	1358	7632	17066	26617	51541	94992	197396	484862	1109734	4879401
Operating Costs/Operating Income (%)														
Cost of Operations	10	80.6	82.1	59.3	70.9	76.5	81.2	78.5	81.8	83.3	82.1	87.3	82.7	78.7
Salaries and Wages	11	3.7	4.6	13.9	5.9	4.5	2.4	4.7	4.1	4.1	4.6	2.5	4.5	2.0
Taxes Paid	12	1.6	2.0	2.7	2.7	1.9	2.4	1.7	1.6	1.2	1.2	1.3	1.3	1.9
Interest Paid	13	2.1	1.4	0.4	1.8	0.6	1.6	1.1	1.6	1.3	2.0	2.2	3.1	1.9
Depreciation	14	4.5	3.9	2.2	3.8	4.3	5.2	3.0	4.3	3.6	3.7	3.2	4.4	5.5
Amortization and Depletion	15	0.3	0.3	0.2	0.1	0.0	0.0	0.2	0.3	0.2	0.4	0.1	0.4	0.2
Pensions and Other Deferred Comp.	16	1.0	3.5	0.5	0.3	0.2	0.9	0.3	0.4	0.3	0.8	0.2	0.6	1.6
Employee Benefits	17	2.1	7.0	1.5	1.4	1.3	0.6	1.4	1.6	1.3	1.3	1.2	1.9	2.7
Advertising	18	0.1	0.0	0.2	0.3	0.1	0.2	0.3	0.1	0.1	0.2	0.0	0.1	0.0
Other Expenses	19	11.6	76.0	20.9	10.4	6.2	7.1	6.5	5.3	6.1	6.4	6.5	6.6	13.3
Officers' Compensation	20	0.7	0.1	4.7	4.5	3.4	1.3	2.2	1.2	0.7	0.6	0.4	0.3	0.3
Operating Margin	21	•	•	•	•	0.9	•	0.1	•	•	•	•	•	•
Operating Margin Before Officers' Comp.	22	2.3	•	2.4	2.4	4.3	2.4	2.3	•	•	•	•	•	•

Selected Average Balance Sheet ($ in Thousands)

Net Receivables 23	2743	0	68	58	1026	2431	4035	7076	13460	26097	58647	189350	612807
Inventories 24	2829	0	19	75	841	913	3610	8165	16635	33671	79218	167606	732282
Net Property, Plant and Equipment 25	6423	0	38	301	1055	2668	4555	10882	22311	55765	92443	412917	2121644
Total Assets 26	16234	0	161	621	3484	7762	15456	33704	68601	151765	301214	1106224	4584791
Notes and Loans Payable 27	4891	0	90	305	1772	4351	5166	15334	24008	61648	101170	348086	982097
All Other Liabilities 28	7756	0	62	40	1190	3731	4221	11706	19364	51373	98494	526360	2685467
Net Worth 29	3586	0	9	277	521	-320	6070	6664	25228	38744	101550	231778	917228

Selected Financial Ratios (Times to 1)

Current Ratio 30	1.6	•	1.2	3.7	2.2	1.2	1.6	1.4	2.0	1.8	1.6	1.4	1.7
Quick Ratio 31	0.8	•	0.9	2.3	1.3	0.9	0.9	0.7	0.9	0.8	0.7	0.7	0.8
Net Sales to Working Capital 32	7.7	•	26.9	8.2	6.0	22.2	7.2	9.7	4.9	6.0	6.9	8.7	7.0
Coverage Ratio 33	•	•	•	0.1	4.2	1.3	1.5	•	0.2	•	0.6	0.5	•
Total Asset Turnover 34	1.2	•	3.5	2.2	2.2	2.1	1.7	1.5	1.4	1.3	1.5	1.0	1.0
Inventory Turnover 35	5.6	•	17.8	12.7	6.9	14.7	5.8	5.1	4.7	4.8	5.1	5.2	5.1
Receivables Turnover 36	8.1	•	9.4	16.4	9.0	10.9	7.1	8.0	7.5	7.5	8.1	6.8	8.5
Total Liabilities to Net Worth 37	3.5	•	16.5	1.2	5.7	•	1.5	4.1	1.7	2.9	2.0	3.8	4.0
Current Assets to Working Capital 38	2.7	•	5.2	1.4	1.9	6.6	2.6	3.5	2.0	2.3	2.6	3.6	2.4
Current Liabilities to Working Capital 39	1.7	•	4.2	0.4	0.9	5.6	1.6	2.5	1.0	1.3	1.6	2.6	1.4
Working Capital to Net Sales 40	0.1	•	0.0	0.1	0.2	0.0	0.1	0.1	0.2	0.2	0.1	0.1	0.1
Inventory to Working Capital 41	1.1	•	1.1	0.5	0.7	1.5	1.0	1.6	0.9	1.0	1.1	1.4	1.0
Total Receipts to Cash Flow 42	30.8	5.2	12.8	16.1	17.1	33.6	18.8	43.5	28.1	37.0	27.0	27.6	379.0
Cost of Goods to Cash Flow 43	24.8	4.3	7.6	11.4	13.1	27.3	14.8	35.6	23.4	30.4	23.6	22.8	298.4
Cash Flow to Total Debt 44	0.1	•	0.3	0.2	0.1	0.1	0.2	0.0	0.1	0.0	0.1	0.0	0.0

Selected Financial Factors (in Percentages)

Debt Ratio 45	77.9	•	94.3	55.4	85.0	104.1	60.7	80.2	63.2	74.5	66.3	79.0	80.0
Return on Total Assets 46	•	•	•	0.2	5.9	4.5	2.7	•	0.3	•	2.0	1.4	•
Return on Equity Before Income Taxes 47	•	•	•	•	29.9	•	2.2	•	•	•	•	•	•
Return on Equity After Income Taxes 48	•	•	•	•	28.1	•	1.3	•	•	•	•	•	•
Profit Margin (Before Income Tax) 49	•	•	•	•	2.1	0.5	0.5	•	•	•	•	•	•
Profit Margin (After Income Tax) 50	•	•	•	•	1.9	0.3	0.3	•	•	•	•	•	•

Manufacturing 331115

Table II
Corporations with Net Income

IRON, STEEL MILLS AND STEEL PRODUCT

MONEY AMOUNTS AND SIZE OF ASSETS IN THOUSANDS OF DOLLARS

Item Description for Accounting Period 7/03 Through 6/04	Total	Zero Assets	Under 500	500 to 1,000	1,000 to 5,000	5,000 to 10,000	10,000 to 25,000	25,000 to 50,000	50,000 to 100,000	100,000 to 250,000	250,000 to 500,000	500,000 to 2,500,000	2,500,000 and over
Number of Enterprises 1	1785	11	1152	107	293	87	65	24	18	18	4	7	•
Revenues ($ in Thousands)													
Net Sales 2	22024093	18958	306530	186594	2340341	1450495	1879135	1215982	1864443	3836846	2153478	6771290	•
Interest 3	129975	3	0	49	251	172	549	692	3228	10671	12710	101648	•
Rents 4	7577	0	0	0	1	34	47	2539	300	1415	422	2819	•
Royalties 5	84482	0	0	0	0	0	89	0	153	2123	13488	68630	•
Other Portfolio Income 6	71278	0	8576	0	1994	12251	900	278	528	1756	6168	38828	•
Other Receipts 7	455736	6805	0	928	8077	1114	6176	6444	13375	24790	33405	354622	•
Total Receipts 8	22773141	25766	315106	187571	2350664	1464066	1886896	1225935	1882027	3877601	2219671	7337837	•
Average Total Receipts 9	12758	2342	274	1753	8023	16828	29029	51081	104557	215422	554918	1048262	•
Operating Costs/Operating Income (%)													
Cost of Operations 10	77.9	93.1	20.5	63.4	75.0	76.9	76.9	78.5	83.0	80.4	88.3	76.2	•
Salaries and Wages 11	4.3	9.4	18.0	0.8	4.8	2.2	4.4	3.6	4.4	4.9	1.9	4.5	•
Taxes Paid 12	1.7	0.1	2.9	3.4	1.9	2.8	1.6	1.7	1.3	1.3	0.7	1.9	•
Interest Paid 13	1.6	0.5	0.9	0.4	0.8	0.6	0.8	1.0	0.6	0.9	1.3	3.5	•
Depreciation 14	3.7	5.4	3.6	5.8	3.0	6.7	2.6	3.7	2.2	3.0	2.4	4.9	•
Amortization and Depletion 15	0.3	•	•	0.0	0.1	•	0.2	0.1	0.0	0.2	0.0	0.7	•
Pensions and Other Deferred Comp. 16	0.6	•	2.3	0.7	0.2	0.3	0.4	0.5	0.2	0.6	0.2	1.1	•
Employee Benefits 17	1.4	0.1	0.1	3.2	1.2	0.1	1.3	1.9	0.9	1.1	0.5	2.4	•
Advertising 18	0.2	•	0.0	0.2	0.1	0.2	0.3	0.1	0.1	0.3	0.0	0.1	•
Other Expenses 19	6.4	12.8	41.2	14.9	5.6	3.6	5.8	4.3	4.4	4.7	5.4	7.8	•
Officers' Compensation 20	1.3	0.2	10.0	7.1	3.6	1.4	2.4	1.5	0.7	0.6	0.4	0.3	•
Operating Margin 21	0.5	•	0.4	0.1	3.8	5.3	3.4	3.1	2.2	2.0	•	•	•
Operating Margin Before Officers' Comp. 22	1.8	•	•	7.2	7.5	6.6	5.8	4.7	2.9	2.7	•	•	•

Selected Average Balance Sheet ($ in Thousands)

	1	2	3	4	5	6	7	8	9	10	11	12
Net Receivables 23	1817	0	20	162	1091	1888	4632	7547	13626	26324	63850	180415
Inventories 24	2534	0	16	70	789	916	3681	8931	21509	33950	74799	210226
Net Property, Plant and Equipment 25	3163	0	20	299	1028	2961	4001	9732	14944	52339	109582	412692
Total Assets 26	9208	0	76	719	3410	7773	15826	33640	65994	139804	300441	1122045
Notes and Loans Payable 27	2292	0	44	109	956	1889	4190	8879	18080	25421	82027	284083
All Other Liabilities 28	2623	0	30	100	519	1174	4328	9673	16037	45111	85922	346275
Net Worth 29	4293	0	2	511	1935	4710	7308	15088	31877	69272	132492	491687

Selected Financial Ratios (Times to 1)

	1	2	3	4	5	6	7	8	9	10	11	12
Current Ratio 30	1.8	•	0.6	3.7	2.6	2.6	1.8	1.7	2.6	2.0	1.8	1.5
Quick Ratio 31	0.9	•	0.4	2.4	1.6	1.8	1.0	0.8	1.2	0.9	0.9	0.8
Net Sales to Working Capital 32	6.0	•	•	6.4	5.7	5.7	6.1	6.6	3.7	5.6	7.3	6.8
Coverage Ratio 33	3.4	32.6	4.4	2.5	6.6	10.7	6.1	5.1	6.4	4.5	2.6	2.4
Total Asset Turnover 34	1.3	•	3.5	2.4	2.3	2.1	1.8	1.5	1.6	1.5	1.8	0.9
Inventory Turnover 35	3.8	•	3.5	15.9	7.6	14.0	6.0	4.5	4.0	5.0	6.4	3.5
Receivables Turnover 36	6.0	•	8.0	15.0	9.0	15.6	7.0	7.2	7.9	7.4	16.9	4.8
Total Liabilities to Net Worth 37	1.1	•	41.6	0.4	0.8	0.7	1.2	1.2	1.1	1.0	1.3	1.3
Current Assets to Working Capital 38	2.3	•	•	1.4	1.6	1.6	2.2	2.5	1.6	2.0	2.2	3.0
Current Liabilities to Working Capital 39	1.3	•	•	0.4	0.6	0.6	1.2	1.5	0.6	1.0	1.2	2.0
Working Capital to Net Sales 40	0.2	•	•	0.2	0.2	0.2	0.2	0.2	0.3	0.2	0.1	0.1
Inventory to Working Capital 41	0.9	•	•	0.4	0.6	0.5	0.8	1.2	0.8	0.8	1.0	1.1
Total Receipts to Cash Flow 42	11.6	4.7	2.9	9.0	12.9	12.8	14.5	16.2	14.9	15.1	9.4	
Cost of Goods to Cash Flow 43	9.1	4.3	0.6	5.7	9.7	9.8	11.3	13.5	12.0	13.3	7.1	
Cash Flow to Total Debt 44	0.2	•	1.2	0.9	0.4	0.4	0.3	0.2	0.2	0.2	0.2	0.2

Selected Financial Factors (in Percentages)

	1	2	3	4	5	6	7	8	9	10	11	12
Debt Ratio 45	53.4	•	97.7	29.0	43.2	39.4	53.8	55.1	51.7	50.5	55.9	56.2
Return on Total Assets 46	7.5	•	14.5	2.6	11.7	14.6	8.4	7.4	5.8	6.1	5.9	7.1
Return on Equity Before Income Taxes 47	11.4	•	476.0	2.2	17.6	21.9	15.1	13.2	10.2	9.5	8.2	9.5
Return on Equity After Income Taxes 48	9.4	•	475.7	2.0	16.9	21.1	13.8	11.9	9.5	7.8	6.1	6.7
Profit Margin (Before Income Tax) 49	3.9	14.3	3.2	0.7	4.3	6.2	3.8	3.9	3.1	3.1	2.0	4.8
Profit Margin (After Income Tax) 50	3.3	14.0	3.2	0.6	4.1	6.0	3.5	3.5	2.9	2.5	1.5	3.4

106

Table I

Corporations with and without Net Income

NONFERROUS METAL PRODUCTION AND PROCESSING

MONEY AMOUNTS AND SIZE OF ASSETS IN THOUSANDS OF DOLLARS

Item Description for Accounting Period 7/03 Through 6/04	Total	Zero Assets	Under 500	500 to 1,000	1,000 to 5,000	5,000 to 10,000	10,000 to 25,000	25,000 to 50,000	50,000 to 100,000	100,000 to 250,000	250,000 to 500,000	500,000 to 2,500,000	2,500,000 and over
Number of Enterprises **1**	1043	60	403	31	296	81	68	40	20	17	15	12	•
Revenues ($ in Thousands)													
Net Sales **2**	43503643	5787	533806	87697	1867754	1487437	2260522	2643236	1623888	3184422	4964189	24844907	•
Interest **3**	945821	0	1	2	624	187	2354	3042	3354	5618	8047	922592	•
Rents **4**	31167	0	0	175	6897	0	758	121	191	206	344	22475	•
Royalties **5**	97760	0	0	0	0	0	132	0	7547	555	368	89159	•
Other Portfolio Income **6**	602286	0	1	6515	1746	266	1605	5726	2929	1700	8206	573592	•
Other Receipts **7**	1220173	2591	0	59	1903	1063	11042	19053	264147	29440	317907	572964	•
Total Receipts **8**	46400850	8378	533808	94448	1878924	1488953	2276413	2671178	1902056	3221941	5299061	27025689	•
Average Total Receipts **9**	44488	140	1325	3047	6348	18382	33477	66779	95103	189526	353271	2252141	•
Operating Costs/Operating Income (%)													
Cost of Operations **10**	82.4	1616.4	80.7	83.0	74.8	80.1	81.2	82.3	74.4	87.0	80.2	83.3	•
Salaries and Wages **11**	3.7	20.5	0.4	2.4	5.2	2.2	3.6	2.9	6.9	2.3	3.7	3.8	•
Taxes Paid **12**	1.1	10.3	2.1	2.2	2.0	1.5	1.4	1.6	1.2	0.8	1.3	0.8	•
Interest Paid **13**	3.8	1.0	0.9	0.7	0.7	0.6	0.9	0.7	1.2	1.9	2.8	5.5	•
Depreciation **14**	4.1	13.4	0.7	•	3.2	1.7	2.8	3.1	3.7	3.7	3.6	4.8	•
Amortization and Depletion **15**	0.9	37.5	0.6	•	0.1	0.1	0.1	0.1	7.6	0.2	0.9	0.8	•
Pensions and Other Deferred Comp. **16**	0.3	0.0	•	•	0.7	1.0	0.4	0.3	0.9	0.1	0.4	0.2	•
Employee Benefits **17**	1.4	2.5	1.3	2.6	2.1	2.6	1.3	1.4	2.1	1.0	3.3	1.0	•
Advertising **18**	0.2	•	0.6	0.2	0.2	0.0	0.2	0.1	0.2	0.0	0.1	0.3	•
Other Expenses **19**	8.6	350.3	3.3	11.6	9.1	3.8	5.5	5.5	17.2	3.2	14.5	8.5	•
Officers' Compensation **20**	0.6	1.5	3.3	6.6	1.5	1.9	1.6	1.6	0.8	0.5	0.5	0.1	•
Operating Margin **21**	•	6.1	•	•	0.5	4.7	1.0	0.1	•	•	•	•	•
Operating Margin Before Officers' Comp. **22**	•	9.4	•	•	2.0	6.5	2.7	1.8	•	•	•	•	•

Selected Average Balance Sheet ($ in Thousands)

Net Receivables 23	21389	0	46	287	546	2878	4527	8719	10804	29916	55149	1639850
Inventories 24	5046	0	27	168	562	1405	3207	8738	9914	24855	55304	175552
Net Property, Plant and Equipment 25	13853	0	192	22	701	2694	4947	11594	19741	53931	104739	855162
Total Assets 26	90356	0	418	810	2147	7783	16321	36528	64325	152562	389952	6706794
Notes and Loans Payable 27	30028	0	173	560	892	3546	5356	10010	12205	67494	147908	2192174
All Other Liabilities 28	21233	0	34	536	578	2929	4863	10189	24297	58968	103952	1493429
Net Worth 29	39096	0	212	-286	677	1309	6102	16328	27823	26099	138091	3021190

Selected Financial Ratios (Times to 1)

Current Ratio 30	1.1	•	5.2	1.4	1.8	1.0	1.5	1.7	1.4	1.2	2.1	1.0
Quick Ratio 31	0.9	•	4.2	1.0	1.0	0.7	0.8	0.9	0.8	0.6	0.9	0.9
Net Sales to Working Capital 32	12.6	•	9.2	13.3	10.7	350.7	10.9	7.4	8.9	22.4	4.1	21.9
Coverage Ratio 33	1.4	•	8.0	•	2.6	8.4	3.0	2.6	1.8	1.3	•	1.6
Total Asset Turnover 34	0.5	•	3.2	3.5	2.9	2.4	2.0	1.8	1.3	1.2	0.8	0.3
Inventory Turnover 35	6.8	•	39.9	13.9	8.4	10.5	8.4	6.2	6.1	6.6	4.8	9.8
Receivables Turnover 36	1.9	•	26.2	19.7	10.2	6.6	8.3	7.5	8.1	7.8	7.6	2.3
Total Liabilities to Net Worth 37	1.3	•	1.0	•	2.2	4.9	1.7	1.2	1.3	4.8	1.8	1.2
Current Assets to Working Capital 38	8.9	•	1.2	3.3	2.3	83.9	3.2	2.4	3.3	7.6	1.9	21.5
Current Liabilities to Working Capital 39	7.9	•	0.2	2.3	1.3	82.9	2.2	1.4	2.3	6.6	0.9	20.5
Working Capital to Net Sales 40	0.1	•	0.1	0.1	0.1	0.0	0.1	0.1	0.1	0.0	0.2	0.0
Inventory to Working Capital 41	1.4	•	0.2	0.8	0.9	23.2	1.1	1.0	1.1	3.2	0.9	2.1
Total Receipts to Cash Flow 42	15.5	•	11.7	25.8	16.2	13.8	16.2	20.9	6.6	31.4	11.9	15.6
Cost of Goods to Cash Flow 43	12.8	•	9.5	21.4	12.1	11.1	13.2	17.2	4.9	27.3	9.6	13.0
Cash Flow to Total Debt 44	0.1	•	0.5	0.1	0.3	0.2	0.2	0.2	0.3	0.0	0.1	0.0

Selected Financial Factors (in Percentages)

Debt Ratio 45	56.7	•	49.3	135.3	68.5	83.2	62.6	55.3	56.7	82.9	64.6	55.0
Return on Total Assets 46	2.4	•	22.1	•	5.2	12.7	5.3	3.5	2.7	2.9	•	2.7
Return on Equity Before Income Taxes 47	1.6	•	38.2	15.4	10.1	66.8	9.5	4.7	2.7	3.7	•	2.1
Return on Equity After Income Taxes 48	0.4	•	38.2	15.8	8.4	66.4	8.9	2.2	0.5	•	•	0.9
Profit Margin (Before Income Tax) 49	1.5	•	6.1	•	1.1	4.8	1.7	1.2	0.9	0.5	•	3.1
Profit Margin (After Income Tax) 50	0.3	•	6.1	•	0.9	4.7	1.6	0.5	0.2	0.1	•	1.4

107

Table II
Corporations with Net Income

NONFERROUS METAL PRODUCTION AND PROCESSING

MONEY AMOUNTS AND SIZE OF ASSETS IN THOUSANDS OF DOLLARS

Item Description for Accounting Period 7/03 Through 6/04	Total	Zero Assets	Under 500	500 to 1,000	1,000 to 5,000	5,000 to 10,000	10,000 to 25,000	25,000 to 50,000	50,000 to 100,000	100,000 to 250,000	250,000 to 500,000	500,000 to 2,500,000	2,500,000 and over
Number of Enterprises **1**	661	•	319	•	197	49	42	20	•	10	•	7	•
Revenues ($ in Thousands)													
Net Sales **2**	32304379	•	466840	•	1629443	1215655	1400036	1364404	•	2244569	•	20757499	•
Interest **3**	829891	•	2	•	610	12	1322	2238	•	5514	•	815870	•
Rents **4**	25683	•	0	•	2382	0	392	110	•	145	•	22233	•
Royalties **5**	96655	•	0	•	0	0	0	0	•	0	•	89109	•
Other Portfolio Income **6**	583634	•	3513	•	843	206	1005	5255	•	337	•	569168	•
Other Receipts **7**	776999	•	0	•	1066	349	5305	13104	•	27284	•	462267	•
Total Receipts **8**	34617241	•	470355	•	1634344	1216222	1408060	1385111	•	2277849	•	22716146	•
Average Total Receipts **9**	52371	•	1474	•	8296	24821	33525	69256	•	227785	•	3245164	•
Operating Costs/Operating Income (%)													
Cost of Operations **10**	80.9	•	81.1	•	75.2	79.4	78.1	79.0	•	85.6	•	82.1	•
Salaries and Wages **11**	4.0	•	0.0	•	4.7	1.7	3.5	3.7	•	2.2	•	4.1	•
Taxes Paid **12**	0.9	•	1.3	•	1.7	1.5	1.3	1.6	•	0.7	•	0.7	•
Interest Paid **13**	3.9	•	1.1	•	0.3	0.4	0.7	0.7	•	0.7	•	5.7	•
Depreciation **14**	3.7	•	0.6	•	3.2	1.1	2.8	2.4	•	2.8	•	4.5	•
Amortization and Depletion **15**	0.9	•	0.7	•	•	0.0	0.0	0.1	•	0.1	•	0.6	•
Pensions and Other Deferred Comp. **16**	0.3	•	•	•	0.7	1.1	0.4	0.3	•	0.2	•	0.2	•
Employee Benefits **17**	1.2	•	0.9	•	1.9	2.7	0.9	1.2	•	0.9	•	0.9	•
Advertising **18**	0.3	•	0.6	•	0.1	0.0	0.2	0.2	•	0.0	•	0.3	•
Other Expenses **19**	7.8	•	2.4	•	7.7	2.3	6.0	6.1	•	2.9	•	8.4	•
Officers' Compensation **20**	0.5	•	3.2	•	1.2	1.6	1.8	1.5	•	0.4	•	0.1	•
Operating Margin **21**	•	•	8.1	•	3.3	8.1	4.3	3.4	•	3.6	•	•	•
Operating Margin Before Officers' Comp. **22**	•	•	11.3	•	4.5	9.6	6.1	4.8	•	4.0	•	•	•

Selected Average Balance Sheet ($ in Thousands)

Net Receivables 23	31410	33	661	4148	4559	9040	38416	2746731
Inventories 24	4611	30	588	1521	3489	10136	23134	271661
Net Property, Plant and Equipment 25	15344	225	776	1814	4332	10700	43900	1213144
Total Assets 26	124107	461	2394	8676	15810	37538	152324	10781881
Notes and Loans Payable 27	39034	218	484	3346	4692	10312	39572	3427331
All Other Liabilities 28	24801	39	507	2184	3806	8780	52657	2085724
Net Worth 29	60272	204	1403	3146	7312	18446	60094	5268826

Selected Financial Ratios (Times to 1)

Current Ratio 30	1.1	4.5	2.3	1.3	1.8	1.8	1.6	1.1
Quick Ratio 31	0.9	3.5	1.4	1.0	1.0	1.0	1.0	0.9
Net Sales to Working Capital 32	12.1	10.8	9.6	16.3	7.3	6.7	7.9	17.9
Coverage Ratio 33	2.4	9.4	12.5	22.1	7.6	7.7	8.8	2.0
Total Asset Turnover 34	0.4	3.2	3.5	2.9	2.1	1.8	1.5	0.3
Inventory Turnover 35	8.6	40.0	10.6	13.0	7.5	5.3	8.3	9.0
Receivables Turnover 36	1.5	28.7	25.0	7.4	7.9	6.5	7.5	1.1
Total Liabilities to Net Worth 37	1.1	1.3	0.7	1.8	1.2	1.0	1.5	1.0
Current Assets to Working Capital 38	9.9	1.3	1.8	3.9	2.2	2.2	2.6	19.8
Current Liabilities to Working Capital 39	8.9	0.3	0.8	2.9	1.2	1.2	1.6	18.8
Working Capital to Net Sales 40	0.1	0.1	0.1	0.1	0.1	0.1	0.1	0.1
Inventory to Working Capital 41	1.1	0.3	0.7	1.0	0.8	0.8	0.9	1.5
Total Receipts to Cash Flow 42	11.1	9.1	12.9	10.9	10.4	12.1	13.4	11.5
Cost of Goods to Cash Flow 43	9.0	7.4	9.7	8.7	8.1	9.5	11.5	9.4
Cash Flow to Total Debt 44	0.1	0.6	0.6	0.4	0.4	0.3	0.2	0.0

Selected Financial Factors (in Percentages)

Debt Ratio 45	51.4	55.7	41.4	63.7	53.7	50.9	60.5	51.1
Return on Total Assets 46	3.7	31.6	13.4	24.2	11.9	10.2	8.5	3.2
Return on Equity Before Income Taxes 47	4.5	63.7	21.0	63.8	22.3	18.1	19.1	3.3
Return on Equity After Income Taxes 48	3.2	63.6	19.7	63.6	21.5	13.7	13.7	2.2
Profit Margin (Before Income Tax) 49	5.5	8.9	3.6	8.1	4.9	4.9	5.1	5.9
Profit Margin (After Income Tax) 50	4.0	8.9	3.4	8.1	4.9	3.7	3.7	3.9

Table I

Corporations with and without Net Income

FOUNDRIES

MONEY AMOUNTS AND SIZE OF ASSETS IN THOUSANDS OF DOLLARS

Item Description for Accounting Period 7/03 Through 6/04	Total	Zero Assets	Under 500	500 to 1,000	1,000 to 5,000	5,000 to 10,000	10,000 to 25,000	25,000 to 50,000	50,000 to 100,000	100,000 to 250,000	250,000 to 500,000	500,000 to 2,500,000	2,500,000 and over
Number of Enterprises 1	1895	4	1458	•	264	65	62	19	9	4	5	5	•
Revenues ($ in Thousands)													
Net Sales 2	14128894	140383	695493	•	1162709	652466	1562754	804681	897195	1102722	2420963	4689528	•
Interest 3	80101	12	6	•	739	667	796	305	280	9772	4360	63166	•
Rents 4	2277	0	0	•	702	149	421	220	112	76	246	350	•
Royalties 5	17568	0	0	•	0	98	0	4	0	0	7681	9785	•
Other Portfolio Income 6	13977	583	0	•	2040	104	1782	1597	2817	83	1836	3139	•
Other Receipts 7	101581	3041	0	•	18911	6738	13598	3041	7864	3484	16490	28410	•
Total Receipts 8	14344398	144019	695499	•	1185101	660222	1579351	809848	908268	1116137	2451576	4794378	•
Average Total Receipts 9	7570	36005	477	•	4489	10157	25473	42624	100919	279034	490315	958876	•
Operating Costs/Operating Income (%)													
Cost of Operations 10	74.2	82.3	56.2	•	70.9	77.4	76.8	76.0	74.9	79.2	81.2	70.9	•
Salaries and Wages 11	6.3	4.1	12.1	•	6.0	4.5	4.7	5.1	4.1	2.7	6.1	8.0	•
Taxes Paid 12	2.4	4.1	3.8	•	4.7	2.2	2.5	2.3	2.4	1.2	2.6	1.7	•
Interest Paid 13	2.5	4.8	1.7	•	1.2	1.7	0.9	1.3	1.1	2.5	2.2	4.3	•
Depreciation 14	4.4	4.9	5.5	•	3.4	3.5	3.9	5.7	4.4	4.2	4.7	4.6	•
Amortization and Depletion 15	0.2	2.0	0.9	•	0.0	0.4	0.1	0.1	0.3	0.5	0.3	0.0	•
Pensions and Other Deferred Comp. 16	0.8	0.3	0.1	•	0.4	0.6	0.5	0.5	0.8	0.5	0.5	1.5	•
Employee Benefits 17	3.0	1.4	2.3	•	4.8	2.9	2.4	3.4	1.3	1.6	1.7	4.3	•
Advertising 18	0.1	0.0	0.2	•	0.1	0.2	0.1	0.2	0.1	0.0	0.1	0.1	•
Other Expenses 19	6.5	13.2	10.9	•	8.8	5.4	6.3	5.4	5.9	10.0	3.1	6.4	•
Officers' Compensation 20	1.5	•	11.4	•	1.5	2.0	2.0	1.8	0.9	0.2	0.4	0.7	•
Operating Margin 21	•	•	•	•	•	•	•	•	3.9	•	•	•	•
Operating Margin Before Officers' Comp. 22	•	•	6.2	•	•	1.3	1.7	•	4.8	•	•	•	•

Selected Average Balance Sheet ($ in Thousands)

Item											
Net Receivables 23	1256	31	0	625	1583	3755	6772	14691	39836	95311	187193
Inventories 24	904	21	0	389	1245	2632	4086	9595	22898	49097	166259
Net Property, Plant and Equipment 25	2010	62	0	972	2369	5237	15150	25281	93530	127194	291691
Total Assets 26	6539	189	0	2545	6798	14659	33291	67700	176978	365406	1263359
Notes and Loans Payable 27	2831	242	0	2086	2194	4373	9684	20091	121245	107961	531510
All Other Liabilities 28	772	43	0	391	1692	3841	7413	14548	44506	109892	-10250
Net Worth 29	2937	-96	0	68	2912	6445	16194	33060	11228	147553	742099

Selected Financial Ratios (Times to 1)

Item											
Current Ratio 30	1.8	2.2		2.3	2.2	1.5	1.8	2.1	1.1	2.1	1.8
Quick Ratio 31	1.0	1.7		1.1	1.5	0.9	1.1	1.4	0.6	1.4	0.9
Net Sales to Working Capital 32	6.3	10.3		5.1	4.9	9.4	6.5	5.4	58.0	4.9	5.5
Coverage Ratio 33	0.8			1.2	1.3	1.9	0.1	5.3	0.4	0.3	1.0
Total Asset Turnover 34	1.1	2.5		1.7	1.5	1.7	1.3	1.5	1.6	1.3	0.7
Inventory Turnover 35	6.1	12.7		8.0	6.2	7.4	7.9	7.8	9.5	8.0	4.0
Receivables Turnover 36	6.4	17.1		6.7	4.8	6.8	6.9	6.0	9.6	6.0	5.5
Total Liabilities to Net Worth 37	1.2			36.4	1.3	1.3	1.1	1.0	14.8	1.5	0.7
Current Assets to Working Capital 38	2.2	1.9		1.8	1.9	3.0	2.3	1.9	16.6	1.9	2.3
Current Liabilities to Working Capital 39	1.2	0.9		0.8	0.9	2.0	1.3	0.9	15.6	0.9	1.3
Working Capital to Net Sales 40	0.2	0.1		0.2	0.2	0.1	0.2	0.2	0.0	0.2	0.2
Inventory to Working Capital 41	0.7	0.4		0.5	0.4	1.0	0.6	0.5	6.2	0.5	0.9
Total Receipts to Cash Flow 42	25.9	75.8		18.4	19.7	17.2	45.3	11.7	13.4		23.8
Cost of Goods to Cash Flow 43	19.2	42.6		13.0	15.2	13.2	34.4	8.8	10.6		16.9
Cash Flow to Total Debt 44	0.1	0.0		0.1	0.1	0.1	0.1	0.2	0.1		0.1

Selected Financial Factors (in Percentages)

Item											
Debt Ratio 45	55.1	151.0		97.3	57.2	56.0	51.4	51.2	93.7	59.6	41.3
Return on Total Assets 46	2.4			2.6	3.4	2.9	0.3	8.8	1.7	0.9	3.0
Return on Equity Before Income Taxes 47		25.7		18.8	1.9	3.1		14.5			
Return on Equity After Income Taxes 48		25.7		10.0		2.0		11.4			
Profit Margin (Before Income Tax) 49				0.3	0.5	0.8		4.8			
Profit Margin (After Income Tax) 50				0.2		0.5		3.8			

MANUFACTURING
331500

Table II
Corporations with Net Income

FOUNDRIES

MONEY AMOUNTS AND SIZE OF ASSETS IN THOUSANDS OF DOLLARS

Item Description for Accounting Period 7/03 Through 6/04	Total	Zero Assets	Under 500	500 to 1,000	1,000 to 5,000	5,000 to 10,000	10,000 to 25,000	25,000 to 50,000	50,000 to 100,000	100,000 to 250,000	250,000 to 500,000	500,000 to 2,500,000	2,500,000 and over
Number of Enterprises **1**	603	•	389	•	109	49	34	11	•	•	•	•	•
Revenues ($ in Thousands)													
Net Sales **2**	7081624	•	123670	•	869148	538092	835361	490920	•	•	•	•	•
Interest **3**	60019	•	0	•	488	503	109	33	•	•	•	•	•
Rents **4**	1500	•	0	•	702	148	348	0	•	•	•	•	•
Royalties **5**	17448	•	0	•	0	0	0	0	•	•	•	•	•
Other Portfolio Income **6**	7802	•	0	•	30	104	1173	366	•	•	•	•	•
Other Receipts **7**	62190	•	0	•	17499	4219	10117	2124	•	•	•	•	•
Total Receipts **8**	7230583	•	123670	•	887867	543066	847108	493443	•	•	•	•	•
Average Total Receipts **9**	11991	•	318	•	8146	11083	24915	44858	•	•	•	•	•
Operating Costs/Operating Income (%)													
Cost of Operations **10**	69.7	•	50.9	•	68.8	76.4	73.2	71.1	•	•	•	•	•
Salaries and Wages **11**	8.5	•	23.8	•	4.2	4.2	5.2	5.6	•	•	•	•	•
Taxes Paid **12**	2.2	•	2.8	•	4.3	2.2	2.5	2.5	•	•	•	•	•
Interest Paid **13**	2.1	•	0.2	•	1.6	0.6	0.8	1.2	•	•	•	•	•
Depreciation **14**	4.5	•	5.7	•	3.5	3.4	4.4	5.4	•	•	•	•	•
Amortization and Depletion **15**	0.1	•	3.1	•	•	0.0	0.1	0.1	•	•	•	•	•
Pensions and Other Deferred Comp. **16**	1.0	•	•	•	0.5	0.6	0.4	0.2	•	•	•	•	•
Employee Benefits **17**	3.4	•	•	•	4.8	3.2	2.0	3.0	•	•	•	•	•
Advertising **18**	0.2	•	0.6	•	0.1	0.2	0.1	0.3	•	•	•	•	•
Other Expenses **19**	5.6	•	8.2	•	9.5	4.6	4.9	5.1	•	•	•	•	•
Officers' Compensation **20**	1.2	•	•	•	1.3	1.9	2.3	1.9	•	•	•	•	•
Operating Margin **21**	1.6	•	4.6	•	1.4	2.9	4.0	3.7	•	•	•	•	•
Operating Margin Before Officers' Comp. **22**	2.7	•	4.6	•	2.7	4.9	6.4	5.6	•	•	•	•	•

Selected Average Balance Sheet ($ in Thousands)

Net Receivables 23	2108	0	1102	1649	3789	7596
Inventories 24	1775	16	445	1444	2367	3053
Net Property, Plant and Equipment 25	2992	29	1665	1966	5638	15232
Total Assets 26	11647	107	3309	6629	14844	33319
Notes and Loans Payable 27	3236	63	1132	939	3974	10776
All Other Liabilities 28	395	6	682	1760	3011	6733
Net Worth 29	8016	38	1495	3931	7859	15810

Selected Financial Ratios (Times to 1)

Current Ratio 30	1.7	8.7	1.4	2.4	2.0	1.7
Quick Ratio 31	1.1	8.7	1.0	1.7	1.2	1.1
Net Sales to Working Capital 32	6.2	6.8	18.0	4.5	6.1	8.1
Coverage Ratio 33	2.7	26.2	3.3	7.9	7.7	4.5
Total Asset Turnover 34	1.0	3.0	2.4	1.7	1.7	1.3
Inventory Turnover 35	4.6	10.2	12.3	5.8	7.6	10.4
Receivables Turnover 36	5.5	9.0	14.5	4.7	7.5	6.8
Total Liabilities to Net Worth 37	0.5	1.8	1.2	0.7	0.9	1.1
Current Assets to Working Capital 38	2.3	1.1	3.8	1.7	2.0	2.5
Current Liabilities to Working Capital 39	1.3	0.1	2.8	0.7	1.0	1.5
Working Capital to Net Sales 40	0.2	0.1	0.1	0.2	0.2	0.1
Inventory to Working Capital 41	0.8		1.0	0.4	0.7	0.6
Total Receipts to Cash Flow 42	14.6	11.4	10.9	13.0	10.8	13.4
Cost of Goods to Cash Flow 43	10.2	5.8	7.5	9.9	7.9	9.5
Cash Flow to Total Debt 44	0.2	0.4	0.4	0.3	0.3	0.2

Selected Financial Factors (in Percentages)

Debt Ratio 45	31.2	64.7	54.8	40.7	47.1	52.6
Return on Total Assets 46	5.8	14.4	12.4	7.3	10.3	7.2
Return on Equity Before Income Taxes 47	5.3	39.2	18.9	10.7	17.0	11.9
Return on Equity After Income Taxes 48	4.4	39.2	18.0	8.6	15.4	11.3
Profit Margin (Before Income Tax) 49	3.6	4.6	3.6	3.8	5.4	4.2
Profit Margin (After Income Tax) 50	3.0	4.6	3.4	3.1	4.9	4.0

Table I

Corporations with and without Net Income

FORGING AND STAMPING

MONEY AMOUNTS AND SIZE OF ASSETS IN THOUSANDS OF DOLLARS

Item Description for Accounting Period 7/03 Through 6/04	Total	Zero Assets	Under 500	500 to 1,000	1,000 to 5,000	5,000 to 10,000	10,000 to 25,000	25,000 to 50,000	50,000 to 100,000	100,000 to 250,000	250,000 to 500,000	500,000 to 2,500,000	2,500,000 and over
Number of Enterprises **1**	3062	·	1417	·	658	215	130	47	29	14	·	·	·
Revenues ($ in Thousands)													
Net Sales **2**	17412997	·	576552	·	2641058	2425425	3235659	2342235	2562563	2743310	·	·	·
Interest **3**	64525	·	361	·	944	640	1325	1354	6465	52999	·	·	·
Rents **4**	5088	·	0	·	55	1015	1022	858	2134	5	·	·	·
Royalties **5**	251	·	0	·	2	0	1	5	3	242	·	·	·
Other Portfolio Income **6**	104305	·	51	·	1134	440	6963	7861	4859	79670	·	·	·
Other Receipts **7**	135380	·	723	·	41895	19907	25980	9406	10130	26769	·	·	·
Total Receipts **8**	17722546	·	577687	·	2685088	2447427	3270950	2361719	2586154	2902995	·	·	·
Average Total Receipts **9**	5788	·	408	·	4081	11383	25161	50249	89178	207357	·	·	·
Operating Costs/Operating Income (%)													
Cost of Operations **10**	71.4	·	52.8	·	67.2	75.7	76.1	73.2	72.0	70.0	·	·	·
Salaries and Wages **11**	5.3	·	5.5	·	6.5	5.0	5.0	4.6	4.7	6.1	·	·	·
Taxes Paid **12**	2.4	·	4.1	·	3.0	2.5	2.3	2.3	2.0	1.8	·	·	·
Interest Paid **13**	1.6	·	0.8	·	0.6	1.2	1.1	1.0	1.5	4.6	·	·	·
Depreciation **14**	4.2	·	3.2	·	2.3	3.7	4.2	4.5	4.6	6.3	·	·	·
Amortization and Depletion **15**	0.3	·	0.0	·	0.0	0.1	0.1	0.2	0.4	1.3	·	·	·
Pensions and Other Deferred Comp. **16**	0.6	·	0.1	·	0.6	0.1	0.6	0.8	0.5	1.0	·	·	·
Employee Benefits **17**	2.2	·	1.2	·	2.7	1.1	2.3	2.1	2.2	3.3	·	·	·
Advertising **18**	0.2	·	0.3	·	0.5	0.1	0.1	0.1	0.2	0.2	·	·	·
Other Expenses **19**	8.3	·	18.1	·	13.1	6.9	5.5	6.4	6.5	7.7	·	·	·
Officers' Compensation **20**	2.8	·	9.3	·	5.6	1.9	1.9	1.8	1.6	0.9	·	·	·
Operating Margin **21**	0.6	·	4.8	·	·	1.7	0.7	3.0	3.7	·	·	·	·
Operating Margin Before Officers' Comp. **22**	3.4	·	14.1	·	3.5	3.5	2.6	4.7	5.3	·	·	·	·

Selected Average Balance Sheet ($ in Thousands)

Net Receivables 23	846	43	•	543	1670	3458	7862	15188	31905
Inventories 24	664	15		463	1461	2935	5350	11338	23266
Net Property, Plant and Equipment 25	1247	35		452	2059	5608	12705	25235	62501
Total Assets 26	3827	151		2299	6322	15351	35891	70150	178498
Notes and Loans Payable 27	1203	34		505	2630	5026	9826	23474	57824
All Other Liabilities 28	887	39		543	1510	3624	7143	15043	48058
Net Worth 29	1737	78		1251	2182	6701	18922	31633	72616

Selected Financial Ratios (Times to 1)

Current Ratio 30	1.8	2.3	•	1.5	1.9	1.8	2.0	1.9	1.6
Quick Ratio 31	1.1	2.0		0.9	1.1	1.0	1.3	1.1	1.0
Net Sales to Working Capital 32	6.4	6.6		9.3	6.3	6.9	5.5	5.3	6.8
Coverage Ratio 33	2.5	7.2		0.2	3.1	2.7	4.7	4.1	1.6
Total Asset Turnover 34	1.5	2.7		1.7	1.8	1.6	1.4	1.3	1.1
Inventory Turnover 35	6.1	14.4		5.8	5.8	6.5	6.8	5.6	5.9
Receivables Turnover 36	6.7	8.7		7.7	5.9	7.1	6.2	6.3	6.9
Total Liabilities to Net Worth 37	1.2	0.9		0.8	1.9	1.3	0.9	1.2	1.5
Current Assets to Working Capital 38	2.2	1.7		2.9	2.1	2.3	2.0	2.2	2.6
Current Liabilities to Working Capital 39	1.2	0.7		1.9	1.1	1.3	1.0	1.2	1.6
Working Capital to Net Sales 40	0.2	0.2		0.1	0.2	0.1	0.2	0.2	0.1
Inventory to Working Capital 41	0.7	0.2		1.1	0.8	0.8	0.6	0.7	0.8
Total Receipts to Cash Flow 42	12.4	6.2		11.5	15.2	18.1	12.2	10.5	11.9
Cost of Goods to Cash Flow 43	8.9	3.3		7.7	11.5	13.7	8.9	7.5	8.3
Cash Flow to Total Debt 44	0.2	0.9		0.3	0.2	0.2	0.2	0.2	0.2

Selected Financial Factors (in Percentages)

Debt Ratio 45	54.6	48.1	•	45.6	65.5	56.3	47.3	54.9	59.3
Return on Total Assets 46	6.0	15.6		0.3	6.8	4.7	6.6	7.6	7.8
Return on Equity Before Income Taxes 47	7.8	25.9		•	13.4	6.8	9.9	12.8	6.9
Return on Equity After Income Taxes 48	7.0	23.8		•	12.8	5.7	8.7	11.4	6.5
Profit Margin (Before Income Tax) 49	2.4	5.0		•	2.6	1.8	3.8	4.6	2.6
Profit Margin (After Income Tax) 50	2.1	4.6		2.5	1.5	3.3	4.1	2.4

Table II
Corporations with Net Income

FORGING AND STAMPING

MONEY AMOUNTS AND SIZE OF ASSETS IN THOUSANDS OF DOLLARS

Item Description for Accounting Period 7/03 Through 6/04	Total	Zero Assets	Under 500	500 to 1,000	1,000 to 5,000	5,000 to 10,000	10,000 to 25,000	25,000 to 50,000	50,000 to 100,000	100,000 to 250,000	250,000 to 500,000	500,000 to 2,500,000	2,500,000 and over
Number of Enterprises 1	1852	3	758	381	411	156	80	31	21	11	•	•	•
Revenues ($ in Thousands)													
Net Sales 2	12604925	64260	245027	467216	1974033	1833738	2145120	1570215	1914929	2390385	•	•	•
Interest 3	62187	0	307	271	775	166	670	978	6264	52756	•	•	•
Rents 4	3323	0	0	0	55	467	773	131	1897	0	•	•	•
Royalties 5	245	0	0	0	0	0	1	0	3	242	•	•	•
Other Portfolio Income 6	96678	3256	51	68	773	440	6607	3224	2638	79619	•	•	•
Other Receipts 7	97021	51	8	179	36923	10170	12071	6600	6223	24798	•	•	•
Total Receipts 8	12864379	67567	245393	467734	2012559	1844981	2165242	1581148	1931954	2547800	•	•	•
Average Total Receipts 9	6946	22522	324	1228	4897	11827	27066	51005	91998	231618	•	•	•
Operating Costs/Operating Income (%)													
Cost of Operations 10	69.7	74.4	43.2	56.4	67.1	73.7	74.3	69.7	70.6	68.9	•	•	•
Salaries and Wages 11	5.4	3.9	12.1	5.7	5.4	5.0	4.8	4.9	4.6	6.6	•	•	•
Taxes Paid 12	2.2	1.7	4.3	3.3	2.5	2.4	2.2	2.2	2.0	1.6	•	•	•
Interest Paid 13	1.7	2.1	0.1	0.4	0.4	1.2	0.9	0.7	1.3	5.1	•	•	•
Depreciation 14	4.0	3.2	3.6	2.5	2.0	3.9	3.7	4.2	4.0	6.4	•	•	•
Amortization and Depletion 15	0.4	0.1	0.0	•	0.0	0.1	0.1	0.2	0.5	1.5	•	•	•
Pensions and Other Deferred Comp. 16	0.6	0.7	•	0.7	0.6	0.1	0.6	0.7	0.4	0.8	•	•	•
Employee Benefits 17	2.1	5.3	1.2	1.6	2.1	1.0	2.0	1.8	2.4	3.1	•	•	•
Advertising 18	0.2	0.0	0.0	0.1	0.5	0.1	0.1	0.1	0.2	0.2	•	•	•
Other Expenses 19	7.5	3.3	12.5	13.5	13.8	5.4	5.0	6.6	4.7	7.6	•	•	•
Officers' Compensation 20	2.9	3.2	11.1	13.0	5.6	2.1	1.9	1.8	1.9	0.9	•	•	•
Operating Margin 21	3.3	2.1	11.8	2.8	0.1	4.9	4.4	7.2	7.3	•	•	•	•
Operating Margin Before Officers' Comp. 22	6.2	5.3	22.9	15.8	5.6	7.0	6.2	9.0	9.1	•	•	•	•

Selected Average Balance Sheet ($ in Thousands)

Net Receivables 23	1033	0	12	161	625	1917	3610	7732	17048	36331
Inventories 24	719	0	16	176	522	1199	2774	5563	10297	24729
Net Property, Plant and Equipment 25	1357	0	37	177	412	1959	5228	11580	21192	65504
Total Assets 26	4559	0	147	789	2750	6247	15110	36704	72220	187534
Notes and Loans Payable 27	1289	0	22	90	399	2395	4357	7114	22178	69413
All Other Liabilities 28	986	0	8	94	647	1424	3252	5753	15149	48993
Net Worth 29	2284	0	118	605	1704	2427	7501	23837	34893	69129

Selected Financial Ratios (Times to 1)

Current Ratio 30	2.0	•	7.8	5.7	1.5	2.1	1.9	2.4	2.2	1.6
Quick Ratio 31	1.3	•	7.2	4.2	0.9	1.3	1.1	1.6	1.3	1.0
Net Sales to Working Capital 32	5.8	•	3.8	2.6	10.7	6.0	6.7	4.4	4.3	7.3
Coverage Ratio 33	4.2	4.4	129.4	8.3	5.5	5.7	6.7	12.7	7.2	1.7
Total Asset Turnover 34	1.5	•	2.2	1.6	1.7	1.9	1.8	1.4	1.3	1.2
Inventory Turnover 35	6.6	•	8.8	3.9	6.2	7.2	7.2	6.3	6.3	6.1
Receivables Turnover 36	6.8	•	7.1	5.3	7.6	6.2	7.5	6.2	6.1	12.0
Total Liabilities to Net Worth 37	1.0	•	0.3	0.3	0.6	1.6	1.0	0.5	1.1	1.7
Current Assets to Working Capital 38	2.0	•	1.1	1.2	3.1	1.9	2.1	1.7	1.9	2.5
Current Liabilities to Working Capital 39	1.0	•	0.1	0.2	2.1	0.9	1.1	0.7	0.9	1.5
Working Capital to Net Sales 40	0.2	•	0.3	0.4	0.1	0.2	0.2	0.2	0.2	0.1
Inventory to Working Capital 41	0.6	•	0.1	0.3	1.0	0.7	0.7	0.5	0.5	0.8
Total Receipts to Cash Flow 42	9.4	10.4	4.9	8.0	8.7	11.8	11.5	8.0	8.4	10.3
Cost of Goods to Cash Flow 43	6.6	7.8	2.1	4.5	5.9	8.7	8.5	5.6	5.9	7.1
Cash Flow to Total Debt 44	0.3	•	2.2	0.8	0.5	0.3	0.3	0.5	0.3	0.2

Selected Financial Factors (in Percentages)

Debt Ratio 45	49.9	•	20.1	23.3	38.0	61.1	50.4	35.1	51.7	63.1
Return on Total Assets 46	10.5	•	26.4	5.1	4.3	12.6	11.1	11.7	11.9	10.4
Return on Equity Before Income Taxes 47	15.9	•	32.8	5.9	5.7	26.8	18.9	16.6	21.2	11.9
Return on Equity After Income Taxes 48	14.8	•	30.1	5.6	5.2	26.0	17.3	15.2	19.5	11.4
Profit Margin (Before Income Tax) 49	5.3	7.3	11.9	2.9	2.0	5.5	5.3	7.8	8.1	3.8
Profit Margin (After Income Tax) 50	5.0	6.3	11.0	2.8	1.9	5.4	4.9	7.2	7.4	3.6

112

Table I

Corporations with and without Net Income

CUTLERY, HARDWARE, SPRING AND WIRE MACHINE SHOPS, NUT, BOLT

MONEY AMOUNTS AND SIZE OF ASSETS IN THOUSANDS OF DOLLARS

Item Description for Accounting Period 7/03 Through 6/04	Total	Zero Assets	Under 500	500 to 1,000	1,000 to 5,000	5,000 to 10,000	10,000 to 25,000	25,000 to 50,000	50,000 to 100,000	100,000 to 250,000	250,000 to 500,000	500,000 to 2,500,000	2,500,000 and over
Number of Enterprises **1**	21680	2260	14290	1779	2755	224	242	62	27	24	7	10	•
Revenues ($ in Thousands)													
Net Sales **2**	47965180	985886	3943288	2770055	9851941	2326750	5500122	2693066	2008856	4130468	2125667	11629081	•
Interest **3**	929446	3617	2020	1032	8264	2513	3035	5996	2103	8523	7131	885211	•
Rents **4**	18531	0	0	694	6988	454	1902	1151	47	4837	474	1984	•
Royalties **5**	203512	8179	0	0	0	0	116	180	460	756	10922	182899	•
Other Portfolio Income **6**	260762	6481	7583	772	116672	8189	18676	5674	17041	16172	20946	42555	•
Other Receipts **7**	627958	7530	29954	12465	39235	6142	27753	10022	21412	141985	4757	326704	•
Total Receipts **8**	50005389	1011693	3982845	2785018	10023100	2344048	5551604	2716089	2049919	4302741	2169897	13068434	•
Average Total Receipts **9**	2307	448	279	1565	3638	10464	22941	43808	75923	179281	309985	1306843	•
Operating Costs/Operating Income (%)													
Cost of Operations **10**	63.1	61.6	47.5	59.2	65.2	65.3	69.3	71.6	69.3	66.7	65.6	59.4	•
Salaries and Wages **11**	8.4	6.9	11.3	5.0	7.3	4.9	6.9	5.8	6.5	9.0	6.1	11.7	•
Taxes Paid **12**	2.5	1.9	3.3	3.9	3.1	3.2	2.5	2.2	2.5	1.9	3.1	1.4	•
Interest Paid **13**	3.6	1.7	1.3	1.5	2.1	0.6	1.1	1.6	1.6	2.1	3.1	9.4	•
Depreciation **14**	4.4	4.1	5.8	5.2	5.2	5.3	4.3	5.1	4.4	4.0	3.9	2.8	•
Amortization and Depletion **15**	0.8	0.1	0.1	0.0	0.1	0.1	0.2	0.4	0.9	0.8	1.0	2.1	•
Pensions and Other Deferred Comp. **16**	0.9	1.6	0.1	0.5	0.6	0.9	0.6	0.5	0.6	0.7	1.1	1.7	•
Employee Benefits **17**	2.3	1.4	1.4	1.7	2.2	3.0	2.2	1.8	2.5	2.2	2.5	2.9	•
Advertising **18**	0.8	0.1	0.5	0.3	0.3	0.5	0.7	0.9	1.1	0.8	1.0	1.6	•
Other Expenses **19**	13.0	17.5	18.6	14.0	9.4	9.4	8.1	8.0	9.0	9.6	13.7	19.2	•
Officers' Compensation **20**	3.7	2.6	8.6	10.6	6.7	4.2	2.6	1.5	1.3	1.0	1.0	0.8	•
Operating Margin **21**	•	0.4	1.5	•	•	2.6	1.4	0.5	0.3	1.2	•	•	•
Operating Margin Before Officers' Comp. **22**	0.5	3.0	10.1	8.7	4.6	6.8	4.0	2.0	1.6	2.2	•	•	•

Selected Average Balance Sheet ($ in Thousands)

Item												
Net Receivables 23	336	0	21	182	445	1240	3267	6659	12233	27207	39092	268085
Inventories 24	282	0	15	125	397	1727	3533	7224	15016	27669	67770	136352
Net Property, Plant and Equipment 25	416	0	43	306	670	2067	4875	10955	17360	38981	68635	181604
Total Assets 26	2206	0	110	750	2095	7232	15095	32576	67608	153410	367700	2377686
Notes and Loans Payable 27	583	0	69	363	1094	1157	4727	11776	18455	41367	113057	358739
All Other Liabilities 28	658	0	12	136	410	1267	3035	7243	15083	34767	89558	937928
Net Worth 29	965	0	29	250	590	4807	7333	13557	34070	77275	165085	1081020

Selected Financial Ratios (Times to 1)

Item												
Current Ratio 30	1.7	•	2.2	1.6	3.4	1.9	2.1	2.1	1.8	1.3	1.5	
Quick Ratio 31	1.0	•	1.5	1.1	2.0	1.0	1.1	1.0	1.0	0.7	1.0	
Net Sales to Working Capital 32	6.4	•	8.6	8.9	3.4	5.8	4.8	4.0	5.7	9.3	5.7	
Coverage Ratio 33	1.3	2.8	2.9	0.0	6.2	3.2	1.9	2.5	3.6	1.0	1.0	
Total Asset Turnover 34	1.0	•	2.5	2.1	1.4	1.5	1.3	1.1	1.1	0.8	0.5	
Inventory Turnover 35	4.9	•	8.9	7.4	5.9	3.9	4.5	4.3	4.2	2.9	5.1	
Receivables Turnover 36	6.5	•	12.7	7.9	8.2	7.0	6.9	5.8	6.6	6.8	4.1	
Total Liabilities to Net Worth 37	1.3	•	2.8	2.0	2.5	1.1	1.4	1.0	1.0	1.2	1.2	
Current Assets to Working Capital 38	2.4	•	1.9	2.6	1.4	2.2	1.9	1.9	2.2	4.0	2.9	
Current Liabilities to Working Capital 39	1.4	•	0.9	1.6	0.4	1.2	0.9	0.9	1.2	3.0	1.9	
Working Capital to Net Sales 40	0.2	•	0.1	0.1	0.3	0.2	0.2	0.2	0.2	0.1	0.2	
Inventory to Working Capital 41	0.8	•	0.5	0.8	0.5	0.9	0.7	0.8	0.9	1.6	0.7	
Total Receipts to Cash Flow 42	9.0	6.5	6.9	12.7	16.7	10.2	11.9	13.1	10.4	7.5	8.8	6.0
Cost of Goods to Cash Flow 43	5.7	4.0	3.3	7.5	10.9	6.7	8.3	9.4	7.2	5.0	5.8	3.6
Cash Flow to Total Debt 44	0.2	•	0.5	0.2	0.4	0.2	0.2	0.2	0.3	0.2	0.1	

Selected Financial Factors (in Percentages)

Item												
Debt Ratio 45	56.3	•	73.5	66.6	71.8	33.5	51.4	58.4	49.6	55.1	54.5	
Return on Total Assets 46	4.7	•	9.4	0.1	2.8	5.6	5.3	3.9	4.4	8.4	2.5	4.5
Return on Equity Before Income Taxes 47	2.6	23.3	•	7.1	•	7.5	4.4	5.2	12.2	•	•	
Return on Equity After Income Taxes 48	1.6	23.0	•	6.6	•	6.1	3.4	3.3	9.0	•	•	
Profit Margin (Before Income Tax) 49	1.1	3.1	2.5	•	3.3	•	1.4	2.4	5.5	•	•	
Profit Margin (After Income Tax) 50	0.7	2.2	2.4	•	3.1	•	1.1	2.0	4.0	•	•	

Table II
Corporations with Net Income

CUTLERY, HARDWARE, SPRING AND WIRE MACHINE SHOPS, NUT, BOLT

MONEY AMOUNTS AND SIZE OF ASSETS IN THOUSANDS OF DOLLARS

Item Description for Accounting Period 7/03 Through 6/04	Total	Zero Assets	Under 500	500 to 1,000	1,000 to 5,000	5,000 to 10,000	10,000 to 25,000	25,000 to 50,000	50,000 to 100,000	100,000 to 250,000	250,000 to 500,000	500,000 to 2,500,000	2,500,000 and over
Number of Enterprises 1	11958	1538	7673	819	1549	146	152	38	18	21	.	.	4
Revenues ($ in Thousands)													
Net Sales 2	30228860	806391	2479158	1499638	5545515	1637948	3826044	1769903	1356817	3831978	.	7475469	.
Interest 3	901910	3480	1397	592	4667	1033	1878	5166	1044	12942	.	869710	.
Rents 4	10824	0	0	694	2059	18	1227	931	8	4992	.	896	.
Royalties 5	189191	8179	0	0	0	0	107	180	430	11453	.	168843	.
Other Portfolio Income 6	219554	6481	3346	612	111756	8088	14821	3035	11645	17296	.	42474	.
Other Receipts 7	487447	2543	24416	10486	16415	4661	13580	7230	12769	136956	.	258389	.
Total Receipts 8	32037786	827074	2508317	1512022	5680412	1651748	3857657	1786445	1382713	4015617	.	8815781	.
Average Total Receipts 9	2679	538	327	1846	3667	11313	25379	47012	76817	191220	.	2203945	.
Operating Costs/Operating Income (%)													
Cost of Operations 10	61.4	61.3	48.2	55.7	60.9	60.6	67.5	69.7	66.4	65.3	.	59.7	.
Salaries and Wages 11	7.9	6.1	8.5	5.5	7.7	3.2	6.7	5.7	6.8	7.4	.	11.0	.
Taxes Paid 12	2.3	2.0	3.1	3.3	3.0	3.1	2.3	2.0	2.5	2.0	.	1.2	.
Interest Paid 13	4.2	2.0	1.2	1.1	1.3	0.3	0.8	1.2	1.2	1.2	.	13.6	.
Depreciation 14	3.8	2.8	3.8	4.4	4.2	5.6	3.7	4.5	4.3	4.0	.	2.9	.
Amortization and Depletion 15	0.7	0.2	0.1	0.0	0.1	0.0	0.1	0.2	0.6	0.5	.	2.4	.
Pensions and Other Deferred Comp. 16	0.9	1.9	0.2	0.9	0.8	1.1	0.6	0.6	0.6	0.8	.	1.5	.
Employee Benefits 17	2.1	1.2	1.2	1.7	2.4	3.1	1.9	2.0	1.7	2.1	.	2.5	.
Advertising 18	0.8	0.1	0.7	0.3	0.3	0.7	0.7	1.1	1.5	0.9	.	1.1	.
Other Expenses 19	12.5	15.0	15.1	13.8	10.1	7.2	7.6	7.4	9.4	10.3	.	19.6	.
Officers' Compensation 20	3.5	2.4	8.8	9.8	6.1	5.1	2.8	1.7	1.6	1.2	.	0.7	.
Operating Margin 21	.	5.1	9.2	3.4	3.0	10.1	5.1	4.2	3.3	4.3	.	.	.
Operating Margin Before Officers' Comp. 22	3.3	7.5	18.0	13.2	9.1	15.2	7.9	5.8	4.9	5.5	.	.	.

Selected Average Balance Sheet ($ in Thousands)

Net Receivables 23	382	0	25	230	431	1283	3460	7430	12851	27827	•	428505
Inventories 24	286	0	15	148	363	1786	3486	6875	14071	23973	•	180658
Net Property, Plant and Equipment 25	408	0	41	212	526	2120	4340	9882	16325	39880	•	276293
Total Assets 26	2694	0	117	758	2084	7738	15045	32402	66703	175208	•	4484378
Notes and Loans Payable 27	483	0	51	271	815	403	3747	8886	13787	28260	•	524010
All Other Liabilities 28	874	0	10	93	361	989	2830	7628	15085	37145	•	1957603
Net Worth 29	1337	0	57	394	908	6347	8468	15888	37831	109802	•	2002764

Selected Financial Ratios (Times to 1)

Current Ratio 30	2.0	•	3.0	2.7	2.1	5.7	2.2	2.3	2.4	2.2	•	1.6
Quick Ratio 31	1.3	•	2.3	1.8	1.4	3.6	1.2	1.2	1.3	1.2	•	1.2
Net Sales to Working Capital 32	5.0	•	7.2	5.7	5.9	2.9	5.1	4.4	3.6	4.4	•	4.8
Coverage Ratio 33	2.4	4.9	9.3	4.7	5.2	40.6	8.8	5.4	5.4	8.4	•	1.2
Total Asset Turnover 34	0.9	•	2.8	2.4	1.7	1.4	1.7	1.4	1.1	1.0	•	0.4
Inventory Turnover 35	5.4	•	10.5	6.9	6.0	3.8	4.9	4.7	3.6	5.0	•	6.2
Receivables Turnover 36	6.4	•	13.5	8.1	8.6	6.7	7.8	7.2	5.7	8.4	•	3.8
Total Liabilities to Net Worth 37	1.0	•	1.1	0.9	1.3	0.2	0.8	1.0	0.8	0.6	•	1.2
Current Assets to Working Capital 38	2.0	•	1.5	1.6	1.9	1.2	1.9	1.7	1.7	1.8	•	2.7
Current Liabilities to Working Capital 39	1.0	•	0.5	0.6	0.9	0.2	0.9	0.7	0.7	0.8	•	1.7
Working Capital to Net Sales 40	0.2	•	0.1	0.2	0.2	0.3	0.2	0.2	0.3	0.2	•	0.2
Inventory to Working Capital 41	0.6	•	0.3	0.5	0.6	0.4	0.8	0.7	0.7	0.7	•	0.5
Total Receipts to Cash Flow 42	6.3	5.3	4.9	7.8	7.7	6.6	8.6	9.2	7.4	5.7	•	5.0
Cost of Goods to Cash Flow 43	3.9	3.3	2.3	4.4	4.7	4.0	5.8	6.4	4.9	3.7	•	3.0
Cash Flow to Total Debt 44	0.3	•	1.1	0.6	0.4	1.2	0.4	0.3	0.4	0.5	•	0.2

Selected Financial Factors (in Percentages)

Debt Ratio 45	50.4	•	51.4	48.0	56.4	18.0	43.7	51.0	43.3	37.3	•	55.3
Return on Total Assets 46	9.5	•	32.0	12.8	11.5	16.2	11.4	9.0	7.4	10.9	•	6.7
Return on Equity Before Income Taxes 47	11.2	•	58.7	19.4	21.3	19.3	17.9	15.0	10.7	15.2	•	2.3
Return on Equity After Income Taxes 48	9.8	•	58.4	17.8	20.6	18.8	15.9	13.6	8.1	11.2	•	1.8
Profit Margin (Before Income Tax) 49	5.9	7.6	10.4	4.2	5.4	10.9	6.0	5.1	5.3	9.2	•	2.5
Profit Margin (After Income Tax) 50	5.2	6.6	10.3	3.8	5.2	10.6	5.4	4.6	4.1	6.8	•	1.9

MANUFACTURING
332300

Table I
Corporations with and without Net Income

ARCHITECTURAL AND STRUCTURAL METALS

MONEY AMOUNTS AND SIZE OF ASSETS IN THOUSANDS OF DOLLARS

Item Description for Accounting Period 7/03 Through 6/04		Total	Zero Assets	Under 500	500 to 1,000	1,000 to 5,000	5,000 to 10,000	10,000 to 25,000	25,000 to 50,000	50,000 to 100,000	100,000 to 250,000	250,000 to 500,000	500,000 to 2,500,000	2,500,000 and over
Number of Enterprises	1	5477	350	2091	1213	1252	325	159	39	15	24	4	5	•
Revenues ($ in Thousands)														
Net Sales	2	33046179	690165	1642062	1843279	5241112	4309066	4487566	2016271	1481113	5923647	1838515	3573383	•
Interest	3	168267	2867	1793	805	3718	3471	4750	2947	965	35178	5656	106118	•
Rents	4	14207	237	346	266	116	696	2176	1035	607	2442	1577	4709	•
Royalties	5	57346	1682	0	519	0	0	0	154	312	744	3462	50472	•
Other Portfolio Income	6	119206	31857	4763	80	22666	1431	7974	3094	6547	5749	1366	33679	•
Other Receipts	7	260111	10620	667	2522	9947	23834	30444	2605	42036	63925	10468	63043	•
Total Receipts	8	33665316	737428	1649631	1847471	5277559	4338498	4532910	2026106	1531580	6031685	1861044	3831404	•
Average Total Receipts	9	6147	2107	789	1523	4215	13349	28509	51951	102105	251320	465261	766281	•
Operating Costs/Operating Income (%)														
Cost of Operations	10	71.5	77.8	65.2	69.0	70.9	76.9	73.1	72.9	69.7	75.0	70.5	61.3	•
Salaries and Wages	11	7.5	5.3	6.2	4.4	6.9	5.4	6.9	6.2	10.2	9.2	8.3	10.6	•
Taxes Paid	12	2.2	2.3	3.6	2.9	2.7	1.9	2.2	2.0	1.9	2.0	1.9	1.9	•
Interest Paid	13	2.0	1.4	0.8	0.6	0.9	0.9	0.9	1.5	0.9	1.8	4.4	7.5	•
Depreciation	14	3.1	1.5	2.4	1.0	2.4	2.6	2.9	2.8	5.9	2.8	3.9	6.0	•
Amortization and Depletion	15	0.3	0.1	0.0	0.0	0.1	0.1	0.1	0.3	0.1	0.6	1.0	0.9	•
Pensions and Other Deferred Comp.	16	0.4	0.7	0.3	0.2	0.3	0.6	0.5	0.3	0.5	0.5	0.5	0.4	•
Employee Benefits	17	2.2	2.2	1.9	3.3	3.3	1.7	1.9	1.3	1.7	2.2	2.4	2.1	•
Advertising	18	0.6	0.3	0.5	0.2	0.5	0.6	0.6	0.4	0.9	0.8	0.7	0.6	•
Other Expenses	19	9.2	12.9	14.2	9.0	10.2	7.2	8.2	7.0	10.2	6.3	7.6	15.2	•
Officers' Compensation	20	2.3	1.2	5.9	5.4	4.3	2.1	2.3	1.3	0.9	0.8	0.6	0.6	•
Operating Margin	21	•	•	3.9	•	•	•	0.5	4.0	•	•	•	•	•
Operating Margin Before Officers' Comp.	22	0.9	•	5.1	9.4	1.9	2.0	2.8	5.3	•	•	•	•	•

Selected Average Balance Sheet ($ in Thousands)

	1	2	3	4	5	6	7	8	9	10	11	12
Net Receivables 23	1003	0	99	265	624	2254	5002	9546	16417	43103	82719	134046
Inventories 24	591	0	31	121	403	1487	2636	6258	13223	23108	50679	84039
Net Property, Plant and Equipment 25	982	0	58	74	446	1484	3894	8840	18191	44207	95581	289303
Total Assets 26	3767	0	250	733	2068	6695	15541	35264	74733	155573	336380	882297
Notes and Loans Payable 27	1378	0	90	203	1037	2202	5339	12331	21802	44962	204512	308931
All Other Liabilities 28	1148	0	86	144	615	1954	4634	10365	18198	63146	96263	243457
Net Worth 29	1241	0	74	387	416	2538	5568	12568	34733	47465	35604	329909

Selected Financial Ratios (Times to 1)

	1	2	3	4	5	6	7	8	9	10	11	12
Current Ratio 30	1.6	•	1.8	3.2	1.5	1.8	1.6	2.0	1.8	1.4	1.5	1.5
Quick Ratio 31	1.0	•	1.4	2.4	0.9	1.1	1.0	1.3	1.0	0.8	1.0	0.9
Net Sales to Working Capital 32	7.5	•	10.1	3.7	9.5	6.4	7.3	4.8	5.5	10.2	8.8	8.3
Coverage Ratio 33	1.2	1.9	0.4	7.8	•	1.7	2.6	3.9	1.5	0.8	0.9	1.1
Total Asset Turnover 34	1.6	•	3.1	2.1	2.0	2.0	1.8	1.5	1.3	1.6	1.4	0.8
Inventory Turnover 35	7.3	•	16.4	8.7	7.4	6.9	7.8	6.0	5.2	8.0	6.4	5.2
Receivables Turnover 36	6.2	•	8.6	5.9	6.9	6.4	5.8	6.1	5.9	5.8	5.3	5.2
Total Liabilities to Net Worth 37	2.0	•	2.4	0.9	4.0	1.6	1.8	1.8	1.2	2.3	8.4	1.7
Current Assets to Working Capital 38	2.6	•	2.3	1.5	2.9	2.3	2.7	2.0	2.3	3.6	2.9	3.0
Current Liabilities to Working Capital 39	1.6	•	1.3	0.5	1.9	1.3	1.7	1.0	1.3	2.6	1.9	2.0
Working Capital to Net Sales 40	0.1	•	0.1	0.3	0.1	0.2	0.1	0.2	0.2	0.1	0.1	0.1
Inventory to Working Capital 41	0.7	•	0.4	0.3	0.9	0.8	0.7	0.6	0.7	0.9	0.8	0.9
Total Receipts to Cash Flow 42	14.2	8.8	10.0	10.2	19.0	16.5	13.8	10.0	11.8	26.2	18.3	9.4
Cost of Goods to Cash Flow 43	10.2	6.8	6.5	7.0	13.5	12.7	10.1	7.3	8.2	19.7	12.9	5.7
Cash Flow to Total Debt 44	0.2	•	0.4	0.4	0.1	0.2	0.2	0.2	0.2	0.1	0.1	0.1

Selected Financial Factors (in Percentages)

	1	2	3	4	5	6	7	8	9	10	11	12
Debt Ratio 45	67.1	•	70.2	47.3	79.9	62.1	64.2	64.4	53.5	69.5	89.4	62.6
Return on Total Assets 46	4.0	•	1.0	9.9	•	3.0	4.2	8.8	1.8	2.4	5.2	6.5
Return on Equity Before Income Taxes 47	2.4	•	16.4	•	3.2	7.2	18.2	1.3	•	•	•	1.2
Return on Equity After Income Taxes 48	0.1	•	16.0	•	1.8	5.3	13.9	0.7	0.7	•	•	•
Profit Margin (Before Income Tax) 49	0.5	1.2	4.2	•	0.6	0.6	1.4	4.4	0.5	•	•	0.6
Profit Margin (After Income Tax) 50	0.0	1.1	4.1	•	0.4	0.4	1.0	3.4	0.2	•	•	•

Table II
Corporations with Net Income

ARCHITECTURAL AND STRUCTURAL METALS

MONEY AMOUNTS AND SIZE OF ASSETS IN THOUSANDS OF DOLLARS

Item Description for Accounting Period 7/03 Through 6/04	Total	Zero Assets	Under 500	500 to 1,000	1,000 to 5,000	5,000 to 10,000	10,000 to 25,000	25,000 to 50,000	50,000 to 100,000	100,000 to 250,000	250,000 to 500,000	500,000 to 2,500,000	2,500,000 and over
Number of Enterprises 1	3553	344	1428	839	643	143	104	24	10	•	•	•	•
Revenues ($ in Thousands)													
Net Sales 2	20401385	287397	1321268	1291212	2709126	2546641	3128922	1399285	1010790	•	•	•	•
Interest 3	136740	1409	317	521	1739	339	2445	1263	964	•	•	•	•
Rents 4	7418	237	0	0	113	696	376	228	561	•	•	•	•
Royalties 5	51512	0	0	519	0	0	0	0	312	•	•	•	•
Other Portfolio Income 6	98342	31853	682	80	21459	582	1899	783	6485	•	•	•	•
Other Receipts 7	155063	788	503	1411	4743	20095	20220	1229	8580	•	•	•	•
Total Receipts 8	20850460	321684	1322770	1293743	2737180	2568353	3153862	1402788	1027692	•	•	•	•
Average Total Receipts 9	5868	935	926	1542	4257	17961	30326	58450	102769	•	•	•	•
Operating Costs/Operating Income (%)													
Cost of Operations 10	69.7	80.9	66.1	65.0	71.1	76.4	70.8	71.2	66.5	•	•	•	•
Salaries and Wages 11	7.0	2.5	3.9	4.6	6.2	5.2	6.7	4.9	11.1	•	•	•	•
Taxes Paid 12	2.0	2.4	3.2	2.4	2.2	1.3	2.1	1.8	2.0	•	•	•	•
Interest Paid 13	1.6	1.0	0.7	0.2	0.6	0.3	0.5	1.2	0.9	•	•	•	•
Depreciation 14	2.8	1.7	2.7	1.0	2.0	1.7	2.7	2.7	3.3	•	•	•	•
Amortization and Depletion 15	0.3	0.2	•	•	0.0	0.1	0.0	0.3	0.2	•	•	•	•
Pensions and Other Deferred Comp. 16	0.4	0.0	0.4	0.2	0.3	0.3	0.5	0.3	0.6	•	•	•	•
Employee Benefits 17	1.8	0.2	1.7	2.4	1.0	1.4	1.8	1.4	1.9	•	•	•	•
Advertising 18	0.6	0.3	0.6	0.1	0.3	0.4	0.6	0.4	1.1	•	•	•	•
Other Expenses 19	8.6	7.9	12.9	8.8	9.5	7.2	7.0	6.4	8.5	•	•	•	•
Officers' Compensation 20	2.3	1.9	5.6	6.9	4.4	1.3	2.3	1.3	1.2	•	•	•	•
Operating Margin 21	3.0	1.0	2.1	8.3	2.4	4.6	5.0	8.1	2.9	•	•	•	•
Operating Margin Before Officers' Comp. 22	5.3	2.8	7.8	15.1	6.8	5.8	7.3	9.4	4.0	•	•	•	•

Selected Average Balance Sheet ($ in Thousands)

Net Receivables 23	911	0	108	240	598	2554	4799	10485	15187
Inventories 24	578	0	38	87	381	2094	2881	6407	14272
Net Property, Plant and Equipment 25	848	0	82	62	380	1055	3793	8348	20095
Total Assets 26	3455	0	272	743	1792	7009	15470	35162	78226
Notes and Loans Payable 27	974	0	98	89	1055	1361	3422	9631	17609
All Other Liabilities 28	1001	0	89	138	516	2225	4026	10810	18360
Net Worth 29	1480	0	85	516	221	3424	8022	14721	42257

Selected Financial Ratios (Times to 1)

Current Ratio 30	2.0	•	1.7	3.2	1.9	2.5	2.1	2.2	2.0
Quick Ratio 31	1.3	•	1.3	2.5	1.3	1.6	1.3	1.3	1.2
Net Sales to Working Capital 32	5.9	•	12.8	3.8	6.9	5.1	5.5	4.6	5.0
Coverage Ratio 33	4.4	13.5	4.1	41.8	6.4	18.2	12.2	8.1	6.2
Total Asset Turnover 34	1.7	•	3.4	2.1	2.4	2.5	1.9	1.7	1.3
Inventory Turnover 35	6.9	•	16.3	11.5	7.9	6.5	7.4	6.5	4.7
Receivables Turnover 36	6.1	•	17.1	6.5	6.3	5.9	5.9	6.2	6.9
Total Liabilities to Net Worth 37	1.3	•	2.2	0.4	7.1	1.0	0.9	1.4	0.9
Current Assets to Working Capital 38	2.0	•	2.5	1.5	2.1	1.7	1.9	1.8	2.0
Current Liabilities to Working Capital 39	1.0	•	1.5	0.5	1.1	0.7	0.9	0.8	1.0
Working Capital to Net Sales 40	0.2	•	0.1	0.3	0.1	0.2	0.2	0.2	0.2
Inventory to Working Capital 41	0.6	•	0.5	0.3	0.5	0.5	0.5	0.5	0.7
Total Receipts to Cash Flow 42	8.9	5.6	8.2	7.1	10.1	9.4	9.2	7.5	9.5
Cost of Goods to Cash Flow 43	6.2	4.6	5.4	4.6	7.2	7.2	6.5	5.4	6.3
Cash Flow to Total Debt 44	0.3	•	0.6	1.0	0.3	0.5	0.4	0.4	0.3

Selected Financial Factors (in Percentages)

Debt Ratio 45	57.2	•	68.7	30.5	87.7	51.2	48.1	58.1	46.0
Return on Total Assets 46	11.4	•	10.1	18.0	9.6	14.6	12.3	15.7	7.0
Return on Equity Before Income Taxes 47	20.5	•	24.3	25.2	65.8	28.2	21.7	32.9	10.9
Return on Equity After Income Taxes 48	17.5	•	23.0	24.8	61.1	25.9	19.7	26.9	10.1
Profit Margin (Before Income Tax) 49	5.3	12.9	2.2	8.5	3.5	5.4	5.8	8.3	4.6
Profit Margin (After Income Tax) 50	4.5	12.7	2.1	8.3	3.2	5.0	5.2	6.8	4.2

116

Table I

Corporations with and without Net Income

BOILER, TANK, AND SHIPPING CONTAINER

MONEY AMOUNTS AND SIZE OF ASSETS IN THOUSANDS OF DOLLARS

Item Description for Accounting Period 7/03 Through 6/04	Total	Zero Assets	Under 500	500 to 1,000	1,000 to 5,000	5,000 to 10,000	10,000 to 25,000	25,000 to 50,000	50,000 to 100,000	100,000 to 250,000	250,000 to 500,000	500,000 to 2,500,000	2,500,000 and over
Number of Enterprises **1**	334	•	53	54	114	42	39	14	6	5	3	•	3
Revenues ($ in Thousands)													
Net Sales **2**	14058374	•	426	114410	350260	720187	964309	749571	647764	623162	2398073	•	7490211
Interest **3**	127636	•	0	47	140	68	1416	575	232	9220	1089	•	114850
Rents **4**	37278	•	0	2863	2680	0	1066	832	0	5236	0	•	24600
Royalties **5**	61270	•	0	0	0	6	244	6	286	0	113	•	60614
Other Portfolio Income **6**	34760	•	3779	0	737	22	1107	149	1296	3184	37	•	24449
Other Receipts **7**	305511	•	5616	1399	350	399	7143	6016	2052	9680	9424	•	263434
Total Receipts **8**	14624829	•	9821	118719	354167	720682	975285	757149	651630	650482	2408736	•	7978158
Average Total Receipts **9**	43787	•	185	2198	3107	17159	25007	54082	108605	130096	802912	•	2659386
Operating Costs/Operating Income (%)													
Cost of Operations **10**	77.6	•	3585.4	56.5	75.1	63.0	73.3	76.7	75.6	73.8	77.6	•	80.5
Salaries and Wages **11**	5.0	•	72.5	14.4	7.2	13.8	5.9	6.0	7.9	4.3	3.3	•	4.0
Taxes Paid **12**	1.9	•	65.3	6.7	2.6	2.4	2.4	1.8	0.8	1.9	1.5	•	1.9
Interest Paid **13**	3.6	•	•	0.3	2.2	0.8	1.0	1.1	0.7	7.4	5.4	•	4.0
Depreciation **14**	4.0	•	•	1.1	4.0	4.1	2.9	2.9	4.6	5.0	5.6	•	3.6
Amortization and Depletion **15**	0.4	•	•	•	0.2	0.5	0.2	0.2	0.6	1.4	0.5	•	0.4
Pensions and Other Deferred Comp. **16**	0.7	•	•	1.6	0.2	0.1	0.5	0.3	0.3	0.1	1.1	•	0.8
Employee Benefits **17**	2.1	•	•	6.5	1.9	1.9	1.8	1.6	0.6	1.2	1.2	•	2.7
Advertising **18**	0.2	•	•	0.4	0.1	1.4	0.8	0.3	0.3	0.5	0.1	•	0.0
Other Expenses **19**	6.5	•	1320.0	4.1	7.7	10.8	8.5	7.5	6.3	8.1	5.4	•	5.9
Officers' Compensation **20**	1.0	•	675.1	4.7	3.3	3.4	2.0	1.4	1.9	0.9	0.2	•	0.6
Operating Margin **21**	•	•	•	3.8	•	•	0.7	0.2	0.3	•	•	•	•
Operating Margin Before Officers' Comp. **22**	•	•	•	8.5	•	1.4	2.7	1.7	2.2	•	•	•	•

Selected Average Balance Sheet ($ in Thousands)

Item	All												
Net Receivables 23	7631	•	115	203	529	2055	4762	8793	20982	12200	70245	•	559532
Inventories 24	4136	•	58	208	534	2269	2625	5070	10692	31313	102527	•	168528
Net Property, Plant and Equipment 25	8779	•	32	196	899	1992	3763	9993	22978	27648	250690	•	472950
Total Assets 26	53355	•	306	973	2228	8494	15471	33085	69306	168165	1038961	•	3900356
Notes and Loans Payable 27	14745	•	219	148	1285	3699	4260	10017	15770	87912	732902	•	521369
All Other Liabilities 28	22879	•	100	133	278	1510	3805	7680	27554	43961	264791	•	2032828
Net Worth 29	15731	•	-13	692	665	3285	7406	15388	25982	36292	41269	•	1346159

Selected Financial Ratios (Times to 1)

Item	All												
Current Ratio 30	1.3	•	0.8	5.6	2.0	1.8	1.9	2.1	1.3	0.8	4.0	•	0.9
Quick Ratio 31	0.7	•	0.4	3.3	1.3	0.9	1.2	1.2	0.8	0.3	0.6	•	0.6
Net Sales to Working Capital 32	10.5	•	•	•	•	3.4	5.2	6.9	5.0	5.4	10.0	•	2.0
Coverage Ratio 33	1.3	•	•	28.5	•	2.8	2.1	2.2	1.6	1.0	0.8	•	1.7
Total Asset Turnover 34	0.8	•	0.0	2.2	1.4	2.0	1.6	1.6	1.6	0.7	0.8	•	0.6
Inventory Turnover 35	7.9	•	5.0	5.8	4.3	4.8	6.9	8.1	7.6	2.9	6.0	•	11.9
Receivables Turnover 36	5.3	•	0.1	20.9	4.7	10.3	5.2	6.7	6.5	8.6	9.7	•	4.2
Total Liabilities to Net Worth 37	2.4	•	•	0.4	2.4	1.6	1.1	1.2	1.7	3.6	24.2	•	1.9
Current Assets to Working Capital 38	4.4	•	•	1.2	2.0	2.3	2.1	1.9	4.0	•	•	•	1.3
Current Liabilities to Working Capital 39	3.4	•	•	0.2	1.0	1.3	1.1	0.9	3.0	•	•	•	0.3
Working Capital to Net Sales 40	0.1	•	•	0.3	0.2	0.1	0.2	0.2	0.1	•	•	•	0.5
Inventory to Working Capital 41	1.0	•	•	0.3	0.6	1.1	0.5	0.5	1.4	•	•	•	0.3
Total Receipts to Cash Flow 42	17.9	•	•	8.9	33.9	16.5	12.1	13.6	18.8	17.1	34.9	•	16.5
Cost of Goods to Cash Flow 43	13.9	•	5.0	25.4	10.4	8.9	10.4	14.3	12.6	27.0	•	•	13.3
Cash Flow to Total Debt 44	0.1	•	•	0.9	0.1	0.2	0.3	0.2	0.1	0.1	0.0	•	0.1

Selected Financial Factors (in Percentages)

Item	All												
Debt Ratio 45	70.5	•	104.3	28.9	70.2	61.3	52.1	53.5	62.5	78.4	96.0	•	65.5
Return on Total Assets 46	3.8	•	•	17.1	•	•	4.4	3.8	2.4	5.4	3.2	•	4.3
Return on Equity Before Income Taxes 47	3.3	•	2088.9	23.2	•	•	5.9	4.3	3.5	•	•	•	5.0
Return on Equity After Income Taxes 48	1.6	•	2088.9	23.2	•	•	4.4	2.2	2.3	•	•	•	3.2
Profit Margin (Before Income Tax) 49	1.2	•	•	7.6	•	•	1.8	1.2	0.8	•	•	•	2.7
Profit Margin (After Income Tax) 50	0.6	•	•	7.6	•	•	1.3	0.6	0.5	•	•	•	1.7

Table II

Corporations with Net Income

BOILER, TANK, AND SHIPPING CONTAINER

MONEY AMOUNTS AND SIZE OF ASSETS IN THOUSANDS OF DOLLARS

Item Description for Accounting Period 7/03 Through 6/04	Total	Zero Assets	Under 500	500 to 1,000	1,000 to 5,000	5,000 to 10,000	10,000 to 25,000	25,000 to 50,000	50,000 to 100,000	100,000 to 250,000	250,000 to 500,000	500,000 to 2,500,000	2,500,000 and over
Number of Enterprises 1	167	·	·	·	68	3	24	9	·	·	3	·	·
Revenues ($ in Thousands)													
Net Sales 2	8395239	·	·	·	218560	72866	624859	489887	·	·	5944569	·	·
Interest 3	117050	·	·	·	111	0	464	100	·	·	110224	·	·
Rents 4	22969	·	·	·	225	0	895	832	·	·	12917	·	·
Royalties 5	59398	·	·	·	0	0	244	0	·	·	58868	·	·
Other Portfolio Income 6	9275	·	·	·	388	22	964	146	·	·	4044	·	·
Other Receipts 7	222086	·	·	·	141	179	5532	2964	·	·	203560	·	·
Total Receipts 8	8826017	·	·	·	219425	73067	632958	493929	·	·	6334182	·	·
Average Total Receipts 9	52850	·	·	·	3227	24356	26373	54881	·	·	2111394	·	·
Operating Costs/Operating Income (%)													
Cost of Operations 10	79.4	·	·	·	68.0	52.3	72.1	75.8	·	·	82.2	·	·
Salaries and Wages 11	4.7	·	·	·	8.4	7.7	6.3	4.5	·	·	3.8	·	·
Taxes Paid 12	2.1	·	·	·	1.9	1.9	2.2	1.8	·	·	2.2	·	·
Interest Paid 13	3.6	·	·	·	3.0	0.2	0.7	1.0	·	·	4.2	·	·
Depreciation 14	2.9	·	·	·	4.7	0.8	2.4	2.8	·	·	3.1	·	·
Amortization and Depletion 15	0.3	·	·	·	0.3	0.0	0.0	0.1	·	·	0.4	·	·
Pensions and Other Deferred Comp. 16	0.7	·	·	·	0.1	0.1	0.6	0.4	·	·	0.8	·	·
Employee Benefits 17	2.0	·	·	·	1.5	0.5	1.7	1.3	·	·	2.2	·	·
Advertising 18	0.2	·	·	·	0.2	0.8	1.1	0.1	·	·	0.0	·	·
Other Expenses 19	4.7	·	·	·	7.2	11.5	6.6	7.2	·	·	3.9	·	·
Officers' Compensation 20	1.1	·	·	·	3.3	5.1	2.0	1.7	·	·	0.6	·	·
Operating Margin 21	·	·	·	·	1.4	19.1	4.2	3.2	·	·	·	·	·
Operating Margin Before Officers' Comp. 22	·	·	·	·	4.7	24.2	6.2	4.9	·	·	·	·	·

Selected Average Balance Sheet ($ in Thousands)

Net Receivables 23	11996	424	1530	4148	8349	556092
Inventories 24	5229	469	4003	2983	5801	148513
Net Property, Plant and Equipment 25	8577	1122	2057	3371	8964	357351
Total Assets 26	59072	2254	7066	14809	31353	2743951
Notes and Loans Payable 27	11394	1718	167	3192	8831	432150
All Other Liabilities 28	34059	212	1294	3919	6141	1772475
Net Worth 29	13620	325	5605	7698	16381	539326

Selected Financial Ratios (Times to 1)

Current Ratio 30	1.0	1.9	3.6	1.8	2.6	0.9
Quick Ratio 31	0.7	1.0	2.2	1.2	1.4	0.7
Net Sales to Working Capital 32	179.0	6.0	7.0	5.9	4.3	
Coverage Ratio 33	2.1	1.6	109.5	8.8	5.0	1.9
Total Asset Turnover 34	0.9	1.4	3.4	1.8	1.7	0.7
Inventory Turnover 35	7.6	4.7	3.2	6.3	7.1	11.0
Receivables Turnover 36	3.8	7.0	6.0	5.3	6.8	7.1
Total Liabilities to Net Worth 37	3.3	5.9	0.3	0.9	0.9	4.1
Current Assets to Working Capital 38	74.7	2.1	1.4	2.2	1.6	
Current Liabilities to Working Capital 39	73.7	1.1	0.4	1.2	0.6	
Working Capital to Net Sales 40	0.0	0.2	0.1	0.2	0.2	
Inventory to Working Capital 41	15.5	0.9	0.4	0.6	0.4	
Total Receipts to Cash Flow 42	14.8	12.5	3.3	9.2	10.5	17.6
Cost of Goods to Cash Flow 43	11.8	8.5	1.7	6.6	8.0	14.5
Cash Flow to Total Debt 44	0.1	0.1	5.0	0.4	0.3	0.1

Selected Financial Factors (in Percentages)

Debt Ratio 45	76.9	85.6	20.7	48.0	47.8	80.3
Return on Total Assets 46	6.3	6.8	67.2	10.9	8.7	5.6
Return on Equity Before Income Taxes 47	14.2	17.7	83.9	18.6	13.3	13.4
Return on Equity After Income Taxes 48	10.3	17.5	83.9	16.3	10.3	8.8
Profit Margin (Before Income Tax) 49	3.8	1.8	19.4	5.5	4.0	3.7
Profit Margin (After Income Tax) 50	2.8	1.8	19.4	4.8	3.1	2.4

Table I

Corporations with and without Net Income

COATING, ENGRAVING, HEAT TREATING, AND ALLIED ACTIVITIES

MONEY AMOUNTS AND SIZE OF ASSETS IN THOUSANDS OF DOLLARS

Item Description for Accounting Period 7/03 Through 6/04	Total	Zero Assets	Under 500	500 to 1,000	1,000 to 5,000	5,000 to 10,000	10,000 to 25,000	25,000 to 50,000	50,000 to 100,000	100,000 to 250,000	250,000 to 500,000	500,000 to 2,500,000	2,500,000 and over
Number of Enterprises 1	3794	•	2982	•	602	64	55	13	7	3	3	•	•
Revenues ($ in Thousands)													
Net Sales 2	9523925	•	2283711	•	2473975	558306	1234717	482718	676872	481718	1240725	•	•
Interest 3	27755	•	552	•	1980	804	1021	566	1218	1610	19975	•	•
Rents 4	15666	•	8579	•	3495	2737	268	0	53	175	359	•	•
Royalties 5	2254	•	113	•	0	0	776	125	0	959	282	•	•
Other Portfolio Income 6	10506	•	170	•	163	1134	2875	1817	1801	1958	551	•	•
Other Receipts 7	86798	•	13430	•	39785	3088	4736	3958	9713	1840	10220	•	•
Total Receipts 8	9666904	•	2306555	•	2519398	566069	1244393	489184	689657	488260	1272112	•	•
Average Total Receipts 9	2548	•	773	•	4185	8845	22625	37630	98522	162753	424037	•	•
Operating Costs/Operating Income (%)													
Cost of Operations 10	55.3	•	33.8	•	55.6	64.5	65.3	62.7	73.7	58.9	63.5	•	•
Salaries and Wages 11	9.6	•	18.6	•	7.3	4.1	7.0	7.6	6.1	7.7	6.6	•	•
Taxes Paid 12	3.6	•	5.3	•	3.9	3.0	2.7	2.9	1.8	4.7	1.7	•	•
Interest Paid 13	1.7	•	0.4	•	1.4	1.5	1.8	1.5	2.4	2.9	3.8	•	•
Depreciation 14	5.1	•	2.2	•	5.7	7.7	5.3	7.0	4.7	7.5	6.4	•	•
Amortization and Depletion 15	0.5	•	0.0	•	0.4	0.1	0.3	0.3	0.3	2.3	1.4	•	•
Pensions and Other Deferred Comp. 16	0.5	•	0.1	•	0.4	1.5	0.5	0.6	0.8	0.8	0.5	•	•
Employee Benefits 17	2.5	•	2.2	•	3.0	2.9	2.8	3.4	2.3	2.6	1.3	•	•
Advertising 18	0.2	•	0.1	•	0.2	0.3	0.2	0.2	0.2	0.3	0.4	•	•
Other Expenses 19	15.9	•	24.2	•	18.9	8.4	9.4	9.5	5.6	13.4	13.5	•	•
Officers' Compensation 20	6.1	•	15.1	•	5.1	4.0	2.6	2.6	1.1	1.3	2.2	•	•
Operating Margin 21	•	•	•	•	•	2.1	2.0	1.6	0.9	•	•	•	•
Operating Margin Before Officers' Comp. 22	5.2	•	13.0	•	3.2	6.1	4.6	4.2	2.0	0.9	0.9	•	•

Selected Average Balance Sheet ($ in Thousands)

Net Receivables 23	367	51	574	942	3382	5175	10954	25913	140438
Inventories 24	131	8	108	642	1810	3677	9616	21151	55930
Net Property, Plant and Equipment 25	710	67	1405	3673	6355	15147	32418	63832	146430
Total Assets 26	1744	183	2644	6737	15106	31578	73156	151251	601665
Notes and Loans Payable 27	703	69	1654	2037	6724	9961	31860	65327	138436
All Other Liabilities 28	486	67	596	1524	3370	5695	22806	23934	230759
Net Worth 29	555	48	394	3176	5012	15923	18490	61989	232471

Selected Financial Ratios (Times to 1)

Current Ratio 30	1.6	1.4	0.9	1.9	1.4	1.8	1.1	2.0	4.6
Quick Ratio 31	1.1	0.9	0.7	1.1	0.9	1.0	0.6	1.5	3.4
Net Sales to Working Capital 32	9.9	27.4	·	8.0	11.3	7.1	35.2	4.9	2.1
Coverage Ratio 33	1.4	·	1.0	3.4	2.5	2.9	2.2	0.6	1.3
Total Asset Turnover 34	1.4	4.2	1.6	1.3	1.5	1.2	1.3	1.1	0.7
Inventory Turnover 35	10.6	31.0	21.1	8.8	8.1	6.3	7.4	4.5	4.7
Receivables Turnover 36	7.9	16.6	7.6	8.6	7.2	6.1	7.9	4.4	5.9
Total Liabilities to Net Worth 37	2.1	2.8	5.7	1.1	2.0	1.0	3.0	1.4	1.6
Current Assets to Working Capital 38	2.8	3.7	·	2.1	3.6	2.2	9.5	2.0	1.3
Current Liabilities to Working Capital 39	1.8	2.7	·	1.1	2.6	1.2	8.5	1.0	0.3
Working Capital to Net Sales 40	0.1	0.0	·	0.1	0.1	0.1	0.0	0.2	0.5
Inventory to Working Capital 41	0.6	0.3	·	0.5	1.0	0.6	3.5	0.4	0.3
Total Receipts to Cash Flow 42	8.3	6.7	7.0	11.2	10.7	9.9	14.4	11.1	7.7
Cost of Goods to Cash Flow 43	4.6	2.3	3.9	7.2	7.0	6.2	10.6	6.6	4.9
Cash Flow to Total Debt 44	0.3	0.8	0.3	0.2	0.2	0.2	0.1	0.2	0.1

Selected Financial Factors (in Percentages)

Debt Ratio 45	68.2	73.9	85.1	52.9	66.8	49.6	74.7	59.0	61.4
Return on Total Assets 46	3.2	·	2.1	6.4	6.9	5.2	7.0	1.9	3.5
Return on Equity Before Income Taxes 47	2.7	·	·	9.6	12.5	6.8	14.8	·	2.3
Return on Equity After Income Taxes 48	1.0	·	·	7.9	11.2	5.9	12.8	·	1.0
Profit Margin (Before Income Tax) 49	0.6	·	·	3.5	2.8	2.9	2.8	·	1.3
Profit Margin (After Income Tax) 50	0.2	·	·	2.9	2.5	2.5	2.4	·	0.6

Table II
Corporations with Net Income

COATING, ENGRAVING, HEAT TREATING, AND ALLIED ACTIVITIES

MONEY AMOUNTS AND SIZE OF ASSETS IN THOUSANDS OF DOLLARS

Item Description for Accounting Period 7/03 Through 6/04	Total	Zero Assets	Under 500	500 to 1,000	1,000 to 5,000	5,000 to 10,000	10,000 to 25,000	25,000 to 50,000	50,000 to 100,000	100,000 to 250,000	250,000 to 500,000	500,000 to 2,500,000	2,500,000 and over
Number of Enterprises **1**	1456	•	1012	3	346	43	41	5	7	•	•	•	•
Revenues ($ in Thousands)													
Net Sales **2**	5612164	•	1457088	4961	1418369	357832	970485	193851	1209578	•	•	•	•
Interest **3**	6111	•	523	6	1386	744	743	186	2524	•	•	•	•
Rents **4**	9826	•	8579	0	939	22	232	0	55	•	•	•	•
Royalties **5**	1253	•	113	0	0	0	734	125	282	•	•	•	•
Other Portfolio Income **6**	6227	•	130	0	109	163	2802	854	2168	•	•	•	•
Other Receipts **7**	41462	•	12568	4	6819	2843	3688	892	14645	•	•	•	•
Total Receipts **8**	5677043	•	1479001	4971	1427622	361604	978684	195908	1229252	•	•	•	•
Average Total Receipts **9**	3899	•	1461	1657	4126	8409	23870	39182	175607	•	•	•	•
Operating Costs/Operating Income (%)													
Cost of Operations **10**	54.9	•	37.7	50.2	53.0	52.9	64.8	62.0	69.3	•	•	•	•
Salaries and Wages **11**	8.4	•	15.9	6.1	6.5	4.6	6.7	6.2	4.5	•	•	•	•
Taxes Paid **12**	3.4	•	4.4	4.7	4.8	3.0	2.6	2.6	1.6	•	•	•	•
Interest Paid **13**	1.2	•	0.0	0.7	1.5	1.3	1.1	0.8	2.2	•	•	•	•
Depreciation **14**	4.0	•	1.8	4.4	4.9	7.6	4.7	7.3	3.4	•	•	•	•
Amortization and Depletion **15**	0.3	•	•	0.1	0.1	0.0	0.1	0.0	1.2	•	•	•	•
Pensions and Other Deferred Comp. **16**	0.6	•	0.1	•	0.6	2.2	0.5	0.9	0.6	•	•	•	•
Employee Benefits **17**	2.5	•	2.4	4.3	2.7	4.4	2.5	3.0	1.8	•	•	•	•
Advertising **18**	0.2	•	0.1	0.2	0.2	0.3	0.3	0.1	0.4	•	•	•	•
Other Expenses **19**	15.2	•	25.8	12.0	17.1	9.2	8.1	6.3	9.2	•	•	•	•
Officers' Compensation **20**	5.9	•	11.8	11.9	5.2	5.5	3.0	2.1	2.7	•	•	•	•
Operating Margin **21**	3.4	•	•	5.4	3.4	8.9	5.6	8.6	3.1	•	•	•	•
Operating Margin Before Officers' Comp. **22**	9.3	•	11.8	17.3	8.6	14.4	8.6	10.7	5.8	•	•	•	•

Selected Average Balance Sheet ($ in Thousands)

Net Receivables 23	422	•	62	192	510	1040	3504	5431	22722
Inventories 24	172	•	8	957	82	229	1453	5094	18987
Net Property, Plant and Equipment 25	960	•	53	211	1801	2976	5987	15467	38645
Total Assets 26	2377	•	188	645	3014	6201	14951	31902	169580
Notes and Loans Payable 27	1084	•	38	199	2076	1712	4888	7292	72967
All Other Liabilities 28	428	•	36	131	534	748	3426	4793	29229
Net Worth 29	865	•	113	316	405	3742	6638	19817	67384

Selected Financial Ratios (Times to 1)

Current Ratio 30	1.6	•	2.6	1.7	0.9	2.1	1.5	2.8	2.5
Quick Ratio 31	1.1	•	2.3	1.4	0.7	1.3	1.1	1.7	1.6
Net Sales to Working Capital 32	10.9	•	24.0	12.2	•	6.5	9.5	4.2	4.1
Coverage Ratio 33	4.9	•	40.5	8.9	3.6	8.9	6.7	12.9	3.2
Total Asset Turnover 34	1.6	•	7.7	2.6	1.4	1.3	1.6	1.2	1.0
Inventory Turnover 35	12.3	•	68.5	0.9	26.5	19.2	10.6	4.7	6.3
Receivables Turnover 36	9.3	•	46.6	0.3	7.3	10.0	8.5	3.8	15.2
Total Liabilities to Net Worth 37	1.7	•	0.7	1.0	6.4	0.7	1.3	0.6	1.5
Current Assets to Working Capital 38	2.7	•	1.6	2.5	•	1.9	2.9	1.5	1.7
Current Liabilities to Working Capital 39	1.7	•	0.6	1.5	•	0.9	1.9	0.5	0.7
Working Capital to Net Sales 40	0.1	•	0.0	0.1	•	0.2	0.1	0.2	0.2
Inventory to Working Capital 41	0.5	•	0.1	0.3	•	0.3	0.7	0.3	0.5
Total Receipts to Cash Flow 42	6.5	•	5.5	6.1	6.0	6.4	8.1	7.1	7.7
Cost of Goods to Cash Flow 43	3.6	•	2.1	3.1	3.2	3.4	5.3	4.4	5.3
Cash Flow to Total Debt 44	0.4	•	3.5	0.8	0.3	0.5	0.4	0.5	0.2

Selected Financial Factors (in Percentages)

Debt Ratio 45	63.6	•	39.9	51.0	86.6	39.7	55.6	37.9	60.3
Return on Total Assets 46	9.2	•	11.4	16.1	7.6	15.0	12.0	12.7	7.0
Return on Equity Before Income Taxes 47	20.1	•	18.5	29.2	40.9	22.1	23.0	18.9	12.1
Return on Equity After Income Taxes 48	17.3	•	17.8	25.9	33.4	20.0	21.7	17.0	9.0
Profit Margin (Before Income Tax) 49	4.5	•	1.5	5.6	4.0	9.9	6.4	9.7	4.7
Profit Margin (After Income Tax) 50	3.9	•	1.4	5.0	3.3	9.0	6.1	8.7	3.5

Table I

Corporations with and without Net Income

OTHER FABRICATED METAL PRODUCT

MONEY AMOUNTS AND SIZE OF ASSETS IN THOUSANDS OF DOLLARS

Item Description for Accounting Period 7/03 Through 6/04		Total	Zero Assets	Under 500	500 to 1,000	1,000 to 5,000	5,000 to 10,000	10,000 to 25,000	25,000 to 50,000	50,000 to 100,000	100,000 to 250,000	250,000 to 500,000	500,000 to 2,500,000	2,500,000 and over
Number of Enterprises	1	19442	1142	11491	1702	3766	682	375	138	51	50	19	15	11
Revenues ($ in Thousands)														
Net Sales	2	134789047	433913	4651371	2835351	17045988	9793478	9299315	6768660	4555753	7919884	7361618	12580779	51542938
Interest	3	2633454	421	3049	1359	6888	2484	6978	8515	3556	35114	27081	377889	2160120
Rents	4	218331	152	1287	0	3170	37	6638	2111	842	2277	7255	8642	185918
Royalties	5	1368506	6600	0	0	0	160	5105	1281	1191	37566	43801	38547	1234254
Other Portfolio Income	6	1488113	2633	13128	40657	132779	11595	32725	18365	5879	57642	32750	39564	1096397
Other Receipts	7	1081332	27664	-43328	6282	74328	5129	71201	41670	27581	58091	114403	88034	610279
Total Receipts	8	141574783	471383	4625507	2883649	17263153	9812883	9421962	6840602	4594802	8110574	7586908	13133455	56829906
Average Total Receipts	9	7282	413	403	1694	4584	14388	25125	49570	90094	162211	399311	875564	5166355
Operating Costs/Operating Income (%)														
Cost of Operations	10	66.0	76.4	43.4	63.6	66.9	73.9	69.5	68.3	69.5	66.3	69.9	67.9	64.0
Salaries and Wages	11	6.9	8.5	16.5	9.1	6.8	6.1	6.8	7.6	7.7	9.0	6.7	6.7	5.7
Taxes Paid	12	2.1	1.7	3.4	4.2	2.8	1.9	2.4	2.1	2.0	2.1	2.2	2.0	1.7
Interest Paid	13	3.5	1.3	1.4	1.0	0.9	0.9	1.0	1.5	1.4	2.5	1.9	6.2	5.7
Depreciation	14	3.5	1.9	3.4	3.8	3.7	2.4	3.3	3.8	3.6	3.7	3.6	3.6	3.7
Amortization and Depletion	15	0.9	0.8	0.1	0.1	0.1	0.0	0.2	0.3	0.3	0.8	0.2	0.6	1.8
Pensions and Other Deferred Comp.	16	1.2	0.0	0.2	0.5	0.6	0.3	0.6	0.7	0.6	0.9	1.1	0.6	2.0
Employee Benefits	17	2.4	1.6	2.1	0.9	1.7	1.5	2.1	2.2	2.0	2.5	2.6	3.3	2.9
Advertising	18	1.4	0.4	0.4	0.4	0.6	0.6	0.5	0.7	0.8	1.1	1.1	1.5	2.3
Other Expenses	19	11.7	20.1	21.6	12.6	10.3	7.1	8.1	9.3	7.7	10.7	11.4	8.5	14.2
Officers' Compensation	20	1.8	1.3	6.3	7.0	4.9	3.4	2.5	1.8	1.0	0.9	0.7	0.5	0.4
Operating Margin	21	•	•	1.2	•	0.6	1.8	3.0	1.6	3.3	•	•	•	•
Operating Margin Before Officers' Comp.	22	0.5	•	7.6	3.8	5.5	5.2	5.5	3.4	4.4	0.4	•	•	•

Selected Average Balance Sheet ($ in Thousands)

Net Receivables 23	1162	0	24	214	609	2057	3727	7346	12859	28664	66495	187426	879268
Inventories 24	777	0	18	199	446	1739	3677	7544	16568	22482	72563	126607	366044
Net Property, Plant and Equipment 25	1324	0	50	213	569	1603	4145	9847	20223	37494	83630	169891	1055741
Total Assets 26	11948	0	128	685	2160	6794	15599	35775	67759	160636	339673	1122866	15574986
Notes and Loans Payable 27	4078	0	95	304	818	2399	4482	11547	19239	48554	100056	327912	5405693
All Other Liabilities 28	1891	0	29	119	498	1612	3700	8470	16606	44426	99956	327870	1892015
Net Worth 29	5979	0	4	263	845	2783	7417	15758	31915	67657	139662	467084	8277279

Selected Financial Ratios (Times to 1)

Current Ratio 30	1.6	•	1.3	2.2	1.9	2.1	1.9	1.9	1.9	2.0	2.2	1.4	1.4
Quick Ratio 31	0.9	•	0.9	1.5	1.2	1.2	1.0	1.0	1.0	1.0	1.1	0.8	0.8
Net Sales to Working Capital 32	6.9	•	27.7	7.1	6.7	5.6	5.5	5.2	5.3	4.2	3.9	7.4	9.7
Coverage Ratio 33	2.2	•	1.5	•	3.0	3.4	5.4	2.7	3.9	1.8	1.9	1.5	2.3
Total Asset Turnover 34	0.6	•	3.2	2.4	2.1	2.1	1.6	1.4	1.3	1.0	1.1	0.7	0.3
Inventory Turnover 35	5.9	•	9.9	5.3	6.8	6.1	4.7	4.4	3.7	4.7	3.7	4.5	8.2
Receivables Turnover 36	6.3	•	19.1	7.0	7.2	7.4	6.8	6.8	6.7	6.5	5.8	4.5	5.9
Total Liabilities to Net Worth 37	1.0	•	29.1	1.6	1.6	1.4	1.3	1.3	1.1	1.4	1.4	1.4	0.9
Current Assets to Working Capital 38	2.7	•	4.5	1.8	2.1	1.9	2.1	2.1	2.1	2.0	1.9	3.7	3.8
Current Liabilities to Working Capital 39	1.7	•	3.5	0.8	1.1	0.9	1.1	1.1	1.1	1.0	0.9	2.7	2.8
Working Capital to Net Sales 40	0.1	•	0.0	0.1	0.1	0.2	0.2	0.2	0.2	0.2	0.3	0.1	0.1
Inventory to Working Capital 41	0.8	•	1.1	0.5	0.6	0.7	0.8	0.8	0.9	0.6	0.7	1.0	0.8
Total Receipts to Cash Flow 42	7.8	9.7	5.6	16.5	11.9	13.3	9.7	10.1	10.0	9.8	9.1	10.1	5.7
Cost of Goods to Cash Flow 43	5.2	7.4	2.4	10.5	8.0	9.9	6.8	6.9	7.0	6.5	6.4	6.9	3.6
Cash Flow to Total Debt 44	0.1	0.6	0.2	0.2	0.3	0.3	0.3	0.2	0.2	0.2	0.2	0.1	0.1

Selected Financial Factors (in Percentages)

Debt Ratio 45	50.0	•	96.7	61.7	60.9	59.0	52.5	56.0	52.9	57.9	58.9	58.4	46.9
Return on Total Assets 46	4.5	•	6.5	•	5.8	6.1	8.4	5.8	7.3	4.4	4.0	6.9	4.0
Return on Equity Before Income Taxes 47	5.0	•	64.3	•	9.8	10.5	14.4	8.3	11.6	4.6	4.5	5.5	4.2
Return on Equity After Income Taxes 48	3.3	•	56.2	•	9.0	9.2	12.7	6.7	9.5	2.7	2.0	3.2	2.6
Profit Margin (Before Income Tax) 49	4.3	•	0.7	•	1.8	2.0	4.3	2.7	4.1	2.0	1.6	3.1	7.5
Profit Margin (After Income Tax) 50	2.8	•	0.6	•	1.7	1.8	3.8	2.2	3.4	1.2	0.7	1.8	4.6

Table II

Corporations with Net Income

OTHER FABRICATED METAL PRODUCT

MONEY AMOUNTS AND SIZE OF ASSETS IN THOUSANDS OF DOLLARS

Item Description for Accounting Period 7/03 Through 6/04	Total	Zero Assets	Under 500	500 to 1,000	1,000 to 5,000	5,000 to 10,000	10,000 to 25,000	25,000 to 50,000	50,000 to 100,000	100,000 to 250,000	250,000 to 500,000	500,000 to 2,500,000	2,500,000 and over
Number of Enterprises **1**	10313	633	5587	•	2330	420	266	89	•	32	11	•	8
Revenues ($ in Thousands)													
Net Sales **2**	103529778	129651	2708736	•	11437890	6821940	7032364	4485284	•	4862741	4397306	•	46889389
Interest **3**	2178134	66	2946	•	3114	1864	4692	3096	•	25188	14295	•	1771720
Rents **4**	205432	140	973	•	2816	23	3911	1081	•	2216	5290	•	185728
Royalties **5**	1184000	0	0	•	0	160	4895	704	•	29590	14428	•	1097494
Other Portfolio Income **6**	1194598	0	12482	•	78132	1053	22795	8785	•	35289	27153	•	968229
Other Receipts **7**	888726	27284	-44520	•	38028	11532	56850	23323	•	17207	53489	•	609563
Total Receipts **8**	109180668	157141	2680617	•	11559980	6836572	7125507	4522273	•	4972231	4511961	•	51522123
Average Total Receipts **9**	10587	248	480	•	4961	16278	26788	50812	•	155382	410178	•	6440265
Operating Costs/Operating Income (%)													
Cost of Operations **10**	63.7	52.8	39.1	•	61.7	73.6	67.4	65.5	•	62.3	63.5	•	62.8
Salaries and Wages **11**	6.6	9.8	13.5	•	7.2	5.4	6.9	7.7	•	8.8	7.8	•	5.7
Taxes Paid **12**	2.0	1.3	3.4	•	2.9	1.6	2.3	2.1	•	2.0	2.1	•	1.7
Interest Paid **13**	3.3	1.2	0.8	•	0.7	0.7	0.8	1.1	•	1.3	1.3	•	5.2
Depreciation **14**	3.3	2.6	2.0	•	3.5	2.2	3.0	3.6	•	3.4	4.0	•	3.2
Amortization and Depletion **15**	0.9	0.1	0.0	•	0.0	0.0	0.1	0.2	•	0.7	0.2	•	1.7
Pensions and Other Deferred Comp. **16**	1.3	0.0	0.2	•	0.8	0.3	0.6	0.8	•	1.1	1.2	•	1.9
Employee Benefits **17**	2.6	2.2	2.4	•	1.9	1.0	2.0	2.1	•	2.7	3.4	•	3.0
Advertising **18**	1.6	0.3	0.3	•	0.6	0.6	0.5	0.7	•	1.3	1.5	•	2.4
Other Expenses **19**	11.7	34.9	23.4	•	10.6	6.1	7.7	8.1	•	9.8	12.0	•	14.2
Officers' Compensation **20**	1.6	1.1	6.1	•	5.2	3.3	2.7	1.9	•	1.1	0.7	•	0.3
Operating Margin **21**	1.3	•	8.7	•	5.0	5.0	5.9	6.2	•	5.3	2.3	•	•
Operating Margin Before Officers' Comp. **22**	3.0	•	14.8	•	10.2	8.3	8.6	8.0	•	6.4	3.0	•	•

Selected Average Balance Sheet ($ in Thousands)

Net Receivables 23	1484	0	29	•	629	2331	3961	7535	•	28839	71487	•	850496
Inventories 24	1061	0	18	•	436	1778	3734	8007	•	23460	85544	•	473562
Net Property, Plant and Equipment 25	1916	0	44	•	583	1713	3902	9732	•	34640	83452	•	1328462
Total Assets 26	19194	0	144	•	2231	7038	15765	36237	•	159920	336912	•	19933535
Notes and Loans Payable 27	6299	0	73	•	634	2263	3741	9576	•	33645	83853	•	6805997
All Other Liabilities 28	2646	0	35	•	486	1778	3540	6799	•	37621	99380	•	2252351
Net Worth 29	10250	0	36	•	1112	2998	8485	19862	•	88654	153678	•	10875187

Selected Financial Ratios (Times to 1)

Current Ratio 30	1.6	•	1.8	•	2.3	2.1	2.2	2.4	•	2.4	2.3	•	1.2
Quick Ratio 31	0.9	•	1.4	•	1.6	1.3	1.2	1.4	•	1.2	1.2	•	0.7
Net Sales to Working Capital 32	7.5	•	13.2	•	5.9	6.1	4.9	4.2	•	3.4	3.9	•	16.0
Coverage Ratio 33	3.2	13.9	10.0	•	9.7	8.2	10.0	7.2	•	6.9	5.0	•	2.7
Total Asset Turnover 34	0.5	•	3.4	•	2.2	2.3	1.7	1.4	•	1.0	1.2	•	0.3
Inventory Turnover 35	6.0	•	10.5	•	6.9	6.7	4.8	4.1	•	4.0	3.0	•	7.8
Receivables Turnover 36	6.6	•	23.4	•	7.3	7.2	6.9	6.4	•	5.9	5.5	•	6.4
Total Liabilities to Net Worth 37	0.9	•	3.0	•	1.0	1.3	0.9	0.8	•	0.8	1.2	•	0.8
Current Assets to Working Capital 38	2.7	•	2.2	•	1.8	1.9	1.9	1.7	•	1.7	1.8	•	5.3
Current Liabilities to Working Capital 39	1.7	•	1.2	•	0.8	0.9	0.9	0.7	•	0.7	0.8	•	4.3
Working Capital to Net Sales 40	0.1	•	0.1	•	0.2	0.2	0.2	0.2	•	0.3	0.3	•	0.1
Inventory to Working Capital 41	0.8	•	0.5	•	0.5	0.6	0.7	0.6	•	0.6	0.7	•	1.3
Total Receipts to Cash Flow 42	6.2	2.4	3.9	•	8.0	9.9	7.7	7.5	•	6.6	6.8	•	5.1
Cost of Goods to Cash Flow 43	3.9	1.3	1.5	•	4.9	7.3	5.2	4.9	•	4.1	4.3	•	3.2
Cash Flow to Total Debt 44	0.2	•	1.2	•	0.5	0.4	0.5	0.4	•	0.3	0.3	•	0.1

Selected Financial Factors (in Percentages)

Debt Ratio 45	46.6	•	74.8	•	50.2	57.4	46.2	45.2	•	44.6	54.4	•	45.4
Return on Total Assets 46	5.6	•	28.6	•	14.9	13.8	13.4	11.4	•	8.6	7.4	•	4.2
Return on Equity Before Income Taxes 47	7.3	•	102.3	•	26.8	28.4	22.5	17.9	•	13.3	13.0	•	4.9
Return on Equity After Income Taxes 48	5.4	•	100.4	•	25.7	26.4	20.4	15.9	•	11.1	9.1	•	3.2
Profit Margin (Before Income Tax) 49	7.4	14.9	7.6	•	6.1	5.2	7.2	7.0	•	7.7	5.0	•	9.0
Profit Margin (After Income Tax) 50	5.5	14.7	7.5	•	5.8	4.9	6.5	6.3	•	6.5	3.5	•	5.9

Table I

Corporations with and without Net Income

AGRICULTURE, CONSTRUCTION, AND MINING MACHINERY

MONEY AMOUNTS AND SIZE OF ASSETS IN THOUSANDS OF DOLLARS

Item Description for Accounting Period 7/03 Through 6/04	Total	Zero Assets	Under 500	500 to 1,000	1,000 to 5,000	5,000 to 10,000	10,000 to 25,000	25,000 to 50,000	50,000 to 100,000	100,000 to 250,000	250,000 to 500,000	500,000 to 2,500,000	2,500,000 and over
Number of Enterprises **1**	2660	105	940	505	808	114	91	30	22	21	6	10	9
Revenues ($ in Thousands)													
Net Sales **2**	71781675	73107	288074	1459616	2623773	1089095	2094906	1384944	1863379	3241295	1875653	10194189	45593645
Interest **3**	2643310	100	0	331	4251	2117	1824	789	5345	15786	6606	73730	2532431
Rents **4**	980435	0	0	135	178	57	3185	51	909	1170	1168	2711	970871
Royalties **5**	440522	0	0	0	0	30	195	229	7125	1248	8657	68473	354566
Other Portfolio Income **6**	752469	1	11800	496	17803	15248	4876	7641	6066	8048	13527	26776	640190
Other Receipts **7**	2094412	10516	1679	260	11416	7768	17396	22078	57723	42615	9566	-13908	1927298
Total Receipts **8**	78692823	83724	301553	1460838	2657421	1114315	2122382	1415732	1940547	3310162	1915177	10351971	52019001
Average Total Receipts **9**	29584	797	321	2893	3289	9775	23323	47191	88207	157627	319196	1035197	5779889
Operating Costs/Operating Income (%)													
Cost of Operations **10**	74.4	64.0	54.4	70.2	70.3	67.3	69.8	69.3	67.3	71.8	80.0	76.2	75.3
Salaries and Wages **11**	6.8	7.5	10.1	7.5	7.9	6.8	7.9	6.6	10.1	8.5	5.4	6.9	6.4
Taxes Paid **12**	1.0	2.0	2.2	0.4	2.5	3.1	1.9	2.2	1.8	1.4	1.1	1.3	0.7
Interest Paid **13**	4.1	2.1	1.1	0.1	0.9	1.2	1.2	1.9	1.4	2.1	2.2	1.9	5.5
Depreciation **14**	3.5	2.8	2.5	2.9	1.6	2.4	2.5	2.7	2.1	2.5	2.3	2.2	4.2
Amortization and Depletion **15**	0.6	2.1	0.2	0.0	0.2	0.0	0.2	0.3	0.6	0.4	0.2	0.4	0.8
Pensions and Other Deferred Comp. **16**	1.7	0.1	•	0.1	0.4	0.1	1.3	0.6	0.7	0.5	1.2	0.7	2.4
Employee Benefits **17**	1.7	0.3	0.8	0.8	1.8	1.5	2.0	1.3	1.9	1.7	1.0	1.6	1.9
Advertising **18**	0.5	0.4	1.0	0.6	0.8	2.4	0.9	1.1	0.9	0.3	0.3	0.7	0.3
Other Expenses **19**	13.7	9.3	18.9	7.8	9.6	11.4	9.5	10.3	10.6	9.9	7.0	9.2	16.2
Officers' Compensation **20**	0.7	3.2	2.2	7.0	3.4	3.7	2.4	1.5	1.2	0.8	0.5	0.4	0.2
Operating Margin **21**	•	6.1	6.5	2.6	0.5	0.1	0.4	2.3	1.3	•	•	•	•
Operating Margin Before Officers' Comp. **22**	•	9.4	8.7	9.6	3.9	3.8	2.8	3.9	2.5	•	0.1	•	•

Selected Average Balance Sheet ($ in Thousands)

Item													
Net Receivables 23	12776	0	38	214	317	946	3641	6661	15994	31062	68837	214112	3265247
Inventories 24	3878	0	42	441	775	2499	5242	7956	17949	35711	91809	164832	566995
Net Property, Plant and Equipment 25	4841	0	32	107	356	926	3182	8231	11174	30928	48695	136521	1034582
Total Assets 26	47934	0	150	871	1961	5966	15052	34088	70041	145594	340730	1108158	11615814
Notes and Loans Payable 27	21668	0	86	130	737	1706	5611	11510	19885	34472	78791	325554	5661638
All Other Liabilities 28	13064	0	15	282	347	945	4424	9326	21632	34532	129540	294240	3178074
Net Worth 29	13201	0	48	459	877	3315	5017	13253	28524	76590	132400	488365	2776103

Selected Financial Ratios (Times to 1)

Item													
Current Ratio 30	1.6	•	3.3	2.6	2.6	2.3	1.7	1.7	1.5	2.1	1.4	1.6	1.6
Quick Ratio 31	1.1	•	1.7	1.3	1.1	0.7	0.8	0.8	0.8	1.0	0.7	0.9	1.1
Net Sales to Working Capital 32	3.4	•	5.1	6.5	4.0	3.9	5.2	5.5	6.1	3.8	7.0	5.4	2.8
Coverage Ratio 33	1.4	10.8	10.9	19.0	3.0	3.0	2.4	3.4	4.9	1.7	1.8	1.5	1.3
Total Asset Turnover 34	0.6	•	2.0	3.3	1.7	1.6	1.5	1.4	1.2	1.1	0.9	0.9	0.4
Inventory Turnover 35	5.2	•	4.0	4.6	2.9	2.6	3.1	4.0	3.2	3.1	2.7	4.7	6.7
Receivables Turnover 36	2.2	•	16.3	11.8	10.1	7.6	6.6	7.1	5.8	4.8	3.6	4.6	1.6
Total Liabilities to Net Worth 37	2.6	•	2.1	0.9	1.2	0.8	2.0	1.6	1.5	0.9	1.6	1.3	3.2
Current Assets to Working Capital 38	2.6	•	1.4	1.6	1.6	1.8	2.4	2.4	3.0	1.9	3.4	2.6	2.8
Current Liabilities to Working Capital 39	1.6	•	0.4	0.6	0.6	0.8	1.4	1.4	2.0	0.9	2.4	1.6	1.8
Working Capital to Net Sales 40	0.3	•	0.2	0.2	0.3	0.3	0.2	0.2	0.2	0.3	0.1	0.2	0.4
Inventory to Working Capital 41	0.5	•	0.7	0.8	0.9	1.2	1.1	1.1	1.3	0.9	1.4	0.8	0.3
Total Receipts to Cash Flow 42	7.6	3.6	5.7	10.6	12.2	9.4	10.4	7.8	6.9	10.9	15.4	12.5	6.5
Cost of Goods to Cash Flow 43	5.7	2.3	3.1	7.5	8.6	6.3	7.2	5.4	4.6	7.8	12.3	9.5	4.9
Cash Flow to Total Debt 44	0.1	•	0.5	0.7	0.2	0.4	0.2	0.3	0.3	0.2	0.1	0.1	0.1

Selected Financial Factors (in Percentages)

Item													
Debt Ratio 45	72.5	•	67.9	47.3	55.3	44.4	66.7	61.1	59.3	47.4	61.1	55.9	76.1
Return on Total Assets 46	3.2	•	25.2	9.3	4.4	5.9	4.4	8.7	8.2	3.8	3.7	2.6	3.0
Return on Equity Before Income Taxes 47	3.3	•	71.2	16.7	6.6	7.0	7.9	15.9	16.1	3.0	4.2	1.8	2.5
Return on Equity After Income Taxes 48	2.0	20.7	70.8	16.3	5.6	6.2	5.3	12.6	12.7	1.8	2.6	0.4	1.3
Profit Margin (Before Income Tax) 49	1.6	20.7	11.2	2.7	1.8	2.4	1.7	4.6	5.4	1.5	1.8	0.9	1.4
Profit Margin (After Income Tax) 50	1.0	15.9	11.1	2.6	1.5	2.2	1.2	3.6	4.3	0.9	1.1	0.2	0.7

Table II

Corporations with Net Income

AGRICULTURE, CONSTRUCTION, AND MINING MACHINERY

MONEY AMOUNTS AND SIZE OF ASSETS IN THOUSANDS OF DOLLARS

Item Description for Accounting Period 7/03 Through 6/04	Total	Zero Assets	Under 500	500 to 1,000	1,000 to 5,000	5,000 to 10,000	10,000 to 25,000	25,000 to 50,000	50,000 to 100,000	100,000 to 250,000	250,000 to 500,000	500,000 to 2,500,000	2,500,000 and over
Number of Enterprises 1	1998	·	647	454	561	110	64	20	·	11	·	5	5
Revenues ($ in Thousands)													
Net Sales 2	55561258	·	252294	1417029	1972927	1046565	1653135	995857	·	1773031	·	6389682	37189038
Interest 3	1895396	·	0	326	2881	2093	1064	484	·	5728	·	40417	1834306
Rents 4	868309	·	0	135	17	57	2484	51	·	585	·	955	861947
Royalties 5	304140	·	0	0	0	57	191	229	·	314	·	3398	284551
Other Portfolio Income 6	697693	·	11800	496	15678	15248	1602	5600	·	4673	·	18656	604992
Other Receipts 7	1826181	·	1664	233	10541	7489	12761	17119	·	35482	·	-32976	1700960
Total Receipts 8	61152977	·	265758	1418219	2002044	1071452	1671237	1019340	·	1819813	·	6420132	42475794
Average Total Receipts 9	30607	·	411	3124	3569	9740	26113	50967	·	165438	·	1284026	8495159
Operating Costs/Operating Income (%)													
Cost of Operations 10	73.5	·	52.1	70.4	72.6	67.2	68.0	67.5	·	72.3	·	75.9	74.3
Salaries and Wages 11	6.6	·	10.8	7.7	5.4	6.4	7.8	6.5	·	8.4	·	6.3	6.3
Taxes Paid 12	0.9	·	1.8	0.3	1.5	3.1	1.9	2.2	·	1.6	·	1.1	0.7
Interest Paid 13	3.3	·	1.3	0.2	0.8	1.1	1.1	0.9	·	1.2	·	1.9	4.3
Depreciation 14	3.5	·	1.9	3.0	1.0	2.3	2.3	2.4	·	2.7	·	2.0	4.2
Amortization and Depletion 15	0.5	·	0.2	0.0	0.2	0.0	0.1	0.2	·	0.2	·	0.1	0.7
Pensions and Other Deferred Comp. 16	1.7	·	·	0.1	0.4	0.1	0.5	0.6	·	0.6	·	0.6	2.3
Employee Benefits 17	1.6	·	0.9	0.6	0.8	1.5	1.8	1.2	·	1.4	·	0.7	1.8
Advertising 18	0.4	·	1.1	0.6	1.0	2.4	0.9	0.9	·	0.9	·	0.9	0.2
Other Expenses 19	14.7	·	12.2	7.7	8.6	11.2	9.2	9.4	·	7.2	·	7.9	17.7
Officers' Compensation 20	0.7	·	2.3	6.8	2.6	3.8	2.6	1.6	·	0.8	·	0.3	0.2
Operating Margin 21	·	·	15.3	2.8	5.0	0.8	3.9	6.6	·	2.7	·	2.4	·
Operating Margin Before Officers' Comp. 22	·	·	17.6	9.6	7.7	4.6	6.5	8.2	·	3.5	·	2.7	·

Selected Average Balance Sheet ($ in Thousands)

Net Receivables 23	11380	27	226	302	930	3753	7408	31804	231914	3971946
Inventories 24	2919	30	322	671	2379	4943	7508	46950	156366	741496
Net Property, Plant and Equipment 25	4844	41	119	331	865	2948	7888	31506	133347	1509216
Total Assets 26	46734	178	880	1760	5880	14956	33127	151039	1162652	15868899
Notes and Loans Payable 27	21276	58	47	763	1497	4317	6623	26211	352803	7744104
All Other Liabilities 28	12130	11	312	341	904	3566	8619	30278	212862	4203659
Net Worth 29	13328	109	521	656	3479	7074	17885	94550	596986	3921135

Selected Financial Ratios (Times to 1)

Current Ratio 30	1.5	5.8	2.3	3.0	2.4	2.0	1.9	2.9	2.2	1.4
Quick Ratio 31	0.9	2.1	1.2	1.4	0.8	0.9	1.0	1.5	1.3	0.9
Net Sales to Working Capital 32	4.5	5.0	7.6	4.6	3.7	4.9	5.1	2.8	4.9	4.4
Coverage Ratio 33	2.0	17.3	19.8	9.1	3.9	5.6	10.9	5.6	2.8	1.6
Total Asset Turnover 34	0.6	2.2	3.5	2.0	1.6	1.7	1.5	1.1	1.1	0.5
Inventory Turnover 35	7.0	6.7	6.8	3.8	2.7	3.6	4.5	2.5	6.2	7.5
Receivables Turnover 36	3.0	24.2	27.6	11.9	8.9	7.5	7.1	4.3	6.3	3.7
Total Liabilities to Net Worth 37	2.5	0.6	0.7	1.7	0.7	1.1	0.9	0.6	0.9	3.0
Current Assets to Working Capital 38	3.1	1.2	1.8	1.5	1.7	2.0	2.1	1.5	1.8	3.7
Current Liabilities to Working Capital 39	2.1	0.2	0.8	0.5	0.7	1.0	1.1	0.5	0.8	2.7
Working Capital to Net Sales 40	0.2	0.2	0.1	0.2	0.3	0.2	0.2	0.4	0.2	0.2
Inventory to Working Capital 41	0.6	0.8	0.8	0.8	1.1	1.0	0.9	0.7	0.6	0.4
Total Receipts to Cash Flow 42	6.4	3.7	10.6	8.2	8.9	7.9	5.9	9.2	10.5	5.6
Cost of Goods to Cash Flow 43	4.7	1.9	7.5	5.9	6.0	5.4	4.0	6.7	8.0	4.2
Cash Flow to Total Debt 44	0.1	1.5	0.8	0.4	0.4	0.4	0.6	0.3	0.2	0.1

Selected Financial Factors (in Percentages)

Debt Ratio 45	71.5	38.7	40.8	62.7	40.8	52.7	46.0	37.4	48.7	75.3
Return on Total Assets 46	3.9	48.0	10.6	14.6	7.0	10.5	14.9	6.8	5.8	3.1
Return on Equity Before Income Taxes 47	6.8	73.8	17.0	34.9	8.7	18.3	25.1	8.9	7.3	4.5
Return on Equity After Income Taxes 48	5.0	73.6	16.5	33.0	8.0	15.7	21.4	7.1	4.9	3.0
Profit Margin (Before Income Tax) 49	3.2	20.6	2.8	6.5	3.2	5.0	9.0	5.2	3.4	2.4
Profit Margin (After Income Tax) 50	2.4	20.6	2.8	6.2	2.9	4.3	7.7	4.2	2.3	1.6

Table I

Corporations with and without Net Income

INDUSTRIAL MACHINERY

MONEY AMOUNTS AND SIZE OF ASSETS IN THOUSANDS OF DOLLARS

Item Description for Accounting Period 7/03 Through 6/04	Total	Zero Assets	Under 500	500 to 1,000	1,000 to 5,000	5,000 to 10,000	10,000 to 25,000	25,000 to 50,000	50,000 to 100,000	100,000 to 250,000	250,000 to 500,000	500,000 to 2,500,000	2,500,000 and over
Number of Enterprises **1**	3214	426	1386	312	631	157	152	65	38	24	8	11	3
Revenues ($ in Thousands)													
Net Sales **2**	33258567	103177	308048	649069	3029708	1647551	3100445	2543669	2467628	3393508	2623426	4922977	8469360
Interest **3**	298022	81	26	110	1106	1321	8772	9744	11685	25539	23214	103949	112475
Rents **4**	39294	3	0	1727	867	986	1663	6077	887	7875	1283	681	17245
Royalties **5**	145391	0	0	0	82	0	1687	4335	18484	13467	10933	39560	56843
Other Portfolio Income **6**	272936	1547	0	13	7042	6595	5154	19924	31868	33527	10062	91026	66179
Other Receipts **7**	423474	4359	2594	5078	88733	10803	20955	47936	51132	42634	8302	97415	43532
Total Receipts **8**	34437684	109167	310668	655997	3127538	1667256	3138676	2631685	2581684	3516550	2677220	5255608	8765634
Average Total Receipts **9**	10715	256	224	2103	4956	10619	20649	40487	67939	146523	334652	477783	2921878
Operating Costs/Operating Income (%)													
Cost of Operations **10**	65.6	68.8	65.0	59.4	58.3	70.0	69.3	65.8	67.3	69.3	65.8	59.0	68.1
Salaries and Wages **11**	12.8	3.8	3.9	5.2	13.4	8.6	9.5	10.6	12.1	15.8	10.3	13.5	15.6
Taxes Paid **12**	2.3	2.7	5.1	3.8	3.7	3.0	2.3	2.4	2.2	1.9	1.5	2.5	1.5
Interest Paid **13**	3.0	6.9	1.3	0.8	1.5	0.9	1.2	1.6	2.3	2.2	5.1	6.0	3.1
Depreciation **14**	4.0	1.8	3.5	2.6	1.9	1.9	2.7	3.4	2.9	3.0	2.5	5.3	6.5
Amortization and Depletion **15**	1.0	0.1	•	0.2	0.1	0.4	0.5	0.7	0.9	1.2	0.6	2.3	1.3
Pensions and Other Deferred Comp. **16**	1.0	0.0	0.0	0.6	0.4	1.0	1.0	0.7	0.7	1.2	1.5	1.6	0.7
Employee Benefits **17**	2.8	0.5	0.2	4.2	2.5	2.9	1.9	2.3	2.7	3.8	3.1	3.3	2.6
Advertising **18**	0.6	1.5	1.8	0.5	1.4	0.4	0.7	0.8	0.4	0.5	0.7	0.7	0.4
Other Expenses **19**	12.0	22.0	18.5	11.5	14.5	6.9	9.6	11.5	9.2	12.6	12.0	12.1	13.3
Officers' Compensation **20**	1.8	2.6	8.1	5.6	5.6	3.7	2.3	1.6	1.7	1.2	1.1	0.7	0.5
Operating Margin **21**	•	•	•	5.5	•	0.4	0.5	•	0.7	•	1.6	•	•
Operating Margin Before Officers' Comp. **22**	•	•	0.7	11.1	2.2	4.0	1.3	0.2	2.4	•	•	•	•

Selected Average Balance Sheet ($ in Thousands)

Item													
Net Receivables 23	2354	0	37	261	725	2940	3874	7755	16497	32440	54876	164633	588354
Inventories 24	1535	0	54	117	701	1964	3959	6759	11799	26038	30728	89282	487047
Net Property, Plant and Equipment 25	2302	0	19	222	542	1143	3202	7553	11689	27013	54243	71728	1162564
Total Assets 26	13851	0	123	770	2685	7946	15582	35515	68896	167686	354444	891430	5734958
Notes and Loans Payable 27	3957	0	31	331	1262	1862	5026	11134	20454	33057	190752	282875	1262609
All Other Liabilities 28	3793	0	108	194	786	1969	4848	9163	18431	61740	134140	333641	972874
Net Worth 29	6101	-16	244	637	4115	5708	15219	30011	72890	29552	274913		3499475

Selected Financial Ratios (Times to 1)

Ratio													
Current Ratio 30	2.1	•	1.8	1.9	2.0	1.5	1.8	1.7	1.7	1.3	1.8	3.3	
Quick Ratio 31	1.4	•	1.3	0.9	1.3	0.8	1.0	1.1	0.9	0.9	1.2	2.5	
Net Sales to Working Capital 32	2.8	•	9.3	5.5	3.7	6.0	4.6	4.1	3.7	9.2	3.5	1.3	
Coverage Ratio 33	0.2	0.3	8.8	2.7	0.9	2.8	1.2	2.3	2.2	•	1.1	1.3	•
Total Asset Turnover 34	0.7	•	2.7	1.8	1.3	1.3	1.1	0.9	0.8	0.9	0.5	0.5	
Inventory Turnover 35	4.4	•	10.6	4.0	3.7	3.6	3.8	3.7	3.8	7.0	3.0	4.0	
Receivables Turnover 36	4.8	•	9.4	6.3	4.1	5.7	5.1	4.4	4.0	5.0	2.4	9.6	
Total Liabilities to Net Worth 37	1.3	•	2.2	3.2	0.9	1.7	1.3	1.3	1.3	11.0	2.2	0.6	
Current Assets to Working Capital 38	1.9	•	2.3	2.1	2.0	3.0	2.3	2.4	2.5	4.0	2.3	1.4	
Current Liabilities to Working Capital 39	0.9	•	1.3	1.1	1.0	2.0	1.3	1.4	1.5	3.0	1.3	0.4	
Working Capital to Net Sales 40	0.4	•	0.1	0.2	0.3	0.2	0.2	0.2	0.3	0.1	0.3	0.8	
Inventory to Working Capital 41	0.4	•	0.5	0.9	0.6	1.2	0.8	0.7	0.6	0.9	0.5	0.2	
Total Receipts to Cash Flow 42	17.5	10.1	18.4	6.2	10.3	14.6	12.7	9.2	10.5	3336.8	14.2	10.0	•
Cost of Goods to Cash Flow 43	11.5	6.9	12.0	3.7	6.0	10.2	8.8	6.0	7.1	2313.1	9.3	5.9	•
Cash Flow to Total Debt 44	0.1	•	0.6	0.2	0.2	0.2	0.8	0.2	0.0	0.1	0.1	•	

Selected Financial Factors (in Percentages)

Factor													
Debt Ratio 45	56.0	•	113.0	68.3	76.3	48.2	63.4	57.1	56.4	56.5	91.7	69.2	39.0
Return on Total Assets 46	0.4	•	•	20.0	2.4	3.2	1.9	4.0	4.7	•	5.2	3.9	•
Return on Equity Before Income Taxes 47	•	•	90.8	56.0	•	4.0	0.9	5.2	5.9	•	5.0	2.9	•
Return on Equity After Income Taxes 48	•	•	90.8	46.4	3.3	•	2.6	3.6	•	•	•	0.0	•
Profit Margin (Before Income Tax) 49	•	•	6.6	•	1.6	2.0	2.7	1.8	0.4	•	0.0	1.8	•
Profit Margin (After Income Tax) 50	•	•	5.4	•	1.3	1.0	1.6	•	•	•	0.0	•	

Table II

Corporations with Net Income

INDUSTRIAL MACHINERY

MONEY AMOUNTS AND SIZE OF ASSETS IN THOUSANDS OF DOLLARS

Item Description for Accounting Period 7/03 Through 6/04	Total	Zero Assets	Under 500	500 to 1,000	1,000 to 5,000	5,000 to 10,000	10,000 to 25,000	25,000 to 50,000	50,000 to 100,000	100,000 to 250,000	250,000 to 500,000	500,000 to 2,500,000	2,500,000 and over
Number of Enterprises **1**	1676	12	797	256	313	138	82	38	21	8	3	7	•
Revenues ($ in Thousands)													
Net Sales **2**	16144562	11144	218658	566244	1727552	1471038	1906652	1602670	1377760	1135421	1019471	5107953	•
Interest **3**	50604	80	0	110	858	760	1960	7098	3639	6461	1913	27726	•
Rents **4**	11792	0	0	0	11	494	871	2571	210	7074	0	562	•
Royalties **5**	38338	0	0	0	82	0	914	875	12827	58	10268	13313	•
Other Portfolio Income **6**	121667	1543	0	0	2856	6425	1284	10997	26444	8739	3856	59522	•
Other Receipts **7**	257292	3597	0	1917	81193	9055	12218	24657	21117	27996	88	75453	•
Total Receipts **8**	16624255	16364	218658	568271	1812552	1487772	1923899	1648868	1441997	1185749	1035596	5284529	•
Average Total Receipts **9**	9919	1364	274	2220	5791	10781	23462	43391	68667	148219	345199	754933	•
Operating Costs/Operating Income (%)													
Cost of Operations **10**	62.7	62.1	66.5	57.5	58.5	69.6	65.9	66.3	63.9	56.7	60.0	61.8	•
Salaries and Wages **11**	10.3	4.8	4.2	5.6	10.5	8.3	9.0	8.6	12.5	15.6	9.1	11.1	•
Taxes Paid **12**	2.4	1.0	5.0	3.6	2.8	2.9	2.2	2.2	1.7	2.2	0.9	2.5	•
Interest Paid **13**	1.5	1.1	•	0.8	0.7	0.8	0.9	1.0	1.5	3.0	0.5	2.5	•
Depreciation **14**	2.6	3.1	0.5	2.8	1.8	1.8	2.6	2.7	2.8	2.8	2.7	2.9	•
Amortization and Depletion **15**	1.0	•	•	0.2	0.2	0.3	0.3	0.4	0.6	1.5	0.2	2.1	•
Pensions and Other Deferred Comp. **16**	1.2	•	•	0.7	0.2	1.0	0.9	0.7	0.6	1.3	2.5	1.9	•
Employee Benefits **17**	2.3	0.6	•	3.8	1.2	3.0	1.8	1.7	3.1	2.6	2.9	2.2	•
Advertising **18**	0.6	0.4	2.3	0.5	0.7	0.3	0.6	0.6	0.4	0.6	0.7	0.8	•
Other Expenses **19**	9.9	19.1	13.0	11.7	13.9	5.4	9.4	9.0	7.3	10.3	9.0	10.8	•
Officers' Compensation **20**	2.3	0.2	7.3	5.1	6.8	3.5	2.3	1.7	2.0	1.2	1.2	0.6	•
Operating Margin **21**	3.2	7.6	1.2	7.6	2.7	3.0	4.1	5.0	3.6	2.2	10.4	0.7	•
Operating Margin Before Officers' Comp. **22**	5.5	7.8	8.6	12.6	9.5	6.5	6.4	6.7	5.6	3.4	11.6	1.2	•

Selected Average Balance Sheet ($ in Thousands)

Net Receivables 23	2071	0	34	194	831	3123	4283	8620	15116	27566	69924	182415	•
Inventories 24	1360	0	53	93	753	1169	3957	6270	10307	26449	35060	102980	•
Net Property, Plant and Equipment 25	1363	0	6	232	434	1116	3285	7053	10048	26378	52133	116433	•
Total Assets 26	10452	0	105	752	2719	7959	15716	36611	66567	157235	314401	1287483	•
Notes and Loans Payable 27	2239	0	1	338	720	1803	3914	6413	13814	41558	16982	279008	•
All Other Liabilities 28	2538	0	1	124	915	1821	4891	9055	17102	52043	113790	260281	•
Net Worth 29	5674	0	103	291	1084	4335	6911	21143	35651	63633	183628	748194	•

Selected Financial Ratios (Times to 1)

Current Ratio 30	1.7	•	94.5	2.4	1.8	2.1	1.9	2.1	1.9	1.6	1.9	1.4	•
Quick Ratio 31	1.1	•	42.8	1.7	1.0	1.4	1.0	1.2	1.3	1.0	1.5	0.9	•
Net Sales to Working Capital 32	5.1	•	2.9	7.7	6.8	3.3	4.6	3.8	3.8	4.5	4.2	7.9	•
Coverage Ratio 33	5.7	51.9	•	10.5	11.2	5.9	6.7	9.3	7.1	3.2	27.7	4.0	•
Total Asset Turnover 34	0.9	•	2.6	2.9	2.0	1.3	1.5	1.2	1.0	0.9	1.1	0.6	•
Inventory Turnover 35	4.4	•	3.5	13.7	4.3	6.3	3.9	4.5	4.1	3.0	5.8	4.4	•
Receivables Turnover 36	4.9	•	6.1	15.1	5.9	5.6	5.8	5.1	4.7	4.2	2.9	4.6	•
Total Liabilities to Net Worth 37	0.8	•	0.0	1.6	1.5	0.8	1.3	0.7	0.9	1.5	0.7	0.7	•
Current Assets to Working Capital 38	2.4	•	1.0	1.7	2.3	1.9	2.2	1.9	2.1	2.6	2.1	3.8	•
Current Liabilities to Working Capital 39	1.4	•	0.0	0.7	1.3	0.9	1.2	0.9	1.1	1.6	1.1	2.8	•
Working Capital to Net Sales 40	0.2	•	0.3	0.1	0.1	0.3	0.2	0.3	0.3	0.2	0.2	0.1	•
Inventory to Working Capital 41	0.7	•	0.5	0.4	0.9	0.6	0.8	0.6	0.6	0.8	0.3	1.1	•
Total Receipts to Cash Flow 42	7.1	1.4	12.4	5.7	5.9	12.3	8.1	6.7	7.2	6.7	5.1	7.3	•
Cost of Goods to Cash Flow 43	4.4	0.9	8.2	3.3	3.4	8.5	5.3	4.4	4.6	3.8	3.0	4.5	•
Cash Flow to Total Debt 44	0.3	•	10.1	0.8	0.6	0.2	0.3	0.4	0.3	0.2	0.5	0.2	•

Selected Financial Factors (in Percentages)

Debt Ratio 45	45.7	•	2.1	61.3	60.1	45.5	56.0	42.2	46.4	59.5	41.6	41.9	•
Return on Total Assets 46	8.2	•	3.2	25.7	17.0	6.7	8.8	10.2	10.6	8.7	14.3	5.6	•
Return on Equity Before Income Taxes 47	12.4	•	3.3	60.2	38.9	10.2	17.0	15.8	17.0	14.8	23.6	7.2	•
Return on Equity After Income Taxes 48	9.6	•	3.3	50.4	36.9	9.5	14.8	12.6	13.4	11.8	15.3	4.9	•
Profit Margin (Before Income Tax) 49	7.3	54.4	1.2	7.9	7.6	4.2	5.1	7.9	9.2	6.6	12.7	7.4	•
Profit Margin (After Income Tax) 50	5.7	50.4	1.2	6.6	7.2	3.9	4.4	6.3	7.3	5.3	8.3	5.0	•

126

Table I

Corporations with and without Net Income

COMMERCIAL AND SERVICE INDUSTRY MACHINERY

MONEY AMOUNTS AND SIZE OF ASSETS IN THOUSANDS OF DOLLARS

Item Description for Accounting Period 7/03 Through 6/04	Total	Zero Assets	Under 500	500 to 1,000	1,000 to 5,000	5,000 to 10,000	10,000 to 25,000	25,000 to 50,000	50,000 to 100,000	100,000 to 250,000	250,000 to 500,000	500,000 to 2,500,000	2,500,000 and over
Number of Enterprises **1**	2048	24	1266	105	397	122	71	17	17	16	•	8	6
Revenues ($ in Thousands)													
Net Sales **2**	42833315	4949	358213	208207	1771521	808456	1589306	558973	1271791	3177438	•	4158278	28926183
Interest **3**	1349609	42	283	150	975	842	2628	800	1889	17423	•	63180	1261397
Rents **4**	622068	0	10805	0	5616	139	1597	1158	7021	6554	•	180190	408988
Royalties **5**	917545	0	0	0	0	0	39	218	222	28605	•	17679	870782
Other Portfolio Income **6**	399698	0	3275	1066	14898	10933	2566	859	10250	94998	•	34254	226596
Other Receipts **7**	1623573	3991	3398	5598	16535	14389	21790	5764	23294	29302	•	124958	1374559
Total Receipts **8**	47745808	8982	375974	215021	1809545	834759	1617926	567772	1314467	3354320	•	4578539	33068505
Average Total Receipts **9**	23313	374	297	2048	4558	6842	22788	33398	77322	209645	•	572317	5511418
Operating Costs/Operating Income (%)													
Cost of Operations **10**	54.9	1.7	51.8	75.0	66.9	69.0	67.6	66.1	58.0	61.9	•	60.0	51.2
Salaries and Wages **11**	16.6	79.0	19.4	6.2	10.0	7.8	9.8	10.9	14.0	11.7	•	15.4	18.6
Taxes Paid **12**	2.2	1.1	3.3	2.2	2.5	1.6	2.4	2.4	2.1	1.3	•	2.7	2.2
Interest Paid **13**	4.6	•	0.3	0.5	0.7	2.2	1.5	1.5	0.8	1.9	•	3.3	5.9
Depreciation **14**	7.8	2.6	4.5	0.3	3.1	3.6	2.6	3.7	3.1	3.7	•	7.2	9.3
Amortization and Depletion **15**	0.9	•	0.2	0.0	0.1	0.2	0.5	1.3	0.8	0.3	•	1.2	1.0
Pensions and Other Deferred Comp. **16**	1.3	•	1.2	•	0.6	0.1	0.7	1.2	1.2	1.0	•	0.5	1.6
Employee Benefits **17**	4.5	14.2	3.3	1.4	2.4	1.5	2.2	2.2	2.9	1.9	•	2.6	5.5
Advertising **18**	1.5	1.1	1.5	0.1	1.0	0.6	0.7	0.8	1.1	2.2	•	0.7	1.7
Other Expenses **19**	15.9	254.8	29.8	18.6	12.6	9.3	12.5	11.1	13.2	11.5	•	15.5	17.0
Officers' Compensation **20**	1.0	•	3.7	8.1	4.7	3.8	2.3	2.0	2.4	1.1	•	0.9	0.4
Operating Margin **21**	•	•	•	•	•	0.3	•	•	0.5	1.2	•	•	•
Operating Margin Before Officers' Comp. **22**	•	•	•	•	•	4.1	0.0	•	2.8	2.3	•	•	•

Selected Average Balance Sheet ($ in Thousands)

Net Receivables 23	6469	0	26	141	521	682	3625	5846	15494	47294	•	216155	1634065
Inventories 24	1768	0	26	351	662	1732	3724	9715	11601	21674	•	68964	244972
Net Property, Plant and Equipment 25	5539	0	17	20	623	1991	3049	6419	11405	26164	•	120146	1488551
Total Assets 26	39579	0	84	652	2642	6715	15878	35015	65536	172913	•	878009	11064366
Notes and Loans Payable 27	15208	0	81	406	934	1597	5682	8121	16286	53011	•	331852	4352297
All Other Liabilities 28	12778	0	52	330	734	1066	17051	8606	22666	53626	•	250080	3507896
Net Worth 29	11593	0	-48	-84	975	4051	-6855	18289	26585	66276	•	296077	3204173

Selected Financial Ratios (Times to 1)

Current Ratio 30	1.1	•	1.5	1.6	1.9	1.9	0.6	1.7	1.6	1.5	•	1.9	1.0
Quick Ratio 31	0.7	•	0.8	1.1	1.0	1.0	0.3	0.8	0.9	0.9	•	1.3	0.7
Net Sales to Working Capital 32	20.3	•	13.0	10.7	5.5	4.0	•	4.2	5.0	6.0	•	3.2	•
Coverage Ratio 33	1.2	•	•	•	•	2.6	0.3	•	5.9	4.5	•	1.0	1.2
Total Asset Turnover 34	0.5	•	3.4	3.0	1.7	1.0	1.4	0.9	1.1	1.1	•	0.6	0.4
Inventory Turnover 35	6.5	•	5.6	4.2	4.5	2.6	4.1	2.2	3.7	5.7	•	4.5	10.1
Receivables Turnover 36	3.3	•	12.7	4.3	7.9	7.4	7.3	4.6	5.5	6.7	•	2.8	2.9
Total Liabilities to Net Worth 37	2.4	•	•	•	1.7	0.7	0.9	0.9	1.5	1.6	•	2.0	2.5
Current Assets to Working Capital 38	12.0	•	2.9	2.8	2.1	2.1	•	2.4	2.6	2.9	•	2.2	•
Current Liabilities to Working Capital 39	11.0	•	1.9	1.8	1.1	1.1	•	1.4	1.6	1.9	•	1.2	•
Working Capital to Net Sales 40	0.0	•	0.1	0.1	0.2	0.3	•	0.2	0.2	0.2	•	0.3	•
Inventory to Working Capital 41	1.7	•	1.4	0.3	0.9	0.8	•	1.0	1.0	0.9	•	0.4	•
Total Receipts to Cash Flow 42	7.9	2.7	16.8	14.7	16.1	10.9	11.0	12.8	7.1	6.2	•	9.6	7.4
Cost of Goods to Cash Flow 43	4.3	0.0	8.7	11.0	10.8	7.5	7.5	8.5	4.1	3.9	•	5.8	3.8
Cash Flow to Total Debt 44	0.1	•	0.1	0.2	0.2	0.2	0.1	0.2	0.3	0.3	•	0.1	0.1

Selected Financial Factors (in Percentages)

Debt Ratio 45	70.7	•	157.0	112.8	63.1	39.7	143.2	47.8	59.4	61.7	•	66.3	71.0
Return on Total Assets 46	3.0	•	•	•	•	5.6	0.5	•	5.4	10.1	•	2.0	3.0
Return on Equity Before Income Taxes 47	1.8	•	83.6	220.6	•	5.7	3.5	•	10.9	20.5	•	0.1	1.5
Return on Equity After Income Taxes 48	0.6	•	84.0	222.8	•	5.1	5.4	•	7.9	14.7	•	•	0.6
Profit Margin (Before Income Tax) 49	1.0	•	•	•	•	3.5	•	•	3.9	6.8	•	0.0	1.0
Profit Margin (After Income Tax) 50	0.3	•	•	•	•	3.1	•	•	2.8	4.9	•	•	0.4

Table II
Corporations with Net Income

COMMERCIAL AND SERVICE INDUSTRY MACHINERY

MONEY AMOUNTS AND SIZE OF ASSETS IN THOUSANDS OF DOLLARS

Item Description for Accounting Period 7/03 Through 6/04	Total	Zero Assets	Under 500	500 to 1,000	1,000 to 5,000	5,000 to 10,000	10,000 to 25,000	25,000 to 50,000	50,000 to 100,000	100,000 to 250,000	250,000 to 500,000	500,000 to 2,500,000	2,500,000 and over
Number of Enterprises **1**	725	•	•	•	193	99	39	•	12	11	•	5	•
Revenues ($ in Thousands)													
Net Sales **2**	26237436	•	•	•	1255488	720389	888788	•	904658	2322713	•	3150762	•
Interest **3**	1283795	•	•	•	498	728	1033	•	1541	15364	•	47668	•
Rents **4**	465214	•	•	•	0	139	242	•	2723	6437	•	180133	•
Royalties **5**	639772	•	•	•	0	0	1	•	0	28605	•	16381	•
Other Portfolio Income **6**	272706	•	•	•	5019	10932	1722	•	5957	93340	•	27067	•
Other Receipts **7**	1317063	•	•	•	14983	8596	4620	•	14630	22726	•	100667	•
Total Receipts **8**	30215986	•	•	•	1275988	740784	896406	•	929509	2489185	•	3522678	•
Average Total Receipts **9**	41677	•	•	•	6611	7483	22985	•	77459	226290	•	704536	•
Operating Costs/Operating Income (%)													
Cost of Operations **10**	52.4	•	•	•	65.5	69.6	68.0	•	55.3	59.7	•	58.2	•
Salaries and Wages **11**	20.5	•	•	•	9.9	5.0	7.5	•	13.7	11.9	•	14.2	•
Taxes Paid **12**	2.5	•	•	•	2.1	1.5	2.3	•	2.2	1.4	•	3.0	•
Interest Paid **13**	5.9	•	•	•	0.1	1.3	0.9	•	0.5	1.6	•	3.0	•
Depreciation **14**	9.2	•	•	•	1.7	3.3	2.2	•	2.7	2.5	•	7.5	•
Amortization and Depletion **15**	0.5	•	•	•	0.1	0.1	0.2	•	0.2	0.1	•	0.9	•
Pensions and Other Deferred Comp. **16**	2.0	•	•	•	0.7	0.1	0.9	•	1.5	1.2	•	0.5	•
Employee Benefits **17**	3.5	•	•	•	2.8	0.9	1.5	•	3.2	1.9	•	2.6	•
Advertising **18**	1.0	•	•	•	1.1	0.6	0.6	•	1.2	2.5	•	0.6	•
Other Expenses **19**	12.9	•	•	•	6.4	7.2	8.4	•	11.9	11.7	•	16.5	•
Officers' Compensation **20**	1.0	•	•	•	4.3	3.8	2.6	•	2.1	0.9	•	0.8	•
Operating Margin **21**	•	•	•	•	5.3	6.6	5.1	•	5.5	4.6	•	•	•
Operating Margin Before Officers' Comp. **22**	•	•	•	•	9.6	10.4	7.7	•	7.6	5.5	•	•	•

Selected Average Balance Sheet ($ in Thousands)

Net Receivables 23	14700	668	755	3970	14642	55179	240467
Inventories 24	3602	885	1871	4157	13942	19189	68203
Net Property, Plant and Equipment 25	7674	429	1887	2672	9413	24777	133337
Total Assets 26	72055	3009	6830	15401	63308	173550	1020883
Notes and Loans Payable 27	32596	286	928	3903	6986	49171	408976
All Other Liabilities 28	18639	781	1041	4377	19998	50050	293621
Net Worth 29	20821	1941	4861	7122	36324	74329	318286

Selected Financial Ratios (Times to 1)

Current Ratio 30	1.5	2.5	2.3	2.0	1.9	1.6	1.6
Quick Ratio 31	1.2	1.5	1.3	1.0	1.0	1.0	1.2
Net Sales to Working Capital 32	4.5	5.0	3.5	4.3	4.1	5.2	4.6
Coverage Ratio 33	1.8	47.5	8.3	7.4	19.0	8.7	2.3
Total Asset Turnover 34	0.5	2.2	1.1	1.5	1.2	1.2	0.6
Inventory Turnover 35	5.3	4.8	2.7	3.7	3.0	6.6	5.4
Receivables Turnover 36	2.5	7.3	7.6	6.3	10.3	6.7	5.2
Total Liabilities to Net Worth 37	2.5	0.5	0.4	1.2	0.7	1.3	2.2
Current Assets to Working Capital 38	2.9	1.7	1.8	2.0	2.1	2.5	2.6
Current Liabilities to Working Capital 39	1.9	0.7	0.8	1.0	1.1	1.5	1.6
Working Capital to Net Sales 40	0.2	0.2	0.3	0.2	0.2	0.2	0.2
Inventory to Working Capital 41	0.4	0.6	0.7	0.8	0.8	0.8	0.5
Total Receipts to Cash Flow 42	7.9	9.5	7.3	7.8	5.4	4.7	6.5
Cost of Goods to Cash Flow 43	4.1	6.2	5.1	5.3	3.0	2.8	3.8
Cash Flow to Total Debt 44	0.1	0.6	0.5	0.4	0.5	0.5	0.1

Selected Financial Factors (in Percentages)

Debt Ratio 45	71.1	35.5	28.8	53.8	42.6	57.2	68.8
Return on Total Assets 46	5.3	15.3	11.3	10.2	10.5	16.4	4.3
Return on Equity Before Income Taxes 47	8.2	23.2	14.0	19.1	17.3	33.8	7.8
Return on Equity After Income Taxes 48	6.2	21.6	13.3	15.8	14.1	26.4	6.7
Profit Margin (Before Income Tax) 49	4.7	6.9	9.3	6.0	8.3	11.9	3.9
Profit Margin (After Income Tax) 50	3.6	6.4	8.9	4.9	6.8	9.3	3.4

Table I
Corporations with and without Net Income

VENTILATION, HEATING, A.C. & COMMERCIAL REFRIGERATION EQUIP.

MONEY AMOUNTS AND SIZE OF ASSETS IN THOUSANDS OF DOLLARS

Item Description for Accounting Period 7/03 Through 6/04	Total	Zero Assets	Under 500	500 to 1,000	1,000 to 5,000	5,000 to 10,000	10,000 to 25,000	25,000 to 50,000	50,000 to 100,000	100,000 to 250,000	250,000 to 500,000	500,000 to 2,500,000	2,500,000 and over
Number of Enterprises **1**	798	49	248	154	141	78	60	34	13	10	•	11	•
Revenues ($ in Thousands)													
Net Sales **2**	29255545	487474	5341	248481	440753	912737	1899423	1779996	1334736	2499916	•	19646688	•
Interest **3**	133472	655	23	122	223	135	1678	1423	2537	2864	•	123811	•
Rents **4**	9387	0	17	444	0	6	732	1027	434	3511	•	3217	•
Royalties **5**	281129	0	0	0	0	135	142	1848	2442	1262	•	275301	•
Other Portfolio Income **6**	222003	5568	2036	55	1	346	3784	9848	5134	6182	•	189049	•
Other Receipts **7**	301417	2591	187	4722	86	13789	20817	12052	7124	18369	•	221679	•
Total Receipts **8**	30202953	496288	7604	253824	441063	927148	1926576	1806194	1352407	2532104	•	20459745	•
Average Total Receipts **9**	37848	10128	31	1648	3128	11887	32110	53123	104031	253210	•	1859977	•
Operating Costs/Operating Income (%)													
Cost of Operations **10**	74.4	67.2	30.7	61.1	66.1	61.3	70.5	66.6	64.8	74.8	•	77.2	•
Salaries and Wages **11**	6.9	4.4	37.3	6.4	6.3	13.9	8.2	8.4	7.0	6.0	•	6.4	•
Taxes Paid **12**	1.3	2.4	10.4	2.5	3.2	2.1	2.4	1.7	1.6	1.7	•	1.0	•
Interest Paid **13**	2.2	0.8	2.5	0.3	1.6	1.3	0.7	0.8	1.0	1.6	•	2.7	•
Depreciation **14**	1.9	0.7	1.9	1.7	1.6	5.6	2.4	2.6	3.2	1.8	•	1.6	•
Amortization and Depletion **15**	0.4	0.0	9.5	•	0.6	0.1	0.1	0.3	0.8	0.6	•	0.4	•
Pensions and Other Deferred Comp. **16**	0.6	0.5	•	0.7	0.1	0.6	0.7	0.7	0.9	0.7	•	0.6	•
Employee Benefits **17**	1.9	3.5	17.8	1.7	0.9	3.5	2.1	2.1	2.4	2.3	•	1.7	•
Advertising **18**	1.2	0.3	1.4	0.8	0.9	0.2	0.6	0.8	1.0	0.6	•	1.5	•
Other Expenses **19**	8.8	30.9	132.8	8.1	10.4	11.3	8.5	7.9	9.7	5.7	•	8.5	•
Officers' Compensation **20**	1.4	4.8	4.0	16.8	6.8	1.4	2.1	2.1	1.5	0.7	•	1.0	•
Operating Margin **21**	•	•	•	•	1.5	0.1	1.8	5.9	6.0	3.4	•	•	•
Operating Margin Before Officers' Comp. **22**	0.4	•	•	16.8	8.3	0.1	3.9	8.0	7.5	4.0	•	•	•

Selected Average Balance Sheet ($ in Thousands)

Net Receivables 23	5824	0	0	128	364	1525	4872	7269	17343	27743	•	310507
Inventories 24	3338	0	1	122	411	753	3820	6717	11911	35585	•	141797
Net Property, Plant and Equipment 25	4844	0	0	185	201	3278	4116	8843	14995	30455	•	227803
Total Assets 26	34748	0	5	642	1551	6817	16701	36186	70810	167660	•	2004466
Notes and Loans Payable 27	9129	0	7	39	715	2324	4271	6206	15895	51128	•	528151
All Other Liabilities 28	15928	0	2	161	236	1392	4211	8039	16480	54019	•	1023876
Net Worth 29	9692	0	-3	441	600	3102	8218	21941	38435	62513	•	452438

Selected Financial Ratios (Times to 1)

Current Ratio 30	1.1	•	1.9	1.9	3.3	1.0	2.1	2.4	2.3	1.3	•	0.9
Quick Ratio 31	0.6	•	1.1	1.1	1.7	0.7	1.3	1.4	1.3	0.5	•	0.5
Net Sales to Working Capital 32	38.3	•	13.1	10.1	4.9	81.3	5.4	4.3	4.6	13.8	•	•
Coverage Ratio 33	2.3	•	•	8.9	2.0	1.2	5.3	10.0	8.2	3.8	•	1.9
Total Asset Turnover 34	1.1	•	4.2	2.5	2.0	1.7	1.9	1.4	1.4	1.5	•	0.9
Inventory Turnover 35	8.2	•	4.7	8.1	5.0	9.5	5.8	5.2	5.6	5.3	•	9.7
Receivables Turnover 36	7.0	•	3.3	10.7	10.5	7.4	6.6	7.0	6.5	8.5	•	6.6
Total Liabilities to Net Worth 37	2.6	•	•	0.5	1.6	1.2	1.0	0.6	0.8	1.7	•	3.4
Current Assets to Working Capital 38	13.2	•	2.1	2.1	1.4	21.9	1.9	1.7	1.8	4.2	•	•
Current Liabilities to Working Capital 39	12.2	•	1.1	1.1	0.4	20.9	0.9	0.7	0.8	3.2	•	•
Working Capital to Net Sales 40	0.0	•	0.1	0.1	0.2	0.0	0.2	0.2	0.2	0.1	•	•
Inventory to Working Capital 41	3.7	•	0.8	0.7	0.6	7.3	0.6	0.6	0.6	1.9	•	•
Total Receipts to Cash Flow 42	10.9	•	14.8	11.4	10.1	10.1	7.4	6.3	12.0	11.5	•	•
Cost of Goods to Cash Flow 43	8.1	•	9.0	7.5	6.2	7.1	5.0	4.1	8.9	8.9	•	•
Cash Flow to Total Debt 44	0.1	•	0.5	0.3	0.3	0.4	0.5	0.5	0.2	0.1	•	•

Selected Financial Factors (in Percentages)

Debt Ratio 45	72.1	•	167.2	31.2	61.3	54.5	50.8	39.4	45.7	62.7	•	77.4
Return on Total Assets 46	5.4	•	•	6.0	6.4	2.6	7.5	12.0	12.2	9.3	•	4.7
Return on Equity Before Income Taxes 47	10.9	•	656.6	7.8	8.2	1.1	12.3	17.8	19.8	18.5	•	9.9
Return on Equity After Income Taxes 48	6.7	•	656.8	6.2	5.7	•	10.0	14.9	13.5	14.7	•	5.3
Profit Margin (Before Income Tax) 49	2.9	•	•	2.1	1.6	0.3	3.2	7.5	7.4	4.6	•	2.5
Profit Margin (After Income Tax) 50	1.8	•	•	1.7	1.1	•	2.6	6.2	5.0	3.7	•	1.3

129

Table II

Corporations with Net Income

VENTILATION, HEATING, A.C. & COMMERCIAL REFRIGERATION EQUIP.

MONEY AMOUNTS AND SIZE OF ASSETS IN THOUSANDS OF DOLLARS

Item Description for Accounting Period 7/03 Through 6/04	Total	Zero Assets	Under 500	500 to 1,000	1,000 to 5,000	5,000 to 10,000	10,000 to 25,000	25,000 to 50,000	50,000 to 100,000	100,000 to 250,000	250,000 to 500,000	500,000 to 2,500,000	2,500,000 and over
Number of Enterprises 1	629	3	•	•	113	•	42	28	•	•	•	5	•
Revenues ($ in Thousands)													
Net Sales 2	19478432	95877	•	•	372640	•	1319416	1588752	•	•	•	12045384	•
Interest 3	97435	9	•	•	165	•	1132	1032	•	•	•	89740	•
Rents 4	4969	0	•	•	0	•	161	913	•	•	•	490	•
Royalties 5	111236	0	•	•	0	•	142	1527	•	•	•	106641	•
Other Portfolio Income 6	188013	5568	•	•	0	•	2184	7856	•	•	•	160805	•
Other Receipts 7	173531	640	•	•	78	•	10554	10361	•	•	•	127006	•
Total Receipts 8	20053616	102094	•	•	372883	•	1333589	1610441	•	•	•	12530066	•
Average Total Receipts 9	31882	34031	•	•	3300	•	31752	57516	•	•	•	2506013	•
Operating Costs/Operating Income (%)													
Cost of Operations 10	73.2	68.8	•	•	62.4	•	68.0	66.4	•	•	•	76.4	•
Salaries and Wages 11	6.2	4.9	•	•	6.3	•	8.2	7.9	•	•	•	5.7	•
Taxes Paid 12	1.2	2.3	•	•	2.9	•	2.2	1.6	•	•	•	0.8	•
Interest Paid 13	1.8	2.3	•	•	1.9	•	0.6	0.8	•	•	•	2.3	•
Depreciation 14	1.5	1.1	•	•	1.8	•	2.4	2.7	•	•	•	1.0	•
Amortization and Depletion 15	0.4	0.0	•	•	0.5	•	0.1	0.3	•	•	•	0.4	•
Pensions and Other Deferred Comp. 16	0.7	1.0	•	•	0.2	•	0.7	0.7	•	•	•	0.7	•
Employee Benefits 17	1.7	1.5	•	•	0.6	•	1.6	2.0	•	•	•	1.6	•
Advertising 18	1.5	0.9	•	•	1.0	•	0.6	0.8	•	•	•	2.0	•
Other Expenses 19	8.1	7.2	•	•	10.7	•	7.9	7.2	•	•	•	8.5	•
Officers' Compensation 20	1.2	3.4	•	•	8.0	•	2.2	1.8	•	•	•	0.4	•
Operating Margin 21	2.3	6.7	•	•	3.7	•	5.4	7.7	•	•	•	0.3	•
Operating Margin Before Officers' Comp. 22	3.5	10.1	•	•	11.7	•	7.6	9.5	•	•	•	0.7	•

Selected Average Balance Sheet ($ in Thousands)

Net Receivables 23	5092	0	364	4555	6891	454853
Inventories 24	2915	0	291	3542	6895	168082
Net Property, Plant and Equipment 25	3254	0	241	3968	9978	212507
Total Assets 26	25783	0	1652	16839	36737	2357598
Notes and Loans Payable 27	5700	0	853	3502	6800	496400
All Other Liabilities 28	13388	0	264	3768	7660	1459652
Net Worth 29	6695	0	534	9569	22277	401546

Selected Financial Ratios (Times to 1)

Current Ratio 30	1.0		2.7	2.5	2.5	0.7
Quick Ratio 31	0.6		1.4	1.5	1.4	0.5
Net Sales to Working Capital 32		6.8	5.9	4.6	4.5	
Coverage Ratio 33	4.3		3.0	11.5	11.9	3.5
Total Asset Turnover 34	1.2		2.0	1.9	1.5	1.0
Inventory Turnover 35	7.8		7.1	6.0	5.5	10.9
Receivables Turnover 36	6.0		12.3	7.0	7.6	10.6
Total Liabilities to Net Worth 37	2.9		2.1	0.8	0.6	4.9
Current Assets to Working Capital 38			1.6	1.6	1.7	
Current Liabilities to Working Capital 39			0.6	0.6	0.7	
Working Capital to Net Sales 40			0.2	0.2	0.2	
Inventory to Working Capital 41			0.7	0.5	0.6	
Total Receipts to Cash Flow 42	8.4	5.2	9.3	7.8	6.9	8.7
Cost of Goods to Cash Flow 43	6.1	3.6	5.8	5.3	4.6	6.6
Cash Flow to Total Debt 44			0.3	0.6	0.6	0.1

Selected Financial Factors (in Percentages)

Debt Ratio 45	74.0		67.7	43.2	39.4	83.0
Return on Total Assets 46	9.4		11.3	13.1	15.5	8.0
Return on Equity Before Income Taxes 47	27.9		23.3	21.1	23.4	33.5
Return on Equity After Income Taxes 48	20.2		19.7	18.2	19.9	22.0
Profit Margin (Before Income Tax) 49	6.0	13.2	3.8	6.4	9.2	5.6
Profit Margin (After Income Tax) 50	4.4	11.8	3.2	5.6	7.8	3.7

Table I
Corporations with and without Net Income

METALWORKING MACHINERY

MONEY AMOUNTS AND SIZE OF ASSETS IN THOUSANDS OF DOLLARS

Item Description for Accounting Period 7/03 Through 6/04	Total	Zero Assets	Under 500	500 to 1,000	1,000 to 5,000	5,000 to 10,000	10,000 to 25,000	25,000 to 50,000	50,000 to 100,000	100,000 to 250,000	250,000 to 500,000	500,000 to 2,500,000	2,500,000 and over
Number of Enterprises **1**	6833	618	3939	734	1194	160	110	48	15	11	•	3	•
Revenues ($ in Thousands)													
Net Sales **2**	19994593	14771	1651888	780278	3892650	1642800	2018299	1751457	1049700	1650750	•	5542002	•
Interest **3**	199294	2	1124	719	2579	1200	1532	3960	1010	49092	•	138076	•
Rents **4**	22935	0	0	4764	5956	5820	1102	658	535	2453	•	1648	•
Royalties **5**	131421	0	0	0	0	727	112	509	325	9047	•	120701	•
Other Portfolio Income **6**	178751	10703	21067	2186	10660	8298	5699	4290	4454	31821	•	79578	•
Other Receipts **7**	266588	858	2678	2496	8498	10725	15065	17472	8606	62626	•	137557	•
Total Receipts **8**	20793582	26334	1676757	790443	3920343	1669570	2041809	1778346	1064630	1805789	•	6019562	•
Average Total Receipts **9**	3043	43	426	1077	3283	10435	18562	37049	70975	164163	•	2006521	•
Operating Costs/Operating Income (%)													
Cost of Operations **10**	66.2	68.0	40.1	59.2	64.0	67.3	69.7	68.8	66.0	71.2	•	72.5	•
Salaries and Wages **11**	7.7	5.1	4.9	7.3	4.9	5.5	7.2	7.4	10.0	13.0	•	9.3	•
Taxes Paid **12**	2.8	2.5	3.5	5.2	4.0	3.3	3.1	3.3	2.6	2.2	•	1.3	•
Interest Paid **13**	3.3	3.6	2.1	1.0	0.9	1.2	1.4	2.1	1.0	6.0	•	7.0	•
Depreciation **14**	4.2	7.6	8.2	3.6	4.7	5.8	4.7	4.9	4.6	3.6	•	1.9	•
Amortization and Depletion **15**	0.4	0.1	0.1	0.0	0.0	0.0	0.1	0.5	0.3	0.3	•	0.9	•
Pensions and Other Deferred Comp. **16**	0.5	0.6	0.5	0.8	0.6	0.7	0.3	0.6	1.6	1.0	•	0.0	•
Employee Benefits **17**	2.3	0.9	2.0	4.4	2.5	3.0	2.7	2.6	2.6	2.1	•	1.5	•
Advertising **18**	0.5	0.4	0.1	0.5	0.3	0.2	0.3	0.4	0.5	0.5	•	0.8	•
Other Expenses **19**	11.6	7.8	32.2	12.4	8.8	6.3	8.3	7.6	9.6	8.1	•	12.8	•
Officers' Compensation **20**	3.4	3.6	8.6	7.9	6.2	4.1	2.9	2.2	1.5	1.3	•	0.5	•
Operating Margin **21**	•	•	•	3.1	•	2.6	•	•	•	•	•	•	•
Operating Margin Before Officers' Comp. **22**	0.6	3.4	6.3	5.5	9.3	6.7	2.1	1.8	1.1	•	•	•	•

Selected Average Balance Sheet ($ in Thousands)

Net Receivables 23	677	0	42	199	497	1671	3809	8337	13911	40960	•	657503
Inventories 24	414	0	16	121	321	1708	2826	6540	11240	41485	•	256645
Net Property, Plant and Equipment 25	586	0	69	112	648	2421	4614	9550	17012	31245	•	308452
Total Assets 26	3266	0	183	660	2032	6630	14792	34038	68871	199190	•	3713327
Notes and Loans Payable 27	1259	0	151	214	468	2313	5349	12471	13718	59989	•	1623532
All Other Liabilities 28	891	0	49	201	310	1745	3312	8525	17741	57635	•	1141286
Net Worth 29	1116	0	-18	245	1254	2572	6131	13042	37412	81565	•	948509

Selected Financial Ratios (Times to 1)

Current Ratio 30	1.7	•	1.3	1.8	2.5	1.5	1.6	1.6	1.8	1.6	•	1.5
Quick Ratio 31	1.0	•	1.0	1.0	1.7	0.9	1.0	1.0	1.1	0.8	•	1.0
Net Sales to Working Capital 32	5.0	•	18.8	4.3	4.6	7.8	5.4	4.9	4.4	4.3	•	4.1
Coverage Ratio 33	1.4	22.4	0.6	•	5.1	4.7	1.2	1.6	2.2	1.0	•	1.0
Total Asset Turnover 34	0.9	•	2.3	1.6	1.6	1.5	1.2	1.1	1.0	0.8	•	0.5
Inventory Turnover 35	4.7	•	10.3	5.2	6.5	4.0	4.5	3.8	4.1	2.6	•	5.2
Receivables Turnover 36	4.2	•	8.8	5.8	6.7	6.0	5.0	4.6	4.5	3.0	•	2.8
Total Liabilities to Net Worth 37	1.9	•	•	1.7	0.6	1.6	1.4	1.6	0.8	1.4	•	2.9
Current Assets to Working Capital 38	2.5	•	4.7	2.2	1.7	2.9	2.6	2.6	2.3	2.7	•	2.8
Current Liabilities to Working Capital 39	1.5	•	3.7	1.2	0.7	1.9	1.6	1.6	1.3	1.7	•	1.8
Working Capital to Net Sales 40	0.2	•	0.1	0.2	0.2	0.1	0.2	0.2	0.2	0.2	•	0.2
Inventory to Working Capital 41	0.7	•	0.7	0.6	0.5	1.0	0.8	0.8	0.6	1.1	•	0.6
Total Receipts to Cash Flow 42	11.5	1.3	8.2	13.9	10.3	12.4	16.6	14.3	11.1	17.5	•	10.5
Cost of Goods to Cash Flow 43	7.6	0.9	3.3	8.2	6.6	8.3	11.6	9.8	7.3	12.4	•	7.6
Cash Flow to Total Debt 44	0.1	0.3	0.2	0.2	0.4	0.2	0.1	0.1	0.2	0.1	•	0.1

Selected Financial Factors (in Percentages)

Debt Ratio 45	65.8	•	109.8	62.9	38.3	61.2	58.6	61.7	45.7	59.1	•	74.5
Return on Total Assets 46	4.2	•	2.8	•	7.6	8.4	2.1	3.5	2.3	4.6	•	3.6
Return on Equity Before Income Taxes 47	3.5	•	19.4	•	9.9	17.0	1.0	3.5	2.3	0.2	•	0.6
Return on Equity After Income Taxes 48	2.7	•	24.7	•	9.6	15.8	0.4	1.9	1.2	0.2	•	•
Profit Margin (Before Income Tax) 49	1.3	77.8	•	•	3.8	4.3	0.3	1.2	1.2	0.1	•	0.3
Profit Margin (After Income Tax) 50	1.0	77.3	•	•	3.7	4.0	0.1	0.7	0.6	•	•	•

131

Table II

Corporations with Net Income

METALWORKING MACHINERY

MONEY AMOUNTS AND SIZE OF ASSETS IN THOUSANDS OF DOLLARS

Item Description for Accounting Period 7/03 Through 6/04		Total	Zero Assets	Under 500	500 to 1,000	1,000 to 5,000	5,000 to 10,000	10,000 to 25,000	25,000 to 50,000	50,000 to 100,000	100,000 to 250,000	250,000 to 500,000	500,000 to 2,500,000	2,500,000 and over
Number of Enterprises	1	4569	618	2323	479	932	108	63	29	7	8	•	•	•
Revenues ($ in Thousands)														
Net Sales	2	13962770	14771	940927	509093	3034400	1199025	1146066	1028796	498100	5591592	•	•	•
Interest	3	184816	2	753	207	1154	925	799	1369	612	178996	•	•	•
Rents	4	7062	0	0	0	1244	2341	16	627	113	2721	•	•	•
Royalties	5	131145	0	0	0	0	727	112	233	325	129747	•	•	•
Other Portfolio Income	6	141040	10703	16484	640	3533	6301	3810	3423	1791	94357	•	•	•
Other Receipts	7	244855	858	1565	755	7456	9283	9122	14857	2731	198227	•	•	•
Total Receipts	8	14671688	26334	959729	510695	3047787	1218602	1159925	1049305	503672	6195640	•	•	•
Average Total Receipts	9	3211	43	413	1066	3270	11283	18412	36183	71953	774455	•	•	•
Operating Costs/Operating Income (%)														
Cost of Operations	10	65.4	68.0	40.6	56.8	60.8	65.6	66.1	67.8	61.9	72.6	•	•	•
Salaries and Wages	11	7.0	5.1	2.8	6.4	5.2	3.5	6.8	6.5	8.4	9.4	•	•	•
Taxes Paid	12	2.6	2.5	3.9	4.5	3.6	3.2	3.0	2.8	3.2	1.3	•	•	•
Interest Paid	13	3.9	3.6	1.5	0.6	0.9	0.9	1.1	1.9	0.5	8.0	•	•	•
Depreciation	14	3.9	7.6	9.4	4.1	5.0	5.2	4.4	4.6	5.1	1.8	•	•	•
Amortization and Depletion	15	0.4	0.1	0.0	•	0.0	0.0	0.1	0.4	0.4	0.8	•	•	•
Pensions and Other Deferred Comp.	16	0.5	0.6	0.1	0.9	0.7	0.5	0.4	0.7	1.9	0.2	•	•	•
Employee Benefits	17	1.8	0.9	2.2	3.7	2.0	2.4	2.6	2.1	1.7	1.2	•	•	•
Advertising	18	0.4	0.4	0.1	0.2	0.3	0.2	0.3	0.3	0.4	0.7	•	•	•
Other Expenses	19	10.4	7.8	20.3	11.4	8.7	6.1	7.1	7.5	8.4	11.9	•	•	•
Officers' Compensation	20	3.6	3.6	12.7	8.5	6.3	4.7	3.2	2.0	1.9	0.6	•	•	•
Operating Margin	21	0.0	•	6.4	2.8	6.5	7.7	5.1	3.5	6.1	•	•	•	•
Operating Margin Before Officers' Comp.	22	3.7	3.4	19.0	11.3	12.8	12.4	8.2	5.5	7.9	•	•	•	•

Selected Average Balance Sheet ($ in Thousands)

Net Receivables 23	764	0	38	189	450	1735	3697	9110	10300	266848
Inventories 24	287	0	5	184	261	1309	2459	5378	13114	55236
Net Property, Plant and Equipment 25	574	0	65	96	625	2134	4108	8786	15817	123461
Total Assets 26	3721	0	174	623	2003	6629	13917	32891	66647	1427418
Notes and Loans Payable 27	1351	0	106	129	425	1718	4055	12469	7238	576920
All Other Liabilities 28	1027	0	18	225	302	1556	2751	7406	8244	455734
Net Worth 29	1343	0	50	268	1276	3355	7111	13016	51164	394764

Selected Financial Ratios (Times to 1)

Current Ratio 30	1.9	•	1.8	2.0	2.7	1.9	1.9	1.7	4.0	1.7
Quick Ratio 31	1.3	•	1.5	1.2	1.9	1.1	1.2	1.0	2.4	1.2
Net Sales to Working Capital 32	4.0	•	8.9	4.0	4.5	5.7	4.5	4.6	2.6	3.3
Coverage Ratio 33	2.3	22.4	6.5	5.9	8.3	11.0	6.9	3.9	14.9	1.3
Total Asset Turnover 34	0.8	•	2.3	1.7	1.6	1.7	1.3	1.1	1.1	0.5
Inventory Turnover 35	7.0	•	30.0	3.3	7.6	5.6	4.9	4.5	3.4	9.2
Receivables Turnover 36	5.5	•	10.9	11.3	7.6	6.6	5.3	4.5	4.2	4.5
Total Liabilities to Net Worth 37	1.8	•	2.5	1.3	0.6	1.0	1.0	1.5	0.3	2.6
Current Assets to Working Capital 38	2.1	•	2.2	2.0	1.6	2.1	2.1	2.5	1.3	2.4
Current Liabilities to Working Capital 39	1.1	•	1.2	1.0	0.6	1.1	1.1	1.5	0.3	1.4
Working Capital to Net Sales 40	0.2	•	0.1	0.2	0.2	0.2	0.2	0.2	0.4	0.3
Inventory to Working Capital 41	0.5	•	0.1	0.7	0.4	0.7	0.6	0.7	0.4	0.5
Total Receipts to Cash Flow 42	8.1	1.3	4.7	10.3	7.8	7.8	9.3	9.0	6.6	9.4
Cost of Goods to Cash Flow 43	5.3	0.9	1.9	5.8	4.7	5.1	6.2	6.1	4.1	6.8
Cash Flow to Total Debt 44	0.2	•	0.7	0.3	0.6	0.4	0.3	0.2	0.7	0.1

Selected Financial Factors (in Percentages)

Debt Ratio 45	63.9	•	71.3	57.0	36.3	49.4	48.9	60.4	23.2	72.3
Return on Total Assets 46	7.4	•	23.0	6.3	12.8	17.2	9.5	8.0	8.2	5.1
Return on Equity Before Income Taxes 47	11.8	•	67.8	12.2	17.6	30.9	16.0	15.1	10.0	4.3
Return on Equity After Income Taxes 48	10.8	•	64.5	11.8	17.3	29.5	15.1	12.5	8.2	3.4
Profit Margin (Before Income Tax) 49	5.2	77.8	8.3	3.1	6.9	9.3	6.2	5.6	7.2	2.4
Profit Margin (After Income Tax) 50	4.8	77.3	7.9	3.0	6.8	8.9	5.9	4.6	5.9	1.9

Table I

Corporations with and without Net Income

ENGINE, TURBINE AND POWER TRANSMISSION EQUIPMENT

MONEY AMOUNTS AND SIZE OF ASSETS IN THOUSANDS OF DOLLARS

Item Description for Accounting Period 7/03 Through 6/04	Total	Zero Assets	Under 500	500 to 1,000	1,000 to 5,000	5,000 to 10,000	10,000 to 25,000	25,000 to 50,000	50,000 to 100,000	100,000 to 250,000	250,000 to 500,000	500,000 to 2,500,000	2,500,000 and over
Number of Enterprises **1**	242	3	•	82	70	21	33	7	4	10	3	6	3
Revenues ($ in Thousands)													
Net Sales **2**	33873968	52905	•	110876	101005	168305	711402	336841	227685	1914187	1015305	4385622	24849836
Interest **3**	603203	277	•	28	77	214	799	1261	2565	21747	6043	54597	515594
Rents **4**	352727	0	•	0	0	787	1081	160	146	1034	265	3200	346054
Royalties **5**	293055	0	•	0	21	0	0	152	3711	13811	2888	13792	258681
Other Portfolio Income **6**	82302	3	•	0	0	161	1402	0	91	6688	4059	14117	55781
Other Receipts **7**	396876	1355	•	97	405	3884	1739	1131	1717	33888	21240	98638	232779
Total Receipts **8**	35602131	54540	•	111001	101508	173351	716423	339545	235915	1991355	1049800	4569966	26258725
Average Total Receipts **9**	147116	18180	•	1354	1450	8255	21710	48506	58979	199136	349933	761661	8752908
Operating Costs/Operating Income (%)													
Cost of Operations **10**	73.8	99.8	•	61.0	91.9	71.3	70.9	77.9	71.3	72.5	75.5	72.0	74.1
Salaries and Wages **11**	15.8	21.9	•	16.3	8.8	2.4	7.0	7.8	6.3	7.7	5.5	11.1	18.2
Taxes Paid **12**	1.5	1.2	•	3.7	2.0	2.0	2.1	1.3	3.7	2.1	2.1	1.2	1.5
Interest Paid **13**	2.3	0.2	•	4.6	1.5	4.6	1.2	1.0	2.9	1.6	0.8	3.3	2.3
Depreciation **14**	3.5	2.8	•	2.4	3.5	2.7	4.4	2.7	4.5	3.8	1.6	3.6	3.5
Amortization and Depletion **15**	0.4	6.5	•	0.2	0.1	0.2	0.2	0.1	0.6	0.7	2.8	1.2	0.1
Pensions and Other Deferred Comp. **16**	3.7	•	•	0.4	0.1	0.0	1.1	0.4	1.9	1.9	0.3	0.7	4.7
Employee Benefits **17**	2.0	1.4	•	3.1	1.6	2.1	2.0	2.6	1.3	2.3	1.1	1.1	2.2
Advertising **18**	0.6	0.6	•	1.1	0.3	0.4	0.6	0.3	0.8	0.7	0.1	0.8	0.6
Other Expenses **19**	2.5	8.0	•	22.5	10.5	8.5	9.4	6.4	7.9	8.2	9.1	7.1	0.6
Officers' Compensation **20**	0.7	0.6	•	4.3	4.9	2.4	2.5	1.2	1.7	0.7	1.0	0.5	0.6
Operating Margin **21**	•	•	•	•	•	3.6	•	•	•	•	0.2	•	•
Operating Margin Before Officers' Comp. **22**	•	•	•	•	•	6.0	1.1	•	•	•	1.2	•	•

Selected Average Balance Sheet ($ in Thousands)

Item													
Net Receivables 23	24516	0	•	198	155	885	3549	13734	9441	30462	47666	181653	1366204
Inventories 24	19025	0	•	194	960	2466	3903	7477	15825	37090	27814	127942	1017450
Net Property, Plant and Equipment 25	22321	0	•	242	706	1572	5186	7613	17634	42649	28309	210165	1077312
Total Assets 26	141050	0	•	683	1881	5944	16489	31809	67790	182438	341237	982861	8012768
Notes and Loans Payable 27	30810	0	•	818	1104	3117	5179	9971	21651	38317	59605	245245	1628453
All Other Liabilities 28	84368	0	•	283	424	1653	4118	15232	21482	57051	130203	491977	5362642
Net Worth 29	25872	0	•	-418	353	1174	7192	6605	24658	87070	151429	245639	1021673

Selected Financial Ratios (Times to 1)

Item													
Current Ratio 30	1.2	•	•	1.0	0.8	1.7	1.9	1.3	2.0	1.8	1.4	1.4	1.1
Quick Ratio 31	0.6	•	•	0.5	0.4	0.8	0.9	0.8	1.0	1.1	0.9	0.8	0.5
Net Sales to Working Capital 32	15.2	•	•	•	•	6.7	4.5	8.6	3.5	4.5	6.4	5.5	42.8
Coverage Ratio 33	0.3	•	•	•	2.4	•	0.1	1.5	1.2	2.2	5.7	1.6	•
Total Asset Turnover 34	1.0	•	•	2.0	0.8	1.3	1.3	1.5	0.8	1.0	1.0	0.7	1.0
Inventory Turnover 35	5.4	•	•	4.3	1.4	2.3	3.9	5.0	2.6	3.7	9.2	4.1	6.0
Receivables Turnover 36	5.1	•	•	13.7	2.1	3.4	6.7	4.2	4.2	5.2	14.2	3.0	5.7
Total Liabilities to Net Worth 37	4.5	•	•	•	4.3	4.1	1.3	3.8	1.7	1.1	1.3	3.0	6.8
Current Assets to Working Capital 38	7.0	•	•	•	•	2.4	2.1	4.3	3.3	2.0	1.2	3.6	18.2
Current Liabilities to Working Capital 39	6.0	•	•	•	•	1.4	1.1	3.3	1.0	1.2	2.6	2.5	17.2
Working Capital to Net Sales 40	0.1	•	•	0.1	0.2	0.9	0.1	0.2	0.3	1.0	0.7	0.2	0.0
Inventory to Working Capital 41	2.0	•	•	1.1	0.9	1.4	•	•	0.9	0.7	0.5	1.2	4.8
Total Receipts to Cash Flow 42	•	•	•	7.5	15.0	26.7	14.0	12.1	9.9	12.5	•	•	•
Cost of Goods to Cash Flow 43	•	•	•	5.3	10.6	20.8	10.0	8.8	7.5	9.0	•	•	•
Cash Flow to Total Debt 44	•	•	•	0.2	0.2	0.1	0.1	0.2	0.2	0.1	•	•	•

Selected Financial Factors (in Percentages)

Item													
Debt Ratio 45	81.7	•	•	161.3	81.2	80.3	56.4	79.2	63.6	52.3	55.6	75.0	87.2
Return on Total Assets 46	0.7	•	•	15.0	0.6	0.1	3.0	•	•	3.7	4.3	3.9	•
Return on Equity Before Income Taxes 47	•	•	•	63.7	45.0	•	•	•	•	1.6	4.2	7.9	6.1
Return on Equity After Income Taxes 48	•	•	•	63.7	35.4	•	•	•	•	0.9	0.4	6.6	2.8
Profit Margin (Before Income Tax) 49	•	•	•	6.6	•	•	•	•	•	0.7	1.9	3.5	2.0
Profit Margin (After Income Tax) 50	•	•	•	5.2	•	•	•	•	•	0.4	0.2	2.9	0.9

Table II

Corporations with Net Income

ENGINE, TURBINE AND POWER TRANSMISSION EQUIPMENT

MONEY AMOUNTS AND SIZE OF ASSETS IN THOUSANDS OF DOLLARS

Item Description for Accounting Period 7/03 Through 6/04		Total	Zero Assets	Under 500	500 to 1,000	1,000 to 5,000	5,000 to 10,000	10,000 to 25,000	25,000 to 50,000	50,000 to 100,000	100,000 to 250,000	250,000 to 500,000	500,000 to 2,500,000	2,500,000 and over
Number of Enterprises	1	59	•	•	•	•	•	19	•	•	•	•	•	•
Revenues ($ in Thousands)														
Net Sales	2	23763564	•	•	•	•	•	411486	•	•	•	•	•	•
Interest	3	515489	•	•	•	•	•	535	•	•	•	•	•	•
Rents	4	348612	•	•	•	•	•	1081	•	•	•	•	•	•
Royalties	5	126506	•	•	•	•	•	0	•	•	•	•	•	•
Other Portfolio Income	6	55355	•	•	•	•	•	1209	•	•	•	•	•	•
Other Receipts	7	103797	•	•	•	•	•	313	•	•	•	•	•	•
Total Receipts	8	24913323	•	•	•	•	•	414624	•	•	•	•	•	•
Average Total Receipts	9	422260	•	•	•	•	•	21822	•	•	•	•	•	•
Operating Costs/Operating Income (%)														
Cost of Operations	10	72.1	•	•	•	•	•	66.3	•	•	•	•	•	•
Salaries and Wages	11	17.4	•	•	•	•	•	6.9	•	•	•	•	•	•
Taxes Paid	12	1.5	•	•	•	•	•	2.2	•	•	•	•	•	•
Interest Paid	13	2.4	•	•	•	•	•	1.0	•	•	•	•	•	•
Depreciation	14	3.9	•	•	•	•	•	3.7	•	•	•	•	•	•
Amortization and Depletion	15	0.2	•	•	•	•	•	0.1	•	•	•	•	•	•
Pensions and Other Deferred Comp.	16	4.8	•	•	•	•	•	1.7	•	•	•	•	•	•
Employee Benefits	17	0.9	•	•	•	•	•	1.8	•	•	•	•	•	•
Advertising	18	0.8	•	•	•	•	•	0.7	•	•	•	•	•	•
Other Expenses	19	•	•	•	•	•	•	8.5	•	•	•	•	•	•
Officers' Compensation	20	0.6	•	•	•	•	•	2.3	•	•	•	•	•	•
Operating Margin	21	•	•	•	•	•	•	4.8	•	•	•	•	•	•
Operating Margin Before Officers' Comp.	22	•	•	•	•	•	•	7.1	•	•	•	•	•	•

Selected Average Balance Sheet ($ in Thousands)

Net Receivables 23	67261	3764
Inventories 24	60587	3765
Net Property, Plant and Equipment 25	63536	4410
Total Assets 26	405561	15344
Notes and Loans Payable 27	56241	4648
All Other Liabilities 28	256681	3544
Net Worth 29	92639	7152

Selected Financial Ratios (Times to 1)

Current Ratio 30	1.4	2.4
Quick Ratio 31	0.7	1.3
Net Sales to Working Capital 32	7.0	3.7
Coverage Ratio 33	2.1	6.7
Total Asset Turnover 34	1.0	1.4
Inventory Turnover 35	4.8	3.8
Receivables Turnover 36	5.2	6.0
Total Liabilities to Net Worth 37	3.4	1.1
Current Assets to Working Capital 38	3.4	1.7
Current Liabilities to Working Capital 39	2.4	0.7
Working Capital to Net Sales 40	0.1	0.3
Inventory to Working Capital 41	1.0	0.6
Total Receipts to Cash Flow 42		8.3
Cost of Goods to Cash Flow 43		5.5
Cash Flow to Total Debt 44		0.3

Selected Financial Factors (in Percentages)

Debt Ratio 45	77.2	53.4
Return on Total Assets 46	5.0	9.2
Return on Equity Before Income Taxes 47	11.4	16.8
Return on Equity After Income Taxes 48	8.5	13.4
Profit Margin (Before Income Tax) 49	2.6	5.5
Profit Margin (After Income Tax) 50	2.0	4.4

Table I
Corporations with and without Net Income

OTHER GENERAL PURPOSE MACHINERY

MONEY AMOUNTS AND SIZE OF ASSETS IN THOUSANDS OF DOLLARS

Item Description for Accounting Period 7/03 Through 6/04	Total	Zero Assets	Under 500	500 to 1,000	1,000 to 5,000	5,000 to 10,000	10,000 to 25,000	25,000 to 50,000	50,000 to 100,000	100,000 to 250,000	250,000 to 500,000	500,000 to 2,500,000	2,500,000 and over
Number of Enterprises 1	6176	270	4255	341	884	174	121	48	25	26	10	14	8
Revenues ($ in Thousands)													
Net Sales 2	53214914	37400	1422059	487482	3144686	1881697	2573343	1974143	2332022	3982284	3783781	7293358	24302658
Interest 3	847740	135	517	518	1366	7007	5247	3693	8134	15081	13798	58228	734016
Rents 4	21865	1	0	761	482	117	2741	1390	747	5880	3457	2318	3970
Royalties 5	567771	0	0	0	0	2	1566	312	7	11851	2056	89861	462116
Other Portfolio Income 6	364519	4	1870	2921	776	1689	11429	9771	2468	32541	12896	97496	190659
Other Receipts 7	929934	211	2524	3618	11658	281794	62267	14793	36556	18775	28498	227588	241652
Total Receipts 8	55946743	37751	1426970	495300	3158968	2172306	2656593	2004102	2379934	4066412	3844486	7768849	25935071
Average Total Receipts 9	9059	140	335	1452	3573	12485	21955	41752	95197	156400	384449	554918	3241884
Operating Costs/Operating Income (%)													
Cost of Operations 10	64.7	46.9	42.2	61.6	67.3	64.1	67.9	70.6	69.7	62.3	71.7	64.3	63.9
Salaries and Wages 11	10.1	17.8	13.3	8.5	9.7	10.5	10.1	8.7	8.1	10.4	6.4	12.5	10.2
Taxes Paid 12	1.9	2.2	3.5	3.6	2.9	2.3	2.5	2.3	1.5	1.9	1.8	2.0	1.6
Interest Paid 13	4.3	3.4	0.9	1.1	1.3	1.7	1.2	1.5	0.8	2.5	1.6	3.0	7.1
Depreciation 14	2.8	2.2	2.4	1.8	3.0	2.6	3.2	2.8	2.5	3.3	3.7	2.3	2.7
Amortization and Depletion 15	1.2	1.9	0.0	0.1	0.1	1.0	0.4	0.5	0.3	1.2	1.0	1.5	1.5
Pensions and Other Deferred Comp. 16	1.1	0.0	0.1	0.3	0.2	0.7	0.7	1.4	0.4	0.6	0.6	1.6	1.4
Employee Benefits 17	3.1	3.7	2.1	3.7	1.9	1.5	2.1	1.9	6.0	3.0	1.9	3.6	3.3
Advertising 18	0.8	0.5	0.8	1.4	0.5	1.0	0.7	0.6	0.6	0.9	0.7	0.4	1.0
Other Expenses 19	13.7	13.9	20.4	13.1	12.4	33.1	11.5	9.5	9.1	10.0	8.7	14.1	14.2
Officers' Compensation 20	1.6	8.1	10.0	8.2	4.6	5.2	2.7	1.8	1.1	2.4	0.9	0.7	0.4
Operating Margin 21	•	•	4.3	•	•	•	•	•	•	1.5	0.9	•	•
Operating Margin Before Officers' Comp. 22	•	7.4	14.2	4.8	0.7	•	•	0.2	1.0	3.8	1.8	•	•

Selected Average Balance Sheet ($ in Thousands)

Line Item													
Net Receivables 23	1860	0	25	127	569	1885	3628	7058	18316	30510	68191	142549	725341
Inventories 24	1135	0	25	348	701	1559	3663	7366	15415	21158	53926	75390	320949
Net Property, Plant and Equipment 25	1329	0	27	136	421	1821	3501	6739	12239	30721	64993	81706	464476
Total Assets 26	17706		96	710	2081	7326	15335	35750	71165	152303	348004	781076	10233013
Notes and Loans Payable 27	4763	0	64	256	1187	2538	5241	12823	15624	51587	79060	204102	2616600
All Other Liabilities 28	5084	0	21	205	605	3429	4481	9888	21106	38584	128139	348688	2674766
Net Worth 29	7860		11	248	289	1359	5613	13039	34435	62131	140804	228286	4941647

Selected Financial Ratios (Times to 1)

Line Item													
Current Ratio 30	1.3	•	2.3	1.9	2.0	1.6	1.8	1.6	1.7	1.9	1.2	1.3	1.1
Quick Ratio 31	0.8	•	1.5	0.7	1.0	0.9	1.0	0.7	1.0	1.1	0.7	0.8	0.7
Net Sales to Working Capital 32	9.7	•	9.4	6.0	4.8	6.2	5.0	6.0	4.7	4.8	11.6	5.9	43.7
Coverage Ratio 33	1.1	•	6.1	•	•	1.0	1.3	1.0	3.5	2.7	2.7	1.5	1.0
Total Asset Turnover 34	0.5	•	3.5	2.0	1.7	1.5	1.4	1.2	1.3	1.0	1.1	0.7	0.3
Inventory Turnover 35	4.9	•	5.6	2.5	3.4	4.4	3.9	3.9	4.2	4.5	5.0	4.4	6.0
Receivables Turnover 36	4.6	•	11.5	7.6	6.7	6.3	5.8	5.8	5.8	5.0	5.7	3.3	4.2
Total Liabilities to Net Worth 37	1.3	•	7.9	1.9	6.2	4.4	1.7	1.7	1.1	1.5	1.5	2.4	1.1
Current Assets to Working Capital 38	4.6	•	1.7	2.1	2.0	2.6	2.3	2.8	2.4	2.1	5.5	4.0	19.6
Current Liabilities to Working Capital 39	3.6	•	0.7	1.1	1.0	1.6	1.3	1.8	1.4	1.1	4.5	3.0	18.6
Working Capital to Net Sales 40	0.1	•	0.1	0.2	0.2	0.2	0.2	0.2	0.2	0.2	0.1	0.2	0.0
Inventory to Working Capital 41	1.2	•	0.6	1.3	0.9	0.9	0.8	1.2	0.9	0.6	1.7	0.8	4.3
Total Receipts to Cash Flow 42	9.2	8.4	5.4	12.6	16.0	7.1	10.7	13.9	10.4	8.2	9.8	7.9	9.2
Cost of Goods to Cash Flow 43	5.9	3.9	2.3	7.8	10.8	4.6	7.3	9.8	7.2	5.1	7.1	5.1	5.9
Cash Flow to Total Debt 44	0.1	•	0.7	0.2	0.1	0.3	0.2	0.2	0.1	0.2	0.1	0.2	0.1

Selected Financial Factors (in Percentages)

Line Item													
Debt Ratio 45	55.6	•	88.7	65.1	86.1	81.5	63.4	63.5	51.6	59.2	59.5	70.8	51.7
Return on Total Assets 46	2.3	•	19.2	•	•	•	2.2	1.7	3.7	6.7	4.6	3.0	2.1
Return on Equity Before Income Taxes 47	0.4	•	142.1	•	•	•	1.4	•	5.4	10.4	7.2	3.4	•
Return on Equity After Income Taxes 48	•	•	142.0	•	•	•	•	•	3.3	6.4	2.7	•	•
Profit Margin (Before Income Tax) 49	0.4	0.3	4.6	•	•	0.4	•	•	2.0	4.2	2.7	1.5	•
Profit Margin (After Income Tax) 50	•	•	4.6	•	•	•	•	•	1.2	2.6	1.0	•	•

Table II
Corporations with Net Income

OTHER GENERAL PURPOSE MACHINERY

MONEY AMOUNTS AND SIZE OF ASSETS IN THOUSANDS OF DOLLARS

Item Description for Accounting Period 7/03 Through 6/04	Total	Zero Assets	Under 500	500 to 1,000	1,000 to 5,000	5,000 to 10,000	10,000 to 25,000	25,000 to 50,000	50,000 to 100,000	100,000 to 250,000	250,000 to 500,000	500,000 to 2,500,000	2,500,000 and over
Number of Enterprises 1	3745	3	2807	157	511	116	74	26	14	20	•	•	•

Revenues ($ in Thousands)

Net Sales 2	30450049	30482	1072702	251390	2233799	1340598	1827949	1147042	1469967	3217308	•	•	•
Interest 3	537444	46	1	125	919	2679	2365	1750	5303	10722	•	•	•
Rents 4	14531	1	0	675	482	0	1093	86	395	4696	•	•	•
Royalties 5	449615	0	0	0	0	0	50	112	7	11848	•	•	•
Other Portfolio Income 6	182429	4	1870	983	305	1343	4893	5850	1726	28375	•	•	•
Other Receipts 7	372130	211	1286	165	8929	4938	18291	5303	22844	17953	•	•	•
Total Receipts 8	32006198	30744	1075859	253338	2244434	1349558	1854641	1160143	1500242	3290902	•	•	•
Average Total Receipts 9	8546	10248	383	1614	4392	11634	25063	44621	107160	164545	•	•	•

Operating Costs/Operating Income (%)

Cost of Operations 10	65.4	46.9	37.3	58.5	66.6	63.8	66.2	67.1	66.2	61.2	•	•	•
Salaries and Wages 11	8.7	14.0	15.8	6.9	8.0	7.2	8.7	7.6	7.6	9.9	•	•	•
Taxes Paid 12	2.1	2.6	2.9	3.4	3.0	2.2	2.5	2.3	1.4	1.9	•	•	•
Interest Paid 13	3.3	4.2	0.5	0.5	0.9	0.4	1.1	1.2	0.8	2.0	•	•	•
Depreciation 14	2.6	2.1	2.9	1.7	1.8	2.5	2.8	2.9	2.8	3.2	•	•	•
Amortization and Depletion 15	0.9	1.9	0.0	•	0.0	0.1	0.3	0.4	0.3	1.1	•	•	•
Pensions and Other Deferred Comp. 16	1.2	0.0	0.1	0.3	0.2	0.5	0.7	0.8	0.5	0.6	•	•	•
Employee Benefits 17	2.3	3.6	1.5	1.8	1.8	1.1	2.0	1.8	8.3	3.0	•	•	•
Advertising 18	1.0	0.3	0.5	0.9	0.4	0.5	0.6	0.6	0.4	1.1	•	•	•
Other Expenses 19	11.3	11.2	18.6	12.9	10.8	6.8	7.7	8.2	8.6	10.0	•	•	•
Officers' Compensation 20	1.7	8.0	8.1	12.2	3.7	5.6	2.1	2.1	1.0	2.6	•	•	•
Operating Margin 21	•	5.3	11.7	1.0	2.8	9.2	5.3	5.0	2.2	3.5	•	•	•
Operating Margin Before Officers' Comp. 22	1.3	13.3	19.8	13.2	6.5	14.9	7.5	7.1	3.2	6.1	•	•	•

Selected Average Balance Sheet ($ in Thousands)

Net Receivables 23	1635	0	28	95	683	2091	3685	6472	19429	30038
Inventories 24	1075	0	9	395	622	1427	3984	7954	13559	22212
Net Property, Plant and Equipment 25	1195	0	35	114	301	1957	3246	7970	13625	30257
Total Assets 26	10092	0	89	702	2061	7417	15127	35316	74821	153794
Notes and Loans Payable 27	2892	0	35	179	671	1130	4304	12600	14975	41235
All Other Liabilities 28	3313	0	14	165	613	1218	3951	5926	18052	44169
Net Worth 29	3887	0	40	358	778	5068	6871	16790	41794	68391

Selected Financial Ratios (Times to 1)

Current Ratio 30	1.3	•	2.1	3.2	2.2	2.6	2.2	1.9	2.0	2.3
Quick Ratio 31	0.8	•	1.9	1.0	1.2	1.5	1.2	1.0	1.2	1.3
Net Sales to Working Capital 32	11.5	•	16.0	4.4	5.1	4.2	4.6	5.2	4.4	4.2
Coverage Ratio 33	2.6	2.5	23.8	4.5	4.7	25.4	7.4	6.2	6.6	4.3
Total Asset Turnover 34	0.8	•	4.3	2.3	2.1	1.6	1.6	1.2	1.4	1.0
Inventory Turnover 35	4.9	•	15.1	2.4	4.7	5.2	4.1	3.7	5.1	4.4
Receivables Turnover 36	4.5	•	12.2	8.3	7.4	6.1	6.4	5.4	7.0	5.4
Total Liabilities to Net Worth 37	1.6	•	1.2	1.0	1.7	0.5	1.2	1.1	0.8	1.2
Current Assets to Working Capital 38	4.7	•	1.9	1.5	1.8	1.6	1.9	2.1	2.0	1.8
Current Liabilities to Working Capital 39	3.7	•	0.9	0.5	0.8	0.6	0.9	1.1	1.0	0.8
Working Capital to Net Sales 40	0.1	•	0.1	0.2	0.2	0.2	0.2	0.2	0.2	0.2
Inventory to Working Capital 41	1.4	•	0.1	0.9	0.7	0.5	0.7	0.8	0.7	0.5
Total Receipts to Cash Flow 42	7.3	6.6	4.2	9.5	8.6	6.6	7.9	7.8	8.5	6.9
Cost of Goods to Cash Flow 43	4.8	3.1	1.6	5.5	5.7	4.2	5.2	5.3	5.6	4.2
Cash Flow to Total Debt 44	0.2	•	1.8	0.5	0.4	0.7	0.4	0.3	0.4	0.3

Selected Financial Factors (in Percentages)

Debt Ratio 45	61.5	•	55.3	48.9	62.3	31.7	54.6	52.5	44.1	55.5
Return on Total Assets 46	7.0	•	53.5	5.3	8.9	16.1	12.9	9.5	7.0	8.9
Return on Equity Before Income Taxes 47	11.2	•	114.7	8.1	18.6	22.6	24.5	16.8	10.7	15.4
Return on Equity After Income Taxes 48	8.1	•	114.6	6.9	14.9	18.6	21.0	14.2	7.6	10.7
Profit Margin (Before Income Tax) 49	5.4	6.1	11.9	1.8	3.3	9.9	6.8	6.4	4.3	6.5
Profit Margin (After Income Tax) 50	3.9	4.8	11.9	1.5	2.7	8.1	5.8	5.4	3.0	4.5

Table I

Corporations with and without Net Income

COMPUTER AND PERIPHERAL EQUIPMENT

MONEY AMOUNTS AND SIZE OF ASSETS IN THOUSANDS OF DOLLARS

Item Description for Accounting Period 7/03 Through 6/04	Total	Zero Assets	Under 500	500 to 1,000	1,000 to 5,000	5,000 to 10,000	10,000 to 25,000	25,000 to 50,000	50,000 to 100,000	100,000 to 250,000	250,000 to 500,000	500,000 to 2,500,000	2,500,000 and over
Number of Enterprises **1**	3475	639	2031	206	229	115	111	52	25	22	15	23	7
Revenues ($ in Thousands)													
Net Sales **2**	195404610	465143	1507037	233588	1203201	1342496	2087245	2038829	1811733	3903328	5121778	19027988	156662243
Interest **3**	2729519	3610	49	17	2928	3374	8348	11354	6420	20025	35807	145101	2492487
Rents **4**	1609598	656	0	0	472	659	1237	542	945	789	719	50302	1553272
Royalties **5**	17723020	6667	0	0	3847	68	1332	8748	24567	16468	97033	310279	17254010
Other Portfolio Income **6**	2592787	1069	0	20	1492	26439	5821	4396	4487	3116	59272	189379	2297294
Other Receipts **7**	6838531	12752	2460	3125	8374	10600	31006	13923	9796	6503	29042	223426	6487525
Total Receipts **8**	226898065	489247	1510202	236750	1220314	1383636	2134989	2077792	1857948	3950229	5343651	19946475	186746831
Average Total Receipts **9**	65294	766	744	1149	5329	12032	19234	39958	74318	179556	356243	867238	26678119
Operating Costs/Operating Income (%)													
Cost of Operations **10**	66.0	70.8	54.0	27.1	58.0	59.6	68.7	62.5	60.5	71.6	64.1	66.5	66.2
Salaries and Wages **11**	14.1	28.9	18.2	15.8	23.8	17.5	19.6	17.3	18.1	10.0	18.0	15.9	13.5
Taxes Paid **12**	1.6	2.5	4.0	2.9	2.9	2.4	2.1	2.2	1.3	1.3	1.8	1.5	1.6
Interest Paid **13**	1.4	0.8	1.9	0.3	0.8	1.6	1.4	1.0	1.0	1.7	1.5	0.9	1.5
Depreciation **14**	4.2	1.9	1.6	1.0	1.7	4.9	2.9	3.3	2.4	2.7	3.1	3.2	4.5
Amortization and Depletion **15**	0.3	1.6	0.3	3.3	1.0	1.1	1.1	1.0	1.8	0.8	1.3	1.0	0.2
Pensions and Other Deferred Comp. **16**	0.5	0.3	0.2	5.8	0.4	0.1	0.3	0.3	0.4	0.4	0.4	0.5	0.5
Employee Benefits **17**	2.2	1.8	5.2	0.4	1.1	2.6	2.0	1.5	2.1	1.5	1.9	1.9	2.3
Advertising **18**	2.0	0.8	0.2	0.1	0.4	0.8	1.0	1.9	0.8	1.5	1.2	1.8	2.1
Other Expenses **19**	17.3	17.5	16.7	25.6	18.2	26.3	14.8	19.0	16.4	11.3	13.2	11.0	18.2
Officers' Compensation **20**	0.4	7.2	3.4	18.1	6.2	3.3	3.8	1.6	1.6	1.1	0.9	0.8	0.2
Operating Margin **21**	•	•	•	•	•	•	•	•	•	•	•	•	•
Operating Margin Before Officers' Comp. **22**	•	•	•	17.8	•	•	•	•	•	•	•	•	•

Selected Average Balance Sheet ($ in Thousands)

Net Receivables 23	11146	0	30	93	698	1698	3489	7413	13170	29359	60716	128852	4667639
Inventories 24	3399	0	8	215	595	1239	2372	3889	9320	21693	35661	54128	1216701
Net Property, Plant and Equipment 25	9550	0	24	122	206	1493	1912	4026	7466	10669	26501	109550	4161770
Total Assets 26	63069	0	89	898	2508	7587	15864	36565	68861	159123	370766	1099396	25374320
Notes and Loans Payable 27	15496	0	183	3274	720	2399	5017	7594	8429	28472	84301	141050	6580691
All Other Liabilities 28	22015	0	99	595	958	3055	5390	11672	23301	54256	122667	328247	9033881
Net Worth 29	25558	0	-192	-2971	829	2133	5457	17299	37131	76394	163797	630100	9759748

Selected Financial Ratios (Times to 1)

Current Ratio 30	1.5	•	0.5	1.0	2.0	1.6	1.9	2.0	2.1	1.9	1.8	2.2	1.4
Quick Ratio 31	0.8	•	0.4	0.4	1.4	1.1	1.4	1.3	1.5	1.3	1.3	1.5	0.7
Net Sales to Working Capital 32	5.5	•	•	•	5.6	6.4	3.6	3.2	3.1	3.6	3.7	2.6	6.6
Coverage Ratio 33	6.4	•	•	4.9	•	•	•	•	•	0.5	•	1.3	8.0
Total Asset Turnover 34	0.9	•	8.3	1.3	2.1	1.5	1.2	1.1	1.1	1.1	0.9	0.8	0.9
Inventory Turnover 35	10.9	•	48.8	1.4	5.1	5.6	5.4	6.3	4.7	5.9	6.1	10.2	12.2
Receivables Turnover 36	3.9	•	39.1	5.3	6.6	7.0	5.3	5.8	3.8	5.1	5.2	6.5	3.6
Total Liabilities to Net Worth 37	1.5	•	•	•	2.0	2.6	1.9	1.1	0.9	1.1	1.3	0.7	1.6
Current Assets to Working Capital 38	3.0	•	•	•	2.0	2.7	2.1	2.0	1.9	2.1	2.2	1.8	3.5
Current Liabilities to Working Capital 39	2.0	•	•	•	1.0	1.7	1.1	1.0	0.9	1.1	1.2	0.8	2.5
Working Capital to Net Sales 40	0.2	•	•	•	0.2	0.2	0.3	0.3	0.3	0.3	0.3	0.4	0.2
Inventory to Working Capital 41	0.3	•	•	•	0.4	0.7	0.4	0.4	0.3	0.4	0.4	0.2	0.4
Total Receipts to Cash Flow 42	4.8	•	29.8	4.4	321.9	•	•	15.7	9.8	14.8	12.7	12.7	4.0
Cost of Goods to Cash Flow 43	3.1	•	16.1	1.2	186.8	•	•	9.8	6.0	10.6	8.1	8.5	2.7
Cash Flow to Total Debt 44	0.3	•	0.1	0.1	0.0	•	0.1	0.1	0.2	0.1	0.1	0.1	0.4

Selected Financial Factors (in Percentages)

Debt Ratio 45	59.5	•	316.4	430.9	66.9	71.9	65.6	52.7	46.1	52.0	55.8	42.7	61.5
Return on Total Assets 46	8.1	•	•	1.8	•	•	•	•	•	0.9	•	0.9	10.4
Return on Equity Before Income Taxes 47	16.8	•	20.8	•	•	•	•	•	•	•	•	0.3	23.7
Return on Equity After Income Taxes 48	10.3	•	20.8	•	•	•	•	•	•	•	•	•	15.9
Profit Margin (Before Income Tax) 49	7.6	•	•	1.1	•	•	•	•	•	•	•	0.3	10.3
Profit Margin (After Income Tax) 50	4.7	•	•	1.1	•	•	•	•	•	•	•	•	6.9

Table II
Corporations with Net Income

COMPUTER AND PERIPHERAL EQUIPMENT

MONEY AMOUNTS AND SIZE OF ASSETS IN THOUSANDS OF DOLLARS

Item Description for Accounting Period 7/03 Through 6/04		Total	Zero Assets	Under 500	500 to 1,000	1,000 to 5,000	5,000 to 10,000	10,000 to 25,000	25,000 to 50,000	50,000 to 100,000	100,000 to 250,000	250,000 to 500,000	500,000 to 2,500,000	2,500,000 and over
Number of Enterprises	1	1576	480	662	200	97	30	44	21	8	13	•	11	•
Revenues ($ in Thousands)														
Net Sales	2	172941544	278766	572556	229427	726035	507044	1339961	1238236	928321	2575532	•	13947507	•
Interest	3	2460444	789	36	2	1371	1634	2093	1719	732	8020	•	60875	•
Rents	4	1450428	6	656	0	0	640	308	90	892	789	•	38243	•
Royalties	5	17579067	0	0	0	3847	0	253	759	24332	8035	•	284664	•
Other Portfolio Income	6	2499821	11	0	20	849	25275	4377	397	65	1796	•	185882	•
Other Receipts	7	6609599	5044	1653	3066	4220	4850	6051	9702	1967	1261	•	69481	•
Total Receipts	8	203533903	284616	574901	232515	736322	539443	1353043	1250903	956309	2595433	•	14588652	•
Average Total Receipts	9	129150	593	868	1163	7591	17981	30751	59567	119539	199649	•	1326059	•
Operating Costs/Operating Income (%)														
Cost of Operations	10	66.2	82.1	67.7	26.4	46.6	42.9	68.6	60.2	65.4	72.2	•	68.1	•
Salaries and Wages	11	13.1	3.3	4.9	12.1	23.6	21.5	9.6	10.0	12.1	9.4	•	13.1	•
Taxes Paid	12	1.6	1.2	2.3	2.6	3.1	1.3	1.3	1.7	0.7	1.3	•	1.4	•
Interest Paid	13	1.4	0.5	1.8	0.0	0.5	1.1	0.5	0.6	1.3	0.3	•	0.3	•
Depreciation	14	4.1	0.5	0.8	0.7	1.1	2.6	1.8	2.2	2.0	2.0	•	2.3	•
Amortization and Depletion	15	0.2	0.1	•	•	0.4	0.4	0.3	0.7	0.2	0.1	•	0.6	•
Pensions and Other Deferred Comp.	16	0.5	0.4	0.3	5.9	0.5	0.2	0.2	0.4	0.6	0.1	•	0.6	•
Employee Benefits	17	2.2	0.6	0.2	0.1	1.0	1.7	1.1	1.1	2.2	1.0	•	1.4	•
Advertising	18	1.9	0.3	0.3	0.1	0.1	0.4	0.7	1.5	0.5	0.9	•	1.2	•
Other Expenses	19	17.5	0.3	12.2	22.1	12.2	24.2	7.7	15.7	12.2	9.6	•	7.8	•
Officers' Compensation	20	0.3	8.8	5.5	17.9	7.7	2.0	2.3	0.9	1.0	1.0	•	0.8	•
Operating Margin	21	•	2.0	4.0	12.2	3.2	1.7	5.9	5.0	1.7	2.2	•	2.5	•
Operating Margin Before Officers' Comp.	22	10.8	10.8	9.5	30.1	11.0	3.7	8.1	5.9	2.7	3.1	•	3.3	•

Selected Average Balance Sheet ($ in Thousands)

Net Receivables 23	22235	0	66	94	913	1842	4456	10155	17349	29672	•	199746
Inventories 24	5280	0	20	202	583	2030	3109	4396	14202	26842	•	83953
Net Property, Plant and Equipment 25	18631	0	40	124	245	1024	1825	4524	11340	11091	•	134193
Total Assets 26	116886	0	159	903	3204	7627	15641	34810	74489	154616	•	1267176
Notes and Loans Payable 27	30190	0	103	28	543	2231	2794	3382	14094	11461	•	117017
All Other Liabilities 28	42175	0	96	79	1007	4662	4502	16503	28787	60131	•	400724
Net Worth 29	44521	0	-40	796	1654	734	8345	14925	31608	83024	•	749435

Selected Financial Ratios (Times to 1)

Current Ratio 30	1.4	•	1.0	9.6	3.2	1.5	2.2	1.8	2.0	1.8	•	2.3
Quick Ratio 31	0.8	•	0.8	4.0	2.3	1.0	1.5	1.1	1.4	1.2	•	1.4
Net Sales to Working Capital 32	6.1	•	236.9	1.7	4.4	8.7	4.9	5.4	5.0	4.2	•	2.9
Coverage Ratio 33	8.6	9.9	3.4	335.9	10.7	8.4	13.6	10.5	4.7	18.4	•	22.8
Total Asset Turnover 34	0.9	•	5.4	1.3	2.3	2.2	1.9	1.7	1.6	1.3	•	1.0
Inventory Turnover 35	13.8	•	28.6	1.5	6.0	3.6	6.7	8.1	5.3	5.3	•	10.3
Receivables Turnover 36	4.9	•	•	5.4	8.5	7.4	6.8	7.3	4.1	5.7	•	6.9
Total Liabilities to Net Worth 37	1.6	•	•	0.1	0.9	9.4	0.9	1.3	1.4	0.9	•	0.7
Current Assets to Working Capital 38	3.2	•	33.2	1.1	1.4	3.2	1.8	2.3	2.0	2.2	•	1.8
Current Liabilities to Working Capital 39	2.2	•	32.2	0.1	0.4	2.2	0.8	1.3	1.0	1.2	•	0.8
Working Capital to Net Sales 40	0.2	•	0.0	0.6	0.2	0.1	0.2	0.2	0.2	0.2	•	0.3
Inventory to Working Capital 41	0.4	•	5.6	0.2	0.3	0.9	0.5	0.6	0.5	0.5	•	0.2
Total Receipts to Cash Flow 42	4.1	26.0	8.0	3.0	7.2	3.9	8.0	5.0	6.5	9.1	•	7.6
Cost of Goods to Cash Flow 43	2.7	21.4	5.4	0.8	3.4	1.7	5.5	3.0	4.2	6.5	•	5.2
Cash Flow to Total Debt 44	0.4	•	0.5	3.5	0.7	0.6	0.5	0.6	0.4	0.3	•	0.3

Selected Financial Factors (in Percentages)

Debt Ratio 45	61.9	•	124.8	11.9	48.4	90.4	46.6	57.1	57.6	46.3	•	40.9
Return on Total Assets 46	11.1	•	33.7	17.3	12.0	20.3	14.4	11.2	9.4	7.8	•	7.8
Return on Equity Before Income Taxes 47	25.7	•	•	19.6	21.2	185.9	25.0	23.7	17.4	13.7	•	12.6
Return on Equity After Income Taxes 48	17.6	•	•	19.6	17.9	184.7	20.9	19.1	12.4	10.3	•	8.9
Profit Margin (Before Income Tax) 49	10.4	4.1	4.4	13.6	4.7	8.1	6.8	6.0	4.7	5.7	•	7.5
Profit Margin (After Income Tax) 50	7.1	3.5	4.4	13.6	4.0	8.0	5.7	4.8	3.4	4.3	•	5.3

138

Table I
Corporations with and without Net Income

COMMUNICATIONS EQUIPMENT

MONEY AMOUNTS AND SIZE OF ASSETS IN THOUSANDS OF DOLLARS

Item Description for Accounting Period 7/03 Through 6/04	Total	Zero Assets	Under 500	500 to 1,000	1,000 to 5,000	5,000 to 10,000	10,000 to 25,000	25,000 to 50,000	50,000 to 100,000	100,000 to 250,000	250,000 to 500,000	500,000 to 2,500,000	2,500,000 and over
Number of Enterprises 1	1788	24	549	496	450	39	102	30	26	29	13	22	9
Revenues ($ in Thousands)													
Net Sales 2	91436907	1133093	283996	340318	1571960	264300	1506937	1066814	1351436	5770155	2520085	14971058	60656754
Interest 3	1580144	4689	125	3052	1965	1407	10063	5530	13348	35424	19003	237659	1247879
Rents 4	449705	1790	0	0	247	131	1604	1152	1021	724	1317	5660	436059
Royalties 5	2721877	89	176	0	0	4031	32	828	14254	18140	2743	134768	2546816
Other Portfolio Income 6	1011049	90910	231	2	1274	1891	3636	3263	93385	28497	13648	359247	415065
Other Receipts 7	1379351	14340	708	2832	61715	1657	30169	19348	8991	6519	44559	-109309	1297822
Total Receipts 8	98579033	1244911	285236	346204	1637161	273417	1552441	1096935	1482435	5859459	2601355	15599083	66600395
Average Total Receipts 9	55134	51871	520	698	3638	7011	15220	36564	57017	202050	200104	709049	7400044
Operating Costs/Operating Income (%)													
Cost of Operations 10	67.6	76.1	56.7	52.7	62.9	65.1	60.7	53.3	55.4	78.3	58.8	59.8	69.7
Salaries and Wages 11	18.3	8.7	9.3	17.9	25.1	52.0	27.2	24.4	20.5	11.1	15.4	15.0	19.5
Taxes Paid 12	1.5	1.2	3.1	3.0	2.7	5.0	3.3	3.1	1.9	1.5	1.6	1.7	1.3
Interest Paid 13	2.7	4.5	1.9	0.5	1.7	5.2	1.4	0.9	2.6	0.6	2.3	2.9	2.9
Depreciation 14	5.2	1.7	0.9	1.1	4.5	8.7	5.0	4.3	5.2	2.4	6.7	6.0	5.3
Amortization and Depletion 15	1.7	1.2	2.3	0.2	1.8	4.2	3.7	1.9	2.2	0.7	2.7	1.9	1.7
Pensions and Other Deferred Comp. 16	1.1	0.2	•	2.9	0.2	0.1	0.3	0.5	0.9	0.3	0.3	2.6	1.0
Employee Benefits 17	2.8	0.6	0.6	0.8	2.7	4.5	3.4	2.5	3.6	1.1	5.8	3.7	2.6
Advertising 18	1.3	0.2	0.2	1.6	0.5	1.9	0.9	0.7	0.7	0.4	0.4	0.9	1.6
Other Expenses 19	16.1	18.3	30.7	15.5	24.9	53.0	23.4	20.6	22.8	12.3	16.2	23.9	13.7
Officers' Compensation 20	0.7	2.0	8.1	9.4	5.4	7.0	4.3	2.8	2.6	0.9	0.8	0.8	0.3
Operating Margin 21	•	•	•	•	•	•	•	•	•	•	•	•	•
Operating Margin Before Officers' Comp. 22	•	•	•	3.6	•	•	•	•	•	•	•	•	•

Selected Average Balance Sheet ($ in Thousands)

Net Receivables 23	12152	0	21	88	484	1146	2284	6512	11463	31087	72398	190175	1628592
Inventories 24	4074	0	71	39	487	1212	2365	5313	8148	17940	12567	76277	442878
Net Property, Plant and Equipment 25	9739	0	9	322	246	1204	2232	5243	10354	10945	30641	185704	1292897
Total Assets 26	102540	0	246	659	1788	7239	15348	35551	65292	156131	336621	1536349	14973368
Notes and Loans Payable 27	17604	0	216	333	815	2188	4991	13371	11705	8849	37962	295408	2475221
All Other Liabilities 28	39558	0	150	174	1139	4807	3569	11964	21334	46798	126655	408237	6288662
Net Worth 29	45379	0	-120	152	-166	245	6787	10216	32252	100484	172004	832704	6209485

Selected Financial Ratios (Times to 1)

Current Ratio 30	1.6	•	0.7	1.6	0.9	1.1	2.0	2.0	2.1	2.5	1.9	2.0	1.5
Quick Ratio 31	1.0	•	0.5	1.4	0.7	1.4	1.3	1.4	1.6	1.5	•	1.2	0.9
Net Sales to Working Capital 32	3.3	•	•	5.6	23.1	2.7	2.8	2.5	3.4	2.1	2.1	•	3.6
Coverage Ratio 33	•	•	•	•	•	•	•	•	•	•	•	•	•
Total Asset Turnover 34	0.5	2.1	2.1	1.0	0.9	1.0	1.0	1.0	0.8	1.3	0.6	0.4	0.5
Inventory Turnover 35	8.5	•	4.1	9.4	4.5	3.6	3.8	3.6	3.5	8.7	9.1	5.3	10.6
Receivables Turnover 36	4.1	•	21.0	7.7	7.5	5.0	6.3	5.5	3.7	6.4	3.1	4.4	3.8
Total Liabilities to Net Worth 37	1.3	•	•	3.3	28.6	1.3	2.5	1.0	0.6	1.0	0.8	•	1.4
Current Assets to Working Capital 38	2.5	•	•	2.6	18.1	2.0	2.0	1.9	1.7	2.1	2.0	•	2.9
Current Liabilities to Working Capital 39	1.5	•	•	1.6	17.1	1.0	1.0	0.9	0.7	1.1	1.0	•	1.9
Working Capital to Net Sales 40	0.3	•	•	0.2	0.0	0.4	0.4	0.4	0.3	0.5	0.5	0.2	0.3
Inventory to Working Capital 41	0.2	•	•	0.3	3.9	0.4	0.3	0.3	0.1	0.2	0.2	•	•
Total Receipts to Cash Flow 42	76.3	8.7	12.0	8.0	•	•	•	26.9	11.4	74.6	19.2	21.9	133.7
Cost of Goods to Cash Flow 43	51.6	6.6	6.3	4.5	•	•	•	14.3	6.3	58.4	11.3	13.1	93.2
Cash Flow to Total Debt 44	0.0	•	0.1	0.2	0.1	0.1	0.1	0.1	0.1	0.0	0.1	0.0	0.0

Selected Financial Factors (in Percentages)

Debt Ratio 45	55.7	•	148.8	76.9	109.3	96.6	55.8	71.3	50.6	35.6	48.9	45.8	58.5
Return on Total Assets 46	•	•	•	•	•	•	•	•	•	•	•	•	•
Return on Equity Before Income Taxes 47	•	•	57.6	•	593.5	•	•	•	•	•	•	•	•
Return on Equity After Income Taxes 48	•	•	57.6	•	610.2	•	•	•	•	•	•	•	•
Profit Margin (Before Income Tax) 49	•	•	•	•	•	•	•	•	•	•	•	•	•
Profit Margin (After Income Tax) 50	•	•	•	•	•	•	•	•	•	•	•	•	•

Table II
Corporations with Net Income

COMMUNICATIONS EQUIPMENT

MONEY AMOUNTS AND SIZE OF ASSETS IN THOUSANDS OF DOLLARS

Item Description for Accounting Period 7/03 Through 6/04	Total	Zero Assets	Under 500	500 to 1,000	1,000 to 5,000	5,000 to 10,000	10,000 to 25,000	25,000 to 50,000	50,000 to 100,000	100,000 to 250,000	250,000 to 500,000	500,000 to 2,500,000	2,500,000 and over
Number of Enterprises **1**	549	3	104	178	172	6	33	12	8	12	6	11	3
Revenues ($ in Thousands)													
Net Sales **2**	43329237	1004206	138753	285946	536448	103070	895742	653480	659783	4216339	1807672	10694049	22333749
Interest **3**	720341	4099	22	292	272	4	1212	894	1624	9652	8766	90169	603335
Rents **4**	376055	1790	0	0	0	0	12	86	0	633	4278	369166	
Royalties **5**	149048	89	0	0	0	0	27	0	13432	3533	2618	118357	10991
Other Portfolio Income **6**	581591	90901	0	0	0	2	1094	631	86624	25022	13604	323704	40008
Other Receipts **7**	1193785	11830	-1	0	54368	184	9560	2542	-812	2481	27970	40716	1044951
Total Receipts **8**	46350057	1112915	138774	286238	591088	103260	907647	657633	760651	4257660	1860719	11271273	24402200
Average Total Receipts **9**	84426	370972	1334	1608	3437	17210	27504	54803	95081	354805	310120	1024661	8134067
Operating Costs/Operating Income (%)													
Cost of Operations **10**	65.9	76.1	29.2	34.6	51.7	54.7	60.3	48.8	45.6	82.7	53.8	60.4	68.2
Salaries and Wages **11**	18.9	7.7	4.6	7.5	16.1	10.7	10.9	16.3	21.5	5.8	12.4	10.0	27.4
Taxes Paid **12**	1.2	1.0	4.3	1.9	2.8	1.9	1.9	2.5	1.1	1.0	1.3	1.4	1.1
Interest Paid **13**	1.5	4.6	•	0.2	1.0	0.1	0.3	0.3	2.7	0.4	2.4	1.3	1.7
Depreciation **14**	4.4	1.6	0.6	0.7	2.5	1.4	1.7	2.9	3.3	1.3	6.9	3.5	5.7
Amortization and Depletion **15**	0.6	0.5	•	•	0.2	0.0	0.1	1.0	0.5	0.3	1.6	0.8	0.5
Pensions and Other Deferred Comp. **16**	1.1	0.2	2.7	•	0.4	0.1	0.4	0.6	1.2	0.2	0.1	3.2	0.5
Employee Benefits **17**	1.6	0.4	•	0.0	0.9	1.5	2.5	1.8	4.1	0.5	7.2	4.2	0.2
Advertising **18**	1.7	0.1	•	0.9	0.5	0.2	0.8	0.7	0.9	0.3	0.4	1.1	2.6
Other Expenses **19**	4.8	15.8	41.8	7.1	17.6	6.5	9.8	11.4	17.8	6.1	11.8	11.3	•
Officers' Compensation **20**	0.7	1.5	12.4	6.1	6.6	3.6	3.2	2.2	2.6	0.4	0.7	0.8	0.1
Operating Margin **21**	•	•	7.1	38.3	•	19.4	8.0	11.5	•	0.9	1.3	2.1	•
Operating Margin Before Officers' Comp. **22**	•	•	19.5	44.4	6.4	22.9	11.2	13.6	1.4	1.3	2.0	2.9	•

Selected Average Balance Sheet ($ in Thousands)

Net Receivables 23	14428	0	84	122	421	2518	3619	7874	11686	42828	68883	282410	1153943
Inventories 24	6730	0	102	88	578	4152	3264	4278	8303	28816	16672	120168	533692
Net Property, Plant and Equipment 25	10656	0	12	75	63	747	1827	8367	9329	12070	44931	109414	1322335
Total Assets 26	111894	0	416	543	1696	7640	13746	38232	67656	162056	354211	1378611	13421319
Notes and Loans Payable 27	8963	0	159	1010	145	2626	1580	22911	9201	38092	122357	914580	
All Other Liabilities 28	30961	0	45	114	365	1971	3654	11517	20205	51535	174666	389180	3510103
Net Worth 29	71970	0	372	269	321	5524	7467	25135	24540	101320	141452	867074	8996636

Selected Financial Ratios (Times to 1)

Current Ratio 30	1.7	•	8.8	2.9	1.1	3.2	2.3	2.3	2.2	1.9	1.4	3.2	1.2
Quick Ratio 31	1.1	•	5.4	2.5	0.5	2.0	1.3	1.6	1.6	1.2	1.0	2.1	0.8
Net Sales to Working Capital 32	4.5	•	3.8	5.3	27.8	4.1	4.4	4.0	3.8	7.2	5.7	1.9	9.8
Coverage Ratio 33	4.0	1.3	•	164.4	10.6	297.4	28.5	35.6	7.3	5.7	2.8	6.8	2.4
Total Asset Turnover 34	0.7	•	3.2	3.0	1.8	2.2	2.0	1.4	1.2	2.2	0.9	0.7	0.6
Inventory Turnover 35	7.7	•	3.8	6.3	2.8	2.3	5.0	6.2	4.5	10.1	9.7	4.9	9.5
Receivables Turnover 36	5.6	•	25.9	16.2	7.2	4.3	7.9	9.4	5.9	7.4	8.7	3.9	5.9
Total Liabilities to Net Worth 37	0.6	•	0.1	1.0	4.3	0.4	0.8	0.5	1.8	0.6	1.5	0.6	0.5
Current Assets to Working Capital 38	2.5	•	1.1	1.5	12.6	1.5	1.8	1.8	1.9	2.1	3.4	1.4	5.4
Current Liabilities to Working Capital 39	1.5	•	0.1	0.5	11.6	0.5	0.8	0.8	0.9	1.1	2.4	0.4	4.4
Working Capital to Net Sales 40	0.2	•	0.3	0.2	0.0	0.2	0.2	0.3	0.3	0.1	0.2	0.5	0.1
Inventory to Working Capital 41	0.3	•	0.4	0.2	6.0	0.4	0.6	0.4	0.3	0.6	0.3	0.2	0.5
Total Receipts to Cash Flow 42	16.3	6.5	2.2	2.3	4.2	4.0	5.7	4.8	3.4	15.2	7.6	6.7	0.5
Cost of Goods to Cash Flow 43	10.8	4.9	0.6	0.8	2.2	2.2	3.5	2.3	1.5	12.5	4.1	4.0	•
Cash Flow to Total Debt 44	0.1	•	13.7	2.6	0.5	2.0	0.8	0.9	0.6	0.4	0.2	0.3	•

Selected Financial Factors (in Percentages)

Debt Ratio 45	35.7	•	10.7	50.4	81.1	27.7	45.7	34.3	63.7	37.5	60.1	37.1	33.0
Return on Total Assets 46	4.3	•	22.9	114.4	20.1	44.1	19.1	17.7	23.6	5.0	5.7	6.3	2.3
Return on Equity Before Income Taxes 47	5.0	•	25.6	229.2	96.4	60.8	33.9	26.1	56.2	6.6	9.1	8.6	1.9
Return on Equity After Income Taxes 48	3.8	•	25.6	229.2	73.9	60.7	30.4	19.0	39.7	4.7	8.8	5.8	1.5
Profit Margin (Before Income Tax) 49	4.6	1.2	7.1	38.4	9.9	19.6	9.3	12.0	16.7	1.9	4.3	7.6	2.4
Profit Margin (After Income Tax) 50	3.4	1.2	7.1	38.4	7.6	19.5	8.4	8.8	11.8	1.4	4.1	5.2	1.8

Table I

Corporations with and without Net Income

AUDIO AND VIDEO EQUIP., REPRODUCING MAGNETIC & OPTICAL MEDIA

MONEY AMOUNTS AND SIZE OF ASSETS IN THOUSANDS OF DOLLARS

Item Description for Accounting Period 7/03 Through 6/04	Total	Zero Assets	Under 500	500 to 1,000	1,000 to 5,000	5,000 to 10,000	10,000 to 25,000	25,000 to 50,000	50,000 to 100,000	100,000 to 250,000	250,000 to 500,000	500,000 to 2,500,000	2,500,000 and over
Number of Enterprises 1	1026	5	315	86	426	67	46	32	16	19	5	9	•
Revenues ($ in Thousands)													
Net Sales 2	20091866	46630	172624	41496	1730860	669846	1021779	1174196	1331085	2781480	963272	10158598	•
Interest 3	256787	5	7	354	1249	1361	1580	6152	2163	17496	6757	219663	•
Rents 4	12516	81	0	625	0	939	828	62	5761	2	324	3894	•
Royalties 5	321408	0	0	494	0	96	75	6240	2165	2187	0	310152	•
Other Portfolio Income 6	162634	0	0	177	26	2926	5105	11580	8906	34140	786	98988	•
Other Receipts 7	546383	69	1421	457	19363	1208	6368	28943	11440	17958	109841	349314	•
Total Receipts 8	21391594	46785	174052	43603	1751498	676376	1035735	1227173	1361520	2853263	1080980	11140609	•
Average Total Receipts 9	20850	9357	553	507	4111	10095	22516	38349	85095	150172	216196	1237845	•
Operating Costs/Operating Income (%)													
Cost of Operations 10	62.3	36.0	18.9	57.3	46.4	67.0	60.1	59.9	72.0	64.2	43.1	66.1	•
Salaries and Wages 11	13.7	28.0	8.9	22.8	22.9	15.3	13.1	19.4	12.3	11.3	28.3	10.9	•
Taxes Paid 12	1.8	2.9	2.7	4.1	3.2	2.9	1.8	2.2	1.4	1.7	2.7	1.4	•
Interest Paid 13	2.1	1.8	2.2	0.7	0.3	0.9	1.7	3.2	1.1	2.0	2.0	2.5	•
Depreciation 14	4.0	2.9	6.2	8.7	1.6	2.5	3.6	6.3	5.3	4.1	7.4	3.8	•
Amortization and Depletion 15	1.4	1.5	0.1	•	0.3	2.0	1.0	2.4	0.9	0.9	3.9	1.4	•
Pensions and Other Deferred Comp. 16	0.5	0.0	0.1	2.1	0.1	0.3	0.3	0.2	0.5	0.6	0.5	0.6	•
Employee Benefits 17	2.2	1.6	1.2	3.1	2.3	1.9	2.1	4.3	1.4	1.4	3.2	2.2	•
Advertising 18	1.9	1.9	1.0	0.4	3.0	0.4	2.2	1.4	1.5	1.4	0.6	2.2	•
Other Expenses 19	17.8	33.1	45.4	26.3	19.7	21.2	16.6	24.1	17.6	13.5	17.8	17.2	•
Officers' Compensation 20	1.6	0.4	11.4	18.2	6.1	3.8	2.5	2.3	0.9	2.0	1.3	0.3	•
Operating Margin 21	•	1.9	•	•	•	•	•	•	•	•	•	•	•
Operating Margin Before Officers' Comp. 22	•	13.3	0.2	•	0.2	•	•	•	•	•	•	•	•

Selected Average Balance Sheet ($ in Thousands)

Net Receivables 23	3508	0	29	105	574	1875	3476	7041	13725	25786	53631	205310
Inventories 24	2332	0	78	180	332	1465	2468	5723	12277	18132	31994	123907
Net Property, Plant and Equipment 25	2887	0	84	2	151	822	2939	8054	7798	22488	35868	187947
Total Assets 26	21796	0	287	669	1869	7090	15578	35801	66029	162235	308009	1489119
Notes and Loans Payable 27	4379	0	154	38	415	957	5056	7750	22729	33919	41792	278076
All Other Liabilities 28	8701	0	32	375	703	2756	6053	19960	30378	50187	103085	614316
Net Worth 29	8715	0	101	255	751	3378	4469	8091	12922	78129	163132	596727

Selected Financial Ratios (Times to 1)

Current Ratio 30	1.3	•	1.7	1.0	2.0	1.9	1.5	1.4	1.8	1.9	1.6	1.1
Quick Ratio 31	0.8	•	0.8	0.8	1.3	1.4	1.0	0.9	1.0	1.3	1.1	0.5
Net Sales to Working Capital 32	7.2	•	7.5	•	5.2	3.5	6.9	6.1	4.3	3.5	4.1	17.5
Coverage Ratio 33	•	•	2.3	•	•	•	•	•	•	0.8	1.7	1.5
Total Asset Turnover 34	0.9	•	1.9	0.7	2.2	1.4	1.4	1.0	1.3	0.9	0.6	0.8
Inventory Turnover 35	5.2	•	1.3	1.5	5.7	4.6	5.4	3.8	4.9	5.2	2.6	6.0
Receivables Turnover 36	5.0	•	8.8	0.7	8.8	6.1	6.5	4.3	5.2	6.2	3.3	4.6
Total Liabilities to Net Worth 37	1.5	•	1.8	1.6	1.5	1.1	2.5	3.4	4.1	1.1	0.9	1.5
Current Assets to Working Capital 38	4.0	•	2.5	•	2.0	2.1	3.0	3.8	2.2	2.2	2.7	10.0
Current Liabilities to Working Capital 39	3.0	•	1.5	•	1.0	1.1	2.0	2.8	1.2	1.2	1.7	9.0
Working Capital to Net Sales 40	0.1	•	0.1	•	0.2	0.3	0.1	0.2	0.2	0.3	0.2	0.1
Inventory to Working Capital 41	0.8	•	1.1	•	0.4	0.4	0.8	0.9	0.6	0.5	0.6	1.8
Total Receipts to Cash Flow 42	8.3	•	2.7	•	9.1	303.5	10.2	•	47.1	9.8	6.2	6.3
Cost of Goods to Cash Flow 43	5.2	4.7	0.5	•	4.2	203.3	6.1	•	33.9	6.3	2.7	4.1
Cash Flow to Total Debt 44	0.2	1.7	1.1	•	0.4	0.0	0.2	•	0.0	0.2	0.2	0.2

Selected Financial Factors (in Percentages)

Debt Ratio 45	60.0	•	64.8	61.8	59.8	52.4	71.3	77.4	80.4	51.8	47.0	59.9
Return on Total Assets 46	•	•	9.5	•	•	•	•	•	•	1.4	2.1	2.8
Return on Equity Before Income Taxes 47	•	•	15.1	•	•	•	•	•	•	•	1.6	2.4
Return on Equity After Income Taxes 48	•	•	7.7	•	•	•	•	•	•	•	•	•
Profit Margin (Before Income Tax) 49	•	•	2.8	•	•	•	•	•	•	•	1.4	1.3
Profit Margin (After Income Tax) 50	•	•	1.4	•	•	•	•	•	•	•	1.3	•

Table II
Corporations with Net Income

AUDIO AND VIDEO EQUIP., REPRODUCING MAGNETIC & OPTICAL MEDIA

MONEY AMOUNTS AND SIZE OF ASSETS IN THOUSANDS OF DOLLARS

Item Description for Accounting Period 7/03 Through 6/04	Total	Zero Assets	Under 500	500 to 1,000	1,000 to 5,000	5,000 to 10,000	10,000 to 25,000	25,000 to 50,000	50,000 to 100,000	100,000 to 250,000	250,000 to 500,000	500,000 to 2,500,000	2,500,000 and over
Number of Enterprises 1	516	•	•	66	157	26	23	12	5	12	•	5	•
Revenues ($ in Thousands)													
Net Sales 2	10478580	•	•	39653	819730	404133	669106	613180	298680	2317901	•	5227679	•
Interest 3	203134	•	•	151	832	411	252	885	644	11693	•	188259	•
Rents 4	5797	•	•	625	0	939	198	62	49	0	•	3843	•
Royalties 5	22597	•	•	0	0	0	69	1097	1551	387	•	19493	•
Other Portfolio Income 6	49152	•	•	177	0	0	1424	329	1224	28901	•	17098	•
Other Receipts 7	330040	•	•	232	9884	82	2684	20257	5859	17240	•	273228	•
Total Receipts 8	11089300	•	•	40838	830446	405565	673733	635810	308007	2376122	•	5729600	•
Average Total Receipts 9	21491	•	•	619	5289	15599	29293	52984	61601	198010	•	1145920	•
Operating Costs/Operating Income (%)													
Cost of Operations 10	61.9	•	•	44.7	58.2	71.8	59.4	51.7	42.5	60.5	•	65.4	•
Salaries and Wages 11	9.2	•	•	9.9	6.1	6.6	10.1	11.2	17.1	11.9	•	8.0	•
Taxes Paid 12	1.2	•	•	2.5	1.9	2.7	1.4	1.6	2.6	1.6	•	0.7	•
Interest Paid 13	2.3	•	•	0.2	0.2	0.1	0.7	1.2	1.4	0.7	•	4.0	•
Depreciation 14	3.1	•	•	8.1	0.7	1.0	2.2	3.9	2.3	4.4	•	3.2	•
Amortization and Depletion 15	0.3	•	•	•	0.0	0.0	1.0	0.4	1.7	0.4	•	0.2	•
Pensions and Other Deferred Comp. 16	0.6	•	•	2.2	0.2	0.4	0.2	0.4	1.0	0.8	•	0.7	•
Employee Benefits 17	1.9	•	•	2.4	1.2	2.0	1.4	5.0	2.1	1.0	•	2.1	•
Advertising 18	2.4	•	•	0.4	0.8	0.2	2.7	1.6	1.3	1.2	•	3.5	•
Other Expenses 19	12.8	•	•	9.1	10.5	6.4	13.2	14.4	13.5	10.4	•	14.2	•
Officers' Compensation 20	1.7	•	•	15.3	6.8	4.6	1.8	2.1	2.0	2.0	•	0.3	•
Operating Margin 21	2.5	•	•	5.3	13.4	4.4	5.7	6.5	12.5	5.2	•	•	•
Operating Margin Before Officers' Comp. 22	4.2	•	•	20.5	20.2	9.0	7.6	8.6	14.6	7.2	•	•	•

Selected Average Balance Sheet ($ in Thousands)

Net Receivables 23	3302	8	699	2637	4306	7541	9042	29727	184888
Inventories 24	2301	50	488	2437	2794	9110	8972	24992	99154
Net Property, Plant and Equipment 25	2980	1	64	611	2089	8450	4400	30872	193881
Total Assets 26	20036	694	1528	6962	15190	38825	64548	181152	1301201
Notes and Loans Payable 27	4539	22	357	291	2694	7887	11353	27725	345371
All Other Liabilities 28	5735	82	835	3106	4304	7553	10394	67689	335908
Net Worth 29	9762	590	336	3565	8192	23385	42801	85738	619922

Selected Financial Ratios (Times to 1)

Current Ratio 30	1.9	4.2	1.3	2.0	2.0	2.3	4.8	2.1	1.7
Quick Ratio 31	1.1	3.5	0.8	1.5	1.2	1.4	3.4	1.4	0.8
Net Sales to Working Capital 32	4.1	2.3	20.8	5.0	5.9	3.7	1.8	3.1	4.4
Coverage Ratio 33	4.6	47.1	94.2	79.9	10.0	9.8	12.4	12.1	2.8
Total Asset Turnover 34	1.0	0.9	3.4	2.2	1.9	1.3	0.9	1.1	0.8
Inventory Turnover 35	5.5	5.4	6.2	4.6	6.2	2.9	2.8	4.7	6.9
Receivables Turnover 36	6.1	143.9	8.6	5.7	7.5	4.9	3.8	7.1	6.0
Total Liabilities to Net Worth 37	1.1	0.2	3.5	1.0	0.9	0.7	0.5	1.1	1.1
Current Assets to Working Capital 38	2.1	1.3	4.8	2.0	2.0	1.8	1.3	1.9	2.3
Current Liabilities to Working Capital 39	1.1	0.3	3.8	1.0	1.0	0.8	0.3	0.9	1.3
Working Capital to Net Sales 40	0.2	0.4	0.0	0.2	0.2	0.3	0.6	0.3	0.2
Inventory to Working Capital 41	0.5	0.2	1.4	0.4	0.7	0.6	0.2	0.5	0.5
Total Receipts to Cash Flow 42	5.2	7.7	4.4	10.1	5.7	4.4	3.7	6.6	4.9
Cost of Goods to Cash Flow 43	3.2	3.4	2.6	7.2	3.4	2.3	1.6	4.0	3.2
Cash Flow to Total Debt 44	0.4	0.8	1.0	0.5	0.7	0.8	0.7	0.3	0.3

Selected Financial Factors (in Percentages)

Debt Ratio 45	51.3	14.9	78.0	48.8	46.1	39.8	33.7	52.7	52.4
Return on Total Assets 46	10.8	7.3	50.8	10.7	13.8	14.9	15.8	9.0	9.2
Return on Equity Before Income Taxes 47	17.4	8.4	228.3	20.7	23.0	22.2	21.9	17.4	12.5
Return on Equity After Income Taxes 48	13.3	7.1	226.2	15.3	19.8	19.9	19.8	12.4	8.3
Profit Margin (Before Income Tax) 49	8.4	8.3	14.7	4.7	6.5	10.2	15.7	7.7	7.4
Profit Margin (After Income Tax) 50	6.4	7.0	14.6	3.5	5.6	9.1	14.2	5.5	4.9

Table I

Corporations with and without Net Income

SEMICONDUCTOR AND OTHER ELECTRONIC COMPONENT

MONEY AMOUNTS AND SIZE OF ASSETS IN THOUSANDS OF DOLLARS

Item Description for Accounting Period 7/03 Through 6/04	Total	Zero Assets	Under 500	500 to 1,000	1,000 to 5,000	5,000 to 10,000	10,000 to 25,000	25,000 to 50,000	50,000 to 100,000	100,000 to 250,000	250,000 to 500,000	500,000 to 2,500,000	2,500,000 and over
Number of Enterprises 1	6047	369	3063	247	1537	358	206	56	48	56	37	51	19
Revenues ($ in Thousands)													
Net Sales 2	144646671	2228166	1591941	342580	6424913	3992674	3666363	1726416	3428386	8443013	9366899	30346251	73089068
Interest 3	2154894	30554	442	624	3098	5608	9591	9397	12506	46195	72234	537471	1427173
Rents 4	87478	339	0	0	1299	1637	2441	4246	1262	1999	15350	19656	39248
Royalties 5	2925056	8578	0	0	73	638	3011	874	26794	49576	199618	502432	2133461
Other Portfolio Income 6	1269838	66146	11496	4833	6240	3159	65120	13943	11711	11617	89971	404647	580959
Other Receipts 7	1468092	30997	2163	2498	39388	30474	74469	16249	21748	137277	157263	700506	255059
Total Receipts 8	152552029	2364780	1606042	350535	6475011	4034190	3820995	1771125	3502407	8689677	9901335	32510963	77524968
Average Total Receipts 9	25228	6409	524	1419	4213	11269	18549	31627	72967	155173	267604	637470	4080261
Operating Costs/Operating Income (%)													
Cost of Operations 10	72.5	76.2	61.4	43.1	61.0	66.3	67.0	67.6	74.7	70.5	73.6	68.7	76.0
Salaries and Wages 11	11.5	6.2	8.6	19.3	14.5	11.6	14.9	15.2	10.9	12.6	13.0	17.6	8.3
Taxes Paid 12	1.4	1.2	2.5	3.4	3.7	3.1	2.5	2.2	1.7	1.7	1.6	1.6	0.8
Interest Paid 13	3.1	2.7	1.2	0.5	1.0	1.0	1.2	2.0	0.8	1.1	1.7	3.0	4.2
Depreciation 14	5.5	7.7	1.0	2.4	4.8	3.7	4.5	5.4	4.5	4.5	4.8	6.5	5.7
Amortization and Depletion 15	1.0	2.6	0.2	1.1	0.3	0.3	0.8	0.2	0.9	0.9	1.1	1.5	0.8
Pensions and Other Deferred Comp. 16	0.5	0.2	0.2	1.6	0.4	0.8	0.4	0.3	0.5	0.4	0.3	0.6	0.6
Employee Benefits 17	2.0	3.5	0.7	0.5	1.8	1.3	2.0	2.3	1.3	1.8	1.6	1.9	2.1
Advertising 18	0.7	0.2	2.9	0.0	0.5	0.7	0.6	0.7	0.5	0.7	0.5	0.5	0.8
Other Expenses 19	13.3	11.8	17.2	43.1	13.7	14.4	13.1	17.1	29.4	12.9	11.8	16.1	11.2
Officers' Compensation 20	1.2	1.5	6.6	12.6	4.6	4.2	3.4	2.4	1.7	1.4	1.3	1.2	0.4
Operating Margin 21	•	•	•	•	•	•	•	•	•	•	•	•	•
Operating Margin Before Officers' Comp. 22	•	4.2	•	•	•	•	•	•	•	•	•	•	•

Selected Average Balance Sheet ($ in Thousands)

Net Receivables 23	6070	0	52	184	561	1607	2787	5456	16116	26613	49546	182287	1094065
Inventories 24	3065	0	34	130	465	1939	2572	5134	9958	21116	31817	62441	534245
Net Property, Plant and Equipment 25	5329	0	9	47	701	1507	3312	6118	13443	31550	39304	166567	904311
Total Assets 26	42966	0	137	686	2363	7274	15390	33598	71727	169245	344804	1207432	8457042
Notes and Loans Payable 27	8281	0	48	186	961	2167	3586	8857	13760	26991	28589	256311	1584003
All Other Liabilities 28	11655	0	66	189	507	1760	5332	8076	22559	38702	100738	327959	2293017
Net Worth 29	23030	0	23	311	895	3347	6472	16665	35409	103552	215477	623162	4580022

Selected Financial Ratios (Times to 1)

Current Ratio 30	1.7	·	1.4	2.3	1.9	2.1	1.6	2.1	2.0	2.5	2.4	2.0	1.4
Quick Ratio 31	1.1	·	1.0	1.8	1.1	1.2	1.1	1.3	1.3	1.6	1.5	1.5	0.9
Net Sales to Working Capital 32	3.4	·	15.3	4.5	5.9	4.3	4.8	3.0	3.1	2.7	2.2	2.0	4.8
Coverage Ratio 33	·	·	·	·	·	·	·	·	·	·	·	·	0.1
Total Asset Turnover 34	0.6	·	3.8	2.0	1.8	1.5	1.2	0.9	1.0	0.9	0.7	0.5	0.5
Inventory Turnover 35	5.7	·	9.5	4.6	5.5	3.8	4.6	4.1	5.4	5.0	5.9	6.5	5.5
Receivables Turnover 36	4.2	·	9.0	8.4	8.4	6.2	6.8	6.0	4.5	5.6	4.7	3.4	3.8
Total Liabilities to Net Worth 37	0.9	·	5.0	1.2	1.6	1.2	1.4	1.0	1.0	0.6	0.6	0.9	0.8
Current Assets to Working Capital 38	2.4	·	3.4	1.8	2.1	1.9	2.7	1.9	2.0	1.7	1.7	2.0	3.2
Current Liabilities to Working Capital 39	1.4	·	2.4	0.8	1.1	0.9	1.7	0.9	1.0	0.7	0.7	1.0	2.2
Working Capital to Net Sales 40	0.3	·	0.1	0.2	0.2	0.2	0.2	0.3	0.3	0.4	0.4	0.5	0.2
Inventory to Working Capital 41	0.4	·	0.9	0.4	0.8	0.6	0.7	0.5	0.4	0.4	0.3	0.2	0.6
Total Receipts to Cash Flow 42	41.6	·	10.5	·	27.0	25.7	37.0	432.7	·	21.7	30.6	·	25.3
Cost of Goods to Cash Flow 43	30.1	·	6.4	·	16.5	17.0	24.8	292.3	·	15.3	22.6	·	19.2
Cash Flow to Total Debt 44	0.0	·	0.4	·	0.1	0.1	0.1	0.0	·	0.1	0.1	·	0.0

Selected Financial Factors (in Percentages)

Debt Ratio 45	46.4	·	83.3	54.6	62.1	54.0	57.9	50.4	50.6	38.8	37.5	48.4	45.8
Return on Total Assets 46	·	·	·	·	·	·	·	·	·	·	·	·	0.2
Return on Equity Before Income Taxes 47	·	·	·	·	·	·	·	·	·	·	·	·	·
Return on Equity After Income Taxes 48	·	·	·	·	·	·	·	·	·	·	·	·	·
Profit Margin (Before Income Tax) 49	·	·	·	·	·	·	·	·	·	·	·	·	·
Profit Margin (After Income Tax) 50	·	·	·	·	·	·	·	·	·	·	·	·	·

143

Table II
Corporations with Net Income

SEMICONDUCTOR AND OTHER ELECTRONIC COMPONENT

MONEY AMOUNTS AND SIZE OF ASSETS IN THOUSANDS OF DOLLARS

Item Description for Accounting Period 7/03 Through 6/04		Total	Zero Assets	Under 500	500 to 1,000	1,000 to 5,000	5,000 to 10,000	10,000 to 25,000	25,000 to 50,000	50,000 to 100,000	100,000 to 250,000	250,000 to 500,000	500,000 to 2,500,000	2,500,000 and over
Number of Enterprises	1	3233	39	1729	200	914	152	106	21	17	23	11	14	7
Revenues ($ in Thousands)														
Net Sales	2	54024452	1531704	1436550	339781	4877577	1636594	2526563	825792	1653295	4220682	3663777	10437318	20874819
Interest	3	531561	1395	420	385	695	2766	3306	2575	2750	16239	18907	137252	344870
Rents	4	48234	137	0	0	308	1522	1653	3572	200	1418	6067	4436	28920
Royalties	5	2318903	642	0	0	0	0	1979	113	26674	11457	147371	147971	2012694
Other Portfolio Income	6	621119	3451	11496	0	2129	147	43510	9161	851	7201	29554	229810	283811
Other Receipts	7	648415	26345	2136	56	17351	2790	41592	3851	1387	89340	9058	383157	71352
Total Receipts	8	58192684	1563674	1450602	340222	4898060	1643819	2618603	845064	1685157	4346337	3844734	11339944	23616466
Average Total Receipts	9	18000	40094	839	1701	5359	10815	24704	40241	99127	188971	349521	809996	3373781
Operating Costs/Operating Income (%)														
Cost of Operations	10	64.3	76.6	61.3	43.0	56.8	57.9	64.1	66.1	70.2	61.9	73.8	59.1	67.1
Salaries and Wages	11	13.7	2.9	7.1	14.7	12.3	9.6	10.9	10.1	7.6	10.9	11.1	19.6	14.6
Taxes Paid	12	1.9	0.6	2.3	3.0	3.8	1.8	2.2	2.1	1.4	1.5	1.4	1.7	1.7
Interest Paid	13	1.1	0.4	1.2	0.2	0.6	0.5	0.9	0.6	0.4	0.8	0.2	1.5	1.3
Depreciation	14	5.3	7.5	0.3	0.9	3.4	2.6	3.0	3.3	2.7	2.9	3.1	5.5	7.4
Amortization and Depletion	15	0.8	0.4	0.0	0.1	0.2	0.2	0.2	0.4	0.5	0.4	0.3	0.8	1.4
Pensions and Other Deferred Comp.	16	0.9	0.1	0.2	1.6	0.3	1.3	0.5	0.3	0.8	0.6	0.3	1.0	1.4
Employee Benefits	17	2.6	2.5	0.6	0.2	1.8	0.5	1.6	2.3	1.1	1.8	0.8	1.4	4.4
Advertising	18	0.7	0.2	3.1	0.0	0.5	1.3	0.6	0.5	0.4	0.7	0.5	0.8	0.6
Other Expenses	19	8.3	4.7	13.8	22.4	10.1	12.5	8.6	8.4	8.7	12.0	6.5	7.3	7.2
Officers' Compensation	20	1.9	0.2	6.5	11.9	4.8	4.6	3.0	1.8	1.7	1.6	1.6	1.3	1.0
Operating Margin	21	•	3.8	3.7	2.0	5.4	7.2	4.5	4.2	4.5	4.9	0.6	•	•
Operating Margin Before Officers' Comp.	22	0.5	4.1	10.2	13.9	10.2	11.8	7.5	6.0	6.2	6.5	2.2	1.3	•

Selected Average Balance Sheet ($ in Thousands)

Net Receivables 23	4063	0	92	223	692	1666	3603	6682	21636	33674	48991	252483	900795
Inventories 24	1236	0	46	102	460	1997	3100	5122	12401	23700	24000	50247	144686
Net Property, Plant and Equipment 25	3484	0	10	51	663	981	3124	4384	10504	27963	27566	221055	834008
Total Assets 26	23578	0	211	651	2271	7661	15491	31430	74978	169658	339349	1353504	6047238
Notes and Loans Payable 27	2016	0	28	159	752	758	3264	4220	6717	15302	12733	135932	384479
All Other Liabilities 28	6165	0	114	201	486	1340	3694	8091	18404	42973	86214	423906	1477592
Net Worth 29	15396	0	69	290	1033	5563	8533	19119	49857	111383	240403	793666	4191167

Selected Financial Ratios (Times to 1)

Current Ratio 30	2.4	•	1.6	2.3	1.9	3.9	2.1	2.5	2.7	2.7	2.7	2.6	2.3
Quick Ratio 31	1.5	•	1.1	1.6	1.1	2.0	1.3	1.6	1.9	1.8	1.8	2.0	1.3
Net Sales to Working Capital 32	2.3	•	11.5	6.2	7.8	2.6	4.4	3.0	2.9	2.7	2.2	1.6	1.9
Coverage Ratio 33	8.1	14.7	5.0	12.1	10.5	16.0	10.0	11.9	16.1	11.7	34.8	7.7	6.5
Total Asset Turnover 34	0.7	•	3.9	2.6	2.4	1.4	1.5	1.3	1.3	1.1	1.0	0.6	0.5
Inventory Turnover 35	8.7	•	11.2	7.2	6.6	3.1	4.9	5.1	5.5	4.8	10.2	8.8	13.8
Receivables Turnover 36	5.6	•	8.7	12.1	9.8	5.5	7.5	7.2	4.6	5.5	9.6	4.1	4.9
Total Liabilities to Net Worth 37	0.5	•	2.1	1.2	1.2	0.8	0.6	0.6	0.5	0.5	0.4	0.7	0.4
Current Assets to Working Capital 38	1.7	•	2.6	1.8	2.1	1.3	1.9	1.7	1.6	1.6	1.6	1.6	1.8
Current Liabilities to Working Capital 39	0.7	•	1.6	0.8	1.1	0.3	0.9	0.7	0.6	0.6	0.6	0.6	0.8
Working Capital to Net Sales 40	0.4	•	0.1	0.2	0.1	0.4	0.2	0.3	0.3	0.4	0.5	0.6	0.5
Inventory to Working Capital 41	0.2	•	0.7	0.5	0.8	0.4	0.6	0.4	0.4	0.3	0.2	0.1	0.1
Total Receipts to Cash Flow 42	8.3	10.6	8.0	6.3	8.3	5.9	7.1	8.5	7.4	5.6	9.7	7.3	10.4
Cost of Goods to Cash Flow 43	5.4	8.1	4.9	2.7	4.7	3.4	4.5	5.6	5.2	3.4	7.2	4.3	7.0
Cash Flow to Total Debt 44	0.2	•	0.7	0.5	0.9	0.5	0.4	0.4	0.5	0.6	0.3	0.2	0.2

Selected Financial Factors (in Percentages)

Debt Ratio 45	34.7	•	67.4	55.4	54.5	27.4	44.9	39.2	33.5	34.3	29.2	41.4	30.7
Return on Total Assets 46	6.1	•	22.8	5.9	15.0	11.4	13.9	8.7	9.0	9.8	5.9	6.3	4.3
Return on Equity Before Income Taxes 47	8.2	•	55.9	12.2	29.7	14.7	22.7	13.1	12.7	13.6	8.1	9.4	5.2
Return on Equity After Income Taxes 48	6.4	•	55.5	10.4	28.6	12.5	20.1	11.0	10.7	11.5	5.7	7.5	3.7
Profit Margin (Before Income Tax) 49	7.5	5.9	4.6	2.1	5.8	7.6	8.1	6.4	6.5	8.3	5.8	10.0	7.4
Profit Margin (After Income Tax) 50	5.9	4.3	4.6	1.8	5.5	6.5	7.2	5.4	5.5	7.0	4.1	7.9	5.2

Table I
Corporations with and without Net Income

NAVIGATIONAL, MEASURING, ELECTROMEDICAL, AND CONTROL

MONEY AMOUNTS AND SIZE OF ASSETS IN THOUSANDS OF DOLLARS

Item Description for Accounting Period 7/03 Through 6/04	Total	Zero Assets	Under 500	500 to 1,000	1,000 to 5,000	5,000 to 10,000	10,000 to 25,000	25,000 to 50,000	50,000 to 100,000	100,000 to 250,000	250,000 to 500,000	500,000 to 2,500,000	2,500,000 and over
Number of Enterprises 1	2810	31	1250	556	490	277	75	36	32	26	14	15	7
Revenues ($ in Thousands)													
Net Sales 2	47756815	187578	367280	850243	2361437	2819429	1461888	1544744	2336014	3181326	4281799	10899897	17465181
Interest 3	349196	2102	234	168	3271	6204	2585	1863	9421	26989	19525	118971	157862
Rents 4	51183	0	1917	265	19	2436	1026	1124	1349	827	2905	15200	24115
Royalties 5	640774	419	0	0	186	4575	2	2446	1109	11765	46325	187334	386614
Other Portfolio Income 6	574343	761	0	100	33444	105085	2196	6941	28343	19358	31211	215288	131619
Other Receipts 7	1254485	7087	0	2428	8843	11851	16049	12772	20783	20626	78649	446943	628451
Total Receipts 8	50626796	197947	369431	853204	2407200	2949580	1483746	1569890	2397019	3260891	4460414	11883633	18793842
Average Total Receipts 9	18017	6385	296	1535	4913	10648	19783	43608	74907	125419	318601	792242	2684835
Operating Costs/Operating Income (%)													
Cost of Operations 10	59.7	60.6	39.5	51.3	59.0	50.1	54.6	55.0	55.3	55.1	59.0	53.5	68.4
Salaries and Wages 11	16.5	17.4	11.9	10.4	14.1	16.9	15.5	14.5	15.1	16.6	16.5	18.0	16.6
Taxes Paid 12	2.4	2.5	3.6	3.2	3.3	3.0	2.5	2.3	2.0	3.1	2.4	2.2	2.1
Interest Paid 13	2.3	0.9	2.0	1.1	1.4	1.9	0.7	1.1	1.1	1.1	1.8	2.2	3.4
Depreciation 14	3.6	2.9	2.2	1.5	2.3	2.4	2.8	2.7	2.3	3.2	2.8	3.4	4.8
Amortization and Depletion 15	1.2	2.1	0.7	0.2	0.4	1.0	0.5	0.7	0.6	1.1	1.4	2.2	1.1
Pensions and Other Deferred Comp. 16	2.3	1.0	0.2	0.3	0.3	0.6	0.6	0.9	0.7	1.5	0.8	2.2	4.1
Employee Benefits 17	3.1	1.9	2.4	1.6	2.4	3.7	2.6	2.5	2.1	3.2	3.0	2.6	3.7
Advertising 18	0.9	1.3	0.1	0.8	0.8	2.0	1.3	1.3	2.6	1.8	0.9	0.5	0.7
Other Expenses 19	14.3	20.5	30.4	16.9	14.9	14.6	13.7	15.8	15.3	15.8	12.4	20.5	9.8
Officers' Compensation 20	2.1	5.2	20.5	10.6	4.9	6.2	3.1	2.0	2.7	2.1	0.9	1.8	0.5
Operating Margin 21	•	•	•	2.2	•	•	2.3	1.1	0.3	•	•	•	•
Operating Margin Before Officers' Comp. 22	•	•	7.1	12.8	1.0	3.7	5.4	3.1	2.9	•	•	•	•

Selected Average Balance Sheet ($ in Thousands)

Item													
Net Receivables 23	4037	0	25	146	1148	1680	3663	7359	14277	28787	85844	206869	593227
Inventories 24	2323	0	20	159	656	1385	3266	6210	11090	22972	32831	86354	361781
Net Property, Plant and Equipment 25	2801	0	11	73	419	1128	2725	6685	7185	24776	48208	151706	432801
Total Assets 26	26055	0	126	671	2760	7079	15217	36462	69902	163019	389138	1223498	5213010
Notes and Loans Payable 27	5576	0	76	286	986	1785	2462	7697	9924	18509	101574	319969	993527
All Other Liabilities 28	10325	0	39	141	957	1695	3728	10548	20259	28878	111110	268321	2901203
Net Worth 29	10155	0	12	243	817	3599	9026	18217	39720	115632	176455	645208	1318281

Selected Financial Ratios (Times to 1)

Item												
Current Ratio 30	0.9	0.8	3.4	2.4	2.3	2.4	1.6	2.5	3.1	1.5	1.7	0.4
Quick Ratio 31	0.6	0.7	2.0	1.5	1.3	1.5	0.9	1.7	2.0	1.1	1.2	0.2
Net Sales to Working Capital 32	•	•	4.1	3.8	3.8	3.3	5.9	2.7	1.9	4.8	3.5	•
Coverage Ratio 33	0.4	•	3.2	•	2.1	6.6	3.4	4.0	0.9	2.3	2.1	•
Total Asset Turnover 34	0.7	2.3	2.3	1.7	1.4	1.3	1.2	1.0	0.8	0.8	0.6	0.5
Inventory Turnover 35	4.4	5.9	4.9	4.3	3.7	3.3	3.8	3.6	2.9	5.5	4.5	4.7
Receivables Turnover 36	4.6	6.7	13.5	4.8	7.9	5.4	5.9	5.1	4.3	3.6	4.8	4.2
Total Liabilities to Net Worth 37	1.6	9.7	1.8	2.4	1.0	0.7	1.0	0.8	0.4	1.2	0.9	3.0
Current Assets to Working Capital 38	•	•	1.4	1.7	1.8	1.7	2.7	1.7	1.5	2.9	2.5	•
Current Liabilities to Working Capital 39	•	•	0.4	0.7	0.8	0.7	1.7	0.7	0.5	1.9	1.5	•
Working Capital to Net Sales 40	•	•	0.2	0.3	0.3	0.3	0.2	0.4	0.5	0.2	0.3	•
Inventory to Working Capital 41	•	0.5	0.5	0.6	0.7	0.5	0.9	0.4	0.4	0.5	0.5	•
Total Receipts to Cash Flow 42	11.6	9.4	6.7	11.6	7.3	6.6	6.1	6.7	9.2	8.3	5.9	•
Cost of Goods to Cash Flow 43	6.9	3.7	3.4	6.8	3.7	3.6	3.4	3.7	5.1	4.9	3.2	•
Cash Flow to Total Debt 44	0.1	0.3	0.5	0.2	0.4	0.5	0.4	0.4	0.3	0.2	0.2	•

Selected Financial Factors (in Percentages)

Item												
Debt Ratio 45	61.0	90.7	63.7	70.4	49.2	40.7	50.0	43.2	29.1	54.7	47.7	74.7
Return on Total Assets 46	0.6	•	8.4	•	5.8	5.9	4.5	4.8	0.7	3.4	2.7	•
Return on Equity Before Income Taxes 47	•	•	15.9	•	6.0	8.4	6.3	6.4	•	4.3	2.7	•
Return on Equity After Income Taxes 48	•	•	14.7	•	4.6	5.6	2.4	4.0	•	2.0	0.3	•
Profit Margin (Before Income Tax) 49	•	•	2.5	•	2.1	3.9	2.7	3.5	•	2.5	2.4	•
Profit Margin (After Income Tax) 50	•	•	2.3	•	1.6	2.6	1.0	2.2	•	1.2	0.2	•

Table II

Corporations with Net Income

NAVIGATIONAL, MEASURING, ELECTROMEDICAL, AND CONTROL

MONEY AMOUNTS AND SIZE OF ASSETS IN THOUSANDS OF DOLLARS

Item Description for Accounting Period 7/03 Through 6/04	Total	Zero Assets	Under 500	500 to 1,000	1,000 to 5,000	5,000 to 10,000	10,000 to 25,000	25,000 to 50,000	50,000 to 100,000	100,000 to 250,000	250,000 to 500,000	500,000 to 2,500,000	2,500,000 and over
Number of Enterprises **1**	1421	·	·	485	290	191	52	26	24	17	·	9	·
Revenues ($ in Thousands)													
Net Sales **2**	32378057	·	·	828239	1287137	2237981	1040311	1233059	1772281	2413325	·	8274185	·
Interest **3**	209903	·	·	115	2983	563	1706	846	7771	14262	·	83179	·
Rents **4**	32329	·	·	0	0	2219	615	1124	987	685	·	15200	·
Royalties **5**	270966	·	·	0	0	0	2	115	1109	7219	·	186985	·
Other Portfolio Income **6**	423339	·	·	100	32055	13824	2048	3186	26209	17321	·	210697	·
Other Receipts **7**	655791	·	·	904	4654	12172	13207	9192	20028	4152	·	102113	·
Total Receipts **8**	33970385	·	·	829358	1326829	2266759	1057889	1247522	1828385	2456964	·	8872359	·
Average Total Receipts **9**	23906	·	·	1710	4575	11868	20344	47982	76183	144527	·	985818	·
Operating Costs/Operating Income (%)													
Cost of Operations **10**	55.8	·	·	52.1	45.2	49.1	51.5	52.5	56.5	54.0	·	52.6	·
Salaries and Wages **11**	14.9	·	·	8.7	16.6	14.6	14.3	13.6	11.7	13.7	·	14.9	·
Taxes Paid **12**	2.3	·	·	3.1	3.3	2.7	2.4	2.2	2.0	2.6	·	2.6	·
Interest Paid **13**	2.0	·	·	1.0	1.1	1.3	0.5	0.9	0.8	0.9	·	2.5	·
Depreciation **14**	3.2	·	·	1.4	2.4	2.1	2.1	2.5	2.4	2.8	·	2.7	·
Amortization and Depletion **15**	1.1	·	·	0.1	0.1	0.1	0.3	0.6	0.6	0.5	·	2.4	·
Pensions and Other Deferred Comp. **16**	1.8	·	·	0.4	0.5	0.7	0.6	1.0	0.9	1.6	·	2.7	·
Employee Benefits **17**	2.7	·	·	1.4	1.7	2.6	2.6	2.3	2.0	3.0	·	1.6	·
Advertising **18**	1.1	·	·	0.7	1.1	1.9	1.5	1.3	3.2	2.2	·	0.5	·
Other Expenses **19**	13.8	·	·	15.4	17.1	13.2	11.0	13.4	14.4	13.1	·	18.9	·
Officers' Compensation **20**	1.9	·	·	10.3	5.3	5.9	3.1	2.1	2.1	2.1	·	1.0	·
Operating Margin **21**	·	·	·	5.3	5.6	5.9	10.1	7.6	3.5	3.5	·	3.5	·
Operating Margin Before Officers' Comp. **22**	1.6	·	·	15.6	10.9	11.8	13.1	9.7	5.6	5.6	·	5.6	·

Selected Average Balance Sheet ($ in Thousands)

Net Receivables 23	4139	163	941	2025	3773	7834	13474	25375	201026
Inventories 24	2773	160	681	1420	3338	5540	9307	19440	84212
Net Property, Plant and Equipment 25	3423	79	541	1416	2248	7499	7760	23359	150727
Total Assets 26	26465	667	2824	7584	14994	36182	69481	152964	1363448
Notes and Loans Payable 27	6752	280	650	1948	1738	6659	8653	17873	343675
All Other Liabilities 28	6295	138	910	1607	3438	10646	16948	26872	301830
Net Worth 29	13418	248	1264	4029	9818	18878	43880	108219	717943

Selected Financial Ratios (Times to 1)

Current Ratio 30	1.5	3.4	3.0	2.8	3.1	1.7	2.6	2.7	2.0
Quick Ratio 31	0.9	2.3	1.8	1.6	1.9	1.0	1.8	1.7	1.4
Net Sales to Working Capital 32	6.5	4.4	3.1	3.3	2.8	5.4	2.7	2.6	3.1
Coverage Ratio 33	4.0	6.2	9.2	6.6	27.1	10.6	10.3	9.7	4.3
Total Asset Turnover 34	0.9	2.6	1.6	1.5	1.3	1.3	1.1	0.9	0.7
Inventory Turnover 35	4.6	5.6	2.9	4.1	3.1	4.5	4.5	3.9	5.7
Receivables Turnover 36	6.3	20.9	4.5	8.9	5.5	6.8	6.3	5.6	6.9
Total Liabilities to Net Worth 37	1.0	1.7	1.2	0.9	0.5	0.9	0.6	0.4	0.9
Current Assets to Working Capital 38	3.2	1.4	1.5	1.5	1.5	2.3	1.6	1.6	2.0
Current Liabilities to Working Capital 39	2.2	0.4	0.5	0.5	0.5	1.3	0.6	0.6	1.0
Working Capital to Net Sales 40	0.2	0.2	0.3	0.3	0.4	0.2	0.4	0.4	0.3
Inventory to Working Capital 41	0.9	0.4	0.5	0.6	0.5	0.8	0.4	0.4	0.4
Total Receipts to Cash Flow 42	6.6	6.0	4.8	5.5	4.8	4.9	5.7	6.5	4.9
Cost of Goods to Cash Flow 43	3.7	3.1	2.2	2.7	2.5	2.6	3.2	3.5	2.6
Cash Flow to Total Debt 44	0.3	0.7	0.6	0.6	0.8	0.6	0.5	0.5	0.3

Selected Financial Factors (in Percentages)

Debt Ratio 45	49.3	62.8	55.3	46.9	34.5	47.8	36.8	29.3	47.3
Return on Total Assets 46	6.7	16.5	15.4	13.0	16.4	12.6	8.9	7.8	7.2
Return on Equity Before Income Taxes 47	9.8	37.3	30.6	20.8	24.1	21.9	12.7	9.8	10.5
Return on Equity After Income Taxes 48	7.4	36.0	26.8	19.0	20.4	16.8	9.8	7.4	6.9
Profit Margin (Before Income Tax) 49	5.8	5.4	8.7	7.2	11.8	8.7	7.5	7.5	8.2
Profit Margin (After Income Tax) 50	4.3	5.2	7.6	6.5	10.0	6.7	5.8	5.6	5.4

ELECTRICAL LIGHTING EQUIPMENT AND HOUSEHOLD APPLIANCE

Table I

Corporations with and without Net Income

MONEY AMOUNTS AND SIZE OF ASSETS IN THOUSANDS OF DOLLARS

Item Description for Accounting Period 7/03 Through 6/04	Total	Zero Assets	Under 500	500 to 1,000	1,000 to 5,000	5,000 to 10,000	10,000 to 25,000	25,000 to 50,000	50,000 to 100,000	100,000 to 250,000	250,000 to 500,000	500,000 to 2,500,000	2,500,000 and over
Number of Enterprises **1**	1542	·	·	·	160	49	53	16	9	18	4	5	4

Revenues ($ in Thousands)

Item	Total	Zero Assets	Under 500	500 to 1,000	1,000 to 5,000	5,000 to 10,000	10,000 to 25,000	25,000 to 50,000	50,000 to 100,000	100,000 to 250,000	250,000 to 500,000	500,000 to 2,500,000	2,500,000 and over
Net Sales **2**	122663933	·	·	·	896735	774650	1426622	1065566	1125133	4497697	1215727	11530377	99947327
Interest **3**	20092637	·	·	·	694	219	964	392	8365	7485	4807	17100	20052362
Rents **4**	29231	·	·	·	285	0	724	475	362	2889	377	15743	8376
Royalties **5**	2468906	·	·	·	0	53	15	946	138	7988	317	50151	2409299
Other Portfolio Income **6**	3798321	·	·	·	11	322	4612	922	259	8224	3464	43536	3732957
Other Receipts **7**	11806479	·	·	·	6194	9120	23787	5633	-1905	31784	30580	66611	11634659
Total Receipts **8**	160859507	·	·	·	903919	784364	1456724	1073934	1132352	4556067	1255272	11723518	137784980
Average Total Receipts **9**	104319	·	·	·	5649	16007	27485	67121	125817	253115	313818	2344704	34446245

Operating Costs/Operating Income (%)

Item	Total	Zero Assets	Under 500	500 to 1,000	1,000 to 5,000	5,000 to 10,000	10,000 to 25,000	25,000 to 50,000	50,000 to 100,000	100,000 to 250,000	250,000 to 500,000	500,000 to 2,500,000	2,500,000 and over
Cost of Operations **10**	58.4	·	·	·	66.9	61.1	65.1	63.3	63.1	64.2	55.5	75.1	56.0
Salaries and Wages **11**	11.7	·	·	·	13.3	7.6	8.6	7.2	8.6	7.0	11.1	5.6	12.8
Taxes Paid **12**	1.1	·	·	·	2.9	2.6	1.9	1.9	1.6	1.4	2.5	1.5	1.0
Interest Paid **13**	19.6	·	·	·	2.5	1.4	1.1	0.9	1.0	1.0	1.9	1.4	23.8
Depreciation **14**	10.0	·	·	·	1.5	2.7	2.7	1.9	1.9	2.3	6.4	2.4	11.7
Amortization and Depletion **15**	1.4	·	·	·	0.4	0.1	0.2	0.5	0.4	0.4	4.2	0.1	1.7
Pensions and Other Deferred Comp. **16**	1.4	·	·	·	0.2	0.1	0.5	3.1	0.7	0.5	0.3	1.0	1.5
Employee Benefits **17**	1.7	·	·	·	2.2	1.8	1.8	1.1	2.3	1.4	1.7	1.3	1.8
Advertising **18**	1.0	·	·	·	0.2	0.6	1.1	1.3	2.9	4.8	8.5	1.1	0.7
Other Expenses **19**	22.4	·	·	·	15.2	18.8	15.0	13.9	11.2	10.4	13.2	10.0	24.9
Officers' Compensation **20**	0.5	·	·	·	1.5	3.4	2.6	1.6	0.9	1.1	0.9	0.2	0.4
Operating Margin **21**	·	·	·	·	·	·	·	3.3	5.5	5.6	·	0.3	·
Operating Margin Before Officers' Comp. **22**	·	·	·	·	·	3.0	2.0	4.9	6.3	6.7	·	0.5	·

Selected Average Balance Sheet ($ in Thousands)

Net Receivables 23	90629	774	2164	3382	11421	20778	38825	32508	259035	34210189
Inventories 24	5598	1208	3209	3837	10071	19509	37063	31538	251072	1432228
Net Property, Plant and Equipment 25	34219	860	1559	3216	5737	14921	32138	58557	251584	12519694
Total Assets 26	566663	3796	8193	15431	34975	74046	161532	356967	1717438	214436945
Notes and Loans Payable 27	222661	2224	1669	4515	8117	17169	30307	76386	295490	85005322
All Other Liabilities 28	123308	1466	2568	4229	12585	20816	45589	155643	578078	46197829
Net Worth 29	220693	106	3956	6687	14273	36061	85636	124937	843869	83233794

Selected Financial Ratios (Times to 1)

Current Ratio 30	0.6	0.9	1.8	1.9	1.5	2.1	2.3	2.0	1.6	0.6
Quick Ratio 31	0.5	0.4	1.0	0.9	0.8	1.1	1.2	1.0	0.8	0.5
Net Sales to Working Capital 32	•	•	5.4	5.8	7.7	4.8	4.8	3.6	9.9	•
Coverage Ratio 33	1.2	•	1.6	2.3	5.3	7.4	8.3	•	2.6	1.2
Total Asset Turnover 34	0.1	1.5	1.9	1.7	1.9	1.7	1.5	0.9	1.3	0.1
Inventory Turnover 35	8.3	3.1	3.0	4.6	4.2	4.0	4.3	5.3	6.9	9.8
Receivables Turnover 36	0.9	6.5	6.3	8.6	5.4	6.5	6.4	18.7	8.0	0.7
Total Liabilities to Net Worth 37	1.6	34.7	1.1	1.3	1.5	1.1	0.9	1.9	1.0	1.6
Current Assets to Working Capital 38	•	•	2.2	2.2	2.9	2.0	1.8	2.0	2.6	•
Current Liabilities to Working Capital 39	•	•	1.2	1.2	1.9	1.0	0.8	1.0	1.6	•
Working Capital to Net Sales 40	•	•	0.2	0.2	0.1	0.2	0.2	0.3	0.1	•
Inventory to Working Capital 41	•	•	0.8	0.9	1.1	0.8	0.7	0.4	1.0	•
Total Receipts to Cash Flow 42	4.6	12.6	5.7	8.5	6.2	6.5	6.2	12.0	9.3	4.2
Cost of Goods to Cash Flow 43	2.7	8.4	3.5	5.5	3.9	4.1	4.0	6.7	7.0	2.4
Cash Flow to Total Debt 44	0.0	0.1	0.7	0.4	0.5	0.5	0.5	0.1	0.3	0.0

Selected Financial Factors (in Percentages)

Debt Ratio 45	61.1	97.2	51.7	56.7	59.2	51.3	47.0	65.0	50.9	61.2
Return on Total Assets 46	3.3	•	4.5	4.6	9.6	11.9	12.4	•	4.9	3.3
Return on Equity Before Income Taxes 47	1.5	•	3.6	5.9	19.0	21.2	20.5	•	6.1	1.3
Return on Equity After Income Taxes 48	1.0	•	2.1	4.2	15.7	19.5	17.6	•	3.6	0.9
Profit Margin (Before Income Tax) 49	4.1	•	0.9	1.5	4.1	6.1	7.0	•	2.2	4.5
Profit Margin (After Income Tax) 50	2.8	•	0.5	1.0	3.4	4.2	5.6	•	1.3	3.1

Table II
Corporations with Net Income

ELECTRICAL LIGHTING EQUIPMENT AND HOUSEHOLD APPLIANCE

MONEY AMOUNTS AND SIZE OF ASSETS IN THOUSANDS OF DOLLARS

Item Description for Accounting Period 7/03 Through 6/04	Total	Zero Assets	Under 500	500 to 1,000	1,000 to 5,000	5,000 to 10,000	10,000 to 25,000	25,000 to 50,000	50,000 to 100,000	100,000 to 250,000	250,000 to 500,000	500,000 to 2,500,000	2,500,000 and over
Number of Enterprises **1**	552	·	406	·	41	23	36	12	·	·	·	·	·
Revenues ($ in Thousands)													
Net Sales **2**	110208471	·	17185	·	304261	517816	987214	804378	·	·	·	·	·
Interest **3**	19624295	·	0	·	2	121	533	314	·	·	·	·	·
Rents **4**	21432	·	0	·	0	0	724	91	·	·	·	·	·
Royalties **5**	2225489	·	0	·	0	0	15	946	·	·	·	·	·
Other Portfolio Income **6**	3750964	·	0	·	11	14	1775	486	·	·	·	·	·
Other Receipts **7**	11745439	·	0	·	2286	8752	18579	5342	·	·	·	·	·
Total Receipts **8**	147576090	·	17185	·	306560	526703	1008840	811557	·	·	·	·	·
Average Total Receipts **9**	267348	·	42	·	7477	22900	28023	67630	·	·	·	·	·
Operating Costs/Operating Income (%)													
Cost of Operations **10**	57.4	·	40.0	·	64.2	63.6	66.1	58.9	·	·	·	·	·
Salaries and Wages **11**	12.3	·	0.1	·	4.1	5.9	8.4	8.2	·	·	·	·	·
Taxes Paid **12**	1.0	·	1.9	·	1.2	2.3	1.8	1.8	·	·	·	·	·
Interest Paid **13**	21.1	·	·	·	0.7	1.5	0.8	0.5	·	·	·	·	·
Depreciation **14**	10.7	·	0.0	·	1.0	2.2	2.1	1.9	·	·	·	·	·
Amortization and Depletion **15**	1.5	·	·	·	0.2	0.0	0.1	0.1	·	·	·	·	·
Pensions and Other Deferred Comp. **16**	1.2	·	·	·	0.0	0.2	0.6	4.0	·	·	·	·	·
Employee Benefits **17**	1.6	·	·	·	1.2	1.3	1.3	1.1	·	·	·	·	·
Advertising **18**	0.9	·	1.5	·	0.2	0.6	1.2	1.5	·	·	·	·	·
Other Expenses **19**	23.5	·	37.0	·	20.6	17.6	9.5	13.9	·	·	·	·	·
Officers' Compensation **20**	0.4	·	·	·	2.8	3.3	3.1	1.7	·	·	·	·	·
Operating Margin **21**	·	·	19.5	·	3.8	1.6	5.0	6.5	·	·	·	·	·
Operating Margin Before Officers' Comp. **22**	·	·	19.5	·	6.7	4.9	8.1	8.1	·	·	·	·	·

Selected Average Balance Sheet ($ in Thousands)

Net Receivables 23	250200	1	874	2666	3630	11662
Inventories 24	13237	14	2589	1845	4183	9226
Net Property, Plant and Equipment 25	91457	0	266	1897	3073	5584
Total Assets 26	1559025	2	3010	7925	15143	34298
Notes and Loans Payable 27	616075	10	377	1409	3656	4915
All Other Liabilities 28	329735	-28	655	2595	3597	12859
Net Worth 29	613214	20	1978	3920	7890	16523

Selected Financial Ratios (Times to 1)

Current Ratio 30	0.6	1.2	1.9	1.7	2.3	1.9
Quick Ratio 31	0.5	0.8	0.7	1.1	1.2	1.1
Net Sales to Working Capital 32	.	123.6	5.9	9.1	4.6	5.5
Coverage Ratio 33	1.2	.	7.5	3.2	10.1	16.4
Total Asset Turnover 34	0.1	23.3	2.5	2.8	1.8	2.0
Inventory Turnover 35	8.7	1.2	1.8	7.8	4.3	4.3
Receivables Turnover 36	0.8	3.6	4.1	7.8	7.5	5.9
Total Liabilities to Net Worth 37	1.5	.	0.5	1.0	0.9	1.1
Current Assets to Working Capital 38	.	5.4	2.1	2.3	1.8	2.1
Current Liabilities to Working Capital 39	.	4.4	1.1	1.3	0.8	1.1
Working Capital to Net Sales 40	.	0.0	0.2	0.1	0.2	0.2
Inventory to Working Capital 41	.	2.0	1.3	0.8	0.7	0.7
Total Receipts to Cash Flow 42	4.3	2.4	4.3	5.3	6.6	5.3
Cost of Goods to Cash Flow 43	2.5	1.0	2.7	3.3	4.4	3.1
Cash Flow to Total Debt 44	0.0	.	1.7	1.1	0.6	0.7

Selected Financial Factors (in Percentages)

Debt Ratio 45	60.7	.	34.3	50.5	47.9	51.8
Return on Total Assets 46	3.3	453.7	13.1	13.5	14.5	15.3
Return on Equity Before Income Taxes 47	1.6	42.2	17.2	18.8	25.0	29.8
Return on Equity After Income Taxes 48	1.2	42.2	13.8	15.6	22.9	26.0
Profit Margin (Before Income Tax) 49	5.0	19.5	4.6	3.3	7.2	7.4
Profit Margin (After Income Tax) 50	3.6	19.5	3.7	2.7	6.6	6.4

Table I

Corporations with and without Net Income

ELECTRICAL EQUIPMENT

MONEY AMOUNTS AND SIZE OF ASSETS IN THOUSANDS OF DOLLARS

Item Description for Accounting Period 7/03 Through 6/04	Total	Zero Assets	Under 500	500 to 1,000	1,000 to 5,000	5,000 to 10,000	10,000 to 25,000	25,000 to 50,000	50,000 to 100,000	100,000 to 250,000	250,000 to 500,000	500,000 to 2,500,000	2,500,000 and over
Number of Enterprises 1	1398	•	•	68	331	59	57	24	12	12	4	6	3
Revenues ($ in Thousands)													
Net Sales 2	30344058	•	•	92106	1636596	539332	1796661	1175224	998170	2041278	1120928	4744289	16065857
Interest 3	328571	•	•	49	2601	390	2842	2006	10229	5706	3615	16497	284636
Rents 4	72279	•	•	0	0	0	772	2908	523	592	0	17	67468
Royalties 5	402348	•	•	61	336	0	36	97	1114	170058	2679	13174	214791
Other Portfolio Income 6	164252	•	•	0	9809	491	4723	3489	3323	23228	14456	11913	90226
Other Receipts 7	387115	•	•	27	998	3682	15189	8117	2748	20992	10457	104302	221083
Total Receipts 8	31698623	•	•	92243	1650340	543895	1820223	1191841	1016107	2261854	1152135	4890192	16944061
Average Total Receipts 9	22674	•	•	1357	4986	9219	31934	49660	84676	188488	288034	815032	5648020
Operating Costs/Operating Income (%)													
Cost of Operations 10	68.6	•	•	42.6	66.9	74.2	74.5	70.8	66.6	61.0	55.3	73.0	68.7
Salaries and Wages 11	7.2	•	•	14.1	8.3	6.6	7.6	9.1	9.8	11.4	12.0	6.8	6.1
Taxes Paid 12	1.9	•	•	3.3	1.9	2.5	2.0	2.1	1.7	2.2	3.1	0.9	2.1
Interest Paid 13	2.8	•	•	0.4	1.0	1.9	0.7	1.6	1.8	1.3	0.4	0.8	4.4
Depreciation 14	2.9	•	•	1.1	1.5	1.8	2.1	3.5	3.7	3.7	5.5	2.5	2.9
Amortization and Depletion 15	1.4	•	•	0.3	0.0	2.0	0.2	0.4	1.4	1.3	0.9	1.2	1.8
Pensions and Other Deferred Comp. 16	1.6	•	•	0.0	1.0	0.5	0.4	0.5	0.7	1.2	2.7	0.2	2.4
Employee Benefits 17	2.2	•	•	2.2	1.1	1.7	1.7	2.4	2.9	2.2	3.4	1.2	2.5
Advertising 18	0.6	•	•	0.4	0.6	0.3	0.4	0.5	0.6	1.0	0.5	1.0	0.4
Other Expenses 19	10.9	•	•	32.9	9.1	11.4	8.2	8.9	10.1	12.3	16.3	11.6	10.4
Officers' Compensation 20	1.1	•	•	8.4	5.9	2.0	1.7	1.2	2.0	1.4	0.8	0.4	0.6
Operating Margin 21	•	•	•	•	2.7	•	0.6	•	•	0.9	•	0.4	•
Operating Margin Before Officers' Comp. 22	•	•	•	2.7	8.6	•	2.3	0.3	0.6	2.3	•	0.8	•

Selected Average Balance Sheet ($ in Thousands)

Net Receivables 23	8664	•	211	721	1358	4450	8029	12108	25619	75998	255310	3011601
Inventories 24	2420	•	288	798	1752	3374	8804	7379	22710	58451	120112	405060
Net Property, Plant and Equipment 25	3611	•	20	331	490	2779	9306	15275	33887	94711	107078	971293
Total Assets 26	42215	•	572	2586	6324	15911	34436	70195	163259	310809	1238052	14837703
Notes and Loans Payable 27	5291	•	137	944	3470	4051	9115	19034	18128	28768	126916	1693183
All Other Liabilities 28	10608	•	71	538	4641	4516	9610	14695	46574	63487	318774	3657329
Net Worth 29	26315	•	364	1104	-1787	7344	15711	36466	98557	218555	792362	9487190

Selected Financial Ratios (Times to 1)

Current Ratio 30	1.4	•	5.6	2.8	0.7	1.9	1.8	1.9	1.9	3.0	1.5	1.2
Quick Ratio 31	1.0	•	2.6	1.4	0.4	1.1	1.0	1.1	1.1	2.1	1.0	0.9
Net Sales to Working Capital 32	6.2	•	3.0	3.8	•	6.3	5.3	5.8	4.5	2.4	5.1	8.2
Coverage Ratio 33	2.5	•	•	4.3	•	4.0	1.4	1.4	10.7	7.1	7.8	1.9
Total Asset Turnover 34	0.5	•	2.4	1.9	1.4	2.0	1.4	1.2	1.0	0.9	0.6	0.4
Inventory Turnover 35	6.2	•	2.0	4.1	3.9	7.0	3.9	7.5	4.6	2.7	4.8	9.1
Receivables Turnover 36	2.5	•	12.8	6.9	4.9	7.5	5.0	8.6	6.3	3.0	3.4	1.8
Total Liabilities to Net Worth 37	0.6	•	0.6	1.3	•	1.2	1.2	0.9	0.7	0.4	0.6	0.6
Current Assets to Working Capital 38	3.8	•	1.2	1.6	•	2.1	2.1	2.2	2.1	1.5	3.2	6.0
Current Liabilities to Working Capital 39	2.8	•	0.2	0.6	•	1.1	1.2	1.1	0.5	2.2	•	5.0
Working Capital to Net Sales 40	0.2	•	0.3	0.3	•	0.2	0.2	0.2	0.4	0.2	0.1	
Inventory to Working Capital 41	0.7	•	0.6	0.7	0.7	•	0.9	0.6	0.6	0.4	0.8	0.6
Total Receipts to Cash Flow 42	8.2	•	4.5	10.1	21.1	11.8	12.5	11.0	4.6	6.3	7.3	8.7
Cost of Goods to Cash Flow 43	5.7	•	1.9	6.8	15.7	8.8	8.8	7.4	2.8	3.5	5.3	6.0
Cash Flow to Total Debt 44	0.2	•	1.4	0.3	0.1	0.3	0.2	0.2	0.6	0.4	0.5	0.1

Selected Financial Factors (in Percentages)

Debt Ratio 45	37.7	•	36.4	57.3	128.3	53.8	54.4	48.0	39.6	29.7	36.0	36.1
Return on Total Assets 46	3.6	•	•	8.7	•	5.6	3.3	3.0	14.0	2.8	3.8	3.1
Return on Equity Before Income Taxes 47	3.4	•	•	15.6	21.0	9.1	2.1	1.6	21.0	3.4	5.2	2.3
Return on Equity After Income Taxes 48	2.2	•	•	14.0	24.8	7.1	0.2	•	13.8	1.4	3.4	1.5
Profit Margin (Before Income Tax) 49	4.1	•	3.5	•	•	2.1	0.7	0.7	12.2	2.7	5.2	4.1
Profit Margin (After Income Tax) 50	2.6	•	3.1	•	•	1.7	0.0	•	8.0	1.1	3.4	2.6

149

Table II
Corporations with Net Income

ELECTRICAL EQUIPMENT

MONEY AMOUNTS AND SIZE OF ASSETS IN THOUSANDS OF DOLLARS

Item Description for Accounting Period 7/03 Through 6/04	Total	Zero Assets	Under 500	500 to 1,000	1,000 to 5,000	5,000 to 10,000	10,000 to 25,000	25,000 to 50,000	50,000 to 100,000	100,000 to 250,000	250,000 to 500,000	500,000 to 2,500,000	2,500,000 and over
Number of Enterprises 1	589	251	•	•	179	18	37	12	•	•	•	•	•
Revenues ($ in Thousands)													
Net Sales 2	27068150	38926	•	•	1235061	282379	1329730	560047	•	•	•	•	•
Interest 3	292462	0	•	•	2435	108	767	1273	•	•	•	•	•
Rents 4	69357	0	•	•	0	0	322	437	•	•	•	•	•
Royalties 5	400880	0	•	•	0	0	36	97	•	•	•	•	•
Other Portfolio Income 6	159430	2557	•	•	9770	376	4057	1345	•	•	•	•	•
Other Receipts 7	375731	-481	•	•	409	966	14005	911	•	•	•	•	•
Total Receipts 8	28366010	41042	•	•	1247675	283829	1348917	564110	•	•	•	•	•
Average Total Receipts 9	48160	164	•	•	6970	15768	36457	47009	•	•	•	•	•
Operating Costs/Operating Income (%)													
Cost of Operations 10	68.4	28.0	•	•	65.5	69.3	76.4	65.8	•	•	•	•	•
Salaries and Wages 11	7.1	1.9	•	•	8.2	4.6	6.8	9.1	•	•	•	•	•
Taxes Paid 12	1.9	1.9	•	•	1.8	2.6	1.7	2.5	•	•	•	•	•
Interest Paid 13	2.5	0.9	•	•	0.2	0.2	0.5	1.1	•	•	•	•	•
Depreciation 14	2.7	2.5	•	•	1.2	1.3	1.7	3.8	•	•	•	•	•
Amortization and Depletion 15	1.4	•	•	•	0.0	•	0.1	0.4	•	•	•	•	•
Pensions and Other Deferred Comp. 16	1.7	•	•	•	0.8	0.8	0.4	0.7	•	•	•	•	•
Employee Benefits 17	2.2	6.6	•	•	1.2	0.5	1.4	1.6	•	•	•	•	•
Advertising 18	0.6	0.0	•	•	0.7	0.1	0.3	0.7	•	•	•	•	•
Other Expenses 19	10.5	57.7	•	•	7.5	10.2	6.2	7.5	•	•	•	•	•
Officers' Compensation 20	0.9	0.3	•	•	5.5	1.6	1.7	1.3	•	•	•	•	•
Operating Margin 21	•	0.2	•	•	7.3	9.0	2.8	5.4	•	•	•	•	•
Operating Margin Before Officers' Comp. 22	0.9	0.5	•	•	12.8	10.6	4.5	6.7	•	•	•	•	•

Selected Average Balance Sheet ($ in Thousands)

Net Receivables 23	19801	0	·	·	1020	2221	4620	7352
Inventories 24	4767	0	·	·	586	3461	3172	9919
Net Property, Plant and Equipment 25	7492	0	·	·	276	608	2469	8825
Total Assets 26	90776	0	·	·	2856	6724	15994	33939
Notes and Loans Payable 27	11019	0	·	·	307	766	3309	6583
All Other Liabilities 28	21311	0	·	·	582	1937	4603	8788
Net Worth 29	58445	0	·	·	1967	4021	8082	18568

Selected Financial Ratios (Times to 1)

Current Ratio 30	1.4	·	·	·	2.9	2.4	2.2	1.8
Quick Ratio 31	1.0	·	·	·	2.0	1.4	1.4	0.9
Net Sales to Working Capital 32	6.0	·	·	·	4.6	4.6	6.1	5.6
Coverage Ratio 33	3.3	7.5	·	·	37.8	55.0	9.6	6.6
Total Asset Turnover 34	0.5	·	·	·	2.4	2.3	2.2	1.4
Inventory Turnover 35	6.6	·	·	·	7.7	3.1	8.7	3.1
Receivables Turnover 36	2.3	·	·	·	6.8	3.3	8.6	4.0
Total Liabilities to Net Worth 37	0.6	·	·	·	0.5	0.7	1.0	0.8
Current Assets to Working Capital 38	3.8	·	·	·	1.5	1.7	1.9	2.2
Current Liabilities to Working Capital 39	2.8	·	·	·	0.5	0.7	0.9	1.2
Working Capital to Net Sales 40	0.2	·	·	·	0.2	0.2	0.2	0.2
Inventory to Working Capital 41	0.6	·	·	·	0.4	0.6	0.5	0.9
Total Receipts to Cash Flow 42	7.5	3.3	·	·	7.9	5.6	11.0	7.9
Cost of Goods to Cash Flow 43	5.2	0.9	·	·	5.2	3.9	8.4	5.2
Cash Flow to Total Debt 44	0.2	·	·	·	1.0	1.0	0.4	0.4

Selected Financial Factors (in Percentages)

Debt Ratio 45	35.6	·	·	·	31.1	40.2	49.5	45.3
Return on Total Assets 46	4.2	·	·	·	20.6	22.4	11.5	10.3
Return on Equity Before Income Taxes 47	4.5	·	·	·	29.1	36.8	20.3	16.0
Return on Equity After Income Taxes 48	3.2	·	·	·	27.4	31.3	17.6	12.8
Profit Margin (Before Income Tax) 49	5.8	5.6	·	·	8.3	9.4	4.6	6.4
Profit Margin (After Income Tax) 50	4.1	5.6	·	·	7.8	8.0	4.0	5.1

Table I

Corporations with and without Net Income

OTHER ELECTRICAL EQUIPMENT AND COMPONENT

MONEY AMOUNTS AND SIZE OF ASSETS IN THOUSANDS OF DOLLARS

Item Description for Accounting Period 7/03 Through 6/04	Total	Zero Assets	Under 500	500 to 1,000	1,000 to 5,000	5,000 to 10,000	10,000 to 25,000	25,000 to 50,000	50,000 to 100,000	100,000 to 250,000	250,000 to 500,000	500,000 to 2,500,000	2,500,000 and over
Number of Enterprises **1**	4191	334	1556	663	839	383	207	91	50	32	17	18	•
Revenues ($ in Thousands)													
Net Sales **2**	43118020	385829	348833	966206	3915720	3775983	4940370	4457096	3827477	4296661	4217030	11996814	•
Interest **3**	381459	656	26	488	1253	1452	10791	5893	13215	35860	24935	286890	•
Rents **4**	26469	7	0	631	1818	464	807	731	3553	1739	378	16340	•
Royalties **5**	126972	1208	0	0	0	114	1579	10286	14737	7682	1216	90151	•
Other Portfolio Income **6**	172266	2468	14	0	2106	12480	16146	13975	21499	35759	22405	45413	•
Other Receipts **7**	803872	24738	507	12172	10003	59825	43332	78357	39435	32225	40092	463189	•
Total Receipts **8**	44629058	414906	349380	979497	3930900	3850318	5013025	4566338	3919916	4409926	4306056	12888797	•
Average Total Receipts **9**	10649	1242	225	1477	4685	10053	24218	50180	78398	137810	253297	716044	•
Operating Costs/Operating Income (%)													
Cost of Operations **10**	65.9	71.1	35.7	60.2	61.9	68.0	67.8	71.3	64.7	69.2	62.6	65.3	•
Salaries and Wages **11**	11.2	8.4	19.0	13.1	11.1	11.8	10.7	9.6	13.3	10.0	9.8	11.8	•
Taxes Paid **12**	2.1	1.7	4.5	1.7	2.8	3.0	2.2	1.9	2.3	1.8	2.3	1.7	•
Interest Paid **13**	2.7	2.8	0.8	3.4	1.2	1.4	1.1	1.4	1.7	2.7	1.9	5.4	•
Depreciation **14**	3.6	4.2	0.7	1.5	2.7	2.6	2.8	3.0	4.9	4.5	5.0	3.8	•
Amortization and Depletion **15**	0.8	0.3	0.0	0.0	0.2	0.4	0.3	0.4	0.6	0.9	1.1	1.4	•
Pensions and Other Deferred Comp. **16**	0.8	0.1	0.0	0.4	1.0	0.4	0.5	0.5	0.7	0.7	0.6	1.5	•
Employee Benefits **17**	2.5	2.0	1.6	0.6	1.9	1.4	2.1	2.1	2.4	2.3	3.6	3.1	•
Advertising **18**	1.1	0.1	0.0	0.8	0.6	0.8	0.7	0.6	0.9	0.5	0.6	2.1	•
Other Expenses **19**	12.6	28.8	35.9	18.4	10.5	10.2	12.2	8.7	12.8	12.8	12.3	13.9	•
Officers' Compensation **20**	2.0	1.5	8.5	3.5	4.8	2.9	2.6	1.9	2.0	1.0	1.2	1.0	•
Operating Margin **21**	•	•	•	•	1.4	•	•	•	•	•	•	•	•
Operating Margin Before Officers' Comp. **22**	•	1.9	•	6.1	0.0	0.0	0.5	0.3	•	•	•	•	•

Selected Average Balance Sheet ($ in Thousands)

Net Receivables 23	1866	0	11	220	727	1281	3777	9425	15242	26653	77532	110291
Inventories 24	1564	0	32	179	801	2015	3742	7610	15064	21459	35858	66846
Net Property, Plant and Equipment 25	1796	0	15	36	497	1414	2977	6584	16563	33880	58094	133614
Total Assets 26	12728	0	84	578	2492	6211	15506	34737	71949	163189	376107	1487493
Notes and Loans Payable 27	3573	0	64	991	682	2440	5814	8450	16801	42903	68916	408588
All Other Liabilities 28	3679	0	61	319	982	1546	4582	10435	19124	39612	94329	442928
Net Worth 29	5476	0	-41	-731	828	2224	5110	15851	36024	80674	212862	635977

Selected Financial Ratios (Times to 1)

Current Ratio 30	1.7	·	0.5	1.3	1.7	1.8	1.9	2.2	2.3	1.8	2.3	1.2
Quick Ratio 31	0.9	·	0.3	0.8	1.1	0.8	1.1	1.3	1.3	1.2	1.5	0.6
Net Sales to Working Capital 32	4.8	·	·	15.1	5.9	5.2	5.1	3.8	3.1	3.7	2.4	9.5
Coverage Ratio 33	0.4	·	·	0.4	2.5	0.3	·	1.8	·	·	1.6	0.4
Total Asset Turnover 34	0.8	·	2.7	2.5	1.9	1.6	1.5	1.4	1.1	0.8	0.7	0.4
Inventory Turnover 35	4.3	·	2.5	4.9	3.6	3.3	4.3	4.6	3.3	4.3	4.3	6.5
Receivables Turnover 36	5.6	·	6.1	7.6	5.6	7.4	6.1	5.7	4.6	4.6	3.6	7.6
Total Liabilities to Net Worth 37	1.3	·	·	·	2.0	1.8	2.0	1.2	1.0	1.0	0.8	1.3
Current Assets to Working Capital 38	2.5	·	·	4.9	2.3	2.2	2.2	1.8	1.8	2.2	1.8	5.2
Current Liabilities to Working Capital 39	1.5	·	·	3.9	1.3	1.2	1.2	0.8	0.8	1.2	0.8	4.2
Working Capital to Net Sales 40	0.2	·	·	0.1	0.2	0.2	0.2	0.3	0.3	0.3	0.4	0.1
Inventory to Working Capital 41	0.7	·	·	1.6	0.8	1.2	0.7	0.6	0.6	0.5	0.4	1.1
Total Receipts to Cash Flow 42	12.8	18.1	8.7	7.6	10.6	15.3	15.5	12.7	16.0	15.1	8.9	13.3
Cost of Goods to Cash Flow 43	8.4	12.8	3.1	4.6	6.6	10.4	10.5	9.1	10.3	10.5	5.6	8.7
Cash Flow to Total Debt 44	0.1	·	0.2	0.1	0.3	0.2	0.1	0.2	0.1	0.1	0.2	0.1

Selected Financial Factors (in Percentages)

Debt Ratio 45	57.0	·	148.6	226.5	66.8	64.2	67.0	54.4	49.9	50.6	43.4	57.2
Return on Total Assets 46	0.8	·	·	3.3	5.5	0.7	·	3.5	·	·	2.1	1.0
Return on Equity Before Income Taxes 47	·	·	35.8	4.2	9.9	·	3.4	·	·	·	1.4	·
Return on Equity After Income Taxes 48	·	·	35.9	4.4	7.5	·	1.0	·	·	·	·	·
Profit Margin (Before Income Tax) 49	·	·	1.8	1.8	·	1.1	·	·	·	·	1.2	·
Profit Margin (After Income Tax) 50	·	·	1.3	·	·	0.3	·	·	·	·	·	·

Table II

Corporations with Net Income

OTHER ELECTRICAL EQUIPMENT AND COMPONENT

MONEY AMOUNTS AND SIZE OF ASSETS IN THOUSANDS OF DOLLARS

Item Description for Accounting Period 7/03 Through 6/04	Total	Zero Assets	Under 500	500 to 1000	251 to 500	501 to 1,000	1,001 to 5,000	5,001 to 10,000	10,001 to 25,000	25,001 to 50,000	50,001 to 100,000	100,001 to 250,000	250,001 and over
Number of Enterprises 1	2579	•	834	•	585	280	137	58	24	17	•	6	•
Revenues ($ in Thousands)													
Net Sales 2	26097255	•	235521	•	2979948	2899662	3606196	3317995	2249743	2538496	•	5666960	•
Interest 3	143219	•	1	•	798	840	2819	3451	4872	13220	•	109368	•
Rents 4	21541	•	0	•	1818	464	571	510	553	1592	•	15157	•
Royalties 5	66614	•	0	•	0	114	1149	19	3526	5280	•	55753	•
Other Portfolio Income 6	96117	•	14	•	1934	5820	11045	8355	11261	21871	•	26627	•
Other Receipts 7	504924	•	2	•	8723	52302	21591	51143	7569	22874	•	318948	•
Total Receipts 8	26929670	•	235538	•	2993221	2959202	3643371	3381473	2277524	2603333	•	6192813	•
Average Total Receipts 9	10442	•	282	•	5117	10569	26594	58301	94897	153137	•	1032136	•
Operating Costs/Operating Income (%)													
Cost of Operations 10	62.5	•	19.4	•	63.3	67.9	65.2	71.5	61.2	67.0	•	54.6	•
Salaries and Wages 11	9.7	•	21.9	•	8.0	11.0	9.5	7.8	11.0	9.0	•	11.5	•
Taxes Paid 12	2.2	•	4.3	•	2.6	2.6	2.1	1.9	2.1	1.6	•	2.3	•
Interest Paid 13	1.7	•	0.0	•	1.0	0.8	0.6	0.7	1.1	1.4	•	4.0	•
Depreciation 14	2.8	•	0.0	•	2.3	2.0	2.3	2.3	3.5	3.3	•	3.4	•
Amortization and Depletion 15	0.4	•	•	•	0.1	0.1	0.1	0.2	0.4	0.9	•	0.4	•
Pensions and Other Deferred Comp. 16	1.1	•	0.0	•	1.3	0.4	0.5	0.5	0.9	0.6	•	2.6	•
Employee Benefits 17	2.1	•	0.0	•	2.0	0.8	1.8	2.0	2.5	1.9	•	3.0	•
Advertising 18	1.3	•	0.0	•	0.4	0.5	0.7	0.6	1.1	0.7	•	3.5	•
Other Expenses 19	11.0	•	35.4	•	7.8	9.1	8.5	6.3	9.7	10.5	•	16.5	•
Officers' Compensation 20	2.1	•	9.8	•	4.3	2.4	2.7	1.5	2.1	0.7	•	1.3	•
Operating Margin 21	3.2	•	9.1	•	6.9	2.4	6.1	4.7	4.5	2.4	•	•	•
Operating Margin Before Officers' Comp. 22	5.3	•	18.9	•	11.2	4.8	8.7	6.1	6.6	3.2	•	•	•

Selected Average Balance Sheet ($ in Thousands)

Net Receivables 23	1649	•	10	•	•	763	1427	3908	10888	15509	24391	•	120636
Inventories 24	1467	•	30	•	•	635	1816	3658	7422	16951	20672	•	92907
Net Property, Plant and Equipment 25	1464	•	0	•	•	531	1428	2942	5531	14555	27419	•	194423
Total Assets 26	10573	•	88	•	•	2611	6192	15168	34418	69768	153776	•	2049226
Notes and Loans Payable 27	2294	•	1	•	•	623	1945	2950	6818	14589	35174	•	470850
All Other Liabilities 28	2919	•	70	•	•	726	1271	4014	9210	15837	31159	•	632399
Net Worth 29	5360	•	17	•	•	1263	2976	8204	18391	39341	87442	•	945977

Selected Financial Ratios (Times to 1)

Current Ratio 30	2.2	•	0.3	•	•	2.2	2.2	2.1	2.5	2.7	2.1	•	1.8
Quick Ratio 31	1.2	•	0.3	•	•	1.5	1.0	1.2	1.5	1.4	1.3	•	0.7
Net Sales to Working Capital 32	4.0	•		•	•	4.9	4.4	4.7	3.7	3.4	3.9	•	4.6
Coverage Ratio 33	4.9	•	2391.6	•	•	8.6	6.3	12.6	10.5	6.3	4.9	•	2.7
Total Asset Turnover 34	1.0	•	3.2	•	•	2.0	1.7	1.7	1.7	1.3	1.0	•	0.5
Inventory Turnover 35	4.3	•	1.8	•	•	5.1	3.9	4.7	5.5	3.4	4.8	•	5.6
Receivables Turnover 36	6.0	•	5.7	•	•	7.0	7.2	6.8	6.6	4.9	6.2	•	9.3
Total Liabilities to Net Worth 37	1.0	•	4.3	•	•	1.1	1.1	0.8	0.9	0.8	0.8	•	1.2
Current Assets to Working Capital 38	1.8	•		•	•	1.9	1.9	1.9	1.7	1.6	1.9	•	2.3
Current Liabilities to Working Capital 39	0.8	•		•	•	0.9	0.9	0.9	0.7	0.6	0.9	•	1.3
Working Capital to Net Sales 40	0.3	•		•	•	0.2	0.2	0.2	0.3	0.3	0.3	•	0.2
Inventory to Working Capital 41	0.6	•		•	•	0.5	0.9	0.7	0.6	0.5	0.5	•	0.5
Total Receipts to Cash Flow 42	6.7	•	4.8	•	•	7.9	8.8	7.3	8.9	7.6	7.5	•	5.0
Cost of Goods to Cash Flow 43	4.2	•	0.9	•	•	5.0	6.0	4.7	6.3	4.7	5.0	•	2.7
Cash Flow to Total Debt 44	0.3	•	0.8	•	•	0.5	0.4	0.5	0.4	0.5	0.4	•	0.2

Selected Financial Factors (in Percentages)

Debt Ratio 45	49.3	•	81.1	•	•	51.7	51.9	45.9	46.6	43.6	43.1	•	53.8
Return on Total Assets 46	7.8	•	29.5	•	•	16.2	8.9	13.4	12.1	9.1	6.5	•	4.9
Return on Equity Before Income Taxes 47	12.2	•	156.2	•	•	29.6	15.6	22.8	20.5	13.6	9.1	•	6.7
Return on Equity After Income Taxes 48	9.7	•	156.1	•	•	27.3	13.5	19.7	17.2	10.9	6.3	•	4.6
Profit Margin (Before Income Tax) 49	6.5	•	9.1	•	•	7.3	4.5	7.1	6.6	5.7	5.3	•	6.7
Profit Margin (After Income Tax) 50	5.1	•	9.1	•	•	6.8	3.9	6.1	5.5	4.6	3.7	•	4.6

152

Table I
Corporations with and without Net Income

MOTOR VEHICLES AND PARTS

MONEY AMOUNTS AND SIZE OF ASSETS IN THOUSANDS OF DOLLARS

Item Description for Accounting Period 7/03 Through 6/04	Total	Zero Assets	Under 500	500 to 1,000	1,000 to 5,000	5,000 to 10,000	10,000 to 25,000	25,000 to 50,000	50,000 to 100,000	100,000 to 250,000	250,000 to 500,000	500,000 to 2,500,000	2,500,000 and over
Number of Enterprises 1	5739	318	3119	665	882	128	229	123	102	80	30	43	20
Revenues ($ in Thousands)													
Net Sales 2	626044127	5355885	2000292	1737494	5526725	2083830	6341555	6608579	12018414	21840538	15024948	44545998	502959869
Interest 3	39334003	3976	41	1225	2553	4339	3910	6416	12968	46959	56812	276127	38918677
Rents 4	21015382	9	0	0	15	49	2093	4953	2076	9618	18847	34546	20943177
Royalties 5	7101472	131	0	0	1154	23	1268	2852	3381	16731	17412	253033	6805488
Other Portfolio Income 6	16565601	28938	7109	2564	4377	14733	9782	7990	8807	42643	54559	121231	16262869
Other Receipts 7	20752759	46638	4365	4136	13154	16556	47233	58913	102046	320721	172573	306889	19659531
Total Receipts 8	730813344	5435577	2011807	1745419	5547978	2119530	6405841	6689703	12147692	22277210	15360850	45522125	605549611
Average Total Receipts 9	127342	17093	645	2625	6290	16559	27973	54388	119095	278465	512028	1058654	30277481
Operating Costs/Operating Income (%)													
Cost of Operations 10	80.7	79.3	81.3	80.5	72.1	83.2	76.1	78.1	79.4	81.3	79.4	77.2	81.3
Salaries and Wages 11	3.4	5.7	4.1	5.4	5.9	5.6	5.3	4.5	3.7	3.9	3.9	5.1	3.1
Taxes Paid 12	0.9	1.1	2.0	2.6	2.2	1.5	2.0	1.8	1.6	1.5	1.5	1.4	0.7
Interest Paid 13	4.9	0.5	0.3	1.6	1.6	0.6	1.0	1.1	1.2	1.3	1.8	2.7	5.6
Depreciation 14	8.1	3.3	1.0	2.5	2.2	2.6	3.1	4.6	4.5	3.6	4.8	3.1	9.2
Amortization and Depletion 15	0.3	0.1	0.2	0.2	0.2	0.2	0.3	0.3	0.4	0.4	0.3	0.7	0.3
Pensions and Other Deferred Comp. 16	2.6	0.3	0.0	0.2	0.4	0.1	0.3	0.4	0.4	0.4	0.5	1.1	3.0
Employee Benefits 17	1.5	1.1	0.9	0.8	1.5	0.8	1.6	2.0	2.3	1.7	1.7	2.7	1.4
Advertising 18	1.6	0.1	0.4	1.6	0.3	0.4	0.5	0.5	0.3	0.2	0.3	0.3	2.0
Other Expenses 19	12.5	5.5	9.1	8.6	10.2	8.0	8.0	6.8	4.9	5.4	5.6	7.1	13.9
Officers' Compensation 20	0.2	0.3	2.5	3.4	3.0	1.2	1.7	0.9	0.8	0.4	0.4	0.3	0.1
Operating Margin 21	•	2.8	•	•	0.5	•	0.2	•	0.7	•	•	•	•
Operating Margin Before Officers' Comp. 22	•	3.0	0.5	•	3.5	•	1.8	0.1	1.4	•	•	•	•

Selected Average Balance Sheet ($ in Thousands)

Net Receivables 23	71784	0	34	153	667	1605	3740	7585	15327	34938	65198	158638	19802032
Inventories 24	5872	0	47	171	739	2497	3760	6601	12203	25677	48124	93315	1101944
Net Property, Plant and Equipment 25	32162	0	25	197	669	2062	4655	12314	26460	48679	109797	205718	8109986
Total Assets 26	230540	0	141	725	2509	7182	15773	35340	72898	152529	341414	1014742	61877191
Notes and Loans Payable 27	89242	0	153	416	1263	2651	5399	12726	24592	45357	126411	376872	24050954
All Other Liabilities 28	96166	0	45	124	1583	3002	4707	9768	22975	55112	99464	335455	26172655
Net Worth 29	45132	0	-57	184	-337	1529	5667	12846	25331	52060	115539	302415	11653582

Selected Financial Ratios (Times to 1)

Current Ratio 30	1.3	•	3.0	1.9	1.3	1.4	1.6	1.4	1.3	1.3	1.4	1.4	1.3
Quick Ratio 31	0.9	•	1.3	0.8	0.8	0.7	0.9	0.8	0.7	0.7	0.8	0.9	0.9
Net Sales to Working Capital 32	4.5	•	9.4	11.5	14.5	13.7	7.5	10.9	14.7	15.6	11.7	10.3	3.9
Coverage Ratio 33	1.1	10.4	•	•	1.5	•	2.2	1.4	2.5	2.5	2.1	1.3	1.0
Total Asset Turnover 34	0.5	•	4.6	3.6	2.5	2.3	1.8	1.5	1.6	1.8	1.5	1.0	0.4
Inventory Turnover 35	15.0	•	11.0	12.3	6.1	5.4	5.6	6.4	7.7	8.6	8.3	8.6	18.5
Receivables Turnover 36	1.6	•	27.8	18.6	11.4	8.3	7.7	7.7	7.9	7.4	8.7	6.7	1.4
Total Liabilities to Net Worth 37	4.1	•	•	2.9	•	3.7	1.8	1.8	1.9	1.9	2.0	2.4	4.3
Current Assets to Working Capital 38	4.6	•	1.5	2.1	4.0	3.8	2.6	3.7	4.6	4.5	3.4	3.6	4.6
Current Liabilities to Working Capital 39	3.6	•	0.5	1.1	3.0	2.8	1.6	2.7	3.6	3.5	2.4	2.6	3.6
Working Capital to Net Sales 40	0.2	•	0.1	0.1	0.1	0.1	0.1	0.1	0.1	0.1	0.1	0.1	0.3
Inventory to Working Capital 41	0.2	•	0.8	0.9	1.5	1.6	1.0	1.3	1.6	1.4	1.1	0.9	0.2
Total Receipts to Cash Flow 42	8.6	12.2	17.9	•	11.6	32.9	13.8	17.1	18.5	16.4	15.7	16.0	7.8
Cost of Goods to Cash Flow 43	7.0	9.6	14.6	•	8.4	27.4	10.5	13.4	14.7	13.3	12.5	12.4	6.3
Cash Flow to Total Debt 44	0.1	•	0.2	•	0.2	0.1	0.2	0.1	0.1	0.2	0.1	0.1	0.1

Selected Financial Factors (in Percentages)

Debt Ratio 45	80.4	•	140.6	74.5	113.4	78.7	64.1	63.6	65.3	65.9	66.2	70.2	81.2
Return on Total Assets 46	2.5	•	•	•	•	6.2	4.0	2.3	4.7	5.8	5.6	3.6	2.4
Return on Equity Before Income Taxes 47	1.0	•	15.7	•	•	•	6.2	1.7	8.1	10.1	8.7	2.9	0.5
Return on Equity After Income Taxes 48	0.2	•	16.2	•	•	•	3.7	•	5.3	7.2	4.6	0.3	•
Profit Margin (Before Income Tax) 49	0.4	4.3	•	•	0.9	•	1.3	0.4	1.8	1.9	2.0	0.8	0.2
Profit Margin (After Income Tax) 50	0.1	3.9	•	•	0.6	•	0.7	•	1.1	1.4	1.1	0.1	•

153

Table II
Corporations with Net Income

MOTOR VEHICLES AND PARTS

MONEY AMOUNTS AND SIZE OF ASSETS IN THOUSANDS OF DOLLARS

Item Description for Accounting Period 7/03 Through 6/04	Total	Zero Assets	Under 500	500 to 1,000	1,000 to 5,000	5,000 to 10,000	10,000 to 25,000	25,000 to 50,000	50,000 to 100,000	100,000 to 250,000	250,000 to 500,000	500,000 to 2,500,000	2,500,000 and over
Number of Enterprises 1	2553	13	1438	149	495	70	143	70	69	56	21	20	9
Revenues ($ in Thousands)													
Net Sales 2	397904592	5217747	1643541	324939	3890996	796980	4402376	4250760	8503533	15704406	10648591	24036198	318485126
Interest 3	22310740	3937	0	1	1531	2567	2559	4132	10235	38323	32684	40170	22174599
Rents 4	10697204	9	0	0	15	33	1544	3864	1041	7703	7151	3585	10672259
Royalties 5	4392650	130	0	0	0	23	1201	2679	2952	14860	5092	196924	4168788
Other Portfolio Income 6	10064627	18806	5612	2236	2955	13299	5650	6141	7543	23150	22837	88100	9869098
Other Receipts 7	14510345	28970	4359	104	6798	8104	33682	20515	75179	262453	87221	90471	13892490
Total Receipts 8	459880158	5268199	1653512	327280	3902295	821006	4447012	4288091	8600483	16050895	10803576	24455448	379262360
Average Total Receipts 9	180133	405246	1150	2197	7883	11729	31098	61258	124645	286623	514456	1222772	42140262
Operating Costs/Operating Income (%)													
Cost of Operations 10	79.7	79.3	82.2	62.4	71.2	73.9	74.9	75.3	78.0	80.1	78.5	78.1	80.2
Salaries and Wages 11	3.5	5.8	3.9	13.2	6.3	5.2	4.9	4.3	3.5	3.8	4.2	4.2	3.3
Taxes Paid 12	0.9	1.1	1.9	2.0	2.0	1.8	1.8	1.9	1.6	1.5	1.5	1.0	0.8
Interest Paid 13	4.5	0.3	0.2	0.6	0.8	0.6	0.7	0.8	0.9	0.8	1.0	0.9	5.4
Depreciation 14	7.5	3.3	0.8	2.5	2.1	3.4	2.4	3.8	3.7	3.3	4.6	2.9	8.6
Amortization and Depletion 15	0.3	0.1	0.0	•	0.2	0.0	0.1	0.2	0.2	0.3	0.2	0.2	0.4
Pensions and Other Deferred Comp. 16	3.5	0.3	0.0	0.0	0.5	0.2	0.2	0.4	0.4	0.4	0.4	0.7	4.3
Employee Benefits 17	1.6	1.1	0.4	0.4	1.9	0.9	1.3	2.0	1.9	1.8	1.5	2.2	1.5
Advertising 18	1.8	0.0	0.1	0.2	0.2	0.8	0.5	0.4	0.3	0.2	0.3	0.2	2.1
Other Expenses 19	10.5	4.8	7.3	14.3	7.0	6.7	7.0	5.8	5.1	5.1	4.6	6.3	11.7
Officers' Compensation 20	0.2	0.1	1.9	3.4	3.2	1.9	1.7	1.0	0.9	0.4	0.4	0.3	0.1
Operating Margin 21	•	3.9	1.2	1.0	4.5	4.4	4.4	4.2	3.5	2.3	2.9	3.0	•
Operating Margin Before Officers' Comp. 22	•	4.0	3.1	4.4	7.7	6.3	6.1	5.2	4.3	2.7	3.3	3.3	•

Selected Average Balance Sheet ($ in Thousands)

Net Receivables 23	95534	0	59	67	753	1129	3956	8976	16387	35776	67857	135691	26098246
Inventories 24	7998	0	78	285	894	1856	4098	7388	13216	24223	51970	105469	1457629
Net Property, Plant and Equipment 25	41950	0	30	71	783	1744	3773	10940	23340	46518	91673	250305	10453543
Total Assets 26	322122	0	171	646	2945	6440	15714	34979	73026	153228	330905	911914	86291525
Notes and Loans Payable 27	117627	0	288	183	1153	2396	3734	9660	18964	36527	73897	237744	32027845
All Other Liabilities 28	139672	0	49	89	741	1721	4582	8885	22117	51815	111339	260864	38083376
Net Worth 29	64824	0	-166	374	1051	2323	7399	16435	31945	64887	145670	413306	16180304

Selected Financial Ratios (Times to 1)

Current Ratio 30	1.4	•	4.0	4.1	2.0	1.7	1.9	1.6	1.5	1.4	1.5	1.6	1.4
Quick Ratio 31	0.9	•	1.8	1.2	1.2	0.9	1.0	0.9	0.8	0.8	0.9	1.0	1.0
Net Sales to Working Capital 32	3.6	•	9.2	5.5	7.9	6.7	6.3	8.3	9.3	12.6	10.1	9.1	3.1
Coverage Ratio 33	1.5	15.3	8.2	4.1	7.1	13.0	9.0	7.4	6.4	6.5	5.4	6.7	1.3
Total Asset Turnover 34	0.5	•	6.7	3.4	2.7	1.8	2.0	1.7	1.7	1.8	1.5	1.3	0.4
Inventory Turnover 35	15.5	•	12.0	4.8	6.3	4.5	5.6	6.2	7.3	9.3	7.7	8.9	19.5
Receivables Turnover 36	1.7	•	27.8	8.6	12.1	7.5	7.8	7.3	8.0	7.8	8.3	7.3	1.5
Total Liabilities to Net Worth 37	4.0	•	0.7	1.8	1.1	1.1	1.3	1.3	1.4	1.3	1.2		4.3
Current Assets to Working Capital 38	3.7	•	1.3	2.0	1.0	2.4	2.1	2.7	3.0	3.6	3.1	2.8	3.8
Current Liabilities to Working Capital 39	2.7	•	0.3	1.0	1.4	1.1	1.7	2.0	2.6	2.1	1.8		2.8
Working Capital to Net Sales 40	0.3	•	0.1	0.1	0.1	0.2	0.1	0.1	0.1	0.1	0.1	0.1	0.3
Inventory to Working Capital 41	0.2	•	0.8	0.8	0.8	1.0	0.8	1.0	1.1	1.0	0.7		0.1
Total Receipts to Cash Flow 42	8.9	12.2	13.3	8.5	10.6	8.1	9.5	10.5	11.6	12.4	9.9		8.6
Cost of Goods to Cash Flow 43	7.1	9.7	5.3	7.6	6.0	7.1	7.9	9.1	9.3	9.8	7.7		6.9
Cash Flow to Total Debt 44	0.1	•	0.9	0.4	0.3	0.4	0.3	0.3	0.3	0.2	0.1		0.1

Selected Financial Factors (in Percentages)

Debt Ratio 45	79.9	•	196.7	42.2	64.3	63.9	52.9	53.0	56.3	57.7	56.0	54.7	81.2
Return on Total Assets 46	3.2	•	13.4	7.7	15.0	14.2	12.1	10.2	9.3	9.8	8.2	8.0	2.8
Return on Equity Before Income Taxes 47	5.2	•	10.1	36.2	36.4	22.9	18.8	17.9	19.6	15.2	15.0		3.3
Return on Equity After Income Taxes 48	3.9	•	8.3	32.9	33.8	19.8	15.0	14.5	16.2	10.6	11.0		2.4
Profit Margin (Before Income Tax) 49	2.2	4.9	1.8	4.8	1.7	7.4	5.5	5.1	4.6	4.5	4.4	5.2	1.5
Profit Margin (After Income Tax) 50	1.6	4.5	1.7	1.4	4.4	6.9	4.8	4.1	3.8	3.8	3.0	3.8	1.1

Table I

Corporations with and without Net Income

AEROSPACE PRODUCT AND PARTS

MONEY AMOUNTS AND SIZE OF ASSETS IN THOUSANDS OF DOLLARS

Item Description for Accounting Period 7/03 Through 6/04	Total	Zero Assets	Under 500	500 to 1,000	1,000 to 5,000	5,000 to 10,000	10,000 to 25,000	25,000 to 50,000	50,000 to 100,000	100,000 to 250,000	250,000 to 500,000	500,000 to 2,500,000	2,500,000 and over
Number of Enterprises 1	1807	•	1260	•	163	91	77	35	16	10	9	11	9
Revenues ($ in Thousands)													
Net Sales 2	180105487	•	405287	•	647959	527950	1344646	1582105	1249328	1590922	2570372	6818136	158508600
Interest 3	2274115	•	514	•	2067	172	1317	2194	2917	3576	40404	18846	1906362
Rents 4	2007137	•	0	•	0	2	696	323	2088	7959	5642	47541	1694406
Royalties 5	1754152	•	0	•	0	0	1	79	1331	0	2621	15536	1734341
Other Portfolio Income 6	1836005	•	16483	•	1847	4190	2670	108991	9423	12439	12917	109155	1516767
Other Receipts 7	1600934	•	0	•	-618	844	37645	6875	21482	4650	19423	20722	1260682
Total Receipts 8	189577830	•	422284	•	651255	533158	1386975	1700567	1288569	1619546	2651379	7029936	166621158
Average Total Receipts 9	104913	•	335	•	3995	5859	18013	48588	80411	161955	294598	639085	18513462
Operating Costs/Operating Income (%)													
Cost of Operations 10	70.6	•	58.7	•	56.3	58.5	70.3	70.0	66.0	70.3	68.5	67.7	70.5
Salaries and Wages 11	11.1	•	1.3	•	11.9	9.3	6.7	7.1	9.5	6.1	7.2	6.9	11.7
Taxes Paid 12	1.4	•	3.1	•	2.9	2.9	2.7	2.1	2.3	2.6	2.6	2.5	1.3
Interest Paid 13	2.7	•	0.7	•	2.0	2.1	2.1	3.1	2.3	1.6	7.7	4.7	2.4
Depreciation 14	3.5	•	7.0	•	4.1	3.1	4.6	2.5	4.5	3.3	3.6	4.1	3.5
Amortization and Depletion 15	0.6	•	0.1	•	0.3	0.1	0.3	0.9	2.8	0.7	1.6	1.0	0.5
Pensions and Other Deferred Comp. 16	1.4	•	0.6	•	0.2	0.4	0.4	0.4	0.6	0.7	0.7	2.3	1.5
Employee Benefits 17	3.5	•	0.4	•	2.5	2.2	2.1	1.9	3.5	2.9	3.2	3.0	3.6
Advertising 18	0.2	•	0.7	•	0.4	0.3	0.4	0.2	0.5	0.2	0.2	0.2	0.2
Other Expenses 19	10.7	•	18.9	•	11.7	16.3	11.3	9.7	10.5	9.3	8.6	8.8	10.6
Officers' Compensation 20	0.4	•	10.7	•	7.8	3.5	2.7	1.6	1.4	2.1	1.3	0.9	0.2
Operating Margin 21	•	•	•	•	•	1.4	•	0.6	•	0.0	•	•	•
Operating Margin Before Officers' Comp. 22	•	•	8.4	•	7.6	4.9	•	2.2	•	2.1	•	•	•

Selected Average Balance Sheet ($ in Thousands)

Net Receivables 23	16823	11	•	564	794	2632	5534	9731	24426	44011	148589	3042666
Inventories 24	11761	37	•	630	2249	4639	10644	16936	50749	56054	156975	1900512
Net Property, Plant and Equipment 25	18375	24	•	1188	687	3376	4763	21341	35061	50614	179213	3262785
Total Assets 26	128384	108	•	3013	8061	15769	35017	72791	149533	331713	1240830	23202347
Notes and Loans Payable 27	35307	67	•	1225	4647	5847	11343	25077	34820	228907	398216	6115985
All Other Liabilities 28	53800	50	•	559	782	3661	8977	19546	44377	65772	468042	9986854
Net Worth 29	39277	-9	•	1229	2632	6261	14698	28169	70336	37034	374572	7099508

Selected Financial Ratios (Times to 1)

Current Ratio 30	1.2	1.3	•	2.8	0.8	2.1	1.8	2.1	2.5	1.9	1.6	1.2
Quick Ratio 31	0.7	0.7	•	1.9	0.4	0.9	0.8	1.1	1.3	1.0	0.9	0.7
Net Sales to Working Capital 32	14.5	17.6	•	3.5	•	3.3	4.9	4.1	2.7	4.8	4.6	18.5
Coverage Ratio 33	0.9	3.6	•	1.1	2.1	0.7	3.6	0.6	1.7	0.8	1.3	0.9
Total Asset Turnover 34	0.8	3.0	•	1.3	0.7	1.1	1.3	1.1	1.1	0.9	0.5	0.8
Inventory Turnover 35	6.0	5.1	•	3.6	1.5	2.6	3.0	3.0	2.2	3.5	2.7	6.5
Receivables Turnover 36	5.4	61.1	•	7.1	4.8	7.3	8.7	5.4	5.9	5.3	3.6	5.3
Total Liabilities to Net Worth 37	2.3	•	•	1.5	2.1	1.5	1.4	1.6	1.1	8.0	2.3	2.3
Current Assets to Working Capital 38	5.5	4.3	•	1.6	•	1.9	2.3	1.9	1.7	2.1	2.7	6.9
Current Liabilities to Working Capital 39	4.5	3.3	•	0.6	•	0.9	1.3	0.9	0.7	1.1	1.7	5.9
Working Capital to Net Sales 40	0.1	0.1	•	0.3	•	0.3	0.2	0.2	0.4	0.2	0.2	0.1
Inventory to Working Capital 41	1.6	2.0	•	0.5	•	0.9	1.1	0.8	0.7	0.8	1.1	1.9
Total Receipts to Cash Flow 42	12.9	8.6	•	10.7	6.1	14.0	12.1	14.4	10.9	24.2	13.2	12.8
Cost of Goods to Cash Flow 43	9.1	5.0	•	6.0	3.5	9.8	8.5	9.5	7.7	16.6	8.9	9.0
Cash Flow to Total Debt 44	0.1	0.3	•	0.2	0.2	0.1	0.2	0.1	0.2	0.0	0.1	0.1

Selected Financial Factors (in Percentages)

Debt Ratio 45	69.4	108.6	•	59.2	67.3	60.3	58.0	61.3	53.0	88.8	69.8	69.4
Return on Total Assets 46	1.8	7.7	•	3.1	3.2	1.7	14.4	1.6	2.9	5.0	3.0	1.6
Return on Equity Before Income Taxes 47	•	•	•	0.9	5.1	•	24.8	•	2.5	•	2.1	•
Return on Equity After Income Taxes 48	•	•	•	0.2	2.9	•	23.1	•	1.7	•	0.5	•
Profit Margin (Before Income Tax) 49	•	1.9	•	0.3	2.3	•	8.1	•	1.1	•	1.3	•
Profit Margin (After Income Tax) 50	•	1.7	•	0.1	1.3	•	7.5	•	0.7	•	0.3	•

Table II
Corporations with Net Income

AEROSPACE PRODUCT AND PARTS

MONEY AMOUNTS AND SIZE OF ASSETS IN THOUSANDS OF DOLLARS

Item Description for Accounting Period 7/03 Through 6/04	Total	Zero Assets	Under 500	500 to 1,000	1,000 to 5,000	5,000 to 10,000	10,000 to 25,000	25,000 to 50,000	50,000 to 100,000	100,000 to 250,000	250,000 to 500,000	500,000 to 2,500,000	2,500,000 and over
Number of Enterprises **1**	851	•	526	•	108	19	44	19	10	6	•	6	6
Revenues ($ in Thousands)													
Net Sales **2**	83377924	•	270157	•	386903	304095	756409	1055847	848193	972331	•	3278282	75095082
Interest **3**	1014240	•	0	•	16	115	333	819	1697	906	•	4648	1001475
Rents **4**	629673	•	0	•	0	0	264	124	569	4793	•	955	617692
Royalties **5**	457039	•	0	•	0	0	1	0	191	0	•	6423	448681
Other Portfolio Income **6**	1047935	•	15916	•	61	4119	1834	104057	9403	11330	•	3770	897393
Other Receipts **7**	506689	•	1	•	-2790	107	25315	10058	1280	2667	•	5083	463506
Total Receipts **8**	87533500	•	288074	•	384190	308436	784156	1173705	861333	992027	•	3299161	78523829
Average Total Receipts **9**	102860	•	544	•	3557	16233	17822	61774	86133	165338	•	549860	13087305
Operating Costs/Operating Income (%)													
Cost of Operations **10**	72.3	•	52.7	•	47.6	56.0	66.2	69.0	64.5	70.1	•	69.1	73.1
Salaries and Wages **11**	6.2	•	1.8	•	12.9	10.3	5.6	6.7	8.2	3.5	•	4.8	6.2
Taxes Paid **12**	1.9	•	3.3	•	2.9	2.4	2.5	1.8	1.9	2.4	•	1.8	1.9
Interest Paid **13**	2.9	•	0.5	•	1.7	0.1	1.0	1.3	1.8	0.4	•	3.0	2.9
Depreciation **14**	2.9	•	9.0	•	4.4	2.4	3.3	2.0	4.0	2.5	•	2.5	2.9
Amortization and Depletion **15**	0.8	•	•	•	0.5	0.1	0.1	0.3	0.2	0.4	•	0.8	0.8
Pensions and Other Deferred Comp. **16**	1.2	•	0.8	•	0.2	0.4	0.4	0.3	0.6	0.7	•	0.6	1.3
Employee Benefits **17**	3.8	•	0.0	•	2.9	1.7	1.8	1.4	1.8	2.2	•	2.4	4.0
Advertising **18**	0.2	•	0.8	•	0.5	0.4	0.3	0.2	0.2	0.1	•	0.3	0.2
Other Expenses **19**	9.5	•	12.6	•	5.9	7.6	9.0	7.8	7.8	9.3	•	8.3	9.6
Officers' Compensation **20**	0.4	•	13.0	•	9.2	4.1	2.9	1.4	1.6	3.0	•	1.0	0.2
Operating Margin **21**	•	•	5.4	•	11.2	14.6	7.0	7.8	7.3	5.4	•	5.4	•
Operating Margin Before Officers' Comp. **22**	•	•	18.4	•	20.4	18.6	9.9	9.3	8.9	8.3	•	6.4	•

Selected Average Balance Sheet ($ in Thousands)

Net Receivables 23	19702	14	611	1900	2713	5947	14201	22050	134394	2539413
Inventories 24	14282	56	554	5052	4358	11455	16394	42094	168747	1632849
Net Property, Plant and Equipment 25	15085	31	1263	1212	2492	3702	21805	26466	145350	1850628
Total Assets 26	112688	111	3027	8120	14990	35521	72276	144142	1146619	14079172
Notes and Loans Payable 27	30417	27	823	296	3217	7766	21970	11765	390563	3700322
All Other Liabilities 28	43590	3	111	1012	2919	8419	16097	32250	387587	5619930
Net Worth 29	38682	80	2093	6812	8854	19336	34208	100128	368468	4758920

Selected Financial Ratios (Times to 1)

Current Ratio 30	1.3	15.8	15.5	6.4	2.8	2.3	2.1	3.1	1.7	1.3
Quick Ratio 31	0.8	5.4	12.0	4.2	1.3	1.0	1.2	1.9	1.0	0.8
Net Sales to Working Capital 32	10.2	6.4	2.2	2.9	2.6	4.0	4.2	2.4	4.1	13.1
Coverage Ratio 33	2.2	23.1	7.2	112.5	11.3	14.9	6.0	15.1	3.0	1.9
Total Asset Turnover 34	0.9	4.6	1.2	2.0	1.1	1.6	1.2	1.1	0.5	0.9
Inventory Turnover 35	5.0	4.9	3.1	1.8	2.6	3.4	3.3	2.7	2.2	5.6
Receivables Turnover 36	3.9	73.5	5.9	3.9	6.2	10.0	4.5	6.4	2.4	3.9
Total Liabilities to Net Worth 37	1.9	0.4	0.4	0.2	0.7	0.8	1.1	0.4	2.1	2.0
Current Assets to Working Capital 38	3.9	1.1	1.1	1.2	1.6	1.8	1.9	1.5	2.4	4.8
Current Liabilities to Working Capital 39	2.9	0.1	0.1	0.2	0.6	0.8	0.9	0.5	1.4	3.8
Working Capital to Net Sales 40	0.1	0.2	0.5	0.3	0.4	0.2	0.2	0.4	0.2	0.1
Inventory to Working Capital 41	0.9	0.7	0.2	0.3	0.7	0.9	0.7	0.4	0.9	1.0
Total Receipts to Cash Flow 42	11.0	5.4	6.6	4.6	5.8	6.8	7.1	6.5	7.8	11.9
Cost of Goods to Cash Flow 43	7.9	2.8	3.2	2.6	3.8	4.7	4.6	4.6	5.4	8.7
Cash Flow to Total Debt 44	0.1	3.1	0.6	2.7	0.5	0.5	0.3	0.6	0.1	0.1

Selected Financial Factors (in Percentages)

Debt Ratio 45	65.7	27.5	30.9	16.1	40.9	45.6	52.7	30.5	67.9	66.2
Return on Total Assets 46	5.4	54.7	14.4	31.7	13.4	31.4	12.5	7.6	4.3	5.0
Return on Equity Before Income Taxes 47	8.5	72.2	18.0	37.5	20.7	53.8	22.0	10.2	9.0	7.1
Return on Equity After Income Taxes 48	6.1	71.0	17.4	33.2	19.1	51.4	18.9	9.2	5.9	4.7
Profit Margin (Before Income Tax) 49	3.3	11.3	10.5	15.9	10.7	18.7	8.9	6.3	6.0	2.7
Profit Margin (After Income Tax) 50	2.4	11.1	10.1	14.1	9.8	17.8	7.6	5.7	4.0	1.8

Table I

Corporations with and without Net Income

SHIP AND BOAT BUILDING

MONEY AMOUNTS AND SIZE OF ASSETS IN THOUSANDS OF DOLLARS

Item Description for Accounting Period 7/03 Through 6/04		Total	Zero Assets	Under 500	500 to 1,000	1,000 to 5,000	5,000 to 10,000	10,000 to 25,000	25,000 to 50,000	50,000 to 100,000	100,000 to 250,000	250,000 to 500,000	500,000 to 2,500,000	2,500,000 and over
Number of Enterprises	1	3012	272	2277	•	285	79	56	24	8	7	•	•	3
Revenues ($ in Thousands)														
Net Sales	2	28132825	138673	1111976	•	1456346	742546	1650466	1832052	799175	2543689	•	•	17857903
Interest	3	30620	50	784	•	4419	296	1302	294	831	4613	•	•	18030
Rents	4	49700	93	0	•	5454	2841	281	30	1	1746	•	•	39254
Royalties	5	7779	0	0	•	0	0	680	0	0	453	•	•	6647
Other Portfolio Income	6	238199	50	123	•	2139	0	648	752	2460	186060	•	•	45969
Other Receipts	7	405118	1253	1150	•	11436	4158	18825	12718	16723	97672	•	•	241180
Total Receipts	8	28864241	140119	1114033	•	1479794	749841	1672202	1845846	819190	2834233	•	•	18208983
Average Total Receipts	9	9583	515	489	•	5192	9492	29861	76910	102399	404890	•	•	6069661
Operating Costs/Operating Income (%)														
Cost of Operations	10	75.8	67.5	59.8	•	65.9	78.0	76.5	75.5	75.3	72.3	•	•	78.1
Salaries and Wages	11	4.1	3.1	10.1	•	6.6	1.6	4.2	3.7	4.5	7.6	•	•	3.1
Taxes Paid	12	2.2	2.0	2.3	•	3.3	1.2	1.8	1.8	2.4	2.3	•	•	2.2
Interest Paid	13	1.0	1.8	0.5	•	0.5	0.9	1.0	0.7	0.8	1.0	•	•	1.1
Depreciation	14	2.3	4.5	1.3	•	2.7	1.3	2.1	2.3	3.6	2.9	•	•	2.3
Amortization and Depletion	15	1.0	0.2	0.3	•	0.1	0.0	0.2	0.2	0.1	0.2	•	•	1.5
Pensions and Other Deferred Comp.	16	0.8	0.1	0.1	•	0.2	0.1	0.2	0.4	1.0	0.5	•	•	1.1
Employee Benefits	17	1.9	0.1	4.2	•	2.5	0.1	1.1	1.9	1.9	2.1	•	•	1.8
Advertising	18	0.6	0.0	0.4	•	1.0	1.4	1.1	1.4	1.1	1.7	•	•	0.3
Other Expenses	19	7.6	29.8	14.9	•	15.2	6.1	9.0	7.3	9.1	12.5	•	•	5.6
Officers' Compensation	20	1.3	0.9	7.2	•	4.4	3.5	2.0	1.1	0.7	0.6	•	•	0.6
Operating Margin	21	1.3	•	•	•	•	5.6	1.0	3.8	•	•	•	•	2.2
Operating Margin Before Officers' Comp.	22	2.6	•	6.2	•	2.0	9.2	2.9	4.8	0.2	•	•	•	2.8

Selected Average Balance Sheet ($ in Thousands)

Net Receivables 23	915	0	28	•	269	729	2680	5788	5081	27472	•	678369
Inventories 24	1420	0	16	•	802	1344	3570	7330	18793	18281	•	1063879
Net Property, Plant and Equipment 25	1409	0	23	•	613	630	3809	11844	25792	73231	•	917051
Total Assets 26	11530	0	126	•	2143	5733	15566	35387	68844	226439	•	9840524
Notes and Loans Payable 27	2180	0	52	•	764	3040	5867	9322	19842	40977	•	1663985
All Other Liabilities 28	3246	0	37	•	868	1230	5493	11262	12978	77177	•	2708637
Net Worth 29	6104	0	36	•	510	1463	4206	14802	36023	108286	•	5467902

Selected Financial Ratios (Times to 1)

Current Ratio 30	1.4	•	2.0	•	1.4	1.7	1.3	1.7	1.9	1.7	•	1.3
Quick Ratio 31	0.4	•	1.6	•	0.7	0.3	0.6	0.8	0.8	0.8	•	0.3
Net Sales to Working Capital 32	8.1	•	13.9	•	13.1	4.6	14.2	8.7	5.5	8.2	•	7.7
Coverage Ratio 33	5.2	•	•	•	•	8.2	3.3	7.9	3.6	9.0	•	5.2
Total Asset Turnover 34	0.8	•	3.9	•	2.4	1.6	1.9	2.2	1.5	1.6	•	0.6
Inventory Turnover 35	5.0	•	18.2	•	4.2	5.5	6.3	7.9	4.0	14.4	•	4.4
Receivables Turnover 36	11.2	•	25.7	•	19.2	11.1	11.3	16.4	16.1	17.6	•	17.5
Total Liabilities to Net Worth 37	0.9	•	2.5	•	3.2	2.9	2.7	1.4	0.9	1.1	•	0.8
Current Assets to Working Capital 38	3.6	•	2.0	•	3.5	2.5	4.2	2.4	2.1	2.5	•	4.0
Current Liabilities to Working Capital 39	2.6	•	1.0	•	2.5	1.5	3.2	1.4	1.1	1.5	•	3.0
Working Capital to Net Sales 40	0.1	•	0.1	•	0.1	0.2	0.1	0.1	0.2	0.1	•	0.1
Inventory to Working Capital 41	1.3	•	0.3	•	1.4	1.1	1.5	1.1	1.0	0.8	•	1.4
Total Receipts to Cash Flow 42	11.3	•	10.1	•	9.8	9.3	11.3	9.1	9.9	9.0	•	12.5
Cost of Goods to Cash Flow 43	8.6	•	6.1	•	6.5	7.2	8.6	6.9	7.5	6.5	•	9.7
Cash Flow to Total Debt 44	0.2	•	0.5	•	0.3	0.2	0.2	0.4	0.3	0.3	•	0.1

Selected Financial Factors (in Percentages)

Debt Ratio 45	47.1	•	71.2	•	76.2	74.5	73.0	58.2	47.7	52.2	•	44.4
Return on Total Assets 46	4.1	•	•	•	•	12.4	6.1	11.1	3.9	14.2	•	3.3
Return on Equity Before Income Taxes 47	6.2	•	•	•	•	42.6	15.8	23.2	5.4	26.4	•	4.8
Return on Equity After Income Taxes 48	4.7	•	•	•	•	41.4	12.3	21.0	1.2	25.0	•	3.4
Profit Margin (Before Income Tax) 49	4.1	•	•	•	•	6.6	2.3	4.5	2.0	7.9	•	4.4
Profit Margin (After Income Tax) 50	3.1	•	•	•	•	6.4	1.8	4.1	0.4	7.4	•	3.1

157

Table II
Corporations with Net Income

SHIP AND BOAT BUILDING

MONEY AMOUNTS AND SIZE OF ASSETS IN THOUSANDS OF DOLLARS

Item Description for Accounting Period 7/03 Through 6/04	Total	Zero Assets	Under 500	500 to 1,000	1,000 to 5,000	5,000 to 10,000	10,000 to 25,000	25,000 to 50,000	50,000 to 100,000	100,000 to 250,000	250,000 to 500,000	500,000 to 2,500,000	2,500,000 and over
Number of Enterprises **1**	1589	•	•	•	216	68	36	16	4	•	•	•	3
Revenues ($ in Thousands)													
Net Sales **2**	26311392	•	•	•	1319855	742546	1275675	1494665	577927	•	•	•	17857903
Interest **3**	29130	•	•	•	4355	296	1188	185	671	•	•	•	18030
Rents **4**	49014	•	•	•	5454	2841	175	0	0	•	•	•	39254
Royalties **5**	7769	•	•	•	0	0	670	0	0	•	•	•	6647
Other Portfolio Income **6**	235321	•	•	•	2139	0	482	315	183	•	•	•	45969
Other Receipts **7**	389979	•	•	•	10955	4158	10337	9283	16021	•	•	•	241180
Total Receipts **8**	27022605	•	•	•	1342758	749841	1288527	1504448	594802	•	•	•	18208983
Average Total Receipts **9**	17006	•	•	•	6216	11027	35792	94028	148700	•	•	•	6069661
Operating Costs/Operating Income (%)													
Cost of Operations **10**	75.5	•	•	•	65.6	78.0	73.8	73.7	77.5	•	•	•	78.1
Salaries and Wages **11**	4.1	•	•	•	6.6	1.6	4.4	3.6	4.1	•	•	•	3.1
Taxes Paid **12**	2.2	•	•	•	3.2	1.2	1.6	1.7	2.0	•	•	•	2.2
Interest Paid **13**	0.9	•	•	•	0.4	0.9	0.9	0.4	0.2	•	•	•	1.1
Depreciation **14**	2.2	•	•	•	2.3	1.3	2.0	2.0	1.9	•	•	•	2.3
Amortization and Depletion **15**	1.1	•	•	•	0.0	0.0	0.2	0.1	0.0	•	•	•	1.5
Pensions and Other Deferred Comp. **16**	0.9	•	•	•	0.1	0.1	0.3	0.5	0.3	•	•	•	1.1
Employee Benefits **17**	1.9	•	•	•	2.5	0.1	0.8	1.9	0.6	•	•	•	1.8
Advertising **18**	0.6	•	•	•	0.9	1.4	1.1	1.4	1.3	•	•	•	0.3
Other Expenses **19**	7.1	•	•	•	13.5	5.9	8.6	7.7	5.0	•	•	•	5.6
Officers' Compensation **20**	1.2	•	•	•	4.7	3.5	1.9	1.1	0.4	•	•	•	0.6
Operating Margin **21**	2.3	•	•	•	0.2	5.8	4.6	5.8	6.7	•	•	•	2.2
Operating Margin Before Officers' Comp. **22**	3.5	•	•	•	4.9	9.4	6.5	6.9	7.1	•	•	•	2.8

Selected Average Balance Sheet ($ in Thousands)

Net Receivables 23	1615	317	847	2746	6192	3491	678369
Inventories 24	2450	755	1083	3194	7686	25762	1063879
Net Property, Plant and Equipment 25	2422	643	731	4773	13544	16769	917051
Total Assets 26	21003	2137	5788	15521	36324	75702	9840524
Notes and Loans Payable 27	3696	669	2578	4110	5663	15599	1663985
All Other Liabilities 28	5857	760	1429	5183	10805	12565	2708637
Net Worth 29	11450	708	1780	6228	19856	47538	5467902

Selected Financial Ratios (Times to 1)

Current Ratio 30	1.4	1.5	1.4	1.5	1.9	2.2	1.3
Quick Ratio 31	0.4	0.7	0.3	0.8	1.0	0.8	0.3
Net Sales to Working Capital 32	8.0	13.8	7.3	11.2	9.4	4.8	7.7
Coverage Ratio 33	6.5	5.4	8.3	7.4	15.8	46.8	5.2
Total Asset Turnover 34	0.8	2.9	1.9	2.3	2.6	1.9	0.6
Inventory Turnover 35	5.1	5.3	7.9	8.2	9.0	4.3	4.4
Receivables Turnover 36	11.6	24.7	17.7	12.9	17.7	36.4	17.5
Total Liabilities to Net Worth 37	0.8	2.0	2.3	1.5	0.8	0.6	0.8
Current Assets to Working Capital 38	3.6	3.0	3.3	2.9	2.1	1.8	4.0
Current Liabilities to Working Capital 39	2.6	2.0	2.3	1.9	1.1	0.8	3.0
Working Capital to Net Sales 40	0.1	0.1	0.1	0.1	0.1	0.2	0.1
Inventory to Working Capital 41	1.2	1.3	1.2	1.0	0.9	1.1	1.4
Total Receipts to Cash Flow 42	10.5	8.5	9.2	8.3	7.4	6.9	12.5
Cost of Goods to Cash Flow 43	8.0	5.6	7.2	6.2	5.4	5.4	9.7
Cash Flow to Total Debt 44	0.2	0.5	0.3	0.5	0.8	0.7	0.1

Selected Financial Factors (in Percentages)

Debt Ratio 45	45.5	66.9	69.2	59.9	45.3	37.2	44.4
Return on Total Assets 46	4.8	6.9	14.6	14.9	17.7	18.7	3.3
Return on Equity Before Income Taxes 47	7.4	17.0	41.7	32.1	30.4	29.2	4.8
Return on Equity After Income Taxes 48	5.9	16.2	40.7	28.4	27.9	22.8	3.4
Profit Margin (Before Income Tax) 49	5.1	2.0	6.8	5.6	6.5	9.6	4.4
Profit Margin (After Income Tax) 50	4.1	1.9	6.6	5.0	5.9	7.5	3.1

158

Table I

Corporations with and without Net Income

OTHER TRANSPORTATION EQUIPMENT AND RAILROAD ROLLING STOCK

MONEY AMOUNTS AND SIZE OF ASSETS IN THOUSANDS OF DOLLARS

Item Description for Accounting Period 7/03 Through 6/04	Total	Zero Assets	Under 500	500 to 1,000	1,000 to 5,000	5,000 to 10,000	10,000 to 25,000	25,000 to 50,000	50,000 to 100,000	100,000 to 250,000	250,000 to 500,000	500,000 to 2,500,000	2,500,000 and over
Number of Enterprises 1	710	•	37	•	244	46	37	15	10	8	6	5	•
Revenues ($ in Thousands)													
Net Sales 2	20727492	•	1079	•	1406492	520819	1139594	1052882	1074363	1798270	2639844	9724160	•
Interest 3	437453	•	6	•	740	74	642	151	1543	7239	10208	394065	•
Rents 4	29942	•	0	•	5686	149	32	236	34	0	678	6063	•
Royalties 5	51238	•	0	•	0	0	290	231	5142	0	481	45094	•
Other Portfolio Income 6	189813	•	0	•	386	326	1729	262	3625	6949	42031	127409	•
Other Receipts 7	196400	•	7	•	4026	1099	1879	4048	4974	24617	47670	84865	•
Total Receipts 8	21632338	•	1092	•	1417330	522467	1144166	1057810	1089681	1837075	2740912	10381656	•
Average Total Receipts 9	30468	•	30	•	5809	11358	30923	70521	108968	229634	456819	2076331	•
Operating Costs/Operating Income (%)													
Cost of Operations 10	68.2	•	95.3	•	72.1	62.2	75.9	77.0	78.3	75.3	77.2	60.2	•
Salaries and Wages 11	6.6	•	•	•	6.7	12.1	5.9	5.3	6.1	5.8	5.6	7.5	•
Taxes Paid 12	1.8	•	46.2	•	2.4	1.9	1.6	2.1	1.5	1.5	1.3	1.9	•
Interest Paid 13	1.9	•	•	•	1.0	0.3	0.6	1.0	1.6	1.6	2.4	2.2	•
Depreciation 14	4.7	•	•	•	3.3	2.0	1.9	2.0	1.5	3.5	4.0	6.8	•
Amortization and Depletion 15	0.6	•	•	•	0.1	0.1	0.1	0.6	0.2	0.6	1.1	0.8	•
Pensions and Other Deferred Comp. 16	0.4	•	•	•	0.2	0.2	0.2	0.4	0.3	0.5	0.5	0.6	•
Employee Benefits 17	3.0	•	0.9	•	1.0	2.6	1.4	1.6	1.7	1.8	1.9	4.5	•
Advertising 18	0.8	•	47.6	•	0.5	0.2	0.7	0.3	0.7	1.0	0.3	1.0	•
Other Expenses 19	10.3	•	2348.2	•	12.1	12.7	7.1	6.4	5.1	8.6	7.8	11.3	•
Officers' Compensation 20	0.9	•	781.6	•	1.4	1.6	1.9	1.6	1.4	0.4	0.4	0.2	•
Operating Margin 21	1.0	•	•	•	•	4.1	2.7	1.7	1.7	•	•	3.1	•
Operating Margin Before Officers' Comp. 22	1.8	•	•	•	0.7	5.6	4.6	3.4	3.1	•	•	3.2	•

Selected Average Balance Sheet ($ in Thousands)

Net Receivables 23	5207	•	13	•	482	3659	8306	16166	23012	63121	486443	•
Inventories 24	3309	•	5	•	604	5096	8914	23261	30079	53636	176133	•
Net Property, Plant and Equipment 25	6857	•	1	•	888	3044	8528	9642	30098	115142	658697	•
Total Assets 26	24898	•	334	•	2719	16262	36237	72691	161066	405985	2179076	•
Notes and Loans Payable 27	6506	•	1208	•	1785	3280	11985	20549	35589	147741	475247	•
All Other Liabilities 28	9708	•	51	•	6457	5882	10746	19321	63830	139659	658912	•
Net Worth 29	8685	•	-924	•	-5523	7100	13505	32821	61647	118585	1044918	•

Selected Financial Ratios (Times to 1)

Current Ratio 30	1.6	•	0.2	•	0.9	3.0	1.7	1.4	2.3	1.1	1.7	1.7
Quick Ratio 31	0.8	•	0.1	•	0.6	1.3	0.8	0.7	1.2	0.4	0.8	0.9
Net Sales to Working Capital 32	6.1	•	•	•	•	3.2	6.9	11.7	4.1	25.1	6.1	4.5
Coverage Ratio 33	4.0	•	•	•	•	1.1	5.7	3.1	2.9	2.0	1.9	5.6
Total Asset Turnover 34	1.2	•	0.1	•	•	2.1	1.9	1.9	1.5	1.4	1.1	0.9
Inventory Turnover 35	6.0	•	5.8	•	6.9	2.1	4.6	6.1	3.6	5.6	6.3	6.6
Receivables Turnover 36	6.2	•	4.5	•	10.8	5.1	8.7	7.7	5.9	9.4	8.5	4.6
Total Liabilities to Net Worth 37	1.9	•	•	•	•	0.7	1.3	1.7	1.2	1.6	2.4	1.1
Current Assets to Working Capital 38	2.6	•	•	•	•	1.5	2.4	3.2	1.8	9.1	2.5	2.4
Current Liabilities to Working Capital 39	1.6	•	•	•	•	0.5	1.4	2.2	0.8	8.1	1.5	1.4
Working Capital to Net Sales 40	0.2	•	•	•	•	0.3	0.1	0.1	0.2	0.0	0.2	0.2
Inventory to Working Capital 41	0.7	•	•	•	•	0.8	1.2	1.4	0.7	3.3	0.8	0.4
Total Receipts to Cash Flow 42	7.2	•	10.4	•	•	7.3	11.0	14.0	15.4	11.7	14.7	5.0
Cost of Goods to Cash Flow 43	4.9	•	7.5	•	•	4.5	8.4	10.8	12.1	8.8	11.4	3.0
Cash Flow to Total Debt 44	0.2	•	0.1	•	•	0.6	0.3	0.2	0.2	0.2	0.1	0.3

Selected Financial Factors (in Percentages)

Debt Ratio 45	65.1	•	376.2	•	303.1	42.2	56.3	62.7	54.8	61.7	70.8	52.0
Return on Total Assets 46	8.6	•	•	•	2.3	8.8	7.0	6.3	7.0	4.5	4.9	10.8
Return on Equity Before Income Taxes 47	18.4	•	101.6	•	•	14.2	13.2	11.4	10.2	5.9	8.1	18.4
Return on Equity After Income Taxes 48	11.4	•	101.6	•	•	14.0	11.9	9.6	7.7	5.1	3.4	11.2
Profit Margin (Before Income Tax) 49	5.5	•	•	•	0.1	4.4	3.0	2.2	3.1	1.6	2.2	9.9
Profit Margin (After Income Tax) 50	3.4	•	•	•	0.0	4.3	2.7	1.9	2.4	1.4	0.9	6.0

Table II

Corporations with Net Income

OTHER TRANSPORTATION EQUIPMENT AND RAILROAD ROLLING STOCK

MONEY AMOUNTS AND SIZE OF ASSETS IN THOUSANDS OF DOLLARS

Item Description for Accounting Period 7/03 Through 6/04	Total	Zero Assets	Under 500	500 to 1,000	1,000 to 5,000	5,000 to 10,000	10,000 to 25,000	25,000 to 50,000	50,000 to 100,000	100,000 to 250,000	250,000 to 500,000	500,000 to 2,500,000	2,500,000 and over
Number of Enterprises **1**	379	•	•	•	82	41	27	11	7	•	•	•	•
Revenues ($ in Thousands)													
Net Sales **2**	13706774	•	•	•	1040305	456932	944575	856996	717997	•	•	•	•
Interest **3**	378493	•	•	•	270	0	292	64	1299	•	•	•	•
Rents **4**	8945	•	•	•	5686	149	12	51	34	•	•	•	•
Royalties **5**	50169	•	•	•	0	0	290	231	4342	•	•	•	•
Other Portfolio Income **6**	61722	•	•	•	386	326	412	22	2124	•	•	•	•
Other Receipts **7**	148164	•	•	•	2964	741	1358	3896	2444	•	•	•	•
Total Receipts **8**	14354267	•	•	•	1049611	458148	946939	861260	728240	•	•	•	•
Average Total Receipts **9**	37874	•	•	•	12800	11174	35072	78296	104034	•	•	•	•
Operating Costs/Operating Income (%)													
Cost of Operations **10**	64.9	•	•	•	62.3	60.3	74.6	78.7	75.5	•	•	•	•
Salaries and Wages **11**	6.0	•	•	•	8.2	12.7	5.6	4.6	5.7	•	•	•	•
Taxes Paid **12**	1.6	•	•	•	2.0	1.7	1.3	1.9	1.5	•	•	•	•
Interest Paid **13**	1.3	•	•	•	0.7	0.3	0.4	0.7	1.1	•	•	•	•
Depreciation **14**	3.7	•	•	•	2.0	1.9	1.9	1.7	1.5	•	•	•	•
Amortization and Depletion **15**	0.6	•	•	•	0.0	0.1	0.1	0.6	0.1	•	•	•	•
Pensions and Other Deferred Comp. **16**	0.4	•	•	•	0.2	0.0	0.2	0.4	0.4	•	•	•	•
Employee Benefits **17**	3.3	•	•	•	0.4	2.2	1.4	1.4	2.0	•	•	•	•
Advertising **18**	1.1	•	•	•	0.5	0.2	0.8	0.3	1.0	•	•	•	•
Other Expenses **19**	9.7	•	•	•	12.5	12.0	6.5	5.8	5.2	•	•	•	•
Officers' Compensation **20**	0.9	•	•	•	1.6	1.5	1.9	1.3	1.0	•	•	•	•
Operating Margin **21**	6.6	•	•	•	9.6	7.0	5.2	2.5	5.0	•	•	•	•
Operating Margin Before Officers' Comp. **22**	7.5	•	•	•	11.2	8.5	7.1	3.8	6.0	•	•	•	•

Selected Average Balance Sheet ($ in Thousands)

Net Receivables 23	7141	580	2036	4094	7713	18261
Inventories 24	3139	705	2334	5028	7734	15526
Net Property, Plant and Equipment 25	6269	961	798	2996	8481	10609
Total Assets 26	27124	3747	5805	15956	36543	71253
Notes and Loans Payable 27	4749	580	453	2811	10630	17649
All Other Liabilities 28	8536	1851	1529	6351	11597	21093
Net Worth 29	13840	1317	3823	6794	14316	32510

Selected Financial Ratios (Times to 1)

Current Ratio 30	1.8	1.3	3.4	1.8	1.3	2.3
Quick Ratio 31	0.9	0.9	1.5	0.9	0.6	1.4
Net Sales to Working Capital 32	4.9	21.6	3.1	7.1	20.4	4.0
Coverage Ratio 33	9.9	15.8	27.1	13.4	5.3	7.0
Total Asset Turnover 34	1.3	3.4	1.9	2.2	2.1	1.4
Inventory Turnover 35	7.5	11.2	2.9	5.2	7.9	5.0
Receivables Turnover 36	5.7	19.3	6.6	9.5	11.0	5.8
Total Liabilities to Net Worth 37	1.0	1.8	0.5	1.3	1.6	1.2
Current Assets to Working Capital 38	2.3	4.5	1.4	2.3	4.8	1.8
Current Liabilities to Working Capital 39	1.3	3.5	0.4	1.3	3.8	0.8
Working Capital to Net Sales 40	0.2	0.0	0.3	0.1	0.0	0.3
Inventory to Working Capital 41	0.5	1.1	0.8	1.1	2.2	0.6
Total Receipts to Cash Flow 42	5.2	4.9	6.0	9.1	13.6	10.3
Cost of Goods to Cash Flow 43	3.4	3.1	3.6	6.8	10.7	7.8
Cash Flow to Total Debt 44	0.5	1.1	0.9	0.4	0.3	0.3

Selected Financial Factors (in Percentages)

Debt Ratio 45	49.0	64.9	34.1	57.4	60.8	54.4
Return on Total Assets 46	16.9	38.0	14.6	12.9	8.0	10.7
Return on Equity Before Income Taxes 47	29.9	101.3	21.3	28.1	16.5	20.1
Return on Equity After Income Taxes 48	21.6	100.3	21.1	26.3	14.3	16.7
Profit Margin (Before Income Tax) 49	11.4	10.5	7.3	5.5	3.0	6.4
Profit Margin (After Income Tax) 50	8.3	10.4	7.2	5.1	2.6	5.3

Table I

Corporations with and without Net Income

FURNITURE AND RELATED PRODUCT MANUFACTURING

MONEY AMOUNTS AND SIZE OF ASSETS IN THOUSANDS OF DOLLARS

Item Description for Accounting Period 7/03 Through 6/04	Total	Zero Assets	Under 500	500 to 1,000	1,000 to 5,000	5,000 to 10,000	10,000 to 25,000	25,000 to 50,000	50,000 to 100,000	100,000 to 250,000	250,000 to 500,000	500,000 to 2,500,000	2,500,000 and over
Number of Enterprises 1	12340	1023	8434	1143	1190	268	170	44	29	17	8	14	·
Revenues ($ in Thousands)													
Net Sales 2	58979714	1368550	4403772	2307852	6900456	4553798	5612704	2908487	3641645	3934462	3640923	19707065	·
Interest 3	99585	2472	715	545	2268	1663	2638	2477	2915	14021	25729	44142	·
Rents 4	63347	0	626	106	242	896	4541	3098	357	2934	6607	43941	·
Royalties 5	64363	8516	0	0	0	0	843	338	283	4662	3821	45901	·
Other Portfolio Income 6	195802	50543	4867	820	24460	2263	5903	4474	3188	11419	7890	79974	·
Other Receipts 7	746762	14473	8536	22493	25135	10233	35234	56069	47855	7464	20297	498972	·
Total Receipts 8	60149573	1444554	4418516	2331816	6952561	4568853	5661863	2974943	3696243	3974962	3705267	20419995	·
Average Total Receipts 9	4874	1412	524	2040	5842	17048	33305	67612	127457	233821	463158	1458571	·
Operating Costs/Operating Income (%)													
Cost of Operations 10	67.5	51.2	54.8	66.3	66.4	66.5	71.7	72.8	72.8	70.0	68.9	68.6	·
Salaries and Wages 11	8.2	13.2	12.0	5.4	8.2	11.1	6.8	6.0	5.8	5.3	6.7	8.8	·
Taxes Paid 12	2.3	1.7	3.4	2.8	2.8	2.2	2.0	2.1	2.3	1.7	2.1	2.2	·
Interest Paid 13	1.3	3.8	0.9	1.1	1.0	0.8	0.9	0.7	1.1	2.5	2.5	1.2	·
Depreciation 14	2.4	1.1	2.3	1.7	2.3	1.6	2.2	2.2	2.2	2.4	2.4	3.1	·
Amortization and Depletion 15	0.3	0.2	0.1	0.0	0.1	0.1	0.2	0.1	0.2	0.7	0.2	0.5	·
Pensions and Other Deferred Comp. 16	0.5	0.3	0.4	0.2	0.3	0.3	0.4	0.4	0.3	0.5	0.6	0.7	·
Employee Benefits 17	2.0	1.4	1.4	1.2	1.2	0.9	1.9	2.1	2.0	2.2	3.1	2.5	·
Advertising 18	1.7	9.5	0.3	0.2	1.2	0.8	1.2	1.5	1.2	1.9	2.0	2.1	·
Other Expenses 19	11.0	22.5	16.4	16.5	13.1	8.8	9.2	10.0	6.7	10.2	10.9	9.8	·
Officers' Compensation 20	2.2	5.6	7.6	3.5	3.0	5.1	2.0	1.8	1.0	1.1	0.8	0.6	·
Operating Margin 21	0.5	·	0.4	1.0	0.4	1.8	1.5	0.4	4.3	1.6	·	0.0	·
Operating Margin Before Officers' Comp. 22	2.8	·	8.0	4.5	3.4	6.9	3.5	2.1	5.3	2.7	0.7	0.6	·

Selected Average Balance Sheet ($ in Thousands)

Net Receivables 23	526	0	46	165	639	1892	3864	7699	15695	29442	55754	161138 •
Inventories 24	497	0	25	205	681	2030	4045	8865	17380	32023	62017	121670 •
Net Property, Plant and Equipment 25	650	0	40	175	504	1476	4472	9400	18873	37426	96883	240119 •
Total Assets 26	2947	137	769	2267	6746	15537	34673	70026	154780	353974		1297602 •
Notes and Loans Payable 27	872	0	75	260	1034	2345	4916	8456	18132	48986	113534	321036 •
All Other Liabilities 28	815	0	45	309	959	2171	3866	8348	15119	42552	63882	349863 •
Net Worth 29	1260	0	16	200	274	2230	6756	17869	36775	63242	176558	626703 •

Selected Financial Ratios (Times to 1)

Current Ratio 30	1.7	•	1.6	1.5	1.4	1.8	1.7	2.2	2.4	1.9	1.9	1.6 •
Quick Ratio 31	0.9	•	1.1	0.7	0.7	0.9	0.9	1.1	1.3	0.8	0.9	0.8 •
Net Sales to Working Capital 32	8.1	•	16.2	11.6	14.1	7.6	8.0	5.8	5.4	5.5	7.3	7.5 •
Coverage Ratio 33	2.9	•	1.8	2.8	2.1	3.6	3.5	4.6	6.5	2.0	1.7	4.2 •
Total Asset Turnover 34	1.6	•	3.8	2.6	2.6	2.5	2.1	1.9	1.8	1.5	1.3	1.1 •
Inventory Turnover 35	6.5	•	11.3	6.5	5.7	5.6	5.8	5.4	5.3	5.1	5.1	7.9 •
Receivables Turnover 36	9.2	•	14.2	11.7	8.9	9.0	8.6	8.2	8.0	8.4	6.3	9.5 •
Total Liabilities to Net Worth 37	1.3	•	7.5	2.8	7.3	2.0	1.3	0.9	0.9	1.4	1.0	1.1 •
Current Assets to Working Capital 38	2.4	•	2.8	3.1	3.8	2.2	2.4	1.8	1.7	2.1	2.2	2.6 •
Current Liabilities to Working Capital 39	1.4	•	1.8	2.1	2.8	1.2	1.4	0.8	0.7	1.1	1.2	1.6 •
Working Capital to Net Sales 40	0.1	•	0.1	0.1	0.1	0.1	0.1	0.2	0.2	0.2	0.1	0.1 •
Inventory to Working Capital 41	0.8	•	0.8	1.0	1.6	0.9	1.0	0.7	0.7	0.8	0.8	0.7 •
Total Receipts to Cash Flow 42	9.3	8.7	8.6	8.2	10.2	13.7	10.3	9.4	9.0	9.1	9.1	8.7 •
Cost of Goods to Cash Flow 43	6.3	4.4	4.7	5.4	6.8	9.1	7.4	6.8	6.6	6.4	6.2	6.0 •
Cash Flow to Total Debt 44	0.3	•	0.5	0.4	0.3	0.3	0.4	0.4	0.2	0.3	0.3	0.2 •

Selected Financial Factors (in Percentages)

Debt Ratio 45	57.2	•	88.2	74.0	87.9	66.9	56.5	48.5	47.5	59.1	50.1	51.7 •
Return on Total Assets 46	6.2	•	6.2	8.3	5.7	7.3	6.9	6.5	12.2	7.7	5.3	5.4 •
Return on Equity Before Income Taxes 47	9.5	•	23.1	20.6	24.8	16.1	11.4	9.8	19.7	9.6	4.3	8.5 •
Return on Equity After Income Taxes 48	6.9	•	19.3	19.6	20.6	15.2	9.4	8.1	17.7	7.2	1.4	5.7 •
Profit Margin (Before Income Tax) 49	2.5	•	0.7	2.0	1.2	2.1	2.3	2.6	5.8	2.6	1.7	3.8 •
Profit Margin (After Income Tax) 50	1.8	•	0.6	1.9	1.0	2.0	1.9	2.2	5.2	2.0	0.5	2.5 •

161

Table II

Corporations with Net Income

FURNITURE AND RELATED PRODUCT MANUFACTURING

MONEY AMOUNTS AND SIZE OF ASSETS IN THOUSANDS OF DOLLARS

Item Description for Accounting Period 7/03 Through 6/04		Total	Zero Assets	Under 500	500 to 1,000	1,000 to 5,000	5,000 to 10,000	10,000 to 25,000	25,000 to 50,000	50,000 to 100,000	100,000 to 250,000	250,000 to 500,000	500,000 to 2,500,000	2,500,000 and over
Number of Enterprises	1	6447	20	4574	826	686	130	128	33	22	12	5	11	•
Revenues ($ in Thousands)														
Net Sales	2	43496550	76232	2216855	1703284	4475201	2298258	4392779	2201480	2882093	2876580	2693387	17680402	•
Interest	3	63601	4	228	530	1805	1423	2109	1958	2082	1874	19815	31772	•
Rents	4	23048	0	247	106	164	661	3008	2968	357	433	6607	8496	•
Royalties	5	38605	0	0	0	0	0	5	338	47	117	3821	34277	•
Other Portfolio Income	6	103646	56	3918	820	24010	297	2424	3713	1867	8177	7890	50475	•
Other Receipts	7	640418	7107	1361	1621	17551	8419	31303	29264	46835	7799	14909	474250	•
Total Receipts	8	44365868	83399	2222609	1706361	4518731	2309058	4431628	2239721	2933281	2894980	2746429	18279672	•
Average Total Receipts	9	6882	4170	486	2066	6587	17762	34622	67870	133331	241248	549286	1661788	•
Operating Costs/Operating Income (%)														
Cost of Operations	10	67.0	56.1	51.8	66.3	63.5	66.4	70.1	72.6	72.0	71.0	66.6	67.1	•
Salaries and Wages	11	7.5	3.5	10.0	7.1	7.6	10.7	6.7	5.6	5.5	5.1	7.1	8.1	•
Taxes Paid	12	2.3	2.9	3.5	3.2	2.5	2.9	2.0	1.9	2.4	1.8	2.2	2.1	•
Interest Paid	13	0.9	0.2	0.6	1.0	1.0	0.3	0.8	0.6	0.8	1.2	0.7	1.1	•
Depreciation	14	2.4	1.4	2.4	2.0	2.5	1.9	2.1	2.0	2.1	2.4	2.3	2.8	•
Amortization and Depletion	15	0.3	•	0.0	0.1	0.0	0.1	0.1	0.1	0.1	0.1	0.1	0.5	•
Pensions and Other Deferred Comp.	16	0.5	0.0	0.1	0.2	0.4	0.3	0.4	0.4	0.3	0.4	0.7	0.7	•
Employee Benefits	17	1.8	1.8	0.9	0.9	0.9	0.4	1.5	2.1	2.0	2.6	3.2	2.1	•
Advertising	18	1.6	1.6	0.2	0.2	1.4	0.8	1.4	1.5	1.1	1.2	2.2	2.2	•
Other Expenses	19	10.6	5.8	14.3	11.4	12.6	8.0	9.0	9.1	5.9	8.2	11.1	11.5	•
Officers' Compensation	20	1.9	8.2	9.2	4.3	3.6	1.8	2.1	1.6	1.1	1.3	0.8	0.6	•
Operating Margin	21	3.2	18.5	7.0	3.4	3.9	6.4	3.8	2.4	6.5	4.7	2.8	1.3	•
Operating Margin Before Officers' Comp.	22	5.1	26.7	16.2	7.6	7.5	8.2	5.9	4.0	7.6	6.0	3.7	1.9	•

Selected Average Balance Sheet ($ in Thousands)

Item													
Net Receivables 23	748	0	44	157	595	2338	3939	7744	15850	32974	60661	178859	•
Inventories 24	682	0	16	167	732	1686	4223	8783	16089	34840	69115	137936	•
Net Property, Plant and Equipment 25	928	0	36	196	573	2093	4439	9503	19438	38537	112501	241607	•
Total Assets 26	3837	0	125	722	2382	7199	15368	35099	71686	157120	338403	1156627	•
Notes and Loans Payable 27	967	0	41	357	929	824	4240	7102	15238	36661	42728	294482	•
All Other Liabilities 28	952	0	46	126	660	1925	3454	8512	13386	44538	58759	297618	•
Net Worth 29	1919	0	38	239	794	4450	7673	19485	43062	75921	236916	564527	•

Selected Financial Ratios (Times to 1)

Item													
Current Ratio 30	1.9	•	1.8	1.7	2.1	2.0	2.0	2.4	2.6	2.0	1.8	1.7	•
Quick Ratio 31	1.1	•	1.4	0.9	1.0	1.5	1.1	1.2	1.5	1.0	0.9	1.0	•
Net Sales to Working Capital 32	7.4	•	13.2	11.0	8.1	8.0	7.0	5.3	5.3	5.7	8.2	7.8	•
Coverage Ratio 33	6.6	153.6	13.1	4.6	6.0	23.4	7.1	7.6	11.0	5.5	7.5	5.3	•
Total Asset Turnover 34	1.8	•	3.9	2.9	2.7	2.5	2.2	1.9	1.8	1.5	1.6	1.4	•
Inventory Turnover 35	6.6	•	15.6	8.2	5.7	7.0	5.7	5.5	5.9	4.9	5.2	7.8	•
Receivables Turnover 36	9.3	•	12.9	16.0	9.0	7.1	8.3	8.1	8.1	8.1	6.5	10.5	•
Total Liabilities to Net Worth 37	1.0	•	2.3	2.0	2.0	0.6	1.0	0.8	0.7	1.1	0.4	1.0	•
Current Assets to Working Capital 38	2.1	•	2.3	2.5	1.9	2.0	2.0	1.7	1.6	2.0	2.2	2.4	•
Current Liabilities to Working Capital 39	1.1	•	1.3	1.5	0.9	1.0	1.0	0.7	0.6	1.0	1.2	1.4	•
Working Capital to Net Sales 40	0.1	•	0.1	0.1	0.1	0.1	0.1	0.2	0.2	0.2	0.1	0.1	•
Inventory to Working Capital 41	0.7	•	0.4	1.1	0.9	0.4	0.8	0.7	0.6	0.9	0.8	0.7	•
Total Receipts to Cash Flow 42	7.4	3.4	5.8	10.2	7.9	7.7	8.3	8.7	7.7	8.2	7.0	6.9	•
Cost of Goods to Cash Flow 43	4.9	1.9	3.0	6.8	5.0	5.1	5.8	6.3	5.6	5.8	4.7	4.6	•
Cash Flow to Total Debt 44	0.5	•	1.0	0.4	0.5	0.8	0.5	0.5	0.6	0.4	0.8	0.4	•

Selected Financial Factors (in Percentages)

Item													
Debt Ratio 45	50.0	•	69.8	66.9	66.7	38.2	50.1	44.5	39.9	51.7	30.0	51.2	•
Return on Total Assets 46	10.9	•	30.4	12.9	16.0	17.7	12.2	9.1	16.6	9.9	8.8	8.2	•
Return on Equity Before Income Taxes 47	18.5	•	92.8	30.5	40.1	27.4	21.0	14.2	25.1	16.8	10.9	13.7	•
Return on Equity After Income Taxes 48	15.2	•	89.8	29.3	37.6	26.4	18.7	12.1	22.9	13.9	7.5	9.7	•
Profit Margin (Before Income Tax) 49	5.3	27.8	7.2	3.5	4.9	6.9	4.7	4.1	8.2	5.3	4.8	4.8	•
Profit Margin (After Income Tax) 50	4.3	21.5	7.0	3.4	4.6	6.7	4.2	3.5	8.2	5.3	4.8	3.4	•

Table I
Corporations with and without Net Income

MEDICAL EQUIPMENT AND SUPPLIES

MONEY AMOUNTS AND SIZE OF ASSETS IN THOUSANDS OF DOLLARS

Item Description for Accounting Period 7/03 Through 6/04	Total	Zero Assets	Under 500	500 to 1,000	1,000 to 5,000	5,000 to 10,000	10,000 to 25,000	25,000 to 50,000	50,000 to 100,000	100,000 to 250,000	250,000 to 500,000	500,000 to 2,500,000	2,500,000 and over
Number of Enterprises 1	8672	1870	4609	540	1001	202	201	88	52	44	29	25	11
Revenues ($ in Thousands)													
Net Sales 2	82056253	764402	1103214	1054199	4257698	1833244	4014468	3811271	3399852	5695395	6669047	19475547	29977914
Interest 3	1289358	2018	6234	409	2011	11716	10613	25964	15059	25965	52939	123462	1012968
Rents 4	43448	0	1050	1	186	430	1318	697	6055	6191	8426	8000	11095
Royalties 5	1758845	82333	0	0	816	27236	4762	7039	8031	9652	71031	107890	1440055
Other Portfolio Income 6	814372	8784	25500	3732	70617	458	26375	21210	78376	109871	133813	153259	182375
Other Receipts 7	2534307	22768	17596	1107	22735	21220	33670	25596	136759	44308	70357	824519	1313676
Total Receipts 8	88496583	880305	1153594	1059448	4354063	1894304	4091206	3891777	3644132	5891382	7005613	20692677	33938083
Average Total Receipts 9	10205	471	250	1962	4350	9378	20354	44225	70079	133895	241573	827707	3085280
Operating Costs/Operating Income (%)													
Cost of Operations 10	49.6	49.5	21.4	30.2	61.3	55.0	51.3	52.5	44.2	47.5	42.8	45.9	53.5
Salaries and Wages 11	16.1	25.7	16.5	33.9	12.2	20.9	17.0	16.6	18.7	16.2	14.5	13.6	17.0
Taxes Paid 12	2.0	2.3	4.6	7.7	3.0	2.6	2.3	2.3	2.1	2.1	2.0	1.7	1.6
Interest Paid 13	3.5	2.8	1.0	1.8	0.7	1.6	1.2	1.4	2.6	2.2	2.7	3.1	5.6
Depreciation 14	3.4	3.5	3.1	2.7	2.0	2.2	3.5	3.2	4.4	3.3	4.2	3.7	3.3
Amortization and Depletion 15	1.5	1.2	0.2	0.2	0.4	0.7	0.8	1.0	1.2	1.4	2.0	1.5	1.9
Pensions and Other Deferred Comp. 16	0.8	0.1	0.4	0.0	0.3	0.3	0.5	0.5	0.8	0.3	1.6	0.8	1.1
Employee Benefits 17	2.3	1.4	2.1	2.1	1.2	2.1	2.3	2.6	2.7	2.4	2.5	2.0	2.6
Advertising 18	1.2	1.0	1.0	0.5	1.7	1.5	1.4	1.7	4.3	1.7	1.5	0.9	0.8
Other Expenses 19	22.1	25.0	34.7	20.5	16.8	21.3	20.0	21.0	21.0	19.1	19.4	23.2	23.3
Officers' Compensation 20	1.9	3.2	24.6	5.7	5.2	2.6	3.8	2.8	2.7	2.1	1.4	1.1	0.6
Operating Margin 21	•	•	•	•	•	•	•	•	•	1.4	5.3	2.5	•
Operating Margin Before Officers' Comp. 22	•	•	15.0	0.3	•	•	•	•	•	3.5	6.7	3.6	•

Selected Average Balance Sheet ($ in Thousands)

Net Receivables 23	2572	0	6	225	730	1500	2942	6783	12301	30367	62295	151204	1124883
Inventories 24	1200	0	13	152	355	1362	2840	4976	8954	16310	30991	102607	362160
Net Property, Plant and Equipment 25	1549	0	26	226	272	880	2700	5645	13223	19578	48708	141193	473402
Total Assets 26	14717	0	63	822	1923	6664	16233	35950	71970	164571	376047	1098250	6168588
Notes and Loans Payable 27	4010	0	46	340	565	2324	3656	10823	18749	32493	81056	266221	1840301
All Other Liabilities 28	4709	0	10	194	593	1257	3900	11025	14790	26868	64782	250175	2545443
Net Worth 29	5999	0	7	288	765	3083	8678	14102	38430	105210	230209	581854	1782844

Selected Financial Ratios (Times to 1)

Current Ratio 30	1.5	•	0.8	1.8	2.0	2.8	2.5	2.1	2.6	2.1	2.3	2.1	1.2
Quick Ratio 31	1.0	•	0.4	1.2	1.4	1.6	1.6	1.3	1.6	1.3	1.5	1.2	0.8
Net Sales to Working Capital 32	4.7	•	3.1	8.1	5.5	2.8	3.0	3.8	3.1	3.2	2.5	4.3	8.7
Coverage Ratio 33	2.2	•	•	•	•	•	•	•	2.3	3.2	5.0	4.1	1.6
Total Asset Turnover 34	0.6	•	3.8	2.4	2.2	1.4	1.2	1.2	0.9	0.8	0.6	0.7	0.4
Inventory Turnover 35	3.9	•	4.1	3.9	3.7	7.3	3.6	4.6	3.2	3.8	3.2	3.5	4.0
Receivables Turnover 36	3.8	•	18.7	11.5	7.7	6.7	6.8	7.4	4.5	4.9	4.4	5.3	2.4
Total Liabilities to Net Worth 37	1.5	•	8.4	1.9	1.5	1.2	0.9	1.5	0.9	0.6	0.6	0.9	2.5
Current Assets to Working Capital 38	2.9	•	•	2.2	2.0	1.6	1.6	1.9	1.6	1.9	1.7	2.0	7.0
Current Liabilities to Working Capital 39	1.9	•	•	1.2	1.0	0.6	0.6	0.9	0.6	0.9	0.7	1.0	6.0
Working Capital to Net Sales 40	0.2	•	•	0.1	0.2	0.4	0.3	0.3	0.3	0.3	0.4	0.2	0.1
Inventory to Working Capital 41	0.6	•	•	0.7	0.5	0.5	0.5	0.5	0.4	0.4	0.4	0.6	1.2
Total Receipts to Cash Flow 42	4.4	•	5.3	9.6	11.7	9.2	6.9	7.0	5.1	4.8	3.6	3.4	4.2
Cost of Goods to Cash Flow 43	2.2	•	2.6	2.9	7.2	5.0	3.6	3.7	2.3	2.3	1.6	1.6	2.3
Cash Flow to Total Debt 44	0.2	•	0.9	0.4	0.3	0.3	0.4	0.3	0.4	0.5	0.4	0.4	0.1

Selected Financial Factors (in Percentages)

Debt Ratio 45	59.2	•	89.3	65.0	53.7	46.5	60.2	60.8	46.6	36.1	38.8	47.0	71.1
Return on Total Assets 46	5.0	•	•	•	•	•	•	•	5.6	5.7	8.4	8.9	4.1
Return on Equity Before Income Taxes 47	6.8	•	•	•	•	•	•	•	6.0	6.2	11.0	12.6	5.5
Return on Equity After Income Taxes 48	3.3	•	•	•	•	•	•	•	2.2	3.5	7.3	7.8	2.6
Profit Margin (Before Income Tax) 49	4.3	5.9	•	•	•	•	•	•	3.5	5.0	11.0	9.4	3.6
Profit Margin (After Income Tax) 50	2.1	3.0	•	•	•	•	•	•	1.3	2.9	7.3	5.9	1.7

Table II

Corporations with Net Income

MEDICAL EQUIPMENT AND SUPPLIES

MONEY AMOUNTS AND SIZE OF ASSETS IN THOUSANDS OF DOLLARS

Item Description for Accounting Period 7/03 Through 6/04	Total	Zero Assets	Under 500	500 to 1,000	1,000 to 5,000	5,000 to 10,000	10,000 to 25,000	25,000 to 50,000	50,000 to 100,000	100,000 to 250,000	250,000 to 500,000	500,000 to 2,500,000	2,500,000 and over
Number of Enterprises **1**	4589	821	2332	•	679	107	106	45	27	28	21	20	•
Revenues ($ in Thousands)													
Net Sales **2**	55324662	377593	673412	•	3283072	1418009	2786366	2199593	2383902	3790200	5329422	17034404	•
Interest **3**	989800	1485	513	•	755	1643	2942	15426	5725	19755	42373	52369	•
Rents **4**	23246	0	0	•	0	430	219	454	99	3306	8354	6444	•
Royalties **5**	1454425	82000	0	•	1	27083	1298	5950	7505	6969	66942	89622	•
Other Portfolio Income **6**	677407	3	0	•	70056	166	7655	18444	60071	108690	132536	146211	•
Other Receipts **7**	1499899	21833	4335	•	14935	16569	17856	15222	21132	26071	75113	778158	•
Total Receipts **8**	59969439	482914	678260	•	3368819	1463900	2816336	2255089	2478434	3954991	5654740	18107208	•
Average Total Receipts **9**	13068	588	291	•	4961	13681	26569	50113	91794	141250	269273	905360	•
Operating Costs/Operating Income (%)													
Cost of Operations **10**	46.8	38.4	13.0	•	57.3	53.9	51.3	50.1	44.8	48.7	42.4	44.3	•
Salaries and Wages **11**	15.0	37.1	13.7	•	9.5	16.2	13.0	13.5	12.6	13.3	14.1	13.7	•
Taxes Paid **12**	2.1	2.0	5.0	•	2.7	2.0	2.1	2.0	1.6	1.9	2.0	1.8	•
Interest Paid **13**	3.3	3.7	0.3	•	0.5	0.9	0.9	1.0	2.8	1.9	1.9	1.6	•
Depreciation **14**	3.3	1.8	1.5	•	1.1	1.5	2.6	3.1	3.1	2.8	4.0	3.6	•
Amortization and Depletion **15**	1.2	0.9	•	•	0.0	0.2	0.3	0.7	0.7	0.9	1.4	1.3	•
Pensions and Other Deferred Comp. **16**	0.9	0.0	0.1	•	0.2	0.4	0.6	0.6	0.9	0.4	1.9	0.8	•
Employee Benefits **17**	2.2	0.9	2.5	•	0.9	1.1	1.7	1.9	2.1	2.7	2.5	2.1	•
Advertising **18**	1.4	0.6	0.1	•	2.0	1.2	1.3	2.2	4.9	1.8	1.4	0.9	•
Other Expenses **19**	19.1	26.9	22.0	•	13.6	16.2	13.3	15.7	14.7	15.7	19.0	23.2	•
Officers' Compensation **20**	1.8	1.5	28.8	•	4.7	2.1	3.3	2.2	2.2	1.3	1.5	1.2	•
Operating Margin **21**	2.8	•	12.9	•	7.5	4.3	9.6	6.9	9.6	8.7	7.9	5.5	•
Operating Margin Before Officers' Comp. **22**	4.6	•	41.7	•	12.2	6.3	12.9	9.1	11.8	9.9	9.4	6.6	•

Selected Average Balance Sheet ($ in Thousands)

Item													
Net Receivables 23	2620	0	6	•	841	2016	3750	7356	13836	34667	68190	152482	•
Inventories 24	1644	0	9	•	363	1528	3455	5345	12511	14091	36131	111546	•
Net Property, Plant and Equipment 25	1921	0	21	•	199	1120	2982	6233	12749	18680	49486	155634	•
Total Assets 26	16695	0	48	•	1851	6835	16150	36114	74463	163011	377481	1072636	•
Notes and Loans Payable 27	3619	0	15	•	420	1637	3802	6571	25085	26977	49740	204480	•
All Other Liabilities 28	5847	0	7	•	579	1412	4008	7594	15738	28548	70530	252116	•
Net Worth 29	7229	0	25	•	852	3786	8340	21949	33639	107486	257211	616040	•

Selected Financial Ratios (Times to 1)

Item													
Current Ratio 30	1.7	•	1.6	•	2.1	2.7	2.5	2.7	2.3	2.3	2.3		•
Quick Ratio 31	1.1	•	1.1	•	1.5	1.4	1.5	1.7	1.5	1.4	1.3		•
Net Sales to Working Capital 32	4.8	•	55.8	•	5.8	4.5	4.1	3.7	3.9	3.0	2.5	4.0	•
Coverage Ratio 33	4.8	8.4	39.9	•	23.0	9.1	13.4	10.2	6.3	8.0	8.6	8.8	•
Total Asset Turnover 34	0.7	•	6.0	•	2.6	1.9	1.6	1.4	1.2	0.8	0.7	0.8	•
Inventory Turnover 35	3.4	•	4.4	•	7.6	4.7	3.9	4.6	3.2	4.7	3.0	3.4	•
Receivables Turnover 36	3.8	•	18.7	•	7.7	7.0	7.0	7.1	4.7	5.1	4.4	11.2	•
Total Liabilities to Net Worth 37	1.3	•	0.9	•	1.2	0.8	0.9	0.6	1.2	0.5	0.5	0.7	•
Current Assets to Working Capital 38	2.5	•	2.8	•	1.9	1.6	1.7	1.6	1.6	1.8	1.8	1.8	•
Current Liabilities to Working Capital 39	1.5	•	1.8	•	0.9	0.6	0.7	0.6	0.6	0.8	0.8	0.8	•
Working Capital to Net Sales 40	0.2	•	0.0	•	0.2	0.2	0.2	0.3	0.3	0.3	0.4	0.3	•
Inventory to Working Capital 41	0.6	•	0.2	•	0.5	0.4	0.6	0.4	0.4	0.4	0.4	0.5	•
Total Receipts to Cash Flow 42	3.6	2.7	3.2	•	5.7	4.5	4.6	4.4	3.9	3.9	3.2	3.0	•
Cost of Goods to Cash Flow 43	1.7	1.0	0.4	•	3.3	2.4	2.3	2.2	1.8	1.9	1.4	1.3	•
Cash Flow to Total Debt 44	0.4	•	4.0	•	0.8	1.0	0.7	0.8	0.6	0.3	0.6	0.7	•

Selected Financial Factors (in Percentages)

Item													
Debt Ratio 45	56.7	•	47.2	•	54.0	44.6	48.4	39.2	54.8	34.1	31.9	42.6	•
Return on Total Assets 46	11.3	•	84.2	•	27.6	16.3	18.7	14.3	20.9	12.5	11.3	11.2	•
Return on Equity Before Income Taxes 47	20.5	•	155.5	•	57.3	26.2	33.6	21.2	39.0	16.6	14.6	17.3	•
Return on Equity After Income Taxes 48	15.0	•	154.6	•	56.4	22.1	30.5	17.6	30.6	12.5	10.0	11.7	•
Profit Margin (Before Income Tax) 49	12.3	27.3	13.6	•	10.1	7.5	10.6	9.5	14.8	13.1	14.8	12.5	•
Profit Margin (After Income Tax) 50	9.0	21.3	13.5	•	9.9	6.3	9.7	7.9	11.6	9.9	10.2	8.4	•

Table I

Corporations with and without Net Income

OTHER MISCELLANEOUS MANUFACTURING

MONEY AMOUNTS AND SIZE OF ASSETS IN THOUSANDS OF DOLLARS

Item Description for Accounting Period 7/03 Through 6/04	Total	Zero Assets	Under 500	500 to 1,000	1,000 to 5,000	5,000 to 10,000	10,000 to 25,000	25,000 to 50,000	50,000 to 100,000	100,000 to 250,000	250,000 to 500,000	500,000 to 2,500,000	2,500,000 and over
Number of Enterprises **1**	26465	1965	19150	2048	2152	387	419	175	72	54	22	15	5
Revenues ($ in Thousands)													
Net Sales **2**	93456418	1060420	7652577	3683986	11930388	4921551	10091399	8748128	6234384	8712675	9211858	8915895	12293155
Interest **3**	867097	3563	1864	1137	4868	3517	16636	7443	12106	29793	111785	75084	599301
Rents **4**	45544	291	2933	405	437	849	2984	1661	1756	5794	19132	9111	190
Royalties **5**	573700	3267	0	289	55	468	3452	17512	18255	4278	19679	58268	448177
Other Portfolio Income **6**	611242	10092	20393	12745	35811	19484	28583	31501	18829	20513	114622	108761	192906
Other Receipts **7**	1733461	40129	24550	30461	49379	13905	107927	48896	72929	86614	45686	132685	1080305
Total Receipts **8**	97290462	1117762	7702317	3729023	12020938	4959774	10250981	8855141	6358259	8859667	9522762	9299804	14614034
Average Total Receipts **9**	3676	569	402	1821	5586	12816	24465	50601	88309	164068	432853	619987	2922807
Operating Costs/Operating Income (%)													
Cost of Operations **10**	63.4	62.5	57.1	60.8	63.4	61.4	67.1	65.5	64.2	63.6	69.5	61.0	61.2
Salaries and Wages **11**	9.4	8.2	10.4	10.6	8.0	10.6	9.0	9.1	8.4	8.7	7.8	8.4	12.9
Taxes Paid **12**	2.0	2.2	2.3	2.8	2.7	1.8	2.1	2.1	1.6	1.7	1.7	1.3	1.8
Interest Paid **13**	2.7	2.8	1.1	1.1	0.9	1.2	1.5	1.8	2.3	2.7	2.8	3.2	7.8
Depreciation **14**	3.0	3.1	1.9	2.1	2.1	2.7	2.8	2.7	3.3	3.9	3.5	3.1	4.1
Amortization and Depletion **15**	0.4	2.8	0.1	0.2	0.1	0.3	0.4	0.5	0.8	0.9	1.0	1.1	•
Pensions and Other Deferred Comp. **16**	0.6	0.4	0.3	0.3	0.8	0.4	0.5	0.6	0.4	0.7	0.5	0.9	0.9
Employee Benefits **17**	1.6	1.2	1.7	0.8	1.3	1.8	1.5	1.8	1.4	1.7	2.2	2.0	1.4
Advertising **18**	1.8	0.6	1.5	1.1	0.8	2.1	1.4	2.0	2.3	1.6	1.1	3.1	2.5
Other Expenses **19**	13.9	23.0	17.2	13.8	14.8	12.8	11.3	10.8	13.0	10.4	7.9	15.1	21.8
Officers' Compensation **20**	2.5	2.5	6.8	7.3	3.7	3.8	2.4	2.5	1.5	1.2	0.7	1.0	0.7
Operating Margin **21**	•	•	•	•	1.4	1.1	0.1	0.7	0.7	2.9	1.0	•	•
Operating Margin Before Officers' Comp. **22**	1.1	•	•	6.4	5.1	4.8	2.5	3.2	2.3	4.1	1.7	0.7	•

Selected Average Balance Sheet ($ in Thousands)

Item													
Net Receivables 23	557	0	38	133	560	2015	3871	8317	15476	27887	59609	152423	489315
Inventories 24	499	0	29	152	784	2251	4043	8183	13867	24389	59603	92127	329984
Net Property, Plant and Equipment 25	503	0	19	201	495	1042	3248	7417	12777	31072	70711	104959	534790
Total Assets 26	3019	0	119	690	2288	7057	15335	33907	70918	148006	383926	946118	4092122
Notes and Loans Payable 27	1045	0	84	298	876	2564	5047	13963	26500	55328	118445	263772	1306641
All Other Liabilities 28	878	0	44	236	604	2414	4204	8661	19507	32350	89039	294208	1374888
Net Worth 29	1097	0	-9	156	807	2078	6084	11283	24912	60328	176443	388138	1410593

Selected Financial Ratios (Times to 1)

Ratio													
Current Ratio 30	1.6	•	1.7	1.2	1.9	1.5	1.7	1.7	1.9	1.7	1.8	1.6	1.2
Quick Ratio 31	0.9	•	1.1	0.6	1.0	0.8	0.9	0.9	1.0	0.9	0.9	1.0	0.7
Net Sales to Working Capital 32	6.4	•	10.5	26.5	7.5	6.9	5.7	5.6	4.6	5.7	5.3	4.6	8.4
Coverage Ratio 33	2.2	•	1.3	1.3	3.3	2.5	2.1	2.1	2.2	2.7	2.5	2.4	1.9
Total Asset Turnover 34	1.2	•	3.3	2.6	2.4	1.8	1.6	1.5	1.2	1.1	1.1	0.6	0.6
Inventory Turnover 35	4.5	•	7.9	7.2	4.5	3.5	4.0	4.0	4.0	4.2	4.9	3.9	4.6
Receivables Turnover 36	6.2	•	11.1	13.7	8.8	6.0	6.1	6.1	5.4	5.6	6.2	3.8	5.2
Total Liabilities to Net Worth 37	1.8	•	•	3.4	1.8	2.4	1.5	2.0	1.8	1.5	1.2	1.4	1.9
Current Assets to Working Capital 38	2.7	•	2.4	6.2	2.1	2.8	2.4	2.4	2.1	2.4	2.3	2.6	5.3
Current Liabilities to Working Capital 39	1.7	•	1.4	5.2	1.1	1.8	1.4	1.4	1.1	1.4	1.3	1.6	4.3
Working Capital to Net Sales 40	0.2	•	0.1	0.0	0.1	0.1	0.2	0.2	0.2	0.2	0.2	0.2	0.1
Inventory to Working Capital 41	0.9	•	0.7	2.4	0.9	1.2	0.9	0.9	0.8	0.8	0.7	0.7	1.1
Total Receipts to Cash Flow 42	7.1	6.8	8.3	9.3	7.5	8.0	9.2	9.3	7.3	7.5	9.6	5.9	4.3
Cost of Goods to Cash Flow 43	4.5	4.3	4.7	5.6	4.7	4.9	6.2	6.1	4.7	4.8	6.7	3.6	2.6
Cash Flow to Total Debt 44	0.3	•	0.4	0.4	0.5	0.3	0.3	0.2	0.3	0.2	0.2	0.2	0.2

Selected Financial Factors (in Percentages)

Factor													
Debt Ratio 45	63.7	•	107.3	77.3	64.7	70.6	60.3	66.7	64.9	59.2	54.0	59.0	65.5
Return on Total Assets 46	6.9	•	4.9	3.8	7.4	5.6	5.0	5.5	6.1	8.1	7.9	4.9	9.1
Return on Equity Before Income Taxes 47	10.2	•	•	3.6	14.5	11.4	6.7	8.7	9.5	12.5	10.4	7.0	12.7
Return on Equity After Income Taxes 48	6.7	•	•	1.0	12.8	9.0	4.9	6.5	7.0	9.6	6.3	3.9	7.2
Profit Margin (Before Income Tax) 49	3.2	•	0.3	0.3	2.1	1.9	1.7	2.0	2.7	4.7	4.4	4.6	7.3
Profit Margin (After Income Tax) 50	2.1	•	0.2	0.1	1.9	1.5	1.2	1.5	2.0	3.6	2.7	2.5	4.1

Table II

Corporations with Net Income

OTHER MISCELLANEOUS MANUFACTURING

MONEY AMOUNTS AND SIZE OF ASSETS IN THOUSANDS OF DOLLARS

Item Description for Accounting Period 7/03 Through 6/04	Total	Zero Assets	Under 500	500 to 1,000	1,000 to 5,000	5,000 to 10,000	10,000 to 25,000	25,000 to 50,000	50,000 to 100,000	100,000 to 250,000	250,000 to 500,000	500,000 to 2,500,000	2,500,000 and over
Number of Enterprises **1**	12751	19	9097	•	1633	290	284	117	48	35	14	10	•
Revenues ($ in Thousands)													
Net Sales **2**	64981734	645910	4218694	•	9826985	4072144	7394253	6186503	4586915	6397645	6006788	7149149	•
Interest **3**	321079	2855	1307	•	3095	1853	10887	4968	7856	14256	56249	72719	•
Rents **4**	32930	0	0	•	437	745	1396	1280	71	3687	16584	8325	•
Royalties **5**	509555	3267	0	•	2	420	1357	6954	12134	758	6236	51400	•
Other Portfolio Income **6**	485726	1841	18741	•	14069	17574	18539	9914	12454	13971	107838	94526	•
Other Receipts **7**	1190224	25154	18423	•	35112	11181	64350	30635	28390	49901	32090	124840	•
Total Receipts **8**	67521248	679027	4257165	•	9879700	4103917	7490782	6240254	4647820	6480218	6225785	7500959	•
Average Total Receipts **9**	5295	35738	468	•	6050	14151	26376	53336	96830	185149	444699	750096	•
Operating Costs/Operating Income (%)													
Cost of Operations **10**	60.4	61.1	50.7	•	62.6	59.9	65.6	63.7	62.0	62.2	66.7	58.3	•
Salaries and Wages **11**	9.7	7.7	9.4	•	7.7	10.0	8.5	8.8	7.5	7.9	7.7	8.8	•
Taxes Paid **12**	2.0	2.2	2.2	•	2.6	1.7	2.1	2.0	1.5	1.5	2.0	1.5	•
Interest Paid **13**	1.8	3.4	1.2	•	0.6	1.1	1.1	1.0	1.8	1.6	1.9	2.7	•
Depreciation **14**	2.7	2.3	1.8	•	1.7	2.4	2.4	2.4	3.0	4.0	3.2	3.2	•
Amortization and Depletion **15**	0.6	0.3	0.1	•	0.1	0.2	0.2	0.3	0.6	0.6	1.0	0.9	•
Pensions and Other Deferred Comp. **16**	0.7	0.5	0.4	•	1.0	0.4	0.5	0.6	0.4	0.7	0.7	1.0	•
Employee Benefits **17**	1.7	1.5	2.3	•	1.2	1.7	1.4	1.5	1.3	1.8	2.3	2.1	•
Advertising **18**	1.9	0.6	1.7	•	0.8	2.0	1.3	1.9	2.3	1.4	1.2	3.5	•
Other Expenses **19**	12.4	15.2	15.9	•	14.4	11.8	9.7	9.0	12.2	9.4	7.6	14.6	•
Officers' Compensation **20**	2.6	2.1	6.8	•	3.6	3.9	2.5	2.9	1.3	1.2	0.7	1.1	•
Operating Margin **21**	3.5	3.0	7.6	•	3.7	4.9	4.7	5.9	6.0	7.8	5.0	2.1	•
Operating Margin Before Officers' Comp. **22**	6.1	5.1	14.4	•	7.4	8.8	7.2	8.8	7.3	9.0	5.6	3.2	•

Selected Average Balance Sheet ($ in Thousands)

Net Receivables 23	759	0	40	558	2138	3984	8170	16849	30443	68819	169547
Inventories 24	724	0	29	790	2213	4084	7813	14643	26860	69599	99027
Net Property, Plant and Equipment 25	636	0	19	451	861	3226	7370	11654	35722	70576	123866
Total Assets 26	4221	0	133	2210	6959	15125	33601	70940	146605	393113	1090342
Notes and Loans Payable 27	1215	0	94	682	2310	4227	8829	24643	41640	72805	312918
All Other Liabilities 28	1207	0	42	544	1946	3755	8000	17412	30459	102671	362590
Net Worth 29	1798	0	-3	984	2702	7142	16772	28885	74506	217637	414833

Selected Financial Ratios (Times to 1)

Current Ratio 30	1.7	•	1.8	2.2	1.9	2.0	2.2	1.9	2.2	2.1	1.6
Quick Ratio 31	0.9	•	1.2	1.1	1.0	1.1	1.2	1.0	1.2	1.1	1.0
Net Sales to Working Capital 32	5.8	•	10.6	7.4	5.5	5.0	4.5	4.9	4.5	4.2	5.0
Coverage Ratio 33	5.3	3.5	7.8	7.7	6.4	6.5	7.6	5.0	6.9	5.5	3.8
Total Asset Turnover 34	1.2	•	3.5	2.7	2.0	1.7	1.6	1.3	1.2	1.1	0.7
Inventory Turnover 35	4.3	•	8.2	4.8	3.8	4.2	4.3	4.0	4.2	4.1	4.2
Receivables Turnover 36	6.1	•	13.6	9.5	6.7	6.5	6.8	5.9	5.7	5.3	8.4
Total Liabilities to Net Worth 37	1.3	•	•	1.2	1.6	1.1	1.0	1.5	1.0	0.8	1.6
Current Assets to Working Capital 38	2.4	•	2.3	1.8	2.2	2.0	1.8	2.1	1.8	1.9	2.7
Current Liabilities to Working Capital 39	1.4	•	1.3	0.8	1.2	1.0	0.8	1.1	0.8	0.9	1.7
Working Capital to Net Sales 40	0.2	•	0.1	0.1	0.2	0.2	0.2	0.2	0.2	0.2	0.2
Inventory to Working Capital 41	0.7	•	0.7	0.8	1.0	0.7	0.7	0.8	0.6	0.6	0.7
Total Receipts to Cash Flow 42	5.8	5.2	5.0	6.6	6.5	7.3	7.2	5.6	5.9	7.1	5.1
Cost of Goods to Cash Flow 43	3.5	3.2	2.5	4.1	3.9	4.8	4.6	3.5	3.7	4.8	3.0
Cash Flow to Total Debt 44	0.4	•	0.7	0.7	0.5	0.4	0.4	0.4	0.4	0.3	0.2

Selected Financial Factors (in Percentages)

Debt Ratio 45	57.4	•	102.6	55.5	61.2	52.8	50.1	59.3	49.2	44.6	62.0
Return on Total Assets 46	11.8	•	33.9	13.3	13.6	12.2	12.3	12.5	13.4	11.5	6.8
Return on Equity Before Income Taxes 47	22.6	•	•	26.0	29.6	21.9	21.4	24.6	22.5	17.0	13.2
Return on Equity After Income Taxes 48	18.1	•	•	24.1	27.2	19.7	19.1	21.3	18.8	11.8	8.8
Profit Margin (Before Income Tax) 49	8.0	8.4	8.5	4.2	5.7	6.0	6.8	7.4	9.2	8.6	7.7
Profit Margin (After Income Tax) 50	6.4	8.0	8.4	3.9	5.2	5.4	6.1	6.4	7.7	6.0	5.1

Table I
Corporations with and without Net Income

MOTOR VEHICLE AND MOTOR VEHICLE PARTS AND SUPPLIES

Money Amounts and Size of Assets in Thousands of Dollars

Item Description for Accounting Period 7/03 Through 6/04		Total	Zero Assets	Under 500	500 to 1,000	1,000 to 5,000	5,000 to 10,000	10,000 to 25,000	25,000 to 50,000	50,000 to 100,000	100,000 to 250,000	250,000 to 500,000	500,000 to 2,500,000	2,500,000 and over
Number of Enterprises	1	16131	1006	9667	2444	2189	357	260	100	45	27	13	16	7
Revenues ($ in Thousands)														
Net Sales	2	212422733	249074	10935661	4183228	10591209	5383379	9086878	7980302	6409229	7858723	10645552	33771851	105327647
Interest	3	1724557	2410	2331	1523	13103	8667	5503	7516	7466	13027	47076	125992	1489943
Rents	4	634054	22	4515	665	6466	1614	5088	11630	3720	913	7128	115526	476767
Royalties	5	95323	0	0	0	0	26	713	2	390	1981	58013	14890	19307
Other Portfolio Income	6	1299153	1284	603	372	4507	4594	23349	12232	3966	13621	15144	277694	939789
Other Receipts	7	2448792	7552	24852	8344	61247	89465	40118	64904	48997	74481	21843	250055	1756933
Total Receipts	8	218622612	260342	10967962	4194132	10676532	5487745	9161649	8076586	6473768	7962746	10794756	34556008	110010386
Average Total Receipts	9	13553	259	1135	1716	4877	15372	35237	80766	143862	294917	830366	2159750	15715769
Operating Costs/Operating Income (%)														
Cost of Operations	10	80.8	68.1	85.0	67.9	71.4	79.2	75.7	77.0	77.0	78.4	86.2	83.9	81.5
Salaries and Wages	11	4.3	9.2	3.8	9.5	9.0	7.5	8.7	7.8	7.9	6.8	4.3	3.4	2.7
Taxes Paid	12	0.8	2.6	0.8	1.9	1.6	1.3	1.3	1.2	1.5	1.1	0.7	0.8	0.5
Interest Paid	13	0.8	0.4	0.3	0.5	0.5	0.7	0.6	0.6	0.6	0.9	0.8	0.4	1.0
Depreciation	14	4.6	0.8	0.5	1.6	0.9	0.9	1.4	1.5	1.5	1.3	1.2	1.8	7.9
Amortization and Depletion	15	0.1	0.1	0.1	0.0	0.1	0.1	0.1	0.1	0.1	0.3	0.2	0.1	0.1
Pensions and Other Deferred Comp.	16	0.2	0.5	0.1	0.3	0.2	0.2	0.2	0.2	0.2	0.1	0.2	0.2	0.2
Employee Benefits	17	0.5	0.7	0.2	0.8	0.5	0.5	0.7	0.9	0.7	1.1	0.6	0.5	0.4
Advertising	18	2.9	1.6	0.3	0.6	0.8	0.5	0.5	0.7	0.6	0.7	0.6	3.4	4.3
Other Expenses	19	5.9	15.4	7.1	11.2	10.8	8.5	8.2	7.2	7.1	7.9	5.1	6.6	4.2
Officers' Compensation	20	0.7	4.1	2.6	4.4	3.4	2.0	1.6	1.4	0.7	0.5	0.3	0.3	0.1
Operating Margin	21	•	•	•	1.3	0.2	•	1.0	1.4	2.0	1.0	•	•	•
Operating Margin Before Officers' Comp.	22	•	0.6	1.8	5.6	3.6	0.7	2.6	2.8	2.7	1.5	0.2	•	•

Selected Average Balance Sheet ($ in Thousands)

Net Receivables 23	2140	0	42	128	450	1848	4159	8895	15134	30888	76961	210449	3471760
Inventories 24	1512	0	67	346	828	3425	6187	12192	24308	52800	88777	276993	1275822
Net Property, Plant and Equipment 25	1797	0	14	74	214	650	1877	5317	10982	18280	58521	129360	3304986
Total Assets 26	7867	0	179	649	1925	6916	15155	33943	65753	156868	321357	931554	11899963
Notes and Loans Payable 27	2857	0	74	183	464	2127	4929	12636	19982	47288	107724	187704	4862009
All Other Liabilities 28	2800	0	65	161	584	2722	5158	9955	18709	48834	99330	446537	4137355
Net Worth 29	2209	0	40	304	877	2066	5068	11351	27062	60745	114303	297313	2899599

Selected Financial Ratios (Times to 1)

Current Ratio 30	1.6	•	2.3	2.4	2.2	1.5	1.6	1.6	1.7	1.5	1.4	1.3	1.6
Quick Ratio 31	0.8	•	1.1	1.0	0.9	0.5	0.7	0.7	0.8	0.7	0.6	0.6	0.9
Net Sales to Working Capital 32	7.1	•	12.9	5.2	5.7	8.3	8.2	8.5	7.0	8.8	15.3	15.9	5.5
Coverage Ratio 33	3.0	3.9	•	3.8	2.8	1.9	3.8	5.0	5.7	3.8	2.7	3.1	2.8
Total Asset Turnover 34	1.7	•	6.3	2.6	2.5	2.2	2.3	2.4	2.2	1.9	2.5	2.3	1.3
Inventory Turnover 35	7.0	•	14.4	3.4	4.2	3.5	4.3	5.0	4.5	4.3	7.9	6.4	9.6
Receivables Turnover 36	6.1	•	29.1	13.4	10.0	8.1	8.7	9.1	10.7	10.0	9.8	9.4	4.3
Total Liabilities to Net Worth 37	2.6	•	3.5	1.1	1.2	2.3	2.0	2.0	1.4	1.6	1.8	2.1	3.1
Current Assets to Working Capital 38	2.8	•	1.8	1.8	1.8	3.2	2.8	2.7	2.4	3.2	3.4	4.7	2.7
Current Liabilities to Working Capital 39	1.8	•	0.8	0.7	0.8	2.2	1.8	1.7	1.4	2.2	2.4	3.7	1.7
Working Capital to Net Sales 40	0.1	•	0.1	0.2	0.2	0.1	0.1	0.1	0.1	0.1	0.1	0.1	0.2
Inventory to Working Capital 41	0.8	•	0.9	1.0	1.0	1.9	1.5	1.3	1.2	1.7	1.4	2.3	0.5
Total Receipts to Cash Flow 42	16.4	8.3	22.4	10.4	11.6	14.6	12.4	12.7	12.5	11.8	19.8	15.8	18.9
Cost of Goods to Cash Flow 43	13.2	5.7	19.1	7.0	8.3	11.5	9.4	9.8	9.6	9.2	17.1	13.2	15.4
Cash Flow to Total Debt 44	0.1	•	0.4	0.5	0.4	0.2	0.3	0.3	0.3	0.3	0.2	0.2	0.1

Selected Financial Factors (in Percentages)

Debt Ratio 45	71.9	77.6	•	53.1	54.4	70.1	66.6	66.6	58.8	61.3	64.4	68.1	75.6
Return on Total Assets 46	3.7	•	•	5.4	3.8	2.8	5.6	7.6	7.9	5.9	5.3	3.1	3.4
Return on Equity Before Income Taxes 47	8.8	•	•	8.5	5.4	4.3	12.4	18.2	15.8	11.2	9.2	6.5	8.8
Return on Equity After Income Taxes 48	4.7	•	•	6.9	4.4	2.3	10.2	16.6	12.3	8.6	6.9	3.0	3.5
Profit Margin (Before Income Tax) 49	1.5	1.1	•	1.5	1.0	0.6	1.8	2.6	3.0	2.3	1.3	0.9	1.7
Profit Margin (After Income Tax) 50	0.8	0.5	•	1.2	0.8	0.3	1.5	2.4	2.3	1.8	1.0	0.4	0.7

Table II

Corporations with Net Income

MOTOR VEHICLE AND MOTOR VEHICLE PARTS AND SUPPLIES

MONEY AMOUNTS AND SIZE OF ASSETS IN THOUSANDS OF DOLLARS

Item Description for Accounting Period 7/03 Through 6/04		Total	Zero Assets	Under 500	500 to 1,000	1,000 to 5,000	5,000 to 10,000	10,000 to 25,000	25,000 to 50,000	50,000 to 100,000	100,000 to 250,000	250,000 to 500,000	500,000 to 2,500,000	2,500,000 and over
Number of Enterprises	1	9937	978	5288	1569	1490	256	199	76	36	•	10	10	•
Revenues ($ in Thousands)														
Net Sales	2	155391551	231787	8379727	3113513	7685497	4227695	7284437	6528745	5544140	•	8635212	19380906	•
Interest	3	816310	2312	643	1424	10770	6018	4040	5175	6872	•	30555	117580	•
Rents	4	618438	22	1106	665	3071	478	3999	6614	2977	•	7128	114699	•
Royalties	5	34428	0	0	0	0	26	240	2	390	•	798	14890	•
Other Portfolio Income	6	472575	1284	83	305	3564	477	12102	6375	1697	•	2893	212770	•
Other Receipts	7	1144156	7438	23857	7063	50648	30337	38928	60643	46659	•	19480	186400	•
Total Receipts	8	158477458	242843	8405416	3122970	7753550	4265031	7343746	6607554	5602735	•	8696066	20027245	•
Average Total Receipts	9	15948	248	1590	1990	5204	16660	36903	86942	155632	•	869607	2002724	•
Operating Costs/Operating Income (%)														
Cost of Operations	10	81.0	67.3	85.3	68.8	73.8	79.9	75.3	76.9	76.8	•	84.6	83.7	•
Salaries and Wages	11	4.6	7.9	4.1	9.1	7.5	6.6	8.7	7.7	7.9	•	4.8	4.5	•
Taxes Paid	12	0.9	2.5	0.8	1.7	1.4	1.3	1.4	1.2	1.6	•	0.7	0.8	•
Interest Paid	13	0.4	0.3	0.3	0.5	0.3	0.6	0.5	0.5	0.5	•	0.5	0.7	•
Depreciation	14	2.3	0.8	0.3	1.3	0.8	0.8	1.0	1.1	1.0	•	1.0	1.7	•
Amortization and Depletion	15	0.1	0.0	0.1	0.0	0.0	0.1	0.0	0.1	0.1	•	0.2	0.1	•
Pensions and Other Deferred Comp.	16	0.2	0.5	0.0	0.3	0.4	0.2	0.2	0.2	0.2	•	0.1	0.2	•
Employee Benefits	17	0.5	0.7	0.2	0.9	0.5	0.4	0.6	0.8	0.7	•	0.7	0.6	•
Advertising	18	2.6	1.7	0.2	0.6	0.8	0.5	0.5	0.6	0.6	•	0.7	2.5	•
Other Expenses	19	5.3	11.8	5.5	10.1	8.8	6.2	7.4	6.7	7.2	•	4.5	5.4	•
Officers' Compensation	20	0.7	4.3	1.9	3.2	3.5	2.1	1.7	1.5	0.7	•	0.3	0.5	•
Operating Margin	21	1.5	2.1	1.3	3.4	2.3	1.4	2.6	2.6	2.8	•	2.0	•	•
Operating Margin Before Officers' Comp.	22	2.2	6.4	3.2	6.7	5.7	3.5	4.3	4.1	3.4	•	2.3	•	•

Selected Average Balance Sheet ($ in Thousands)

Net Receivables 23	1802	0	58	148	466	2156	4289	9387	15625	71639	261308	•
Inventories 24	1767	0	76	388	939	3733	6552	13124	24548	78482	293730	•
Net Property, Plant and Equipment 25	1060	0	13	66	132	596	1572	4855	7990	51274	119534	•
Total Assets 26	7250	0	225	664	1970	6829	15081	33935	65931	323013	908996	•
Notes and Loans Payable 27	1842	0	73	163	333	1853	4240	10807	16183	83261	215695	•
All Other Liabilities 28	2599	0	92	166	517	2544	5171	10300	20162	102664	370652	•
Net Worth 29	2810	0	59	336	1120	2431	5670	12828	29586	137088	322649	•

Selected Financial Ratios (Times to 1)

Current Ratio 30	1.5	•	2.1	2.4	2.6	1.6	1.7	1.6	1.9	1.6	1.5
Quick Ratio 31	0.7	•	1.0	0.9	1.0	0.6	0.7	0.8	0.9	0.8	0.8
Net Sales to Working Capital 32	9.6	•	14.9	5.8	5.1	7.9	7.2	8.3	6.5	12.9	9.6
Coverage Ratio 33	8.9	23.6	7.4	9.1	11.1	5.1	7.1	8.1	8.9	6.8	4.8
Total Asset Turnover 34	2.2	•	7.1	3.0	2.6	2.4	2.4	2.5	2.3	2.7	2.1
Inventory Turnover 35	7.2	•	17.7	3.5	4.1	3.5	4.2	5.0	4.8	9.3	5.5
Receivables Turnover 36	7.7	•	33.5	13.1	9.4	7.1	8.7	9.0	11.1	24.1	6.6
Total Liabilities to Net Worth 37	1.6	•	2.8	1.0	0.8	1.8	1.7	1.6	1.2	1.4	1.8
Current Assets to Working Capital 38	3.2	•	1.9	1.7	1.6	2.8	2.5	2.6	2.1	2.7	3.2
Current Liabilities to Working Capital 39	2.2	•	0.9	0.7	0.6	1.8	1.5	1.6	1.1	1.7	2.2
Working Capital to Net Sales 40	0.1	•	0.1	0.2	0.2	0.1	0.1	0.1	0.2	0.1	0.1
Inventory to Working Capital 41	1.1	•	0.9	1.0	0.9	1.5	1.3	1.3	1.0	1.2	1.2
Total Receipts to Cash Flow 42	13.3	7.0	18.4	8.7	10.7	14.9	11.2	11.6	11.2	16.7	15.6
Cost of Goods to Cash Flow 43	10.8	4.7	15.7	6.0	7.9	11.9	8.4	8.9	8.6	14.1	13.1
Cash Flow to Total Debt 44	0.3	•	0.5	0.7	0.6	0.3	0.3	0.4	0.4	0.3	0.2

Selected Financial Factors (in Percentages)

Debt Ratio 45	61.2	•	73.5	49.5	43.2	64.4	62.4	62.2	55.1	57.6	64.5
Return on Total Assets 46	8.4	•	13.2	12.6	9.1	6.9	9.4	10.9	10.0	8.3	6.9
Return on Equity Before Income Taxes 47	19.1	•	43.0	22.1	14.5	15.6	21.4	25.2	19.8	16.7	15.5
Return on Equity After Income Taxes 48	13.9	•	42.0	19.9	13.3	13.2	18.9	23.4	15.8	14.2	10.4
Profit Margin (Before Income Tax) 49	3.4	6.9	1.6	3.7	3.2	2.3	3.3	3.8	3.8	2.7	2.6
Profit Margin (After Income Tax) 50	2.5	6.3	1.6	3.4	2.9	1.9	2.9	3.5	3.0	2.3	1.7

168

Table I

Corporations with and without Net Income

LUMBER AND OTHER CONSTRUCTION MATERIALS

MONEY AMOUNTS AND SIZE OF ASSETS IN THOUSANDS OF DOLLARS

Item Description for Accounting Period 7/03 Through 6/04	Total	Zero Assets	Under 500	500 to 1,000	1,000 to 5,000	5,000 to 10,000	10,000 to 25,000	25,000 to 50,000	50,000 to 100,000	100,000 to 250,000	250,000 to 500,000	500,000 to 2,500,000	2,500,000 and over
Number of Enterprises **1**	15131	1466	7735	1126	3210	1054	360	115	41	15	3	5	•
Revenues ($ in Thousands)													
Net Sales **2**	98621327	479898	4297243	2676288	22512113	19340316	15260143	11346112	7375744	4726457	2009543	8597469	•
Interest **3**	137114	198	6364	2561	21550	7602	8966	7149	10718	7267	11644	53094	•
Rents **4**	126962	0	0	8120	5062	4022	9681	1716	2084	3364	0	92914	•
Royalties **5**	6801	0	0	0	0	25	25	0	3	1179	0	5569	•
Other Portfolio Income **6**	127945	1106	10437	1761	14068	22675	14716	24968	6308	10122	12315	9466	•
Other Receipts **7**	592637	4620	30592	10679	128113	110392	82556	65048	33743	38155	2401	86340	•
Total Receipts **8**	99612786	485822	4344636	2699409	22680906	19485032	15376087	11444993	7428600	4786544	2035903	8844852	•
Average Total Receipts **9**	6583	331	562	2397	7066	18487	42711	99522	181185	319103	678634	1768970	•
Operating Costs/Operating Income (%)													
Cost of Operations **10**	79.0	62.8	66.4	76.4	77.8	80.2	79.4	82.6	80.5	77.8	77.4	82.2	•
Salaries and Wages **11**	6.8	14.7	7.8	5.8	7.2	5.6	7.5	6.3	7.3	8.1	7.4	5.8	•
Taxes Paid **12**	1.2	3.6	1.7	1.6	1.2	1.2	1.2	0.9	1.1	1.0	1.6	1.2	•
Interest Paid **13**	0.7	0.4	0.3	0.5	0.6	0.6	0.5	0.6	0.6	1.0	2.1	1.4	•
Depreciation **14**	1.3	0.8	1.5	1.0	1.0	1.0	1.1	0.9	1.4	1.9	2.6	2.9	•
Amortization and Depletion **15**	0.1	0.5	0.1	0.0	0.0	0.1	0.0	0.0	0.1	0.3	0.4	0.3	•
Pensions and Other Deferred Comp. **16**	0.3	0.2	1.5	0.4	0.4	0.2	0.3	0.2	0.3	0.3	0.5	0.3	•
Employee Benefits **17**	0.7	0.3	0.6	0.6	0.6	0.8	0.7	0.6	0.8	0.7	1.6	1.0	•
Advertising **18**	0.3	0.2	0.7	0.4	0.4	0.2	0.3	0.3	0.3	0.3	0.1	0.1	•
Other Expenses **19**	6.2	13.9	12.9	7.9	6.0	5.7	5.7	5.3	5.7	7.0	5.4	6.0	•
Officers' Compensation **20**	2.0	5.1	5.5	4.2	2.8	2.2	1.5	0.8	0.7	0.6	0.2	0.9	•
Operating Margin **21**	1.4	•	0.8	1.3	2.2	2.2	1.9	1.5	1.3	1.1	0.8	•	•
Operating Margin Before Officers' Comp. **22**	3.4	2.7	6.4	5.5	5.1	4.4	3.4	2.3	2.0	1.7	1.0	•	•

Selected Average Balance Sheet ($ in Thousands)

Net Receivables 23	788	0	•	30	264	803	2183	5196	11829	22179	56351	105885	241245
Inventories 24	623	0	•	27	294	825	1689	4690	9658	18062	28292	69228	58185
Net Property, Plant and Equipment 25	463	0	•	23	67	254	1054	2229	5030	13056	27545	91207	446190
Total Assets 26	2417	0	•	119	706	2189	6447	15083	34218	67805	162121	333751	1090670
Notes and Loans Payable 27	834	0	•	70	204	586	2178	4743	11274	23171	61652	141292	473369
All Other Liabilities 28	649	0	•	26	187	641	1600	4022	8900	16545	53741	107295	277163
Net Worth 29	934	0	•	23	315	963	2669	6319	14044	28090	46728	85163	340139

Selected Financial Ratios (Times to 1)

Current Ratio 30	1.8		•	2.6	2.3	2.1	2.1	1.8	1.7	2.2	1.4	1.7	1.1
Quick Ratio 31	1.0		•	1.6	1.4	1.2	1.1	0.9	0.9	1.2	0.9	1.1	0.7
Net Sales to Working Capital 32	8.7		•	10.4	7.0	7.5	7.3	8.4	9.2	6.9	11.3	8.4	69.0
Coverage Ratio 33	4.8		•	7.2	5.0	8.1	5.7	5.9	4.9	4.1	3.4	2.0	1.9
Total Asset Turnover 34	2.7		•	4.7	3.4	3.2	2.8	2.8	2.9	2.7	1.9	2.0	1.6
Inventory Turnover 35	8.3		•	13.7	6.2	6.6	8.7	7.2	8.4	8.0	8.7	7.5	24.3
Receivables Turnover 36	9.1		•	21.4	7.5	8.2	10.7	8.7	9.2	9.2	7.1	5.8	9.6
Total Liabilities to Net Worth 37	1.6		•	4.1	1.2	1.3	1.4	1.4	1.4	1.4	2.5	2.9	2.2
Current Assets to Working Capital 38	2.3		•	1.6	1.8	1.9	1.9	2.3	2.3	1.8	3.6	2.4	17.5
Current Liabilities to Working Capital 39	1.3		•	0.6	0.8	0.9	0.9	1.3	1.3	0.8	2.6	1.4	16.5
Working Capital to Net Sales 40	0.1		•	0.1	0.1	0.1	0.1	0.1	0.1	0.1	0.1	0.1	0.0
Inventory to Working Capital 41	0.9		•	0.6	0.6	0.8	0.8	1.0	0.9	0.8	1.2	0.8	3.1
Total Receipts to Cash Flow 42	14.7	9.3		9.4	13.5	14.0	15.0	15.1	17.1	17.1	12.8	15.9	17.4
Cost of Goods to Cash Flow 43	11.6	5.8		6.2	10.3	10.9	12.1	12.0	14.1	13.7	9.9	12.3	14.3
Cash Flow to Total Debt 44	0.3		•	0.6	0.4	0.4	0.3	0.3	0.3	0.3	0.2	0.2	0.1

Selected Financial Factors (in Percentages)

Debt Ratio 45	61.3		•	80.4	55.4	56.0	58.6	58.1	59.0	58.6	71.2	74.5	68.8
Return on Total Assets 46	8.5		•	10.6	9.0	10.9	10.1	8.9	8.4	7.1	6.4	8.5	4.2
Return on Equity Before Income Taxes 47	17.3		•	46.4	16.2	21.6	20.1	17.6	16.4	12.9	15.8	16.9	6.4
Return on Equity After Income Taxes 48	15.4		•	43.5	15.0	20.8	18.7	15.7	14.8	11.3	13.0	13.9	2.2
Profit Margin (Before Income Tax) 49	2.5		•	2.0	2.1	3.0	2.9	2.6	2.3	2.0	2.3	2.2	1.3
Profit Margin (After Income Tax) 50	2.2		•	1.8	2.0	2.9	2.7	2.3	2.1	1.8	1.9	1.8	0.4

Table II
Corporations with Net Income

LUMBER AND OTHER CONSTRUCTION MATERIALS

MONEY AMOUNTS AND SIZE OF ASSETS IN THOUSANDS OF DOLLARS

Item Description for Accounting Period 7/03 Through 6/04	Total	Zero Assets	Under 500	500 to 1,000	1,000 to 5,000	5,000 to 10,000	10,000 to 25,000	25,000 to 50,000	50,000 to 100,000	100,000 to 250,000	250,000 to 500,000	500,000 to 2,500,000	2,500,000 and over
Number of Enterprises **1**	10091	1024	4244	930	2477	965	303	96	33	•	•	•	•
Revenues ($ in Thousands)													
Net Sales **2**	82599217	289654	2832288	2239426	19118553	17976786	13444636	9177359	6639498	•	•	•	•
Interest **3**	70597	196	585	2471	15003	6783	6987	4004	9944	•	•	•	•
Rents **4**	28460	0	0	8119	3896	3996	5483	1212	1735	•	•	•	•
Royalties **5**	5617	0	0	0	0	25	25	0	0	•	•	•	•
Other Portfolio Income **6**	101040	620	431	624	9210	22067	11968	24108	2961	•	•	•	•
Other Receipts **7**	452402	2492	27726	6933	101896	107408	73076	60035	30149	•	•	•	•
Total Receipts **8**	83257333	292962	2861030	2257573	19248858	18117065	13542175	9266718	6684287	•	•	•	•
Average Total Receipts **9**	8251	286	674	2427	7771	18774	44694	96528	202554	•	•	•	•
Operating Costs/Operating Income (%)													
Cost of Operations **10**	78.3	65.9	64.2	75.5	77.1	80.2	79.3	81.4	80.7	•	•	•	•
Salaries and Wages **11**	7.0	4.6	9.2	6.0	7.4	5.5	7.4	6.8	7.3	•	•	•	•
Taxes Paid **12**	1.2	1.3	1.4	1.7	1.1	1.1	1.1	0.9	1.1	•	•	•	•
Interest Paid **13**	0.5	0.4	0.3	0.5	0.3	0.6	0.5	0.6	0.6	•	•	•	•
Depreciation **14**	1.2	1.2	1.2	1.1	1.0	0.9	1.0	0.9	1.1	•	•	•	•
Amortization and Depletion **15**	0.1	0.8	0.0	0.0	0.0	0.1	0.0	0.0	0.1	•	•	•	•
Pensions and Other Deferred Comp. **16**	0.3	0.1	1.0	0.4	0.4	0.2	0.3	0.2	0.3	•	•	•	•
Employee Benefits **17**	0.7	0.3	0.6	0.7	0.6	0.8	0.6	0.6	0.7	•	•	•	•
Advertising **18**	0.3	0.3	0.7	0.2	0.4	0.2	0.3	0.3	0.3	•	•	•	•
Other Expenses **19**	5.9	12.2	11.2	7.6	5.8	5.7	5.5	5.3	5.4	•	•	•	•
Officers' Compensation **20**	1.9	7.9	4.5	4.2	2.5	2.2	1.5	0.9	0.7	•	•	•	•
Operating Margin **21**	2.6	5.0	5.7	2.1	3.4	2.5	2.5	2.1	1.8	•	•	•	•
Operating Margin Before Officers' Comp. **22**	4.5	12.8	10.3	6.4	5.8	4.7	4.0	3.0	2.4	•	•	•	•

Selected Average Balance Sheet ($ in Thousands)

Net Receivables 23	981	0	31	278	831	2231	5450	11998	23815
Inventories 24	762	0	24	234	851	1584	4746	9748	18860
Net Property, Plant and Equipment 25	468	0	15	70	248	989	2184	4574	12392
Total Assets 26	2768	0	105	714	2190	6434	15032	33874	67512
Notes and Loans Payable 27	848	0	30	192	514	2117	4526	10980	22537
All Other Liabilities 28	764	0	23	207	619	1561	3952	9404	16910
Net Worth 29	1156	0	52	315	1058	2757	6553	13490	28065

Selected Financial Ratios (Times to 1)

Current Ratio 30	1.9	•	2.9	2.3	2.2	2.1	1.8	1.7	2.1
Quick Ratio 31	1.1	•	2.1	1.4	1.3	1.2	1.0	0.9	1.1
Net Sales to Working Capital 32	8.2	•	11.8	6.9	7.5	7.1	8.4	9.0	7.5
Coverage Ratio 33	7.3	15.0	24.2	7.3	12.7	6.4	7.9	6.1	5.0
Total Asset Turnover 34	3.0	•	6.3	3.4	3.5	2.9	3.0	2.8	3.0
Inventory Turnover 35	8.4	•	17.9	7.8	7.0	9.4	7.4	8.0	8.6
Receivables Turnover 36	9.2	•	22.4	7.6	8.7	11.3	8.7	9.0	9.7
Total Liabilities to Net Worth 37	1.4	•	1.0	1.3	1.1	1.3	1.3	1.5	1.4
Current Assets to Working Capital 38	2.1	•	1.5	1.8	1.8	1.9	2.2	2.4	1.9
Current Liabilities to Working Capital 39	1.1	•	0.5	0.8	0.8	0.9	1.2	1.4	0.9
Working Capital to Net Sales 40	0.1	•	0.1	0.1	0.1	0.1	0.1	0.1	0.1
Inventory to Working Capital 41	0.8	•	0.3	0.6	0.7	0.8	0.9	1.0	0.8
Total Receipts to Cash Flow 42	13.3	6.1	6.9	12.4	12.4	14.5	14.1	15.3	16.6
Cost of Goods to Cash Flow 43	10.4	4.0	4.4	9.4	9.5	11.6	11.2	12.4	13.4
Cash Flow to Total Debt 44	0.4	•	1.8	0.5	0.6	0.4	0.4	0.3	0.3

Selected Financial Factors (in Percentages)

Debt Ratio 45	58.2	•	50.9	55.9	51.7	57.2	56.4	60.2	58.4
Return on Total Assets 46	11.9	•	44.6	11.4	15.4	11.3	10.8	10.5	9.0
Return on Equity Before Income Taxes 47	24.6	•	87.1	22.4	29.4	22.2	21.7	21.9	17.4
Return on Equity After Income Taxes 48	22.4	•	84.7	20.9	28.5	20.7	19.5	20.1	15.4
Profit Margin (Before Income Tax) 49	3.5	6.1	6.8	2.9	4.0	3.3	3.2	3.1	2.4
Profit Margin (After Income Tax) 50	3.2	5.7	6.6	2.7	3.9	3.1	2.9	2.8	2.2

Table I

Corporations with and without Net Income

PROFESSIONAL AND COMMERCIAL EQUIPMENT AND SUPPLIES

MONEY AMOUNTS AND SIZE OF ASSETS IN THOUSANDS OF DOLLARS

Item Description for Accounting Period 7/03 Through 6/04	Total	Zero Assets	Under 500	500 to 1,000	1,000 to 5,000	5,000 to 10,000	10,000 to 25,000	25,000 to 50,000	50,000 to 100,000	100,000 to 250,000	250,000 to 500,000	500,000 to 2,500,000	2,500,000 and over
Number of Enterprises **1**	31492	3764	20855	2569	3316	507	269	92	52	27	21	13	6
Revenues ($ in Thousands)													
Net Sales **2**	165563377	3884146	9816562	5930081	19268706	20648045	10924723	6857284	8474899	7549404	12942179	23959258	35308089
Interest **3**	324524	1070	1956	2804	10436	5435	6861	13293	10968	7742	49477	117199	97284
Rents **4**	212639	0	18	3072	4324	499	2582	1302	4280	632	24494	24189	147246
Royalties **5**	154586	0	0	846	14	1261	1783	5599	5176	8753	58567	71244	1343
Other Portfolio Income **6**	107193	51	691	1230	14770	7688	9560	5417	14439	2269	31771	6206	13100
Other Receipts **7**	1104519	15977	64519	65689	135823	130493	80069	59588	37634	62752	88473	182824	180680
Total Receipts **8**	167466838	3901244	9883746	6003722	19434073	20793421	11025578	6942483	8547396	7631552	13194961	24360920	35747742
Average Total Receipts **9**	5318	1036	474	2337	5861	41013	40987	75462	164373	282650	628331	1873917	5957957
Operating Costs/Operating Income (%)													
Cost of Operations **10**	77.2	89.5	65.4	69.7	69.8	89.0	76.6	74.4	81.2	74.3	79.2	79.2	75.9
Salaries and Wages **11**	7.8	5.1	9.1	9.2	11.3	4.9	8.8	9.2	6.4	7.1	8.0	8.0	6.8
Taxes Paid **12**	1.0	1.5	1.6	1.3	1.7	0.5	1.1	1.2	0.8	1.1	0.8	0.8	0.8
Interest Paid **13**	0.7	0.2	0.5	0.5	0.5	0.2	0.5	0.7	0.6	0.4	0.8	0.9	1.4
Depreciation **14**	2.1	0.6	1.0	0.6	1.3	0.4	0.9	1.3	1.1	0.9	2.5	0.9	5.9
Amortization and Depletion **15**	0.2	0.6	0.1	0.0	0.1	0.0	0.2	0.2	0.2	0.3	0.7	0.4	0.2
Pensions and Other Deferred Comp. **16**	0.3	0.0	0.3	0.1	0.4	0.1	0.2	0.3	0.1	0.2	0.3	0.3	0.4
Employee Benefits **17**	0.8	0.2	0.4	0.5	1.0	0.3	0.7	0.8	0.7	1.1	0.9	1.0	0.9
Advertising **18**	0.8	0.3	1.1	0.5	0.6	0.2	0.7	0.8	0.7	1.6	0.9	0.7	1.1
Other Expenses **19**	7.9	10.4	14.7	11.8	9.4	3.5	8.9	8.4	8.5	9.1	6.9	6.0	7.8
Officers' Compensation **20**	1.4	0.7	5.8	4.2	3.7	0.7	1.5	1.1	0.6	0.6	0.4	0.4	0.1
Operating Margin **21**	•	•	•	1.4	0.2	0.1	•	1.5	•	3.3	•	1.3	•
Operating Margin Before Officers' Comp. **22**	1.2	•	5.8	5.6	3.8	0.8	1.5	2.6	•	3.9	•	1.8	•

Selected Average Balance Sheet ($ in Thousands)

Net Receivables 23	714	0	17	246	790	2309	5652	10692	23652	42106	130274	369038	886106
Inventories 24	395	0	23	172	415	2281	4300	8442	16326	36113	53963	142398	372439
Net Property, Plant and Equipment 25	197	0	10	86	294	619	1371	4194	6308	13554	28552	97772	193595
Total Assets 26	2465	0	83	715	2156	6620	15560	36218	72458	146771	360809	1170584	4250448
Notes and Loans Payable 27	666	0	75	192	711	1748	3925	8589	17570	32555	64099	124888	1511418
All Other Liabilities 28	997	0	39	289	963	3375	7368	15451	32838	53782	195626	506392	1279504
Net Worth 29	802	0	-31	234	482	1497	4267	12178	22050	60433	101084	539305	1459526

Selected Financial Ratios (Times to 1)

Current Ratio 30	1.3	•	1.0	1.6	1.4	1.4	1.4	1.4	1.3	1.7	1.2	1.8	1.1
Quick Ratio 31	0.8	•	0.6	1.0	0.9	0.7	0.8	0.8	0.7	0.9	0.7	1.3	0.6
Net Sales to Working Capital 32	14.1	•	192.7	11.4	12.9	28.0	12.0	9.7	14.1	6.7	17.1	6.8	27.7
Coverage Ratio 33	2.4	•	2.4	6.0	3.0	4.9	2.7	4.9	0.7	12.7	2.1	4.4	1.0
Total Asset Turnover 34	2.1	•	5.7	3.2	2.7	6.2	2.6	2.1	2.2	1.9	1.7	1.6	1.4
Inventory Turnover 35	10.3	•	13.2	9.3	9.8	15.9	7.2	6.6	8.1	5.8	9.0	10.3	12.0
Receivables Turnover 36	7.6	•	21.6	9.1	8.2	16.5	7.6	7.4	7.2	6.0	5.9	4.9	6.9
Total Liabilities to Net Worth 37	2.1	•	2.1	3.5	3.4	2.6	2.0	2.3	1.4	2.6	1.2	1.9	
Current Assets to Working Capital 38	3.9	•	26.2	2.7	3.7	3.8	3.7	3.3	4.7	2.5	6.8	2.3	8.2
Current Liabilities to Working Capital 39	2.9	•	25.2	1.7	2.7	2.8	2.7	2.3	3.7	1.5	5.8	1.3	7.2
Working Capital to Net Sales 40	0.1	•	0.0	0.1	0.1	0.0	0.1	0.1	0.1	0.1	0.1	0.1	0.0
Inventory to Working Capital 41	1.1	•	9.9	0.8	0.9	1.6	1.3	1.1	1.5	0.8	1.7	0.5	2.0
Total Receipts to Cash Flow 42	13.5	•	8.5	7.9	11.9	26.7	12.0	10.0	13.5	8.1	16.5	12.7	15.5
Cost of Goods to Cash Flow 43	10.4	•	5.6	5.5	8.3	23.8	9.2	7.5	11.0	6.0	13.1	10.0	11.8
Cash Flow to Total Debt 44	0.2	•	0.5	0.6	0.3	0.3	0.3	0.3	0.2	0.4	0.1	0.2	0.1

Selected Financial Factors (in Percentages)

Debt Ratio 45	67.5	•	137.7	67.3	77.6	77.4	72.6	66.4	69.6	58.8	72.0	53.9	65.7
Return on Total Assets 46	3.7	•	6.6	10.3	4.1	5.9	3.6	7.2	0.9	9.0	2.8	6.2	2.0
Return on Equity Before Income Taxes 47	6.7	•	•	26.3	12.3	20.7	8.2	16.9	•	20.2	5.3	10.4	0.1
Return on Equity After Income Taxes 48	4.0	•		24.7	10.6	17.9	5.5	13.1	•	16.0	1.3	6.8	•
Profit Margin (Before Income Tax) 49	1.0	•	0.7	2.7	1.0	0.8	0.9	2.8	•	4.4	0.9	3.0	0.0
Profit Margin (After Income Tax) 50	0.6	•	0.6	2.5	0.9	0.7	0.6	2.1	•	3.5	0.2	2.0	•

Table II
Corporations with Net Income

PROFESSIONAL AND COMMERCIAL EQUIPMENT AND SUPPLIES

MONEY AMOUNTS AND SIZE OF ASSETS IN THOUSANDS OF DOLLARS

Item Description for Accounting Period 7/03 Through 6/04	Total	Zero Assets	Under 500	500 to 1,000	1,000 to 5,000	5,000 to 10,000	10,000 to 25,000	25,000 to 50,000	50,000 to 100,000	100,000 to 250,000	250,000 to 500,000	500,000 to 2,500,000	2,500,000 and over
Number of Enterprises 1	17460	1347	11355	1906	2141	384	181	64	31	23	15	9	3
Revenues ($ in Thousands)													
Net Sales 2	111259023	3080437	6111463	4217341	14024920	9584243	7939523	5071392	5546527	6690431	9893167	20509715	18589862
Interest 3	217477	96	54	2087	6906	3523	3546	8075	5961	6208	24592	114162	42267
Rents 4	158636	0	0	4	4096	374	1507	233	2718	545	3633	157	145370
Royalties 5	96735	0	0	846	0	942	605	5599	555	3491	16108	68590	0
Other Portfolio Income 6	82722	40	147	561	11466	7688	3476	1560	11281	2269	31433	5629	7171
Other Receipts 7	646966	4820	21857	43412	120540	87175	55781	52285	31696	52085	80083	50313	46920
Total Receipts 8	112461559	3085393	6133521	4264251	14167928	9683945	8004438	5139144	5598738	6755029	10049016	20748566	18831590
Average Total Receipts 9	6441	2291	540	2237	6617	25219	44223	80299	180604	293697	669934	2305396	6277197
Operating Costs/Operating Income (%)													
Cost of Operations 10	76.4	94.2	62.3	63.9	70.6	79.5	75.8	73.2	80.5	74.3	80.8	78.8	79.2
Salaries and Wages 11	7.4	1.6	7.9	10.0	10.2	8.3	8.7	9.0	6.6	6.8	6.2	8.2	4.4
Taxes Paid 12	1.0	0.2	1.6	1.4	1.5	0.8	1.1	1.2	0.9	1.0	0.8	0.8	0.8
Interest Paid 13	0.5	0.1	0.5	0.5	0.3	0.3	0.5	0.6	0.4	0.4	0.6	0.9	0.5
Depreciation 14	1.2	0.2	1.1	0.5	0.7	0.8	0.9	1.3	0.7	0.9	1.4	0.7	3.3
Amortization and Depletion 15	0.2	0.1	0.0	0.0	0.0	0.0	0.2	0.1	0.2	0.3	0.3	0.4	0.1
Pensions and Other Deferred Comp. 16	0.2	0.0	0.4	0.2	0.4	0.2	0.2	0.3	0.1	0.2	0.2	0.2	0.2
Employee Benefits 17	0.6	0.1	0.4	0.5	0.8	0.5	0.7	0.8	0.9	1.1	0.7	0.7	0.4
Advertising 18	0.9	0.3	1.5	0.6	0.5	0.4	0.5	0.7	0.3	1.2	1.0	0.7	2.1
Other Expenses 19	7.7	2.5	12.3	13.0	8.4	6.0	7.8	7.5	6.5	9.2	6.9	5.6	8.6
Officers' Compensation 20	1.5	0.0	7.0	5.0	3.5	1.3	1.5	1.0	0.7	0.6	0.4	0.4	0.2
Operating Margin 21	2.3	0.7	5.0	4.3	3.0	1.8	2.1	4.2	2.3	4.1	0.7	2.7	0.2
Operating Margin Before Officers' Comp. 22	3.8	0.8	12.0	9.3	6.5	3.1	3.6	5.2	2.9	4.8	1.1	3.0	0.4

Selected Average Balance Sheet ($ in Thousands)

Line Item													
Net Receivables 23	874	0	23	262	832	2133	6033	10463	25504	41271	107674	425264	984790
Inventories 24	510	0	25	149	443	2136	4500	8821	17011	32612	56230	162868	480336
Net Property, Plant and Equipment 25	195	0	9	84	173	711	1400	4523	5309	14982	29026	52815	178300
Total Assets 26	2743	0	90	711	2015	6631	15492	35991	70694	144885	346694	1377574	3474305
Notes and Loans Payable 27	631	0	66	194	462	1676	3720	8093	16086	32428	64108	139166	1208122
All Other Liabilities 28	1041	0	35	266	863	3107	6544	15171	28547	55563	137627	594296	833783
Net Worth 29	1070	0	-11	252	690	1848	5228	12726	26061	56894	144959	644113	1432401

Selected Financial Ratios (Times to 1)

Line Item													
Current Ratio 30	1.6	•	1.7	1.6	1.7	1.4	1.5	1.6	1.4	1.6	1.4	2.0	1.4
Quick Ratio 31	0.9	•	1.1	1.0	1.2	0.7	0.9	0.9	0.8	0.9	0.8	1.4	0.7
Net Sales to Working Capital 32	9.8	•	18.2	10.9	9.7	16.1	10.4	8.6	11.4	7.2	11.0	6.3	10.6
Coverage Ratio 33	7.5	16.3	12.2	12.3	13.2	9.9	7.3	9.9	8.7	15.5	5.4	5.2	4.2
Total Asset Turnover 34	2.3	•	6.0	3.1	3.3	3.8	2.8	2.2	2.5	2.0	1.9	1.7	1.8
Inventory Turnover 35	9.5	•	13.6	9.5	10.4	9.3	7.4	6.6	8.5	6.6	9.5	11.0	10.2
Receivables Turnover 36	7.0	•	20.0	9.7	8.2	11.2	7.7	8.0	7.8	6.8	6.7	10.7	12.6
Total Liabilities to Net Worth 37	1.6	•	•	1.8	1.9	2.6	2.0	1.8	1.7	1.5	1.4	1.1	1.4
Current Assets to Working Capital 38	2.8	•	2.4	2.6	2.5	3.5	3.0	2.8	3.4	2.6	3.8	2.0	3.6
Current Liabilities to Working Capital 39	1.8	•	1.4	1.6	1.5	2.5	2.0	1.8	2.4	1.6	2.8	1.0	2.6
Working Capital to Net Sales 40	0.1	•	0.1	0.1	0.1	0.1	0.1	0.1	0.1	0.1	0.1	0.2	0.1
Inventory to Working Capital 41	0.8	•	0.7	0.7	0.6	1.5	1.0	1.0	1.2	0.9	1.1	0.5	0.8
Total Receipts to Cash Flow 42	10.2	32.6	7.1	6.0	9.4	12.4	10.5	8.4	11.4	7.7	12.1	11.9	11.0
Cost of Goods to Cash Flow 43	7.8	30.7	4.4	3.9	6.6	9.9	7.9	6.1	9.2	5.7	9.8	9.4	8.7
Cash Flow to Total Debt 44	0.4	•	0.7	0.8	0.5	0.4	0.4	0.4	0.4	0.4	0.3	0.3	0.3

Selected Financial Factors (in Percentages)

Line Item													
Debt Ratio 45	61.0	•	112.1	64.6	65.8	72.1	66.3	64.6	63.1	60.7	58.2	53.2	58.8
Return on Total Assets 46	9.1	•	35.1	18.2	14.1	11.9	9.6	13.5	9.3	11.0	6.2	7.9	3.6
Return on Equity Before Income Taxes 47	20.3	•	•	47.3	38.2	38.3	24.6	34.3	22.2	26.1	12.1	13.6	6.6
Return on Equity After Income Taxes 48	16.6	•	•	45.3	36.3	35.3	21.2	29.1	16.4	21.0	8.2	9.3	4.4
Profit Margin (Before Income Tax) 49	3.4	0.9	5.4	4.0	2.8	2.9	5.5	3.2	5.1	2.7	3.8		1.5
Profit Margin (After Income Tax) 50	2.8	0.8	5.3	3.8	2.6	2.5	4.7	2.4	4.1	1.8	2.6		1.0

172

Table I

Corporations with and without Net Income

METAL AND MINERAL (EXCEPT PETROLEUM)

MONEY AMOUNTS AND SIZE OF ASSETS IN THOUSANDS OF DOLLARS

Item Description for Accounting Period 7/03 Through 6/04	Total	Zero Assets	Under 500	500 to 1,000	1,000 to 5,000	5,000 to 10,000	10,000 to 25,000	25,000 to 50,000	50,000 to 100,000	100,000 to 250,000	250,000 to 500,000	500,000 to 2,500,000	2,500,000 and over
Number of Enterprises **1**	5884	692	3144	578	765	361	186	63	44	22	16	12	•
Revenues ($ in Thousands)													
Net Sales **2**	87061695	1168138	1145230	1274542	4667580	6489475	6813554	4976376	6748312	6503930	8032084	39242473	•
Interest **3**	671702	315	345	756	1787	5987	4406	4390	8590	24524	28889	591714	•
Rents **4**	51858	62	0	0	6589	234	1185	1217	1924	536	15318	24792	•
Royalties **5**	2928	0	0	10	0	0	511	0	3	61	517	1825	•
Other Portfolio Income **6**	111813	0	362	2042	1495	1581	8163	6899	7445	8505	35142	40176	•
Other Receipts **7**	330469	2115	146	4670	33690	18428	16841	35432	26283	19434	133435	40000	•
Total Receipts **8**	88230465	1170630	1146083	1282020	4711141	6515705	6844660	5024314	6792557	6556990	8245385	39940980	•
Average Total Receipts **9**	14995	1692	365	2218	6158	18049	36799	79751	154376	298045	515337	3328415	•
Operating Costs/Operating Income (%)													
Cost of Operations **10**	88.5	83.4	67.3	75.7	78.2	85.4	85.2	87.2	89.7	89.1	82.4	93.2	•
Salaries and Wages **11**	3.5	1.4	4.2	4.4	6.5	4.4	4.6	3.6	3.0	3.2	5.5	2.5	•
Taxes Paid **12**	0.7	1.6	1.3	1.3	1.2	0.8	0.8	0.9	0.7	0.9	1.2	0.4	•
Interest Paid **13**	1.3	0.7	1.5	0.6	0.6	0.5	0.6	0.7	0.9	0.5	0.9	2.0	•
Depreciation **14**	1.0	1.1	1.9	1.2	1.6	1.1	0.8	1.0	0.7	0.8	2.0	0.8	•
Amortization and Depletion **15**	0.2	0.1	0.1	0.0	0.1	0.0	0.1	0.1	0.1	0.1	0.3	0.3	•
Pensions and Other Deferred Comp. **16**	0.2	0.7	0.2	0.2	0.4	0.2	0.2	0.3	0.1	0.3	0.4	0.1	•
Employee Benefits **17**	0.7	0.1	1.1	0.5	0.8	0.5	0.5	0.5	0.6	0.7	1.8	0.7	•
Advertising **18**	0.1	0.2	0.3	0.2	0.1	0.1	0.1	0.1	0.1	0.0	0.1	0.0	•
Other Expenses **19**	4.3	11.6	14.3	10.0	7.3	4.4	5.5	3.8	3.5	4.3	6.3	2.8	•
Officers' Compensation **20**	0.8	3.9	7.6	4.8	2.6	1.3	1.4	1.2	0.8	0.5	0.3	0.1	•
Operating Margin **21**	•	•	0.3	1.0	0.5	1.3	0.3	0.8	•	•	•	•	•
Operating Margin Before Officers' Comp. **22**	•	•	7.8	5.8	3.1	2.6	1.7	2.0	•	•	•	•	•

Selected Average Balance Sheet ($ in Thousands)

Net Receivables 23	2180	0	37	241	663	1894	5023	10905	21754	38664	86592	547271	•
Inventories 24	1685	0	30	143	916	1667	6237	13178	27198	37337	91863	246286	•
Net Property, Plant and Equipment 25	1101	0	25	64	260	547	1716	4649	9886	17302	62981	294178	•
Total Assets 26	7417	0	137	706	2429	6104	15608	35799	67295	145301	338465	1833926	•
Notes and Loans Payable 27	2890	0	77	186	877	2261	6095	10522	28385	36859	101006	807871	•
All Other Liabilities 28	2550	0	27	238	836	1703	5219	11865	19520	50619	92816	695810	•
Net Worth 29	1978	0	33	282	717	2139	4294	13413	19390	57824	144643	330245	•

Selected Financial Ratios (Times to 1)

Current Ratio 30	1.4	•	2.2	1.4	1.6	1.7	1.5	1.7	1.5	1.7	1.8	1.2	•
Quick Ratio 31	0.8	•	1.5	0.9	1.0	0.9	0.7	0.8	0.7	0.8	0.9	0.7	•
Net Sales to Working Capital 32	10.2	•	7.3	16.8	10.6	8.6	8.3	7.2	9.4	6.3	5.5	16.7	•
Coverage Ratio 33	1.0	•	1.2	3.3	3.5	4.6	2.2	3.8	1.5	2.0	2.9	0.4	•
Total Asset Turnover 34	2.0	•	2.7	3.1	2.5	2.9	2.3	2.2	2.3	2.0	1.5	1.8	•
Inventory Turnover 35	7.8	•	8.2	11.7	5.2	9.2	5.0	5.2	5.1	7.1	4.5	12.4	•
Receivables Turnover 36	6.8	•	10.4	10.9	6.4	10.9	7.3	7.5	6.6	8.8	7.1	5.8	•
Total Liabilities to Net Worth 37	2.8	•	3.1	1.5	2.4	1.9	2.6	1.7	2.5	1.5	1.3	4.6	•
Current Assets to Working Capital 38	3.3	•	1.9	3.6	2.7	2.5	2.8	2.5	3.2	2.3	2.3	5.2	•
Current Liabilities to Working Capital 39	2.3	•	0.9	2.6	1.7	1.5	1.8	1.5	2.2	1.3	1.3	4.2	•
Working Capital to Net Sales 40	0.1	•	0.1	0.1	0.1	0.1	0.1	0.1	0.1	0.2	0.2	0.1	•
Inventory to Working Capital 41	1.2	•	0.5	1.1	1.0	1.1	1.3	1.2	1.5	1.0	1.0	1.3	•
Total Receipts to Cash Flow 42	32.8	16.8	9.2	10.5	15.0	21.6	20.8	20.9	32.8	23.8	16.8	191.1	•
Cost of Goods to Cash Flow 43	29.1	14.0	6.2	8.0	11.7	18.5	17.7	18.3	29.4	21.2	13.8	178.1	•
Cash Flow to Total Debt 44	0.1	•	0.4	0.5	0.2	0.2	0.2	0.2	0.1	0.1	0.2	0.0	•

Selected Financial Factors (in Percentages)

Debt Ratio 45	73.3	•	75.5	60.0	70.5	64.9	72.5	62.5	71.2	60.2	57.3	82.0	•
Return on Total Assets 46	2.6	•	5.0	6.2	5.1	6.6	3.2	5.4	3.1	2.0	3.7	1.4	•
Return on Equity Before Income Taxes 47	•	•	3.8	10.8	12.4	14.7	6.4	10.6	3.6	2.6	5.7	•	•
Return on Equity After Income Taxes 48	•	•	2.0	10.5	10.5	13.8	4.4	8.3	2.0	1.2	3.4	•	•
Profit Margin (Before Income Tax) 49	•	•	0.3	1.4	1.5	1.7	0.8	1.8	0.5	0.5	1.6	•	•
Profit Margin (After Income Tax) 50	•	•	0.2	1.3	1.2	1.6	0.5	1.4	0.3	0.2	1.0	•	•

Table II

Corporations with Net Income

METAL AND MINERAL (EXCEPT PETROLEUM)

MONEY AMOUNTS AND SIZE OF ASSETS IN THOUSANDS OF DOLLARS

Item Description for Accounting Period 7/03 Through 6/04		Total	Zero Assets	Under 500	500 to 1,000	1,000 to 5,000	5,000 to 10,000	10,000 to 25,000	25,000 to 50,000	50,000 to 100,000	100,000 to 250,000	250,000 to 500,000	500,000 to 2,500,000	2,500,000 and over
Number of Enterprises	1	3925	252	2079	494	520	331	143	46	30	14	10	4	•
Revenues ($ in Thousands)														
Net Sales	2	49954104	19450	912737	1137658	3341171	5722417	5354000	3736758	5291462	4560675	5042267	14835507	•
Interest	3	71437	311	199	83	1371	4958	2793	3690	7618	15416	16466	18531	•
Rents	4	37089	0	0	0	5836	208	990	1212	1759	259	8769	18057	•
Royalties	5	567	0	0	10	0	0	511	0	0	0	46	0	•
Other Portfolio Income	6	51811	0	0	2042	1299	1581	3585	6392	3154	7531	14759	11466	•
Other Receipts	7	295458	14	114	4670	34115	17433	20852	28791	18601	16796	103358	50720	•
Total Receipts	8	50410466	19775	913050	1144463	3383792	5746597	5382731	3776843	5322594	4600677	5185665	14934281	•
Average Total Receipts	9	12843	78	439	2317	6507	17361	37641	82105	177420	328620	518566	3733570	•
Operating Costs/Operating Income (%)														
Cost of Operations	10	87.4	73.5	69.3	75.6	74.4	84.7	83.7	87.5	89.9	91.0	82.5	94.3	•
Salaries and Wages	11	3.7	6.5	3.3	4.8	7.6	4.6	4.7	3.4	2.8	2.1	4.9	2.5	•
Taxes Paid	12	0.7	2.4	1.1	1.3	1.5	0.8	0.8	0.8	0.5	0.8	1.2	0.4	•
Interest Paid	13	0.5	0.2	1.8	0.6	0.6	0.5	0.6	0.5	0.7	0.3	0.6	0.3	•
Depreciation	14	0.9	0.5	2.1	0.7	1.7	1.2	0.8	0.6	0.5	0.5	2.0	0.4	•
Amortization and Depletion	15	0.1	•	0.1	0.0	0.1	0.0	0.1	0.0	0.0	0.0	0.3	0.1	•
Pensions and Other Deferred Comp.	16	0.2	0.3	0.2	0.2	0.3	0.2	0.2	0.3	0.1	0.3	0.4	0.1	•
Employee Benefits	17	0.6	•	0.5	0.6	1.0	0.5	0.5	0.3	0.3	0.4	1.5	0.4	•
Advertising	18	0.1	0.3	0.2	0.2	0.1	0.1	0.1	0.1	0.0	0.0	0.1	0.0	•
Other Expenses	19	3.9	8.4	12.3	9.5	8.0	4.2	5.1	3.0	3.1	3.1	5.7	1.6	•
Officers' Compensation	20	1.0	1.5	6.2	4.8	2.9	1.3	1.4	1.3	0.8	0.5	0.3	0.2	•
Operating Margin	21	1.0	6.5	3.0	1.9	1.7	1.9	2.0	2.1	1.1	0.9	0.5	•	
Operating Margin Before Officers' Comp.	22	2.0	8.0	9.2	6.6	4.6	3.2	3.4	3.4	2.0	1.3	0.8	•	

Selected Average Balance Sheet ($ in Thousands)

	C1	C2	C3	C4	C5	C6	C7	C8	C9	C10	C11	C12
Net Receivables 23	1527	0	255	660	1715	5300	11415	23332	41029	75229	391894	•
Inventories 24	1555	0	132	966	1652	6164	13910	32192	39290	81903	269968	•
Net Property, Plant and Equipment 25	626	0	45	258	581	1619	3484	6136	11853	56002	188691	•
Total Assets 26	5068	141	705	2619	6016	15626	35305	66070	136067	332074	1207772	•
Notes and Loans Payable 27	1551	0	179	707	2211	5196	8169	25101	22371	105493	364013	•
All Other Liabilities 28	1615	0	264	720	1591	4617	13113	19742	62963	78360	435836	•
Net Worth 29	1902	0	262	1192	2214	5813	14023	21227	50732	148222	407922	•

Selected Financial Ratios (Times to 1)

	C1	C2	C3	C4	C5	C6	C7	C8	C9	C10	C11	C12
Current Ratio 30	1.6	•	2.4	1.3	1.7	1.7	1.8	1.6	1.6	1.8	1.3	•
Quick Ratio 31	0.8	•	1.7	0.8	0.9	0.8	0.9	0.8	0.7	0.8	0.7	•
Net Sales to Working Capital 32	9.2	•	8.2	24.1	8.0	6.9	6.7	8.0	7.0	5.9	20.8	•
Coverage Ratio 33	4.7	41.7	2.7	5.0	5.7	5.3	7.1	3.6	6.3	6.2	2.2	•
Total Asset Turnover 34	2.5	•	3.1	3.3	2.5	2.9	2.4	2.3	2.7	2.4	1.5	•
Inventory Turnover 35	7.2	•	12.3	13.2	4.9	8.9	5.1	4.9	7.5	5.1	13.0	•
Receivables Turnover 36	8.5	•	11.6	12.4	6.2	11.7	7.4	7.6	6.7	10.0	8.1	•
Total Liabilities to Net Worth 37	1.7	•	5.4	1.7	1.2	1.7	1.5	2.1	1.7	1.2	2.0	•
Current Assets to Working Capital 38	2.7	•	1.7	4.9	2.4	2.3	2.3	2.5	2.6	2.3	4.7	•
Current Liabilities to Working Capital 39	1.7	•	0.7	3.9	1.4	1.3	1.3	1.5	1.6	1.3	3.7	•
Working Capital to Net Sales 40	0.1	•	0.1	0.0	0.1	0.1	0.1	0.1	0.1	0.2	0.0	•
Inventory to Working Capital 41	1.1	•	0.4	1.5	0.8	1.0	1.1	1.2	1.0	1.1	1.4	•
Total Receipts to Cash Flow 42	21.5	6.7	8.5	9.9	11.8	20.2	18.4	24.7	23.6	13.3	70.1	•
Cost of Goods to Cash Flow 43	18.8	4.9	5.9	7.5	8.7	17.1	16.1	22.3	21.5	11.0	66.1	•
Cash Flow to Total Debt 44	0.2	•	0.4	0.5	0.4	0.2	0.2	0.2	0.2	0.2	0.1	•

Selected Financial Factors (in Percentages)

	C1	C2	C3	C4	C5	C6	C7	C8	C9	C10	C11	C12
Debt Ratio 45	62.5	•	84.3	62.8	54.5	63.2	60.3	67.9	62.7	55.4	66.2	•
Return on Total Assets 46	6.0	•	14.9	9.4	8.8	8.1	8.5	6.4	4.9	6.1	2.2	•
Return on Equity Before Income Taxes 47	12.5	•	59.6	20.1	15.9	18.3	18.3	14.5	11.0	11.5	3.5	•
Return on Equity After Income Taxes 48	10.4	•	55.4	19.7	14.2	17.4	15.2	12.3	8.4	7.9	2.3	•
Profit Margin (Before Income Tax) 49	1.9	8.2	3.0	2.3	2.9	2.3	3.2	1.7	1.7	3.4	0.4	•
Profit Margin (After Income Tax) 50	1.6	6.2	2.8	2.2	2.6	2.2	2.6	1.5	1.3	2.3	0.3	•

Table I

Corporations with and without Net Income

ELECTRICAL GOODS

MONEY AMOUNTS AND SIZE OF ASSETS IN THOUSANDS OF DOLLARS

Item Description for Accounting Period 7/03 Through 6/04	Total	Zero Assets	Under 500	500 to 1,000	1,000 to 5,000	5,000 to 10,000	10,000 to 25,000	25,000 to 50,000	50,000 to 100,000	100,000 to 250,000	250,000 to 500,000	500,000 to 2,500,000	2,500,000 and over
Number of Enterprises **1**	21925	1713	13317	1727	3802	649	386	150	82	46	22	26	5
Revenues ($ in Thousands)													
Net Sales **2**	212190269	2201464	6401768	3138320	23306791	10328435	14502804	12092012	11796308	17301477	13978575	50878295	46264020
Interest **3**	414066	3256	3389	3524	7601	4738	9547	8862	15621	20668	15158	198495	123207
Rents **4**	167786	311	31	0	2105	4336	2548	2014	21890	1027	4032	38303	91189
Royalties **5**	556482	0	0	0	178	2726	3810	12022	8863	22035	9700	66836	430313
Other Portfolio Income **6**	261316	1189	8648	4478	31633	4978	14013	14266	5576	3031	9232	38136	66138
Other Receipts **7**	2670002	16538	198037	29990	142439	47236	118835	148207	71035	177569	92984	558566	1068562
Total Receipts **8**	216259921	2222758	6611873	3176312	23490747	10392449	14651557	12277383	11919293	17525807	14169681	51778631	48043429
Average Total Receipts **9**	9864	1298	496	1839	6179	16013	37957	81849	145357	380996	644076	1991486	9608686
Operating Costs/Operating Income (%)													
Cost of Operations **10**	79.8	81.6	58.8	70.3	74.6	78.9	79.8	79.3	82.6	86.9	87.6	84.5	75.3
Salaries and Wages **11**	6.9	6.8	12.4	10.6	8.1	8.4	7.8	8.3	6.4	4.5	4.8	6.0	7.1
Taxes Paid **12**	0.9	1.3	2.1	1.6	1.3	1.3	1.1	1.1	0.9	0.6	0.7	0.6	0.8
Interest Paid **13**	0.7	0.5	1.0	0.5	0.4	0.5	0.5	0.5	0.4	0.5	0.5	1.1	0.7
Depreciation **14**	0.9	1.0	1.0	0.9	0.5	0.7	0.8	0.9	0.8	0.5	0.6	1.1	1.2
Amortization and Depletion **15**	1.4	3.2	0.5	0.1	0.0	0.2	0.2	0.1	0.2	0.0	0.5	0.2	5.6
Pensions and Other Deferred Comp. **16**	0.3	0.2	0.5	0.3	0.4	0.2	0.2	0.2	0.2	0.1	0.1	0.2	0.6
Employee Benefits **17**	0.7	0.7	1.3	0.6	0.7	0.5	0.6	0.8	0.7	0.4	0.4	0.9	0.9
Advertising **18**	1.5	0.4	0.5	0.4	0.5	0.5	0.5	0.8	0.8	1.0	0.6	1.1	4.3
Other Expenses **19**	7.0	9.6	19.2	10.4	9.8	7.9	6.5	7.1	6.5	5.3	4.5	5.7	6.6
Officers' Compensation **20**	1.1	1.9	7.2	6.2	3.2	1.6	1.5	1.1	0.6	0.4	0.4	0.1	0.1
Operating Margin **21**	•	•	•	•	0.5	•	0.5	•	•	•	•	•	•
Operating Margin Before Officers' Comp. **22**	•	•	2.6	4.2	3.7	1.0	1.9	0.9	0.5	0.1	•	•	•

Selected Average Balance Sheet ($ in Thousands)

Net Receivables 23	1441	0	38	235	745	2277	5551	12712	24710	59240	108645	284435	1554950
Inventories 24	1023	0	31	260	599	2139	4789	10099	18754	41721	61651	198435	910937
Net Property, Plant and Equipment 25	396	0	16	47	185	497	1334	3405	5594	9507	17469	89844	541211
Total Assets 26	5213	0	138	750	2081	7071	15318	34796	68029	162325	366999	1053342	7803799
Notes and Loans Payable 27	1290	0	86	202	608	2120	4139	6867	11680	33083	64299	184639	2355643
All Other Liabilities 28	2193	0	66	306	890	2544	6789	14031	31459	76464	151930	454272	3134201
Net Worth 29	1730	0	-14	241	583	2408	4390	13898	24891	52778	150771	414432	2313955

Selected Financial Ratios (Times to 1)

Current Ratio 30	1.5	•	1.8	2.0	1.7	2.0	1.5	1.7	1.6	1.4	1.5	1.4	1.3
Quick Ratio 31	0.8	•	1.1	1.0	1.0	1.0	0.8	1.0	0.9	0.8	1.0	0.7	0.6
Net Sales to Working Capital 32	8.9	•	9.9	5.5	8.3	5.2	9.0	6.8	7.2	10.4	7.7	12.0	9.0
Coverage Ratio 33	1.9	•	•	•	4.0	1.0	4.1	3.9	3.4	3.1	2.6	1.3	1.9
Total Asset Turnover 34	1.9	•	3.5	2.4	2.9	2.3	2.5	2.3	2.1	2.3	1.7	1.9	1.2
Inventory Turnover 35	7.6	•	9.1	4.9	7.6	5.9	6.3	6.3	6.3	7.8	9.0	8.3	7.7
Receivables Turnover 36	7.1	•	14.7	8.2	9.1	7.3	7.1	6.6	6.3	7.3	6.6	7.4	5.9
Total Liabilities to Net Worth 37	2.0	•	•	2.1	2.6	1.9	2.5	1.5	1.7	2.1	1.4	1.5	2.4
Current Assets to Working Capital 38	3.2	•	2.3	2.0	2.4	2.0	3.0	2.4	2.7	3.5	3.0	3.8	4.4
Current Liabilities to Working Capital 39	2.2	•	1.3	1.0	1.4	1.0	2.0	1.4	1.7	2.5	2.0	2.8	3.4
Working Capital to Net Sales 40	0.1	•	0.1	0.2	0.1	0.2	0.1	0.1	0.1	0.1	0.1	0.1	0.1
Inventory to Working Capital 41	1.0	•	0.8	0.8	0.9	0.8	1.1	0.9	0.9	1.2	0.8	1.3	0.8
Total Receipts to Cash Flow 42	16.4	321.3	7.3	14.2	10.6	17.4	15.2	14.6	16.2	18.5	24.7	21.6	17.1
Cost of Goods to Cash Flow 43	13.1	262.0	4.3	10.0	7.9	13.7	12.1	11.6	13.4	16.1	21.6	18.3	12.9
Cash Flow to Total Debt 44	0.2	•	0.4	0.3	0.4	0.2	0.2	0.3	0.2	0.2	0.1	0.1	0.1

Selected Financial Factors (in Percentages)

Debt Ratio 45	66.8	•	110.1	67.8	72.0	66.0	71.3	60.1	63.4	67.5	58.9	60.7	70.3
Return on Total Assets 46	2.4	•	•	•	4.7	1.3	5.0	4.2	2.9	3.3	2.2	2.7	1.7
Return on Equity Before Income Taxes 47	3.4	•	42.9	•	12.6	0.2	13.2	7.9	5.6	6.9	3.3	1.7	2.6
Return on Equity After Income Taxes 48	2.1	•	45.8	•	11.0	•	10.7	6.2	3.8	4.8	2.5	0.3	2.0
Profit Margin (Before Income Tax) 49	0.6	•	•	•	1.2	0.0	1.5	1.4	1.0	1.0	0.8	0.4	0.7
Profit Margin (After Income Tax) 50	0.4	•	•	•	1.0	•	1.2	1.1	0.7	0.7	0.6	0.1	0.5

Table II

Corporations with Net Income

ELECTRICAL GOODS

MONEY AMOUNTS AND SIZE OF ASSETS IN THOUSANDS OF DOLLARS

Item Description for Accounting Period 7/03 Through 6/04	Total	Zero Assets	Under 500	500 to 1,000	1,000 to 5,000	5,000 to 10,000	10,000 to 25,000	25,000 to 50,000	50,000 to 100,000	100,000 to 250,000	250,000 to 500,000	500,000 to 2,500,000	2,500,000 and over
Number of Enterprises **1**	14069	867	8096	1063	3120	417	276	107	55	35	•	16	•
Revenues ($ in Thousands)													
Net Sales **2**	161792836	1620542	3614981	2054460	19217618	7631260	11341276	9680292	9244910	14539424	•	36187991	•
Interest **3**	322130	2498	2879	3305	6105	3050	5964	5904	4618	15128	•	167506	•
Rents **4**	127621	311	0	0	1143	2815	1554	1374	11754	280	•	18072	•
Royalties **5**	477036	0	0	0	0	0	28	0	8063	2523	•	28116	•
Other Portfolio Income **6**	224305	1189	4267	3737	31378	3013	9795	2546	5260	2184	•	25756	•
Other Receipts **7**	2157397	3756	175161	23036	134632	40454	99473	128148	54482	137658	•	264117	•
Total Receipts **8**	165101325	1628296	3797288	2084538	19390876	7680592	11458090	9818264	9329087	14697197	•	36691558	•
Average Total Receipts **9**	11735	1878	469	1961	6215	18419	41515	91759	169620	419920	•	2293222	•
Operating Costs/Operating Income (%)													
Cost of Operations **10**	79.3	81.8	50.8	74.9	72.8	78.6	79.7	79.6	82.9	87.7	•	86.0	•
Salaries and Wages **11**	6.4	4.4	14.1	8.1	8.5	7.8	7.4	7.7	6.2	3.7	•	4.8	•
Taxes Paid **12**	0.9	0.6	2.2	1.4	1.4	1.2	1.0	1.1	0.9	0.5	•	0.5	•
Interest Paid **13**	0.5	0.1	0.4	0.2	0.3	0.4	0.4	0.4	0.3	0.4	•	1.1	•
Depreciation **14**	0.8	0.3	1.0	0.7	0.5	0.6	0.7	0.7	0.7	0.5	•	1.0	•
Amortization and Depletion **15**	1.7	0.8	0.0	0.1	0.0	0.1	0.1	0.1	0.1	0.1	•	0.2	•
Pensions and Other Deferred Comp. **16**	0.3	0.3	0.9	0.4	0.4	0.2	0.2	0.2	0.2	0.1	•	0.1	•
Employee Benefits **17**	0.7	0.4	1.0	0.5	0.7	0.5	0.5	0.6	0.6	0.4	•	0.8	•
Advertising **18**	1.8	0.3	0.5	0.4	0.5	0.5	0.4	0.6	0.7	0.9	•	0.9	•
Other Expenses **19**	6.3	6.0	18.2	7.6	9.7	6.3	5.8	6.2	5.4	4.6	•	3.9	•
Officers' Compensation **20**	1.1	2.0	9.4	5.5	3.3	1.7	1.4	1.1	0.6	0.3	•	0.1	•
Operating Margin **21**	0.3	2.9	1.5	0.3	2.0	2.2	2.4	1.6	1.6	0.9	•	0.7	•
Operating Margin Before Officers' Comp. **22**	1.3	4.9	10.9	5.8	5.3	3.9	3.8	2.8	2.2	1.2	•	0.8	•

Selected Average Balance Sheet ($ in Thousands)

Net Receivables 23	1596	0	30	198	740	2834	5855	13784	26935	61631	296491	•
Inventories 24	1085	0	19	230	578	2046	4911	10005	19725	44021	304000	•
Net Property, Plant and Equipment 25	443	0	19	34	171	442	1255	3184	5767	10541	79514	•
Total Assets 26	5616	0	129	732	2071	7005	15393	34606	69871	163531	1169693	•
Notes and Loans Payable 27	1281	0	23	96	559	1918	3519	6870	9573	29537	177366	•
All Other Liabilities 28	2338	0	30	268	731	2445	5990	14287	31965	78667	484734	•
Net Worth 29	1996	0	76	368	781	2642	5884	13450	28333	55327	507593	•

Selected Financial Ratios (Times to 1)

Current Ratio 30	1.4	•	2.6	3.1	1.8	2.0	1.7	1.7	1.6	1.4	1.3	•
Quick Ratio 31	0.7	•	1.8	1.5	1.0	1.1	0.9	1.0	1.0	0.8	0.7	•
Net Sales to Working Capital 32	9.9	•	7.7	4.4	7.6	6.0	7.9	7.3	7.8	11.2	13.9	•
Coverage Ratio 33	5.6	29.8	19.5	12.0	9.5	9.0	9.8	8.3	11.0	6.3	2.9	•
Total Asset Turnover 34	2.0	•	3.5	2.6	3.0	2.6	2.7	2.6	2.4	2.5	1.9	•
Inventory Turnover 35	8.4	•	12.2	6.3	7.8	7.0	6.7	7.2	7.1	8.3	6.4	•
Receivables Turnover 36	7.9	•	18.0	9.2	9.6	7.2	7.5	7.3	7.3	7.7	5.3	•
Total Liabilities to Net Worth 37	1.8	•	0.7	1.0	1.7	1.7	1.6	1.6	1.5	2.0	1.3	•
Current Assets to Working Capital 38	3.4	•	1.6	1.5	2.2	2.0	2.5	2.4	2.6	3.5	4.1	•
Current Liabilities to Working Capital 39	2.4	•	0.6	0.5	1.2	1.0	1.5	1.4	1.6	2.5	3.1	•
Working Capital to Net Sales 40	0.1	•	0.1	0.2	0.1	0.2	0.1	0.1	0.1	0.1	0.1	•
Inventory to Working Capital 41	1.0	•	0.5	0.6	0.8	0.8	1.0	0.9	0.9	1.3	1.4	•
Total Receipts to Cash Flow 42	13.8	11.7	4.7	13.4	9.3	13.2	12.6	12.7	14.6	16.7	20.7	•
Cost of Goods to Cash Flow 43	11.0	9.6	2.4	10.0	6.7	10.4	10.0	10.1	12.1	14.6	17.8	•
Cash Flow to Total Debt 44	0.2	•	1.8	0.4	0.5	0.3	0.3	0.3	0.3	0.2	0.2	•

Selected Financial Factors (in Percentages)

Debt Ratio 45	64.5	•	41.1	49.7	62.3	62.3	61.8	61.1	59.5	66.2	56.6	•
Return on Total Assets 46	5.7	•	24.0	5.2	9.4	8.3	10.2	9.1	6.6	5.9	6.2	•
Return on Equity Before Income Taxes 47	13.3	•	38.6	9.5	22.2	19.7	24.0	20.6	14.8	14.8	9.4	•
Return on Equity After Income Taxes 48	11.5	•	37.7	8.0	20.7	17.2	21.4	18.2	12.4	12.2	7.5	•
Profit Margin (Before Income Tax) 49	2.3	3.4	6.6	1.8	2.8	2.8	3.4	3.1	2.5	2.0	2.1	•
Profit Margin (After Income Tax) 50	2.0	3.2	6.4	1.5	2.6	2.5	3.1	2.7	2.1	1.6	1.7	•

Table I

Corporations with and without Net Income

HARDWARE, PLUMBING, HEATING EQUIPMENT, AND SUPPLIES

MONEY AMOUNTS AND SIZE OF ASSETS IN THOUSANDS OF DOLLARS

Item Description for Accounting Period 7/03 Through 6/04		Total	Zero Assets	Under 500	500 to 1,000	1,000 to 5,000	5,000 to 10,000	10,000 to 25,000	25,000 to 50,000	50,000 to 100,000	100,000 to 250,000	250,000 to 500,000	500,000 to 2,500,000	2,500,000 and over
Number of Enterprises	1	12741	823	6806	1584	2587	517	290	72	38	11	5	8	•
Revenues ($ in Thousands)														
Net Sales	2	78931603	861374	3055941	3228132	15228988	8043112	10255832	5989070	5858007	3461051	2681909	20268188	•
Interest	3	169472	306	1632	1550	13278	6997	8991	5500	6705	4538	282	119694	•
Rents	4	27251	506	3931	800	3512	2751	2056	1601	3515	0	1969	6610	•
Royalties	5	56003	9040	0	0	0	1	776	31	895	4982	0	40278	•
Other Portfolio Income	6	42406	713	4538	642	8517	7133	7957	3293	2723	68	3374	3447	•
Other Receipts	7	1706589	8330	4105	171169	602079	59095	81348	64094	37781	89167	108528	480893	•
Total Receipts	8	80933324	880269	3070147	3402293	15856374	8119089	10356960	6063589	5909626	3559806	2796062	20919110	•
Average Total Receipts	9	6352	1070	451	2148	6129	15704	35714	84217	155516	323619	559212	2614889	•
Operating Costs/Operating Income (%)														
Cost of Operations	10	74.9	68.5	59.8	70.2	73.6	72.9	75.0	77.1	79.7	73.9	70.5	78.6	•
Salaries and Wages	11	9.8	9.5	11.3	11.9	11.1	10.5	10.1	9.0	7.9	8.9	11.6	8.7	•
Taxes Paid	12	1.4	1.1	2.3	1.8	1.6	1.4	1.3	1.3	1.2	1.3	1.4	1.2	•
Interest Paid	13	1.0	1.9	0.3	0.6	0.6	0.8	0.6	0.6	0.8	0.9	1.6	1.9	•
Depreciation	14	1.0	0.7	0.6	0.7	1.4	0.9	0.7	0.8	1.0	1.3	1.4	0.8	•
Amortization and Depletion	15	0.2	0.4	0.1	0.1	0.1	0.0	0.3	0.0	0.2	0.3	0.4	0.3	•
Pensions and Other Deferred Comp.	16	0.4	1.1	1.0	0.7	0.4	0.5	0.3	0.4	0.3	0.4	0.3	0.2	•
Employee Benefits	17	0.9	0.7	0.7	1.4	0.9	1.2	0.8	0.9	0.7	1.1	1.9	0.7	•
Advertising	18	0.4	0.4	0.3	0.2	0.6	0.3	0.5	0.6	0.4	0.9	0.2	0.2	•
Other Expenses	19	8.8	12.0	17.3	9.7	9.8	7.8	7.1	6.9	6.1	9.5	8.6	8.9	•
Officers' Compensation	20	2.1	3.3	9.2	7.3	4.0	2.2	2.0	0.9	0.8	0.6	0.2	0.1	•
Operating Margin	21	•	0.3	•	•	•	1.3	1.2	1.4	1.0	0.9	1.8	•	•
Operating Margin Before Officers' Comp.	22	1.2	3.6	6.5	2.7	•	3.5	3.2	2.3	1.8	1.5	2.0	•	•

Selected Average Balance Sheet ($ in Thousands)

Net Receivables 23	816	0	35	245	792	2061	5038	11313	21374	38327	62709	354183	•
Inventories 24	889	0	42	265	883	2885	5513	11722	21510	55449	73561	325838	•
Net Property, Plant and Equipment 25	294	0	7	57	238	614	1355	3810	9334	18634	51038	148259	•
Total Assets 26	2645	0	106	686	2436	6552	14973	35395	66189	154107	326421	1183197	•
Notes and Loans Payable 27	867	0	41	180	571	2038	4346	12436	18103	54932	67072	520852	•
All Other Liabilities 28	844	0	61	269	806	1962	4413	9146	22199	42229	103691	380837	•
Net Worth 29	934	0	4	237	1059	2552	6214	13813	25888	56946	155658	281507	•

Selected Financial Ratios (Times to 1)

Current Ratio 30	1.8	•	1.4	1.7	1.9	1.8	1.8	2.1	1.8	1.8	1.7	1.8	•
Quick Ratio 31	0.9	•	0.8	0.9	1.0	0.8	0.9	1.1	0.9	0.7	0.8	0.9	•
Net Sales to Working Capital 32	7.0	•	16.8	8.9	6.4	6.1	6.5	5.7	7.2	6.1	8.2	7.7	•
Coverage Ratio 33	2.6	2.3	•	2.2	1.0	3.8	4.5	5.5	3.2	5.4	4.7	1.8	•
Total Asset Turnover 34	2.3	•	4.2	3.0	2.4	2.4	2.4	2.4	2.3	2.0	1.6	2.1	•
Inventory Turnover 35	5.2	•	6.5	5.4	4.9	3.9	4.8	5.5	5.7	4.2	5.1	6.1	•
Receivables Turnover 36	7.8	•	11.7	8.6	8.1	7.4	7.4	7.5	7.3	7.7	7.3	7.3	•
Total Liabilities to Net Worth 37	1.8	•	27.7	1.9	1.3	1.6	1.4	1.6	1.6	1.7	1.1	3.2	•
Current Assets to Working Capital 38	2.2	•	3.5	2.5	2.1	2.2	2.3	1.9	2.3	2.2	2.3	2.3	•
Current Liabilities to Working Capital 39	1.2	•	2.5	1.5	1.1	1.2	1.3	0.9	1.3	1.2	1.3	1.3	•
Working Capital to Net Sales 40	0.1	•	0.1	0.1	0.2	0.2	0.2	0.2	0.1	0.2	0.1	0.1	•
Inventory to Working Capital 41	1.0	•	1.3	1.0	1.0	1.2	1.0	0.8	1.0	1.0	1.2	1.0	•
Total Receipts to Cash Flow 42	12.2	7.6	8.6	14.4	14.3	12.6	13.6	12.9	16.0	9.0	8.1	11.6	•
Cost of Goods to Cash Flow 43	9.2	5.2	5.1	10.1	10.5	9.2	10.2	9.9	12.7	6.7	5.7	9.1	•
Cash Flow to Total Debt 44	0.3	•	0.5	0.3	0.3	0.3	0.3	0.3	0.2	0.4	0.4	0.2	•

Selected Financial Factors (in Percentages)

Debt Ratio 45	64.7	•	96.5	65.5	56.5	61.1	58.5	61.0	60.9	63.0	52.3	76.2	•
Return on Total Assets 46	6.1	•	•	4.0	1.4	7.3	6.6	7.5	6.3	9.5	12.6	7.3	•
Return on Equity Before Income Taxes 47	10.5	•	•	6.3	0.0	13.7	12.5	15.8	11.0	20.9	20.8	13.6	•
Return on Equity After Income Taxes 48	8.0	•	•	4.1	•	12.8	10.6	12.0	9.2	16.2	20.2	8.7	•
Profit Margin (Before Income Tax) 49	1.6	2.5	0.7	0.7	0.0	2.3	2.2	2.6	1.9	3.8	6.0	1.5	•
Profit Margin (After Income Tax) 50	1.2	1.2	0.5	0.5	•	2.1	1.9	2.0	1.5	2.9	5.9	1.0	•

Table II
Corporations with Net Income

HARDWARE, PLUMBING, HEATING EQUIPMENT, AND SUPPLIES

MONEY AMOUNTS AND SIZE OF ASSETS IN THOUSANDS OF DOLLARS

Item Description for Accounting Period 7/03 Through 6/04	Total	Zero Assets	Under 500	500 to 1,000	1,000 to 5,000	5,000 to 10,000	10,000 to 25,000	25,000 to 50,000	50,000 to 100,000	100,000 to 250,000	250,000 to 500,000	500,000 to 2,500,000	2,500,000 and over
Number of Enterprises **1**	7084	81	3223	1195	1763	462	254	57	29	·	·	5	·
Revenues ($ in Thousands)													
Net Sales **2**	65199027	733891	1398729	2599897	11595969	7300738	9328687	5210425	4402135	·	·	17191311	·
Interest **3**	139617	202	59	928	8248	4830	8676	3994	4647	·	·	105973	·
Rents **4**	14628	273	339	800	2720	1654	1611	1443	546	·	·	4041	·
Royalties **5**	50713	9040	0	0	0	1	672	31	0	·	·	35988	·
Other Portfolio Income **6**	32847	577	3854	475	5119	6996	6528	2995	1491	·	·	3023	·
Other Receipts **7**	1546912	1479	318	168246	561829	58280	72234	54099	29779	·	·	404243	·
Total Receipts **8**	66983744	745462	1403299	2770346	12173885	7372499	9418408	5272987	4438598	·	·	17744579	·
Average Total Receipts **9**	9456	9203	435	2318	6905	15958	37080	92509	153055	·	·	3548916	·
Operating Costs/Operating Income (%)													
Cost of Operations **10**	75.3	68.6	52.5	69.4	73.0	72.7	74.7	76.9	77.1	·	·	81.1	·
Salaries and Wages **11**	9.8	10.1	9.8	12.1	11.1	10.6	9.8	8.9	8.5	·	·	8.9	·
Taxes Paid **12**	1.4	1.2	2.0	1.8	1.6	1.4	1.3	1.3	1.3	·	·	1.2	·
Interest Paid **13**	0.9	1.7	0.2	0.5	0.4	0.8	0.6	0.5	0.7	·	·	1.5	·
Depreciation **14**	0.9	0.5	0.5	0.6	1.5	0.9	0.7	0.8	1.0	·	·	0.7	·
Amortization and Depletion **15**	0.1	0.0	·	0.1	0.0	0.0	0.1	0.0	0.2	·	·	0.2	·
Pensions and Other Deferred Comp. **16**	0.4	1.1	0.5	0.8	0.3	0.6	0.3	0.5	0.3	·	·	0.2	·
Employee Benefits **17**	0.9	0.7	0.3	1.4	0.8	1.2	0.8	0.8	0.7	·	·	0.6	·
Advertising **18**	0.4	0.4	0.3	0.2	0.7	0.3	0.5	0.6	0.4	·	·	0.2	·
Other Expenses **19**	7.7	7.2	19.9	9.6	9.0	7.4	6.7	6.2	6.6	·	·	6.6	·
Officers' Compensation **20**	2.1	3.8	10.2	7.8	4.3	2.2	2.0	1.0	0.9	·	·	0.1	·
Operating Margin **21**	0.1	4.6	3.7	·	·	1.8	2.3	2.6	2.3	·	·	·	·
Operating Margin Before Officers' Comp. **22**	2.2	8.4	13.9	3.4	1.5	4.1	4.3	3.6	3.1	·	·	·	·

Selected Average Balance Sheet ($ in Thousands)

Net Receivables 23	1212	0	36	261	825	2038	5171	12312	21656	•	•	492899
Inventories 24	1223	0	39	163	962	2478	5506	12868	20899	•	•	391062
Net Property, Plant and Equipment 25	436	0	6	47	283	637	1307	4165	9060	•	•	196057
Total Assets 26	3781	0	92	704	2451	6510	15045	35446	64992	•	•	1546367
Notes and Loans Payable 27	1197	0	22	137	557	2118	4232	9007	19151	•	•	659887
All Other Liabilities 28	1138	0	33	304	873	1673	4208	9461	18144	•	•	463386
Net Worth 29	1447	0	37	263	1021	2718	6605	16979	27697	•	•	423094

Selected Financial Ratios (Times to 1)

Current Ratio 30	1.9	•	2.3	1.7	1.8	2.0	1.9	2.1	1.9	•	•	1.9
Quick Ratio 31	0.9	•	1.6	1.0	0.9	0.8	0.9	1.1	0.9	•	•	1.0
Net Sales to Working Capital 32	6.9	•	9.1	9.4	7.4	5.8	6.2	6.1	6.3	•	•	7.1
Coverage Ratio 33	4.3	4.7	17.8	5.2	5.8	4.8	6.9	9.0	5.6	•	•	2.2
Total Asset Turnover 34	2.4	•	4.7	3.1	2.7	2.4	2.4	2.6	2.3	•	•	2.2
Inventory Turnover 35	5.7	•	5.9	9.3	5.0	4.6	5.0	5.5	5.6	•	•	7.1
Receivables Turnover 36	8.1	•	10.2	10.9	8.0	9.1	7.7	7.5	7.4	•	•	7.6
Total Liabilities to Net Worth 37	1.6	•	1.5	1.7	1.4	1.4	1.3	1.1	1.3	•	•	2.7
Current Assets to Working Capital 38	2.1	•	1.8	2.5	2.3	2.0	2.1	1.9	2.1	•	•	2.1
Current Liabilities to Working Capital 39	1.1	•	0.8	1.5	1.3	1.0	1.1	0.9	1.1	•	•	1.1
Working Capital to Net Sales 40	0.1	•	0.1	0.1	0.1	0.2	0.2	0.2	0.2	•	•	0.1
Inventory to Working Capital 41	1.0	•	0.5	1.0	1.0	1.1	1.0	0.9	1.0	•	•	0.9
Total Receipts to Cash Flow 42	11.6	8.3	4.7	11.7	11.1	12.2	12.3	12.2	12.7	•	•	14.7
Cost of Goods to Cash Flow 43	8.7	5.7	2.5	8.1	8.1	8.9	9.2	9.3	9.8	•	•	11.9
Cash Flow to Total Debt 44	0.3	•	1.7	0.4	0.4	0.3	0.4	0.4	0.3	•	•	0.2

Selected Financial Factors (in Percentages)

Debt Ratio 45	61.7	•	59.6	62.6	58.4	58.2	56.1	52.1	57.4	•	•	72.6
Return on Total Assets 46	9.1	•	20.4	8.5	7.0	8.7	9.4	11.1	8.8	•	•	7.5
Return on Equity Before Income Taxes 47	18.4	•	47.6	18.3	13.9	16.5	18.3	20.7	16.9	•	•	15.1
Return on Equity After Income Taxes 48	15.4	•	46.4	15.7	12.0	15.5	16.3	16.8	14.6	•	•	9.9
Profit Margin (Before Income Tax) 49	2.9	6.2	4.1	2.2	2.2	2.8	3.3	3.8	3.1	•	•	1.9
Profit Margin (After Income Tax) 50	2.4	4.6	4.0	1.9	1.9	2.7	2.9	3.1	2.7	•	•	1.2

178

Table I

Corporations with and without Net Income

MACHINERY, EQUIPMENT, AND SUPPLIES

MONEY AMOUNTS AND SIZE OF ASSETS IN THOUSANDS OF DOLLARS

Item Description for Accounting Period 7/03 Through 6/04	Total	Zero Assets	Under 500	500 to 1,000	1,000 to 5,000	5,000 to 10,000	10,000 to 25,000	25,000 to 50,000	50,000 to 100,000	100,000 to 250,000	250,000 to 500,000	500,000 to 2,500,000	2,500,000 and over
Number of Enterprises 1	49415	3050	31135	4344	8558	1235	689	189	77	69	23	15	•
Revenues ($ in Thousands)													
Net Sales 2	171080951	2800471	15042084	6709934	43597734	21058493	19719023	11429040	7865516	13562818	9201332	20094505	•
Interest 3	428620	1813	4146	6682	30791	15964	23599	19168	22507	52110	40742	211098	•
Rents 4	213495	864	483	1065	21956	16574	16315	9867	8796	35874	12671	89030	•
Royalties 5	49188	0	0	0	0	0	5626	544	34150	310	519	8040	•
Other Portfolio Income 6	837258	13897	9721	17099	74650	53596	132253	70350	72496	152739	155776	84685	•
Other Receipts 7	1810557	9456	262029	20046	354778	181946	220162	125482	118428	201116	178608	138503	•
Total Receipts 8	174420069	2826501	15318463	6754826	44079909	21326573	20116978	11654451	8121893	14004967	9589648	20625861	•
Average Total Receipts 9	3530	927	492	1555	5133	17268	29197	61664	105479	202971	416941	1375057	•
Operating Costs/Operating Income (%)													
Cost of Operations 10	74.1	91.1	70.4	63.8	73.4	78.4	76.2	76.8	73.6	76.3	69.9	71.8	•
Salaries and Wages 11	8.5	2.9	7.0	9.7	9.0	8.0	8.8	8.3	9.2	7.7	7.9	9.5	•
Taxes Paid 12	1.3	0.4	1.5	1.9	1.5	1.1	1.2	1.2	1.4	1.1	1.1	1.5	•
Interest Paid 13	1.1	0.2	0.9	0.9	0.8	0.6	0.9	0.9	1.1	1.3	3.7	1.3	•
Depreciation 14	2.3	0.8	1.1	2.3	1.3	1.1	2.5	2.2	3.3	4.9	7.0	2.0	•
Amortization and Depletion 15	0.2	0.0	0.1	0.1	0.1	0.1	0.1	0.1	0.3	0.6	0.4	0.4	•
Pensions and Other Deferred Comp. 16	0.4	0.0	0.2	0.3	0.5	0.3	0.3	0.4	0.3	0.2	0.3	0.6	•
Employee Benefits 17	1.0	0.1	0.7	0.8	0.8	0.7	0.9	0.9	1.2	1.6	1.6	1.4	•
Advertising 18	0.6	0.1	1.2	0.9	0.5	0.5	0.5	0.5	0.5	0.3	0.3	0.6	•
Other Expenses 19	9.0	4.0	12.1	14.3	9.1	6.9	7.6	7.7	9.8	8.4	14.5	7.6	•
Officers' Compensation 20	2.1	0.3	5.1	6.0	2.8	2.0	1.6	1.2	0.9	0.6	0.6	0.4	•
Operating Margin 21	•	0.1	•	•	0.4	0.4	•	•	•	•	•	2.7	•
Operating Margin Before Officers' Comp. 22	1.7	0.4	4.7	5.0	3.3	2.4	0.9	1.0	•	•	•	3.2	•

Selected Average Balance Sheet ($ in Thousands)

Net Receivables 23	491	0	36	156	617	2024	3807	8223	17318	35452	72211	335865	•
Inventories 24	618	0	35	240	869	3100	5937	12913	20159	48023	87665	247140	•
Net Property, Plant and Equipment 25	274	0	16	116	252	677	2346	4560	14477	28509	87240	132994	•
Total Assets 26	1849	0	119	692	2183	7116	15032	33625	67792	149326	334333	1146326	•
Notes and Loans Payable 27	628	0	79	266	727	2197	5264	11513	19452	51574	118262	324115	•
All Other Liabilities 28	578	0	38	205	729	2512	4765	11466	20731	47174	117315	275071	•
Net Worth 29	643	0	2	220	727	2407	5003	10645	27609	50578	98756	547139	•

Selected Financial Ratios (Times to 1)

Current Ratio 30	1.6	•	1.8	2.0	1.7	1.5	1.5	1.5	1.6	1.5	1.3	2.0	•
Quick Ratio 31	0.8	•	1.1	1.0	0.8	0.6	0.7	0.6	0.8	0.6	0.6	1.1	•
Net Sales to Working Capital 32	6.7	•	11.6	5.8	7.1	8.4	7.5	6.8	6.2	6.0	8.3	3.6	•
Coverage Ratio 33	2.5	6.4	2.5	0.7	3.0	3.9	2.5	2.9	2.7	1.1	0.4	5.2	•
Total Asset Turnover 34	1.9	•	4.0	2.2	2.3	2.4	1.9	1.8	1.5	1.3	1.2	1.2	•
Inventory Turnover 35	4.2	•	9.9	4.1	4.3	4.3	3.7	3.6	3.7	3.1	3.2	3.9	•
Receivables Turnover 36	7.3	•	13.9	8.6	8.7	8.9	7.6	7.3	6.0	5.8	5.9	4.0	•
Total Liabilities to Net Worth 37	1.9	•	51.9	2.1	2.0	2.0	2.0	2.2	1.5	2.0	2.4	1.1	•
Current Assets to Working Capital 38	2.6	•	2.2	2.0	2.4	2.9	3.0	2.9	2.8	3.0	4.0	2.0	•
Current Liabilities to Working Capital 39	1.6	•	1.2	1.0	1.4	1.9	2.0	1.9	1.8	2.0	3.0	1.0	•
Working Capital to Net Sales 40	0.1	•	0.1	0.2	0.1	0.1	0.1	0.1	0.2	0.2	0.1	0.3	•
Inventory to Working Capital 41	1.2	•	0.8	0.8	1.2	1.5	1.5	1.5	1.2	1.5	2.0	0.6	•
Total Receipts to Cash Flow 42	12.0	25.2	9.5	9.6	11.4	14.4	14.1	12.9	11.6	15.6	22.8	8.7	•
Cost of Goods to Cash Flow 43	8.9	23.0	6.7	6.1	8.3	11.3	10.7	9.9	8.6	11.9	15.9	6.3	•
Cash Flow to Total Debt 44	0.2	•	0.4	0.3	0.3	0.3	0.2	0.2	0.2	0.1	0.1	0.3	•

Selected Financial Factors (in Percentages)

Debt Ratio 45	65.2	•	98.1	68.2	66.7	66.2	66.7	68.3	59.3	66.1	70.5	52.3	•
Return on Total Assets 46	5.0	•	9.5	1.4	5.3	5.3	4.2	4.8	4.3	1.9	2.0	7.8	•
Return on Equity Before Income Taxes 47	8.6	•	299.8	•	10.7	11.6	7.5	10.0	6.6	0.5	•	13.2	•
Return on Equity After Income Taxes 48	6.0	•	273.7	•	9.6	9.9	5.7	7.6	4.1	•	•	7.8	•
Profit Margin (Before Income Tax) 49	1.6	1.0	1.4	•	1.5	1.6	1.3	1.8	1.8	•	•	5.4	•
Profit Margin (After Income Tax) 50	1.1	0.8	1.3	•	1.4	1.4	1.0	1.3	1.1	0.1	•	3.2	•

179

Table II

Corporations with Net Income

MACHINERY, EQUIPMENT, AND SUPPLIES

MONEY AMOUNTS AND SIZE OF ASSETS IN THOUSANDS OF DOLLARS

Item Description for Accounting Period 7/03 Through 6/04		Total	Zero Assets	Under 500	500 to 1,000	1,000 to 5,000	5,000 to 10,000	10,000 to 25,000	25,000 to 50,000	50,000 to 100,000	100,000 to 250,000	250,000 to 500,000	500,000 to 2,500,000	2,500,000 and over
Number of Enterprises	1	28642	947	17580	2695	5727	973	465	137	52	40	13	12	•
Revenues ($ in Thousands)														
Net Sales	2	128256933	2592567	10210728	4399463	33520968	16870465	14087697	8975653	5750723	8375240	5839452	17633976	•
Interest	3	246389	1579	2157	6166	22225	12559	13501	14228	11894	23902	7749	130429	•
Rents	4	171956	801	188	1065	15719	16366	11322	6767	4900	21638	12594	80596	•
Royalties	5	45509	0	0	0	0	0	2658	528	34067	126	484	7646	•
Other Portfolio Income	6	516503	13890	5508	14505	60547	45617	79735	61394	30277	77720	49520	77787	•
Other Receipts	7	1274313	8811	173729	12543	251006	170791	161091	110876	72043	139044	60440	113943	•
Total Receipts	8	130511603	2617648	10392310	4433742	33870465	17115798	14356004	9169446	5903904	8637670	5970239	18044377	•
Average Total Receipts	9	4557	2764	591	1645	5914	17591	30873	66930	113537	215942	459249	1503698	•
Operating Costs/Operating Income (%)														
Cost of Operations	10	74.0	92.6	70.1	60.6	73.4	77.6	75.4	76.9	73.0	75.3	76.9	70.7	•
Salaries and Wages	11	8.2	2.1	6.2	9.3	8.5	8.1	8.5	8.0	8.9	7.9	7.8	9.6	•
Taxes Paid	12	1.3	0.3	1.5	1.8	1.4	1.2	1.2	1.2	1.3	1.0	0.9	1.6	•
Interest Paid	13	0.8	0.1	0.7	0.8	0.6	0.5	0.7	0.8	0.8	1.2	1.2	1.1	•
Depreciation	14	1.7	0.6	0.8	1.5	1.0	1.1	2.0	1.9	2.8	4.6	3.5	1.9	•
Amortization and Depletion	15	0.1	0.0	0.1	0.0	0.1	0.0	0.1	0.1	0.1	0.1	0.3	0.4	•
Pensions and Other Deferred Comp.	16	0.4	0.0	0.3	0.4	0.5	0.3	0.4	0.4	0.2	0.2	0.4	0.6	•
Employee Benefits	17	0.9	0.1	0.6	0.8	0.7	0.8	0.9	0.8	0.9	1.7	1.6	1.3	•
Advertising	18	0.5	0.0	0.4	0.8	0.5	0.5	0.5	0.5	0.5	0.5	0.2	0.5	•
Other Expenses	19	7.7	2.8	10.0	13.0	8.4	6.4	7.0	7.1	9.4	7.2	6.3	6.6	•
Officers' Compensation	20	2.0	0.2	5.1	6.6	2.6	2.2	1.6	1.1	0.9	0.7	0.5	0.5	•
Operating Margin	21	2.4	1.3	4.1	4.4	2.4	1.4	1.8	1.2	1.3	•	0.5	5.1	•
Operating Margin Before Officers' Comp.	22	4.4	1.5	9.2	10.9	5.0	3.6	3.4	2.2	2.2	0.3	1.0	5.6	•

Selected Average Balance Sheet ($ in Thousands)

	1	2	3	4	5	6	7	8	9	10	11	12
Net Receivables 23	578	0	36	169	659	2130	3958	8196	18171	34863	72103	280131
Inventories 24	716	0	36	195	915	2981	5772	11855	18142	45860	99375	235827
Net Property, Plant and Equipment 25	280	0	14	103	208	575	2085	4530	12035	30189	45134	144855
Total Assets 26	2210		132	684	2270	7144	14992	33678	67855	155434	315356	1146335
Notes and Loans Payable 27	654	0	59	219	647	2079	4642	11168	17371	45661	109480	293491
All Other Liabilities 28	652	0	36	160	737	2494	4818	10636	20766	49223	103857	237991
Net Worth 29	905	0	37	305	886	2570	5531	11874	29719	60551	102020	614854

Selected Financial Ratios (Times to 1)

	1	2	3	4	5	6	7	8	9	10	11	12
Current Ratio 30	1.7	•	2.2	2.3	1.8	1.6	1.6	1.6	1.8	1.5	1.4	2.1
Quick Ratio 31	0.8	•	1.3	1.4	0.9	0.7	0.7	0.7	0.9	0.6	0.5	1.1
Net Sales to Working Capital 32	6.4	•	10.5	5.5	6.9	7.9	6.8	6.7	5.4	5.8	7.8	3.9
Coverage Ratio 33	6.4	30.7	9.0	7.8	6.5	6.6	6.2	5.3	6.0	3.4	3.3	8.1
Total Asset Turnover 34	2.0	•	4.4	2.4	2.6	2.4	2.0	1.9	1.6	1.3	1.4	1.3
Inventory Turnover 35	4.6	•	11.3	5.1	4.7	4.5	4.0	4.3	4.4	3.4	3.5	4.4
Receivables Turnover 36	8.5	•	18.0	9.2	9.3	9.3	8.0	8.6	6.7	7.3	6.9	5.8
Total Liabilities to Net Worth 37	1.4	•	2.6	1.2	1.6	1.8	1.7	1.8	1.3	1.6	2.1	0.9
Current Assets to Working Capital 38	2.3	•	1.8	1.8	2.2	2.8	2.7	2.6	2.3	2.9	3.5	1.9
Current Liabilities to Working Capital 39	1.3	•	0.8	0.8	1.2	1.8	1.7	1.6	1.3	1.9	2.5	0.9
Working Capital to Net Sales 40	0.2	•	0.1	0.2	0.1	0.1	0.1	0.1	0.2	0.2	0.1	0.3
Inventory to Working Capital 41	1.1	•	0.6	0.6	1.1	1.4	1.4	1.4	1.0	1.4	2.0	0.7
Total Receipts to Cash Flow 42	10.0	23.9	7.4	6.7	9.8	13.0	11.1	11.4	9.9	12.3	13.6	8.0
Cost of Goods to Cash Flow 43	7.4	22.1	5.2	4.1	7.2	10.1	8.3	8.8	7.2	9.3	10.4	5.6
Cash Flow to Total Debt 44	0.3	•	0.8	0.6	0.4	0.3	0.3	0.3	0.3	0.2	0.2	0.3

Selected Financial Factors (in Percentages)

	1	2	3	4	5	6	7	8	9	10	11	12
Debt Ratio 45	59.1	•	72.1	55.4	61.0	64.0	63.1	64.7	56.2	61.0	67.6	46.4
Return on Total Assets 46	9.9	•	29.2	14.1	10.5	8.1	8.9	7.9	7.7	5.3	5.6	10.9
Return on Equity Before Income Taxes 47	20.3	•	92.9	27.6	22.8	19.0	20.3	18.2	14.7	9.5	12.1	17.8
Return on Equity After Income Taxes 48	17.2	•	90.1	25.9	21.5	17.0	17.9	15.2	11.2	8.2	9.3	11.9
Profit Margin (Before Income Tax) 49	4.1	2.3	5.9	5.2	3.4	2.8	3.7	3.3	3.9	2.8	2.8	7.5
Profit Margin (After Income Tax) 50	3.5	2.1	5.7	4.8	3.3	2.5	3.3	2.8	3.0	2.4	2.1	5.0

Table I
Corporations with and without Net Income

FURNITURE, SPORTS, TOYS, JEWELRY, OTHER DURABLE GOODS

MONEY AMOUNTS AND SIZE OF ASSETS IN THOUSANDS OF DOLLARS

Item Description for Accounting Period 7/03 Through 6/04	Total	Zero Assets	Under 500	500 to 1,000	1,000 to 5,000	5,000 to 10,000	10,000 to 25,000	25,000 to 50,000	50,000 to 100,000	100,000 to 250,000	250,000 to 500,000	500,000 to 2,500,000	2,500,000 and over
Number of Enterprises **1**	67492	6239	46037	6105	6685	1269	732	232	90	63	27	14	•
Revenues ($ in Thousands)													
Net Sales **2**	195806895	3042306	17707664	10128311	38863067	18103476	23831204	18159022	12118941	14093134	13185602	26574168	•
Interest **3**	315840	7179	6594	8052	15447	8248	14889	15314	13258	80007	60649	86204	•
Rents **4**	114411	40	1639	1829	9594	8106	7832	3296	6997	3704	36041	35334	•
Royalties **5**	353896	1591	0	3222	2911	5366	6593	11300	27585	45039	47234	203055	•
Other Portfolio Income **6**	397677	73520	11654	14545	29808	35809	12393	25614	18236	83907	67836	24354	•
Other Receipts **7**	1863380	20072	195236	152097	281899	69242	179111	139503	81938	334127	268587	141566	•
Total Receipts **8**	19852099	3114708	17922787	10308056	39202726	18230247	24052022	18354049	12266955	14639918	13665949	27064681	•
Average Total Receipts **9**	2946	504	389	1688	5864	14366	32858	79112	136300	232380	506146	1933192	•
Operating Costs/Operating Income (%)													
Cost of Operations **10**	75.3	82.8	59.6	69.4	72.4	77.9	77.4	78.4	79.4	75.1	79.3	82.3	•
Salaries and Wages **11**	6.6	3.7	8.0	6.6	8.2	5.8	6.8	6.1	6.2	6.7	5.9	5.2	•
Taxes Paid **12**	1.2	0.9	1.7	1.5	1.5	1.4	1.2	1.0	1.2	1.1	1.0	0.6	•
Interest Paid **13**	0.8	0.9	0.6	0.5	0.6	0.6	0.7	0.7	0.7	1.4	1.3	0.9	•
Depreciation **14**	1.0	1.1	1.3	0.9	0.9	1.0	0.9	0.8	1.1	1.4	1.5	0.8	•
Amortization and Depletion **15**	0.2	1.3	0.1	0.0	0.1	0.0	0.1	0.2	0.5	0.4	0.4	0.5	•
Pensions and Other Deferred Comp. **16**	0.3	0.0	0.5	0.6	0.3	0.3	0.2	0.1	0.2	0.2	0.2	0.3	•
Employee Benefits **17**	0.5	0.4	0.5	0.5	0.4	0.5	0.5	0.5	0.7	1.0	0.9	0.4	•
Advertising **18**	1.4	0.9	1.0	0.8	1.0	0.7	1.2	1.4	1.4	2.3	2.1	2.6	•
Other Expenses **19**	9.7	9.5	19.6	14.1	10.6	7.7	8.2	8.1	7.5	9.8	8.2	5.5	•
Officers' Compensation **20**	2.4	3.2	7.3	4.2	3.1	3.0	1.7	1.3	1.1	0.8	0.5	0.7	•
Operating Margin **21**	0.4	•	•	0.8	0.9	1.2	1.2	1.4	0.2	•	•	0.0	•
Operating Margin Before Officers' Comp. **22**	2.8	•	7.2	5.0	4.0	4.2	2.9	2.7	1.3	0.5	0.7	0.7	•

Selected Average Balance Sheet ($ in Thousands)

Net Receivables 23	368	0	21	195	617	2045	5310	11121	19811	42049	84543	199534
Inventories 24	398	0	33	282	849	2581	5527	11015	20829	29862	65464	180442
Net Property, Plant and Equipment 25	156	0	19	64	289	893	1395	2950	9029	15212	36825	125732
Total Assets 26	1416	0	107	704	2272	6739	15269	34501	67908	148357	359259	1301427
Notes and Loans Payable 27	433	0	59	256	652	2105	4658	10800	21685	50033	93885	309817
All Other Liabilities 28	522	0	36	286	939	2482	5983	12043	23632	50552	105829	503941
Net Worth 29	461	0	13	162	681	2152	4628	11658	22591	47772	159546	487669

Selected Financial Ratios (Times to 1)

Current Ratio 30	1.6	•	2.0	1.7	1.6	1.6	1.5	1.6	1.6	1.7	1.4	1.3
Quick Ratio 31	0.8	•	1.1	0.9	0.8	0.8	0.8	0.8	0.8	1.0	0.7	0.6
Net Sales to Working Capital 32	8.2	•	9.8	6.7	8.6	6.8	7.4	7.6	7.1	5.4	9.7	13.1
Coverage Ratio 33	3.6	•	2.7	5.8	3.9	4.1	4.3	4.6	3.1	3.6	2.9	3.5
Total Asset Turnover 34	2.0	•	3.6	2.4	2.6	2.1	2.1	2.3	2.0	1.5	1.4	1.5
Inventory Turnover 35	5.5	•	6.9	4.1	5.0	4.3	4.6	5.6	5.1	5.6	5.9	8.7
Receivables Turnover 36	7.9	•	18.5	8.9	9.3	6.7	6.2	7.4	6.4	6.2	6.1	8.4
Total Liabilities to Net Worth 37	2.1	•	7.5	3.3	2.3	2.1	2.3	2.0	2.0	2.1	1.3	1.7
Current Assets to Working Capital 38	2.8	•	2.0	2.4	2.7	2.6	2.9	2.7	2.6	2.4	3.7	4.3
Current Liabilities to Working Capital 39	1.8	•	1.0	1.4	1.7	1.6	1.9	1.7	1.6	1.4	2.7	3.3
Working Capital to Net Sales 40	0.1	•	0.1	0.1	0.1	0.1	0.1	0.1	0.1	0.2	0.1	0.1
Inventory to Working Capital 41	1.1	•	0.9	1.1	1.2	1.2	1.2	1.1	1.1	0.8	1.2	1.2
Total Receipts to Cash Flow 42	10.9	17.2	6.6	7.5	10.9	13.4	11.8	11.0	14.5	9.0	11.4	16.1
Cost of Goods to Cash Flow 43	8.2	14.2	3.9	5.2	7.9	10.4	9.1	8.6	11.5	6.8	9.1	13.3
Cash Flow to Total Debt 44	0.3	•	0.6	0.4	0.3	0.2	0.3	0.3	0.2	0.2	0.2	0.1

Selected Financial Factors (in Percentages)

Debt Ratio 45	67.4	•	88.2	77.0	70.0	68.1	69.7	66.2	66.7	67.8	55.6	62.5
Return on Total Assets 46	5.7	•	6.1	7.4	6.0	5.2	5.9	7.2	4.2	7.8	5.0	4.4
Return on Equity Before Income Taxes 47	12.8	•	32.4	26.6	15.0	12.2	15.0	16.6	8.5	17.6	7.4	8.3
Return on Equity After Income Taxes 48	10.5	•	28.3	25.3	13.9	10.0	13.1	14.6	5.3	13.5	4.6	6.6
Profit Margin (Before Income Tax) 49	2.0	•	1.1	2.6	1.8	1.8	2.1	2.5	1.4	3.8	2.4	2.1
Profit Margin (After Income Tax) 50	1.7	•	0.9	2.5	1.6	1.5	1.9	2.2	0.9	2.9	1.5	1.7

181

Table II
Corporations with Net Income

FURNITURE, SPORTS, TOYS, JEWELRY, OTHER DURABLE GOODS

MONEY AMOUNTS AND SIZE OF ASSETS IN THOUSANDS OF DOLLARS

Item Description for Accounting Period 7/03 Through 6/04	Total	Zero Assets	Under 500	500 to 1,000	1,000 to 5,000	5,000 to 10,000	10,000 to 25,000	25,000 to 50,000	50,000 to 100,000	100,000 to 250,000	250,000 to 500,000	500,000 to 2,500,000	2,500,000 and over
Number of Enterprises **1**	36400	1749	23675	4379	4774	936	570	172	65	51	19	11	•
Revenues ($ in Thousands)													
Net Sales **2**	150674402	935815	12027283	7979820	31564162	14698169	19419981	12938697	9257796	11956197	10756434	19140048	•
Interest **3**	189959	79	4765	6724	11131	6694	11363	7273	8968	32541	36841	63581	•
Rents **4**	81217	0	1639	984	7378	6392	5087	2876	6147	2801	30011	17901	•
Royalties **5**	286836	1591	0	3222	2372	5207	4202	6066	24277	43591	39065	157244	•
Other Portfolio Income **6**	330622	72983	524	8973	17454	33833	8474	22941	16304	77357	50781	20996	•
Other Receipts **7**	1522719	23524	81456	137577	221798	53141	126555	127207	58960	315926	238793	137783	•
Total Receipts **8**	153085755	1033992	12115667	8137300	31824295	14803436	19575662	13105060	9372452	12428413	11151925	19537553	•
Average Total Receipts **9**	4206	591	512	1858	6666	15816	34343	76192	144192	243694	586943	1776141	•
Operating Costs/Operating Income (%)													
Cost of Operations **10**	74.9	69.1	57.3	70.2	71.7	78.0	77.2	76.7	80.6	76.4	78.1	82.0	•
Salaries and Wages **11**	6.5	3.3	8.9	5.8	8.1	5.4	6.5	6.2	4.8	6.0	5.9	5.2	•
Taxes Paid **12**	1.2	1.0	1.7	1.3	1.4	1.3	1.1	1.1	1.2	0.9	1.1	0.6	•
Interest Paid **13**	0.7	0.4	0.4	0.4	0.5	0.5	0.6	0.6	0.5	1.2	1.1	1.0	•
Depreciation **14**	0.9	2.1	1.2	0.9	0.7	0.8	0.8	0.8	1.1	1.3	1.6	0.8	•
Amortization and Depletion **15**	0.2	0.1	0.0	0.0	0.1	0.0	0.1	0.1	0.1	0.4	0.3	0.6	•
Pensions and Other Deferred Comp. **16**	0.3	0.1	0.4	0.7	0.3	0.3	0.2	0.2	0.1	0.2	0.2	0.4	•
Employee Benefits **17**	0.5	0.5	0.4	0.3	0.4	0.4	0.5	0.5	0.5	0.8	0.9	0.5	•
Advertising **18**	1.5	1.0	0.8	0.6	1.0	0.5	1.1	1.4	1.4	2.2	2.3	3.3	•
Other Expenses **19**	8.4	10.6	16.1	12.9	9.7	6.5	7.4	7.2	6.2	8.7	8.3	3.9	•
Officers' Compensation **20**	2.3	2.8	6.6	3.8	3.2	3.2	1.6	1.4	1.1	0.7	0.5	0.7	•
Operating Margin **21**	2.7	9.1	6.1	3.0	3.0	3.2	2.9	3.9	2.3	1.2	•	1.0	•
Operating Margin Before Officers' Comp. **22**	5.0	11.9	12.7	6.8	6.2	6.3	4.5	5.3	3.4	2.0	0.3	1.6	•

Selected Average Balance Sheet ($ in Thousands)

Item													
Net Receivables 23	521	0	26	216	679	2171	5480	11316	20188	43144	88756	168739	•
Inventories 24	552	0	36	254	914	2737	5576	12097	21917	29429	72518	146869	•
Net Property, Plant and Equipment 25	193	0	26	58	277	731	1279	2841	9281	13884	43643	72534	•
Total Assets 26	1959	0	132	728	2474	6557	15246	34365	68049	151322	352808	1238842	•
Notes and Loans Payable 27	524	0	58	224	615	1530	4195	9496	18344	50495	81317	276339	•
All Other Liabilities 28	690	0	37	275	991	2366	5885	12015	21514	48784	102204	440610	•
Net Worth 29	745	0	37	229	868	2661	5166	12854	28191	52043	169287	521893	•

Selected Financial Ratios (Times to 1)

Item													
Current Ratio 30	1.7	•	2.1	2.0	1.7	1.9	1.6	1.6	1.8	1.8	1.6	1.4	•
Quick Ratio 31	0.9	•	1.2	1.1	0.8	1.0	0.8	0.8	0.9	1.0	0.9	0.5	•
Net Sales to Working Capital 32	7.5	•	10.4	6.0	8.1	6.0	7.0	6.9	6.4	5.5	8.0	11.9	•
Coverage Ratio 33	7.5	51.3	16.5	12.3	8.1	9.4	7.4	10.0	7.9	5.4	4.3	4.6	
Total Asset Turnover 34	2.1	•	3.9	2.5	2.7	2.4	2.2	2.2	2.1	1.5	1.6	1.4	•
Inventory Turnover 35	5.6	•	8.0	5.0	5.2	4.5	4.7	4.8	5.2	6.1	6.1	9.7	•
Receivables Turnover 36	8.2	•	20.0	9.8	9.7	6.7	6.3	6.6	7.0	6.4	6.4	11.9	•
Total Liabilities to Net Worth 37	1.6	•	2.6	2.2	1.8	1.5	2.0	1.7	1.4	1.9	1.1	1.4	•
Current Assets to Working Capital 38	2.5	•	1.9	2.0	2.5	2.1	2.6	2.6	2.2	2.3	2.7	3.8	•
Current Liabilities to Working Capital 39	1.5	•	0.9	1.0	1.5	1.1	1.6	1.6	1.2	1.3	1.7	2.8	•
Working Capital to Net Sales 40	0.1	•	0.1	0.2	0.1	0.2	0.1	0.1	0.2	0.2	0.1	0.1	•
Inventory to Working Capital 41	1.0	•	0.7	0.8	1.1	1.0	1.1	1.1	0.9	0.8	0.9	1.0	•
Total Receipts to Cash Flow 42	9.6	3.7	5.4	6.7	9.7	11.5	10.7	9.2	12.5	8.6	10.2	17.1	
Cost of Goods to Cash Flow 43	7.2	2.5	3.1	4.7	6.9	9.0	8.3	7.1	10.1	6.5	8.0	14.0	
Cash Flow to Total Debt 44	0.4	•	1.0	0.5	0.4	0.4	0.3	0.4	0.3	0.3	0.3	0.1	•

Selected Financial Factors (in Percentages)

Item													
Debt Ratio 45	62.0	•	71.9	68.6	64.9	59.4	66.1	62.6	58.6	65.6	52.0	57.9	•
Return on Total Assets 46	10.6	•	28.1	13.6	11.6	10.3	9.4	12.5	8.4	10.1	7.5	6.2	•
Return on Equity Before Income Taxes 47	24.2	•	93.9	39.7	29.1	22.7	24.1	30.2	17.8	23.9	11.9	11.5	•
Return on Equity After Income Taxes 48	21.6	•	91.2	38.4	27.9	20.3	21.9	27.8	14.2	19.2	8.3	9.4	•
Profit Margin (Before Income Tax) 49	4.4	19.6	6.8	5.0	3.8	3.9	3.7	5.2	3.5	5.3	3.6	3.5	
Profit Margin (After Income Tax) 50	3.9	19.2	6.6	4.8	3.7	3.4	3.3	4.7	2.8	4.3	2.5	2.8	

Table I

Corporations with and without Net Income

PAPER AND PAPER PRODUCT

MONEY AMOUNTS AND SIZE OF ASSETS IN THOUSANDS OF DOLLARS

Item Description for Accounting Period 7/03 Through 6/04	Total	Zero Assets	Under 500	500 to 1,000	1,000 to 5,000	5,000 to 10,000	10,000 to 25,000	25,000 to 50,000	50,000 to 100,000	100,000 to 250,000	250,000 to 500,000	500,000 to 2,500,000	2,500,000 and over
Number of Enterprises **1**	9464	915	6537	792	925	103	112	40	20	14	·	4	·
Revenues ($ in Thousands)													
Net Sales **2**	46388359	276726	3024453	1479021	8233581	1789236	6035280	4483236	4384683	7599112	·	9083030	·
Interest **3**	24808	124	365	1664	1285	1351	2443	1695	2638	2939	·	10304	·
Rents **4**	12515	15	0	0	5402	108	691	759	773	113	·	4654	·
Royalties **5**	9647	0	0	0	0	0	4679	0	2098	2870	·	0	·
Other Portfolio Income **6**	36800	0	2951	202	954	2319	1625	3128	1051	12605	·	11963	·
Other Receipts **7**	222622	6539	24063	5324	79441	6577	18779	11204	17640	36190	·	16868	·
Total Receipts **8**	46694751	283404	3051832	1486211	8320663	1799591	6063497	4500022	4408883	7653829	·	9126819	·
Average Total Receipts **9**	4934	310	467	1877	8995	17472	54138	112501	220444	546702	·	2281705	·
Operating Costs/Operating Income (%)													
Cost of Operations **10**	82.0	94.4	66.9	67.0	78.8	63.9	84.5	83.7	87.1	86.9	·	86.6	·
Salaries and Wages **11**	5.7	1.7	4.9	6.9	6.9	13.3	5.8	6.4	4.5	4.8	·	4.3	·
Taxes Paid **12**	0.8	0.4	1.2	2.0	1.0	2.2	0.8	0.8	0.6	0.6	·	0.4	·
Interest Paid **13**	0.8	0.3	0.9	0.4	0.5	0.6	0.4	0.6	0.5	1.1	·	1.2	·
Depreciation **14**	0.8	0.2	1.0	1.7	0.6	0.8	0.7	0.7	0.4	0.5	·	1.2	·
Amortization and Depletion **15**	0.2	0.1	0.0	0.0	0.1	0.0	0.0	0.2	0.1	0.2	·	0.4	·
Pensions and Other Deferred Comp. **16**	0.3	1.6	0.1	0.1	0.5	0.1	0.2	0.2	0.1	0.2	·	0.4	·
Employee Benefits **17**	0.5	0.2	0.6	0.5	0.7	0.6	0.4	0.5	0.3	0.5	·	0.5	·
Advertising **18**	0.3	0.1	0.6	0.3	0.2	0.1	0.3	0.3	0.1	0.1	·	0.4	·
Other Expenses **19**	6.5	6.3	18.4	13.2	6.4	10.1	4.9	5.4	5.1	4.4	·	5.1	·
Officers' Compensation **20**	1.9	1.3	7.1	5.8	4.3	2.1	1.2	0.8	0.9	0.4	·	0.2	·
Operating Margin **21**	0.2	·	·	2.3	·	6.2	0.8	0.4	0.5	0.3	·	·	·
Operating Margin Before Officers' Comp. **22**	2.2	·	5.3	8.1	4.3	8.3	2.0	1.3	1.3	0.7	·	·	·

Selected Average Balance Sheet ($ in Thousands)

	1	2	3	4	5	6	7	8	9	10	11
Net Receivables 23	589	0	36	263	866	2036	7176	12759	32416	72588	286198
Inventories 24	361	0	12	227	567	2402	3611	9976	12392	29568	230061
Net Property, Plant and Equipment 25	179	0	11	41	165	676	1728	3229	5460	18666	168061
Total Assets 26	1605	0	94	741	2097	6563	15393	35407	70720	187429	1047653
Notes and Loans Payable 27	619	0	63	133	903	1134	4356	12718	20807	81393	460614
All Other Liabilities 28	584	0	66	122	819	2065	6336	12018	29254	62945	341793
Net Worth 29	401	0	-35	486	375	3363	4701	10671	20658	43091	245246

Selected Financial Ratios (Times to 1)

	1	2	3	4	5	6	7	8	9	10	11
Current Ratio 30	1.5	•	0.9	4.6	1.6	2.2	1.5	1.5	1.4	1.7	1.3
Quick Ratio 31	0.9	•	0.8	2.9	1.0	1.3	1.0	0.8	0.9	1.2	0.7
Net Sales to Working Capital 32	13.0	•	•	3.7	15.1	6.2	12.9	12.8	12.9	10.8	17.4
Coverage Ratio 33	2.2	•	0.0	8.9	3.2	12.9	4.3	2.4	2.9	1.9	0.7
Total Asset Turnover 34	3.1	•	4.9	2.5	4.2	2.6	3.5	3.2	3.1	2.9	2.2
Inventory Turnover 35	11.1	•	26.4	5.5	12.4	4.6	12.6	9.4	15.4	16.0	8.5
Receivables Turnover 36	7.9	•	12.4	7.8	10.5	5.7	8.0	7.7	7.2	8.1	6.2
Total Liabilities to Net Worth 37	3.0	•	•	0.5	4.6	1.0	2.3	2.3	2.4	3.3	3.3
Current Assets to Working Capital 38	3.0	•	•	1.3	2.8	1.8	3.0	3.1	3.4	2.5	4.2
Current Liabilities to Working Capital 39	2.0	•	•	0.3	1.8	0.8	2.0	2.1	2.4	1.5	3.2
Working Capital to Net Sales 40	0.1	•	•	0.3	0.1	0.2	0.1	0.1	0.1	0.1	0.1
Inventory to Working Capital 41	0.9	•	•	0.5	1.0	0.5	0.9	1.1	0.9	0.6	1.3
Total Receipts to Cash Flow 42	17.5	102.4	7.0	7.9	18.1	7.4	20.5	23.2	20.0	24.8	28.1
Cost of Goods to Cash Flow 43	14.4	96.7	4.7	5.3	14.3	4.7	17.4	19.5	17.4	21.5	24.3
Cash Flow to Total Debt 44	0.2	0.5	0.9	0.3	0.7	0.2	0.2	0.2	0.2	0.2	0.1

Selected Financial Factors (in Percentages)

	1	2	3	4	5	6	7	8	9	10	11
Debt Ratio 45	75.0	137.4	70.8	34.4	82.1	48.8	69.5	69.9	70.8	77.0	76.6
Return on Total Assets 46	5.0	0.2	•	7.9	6.5	19.4	5.8	4.3	4.9	6.2	1.9
Return on Equity Before Income Taxes 47	10.9	•	11.6	10.8	24.9	35.0	14.4	8.5	10.9	12.9	•
Return on Equity After Income Taxes 48	7.8	•	11.8	9.8	21.7	33.9	12.4	7.4	10.1	9.5	•
Profit Margin (Before Income Tax) 49	0.9	•	2.8	1.1	6.8	1.3	0.8	1.0	1.0	•	•
Profit Margin (After Income Tax) 50	0.6	•	2.6	0.9	6.6	1.1	0.7	1.0	0.8	•	•

Table II
Corporations with Net Income

PAPER AND PAPER PRODUCT

MONEY AMOUNTS AND SIZE OF ASSETS IN THOUSANDS OF DOLLARS

Item Description for Accounting Period 7/03 Through 6/04	Total	Zero Assets	Under 500	500 to 1,000	1,000 to 5,000	5,000 to 10,000	10,000 to 25,000	25,000 to 50,000	50,000 to 100,000	100,000 to 250,000	250,000 to 500,000	500,000 to 2,500,000	2,500,000 and over
Number of Enterprises 1	4141	278	2420	682	525	92	89	27	14	10	3	•	•
Revenues ($ in Thousands)													
Net Sales 2	32089090	22185	1802316	1280833	6294000	1484849	4928421	3064964	3586202	5183407	4441913	•	•
Interest 3	16746	0	132	793	721	1351	2049	1461	1435	1944	6861	•	•
Rents 4	4691	0	0	0	2036	108	370	759	773	105	540	•	•
Royalties 5	9636	0	0	0	0	0	4668	0	2098	2818	52	•	•
Other Portfolio Income 6	23773	0	82	45	338	2319	1573	3069	1007	11119	4221	•	•
Other Receipts 7	151362	0	17904	5054	48714	6213	15076	4948	16694	33495	3265	•	•
Total Receipts 8	32295298	22185	1820434	1286725	6345809	1494840	4952157	3075201	3608209	5232888	4456852	•	•
Average Total Receipts 9	7799	80	752	1887	12087	16248	55642	113896	257729	523289	1485617	•	•
Operating Costs/Operating Income (%)													
Cost of Operations 10	81.6	56.4	69.0	66.6	80.2	62.7	84.1	84.4	87.1	88.5	82.3	•	•
Salaries and Wages 11	5.8	3.9	3.6	7.3	6.4	13.0	5.8	6.0	4.3	4.5	5.5	•	•
Taxes Paid 12	0.9	0.6	0.9	1.8	0.9	2.4	0.8	0.7	0.5	0.5	0.8	•	•
Interest Paid 13	0.5	0.9	0.3	0.3	0.4	0.6	0.4	0.4	0.5	0.7	0.8	•	•
Depreciation 14	0.6	0.4	0.4	1.3	0.5	0.9	0.6	0.6	0.4	0.4	0.6	•	•
Amortization and Depletion 15	0.1	•	0.0	0.0	0.0	0.0	0.0	0.2	0.0	0.1	0.3	•	•
Pensions and Other Deferred Comp. 16	0.2	•	0.2	0.1	0.4	0.1	0.3	0.2	0.1	0.1	0.4	•	•
Employee Benefits 17	0.4	0.6	0.4	0.4	0.6	0.2	0.4	0.4	0.2	0.4	0.6	•	•
Advertising 18	0.2	0.8	0.8	0.3	0.1	0.1	0.4	0.1	0.1	0.0	0.1	•	•
Other Expenses 19	5.9	15.6	16.9	13.5	5.6	9.4	4.5	4.3	5.0	4.1	4.2	•	•
Officers' Compensation 20	1.8	•	5.4	5.5	3.6	2.4	1.2	0.8	0.8	0.4	0.2	•	•
Operating Margin 21	2.0	21.2	1.9	2.8	1.3	8.1	1.6	2.0	1.0	0.2	4.3	•	•
Operating Margin Before Officers' Comp. 22	3.8	21.2	7.3	8.3	4.8	10.5	2.8	2.9	1.8	0.6	4.4	•	•

Selected Average Balance Sheet ($ in Thousands)

	•	•	•	•	•	•	•	•	•	•	•
Net Receivables 23	873	0	55	282	996	1910	7213	13006	35459	64350	151927
Inventories 24	530	0	10	238	834	2582	3636	11066	12585	22124	110545
Net Property, Plant and Equipment 25	190	0	11	30	121	730	1770	3031	6070	13718	48368
Total Assets 26	2259	0	147	734	2294	6612	15444	35557	70948	153010	609790
Notes and Loans Payable 27	649	0	19	113	867	986	3828	11320	14498	52900	213743
All Other Liabilities 28	828	0	111	127	855	1484	6421	12086	32692	62806	167903
Net Worth 29	782	0	16	494	572	4142	5196	12150	23758	37303	228144

Selected Financial Ratios (Times to 1)

	•	•	•	•	•	•	•	•	•	•	•
Current Ratio 30	1.7	•	0.8	4.9	1.6	3.0	1.5	1.5	1.5	1.7	1.6
Quick Ratio 31	1.1	•	0.7	3.1	1.0	1.7	1.0	0.9	1.0	1.2	0.9
Net Sales to Working Capital 32	11.7	•	•	3.5	15.5	4.7	12.9	12.4	12.7	11.8	11.9
Coverage Ratio 33	6.3	24.0	10.6	11.1	6.9	14.6	6.9	6.5	4.5	2.6	6.6
Total Asset Turnover 34	3.4	•	5.1	2.6	5.2	2.4	3.6	3.2	3.6	3.4	2.4
Inventory Turnover 35	11.9	•	50.6	5.3	11.5	3.9	12.8	8.7	17.7	20.7	11.0
Receivables Turnover 36	8.5	•	12.6	13.3	10.8	5.0	8.4	6.8	7.6	9.1	8.4
Total Liabilities to Net Worth 37	1.9	•	8.2	0.5	3.0	0.6	2.0	1.9	2.0	3.1	1.7
Current Assets to Working Capital 38	2.5	•	•	1.3	2.5	1.5	3.0	3.0	3.0	2.5	2.6
Current Liabilities to Working Capital 39	1.5	•	•	0.3	1.5	0.5	2.0	2.0	2.0	1.5	1.6
Working Capital to Net Sales 40	0.1	•	•	0.3	0.1	0.2	0.1	0.1	0.1	0.1	0.1
Inventory to Working Capital 41	0.7	•	•	0.4	1.0	0.4	0.9	1.0	0.7	0.6	0.7
Total Receipts to Cash Flow 42	14.3	2.8	5.6	7.5	17.0	6.8	18.5	19.0	17.8	27.1	13.5
Cost of Goods to Cash Flow 43	11.7	1.6	3.9	5.0	13.6	4.3	15.6	16.0	15.5	24.0	11.1
Cash Flow to Total Debt 44	0.4	•	1.0	1.0	0.4	1.0	0.3	0.3	0.3	0.2	0.3

Selected Financial Factors (in Percentages)

	•	•	•	•	•	•	•	•	•	•	•
Debt Ratio 45	65.4	•	89.1	32.7	75.1	37.4	66.4	65.8	66.5	75.6	62.6
Return on Total Assets 46	10.9	•	16.6	9.3	12.8	23.1	8.7	9.0	7.5	6.3	13.2
Return on Equity Before Income Taxes 47	26.6	•	138.1	12.6	43.9	34.3	22.2	22.2	17.5	16.0	29.8
Return on Equity After Income Taxes 48	22.9	•	136.5	11.5	40.1	33.4	19.9	20.8	16.5	11.8	20.3
Profit Margin (Before Income Tax) 49	2.7	21.2	3.0	3.3	2.1	8.8	2.1	2.4	1.6	1.2	4.6
Profit Margin (After Income Tax) 50	2.3	20.7	2.9	3.0	1.9	8.6	1.9	2.2	1.5	0.8	3.1

184

Table I

Corporations with and without Net Income

DRUGS AND DRUGGISTS' SUNDRIES

MONEY AMOUNTS AND SIZE OF ASSETS IN THOUSANDS OF DOLLARS

Item Description for Accounting Period 7/03 Through 6/04	Total	Zero Assets	Under 500	500 to 1,000	1,000 to 5,000	5,000 to 10,000	10,000 to 25,000	25,000 to 50,000	50,000 to 100,000	100,000 to 250,000	250,000 to 500,000	500,000 to 2,500,000	2,500,000 and over
Number of Enterprises 1	4668	450	2291	1045	346	309	92	41	29	23	11	21	10
Revenues ($ in Thousands)													
Net Sales 2	260294387	1731147	725164	2820014	2106488	4535501	3859832	3098576	5556986	8274669	7577786	34772398	185235826
Interest 3	529381	20381	15	1035	1062	3235	3641	3754	5785	11612	7156	115959	355747
Rents 4	440736	0	0	0	638	19	1115	828	791	742	1309	3686	431609
Royalties 5	2125471	8958	0	0	0	33	1198	4897	9499	34732	22929	1088331	954892
Other Portfolio Income 6	1274780	274628	3	0	314	40872	9971	17051	59979	2788	2507	116354	750313
Other Receipts 7	3545716	-3357	8754	763	32417	21655	37083	42152	126811	50576	-14540	508121	2735280
Total Receipts 8	268210471	2031757	733936	2821812	2140919	4601315	3912840	3167258	5759851	8375119	7597147	36604849	190463667
Average Total Receipts 9	57457	4515	320	2700	6188	14891	42531	77250	198616	364136	690650	1743088	19046367
Operating Costs/Operating Income (%)													
Cost of Operations 10	84.7	64.2	64.4	82.1	69.9	74.7	77.3	73.4	82.0	78.9	77.8	63.7	90.4
Salaries and Wages 11	3.8	11.0	1.3	3.2	8.8	4.5	7.0	7.3	4.9	4.2	8.0	6.0	3.0
Taxes Paid 12	0.5	0.9	2.2	1.1	1.4	1.0	0.9	1.0	0.5	0.9	0.9	0.9	0.3
Interest Paid 13	0.6	1.1	0.7	0.1	0.8	1.4	0.5	0.6	0.4	0.8	0.5	1.4	0.4
Depreciation 14	0.6	0.5	1.7	0.3	0.7	1.1	0.7	1.0	0.5	0.6	0.8	1.0	0.5
Amortization and Depletion 15	0.4	0.7	0.2	0.1	0.1	0.1	0.3	0.3	0.3	0.6	0.7	0.6	0.4
Pensions and Other Deferred Comp. 16	0.1	0.1	0.1	0.1	0.1	0.3	0.2	0.3	0.1	0.2	0.1	0.2	0.1
Employee Benefits 17	0.4	0.7	2.1	0.2	0.6	0.3	0.5	0.7	0.5	0.4	0.5	0.7	0.3
Advertising 18	1.1	1.7	1.3	0.4	3.3	2.1	1.5	2.6	2.6	1.2	1.0	2.1	0.8
Other Expenses 19	6.5	18.5	19.9	6.2	13.3	11.7	8.9	10.5	8.5	9.7	8.3	18.1	3.5
Officers' Compensation 20	0.4	0.2	13.3	2.1	5.1	2.3	2.0	1.2	0.7	0.6	0.3	0.3	0.2
Operating Margin 21	0.9	0.2	•	4.2	•	0.8	0.3	1.1	•	1.9	1.4	5.0	0.2
Operating Margin Before Officers' Comp. 22	1.3	0.5	6.2	6.3	1.0	3.0	2.3	2.3	•	2.5	1.7	5.3	0.3

Selected Average Balance Sheet ($ in Thousands)

Net Receivables 23	6377	0	27	340	684	2017	4400	10180	22706	34430	47128	179216	2193801
Inventories 24	5887	0	23	119	968	1699	4316	8168	17720	33480	81700	129181	2081491
Net Property, Plant and Equipment 25	1728	0	12	35	273	467	1321	3215	5362	10145	27365	93875	484684
Total Assets 26	29347	0	99	811	2553	6681	16009	34205	73866	156304	345323	1061912	9825723
Notes and Loans Payable 27	4984	0	63	406	1106	2956	4653	12660	15841	50362	83352	327824	1103856
All Other Liabilities 28	12715	0	61	345	2488	3030	6014	12816	29607	47125	92166	346636	4574188
Net Worth 29	11647	0	-24	59	-1040	695	5342	8729	28418	58817	169804	387452	4147680

Selected Financial Ratios (Times to 1)

Current Ratio 30	1.4	•	1.0	1.8	0.9	1.3	1.5	1.2	1.4	1.3	1.7	1.5	1.4
Quick Ratio 31	0.8	•	0.5	1.1	0.5	0.6	0.8	0.7	0.8	0.7	0.9	0.8	0.8
Net Sales to Working Capital 32	10.5	•	•	8.3	•	10.0	10.4	17.3	12.0	16.0	9.8	8.1	10.6
Coverage Ratio 33	8.3	16.9	•	46.5	•	2.6	4.0	6.4	8.8	4.7	4.3	8.5	9.3
Total Asset Turnover 34	1.9	•	3.2	3.3	2.4	2.2	2.6	2.2	2.6	2.3	2.0	1.6	1.9
Inventory Turnover 35	8.0	•	8.8	18.5	4.4	6.4	7.5	6.8	8.9	8.5	6.6	8.2	8.0
Receivables Turnover 36	9.2	•	8.8	10.8	6.2	10.0	9.4	8.4	8.4	10.6	9.8	10.9	8.8
Total Liabilities to Net Worth 37	1.5	•	•	12.6	•	8.6	2.0	2.9	1.6	1.7	1.0	1.7	1.4
Current Assets to Working Capital 38	3.3	•	•	2.2	•	3.9	3.0	5.5	3.4	4.1	2.5	2.9	3.3
Current Liabilities to Working Capital 39	2.3	•	•	1.2	•	2.9	2.0	4.5	2.4	3.1	1.5	1.9	2.3
Working Capital to Net Sales 40	0.1	•	•	0.1	•	0.1	0.1	0.1	0.1	0.1	0.1	0.1	0.1
Inventory to Working Capital 41	1.2	•	•	0.6	•	1.5	1.1	2.1	1.1	1.5	0.9	0.8	1.2
Total Receipts to Cash Flow 42	10.3	•	8.8	10.9	11.6	8.3	11.1	8.4	10.2	8.2	10.9	3.7	16.6
Cost of Goods to Cash Flow 43	8.7	1.9	5.7	8.9	8.1	6.2	8.5	6.1	8.4	6.5	8.5	2.3	15.0
Cash Flow to Total Debt 44	0.3	•	0.3	0.3	0.1	0.3	0.4	0.4	0.4	0.5	0.4	0.7	0.2

Selected Financial Factors (in Percentages)

Debt Ratio 45	60.3	•	124.4	92.7	140.8	89.6	66.6	74.5	61.5	62.4	50.8	63.5	57.8
Return on Total Assets 46	8.7	•	•	14.6	•	7.9	5.7	8.6	8.2	9.1	4.2	18.2	6.6
Return on Equity Before Income Taxes 47	19.4	•	77.9	194.8	14.2	46.9	12.8	28.4	19.0	19.0	6.6	43.9	14.0
Return on Equity After Income Taxes 48	13.1	•	78.9	189.7	17.9	35.6	10.2	25.0	14.3	14.7	3.8	28.4	9.5
Profit Margin (Before Income Tax) 49	4.0	17.6	•	4.3	•	2.2	1.6	3.3	2.8	3.1	1.6	10.3	3.1
Profit Margin (After Income Tax) 50	2.7	15.2	•	4.2	•	1.7	1.3	2.9	2.1	2.4	0.9	6.6	2.1

Table II
Corporations with Net Income

DRUGS AND DRUGGISTS' SUNDRIES

MONEY AMOUNTS AND SIZE OF ASSETS IN THOUSANDS OF DOLLARS

Item Description for Accounting Period 7/03 Through 6/04	Total	Zero Assets	Under 500	500 to 1,000	1,000 to 5,000	5,000 to 10,000	10,000 to 25,000	25,000 to 50,000	50,000 to 100,000	100,000 to 250,000	250,000 to 500,000	500,000 to 2,500,000	2,500,000 and over
Number of Enterprises **1**	1659	165	191	800	180	152	64	32	23	19	7	16	10
Revenues ($ in Thousands)													
Net Sales **2**	250594966	881138	139665	2695470	1344656	2797477	3321184	2445024	5163008	7586668	7054704	31930146	185235826
Interest **3**	494496	18604	9	1005	258	1185	1819	3136	5005	4534	4409	98784	355747
Rents **4**	438499	0	0	0	602	19	15	828	39	694	1008	3686	431609
Royalties **5**	2057323	6378	0	0	0	33	120	0	4485	13430	0	1077985	954892
Other Portfolio Income **6**	1212391	271188	3	0	16	91	7665	16966	59973	2788	1463	101921	750313
Other Receipts **7**	3236119	108	7464	763	9988	15852	25736	16006	65190	41421	11234	307081	2735280
Total Receipts **8**	258033794	1177416	147141	2697238	1355520	2814657	3356539	2481960	5297700	7649535	7072818	33519603	190463667
Average Total Receipts **9**	155536	7136	770	3372	7531	18517	52446	77561	230335	402607	1010403	2094975	19046367
Operating Costs/Operating Income (%)													
Cost of Operations **10**	85.6	40.6	50.0	83.0	69.5	81.1	79.9	72.6	84.4	80.9	81.1	64.9	90.4
Salaries and Wages **11**	3.5	16.9	0.7	2.5	6.3	3.1	5.8	7.3	3.2	3.4	6.8	5.1	3.0
Taxes Paid **12**	0.4	1.3	3.4	1.1	1.3	0.9	0.8	1.0	0.4	0.8	0.5	0.9	0.3
Interest Paid **13**	0.5	0.0	0.1	0.1	0.5	0.4	0.4	0.5	0.3	0.6	0.3	1.1	0.4
Depreciation **14**	0.6	0.3	0.9	0.2	0.4	0.4	0.6	0.9	0.4	0.5	0.7	0.9	0.5
Amortization and Depletion **15**	0.4	0.4	0.0	0.0	0.0	0.1	0.1	0.3	0.2	0.5	0.2	0.5	0.4
Pensions and Other Deferred Comp. **16**	0.1	0.0	3.1	0.1	0.0	0.2	0.1	0.3	0.1	0.1	0.1	0.2	0.1
Employee Benefits **17**	0.4	0.7	0.0	0.1	0.4	0.2	0.4	0.8	0.3	0.4	0.3	0.7	0.3
Advertising **18**	0.9	1.7	0.5	0.3	2.8	0.9	0.8	2.0	2.2	0.8	0.8	1.5	0.8
Other Expenses **19**	5.8	29.6	26.2	5.1	9.7	5.8	6.6	9.0	6.3	8.4	5.8	16.7	3.5
Officers' Compensation **20**	0.3	0.2	14.6	2.0	4.3	1.5	1.8	1.3	0.6	0.4	0.3	0.3	0.2
Operating Margin **21**	1.5	8.3	0.6	5.5	4.8	5.6	2.8	3.9	1.5	3.1	3.1	7.3	0.2
Operating Margin Before Officers' Comp. **22**	1.8	8.5	15.2	7.5	9.1	7.1	4.6	5.1	2.2	3.6	3.4	7.6	0.3

Selected Average Balance Sheet ($ in Thousands)

Line Item													
Net Receivables **23**	17076	0	102	240	865	2101	5024	10146	24392	37746	65570	207633	2193801
Inventories **24**	15689	0	107	130	1081	1467	4884	8466	17531	35997	115213	137136	2155333
Net Property, Plant and Equipment **25**	4400	0	26	28	128	321	1328	3281	3204	10402	35397	102792	484684
Total Assets **26**	77107	0	299	813	2198	6249	15619	33908	75302	160271	338124	1148850	9825723
Notes and Loans Payable **27**	12259	0	18	334	529	1644	4079	10839	15696	51158	94645	380020	1103856
All Other Liabilities **28**	33811	0	107	325	792	2779	6188	10555	32599	49483	114291	392581	4574188
Net Worth **29**	31037	0	174	154	876	1826	5352	12514	27007	59631	129188	376249	4147680

Selected Financial Ratios (Times to 1)

Line Item													
Current Ratio **30**	1.4	•	2.0	2.1	1.8	1.6	1.5	1.4	1.3	1.7	1.6	1.4	1.4
Quick Ratio **31**	0.8	•	1.2	1.1	1.0	0.8	0.8	0.8	0.7	1.0	0.7	0.8	0.8
Net Sales to Working Capital **32**	10.8	•	5.6	9.1	7.4	10.8	8.8	14.6	16.1	11.3	11.5	11.5	10.6
Coverage Ratio **33**	10.7	934.2	100.6	18.2	11.5	11.8	12.7	11.6	15.7	7.2	11.3	12.2	9.3
Total Asset Turnover **34**	2.0	•	2.4	4.1	2.9	3.3	2.3	3.0	3.0	2.5	1.7	1.7	1.9
Inventory Turnover **35**	8.2	•	3.4	21.6	10.2	8.5	6.6	10.8	9.0	7.1	9.4	9.4	7.8
Receivables Turnover **36**	9.3	•	3.1	23.8	10.6	10.5	8.6	9.9	11.0	10.4	11.6	11.6	16.9
Total Liabilities to Net Worth **37**	1.5	•	0.7	4.3	2.4	1.9	1.7	1.8	1.7	1.6	2.1	2.1	1.4
Current Assets to Working Capital **38**	3.3	•	2.0	1.9	2.2	2.7	2.8	3.7	4.0	2.4	3.6	3.6	3.3
Current Liabilities to Working Capital **39**	2.3	•	1.0	0.9	1.2	1.7	1.8	2.7	3.0	1.4	2.6	2.6	2.3
Working Capital to Net Sales **40**	0.1	•	0.2	0.1	0.1	0.1	0.1	0.1	0.1	0.1	0.1	0.1	0.1
Inventory to Working Capital **41**	1.2	•	0.8	0.7	0.5	1.1	1.1	1.3	1.5	0.9	1.0	1.0	1.2
Total Receipts to Cash Flow **42**	10.4	1.5	3.3	10.5	8.7	11.0	8.0	10.9	8.5	11.7	3.6	3.6	16.6
Cost of Goods to Cash Flow **43**	8.9	0.6	1.7	8.8	7.0	8.8	5.8	9.2	6.8	9.5	2.3	2.3	15.0
Cash Flow to Total Debt **44**	0.3	•	1.8	0.5	0.5	0.5	0.4	0.4	0.5	0.4	0.7	0.7	0.2

Selected Financial Factors (in Percentages)

Line Item													
Debt Ratio **45**	59.7	•	41.8	81.1	60.1	70.8	65.7	63.1	64.1	62.8	61.8	67.2	57.8
Return on Total Assets **46**	10.0	•	14.8	23.5	20.9	19.4	13.9	13.2	13.7	11.5	11.0	23.3	6.6
Return on Equity Before Income Taxes **47**	22.4	•	25.2	122.7	62.6	47.8	37.1	32.9	35.9	26.6	26.3	65.3	14.0
Return on Equity After Income Taxes **48**	15.9	•	23.5	120.2	53.9	39.5	33.4	29.8	29.6	21.4	20.7	44.2	9.5
Profit Margin (Before Income Tax) **49**	4.6	41.8	6.0	5.6	6.2	5.6	3.8	5.4	4.3	4.0	3.4	12.3	3.1
Profit Margin (After Income Tax) **50**	3.3	37.3	5.6	5.5	5.3	4.6	3.4	4.9	3.6	3.2	2.6	8.3	2.1

Table I

Corporations with and without Net Income

APPAREL, PIECE GOODS, AND NOTIONS

MONEY AMOUNTS AND SIZE OF ASSETS IN THOUSANDS OF DOLLARS

Item Description for Accounting Period 7/03 Through 6/04	Total	Zero Assets	Under 500	500 to 1,000	1,000 to 5,000	5,000 to 10,000	10,000 to 25,000	25,000 to 50,000	50,000 to 100,000	100,000 to 250,000	250,000 to 500,000	500,000 to 2,500,000	2,500,000 and over
Number of Enterprises **1**	25118	3104	17279	1899	2022	387	260	80	45	25	7	9	•
Revenues ($ in Thousands)													
Net Sales **2**	80212458	1765377	8053736	4111985	11678698	7801011	9980694	6026331	5260702	5432970	3847201	16253754	•
Interest **3**	138076	3150	1720	2207	7141	887	3603	6107	4977	7982	16033	84271	•
Rents **4**	32451	52	2480	0	1094	318	2138	961	2167	12035	3639	7567	•
Royalties **5**	782152	5866	0	0	2759	1419	6857	14454	12350	31579	44350	662519	•
Other Portfolio Income **6**	299506	561	1759	2284	13654	8067	2745	9490	2358	102346	751	155490	•
Other Receipts **7**	1903073	42797	206149	17408	535880	210718	93498	55128	61859	60856	13804	604973	•
Total Receipts **8**	83367716	1817803	8265844	4133884	12239226	8022420	10089535	6112471	5344413	5647768	3925778	17768574	•
Average Total Receipts **9**	3319	586	478	2177	6053	20730	38806	76406	118765	225911	560825	1974286	•
Operating Costs/Operating Income (%)													
Cost of Operations **10**	69.5	72.1	70.3	72.9	75.6	72.5	74.0	69.7	69.2	60.2	76.6	60.8	•
Salaries and Wages **11**	8.5	6.9	5.7	4.6	7.7	9.4	7.4	8.2	8.1	9.7	7.5	12.1	•
Taxes Paid **12**	2.3	1.6	2.2	1.2	2.9	1.7	2.4	3.1	2.0	3.3	2.0	2.2	•
Interest Paid **13**	1.0	0.8	0.3	0.5	0.8	0.8	0.8	0.8	1.0	1.7	2.1	1.7	•
Depreciation **14**	1.1	0.7	1.0	0.5	0.4	0.4	0.5	0.8	1.5	1.5	1.3	2.4	•
Amortization and Depletion **15**	0.2	1.2	0.0	0.0	0.1	0.0	0.1	0.2	0.2	0.3	0.5	0.2	•
Pensions and Other Deferred Comp. **16**	0.3	0.1	0.1	0.5	0.4	0.1	0.2	0.3	0.4	0.7	0.3	0.3	•
Employee Benefits **17**	0.5	0.9	0.3	0.3	0.3	0.5	0.4	0.4	0.9	0.8	0.7	0.5	•
Advertising **18**	1.8	1.9	0.7	1.9	0.6	0.9	0.8	1.2	2.3	2.6	1.6	4.1	•
Other Expenses **19**	12.9	13.0	17.4	14.5	11.2	11.2	8.8	10.2	10.4	14.8	9.5	17.0	•
Officers' Compensation **20**	2.5	2.1	4.5	4.4	3.5	2.9	2.4	2.3	1.4	1.5	0.7	1.2	•
Operating Margin **21**	•	•	•	•	•	•	2.2	2.7	2.4	2.8	•	•	•
Operating Margin Before Officers' Comp. **22**	1.8	1.0	2.1	3.1	0.0	2.6	4.6	5.0	3.9	4.3	•	1.2	•

Selected Average Balance Sheet ($ in Thousands)

	Total										
Net Receivables 23	436	24	243	643	3079	4595	10428	16338	36086	86897	368816	•
Inventories 24	397	39	154	626	2557	5667	11240	20971	36615	81998	216619	•
Net Property, Plant and Equipment 25	180	13	36	119	465	1011	2361	8065	21323	38729	244450	•
Total Assets 26	1770	116	658	1994	7411	15443	34725	68046	154869	405523	1972951	•
Notes and Loans Payable 27	458	56	252	625	1814	5049	10811	21478	41747	232047	254644	•
All Other Liabilities 28	660	48	297	1108	3196	5225	10463	19030	35171	362105	582389	•
Net Worth 29	652	12	109	261	2401	5169	13451	27539	77951	-188628	1135918	•

Selected Financial Ratios (Times to 1)

	Total										
Current Ratio 30	1.5	1.5	1.7	1.4	1.6	1.7	1.6	1.8	2.4	0.5	2.3	•
Quick Ratio 31	0.9	0.8	1.1	0.8	0.8	0.8	0.8	0.8	1.3	0.2	1.4	•
Net Sales to Working Capital 32	7.7	13.7	9.4	13.1	8.4	7.1	7.0	5.3	3.5	•	3.5	•
Coverage Ratio 33	4.4	3.4	1.9	2.8	4.3	5.0	6.1	5.0	4.9	0.8	5.7	•
Total Asset Turnover 34	1.8	4.0	3.3	2.9	2.7	2.5	2.2	1.7	1.4	1.4	0.9	•
Inventory Turnover 35	5.6	8.4	10.2	7.0	5.7	5.0	4.7	3.9	3.6	5.1	5.1	•
Receivables Turnover 36	7.7	19.4	11.1	7.8	8.3	8.1	7.2	6.9	6.0	6.1	5.7	•
Total Liabilities to Net Worth 37	1.7	8.4	5.0	6.6	2.1	2.0	1.6	1.5	1.0	•	0.7	•
Current Assets to Working Capital 38	2.8	2.8	2.5	3.8	2.8	2.4	2.5	2.3	1.7	•	1.8	•
Current Liabilities to Working Capital 39	1.8	1.8	1.5	2.8	1.8	1.4	1.5	1.3	0.7	•	0.8	•
Working Capital to Net Sales 40	0.1	0.1	0.1	0.1	0.1	0.1	0.1	0.2	0.3	•	0.3	•
Inventory to Working Capital 41	0.9	1.1	0.8	1.2	1.0	1.0	1.0	0.9	0.6	•	0.4	•
Total Receipts to Cash Flow 42	7.5	8.1	9.6	9.7	8.3	9.8	8.1	8.3	6.0	17.0	4.8	•
Cost of Goods to Cash Flow 43	5.2	5.7	7.0	7.3	6.0	7.2	5.6	5.7	3.6	13.0	2.9	•
Cash Flow to Total Debt 44	0.4	0.4	0.4	0.3	0.5	0.4	0.4	0.3	0.5	0.1	0.4	•

Selected Financial Factors (in Percentages)

	Total										
Debt Ratio 45	63.1	89.4	83.4	86.9	67.6	66.5	61.3	59.5	49.7	146.5	42.4	•
Return on Total Assets 46	8.2	2.1	•	6.2	8.9	10.2	10.8	8.6	12.0	2.2	8.8	•
Return on Equity Before Income Taxes 47	17.1	9.4	•	30.3	21.0	24.4	23.4	17.1	19.0	1.3	12.6	•
Return on Equity After Income Taxes 48	12.8	6.5	•	26.0	19.7	22.4	21.2	13.5	14.4	2.2	8.2	•
Profit Margin (Before Income Tax) 49	3.5	1.8	0.2	1.4	2.5	3.3	4.2	4.0	6.8	•	7.9	•
Profit Margin (After Income Tax) 50	2.6	0.7	0.2	1.2	2.3	3.0	3.8	3.2	5.1	•	5.2	•

187

Table II
Corporations with Net Income

APPAREL, PIECE GOODS, AND NOTIONS

MONEY AMOUNTS AND SIZE OF ASSETS IN THOUSANDS OF DOLLARS

Item Description for Accounting Period 7/03 Through 6/04	Total	Zero Assets	Under 500	500 to 1,000	1,000 to 5,000	5,000 to 10,000	10,000 to 25,000	25,000 to 50,000	50,000 to 100,000	100,000 to 250,000	250,000 to 500,000	500,000 to 2,500,000	2,500,000 and over
Number of Enterprises **1**	13581	874	9237	1346	1502	288	211	58	31	20	4	9	•
Revenues ($ in Thousands)													
Net Sales **2**	66787609	1418147	5782623	3096403	9802263	6799270	8351316	4688328	4003158	4991649	1600697	16253754	•
Interest **3**	113929	347	1094	1527	6124	614	2468	3457	4778	6375	2874	84271	•
Rents **4**	26004	0	2135	0	449	134	849	682	1772	8826	3588	7567	•
Royalties **5**	735870	5866	0	0	0	35	2787	10832	5680	30489	17661	662519	•
Other Portfolio Income **6**	293290	517	1755	0	12941	7684	1182	9198	1425	102346	751	155490	•
Other Receipts **7**	1662037	22973	149131	13105	495556	198071	65571	45060	45751	17226	4624	604973	•
Total Receipts **8**	69618739	1447850	5936738	3111035	10317333	7005808	8424173	4757557	4062564	5156911	1630195	17768574	•
Average Total Receipts **9**	5126	1657	643	2311	6869	24326	39925	82027	131050	257846	407549	1974286	•
Operating Costs/Operating Income (%)													
Cost of Operations **10**	67.9	69.2	69.2	68.8	76.2	71.4	73.5	68.5	68.0	60.6	60.7	60.8	•
Salaries and Wages **11**	8.6	7.3	3.7	4.7	7.6	9.7	7.2	7.8	7.2	8.9	12.1	12.1	•
Taxes Paid **12**	2.4	1.5	2.3	1.3	3.1	1.7	2.5	3.2	2.0	3.3	2.4	2.2	•
Interest Paid **13**	1.0	0.8	0.2	0.4	0.7	0.7	0.7	0.7	0.8	1.5	0.6	1.7	•
Depreciation **14**	1.1	0.7	0.9	0.5	0.3	0.3	0.4	0.7	1.3	1.3	2.2	2.4	•
Amortization and Depletion **15**	0.1	0.4	0.0	0.0	0.0	0.0	0.0	0.1	0.2	0.2	0.3	0.2	•
Pensions and Other Deferred Comp. **16**	0.3	0.1	0.1	0.6	0.4	0.1	0.2	0.3	0.5	0.5	0.5	0.3	•
Employee Benefits **17**	0.5	0.9	0.3	0.3	0.3	0.5	0.3	0.4	0.8	0.8	1.0	0.5	•
Advertising **18**	2.0	1.9	0.8	2.5	0.6	0.9	0.7	1.2	2.5	2.6	2.5	4.1	•
Other Expenses **19**	12.5	9.1	15.7	14.4	9.9	10.6	8.0	9.4	9.7	13.4	15.8	17.0	•
Officers' Compensation **20**	2.5	1.7	4.3	5.5	3.5	3.1	2.5	2.3	1.3	1.6	1.5	1.2	•
Operating Margin **21**	1.1	6.5	2.7	1.0	•	1.0	3.9	5.3	5.7	5.4	0.3	•	•
Operating Margin Before Officers' Comp. **22**	3.6	8.2	6.9	6.6	0.9	4.1	6.3	7.7	7.1	6.9	1.9	1.2	•

Selected Average Balance Sheet ($ in Thousands)

Net Receivables 23	671	0	28	240	723	3035	4667	10716	18405	43333	50123	368816
Inventories 24	583	0	52	188	555	2880	5964	11528	21859	37690	89252	230979
Net Property, Plant and Equipment 25	275	0	17	38	111	417	824	2138	7323	15657	53179	244450
Total Assets 26	2735	0	150	649	2003	7560	15420	34212	69992	156517	352587	1972951
Notes and Loans Payable 27	579	0	59	257	695	1604	4685	8849	19120	33909	102134	254644
All Other Liabilities 28	872	0	37	278	1181	3583	4902	10308	19834	32444	47968	582389
Net Worth 29	1283	0	54	113	127	2373	5833	15055	31038	90165	202485	1135918

Selected Financial Ratios (Times to 1)

Current Ratio 30	1.9	•	2.4	1.8	1.4	1.5	1.8	1.8	1.8	2.8	2.2	2.3
Quick Ratio 31	1.1	•	1.3	1.2	0.8	0.8	0.8	0.9	0.8	1.6	0.9	1.4
Net Sales to Working Capital 32	5.7	•	8.7	8.5	13.9	10.3	6.5	6.4	5.3	3.3	3.7	3.5
Coverage Ratio 33	6.9	12.1	34.9	5.2	4.7	6.5	7.5	11.1	9.6	6.9	4.9	5.7
Total Asset Turnover 34	1.8	•	4.2	3.5	3.3	3.1	2.6	2.4	1.8	1.6	1.1	0.9
Inventory Turnover 35	5.7	•	8.3	8.4	9.0	5.9	4.9	4.8	4.0	4.0	2.7	4.8
Receivables Turnover 36	8.3	•	19.6	19.1	8.7	10.9	8.2	7.4	6.8	6.2	5.7	9.8
Total Liabilities to Net Worth 37	1.1	•	1.8	4.7	14.8	2.2	1.6	1.3	1.3	0.7	0.7	0.7
Current Assets to Working Capital 38	2.1	•	1.7	2.2	3.8	3.0	2.2	2.2	2.2	1.6	1.9	1.8
Current Liabilities to Working Capital 39	1.1	•	0.7	1.2	2.8	2.0	1.2	1.2	1.2	0.6	0.9	0.8
Working Capital to Net Sales 40	0.2	•	0.1	0.1	0.1	0.1	0.2	0.2	0.2	0.3	0.3	0.3
Inventory to Working Capital 41	0.7	•	0.8	0.7	1.1	1.1	1.0	0.9	0.9	0.5	0.7	0.4
Total Receipts to Cash Flow 42	6.6	6.1	6.4	7.9	9.4	7.6	8.9	6.9	6.8	5.6	8.2	4.8
Cost of Goods to Cash Flow 43	4.5	4.3	4.4	5.4	7.2	5.5	6.5	4.7	4.6	3.4	5.0	2.9
Cash Flow to Total Debt 44	0.5	•	1.0	0.5	0.4	0.6	0.5	0.6	0.5	0.7	0.3	0.4

Selected Financial Factors (in Percentages)

Debt Ratio 45	53.1	•	63.8	82.5	93.7	68.6	62.2	56.0	55.7	42.4	42.6	42.4
Return on Total Assets 46	11.9	•	23.0	6.6	11.1	14.8	14.0	17.8	14.9	16.4	3.5	8.8
Return on Equity Before Income Taxes 47	21.7	•	61.6	30.7	138.4	39.8	32.0	36.9	30.1	24.3	4.8	12.6
Return on Equity After Income Taxes 48	17.6	•	60.4	28.9	126.5	38.0	29.8	34.2	25.4	19.3	3.3	8.2
Profit Margin (Before Income Tax) 49	5.7	8.5	5.3	1.5	2.7	4.0	4.7	6.9	7.2	8.8	2.4	7.9
Profit Margin (After Income Tax) 50	4.6	7.1	5.2	1.4	2.5	3.8	4.4	6.4	6.1	7.0	1.7	5.2

Table I

Corporations with and without Net Income

GROCERY AND RELATED PRODUCT

MONEY AMOUNTS AND SIZE OF ASSETS IN THOUSANDS OF DOLLARS

Item Description for Accounting Period 7/03 Through 6/04		Total	Zero Assets	Under 500	500 to 1,000	1,000 to 5,000	5,000 to 10,000	10,000 to 25,000	25,000 to 50,000	50,000 to 100,000	100,000 to 250,000	250,000 to 500,000	500,000 to 2,500,000	2,500,000 and over
Number of Enterprises	1	33120	2355	21923	2152	5114	792	490	154	68	34	16	20	•
Revenues ($ in Thousands)														
Net Sales	2	353082560	1171825	15996088	8691707	61859666	28264926	32158510	23579774	19226930	20577900	26407388	115147845	•
Interest	3	609639	2425	9743	1561	12356	11337	9864	11427	5489	20426	21737	503275	•
Rents	4	278655	560	396	3999	16666	9968	7488	4422	2255	24162	12804	195936	•
Royalties	5	784007	0	0	8282	0	300	1698	1637	13	2420	0	769657	•
Other Portfolio Income	6	214204	24628	40001	3460	39854	11261	4757	9562	3316	6464	24616	46282	•
Other Receipts	7	3607440	15690	108244	14004	222165	143465	201039	174680	178504	206306	324809	2018537	•
Total Receipts	8	358576505	1215128	16154472	8723013	62150707	28441257	32383356	23781502	19416507	20837678	26791354	118681532	•
Average Total Receipts	9	10827	516	737	4053	12153	35911	66088	154425	285537	612873	1674460	5934077	•
Operating Costs/Operating Income (%)														
Cost of Operations	10	85.4	80.2	77.3	81.8	86.3	86.6	85.2	86.0	89.2	86.9	84.0	85.4	•
Salaries and Wages	11	4.9	4.6	5.0	5.3	3.8	3.6	5.0	5.2	3.7	4.1	6.4	5.6	•
Taxes Paid	12	0.8	0.6	1.0	1.1	0.7	0.7	1.0	0.7	0.5	1.6	0.8	0.7	•
Interest Paid	13	0.5	1.7	0.3	0.3	0.3	0.3	0.4	0.4	0.3	0.5	0.6	0.8	•
Depreciation	14	0.9	1.5	1.1	0.6	0.7	0.7	0.7	0.7	0.7	0.8	1.2	1.0	•
Amortization and Depletion	15	0.1	0.7	0.1	0.0	0.0	0.0	0.1	0.1	0.1	0.1	0.2	0.1	•
Pensions and Other Deferred Comp.	16	0.2	0.3	0.2	0.1	0.2	0.2	0.2	0.2	0.1	0.2	0.3	0.4	•
Employee Benefits	17	0.5	1.0	0.4	0.2	0.4	0.4	0.5	0.5	0.4	0.5	0.8	0.7	•
Advertising	18	0.3	0.3	0.2	0.2	0.3	0.3	0.4	0.5	0.7	0.6	0.3	0.3	•
Other Expenses	19	6.1	9.9	9.7	6.9	5.5	5.7	4.8	4.7	3.6	4.6	5.7	7.4	•
Officers' Compensation	20	0.9	0.4	3.9	3.1	1.7	1.2	1.0	0.6	0.8	0.4	0.3	0.1	•
Operating Margin	21	•	•	0.8	0.4	0.6	0.5	0.9	0.4	•	•	•	•	•
Operating Margin Before Officers' Comp.	22	0.2	•	4.7	3.5	2.2	1.6	1.9	1.1	0.7	0.1	•	•	•

Selected Average Balance Sheet ($ in Thousands)

Net Receivables 23	681	0	24	218	797	2699	5269	10649	20028	36384	88285	355556
Inventories 24	530	0	24	176	448	1552	3828	8782	18889	46136	67878	216730
Net Property, Plant and Equipment 25	494	0	32	86	320	1009	2586	5826	10974	31650	108899	364132
Total Assets 26	2456	0	126	652	2142	6774	15463	34339	70459	152657	391215	1588564
Notes and Loans Payable 27	833	0	67	185	695	1664	4738	10366	21072	50667	115359	595420
All Other Liabilities 28	926	0	38	250	765	2841	5536	12339	26331	58830	172451	599068
Net Worth 29	697	0	20	216	682	2270	5189	11634	23056	43159	103405	394076

Selected Financial Ratios (Times to 1)

Current Ratio 30	1.4	•	1.4	1.8	1.6	1.4	1.5	1.6	1.4	1.5	1.3	1.2
Quick Ratio 31	0.8	•	1.0	1.1	1.1	0.9	0.9	0.8	0.7	0.7	0.7	0.7
Net Sales to Working Capital 32	25.5	•	37.0	18.6	19.3	24.4	17.8	16.7	18.4	18.8	39.4	45.0
Coverage Ratio 33	2.7	2.6	6.2	3.8	5.1	5.4	5.6	4.5	3.5	2.9	2.4	1.4
Total Asset Turnover 34	4.3	•	5.8	6.2	5.6	5.3	4.2	4.5	4.0	4.0	4.2	3.6
Inventory Turnover 35	17.2	•	23.6	18.8	23.3	19.9	14.6	15.0	13.4	11.4	20.4	22.7
Receivables Turnover 36	16.6	•	28.5	15.1	15.7	13.6	13.3	15.1	13.6	15.9	21.3	23.5
Total Liabilities to Net Worth 37	2.5	•	5.3	2.0	2.1	2.0	2.0	2.0	2.1	2.5	2.8	3.0
Current Assets to Working Capital 38	3.6	•	3.3	2.3	2.6	3.5	3.1	2.7	3.2	3.2	4.5	6.2
Current Liabilities to Working Capital 39	2.6	•	2.3	1.3	1.6	2.5	2.1	1.7	2.2	2.2	3.5	5.2
Working Capital to Net Sales 40	0.0	•	0.0	0.1	0.1	0.0	0.1	0.1	0.1	0.1	0.0	0.0
Inventory to Working Capital 41	1.3	•	1.0	0.7	0.7	1.0	1.1	1.0	1.3	1.5	1.9	2.2
Total Receipts to Cash Flow 42	18.0	11.6	10.9	16.2	19.3	20.1	19.0	20.0	27.6	21.4	19.8	16.4
Cost of Goods to Cash Flow 43	15.4	9.3	8.4	13.2	16.7	17.4	16.2	17.2	24.6	18.6	16.6	14.0
Cash Flow to Total Debt 44	0.3	•	0.6	0.6	0.4	0.4	0.3	0.3	0.2	0.3	0.3	0.3

Selected Financial Factors (in Percentages)

Debt Ratio 45	71.6	•	84.2	66.8	68.2	66.5	66.4	66.1	67.3	71.7	73.6	75.2
Return on Total Assets 46	6.2	•	12.3	6.5	7.2	7.1	8.4	7.3	4.7	6.1	6.5	4.4
Return on Equity Before Income Taxes 47	13.8	•	65.0	14.5	18.2	17.3	20.5	16.9	10.3	14.1	14.2	5.5
Return on Equity After Income Taxes 48	10.4	2.6	62.7	14.0	16.4	15.3	18.7	14.8	8.6	11.6	10.1	•
Profit Margin (Before Income Tax) 49	0.9	2.6	1.8	0.8	1.0	1.1	1.6	1.3	0.8	0.9	0.9	0.4
Profit Margin (After Income Tax) 50	0.7	2.1	1.7	0.7	0.9	1.0	1.5	1.1	0.7	0.8	0.6	•

Table II
Corporations with Net Income

GROCERY AND RELATED PRODUCT

MONEY AMOUNTS AND SIZE OF ASSETS IN THOUSANDS OF DOLLARS

Item Description for Accounting Period 7/03 Through 6/04		Total	Zero Assets	Under 500	500 to 1,000	1,000 to 5,000	5,000 to 10,000	10,000 to 25,000	25,000 to 50,000	50,000 to 100,000	100,000 to 250,000	250,000 to 500,000	500,000 to 2,500,000	2,500,000 and over
Number of Enterprises	1	21566	911	14238	1472	3705	607	402	129	52	26	13	11	•
Revenues ($ in Thousands)														
Net Sales	2	273986488	604906	11881732	6333546	51899582	22139013	27231530	18822640	14752288	17089326	21638962	81592963	•
Interest	3	365925	1971	9299	273	10140	10381	6229	10847	4980	12774	16827	282205	•
Rents	4	170737	2	396	2314	15068	8742	7005	4392	1871	10414	5151	115382	•
Royalties	5	768447	0	0	0	0	0	1698	1637	13	1904	0	763195	•
Other Portfolio Income	6	139908	1323	26324	2963	29339	8877	4145	9287	1873	5803	23811	26160	•
Other Receipts	7	2846702	12776	35394	4019	207178	120489	165367	118914	173154	153433	165885	1690095	•
Total Receipts	8	277278207	620978	11953145	6343115	52161307	22287502	27415974	18967717	14934179	17273654	21850636	84470000	•
Average Total Receipts	9	12904	682	840	4309	14079	36717	68199	147037	287196	664371	1680818	7679091	•
Operating Costs/Operating Income (%)														
Cost of Operations	10	85.1	80.4	75.7	81.8	87.1	85.6	84.8	84.2	88.7	86.6	84.5	85.0	•
Salaries and Wages	11	4.9	2.9	4.1	5.1	3.2	3.6	4.9	5.8	3.8	4.1	6.1	6.2	•
Taxes Paid	12	0.8	0.7	0.9	1.0	0.6	0.8	1.0	0.8	0.5	1.8	0.8	0.8	•
Interest Paid	13	0.5	0.3	0.2	0.2	0.2	0.2	0.3	0.4	0.4	0.5	0.6	0.9	•
Depreciation	14	0.9	1.3	1.0	0.3	0.7	0.7	0.7	0.7	0.7	0.8	1.1	1.2	•
Amortization and Depletion	15	0.1	0.0	0.1	0.0	0.0	0.0	0.0	0.1	0.1	0.0	0.1	0.1	•
Pensions and Other Deferred Comp.	16	0.3	0.6	0.3	0.1	0.2	0.2	0.2	0.2	0.1	0.2	0.2	0.5	•
Employee Benefits	17	0.4	0.5	0.3	0.2	0.2	0.4	0.5	0.5	0.4	0.5	0.7	0.6	•
Advertising	18	0.3	0.3	0.2	0.2	0.1	0.3	0.4	0.6	0.8	0.7	0.2	0.3	•
Other Expenses	19	5.3	6.8	9.1	5.7	4.7	6.1	4.6	4.9	3.7	4.4	4.9	5.8	•
Officers' Compensation	20	0.9	0.3	3.9	3.2	1.5	1.2	1.0	0.7	1.0	0.4	0.3	0.1	•
Operating Margin	21	0.4	5.9	4.2	2.2	1.5	1.0	1.6	1.1	0.0	0.2	0.3	•	•
Operating Margin Before Officers' Comp.	22	1.3	6.2	8.1	5.4	2.9	2.2	2.6	1.8	1.0	0.6	0.6	•	•

Selected Average Balance Sheet ($ in Thousands)

	•	•	•	•	•	•	•	•	•	•	•	•
Net Receivables 23	801	0	24	216	869	2556	5411	10506	21251	38461	97467	448789
Inventories 24	604	0	19	203	459	1525	3840	8871	20639	50836	83224	342734
Net Property, Plant and Equipment 25	597	0	29	50	325	1079	2404	5726	10998	31447	104476	551721
Total Assets 26	2785	0	127	653	2210	6774	15301	34405	69800	154601	370269	1993548
Notes and Loans Payable 27	851	0	40	150	595	1472	4341	9475	20973	50409	101510	706783
All Other Liabilities 28	1007	0	31	180	769	2753	5391	11988	25883	63291	162047	697943
Net Worth 29	927	0	56	323	846	2548	5569	12942	22945	40900	106712	588822

Selected Financial Ratios (Times to 1)

Current Ratio 30	1.5	•	2.0	2.6	1.7	1.5	1.5	1.6	1.5	1.5	1.3	1.2
Quick Ratio 31	0.8	•	1.4	1.7	1.1	1.0	0.9	0.9	0.8	0.7	0.7	0.7
Net Sales to Working Capital 32	22.6	•	24.1	12.7	19.8	22.0	16.5	15.1	16.2	19.4	32.5	37.6
Coverage Ratio 33	5.2	28.9	24.0	16.5	12.7	9.0	8.1	6.0	4.7	3.5	3.1	3.3
Total Asset Turnover 34	4.6	•	6.6	6.6	6.3	5.4	4.4	4.2	4.1	4.3	4.5	3.7
Inventory Turnover 35	17.9	•	33.6	17.4	26.6	20.5	15.0	13.8	12.2	11.2	16.9	18.4
Receivables Turnover 36	18.2	•	33.9	14.1	16.7	28.5	13.4	14.7	13.2	16.3	34.2	26.5
Total Liabilities to Net Worth 37	2.0	•	1.3	1.0	1.6	1.7	1.7	1.7	2.0	2.8	2.5	2.4
Current Assets to Working Capital 38	3.2	•	2.0	1.6	2.4	3.1	2.8	2.6	2.9	3.2	4.0	5.1
Current Liabilities to Working Capital 39	2.2	•	1.0	0.6	1.4	2.1	1.8	1.6	1.9	2.2	3.0	4.1
Working Capital to Net Sales 40	0.0	•	0.0	0.1	0.1	0.0	0.1	0.1	0.1	0.1	0.0	0.0
Inventory to Working Capital 41	1.2	•	0.5	0.5	0.7	0.9	1.0	1.0	1.2	1.6	1.6	2.1
Total Receipts to Cash Flow 42	16.6	7.1	8.2	15.3	18.0	17.5	17.3	17.5	24.2	20.8	20.9	15.5
Cost of Goods to Cash Flow 43	14.1	5.7	6.2	12.5	15.7	15.0	14.7	14.7	21.4	18.0	17.7	13.1
Cash Flow to Total Debt 44	0.4	•	1.4	0.9	0.6	0.5	0.4	0.4	0.3	0.3	0.3	0.3

Selected Financial Factors (in Percentages)

Debt Ratio 45	66.7	•	55.9	50.5	61.7	62.4	63.6	62.4	67.1	73.5	71.2	70.5
Return on Total Assets 46	11.1	•	32.8	16.6	13.5	10.1	11.5	9.3	6.7	7.5	8.5	10.5
Return on Equity Before Income Taxes 47	27.0	•	71.2	31.5	32.4	23.9	27.7	20.6	16.1	20.4	19.9	24.6
Return on Equity After Income Taxes 48	23.1	•	69.9	31.0	30.4	21.6	25.6	18.4	13.9	16.9	15.0	17.7
Profit Margin (Before Income Tax) 49	2.0	8.6	4.8	2.4	2.0	1.7	2.3	1.8	1.3	1.3	1.3	2.0
Profit Margin (After Income Tax) 50	1.7	7.5	4.7	2.3	1.8	1.5	2.1	1.6	1.1	1.1	1.0	1.4

Table I
Corporations with and without Net Income

FARM PRODUCT RAW MATERIAL

MONEY AMOUNTS AND SIZE OF ASSETS IN THOUSANDS OF DOLLARS

Item Description for Accounting Period 7/03 Through 6/04	Total	Zero Assets	Under 500	500 to 1,000	1,000 to 5,000	5,000 to 10,000	10,000 to 25,000	25,000 to 50,000	50,000 to 100,000	100,000 to 250,000	250,000 to 500,000	500,000 to 2,500,000	2,500,000 and over
Number of Enterprises 1	5386	19	2871	871	1170	281	97	32	18	15	5	4	3
Revenues ($ in Thousands)													
Net Sales 2	98111321	142518	1377902	3258768	12951632	5055954	4982578	2725771	2262543	8587805	4841388	3146970	48777493
Interest 3	820937	24	1718	3361	5570	3481	3432	4675	3971	9034	24205	6378	755087
Rents 4	108919	14	5	4747	1394	625	1762	4959	4118	1794	4547	255	84699
Royalties 5	74316	0	0	0	0	0	4254	2945	257	8024	9449	1356	48030
Other Portfolio Income 6	982700	2	27514	410	5876	3745	2859	1449	6736	16587	5050	811	911661
Other Receipts 7	1458305	2501	13290	89013	113948	110238	82486	25225	54755	41604	45059	25740	854447
Total Receipts 8	101556498	145059	1420429	3356299	13078420	5174043	5077371	2765024	2332380	8664848	4929698	3181510	51431417
Average Total Receipts 9	18856	7635	495	3853	11178	18413	52344	86407	129577	577657	985940	795378	17143806
Operating Costs/Operating Income (%)													
Cost of Operations 10	91.4	94.6	73.8	86.7	89.8	88.9	90.9	88.5	86.9	94.8	94.2	91.5	92.4
Salaries and Wages 11	2.4	1.9	3.1	3.2	2.6	2.8	3.2	3.4	2.4	1.5	2.5	4.0	2.1
Taxes Paid 12	0.6	0.5	1.0	0.6	0.6	0.7	0.5	0.6	0.8	0.2	0.4	0.3	0.6
Interest Paid 13	1.3	0.1	0.9	0.6	0.4	0.4	0.5	0.5	0.9	0.3	0.6	1.6	2.1
Depreciation 14	1.2	0.5	2.0	1.1	0.8	0.8	0.9	1.3	1.7	0.4	0.7	1.0	1.5
Amortization and Depletion 15	0.1	0.0	0.1	0.0	0.0	0.0	0.1	0.0	0.0	0.1	0.0	0.1	0.1
Pensions and Other Deferred Comp. 16	0.2	0.0	0.4	0.1	0.1	0.4	0.1	0.1	0.2	0.1	0.1	0.0	0.4
Employee Benefits 17	0.4	0.1	0.2	0.2	0.3	0.1	0.3	0.3	0.5	0.2	0.3	0.8	0.5
Advertising 18	0.1	0.1	0.3	0.3	0.1	0.2	0.2	0.2	0.2	0.1	0.0	0.1	0.1
Other Expenses 19	3.7	2.2	15.5	6.7	4.2	3.5	3.7	4.7	6.6	2.1	2.5	3.1	3.4
Officers' Compensation 20	0.7	0.4	3.6	2.4	0.9	1.9	0.6	0.8	0.7	0.3	0.1	0.5	0.5
Operating Margin 21	•	•	•	•	0.2	0.2	•	•	•	•	•	•	•
Operating Margin Before Officers' Comp. 22	•	0.1	2.7	0.5	1.1	2.1	•	0.4	0.2	•	•	•	•

Selected Average Balance Sheet ($ in Thousands)

Item													
Net Receivables 23	5962	0	36	201	673	2188	4846	8513	15111	42875	111226	122154	9241815
Inventories 24	1677	0	3	67	444	1427	3656	8160	20958	44997	62991	273871	1656229
Net Property, Plant and Equipment 25	1244	0	34	198	453	1098	2714	6765	13199	17493	39283	72543	1375400
Total Assets 26	15303	0	143	699	2268	6742	15020	33842	65317	145239	368096	816440	21951718
Notes and Loans Payable 27	4383	0	90	237	968	1466	4917	8505	21324	49149	227429	419245	5636947
All Other Liabilities 28	7092	0	34	224	770	2988	6480	11938	20315	50806	87383	303553	10791508
Net Worth 29	3828	0	18	238	530	2287	3622	13399	23678	45284	53284	93642	5523263

Selected Financial Ratios (Times to 1)

Item													
Current Ratio 30	1.2	•	1.8	1.7	1.6	1.3	1.3	1.5	1.5	1.5	1.3	1.6	1.2
Quick Ratio 31	0.8	•	1.7	1.5	0.9	0.8	0.8	0.8	0.7	0.7	0.5	0.4	0.8
Net Sales to Working Capital 32	10.7	•	14.7	22.1	18.3	17.4	19.6	11.4	9.9	14.4	13.9	3.2	9.2
Coverage Ratio 33	2.9	12.8	3.4	2.9	3.6	7.1	3.3	3.3	3.5	3.3	1.7	•	3.0
Total Asset Turnover 34	1.2	•	3.4	5.4	4.9	2.7	3.4	2.5	1.9	3.9	2.6	1.0	0.7
Inventory Turnover 35	9.9	•	119.4	48.3	22.4	11.2	12.8	9.2	5.2	12.1	14.5	2.6	9.1
Receivables Turnover 36	4.0	•	17.8	22.5	16.1	9.5	10.3	9.6	6.8	15.7	8.9	8.0	2.4
Total Liabilities to Net Worth 37	3.0	•	6.8	1.9	3.3	1.9	3.1	1.5	1.8	2.2	5.9	7.7	3.0
Current Assets to Working Capital 38	5.7	•	2.3	2.4	2.7	4.6	4.2	3.2	3.2	2.9	4.1	2.8	7.6
Current Liabilities to Working Capital 39	4.7	•	1.3	1.4	1.7	3.6	3.2	2.2	2.2	1.9	3.1	1.8	6.6
Working Capital to Net Sales 40	0.1	•	0.1	0.0	0.1	0.1	0.1	0.1	0.1	0.1	0.1	0.3	0.1
Inventory to Working Capital 41	1.1	•	0.1	0.2	0.7	1.3	1.5	1.2	1.2	1.3	1.0	1.5	1.0
Total Receipts to Cash Flow 42	24.2	35.6	7.3	15.4	21.7	17.9	25.8	21.4	12.9	42.6	48.4	•	24.5
Cost of Goods to Cash Flow 43	22.1	33.7	5.4	13.3	19.5	15.9	23.5	18.9	11.2	40.4	45.6	•	22.6
Cash Flow to Total Debt 44	0.1	•	0.5	0.5	0.3	0.2	0.2	0.2	0.2	0.1	0.1	•	0.0

Selected Financial Factors (in Percentages)

Item													
Debt Ratio 45	75.0	•	87.1	66.0	76.6	66.1	75.9	60.4	63.7	68.8	85.5	88.5	74.8
Return on Total Assets 46	4.6	•	10.5	8.6	7.9	7.9	5.3	3.8	6.0	4.5	2.5	•	4.5
Return on Equity Before Income Taxes 47	12.0	•	57.2	16.6	24.4	20.1	15.4	6.8	11.9	10.0	7.0	•	11.9
Return on Equity After Income Taxes 48	8.2	•	47.4	13.4	23.3	19.0	12.9	4.8	8.0	6.5	5.3	•	7.7
Profit Margin (Before Income Tax) 49	2.5	1.5	2.2	1.1	1.2	2.6	1.1	1.1	2.2	0.8	0.4	•	4.1
Profit Margin (After Income Tax) 50	1.7	1.0	1.8	0.9	1.1	2.4	0.9	0.8	1.5	0.5	0.3	•	2.6

Table II

Corporations with Net Income

FARM PRODUCT RAW MATERIAL

MONEY AMOUNTS AND SIZE OF ASSETS IN THOUSANDS OF DOLLARS

Item Description for Accounting Period 7/03 Through 6/04	Total	Zero Assets	Under 500	500 to 1,000	1,000 to 5,000	5,000 to 10,000	10,000 to 25,000	25,000 to 50,000	50,000 to 100,000	100,000 to 250,000	250,000 to 500,000	500,000 to 2,500,000	2,500,000 and over
Number of Enterprises **1**	3462	•	1626	567	911	211	69	27	14	10	5	•	•
Revenues ($ in Thousands)													
Net Sales **2**	78135007	•	939136	2669476	11137381	3533622	3667160	2219368	1419163	6032203	4841388	•	•
Interest **3**	679346	•	1680	2766	3615	3027	2974	3896	3536	1792	24205	•	•
Rents **4**	101597	•	5	3001	459	625	1690	2897	2502	1786	4547	•	•
Royalties **5**	68706	•	0	0	0	0	1	2945	257	8024	9449		•
Other Portfolio Income **6**	894979	•	21842	276	5672	2291	2533	1139	6526	2942	5050	•	•
Other Receipts **7**	1369219	•	13073	82724	101523	108513	71169	18272	51434	30672	45059	•	•
Total Receipts **8**	81248854	•	975736	2758243	11248650	3648078	3745527	2248517	1483418	6077419	4929698	•	•
Average Total Receipts **9**	23469	•	600	4865	12348	17289	54283	83278	105958	607742	985940	•	•
Operating Costs/Operating Income (%)													
Cost of Operations **10**	91.2	•	68.8	87.5	90.4	85.2	90.6	88.4	86.7	93.9	94.2	•	•
Salaries and Wages **11**	2.4	•	4.4	3.0	2.4	3.8	3.2	3.2	2.8	1.8	2.5	•	•
Taxes Paid **12**	0.6	•	1.1	0.6	0.4	0.9	0.5	0.6	0.8	0.2	0.4	•	•
Interest Paid **13**	1.3	•	1.3	0.6	0.4	0.4	0.4	0.5	1.2	0.3	0.6	•	•
Depreciation **14**	1.3	•	2.8	0.9	0.6	1.0	0.8	1.2	1.6	0.5	0.7	•	•
Amortization and Depletion **15**	0.1	•	0.2	•	0.0	0.1	0.0	0.0	0.0	0.1	0.0	•	•
Pensions and Other Deferred Comp. **16**	0.3	•	0.0	0.1	0.1	0.5	0.2	0.1	0.0	0.1	0.1	•	•
Employee Benefits **17**	0.4	•	0.2	0.1	0.2	0.2	0.2	0.3	0.2	0.3	0.1	•	•
Advertising **18**	0.1	•	0.2	0.3	0.1	0.3	0.1	0.2	0.1	0.1	0.0	•	•
Other Expenses **19**	3.5	•	13.9	5.2	3.8	4.3	3.6	4.5	5.8	2.0	2.5	•	•
Officers' Compensation **20**	0.7	•	2.7	1.7	0.9	2.1	0.7	0.7	0.7	0.3	0.1	•	•
Operating Margin **21**	•	•	4.4	0.0	0.7	1.3	•	0.3	•	0.6	•	•	•
Operating Margin Before Officers' Comp. **22**	•	•	7.2	1.8	1.6	3.3	0.3	1.0	0.4	0.8	•	•	•

Selected Average Balance Sheet ($ in Thousands)

Net Receivables 23	6984	15	177	643	1298	4779	8518	15704	30953	111226
Inventories 24	1747	3	29	403	1654	3824	7742	21403	47371	70007
Net Property, Plant and Equipment 25	1593	58	168	379	1228	2437	6297	13036	23824	39283
Total Assets 26	17958	143	660	2299	6799	15340	33251	65175	141108	368096
Notes and Loans Payable 27	4138	67	173	986	1153	4582	8347	23116	41451	227429
All Other Liabilities 28	8368	19	177	734	2804	6752	11519	20406	52817	87383
Net Worth 29	5453	57	309	578	2842	4006	13385	21652	46841	53284

Selected Financial Ratios (Times to 1)

Current Ratio 30	1.2	1.5	2.0	1.7	1.4	1.4	1.5	1.3	1.5	1.3
Quick Ratio 31	0.8	1.5	1.7	0.9	0.8	0.8	0.8	0.6	0.5	0.5
Net Sales to Working Capital 32	11.5	36.8	21.6	16.5	14.3	16.6	11.2	11.5	17.0	13.9
Coverage Ratio 33	3.8	7.6	6.6	5.3	11.4	5.3	4.5	4.6	6.0	1.7
Total Asset Turnover 34	1.3	4.0	7.1	5.3	2.5	3.5	2.5	1.6	4.3	2.6
Inventory Turnover 35	11.8	134.9	144.1	27.5	8.6	12.6	9.4	4.1	12.0	13.0
Receivables Turnover 36	4.0	25.0	29.2	18.1	10.7	10.0	9.0	5.8	13.1	17.4
Total Liabilities to Net Worth 37	2.3	1.5	1.1	3.0	1.4	2.8	1.5	2.0	2.0	5.9
Current Assets to Working Capital 38	5.4	3.1	2.0	2.4	3.8	3.6	3.2	4.3	3.0	4.1
Current Liabilities to Working Capital 39	4.4	2.1	1.0	1.4	2.8	2.6	2.2	3.3	2.0	3.1
Working Capital to Net Sales 40	0.1	0.0	0.0	0.1	0.1	0.1	0.1	0.1	0.1	0.1
Inventory to Working Capital 41	1.1	0.0	0.2	0.6	1.4	1.2	1.1	1.7	1.6	1.0
Total Receipts to Cash Flow 42	20.9	5.3	13.1	20.4	12.1	22.3	18.6	11.3	33.5	48.4
Cost of Goods to Cash Flow 43	19.1	3.7	11.4	18.4	10.3	20.2	16.4	9.8	31.5	45.6
Cash Flow to Total Debt 44	0.1	1.3	1.0	0.3	0.3	0.2	0.2	0.2	0.2	0.1

Selected Financial Factors (in Percentages)

Debt Ratio 45	69.6	60.1	53.1	74.8	58.2	73.9	59.7	66.8	66.8	85.5
Return on Total Assets 46	6.1	38.7	28.1	11.3	12.2	7.5	5.2	8.4	6.8	2.5
Return on Equity Before Income Taxes 47	14.9	84.0	50.9	36.4	26.6	23.3	10.0	19.8	17.2	7.0
Return on Equity After Income Taxes 48	10.7	78.4	47.2	35.2	25.5	20.1	7.7	14.3	12.1	5.3
Profit Margin (Before Income Tax) 49	3.6	8.3	3.3	1.7	4.5	1.8	1.6	4.2	1.3	0.4
Profit Margin (After Income Tax) 50	2.6	7.8	3.1	1.7	4.3	1.5	1.2	3.1	0.9	0.3

Table I

Corporations with and without Net Income

CHEMICAL AND ALLIED PRODUCTS

MONEY AMOUNTS AND SIZE OF ASSETS IN THOUSANDS OF DOLLARS

Item Description for Accounting Period 7/03 Through 6/04	Total	Zero Assets	Under 500	500 to 1,000	1,000 to 5,000	5,000 to 10,000	10,000 to 25,000	25,000 to 50,000	50,000 to 100,000	100,000 to 250,000	250,000 to 500,000	500,000 to 2,500,000	2,500,000 and over
Number of Enterprises **1**	10573	705	7099	690	1541	264	163	50	32	13	5	11	•
Revenues ($ in Thousands)													
Net Sales **2**	57206702	330870	2171156	1756834	11114469	5724099	6311162	4195043	4444081	2706973	2946171	15505844	•
Interest **3**	98068	498	335	758	6725	5121	2933	1739	7163	34089	13420	25289	•
Rents **4**	38363	0	0	0	2728	454	1166	1549	769	7738	530	23429	•
Royalties **5**	71374	0	0	0	0	0	110	573	0	681	34069	35940	•
Other Portfolio Income **6**	238254	0	296	16698	4493	5378	1337	2503	1708	5424	7458	192959	•
Other Receipts **7**	1253206	23287	15943	2887	53342	37029	57565	30916	172156	42313	45697	772069	•
Total Receipts **8**	58905967	354655	2187730	1777177	11181757	5772081	6374273	4232323	4625877	2797218	3047345	16555530	•
Average Total Receipts **9**	5571	503	308	2576	7256	21864	39106	84646	144559	215171	609469	1505048	•
Operating Costs/Operating Income (%)													
Cost of Operations **10**	75.7	54.0	64.3	57.5	78.4	79.2	80.9	83.4	84.3	78.8	83.5	67.8	•
Salaries and Wages **11**	6.6	8.7	6.0	15.0	6.9	5.8	6.0	4.9	4.4	5.4	4.8	7.7	•
Taxes Paid **12**	1.1	1.7	1.8	2.1	1.0	1.1	0.9	0.9	0.9	1.3	0.6	1.3	•
Interest Paid **13**	1.0	1.0	0.4	0.3	0.3	0.4	0.4	0.5	0.8	2.4	0.9	2.0	•
Depreciation **14**	1.8	3.2	0.7	1.8	0.9	1.0	1.2	0.7	1.8	2.4	1.1	3.3	•
Amortization and Depletion **15**	0.3	0.4	0.0	0.0	0.1	0.0	0.1	0.1	0.1	0.5	0.2	1.0	•
Pensions and Other Deferred Comp. **16**	0.5	0.1	0.8	0.3	0.4	0.5	0.3	0.2	0.3	0.2	0.2	0.9	•
Employee Benefits **17**	1.0	1.5	1.0	1.7	0.5	0.6	0.5	0.4	0.8	0.7	0.9	2.0	•
Advertising **18**	0.7	0.7	0.2	0.3	0.4	0.1	0.2	0.3	0.1	0.6	0.1	1.9	•
Other Expenses **19**	9.9	36.6	13.0	14.2	6.9	8.0	6.9	5.1	8.7	8.5	7.6	14.7	•
Officers' Compensation **20**	1.8	4.2	9.4	9.0	2.1	1.6	1.6	1.2	0.9	0.9	0.5	0.7	•
Operating Margin **21**	•	•	2.5	•	2.1	1.7	0.8	2.3	•	•	•	•	•
Operating Margin Before Officers' Comp. **22**	1.4	•	11.9	6.7	4.2	3.3	2.5	3.5	•	•	0.1	•	•

Selected Average Balance Sheet ($ in Thousands)

Net Receivables 23	663	0	13	254	770	2617	5310	11861	24234	36128	85272	157517
Inventories 24	484	0	14	124	376	2386	3868	8687	13020	26894	45729	150509
Net Property, Plant and Equipment 25	662	0	9	111	270	703	2204	3464	14044	34416	57871	412696
Total Assets 26	3032	0	72	718	2258	7326	15051	34962	68859	152985	363251	1402195
Notes and Loans Payable 27	820	0	37	143	508	2058	4230	7873	20275	45774	53706	398952
All Other Liabilities 28	1075	0	16	289	911	3308	5568	12059	27736	43944	145096	462232
Net Worth 29	1136	0	19	287	838	1960	5254	15030	20849	63266	164449	541011

Selected Financial Ratios (Times to 1)

Current Ratio 30	1.4	•	1.6	1.7	1.7	1.4	1.4	1.5	1.4	1.4	1.5	1.2
Quick Ratio 31	0.8	•	1.2	1.2	1.2	0.8	0.9	0.9	0.9	0.7	1.0	0.6
Net Sales to Working Capital 32	12.7	•	16.5	11.9	10.3	13.4	11.2	10.5	11.3	9.7	11.3	19.0
Coverage Ratio 33	3.6	•	10.3	•	8.8	7.1	5.1	8.2	2.1	1.8	4.4	2.8
Total Asset Turnover 34	1.8	•	4.3	3.5	3.2	3.0	2.6	2.4	2.0	1.4	1.6	1.0
Inventory Turnover 35	8.5	•	13.6	11.8	15.1	7.2	8.1	8.1	9.0	6.1	10.8	6.4
Receivables Turnover 36	8.3	•	17.7	10.0	10.1	8.2	7.6	7.1	6.7	6.2	4.9	9.3
Total Liabilities to Net Worth 37	1.7	•	2.7	1.5	1.7	2.7	1.9	1.3	2.3	1.4	1.2	1.6
Current Assets to Working Capital 38	3.4	•	2.7	2.5	2.5	3.7	3.2	3.0	3.7	3.7	2.9	5.2
Current Liabilities to Working Capital 39	2.4	•	1.7	1.5	1.5	2.7	2.2	2.0	2.7	2.7	1.9	4.2
Working Capital to Net Sales 40	0.1	•	0.1	0.1	0.1	0.1	0.1	0.1	0.1	0.1	0.1	0.1
Inventory to Working Capital 41	1.1	•	0.6	0.6	0.5	1.5	1.1	1.1	1.1	1.3	0.9	2.1
Total Receipts to Cash Flow 42	9.7	3.5	7.8	10.8	11.7	11.5	13.5	13.8	11.8	11.8	11.0	6.9
Cost of Goods to Cash Flow 43	7.4	1.9	5.0	6.2	9.2	9.1	10.9	11.5	9.9	9.3	9.2	4.7
Cash Flow to Total Debt 44	0.3	•	0.7	0.5	0.4	0.4	0.3	0.3	0.2	0.2	0.3	0.2

Selected Financial Factors (in Percentages)

Debt Ratio 45	62.5	•	73.3	60.1	62.9	73.2	65.1	57.0	69.7	58.6	54.7	61.4
Return on Total Assets 46	6.4	•	15.6	•	9.8	8.7	5.9	8.8	3.3	6.0	6.4	5.7
Return on Equity Before Income Taxes 47	12.4	•	52.7	•	23.4	28.0	13.5	18.0	5.8	6.6	10.9	9.5
Return on Equity After Income Taxes 48	9.6	•	50.2	•	21.1	25.2	11.6	16.1	3.6	5.3	8.2	6.2
Profit Margin (Before Income Tax) 49	2.6	•	3.3	•	2.7	2.5	1.8	3.2	0.9	2.0	3.1	3.7
Profit Margin (After Income Tax) 50	2.0	•	3.2	•	2.4	2.3	1.6	2.9	0.5	1.6	2.3	2.4

Table II
Corporations with Net Income

CHEMICAL AND ALLIED PRODUCTS

MONEY AMOUNTS AND SIZE OF ASSETS IN THOUSANDS OF DOLLARS

Item Description for Accounting Period 7/03 Through 6/04	Total	Zero Assets	Under 500	500 to 1,000	1,000 to 5,000	5,000 to 10,000	10,000 to 25,000	25,000 to 50,000	50,000 to 100,000	100,000 to 250,000	250,000 to 500,000	500,000 to 2,500,000	2,500,000 and over
Number of Enterprises **1**	6339	685	3704	319	1190	239	120	39	23	10	•	•	•
Revenues ($ in Thousands)													
Net Sales **2**	45502918	151260	1305804	859791	10094376	5245234	5094960	3265200	3387494	2124921	•	•	•
Interest **3**	58722	376	216	583	5044	4370	2390	1478	4602	5060	•	•	•
Rents **4**	36538	0	0	0	1888	454	1044	1460	438	7737	•	•	•
Royalties **5**	66382	0	0	0	0	0	1	360	0	0			
Other Portfolio Income **6**	206288	0	296	16682	4237	4389	349	2428	1076	3435	•	•	•
Other Receipts **7**	1032062	20801	166	2613	43863	36826	36012	27093	31190	25655	•	•	•
Total Receipts **8**	46902910	172437	1306482	879669	10149408	5291273	5134756	3298019	3424800	2166808	•	•	•
Average Total Receipts **9**	7399	252	353	2758	8529	22139	42790	84565	148904	216681	•	•	•
Operating Costs/Operating Income (%)													
Cost of Operations **10**	77.2	48.2	62.4	63.9	78.7	79.4	81.7	82.8	84.8	79.3	•	•	•
Salaries and Wages **11**	5.8	13.4	4.5	10.8	6.6	5.7	5.2	4.8	4.6	5.1	•	•	•
Taxes Paid **12**	1.0	2.9	1.5	1.9	0.9	1.1	0.8	0.9	0.8	1.1	•	•	•
Interest Paid **13**	0.6	0.1	0.0	0.3	0.3	0.3	0.3	0.4	0.4	1.3	•	•	•
Depreciation **14**	1.3	6.2	0.4	2.1	0.9	1.0	0.8	0.6	1.2	2.4	•	•	•
Amortization and Depletion **15**	0.3	0.5	0.0	0.0	0.1	0.0	0.0	0.1	0.0	0.5	•	•	•
Pensions and Other Deferred Comp. **16**	0.5	0.2	1.2	0.6	0.4	0.5	0.2	0.3	0.4	0.2	•	•	•
Employee Benefits **17**	0.9	2.2	0.7	1.1	0.5	0.5	0.4	0.4	0.7	0.7	•	•	•
Advertising **18**	0.8	1.2	0.1	0.3	0.4	0.1	0.3	0.2	0.2	0.7	•	•	•
Other Expenses **19**	8.9	22.8	11.4	12.0	6.7	7.6	6.1	4.8	4.8	6.9	•	•	•
Officers' Compensation **20**	1.5	9.2	8.3	5.7	1.9	1.6	1.7	1.3	1.0	0.6	•	•	•
Operating Margin **21**	1.1	•	9.3	1.3	2.7	2.1	2.4	3.5	1.1	1.3	•	•	•
Operating Margin Before Officers' Comp. **22**	2.6	2.3	17.6	7.1	4.6	3.7	4.0	4.9	2.1	1.9	•	•	•

Selected Average Balance Sheet ($ in Thousands)

Net Receivables 23	889	0	3	246	851	2618	5746	12300	25783	38911
Inventories 24	577	0	8	95	363	2356	4068	10035	14700	24120
Net Property, Plant and Equipment 25	662	0	9	75	303	722	1646	2612	11122	37787
Total Assets 26	3550	0	61	691	2394	7246	14904	34721	66965	157860
Notes and Loans Payable 27	760	0	17	55	540	1848	3547	7206	14308	45227
All Other Liabilities 28	1254	0	-2	169	956	3283	5622	11996	30654	39599
Net Worth 29	1535	0	45	466	898	2115	5735	15519	22003	73033

Selected Financial Ratios (Times to 1)

Current Ratio 30	1.4	•	3.6	2.9	1.6	1.4	1.6	1.6	1.4	1.3
Quick Ratio 31	0.9	•	2.8	2.3	1.2	0.8	1.0	0.9	0.9	0.7
Net Sales to Working Capital 32	13.0	•	12.3	7.7	12.1	13.7	9.6	9.0	11.3	10.7
Coverage Ratio 33	8.1	51.7	304.8	12.2	10.6	10.4	10.4	13.2	6.1	3.8
Total Asset Turnover 34	2.0	•	5.8	3.9	3.5	3.0	2.8	2.4	2.2	1.3
Inventory Turnover 35	9.6	•	27.2	18.1	18.4	7.4	8.5	6.9	8.5	7.0
Receivables Turnover 36	8.5	•	47.5	21.9	11.5	8.2	7.6	6.7	7.1	6.9
Total Liabilities to Net Worth 37	1.3	•	0.3	0.5	1.7	2.4	1.6	1.2	2.0	1.2
Current Assets to Working Capital 38	3.4	•	1.4	1.5	2.6	3.7	2.7	2.8	3.7	4.1
Current Liabilities to Working Capital 39	2.4	•	0.4	0.5	1.6	2.7	1.7	1.8	2.7	3.1
Working Capital to Net Sales 40	0.1	•	0.1	0.1	0.1	0.1	0.1	0.1	0.1	0.1
Inventory to Working Capital 41	1.1	•	0.2	0.3	0.5	1.5	0.9	1.1	1.2	1.5
Total Receipts to Cash Flow 42	9.1	3.6	5.4	10.0	11.2	11.5	12.3	12.0	17.1	11.9
Cost of Goods to Cash Flow 43	7.0	1.7	3.4	6.4	8.8	9.1	10.1	10.0	14.5	9.4
Cash Flow to Total Debt 44	0.4	4.3	1.2	0.5	0.4	0.4	0.4	0.4	0.2	0.2

Selected Financial Factors (in Percentages)

Debt Ratio 45	56.8	•	25.1	32.5	62.5	70.8	61.5	55.3	67.1	53.7
Return on Total Assets 46	9.7	•	54.7	15.5	12.7	10.1	10.0	11.9	5.9	6.5
Return on Equity Before Income Taxes 47	19.7	•	72.7	21.1	30.8	31.3	23.5	24.5	15.0	10.3
Return on Equity After Income Taxes 48	16.3	•	70.7	17.7	28.0	28.4	21.1	22.1	12.2	8.8
Profit Margin (Before Income Tax) 49	4.2	7.1	9.4	3.6	3.3	3.0	3.2	4.5	2.2	3.5
Profit Margin (After Income Tax) 50	3.5	6.7	9.1	3.1	3.0	2.7	2.9	4.1	1.8	3.0

Table I

Corporations with and without Net Income

PETROLEUM AND PETROLEUM PRODUCTS

MONEY AMOUNTS AND SIZE OF ASSETS IN THOUSANDS OF DOLLARS

Item Description for Accounting Period 7/03 Through 6/04	Total	Zero Assets	Under 500	500 to 1,000	1,000 to 5,000	5,000 to 10,000	10,000 to 25,000	25,000 to 50,000	50,000 to 100,000	100,000 to 250,000	250,000 to 500,000	500,000 to 2,500,000	2,500,000 and over
Number of Enterprises 1	8556	22	4609	652	2235	540	318	107	25	23	13	8	4
Revenues ($ in Thousands)													
Net Sales 2	249813293	32510283	5480573	2660052	30295106	22498503	25228295	19308971	11780722	19719614	29782210	28122880	22426086
Interest 3	301106	10165	4695	1697	16870	7158	12351	6166	3830	5378	11294	68246	153253
Rents 4	227827	0	4690	307	30480	27166	39114	21966	3674	8164	59814	13897	18555
Royalties 5	59605	0	0	0	289	1630	578	0	0	222	1182	154	55549
Other Portfolio Income 6	1237725	41268	56468	11001	34223	19091	46919	16985	8044	31630	2932	82793	886371
Other Receipts 7	1553946	36033	9913	31064	191413	116334	137206	94113	72745	64498	53639	206366	540623
Total Receipts 8	253193502	32597749	5556339	2704121	30568381	22669882	25464463	19448201	11869015	19829506	29911071	28494336	24080437
Average Total Receipts 9	29593	1481716	1206	4147	13677	41981	80077	181759	474761	862152	2300852	3561792	6020109
Operating Costs/Operating Income (%)													
Cost of Operations 10	91.2	99.4	83.1	90.1	88.7	87.4	90.4	92.4	95.3	95.1	98.2	97.3	65.9
Salaries and Wages 11	2.0	0.4	7.5	2.1	3.7	2.8	2.9	2.3	1.5	1.4	0.6	0.5	2.8
Taxes Paid 12	1.0	0.0	1.3	1.5	0.7	4.6	1.2	0.5	0.3	0.2	0.2	0.2	2.8
Interest Paid 13	0.6	0.1	0.3	0.2	0.2	0.3	0.3	0.3	0.2	0.3	0.1	0.6	4.4
Depreciation 14	1.0	0.0	0.6	0.9	0.9	0.9	1.1	1.1	0.6	0.5	0.3	0.7	4.7
Amortization and Depletion 15	0.2	0.0	0.1	0.0	0.0	0.0	0.0	0.0	0.0	0.1	0.0	0.1	2.2
Pensions and Other Deferred Comp. 16	0.1	0.0	0.2	0.0	0.1	0.1	0.0	0.1	0.1	0.0	0.0	0.1	0.3
Employee Benefits 17	0.2	0.0	0.1	0.3	0.2	0.2	0.2	0.2	0.1	0.2	0.1	0.0	0.4
Advertising 18	0.1	0.0	0.1	0.1	0.1	0.1	0.1	0.1	0.1	0.0	0.0	0.0	0.0
Other Expenses 19	3.5	0.1	5.1	3.1	4.6	2.8	3.5	2.9	1.8	1.5	0.9	1.0	16.7
Officers' Compensation 20	0.4	0.0	1.9	2.5	1.3	0.5	0.5	0.4	0.2	0.2	0.1	0.1	0.3
Operating Margin 21	•	•	•	•	•	0.3	•	•	•	0.4	•	•	•
Operating Margin Before Officers' Comp. 22	0.1	•	1.6	1.6	0.7	0.8	0.0	0.1	0.1	0.6	•	•	•

Selected Average Balance Sheet ($ in Thousands)

Net Receivables 23	2258	0	38	209	770	2009	4490	9835	28365	51469	100860	325163	1979685
Inventories 24	642	0	21	130	303	521	1583	3828	9886	20113	79174	102711	219656
Net Property, Plant and Equipment 25	4297	0	48	174	524	2077	4862	12906	15223	35904	57063	302084	6710759
Total Assets 26	10272	0	169	680	2124	6796	15274	34656	68184	145741	342618	1095210	12853438
Notes and Loans Payable 27	2692	0	84	137	634	1980	4933	12565	15951	38744	88364	320938	3037540
All Other Liabilities 28	3301	0	26	210	756	2118	5661	12031	33604	65479	189441	458408	3397612
Net Worth 29	4279	0	59	333	734	2697	4680	10060	18630	41518	64813	315864	6418286

Selected Financial Ratios (Times to 1)

Current Ratio 30	1.5	•	3.1	1.9	1.5	1.7	1.2	1.2	1.2	1.2	1.2	1.3	2.1
Quick Ratio 31	1.1	•	2.3	1.4	1.0	1.3	0.9	0.8	0.9	0.8	0.6	0.9	1.9
Net Sales to Working Capital 32	25.0	•	17.7	21.3	27.8	24.0	50.9	66.6	68.5	66.9	53.1	30.6	4.7
Coverage Ratio 33	2.8	2.1	4.7	4.7	2.2	4.8	2.6	2.4	5.1	4.7	0.7	2.1	2.9
Total Asset Turnover 34	2.8	•	7.0	6.0	6.4	6.1	5.2	5.2	6.9	5.9	6.7	3.2	0.4
Inventory Turnover 35	41.5	•	48.1	28.3	39.6	69.8	45.3	43.5	45.4	40.6	28.4	33.3	16.8
Receivables Turnover 36	10.6	•	30.5	16.0	16.2	24.8	18.8	19.2	16.6	17.8	22.3	12.1	1.8
Total Liabilities to Net Worth 37	1.4	•	1.9	1.0	1.9	1.5	2.3	2.4	2.7	2.5	4.3	2.5	1.0
Current Assets to Working Capital 38	3.1	•	1.5	2.1	2.9	2.4	5.3	6.5	6.7	6.8	5.7	4.9	1.9
Current Liabilities to Working Capital 39	2.1	•	0.5	1.1	1.9	1.4	4.3	5.5	5.7	5.8	4.7	3.9	0.9
Working Capital to Net Sales 40	0.0	•	0.1	0.0	0.0	0.0	0.0	0.0	0.0	0.0	0.0	0.0	0.2
Inventory to Working Capital 41	0.5	•	0.3	0.5	0.6	0.3	1.1	1.5	1.3	1.5	2.3	0.9	0.1
Total Receipts to Cash Flow 42	26.6	749.9	23.5	36.8	28.8	32.6	34.6	39.6	56.4	50.8	232.9	75.6	4.5
Cost of Goods to Cash Flow 43	24.3	745.2	19.5	33.2	25.6	28.5	31.3	36.6	53.8	48.3	228.7	73.6	3.0
Cash Flow to Total Debt 44	0.2	•	0.5	0.3	0.3	0.3	0.2	0.2	0.2	0.2	0.0	0.1	0.2

Selected Financial Factors (in Percentages)

Debt Ratio 45	58.3	•	64.9	51.0	65.4	60.3	69.4	71.0	72.7	71.5	81.1	71.2	50.1
Return on Total Assets 46	5.2	•	9.7	5.6	3.4	8.3	4.3	4.2	5.6	7.0	0.7	4.1	5.6
Return on Equity Before Income Taxes 47	8.1	•	21.7	9.0	5.5	16.4	8.6	8.4	16.5	19.5	•	7.5	7.3
Return on Equity After Income Taxes 48	6.3	•	18.2	8.4	4.7	15.3	6.8	6.7	13.7	15.6	•	4.4	5.7
Profit Margin (Before Income Tax) 49	1.2	0.1	1.1	0.7	0.3	1.1	0.5	0.5	0.7	0.9	•	0.7	8.3
Profit Margin (After Income Tax) 50	0.9	0.0	0.9	0.7	0.3	1.0	0.4	0.4	0.5	0.8	•	0.4	6.5

Table II
Corporations with Net Income

PETROLEUM AND PETROLEUM PRODUCTS

MONEY AMOUNTS AND SIZE OF ASSETS IN THOUSANDS OF DOLLARS

Item Description for Accounting Period 7/03 Through 6/04	Total	Zero Assets	Under 500	500 to 1,000	1,000 to 5,000	5,000 to 10,000	10,000 to 25,000	25,000 to 50,000	50,000 to 100,000	100,000 to 250,000	250,000 to 500,000	500,000 to 2,500,000	2,500,000 and over
Number of Enterprises 1	5437	18	2664	352	1595	446	231	75	19	19	8	5	4
Revenues ($ in Thousands)													
Net Sales 2	176491745	18829715	3410666	1717517	22423274	18844574	19420126	14919139	10055083	17179547	18007616	9258401	22426086
Interest 3	271585	737	3090	1165	13646	6098	10279	5345	2401	5366	4628	65577	153253
Rents 4	190961	0	4133	0	25228	14682	32553	14105	3222	8164	56596	13724	18555
Royalties 5	59420	0	0	0	289	1630	547	0	222	1182	0		55549
Other Portfolio Income 6	1189485	41238	53449	3088	24970	14066	40168	14206	3542	31630	898	75858	886371
Other Receipts 7	1303677	542	8256	28112	86202	101441	110336	64629	64354	58294	44193	196696	540623
Total Receipts 8	179506873	18872232	3479594	1749882	22573609	18982491	19614009	15017424	10128602	17283223	18115113	9610256	24080437
Average Total Receipts 9	33016	1048457	1306	4971	14153	42562	84909	200232	533084	909643	2264389	1922051	6020109
Operating Costs/Operating Income (%)													
Cost of Operations 10	89.4	99.3	77.4	89.6	89.1	86.6	90.9	93.2	96.1	95.0	97.8	94.8	65.9
Salaries and Wages 11	2.1	0.3	11.1	1.6	3.2	2.8	2.8	2.0	1.1	1.4	0.5	0.6	2.8
Taxes Paid 12	1.2	0.0	1.4	0.7	0.6	5.3	0.9	0.4	0.2	0.2	0.2	0.5	2.8
Interest Paid 13	0.8	0.0	0.3	0.2	0.2	0.3	0.3	0.3	0.1	0.2	0.1	1.3	4.4
Depreciation 14	1.2	0.0	0.7	1.1	1.0	0.8	1.0	0.9	0.5	0.5	0.3	1.3	4.7
Amortization and Depletion 15	0.3	0.0	0.1	0.0	0.0	0.0	0.0	0.0	0.0	0.1	0.0	0.2	2.2
Pensions and Other Deferred Comp. 16	0.1	0.0	0.3	0.0	0.1	0.1	0.1	0.1	0.1	0.0	0.0	0.1	0.3
Employee Benefits 17	0.2	0.0	0.1	0.3	0.2	0.1	0.2	0.1	0.1	0.2	0.1	0.1	0.4
Advertising 18	0.1	0.0	0.1	0.2	0.1	0.1	0.1	0.1	0.1	0.0	0.0	0.0	0.0
Other Expenses 19	4.1	0.1	5.9	3.2	4.2	2.8	3.2	2.4	1.3	1.5	1.0	1.8	16.7
Officers' Compensation 20	0.5	0.0	2.3	2.5	1.3	0.5	0.5	0.3	0.2	0.2	0.2	0.2	0.3
Operating Margin 21	0.1	0.2	0.4	0.6	•	0.6	0.1	0.1	0.1	0.7	•	•	•
Operating Margin Before Officers' Comp. 22	0.5	0.2	2.7	3.1	1.3	1.1	0.6	0.4	0.3	0.9	•	•	•

Selected Average Balance Sheet ($ in Thousands)

Net Receivables 23	3058	0	41	197	892	2060	4936	10904	33713	54012	101427	350700	1979685
Inventories 24	711	0	12	155	267	498	1528	3402	9092	18466	82566	73445	135038
Net Property, Plant and Equipment 25	6238	0	24	183	498	1941	4419	12014	11480	36257	60529	394166	6710759
Total Assets 26	14333	0	175	673	2172	6896	15306	34915	67797	144630	333894	1282129	12853438
Notes and Loans Payable 27	3602	0	67	178	586	1887	4261	10847	13100	36439	94638	383721	3037540
All Other Liabilities 28	4395	0	27	218	789	2100	5645	12834	36780	66674	177305	461673	3397612
Net Worth 29	6337	0	81	277	797	2910	5400	11234	17917	41517	61952	436735	6418286

Selected Financial Ratios (Times to 1)

Current Ratio 30	1.6	·	4.5	1.7	1.5	1.8	1.3	1.3	1.2	1.3	1.4	1.2	2.1
Quick Ratio 31	1.3	·	3.5	1.2	1.1	1.4	1.0	0.9	0.9	0.9	0.8	1.0	1.9
Net Sales to Working Capital 32	19.1	·	13.2	28.1	29.4	21.0	37.6	50.8	76.0	50.8	29.2	17.1	4.7
Coverage Ratio 33	3.5	·	8.9	11.5	3.7	6.1	5.4	3.8	9.8	7.2	3.9	3.0	2.9
Total Asset Turnover 34	2.3	19.5	7.3	7.3	6.5	6.1	5.5	5.7	7.8	6.3	6.7	1.4	0.4
Inventory Turnover 35	40.9	·	84.6	28.3	46.9	73.4	50.0	54.5	56.0	46.5	26.7	23.9	27.3
Receivables Turnover 36	10.1	·	38.2	18.8	17.1	25.9	19.5	20.4	16.5	19.1	30.7	10.6	5.7
Total Liabilities to Net Worth 37	1.3	·	1.2	1.4	1.7	1.4	1.8	2.1	2.8	2.5	4.4	1.9	1.0
Current Assets to Working Capital 38	2.7	·	1.3	2.4	3.1	2.2	4.0	4.8	7.2	5.0	3.3	5.1	1.9
Current Liabilities to Working Capital 39	1.7	·	0.3	1.4	2.1	1.2	3.0	3.8	6.2	4.0	2.3	4.1	0.9
Working Capital to Net Sales 40	0.1	·	0.1	0.0	0.0	0.0	0.0	0.0	0.0	0.0	0.0	0.1	0.2
Inventory to Working Capital 41	0.4	·	0.2	0.6	0.6	0.3	0.8	1.0	1.3	0.9	1.5	0.7	0.1
Total Receipts to Cash Flow 42	20.1	262.4	18.0	21.4	28.5	30.6	31.2	40.0	57.0	44.1	122.5	26.3	4.5
Cost of Goods to Cash Flow 43	18.0	260.4	13.9	19.1	25.4	26.5	28.4	37.3	54.8	41.9	119.9	24.9	3.0
Cash Flow to Total Debt 44	0.2	·	0.8	0.6	0.4	0.3	0.2	0.2	0.0	0.0	0.1	0.1	0.2

Selected Financial Factors (in Percentages)

Debt Ratio 45	55.8	·	53.8	58.8	63.3	57.8	64.7	67.8	73.6	71.3	81.4	65.9	50.1
Return on Total Assets 46	6.2	·	20.2	19.5	5.7	9.7	7.5	6.1	7.5	9.3	3.7	5.9	5.6
Return on Equity Before Income Taxes 47	10.0	·	38.7	43.3	11.3	19.2	17.2	13.9	25.6	28.0	14.7	11.6	7.3
Return on Equity After Income Taxes 48	8.0	·	34.2	41.8	10.3	17.9	15.1	11.7	21.7	23.3	11.7	8.1	5.7
Profit Margin (Before Income Tax) 49	2.0	0.5	2.4	2.5	0.6	1.3	1.1	0.8	0.9	1.3	0.4	2.7	8.3
Profit Margin (After Income Tax) 50	1.6	0.3	2.2	2.4	0.6	1.2	1.0	0.7	0.7	1.1	0.3	1.9	6.5

Table I

Corporations with and without Net Income

BEER, WINE, AND DISTILLED ALCOHOLIC BEVERAGE

MONEY AMOUNTS AND SIZE OF ASSETS IN THOUSANDS OF DOLLARS

Item Description for Accounting Period 7/03 Through 6/04		Total	Zero Assets	Under 500	500 to 1,000	1,000 to 5,000	5,000 to 10,000	10,000 to 25,000	25,000 to 50,000	50,000 to 100,000	100,000 to 250,000	250,000 to 500,000	500,000 to 2,500,000	2,500,000 and over
Number of Enterprises	1	3835	271	1729	163	1007	286	226	83	33	24	6	6	•
Revenues ($ in Thousands)														
Net Sales	2	6668815	83665	712611	261376	12379338	5660679	11275983	7290421	5400169	7406543	5661559	10556472	•
Interest	3	36474	2198	2850	493	2415	1828	1323	1480	1195	2673	2025	17996	•
Rents	4	82366	0	0	0	6779	2489	694	1436	4839	1183	13764	51182	•
Royalties	5	241324	7	0	0	0	0	4833	0	0	8	32459	204015	•
Other Portfolio Income	6	186513	247	6607	0	18853	2763	10091	6484	4056	13183	2201	122029	•
Other Receipts	7	818358	41398	4725	-1	56496	85971	120063	165766	72766	75576	42296	153299	•
Total Receipts	8	68053850	127515	726793	261868	12463881	5753730	11412987	7465587	5483025	7499166	5754304	11104993	•
Average Total Receipts	9	17745	471	420	1607	12377	20118	50500	89947	166152	312465	959051	1850832	•
Operating Costs/Operating Income (%)														
Cost of Operations	10	74.5	67.8	59.8	57.3	75.5	73.2	74.3	75.6	75.2	71.9	76.7	74.9	•
Salaries and Wages	11	8.6	10.7	8.8	13.8	9.1	9.8	8.3	8.6	8.7	7.7	6.9	8.9	•
Taxes Paid	12	3.1	4.1	1.6	2.2	1.5	3.1	3.5	3.1	2.0	3.2	5.4	3.7	•
Interest Paid	13	0.7	9.9	0.4	0.8	0.5	0.6	0.5	0.6	0.6	0.5	0.8	1.6	•
Depreciation	14	0.9	0.2	0.3	1.6	0.8	0.9	0.9	1.0	1.3	0.6	0.8	0.7	•
Amortization and Depletion	15	0.4	1.9	0.0	•	0.1	0.1	0.4	0.5	0.3	0.3	0.5	0.9	•
Pensions and Other Deferred Comp.	16	0.4	0.3	1.3	0.9	0.4	0.8	0.4	0.3	0.3	0.3	0.6	0.2	•
Employee Benefits	17	0.8	1.1	0.7	0.8	1.0	0.7	1.0	0.8	0.7	0.6	0.8	0.8	•
Advertising	18	1.4	0.4	0.7	1.1	0.7	0.7	1.0	1.3	1.6	2.2	1.0	2.5	•
Other Expenses	19	6.3	4.2	14.5	13.1	6.5	6.8	5.7	6.0	5.3	6.7	4.9	7.1	•
Officers' Compensation	20	1.3	0.7	4.9	8.3	2.2	2.0	1.5	1.0	1.4	0.8	0.5	0.3	•
Operating Margin	21	1.6	•	7.0	0.2	1.7	1.2	2.4	1.1	2.6	5.1	1.2	•	•
Operating Margin Before Officers' Comp.	22	3.0	•	11.9	8.5	4.0	3.2	3.9	2.1	4.0	5.9	1.7	•	•

Selected Average Balance Sheet ($ in Thousands)

Net Receivables 23	1203	0	14	29	421	961	2642	5764	11844	32335	60914	212692	•
Inventories 24	1508	0	32	115	729	2185	2833	5694	16232	29950	66682	263449	•
Net Property, Plant and Equipment 25	889	0	6	100	500	1040	2543	5327	13208	11483	42485	99623	•
Total Assets 26	6878	0	172	656	2626	6750	15515	33297	69431	147920	359293	1188888	•
Notes and Loans Payable 27	2088	0	90	248	882	1869	4733	10307	24706	42550	117528	320230	•
All Other Liabilities 28	2383	0	40	233	795	1688	3336	8001	17413	41197	106232	688049	•
Net Worth 29	2408	0	41	174	948	3193	7446	14989	27312	64173	135533	180609	•

Selected Financial Ratios (Times to 1)

Current Ratio 30	1.6	•	3.1	1.7	1.5	2.1	1.7	1.7	1.6	1.7	1.5	1.5	•
Quick Ratio 31	0.8	•	2.0	1.3	0.7	1.1	0.9	0.9	0.8	0.9	0.6	0.6	•
Net Sales to Working Capital 32	12.5	•	4.7	8.2	23.0	9.6	15.5	12.5	11.2	9.2	15.5	9.9	•
Coverage Ratio 33	6.0	6.2	25.5	1.5	5.9	5.4	8.3	7.0	7.4	12.6	4.5	3.5	•
Total Asset Turnover 34	2.5	•	2.4	2.4	4.7	2.9	3.2	2.6	2.4	2.1	2.6	1.5	•
Inventory Turnover 35	8.6	•	7.6	8.0	12.7	6.6	13.1	11.7	7.6	7.4	10.9	5.0	•
Receivables Turnover 36	14.7	•	31.4	13.0	28.8	16.2	19.1	16.1	13.3	10.4	18.3	8.5	•
Total Liabilities to Net Worth 37	1.9	•	3.1	2.8	1.8	1.1	1.1	1.2	1.5	1.3	1.7	5.6	•
Current Assets to Working Capital 38	2.6	•	1.5	2.5	3.0	1.9	2.4	2.5	2.6	2.4	3.0	3.0	•
Current Liabilities to Working Capital 39	1.6	•	0.5	1.5	2.0	0.9	1.4	1.5	1.6	1.4	2.0	2.0	•
Working Capital to Net Sales 40	0.1	•	0.2	0.1	0.0	0.1	0.1	0.1	0.1	0.1	0.1	0.1	•
Inventory to Working Capital 41	1.1	•	0.5	0.5	1.4	0.9	0.9	0.9	1.0	1.0	1.3	1.5	•
Total Receipts to Cash Flow 42	11.7	1.9	4.7	9.7	13.8	12.4	13.0	12.2	12.1	8.3	14.4	11.0	•
Cost of Goods to Cash Flow 43	8.7	1.3	2.8	5.5	10.4	9.1	9.7	9.2	9.1	6.0	11.1	8.3	•
Cash Flow to Total Debt 44	0.3	•	0.7	0.3	0.5	0.4	0.5	0.4	0.3	0.4	0.3	0.2	•

Selected Financial Factors (in Percentages)

Debt Ratio 45	65.0	•	75.9	73.4	63.9	52.7	52.0	55.0	60.7	56.6	62.3	84.8	•
Return on Total Assets 46	11.4	•	22.5	2.8	13.7	10.1	13.1	10.8	11.2	14.4	9.6	8.2	•
Return on Equity Before Income Taxes 47	27.1	•	89.6	3.8	31.4	17.4	24.1	20.5	24.7	30.6	19.7	38.8	•
Return on Equity After Income Taxes 48	24.0	•	87.4	3.2	29.5	16.5	23.4	18.9	27.6	14.1	29.1		•
Profit Margin (Before Income Tax) 49	3.8	51.1	9.0	0.4	2.4	2.8	3.6	3.5	4.1	6.4	2.8	4.0	•
Profit Margin (After Income Tax) 50	3.3	34.6	8.8	0.3	2.3	2.7	3.5	3.2	3.9	5.7	2.0	3.0	•

Table II
Corporations with Net Income

BEER, WINE, AND DISTILLED ALCOHOLIC BEVERAGE

MONEY AMOUNTS AND SIZE OF ASSETS IN THOUSANDS OF DOLLARS

Item Description for Accounting Period 7/03 Through 6/04	Total	Zero Assets	Under 500	500 to 1,000	1,000 to 5,000	5,000 to 10,000	10,000 to 25,000	25,000 to 50,000	50,000 to 100,000	100,000 to 250,000	250,000 to 500,000	500,000 to 2,500,000	2,500,000 and over
Number of Enterprises **1**	2571	•	1216	110	660	256	198	68	29	21	•	•	6

Revenues ($ in Thousands)

Net Sales **2**	59322123	•	378216	197688	9576596	5288978	10293387	6399170	4874821	6576010	•	•	10556472
Interest **3**	31122	•	1253	243	1261	1322	987	1303	915	1833	•	•	17996
Rents **4**	68775	•	0	0	6779	2489	682	1436	4551	1067	•	•	51182
Royalties **5**	239154	•	0	0	0	0	4833	0	0	8	•	•	204015
Other Portfolio Income **6**	166885	•	6599	0	16440	2263	6694	5918	3277	1422	•	•	122029
Other Receipts **7**	804695	•	848	0	54162	98662	116703	143309	69593	84515	•	•	153299
Total Receipts **8**	60632754	•	386916	197931	9655238	5391714	10423286	6551136	4953157	6664855	•	•	11104993
Average Total Receipts **9**	23583	•	318	1799	14629	21061	52643	96340	170799	317374	•	•	1850832

Operating Costs/Operating Income (%)

Cost of Operations **10**	74.2	•	45.5	51.4	74.3	73.8	74.1	75.8	75.8	71.7	•	•	74.9
Salaries and Wages **11**	8.5	•	13.3	15.7	9.3	9.7	8.3	8.4	8.1	7.2	•	•	8.9
Taxes Paid **12**	3.1	•	1.7	2.3	1.4	3.1	3.5	2.9	1.7	3.2	•	•	3.7
Interest Paid **13**	0.7	•	0.2	0.8	0.5	0.6	0.5	0.5	0.6	0.4	•	•	1.6
Depreciation **14**	0.9	•	0.5	1.8	0.9	0.9	0.9	0.9	1.2	0.7	•	•	0.7
Amortization and Depletion **15**	0.4	•	0.1	•	0.1	0.1	0.4	0.5	0.3	0.3	•	•	0.9
Pensions and Other Deferred Comp. **16**	0.4	•	0.0	1.1	0.5	0.8	0.4	0.3	0.3	0.3	•	•	0.2
Employee Benefits **17**	0.8	•	0.0	1.0	1.0	0.7	1.0	0.7	0.6	0.6	•	•	0.8
Advertising **18**	1.4	•	1.3	0.9	0.7	0.7	0.9	1.3	1.8	2.3	•	•	2.5
Other Expenses **19**	6.1	•	15.5	14.7	6.1	6.2	5.6	5.9	4.9	6.5	•	•	7.1
Officers' Compensation **20**	1.3	•	2.8	9.8	2.5	2.0	1.4	0.9	1.5	0.8	•	•	0.3
Operating Margin **21**	2.2	•	19.1	0.4	2.9	1.5	3.0	1.8	3.2	6.1	•	•	•
Operating Margin Before Officers' Comp. **22**	3.5	•	21.9	10.3	5.3	3.5	4.4	2.8	4.7	6.9	•	•	•

Selected Average Balance Sheet ($ in Thousands)

Net Receivables 23	1584	17	43	329	969	2644	6194	11878	31578	212692
Inventories 24	1992	12	110	778	2025	2891	6124	16490	29431	263449
Net Property, Plant and Equipment 25	1191	7	35	665	1067	2549	5232	13285	11558	99623
Total Assets 26	8973	131	697	2703	6675	15515	33428	68014	145201	1188888
Notes and Loans Payable 27	2514	41	273	978	1724	4491	9566	22245	33629	320230
All Other Liabilities 28	3129	10	344	600	1721	3189	8389	17823	42555	688049
Net Worth 29	3329	80	80	1125	3230	7835	15473	27946	69017	180609

Selected Financial Ratios (Times to 1)

Current Ratio 30	1.7	6.9	1.5	1.6	2.0	1.8	1.7	1.7	1.7	1.5
Quick Ratio 31	0.8	5.1	1.2	0.7	1.1	1.1	0.9	0.9	0.9	0.6
Net Sales to Working Capital 32	12.4	4.5	8.9	25.2	10.7	14.5	13.0	11.1	9.7	9.9
Coverage Ratio 33	7.7	124.1	1.7	9.2	6.9	10.2	9.4	8.6	18.3	3.5
Total Asset Turnover 34	2.6	2.4	2.6	5.4	3.1	3.4	2.8	2.5	2.2	1.5
Inventory Turnover 35	8.6	12.3	8.4	13.9	7.5	13.3	11.7	7.7	7.6	5.0
Receivables Turnover 36	14.7	18.3	83.6	37.3	17.2	19.3	16.1	13.1	11.1	8.5
Total Liabilities to Net Worth 37	1.7	0.6	7.7	1.4	1.1	1.0	1.2	1.4	1.1	5.6
Current Assets to Working Capital 38	2.5	1.2	2.9	2.5	2.0	2.2	2.4	2.5	2.5	3.0
Current Liabilities to Working Capital 39	1.5	0.2	1.9	1.5	1.0	1.2	1.4	1.5	1.5	2.0
Working Capital to Net Sales 40	0.1	0.2	0.1	0.0	0.1	0.1	0.1	0.1	0.1	0.1
Inventory to Working Capital 41	1.1	0.3	0.5	1.3	0.8	0.8	0.9	0.9	1.0	1.5
Total Receipts to Cash Flow 42	10.9	3.0	8.7	12.5	11.9	12.2	11.3	11.7	7.6	11.0
Cost of Goods to Cash Flow 43	8.1	1.4	4.5	9.3	8.7	9.0	8.6	8.9	5.5	8.3
Cash Flow to Total Debt 44	0.4	2.0	0.3	0.7	0.5	0.6	0.5	0.4	0.5	0.2

Selected Financial Factors (in Percentages)

Debt Ratio 45	62.9	38.9	88.5	58.4	51.6	49.5	53.7	58.9	52.5	84.8
Return on Total Assets 46	13.4	51.1	3.5	22.2	12.7	15.7	13.3	13.3	16.9	8.2
Return on Equity Before Income Taxes 47	31.3	83.0	12.4	47.6	22.4	28.0	25.6	28.7	33.7	38.8
Return on Equity After Income Taxes 48	28.0	81.5	10.5	45.2	21.4	27.2	23.7	27.2	30.5	29.1
Profit Margin (Before Income Tax) 49	4.5	21.4	0.6	3.7	3.5	4.2	4.2	4.8	7.4	4.0
Profit Margin (After Income Tax) 50	4.0	21.0	0.5	3.5	3.4	4.1	3.9	4.5	6.7	3.0

Table I
Corporations with and without Net Income

MISCELLANEOUS NONDURABLE GOODS

MONEY AMOUNTS AND SIZE OF ASSETS IN THOUSANDS OF DOLLARS

Item Description for Accounting Period 7/03 Through 6/04	Total	Zero Assets	Under 500	500 to 1,000	1,000 to 5,000	5,000 to 10,000	10,000 to 25,000	25,000 to 50,000	50,000 to 100,000	100,000 to 250,000	250,000 to 500,000	500,000 to 2,500,000	2,500,000 and over
Number of Enterprises **1**	37886	5509	24614	3505	3120	597	337	91	57	31	10	15	•
Revenues ($ in Thousands)													
Net Sales **2**	134795635	1666502	13729504	9268755	23031336	17382612	14670828	8188363	8913613	9092184	8461596	20390342	•
Interest **3**	270129	2348	4762	7646	32531	8976	10906	6389	7903	48275	28704	111690	•
Rents **4**	50117	17	2876	513	8428	3073	6025	625	2290	4648	649	20975	•
Royalties **5**	47755	0	0	0	0	4605	2604	0	2328	6015	683	31520	•
Other Portfolio Income **6**	479788	12037	35573	3995	26712	7590	24227	8981	6768	87203	2157	264547	•
Other Receipts **7**	2284984	55433	40942	35045	105633	32252	178525	69594	108909	105955	182965	1369725	•
Total Receipts **8**	137928408	1736337	13813657	9315954	23204640	17439108	14893115	8273952	9041811	9344280	8676754	22188799	•
Average Total Receipts **9**	3641	315	561	2658	7437	29211	44193	90923	158628	301428	867675	1479253	•
Operating Costs/Operating Income (%)													
Cost of Operations **10**	78.6	73.0	75.3	73.0	80.7	86.9	79.4	81.4	79.6	73.9	88.5	70.5	•
Salaries and Wages **11**	6.1	9.9	4.9	6.7	5.3	3.9	6.8	6.1	6.3	9.1	3.8	8.4	•
Taxes Paid **12**	1.5	2.7	1.2	3.2	1.5	1.2	1.9	1.2	1.2	1.1	0.5	1.5	•
Interest Paid **13**	0.7	2.6	0.3	0.4	0.3	0.4	0.5	0.6	1.0	1.0	0.9	1.6	•
Depreciation **14**	1.1	0.9	0.8	0.8	0.7	0.4	0.9	0.9	1.0	1.3	0.4	3.1	•
Amortization and Depletion **15**	0.2	0.5	0.1	0.0	0.1	0.0	0.2	0.1	0.4	0.4	0.2	0.8	•
Pensions and Other Deferred Comp. **16**	0.3	0.5	0.4	0.3	0.2	0.1	0.2	0.2	0.2	0.3	0.1	0.5	•
Employee Benefits **17**	0.6	0.4	0.6	0.4	0.4	0.3	0.5	0.5	0.7	0.7	0.4	1.1	•
Advertising **18**	0.7	0.3	0.5	0.4	0.7	0.4	0.6	1.4	1.7	1.2	0.1	0.7	•
Other Expenses **19**	8.2	19.3	11.8	9.5	7.8	5.1	7.3	5.9	5.8	9.8	4.8	10.9	•
Officers' Compensation **20**	1.6	2.1	4.6	3.1	2.2	0.8	1.4	1.1	0.8	0.9	0.6	0.6	•
Operating Margin **21**	0.3	•	•	2.2	0.2	0.4	0.3	0.7	1.3	0.3	•	0.4	•
Operating Margin Before Officers' Comp. **22**	1.9	•	4.1	5.3	2.4	1.2	1.7	1.7	2.1	1.2	0.3	1.0	•

Selected Average Balance Sheet ($ in Thousands)

Net Receivables 23	361	0	25	223	696	2187	4777	10856	15506	40174	109036	198185
Inventories 24	331	0	27	189	649	2120	4466	10863	16329	30945	74043	185844
Net Property, Plant and Equipment 25	232	0	18	116	288	563	2110	3612	9572	20092	20972	286515
Total Assets 26	1558	0	122	763	2143	6588	15499	33361	69921	159956	374329	1451261
Notes and Loans Payable 27	415	0	68	231	654	1847	4491	11871	21862	39974	109930	262729
All Other Liabilities 28	532	0	42	233	845	3105	5359	11400	27344	55112	159172	407777
Net Worth 29	610	0	13	299	643	1636	5649	10090	20714	64870	105226	780755

Selected Financial Ratios (Times to 1)

Current Ratio 30	1.5	•	1.7	2.0	1.6	1.3	1.6	1.5	1.6	1.5	1.1	1.3
Quick Ratio 31	0.8	•	0.9	1.2	0.9	0.7	0.9	0.8	0.8	0.9	0.7	0.6
Net Sales to Working Capital 32	12.1	•	15.3	9.6	12.0	22.5	10.1	9.7	9.2	8.4	41.2	9.9
Coverage Ratio 33	4.6	•	1.2	7.2	3.9	2.7	4.4	3.7	3.8	4.0	3.5	7.1
Total Asset Turnover 34	2.3	•	4.6	3.5	3.4	4.4	2.8	2.7	2.2	1.8	2.3	0.9
Inventory Turnover 35	8.5	•	15.5	10.2	9.2	11.9	7.7	6.7	7.6	7.0	10.1	5.2
Receivables Turnover 36	9.6	•	24.0	11.5	9.7	13.6	9.3	7.9	10.2	7.4	6.7	6.8
Total Liabilities to Net Worth 37	1.6	•	8.6	1.6	2.3	3.0	1.7	2.3	2.4	1.5	2.6	0.9
Current Assets to Working Capital 38	3.2	•	2.3	2.0	2.7	4.1	2.7	2.8	2.8	2.9	10.6	4.1
Current Liabilities to Working Capital 39	2.2	•	1.3	1.0	1.7	3.1	1.7	1.8	1.8	1.9	9.6	3.1
Working Capital to Net Sales 40	0.1	•	0.1	0.1	0.1	0.0	0.1	0.1	0.1	0.1	0.0	0.1
Inventory to Working Capital 41	1.1	•	1.0	0.7	0.9	1.7	1.0	1.1	1.0	0.8	2.9	1.6
Total Receipts to Cash Flow 42	11.3	14.8	11.1	10.4	13.7	20.6	13.3	15.9	13.5	9.1	17.8	5.9
Cost of Goods to Cash Flow 43	8.9	10.8	8.4	7.6	11.0	17.9	10.5	12.9	10.8	6.7	15.7	4.2
Cash Flow to Total Debt 44	0.3	•	0.5	0.5	0.4	0.3	0.3	0.2	0.2	0.3	0.2	0.3

Selected Financial Factors (in Percentages)

Debt Ratio 45	60.8	•	89.6	60.8	70.0	75.2	63.6	69.8	70.4	59.4	71.9	46.2
Return on Total Assets 46	7.8	•	1.8	10.9	4.6	5.0	6.6	6.2	8.2	7.6	7.0	10.9
Return on Equity Before Income Taxes 47	15.7	•	2.5	24.0	11.3	12.8	14.0	15.0	20.3	14.1	17.9	17.4
Return on Equity After Income Taxes 48	12.9	•	•	23.5	9.2	11.1	11.6	12.2	14.9	12.1	14.2	14.4
Profit Margin (Before Income Tax) 49	2.7	•	0.1	2.7	1.0	0.7	1.8	1.7	2.7	3.1	2.2	10.0
Profit Margin (After Income Tax) 50	2.2	•	•	2.7	0.8	0.6	1.5	1.4	2.0	2.7	1.8	8.3

Table II
Corporations with Net Income

MISCELLANEOUS NONDURABLE GOODS

MONEY AMOUNTS AND SIZE OF ASSETS IN THOUSANDS OF DOLLARS

Item Description for Accounting Period 7/03 Through 6/04	Total	Zero Assets	Under 500	500 to 1,000	1,000 to 5,000	5,000 to 10,000	10,000 to 25,000	25,000 to 50,000	50,000 to 100,000	100,000 to 250,000	250,000 to 500,000	500,000 to 2,500,000	2,500,000 and over
Number of Enterprises 1	18131	1437	11232	2255	2341	452	254	72	40	24	•	•	•
Revenues ($ in Thousands)													
Net Sales 2	108821565	698642	8191578	6878121	19398530	14377291	12288326	6638540	7286256	7318921	•	•	•
Interest 3	158327	470	3350	7402	16353	7336	7642	5346	5414	20261	•	•	•
Rents 4	28133	17	1602	513	7858	1009	5632	561	1897	4525	•	•	•
Royalties 5	40565	0	0	0	0	4605	1078	0	1413	2567	•	•	•
Other Portfolio Income 6	441883	7773	34573	2878	22979	7269	21936	8626	4370	86950	•	•	•
Other Receipts 7	2095187	54285	12518	14209	71850	29159	159501	62961	101449	105875	•	•	•
Total Receipts 8	111585660	761187	8243621	6903123	19517570	14426669	12484115	6716034	7400799	7539099	•	•	•
Average Total Receipts 9	6154	530	734	3061	8337	31917	49150	93278	185020	314129	•	•	•
Operating Costs/Operating Income (%)													
Cost of Operations 10	78.9	57.2	75.5	71.9	81.4	86.7	81.0	82.2	79.6	71.9	•	•	•
Salaries and Wages 11	5.8	9.7	3.5	6.7	4.7	3.5	5.8	5.9	6.0	9.5	•	•	•
Taxes Paid 12	1.4	2.1	0.9	4.0	1.3	1.2	1.6	0.7	1.2	1.1	•	•	•
Interest Paid 13	0.5	2.1	0.3	0.4	0.3	0.4	0.4	0.5	0.7	0.8	•	•	•
Depreciation 14	1.0	0.9	0.7	0.6	0.6	0.4	0.7	0.7	0.8	1.4	•	•	•
Amortization and Depletion 15	0.2	0.8	0.1	0.0	0.0	0.0	0.1	0.1	0.2	0.4	•	•	•
Pensions and Other Deferred Comp. 16	0.2	0.6	0.3	0.3	0.2	0.1	0.2	0.2	0.2	0.3	•	•	•
Employee Benefits 17	0.5	0.5	0.4	0.4	0.3	0.3	0.4	0.5	0.7	0.7	•	•	•
Advertising 18	0.7	0.5	0.6	0.4	0.7	0.4	0.5	0.6	2.0	1.2	•	•	•
Other Expenses 19	7.1	16.0	9.8	7.6	6.7	5.1	6.0	5.6	5.2	10.0	•	•	•
Officers' Compensation 20	1.5	3.6	4.2	3.4	2.1	0.8	1.4	1.2	0.8	1.0	•	•	•
Operating Margin 21	2.2	6.1	3.7	4.4	1.7	1.1	1.9	1.7	2.5	1.8	•	•	•
Operating Margin Before Officers' Comp. 22	3.7	9.6	7.8	7.8	3.7	1.9	3.3	2.8	3.3	2.8	•	•	•

Selected Average Balance Sheet ($ in Thousands)

Net Receivables 23	589	0	36	212	727	2335	4955	10778	14066	40828
Inventories 24	538	0	27	213	606	2190	4617	10724	17239	25553
Net Property, Plant and Equipment 25	315	0	23	116	221	585	1813	3087	8524	19593
Total Assets 26	2435	0	140	745	2127	6689	15218	33390	68448	152655
Notes and Loans Payable 27	491	0	50	180	485	1786	3722	10762	17455	29860
All Other Liabilities 28	810	0	38	234	756	2917	5276	11128	24041	53176
Net Worth 29	1134	0	52	331	886	1986	6219	11500	26952	69619

Selected Financial Ratios (Times to 1)

Current Ratio 30	1.7	·	1.9	2.3	1.8	1.4	1.7	1.6	1.7	1.7
Quick Ratio 31	0.9	·	1.2	1.4	1.1	0.8	1.0	0.8	0.8	1.0
Net Sales to Working Capital 32	9.7	·	16.1	9.4	11.0	21.6	9.6	8.8	9.2	7.5
Coverage Ratio 33	10.4	8.3	13.3	14.2	8.9	5.0	10.2	6.2	7.3	7.1
Total Asset Turnover 34	2.5	·	5.2	4.1	3.9	4.8	3.2	2.8	2.7	2.0
Inventory Turnover 35	8.8	·	20.4	10.3	11.1	12.6	8.5	7.1	8.4	8.6
Receivables Turnover 36	10.4	·	23.3	12.4	10.7	27.2	9.9	8.4	13.3	8.8
Total Liabilities to Net Worth 37	1.1	·	1.7	1.2	1.4	2.4	1.4	1.9	1.5	1.2
Current Assets to Working Capital 38	2.5	·	2.1	1.8	2.2	3.7	2.4	2.6	2.5	2.5
Current Liabilities to Working Capital 39	1.5	·	1.1	0.8	1.2	2.7	1.4	1.6	1.5	1.5
Working Capital to Net Sales 40	0.1	·	0.1	0.1	0.1	0.0	0.1	0.1	0.1	0.1
Inventory to Working Capital 41	0.9	·	0.7	0.7	0.7	1.5	0.9	1.1	0.9	0.7
Total Receipts to Cash Flow 42	9.7	4.3	8.5	9.7	12.7	18.2	12.1	14.0	11.9	7.9
Cost of Goods to Cash Flow 43	7.7	2.4	6.4	7.0	10.3	15.8	9.8	11.5	9.5	5.7
Cash Flow to Total Debt 44	0.5	·	1.0	0.8	0.5	0.4	0.4	0.3	0.4	0.5

Selected Financial Factors (in Percentages)

Debt Ratio 45	53.4	·	63.1	55.5	58.3	70.3	59.1	65.6	60.6	54.4
Return on Total Assets 46	13.3	·	24.1	21.2	10.0	8.4	12.5	9.3	12.6	11.2
Return on Equity Before Income Taxes 47	25.8	·	60.6	44.2	21.2	22.7	27.5	22.6	27.7	21.1
Return on Equity After Income Taxes 48	22.7	·	58.8	43.4	19.3	20.9	24.6	19.5	21.8	18.7
Profit Margin (Before Income Tax) 49	4.9	15.0	4.3	4.8	2.3	1.4	3.5	2.8	4.1	4.8
Profit Margin (After Income Tax) 50	4.3	12.1	4.2	4.7	2.1	1.3	3.2	2.4	3.2	4.3

200

Table I

Corporations with and without Net Income

WHOLESALE ELECTRONIC MARKETS AND AGENTS AND BROKERS

MONEY AMOUNTS AND SIZE OF ASSETS IN THOUSANDS OF DOLLARS

Item Description for Accounting Period 7/03 Through 6/04	Total	Zero Assets	Under 500	500 to 1,000	1,000 to 5,000	5,000 to 10,000	10,000 to 25,000	25,000 to 50,000	50,000 to 100,000	100,000 to 250,000	250,000 to 500,000	500,000 to 2,500,000	2,500,000 and over
Number of Enterprises 1	7333	710	6458	·	156	·	8	·	·	·	·	·	·
Revenues ($ in Thousands)													
Net Sales 2	1514467	31541	884272	·	69651	·	529004	·	·	·	·	·	·
Interest 3	1275	9	803	·	4	·	460	·	·	·	·	·	·
Rents 4	129	0	4	·	0	·	125	·	·	·	·	·	·
Royalties 5	181	0	0	·	0	·	181	·	·	·	·	·	·
Other Portfolio Income 6	39	0	14	·	25	·	0	·	·	·	·	·	·
Other Receipts 7	136794	1584	94852	·	39421	·	935	·	·	·	·	·	·
Total Receipts 8	1652885	33134	979945	·	109101	·	530705	·	·	·	·	·	·
Average Total Receipts 9	225	47	152	·	699	·	66338	·	·	·	·	·	·
Operating Costs/Operating Income (%)													
Cost of Operations 10	8.1	·	·	·	·	·	23.1	·	·	·	·	·	·
Salaries and Wages 11	29.0	45.2	23.3	·	16.7	·	39.2	·	·	·	·	·	·
Taxes Paid 12	3.6	4.4	3.5	·	3.1	·	3.8	·	·	·	·	·	·
Interest Paid 13	1.0	0.5	0.9	·	0.6	·	1.2	·	·	·	·	·	·
Depreciation 14	2.1	0.9	2.2	·	0.9	·	2.3	·	·	·	·	·	·
Amortization and Depletion 15	0.7	0.1	0.0	·	6.4	·	1.0	·	·	·	·	·	·
Pensions and Other Deferred Comp. 16	2.5	3.2	1.3	·	17.6	·	2.6	·	·	·	·	·	·
Employee Benefits 17	3.5	3.4	3.5	·	4.1	·	3.4	·	·	·	·	·	·
Advertising 18	1.1	3.6	1.7	·	0.3	·	0.1	·	·	·	·	·	·
Other Expenses 19	33.3	43.0	38.5	·	42.3	·	22.8	·	·	·	·	·	·
Officers' Compensation 20	17.2	15.9	26.8	·	22.4	·	0.7	·	·	·	·	·	·
Operating Margin 21	·	·	·	·	·	·	·	·	·	·	·	·	·
Operating Margin Before Officers' Comp. 22	15.2	·	25.2	·	8.0	·	0.5	·	·	·	·	·	·

Selected Average Balance Sheet ($ in Thousands)

Net Receivables 23	23	0	0	469	11824
Inventories 24	2	0	0		1582
Net Property, Plant and Equipment 25	17	0	9	5	7424
Total Assets 26	122	0	50	1689	38422
Notes and Loans Payable 27	83	0	38	1035	25629
All Other Liabilities 28	25	0	3	430	12118
Net Worth 29	14	0	10	224	676

Selected Financial Ratios (Times to 1)

Current Ratio 30	1.2		2.3	0.7	1.0
Quick Ratio 31	1.1		2.3	0.6	0.8
Net Sales to Working Capital 32	22.0		8.1		
Coverage Ratio 33	8.2		11.1	66.8	1.1
Total Asset Turnover 34	1.7		2.7	0.3	1.7
Inventory Turnover 35	9.7				9.7
Receivables Turnover 36	13.2		65501.6	1.0	11.2
Total Liabilities to Net Worth 37	7.7		4.2	6.5	55.9
Current Assets to Working Capital 38	6.0		1.7		
Current Liabilities to Working Capital 39	5.0		0.7		
Working Capital to Net Sales 40	0.0		0.1		
Inventory to Working Capital 41	0.2				
Total Receipts to Cash Flow 42	3.1	4.2	2.5	1.7	5.8
Cost of Goods to Cash Flow 43	0.2				1.3
Cash Flow to Total Debt 44	0.6		1.3	0.2	0.3

Selected Financial Factors (in Percentages)

Debt Ratio 45	88.6		80.9	86.7	98.2
Return on Total Assets 46	13.6		27.8	11.3	2.2
Return on Equity Before Income Taxes 47	104.6		132.0	84.2	10.5
Return on Equity After Income Taxes 48	100.6		129.7	79.4	
Profit Margin (Before Income Tax) 49	7.1		9.3	42.2	0.1
Profit Margin (After Income Tax) 50	6.8		9.1	39.8	

Table II
Corporations with Net Income

WHOLESALE ELECTRONIC MARKETS AND AGENTS AND BROKERS

MONEY AMOUNTS AND SIZE OF ASSETS IN THOUSANDS OF DOLLARS

Item Description for Accounting Period 7/03 Through 6/04		Total	Zero Assets	Under 500	500 to 1000	251 to 500	501 to 1,000	1,001 to 5,000	5,001 to 10,000	10,001 to 25,000	25,001 to 50,000	50,001 to 100,000	100,001 to 250,000	250,001 and over
Number of Enterprises	1	2970	•	2827	•	139	•	4	•	•	•	•	•	•
Revenues ($ in Thousands)														
Net Sales	2	1040429	•	527144	•	49800	•	463485	•	•	•	•	•	•
Interest	3	413	•	20	•	4	•	389	•	•	•	•	•	•
Rents	4	100	•	0	•	0	•	100	•	•	•	•	•	•
Royalties	5	181	•	0	•	0	•	181	•	•	•	•	•	•
Other Portfolio Income	6	39	•	14	•	25	•	0	•	•	•	•	•	•
Other Receipts	7	130213	•	90052	•	39421	•	740	•	•	•	•	•	•
Total Receipts	8	1171375	•	617230	•	89250	•	464895	•	•	•	•	•	•
Average Total Receipts	9	394	•	218	•	642	•	116224	•	•	•	•	•	•
Operating Costs/Operating Income (%)														
Cost of Operations	10	7.1	•	•	•	•	•	15.9	•	•	•	•	•	•
Salaries and Wages	11	29.5	•	19.0	•	14.3	•	42.9	•	•	•	•	•	•
Taxes Paid	12	3.9	•	3.7	•	3.6	•	4.2	•	•	•	•	•	•
Interest Paid	13	1.0	•	1.1	•	0.0	•	0.9	•	•	•	•	•	•
Depreciation	14	1.7	•	1.4	•	0.1	•	2.2	•	•	•	•	•	•
Amortization and Depletion	15	0.9	•	0.0	•	9.0	•	1.0	•	•	•	•	•	•
Pensions and Other Deferred Comp.	16	3.3	•	1.5	•	24.6	•	3.0	•	•	•	•	•	•
Employee Benefits	17	4.5	•	5.1	•	5.7	•	3.8	•	•	•	•	•	•
Advertising	18	1.4	•	2.8	•	•	•	0.1	•	•	•	•	•	•
Other Expenses	19	27.2	•	30.5	•	18.7	•	24.4	•	•	•	•	•	•
Officers' Compensation	20	16.6	•	29.1	•	30.2	•	0.8	•	•	•	•	•	•
Operating Margin	21	2.9	•	5.9	•	•	•	0.6	•	•	•	•	•	•
Operating Margin Before Officers' Comp.	22	19.5	•	34.9	•	24.0	•	1.5	•	•	•	•	•	•

Selected Average Balance Sheet ($ in Thousands)

Net Receivables 23	25	0	177	12146
Inventories 24	3	0	0	2238
Net Property, Plant and Equipment 25	31	14	1	12999
Total Assets 26	229	83	1532	58516
Notes and Loans Payable 27	146	38	1106	43054
All Other Liabilities 28	20	2	109	9555
Net Worth 29	63	42	318	5906

Selected Financial Ratios (Times to 1)

Current Ratio 30	1.2	2.1	0.5	1.1
Quick Ratio 31	1.1	2.0	0.5	0.8
Net Sales to Working Capital 32	21.5	7.4		59.2
Coverage Ratio 33	17.0	22.0	9092.0	2.0
Total Asset Turnover 34	1.5	2.2	0.2	2.0
Inventory Turnover 35	8.3			8.3
Receivables Turnover 36	28.4	210857.6	4.0	19.1
Total Liabilities to Net Worth 37	2.6	1.0	3.8	8.9
Current Assets to Working Capital 38	5.2	2.0		10.3
Current Liabilities to Working Capital 39	4.2	1.0		9.3
Working Capital to Net Sales 40	0.0	0.1		0.0
Inventory to Working Capital 41	0.2			1.1
Total Receipts to Cash Flow 42	2.7	2.1	1.1	5.2
Cost of Goods to Cash Flow 43	0.2			0.8
Cash Flow to Total Debt 44	0.8	2.2	0.3	0.4

Selected Financial Factors (in Percentages)

Debt Ratio 45	72.4	48.8	79.2	89.9
Return on Total Assets 46	25.2	54.0	17.1	3.7
Return on Equity Before Income Taxes 47	86.0	100.8	82.3	18.2
Return on Equity After Income Taxes 48	83.8	99.6	78.4	13.9
Profit Margin (Before Income Tax) 49	15.5	22.9	73.0	0.9
Profit Margin (After Income Tax) 50	15.1	22.7	69.6	0.7

Table I
Corporations with and without Net Income

NEW AND USED CAR DEALERS

MONEY AMOUNTS AND SIZE OF ASSETS IN THOUSANDS OF DOLLARS

Item Description for Accounting Period 7/03 Through 6/04	Total	Zero Assets	Under 500	500 to 1,000	1,000 to 5,000	5,000 to 10,000	10,000 to 25,000	25,000 to 50,000	50,000 to 100,000	100,000 to 250,000	250,000 to 500,000	500,000 to 2,500,000	2,500,000 and over
Number of Enterprises **1**	46302	2210	22041	3993	8479	5164	3534	677	147	41	6	10	•
Revenues ($ in Thousands)													
Net Sales **2**	660871773	1396804	21528596	13051452	91000755	146396107	205621778	80908705	30531231	16326944	5629572	48479830	•
Interest **3**	1555927	1106	15734	27722	146789	155498	194109	88442	31743	120418	24063	750305	•
Rents **4**	236640	318	6628	0	30591	25210	33013	26725	24943	55619	1353	32240	•
Royalties **5**	134009	0	0	0	0	44	3	72	0	4366	0	129525	•
Other Portfolio Income **6**	598351	9458	47515	5909	82578	80073	94707	45891	82964	74260	10194	64798	•
Other Receipts **7**	11899621	19885	334976	53769	1647269	2640073	3737569	1531673	600174	354414	86758	893062	•
Total Receipts **8**	675296321	1427571	21933449	13138852	92907982	149297005	209681179	82601508	31271055	16936021	5751940	50349760	•
Average Total Receipts **9**	14585	646	995	3290	10957	28911	59333	122011	212728	413074	958657	5034976	•
Operating Costs/Operating Income (%)													
Cost of Operations **10**	88.2	87.7	86.1	88.5	87.4	89.0	88.9	89.0	87.6	86.2	87.9	85.3	•
Salaries and Wages **11**	4.9	4.1	3.1	3.2	4.8	4.7	4.9	4.9	5.4	5.6	5.0	6.4	•
Taxes Paid **12**	0.8	0.6	1.4	1.0	0.8	0.8	0.7	0.7	0.8	0.9	0.9	1.2	•
Interest Paid **13**	0.6	0.7	0.7	0.5	0.5	0.4	0.3	0.4	0.5	0.7	0.8	2.2	•
Depreciation **14**	0.5	0.2	0.2	0.3	0.3	0.4	0.4	0.6	1.1	1.3	1.4	1.3	•
Amortization and Depletion **15**	0.1	0.0	0.1	0.0	0.0	0.0	0.0	0.0	0.1	0.1	0.1	0.4	•
Pensions and Other Deferred Comp. **16**	0.1	0.0	0.1	0.0	0.1	0.1	0.1	0.1	0.1	0.1	0.1	0.0	•
Employee Benefits **17**	0.4	0.3	0.2	0.1	0.5	0.5	0.4	0.4	0.4	0.6	0.4	0.4	•
Advertising **18**	1.1	1.1	0.8	0.6	1.2	1.3	1.1	1.1	1.2	1.2	0.8	1.1	•
Other Expenses **19**	3.8	11.0	7.0	4.4	4.3	3.6	3.4	3.3	3.5	5.1	3.5	4.2	•
Officers' Compensation **20**	0.8	0.5	1.5	1.2	1.2	0.9	0.7	0.6	0.7	0.6	0.3	0.1	•
Operating Margin **21**	•	•	•	0.2	•	•	•	•	•	•	•	•	•
Operating Margin Before Officers' Comp. **22**	•	•	0.3	1.5	0.0	•	•	•	•	•	•	•	•

Selected Average Balance Sheet ($ in Thousands)

Net Receivables 23	495	0	19	154	354	695	1668	4146	7600	29520	21866	414578	•
Inventories 24	2106	0	82	332	1922	4537	8540	16823	28375	49201	126867	614979	•
Net Property, Plant and Equipment 25	411	0	15	35	179	533	1343	4158	10960	23567	94777	357002	•
Total Assets 26	3930	0	146	681	2703	7161	14848	33378	64757	152384	329689	2331440	•
Notes and Loans Payable 27	2653	0	109	378	1792	5474	10960	23772	44519	92603	187369	918440	•
All Other Liabilities 28	511	0	23	148	314	736	1345	3414	7527	22427	66458	660412	•
Net Worth 29	766	0	14	155	597	951	2544	6192	12712	37354	75862	752588	•

Selected Financial Ratios (Times to 1)

Current Ratio 30	1.2	•	2.1	2.2	1.4	1.2	1.2	1.2	1.2	1.3	1.3	1.0	•
Quick Ratio 31	0.3	•	0.7	0.8	0.3	0.3	0.3	0.3	0.3	0.5	0.3	0.4	•
Net Sales to Working Capital 32	24.5	•	15.4	9.7	15.5	25.8	27.4	27.2	28.5	17.8	22.1	•	•
Coverage Ratio 33	2.5	•	1.9	2.9	2.8	2.3	3.7	3.4	3.3	3.1	2.3	1.5	•
Total Asset Turnover 34	3.6	•	6.7	4.8	4.0	4.0	3.9	3.6	3.2	2.6	2.8	2.1	•
Inventory Turnover 35	6.0	•	10.3	8.7	4.9	5.6	6.1	6.3	6.4	7.0	6.5	6.7	•
Receivables Turnover 36	29.5	•	56.0	22.1	29.2	41.4	36.2	30.1	28.0	17.1	17.4	12.0	•
Total Liabilities to Net Worth 37	4.1	•	9.5	3.4	3.5	6.5	4.8	4.4	4.1	3.1	3.3	2.1	•
Current Assets to Working Capital 38	5.4	•	1.9	1.9	3.5	5.8	5.9	6.1	6.5	4.8	4.6	•	•
Current Liabilities to Working Capital 39	4.4	•	0.9	0.9	2.5	4.8	4.9	5.1	5.5	3.8	3.6	•	•
Working Capital to Net Sales 40	0.0	•	0.1	0.1	0.1	0.0	0.0	0.0	0.0	0.1	0.0	•	•
Inventory to Working Capital 41	3.8	•	1.3	1.1	2.6	4.4	4.4	4.2	4.4	2.6	3.1	•	•
Total Receipts to Cash Flow 42	28.0	27.3	17.0	23.8	24.3	33.9	30.6	29.9	26.8	19.2	26.6	23.7	•
Cost of Goods to Cash Flow 43	24.7	23.9	14.7	21.0	21.3	30.2	27.2	26.6	23.5	16.5	23.4	20.2	•
Cash Flow to Total Debt 44	0.2	•	0.4	0.3	0.2	0.1	0.2	0.1	0.1	0.1	0.1	0.1	•

Selected Financial Factors (in Percentages)

Debt Ratio 45	80.5	•	90.4	77.3	77.9	86.7	82.9	81.5	80.4	75.5	77.0	67.7	•
Return on Total Assets 46	5.1	•	8.7	6.6	5.7	3.6	4.9	5.0	5.3	5.4	4.9	7.0	•
Return on Equity Before Income Taxes 47	16.0	•	44.3	19.0	16.7	15.4	21.0	19.1	18.7	14.9	11.9	7.1	•
Return on Equity After Income Taxes 48	14.2	•	43.2	18.2	15.4	14.4	19.9	17.9	16.9	11.2	8.6	4.1	•
Profit Margin (Before Income Tax) 49	0.9	•	0.6	0.9	0.9	0.5	0.9	1.0	1.1	1.4	1.0	1.1	•
Profit Margin (After Income Tax) 50	0.8	•	0.6	0.9	0.9	0.5	0.9	0.9	1.0	1.1	0.7	0.6	•

Table II

Corporations with Net Income

NEW AND USED CAR DEALERS

MONEY AMOUNTS AND SIZE OF ASSETS IN THOUSANDS OF DOLLARS

Item Description for Accounting Period 7/03 Through 6/04	Total	Zero Assets	Under 500	500 to 1,000	1,000 to 5,000	5,000 to 10,000	10,000 to 25,000	25,000 to 50,000	50,000 to 100,000	100,000 to 250,000	250,000 to 500,000	500,000 to 2,500,000	2,500,000 and over
Number of Enterprises **1**	26273	799	9849	2841	5784	3656	2667	510	118	•	6	•	•
Revenues ($ in Thousands)													
Net Sales **2**	518483397	824522	12173584	9752449	70672583	107025701	163754199	63491888	25680411	•	5629572	•	•
Interest **3**	1387377	526	13289	21196	113162	110486	147991	65091	26697	•	24063	•	•
Rents **4**	161641	318	6628	0	20475	10714	23123	16971	11356	•	1353	•	•
Royalties **5**	134009	0	0	0	0	44	3	72	0	•	0	•	•
Other Portfolio Income **6**	430910	9423	25427	5909	78110	70887	63465	30198	22409	•	10194	•	•
Other Receipts **7**	9455277	16574	93386	39298	1302595	1979251	3018571	1195146	520457	•	86758	•	•
Total Receipts **8**	530052611	851363	12312314	9818852	72186925	109197083	167007352	64799366	26261330	•	5751940	•	•
Average Total Receipts **9**	20175	1066	1250	3456	12480	29868	62620	127058	222554	•	958657	•	•
Operating Costs/Operating Income (%)													
Cost of Operations **10**	88.1	83.4	85.6	87.7	87.6	88.8	88.8	88.8	87.6	•	87.9	•	•
Salaries and Wages **11**	4.9	5.5	2.1	3.0	4.9	4.5	4.9	4.8	5.4	•	5.0	•	•
Taxes Paid **12**	0.8	0.5	1.4	0.9	0.8	0.8	0.7	0.7	0.8	•	0.9	•	•
Interest Paid **13**	0.5	0.4	0.5	0.5	0.4	0.4	0.3	0.4	0.4	•	0.8	•	•
Depreciation **14**	0.4	0.2	0.2	0.3	0.3	0.3	0.4	0.5	0.6	•	1.4	•	•
Amortization and Depletion **15**	0.1	0.0	0.0	0.0	0.0	0.0	0.0	0.0	0.0	•	0.1	•	•
Pensions and Other Deferred Comp. **16**	0.1	0.0	0.1	0.1	0.1	0.1	0.1	0.1	0.1	•	0.1	•	•
Employee Benefits **17**	0.4	0.4	0.2	0.1	0.4	0.5	0.4	0.4	0.4	•	0.4	•	•
Advertising **18**	1.1	1.2	0.7	0.7	1.2	1.2	1.1	1.0	1.2	•	0.8	•	•
Other Expenses **19**	3.6	7.7	5.9	4.5	3.5	3.4	3.2	3.1	3.5	•	3.5	•	•
Officers' Compensation **20**	0.8	0.6	1.3	1.3	1.3	0.9	0.7	0.6	0.7	•	0.3	•	•
Operating Margin **21**	•	•	1.9	1.1	•	•	•	•	•	•	•	•	•
Operating Margin Before Officers' Comp. **22**	0.0	0.4	3.2	2.4	0.8	0.1	0.1	0.0	•	•	•	•	•

Selected Average Balance Sheet ($ in Thousands)

Net Receivables 23	693	0	24	155	374	693	1698	4227	7487	•	21866
Inventories 24	2850	0	115	345	2008	4692	8781	17379	30670	•	129825
Net Property, Plant and Equipment 25	538	0	17	26	167	555	1308	4114	9944	•	94777
Total Assets 26	5328	0	192	683	2877	7064	14955	33504	64786	•	329689
Notes and Loans Payable 27	3372	0	104	283	1811	5152	10704	23208	42566	•	187369
All Other Liabilities 28	719	0	36	158	319	642	1344	3250	8135	•	66458
Net Worth 29	1237	0	51	242	747	1270	2907	7045	14085	•	75862

Selected Financial Ratios (Times to 1)

Current Ratio 30	1.3	•	2.6	2.4	1.4	1.2	1.2	1.2	1.2	•	1.3
Quick Ratio 31	0.3	•	0.7	0.9	0.3	0.3	0.3	0.4	0.4	•	0.3
Net Sales to Working Capital 32	22.4	•	11.6	9.1	15.7	24.2	25.0	23.4	24.4	•	22.1
Coverage Ratio 33	3.7	8.1	6.7	4.7	5.5	4.1	5.6	4.9	4.5	•	2.3
Total Asset Turnover 34	3.7	•	6.4	5.0	4.2	4.1	4.1	3.7	3.4	•	2.8
Inventory Turnover 35	6.1	•	9.2	8.7	5.3	5.5	6.2	6.4	6.2	•	6.4
Receivables Turnover 36	28.7	•	57.5	21.7	32.1	84.5	36.7	30.5	28.3	•	85.8
Total Liabilities to Net Worth 37	3.3	•	2.7	1.8	2.9	4.6	4.1	3.8	3.6	•	3.3
Current Assets to Working Capital 38	4.8	•	1.6	1.7	3.3	5.2	5.2	5.1	5.4	•	4.6
Current Liabilities to Working Capital 39	3.8	•	0.6	0.7	2.3	4.2	4.2	4.1	4.4	•	3.6
Working Capital to Net Sales 40	0.0	•	0.1	0.1	0.1	0.0	0.0	0.0	0.0	•	0.0
Inventory to Working Capital 41	3.4	•	1.1	1.0	2.5	3.9	3.8	3.5	3.7	•	3.1
Total Receipts to Cash Flow 42	25.2	16.5	14.1	19.9	23.9	28.5	27.7	26.9	24.3	•	26.6
Cost of Goods to Cash Flow 43	22.2	13.7	12.1	17.5	21.0	25.3	24.6	23.9	21.3	•	23.4
Cash Flow to Total Debt 44	0.2	•	0.6	0.4	0.2	0.2	0.2	0.2	0.2	•	0.1

Selected Financial Factors (in Percentages)

Debt Ratio 45	76.8	•	73.2	64.6	74.0	82.0	80.6	79.0	78.3	•	77.0
Return on Total Assets 46	7.3	•	22.8	11.1	8.9	6.3	6.7	6.9	6.7	•	4.9
Return on Equity Before Income Taxes 47	23.1	•	72.3	24.6	28.0	26.8	28.5	26.2	23.7	•	11.9
Return on Equity After Income Taxes 48	21.3	•	71.7	23.8	26.7	25.7	27.3	24.8	21.7	•	8.6
Profit Margin (Before Income Tax) 49	1.4	3.1	3.0	1.7	1.7	1.2	1.3	1.5	1.5	•	1.0
Profit Margin (After Income Tax) 50	1.3	2.8	3.0	1.7	1.6	1.1	1.3	1.4	1.4	•	0.7

Table I
Corporations with and without Net Income

OTHER MOTOR VEHICLE AND PARTS DEALERS

MONEY AMOUNTS AND SIZE OF ASSETS IN THOUSANDS OF DOLLARS

Item Description for Accounting Period 7/03 Through 6/04	Total	Zero Assets	Under 500	500 to 1,000	1,000 to 5,000	5,000 to 10,000	10,000 to 25,000	25,000 to 50,000	50,000 to 100,000	100,000 to 250,000	250,000 to 500,000	500,000 to 2,500,000	2,500,000 and over
Number of Enterprises 1	44669	4157	27170	4960	7069	802	363	77	39	21	4	6	•
Revenues ($ in Thousands)													
Net Sales 2	124129608	505805	15949286	8543442	38426870	12211114	13398019	6471385	5382567	5751227	2882740	14607152	•
Interest 3	122293	194	5732	7664	27262	14821	18364	10420	4450	14496	13407	5483	•
Rents 4	95645	0	7575	1625	22411	3238	10387	10162	16790	3235	3591	16629	•
Royalties 5	245631	0	0	0	0	660	4	65	5229	478	1373	237822	•
Other Portfolio Income 6	185668	4179	36512	7759	44992	11271	22753	12152	29700	14898	832	623	•
Other Receipts 7	2682543	4133	106613	84814	365687	191637	166717	64451	81681	52163	31493	1533155	•
Total Receipts 8	127461388	514311	16105718	8645304	38887222	12432741	13616244	6568635	5520417	5836497	2933436	16400864	•
Average Total Receipts 9	2853	124	593	1743	5501	15502	37510	85307	141549	277928	733359	2733477	•
Operating Costs/Operating Income (%)													
Cost of Operations 10	72.7	69.4	68.9	69.9	76.2	78.5	81.4	80.7	74.9	73.5	57.1	55.2	•
Salaries and Wages 11	9.3	4.3	8.2	9.4	7.9	7.2	7.0	7.2	9.4	8.5	18.2	17.8	•
Taxes Paid 12	1.9	2.3	2.5	2.0	1.5	1.4	1.2	1.2	1.4	1.4	2.1	4.3	•
Interest Paid 13	1.0	2.0	0.8	1.0	1.0	1.0	0.9	0.9	1.1	1.0	0.9	1.7	•
Depreciation 14	1.5	2.2	1.2	1.2	0.9	2.0	1.3	1.7	2.5	3.3	1.4	2.3	•
Amortization and Depletion 15	0.1	0.0	0.1	0.1	0.0	0.0	0.0	0.1	0.1	0.3	0.8	0.0	•
Pensions and Other Deferred Comp. 16	0.2	0.0	0.1	0.1	0.2	0.2	0.2	0.2	0.2	0.5	0.3	0.2	•
Employee Benefits 17	0.7	0.2	0.4	0.5	0.5	0.7	0.7	0.8	0.7	1.0	1.0	1.8	•
Advertising 18	1.1	0.9	1.2	1.2	1.2	1.0	0.9	0.8	1.0	0.9	1.8	1.5	•
Other Expenses 19	10.2	21.8	12.8	10.2	7.7	6.6	5.8	6.1	7.8	8.0	16.9	22.4	•
Officers' Compensation 20	1.9	1.9	4.6	2.9	2.1	1.6	1.1	0.7	1.0	0.3	0.3	0.2	•
Operating Margin 21	•	•	•	1.6	0.8	•	•	•	•	1.1	•	•	•
Operating Margin Before Officers' Comp. 22	1.2	•	3.8	4.4	2.8	1.3	0.8	0.2	0.9	1.7	0.9	0.2	•

Selected Average Balance Sheet ($ in Thousands)

Net Receivables 23	123	0	17	60	188	663	1764	5362	8966	27763	72133	99937
Inventories 24	591	0	63	417	1264	3944	8217	16351	29899	44133	78139	643824
Net Property, Plant and Equipment 25	216	0	25	108	263	1304	2243	7095	13337	40592	43895	436741
Total Assets 26	1199	0	138	689	2124	7117	14662	34578	68907	164946	329473	1699901
Notes and Loans Payable 27	512	0	83	304	805	3391	8061	18211	32688	66653	107906	541851
All Other Liabilities 28	358	0	41	110	753	1638	4002	8793	19720	30627	75967	645480
Net Worth 29	329	0	15	275	565	2087	2598	7574	16500	67666	145600	512570

Selected Financial Ratios (Times to 1)

Current Ratio 30	1.5	•	2.1	2.8	1.6	1.4	1.4	1.2	1.3	1.3	1.9	1.1
Quick Ratio 31	0.4	•	0.8	0.7	0.3	0.3	0.3	0.4	0.4	0.5	0.9	0.2
Net Sales to Working Capital 32	10.2	•	11.3	5.1	8.2	9.8	11.7	18.6	12.1	13.3	8.5	33.9
Coverage Ratio 33	2.9	•	1.2	3.8	3.0	2.6	2.5	2.0	3.3	3.6	2.1	3.9
Total Asset Turnover 34	2.3	•	4.2	2.5	2.6	2.1	2.5	2.4	2.0	1.7	2.2	1.4
Inventory Turnover 35	3.4	•	6.4	2.9	3.3	3.0	3.7	4.1	3.5	4.6	5.3	2.1
Receivables Turnover 36	24.5	•	37.0	24.9	32.2	22.9	20.6	16.0	15.0	11.7	10.6	37.7
Total Liabilities to Net Worth 37	2.6	•	8.3	1.5	2.8	2.4	4.6	3.6	3.2	1.4	1.3	2.3
Current Assets to Working Capital 38	3.1	•	1.9	1.6	2.7	3.5	3.6	5.4	4.0	4.4	2.1	13.0
Current Liabilities to Working Capital 39	2.1	•	0.9	0.6	1.7	2.5	2.6	4.4	3.0	3.4	1.1	12.0
Working Capital to Net Sales 40	0.1	•	0.1	0.2	0.1	0.1	0.1	0.1	0.1	0.1	0.1	0.0
Inventory to Working Capital 41	2.3	•	1.1	1.1	2.1	2.6	2.6	3.6	2.6	2.4	1.0	10.1
Total Receipts to Cash Flow 42	11.0	12.2	11.6	10.0	13.5	15.9	19.2	19.7	12.6	11.5	8.1	4.7
Cost of Goods to Cash Flow 43	8.0	8.5	8.0	7.0	10.3	12.5	15.6	15.9	9.4	8.4	4.6	2.6
Cash Flow to Total Debt 44	0.3	•	0.4	0.4	0.3	0.2	0.2	0.2	0.2	0.2	0.5	0.4

Selected Financial Factors (in Percentages)

Debt Ratio 45	72.6	•	89.3	60.1	73.4	70.7	82.3	78.1	76.1	59.0	55.8	69.8
Return on Total Assets 46	7.0	•	4.4	9.3	7.5	5.3	5.5	4.7	7.1	6.0	4.2	9.5
Return on Equity Before Income Taxes 47	16.8	•	7.7	17.2	18.8	11.2	18.6	10.9	20.7	10.5	5.0	23.5
Return on Equity After Income Taxes 48	13.6	•	6.0	16.3	17.9	9.7	15.8	9.3	19.2	7.6	3.3	14.3
Profit Margin (Before Income Tax) 49	2.0	•	0.2	2.7	2.0	1.5	1.3	1.0	2.5	2.6	1.0	4.9
Profit Margin (After Income Tax) 50	1.6	•	0.2	2.6	1.9	1.3	1.1	0.8	2.3	1.9	0.7	3.0

Table II
Corporations with Net Income

OTHER MOTOR VEHICLE AND PARTS DEALERS

MONEY AMOUNTS AND SIZE OF ASSETS IN THOUSANDS OF DOLLARS

Item Description for Accounting Period 7/03 Through 6/04	Total	Zero Assets	Under 500	500 to 1,000	1,000 to 5,000	5,000 to 10,000	10,000 to 25,000	25,000 to 50,000	50,000 to 100,000	100,000 to 250,000	250,000 to 500,000	500,000 to 2,500,000	2,500,000 and over
Number of Enterprises **1**	27530	1647	15649	4003	5181	662	278	56	31	•	•	•	•
Revenues ($ in Thousands)													
Net Sales **2**	98778307	238988	10023849	6871530	31771053	10666001	10764124	5050453	4432072	•	•	•	•
Interest **3**	100133	0	4387	6166	19333	12328	13991	7865	3344	•	•	•	•
Rents **4**	66144	0	7575	1269	16573	2408	6809	10134	1922	•	•	•	•
Royalties **5**	242338	0	0	0	0	660	0	65	3313	•	•	•	•
Other Portfolio Income **6**	134137	4179	19500	7740	33972	8772	16382	8861	20449	•	•	•	•
Other Receipts **7**	2494871	2556	60496	82008	309570	173431	129769	54742	79122	•	•	•	•
Total Receipts **8**	101815930	245723	10115807	6968713	32150501	10863600	10931075	5132120	4540222	•	•	•	•
Average Total Receipts **9**	3698	149	646	1741	6205	16410	39320	91645	146459	•	•	•	•
Operating Costs/Operating Income (%)													
Cost of Operations **10**	72.5	65.1	65.0	70.2	75.8	79.1	80.8	81.4	74.3	•	•	•	•
Salaries and Wages **11**	9.2	6.9	9.4	8.9	7.9	7.0	7.0	7.1	9.8	•	•	•	•
Taxes Paid **12**	1.9	1.8	2.3	1.9	1.5	1.5	1.2	1.2	1.3	•	•	•	•
Interest Paid **13**	1.0	3.2	0.7	0.9	0.8	0.9	0.8	0.8	1.0	•	•	•	•
Depreciation **14**	1.3	0.5	1.3	1.2	0.8	1.0	1.1	1.3	2.2	•	•	•	•
Amortization and Depletion **15**	0.1	0.0	0.0	0.2	0.0	0.0	0.0	0.0	0.1	•	•	•	•
Pensions and Other Deferred Comp. **16**	0.2	0.0	0.1	0.1	0.2	0.2	0.1	0.2	0.2	•	•	•	•
Employee Benefits **17**	0.7	0.2	0.3	0.6	0.5	0.7	0.6	0.9	0.7	•	•	•	•
Advertising **18**	1.1	1.2	1.1	1.1	1.1	1.0	0.9	0.8	1.2	•	•	•	•
Other Expenses **19**	9.9	17.7	12.0	10.2	7.4	6.5	5.6	5.5	7.2	•	•	•	•
Officers' Compensation **20**	1.7	0.5	4.5	2.4	2.1	1.5	1.1	0.7	1.1	•	•	•	•
Operating Margin **21**	0.4	2.8	3.1	2.5	1.8	1.8	0.7	0.1	0.9	•	•	•	•
Operating Margin Before Officers' Comp. **22**	2.1	3.3	7.6	4.9	3.9	2.1	1.8	0.8	2.0	•	•	•	•

Selected Average Balance Sheet ($ in Thousands)

	•	•	•	•	•	•	•	•	•
Net Receivables 23	155	0	14	59	205	695	1717	4951	9059
Inventories 24	749	0	56	365	1318	4344	8154	16903	28961
Net Property, Plant and Equipment 25	233	0	31	101	263	914	2120	6151	14231
Total Assets 26	1488	0	142	698	2241	7117	14545	34172	68688
Notes and Loans Payable 27	614	0	61	288	815	3648	7561	17363	34578
All Other Liabilities 28	419	0	30	100	748	1595	3318	8851	18112
Net Worth 29	455	0	51	310	678	1874	3666	7958	15998

Selected Financial Ratios (Times to 1)

	•	•	•	•	•	•	•	•	•
Current Ratio 30	1.5	•	2.5	3.4	1.7	1.4	1.4	1.3	1.3
Quick Ratio 31	0.4	•	1.0	1.0	0.3	0.3	0.3	0.3	0.4
Net Sales to Working Capital 32	9.7	•	11.3	4.5	8.1	9.3	12.1	17.0	12.2
Coverage Ratio 33	4.7	2.8	6.7	5.5	4.7	3.7	3.8	3.1	4.4
Total Asset Turnover 34	2.4	•	4.5	2.5	2.7	2.3	2.7	2.6	2.1
Inventory Turnover 35	3.5	•	7.4	3.3	3.5	2.9	3.8	4.3	3.7
Receivables Turnover 36	25.8	•	43.6	29.2	33.1	46.4	23.8	18.4	17.0
Total Liabilities to Net Worth 37	2.3	•	1.8	1.3	2.3	2.8	3.0	3.3	3.3
Current Assets to Working Capital 38	3.0	•	1.6	1.4	2.5	3.3	3.6	4.8	3.9
Current Liabilities to Working Capital 39	2.0	•	0.6	0.4	1.5	2.3	2.6	3.8	2.9
Working Capital to Net Sales 40	0.1	•	0.1	0.2	0.1	0.1	0.1	0.1	0.1
Inventory to Working Capital 41	2.1	•	1.0	1.0	1.9	2.5	2.6	3.4	2.5
Total Receipts to Cash Flow 42	9.4	7.5	8.1	9.1	12.3	14.0	16.9	18.6	11.6
Cost of Goods to Cash Flow 43	6.8	4.9	5.3	6.4	9.3	11.1	13.7	15.2	8.6
Cash Flow to Total Debt 44	0.4	•	0.9	0.5	0.3	0.2	0.2	0.2	0.2

Selected Financial Factors (in Percentages)

	•	•	•	•	•	•	•	•	•
Debt Ratio 45	69.4	•	64.4	55.6	69.7	73.7	74.8	76.7	76.7
Return on Total Assets 46	10.7	•	21.6	11.7	10.5	7.9	8.0	6.8	9.0
Return on Equity Before Income Taxes 47	27.6	•	51.5	21.7	27.3	21.8	23.3	19.7	30.0
Return on Equity After Income Taxes 48	23.9	•	50.6	20.7	26.3	19.9	20.8	17.7	28.1
Profit Margin (Before Income Tax) 49	3.5	5.6	4.1	3.9	3.0	2.5	2.2	1.7	3.4
Profit Margin (After Income Tax) 50	3.0	5.3	4.0	3.7	2.9	2.3	2.0	1.6	3.1

Table I

Corporations with and without Net Income

FURNITURE AND HOME FURNISHINGS STORES

MONEY AMOUNTS AND SIZE OF ASSETS IN THOUSANDS OF DOLLARS

Item Description for Accounting Period 7/03 Through 6/04	Total	Zero Assets	Under 500	500 to 1,000	1,000 to 5,000	5,000 to 10,000	10,000 to 25,000	25,000 to 50,000	50,000 to 100,000	100,000 to 250,000	250,000 to 500,000	500,000 to 2,500,000	2,500,000 and over
Number of Enterprises **1**	38666	2895	28607	3599	3084	228	166	37	19	20	3	9	•
Revenues ($ in Thousands)													
Net Sales **2**	73932551	442587	14644919	6788080	13257012	3868712	6676003	3434810	3061770	6776768	1958489	13023401	•
Interest **3**	271416	2	4198	17853	35298	6848	7054	7361	24684	50653	47437	70027	•
Rents **4**	36173	0	1751	605	6092	4494	2455	661	382	4527	2095	13111	•
Royalties **5**	71273	0	0	0	222	0	20	14	0	3890	0	67127	•
Other Portfolio Income **6**	114169	0	30383	11286	11892	2633	8697	1082	1387	5280	33308	8221	•
Other Receipts **7**	888858	5708	45405	47967	86373	54096	107730	73251	28775	138433	24916	276205	•
Total Receipts **8**	75314440	448297	14726656	6865791	13396889	3936783	6801959	3517179	3116998	6979551	2066245	13458092	•
Average Total Receipts **9**	1948	155	515	1908	4344	17267	40976	95059	164053	348978	688748	1495344	•
Operating Costs/Operating Income (%)													
Cost of Operations **10**	59.1	58.0	62.0	61.0	63.0	60.4	62.4	58.4	59.3	55.1	58.9	51.1	•
Salaries and Wages **11**	12.2	12.1	7.9	11.5	11.9	13.5	13.0	14.7	14.1	13.2	13.9	14.7	•
Taxes Paid **12**	2.3	1.8	2.2	3.0	2.2	1.9	1.9	2.2	2.0	2.3	2.4	2.8	•
Interest Paid **13**	0.7	0.6	0.5	0.6	0.7	0.4	0.6	0.5	1.1	0.9	0.5	0.9	•
Depreciation **14**	1.6	2.7	0.8	0.9	1.1	1.1	1.4	1.7	1.3	1.8	2.8	3.3	•
Amortization and Depletion **15**	0.2	0.3	0.1	0.0	0.1	0.1	0.0	0.1	0.4	0.6	0.0	0.4	•
Pensions and Other Deferred Comp. **16**	0.2	0.0	0.0	0.2	0.2	0.2	0.2	0.1	0.2	0.2	0.3	0.3	•
Employee Benefits **17**	0.9	0.7	0.5	1.2	0.7	0.6	0.9	1.1	0.5	0.9	2.3	1.6	•
Advertising **18**	4.1	2.5	2.9	4.0	3.8	4.3	4.8	4.1	5.0	7.0	6.0	3.4	•
Other Expenses **19**	16.1	26.2	17.2	12.9	13.9	16.2	13.0	16.3	14.8	18.2	12.3	19.7	•
Officers' Compensation **20**	2.7	2.5	5.3	4.4	3.2	2.5	1.4	0.9	0.8	0.7	1.0	1.4	•
Operating Margin **21**	•	0.5	0.3	•	•	•	0.4	•	0.5	•	•	0.6	•
Operating Margin Before Officers' Comp. **22**	2.7	•	5.8	4.7	2.5	1.2	1.8	0.8	1.3	•	0.5	2.0	•

Selected Average Balance Sheet ($ in Thousands)

Net Receivables 23	124	0	19	144	333	935	2895	5482	11778	19340	76623	110524
Inventories 24	325	0	57	304	916	3148	5208	14113	23654	43204	149144	349970
Net Property, Plant and Equipment 25	209	0	25	121	347	1395	2971	8975	16167	45506	115757	350623
Total Assets 26	948	0	132	713	1923	6399	15057	35520	73950	160032	410440	1472757
Notes and Loans Payable 27	255	0	68	251	550	2325	3746	8862	21587	49436	67986	246503
All Other Liabilities 28	385	0	41	203	663	3410	5908	14126	25512	56960	105509	744031
Net Worth 29	308	0	23	259	709	665	5403	12532	26852	53636	236945	482223

Selected Financial Ratios (Times to 1)

Current Ratio 30	1.6	•	2.0	2.4	1.9	1.1	1.5	1.4	1.4	1.4	2.5	1.5
Quick Ratio 31	0.6	•	0.8	1.0	0.6	0.4	0.6	0.5	0.6	0.6	1.0	0.5
Net Sales to Working Capital 32	8.2	•	11.1	5.8	6.4	31.1	11.2	15.3	13.6	11.4	4.3	5.7
Coverage Ratio 33	3.6	•	3.0	3.4	1.5	1.9	5.0	6.0	3.1	3.2	11.6	5.3
Total Asset Turnover 34	2.0	•	3.9	2.6	2.2	2.7	2.7	2.6	2.2	2.1	1.6	1.0
Inventory Turnover 35	3.5	•	5.6	3.8	3.0	3.3	4.8	3.8	4.0	4.3	2.6	2.1
Receivables Turnover 36	15.5	•	26.5	12.9	11.0	14.5	14.1	15.3	12.8	19.7	7.1	20.0
Total Liabilities to Net Worth 37	2.1	•	4.7	1.8	1.7	8.6	1.8	1.8	1.8	2.0	0.7	2.1
Current Assets to Working Capital 38	2.6	•	2.0	1.7	2.2	8.4	3.0	3.8	3.5	3.3	1.7	3.0
Current Liabilities to Working Capital 39	1.6	•	1.0	0.7	1.2	7.4	2.0	2.8	2.5	2.3	0.7	2.0
Working Capital to Net Sales 40	0.1	•	0.1	0.2	0.2	0.0	0.1	0.1	0.1	0.1	0.2	0.2
Inventory to Working Capital 41	1.4	•	1.2	0.9	1.3	5.2	1.6	2.1	1.9	1.7	0.9	1.5
Total Receipts to Cash Flow 42	8.7	8.2	9.2	10.2	12.0	10.0	9.8	8.1	9.1	7.2	6.6	6.5
Cost of Goods to Cash Flow 43	5.1	4.7	5.7	6.2	7.6	6.0	6.1	4.8	5.4	4.0	3.9	3.3
Cash Flow to Total Debt 44	0.3	•	0.5	0.4	0.3	0.3	0.4	0.5	0.4	0.4	0.6	0.2

Selected Financial Factors (in Percentages)

Debt Ratio 45	67.5	•	82.5	63.7	63.1	89.6	64.1	64.7	63.7	66.5	42.3	67.3
Return on Total Assets 46	5.0	•	6.3	5.4	2.5	2.3	7.4	7.2	7.3	6.2	8.8	4.7
Return on Equity Before Income Taxes 47	11.2	•	24.2	10.5	2.3	10.3	16.6	17.0	13.4	12.6	14.0	11.5
Return on Equity After Income Taxes 48	7.6	•	22.7	10.0	0.9	7.0	15.6	15.2	12.4	9.7	10.7	4.8
Profit Margin (Before Income Tax) 49	1.8	•	1.1	1.4	0.4	0.4	2.2	2.3	2.2	2.0	5.1	3.8
Profit Margin (After Income Tax) 50	1.2	•	1.0	1.4	0.1	0.3	2.1	2.1	2.1	1.5	3.9	1.6

Table II
Corporations with Net Income

FURNITURE AND HOME FURNISHINGS STORES

MONEY AMOUNTS AND SIZE OF ASSETS IN THOUSANDS OF DOLLARS

Item Description for Accounting Period 7/03 Through 6/04	Total	Zero Assets	Under 500	500 to 1,000	1,000 to 5,000	5,000 to 10,000	10,000 to 25,000	25,000 to 50,000	50,000 to 100,000	100,000 to 250,000	250,000 to 500,000	500,000 to 2,500,000	2,500,000 and over
Number of Enterprises 1	19211	1093	13622	2107	2035	171	117	30	12	12	·	·	·
Revenues ($ in Thousands)													
Net Sales 2	55475514	302003	9346317	4672335	9450263	3174368	4929891	2932194	2332883	3683536			
Interest 3	233506	0	3130	8823	25056	2205	2928	7182	21222	46069			
Rents 4	28042	0	1751	0	1575	4120	1277	323	269	3521			
Royalties 5	67141	0	0	0	0	0	0	14	0	0			
Other Portfolio Income 6	87735	0	30055	1679	2860	1712	2883	1056	1377	4582			
Other Receipts 7	657534	5706	25334	20558	58210	46732	85037	70467	23299	96756			
Total Receipts 8	56549472	307709	9406587	4703395	9537964	3229137	5022016	3011236	2379050	3834464			
Average Total Receipts 9	2944	282	691	2232	4687	18884	42923	100375	198254	319539			
Operating Costs/Operating Income (%)													
Cost of Operations 10	57.9	55.8	60.9	60.7	61.1	59.8	61.7	57.4	62.3	52.5			
Salaries and Wages 11	12.4	16.2	7.0	11.1	12.4	13.8	12.9	14.3	14.6	14.5			
Taxes Paid 12	2.3	1.1	2.1	3.3	2.1	1.8	1.8	2.2	2.0	2.1			
Interest Paid 13	0.6	0.1	0.5	0.6	0.5	0.4	0.3	0.4	0.5	0.5			
Depreciation 14	1.7	1.9	0.8	0.9	1.1	0.9	1.0	1.7	1.1	1.7			
Amortization and Depletion 15	0.1	0.1	0.2	0.0	0.1	0.0	0.0	0.1	0.0	0.0			
Pensions and Other Deferred Comp. 16	0.2	·	0.1	0.3	0.2	0.2	0.2	0.2	0.2	0.3			
Employee Benefits 17	0.9	0.5	0.4	1.2	0.4	0.6	0.8	1.0	0.5	1.0			
Advertising 18	4.0	2.8	3.2	3.8	3.7	4.1	5.0	4.4	4.1	6.4			
Other Expenses 19	14.4	16.6	14.1	11.4	12.9	15.7	12.4	16.5	11.9	18.1			
Officers' Compensation 20	2.6	1.1	5.7	3.7	3.3	2.3	1.5	0.9	0.8	0.8			
Operating Margin 21	2.9	3.7	5.0	2.9	2.3	0.5	2.4	0.8	2.0	2.0			
Operating Margin Before Officers' Comp. 22	5.5	4.8	10.8	6.6	5.6	2.8	3.8	1.7	2.8	2.8			

Selected Average Balance Sheet ($ in Thousands)

Net Receivables 23	194	0	19	193	333	956	3007	5531	14023	26016
Inventories 24	483	0	58	312	945	2945	5353	14276	33957	35046
Net Property, Plant and Equipment 25	338	0	34	157	342	1218	2684	8380	19450	44160
Total Assets 26	1420	0	160	750	1916	6205	14973	35469	77478	152511
Notes and Loans Payable 27	329	0	62	199	468	1955	3051	7648	23240	42921
All Other Liabilities 28	510	0	51	198	600	3021	5804	14654	24773	45717
Net Worth 29	581	0	48	352	848	1229	6118	13167	29464	63873

Selected Financial Ratios (Times to 1)

Current Ratio 30	1.7	•	1.9	2.4	2.2	1.0	1.6	1.4	1.6	1.7
Quick Ratio 31	0.6	•	0.7	1.1	0.7	0.3	0.7	0.5	0.5	0.9
Net Sales to Working Capital 32	7.9	•	13.8	6.7	6.0	97.6	10.2	14.9	10.0	8.0
Coverage Ratio 33	9.7	53.8	11.6	6.7	7.6	7.3	13.1	10.6	8.7	12.9
Total Asset Turnover 34	2.0	•	4.3	3.0	2.4	3.0	2.8	2.8	2.5	2.0
Inventory Turnover 35	3.5	•	7.2	4.3	3.0	3.8	4.9	3.9	3.6	4.6
Receivables Turnover 36	15.3	•	34.3	12.8	10.7	16.8	13.7	18.6	11.8	23.6
Total Liabilities to Net Worth 37	1.4	•	2.4	1.1	1.3	4.0	1.4	1.7	1.6	1.4
Current Assets to Working Capital 38	2.5	•	2.2	1.7	1.9	24.9	2.7	3.6	2.5	2.5
Current Liabilities to Working Capital 39	1.5	•	1.2	0.7	0.9	23.9	1.7	2.6	1.5	1.5
Working Capital to Net Sales 40	0.1	•	0.1	0.1	0.2	0.0	0.1	0.1	0.1	0.1
Inventory to Working Capital 41	1.3	•	1.2	0.9	1.1	15.5	1.4	2.1	1.6	0.9
Total Receipts to Cash Flow 42	7.4	6.6	7.1	9.1	9.4	8.4	8.5	7.3	8.9	5.1
Cost of Goods to Cash Flow 43	4.3	3.7	4.3	5.5	5.8	5.0	5.2	4.2	5.5	2.7
Cash Flow to Total Debt 44	0.5	•	0.9	0.6	0.5	0.4	0.6	0.6	0.5	0.7

Selected Financial Factors (in Percentages)

Debt Ratio 45	59.1	•	70.3	53.0	55.7	80.2	59.1	62.9	62.0	58.1
Return on Total Assets 46	11.0	•	26.6	12.2	9.0	7.6	12.9	10.6	11.2	13.1
Return on Equity Before Income Taxes 47	24.1	•	81.9	22.1	17.7	33.2	29.1	25.9	26.0	28.8
Return on Equity After Income Taxes 48	20.3	•	80.3	21.4	15.9	30.8	27.8	23.9	24.4	24.7
Profit Margin (Before Income Tax) 49	4.8	5.6	5.7	3.5	3.2	2.2	4.2	3.5	3.9	6.0
Profit Margin (After Income Tax) 50	4.1	5.5	5.6	3.4	2.9	2.0	4.0	3.2	3.7	5.1

Table I

Corporations with and without Net Income

ELECTRONICS AND APPLIANCE STORES

MONEY AMOUNTS AND SIZE OF ASSETS IN THOUSANDS OF DOLLARS

Item Description for Accounting Period 7/03 Through 6/04	Total	Zero Assets	Under 500	500 to 1,000	1,000 to 5,000	5,000 to 10,000	10,000 to 25,000	25,000 to 50,000	50,000 to 100,000	100,000 to 250,000	250,000 to 500,000	500,000 to 2,500,000	2,500,000 and over
Number of Enterprises **1**	34785	4939	24553	2324	2532	205	137	34	19	22	8	11	•
Revenues ($ in Thousands)													
Net Sales **2**	107286940	956978	11958043	3947358	15205422	3600746	5716550	2655747	3002887	5364965	6387187	48491057	•
Interest **3**	642800	1258	2217	4373	4699	2417	3272	5899	3040	42981	10385	562259	•
Rents **4**	66697	559	4043	4790	3531	113	4181	0	180	199	5612	43489	•
Royalties **5**	138211	0	0	0	43751	0	4134	3298	347	45094	27064	14524	•
Other Portfolio Income **6**	257145	7707	15715	13887	16315	7751	6016	820	568	61568	16399	110401	•
Other Receipts **7**	1414532	34528	85189	45165	164608	18299	61420	34575	28483	48482	82486	811295	•
Total Receipts **8**	109806325	1001030	12065207	4015573	15438326	3629326	5795573	2700339	3035505	5563289	6529133	50033025	•
Average Total Receipts **9**	3157	203	491	1728	6097	17704	42303	79422	159763	252877	816142	4548457	•
Operating Costs/Operating Income (%)													
Cost of Operations **10**	69.2	65.8	50.1	64.7	72.3	62.8	71.3	69.8	74.7	66.6	74.8	72.9	•
Salaries and Wages **11**	11.6	13.2	16.6	13.8	11.2	14.2	11.7	14.4	10.8	15.4	11.5	9.7	•
Taxes Paid **12**	1.8	1.9	2.9	2.1	1.5	1.6	1.5	1.5	1.3	1.8	1.1	1.8	•
Interest Paid **13**	0.6	0.5	0.5	0.4	0.6	0.6	0.4	0.5	0.4	1.3	0.7	0.5	•
Depreciation **14**	1.5	1.5	1.2	1.5	0.9	1.5	1.1	0.9	2.1	2.9	1.9	1.6	•
Amortization and Depletion **15**	0.2	0.2	0.1	0.2	0.0	0.4	0.2	0.5	0.3	0.7	0.8	0.1	•
Pensions and Other Deferred Comp. **16**	0.1	0.0	0.2	0.3	0.1	0.5	0.2	0.2	0.1	0.1	0.1	0.1	•
Employee Benefits **17**	0.6	1.4	0.9	1.0	0.6	1.2	0.7	1.0	0.7	0.9	0.3	0.4	•
Advertising **18**	2.1	4.2	1.9	1.9	1.9	2.1	1.4	0.9	1.6	2.0	2.0	2.4	•
Other Expenses **19**	11.4	18.5	18.7	11.9	8.5	8.5	8.8	11.9	6.5	12.5	10.2	11.2	•
Officers' Compensation **20**	1.8	0.8	6.9	5.4	2.5	3.3	2.0	1.9	1.0	0.9	1.0	0.1	•
Operating Margin **21**	•	•	0.0	•	•	3.2	0.7	•	0.5	•	•	•	•
Operating Margin Before Officers' Comp. **22**	0.8	•	6.9	2.1	2.3	6.5	2.7	•	1.5	•	•	•	•

Selected Average Balance Sheet ($ in Thousands)

Net Receivables 23	206	0	17	134	488	995	4408	11375	16097	48477	83600	177535
Inventories 24	270	0	39	150	523	1183	2627	3313	12864	19861	106821	410214
Net Property, Plant and Equipment 25	206	0	20	147	296	632	1704	2370	11629	22086	71893	349599
Total Assets 26	1252	0	124	676	1926	6630	15089	33516	67067	158976	363961	1982845
Notes and Loans Payable 27	237	0	69	207	592	1943	4293	11458	11914	15706	89426	173122
All Other Liabilities 28	618	0	65	275	884	2361	7491	16719	27183	93686	226374	960386
Net Worth 29	397	0	-10	194	449	2327	3305	5339	27970	49584	48162	849338

Selected Financial Ratios (Times to 1)

Current Ratio 30	1.4	•	1.2	1.6	1.4	2.0	1.3	1.4	1.3	1.2	1.1	1.5
Quick Ratio 31	0.7	•	0.6	1.0	0.8	1.1	0.8	1.0	0.9	0.8	0.6	0.7
Net Sales to Working Capital 32	13.2	•	35.6	10.2	13.4	7.5	18.0	12.4	13.9	15.7	24.2	11.0
Coverage Ratio 33	3.5	•	2.8	•	3.2	7.7	6.2	•	5.0	•	•	5.8
Total Asset Turnover 34	2.5	•	3.9	2.5	3.1	2.6	2.8	2.3	2.4	1.5	2.2	2.2
Inventory Turnover 35	7.9	•	6.2	7.3	8.3	9.3	11.3	16.5	9.2	8.2	5.6	7.8
Receivables Turnover 36	14.9	•	27.7	13.6	12.7	9.6	9.2	8.0	8.1	6.8	10.6	22.2
Total Liabilities to Net Worth 37	2.2	•	•	2.5	3.3	1.8	3.6	5.3	1.4	2.2	6.6	1.3
Current Assets to Working Capital 38	3.5	•	6.2	2.7	3.3	2.0	4.8	3.8	3.9	7.1	7.8	3.0
Current Liabilities to Working Capital 39	2.5	•	5.2	1.7	2.3	1.0	3.8	2.8	2.9	6.1	6.8	2.0
Working Capital to Net Sales 40	0.1	•	0.0	0.1	0.1	0.1	0.1	0.1	0.1	0.1	0.0	0.1
Inventory to Working Capital 41	1.3	•	2.9	1.0	1.3	0.6	1.2	0.6	1.1	1.0	3.1	1.3
Total Receipts to Cash Flow 42	10.7	13.6	6.7	15.1	13.0	9.8	11.3	13.6	16.1	15.4	30.7	9.9
Cost of Goods to Cash Flow 43	7.4	8.9	3.3	9.8	9.4	6.1	8.0	9.5	12.0	10.3	23.0	7.2
Cash Flow to Total Debt 44	0.3	•	0.5	0.2	0.3	0.4	0.3	0.2	0.3	0.1	0.1	0.4

Selected Financial Factors (in Percentages)

Debt Ratio 45	68.3	•	108.2	71.3	76.7	64.9	78.1	84.1	58.3	68.8	86.8	57.2
Return on Total Assets 46	4.8	•	5.6	•	5.9	12.6	6.7	•	4.7	•	•	6.5
Return on Equity Before Income Taxes 47	10.8	•	•	•	17.2	31.1	25.8	•	9.0	•	•	12.5
Return on Equity After Income Taxes 48	6.9	•	•	•	15.0	29.9	22.4	•	8.1	•	•	7.8
Profit Margin (Before Income Tax) 49	1.4	•	0.9	•	1.3	4.1	2.0	•	1.6	•	•	2.4
Profit Margin (After Income Tax) 50	0.9	•	0.9	•	1.1	4.0	1.8	•	1.4	•	•	1.5

Table II

Corporations with Net Income

Electronics and Appliance Stores

Money Amounts and Size of Assets in Thousands of Dollars

Item Description for Accounting Period 7/03 Through 6/04	Total	Zero Assets	Under 500	500 to 1,000	1,000 to 5,000	5,000 to 10,000	10,000 to 25,000	25,000 to 50,000	50,000 to 100,000	100,000 to 250,000	250,000 to 500,000	500,000 to 2,500,000	2,500,000 and over
Number of Enterprises **1**	15777	1380	11026	1168	1885	166	100	22	7	11	•	•	•
Revenues ($ in Thousands)													
Net Sales **2**	87829229	256497	6845001	1828259	12131511	3162578	4624383	2310285	1688257	3833828	•	•	•
Interest **3**	577125	1178	1044	4070	2872	827	2263	2430	586	26533	•	•	•
Rents **4**	55774	0	389	3801	3531	0	3530	0	180	57	•	•	•
Royalties **5**	24662	0	0	0	0	0	4134	3298	0	2707	•	•	•
Other Portfolio Income **6**	148931	6545	84	1033	10187	2656	3476	95	99	511	•	•	•
Other Receipts **7**	1206002	5759	65238	30316	147729	17614	26733	19004	24399	42153	•	•	•
Total Receipts **8**	89841723	269979	6911756	1867479	12295830	3183675	4664519	2335112	1713521	3905789	•	•	•
Average Total Receipts **9**	5694	196	627	1599	6523	19179	46645	106141	244789	355072	•	•	•
Operating Costs/Operating Income (%)													
Cost of Operations **10**	70.1	58.5	41.2	56.3	71.9	68.1	71.4	73.7	79.1	70.2	•	•	•
Salaries and Wages **11**	10.4	9.2	17.6	16.3	10.6	11.3	10.4	10.8	7.9	10.3	•	•	•
Taxes Paid **12**	1.7	1.9	2.7	2.4	1.5	1.4	1.4	1.2	0.9	1.2	•	•	•
Interest Paid **13**	0.5	0.5	0.5	0.5	0.6	0.5	0.3	0.3	0.2	1.1	•	•	•
Depreciation **14**	1.4	2.3	1.1	1.8	0.9	1.2	1.0	0.6	0.7	3.0	•	•	•
Amortization and Depletion **15**	0.1	0.0	0.1	0.2	0.0	0.4	0.1	0.1	0.0	0.5	•	•	•
Pensions and Other Deferred Comp. **16**	0.1	•	0.3	0.7	0.1	0.5	0.2	0.2	0.1	0.1	•	•	•
Employee Benefits **17**	0.5	0.1	1.0	0.9	0.5	1.1	0.6	0.5	0.5	0.5	•	•	•
Advertising **18**	2.1	0.6	1.2	1.2	2.1	1.7	1.6	0.8	1.0	2.2	•	•	•
Other Expenses **19**	10.2	16.7	18.6	11.6	7.7	6.1	7.7	7.0	4.5	7.1	•	•	•
Officers' Compensation **20**	1.5	1.3	8.3	6.0	2.3	2.4	2.0	1.5	0.9	0.4	•	•	•
Operating Margin **21**	1.4	8.9	7.5	2.0	1.9	5.2	3.3	3.3	4.4	3.3	•	•	•
Operating Margin Before Officers' Comp. **22**	2.8	10.2	15.9	8.0	4.2	7.7	5.3	4.8	5.3	3.7	•	•	•

Selected Average Balance Sheet ($ in Thousands)

Net Receivables 23	308	0	14	181	484	930	4457	14406	12443	35815
Inventories 24	489	0	43	186	516	1215	3115	4511	18561	21257
Net Property, Plant and Equipment 25	362	0	25	88	319	638	1743	2594	16052	29017
Total Assets 26	2025	0	148	700	1985	6607	15165	34301	75891	157138
Notes and Loans Payable 27	311	0	54	234	536	2144	2506	5514	10254	20196
All Other Liabilities 28	913	0	72	307	872	1710	6877	19294	30455	76019
Net Worth 29	801	0	23	159	577	2753	5782	9493	35182	60924

Selected Financial Ratios (Times to 1)

Current Ratio 30	1.6	•	1.1	1.7	1.6	2.3	1.6	1.2	1.6	1.3
Quick Ratio 31	0.8	•	0.6	1.1	0.9	1.1	1.0	0.9	0.9	0.8
Net Sales to Working Capital 32	10.6	•	64.5	7.1	11.9	7.3	10.1	21.2	11.6	15.7
Coverage Ratio 33	8.5	31.6	19.7	8.7	6.6	12.1	14.0	15.3	31.6	5.8
Total Asset Turnover 34	2.7	•	4.2	2.2	3.2	2.9	3.0	3.1	3.2	2.2
Inventory Turnover 35	8.0	•	5.9	4.7	9.0	10.7	10.6	17.1	10.3	11.5
Receivables Turnover 36	19.2	•	32.1	9.6	14.0	15.7	10.2	10.3	38.8	13.3
Total Liabilities to Net Worth 37	1.5	•	5.5	3.4	2.4	1.4	1.6	2.6	1.2	1.6
Current Assets to Working Capital 38	2.7	•	9.5	2.3	2.8	1.7	2.6	5.4	2.7	4.6
Current Liabilities to Working Capital 39	1.7	•	8.5	1.3	1.8	0.7	1.6	4.4	1.7	3.6
Working Capital to Net Sales 40	0.1	•	0.0	0.1	0.1	0.1	0.1	0.0	0.1	0.1
Inventory to Working Capital 41	1.1	•	3.9	0.8	1.1	0.6	0.7	1.1	0.9	1.0
Total Receipts to Cash Flow 42	9.3	4.5	4.4	8.4	11.0	9.7	9.8	10.8	10.9	9.6
Cost of Goods to Cash Flow 43	6.5	2.6	1.8	4.7	6.6	6.6	7.0	8.0	8.6	6.7
Cash Flow to Total Debt 44	0.5	•	1.1	0.3	0.4	0.5	0.5	0.4	0.5	0.4

Selected Financial Factors (in Percentages)

Debt Ratio 45	60.5	•	84.7	77.2	70.9	58.3	61.9	72.3	53.6	61.2
Return on Total Assets 46	11.3	•	37.5	10.5	12.4	18.6	13.6	14.3	19.2	13.9
Return on Equity Before Income Taxes 47	25.2	•	232.3	40.9	36.2	40.9	33.2	48.2	40.2	29.6
Return on Equity After Income Taxes 48	21.0	•	231.4	37.9	33.9	39.7	30.6	42.4	38.3	27.0
Profit Margin (Before Income Tax) 49	3.6	14.2	8.5	4.2	3.2	5.9	4.2	4.4	5.9	5.2
Profit Margin (After Income Tax) 50	3.0	14.0	8.5	3.9	3.0	5.7	3.8	3.8	5.6	4.7

Table I

Corporations with and without Net Income

HOMES CENTERS; PAINT AND WALLPAPER STORES

MONEY AMOUNTS AND SIZE OF ASSETS IN THOUSANDS OF DOLLARS

Item Description for Accounting Period 7/03 Through 6/04	Total	Zero Assets	Under 500	500 to 1,000	1,000 to 5,000	5,000 to 10,000	10,000 to 25,000	25,000 to 50,000	50,000 to 100,000	100,000 to 250,000	250,000 to 500,000	500,000 to 2,500,000	2,500,000 and over
Number of Enterprises **1**	3678	•	2566	561	457	•	31	11	10	•	•	•	3
Revenues ($ in Thousands)													
Net Sales **2**	111159721	•	2300673	976556	2406323	•	1068001	875796	2593305	•	•	•	100385286
Interest **3**	476252	•	800	2188	2704	•	2407	266	32965	•	•	•	433541
Rents **4**	20218	•	0	1885	1458	•	247	84	3389	•	•	•	12142
Royalties **5**	2445678	•	0	0	0	•	1307	0	0	•	•	•	2444371
Other Portfolio Income **6**	108384	•	23	89	1672	•	12455	2057	12962	•	•	•	78734
Other Receipts **7**	1210218	•	14212	2538	5886	•	14408	7892	101978	•	•	•	1064750
Total Receipts **8**	115420471	•	2315708	983256	2418043	•	1098825	886095	2744599	•	•	•	104418824
Average Total Receipts **9**	31381	•	902	1753	5291	•	35446	80554	274460	•	•	•	34806275
Operating Costs/Operating Income (%)													
Cost of Operations **10**	68.4	•	63.9	69.9	67.4	•	71.9	72.5	70.2	•	•	•	68.4
Salaries and Wages **11**	11.8	•	10.9	10.9	11.2	•	11.7	12.6	13.5	•	•	•	11.8
Taxes Paid **12**	1.9	•	5.0	2.4	2.5	•	1.6	1.6	1.4	•	•	•	1.9
Interest Paid **13**	0.7	•	0.3	1.0	0.5	•	1.2	0.4	1.2	•	•	•	0.7
Depreciation **14**	2.9	•	0.5	1.1	1.0	•	1.4	1.6	2.1	•	•	•	3.1
Amortization and Depletion **15**	0.0	•	0.0	0.2	0.1	•	0.0	0.0	0.2	•	•	•	0.0
Pensions and Other Deferred Comp. **16**	0.1	•	0.0	0.1	0.3	•	0.2	0.2	0.2	•	•	•	0.1
Employee Benefits **17**	0.4	•	0.5	0.4	1.0	•	0.9	1.2	1.7	•	•	•	0.3
Advertising **18**	0.4	•	0.9	1.0	0.7	•	1.2	0.8	0.5	•	•	•	0.3
Other Expenses **19**	9.7	•	13.1	11.2	8.8	•	8.7	7.9	11.1	•	•	•	9.6
Officers' Compensation **20**	0.3	•	3.2	2.3	3.6	•	1.2	0.9	0.4	•	•	•	0.1
Operating Margin **21**	3.4	•	1.5	•	3.0	•	•	0.4	•	•	•	•	3.7
Operating Margin Before Officers' Comp. **22**	3.7	•	4.7	1.6	6.6	•	1.1	1.3	3.8	•	•	•	3.8

Selected Average Balance Sheet ($ in Thousands)

Net Receivables 23	892	46	134	586	2615	6673	39626	746530
Inventories 24	4050	88	222	748	5622	10796	28598	4502835
Net Property, Plant and Equipment 25	7443	10	219	193	3274	7106	36642	8847860
Total Assets 26	29403	171	690	1912	14418	31091	184120	34526736
Notes and Loans Payable 27	4199	61	325	490	5592	7603	50473	4677982
All Other Liabilities 28	4950	76	192	309	2647	5727	52525	5687539
Net Worth 29	20254	34	172	1113	6179	17760	81122	24161215

Selected Financial Ratios (Times to 1)

Current Ratio 30	1.4	1.9	1.7	4.6	2.0	2.6	1.9	1.3
Quick Ratio 31	0.5	0.7	0.6	2.5	0.7	1.1	1.2	0.4
Net Sales to Working Capital 32	15.8	12.6	9.7	4.1	7.5	6.8	5.5	18.7
Coverage Ratio 33	11.3	7.6	1.0	8.4	3.2	4.6	3.8	12.1
Total Asset Turnover 34	1.0	5.2	2.5	2.8	2.4	2.6	1.4	1.0
Inventory Turnover 35	5.1	6.5	5.5	4.8	4.4	5.3	6.4	5.1
Receivables Turnover 36	36.9	23.3	18.4	9.6	13.4	12.9	9.0	47.1
Total Liabilities to Net Worth 37	0.5	4.0	3.0	0.7	1.3	0.8	1.3	0.4
Current Assets to Working Capital 38	3.4	2.2	2.4	1.3	2.0	1.6	2.1	3.9
Current Liabilities to Working Capital 39	2.4	1.2	1.4	0.3	1.0	0.6	1.1	2.9
Working Capital to Net Sales 40	0.1	0.1	0.1	0.2	0.1	0.1	0.2	0.1
Inventory to Working Capital 41	2.2	1.3	1.5	0.5	1.2	0.9	0.7	2.6
Total Receipts to Cash Flow 42	6.8	10.7	13.6	10.0	11.3	15.0	8.6	6.5
Cost of Goods to Cash Flow 43	4.7	6.8	9.5	6.7	8.1	10.8	6.1	4.5
Cash Flow to Total Debt 44	0.5	0.6	0.2	0.7	0.4	0.4	0.3	0.5

Selected Financial Factors (in Percentages)

Debt Ratio 45	31.1	80.1	75.0	41.8	57.1	42.9	55.9	30.0
Return on Total Assets 46	8.1	12.8	2.7	10.8	9.5	5.1	6.5	8.2
Return on Equity Before Income Taxes 47	10.8	55.7	0.3	16.3	15.2	7.0	10.9	10.7
Return on Equity After Income Taxes 48	7.4	54.2		15.6	14.8	6.0	7.9	7.3
Profit Margin (Before Income Tax) 49	7.2	2.1	0.0	3.5	2.7	1.6	3.4	7.7
Profit Margin (After Income Tax) 50	4.9	2.1		3.3	2.6	1.3	2.5	5.2

Table II
Corporations with Net Income

HOMES CENTERS; PAINT AND WALLPAPER STORES

MONEY AMOUNTS AND SIZE OF ASSETS IN THOUSANDS OF DOLLARS

Item Description for Accounting Period 7/03 Through 6/04	Total	Zero Assets	Under 500	500 to 1,000	1,000 to 5,000	5,000 to 10,000	10,000 to 25,000	25,000 to 50,000	50,000 to 100,000	100,000 to 250,000	250,000 to 500,000	500,000 to 2,500,000	2,500,000 and over
Number of Enterprises **1**	2883	•	2095	289	427	28	24	•	•	•	•	•	3
Revenues ($ in Thousands)													
Net Sales **2**	109781609	•	2024556	467637	2258454	399964	912083	•	•	•	•	•	100385286
Interest **3**	473709	•	800	2188	2603	1381	1574	•	•	•	•	•	433541
Rents **4**	19358	•	0	1874	1458	403	41	•	•	•	•	•	12142
Royalties **5**	2445678	•	0	0	0	0	1307	•	•	•	•	•	2444371
Other Portfolio Income **6**	107208	•	23	89	1670	393	11937	•	•	•	•	•	78734
Other Receipts **7**	1192349	•	13799	2162	1979	223	13751	•	•	•	•	•	1064750
Total Receipts **8**	114019911	•	2039178	473950	2266164	402364	940693	•	•	•	•	•	104418824
Average Total Receipts **9**	39549	•	973	1640	5307	14370	39196	•	•	•	•	•	34806275
Operating Costs/Operating Income (%)													
Cost of Operations **10**	68.4	•	64.1	75.0	67.3	71.8	72.0	•	•	•	•	•	68.4
Salaries and Wages **11**	11.8	•	10.1	9.7	10.9	12.0	11.9	•	•	•	•	•	11.8
Taxes Paid **12**	1.9	•	5.2	1.6	2.5	1.7	1.6	•	•	•	•	•	1.9
Interest Paid **13**	0.7	•	0.3	0.3	0.5	0.3	1.3	•	•	•	•	•	0.7
Depreciation **14**	2.9	•	0.5	0.9	1.0	1.7	1.3	•	•	•	•	•	3.1
Amortization and Depletion **15**	0.0	•	•	0.5	0.1	0.0	0.0	•	•	•	•	•	0.0
Pensions and Other Deferred Comp. **16**	0.1	•	0.1	0.2	0.4	0.5	0.2	•	•	•	•	•	0.1
Employee Benefits **17**	0.3	•	0.4	0.2	0.9	1.5	0.9	•	•	•	•	•	0.3
Advertising **18**	0.4	•	0.9	1.4	0.7	1.0	1.1	•	•	•	•	•	0.3
Other Expenses **19**	9.6	•	13.1	7.6	8.5	4.9	7.9	•	•	•	•	•	9.6
Officers' Compensation **20**	0.3	•	3.0	2.6	3.8	2.9	1.3	•	•	•	•	•	0.1
Operating Margin **21**	3.5	•	2.4	0.0	3.4	1.7	0.4	•	•	•	•	•	3.7
Operating Margin Before Officers' Comp. **22**	3.8	•	5.4	2.6	7.2	4.6	1.8	•	•	•	•	•	3.8

Selected Average Balance Sheet ($ in Thousands)

Net Receivables 23	1107	48	144	579	999	3062		746530
Inventories 24	5085	88	193	725	3425	5918		4502835
Net Property, Plant and Equipment 25	9460	10	241	205	1508	3275		8847860
Total Assets 26	37301	180	674	1953	6592	14245		34526736
Notes and Loans Payable 27	5244	65	224	523	1451	5908		4677982
All Other Liabilities 28	6267	81	101	309	1336	2536		5687539
Net Worth 29	25789	34	349	1121	3805	5801		24161215

Selected Financial Ratios (Times to 1)

Current Ratio 30	1.4	1.9	3.1	4.6	1.9	2.1		1.3
Quick Ratio 31	0.4	0.7	1.4	2.5	0.7	0.9		0.4
Net Sales to Working Capital 32	16.0	12.2	6.6	4.1	7.2	7.1		18.7
Coverage Ratio 33	11.6	11.2	5.2	8.5	8.2	3.8		12.1
Total Asset Turnover 34	1.0	5.4	2.4	2.7	2.2	2.7		1.0
Inventory Turnover 35	5.1	7.1	6.3	4.9	3.0	4.6		5.1
Receivables Turnover 36	37.7	24.4	22.4	9.9	8.7	12.6		47.1
Total Liabilities to Net Worth 37	0.4	4.4	0.9	0.7	0.7	1.5		0.4
Current Assets to Working Capital 38	3.4	2.1	1.5	1.3	2.1	1.9		3.9
Current Liabilities to Working Capital 39	2.4	1.1	0.5	0.3	1.1	0.9		2.9
Working Capital to Net Sales 40	0.1	0.1	0.2	0.2	0.1	0.1		0.1
Inventory to Working Capital 41	2.2	1.3	0.8	0.6	1.3	1.0		2.6
Total Receipts to Cash Flow 42	6.7	9.8	13.3	9.9	18.6	11.1		6.5
Cost of Goods to Cash Flow 43	4.6	6.3	10.0	6.6	13.3	8.0		4.5
Cash Flow to Total Debt 44	0.5	0.7	0.4	0.6	0.3	0.4		0.5

Selected Financial Factors (in Percentages)

Debt Ratio 45	30.9	81.3	48.2	42.6	42.3	59.3		30.0
Return on Total Assets 46	8.2	18.3	4.0	11.4	5.4	13.0		8.2
Return on Equity Before Income Taxes 47	10.8	89.4	6.3	17.6	8.2	23.5		10.7
Return on Equity After Income Taxes 48	7.4	87.6	5.8	16.9	5.4	22.9		7.3
Profit Margin (Before Income Tax) 49	7.3	3.1	1.4	3.7	2.2	3.6		7.7
Profit Margin (After Income Tax) 50	5.0	3.0	1.3	3.6	1.4	3.5		5.2

Table I

Corporations with and without Net Income

HARDWARE STORES

MONEY AMOUNTS AND SIZE OF ASSETS IN THOUSANDS OF DOLLARS

Item Description for Accounting Period 7/03 Through 6/04		Total	Zero Assets	Under 500	500 to 1,000	1,000 to 5,000	5,000 to 10,000	10,000 to 25,000	25,000 to 50,000	50,000 to 100,000	100,000 to 250,000	250,000 to 500,000	500,000 to 2,500,000	2,500,000 and over
Number of Enterprises	1	8786	1650	3430	1778	1732	137	46	14	•	•	•	•	•
Revenues ($ in Thousands)														
Net Sales	2	17061506	140178	2867859	2704754	6405503	1766004	1587887	1589321	•	•	•	•	•
Interest	3	19814	0	3994	4460	8422	706	1129	1103	•	•	•	•	•
Rents	4	12619	0	5588	1889	1645	0	1914	1583	•	•	•	•	•
Royalties	5	23	0	0	19	4	0	0	0					
Other Portfolio Income	6	28262	0	3416	14314	7160	1110	2055	210	•	•	•	•	•
Other Receipts	7	163481	9	20873	24135	61064	30462	12602	14333					
Total Receipts	8	17285705	140187	2901730	2749571	6483798	1798282	1605587	1606550					
Average Total Receipts	9	1967	85	846	1546	3744	13126	34904	114754	•	•	•	•	•
Operating Costs/Operating Income (%)														
Cost of Operations	10	63.9	65.1	59.1	64.2	64.0	58.9	69.7	71.3	•	•	•	•	•
Salaries and Wages	11	13.5	5.9	14.0	11.3	14.4	17.1	12.3	10.6	•	•	•	•	•
Taxes Paid	12	2.3	2.7	2.5	2.3	2.4	2.4	1.8	1.7	•	•	•	•	•
Interest Paid	13	0.7	0.9	0.7	0.6	1.0	0.3	0.5	0.5	•	•	•	•	•
Depreciation	14	1.6	1.1	1.8	1.7	1.6	1.8	1.2	1.2	•	•	•	•	•
Amortization and Depletion	15	0.0	0.0	0.0	0.0	0.1	0.0	0.0	0.0	•	•	•	•	•
Pensions and Other Deferred Comp.	16	0.3	0.0	0.2	0.2	0.3	0.3	0.5	0.4	•	•	•	•	•
Employee Benefits	17	1.1	0.1	1.3	0.9	1.0	1.1	1.2	1.3	•	•	•	•	•
Advertising	18	1.6	0.6	1.6	1.8	1.4	1.6	1.6	2.3	•	•	•	•	•
Other Expenses	19	11.4	30.1	15.1	12.2	10.7	10.0	7.8	9.4	•	•	•	•	•
Officers' Compensation	20	3.2	1.3	5.8	4.9	2.8	2.0	1.1	0.7	•	•	•	•	•
Operating Margin	21	0.4	•	•	•	0.3	4.5	2.4	0.6	•	•	•	•	•
Operating Margin Before Officers' Comp.	22	3.6	•	3.7	4.7	3.1	6.5	3.5	1.3	•	•	•	•	•

Selected Average Balance Sheet ($ in Thousands)

Net Receivables 23	106	0	41	105	212	672	2516	1675
Inventories 24	356	0	189	333	658	1792	5729	13567
Net Property, Plant and Equipment 25	186	0	37	105	376	2705	3706	9086
Total Assets 26	850	0	311	658	1764	6879	14293	41226
Notes and Loans Payable 27	307	0	177	215	783	607	3360	7865
All Other Liabilities 28	169	0	71	86	359	853	3207	14411
Net Worth 29	374	0	63	356	622	5419	7726	18951

Selected Financial Ratios (Times to 1)

Current Ratio 30	2.7	•	2.1	6.8	2.6	3.8	2.0	1.8
Quick Ratio 31	0.9	•	0.6	2.3	0.9	1.1	0.7	0.5
Net Sales to Working Capital 32	5.4	•	6.7	3.7	5.2	4.9	7.9	9.3
Coverage Ratio 33	3.4	•	•	3.4	2.6	19.2	8.6	4.7
Total Asset Turnover 34	2.3	•	2.7	2.3	2.1	1.9	2.4	2.8
Inventory Turnover 35	3.5	•	2.6	2.9	3.6	4.2	4.2	6.0
Receivables Turnover 36	18.9	•	21.3	14.5	19.2	15.4	14.3	79.2
Total Liabilities to Net Worth 37	1.3	•	3.9	0.8	1.8	0.3	0.9	1.2
Current Assets to Working Capital 38	1.6	•	1.9	1.2	1.6	1.4	2.0	2.2
Current Liabilities to Working Capital 39	0.6	•	0.9	0.2	0.6	0.4	1.0	1.2
Working Capital to Net Sales 40	0.2	•	0.1	0.3	0.2	0.2	0.1	0.1
Inventory to Working Capital 41	1.0	•	1.4	0.8	1.0	0.6	1.2	1.5
Total Receipts to Cash Flow 42	11.7	7.1	13.7	11.0	13.3	7.3	11.6	12.8
Cost of Goods to Cash Flow 43	7.5	4.6	8.1	7.1	8.5	4.3	8.1	9.2
Cash Flow to Total Debt 44	0.3	•	0.2	0.5	0.2	1.2	0.5	0.4

Selected Financial Factors (in Percentages)

Debt Ratio 45	56.0	•	79.6	45.9	64.8	21.2	45.9	54.0
Return on Total Assets 46	5.6	•	•	5.0	5.2	12.3	9.5	5.8
Return on Equity Before Income Taxes 47	8.9	•	•	6.5	9.1	14.8	15.6	9.8
Return on Equity After Income Taxes 48	8.0	•	•	6.1	7.7	14.7	14.5	7.9
Profit Margin (Before Income Tax) 49	1.7	•	•	1.5	1.5	6.2	3.5	1.6
Profit Margin (After Income Tax) 50	1.5	•	•	1.4	1.3	6.2	3.3	1.3

Table II
Corporations with Net Income

HARDWARE STORES

MONEY AMOUNTS AND SIZE OF ASSETS IN THOUSANDS OF DOLLARS

Item Description for Accounting Period 7/03 Through 6/04	Total	Zero Assets	Under 500	500 to 1,000	1,000 to 5,000	5,000 to 10,000	10,000 to 25,000	25,000 to 50,000	50,000 to 100,000	100,000 to 250,000	250,000 to 500,000	500,000 to 2,500,000	2,500,000 and over
Number of Enterprises **1**	5435	634	1879	1236	1498	•	39					•	•
Revenues ($ in Thousands)													
Net Sales **2**	13417867	42727	1356695	1835331	5509910	•	1395645	•	•	•	•	•	•
Interest **3**	13377	0	2148	1457	7015	•	948	•	•	•	•	•	•
Rents **4**	4914	0	3	617	1622	•	1089	•	•	•	•	•	•
Royalties **5**	4	0	0	0	4		0						
Other Portfolio Income **6**	26886	0	3151	13683	7129	•	1608	•	•	•	•	•	•
Other Receipts **7**	138197	0	16731	15522	50793	•	11258	•	•	•	•	•	•
Total Receipts **8**	13601245	42727	1378728	1866610	5576473	•	1410548	•	•	•	•	•	•
Average Total Receipts **9**	2503	67	734	1510	3723	•	36168	•	•	•	•	•	•
Operating Costs/Operating Income (%)													
Cost of Operations **10**	64.3	62.4	54.3	65.3	64.6	•	70.0	•	•	•	•	•	•
Salaries and Wages **11**	13.1	•	13.9	10.3	13.8	•	11.8	•	•	•	•	•	•
Taxes Paid **12**	2.2	0.4	2.4	2.1	2.5	•	1.7	•	•	•	•	•	•
Interest Paid **13**	0.6	0.1	0.9	0.5	0.8	•	0.4	•	•	•	•	•	•
Depreciation **14**	1.6	0.2	2.8	1.2	1.6	•	1.1	•	•	•	•	•	•
Amortization and Depletion **15**	0.0	•	0.0	0.0	0.1	•	0.0	•	•	•	•	•	•
Pensions and Other Deferred Comp. **16**	0.3	•	0.2	0.0	0.3	•	0.5	•	•	•	•	•	•
Employee Benefits **17**	0.9	•	1.1	0.7	0.8	•	1.2	•	•	•	•	•	•
Advertising **18**	1.6	0.3	2.1	1.7	1.4	•	1.4	•	•	•	•	•	•
Other Expenses **19**	10.2	26.9	16.2	11.7	9.4	•	7.3	•	•	•	•	•	•
Officers' Compensation **20**	2.9	•	5.5	4.8	3.0	•	1.0	•	•	•	•	•	•
Operating Margin **21**	2.1	9.7	0.8	1.6	1.6	•	3.4	•	•	•	•	•	•
Operating Margin Before Officers' Comp. **22**	5.0	9.7	6.3	6.4	4.7	•	4.4	•	•	•	•	•	•

Selected Average Balance Sheet ($ in Thousands)

Net Receivables 23	134	0	35	101	216	2569
Inventories 24	423	0	150	338	620	5771
Net Property, Plant and Equipment 25	257	0	43	87	384	3608
Total Assets 26	1111	0	302	649	1759	14177
Notes and Loans Payable 27	306	0	91	177	652	3098
All Other Liabilities 28	182	0	42	67	281	2798
Net Worth 29	623	0	170	404	826	8281

Selected Financial Ratios (Times to 1)

Current Ratio 30	3.0		2.8	7.1	2.9	2.3
Quick Ratio 31	1.0		0.7	2.2	1.0	0.9
Net Sales to Working Capital 32	5.0		5.3	3.4	4.7	7.2
Coverage Ratio 33	6.5	118.9	3.7	7.4	4.4	11.2
Total Asset Turnover 34	2.2		2.4	2.3	2.1	2.5
Inventory Turnover 35	3.7		2.6	2.9	3.8	4.3
Receivables Turnover 36	20.5		20.9	29.4	21.0	15.0
Total Liabilities to Net Worth 37	0.8		0.8	0.6	1.1	0.7
Current Assets to Working Capital 38	1.5		1.6	1.2	1.5	1.8
Current Liabilities to Working Capital 39	0.5		0.6	0.2	0.5	0.8
Working Capital to Net Sales 40	0.2		0.2	0.3	0.2	0.1
Inventory to Working Capital 41	0.9		1.1	0.8	1.0	1.1
Total Receipts to Cash Flow 42	10.2	3.3	9.8	9.9	11.4	10.8
Cost of Goods to Cash Flow 43	6.6	2.1	5.3	6.5	7.4	7.5
Cash Flow to Total Debt 44	0.5		0.6	0.6	0.3	0.6

Selected Financial Factors (in Percentages)

Debt Ratio 45	44.0		43.9	37.7	53.0	41.6
Return on Total Assets 46	9.2		8.0	8.7	7.7	12.3
Return on Equity Before Income Taxes 47	13.9		10.3	12.1	12.7	19.2
Return on Equity After Income Taxes 48	13.0		9.3	11.5	11.5	18.0
Profit Margin (Before Income Tax) 49	3.5	9.7	2.4	3.3	2.9	4.4
Profit Margin (After Income Tax) 50	3.3	9.7	2.2	3.1	2.6	4.2

Table I

Corporations with and without Net Income

OTHER BUILDING MATERIAL DEALERS

MONEY AMOUNTS AND SIZE OF ASSETS IN THOUSANDS OF DOLLARS

Item Description for Accounting Period 7/03 Through 6/04	Total	Zero Assets	Under 500	500 to 1,000	1,000 to 5,000	5,000 to 10,000	10,000 to 25,000	25,000 to 50,000	50,000 to 100,000	100,000 to 250,000	250,000 to 500,000	500,000 to 2,500,000	2,500,000 and over
Number of Enterprises 1	15450	586	9012	2223	3030	361	167	48	11	7	3	3	•
Revenues ($ in Thousands)													
Net Sales 2	5642443	465937	5457510	5037359	15344585	7720612	6293334	4427310	2196409	2438979	1848770	5611637	•
Interest 3	100797	126	309	2416	22445	4871	5750	5472	1270	3650	8471	46017	•
Rents 4	31493	0	2162	1474	6695	165	4605	4548	1047	10451	189	157	•
Royalties 5	1470	0	0	0	0	0	28	0	0	13	1429	0	•
Other Portfolio Income 6	86784	12486	1254	617	19866	852	9195	4857	2436	26619	5448	3152	•
Other Receipts 7	383592	2600	37559	42487	97854	27179	47278	44800	19703	39630	14390	10115	•
Total Receipts 8	57446579	481149	5498794	5084353	15491445	7753679	6360190	4486987	2220865	2519342	1877697	5671078	•
Average Total Receipts 9	3718	821	610	2287	5113	21478	38085	93479	201897	359906	626232	1890359	•
Operating Costs/Operating Income (%)													
Cost of Operations 10	73.4	64.5	66.0	70.6	71.2	78.5	75.1	77.0	76.4	76.1	76.0	74.6	•
Salaries and Wages 11	9.2	14.7	8.9	8.3	9.2	7.7	9.8	9.5	9.4	11.1	8.1	10.4	•
Taxes Paid 12	1.7	1.4	2.0	2.4	2.0	1.4	1.6	1.4	1.3	1.7	1.3	0.9	•
Interest Paid 13	0.7	0.3	0.7	0.4	0.5	0.5	0.5	0.5	0.4	1.2	1.5	1.4	•
Depreciation 14	1.4	0.7	1.6	0.8	1.4	1.3	1.7	1.3	1.2	1.5	2.6	1.5	•
Amortization and Depletion 15	0.1	0.1	0.2	0.0	0.1	0.0	0.0	0.0	0.0	0.3	0.4	0.5	•
Pensions and Other Deferred Comp. 16	0.3	0.0	0.1	0.4	0.3	0.2	0.3	0.4	0.5	0.3	0.1	0.2	•
Employee Benefits 17	0.9	1.0	0.2	1.0	1.1	0.6	0.9	0.8	0.7	1.3	0.8	1.4	•
Advertising 18	0.6	0.5	1.5	0.7	0.8	0.4	0.6	0.4	0.6	0.4	0.5	0.3	•
Other Expenses 19	8.1	14.2	14.5	8.3	8.5	6.3	6.2	6.4	6.5	8.4	7.2	6.8	•
Officers' Compensation 20	2.1	4.5	3.4	4.3	3.1	1.0	1.6	0.9	0.9	0.6	0.2	0.3	•
Operating Margin 21	1.5	•	0.9	2.7	1.9	2.0	1.6	1.4	2.1	•	1.4	1.6	•
Operating Margin Before Officers' Comp. 22	3.6	2.5	4.3	7.0	5.0	2.9	3.2	2.3	3.0	1.6	1.4	1.9	•

Selected Average Balance Sheet ($ in Thousands)

Net Receivables 23	408	0	31	215	546	2542	4862	11571	24470	38569	137479	216263	•
Inventories 24	400	0	48	276	686	2246	3784	7662	17833	40822	73913	182029	•
Net Property, Plant and Equipment 25	252	0	37	47	298	1547	3210	7666	16736	31040	78470	149776	•
Total Assets 26	1413	0	150	707	2006	7333	14891	34306	69487	157178	407606	990005	•
Notes and Loans Payable 27	362	0	80	161	419	2380	4391	9576	17252	45390	67590	160395	•
All Other Liabilities 28	392	0	32	182	573	2024	4007	8582	19531	40527	118737	320260	•
Net Worth 29	660	0	38	364	1014	2930	6493	16148	32704	71261	221278	509349	•

Selected Financial Ratios (Times to 1)

Current Ratio 30	2.0	•	1.6	2.7	2.4	1.7	1.8	1.9	2.1	2.0	1.9	1.7	•
Quick Ratio 31	1.1	•	0.8	1.4	1.3	1.0	1.0	1.1	1.3	1.1	1.2	0.9	•
Net Sales to Working Capital 32	7.5	•	15.7	5.8	5.6	9.5	8.3	8.1	7.9	7.7	5.0	10.2	•
Coverage Ratio 33	4.9	5.1	3.4	10.5	6.4	5.4	6.4	6.4	8.6	1.5	2.9	2.9	•
Total Asset Turnover 34	2.6	•	4.0	3.2	2.5	2.9	2.5	2.7	2.9	2.2	1.5	1.9	•
Inventory Turnover 35	6.7	•	8.3	5.8	5.3	7.5	7.5	9.3	8.6	6.5	6.3	7.7	•
Receivables Turnover 36	9.3	•	17.8	9.7	9.3	8.7	8.3	8.8	7.7	7.3	6.8	9.4	•
Total Liabilities to Net Worth 37	1.1	•	2.9	0.9	1.0	1.5	1.3	1.1	1.1	1.2	0.8	0.9	•
Current Assets to Working Capital 38	2.0	•	2.6	1.6	1.7	2.4	2.3	2.1	1.9	2.0	2.1	2.4	•
Current Liabilities to Working Capital 39	1.0	•	1.6	0.6	0.7	1.4	1.3	1.1	0.9	1.0	1.1	1.4	•
Working Capital to Net Sales 40	0.1	•	0.1	0.2	0.2	0.1	0.1	0.1	0.1	0.1	0.2	0.1	•
Inventory to Working Capital 41	0.8	•	1.3	0.7	0.8	1.0	0.9	0.7	0.6	0.8	0.7	1.0	•
Total Receipts to Cash Flow 42	12.1	9.5	8.4	10.9	11.5	14.4	14.3	13.9	12.4	18.5	11.2	13.2	•
Cost of Goods to Cash Flow 43	8.9	6.1	5.5	7.7	8.2	11.3	10.7	10.7	9.5	14.1	8.5	9.8	•
Cash Flow to Total Debt 44	0.4	•	0.6	0.4	0.4	0.3	0.3	0.4	0.4	0.2	0.3	0.3	•

Selected Financial Factors (in Percentages)

Debt Ratio 45	53.3	•	74.5	48.5	49.5	60.1	56.4	52.9	52.9	54.7	45.7	48.6	•
Return on Total Assets 46	8.5	•	9.7	12.8	8.4	8.6	8.0	8.8	10.3	3.8	6.8	7.7	•
Return on Equity Before Income Taxes 47	14.5	•	26.8	22.5	14.1	17.6	15.5	15.7	19.4	2.8	8.2	9.8	•
Return on Equity After Income Taxes 48	13.0	•	23.9	21.6	13.0	16.1	14.3	13.7	16.7	0.2	7.6	7.6	•
Profit Margin (Before Income Tax) 49	2.6	1.3	1.7	3.6	2.8	2.4	2.7	2.7	3.2	0.6	3.0	2.7	•
Profit Margin (After Income Tax) 50	2.3	1.3	1.5	3.5	2.6	2.2	2.4	2.7	2.7	0.0	2.7	2.1	•

Table II
Corporations with Net Income

OTHER BUILDING MATERIAL DEALERS

MONEY AMOUNTS AND SIZE OF ASSETS IN THOUSANDS OF DOLLARS

Item Description for Accounting Period 7/03 Through 6/04	Total	Zero Assets	Under 500	500 to 1,000	1,000 to 5,000	5,000 to 10,000	10,000 to 25,000	25,000 to 50,000	50,000 to 100,000	100,000 to 250,000	250,000 to 500,000	500,000 to 2,500,000	2,500,000 and over
Number of Enterprises **1**	9829	147	4897	1796	2461	322	142	43	•	•	3	3	3
Revenues ($ in Thousands)													
Net Sales **2**	48687115	423973	4131827	4164925	12916447	7129146	5543993	3323474	•	•	1848770	5611637	•
Interest **3**	94981	125	267	1157	19305	4869	5041	5076	•	•	8471	46017	•
Rents **4**	19218	0	2162	1422	5591	165	4259	4039	•	•	189	157	•
Royalties **5**	1457	0	0	0	0	0	28	0	•	•	1429	0	•
Other Portfolio Income **6**	76310	12486	1254	617	15978	630	5462	3516	•	•	5448	3152	•
Other Receipts **7**	304658	2587	36501	25812	68102	26834	43398	22609	•	•	14390	10115	•
Total Receipts **8**	49183739	439171	4172011	4193933	13025423	7161644	5602181	3358714	•	•	1877697	5671078	•
Average Total Receipts **9**	5004	2988	852	2335	5293	22241	39452	78110	•	•	626232	1890359	•
Operating Costs/Operating Income (%)													
Cost of Operations **10**	73.0	62.7	68.2	69.4	71.2	77.5	75.0	72.4	•	•	76.0	74.6	•
Salaries and Wages **11**	9.1	15.8	7.9	7.6	8.5	8.2	9.8	11.1	•	•	8.1	10.4	•
Taxes Paid **12**	1.7	1.4	2.0	2.5	1.9	1.4	1.6	1.6	•	•	1.3	0.9	•
Interest Paid **13**	0.6	0.3	0.5	0.4	0.4	0.5	0.4	0.6	•	•	1.5	1.4	•
Depreciation **14**	1.4	0.7	1.3	0.6	1.3	1.4	1.5	1.6	•	•	2.6	1.5	•
Amortization and Depletion **15**	0.1	0.1	0.0	0.0	0.1	0.0	0.0	0.1	•	•	0.4	0.5	•
Pensions and Other Deferred Comp. **16**	0.3	•	0.0	0.5	0.4	0.2	0.3	0.5	•	•	0.1	0.2	•
Employee Benefits **17**	0.9	1.1	0.2	1.0	1.0	0.5	0.9	0.9	•	•	0.8	1.4	•
Advertising **18**	0.6	0.5	1.0	0.6	0.8	0.4	0.7	0.5	•	•	0.5	0.3	•
Other Expenses **19**	7.9	13.7	13.0	8.4	8.4	6.7	6.0	7.0	•	•	7.2	6.8	•
Officers' Compensation **20**	2.0	4.6	2.4	4.6	3.1	1.0	1.5	1.1	•	•	0.2	0.3	•
Operating Margin **21**	2.5	•	3.3	4.4	2.9	2.2	2.2	2.7	•	•	1.4	1.6	•
Operating Margin Before Officers' Comp. **22**	4.5	3.7	5.8	9.0	6.0	3.3	3.7	3.8	•	•	1.6	1.9	•

Selected Average Balance Sheet ($ in Thousands)

Net Receivables 23	553	0	44	229	550	2589	4916	10090	·	137479	216263
Inventories 24	529	0	63	248	687	2251	3898	8470	·	73913	182029
Net Property, Plant and Equipment 25	334	0	47	35	282	1656	2814	7823	·	78470	149776
Total Assets 26	1943	0	197	713	2066	7580	14827	33501	·	407606	990005
Notes and Loans Payable 27	454	0	99	165	384	2442	4110	8768	·	67590	160395
All Other Liabilities 28	535	0	40	176	596	1996	4035	7495	·	118737	320260
Net Worth 29	954	0	58	372	1086	3142	6683	17238	·	221278	509349

Selected Financial Ratios (Times to 1)

Current Ratio 30	2.1	·	2.1	2.8	2.5	1.8	1.7	2.2	·	1.9	1.7
Quick Ratio 31	1.1	·	1.0	1.5	1.3	1.0	1.0	1.2	·	1.2	0.9
Net Sales to Working Capital 32	7.1	·	11.5	5.6	5.4	9.3	8.4	6.4	·	5.0	10.2
Coverage Ratio 33	6.6	9.0	9.4	14.6	9.3	6.0	8.8	7.7	·	2.9	2.9
Total Asset Turnover 34	2.5	·	4.3	3.3	2.5	2.9	2.6	2.3	·	1.5	1.9
Inventory Turnover 35	6.8	·	9.2	6.5	5.4	7.6	7.5	6.6	·	6.3	7.7
Receivables Turnover 36	9.5	·	19.8	10.3	9.7	9.1	8.5	15.3	·	6.8	9.4
Total Liabilities to Net Worth 37	1.0	·	2.4	0.9	0.9	1.4	1.2	0.9	·	0.8	0.9
Current Assets to Working Capital 38	1.9	·	1.9	1.5	1.7	2.3	2.3	1.8	·	2.1	2.4
Current Liabilities to Working Capital 39	0.9	·	0.9	0.5	0.7	1.3	1.3	0.8	·	1.1	1.4
Working Capital to Net Sales 40	0.1	·	0.1	0.2	0.2	0.1	0.1	0.2	·	0.2	0.1
Inventory to Working Capital 41	0.8	·	1.0	0.7	0.8	0.9	1.0	0.7	·	0.7	1.0
Total Receipts to Cash Flow 42	11.1	8.2	7.3	9.4	10.6	13.5	13.4	11.7	·	11.2	13.2
Cost of Goods to Cash Flow 43	8.1	5.2	5.0	6.5	7.5	10.4	10.0	8.5	·	8.5	9.8
Cash Flow to Total Debt 44	0.5	·	0.8	0.7	0.5	0.4	0.4	0.4	·	0.3	0.3

Selected Financial Factors (in Percentages)

Debt Ratio 45	50.9	·	70.4	47.9	47.4	58.5	54.9	48.5	·	45.7	48.6
Return on Total Assets 46	10.5	·	20.5	17.6	10.5	9.5	9.6	10.0	·	6.8	7.7
Return on Equity Before Income Taxes 47	18.2	·	61.9	31.5	17.9	19.0	18.9	17.0	·	8.2	9.8
Return on Equity After Income Taxes 48	16.6	·	58.5	30.5	16.7	17.5	17.6	14.9	·	7.6	7.6
Profit Margin (Before Income Tax) 49	3.5	2.7	4.3	5.1	3.7	2.7	3.2	3.8	·	3.0	2.7
Profit Margin (After Income Tax) 50	3.2	2.7	4.0	4.9	3.4	2.5	3.0	3.3	·	2.7	2.1

Table I

Corporations with and without Net Income

LAWN AND GARDEN EQUIPMENT AND SUPPLIES STORES

MONEY AMOUNTS AND SIZE OF ASSETS IN THOUSANDS OF DOLLARS

Item Description for Accounting Period 7/03 Through 6/04	Total	Zero Assets	Under 500	500 to 1,000	1,000 to 5,000	5,000 to 10,000	10,000 to 25,000	25,000 to 50,000	50,000 to 100,000	100,000 to 250,000	250,000 to 500,000	500,000 to 2,500,000	2,500,000 and over
Number of Enterprises **1**	11182	•	8385	1362	904	•	29	5	4	•	•	•	•
Revenues ($ in Thousands)													
Net Sales **2**	14111118	•	3489961	3411776	4167349	•	956606	265111	612775	•	•	•	•
Interest **3**	8716	•	1536	375	4689	•	786	265	172	•	•	•	•
Rents **4**	8862	•	126	501	6636	•	579	67	799	•	•	•	•
Royalties **5**	53	•	0	0	0	•	48	0	0	•	•	•	•
Other Portfolio Income **6**	18829	•	11990	1508	1948	•	450	1916	124	•	•	•	•
Other Receipts **7**	239251	•	136094	48010	40861	•	7831	508	3252	•	•	•	•
Total Receipts **8**	14386829	•	3639707	3462170	4221483	•	966300	267867	617122	•	•	•	•
Average Total Receipts **9**	1287	•	434	2542	4670	•	33321	53573	154280	•	•	•	•
Operating Costs/Operating Income (%)													
Cost of Operations **10**	70.5	•	68.0	63.4	77.3	•	73.2	59.0	68.5	•	•	•	•
Salaries and Wages **11**	11.2	•	11.9	14.9	8.3	•	8.5	15.8	12.1	•	•	•	•
Taxes Paid **12**	2.4	•	3.1	3.4	1.4	•	1.3	1.6	2.1	•	•	•	•
Interest Paid **13**	0.9	•	0.7	0.6	0.9	•	1.0	1.4	1.9	•	•	•	•
Depreciation **14**	1.4	•	1.3	1.4	1.5	•	1.4	3.7	2.5	•	•	•	•
Amortization and Depletion **15**	0.0	•	0.0	0.0	0.0	•	0.0	0.7	0.0	•	•	•	•
Pensions and Other Deferred Comp. **16**	0.3	•	0.0	0.2	0.6	•	0.2	0.2	0.1	•	•	•	•
Employee Benefits **17**	0.5	•	0.1	0.5	0.4	•	0.6	1.9	1.3	•	•	•	•
Advertising **18**	1.2	•	1.0	1.1	1.2	•	1.2	2.4	2.9	•	•	•	•
Other Expenses **19**	10.3	•	14.3	9.9	7.3	•	10.3	12.6	15.5	•	•	•	•
Officers' Compensation **20**	3.3	•	6.1	2.6	2.4	•	1.4	1.3	0.6	•	•	•	•
Operating Margin **21**	•	•	•	1.9	•	•	0.7	•	•	•	•	•	•
Operating Margin Before Officers' Comp. **22**	1.5	•	4.6	•	1.1	•	2.1	0.7	•	•	•	•	•

Selected Average Balance Sheet ($ in Thousands)

Item							
Net Receivables 23	65	16	111	210	4020	1755	13748
Inventories 24	249	62	278	1256	6012	9320	28634
Net Property, Plant and Equipment 25	111	32	226	455	2838	10487	18628
Total Assets 26	501	125	752	2258	15150	28441	69795
Notes and Loans Payable 27	247	98	246	786	16064	11762	30822
All Other Liabilities 28	162	43	180	724	8551	7836	32911
Net Worth 29	92	-16	326	748	-9465	8843	6062

Selected Financial Ratios (Times to 1)

Item							
Current Ratio 30	1.4	1.4	2.3	1.6	0.7	1.1	1.0
Quick Ratio 31	0.4	0.5	1.0	0.3	0.3	0.2	0.3
Net Sales to Working Capital 32	12.0	17.8	8.7	7.8		34.0	512.8
Coverage Ratio 33	1.2		7.0	1.0	2.7	1.3	
Total Asset Turnover 34	2.5	3.3	3.3	2.0	2.2	1.9	2.2
Inventory Turnover 35	3.6	4.6	5.7	2.8	4.0	3.4	3.7
Receivables Turnover 36	19.5	17.2	30.3	21.7	9.5	19.1	12.2
Total Liabilities to Net Worth 37	4.5		1.3	2.0		2.2	10.5
Current Assets to Working Capital 38	3.3	3.7	1.8	2.8		8.4	158.5
Current Liabilities to Working Capital 39	2.3	2.7	0.8	1.8		7.4	157.5
Working Capital to Net Sales 40	0.1	0.1	0.1	0.1		0.0	0.0
Inventory to Working Capital 41	2.2	2.4	0.9	2.2		6.5	103.8
Total Receipts to Cash Flow 42	14.1	14.1	10.1	18.3	10.1	12.5	194.2
Cost of Goods to Cash Flow 43	9.9	9.6	6.4	14.1	7.4	7.4	132.9
Cash Flow to Total Debt 44	0.2	0.2	0.6	0.2	0.1	0.2	0.0

Selected Financial Factors (in Percentages)

Item							
Debt Ratio 45	81.7	113.0	56.6	66.9	162.5	68.9	91.3
Return on Total Assets 46	2.6		13.3	1.9	5.9	3.4	
Return on Equity Before Income Taxes 47	2.5	56.3	26.2			2.5	
Return on Equity After Income Taxes 48	0.5	56.7	25.3			2.5	
Profit Margin (Before Income Tax) 49	0.2		3.4		1.7	0.4	
Profit Margin (After Income Tax) 50	0.0		3.3		1.5	0.4	

Table II
Corporations with Net Income

LAWN AND GARDEN EQUIPMENT AND SUPPLIES STORES

MONEY AMOUNTS AND SIZE OF ASSETS IN THOUSANDS OF DOLLARS

Item Description for Accounting Period 7/03 Through 6/04	Total	Zero Assets	Under 500	500 to 1,000	1,000 to 5,000	5,000 to 10,000	10,000 to 25,000	25,000 to 50,000	50,000 to 100,000	100,000 to 250,000	250,000 to 500,000	500,000 to 2,500,000	2,500,000 and over
Number of Enterprises 1	6702	9	4815	1201	581	·	25	·	·	·	·	·	·
Revenues ($ in Thousands)													
Net Sales 2	10597106	22199	2151863	3259804	2799820	·	858445	·	·	·	·	·	·
Interest 3	6921	1	1149	374	3946	·	206	·	·	·	·	·	·
Rents 4	5464	44	0	501	4230	·	579	·	·	·	·	·	·
Royalties 5	53	5	0	0	0	·	48	·	·	·	·	·	·
Other Portfolio Income 6	12286	0	6999	1508	1340	·	448	·	·	·	·	·	·
Other Receipts 7	205716	550	134492	48010	15482	·	4384	·	·	·	·	·	·
Total Receipts 8	10827546	22799	2294503	3310197	2824818	·	864110	·	·	·	·	·	·
Average Total Receipts 9	1616	2533	477	2756	4862	·	34564	·	·	·	·	·	·
Operating Costs/Operating Income (%)													
Cost of Operations 10	69.3	60.1	66.9	63.7	74.0	·	72.7	·	·	·	·	·	·
Salaries and Wages 11	11.0	6.8	11.0	14.8	8.5	·	8.3	·	·	·	·	·	·
Taxes Paid 12	2.3	0.6	3.2	3.4	1.3	·	1.3	·	·	·	·	·	·
Interest Paid 13	0.7	0.1	0.9	0.6	0.7	·	0.9	·	·	·	·	·	·
Depreciation 14	1.3	1.0	1.5	1.3	1.3	·	1.3	·	·	·	·	·	·
Amortization and Depletion 15	0.0	·	0.0	0.0	0.0	·	0.0	·	·	·	·	·	·
Pensions and Other Deferred Comp. 16	0.3	2.1	0.0	0.2	0.8	·	0.2	·	·	·	·	·	·
Employee Benefits 17	0.5	1.5	0.1	0.4	0.4	·	0.6	·	·	·	·	·	·
Advertising 18	1.0	0.0	0.8	1.2	1.0	·	1.2	·	·	·	·	·	·
Other Expenses 19	9.0	28.0	11.6	9.3	7.5	·	10.4	·	·	·	·	·	·
Officers' Compensation 20	3.4	0.6	6.4	2.6	3.1	·	1.3	·	·	·	·	·	·
Operating Margin 21	1.1	·	·	2.4	1.4	·	1.8	·	·	·	·	·	·
Operating Margin Before Officers' Comp. 22	4.6	·	4.1	5.0	4.4	·	3.1	·	·	·	·	·	·

Selected Average Balance Sheet ($ in Thousands)

Net Receivables 23	84	0	16	121	239	•	4018
Inventories 24	298	0	72	253	1310	•	5903
Net Property, Plant and Equipment 25	119	0	37	192	432	•	2789
Total Assets 26	600	0	154	768	2310	•	14642
Notes and Loans Payable 27	205	0	68	246	660	•	5150
All Other Liabilities 28	184	0	52	179	715	•	5334
Net Worth 29	211	0	34	344	936	•	4158

Selected Financial Ratios (Times to 1)

Current Ratio 30	1.7	•	1.7	2.5	1.5	•	1.4
Quick Ratio 31	0.5	•	0.5	1.1	0.4	•	0.6
Net Sales to Working Capital 32	8.6	•	10.1	8.0	8.4	•	10.6
Coverage Ratio 33	5.7	16.7	6.1	8.1	4.3	•	3.7
Total Asset Turnover 34	2.6	•	2.9	3.5	2.1	•	2.3
Inventory Turnover 35	3.7	•	4.2	6.8	2.7	•	4.2
Receivables Turnover 36	20.0	•	22.6	31.6	18.1	•	10.1
Total Liabilities to Net Worth 37	1.8	•	3.6	1.2	1.5	•	2.5
Current Assets to Working Capital 38	2.4	•	2.4	1.7	2.9	•	3.4
Current Liabilities to Working Capital 39	1.4	•	1.4	0.7	1.9	•	2.4
Working Capital to Net Sales 40	0.1	•	0.1	0.1	0.1	•	0.1
Inventory to Working Capital 41	1.6	•	1.5	0.9	2.2	•	1.8
Total Receipts to Cash Flow 42	10.3	3.5	8.1	9.8	12.7	•	9.3
Cost of Goods to Cash Flow 43	7.2	2.1	5.4	6.3	9.4	•	6.8
Cash Flow to Total Debt 44	0.4	•	0.5	0.7	0.3	•	0.4

Selected Financial Factors (in Percentages)

Debt Ratio 45	64.9	•	78.2	55.2	59.5	•	71.6
Return on Total Assets 46	10.6	•	15.1	16.1	6.1	•	7.8
Return on Equity Before Income Taxes 47	24.9	•	57.6	31.4	11.6	•	20.1
Return on Equity After Income Taxes 48	23.5	•	57.2	30.5	9.4	•	18.3
Profit Margin (Before Income Tax) 49	3.3	1.8	4.3	4.0	2.3	•	2.4
Profit Margin (After Income Tax) 50	3.1	1.3	4.3	3.9	1.8	•	2.2

Table I

Corporations with and without Net Income

FOOD AND BEVERAGE STORES

MONEY AMOUNTS AND SIZE OF ASSETS IN THOUSANDS OF DOLLARS

Item Description for Accounting Period 7/03 Through 6/04	Total	Zero Assets	Under 500	500 to 1,000	1,000 to 5,000	5,000 to 10,000	10,000 to 25,000	25,000 to 50,000	50,000 to 100,000	100,000 to 250,000	250,000 to 500,000	500,000 to 2,500,000	2,500,000 and over
Number of Enterprises **1**	75762	5275	61124	4920	3663	384	204	68	51	28	14	21	9
Revenues ($ in Thousands)													
Net Sales **2**	45804866	1291672	39185924	14605511	29601652	13452453	13740837	9179058	13327176	13561731	13943858	65516308	223398686
Interest **3**	960957	57	4819	5257	10727	5233	5668	4235	7971	9483	22861	89493	795154
Rents **4**	1030099	1228	5851	6301	40638	11101	18735	11690	14636	9370	22841	159861	727848
Royalties **5**	1126477	0	0	0	36	0	78	0	0	21964	18313	130352	955735
Other Portfolio Income **6**	529662	33477	42938	6659	69389	8331	18896	6417	3623	11343	6386	216534	105667
Other Receipts **7**	7777478	35268	535874	106778	269583	194298	163020	121609	145312	128586	190420	538810	5347918
Total Receipts **8**	462229539	1361702	39775406	14730506	29992025	13671416	13947234	9323009	13499718	13742477	14204679	66651358	231331008
Average Total Receipts **9**	6101	258	651	2994	8188	35603	68369	137103	264681	490803	1014620	3173874	25703445
Operating Costs/Operating Income (%)													
Cost of Operations **10**	74.0	75.7	73.4	74.5	75.6	79.5	75.8	75.5	72.2	73.3	72.5	71.4	74.4
Salaries and Wages **11**	10.2	7.9	7.9	9.2	9.1	7.7	10.2	10.1	10.7	11.8	12.2	11.2	10.5
Taxes Paid **12**	1.7	2.6	2.2	1.5	1.6	1.3	1.5	1.5	2.1	1.8	1.6	2.0	1.5
Interest Paid **13**	1.0	0.4	0.4	0.6	0.4	0.4	0.4	0.5	0.4	0.6	0.6	0.9	1.4
Depreciation **14**	2.1	0.8	1.1	1.6	1.2	0.9	1.5	1.7	1.9	1.8	2.3	2.5	2.5
Amortization and Depletion **15**	0.1	0.3	0.4	0.1	0.1	0.1	0.1	0.1	0.1	0.1	0.1	0.1	0.1
Pensions and Other Deferred Comp. **16**	0.4	0.0	0.0	0.0	0.1	0.1	0.2	0.4	0.4	0.4	0.5	0.4	0.5
Employee Benefits **17**	1.4	0.3	0.4	0.3	0.8	0.8	1.0	1.3	1.2	1.5	1.4	1.9	1.6
Advertising **18**	0.8	0.6	0.7	0.9	1.0	0.5	0.9	0.7	1.1	0.9	0.7	0.9	0.7
Other Expenses **19**	9.3	25.0	12.4	9.6	8.7	7.2	8.4	8.2	9.5	7.5	8.0	8.4	9.3
Officers' Compensation **20**	0.5	2.6	2.7	1.9	1.3	0.8	0.6	0.6	0.5	0.4	0.2	0.1	0.1
Operating Margin **21**	•	•	•	•	0.2	0.6	•	•	0.1	•	•	0.1	0.1
Operating Margin Before Officers' Comp. **22**	•	•	1.1	1.7	1.5	1.3	•	•	0.5	0.3	•	0.2	•

Selected Average Balance Sheet ($ in Thousands)

Net Receivables 23	123	0	4	31	145	386	1043	2474	3189	6474	19202	52150	687502
Inventories 24	357	0	34	155	407	1579	3365	6696	12371	25149	35411	193386	1670039
Net Property, Plant and Equipment 25	903	0	32	290	666	2659	5818	14142	30696	66478	126153	580537	4672698
Total Assets 26	2165	0	109	676	1912	6986	15441	35166	67538	143597	353024	1175068	11301067
Notes and Loans Payable 27	706	0	76	388	706	2397	5741	10945	21584	38555	85443	397748	3311736
All Other Liabilities 28	879	0	19	124	441	1816	4618	10153	21020	44475	124018	356432	5482136
Net Worth 29	580	0	15	164	765	2772	5081	14069	24934	60566	143564	420887	2507196

Selected Financial Ratios (Times to 1)

Current Ratio 30	0.9	•	2.1	1.7	1.9	1.4	1.3	1.3	1.1	1.0	1.2	1.3	0.7
Quick Ratio 31	0.3	•	0.7	0.7	0.9	0.7	0.6	0.6	0.4	0.4	0.5	0.5	0.2
Net Sales to Working Capital 32	•	•	23.3	29.1	17.2	33.9	41.5	42.6	112.0	249.6	65.7	36.8	•
Coverage Ratio 33	2.2	•	0.7	2.0	4.7	6.3	2.8	2.7	4.0	3.0	3.5	3.1	1.8
Total Asset Turnover 34	2.7	•	5.9	4.4	4.2	5.0	4.4	3.8	3.9	3.4	2.8	2.7	2.2
Inventory Turnover 35	12.3	•	13.7	14.2	15.0	17.6	15.2	15.2	15.2	14.1	20.4	11.5	11.1
Receivables Turnover 36	47.6	•	174.4	77.6	55.8	97.1	65.7	56.4	61.9	72.8	77.4	55.2	35.7
Total Liabilities to Net Worth 37	2.7	•	6.4	3.1	1.5	2.0	1.5	1.7	1.4	1.5	1.8		3.5
Current Assets to Working Capital 38	•	•	1.9	2.5	2.1	3.3	4.4	4.6	10.2	24.0	6.9	4.4	•
Current Liabilities to Working Capital 39	•	•	0.9	1.5	1.1	2.3	3.4	3.6	9.2	23.0	5.9	3.4	•
Working Capital to Net Sales 40	•	•	0.0	0.0	0.0	0.0	0.0	0.0	0.0	0.0	0.0	0.0	•
Inventory to Working Capital 41	•	•	1.2	1.3	0.8	1.5	2.0	2.1	5.0	11.8	3.1	2.2	•
Total Receipts to Cash Flow 42	13.6	13.8	13.3	14.3	13.4	14.2	16.0	16.1	13.8	17.9	15.4	13.7	13.0
Cost of Goods to Cash Flow 43	10.0	10.5	9.8	10.7	10.1	11.3	12.1	12.2	9.9	13.1	11.2	9.8	9.7
Cash Flow to Total Debt 44	0.3	•	0.5	0.5	0.6	0.4	0.4	0.4	0.0	0.3	0.3	0.3	0.2

Selected Financial Factors (in Percentages)

Debt Ratio 45	73.2	•	86.4	75.7	60.0	60.3	67.1	60.0	63.1	57.8	59.3	64.2	77.8
Return on Total Assets 46	5.8	•	1.4	5.6	8.2	13.0	5.2	5.3	6.9	6.2	6.4	7.3	5.5
Return on Equity Before Income Taxes 47	11.7	•	•	11.4	16.2	27.5	10.2	8.3	14.1	9.8	11.2	13.8	11.0
Return on Equity After Income Taxes 48	8.1	•	•	10.8	14.8	25.8	8.7	6.7	12.2	7.8	7.8	9.9	6.7
Profit Margin (Before Income Tax) 49	1.1	•	0.6	0.6	1.5	2.2	0.8	0.9	1.3	1.2	1.6	1.9	1.1
Profit Margin (After Income Tax) 50	0.8	•	0.6	0.6	1.4	2.0	0.7	0.7	1.2	1.0	1.1	1.3	0.7

219

Table II
Corporations with Net Income

FOOD AND BEVERAGE STORES

MONEY AMOUNTS AND SIZE OF ASSETS IN THOUSANDS OF DOLLARS

Item Description for Accounting Period 7/03 Through 6/04	Total	Zero Assets	Under 500	500 to 1,000	1,000 to 5,000	5,000 to 10,000	10,000 to 25,000	25,000 to 50,000	50,000 to 100,000	100,000 to 250,000	250,000 to 500,000	500,000 to 2,500,000	2,500,000 and over
Number of Enterprises **1**	35395	987	28607	2935	2214	378	132	48	36	21	10	•	•
Revenues ($ in Thousands)													
Net Sales **2**	329306679	489901	22869146	10306869	21821234	13212375	10062468	6914824	10410454	10200030	12312171	•	•
Interest **3**	394641	28	3638	2934	8245	5011	3793	3051	4913	5558	4031	•	•
Rents **4**	651050	682	949	2229	22134	10905	8915	9156	9374	8883	14731	•	•
Royalties **5**	1085622	0	0	0	36	0	0	0	0	0	0	•	•
Other Portfolio Income **6**	235094	29946	20016	5154	59647	7159	13688	4324	1685	10004	2835	•	•
Other Receipts **7**	5671777	16952	310259	87913	164882	190445	109158	101764	111589	75874	169122	•	•
Total Receipts **8**	337344863	537509	23204008	10405099	22076178	13425895	10198022	7033119	10538015	10300349	12502890	•	•
Average Total Receipts **9**	9531	545	811	3545	9971	35518	77258	146523	292723	490493	1250289	•	•
Operating Costs/Operating Income (%)													
Cost of Operations **10**	73.2	78.3	73.0	76.1	76.4	79.6	76.0	74.9	72.5	72.8	72.4	•	•
Salaries and Wages **11**	10.3	5.9	7.3	8.2	8.0	7.6	9.9	10.4	10.9	11.8	12.4	•	•
Taxes Paid **12**	1.7	3.0	2.2	1.4	1.4	1.3	1.5	1.6	1.8	1.7	1.5	•	•
Interest Paid **13**	0.8	0.3	0.3	0.5	0.3	0.4	0.3	0.4	0.4	0.2	0.4	•	•
Depreciation **14**	2.3	0.5	0.9	1.0	0.9	0.9	1.3	1.6	1.7	1.8	2.3	•	•
Amortization and Depletion **15**	0.1	0.2	0.1	0.1	0.1	0.1	0.1	0.1	0.1	0.0	0.1	•	•
Pensions and Other Deferred Comp. **16**	0.4	0.0	0.0	0.1	0.1	0.1	0.2	0.2	0.4	0.5	0.5	•	•
Employee Benefits **17**	1.5	0.3	0.2	0.3	0.7	0.8	0.9	1.4	1.2	1.4	1.3	•	•
Advertising **18**	0.7	0.3	0.7	0.8	1.0	0.5	0.8	0.8	1.1	0.9	0.7	•	•
Other Expenses **19**	8.8	9.5	11.3	8.7	8.1	7.2	7.8	7.7	8.8	7.3	7.8	•	•
Officers' Compensation **20**	0.5	1.5	2.4	1.7	1.4	0.8	0.6	0.6	0.5	0.4	0.2	•	•
Operating Margin **21**	•	0.1	1.5	1.3	1.7	0.7	0.7	0.4	0.7	1.1	0.5	•	•
Operating Margin Before Officers' Comp. **22**	0.2	1.6	3.9	3.0	3.1	1.4	1.3	1.0	1.2	1.5	0.7	•	•

Selected Average Balance Sheet ($ in Thousands)

Item												
Net Receivables 23	188	0	5	22	189	383	1106	2033	3381	5901	24695	•
Inventories 24	622	0	46	151	467	1581	3779	7158	13242	25311	55005	•
Net Property, Plant and Equipment 25	1564	0	29	243	545	2656	5722	13629	28987	65720	127458	•
Total Assets 26	3469	0	119	677	2042	6972	15792	35032	69728	141913	345942	•
Notes and Loans Payable 27	1117	0	59	266	507	2345	4485	9817	20378	23450	72032	•
All Other Liabilities 28	1281	0	18	124	433	1812	4507	9920	22655	40602	125233	•
Net Worth 29	1071	0	42	287	1102	2816	6801	15296	26695	77862	148678	•

Selected Financial Ratios (Times to 1)

Item												
Current Ratio 30	1.0	•	2.7	1.9	2.4	1.4	1.5	1.3	1.2	1.4	1.2	•
Quick Ratio 31	0.3	•	1.0	0.8	1.2	0.7	0.7	0.6	0.5	0.6	0.6	•
Net Sales to Working Capital 32	•	•	18.0	28.7	14.0	34.2	31.3	41.6	73.8	32.4	50.8	•
Coverage Ratio 33	3.7	36.3	10.5	5.3	10.6	6.7	7.2	6.1	5.8	10.3	6.0	•
Total Asset Turnover 34	2.7	•	6.7	5.2	4.8	5.0	4.8	4.1	4.1	3.4	3.6	•
Inventory Turnover 35	10.9	•	12.7	17.7	16.1	17.6	15.3	15.1	15.8	14.0	16.2	•
Receivables Turnover 36	44.1	•	168.6	133.4	57.6	182.4	70.1	141.7	71.0	72.9	99.7	•
Total Liabilities to Net Worth 37	2.2	•	1.9	1.4	0.9	1.5	1.3	1.3	1.6	0.8	1.3	•
Current Assets to Working Capital 38	•	•	1.6	2.2	1.7	3.3	3.2	4.3	6.7	3.3	5.4	•
Current Liabilities to Working Capital 39	•	•	0.6	1.2	0.7	2.3	2.2	3.3	5.7	2.3	4.4	•
Working Capital to Net Sales 40	•	•	0.1	0.0	0.1	0.0	0.0	0.0	0.0	0.0	0.0	•
Inventory to Working Capital 41	•	•	1.0	1.2	0.7	1.5	1.5	2.1	3.3	1.5	2.3	•
Total Receipts to Cash Flow 42	12.3	6.2	9.9	12.4	12.0	14.1	14.1	14.0	13.7	15.2	14.8	•
Cost of Goods to Cash Flow 43	9.0	4.9	7.2	9.4	9.1	11.2	10.7	10.5	10.0	11.0	10.7	•
Cash Flow to Total Debt 44	0.3	•	1.0	0.7	0.9	0.6	0.6	0.5	0.5	0.5	0.4	•

Selected Financial Factors (in Percentages)

Item												
Debt Ratio 45	69.1	•	65.1	57.6	46.0	59.6	56.9	56.3	61.7	45.1	57.0	•
Return on Total Assets 46	7.9	•	22.4	14.3	15.1	13.5	11.4	10.1	9.7	7.9	8.6	•
Return on Equity Before Income Taxes 47	18.6	•	57.9	27.4	25.3	28.4	22.9	19.3	21.0	12.9	16.6	•
Return on Equity After Income Taxes 48	14.5	•	57.0	26.7	23.8	26.7	21.2	17.2	18.5	10.8	12.0	•
Profit Margin (Before Income Tax) 49	2.1	9.9	3.0	2.2	2.8	2.3	2.0	2.1	1.9	2.1	2.0	•
Profit Margin (After Income Tax) 50	1.7	9.6	3.0	2.2	2.7	2.2	1.9	1.8	1.7	1.7	1.4	•

Table I

Corporations with and without Net Income

BEER, WINE, AND LIQUOR STORES

MONEY AMOUNTS AND SIZE OF ASSETS IN THOUSANDS OF DOLLARS

Item Description for Accounting Period 7/03 Through 6/04	Total	Zero Assets	Under 500	500 to 1,000	1,000 to 5,000	5,000 to 10,000	10,000 to 25,000	25,000 to 50,000	50,000 to 100,000	100,000 to 250,000	250,000 to 500,000	500,000 to 2,500,000	2,500,000 and over
Number of Enterprises 1	15130	396	12846	1208	603	51	20	6	•	•	•	•	•
Revenues ($ in Thousands)													
Net Sales 2	17822235	0	9345474	2725056	2436806	1557730	716396	1040773	•	•	•	•	•
Interest 3	5131	0	1136	2503	866	11	367	248	•	•	•	•	•
Rents 4	1169	0	0	0	0	0	662	506	•	•	•	•	•
Royalties 5	0	0	0	0	0	0	0	0	•	•	•	•	•
Other Portfolio Income 6	8602	0	785	134	6586	2	350	746	•	•	•	•	•
Other Receipts 7	268219	0	138902	20057	100532	656	4465	3607	•	•	•	•	•
Total Receipts 8	18105356	0	9486297	2747750	2544790	1558399	722240	1045880	•	•	•	•	•
Average Total Receipts 9	1197	0	738	2275	4220	30557	36112	174313	•	•	•	•	•
Operating Costs/Operating Income (%)													
Cost of Operations 10	78.5	•	78.5	80.2	75.0	82.9	77.1	77.0	•	•	•	•	•
Salaries and Wages 11	5.6	•	4.8	4.5	8.8	5.4	7.7	7.8	•	•	•	•	•
Taxes Paid 12	2.4	•	2.8	2.9	1.9	0.6	1.5	1.2	•	•	•	•	•
Interest Paid 13	0.7	•	0.8	0.9	0.5	0.3	0.7	0.4	•	•	•	•	•
Depreciation 14	0.7	•	0.7	0.6	0.7	0.8	0.9	1.6	•	•	•	•	•
Amortization and Depletion 15	0.3	•	0.2	0.5	0.4	0.0	0.3	0.1	•	•	•	•	•
Pensions and Other Deferred Comp. 16	0.1	•	0.0	0.0	0.4	0.5	0.1	0.1	•	•	•	•	•
Employee Benefits 17	0.4	•	0.3	0.1	0.4	0.7	0.5	1.1	•	•	•	•	•
Advertising 18	0.6	•	0.4	0.7	1.0	0.4	1.4	1.2	•	•	•	•	•
Other Expenses 19	8.4	•	9.3	7.5	9.9	3.2	6.8	8.4	•	•	•	•	•
Officers' Compensation 20	2.5	•	3.4	1.6	1.9	1.1	2.1	0.6	•	•	•	•	•
Operating Margin 21	•	•	•	0.5	•	4.1	1.0	0.5	•	•	•	•	•
Operating Margin Before Officers' Comp. 22	2.3	•	2.3	2.1	1.0	5.2	3.1	1.2	•	•	•	•	•

Selected Average Balance Sheet ($ in Thousands)

Net Receivables 23	15	0	5	9	40	2011	410	2878
Inventories 24	160	0	89	389	769	2130	5833	21051
Net Property, Plant and Equipment 25	68	0	42	119	172	1509	2966	16236
Total Assets 26	357	0	205	743	1464	7062	14923	54741
Notes and Loans Payable 27	190	0	132	460	688	1052	4896	9209
All Other Liabilities 28	81	0	35	191	327	3077	4128	17918
Net Worth 29	87	0	39	92	448	2933	5899	27614

Selected Financial Ratios (Times to 1)

Current Ratio 30	2.5	•	3.4	2.0	2.4	1.6	1.8	1.7
Quick Ratio 31	0.7	•	1.0	0.5	0.8	0.7	0.4	0.3
Net Sales to Working Capital 32	8.6	•	7.8	10.5	6.4	18.0	9.2	13.6
Coverage Ratio 33	3.0	•	1.5	2.6	7.5	13.1	3.6	3.8
Total Asset Turnover 34	3.3	•	3.5	3.0	2.8	4.3	2.4	3.2
Inventory Turnover 35	5.8	•	6.4	4.6	3.9	11.9	4.7	6.3
Receivables Turnover 36	106.5	•	223.1	267.6	61.3	29.3	95.0	70.2
Total Liabilities to Net Worth 37	3.1	•	4.3	7.1	2.3	1.4	1.5	1.0
Current Assets to Working Capital 38	1.7	•	1.4	2.0	1.7	2.8	2.3	2.4
Current Liabilities to Working Capital 39	0.7	•	0.4	1.0	0.7	1.8	1.3	1.4
Working Capital to Net Sales 40	0.1	•	0.1	0.1	0.2	0.1	0.1	0.1
Inventory to Working Capital 41	1.1	•	1.0	1.5	1.1	1.5	1.5	1.9
Total Receipts to Cash Flow 42	14.8	•	15.4	16.7	10.1	15.1	17.7	19.2
Cost of Goods to Cash Flow 43	11.6	•	12.1	13.4	7.6	12.5	13.6	14.8
Cash Flow to Total Debt 44	0.3	•	0.3	0.2	0.4	0.5	0.2	0.3

Selected Financial Factors (in Percentages)

Debt Ratio 45	75.7	•	81.0	87.7	69.4	58.5	60.5	49.6
Return on Total Assets 46	6.8	•	4.0	6.8	11.3	19.4	5.8	4.4
Return on Equity Before Income Taxes 47	18.5	•	6.6	33.5	31.9	43.1	10.7	6.5
Return on Equity After Income Taxes 48	17.3	•	6.2	31.4	29.6	42.7	9.6	4.5
Profit Margin (Before Income Tax) 49	1.4	•	0.4	1.4	3.5	4.1	1.8	1.0
Profit Margin (After Income Tax) 50	1.3	•	0.3	1.3	3.3	4.1	1.6	0.7

221

Table II
Corporations with Net Income

BEER, WINE, AND LIQUOR STORES

MONEY AMOUNTS AND SIZE OF ASSETS IN THOUSANDS OF DOLLARS

Item Description for Accounting Period 7/03 Through 6/04		Total	Zero Assets	Under 500	500 to 1,000	1,000 to 5,000	5,000 to 10,000	10,000 to 25,000	25,000 to 50,000	50,000 to 100,000	100,000 to 250,000	250,000 to 500,000	500,000 to 2,500,000	2,500,000 and over
Number of Enterprises	1	8276	•	6792	953	462	•	15	•	•	•	•	•	•
Revenues ($ in Thousands)														
Net Sales	2	13189530	•	5667233	2485287	2092281	•	582054	•	•	•	•	•	•
Interest	3	4994	•	1041	2503	858	•	343	•	•	•	•	•	•
Rents	4	506	•	0	0	0	•	0	•	•	•	•	•	•
Royalties	5	0	•	0	0	0	•	0	•	•	•	•	•	•
Other Portfolio Income	6	7791	•	0	134	6586	•	339	•	•	•	•	•	•
Other Receipts	7	202617	•	84064	13426	98233	•	2790	•	•	•	•	•	•
Total Receipts	8	13405438	•	5752338	2501350	2197958	•	585526	•	•	•	•	•	•
Average Total Receipts	9	1620	•	847	2625	4757	•	39035	•	•	•	•	•	•
Operating Costs/Operating Income (%)														
Cost of Operations	10	78.6	•	78.9	79.4	74.3	•	77.7	•	•	•	•	•	•
Salaries and Wages	11	5.4	•	3.9	4.4	9.2	•	7.0	•	•	•	•	•	•
Taxes Paid	12	2.2	•	2.6	3.2	1.6	•	1.5	•	•	•	•	•	•
Interest Paid	13	0.5	•	0.5	0.6	0.4	•	0.6	•	•	•	•	•	•
Depreciation	14	0.6	•	0.4	0.5	0.5	•	0.7	•	•	•	•	•	•
Amortization and Depletion	15	0.2	•	0.1	0.5	0.3	•	0.2	•	•	•	•	•	•
Pensions and Other Deferred Comp.	16	0.2	•	0.1	0.0	0.5	•	0.1	•	•	•	•	•	•
Employee Benefits	17	0.3	•	0.2	0.0	0.4	•	0.5	•	•	•	•	•	•
Advertising	18	0.6	•	0.4	0.7	1.1	•	1.4	•	•	•	•	•	•
Other Expenses	19	7.5	•	7.6	7.7	10.3	•	5.7	•	•	•	•	•	•
Officers' Compensation	20	2.6	•	4.2	1.5	1.7	•	2.3	•	•	•	•	•	•
Operating Margin	21	1.4	•	1.2	1.4	•	•	2.3	•	•	•	•	•	•
Operating Margin Before Officers' Comp.	22	4.1	•	5.4	2.9	1.5	•	4.6	•	•	•	•	•	•

Selected Average Balance Sheet ($ in Thousands)

Net Receivables 23	19	1	11	50	368
Inventories 24	214	106	419	841	5802
Net Property, Plant and Equipment 25	69	37	35	181	2229
Total Assets 26	435	207	728	1489	14671
Notes and Loans Payable 27	177	89	438	636	4676
All Other Liabilities 28	101	31	184	325	4107
Net Worth 29	158	87	105	528	5887

Selected Financial Ratios (Times to 1)

Current Ratio 30	2.6	4.2	2.2	2.5	2.0
Quick Ratio 31	0.8	1.3	0.6	0.7	0.4
Net Sales to Working Capital 32	8.6	7.6	10.1	6.3	8.3
Coverage Ratio 33	7.7	6.9	4.4	12.3	6.1
Total Asset Turnover 34	3.7	4.0	3.6	3.0	2.6
Inventory Turnover 35	5.8	6.2	4.9	4.0	5.2
Receivables Turnover 36	111.1	545.5	459.9	58.4	133.2
Total Liabilities to Net Worth 37	1.8	1.4	5.9	1.8	1.5
Current Assets to Working Capital 38	1.6	1.3	1.8	1.7	2.0
Current Liabilities to Working Capital 39	0.6	0.3	0.8	0.7	1.0
Working Capital to Net Sales 40	0.1	0.1	0.1	0.2	0.1
Inventory to Working Capital 41	1.1	0.9	1.3	1.1	1.4
Total Receipts to Cash Flow 42	12.9	13.4	14.7	8.5	16.6
Cost of Goods to Cash Flow 43	10.1	10.6	11.7	6.3	12.9
Cash Flow to Total Debt 44	0.4	0.5	0.3	0.6	0.3

Selected Financial Factors (in Percentages)

Debt Ratio 45	63.8	57.9	85.5	64.5	59.9
Return on Total Assets 46	12.9	12.7	9.4	16.1	8.9
Return on Equity Before Income Taxes 47	30.9	25.7	50.5	41.7	18.6
Return on Equity After Income Taxes 48	29.7	25.3	48.1	39.2	17.2
Profit Margin (Before Income Tax) 49	3.1	2.7	2.0	4.9	2.8
Profit Margin (After Income Tax) 50	2.9	2.6	1.9	4.6	2.6

Table I

Corporations with and without Net Income

HEALTH AND PERSONAL CARE STORES

MONEY AMOUNTS AND SIZE OF ASSETS IN THOUSANDS OF DOLLARS

Item Description for Accounting Period 7/03 Through 6/04	Total	Zero Assets	Under 500	500 to 1,000	1,000 to 5,000	5,000 to 10,000	10,000 to 25,000	25,000 to 50,000	50,000 to 100,000	100,000 to 250,000	250,000 to 500,000	500,000 to 2,500,000	2,500,000 and over
Number of Enterprises **1**	34994	3184	25699	4093	1716	170	61	25	18	14	4	5	5
Revenues ($ in Thousands)													
Net Sales **2**	220546445	16061194	22393624	15828723	9613835	3893215	2254688	2229917	3026438	6673194	1093716	9158393	128319510
Interest **3**	482088	161858	2906	4329	7030	535	1865	979	1551	8505	7468	50993	234069
Rents **4**	118773	489	454	3018	7720	3824	440	126	1015	2146	0	23264	76278
Royalties **5**	198713	100224	3406	0	0	78	0	3349	744	1550	36693	51957	712
Other Portfolio Income **6**	132153	56490	2087	3621	17112	2682	941	636	13367	4638	2090	8477	20015
Other Receipts **7**	2055540	66350	58984	69782	71530	22110	30536	24774	39634	78736	4186	190487	1398425
Total Receipts **8**	223533712	16446605	22461461	15909473	9717227	3922444	2288470	2259781	3082749	6768769	1144153	9483571	130049009
Average Total Receipts **9**	6388	5165	874	3887	5663	23073	37516	90391	171264	483484	286038	1896714	26009802
Operating Costs/Operating Income (%)													
Cost of Operations **10**	77.4	85.2	70.9	76.7	69.2	57.3	64.8	64.3	62.3	73.1	44.7	62.0	81.3
Salaries and Wages **11**	8.5	4.0	7.4	7.1	12.7	17.8	11.7	13.4	15.1	12.0	6.1	15.9	7.9
Taxes Paid **12**	1.0	0.6	1.6	1.3	1.6	1.5	1.6	1.6	2.0	1.7	1.9	2.3	0.7
Interest Paid **13**	0.6	1.0	0.3	0.2	0.4	0.5	0.5	0.9	0.9	1.4	2.4	1.3	0.5
Depreciation **14**	1.0	0.4	0.6	0.4	1.0	1.0	1.3	1.0	1.8	1.3	4.3	2.5	1.0
Amortization and Depletion **15**	0.2	0.1	0.0	0.1	0.1	0.1	0.3	0.5	0.5	0.5	0.4	0.4	0.2
Pensions and Other Deferred Comp. **16**	0.2	0.0	0.2	0.5	0.3	0.2	0.1	0.2	0.3	0.1	0.2	0.4	0.2
Employee Benefits **17**	0.6	0.5	0.3	0.2	0.7	0.4	0.8	0.7	1.4	1.1	0.6	1.3	0.5
Advertising **18**	0.9	0.9	1.0	0.4	1.2	3.4	3.0	1.3	2.2	1.2	1.9	2.2	0.7
Other Expenses **19**	7.3	6.9	10.2	5.9	8.9	13.9	12.8	12.4	12.3	9.6	38.6	12.6	5.7
Officers' Compensation **20**	1.1	0.3	4.6	4.7	3.1	0.8	1.2	1.3	0.9	0.4	0.3	0.4	0.1
Operating Margin **21**	1.1	0.0	2.8	2.7	0.9	3.1	1.9	2.5	0.2	•	•	•	1.1
Operating Margin Before Officers' Comp. **22**	2.2	0.4	7.3	7.4	4.0	3.9	3.1	3.8	1.1	•	•	•	1.2

Selected Average Balance Sheet ($ in Thousands)

Net Receivables 23	220	0	19	73	308	1840	3344	8455	9915	25306	3109	59458	964662
Inventories 24	483	0	60	214	473	1421	3701	10129	15919	51141	49661	249783	2100864
Net Property, Plant and Equipment 25	389	0	28	81	229	1089	2388	4586	16714	32356	43203	283129	1875826
Total Assets 26	1918	0	153	696	1659	6681	14891	35535	70514	155560	367784	1128246	8800531
Notes and Loans Payable 27	369	0	57	190	307	2231	4307	9887	20112	90230	39692	311316	1179650
All Other Liabilities 28	603	0	45	191	490	3324	10137	13576	23571	56813	135380	264030	2742237
Net Worth 29	947	0	51	316	861	1126	446	12072	26831	8517	192712	552900	4878643

Selected Financial Ratios (Times to 1)

Current Ratio 30	1.7	•	2.5	2.4	2.3	1.9	0.8	1.2	1.5	1.7	0.9	2.1	1.6
Quick Ratio 31	0.7	•	1.1	1.1	1.3	1.1	0.4	0.6	0.6	0.6	0.1	0.4	0.6
Net Sales to Working Capital 32	16.4	•	12.8	14.0	8.0	10.0	20.7	•	14.1	12.8	•	6.7	18.4
Coverage Ratio 33	5.3	3.4	12.2	19.4	6.5	8.6	7.8	5.2	3.2	0.4	2.3	2.8	5.7
Total Asset Turnover 34	3.3	•	5.7	5.6	3.4	3.4	2.5	2.5	2.4	3.1	0.7	1.6	2.9
Inventory Turnover 35	10.1	•	10.3	13.8	8.2	9.2	6.5	5.7	6.6	6.8	2.5	4.6	9.9
Receivables Turnover 36	28.9	•	42.4	51.2	16.3	12.8	11.1	9.6	17.2	18.6	19.7	15.7	30.0
Total Liabilities to Net Worth 37	1.0	•	2.0	1.2	0.9	4.9	32.4	1.9	1.6	17.3	0.9	1.0	0.8
Current Assets to Working Capital 38	2.5	•	1.7	1.7	1.8	2.1	•	5.0	3.2	2.4	•	1.9	2.8
Current Liabilities to Working Capital 39	1.5	•	0.7	0.7	0.8	1.1	•	4.0	2.2	1.4	•	0.9	1.8
Working Capital to Net Sales 40	0.1	•	0.1	0.1	0.1	0.1	•	0.0	0.1	0.1	•	0.1	0.1
Inventory to Working Capital 41	1.3	•	0.9	0.8	0.6	0.7	•	2.0	1.4	1.4	•	0.9	1.6
Total Receipts to Cash Flow 42	14.1	13.3	10.2	14.5	12.1	6.5	7.5	7.5	10.5	21.2	3.5	10.8	17.4
Cost of Goods to Cash Flow 43	10.9	11.3	7.2	11.1	8.4	3.7	4.9	4.8	6.5	15.5	1.6	6.7	14.2
Cash Flow to Total Debt 44	0.5	•	0.8	0.7	0.6	0.6	0.3	0.5	0.4	0.2	0.4	0.3	0.4

Selected Financial Factors (in Percentages)

Debt Ratio 45	50.6	•	66.5	54.7	48.1	83.1	97.0	66.0	61.9	94.5	47.6	51.0	44.6
Return on Total Assets 46	10.1	•	19.0	18.8	7.7	14.7	9.7	12.1	7.1	1.5	4.2	5.7	8.8
Return on Equity Before Income Taxes 47	16.6	•	52.0	39.4	12.6	77.4	281.3	28.7	12.7	•	4.5	7.4	13.0
Return on Equity After Income Taxes 48	12.4	•	50.3	38.2	11.4	73.6	241.5	23.7	11.1	•	4.4	4.4	8.6
Profit Margin (Before Income Tax) 49	2.5	2.4	3.1	3.2	1.9	3.8	3.4	3.9	2.0	•	3.2	2.2	2.5
Profit Margin (After Income Tax) 50	1.9	1.7	3.0	3.1	1.8	3.6	2.9	3.2	1.8	•	3.1	1.3	1.6

Table II
Corporations with Net Income

HEALTH AND PERSONAL CARE STORES

MONEY AMOUNTS AND SIZE OF ASSETS IN THOUSANDS OF DOLLARS

Item Description for Accounting Period 7/03 Through 6/04	Total	Zero Assets	Under 500	500 to 1,000	1,000 to 5,000	5,000 to 10,000	10,000 to 25,000	25,000 to 50,000	50,000 to 100,000	100,000 to 250,000	250,000 to 500,000	500,000 to 2,500,000	2,500,000 and over
Number of Enterprises **1**	24525	1661	17513	3710	1401	146	40	19	13	10	•	•	5
Revenues ($ in Thousands)													
Net Sales **2**	204349853	13507771	17362112	14702984	8305822	3243152	1635890	1715616	2680803	4135851	•	•	128319510
Interest **3**	304096	3937	2780	2927	2841	396	241	776	825	3297	•	•	234069
Rents **4**	101360	425	454	3013	6578	3818	438	33	1015	2146	•	•	76278
Royalties **5**	42713	70	0	0	0	0	0	3349	0	0	•	•	712
Other Portfolio Income **6**	79856	23565	1939	2095	16250	2427	338	268	3520	3897	•	•	20015
Other Receipts **7**	1709373	1283	54704	31913	24848	20837	27568	21036	15930	53995	•	•	1398425
Total Receipts **8**	206587251	13537051	17421989	14742932	8356339	3270630	1664475	1741078	2702093	4199186	•	•	130049009
Average Total Receipts **9**	8424	8150	995	3974	5965	22402	41612	91636	207853	419919	•	•	26009802
Operating Costs/Operating Income (%)													
Cost of Operations **10**	78.3	88.8	71.5	76.9	70.1	56.5	62.9	63.4	65.6	68.8	•	•	81.3
Salaries and Wages **11**	8.2	2.6	6.6	6.9	12.6	19.5	11.0	12.7	13.7	12.1	•	•	7.9
Taxes Paid **12**	1.0	0.4	1.4	1.2	1.6	1.6	1.6	1.5	1.9	1.9	•	•	0.7
Interest Paid **13**	0.5	0.3	0.2	0.2	0.3	0.5	0.4	0.3	0.6	1.4	•	•	0.5
Depreciation **14**	0.9	0.3	0.6	0.4	0.8	1.1	0.9	1.1	1.6	1.6	•	•	1.0
Amortization and Depletion **15**	0.2	0.0	0.0	0.1	0.0	0.1	0.3	0.3	0.3	0.5	•	•	0.2
Pensions and Other Deferred Comp. **16**	0.2	0.0	0.2	0.4	0.3	0.2	0.2	0.2	0.3	0.1	•	•	0.2
Employee Benefits **17**	0.5	0.4	0.3	0.2	0.6	0.3	0.8	0.6	1.4	1.3	•	•	0.5
Advertising **18**	0.8	0.5	0.9	0.3	0.6	1.9	3.7	1.1	1.1	1.5	•	•	0.7
Other Expenses **19**	6.5	3.4	9.1	5.6	7.2	12.5	12.9	12.5	9.4	9.2	•	•	5.7
Officers' Compensation **20**	0.9	0.3	4.3	4.2	3.1	0.8	1.5	1.4	0.8	0.6	•	•	0.1
Operating Margin **21**	2.0	3.0	4.8	3.5	2.8	4.8	3.9	5.0	3.4	0.9	•	•	1.1
Operating Margin Before Officers' Comp. **22**	2.9	3.3	9.1	7.8	5.9	5.7	5.4	6.4	4.2	1.5	•	•	1.2

Selected Average Balance Sheet ($ in Thousands)

Net Receivables 23	293	0	22	73	302	2010	3695	8396	11598	26933	•	964662
Inventories 24	583	0	66	191	426	1309	4171	9314	16748	58438	•	2176187
Net Property, Plant and Equipment 25	514	0	25	87	211	1121	1752	5387	18192	36220	•	1875826
Total Assets 26	2521	0	169	707	1608	6576	14864	33896	74881	166172	•	8800531
Notes and Loans Payable 27	402	0	42	144	263	1948	2796	4012	18586	81569	•	1179650
All Other Liabilities 28	776	0	49	186	454	3141	6259	13225	24289	49100	•	2742237
Net Worth 29	1344	0	78	377	891	1487	5808	16659	32006	35503	•	4878643

Selected Financial Ratios (Times to 1)

Current Ratio 30	1.7	•	2.8	2.5	2.5	2.0	1.5	1.6	1.9	1.8	•	1.6
Quick Ratio 31	0.7	•	1.3	1.2	1.4	1.3	0.8	0.8	0.8	0.6	•	0.6
Net Sales to Working Capital 32	16.3	•	12.1	13.9	8.0	9.4	12.2	11.6	10.2	10.7	•	18.4
Coverage Ratio 33	7.2	13.7	25.1	21.8	13.0	11.9	16.7	22.2	7.7	2.8	•	5.7
Total Asset Turnover 34	3.3	•	5.9	5.6	3.7	3.4	2.8	2.7	2.8	2.5	•	2.9
Inventory Turnover 35	11.2	•	10.7	16.0	9.7	9.6	6.2	6.1	8.1	4.9	•	9.6
Receivables Turnover 36	30.9	•	43.2	57.3	18.9	22.1	10.6	10.2	21.8	14.5	•	53.2
Total Liabilities to Net Worth 37	0.9	•	1.2	0.9	0.8	3.4	1.6	1.0	1.3	3.7	•	0.8
Current Assets to Working Capital 38	2.4	•	1.6	1.7	1.7	2.0	3.0	2.8	2.1	2.3	•	2.8
Current Liabilities to Working Capital 39	1.4	•	0.6	0.7	0.7	1.0	2.0	1.8	1.1	1.3	•	1.8
Working Capital to Net Sales 40	0.1	•	0.1	0.1	0.1	0.1	0.1	0.1	0.1	0.1	•	0.1
Inventory to Working Capital 41	1.3	•	0.8	0.8	0.6	0.6	1.2	1.1	1.0	1.4	•	1.6
Total Receipts to Cash Flow 42	14.2	17.5	8.9	13.8	12.1	6.2	6.2	6.2	10.4	13.0	•	17.4
Cost of Goods to Cash Flow 43	11.1	15.6	6.4	10.6	8.5	3.5	3.9	4.0	6.8	9.0	•	14.2
Cash Flow to Total Debt 44	0.5	•	1.2	0.9	0.7	0.7	0.7	0.8	0.5	0.2	•	0.4

Selected Financial Factors (in Percentages)

Debt Ratio 45	46.7	•	54.0	46.7	44.6	77.4	60.9	50.9	57.3	78.6	•	44.6
Return on Total Assets 46	11.7	•	31.5	22.2	13.7	20.9	16.6	18.2	13.3	9.4	•	8.8
Return on Equity Before Income Taxes 47	18.9	•	65.6	39.8	22.8	84.8	40.0	35.3	27.0	28.1	•	13.0
Return on Equity After Income Taxes 48	14.6	•	64.0	38.6	21.4	81.5	35.3	30.6	25.2	19.9	•	8.6
Profit Margin (Before Income Tax) 49	3.0	3.2	5.2	3.8	3.4	5.7	5.7	6.5	4.2	2.4	•	2.5
Profit Margin (After Income Tax) 50	2.4	2.3	5.0	3.7	3.2	5.5	5.0	5.6	3.9	1.7	•	1.6

Table I

Corporations with and without Net Income

GASOLINE STATIONS

MONEY AMOUNTS AND SIZE OF ASSETS IN THOUSANDS OF DOLLARS

Item Description for Accounting Period 7/03 Through 6/04	Total	Zero Assets	Under 500	500 to 1,000	1,000 to 5,000	5,000 to 10,000	10,000 to 25,000	25,000 to 50,000	50,000 to 100,000	100,000 to 250,000	250,000 to 500,000	500,000 to 2,500,000	2,500,000 and over
Number of Enterprises **1**	34717	1602	24801	4719	3008	297	178	57	26	13	7	9	•
Revenues ($ in Thousands)													
Net Sales **2**	159360648	6532611	43595470	13491567	20212521	9539028	12220231	9397466	5447846	6330428	9627633	22965847	•
Interest **3**	55523	1	3778	4166	11535	9021	5378	3885	1783	2246	7912	5817	•
Rents **4**	129954	11124	9923	16603	12177	12196	11610	12226	5356	6726	9254	22758	•
Royalties **5**	45911	26879	0	0	0	0	335	383	514	25	0	17774	•
Other Portfolio Income **6**	371664	7914	43482	34772	70620	88948	32439	11872	9360	5441	39404	27412	•
Other Receipts **7**	1293784	100094	323198	131542	106172	60863	107132	46395	64790	124125	58864	170611	•
Total Receipts **8**	161257484	6678623	43975851	13678650	20413025	9710056	12377125	9472227	5529649	6468991	9743067	23210219	•
Average Total Receipts **9**	4645	4169	1773	2899	6786	32694	69534	166179	212679	497615	1391867	2578913	•
Operating Costs/Operating Income (%)													
Cost of Operations **10**	85.9	84.7	86.1	85.1	86.8	82.5	87.4	86.3	86.4	86.7	85.6	85.7	•
Salaries and Wages **11**	4.3	5.6	3.2	4.5	4.1	5.6	4.2	4.1	4.6	5.1	5.1	5.4	•
Taxes Paid **12**	1.2	1.0	1.4	1.2	1.1	2.6	1.0	2.0	0.8	0.8	0.7	0.9	•
Interest Paid **13**	0.6	0.4	0.2	0.7	1.0	0.7	0.6	0.5	0.9	0.6	0.4	0.7	•
Depreciation **14**	1.5	1.7	0.7	1.6	1.6	1.5	1.5	1.6	1.8	1.8	2.1	2.4	•
Amortization and Depletion **15**	0.1	0.4	0.1	0.2	0.1	0.2	0.1	0.1	0.1	0.1	0.1	0.1	•
Pensions and Other Deferred Comp. **16**	0.1	0.0	0.0	0.1	0.0	0.0	0.1	0.0	0.1	0.2	0.3	0.1	•
Employee Benefits **17**	0.2	0.2	0.1	0.1	0.1	0.4	0.2	0.2	0.4	0.3	0.5	0.4	•
Advertising **18**	0.2	0.2	0.1	0.1	0.2	0.1	0.2	0.1	0.2	0.2	0.4	0.2	•
Other Expenses **19**	5.8	7.3	7.3	6.0	5.0	6.9	5.3	4.7	5.5	4.9	4.7	4.0	•
Officers' Compensation **20**	0.6	0.1	1.2	0.9	0.8	0.5	0.4	0.3	0.3	0.2	0.2	0.1	•
Operating Margin **21**	•	•	•	•	•	•	•	0.1	•	•	•	0.0	•
Operating Margin Before Officers' Comp. **22**	0.1	0.9	0.4	0.4	•	•	•	0.4	0.2	•	0.2	0.1	•

Selected Average Balance Sheet ($ in Thousands)

Net Receivables 23	91	0	16	51	206	806	1390	3054	6611	8524	39892	74651
Inventories 24	110	0	47	59	153	710	1430	3032	4738	16958	37737	72118
Net Property, Plant and Equipment 25	480	0	63	366	1041	3265	8431	20317	30819	62796	176078	420613
Total Assets 26	961	0	192	703	1794	6559	15145	34581	68671	142142	325924	816996
Notes and Loans Payable 27	451	0	107	389	1099	3047	7116	14962	28915	54505	110346	289182
All Other Liabilities 28	237	0	30	124	327	2000	3937	9596	20209	39783	106319	253108
Net Worth 29	273	0	55	190	369	1511	4092	10024	19547	47855	109258	274707

Selected Financial Ratios (Times to 1)

Current Ratio 30	1.4	•	3.0	1.6	1.8	1.2	1.1	1.1	1.0	1.0	0.9	1.2
Quick Ratio 31	0.8	•	1.4	1.1	1.2	0.8	0.7	0.7	0.5	0.5	0.5	0.7
Net Sales to Working Capital 32	47.1	•	27.3	32.9	26.8	72.7	133.5	179.7	419.4	302.5	•	56.5
Coverage Ratio 33	2.2	2.0	3.3	2.3	1.1	2.2	1.4	2.7	1.6	3.1	4.3	2.5
Total Asset Turnover 34	4.8	•	9.2	4.1	3.7	4.9	4.5	4.8	3.1	3.4	4.2	3.1
Inventory Turnover 35	35.9	•	31.9	41.4	38.1	37.3	42.0	46.9	38.2	24.9	31.2	30.3
Receivables Turnover 36	55.1	•	116.5	78.2	39.1	43.9	50.3	64.0	33.5	42.2	24.9	43.8
Total Liabilities to Net Worth 37	2.5	•	2.5	2.7	3.9	3.3	2.7	2.4	2.5	2.0	2.0	2.0
Current Assets to Working Capital 38	3.4	•	1.5	2.6	2.2	5.4	9.4	12.0	44.2	27.1	•	5.9
Current Liabilities to Working Capital 39	2.4	•	0.5	1.6	1.2	4.4	8.4	11.0	43.2	26.1	•	4.9
Working Capital to Net Sales 40	0.0	•	0.0	0.0	0.0	0.0	0.0	0.0	0.0	0.0	•	0.0
Inventory to Working Capital 41	1.1	•	0.7	0.8	0.5	1.7	2.9	3.4	9.7	9.4	•	1.9
Total Receipts to Cash Flow 42	24.5	23.5	23.0	21.5	27.2	21.8	26.6	24.4	23.5	21.5	25.3	30.1
Cost of Goods to Cash Flow 43	21.1	19.9	19.8	18.3	23.6	18.0	23.3	21.0	20.3	18.7	21.7	25.8
Cash Flow to Total Debt 44	0.3	•	0.6	0.3	0.2	0.3	0.2	0.3	0.2	0.2	0.3	0.2

Selected Financial Factors (in Percentages)

Debt Ratio 45	71.6	•	71.5	73.0	79.5	77.0	73.0	71.0	71.5	66.3	66.5	66.4
Return on Total Assets 46	5.8	•	6.9	6.7	4.1	7.1	4.0	6.5	4.3	6.2	6.3	5.5
Return on Equity Before Income Taxes 47	11.1	•	16.8	14.0	1.6	16.8	4.4	14.1	5.8	12.6	14.4	9.9
Return on Equity After Income Taxes 48	9.5	•	15.9	13.2	0.5	15.1	3.3	13.4	4.5	11.2	10.4	8.5
Profit Margin (Before Income Tax) 49	0.7	0.4	0.5	0.9	0.1	0.8	0.3	0.9	0.5	1.2	1.1	1.1
Profit Margin (After Income Tax) 50	0.6	0.2	0.5	0.9	0.0	0.7	0.2	0.8	0.4	1.1	0.8	0.9

Table II

Corporations with Net Income

GASOLINE STATIONS

MONEY AMOUNTS AND SIZE OF ASSETS IN THOUSANDS OF DOLLARS

Item Description for Accounting Period 7/03 Through 6/04	Total	Zero Assets	Under 500	500 to 1,000	1,000 to 5,000	5,000 to 10,000	10,000 to 25,000	25,000 to 50,000	50,000 to 100,000	100,000 to 250,000	250,000 to 500,000	500,000 to 2,500,000	2,500,000 and over
Number of Enterprises **1**	17664	9	13299	2576	1341	245	111	45	17	6	•	•	•
Revenues ($ in Thousands)													
Net Sales **2**	117511115	5742384	29629629	8944578	12977722	7092876	8183399	8220999	3768213	2963555	•	•	•
Interest **3**	45396	1	2861	3709	8360	6982	4679	2991	1429	1000	•	•	•
Rents **4**	85132	11124	706	5147	9469	8102	7405	11171	4202	2502	•	•	•
Royalties **5**	40527	26879	0	0	0	0	157	1	514	0	•	•	•
Other Portfolio Income **6**	270835	7914	43481	34732	68534	12165	26128	11171	3158	882	•	•	•
Other Receipts **7**	991474	69696	220288	94684	87805	52241	78380	34829	46587	85846	•	•	•
Total Receipts **8**	118944479	5857998	29896965	9082850	13151890	7172366	8300148	8281162	3824103	3053785	•	•	•
Average Total Receipts **9**	6734	650889	2248	3526	9808	29275	74776	184026	224947	508964	•	•	•
Operating Costs/Operating Income (%)													
Cost of Operations **10**	86.0	82.9	85.9	86.6	87.3	81.5	87.2	86.9	86.7	89.1	•	•	•
Salaries and Wages **11**	4.2	6.3	2.9	3.5	4.2	5.7	4.1	3.9	4.2	4.0	•	•	•
Taxes Paid **12**	1.2	1.1	1.2	0.9	1.1	2.8	1.2	1.6	0.8	0.5	•	•	•
Interest Paid **13**	0.4	0.5	0.2	0.5	0.6	0.5	0.4	0.4	0.9	0.4	•	•	•
Depreciation **14**	1.5	2.0	0.7	0.9	1.2	1.6	1.4	1.4	1.6	1.7	•	•	•
Amortization and Depletion **15**	0.1	0.5	0.1	0.2	0.1	0.1	0.1	0.1	0.1	0.0	•	•	•
Pensions and Other Deferred Comp. **16**	0.1	0.0	0.0	0.1	0.0	0.0	0.1	0.0	0.1	0.2	•	•	•
Employee Benefits **17**	0.2	0.3	0.1	0.1	0.2	0.3	0.1	0.2	0.4	0.0	•	•	•
Advertising **18**	0.2	0.2	0.1	0.0	0.2	0.1	0.1	0.1	0.1	0.1	•	•	•
Other Expenses **19**	5.3	7.3	6.9	5.6	4.6	6.2	5.3	4.6	4.5	3.2	•	•	•
Officers' Compensation **20**	0.6	•	1.2	0.6	0.8	0.6	0.4	0.4	0.3	0.2	•	•	•
Operating Margin **21**	0.3	•	0.8	0.9	•	0.6	•	0.5	0.4	0.6	•	•	•
Operating Margin Before Officers' Comp. **22**	0.9	•	1.9	1.5	0.7	1.1	0.0	0.8	0.8	0.8	•	•	•

Selected Average Balance Sheet ($ in Thousands)

Net Receivables 23	135	0	17	19	393	802	1529	3471	7455	9146
Inventories 24	133	0	56	62	173	556	1367	2805	4763	17784
Net Property, Plant and Equipment 25	594	0	51	318	928	2950	7700	19125	29956	62765
Total Assets 26	1256	0	207	675	1959	6531	15001	34369	70519	129168
Notes and Loans Payable 27	467	0	85	302	890	2663	5730	12107	26486	30374
All Other Liabilities 28	334	0	34	90	409	1615	4244	10708	20375	28748
Net Worth 29	454	0	88	284	660	2253	5027	11554	23657	70046

Selected Financial Ratios (Times to 1)

Current Ratio 30	1.4	•	3.5	2.3	1.8	1.5	1.1	1.1	1.2	1.5
Quick Ratio 31	0.8	•	1.5	1.3	1.4	0.9	0.7	0.7	0.6	0.8
Net Sales to Working Capital 32	46.5	•	26.5	27.6	26.5	37.4	116.1	148.8	47.2	30.7
Coverage Ratio 33	4.4	3.0	10.3	5.6	3.2	4.8	3.2	4.1	3.1	10.1
Total Asset Turnover 34	5.3	•	10.8	5.1	4.9	4.4	4.9	5.3	3.1	3.8
Inventory Turnover 35	43.1	•	33.9	48.3	48.8	42.5	47.0	56.6	40.3	24.7
Receivables Turnover 36	64.2	•	132.6	187.9	37.5	56.5	53.6	72.3	40.1	46.3
Total Liabilities to Net Worth 37	1.8	•	1.4	1.4	2.0	1.9	2.0	2.0	2.0	0.8
Current Assets to Working Capital 38	3.3	•	1.4	1.8	2.2	3.2	8.4	10.0	5.4	2.8
Current Liabilities to Working Capital 39	2.3	•	0.4	0.8	1.2	2.2	7.4	9.0	4.4	1.8
Working Capital to Net Sales 40	0.0	•	0.0	0.0	0.0	0.0	0.0	0.0	0.0	0.0
Inventory to Working Capital 41	1.1	•	0.7	0.6	0.4	1.0	2.4	2.7	1.1	0.7
Total Receipts to Cash Flow 42	21.8	20.6	19.3	17.0	23.3	17.7	22.4	23.2	19.8	16.7
Cost of Goods to Cash Flow 43	18.7	17.1	16.5	14.7	20.3	14.4	19.5	20.1	17.2	14.9
Cash Flow to Total Debt 44	0.4	•	1.0	0.5	0.3	0.4	0.3	0.3	0.2	0.5

Selected Financial Factors (in Percentages)

Debt Ratio 45	63.8	•	57.7	58.0	66.3	65.5	66.5	66.4	66.5	45.8
Return on Total Assets 46	10.4	•	20.0	15.3	9.0	9.5	7.1	8.4	8.7	15.5
Return on Equity Before Income Taxes 47	22.2	•	42.7	30.0	18.3	21.9	14.8	18.9	17.6	25.8
Return on Equity After Income Taxes 48	20.3	•	41.6	29.0	17.0	20.5	13.4	18.1	16.0	24.1
Profit Margin (Before Income Tax) 49	1.5	0.9	1.7	2.4	1.2	1.7	1.0	1.2	1.9	3.7
Profit Margin (After Income Tax) 50	1.4	0.6	1.6	2.4	1.2	1.6	0.9	1.1	1.7	3.4

Table I

Corporations with and without Net Income

CLOTHING AND CLOTHING ACCESSORIES STORES

MONEY AMOUNTS AND SIZE OF ASSETS IN THOUSANDS OF DOLLARS

Item Description for Accounting Period 7/03 Through 6/04	Total	Zero Assets	Under 500	500 to 1,000	1,000 to 5,000	5,000 to 10,000	10,000 to 25,000	25,000 to 50,000	50,000 to 100,000	100,000 to 250,000	250,000 to 500,000	500,000 to 2,500,000	2,500,000 and over
Number of Enterprises 1	53269	3845	41975	4404	2456	284	142	55	32	27	23	20	5
Revenues ($ in Thousands)													
Net Sales 2	145812336	1328270	15178174	5811415	7261780	3640050	4661614	4155781	5275580	8616158	14532345	35557771	39793399
Interest 3	742605	766	4040	2052	8982	4768	12099	3472	2986	21282	59940	191555	430662
Rents 4	149782	0	0	294	6732	1130	2465	3461	8	2327	32841	42917	57608
Royalties 5	1177452	0	10232	0	0	0	830	2761	10575	5836	137347	492945	516926
Other Portfolio Income 6	363761	0	22306	1026	1780	678	1540	6273	1122	2468	15794	61491	249285
Other Receipts 7	2642529	13323	33553	33534	52600	23964	38949	137494	113789	69772	164573	697303	1263672
Total Receipts 8	150888465	1342359	15248305	5848321	7331874	3670590	4717497	4309242	5404060	8717843	14942840	37043982	42311552
Average Total Receipts 9	2833	349	363	1328	2985	12925	33222	78350	168877	322883	649689	1852199	8462310
Operating Costs/Operating Income (%)													
Cost of Operations 10	54.9	56.4	55.3	57.9	56.5	50.2	56.9	57.9	54.5	55.5	52.8	55.9	53.8
Salaries and Wages 11	14.3	11.7	10.2	13.6	14.0	16.4	13.8	15.7	15.7	14.9	14.9	13.8	15.8
Taxes Paid 12	2.3	2.1	2.6	2.2	2.3	3.1	2.1	2.7	2.7	2.6	2.3	2.1	2.2
Interest Paid 13	1.0	0.7	0.6	0.7	0.8	0.7	0.6	1.0	0.7	0.9	0.6	0.7	1.6
Depreciation 14	2.6	1.3	0.8	0.6	1.2	2.6	1.5	2.1	2.3	3.0	3.2	3.3	3.2
Amortization and Depletion 15	0.3	0.5	0.2	0.1	0.1	0.0	0.1	0.2	0.3	0.3	0.1	0.3	0.6
Pensions and Other Deferred Comp. 16	0.2	0.0	0.3	0.1	0.6	0.2	0.2	0.1	0.1	0.1	0.2	0.3	0.2
Employee Benefits 17	1.0	1.9	0.5	0.7	0.7	0.4	0.7	1.1	1.1	0.9	1.0	1.2	1.3
Advertising 18	2.5	0.6	2.4	2.4	3.4	3.2	3.5	2.9	2.3	2.1	2.5	2.6	2.3
Other Expenses 19	18.7	21.3	21.4	15.4	16.0	20.1	18.8	19.8	21.8	20.3	20.5	19.6	16.2
Officers' Compensation 20	1.8	4.5	5.9	5.1	5.4	1.5	2.5	1.4	1.1	0.7	1.0	0.8	0.6
Operating Margin 21	0.3	•	•	1.2	•	1.4	•	•	•	•	0.9	•	2.2
Operating Margin Before Officers' Comp. 22	2.1	3.5	5.6	6.3	4.5	3.0	1.7	•	•	1.9	1.9	0.3	2.8

Selected Average Balance Sheet ($ in Thousands)

Item	1	2	3	4	5	6	7	8	9	10	11	12	13
Net Receivables 23	106	0	6	36	87	1069	1770	3142	3644	8840	23948	64390	422233
Inventories 24	527	0	74	432	978	3583	7468	13963	29340	61672	99744	352423	1170474
Net Property, Plant and Equipment 25	373	0	10	52	281	1268	2788	6826	16564	51538	101234	259564	1596037
Total Assets 26	1635	0	125	682	1718	6897	16106	35438	72021	169531	350362	1167444	6027532
Notes and Loans Payable 27	339	0	55	217	487	1867	5045	13069	17120	40064	50984	141966	1193889
All Other Liabilities 28	649	0	38	201	513	2720	6083	14518	31035	53551	115847	382414	3127981
Net Worth 29	647	0	32	264	718	2310	4978	7850	23866	75916	183531	643065	1705662

Selected Financial Ratios (Times to 1)

Item	1	2	3	4	5	6	7	8	9	10	11	12	13
Current Ratio 30	2.0	•	2.1	3.0	1.6	2.1	1.6	1.3	1.4	1.6	2.0	1.8	2.2
Quick Ratio 31	0.7	•	0.5	0.6	0.5	0.5	0.5	0.5	0.3	0.4	0.8	0.4	1.3
Net Sales to Working Capital 32	5.8	•	6.8	3.3	6.6	4.4	7.5	12.8	12.8	9.9	6.2	6.8	4.5
Coverage Ratio 33	5.2	1.1	1.3	3.5	4.3	1.1	1.6	•	0.9	1.1	7.3	6.4	6.8
Total Asset Turnover 34	1.7	•	2.9	1.9	1.9	1.7	2.0	2.1	2.3	1.9	1.8	1.5	1.3
Inventory Turnover 35	2.9	•	2.7	1.8	1.8	1.7	2.5	3.1	3.1	2.9	3.3	2.8	3.7
Receivables Turnover 36	26.1	•	51.6	35.6	13.5	32.8	18.4	24.5	34.5	37.6	22.2	30.1	20.0
Total Liabilities to Net Worth 37	1.5	•	2.9	1.6	2.0	1.4	2.2	3.5	2.0	1.2	0.9	0.8	2.5
Current Assets to Working Capital 38	2.0	•	1.9	1.5	2.8	1.9	2.7	4.1	3.7	2.7	2.0	2.2	1.8
Current Liabilities to Working Capital 39	1.0	•	0.9	0.5	1.8	0.9	1.7	3.1	2.7	1.7	1.0	1.2	0.8
Working Capital to Net Sales 40	0.2	•	0.1	0.3	0.2	0.2	0.1	0.1	0.1	0.1	0.2	0.1	0.2
Inventory to Working Capital 41	1.1	•	1.4	1.2	1.8	1.4	1.7	2.3	2.4	1.9	1.0	1.4	0.6
Total Receipts to Cash Flow 42	7.5	9.7	8.4	9.2	7.9	10.7	9.3	11.7	8.1	10.0	7.2	7.9	5.9
Cost of Goods to Cash Flow 43	4.1	5.5	4.6	5.3	4.0	6.1	5.3	6.8	4.4	5.6	3.8	4.4	3.2
Cash Flow to Total Debt 44	0.4	•	0.5	0.3	0.4	0.3	0.3	0.2	0.4	0.3	0.5	0.4	0.3

Selected Financial Factors (in Percentages)

Item	1	2	3	4	5	6	7	8	9	10	11	12	13
Debt Ratio 45	60.4	•	74.4	61.3	66.5	69.1	58.2	77.8	66.9	55.2	47.6	44.9	71.7
Return on Total Assets 46	8.2	•	2.4	4.9	5.5	2.0	1.5	•	1.4	1.7	7.6	6.8	14.5
Return on Equity Before Income Taxes 47	16.7	•	2.1	9.0	12.6	2.4	0.2	•	•	0.2	12.5	10.4	43.7
Return on Equity After Income Taxes 48	10.3	0.6	0.6	8.2	11.8	0.5	•	•	•	•	7.6	6.3	28.4
Profit Margin (Before Income Tax) 49	4.0	0.1	0.2	1.8	2.3	0.4	0.0	•	•	0.0	3.6	3.7	9.4
Profit Margin (After Income Tax) 50	2.4	•	0.1	1.6	2.1	0.1	•	•	•	•	2.2	2.3	6.1

Table II

Corporations with Net Income

CLOTHING AND CLOTHING ACCESSORIES STORES

MONEY AMOUNTS AND SIZE OF ASSETS IN THOUSANDS OF DOLLARS

Item Description for Accounting Period 7/03 Through 6/04	Total	Zero Assets	Under 500	500 to 1,000	1,000 to 5,000	5,000 to 10,000	10,000 to 25,000	25,000 to 50,000	50,000 to 100,000	100,000 to 250,000	250,000 to 500,000	500,000 to 2,500,000	2,500,000 and over
Number of Enterprises **1**	30904	1308	24211	3305	1666	210	101	32	18	15	18	14	5
Revenues ($ in Thousands)													
Net Sales **2**	116076976	603587	9335466	4850582	5491896	2912414	3372563	2487406	2941512	5147484	11746309	27394359	39793399
Interest **3**	691762	653	2861	1286	6166	950	7750	1328	1646	2574	58907	176977	430662
Rents **4**	133625	0	0	125	5071	426	2137	454	8	2327	27268	38201	57608
Royalties **5**	1002516	0	39	0	0	0	632	0	8913	5809	133421	336776	516926
Other Portfolio Income **6**	283352	0	1111	628	1266	671	359	1910	174	1486	15431	11032	249285
Other Receipts **7**	2321124	1173	6950	6260	42407	9680	24951	31813	104219	6392	155223	668384	1263672
Total Receipts **8**	120509355	605413	9346427	4858881	5546806	2924141	3408392	2522911	3056472	5166072	12136559	28625729	42311552
Average Total Receipts **9**	3899	463	386	1470	3329	13924	33746	78841	169804	344405	674253	2044695	8462310
Operating Costs/Operating Income (%)													
Cost of Operations **10**	54.1	53.0	53.1	57.8	56.6	48.2	57.5	58.6	47.8	57.5	51.7	54.6	53.8
Salaries and Wages **11**	14.2	11.8	9.2	12.7	12.7	16.6	12.5	14.2	16.7	12.8	14.8	13.9	15.8
Taxes Paid **12**	2.2	1.9	2.7	2.1	2.2	2.9	2.0	2.5	2.7	2.3	2.4	1.9	2.2
Interest Paid **13**	0.9	0.0	0.5	0.6	0.6	0.5	0.6	0.6	0.4	0.6	0.4	0.5	1.6
Depreciation **14**	2.7	1.6	0.5	0.5	1.0	2.9	1.3	2.1	2.4	3.1	3.3	3.5	3.2
Amortization and Depletion **15**	0.3	0.0	0.1	0.1	0.1	0.0	0.1	0.1	0.1	0.2	0.1	0.4	0.6
Pensions and Other Deferred Comp. **16**	0.2	0.0	0.1	0.1	0.7	0.3	0.2	0.1	0.2	0.1	0.2	0.3	0.2
Employee Benefits **17**	1.0	0.4	0.3	0.7	0.5	0.3	0.6	0.7	1.1	0.6	1.0	1.2	1.3
Advertising **18**	2.4	0.1	2.1	2.3	3.6	3.2	3.5	1.4	3.1	1.9	2.3	2.4	2.3
Other Expenses **19**	17.8	20.4	20.6	14.4	14.2	19.6	14.9	14.9	22.8	15.3	20.6	19.5	16.2
Officers' Compensation **20**	1.6	1.6	5.1	5.0	5.8	1.0	2.9	1.5	1.4	0.6	1.1	0.8	0.6
Operating Margin **21**	2.5	9.2	5.8	3.7	1.9	4.5	3.9	3.3	1.3	5.0	2.0	1.0	2.2
Operating Margin Before Officers' Comp. **22**	4.1	10.8	10.9	8.7	7.8	5.5	6.8	4.8	2.8	5.6	3.1	1.9	2.8

Selected Average Balance Sheet ($ in Thousands)

Net Receivables 23	145	0	8	36	80	1235	1971	3830	2208	7755	29061	46815	422233
Inventories 24	699	0	76	399	955	3124	7125	15403	28649	67100	87854	409482	1170474
Net Property, Plant and Equipment 25	534	0	7	42	274	1299	2671	6858	17879	48148	102194	292875	1596037
Total Assets 26	2234	0	128	656	1760	6876	15830	35350	69371	170126	366981	1151404	6027532
Notes and Loans Payable 27	371	0	32	163	483	1195	3617	6510	11230	33367	24675	101253	1193889
All Other Liabilities 28	913	0	40	157	546	2840	5395	11869	28106	44488	116798	384128	3127981
Net Worth 29	949	0	55	336	731	2841	6818	16972	30036	92272	225508	666024	1705662

Selected Financial Ratios (Times to 1)

Current Ratio 30	2.1	•	2.2	3.3	2.1	1.5	1.8	1.9	1.5	2.0	2.1	2.0	2.2
Quick Ratio 31	0.8	•	0.7	0.7	0.5	0.6	0.5	0.6	0.4	0.5	1.0	0.4	1.3
Net Sales to Working Capital 32	5.4	•	6.3	3.5	4.6	7.4	6.4	6.8	10.6	7.3	5.6	6.6	4.5
Coverage Ratio 33	8.6	437.6	14.1	7.7	6.0	11.4	9.6	9.4	14.7	10.6	14.2	12.6	6.8
Total Asset Turnover 34	1.7	•	3.0	2.2	1.9	2.0	2.1	2.2	2.4	2.0	1.8	1.7	1.3
Inventory Turnover 35	2.9	•	2.7	2.1	2.0	2.1	2.7	3.0	2.7	2.9	3.8	2.6	3.7
Receivables Turnover 36	25.9	•	45.5	38.6	44.9	22.5	17.3	20.2	44.3	47.6	24.7	83.6	20.0
Total Liabilities to Net Worth 37	1.4	•	1.3	1.0	1.4	1.4	1.3	1.1	1.3	0.8	0.6	0.7	2.5
Current Assets to Working Capital 38	1.9	•	1.8	1.4	1.9	2.9	2.3	2.2	3.1	2.0	1.9	2.0	1.8
Current Liabilities to Working Capital 39	0.9	•	0.8	0.4	0.9	1.9	1.3	1.2	2.1	1.0	0.9	1.0	0.8
Working Capital to Net Sales 40	0.2	•	0.2	0.3	0.2	0.1	0.2	0.1	0.1	0.1	0.2	0.2	0.2
Inventory to Working Capital 41	1.0	•	1.2	1.1	1.4	1.7	1.4	1.2	2.0	1.3	0.8	1.4	0.6
Total Receipts to Cash Flow 42	6.4	4.9	5.9	8.1	8.6	6.7	7.2	8.3	5.4	7.5	6.5	6.5	5.9
Cost of Goods to Cash Flow 43	3.5	2.6	3.1	4.7	4.9	3.2	4.1	4.9	2.6	4.3	3.4	3.6	3.2
Cash Flow to Total Debt 44	0.5	•	0.9	0.6	0.4	0.5	0.5	0.5	0.8	0.6	0.7	0.6	0.3

Selected Financial Factors (in Percentages)

Debt Ratio 45	57.5	•	56.7	48.9	58.5	58.7	56.9	52.0	56.7	45.8	38.6	42.2	71.7
Return on Total Assets 46	12.6	•	19.3	9.9	6.6	10.8	11.7	11.5	13.4	11.9	10.0	10.3	14.5
Return on Equity Before Income Taxes 47	26.2	•	41.3	16.8	13.1	23.9	24.2	21.4	28.9	19.9	15.1	16.3	43.7
Return on Equity After Income Taxes 48	18.6	•	39.8	15.9	11.9	23.0	22.3	18.7	23.5	14.2	10.0	10.8	28.4
Profit Margin (Before Income Tax) 49	6.6	9.5	5.9	3.8	2.9	4.9	4.9	4.7	5.3	5.3	5.2	5.6	9.4
Profit Margin (After Income Tax) 50	4.7	6.6	5.7	3.6	2.6	4.7	4.5	4.1	4.3	3.8	3.5	3.7	6.1

Table I

Corporations with and without Net Income

SPORTING GOODS, HOBBY, BOOK, AND MUSIC STORES

MONEY AMOUNTS AND SIZE OF ASSETS IN THOUSANDS OF DOLLARS

Item Description for Accounting Period 7/03 Through 6/04		Total	Zero Assets	Under 500	500 to 1,000	1,000 to 5,000	5,000 to 10,000	10,000 to 25,000	25,000 to 50,000	50,000 to 100,000	100,000 to 250,000	250,000 to 500,000	500,000 to 2,500,000	2,500,000 and over
Number of Enterprises	1	34259	5087	23838	2902	2091	198	72	19	15	12	11	13	•
Revenues ($ in Thousands)														
Net Sales	2	76305383	2464116	7513548	4442511	8948859	3717342	2414284	1513696	1780645	3555430	9461313	30493638	•
Interest	3	102872	1156	1421	3788	9857	665	3396	777	2700	762	9750	68600	•
Rents	4	34114	2290	1546	0	1561	2075	825	1338	781	0	5335	18364	•
Royalties	5	506436	25419	0	166	0	0	2158	0	110	11097	80744	386743	•
Other Portfolio Income	6	85851	4699	493	447	5000	13256	1378	28267	509	697	15253	15850	•
Other Receipts	7	1070153	91887	68707	11433	51717	10741	30827	86448	5125	24872	268963	419435	•
Total Receipts	8	78104809	2589567	7585715	4458345	9016994	3744079	2452868	1630526	1789870	3592858	9841358	31402630	•
Average Total Receipts	9	2280	509	318	1536	4312	18909	34068	85817	119325	299405	894669	2415587	•
Operating Costs/Operating Income (%)														
Cost of Operations	10	62.6	64.3	59.6	61.1	63.0	68.6	61.9	65.3	63.9	60.3	65.4	61.9	•
Salaries and Wages	11	12.1	14.0	8.2	11.2	12.8	10.2	13.1	13.0	12.9	13.2	11.4	12.9	•
Taxes Paid	12	2.2	2.8	2.1	3.1	2.0	1.8	1.9	2.2	1.9	2.3	2.0	2.2	•
Interest Paid	13	1.1	0.6	1.2	0.8	0.8	0.7	0.7	1.5	0.6	0.6	1.0	1.3	•
Depreciation	14	2.1	2.4	1.4	0.9	1.3	1.4	1.3	2.1	1.6	2.9	1.9	2.9	•
Amortization and Depletion	15	0.2	0.0	0.3	0.1	0.0	0.2	0.6	0.2	0.1	0.9	0.1	0.2	•
Pensions and Other Deferred Comp.	16	0.2	0.1	0.1	0.2	0.4	0.1	0.2	0.2	0.2	0.2	0.1	0.2	•
Employee Benefits	17	0.7	0.9	0.9	0.4	0.6	0.5	0.6	0.7	0.7	1.1	0.9	0.6	•
Advertising	18	2.1	3.1	1.7	2.8	1.7	2.0	3.8	2.9	4.5	2.3	3.0	1.5	•
Other Expenses	19	16.1	21.4	19.5	13.7	13.3	11.2	15.0	20.3	12.0	13.8	15.7	17.1	•
Officers' Compensation	20	1.7	0.7	5.8	4.5	3.3	1.1	2.0	1.0	1.1	1.1	0.8	0.4	•
Operating Margin	21	•	•	•	1.1	0.8	2.2	•	•	0.6	1.4	•	•	•
Operating Margin Before Officers' Comp.	22	0.7	•	5.0	5.6	4.1	3.4	1.0	•	1.7	2.5	•	•	•

Selected Average Balance Sheet ($ in Thousands)

	•	•	•	•	•	•	•	•	•	•	•	•
Net Receivables 23	74	0	5	30	270	530	1855	7190	8579	13300	36401	53762
Inventories 24	518	0	74	344	1029	3366	6112	14559	34385	71239	171136	630443
Net Property, Plant and Equipment 25	283	0	19	110	272	1213	2740	4780	8980	38511	89511	480525
Total Assets 26	1254	0	125	678	2030	7872	14763	34076	63788	149725	369140	1822218
Notes and Loans Payable 27	377	0	66	284	845	1860	3877	10622	14778	37446	70912	495630
All Other Liabilities 28	446	0	43	190	494	2648	7484	12602	16533	59678	161571	663458
Net Worth 29	432	0	17	204	691	3364	3402	10853	32477	52601	136658	663131

Selected Financial Ratios (Times to 1)

	•	•	•	•	•	•	•	•	•	•	•	•
Current Ratio 30	1.7	•	1.9	2.5	2.3	1.3	1.4	1.7	2.0	1.7	1.5	1.6
Quick Ratio 31	0.4	•	0.5	0.6	0.8	0.3	0.5	0.8	0.7	0.4	0.3	0.3
Net Sales to Working Capital 32	6.9	•	6.9	5.3	4.8	16.5	10.8	7.6	5.3	7.1	9.6	6.3
Coverage Ratio 33	2.3	•	1.1	2.8	2.9	5.0	1.8	•	2.8	5.3	2.6	2.4
Total Asset Turnover 34	1.8	•	2.5	2.3	2.1	2.4	2.3	2.3	1.9	2.0	2.3	1.3
Inventory Turnover 35	2.7	•	2.5	2.7	2.6	3.8	3.4	3.6	2.2	2.5	3.3	2.3
Receivables Turnover 36	30.9	•	67.4	40.7	17.8	33.9	18.0	13.6	16.1	23.4	24.6	40.9
Total Liabilities to Net Worth 37	1.9	•	6.5	2.3	1.9	1.3	3.3	2.1	1.0	1.8	1.7	1.7
Current Assets to Working Capital 38	2.4	•	2.2	1.7	1.8	4.5	3.4	2.3	2.0	2.5	2.9	2.6
Current Liabilities to Working Capital 39	1.4	•	1.2	0.7	0.8	3.5	2.4	1.3	1.0	1.5	1.9	1.6
Working Capital to Net Sales 40	0.1	•	0.1	0.2	0.2	0.1	0.1	0.1	0.2	0.1	0.1	0.2
Inventory to Working Capital 41	1.6	•	1.6	1.3	1.1	3.1	2.1	1.1	1.1	1.8	2.2	1.7
Total Receipts to Cash Flow 42	9.8	13.8	8.3	10.5	10.4	12.5	10.9	9.9	14.7	10.8	9.4	9.2
Cost of Goods to Cash Flow 43	6.1	8.9	5.0	6.4	6.6	8.6	6.8	6.5	9.4	6.5	6.2	5.7
Cash Flow to Total Debt 44	0.3	•	0.3	0.3	0.3	0.3	0.3	0.3	0.3	0.3	0.4	0.2

Selected Financial Factors (in Percentages)

	•	•	•	•	•	•	•	•	•	•	•	•
Debt Ratio 45	65.6	•	86.6	69.9	65.9	57.3	77.0	68.2	49.1	64.9	63.0	63.6
Return on Total Assets 46	4.2	•	3.3	5.3	4.9	8.8	3.0	•	3.2	6.0	6.0	4.1
Return on Equity Before Income Taxes 47	6.9	•	2.4	11.3	9.4	16.6	5.9	•	4.1	13.9	9.8	6.7
Return on Equity After Income Taxes 48	4.6	•	1.6	10.4	8.2	15.5	2.3	•	2.0	10.8	6.7	4.3
Profit Margin (Before Income Tax) 49	1.3	•	0.1	1.5	1.5	3.0	0.6	•	1.1	2.5	1.6	1.9
Profit Margin (After Income Tax) 50	0.9	•	0.1	1.4	1.3	2.8	0.2	•	0.6	1.9	1.1	1.2

Table II

Corporations with Net Income

SPORTING GOODS, HOBBY, BOOK, AND MUSIC STORES

MONEY AMOUNTS AND SIZE OF ASSETS IN THOUSANDS OF DOLLARS

Item Description for Accounting Period 7/03 Through 6/04	Total	Zero Assets	Under 500	500 to 1,000	1,000 to 5,000	5,000 to 10,000	10,000 to 25,000	25,000 to 50,000	50,000 to 100,000	100,000 to 250,000	250,000 to 500,000	500,000 to 2,500,000	2,500,000 and over
Number of Enterprises **1**	17274	2437	10950	2032	1565	184	57	12	9	•	7	•	•
Revenues ($ in Thousands)													
Net Sales **2**	49040143	189652	3299336	2718685	7296574	3579147	1814103	918225	1238140	•	5289841	•	•
Interest **3**	31666	1	610	2186	7204	640	1537	587	2632	•	6444	•	•
Rents **4**	11877	0	805	0	1355	1795	295	958	781	•	3	•	•
Royalties **5**	29624	0	0	0	0	0	2158	0	110	•	0	•	•
Other Portfolio Income **6**	41274	1510	0	395	4449	13256	1345	2177	485	•	2218	•	•
Other Receipts **7**	419913	24242	60687	6838	34496	-2075	22977	11295	4460	•	40467	•	•
Total Receipts **8**	49574497	215405	3361438	2728104	7344078	3592763	1842415	933242	1246608	•	5333973	•	•
Average Total Receipts **9**	2870	88	307	1343	4693	19526	32323	77770	138512	•	762710	•	•
Operating Costs/Operating Income (%)													
Cost of Operations **10**	61.0	60.1	58.4	60.1	62.4	68.9	61.1	59.9	60.3	•	66.2	•	•
Salaries and Wages **11**	12.2	6.9	6.8	10.1	12.3	10.0	13.0	11.5	14.4	•	10.6	•	•
Taxes Paid **12**	2.1	3.8	1.7	3.6	2.0	1.8	1.7	1.9	1.9	•	1.7	•	•
Interest Paid **13**	0.7	0.3	0.6	0.8	0.5	0.7	0.6	0.4	0.5	•	1.0	•	•
Depreciation **14**	2.1	0.2	1.1	1.0	1.1	1.4	1.1	1.7	1.5	•	2.1	•	•
Amortization and Depletion **15**	0.2	•	0.1	0.1	0.0	0.2	0.2	0.2	0.1	•	0.1	•	•
Pensions and Other Deferred Comp. **16**	0.2	•	0.1	0.1	0.4	0.1	0.2	0.2	0.2	•	0.2	•	•
Employee Benefits **17**	0.7	0.0	0.7	0.2	0.4	0.5	0.7	0.4	0.7	•	1.1	•	•
Advertising **18**	2.0	2.0	1.0	2.7	1.7	1.9	4.4	3.4	5.5	•	3.1	•	•
Other Expenses **19**	14.2	17.6	18.1	11.9	13.1	10.4	12.3	15.2	10.9	•	10.1	•	•
Officers' Compensation **20**	1.6	4.7	4.5	4.9	3.2	1.1	2.2	1.1	1.3	•	0.3	•	•
Operating Margin **21**	2.9	4.4	6.7	4.3	2.8	3.1	2.4	4.0	2.6	•	3.5	•	•
Operating Margin Before Officers' Comp. **22**	4.6	9.1	11.3	9.2	6.0	4.2	4.6	5.0	3.9	•	3.8	•	•

Selected Average Balance Sheet ($ in Thousands)

Net Receivables 23	103	0	5	36	231	531	1874	4617	6790	51601	•
Inventories 24	743	0	70	303	1042	2870	5743	14440	44245	184744	•
Net Property, Plant and Equipment 25	263	0	22	94	253	1224	2258	4729	10440	80857	•
Total Assets 26	1463	0	121	681	1828	7895	14600	34771	66482	358300	•
Notes and Loans Payable 27	329	0	43	226	581	1927	3653	9643	10257	67824	•
All Other Liabilities 28	518	0	35	154	455	2380	4587	13238	18791	125781	•
Net Worth 29	616	0	43	301	792	3588	6360	11890	37434	164695	•

Selected Financial Ratios (Times to 1)

Current Ratio 30	1.9	•	2.5	2.9	2.2	1.4	1.8	1.7	2.1	2.0	•
Quick Ratio 31	0.5	•	0.9	0.8	0.8	0.3	0.5	0.6	0.7	0.5	•
Net Sales to Working Capital 32	6.1	55.8	5.5	4.2	5.7	14.8	7.4	7.2	5.6	5.9	•
Coverage Ratio 33	6.5	55.8	16.5	6.8	8.0	5.8	7.1	16.0	7.3	5.5	•
Total Asset Turnover 34	1.9	•	2.5	2.0	2.6	2.5	2.2	2.2	2.1	2.1	•
Inventory Turnover 35	2.3	•	2.5	2.7	2.8	4.7	3.4	3.2	1.9	2.7	•
Receivables Turnover 36	28.8	•	62.0	31.1	20.4	53.2	19.3	17.6	18.1	29.3	•
Total Liabilities to Net Worth 37	1.4	•	1.8	1.3	1.3	1.2	1.3	1.9	0.8	1.2	•
Current Assets to Working Capital 38	2.2	•	1.7	1.5	1.8	3.8	2.3	2.4	1.9	2.0	•
Current Liabilities to Working Capital 39	1.2	•	0.7	0.5	0.8	2.8	1.3	1.4	0.9	1.0	•
Working Capital to Net Sales 40	0.2	•	0.2	0.2	0.2	0.1	0.1	0.1	0.2	0.2	•
Inventory to Working Capital 41	1.5	•	1.1	1.1	1.1	2.7	1.4	1.2	1.1	1.4	•
Total Receipts to Cash Flow 42	8.8	3.4	4.7	8.2	8.7	12.0	8.6	6.4	11.9	9.9	•
Cost of Goods to Cash Flow 43	5.4	2.0	2.7	4.9	5.5	8.3	5.3	3.8	7.2	6.6	•
Cash Flow to Total Debt 44	0.4	•	0.8	0.4	0.5	0.4	0.4	0.5	0.4	0.4	•

Selected Financial Factors (in Percentages)

Debt Ratio 45	57.9	•	64.5	55.7	56.7	54.6	56.4	65.8	43.7	54.0	•
Return on Total Assets 46	9.2	•	22.7	10.8	10.1	10.4	10.0	13.2	8.0	11.5	•
Return on Equity Before Income Taxes 47	18.5	•	60.2	20.8	20.5	19.0	19.7	36.1	12.2	20.5	•
Return on Equity After Income Taxes 48	15.4	•	59.5	20.0	19.1	17.9	17.2	33.3	9.3	16.4	•
Profit Margin (Before Income Tax) 49	4.0	17.9	8.6	4.7	3.5	3.5	3.9	5.6	3.3	4.5	•
Profit Margin (After Income Tax) 50	3.3	17.9	8.5	4.5	3.2	3.3	3.4	5.2	2.5	3.6	•

Table I
Corporations with and without Net Income

GENERAL MERCHANDISE STORES

MONEY AMOUNTS AND SIZE OF ASSETS IN THOUSANDS OF DOLLARS

Item Description for Accounting Period 7/03 Through 6/04	Total	Zero Assets	Under 500	500 to 1,000	1,000 to 5,000	5,000 to 10,000	10,000 to 25,000	25,000 to 50,000	50,000 to 100,000	100,000 to 250,000	250,000 to 500,000	500,000 to 2,500,000	2,500,000 and over
Number of Enterprises **1**	11118	667	9077	487	708	75	33	17	13	7	8	10	16
Revenues ($ in Thousands)													
Net Sales **2**	556417559	13044528	3120646	487784	5281297	3898618	1024928	1428441	1521140	1947612	4588813	24655159	495418593
Interest **3**	4438278	64503	725	1157	1475	1525	813	1612	17250	3724	38175	114255	4193063
Rents **4**	816724	136	503	0	4468	361	1260	184	9141	5935	2099	32312	760327
Royalties **5**	1727288	0	0	0	70	0	7097	0	0	0	1106	44963	1674052
Other Portfolio Income **6**	5169922	125942	192	30	3523	984	798	1423	3374	365	317	18913	5014061
Other Receipts **7**	13070488	58875	5070	22086	9111	35606	10709	29119	974934	106122	37283	551722	11229850
Total Receipts **8**	581640259	13293984	3127136	511057	5299944	3937094	1045605	1460779	2525839	2063758	4667793	25417324	518289946
Average Total Receipts **9**	52315	19931	345	1049	7486	52495	31685	85928	194295	294823	583474	2541732	32393122
Operating Costs/Operating Income (%)													
Cost of Operations **10**	71.5	65.8	59.1	77.6	60.5	81.9	66.6	67.6	61.6	59.9	65.6	69.7	72.1
Salaries and Wages **11**	11.1	9.8	9.3	8.3	14.7	8.2	13.4	13.5	14.4	14.6	13.0	10.8	11.1
Taxes Paid **12**	1.7	1.4	2.7	1.2	2.5	0.9	1.8	2.1	2.5	2.8	1.5	1.7	1.7
Interest Paid **13**	1.4	0.9	0.2	1.9	0.5	0.3	0.5	0.5	0.4	0.4	1.3	0.7	1.5
Depreciation **14**	2.1	3.0	1.0	1.1	0.7	0.6	1.3	1.6	2.0	1.6	3.0	2.1	2.2
Amortization and Depletion **15**	0.1	0.0	0.1	0.5	0.0	0.0	0.2	0.1	0.0	0.1	0.4	0.1	0.1
Pensions and Other Deferred Comp. **16**	0.5	1.5	0.0	0.3	0.4	0.1	0.2	0.3	0.2	0.3	0.3	0.4	0.5
Employee Benefits **17**	0.9	0.6	0.3	0.5	0.7	0.8	0.9	0.8	1.1	1.0	1.5	1.5	0.8
Advertising **18**	1.5	0.0	0.6	0.2	1.6	0.5	1.4	1.8	3.3	1.5	1.9	1.8	1.5
Other Expenses **19**	9.8	10.9	19.4	11.4	15.8	8.3	11.6	11.5	82.9	16.7	11.7	11.5	9.3
Officers' Compensation **20**	0.1	0.2	5.1	1.9	1.6	1.0	1.2	0.5	0.7	1.7	0.5	0.3	0.1
Operating Margin **21**	•	5.7	2.1	•	1.2	•	0.7	•	•	•	•	•	•
Operating Margin Before Officers' Comp. **22**	•	5.9	7.2	•	2.7	•	1.8	0.1	•	1.0	•	•	•

Selected Average Balance Sheet ($ in Thousands)

Net Receivables 23	2641	0	7	5	169	1119	1357	3355	6726	14909	31631	82124	1732630
Inventories 24	5933	0	60	269	1158	2338	8055	15402	16820	93264	126380	388635	3624718
Net Property, Plant and Equipment 25	7341	0	30	138	315	1404	3031	7727	18081	34184	86944	336859	4761073
Total Assets 26	25960	0	137	677	2123	8848	15173	36875	74840	143739	340923	1174997	16706334
Notes and Loans Payable 27	6670	0	70	326	545	2295	3404	10084	9199	18638	59028	246720	4333126
All Other Liabilities 28	8768	0	28	44	507	6177	3381	12572	136980	50217	93975	427824	5555883
Net Worth 29	10522	0	39	307	1070	376	8387	14219	-71339	74884	187920	500453	6817325

Selected Financial Ratios (Times to 1)

Current Ratio 30	1.4	•	2.8	4.4	3.0	1.1	2.4	1.9	0.5	2.3	2.0	1.4	1.3
Quick Ratio 31	0.5	•	0.9	1.0	0.7	0.5	0.8	0.7	0.2	0.9	0.4	0.4	0.6
Net Sales to Working Capital 32	16.5	•	5.8	3.9	7.1	74.8	4.9	6.8	5.0	6.3	13.9	16.8	
Coverage Ratio 33	3.7	9.6	10.5	0.9	3.9	•	6.1	4.5	12.6	1.9	4.6	3.6	
Total Asset Turnover 34	1.9	•	2.5	1.5	3.5	5.9	2.0	2.3	1.6	1.9	1.7	2.1	1.9
Inventory Turnover 35	6.0	•	3.4	2.9	3.9	18.2	2.6	3.7	4.3	1.8	3.0	4.4	6.2
Receivables Turnover 36	11.3	•	97.3	34.6	53.4	60.1	18.6	26.3	16.7	14.6	17.0	25.4	10.4
Total Liabilities to Net Worth 37	1.5	•	2.5	1.2	1.0	22.5	0.8	1.6	0.9	0.9	0.8	1.3	1.5
Current Assets to Working Capital 38	3.8	•	1.6	1.3	1.5	10.2	1.7	2.1	1.8	1.8	2.0	3.3	3.9
Current Liabilities to Working Capital 39	2.8	•	0.6	0.3	0.5	9.2	0.7	1.1	0.8	0.8	1.0	2.3	2.9
Working Capital to Net Sales 40	0.1	•	0.2	0.3	0.1	0.0	0.2	0.1	0.2	0.2	0.1	0.1	
Inventory to Working Capital 41	2.0	•	1.0	0.8	1.1	5.1	1.1	1.2	•	1.0	1.4	2.1	2.1
Total Receipts to Cash Flow 42	10.3	8.1	8.7	15.3	9.2	34.0	10.6	13.5	1.4	6.5	11.5	9.5	10.6
Cost of Goods to Cash Flow 43	7.4	5.3	5.1	11.9	5.6	27.9	7.0	9.1	0.9	3.9	7.5	6.6	7.6
Cash Flow to Total Debt 44	0.3	•	0.4	0.2	0.8	0.2	0.4	0.3	0.6	0.6	0.3	0.4	0.3

Selected Financial Factors (in Percentages)

Debt Ratio 45	59.5	•	71.6	54.7	49.6	95.7	44.7	61.4	195.3	47.9	44.9	57.4	59.2
Return on Total Assets 46	10.1	•	6.5	2.6	7.1	•	6.5	5.3	•	10.9	4.0	6.8	10.0
Return on Equity Before Income Taxes 47	18.1	•	20.6	•	10.5	•	9.9	10.7	5.2	19.3	3.5	12.5	17.7
Return on Equity After Income Taxes 48	11.3	•	19.5	•	9.5	•	8.5	8.6	6.0	16.8	1.9	8.1	10.6
Profit Margin (Before Income Tax) 49	3.8	7.6	2.3	•	1.5	•	2.7	1.8	•	5.2	1.1	2.5	3.9
Profit Margin (After Income Tax) 50	2.4	7.6	2.2	•	1.4	•	2.3	1.5	0.6	4.5	0.6	1.7	2.3

Table II
Corporations with Net Income

GENERAL MERCHANDISE STORES

MONEY AMOUNTS AND SIZE OF ASSETS IN THOUSANDS OF DOLLARS

Item Description for Accounting Period 7/03 Through 6/04	Total	Zero Assets	Under 500	500 to 1,000	1,000 to 5,000	5,000 to 10,000	10,000 to 25,000	25,000 to 50,000	50,000 to 100,000	100,000 to 250,000	250,000 to 500,000	500,000 to 2,500,000	2,500,000 and over
Number of Enterprises 1	7451	404	•	173	607	12	26	•	8	7	•	10	13
Revenues ($ in Thousands)													
Net Sales 2	488812175	12968122	•	84996	4579232	170464	867769	•	1308743	1947612	•	24655159	435736084
Interest 3	3896318	64496	•	1	1359	354	387	•	12012	3724	•	114255	3683338
Rents 4	725287	136	•	0	5	110	1260	•	8465	5935	•	32312	674961
Royalties 5	1721085	0	•	0	70	0	7097	•	0	0	•	44963	1667848
Other Portfolio Income 6	5118142	125942	•	0	1566	4	242	•	2759	365	•	18913	4967402
Other Receipts 7	10577970	42123	•	21467	3706	3622	8006	•	12077	106122	•	551722	9791244
Total Receipts 8	510850977	13200819	•	106464	4585938	174554	884761	•	1344056	2063758	•	25417324	456520877
Average Total Receipts 9	68561	32675	•	615	7555	14546	34029	•	168007	294823	•	2541732	35116991
Operating Costs/Operating Income (%)													
Cost of Operations 10	71.5	65.9	•	78.2	60.2	58.6	66.6	•	62.8	59.9	•	69.7	72.1
Salaries and Wages 11	10.9	9.9	•	13.2	13.7	10.1	13.0	•	13.2	14.6	•	10.8	10.9
Taxes Paid 12	1.7	1.4	•	2.3	2.4	2.2	1.8	•	2.0	2.8	•	1.7	1.7
Interest Paid 13	1.5	0.9	•	4.3	0.5	1.0	0.5	•	0.4	0.4	•	0.7	1.6
Depreciation 14	2.2	3.0	•	0.2	0.6	4.5	1.3	•	1.6	1.6	•	2.1	2.2
Amortization and Depletion 15	0.1	0.0	•	2.7	0.0	0.0	0.2	•	0.0	0.1	•	0.1	0.1
Pensions and Other Deferred Comp. 16	0.6	1.5	•	•	0.4	0.2	0.3	•	0.3	0.3	•	0.4	0.6
Employee Benefits 17	0.8	0.6	•	0.5	0.5	0.1	1.0	•	1.2	1.0	•	1.5	0.8
Advertising 18	1.3	0.0	•	0.1	1.5	1.3	1.4	•	2.8	1.5	•	1.8	1.3
Other Expenses 19	8.7	10.6	•	20.3	14.6	15.9	10.5	•	14.4	16.7	•	11.5	8.3
Officers' Compensation 20	0.1	0.2	•	2.5	1.3	1.9	1.3	•	0.6	1.7	•	0.3	0.1
Operating Margin 21	0.5	5.9	•	•	4.2	4.3	2.1	•	0.7	•	•	•	0.4
Operating Margin Before Officers' Comp. 22	0.7	6.1	•	•	5.5	6.2	3.4	•	1.3	1.0	•	•	0.5

Selected Average Balance Sheet ($ in Thousands)

Net Receivables 23	3621	0	185	481	1120	•	9959	14909	•	82124	1971088
Inventories 24	7180	401	1036	631	8228	•	23247	88858	•	388635	3598758
Net Property, Plant and Equipment 25	10004	7	249	1852	3066	•	18708	34184	•	336859	5367848
Total Assets 26	35116	566	2086	5772	15186	•	74071	143739	•	1174997	18710317
Notes and Loans Payable 27	8787	415	493	1197	3343	•	11220	18638	•	246720	4732564
All Other Liabilities 28	11076	35	443	1252	3189	•	17960	50217	•	427824	5904333
Net Worth 29	15252	117	1150	3323	8654	•	44891	74884	•	500453	8073420

Selected Financial Ratios (Times to 1)

Current Ratio 30	1.4	•	1.3	3.6	2.4	2.5	•	2.6	2.3	•	1.4	1.3
Quick Ratio 31	0.6	•	0.3	0.9	1.7	0.8	•	0.9	0.9	•	0.4	0.6
Net Sales to Working Capital 32	16.7	•	11.7	6.5	9.3	5.1	•	5.9	5.0	•	13.9	17.5
Coverage Ratio 33	4.3	9.7	1.2	8.9	7.9	8.8	•	9.7	12.6	•	4.6	4.2
Total Asset Turnover 34	1.9	•	0.9	3.6	2.5	2.2	•	2.2	1.9	•	2.1	1.8
Inventory Turnover 35	6.5	•	1.0	4.4	13.2	2.7	•	4.4	1.9	•	4.4	6.7
Receivables Turnover 36	10.7	•	7.5	51.9	59.1	24.2	•	32.9	15.2	•	25.4	9.8
Total Liabilities to Net Worth 37	1.3	•	3.9	0.8	0.7	0.8	•	0.6	0.9	•	1.3	1.3
Current Assets to Working Capital 38	3.8	•	3.9	1.4	1.7	1.7	•	1.6	1.8	•	3.3	4.0
Current Liabilities to Working Capital 39	2.8	•	2.9	0.4	0.7	0.7	•	0.6	0.8	•	2.3	3.0
Working Capital to Net Sales 40	0.1	•	0.1	0.2	0.1	0.2	•	0.2	0.2	•	0.1	0.1
Inventory to Working Capital 41	2.0	•	2.6	1.0	0.4	1.1	•	0.8	1.0	•	2.1	2.1
Total Receipts to Cash Flow 42	9.8	8.1	11.8	7.7	6.3	9.6	•	8.2	6.5	•	9.5	9.9
Cost of Goods to Cash Flow 43	7.0	5.3	9.3	4.6	3.7	6.4	•	5.1	3.9	•	6.6	7.2
Cash Flow to Total Debt 44	0.3	•	0.1	1.1	0.9	0.5	•	0.7	0.6	•	0.4	0.3

Selected Financial Factors (in Percentages)

Debt Ratio 45	56.6	•	79.4	44.9	42.4	43.0	•	39.4	47.9	•	57.4	56.9
Return on Total Assets 46	12.4	•	4.5	17.7	19.0	10.1	•	8.5	10.9	•	6.8	12.3
Return on Equity Before Income Taxes 47	22.0	•	3.7	28.5	28.8	15.7	•	12.6	19.3	•	12.5	21.7
Return on Equity After Income Taxes 48	15.0	•	3.7	27.4	23.0	14.0	•	10.5	16.8	•	8.1	14.3
Profit Margin (Before Income Tax) 49	5.1	7.7	0.9	4.3	6.7	4.1	•	3.4	5.2	•	2.5	5.2
Profit Margin (After Income Tax) 50	3.5	7.7	0.9	4.2	5.4	3.6	•	2.9	4.5	•	1.7	3.5

Table I

Corporations with and without Net Income

MISCELLANEOUS STORE RETAILERS

MONEY AMOUNTS AND SIZE OF ASSETS IN THOUSANDS OF DOLLARS

Item Description for Accounting Period 7/03 Through 6/04		Total	Zero Assets	Under 500	500 to 1,000	1,000 to 5,000	5,000 to 10,000	10,000 to 25,000	25,000 to 50,000	50,000 to 100,000	100,000 to 250,000	250,000 to 500,000	500,000 to 2,500,000	2,500,000 and over
Number of Enterprises	1	99490	10822	77430	5738	4879	301	204	57	21	19	4	12	4
Revenues ($ in Thousands)														
Net Sales	2	129282865	677446	31167900	10285187	19916126	3411187	6030111	3756491	2414304	5208052	1708031	16922803	27785229
Interest	3	229160	172	11671	8727	31664	8018	15886	5673	9961	12631	24751	41488	58519
Rents	4	213874	0	3020	20055	11593	375	5496	2411	7049	2158	1132	145153	15431
Royalties	5	168553	0	0	0	2558	0	163	0	601	21445	5871	12711	125204
Other Portfolio Income	6	265422	9099	68862	10495	18695	8809	23618	12911	14197	3063	470	18585	76617
Other Receipts	7	2232077	13970	162673	55334	373795	42190	85867	65360	24012	57247	36340	445408	869881
Total Receipts	8	132391951	700687	31414126	10379798	20354431	3470579	6161141	3842846	2470124	5304596	1776595	17586148	28930881
Average Total Receipts	9	1331	65	406	1809	4172	11530	30202	67418	117625	279189	444149	1465512	7232720
Operating Costs/Operating Income (%)														
Cost of Operations	10	62.1	45.2	59.0	63.3	65.6	64.3	66.2	63.8	62.6	60.3	46.3	49.8	70.2
Salaries and Wages	11	12.2	9.2	10.5	11.3	11.2	13.5	12.5	13.6	10.6	12.7	15.1	16.4	11.9
Taxes Paid	12	2.1	4.1	2.7	2.1	2.2	1.9	1.8	1.9	1.4	2.2	1.6	2.5	1.4
Interest Paid	13	1.2	1.4	0.7	0.9	1.1	1.6	1.1	0.9	0.9	1.2	3.0	1.2	1.9
Depreciation	14	2.2	1.2	1.2	1.2	1.2	1.4	1.9	2.1	1.3	2.5	4.4	6.7	1.6
Amortization and Depletion	15	0.3	5.7	0.1	0.2	0.1	0.1	0.3	0.3	0.4	0.1	1.1	0.5	0.5
Pensions and Other Deferred Comp.	16	0.2	0.0	0.2	0.2	0.3	0.1	0.3	0.3	0.1	0.1	0.1	0.2	0.1
Employee Benefits	17	0.9	1.2	0.5	0.5	0.9	0.9	1.0	0.8	0.9	1.1	3.0	1.8	0.9
Advertising	18	2.1	1.9	1.4	1.2	1.0	1.2	1.6	1.3	4.5	2.5	1.5	3.2	3.5
Other Expenses	19	15.2	42.1	18.6	15.4	14.9	12.2	13.3	14.4	15.0	13.6	26.2	15.6	10.9
Officers' Compensation	20	2.6	8.3	5.3	4.3	3.6	2.7	1.7	1.2	1.0	0.9	1.5	0.7	0.2
Operating Margin	21	•	•	•	•	•	0.1	•	•	1.3	2.7	•	1.5	•
Operating Margin Before Officers' Comp.	22	1.6	•	5.0	3.5	1.5	2.7	0.6	•	2.4	3.5	•	2.1	•

Selected Average Balance Sheet ($ in Thousands)

Net Receivables 23	166	0	15	91	315	1257	2482	5521	11465	11856	21480	88953	2622808
Inventories 24	183	0	42	280	733	3155	5135	13760	25086	52958	88466	285753	824327
Net Property, Plant and Equipment 25	123	0	17	136	312	866	2763	6282	9839	24403	82728	320152	643305
Total Assets 26	703	0	109	667	1856	6540	14564	36230	66834	152075	351377	1017942	5931571
Notes and Loans Payable 27	209	0	62	285	642	2719	5623	12458	20489	36324	143501	198299	1118275
All Other Liabilities 28	275	0	29	144	515	2097	4684	9646	21395	44132	70165	351409	3457534
Net Worth 29	220	0	18	238	700	1724	4257	14126	24950	71620	137711	468233	1355761

Selected Financial Ratios (Times to 1)

Current Ratio 30	1.8	•	2.2	2.0	1.9	1.5	1.5	2.0	1.6	1.5	2.2	1.4	1.9
Quick Ratio 31	0.9	•	1.0	0.7	0.7	0.6	0.6	0.7	0.5	0.4	0.7	0.5	1.5
Net Sales to Working Capital 32	6.2	•	9.1	7.6	6.1	6.2	8.4	4.9	6.9	10.0	4.7	10.8	3.5
Coverage Ratio 33	2.3	•	1.7	1.2	1.1	2.1	1.4	2.8	4.9	4.7	1.1	5.6	2.0
Total Asset Turnover 34	1.8	•	3.7	2.7	2.2	1.7	2.0	1.8	1.7	1.8	1.2	1.4	1.2
Inventory Turnover 35	4.4	•	5.6	4.1	3.7	2.3	3.8	3.1	2.9	3.1	2.2	2.5	5.9
Receivables Turnover 36	10.0	•	27.5	21.2	13.1	8.5	11.8	12.7	8.6	19.8	23.5	6.3	5.3
Total Liabilities to Net Worth 37	2.2	•	4.9	1.8	1.7	2.8	2.4	1.6	1.7	1.1	1.6	1.2	3.4
Current Assets to Working Capital 38	2.2	•	1.8	2.0	2.1	2.8	2.9	2.0	2.8	3.1	1.8	3.2	2.1
Current Liabilities to Working Capital 39	1.2	•	0.8	1.0	1.1	1.8	1.9	1.0	1.8	2.1	0.8	2.2	1.1
Working Capital to Net Sales 40	0.2	•	0.1	0.1	0.2	0.2	0.1	0.2	0.1	0.1	0.2	0.1	0.3
Inventory to Working Capital 41	0.9	•	1.0	1.2	1.1	1.4	1.4	1.0	1.5	1.7	1.1	1.3	0.4
Total Receipts to Cash Flow 42	9.4	14.4	8.6	11.1	9.1	10.8	11.2	9.1	7.2	8.9	4.9	7.0	13.6
Cost of Goods to Cash Flow 43	5.8	6.5	5.1	7.0	6.0	6.9	7.4	5.8	4.5	5.4	2.3	3.5	9.5
Cash Flow to Total Debt 44	0.3	•	0.5	0.4	0.4	0.2	0.3	0.3	0.4	0.4	0.4	0.4	0.1

Selected Financial Factors (in Percentages)

Debt Ratio 45	68.7	•	83.2	64.3	62.3	73.6	70.8	61.0	62.7	52.9	60.8	54.0	77.1
Return on Total Assets 46	5.1	•	4.7	3.0	2.6	6.0	3.0	4.6	7.9	10.4	3.9	9.1	4.5
Return on Equity Before Income Taxes 47	9.2	•	11.9	1.3	0.6	11.8	2.9	7.5	16.8	17.4	0.6	16.2	9.8
Return on Equity After Income Taxes 48	6.0	•	10.3	0.5	•	7.9	0.5	6.1	15.4	13.6	•	11.0	6.0
Profit Margin (Before Income Tax) 49	1.6	•	0.5	0.2	0.1	1.8	0.4	1.6	3.7	4.5	0.2	5.4	1.9
Profit Margin (After Income Tax) 50	1.0	•	0.5	0.1	•	1.2	0.1	1.3	3.3	3.5	•	3.6	1.2

233

Table II

Corporations with Net Income

MISCELLANEOUS STORE RETAILERS

MONEY AMOUNTS AND SIZE OF ASSETS IN THOUSANDS OF DOLLARS

Item Description for Accounting Period 7/03 Through 6/04	Total	Zero Assets	Under 500	500 to 1,000	1,000 to 5,000	5,000 to 10,000	10,000 to 25,000	25,000 to 50,000	50,000 to 100,000	100,000 to 250,000	250,000 to 500,000	500,000 to 2,500,000	2,500,000 and over
Number of Enterprises **1**	50768	3928	38904	4071	3440	198	140	42	14	15	•	•	•
Revenues ($ in Thousands)													
Net Sales **2**	100949061	235333	21018487	7618371	13840660	2545640	4323730	2840750	2003812	4628810	•	•	•
Interest **3**	165297	14	4411	5591	26482	5111	14782	4527	3374	10519	•	•	•
Rents **4**	181463	0	0	7228	9277	375	4981	982	1094	2158	•	•	•
Royalties **5**	110834	0	0	0	0	0	163	0	38	19561	•	•	•
Other Portfolio Income **6**	193446	0	39265	7383	13295	7153	22381	8604	13265	2872	•	•	•
Other Receipts **7**	1466657	6171	131653	32136	140920	35179	67418	45260	10852	21786	•	•	•
Total Receipts **8**	103066758	241518	21193816	7670709	14030634	2593458	4433455	2900123	2032435	4685706	•	•	•
Average Total Receipts **9**	2030	61	545	1884	4079	13098	31668	69051	145174	312380	•	•	•
Operating Costs/Operating Income (%)													
Cost of Operations **10**	61.9	36.5	59.3	65.0	64.3	64.7	65.7	63.7	61.5	58.7	•	•	•
Salaries and Wages **11**	11.9	7.7	9.6	10.1	10.6	12.8	11.4	13.0	10.1	13.6	•	•	•
Taxes Paid **12**	2.0	2.4	2.6	2.0	2.3	2.0	1.7	1.8	1.3	2.2	•	•	•
Interest Paid **13**	1.2	0.7	0.4	0.9	0.7	1.3	0.9	0.7	0.6	1.3	•	•	•
Depreciation **14**	2.3	0.3	0.9	1.0	1.2	1.1	1.7	1.4	1.1	2.7	•	•	•
Amortization and Depletion **15**	0.3	0.0	0.0	0.1	0.0	0.0	0.1	0.1	0.2	0.1	•	•	•
Pensions and Other Deferred Comp. **16**	0.2	0.0	0.3	0.2	0.3	0.1	0.3	0.3	0.0	0.2	•	•	•
Employee Benefits **17**	1.0	•	0.6	0.4	0.9	0.9	0.9	0.6	0.8	1.1	•	•	•
Advertising **18**	2.0	1.5	1.1	1.0	1.1	0.9	1.7	1.2	5.1	2.7	•	•	•
Other Expenses **19**	13.1	36.0	15.8	13.5	12.1	10.5	11.3	13.0	14.2	12.3	•	•	•
Officers' Compensation **20**	2.3	1.2	5.3	3.9	3.7	3.0	2.0	1.3	1.0	0.9	•	•	•
Operating Margin **21**	1.9	13.5	4.1	1.9	2.6	2.7	2.2	2.7	4.1	4.3	•	•	•
Operating Margin Before Officers' Comp. **22**	4.1	14.8	9.5	5.8	6.3	5.7	4.3	4.0	5.1	5.2	•	•	•

Selected Average Balance Sheet ($ in Thousands)

Net Receivables 23	291	0	21	103	302	1380	2671	5131	10896
Inventories 24	244	0	42	276	687	3038	4858	11030	25028
Net Property, Plant and Equipment 25	186	0	19	114	269	821	2704	4979	7122
Total Assets 26	1085	0	124	662	1873	6379	14624	35414	65897
Notes and Loans Payable 27	287	0	50	252	590	2123	4801	10116	13944
All Other Liabilities 28	440	0	31	143	491	2087	4339	10475	25846
Net Worth 29	359	0	43	266	793	2169	5483	14823	26108

(final column: Net Receivables 23: 10954; Inventories 24: 50240; Net Property, Plant and Equipment 25: 30525; Total Assets 26: 150451; Notes and Loans Payable 27: 41469; All Other Liabilities 28: 47439; Net Worth 29: 61543)

Selected Financial Ratios (Times to 1)

Current Ratio 30	1.9	·	2.5	2.1	1.6	1.6	1.8	1.6	1.6
Quick Ratio 31	1.1	·	1.2	0.8	0.7	0.7	0.6	0.5	0.4
Net Sales to Working Capital 32	5.8	·	9.5	7.4	6.7	8.2	6.3	8.3	9.3
Coverage Ratio 33	4.6	23.3	12.1	4.0	4.5	6.4	7.4	9.9	5.4
Total Asset Turnover 34	1.8	·	4.3	2.8	2.0	2.1	1.9	2.2	2.1
Inventory Turnover 35	5.1	·	7.6	4.4	2.7	4.2	3.9	3.5	3.6
Receivables Turnover 36	9.3	·	26.9	21.4	8.3	11.6	15.4	11.6	26.0
Total Liabilities to Net Worth 37	2.0	·	1.9	1.5	1.9	1.7	1.4	1.5	1.4
Current Assets to Working Capital 38	2.1	·	1.7	1.9	2.6	2.7	2.3	2.8	2.7
Current Liabilities to Working Capital 39	1.1	·	0.7	0.9	1.6	1.7	1.3	1.8	1.7
Working Capital to Net Sales 40	0.2	·	0.1	0.1	0.2	0.1	0.2	0.1	0.1
Inventory to Working Capital 41	0.8	·	0.8	1.1	1.2	1.3	1.2	1.6	1.7
Total Receipts to Cash Flow 42	8.3	2.7	6.9	9.5	9.4	8.3	7.1	6.4	8.9
Cost of Goods to Cash Flow 43	5.1	1.0	4.1	6.2	6.1	5.4	4.6	3.9	5.2
Cash Flow to Total Debt 44	0.3	1.0	0.5	0.5	0.3	0.4	0.5	0.6	0.4

Selected Financial Factors (in Percentages)

Debt Ratio 45	67.0	·	65.2	59.7	57.7	66.0	62.5	58.1	60.4
Return on Total Assets 46	9.8	·	23.5	9.8	10.2	11.9	11.9	10.5	13.3
Return on Equity Before Income Taxes 47	23.3	·	62.1	18.3	20.3	27.2	26.8	21.8	30.1
Return on Equity After Income Taxes 48	19.5	·	60.7	17.3	18.8	22.5	24.0	20.0	28.1
Profit Margin (Before Income Tax) 49	4.2	16.2	5.0	2.6	4.0	4.6	4.8	4.8	5.5
Profit Margin (After Income Tax) 50	3.5	16.1	4.9	2.5	3.7	3.8	4.3	4.4	5.1

(final column: Debt Ratio 45: 59.1; Return on Total Assets 46: 13.9; Return on Equity Before Income Taxes 47: 27.7; Return on Equity After Income Taxes 48: 22.1; Profit Margin (Before Income Tax) 49: 5.5; Profit Margin (After Income Tax) 50: 4.4)

Table I

Corporations with and without Net Income

NONSTORE RETAILERS

MONEY AMOUNTS AND SIZE OF ASSETS IN THOUSANDS OF DOLLARS

Item Description for Accounting Period 7/03 Through 6/04	Total	Zero Assets	Under 500	500 to 1,000	1,000 to 5,000	5,000 to 10,000	10,000 to 25,000	25,000 to 50,000	50,000 to 100,000	100,000 to 250,000	250,000 to 500,000	500,000 to 2,500,000	2,500,000 and over
Number of Enterprises 1	42739	5335	31107	2699	2971	315	151	66	38	27	12	15	3
Revenues ($ in Thousands)													
Net Sales 2	107968855	1413837	13818588	6957241	21979670	7274496	6583989	4936077	4954299	7986206	8470800	17872664	5720988
Interest 3	429458	304	1940	3985	9724	8093	4394	12743	11407	21444	122903	133308	99213
Rents 4	147137	1729	3191	6422	6435	5977	1847	6060	8988	7489	41148	38924	18927
Royalties 5	194621	3218	0	0	14429	947	1994	2243	21255	11372	2483	104707	31973
Other Portfolio Income 6	234713	8615	54333	44044	18627	9933	38866	9716	2326	23547	1775	19108	3822
Other Receipts 7	2313784	17839	72442	63875	119998	54694	55358	81566	108309	228471	88495	1213795	208944
Total Receipts 8	111288568	1445542	13950494	7075567	22148883	7354140	6686448	5048405	5106584	8278529	8727604	19382506	6083867
Average Total Receipts 9	2604	271	448	2622	7455	23346	44281	76491	134384	306612	727300	1292167	2027956
Operating Costs/Operating Income (%)													
Cost of Operations 10	65.1	63.1	61.3	69.9	71.4	64.6	65.9	60.3	61.3	62.1	61.7	71.7	40.2
Salaries and Wages 11	8.9	6.2	6.9	8.8	7.0	8.5	9.3	9.5	11.0	8.0	6.4	10.2	21.0
Taxes Paid 12	1.5	1.0	2.3	2.3	1.5	1.2	1.3	1.4	1.6	1.1	1.0	1.0	1.5
Interest Paid 13	1.0	1.0	0.5	1.5	0.6	0.6	0.6	0.6	1.1	0.9	1.2	2.1	0.9
Depreciation 14	2.0	3.1	2.0	2.7	2.0	1.6	1.8	2.3	2.0	1.7	1.7	1.5	3.7
Amortization and Depletion 15	0.5	1.8	0.1	0.2	0.2	0.2	0.3	0.3	0.7	0.8	0.5	1.1	0.4
Pensions and Other Deferred Comp. 16	0.2	0.0	0.1	0.2	0.2	0.4	0.2	0.3	0.3	0.2	0.3	0.3	0.2
Employee Benefits 17	0.9	0.5	0.4	1.0	0.6	0.7	0.8	1.2	1.1	0.7	0.8	1.3	2.4
Advertising 18	3.4	1.8	1.3	0.6	2.0	5.1	4.2	7.0	4.7	4.3	5.8	2.1	9.6
Other Expenses 19	18.3	21.5	18.0	11.4	10.4	15.1	14.8	16.4	17.7	16.9	21.8	31.1	24.0
Officers' Compensation 20	2.3	5.5	6.2	3.8	2.5	1.8	1.4	1.1	0.8	0.7	0.5	1.4	1.3
Operating Margin 21	•	•	0.8	•	1.7	0.2	•	•	•	2.5	•	•	•
Operating Margin Before Officers' Comp. 22	•	•	7.0	1.5	4.2	2.0	0.7	•	•	3.2	•	•	•

Selected Average Balance Sheet ($ in Thousands)

Net Receivables 23	183	0	16	143	452	1461	3621	5214	15921	25871	74382	55754	407476
Inventories 24	166	0	16	134	367	1095	2954	6080	9097	30529	44399	123972	268993
Net Property, Plant and Equipment 25	193	0	23	235	466	1378	3005	6492	9670	21698	38943	104779	413316
Total Assets 26	1271	0	88	747	2149	6892	15430	34139	70593	163347	338212	948857	3680867
Notes and Loans Payable 27	403	0	45	768	714	1773	5033	7699	18050	41452	62179	295607	946653
All Other Liabilities 28	407	0	30	211	803	2859	6751	12007	24679	46941	118683	331181	741471
Net Worth 29	460	0	13	-231	632	2260	3646	14433	27864	74954	157350	322069	1992743

Selected Financial Ratios (Times to 1)

Current Ratio 30	1.5	•	1.5	1.2	1.3	1.4	1.5	1.7	1.4	1.6	2.1	1.3	1.5
Quick Ratio 31	0.9	•	1.0	0.7	0.8	0.9	0.9	0.9	0.9	0.9	1.2	0.6	1.1
Net Sales to Working Capital 32	12.1	•	23.3	36.9	22.6	16.0	13.4	8.7	11.2	8.1	6.4	12.1	4.0
Coverage Ratio 33	•	•	4.2	0.6	5.5	3.4	2.5	4.1	1.8	7.5	2.1	•	2.4
Total Asset Turnover 34	2.0	•	5.1	3.4	3.4	3.4	2.8	2.2	1.8	1.8	2.1	1.3	0.5
Inventory Turnover 35	9.9	•	17.5	13.4	14.4	13.6	9.7	7.4	8.8	6.0	9.8	6.9	2.9
Receivables Turnover 36	14.4	•	29.4	17.8	18.4	20.0	12.5	12.0	9.5	9.9	10.3	13.1	9.4
Total Liabilities to Net Worth 37	1.8	•	5.8	•	2.4	2.0	3.2	1.4	1.5	1.2	1.1	1.9	0.8
Current Assets to Working Capital 38	3.2	•	2.9	5.5	4.2	3.3	3.2	2.4	3.5	2.7	1.9	3.9	3.2
Current Liabilities to Working Capital 39	2.2	•	1.9	4.5	3.2	2.3	2.2	1.4	2.5	1.7	0.9	2.9	2.2
Working Capital to Net Sales 40	0.1	•	0.0	0.0	0.0	0.1	0.1	0.1	0.1	0.1	0.2	0.1	0.3
Inventory to Working Capital 41	0.8	•	0.9	1.9	1.4	0.7	1.0	0.7	0.7	0.8	0.5	1.0	0.6
Total Receipts to Cash Flow 42	7.9	6.8	5.9	12.2	8.7	6.8	7.6	6.2	6.1	4.8	4.7	•	4.7
Cost of Goods to Cash Flow 43	5.2	4.3	3.6	8.5	6.2	4.4	5.0	3.7	3.8	3.0	2.9	•	1.9
Cash Flow to Total Debt 44	0.4	•	1.0	0.2	0.6	0.7	0.5	0.6	0.5	0.7	0.8	•	0.2

Selected Financial Factors (in Percentages)

Debt Ratio 45	63.8	•	85.3	130.9	70.6	67.2	76.4	57.7	60.5	54.1	53.5	66.1	45.9
Return on Total Assets 46	•	•	11.2	2.8	10.5	6.3	4.5	5.5	3.5	12.9	5.3	•	1.1
Return on Equity Before Income Taxes 47	•	•	57.8	7.1	29.3	13.5	11.4	9.8	3.9	24.4	6.1	•	1.2
Return on Equity After Income Taxes 48	•	•	55.6	8.0	26.1	11.6	8.0	8.0	2.6	22.8	2.3	•	•
Profit Margin (Before Income Tax) 49	•	•	1.7	•	2.5	1.3	1.0	1.9	0.8	6.2	1.4	•	1.2
Profit Margin (After Income Tax) 50	•	•	1.6	•	2.2	1.1	0.7	1.6	0.5	5.8	0.5	•	•

Table II

Corporations with Net Income

NONSTORE RETAILERS

MONEY AMOUNTS AND SIZE OF ASSETS IN THOUSANDS OF DOLLARS

Item Description for Accounting Period 7/03 Through 6/04	Total	Zero Assets	Under 500	500 to 1,000	1,000 to 5,000	5,000 to 10,000	10,000 to 25,000	25,000 to 50,000	50,000 to 100,000	100,000 to 250,000	250,000 to 500,000	500,000 to 2,500,000	2,500,000 and over
Number of Enterprises **1**	24014	2737	17103	1493	2268	217	92	42	24	19	8	11	•
Revenues ($ in Thousands)													
Net Sales **2**	72491268	1011725	9109024	4475688	18198442	5362359	4552010	3837668	3149041	5889802	5961895	10943613	•
Interest **3**	317983	70	1678	2784	8161	4261	1470	5310	10442	14229	120515	149064	•
Rents **4**	74922	0	3191	6331	6274	3097	1657	1745	8466	4252	1200	38709	•
Royalties **5**	135158	0	0	0	11579	947	1	2169	21237	5423	2483	91320	•
Other Portfolio Income **6**	152597	7566	43317	816	15192	9361	29618	6951	2318	23355	553	13551	•
Other Receipts **7**	1083877	9924	48926	10346	82724	47469	40445	66821	62322	218135	49065	447699	•
Total Receipts **8**	74255805	1029285	9206136	4495965	18322372	5427494	4625201	3920664	3253826	6155196	6135711	11683956	•
Average Total Receipts **9**	3092	376	538	3011	8079	25011	50274	93349	135576	323958	766964	1062178	•
Operating Costs/Operating Income (%)													
Cost of Operations **10**	64.5	63.3	59.0	70.9	71.8	65.4	66.9	58.5	59.7	58.7	67.7	57.9	•
Salaries and Wages **11**	7.6	3.2	6.6	8.6	6.3	8.2	7.9	7.8	10.8	7.2	5.8	10.3	•
Taxes Paid **12**	1.3	0.8	1.6	1.8	1.2	1.2	1.1	1.2	1.6	1.0	0.9	1.4	•
Interest Paid **13**	0.6	1.0	0.3	0.5	0.4	0.3	0.6	0.4	1.0	0.8	0.7	1.4	•
Depreciation **14**	1.6	1.2	1.5	2.0	1.4	1.4	1.5	1.8	1.6	1.5	1.1	2.2	•
Amortization and Depletion **15**	0.3	0.7	0.1	0.1	0.1	0.1	0.3	0.2	0.6	0.4	0.2	0.8	•
Pensions and Other Deferred Comp. **16**	0.3	0.0	0.1	0.3	0.3	0.5	0.2	0.3	0.4	0.2	0.3	0.4	•
Employee Benefits **17**	0.7	0.2	0.3	0.7	0.5	0.6	0.6	1.0	1.0	0.6	0.4	1.6	•
Advertising **18**	3.4	2.0	1.6	0.6	2.3	5.5	4.0	8.6	3.5	5.4	6.4	2.2	•
Other Expenses **19**	13.6	13.8	16.1	7.8	9.5	11.4	12.5	15.6	18.3	17.4	15.4	17.3	•
Officers' Compensation **20**	2.4	5.8	6.2	2.8	2.4	1.9	1.3	1.0	1.0	0.5	0.6	2.5	•
Operating Margin **21**	3.6	7.8	6.5	3.9	3.7	3.6	3.1	3.5	0.5	6.3	0.5	2.1	•
Operating Margin Before Officers' Comp. **22**	6.1	13.7	12.7	6.7	6.2	5.5	4.4	4.5	1.5	6.8	1.1	4.6	•

Selected Average Balance Sheet ($ in Thousands)

Net Receivables 23	221	0	18	206	206	502	1702	4125	6003	18058	31263	76024	84820
Inventories 24	206	0	20	171	171	390	1016	3438	6141	10526	33394	45654	129546
Net Property, Plant and Equipment 25	206	0	22	227	227	357	1326	2592	5916	9382	22099	33016	156832
Total Assets 26	1322	0	108	757	757	2226	7214	15818	34318	71244	162374	309420	1090824
Notes and Loans Payable 27	250	0	32	179	179	545	1128	4593	6347	16566	41530	44397	132918
All Other Liabilities 28	401	0	24	212	212	832	2280	5730	10617	21123	43009	85825	321448
Net Worth 29	672	0	51	366	366	848	3806	5495	17354	33555	77836	179198	636457

Selected Financial Ratios (Times to 1)

Current Ratio 30	1.7	•	2.1	2.1	1.4	2.0	1.6	1.9	1.9	1.6	1.5	2.6	1.7
Quick Ratio 31	1.0	•	1.3	1.2	0.9	1.4	0.9	1.0	1.0	1.0	0.8	1.4	0.8
Net Sales to Working Capital 32	9.5	•	13.9	11.0	17.2	9.4	11.9	8.8	7.7	8.8	5.7	5.7	5.5
Coverage Ratio 33	10.5	10.6	25.0	9.0	11.7	17.6	8.6	14.5	5.0	15.1	5.7	7.5	
Total Asset Turnover 34	2.3	•	4.9	4.0	3.6	3.4	3.1	2.7	1.8	1.9	2.4	0.9	
Inventory Turnover 35	9.5	•	16.1	12.4	14.8	15.9	9.6	8.7	7.4	5.5	11.0	4.4	
Receivables Turnover 36	14.9	•	31.2	16.6	19.6	19.4	12.7	13.4	8.9	9.9	10.9	11.4	
Total Liabilities to Net Worth 37	1.0	•	1.1	1.1	1.6	0.9	1.9	1.0	1.1	1.1	0.7	0.7	
Current Assets to Working Capital 38	2.4	•	1.9	1.9	3.3	2.0	2.8	2.1	2.5	2.9	1.6	2.4	
Current Liabilities to Working Capital 39	1.4	•	0.9	0.9	2.3	1.0	1.8	1.1	1.5	1.9	0.6	1.4	
Working Capital to Net Sales 40	0.1	•	0.1	0.1	0.1	0.1	0.1	0.1	0.1	0.1	0.2	0.2	
Inventory to Working Capital 41	0.7	•	0.6	0.6	1.1	0.3	0.9	0.6	0.5	1.0	0.5	0.8	
Total Receipts to Cash Flow 42	5.6	4.5	4.7	9.3	7.9	6.8	6.5	5.1	4.8	3.8	5.7	4.1	
Cost of Goods to Cash Flow 43	3.6	2.9	2.8	6.6	5.7	4.4	4.4	3.0	2.9	2.2	3.9	2.4	
Cash Flow to Total Debt 44	0.8	•	2.0	0.8	0.7	1.1	0.7	1.1	0.7	1.0	1.0	0.5	

Selected Financial Factors (in Percentages)

Debt Ratio 45	49.2	•	52.3	51.7	61.9	47.2	65.3	49.4	52.9	52.1	42.1	41.7	
Return on Total Assets 46	15.4	•	38.6	19.3	17.4	17.6	16.7	16.4	8.8	22.0	10.0	9.4	
Return on Equity Before Income Taxes 47	27.4	•	77.7	35.6	41.7	31.4	42.6	30.2	15.0	42.9	14.3	14.0	
Return on Equity After Income Taxes 48	24.2	•	76.7	34.7	38.6	29.7	38.8	27.8	13.2	40.7	9.3	10.3	
Profit Margin (Before Income Tax) 49	6.1	9.6	7.5	4.3	4.4	4.8	4.7	5.7	3.8	10.8	3.4	9.0	
Profit Margin (After Income Tax) 50	5.4	8.6	7.4	4.2	4.1	4.6	4.3	5.3	3.4	10.2	2.2	6.6	

Table I

Corporations with and without Net Income

AIR TRANSPORTATION

MONEY AMOUNTS AND SIZE OF ASSETS IN THOUSANDS OF DOLLARS

Item Description for Accounting Period 7/03 Through 6/04	Total	Zero Assets	Under 500	500 to 1,000	1,000 to 5,000	5,000 to 10,000	10,000 to 25,000	25,000 to 50,000	50,000 to 100,000	100,000 to 250,000	250,000 to 500,000	500,000 to 2,500,000	2,500,000 and over
Number of Enterprises **1**	9594	1431	5949	522	1270	203	128	41	12	11	4	15	8
Revenues ($ in Thousands)													
Net Sales **2**	108034038	969554	1873578	56486	1370160	1242908	1835777	1216833	1070532	2391397	1837242	15013132	79156440
Interest **3**	519592	474	1651	0	4166	221	2188	2694	2202	5437	2191	86841	411527
Rents **4**	231155	2	0	0	114	296	218	584	0	1834	83	14622	213403
Royalties **5**	28591	0	0	0	0	0	11	0	0	0	0	25784	2797
Other Portfolio Income **6**	3564911	29546	125941	0	37508	6094	17589	12479	14772	25845	5458	117569	3172113
Other Receipts **7**	3347723	6288	24540	0	10086	19400	56975	40162	12602	112121	12773	382604	2670167
Total Receipts **8**	115726010	1005864	2025710	56486	1422034	1268919	1912758	1272752	1100108	2536634	1857747	15640552	85626447
Average Total Receipts **9**	12062	703	341	108	1120	6251	14943	31043	91676	230603	464437	1042703	10703306
Operating Costs/Operating Income (%)													
Cost of Operations **10**	32.5	55.0	21.1	•	43.6	44.3	44.8	59.9	28.8	35.6	40.2	10.4	35.3
Salaries and Wages **11**	20.7	15.5	4.4	2.7	15.2	9.2	14.1	6.0	13.6	15.1	18.7	20.8	22.2
Taxes Paid **12**	3.0	1.4	1.0	0.9	2.4	3.2	2.3	2.1	1.8	2.4	1.5	3.6	3.0
Interest Paid **13**	3.5	0.7	0.5	40.4	4.1	3.7	2.7	1.4	1.4	1.1	1.2	3.2	3.8
Depreciation **14**	9.9	10.4	3.9	76.5	21.2	24.9	13.5	7.7	4.1	5.5	8.1	11.0	9.5
Amortization and Depletion **15**	0.6	0.1	0.0	•	0.0	0.1	0.2	0.3	0.6	0.3	0.4	1.1	0.5
Pensions and Other Deferred Comp. **16**	1.0	1.9	0.8	•	0.2	0.1	0.2	0.4	0.2	1.5	0.1	1.2	1.1
Employee Benefits **17**	3.3	1.9	0.4	•	0.9	0.5	1.6	1.2	0.9	2.5	1.3	2.7	3.7
Advertising **18**	0.9	0.6	0.3	•	0.7	0.2	0.4	0.4	0.1	0.9	0.3	0.8	1.0
Other Expenses **19**	37.2	30.2	62.5	112.0	35.4	31.3	37.1	29.3	45.7	33.8	29.9	51.7	34.3
Officers' Compensation **20**	0.4	2.5	3.3	•	2.5	1.9	1.1	1.0	1.1	0.6	0.4	0.5	0.2
Operating Margin **21**	•	•	1.6	•	•	•	•	•	1.5	0.7	•	•	•
Operating Margin Before Officers' Comp. **22**	•	•	4.9	•	•	•	1.3	•	2.6	1.3	•	•	•

Selected Average Balance Sheet ($ in Thousands)

	1	2	3	4	5	6	7	8	9	10	11	12	13
Net Receivables 23	649	0	14	364	130	1324	1803	3244	6598	26183	27901	55883	480392
Inventories 24	240	0	0	0	38	75	445	891	1502	8580	24699	17314	209322
Net Property, Plant and Equipment 25	9452	0	50	243	1282	3832	9499	14990	26585	57720	134943	511510	9607212
Total Assets 26	15801	0	92	682	1955	6042	15738	34938	64620	144973	342347	1057019	15491665
Notes and Loans Payable 27	6434	0	83	1362	1349	5739	9572	13263	28560	58012	72724	480836	5923888
All Other Liabilities 28	9007	0	36	194	329	1525	6781	6934	22147	71148	189667	339414	9664873
Net Worth 29	360	0	-26	-875	277	-1221	-615	14741	13914	15813	79956	236769	-97096

Selected Financial Ratios (Times to 1)

	1	2	3	4	5	6	7	8	9	10	11	12	13
Current Ratio 30	0.9	•	1.0	2.2	1.1	1.2	0.9	1.7	1.1	1.0	1.2	1.3	0.8
Quick Ratio 31	0.6	•	0.9	2.2	1.0	1.0	0.6	1.2	0.6	0.7	0.8	0.9	0.5
Net Sales to Working Capital 32	•	•	•	0.4	18.5	15.2	•	5.5	24.8	110.7	16.3	12.7	•
Coverage Ratio 33	•	•	20.5	•	•	•	•	•	4.1	7.1	0.2	0.1	•
Total Asset Turnover 34	0.7	•	3.4	0.2	0.6	1.0	0.9	0.8	1.4	1.5	1.3	0.9	0.6
Inventory Turnover 35	15.2	•	•	•	12.4	35.9	14.4	20.0	17.1	9.0	7.5	6.0	16.7
Receivables Turnover 36	17.1	•	19.6	0.4	7.4	6.3	7.5	9.6	12.5	8.3	12.9	17.6	20.1
Total Liabilities to Net Worth 37	42.9	•	•	•	6.1	•	•	1.4	3.6	8.2	3.3	3.5	•
Current Assets to Working Capital 38	•	•	•	1.8	8.8	5.4	1.8	2.5	9.5	35.5	6.0	4.9	•
Current Liabilities to Working Capital 39	•	•	•	0.8	7.8	4.4	0.8	1.5	8.5	34.5	5.0	3.9	•
Working Capital to Net Sales 40	•	•	•	2.2	0.1	0.1	0.2	0.2	0.0	0.0	0.1	0.1	•
Inventory to Working Capital 41	•	•	•	•	0.1	0.2	0.1	0.1	0.7	4.0	0.6	0.3	•
Total Receipts to Cash Flow 42	6.1	517.4	1.5	•	•	25.4	9.9	10.0	3.7	4.4	6.8	3.7	7.2
Cost of Goods to Cash Flow 43	2.0	284.7	0.3	•	•	11.2	4.4	6.0	1.1	1.6	2.7	0.4	2.6
Cash Flow to Total Debt 44	0.1	•	1.7	•	•	0.0	0.1	0.1	0.5	0.4	0.3	0.3	0.1

Selected Financial Factors (in Percentages)

	1	2	3	4	5	6	7	8	9	10	11	12	13
Debt Ratio 45	97.7	•	128.5	228.2	85.8	120.2	103.9	57.8	78.5	89.1	76.6	77.6	100.6
Return on Total Assets 46	34.7	•	•	•	•	•	•	7.8	11.9	•	•	0.2	0.3
Return on Equity Before Income Taxes 47	16.4	•	•	•	•	320.3	•	86.1	27.4	•	93.5	•	666.3
Return on Equity After Income Taxes 48	16.4	•	•	•	•	329.2	•	86.3	26.8	•	83.5	•	670.9
Profit Margin (Before Income Tax) 49	9.7	•	•	•	•	•	•	•	4.3	•	•	•	6.8
Profit Margin (After Income Tax) 50	9.7	•	•	•	•	•	•	•	4.2	•	•	•	6.1

Table II

Corporations with Net Income

AIR TRANSPORTATION

MONEY AMOUNTS AND SIZE OF ASSETS IN THOUSANDS OF DOLLARS

Item Description for Accounting Period 7/03 Through 6/04	Total	Zero Assets	Under 500	500 to 1,000	1,000 to 5,000	5,000 to 10,000	10,000 to 25,000	25,000 to 50,000	50,000 to 100,000	100,000 to 250,000	250,000 to 500,000	500,000 to 2,500,000	2,500,000 and over
Number of Enterprises 1	4311	527	3294	•	363	52	32	15	7	11	•	7	3
Revenues ($ in Thousands)													
Net Sales 2	39958091	44445	1739574	•	877070	425474	806745	739033	647897	3332616	•	7677659	23307579
Interest 3	175050	1	1520	•	1384	14	723	1097	157	6207	•	49571	114377
Rents 4	96089	0	0	•	114	281	0	168	0	1845	•	7280	86400
Royalties 5	311	0	0	•	0	0	0	0	0	0	•	311	0
Other Portfolio Income 6	1623139	29545	125537	•	36692	0	4200	1698	13640	24095	•	28122	1359609
Other Receipts 7	1553403	5471	21429	•	8323	10940	11146	30107	3601	110830	•	171885	1179672
Total Receipts 8	43046083	79462	1888060	•	923583	436709	822814	772103	665295	3475593	•	7934828	26047637
Average Total Receipts 9	9985	151	573	•	2544	8398	25713	51474	95042	315963	•	1133547	8682546
Operating Costs/Operating Income (%)													
Cost of Operations 10	16.2	0.2	17.1	•	43.8	59.2	42.0	60.8	22.3	41.3	•	15.6	8.5
Salaries and Wages 11	21.4	11.1	4.1	•	10.7	5.8	12.9	5.2	13.6	14.0	•	20.9	25.7
Taxes Paid 12	2.7	1.5	0.9	•	1.6	3.1	1.9	2.0	1.6	2.0	•	3.0	2.9
Interest Paid 13	2.7	4.2	0.3	•	0.5	2.6	1.1	0.3	1.1	0.7	•	3.1	3.3
Depreciation 14	8.0	12.9	2.1	•	2.6	9.4	5.2	2.4	3.6	3.4	•	5.8	10.5
Amortization and Depletion 15	0.4	2.2	0.0	•	•	0.1	0.0	0.3	0.8	0.2	•	1.1	0.2
Pensions and Other Deferred Comp. 16	1.3	•	0.8	•	0.3	0.0	0.2	0.4	0.2	1.1	•	0.2	1.9
Employee Benefits 17	3.7	0.0	0.5	•	0.6	0.1	1.4	1.4	0.8	2.1	•	2.8	4.9
Advertising 18	1.0	0.5	0.4	•	0.1	0.0	0.3	0.3	0.1	0.8	•	0.7	1.3
Other Expenses 19	47.1	70.7	62.9	•	29.2	18.5	30.9	25.2	44.6	31.2	•	46.9	50.7
Officers' Compensation 20	0.6	•	3.6	•	3.3	0.2	1.4	1.1	1.2	0.5	•	0.5	0.4
Operating Margin 21	•	7.4	•	•	7.3	1.1	2.7	0.5	10.2	2.9	•	•	•
Operating Margin Before Officers' Comp. 22	11.0	•	•	•	10.6	1.3	4.1	1.6	11.3	3.4	•	•	•

Selected Average Balance Sheet ($ in Thousands)

Net Receivables 23	503	0	17	•	336	4511	3147	3515	6978	29767	•	40614	313403
Inventories 24	123	0	0	•	28	90	919	880	3271	8135	•	22024	123196
Net Property, Plant and Equipment 25	5081	0	46	•	386	743	6776	10707	23429	46576	•	345376	6034228
Total Assets 26	10119	0	110	•	2146	6327	14641	33440	61736	174422	•	892141	10862181
Notes and Loans Payable 27	3984	0	68	•	633	5112	5950	7547	16046	43344	•	422895	4200581
All Other Liabilities 28	4775	0	57	•	455	1086	3826	11013	14097	112504	•	308987	5462560
Net Worth 29	1360	0	-15	•	1058	129	4866	14880	31593	18574	•	160259	1199040

Selected Financial Ratios (Times to 1)

Current Ratio 30	1.2	•	1.0	•	2.8	5.1	1.4	1.3	1.8	1.0	•	1.6	1.0
Quick Ratio 31	0.8	•	0.9	•	2.5	4.3	1.1	1.0	1.1	0.7	•	1.1	0.7
Net Sales to Working Capital 32	20.3	•	•	•	2.4	1.8	12.5	11.1	7.9	•	•	6.9	460.3
Coverage Ratio 33	2.3	19.1	61.4	•	27.4	2.4	5.1	15.2	12.6	11.3	•	1.9	1.5
Total Asset Turnover 34	0.9	•	4.8	•	1.1	1.3	1.7	1.5	1.5	1.7	•	1.2	0.7
Inventory Turnover 35	12.1	•	•	•	37.6	53.7	11.5	34.1	6.3	15.4	•	7.8	5.3
Receivables Turnover 36	25.0	•	23.0	•	5.8	2.6	6.7	13.4	22.7	13.1	•	37.5	•
Total Liabilities to Net Worth 37	6.4	•	•	•	1.0	48.1	2.0	1.2	1.0	8.4	•	4.6	8.1
Current Assets to Working Capital 38	7.2	•	•	•	1.6	1.2	3.4	3.9	2.2	•	•	2.6	165.5
Current Liabilities to Working Capital 39	6.2	•	•	•	0.6	0.2	2.4	2.9	1.2	•	•	1.6	164.5
Working Capital to Net Sales 40	0.0	•	•	•	0.4	0.6	0.1	0.1	0.1	•	•	0.1	0.0
Inventory to Working Capital 41	0.4	•	•	•	0.0	0.0	0.4	0.1	0.3	•	•	0.2	7.3
Total Receipts to Cash Flow 42	3.2	0.8	1.4	•	3.3	5.6	4.4	5.9	2.7	5.0	•	3.9	3.1
Cost of Goods to Cash Flow 43	0.5	0.0	0.2	•	1.4	3.3	1.9	3.6	0.6	2.1	•	0.6	0.3
Cash Flow to Total Debt 44	0.3	•	3.1	•	0.7	0.2	0.6	0.5	1.2	0.4	•	0.4	0.3

Selected Financial Factors (in Percentages)

Debt Ratio 45	86.6	•	113.7	•	50.7	98.0	66.8	55.5	48.8	89.4	•	82.0	89.0
Return on Total Assets 46	5.7	•	77.8	•	14.7	8.1	10.1	7.8	20.9	13.6	•	7.3	3.4
Return on Equity Before Income Taxes 47	23.9	•	•	•	28.8	234.6	24.4	16.5	37.6	116.7	•	19.6	9.8
Return on Equity After Income Taxes 48	21.9	•	•	•	28.1	226.2	19.9	12.9	37.2	102.6	•	16.5	8.8
Profit Margin (Before Income Tax) 49	3.5	75.6	15.9	•	12.6	3.7	4.7	5.0	12.8	7.2	•	2.9	1.5
Profit Margin (After Income Tax) 50	3.2	75.6	15.9	•	12.3	3.6	3.8	3.9	12.7	6.3	•	2.4	1.4

238

Table I

Corporations with and without Net Income

RAIL TRANSPORTATION

MONEY AMOUNTS AND SIZE OF ASSETS IN THOUSANDS OF DOLLARS

Item Description for Accounting Period 7/03 Through 6/04	Total	Zero Assets	Under 500	500 to 1,000	1,000 to 5,000	5,000 to 10,000	10,000 to 25,000	25,000 to 50,000	50,000 to 100,000	100,000 to 250,000	250,000 to 500,000	500,000 to 2,500,000	2,500,000 and over
Number of Enterprises **1**	469	10	279	•	84	31	20	13	10	6	4	4	8
Revenues ($ in Thousands)													
Net Sales **2**	45038356	52355	165493	•	382379	12659	175141	241550	273343	326495	634164	1351020	41423756
Interest **3**	1072337	2776	1576	•	2604	825	553	1089	1690	4356	5909	10612	1040346
Rents **4**	670011	165	0	•	348	66	2203	1850	6360	3855	20224	85369	549571
Royalties **5**	18400	0	0	•	94	0	0	12	240	0	0	0	18054
Other Portfolio Income **6**	513122	2110	0	•	3682	34	1332	2174	9854	6546	4052	82267	401071
Other Receipts **7**	2657746	-7374	44	•	7720	68	6790	8800	7377	477	21347	37924	2574574
Total Receipts **8**	49969972	50032	167113	•	396827	13652	186019	255475	298864	341729	685696	1567192	46007372
Average Total Receipts **9**	106546	5003	599	•	4724	440	9301	19652	29886	56955	171424	391798	5750922
Operating Costs/Operating Income (%)													
Cost of Operations **10**	31.8	35.5	4.6	•	3.7	43.9	25.3	22.1	18.7	43.2	25.4	2.7	33.2
Salaries and Wages **11**	20.5	10.4	4.5	•	23.3	10.6	11.8	18.1	20.6	9.0	14.3	23.7	20.7
Taxes Paid **12**	6.2	6.5	3.2	•	3.3	3.1	6.0	3.9	6.7	5.5	3.4	8.3	6.2
Interest Paid **13**	7.4	19.9	6.2	•	1.4	0.1	2.0	2.4	4.5	3.2	6.3	5.7	7.6
Depreciation **14**	11.6	5.3	1.6	•	7.3	36.3	9.5	12.1	16.5	9.7	12.1	17.2	11.5
Amortization and Depletion **15**	0.2	0.2	•	•	0.1	0.1	0.1	0.2	0.1	0.4	1.1	0.3	0.2
Pensions and Other Deferred Comp. **16**	0.8	•	•	•	0.0	8.2	0.6	1.3	1.5	0.6	1.3	2.1	0.7
Employee Benefits **17**	4.2	15.1	0.9	•	1.5	8.0	1.6	3.3	4.4	6.5	5.8	3.2	4.2
Advertising **18**	0.1	0.0	0.0	•	0.7	0.0	0.4	0.2	0.3	0.0	0.0	0.1	0.1
Other Expenses **19**	26.9	8.9	74.8	•	59.3	70.0	28.7	25.3	37.5	21.8	31.5	47.6	25.6
Officers' Compensation **20**	0.3	14.5	•	•	0.8	•	2.8	2.2	1.6	1.2	1.3	0.6	0.2
Operating Margin **21**	•	•	4.2	•	•	•	11.3	9.1	•	•	•	•	•
Operating Margin Before Officers' Comp. **22**	•	4.2	4.2	•	•	•	14.0	11.3	•	0.0	•	•	•

Selected Average Balance Sheet ($ in Thousands)

Net Receivables 23	12413	0	•	433	635	1977	3616	6826	15158	29266	61940	642062
Inventories 24	1881	0	•	27	27	246	283	2242	1368	3976	2721	101451
Net Property, Plant and Equipment 25	232040	0	•	1362	3110	8915	22955	45846	74072	227751	764106	12904910
Total Assets 26	380395	0	•	2998	6149	15037	34058	71031	128410	350462	996532	21281065
Notes and Loans Payable 27	81872	0	•	1170	356	3592	9989	23709	26969	143121	240436	4517688
All Other Liabilities 28	137762	0	•	1021	2502	4207	8805	29473	42753	95596	390585	7718183
Net Worth 29	160762	0	•	808	3290	7238	15264	17848	58689	111745	365511	9045194

Selected Financial Ratios (Times to 1)

Current Ratio 30	0.7	8.8	•	0.8	2.1	1.3	1.9	0.5	1.0	0.8	0.7	0.6
Quick Ratio 31	0.5	4.9	•	0.6	2.1	1.1	1.5	0.4	0.8	0.6	0.5	0.5
Net Sales to Working Capital 32	•	3.0	•	•	0.3	9.7	3.7	•	•	•	•	•
Coverage Ratio 33	1.1	1.8	•	2.5	•	10.0	7.3	0.3	2.1	1.9	1.8	1.1
Total Asset Turnover 34	0.3	1.6	•	1.5	0.1	0.6	0.5	0.4	0.4	0.5	0.3	0.2
Inventory Turnover 35	16.2	5.8	•	6.1	6.6	9.0	14.5	2.3	17.2	10.1	3.4	17.0
Receivables Turnover 36	8.1	11.2	•	13.1	1.0	4.2	6.0	3.7	4.3	5.3	5.7	8.5
Total Liabilities to Net Worth 37	1.4	0.2	•	2.7	0.9	1.1	1.2	3.0	1.2	2.1	1.7	1.4
Current Assets to Working Capital 38	•	1.1	•	•	1.9	4.6	2.1	•	•	•	•	•
Current Liabilities to Working Capital 39	•	0.1	•	•	0.9	3.6	1.1	•	•	•	•	•
Working Capital to Net Sales 40	•	0.3	•	•	3.7	0.1	0.3	•	•	•	•	•
Inventory to Working Capital 41	•	•	•	•	0.0	0.3	0.1	•	•	•	•	•
Total Receipts to Cash Flow 42	5.8	1.3	•	2.2	•	2.7	3.2	4.2	6.1	3.9	3.4	6.2
Cost of Goods to Cash Flow 43	1.8	0.1	•	0.1	•	0.7	0.7	0.8	2.6	1.0	0.1	2.1
Cash Flow to Total Debt 44	0.1	6.6	•	0.9	•	0.4	0.3	0.1	0.1	0.2	0.2	0.1

Selected Financial Factors (in Percentages)

Debt Ratio 45	57.7	18.8	•	73.1	46.5	51.9	55.2	74.9	54.3	68.1	63.3	57.5
Return on Total Assets 46	2.1	18.5	•	5.4	•	11.3	9.4	0.6	2.8	5.3	3.5	2.1
Return on Equity Before Income Taxes 47	0.7	10.4	•	11.9	•	21.2	18.1	•	3.2	7.6	4.2	0.5
Return on Equity After Income Taxes 48	0.2	10.3	•	8.2	•	19.6	13.5	•	1.5	6.6	4.2	0.0
Profit Margin (Before Income Tax) 49	1.1	5.2	•	2.1	•	17.5	14.9	•	3.5	5.4	4.6	0.8
Profit Margin (After Income Tax) 50	0.3	5.1	•	1.5	•	16.2	11.1	•	1.6	4.7	4.6	0.0

239

Table II
Corporations with Net Income

RAIL TRANSPORTATION

MONEY AMOUNTS AND SIZE OF ASSETS IN THOUSANDS OF DOLLARS

Item Description for Accounting Period 7/03 Through 6/04	Total	Zero Assets	Under 500	500 to 1,000	1,000 to 5,000	5,000 to 10,000	10,000 to 25,000	25,000 to 50,000	50,000 to 100,000	100,000 to 250,000	250,000 to 500,000	500,000 to 2,500,000	2,500,000 and over
Number of Enterprises 1	389	•	279	•	68	•	14	10	5	3	•	•	4
Revenues ($ in Thousands)													
Net Sales 2	32038412	•	165493	•	343195	•	148511	219336	154853	144996	•	•	29348268
Interest 3	804036	•	1576	•	2609	•	542	988	688	4228	•	•	778162
Rents 4	437573	•	0	•	414	•	2157	1575	2378	1546	•	•	346091
Royalties 5	16621	•	0	•	94	•	0	12	214	0	•	•	16301
Other Portfolio Income 6	401522	•	0	•	3716	•	1108	2077	2021	3759	•	•	310199
Other Receipts 7	1502848	•	44	•	11067	•	5777	8800	1276	458	•	•	1421927
Total Receipts 8	35201012	•	167113	•	361095	•	158095	232788	161430	154987	•	•	32220948
Average Total Receipts 9	90491	•	599	•	5310	•	11292	23279	32286	51662	•	•	8055237
Operating Costs/Operating Income (%)													
Cost of Operations 10	33.4	•	4.6	•	5.4	•	25.4	23.5	13.9	9.7	•	•	35.3
Salaries and Wages 11	18.4	•	4.5	•	24.3	•	11.5	17.4	19.4	20.3	•	•	18.3
Taxes Paid 12	5.8	•	3.2	•	2.9	•	6.4	3.6	8.2	8.0	•	•	5.8
Interest Paid 13	7.1	•	6.2	•	1.1	•	1.5	2.3	1.0	4.7	•	•	7.5
Depreciation 14	11.1	•	1.6	•	7.4	•	8.0	11.0	15.0	10.9	•	•	11.0
Amortization and Depletion 15	0.2	•	•	•	0.0	•	0.0	0.2	0.1	0.0	•	•	0.2
Pensions and Other Deferred Comp. 16	0.8	•	•	•	0.0	•	0.5	1.3	1.4	1.4	•	•	0.8
Employee Benefits 17	3.2	•	0.9	•	1.6	•	1.7	2.9	3.3	11.4	•	•	3.2
Advertising 18	0.0	•	0.0	•	0.8	•	0.1	0.2	0.3	•	•	•	0.0
Other Expenses 19	26.0	•	74.8	•	56.8	•	26.7	24.6	24.6	25.4	•	•	24.6
Officers' Compensation 20	0.2	•	•	•	0.9	•	2.5	2.0	2.3	2.2	•	•	0.2
Operating Margin 21	•	•	4.2	•	•	•	15.7	11.1	10.5	6.0	•	•	•
Operating Margin Before Officers' Comp. 22	•	•	4.2	•	•	•	18.2	13.1	12.8	8.2	•	•	•

Selected Average Balance Sheet ($ in Thousands)

Net Receivables 23	7838	66	464	2479	3584	3328	8124	648889
Inventories 24	1563	0	39	274	295	2062	571	140940
Net Property, Plant and Equipment 25	197271	107	1157	9070	23770	57235	88323	18184674
Total Assets 26	288705	366	2985	15890	35765	75606	145225	26629287
Notes and Loans Payable 27	64306	43	922	3744	10791	8602	31396	5939760
All Other Liabilities 28	105980	25	954	4554	8701	17010	43736	9778435
Net Worth 29	118419	297	1109	7592	16273	49994	70093	10911092

Selected Financial Ratios (Times to 1)

Current Ratio 30	0.6	8.8	1.0	1.3	2.0	1.0	1.0	0.6
Quick Ratio 31	0.3	4.9	0.7	1.1	1.5	0.6	0.7	0.3
Net Sales to Working Capital 32	•	3.0	•	8.4	3.7	•	95.5	•
Coverage Ratio 33	1.5	1.8	5.0	15.7	8.6	15.7	3.7	1.4
Total Asset Turnover 34	0.3	1.6	1.7	0.7	0.6	0.4	0.3	0.3
Inventory Turnover 35	17.6	•	6.9	9.8	17.5	2.1	8.2	18.4
Receivables Turnover 36	8.5	17.9	12.8	4.2	12.2	7.2	11.9	8.7
Total Liabilities to Net Worth 37	1.4	0.2	1.7	1.1	1.2	0.5	1.1	1.4
Current Assets to Working Capital 38	•	1.1	•	4.0	2.0	•	32.1	•
Current Liabilities to Working Capital 39	•	0.1	•	3.0	1.0	•	31.1	•
Working Capital to Net Sales 40	•	0.3	•	0.1	0.3	•	0.0	•
Inventory to Working Capital 41	•	•	•	0.2	0.1	•	1.1	•
Total Receipts to Cash Flow 42	5.0	1.3	2.2	2.5	2.9	3.1	4.2	5.4
Cost of Goods to Cash Flow 43	1.7	0.1	0.1	0.6	0.7	0.4	0.4	1.9
Cash Flow to Total Debt 44	0.1	6.6	1.2	0.5	0.4	0.4	0.2	0.1

Selected Financial Factors (in Percentages)

Debt Ratio 45	59.0	18.8	62.8	52.2	54.5	33.9	51.7	59.0
Return on Total Assets 46	3.1	18.5	8.9	15.8	11.9	6.5	5.8	2.9
Return on Equity Before Income Taxes 47	2.6	10.4	19.0	30.9	23.2	9.1	8.9	2.1
Return on Equity After Income Taxes 48	1.8	10.3	14.4	28.7	17.6	6.3	6.3	1.4
Profit Margin (Before Income Tax) 49	3.7	5.2	4.2	22.1	17.2	14.8	12.9	3.1
Profit Margin (After Income Tax) 50	2.6	5.1	3.2	20.6	13.0	10.1	8.5	2.0

Table I

Corporations with and without Net Income

WATER TRANSPORTATION

MONEY AMOUNTS AND SIZE OF ASSETS IN THOUSANDS OF DOLLARS

Item Description for Accounting Period 7/03 Through 6/04	Total	Zero Assets	Under 500	500 to 1,000	1,000 to 5,000	5,000 to 10,000	10,000 to 25,000	25,000 to 50,000	50,000 to 100,000	100,000 to 250,000	250,000 to 500,000	500,000 to 2,500,000	2,500,000 and over
Number of Enterprises **1**	3176	42	1794	539	610	56	54	28	19	16	7	12	•

Revenues ($ in Thousands)

Net Sales **2**	20075774	156813	2774315	1804905	404568	477695	1003124	906949	1152882	1383068	813144	9198310	•
Interest **3**	101484	2020	822	642	1217	664	2199	4868	2046	2607	11301	73099	•
Rents **4**	98509	346	6281	0	20	551	2309	4277	632	2153	391	81550	•
Royalties **5**	7	0	0	0	0	0	0	0	0	7	0	0	•
Other Portfolio Income **6**	243984	780	48838	7025	4163	345	7384	3560	5537	21179	1405	143766	•
Other Receipts **7**	378763	-5177	84073	797	7597	16018	23364	7813	10481	22480	3130	208188	•
Total Receipts **8**	20898521	154782	2914329	1813369	417565	495273	1038380	927467	1171578	1431494	829371	9704913	•
Average Total Receipts **9**	6580	3685	1624	3364	685	8844	19229	33124	61662	89468	118482	808743	•

Operating Costs/Operating Income (%)

Cost of Operations **10**	51.8	62.3	89.2	58.4	52.9	51.0	53.8	50.3	40.6	42.5	35.0	43.2	•
Salaries and Wages **11**	9.9	14.8	3.2	13.1	7.8	8.5	10.5	12.0	9.7	8.6	7.7	11.4	•
Taxes Paid **12**	1.8	1.9	0.6	2.4	2.2	2.0	2.7	2.3	2.1	1.5	2.0	1.9	•
Interest Paid **13**	2.8	18.1	0.0	0.5	3.5	3.6	2.2	3.0	3.1	3.4	9.0	3.0	•
Depreciation **14**	8.0	8.8	0.3	1.2	27.9	4.7	7.7	6.7	9.6	11.9	19.0	9.3	•
Amortization and Depletion **15**	0.4	1.2	0.0	0.0	0.0	0.0	0.1	0.1	0.2	0.2	0.5	0.7	•
Pensions and Other Deferred Comp. **16**	0.8	•	0.7	0.5	0.2	0.1	0.6	0.3	0.4	0.4	0.6	1.1	•
Employee Benefits **17**	2.3	2.0	0.5	1.0	1.0	2.9	1.3	4.9	1.6	1.7	1.7	3.2	•
Advertising **18**	0.3	0.7	0.0	1.4	0.2	0.0	0.5	0.2	0.3	0.1	0.4	0.1	•
Other Expenses **19**	24.3	42.4	7.1	14.5	15.2	28.6	18.9	19.4	34.7	28.0	27.8	30.1	•
Officers' Compensation **20**	1.6	2.4	3.1	2.2	10.2	0.8	2.2	1.8	1.3	0.9	0.9	0.9	•
Operating Margin **21**	•	•	•	4.6	•	•	•	•	•	0.9	•	•	•
Operating Margin Before Officers' Comp. **22**	•	•	•	6.8	•	•	1.8	1.0	1.8	•	•	•	•

Selected Average Balance Sheet ($ in Thousands)

Net Receivables 23	773	0	14	59	141	283	2242	4774	10477	10108	28030	123784
Inventories 24	67	0	0	0	20	52	307	135	413	1812	1320	11009
Net Property, Plant and Equipment 25	3721	0	3	344	1151	2148	8323	19916	39992	89057	155844	543537
Total Assets 26	7558	0	125	637	2065	7211	15682	35334	70178	143175	317647	1174198
Notes and Loans Payable 27	2978	0	10	289	1111	3899	6697	18322	33354	50649	141429	423870
All Other Liabilities 28	1885	0	46	181	216	240	3361	5887	19334	29549	80511	325859
Net Worth 29	2695	0	69	167	738	3072	5724	11125	17490	62978	95706	424469

Selected Financial Ratios (Times to 1)

Current Ratio 30	1.2	•	2.1	0.8	1.7	0.8	1.2	1.2	1.0	1.2	1.4	1.2
Quick Ratio 31	0.8	•	2.0	0.5	1.4	0.7	0.8	1.0	0.7	0.9	1.0	0.8
Net Sales to Working Capital 32	22.4	•	26.9	•	4.7	•	25.1	17.6	197.5	23.3	5.3	21.2
Coverage Ratio 33	1.5	•	13.9	10.6	•	1.4	2.4	1.5	0.3	2.3	0.9	1.8
Total Asset Turnover 34	0.8	•	12.4	5.3	0.3	1.2	1.2	0.9	0.9	0.6	0.4	0.7
Inventory Turnover 35	48.6	•	•	•	17.5	84.0	32.5	120.8	59.7	20.3	30.8	30.1
Receivables Turnover 36	8.0	•	97.2	52.9	3.2	4.4	7.2	7.2	5.7	6.0	5.9	6.7
Total Liabilities to Net Worth 37	1.8	•	0.8	2.8	1.8	1.3	1.7	2.2	3.0	1.3	2.3	1.8
Current Assets to Working Capital 38	6.1	•	1.9	•	2.4	•	7.0	5.5	70.6	7.4	3.6	6.7
Current Liabilities to Working Capital 39	5.1	•	0.9	•	1.4	•	6.0	4.5	69.6	6.4	2.6	5.7
Working Capital to Net Sales 40	0.0	•	0.0	•	0.2	•	0.0	0.0	0.0	0.0	0.2	0.0
Inventory to Working Capital 41	0.2	•	•	•	0.0	•	0.4	0.1	1.6	0.4	0.1	0.3
Total Receipts to Cash Flow 42	5.6	•	27.4	7.0	•	4.2	7.2	8.5	4.0	4.0	4.7	4.3
Cost of Goods to Cash Flow 43	2.9	•	24.5	4.1	•	2.1	3.9	4.3	1.6	1.7	1.6	1.8
Cash Flow to Total Debt 44	0.2	•	1.0	1.0	0.5	0.3	0.3	0.2	0.3	0.3	0.1	0.2

Selected Financial Factors (in Percentages)

Debt Ratio 45	64.3	•	44.8	73.8	64.2	57.4	63.5	68.5	75.1	56.0	69.9	63.9
Return on Total Assets 46	3.4	•	4.4	29.4	•	6.0	6.2	4.1	0.9	4.7	2.9	3.6
Return on Equity Before Income Taxes 47	2.9	•	7.4	101.5	4.1	•	10.1	4.3	•	6.1	•	4.6
Return on Equity After Income Taxes 48	0.8	•	6.4	98.8	2.7	•	8.3	3.8	•	3.7	•	2.0
Profit Margin (Before Income Tax) 49	1.3	•	0.3	5.1	1.5	•	3.1	1.5	•	4.4	•	2.5
Profit Margin (After Income Tax) 50	0.3	•	0.3	4.9	1.0	•	2.5	1.3	•	2.7	•	1.1

Table II

Corporations with Net Income

WATER TRANSPORTATION

MONEY AMOUNTS AND SIZE OF ASSETS IN THOUSANDS OF DOLLARS

Item Description for Accounting Period 7/03 Through 6/04	Total	Zero Assets	Under 500	500 to 1,000	1,000 to 5,000	5,000 to 10,000	10,000 to 25,000	25,000 to 50,000	50,000 to 100,000	100,000 to 250,000	250,000 to 500,000	500,000 to 2,500,000	2,500,000 and over
Number of Enterprises 1	1509	12	733	448	191	53	33	12	6	9	4	8	•
Revenues ($ in Thousands)													
Net Sales 2	16795194	12973	2704592	1674939	319619	439819	709492	593168	619302	946817	524379	8250094	•
Interest 3	78400	0	591	642	461	275	1428	4374	547	2538	5220	62324	•
Rents 4	92167	0	6281	0	0	551	860	0	382	2153	391	81550	•
Royalties 5	0	0	0	0	0	0	0	0	0	0	0	0	•
Other Portfolio Income 6	162909	705	45940	6960	1607	345	5573	674	528	14781	171	85623	•
Other Receipts 7	370645	4723	82251	699	1777	3110	19683	4767	6150	11882	2351	233253	•
Total Receipts 8	17499315	18401	2839655	1683240	323464	444100	737036	602983	626909	978171	532512	8712844	•
Average Total Receipts 9	11597	1533	3874	3757	1694	8379	22334	50249	104485	108686	133128	1089106	•
Operating Costs/Operating Income (%)													
Cost of Operations 10	53.3	9.5	91.4	61.1	55.7	55.2	53.5	47.6	40.1	34.4	37.2	43.6	•
Salaries and Wages 11	9.8	44.1	2.9	14.2	3.7	6.1	10.9	14.7	10.5	9.9	6.6	11.3	•
Taxes Paid 12	1.7	3.2	0.5	2.0	1.6	1.8	2.7	2.0	1.7	1.6	2.5	2.0	•
Interest Paid 13	1.9	8.8	0.0	0.5	3.2	3.7	1.4	2.0	1.2	2.6	3.1	2.6	•
Depreciation 14	4.8	10.7	0.2	1.1	5.5	3.6	5.2	3.5	3.5	10.2	6.6	6.5	•
Amortization and Depletion 15	0.2	0.0	0.0	0.0	•	0.1	0.1	0.1	0.3	0.3	0.5	0.4	•
Pensions and Other Deferred Comp. 16	0.8	•	0.4	0.6	0.2	0.1	0.7	0.1	0.5	0.4	0.8	1.1	•
Employee Benefits 17	2.4	0.2	0.4	1.0	0.4	1.2	1.3	6.7	1.5	1.6	2.5	3.4	•
Advertising 18	0.2	0.0	0.0	0.6	0.1	0.1	0.5	0.1	0.0	0.1	0.7	0.1	•
Other Expenses 19	23.4	17.3	6.0	11.6	6.1	23.9	17.7	18.4	35.4	32.2	36.4	30.4	•
Officers' Compensation 20	1.5	12.3	2.5	2.3	4.0	0.8	2.6	1.4	1.3	0.9	0.8	0.9	•
Operating Margin 21	•	•	•	5.2	19.4	3.5	3.6	3.4	3.9	5.7	2.4	•	•
Operating Margin Before Officers' Comp. 22	1.4	6.2	•	7.5	23.4	4.3	6.2	4.8	5.3	6.7	3.2	•	•

Selected Average Balance Sheet ($ in Thousands)

	1	2	3	4	5	6	7	8	9	10	11	12
Net Receivables 23	1200	0	34	70	133	255	2888	7992	19270	9473	44316	143356
Inventories 24	99		0	0	0	0	145	82	427	2994	2899	13543
Net Property, Plant and Equipment 25	4700	0	4	284	1219	2154	7123	14981	25685	92573	122239	590508
Total Assets 26	9671		216	617	1735	7227	15555	34852	69436	148491	306784	1191596
Notes and Loans Payable 27	3391	0	20	221	771	3640	4900	14016	17700	40920	51262	456859
All Other Liabilities 28	3117		113	202	248	62	3964	9185	29516	34008	127082	405907
Net Worth 29	3162		83	194	716	3525	6690	11651	22221	73563	128440	328831

Selected Financial Ratios (Times to 1)

	1	2	3	4	5	6	7	8	9	10	11	12
Current Ratio 30	1.1	•	1.5	0.9	1.7	0.9	1.2	1.4	1.3	1.7	1.3	1.0
Quick Ratio 31	0.8	•	1.4	0.6	1.0	0.8	0.9	1.1	1.1	1.3	0.9	0.7
Net Sales to Working Capital 32	37.9	•	64.9	•	9.1	•	20.0	10.4	15.8	8.0	4.7	492.8
Coverage Ratio 33	3.7	5.0	26.0	12.4	7.5	2.2	6.4	3.6	5.3	4.5	2.3	3.0
Total Asset Turnover 34	1.2	•	17.1	6.1	1.0	1.1	1.4	1.4	1.5	0.7	0.4	0.9
Inventory Turnover 35	59.9	•	219.0	•	•	•	79.4	287.0	97.1	12.1	16.8	33.2
Receivables Turnover 36	9.7	•	49.5	5.5	4.1	•	10.4	12.4	5.0	5.7	5.9	8.3
Total Liabilities to Net Worth 37	2.1	•	1.6	2.2	1.4	1.1	1.3	2.0	2.1	1.0	1.4	2.6
Current Assets to Working Capital 38	8.4	•	3.2	•	2.4	•	5.7	3.6	4.6	2.5	4.3	119.1
Current Liabilities to Working Capital 39	7.4	•	2.2	•	1.4	•	4.7	2.6	3.6	1.5	3.3	118.1
Working Capital to Net Sales 40	0.0	•	0.0	•	0.1	•	0.1	0.1	0.1	0.1	0.2	0.0
Inventory to Working Capital 41	0.3	•	0.0	•	•	•	0.2	0.0	0.1	0.2	0.1	6.7
Total Receipts to Cash Flow 42	4.6	2.5	35.1	6.9	4.0	3.7	5.1	7.2	2.7	3.1	2.8	3.7
Cost of Goods to Cash Flow 43	2.4	0.2	32.1	4.2	2.2	2.0	2.7	3.4	1.1	1.1	1.0	1.6
Cash Flow to Total Debt 44	0.4	•	0.8	1.3	0.4	0.6	0.5	0.3	0.8	0.5	0.3	0.3

Selected Financial Factors (in Percentages)

	1	2	3	4	5	6	7	8	9	10	11	12
Debt Ratio 45	67.3	•	61.4	68.6	58.7	51.2	57.0	66.6	68.0	50.5	58.1	72.4
Return on Total Assets 46	8.2	•	11.6	37.4	23.0	9.4	12.2	9.9	9.4	8.3	3.0	7.0
Return on Equity Before Income Taxes 47	18.2	•	29.0	109.4	48.2	10.6	24.0	21.3	23.9	13.0	4.1	16.9
Return on Equity After Income Taxes 48	14.4	•	27.0	106.6	48.0	9.3	21.5	20.4	17.0	9.3	3.1	12.0
Profit Margin (Before Income Tax) 49	5.2	35.6	0.7	5.7	20.6	4.5	7.5	5.0	5.2	9.1	4.0	5.4
Profit Margin (After Income Tax) 50	4.1	34.6	0.6	5.5	20.5	4.0	6.7	4.8	3.7	6.5	3.0	3.8

Table I
Corporations with and without Net Income

TRUCK TRANSPORTATION

MONEY AMOUNTS AND SIZE OF ASSETS IN THOUSANDS OF DOLLARS

Item Description for Accounting Period 7/03 Through 6/04	Total	Zero Assets	Under 500	500 to 1,000	1,000 to 5,000	5,000 to 10,000	10,000 to 25,000	25,000 to 50,000	50,000 to 100,000	100,000 to 250,000	250,000 to 500,000	500,000 to 2,500,000	2,500,000 and over
Number of Enterprises 1	96319	13997	70063	5446	5573	645	367	92	62	37	15	21	•

Revenues ($ in Thousands)

	Total	Zero Assets	Under 500	500 to 1,000	1,000 to 5,000	5,000 to 10,000	10,000 to 25,000	25,000 to 50,000	50,000 to 100,000	100,000 to 250,000	250,000 to 500,000	500,000 to 2,500,000	2,500,000 and over
Net Sales 2	176850768	5545917	33248170	13047747	34762311	9305888	14205958	6716465	7783446	8948995	8625927	34659945	•
Interest 3	266106	2939	7402	9477	16999	8927	10218	7640	4160	26904	26519	144922	•
Rents 4	268828	3458	3229	3558	42972	8016	19275	19156	12306	1537	6517	148803	•
Royalties 5	123568	1084	0	96	723	0	48	5	6	0	52599	69006	•
Other Portfolio Income 6	1459689	70640	360533	120219	161561	74906	94856	34326	74032	54541	97965	316109	•
Other Receipts 7	2321956	56195	113713	28805	199750	94922	116585	80230	25295	207926	32594	1365943	•
Total Receipts 8	181290915	5680233	33733047	13209902	35184316	9492659	14446940	6857822	7899245	9239903	8842121	36704728	•
Average Total Receipts 9	1882	406	481	2426	6313	14717	39365	74542	127407	249727	589475	1747844	•

Operating Costs/Operating Income (%)

	Total	Zero Assets	Under 500	500 to 1,000	1,000 to 5,000	5,000 to 10,000	10,000 to 25,000	25,000 to 50,000	50,000 to 100,000	100,000 to 250,000	250,000 to 500,000	500,000 to 2,500,000	2,500,000 and over
Cost of Operations 10	31.4	11.5	31.3	20.3	37.9	36.7	39.9	33.3	30.0	27.1	37.1	27.2	•
Salaries and Wages 11	20.0	30.4	15.0	25.5	17.4	16.7	16.0	19.5	21.6	20.0	22.0	25.2	•
Taxes Paid 12	4.0	5.4	3.4	4.2	3.4	3.5	4.2	4.1	4.6	4.7	4.1	4.7	•
Interest Paid 13	1.1	1.6	1.0	1.1	1.0	1.1	1.0	1.1	1.4	1.3	1.6	1.2	•
Depreciation 14	5.6	2.2	5.0	6.7	5.4	5.3	5.2	6.0	7.3	7.1	7.6	5.6	•
Amortization and Depletion 15	0.1	0.3	0.0	0.0	0.1	0.1	0.1	0.1	0.2	0.2	0.2	0.3	•
Pensions and Other Deferred Comp. 16	0.7	3.8	0.1	0.4	0.3	0.2	0.3	0.4	0.3	0.3	0.8	1.6	•
Employee Benefits 17	2.8	5.2	1.3	2.7	1.7	2.0	2.0	2.2	3.4	2.9	3.6	5.3	•
Advertising 18	0.2	0.1	0.2	0.1	0.2	0.2	0.2	0.3	0.2	0.3	0.1	0.2	•
Other Expenses 19	33.5	40.6	38.7	37.5	30.8	33.2	30.5	33.8	31.3	36.9	22.0	32.4	•
Officers' Compensation 20	1.9	1.6	4.1	2.4	2.4	1.9	1.2	0.8	0.7	0.6	0.7	0.4	•
Operating Margin 21	•	•	•	•	•	•	•	•	•	•	0.3	•	•
Operating Margin Before Officers' Comp. 22	0.5	•	3.8	1.3	1.8	1.1	0.7	•	•	•	1.0	•	•

Selected Average Balance Sheet ($ in Thousands)

Net Receivables 23	172	0	14	103	601	1394	4249	9104	13455	30957	61224	261860	•
Inventories 24	7	0	2	7	17	76	166	571	917	1416	1843	8481	•
Net Property, Plant and Equipment 25	353	0	44	392	837	2770	7058	17055	39072	80948	191139	469634	•
Total Assets 26	816	0	86	700	2057	6822	15246	34639	69340	156061	349776	1373979	•
Notes and Loans Payable 27	347	0	77	427	1013	3296	6760	14024	32935	54695	120022	392696	•
All Other Liabilities 28	224	0	17	87	459	1485	3671	8945	15885	41140	97856	486900	•
Net Worth 29	246	0	-9	186	584	2041	4815	11670	20520	60227	131898	494384	•

Selected Financial Ratios (Times to 1)

Current Ratio 30	1.2	•	1.0	1.3	1.2	1.0	1.2	1.1	1.0	1.4	1.5	1.3	•
Quick Ratio 31	1.0	•	0.8	1.0	1.1	0.7	1.0	0.9	0.8	1.0	1.2	1.0	•
Net Sales to Working Capital 32	37.1	•	•	38.3	39.6	•	30.9	42.8	•	16.8	14.6	18.3	•
Coverage Ratio 33	2.0	0.8	2.2	1.1	1.6	2.1	2.2	1.6	1.4	2.3	2.8	2.7	•
Total Asset Turnover 34	2.2	•	5.5	3.4	3.0	2.1	2.5	2.1	1.8	1.5	1.6	1.2	•
Inventory Turnover 35	77.7	•	96.7	70.9	142.4	69.4	93.1	42.6	41.1	46.4	115.6	52.9	•
Receivables Turnover 36	11.1	•	35.0	18.2	11.6	9.8	9.5	8.2	9.6	8.2	9.0	6.7	•
Total Liabilities to Net Worth 37	2.3	•	•	2.8	2.5	2.3	2.2	2.0	2.4	1.6	1.7	1.8	•
Current Assets to Working Capital 38	6.0	•	•	4.0	6.2	•	5.4	8.0	•	3.7	2.9	4.8	•
Current Liabilities to Working Capital 39	5.0	•	•	3.0	5.2	•	4.4	7.0	•	2.7	1.9	3.8	•
Working Capital to Net Sales 40	0.0	•	•	0.0	0.0	•	0.0	0.0	•	0.1	0.1	0.1	•
Inventory to Working Capital 41	0.2	•	•	0.1	0.1	•	0.1	0.2	•	0.1	0.1	0.1	•
Total Receipts to Cash Flow 42	3.9	3.1	3.4	3.2	4.4	4.3	4.6	4.6	4.4	4.3	4.9	3.6	•
Cost of Goods to Cash Flow 43	1.2	0.4	1.1	0.7	1.7	1.6	1.8	1.5	1.3	1.2	1.8	1.0	•
Cash Flow to Total Debt 44	0.8	•	1.5	1.5	1.0	0.7	0.8	0.7	0.6	0.6	0.5	0.5	•

Selected Financial Factors (in Percentages)

Debt Ratio 45	69.9	•	110.0	73.5	71.6	70.1	68.4	66.3	70.4	61.4	62.3	64.0	•
Return on Total Assets 46	5.2	•	12.2	4.3	4.9	4.8	5.5	3.7	3.5	4.8	7.2	3.8	•
Return on Equity Before Income Taxes 47	8.7	•	•	1.9	6.5	8.5	9.5	3.9	3.4	7.0	12.3	6.7	•
Return on Equity After Income Taxes 48	6.5	•	•	0.7	5.0	6.4	8.0	2.5	2.4	5.2	8.0	4.5	•
Profit Margin (Before Income Tax) 49	1.2	•	1.2	0.1	0.6	1.2	1.2	0.6	0.6	1.7	2.8	2.0	•
Profit Margin (After Income Tax) 50	0.9	•	1.1	0.1	0.5	0.9	1.0	0.4	0.4	1.3	1.8	1.4	•

Table II

Corporations with Net Income

TRUCK TRANSPORTATION

MONEY AMOUNTS AND SIZE OF ASSETS IN THOUSANDS OF DOLLARS

Item Description for Accounting Period 7/03 Through 6/04	Total	Zero Assets	Under 500	500 to 1,000	1,000 to 5,000	5,000 to 10,000	10,000 to 25,000	25,000 to 50,000	50,000 to 100,000	100,000 to 250,000	250,000 to 500,000	500,000 to 2,500,000	2,500,000 and over
Number of Enterprises 1	52315	6068	39951	2275	3252	407	224	49	41	22	10	17	·
Revenues ($ in Thousands)													
Net Sales 2	113499244	1126076	20221654	6618285	20760664	6861509	9427767	3518402	5261342	5634553	6181260	27887732	·
Interest 3	180013	1747	3012	6425	14495	6175	8001	2378	3759	10992	21443	101587	·
Rents 4	163646	5	2170	1676	35917	6711	15165	10731	12196	783	5527	72764	·
Royalties 5	76297	0	0	96	0	0	48	5	6	0	52599	23543	·
Other Portfolio Income 6	1075046	58007	242970	74953	101860	43487	56020	19833	58143	29821	88671	301283	·
Other Receipts 7	1873746	11894	40823	12684	129914	45388	94445	36915	17306	190394	28951	1265032	·
Total Receipts 8	116867992	1197729	20510629	6714119	21042850	6963270	9601446	3558264	5352752	5866543	6378451	29651941	·
Average Total Receipts 9	2234	197	513	2951	6471	17109	42864	73230	130555	266661	637845	1744232	·
Operating Costs/Operating Income (%)													
Cost of Operations 10	31.0	37.8	34.1	21.1	30.8	38.6	41.9	32.7	35.1	23.5	46.1	22.4	·
Salaries and Wages 11	19.6	4.0	11.4	32.0	19.4	16.0	14.7	19.6	20.6	20.6	17.7	26.0	·
Taxes Paid 12	3.9	2.8	3.0	3.7	3.6	3.2	4.0	4.6	4.3	5.0	3.4	4.9	·
Interest Paid 13	0.9	1.6	1.0	0.5	0.8	0.6	0.8	1.0	1.1	1.4	1.1	1.0	·
Depreciation 14	5.1	4.0	4.3	3.5	4.7	4.0	3.9	5.6	6.3	7.0	7.4	6.1	·
Amortization and Depletion 15	0.1	0.0	0.0	0.1	0.1	0.0	0.1	0.1	0.1	0.2	0.1	0.4	·
Pensions and Other Deferred Comp. 16	0.5	0.0	0.1	0.3	0.4	0.1	0.3	0.5	0.2	0.3	0.4	1.4	·
Employee Benefits 17	2.7	0.3	1.5	3.6	1.8	2.1	1.7	2.2	2.7	3.0	2.4	4.8	·
Advertising 18	0.2	0.2	0.2	0.1	0.3	0.2	0.2	0.3	0.2	0.3	0.2	0.2	·
Other Expenses 19	33.1	40.6	36.1	30.9	33.3	31.4	29.6	31.5	28.3	38.1	18.7	35.9	·
Officers' Compensation 20	2.0	3.4	4.2	2.1	3.3	2.2	1.2	0.8	0.7	0.6	0.8	0.4	·
Operating Margin 21	0.8	5.4	4.1	2.2	1.7	1.5	1.6	1.2	0.4	0.1	1.6	·	·
Operating Margin Before Officers' Comp. 22	2.7	8.8	8.3	4.3	5.0	3.7	2.8	2.0	1.1	0.7	2.4	·	·

Selected Average Balance Sheet ($ in Thousands)

Net Receivables 23	216	0	17	142	687	1669	4636	7826	14656	34110	70060	230209	•
Inventories 24	7	0	0	14	54	200	515	1076	1160	3103	7643		•
Net Property, Plant and Equipment 25	405	0	38	231	729	2231	6189	17188	38482	92377	199730	470979	•
Total Assets 26	962	0	85	690	2132	7208	14967	34612	69371	173086	352727	1191998	•
Notes and Loans Payable 27	333	0	67	302	753	2993	5473	11337	29172	48569	99217	314094	•
All Other Liabilities 28	270	0	18	112	512	1455	3879	9132	18334	47555	87770	406085	•
Net Worth 29	359	-0	0	276	867	2760	5614	14143	21865	76962	165739	471819	•

Selected Financial Ratios (Times to 1)

Current Ratio 30	1.4	•	1.0	2.5	1.6	1.2	1.4	1.2	1.2	1.5	1.7	1.5	•
Quick Ratio 31	1.1	•	0.8	2.0	1.4	0.9	1.1	1.0	0.9	1.1	1.3	1.1	•
Net Sales to Working Capital 32	19.3	•	•	13.9	14.4	28.4	21.8	32.6	35.8	13.7	12.7	12.9	•
Coverage Ratio 33	5.0	8.5	6.7	8.0	4.9	5.7	5.3	4.3	2.9	4.0	5.3	3.9	•
Total Asset Turnover 34	2.3	•	6.0	4.2	3.0	2.3	2.8	2.1	1.8	1.5	1.8	1.4	•
Inventory Turnover 35	89.9	•	673.2	144.8	139.1	120.1	88.0	45.7	41.9	51.8	91.9	48.1	•
Receivables Turnover 36	10.7	•	32.2	14.3	10.5	9.4	9.7	18.4	10.2	7.5	17.6	8.0	•
Total Liabilities to Net Worth 37	1.7	•	•	1.5	1.6	1.6	1.7	1.4	2.2	1.2	1.1	1.5	•
Current Assets to Working Capital 38	3.4	•	•	1.7	2.7	5.9	3.8	5.9	6.3	3.2	2.5	3.1	•
Current Liabilities to Working Capital 39	2.4	•	•	0.7	1.7	4.9	2.8	4.9	5.3	2.2	1.5	2.1	•
Working Capital to Net Sales 40	0.1	•	•	0.1	0.1	0.0	0.0	0.0	0.0	0.1	0.1	0.1	•
Inventory to Working Capital 41	0.1	•	•	0.0	0.0	0.2	0.1	0.2	0.5	0.0	0.1	0.1	•
Total Receipts to Cash Flow 42	3.6	2.2	3.1	3.6	3.6	4.1	4.2	4.4	4.7	4.0	5.1	3.2	•
Cost of Goods to Cash Flow 43	1.1	0.8	1.1	0.8	1.1	1.6	1.7	1.5	1.7	0.9	2.4	0.7	•
Cash Flow to Total Debt 44	1.0	•	1.9	2.0	1.4	0.9	1.1	0.8	0.6	0.7	0.6	0.7	•

Selected Financial Factors (in Percentages)

Debt Ratio 45	62.7	•	100.2	60.0	59.3	61.7	62.5	59.1	68.5	55.5	53.0	60.4	•
Return on Total Assets 46	10.5	•	39.0	17.6	11.6	8.5	11.9	8.5	5.9	8.3	10.3	5.3	•
Return on Equity Before Income Taxes 47	22.5	•	•	38.5	22.7	18.4	25.8	16.0	12.3	13.9	17.8	9.9	•
Return on Equity After Income Taxes 48	19.7	•	•	36.6	21.1	15.8	23.7	13.8	10.9	11.6	12.6	7.2	•
Profit Margin (Before Income Tax) 49	3.7	11.7	5.6	3.6	3.1	3.0	3.4	3.1	2.1	4.2	4.8	2.9	•
Profit Margin (After Income Tax) 50	3.3	11.4	5.4	3.5	2.9	2.6	3.2	2.7	1.9	3.5	3.4	2.1	•

Table I

Corporations with and without Net Income

TRANSIT AND GROUND PASSENGER TRANSPORTATION

MONEY AMOUNTS AND SIZE OF ASSETS IN THOUSANDS OF DOLLARS

Item Description for Accounting Period 7/03 Through 6/04	Total	Zero Assets	Under 500	500 to 1,000	1,000 to 5,000	5,000 to 10,000	10,000 to 25,000	25,000 to 50,000	50,000 to 100,000	100,000 to 250,000	250,000 to 500,000	500,000 to 2,500,000	2,500,000 and over
Number of Enterprises **1**	25396	•	20582	•	1247	146	47	16	5	3	3	3	•
Revenues ($ in Thousands)													
Net Sales **2**	21824553	•	3251268	•	5912846	1729694	1076241	723138	412230	545559	1427573	6013486	•
Interest **3**	265186	•	170	•	2697	1555	1641	3634	1196	765	27416	225772	•
Rents **4**	47546	•	497	•	17565	1452	599	3356	219	0	19121	4737	•
Royalties **5**	3	•	0	•	0	0	0	0	0	0	3	0	•
Other Portfolio Income **6**	230227	•	3868	•	41051	19420	5855	5889	847	4481	142098	2657	•
Other Receipts **7**	198957	•	15105	•	25886	6398	6847	31579	2539	522	50853	55979	•
Total Receipts **8**	22566472	•	3270908	•	6000045	1758519	1091183	767596	417031	551327	1667064	6302631	•
Average Total Receipts **9**	889	•	159	•	4812	12045	23217	47975	83406	183776	555688	2100877	•
Operating Costs/Operating Income (%)													
Cost of Operations **10**	30.3	•	21.9	•	42.9	47.0	47.7	38.1	51.7	27.1	28.3	15.6	•
Salaries and Wages **11**	20.8	•	15.3	•	15.4	12.5	14.4	25.7	13.7	22.0	27.1	31.2	•
Taxes Paid **12**	4.2	•	3.2	•	3.7	4.2	4.5	3.5	6.7	1.7	7.2	5.0	•
Interest Paid **13**	3.5	•	2.5	•	1.6	1.6	1.2	1.4	1.6	5.6	8.3	5.9	•
Depreciation **14**	6.9	•	6.5	•	5.0	13.5	9.1	7.9	5.5	6.4	8.3	6.1	•
Amortization and Depletion **15**	1.1	•	0.7	•	0.3	0.0	0.1	0.4	0.2	0.7	5.7	1.7	•
Pensions and Other Deferred Comp. **16**	0.7	•	0.1	•	0.6	0.6	1.2	0.5	0.4	0.3	0.6	1.2	•
Employee Benefits **17**	1.8	•	0.5	•	0.6	2.0	3.0	6.5	3.3	4.0	6.4	1.6	•
Advertising **18**	0.6	•	1.5	•	0.5	0.4	0.4	0.4	0.5	0.4	0.5	0.4	•
Other Expenses **19**	31.6	•	43.5	•	25.6	18.4	17.7	17.6	15.4	32.0	33.8	36.1	•
Officers' Compensation **20**	2.1	•	5.0	•	3.3	1.7	1.6	1.1	1.5	1.6	•	0.0	•
Operating Margin **21**	•	•	•	•	0.4	•	0.4	0.4	0.5	•	•	•	•
Operating Margin Before Officers' Comp. **22**	4.3	•	4.3	•	3.7	•	0.8	•	1.0	•	•	3.7	•

Selected Average Balance Sheet ($ in Thousands)

Line Item										
Net Receivables 23	75	7	454	884	2275	4893	11556	18920	47040	199652
Inventories 24	6	0	15	155	231	781	1628	322	5907	20248
Net Property, Plant and Equipment 25	231	19	846	5438	7895	12068	31105	53687	163289	708755
Total Assets 26	578	73	2052	7798	15466	34260	73251	157773	345963	1987249
Notes and Loans Payable 27	291	57	1338	4496	6843	13098	29797	81614	161637	758575
All Other Liabilities 28	108	12	450	1960	2589	7695	16823	47878	102017	268681
Net Worth 29	179	3	264	1342	6034	13467	26631	28281	82309	959992

Selected Financial Ratios (Times to 1)

Line Item										
Current Ratio 30	1.3	1.4	1.4	0.7	1.1	1.3	1.4	1.0	0.8	2.1
Quick Ratio 31	0.9	1.1	1.1	0.5	0.8	0.9	1.0	0.8	0.6	1.2
Net Sales to Working Capital 32	19.4	30.8	21.7	•	36.7	17.5	13.4	•	•	6.7
Coverage Ratio 33	0.9	1.0	2.2	0.8	1.5	3.3	1.4	0.9	•	1.0
Total Asset Turnover 34	1.5	2.2	2.3	1.5	1.5	1.3	1.1	1.2	1.4	1.0
Inventory Turnover 35	42.1	553.4	132.8	36.0	47.4	22.0	26.2	153.4	22.8	15.4
Receivables Turnover 36	11.4	23.3	11.7	11.0	9.7	8.5	6.0	19.2	9.3	9.5
Total Liabilities to Net Worth 37	2.2	20.8	6.8	4.8	1.6	1.5	1.8	4.6	3.2	1.1
Current Assets to Working Capital 38	3.9	3.3	3.7	•	8.6	4.6	3.5	•	•	1.9
Current Liabilities to Working Capital 39	2.9	2.3	2.7	•	7.6	3.6	2.5	•	•	0.9
Working Capital to Net Sales 40	0.1	0.0	0.0	•	0.0	0.1	0.1	•	•	0.2
Inventory to Working Capital 41	0.1	0.0	0.0	•	0.3	0.3	0.3	•	•	0.1
Total Receipts to Cash Flow 42	4.3	2.8	5.9	6.5	8.1	7.0	11.7	3.8	16.5	3.2
Cost of Goods to Cash Flow 43	1.3	0.6	2.5	3.1	3.9	2.6	6.1	1.0	4.7	0.5
Cash Flow to Total Debt 44	0.5	0.8	0.4	0.3	0.3	0.3	0.2	0.4	0.1	0.6

Selected Financial Factors (in Percentages)

Line Item										
Debt Ratio 45	69.1	95.4	87.1	82.8	61.0	60.7	63.6	82.1	76.2	51.7
Return on Total Assets 46	4.8	5.3	8.2	2.0	2.6	6.1	2.5	5.5	•	6.0
Return on Equity Before Income Taxes 47	•	•	34.2	•	2.2	10.8	1.9	•	•	0.2
Return on Equity After Income Taxes 48	•	•	33.9	•	1.2	9.1	•	•	•	0.2
Profit Margin (Before Income Tax) 49	•	1.9	1.9	•	0.6	3.2	0.6	•	•	0.1
Profit Margin (After Income Tax) 50	•	1.9	1.9	0.3	0.3	2.7	•	•	•	0.1

Table II

Corporations with Net Income

TRANSIT AND GROUND PASSENGER TRANSPORTATION

MONEY AMOUNTS AND SIZE OF ASSETS IN THOUSANDS OF DOLLARS

Item Description for Accounting Period 7/03 Through 6/04	Total	Zero Assets	Under 500	500 to 1,000	1,000 to 5,000	5,000 to 10,000	10,000 to 25,000	25,000 to 50,000	50,000 to 100,000	100,000 to 250,000	250,000 to 500,000	500,000 to 2,500,000	2,500,000 and over
Number of Enterprises 1	13213	1012	10981	•	951	101	27	11	•	•	•	•	•
Revenues ($ in Thousands)													
Net Sales 2	15108039	89728	2411499	•	4774961	1253886	778020	586352	•	•	•	•	•
Interest 3	216932	0	125	•	1831	970	1432	3502	•	•	•	•	•
Rents 4	9024	0	0	•	228	1452	415	2192	•	•	•	•	•
Royalties 5	0	0	0	•	0	0	0	0	•	•	•	•	•
Other Portfolio Income 6	68895	1299	3473	•	39381	18054	3123	1790	•	•	•	•	•
Other Receipts 7	85926	0	11876	•	11717	3709	4848	4270	•	•	•	•	•
Total Receipts 8	15488816	91027	2429973	•	4828118	1278071	787838	598106	•	•	•	•	•
Average Total Receipts 9	1172	90	221	•	5077	12654	29179	54373	•	•	•	•	•
Operating Costs/Operating Income (%)													
Cost of Operations 10	26.2	•	20.9	•	40.3	46.7	49.1	43.0	•	•	•	•	•
Salaries and Wages 11	22.6	•	14.9	•	15.0	13.2	14.7	21.2	•	•	•	•	•
Taxes Paid 12	4.1	1.5	3.0	•	3.9	3.8	4.1	3.4	•	•	•	•	•
Interest Paid 13	3.0	4.5	1.8	•	1.6	1.3	1.0	1.1	•	•	•	•	•
Depreciation 14	5.8	1.2	5.7	•	5.1	12.9	6.6	6.9	•	•	•	•	•
Amortization and Depletion 15	0.4	•	0.0	•	0.3	0.0	0.1	0.4	•	•	•	•	•
Pensions and Other Deferred Comp. 16	0.9	•	0.2	•	0.8	0.8	1.4	0.6	•	•	•	•	•
Employee Benefits 17	1.2	1.3	0.6	•	0.5	2.5	3.1	3.8	•	•	•	•	•
Advertising 18	0.6	•	1.6	•	0.4	0.2	0.4	0.2	•	•	•	•	•
Other Expenses 19	32.8	80.6	42.4	•	26.2	17.2	16.8	16.1	•	•	•	•	•
Officers' Compensation 20	2.4	1.8	4.4	•	3.8	1.7	1.4	1.2	•	•	•	•	•
Operating Margin 21	0.2	9.2	4.4	•	2.1	•	1.3	2.1	•	•	•	•	•
Operating Margin Before Officers' Comp. 22	2.5	11.0	8.8	•	5.9	1.4	2.8	3.3	•	•	•	•	•

Selected Average Balance Sheet ($ in Thousands)

Net Receivables 23	91	0	10	444	1001	2542	3608
Inventories 24	5	0	0	9	99	125	1174
Net Property, Plant and Equipment 25	265	0	26	830	5836	6661	11840
Total Assets 26	647	0	83	2104	7996	16011	36663
Notes and Loans Payable 27	310	0	54	1405	4416	6314	12259
All Other Liabilities 28	116	0	14	359	2399	3031	7545
Net Worth 29	221	0	16	339	1180	6667	16859

Selected Financial Ratios (Times to 1)

Current Ratio 30	1.5	•	1.6	1.4	0.5	1.3	1.2
Quick Ratio 31	1.0	•	1.2	1.1	0.4	0.8	0.8
Net Sales to Working Capital 32	14.4	•	24.0	19.6	•	20.1	24.1
Coverage Ratio 33	1.9	3.4	3.7	3.0	2.3	3.6	4.7
Total Asset Turnover 34	1.8	•	2.6	2.4	1.6	1.8	1.5
Inventory Turnover 35	64.1	•	392.4	221.0	58.8	113.2	19.5
Receivables Turnover 36	15.4	•	22.6	12.4	10.7	10.6	10.3
Total Liabilities to Net Worth 37	1.9	•	4.2	5.2	5.8	1.4	1.2
Current Assets to Working Capital 38	3.0	•	2.6	3.3	•	4.4	5.2
Current Liabilities to Working Capital 39	2.0	•	1.6	2.3	•	3.4	4.2
Working Capital to Net Sales 40	0.1	•	0.0	0.1	•	0.0	0.0
Inventory to Working Capital 41	0.1	•	0.0	0.0	•	0.1	0.5
Total Receipts to Cash Flow 42	3.6	1.2	2.5	5.7	6.1	7.5	6.7
Cost of Goods to Cash Flow 43	0.9	•	0.5	2.3	2.8	3.7	2.9
Cash Flow to Total Debt 44	0.8	•	1.3	0.5	0.3	0.4	0.4

Selected Financial Factors (in Percentages)

Debt Ratio 45	65.9	•	80.9	83.9	85.2	58.4	54.0
Return on Total Assets 46	10.0	•	18.1	11.6	4.5	6.4	7.8
Return on Equity Before Income Taxes 47	14.0	•	69.5	48.2	17.1	11.1	13.3
Return on Equity After Income Taxes 48	13.2	•	68.3	47.9	15.5	9.6	11.5
Profit Margin (Before Income Tax) 49	2.7	10.6	5.0	3.3	1.6	2.6	4.2
Profit Margin (After Income Tax) 50	2.6	10.6	4.9	3.2	1.5	2.2	3.6

Table I
Corporations with and without Net Income

PIPELINE TRANSPORTATION

MONEY AMOUNTS AND SIZE OF ASSETS IN THOUSANDS OF DOLLARS

Item Description for Accounting Period 7/03 Through 6/04	Total	Zero Assets	Under 500	500 to 1,000	1,000 to 5,000	5,000 to 10,000	10,000 to 25,000	25,000 to 50,000	50,000 to 100,000	100,000 to 250,000	250,000 to 500,000	500,000 to 2,500,000	2,500,000 and over
Number of Enterprises **1**	463	•	•	•	193	23	13	10	6	8	3	•	6
Revenues ($ in Thousands)													
Net Sales **2**	4494774	•	•	•	82838	115062	283118	580323	284889	210651	431203	•	2047957
Interest **3**	31250	•	•	•	1171	175	150	965	570	5247	327	•	22646
Rents **4**	6784	•	•	•	0	178	2	94	14	5727	0	•	769
Royalties **5**	0	•	•	•	0	0	0	0	0	0	0	•	0
Other Portfolio Income **6**	76239	•	•	•	0	2561	293	38618	307	105	895	•	262
Other Receipts **7**	212740	•	•	•	14937	1000	1400	2250	145095	44949	1466	•	1503
Total Receipts **8**	4821787	•	•	•	98946	118976	284963	622250	430875	266679	433891	•	2073137
Average Total Receipts **9**	10414	•	•	•	513	5173	21920	62225	71812	33335	144630	•	345523
Operating Costs/Operating Income (%)													
Cost of Operations **10**	34.5	•	•	•	2.8	28.2	64.9	49.9	33.8	2.0	8.9	•	35.8
Salaries and Wages **11**	8.6	•	•	•	18.6	1.5	2.0	2.8	35.4	3.5	2.9	•	6.9
Taxes Paid **12**	3.8	•	•	•	3.4	5.4	2.3	3.7	4.7	3.7	4.3	•	4.1
Interest Paid **13**	7.9	•	•	•	8.2	0.3	1.3	1.0	2.1	18.9	5.8	•	12.7
Depreciation **14**	14.5	•	•	•	41.7	14.9	3.3	3.1	9.5	17.8	28.8	•	18.3
Amortization and Depletion **15**	0.6	•	•	•	1.6	0.1	0.1	0.0	1.6	1.9	0.1	•	0.5
Pensions and Other Deferred Comp. **16**	0.5	•	•	•	1.4	•	0.1	0.2	0.0	0.4	0.3	•	0.9
Employee Benefits **17**	0.8	•	•	•	1.2	0.2	0.2	0.7	0.7	0.3	0.5	•	1.2
Advertising **18**	0.1	•	•	•	•	•	0.0	0.0	0.0	0.0	0.0	•	0.1
Other Expenses **19**	24.3	•	•	•	13.5	38.1	14.4	23.8	56.4	58.5	36.0	•	16.6
Officers' Compensation **20**	0.6	•	•	•	•	0.1	0.5	0.5	0.2	0.1	0.2	•	0.3
Operating Margin **21**	3.9	•	•	•	7.6	11.1	10.9	14.2	•	•	12.2	•	2.6
Operating Margin Before Officers' Comp. **22**	4.5	•	•	•	7.6	11.2	11.4	14.7	•	•	12.4	•	2.9

Selected Average Balance Sheet ($ in Thousands)

Net Receivables 23	1938	477	1252	3438	4925	5929	27106	14426	57426
Inventories 24	148	0	96	329	1276	170	485	5243	127
Net Property, Plant and Equipment 25	16238	1509	4221	8681	17981	32886	78280	265759	868059
Total Assets 26	27561	3838	8129	15668	34569	67071	160440	326174	1406878
Notes and Loans Payable 27	11271	1323	417	5137	8464	20234	67368	226275	570526
All Other Liabilities 28	8683	1616	1677	3481	8860	32834	52970	63747	449358
Net Worth 29	7606	899	6035	7050	17244	14002	40102	36152	386994

Selected Financial Ratios (Times to 1)

Current Ratio 30	0.9	2.7	1.1	1.1	1.6	0.8	0.9	0.3	1.0
Quick Ratio 31	0.7	2.6	0.9	1.0	1.2	0.7	0.7	0.2	0.8
Net Sales to Working Capital 32	•	1.1	30.4	31.4	12.5	•	•	•	1.3
Coverage Ratio 33	2.4	4.3	43.6	9.9	21.8	4.3	2.0	3.2	1.3
Total Asset Turnover 34	0.4	0.1	0.6	1.4	1.7	0.7	0.2	0.4	0.2
Inventory Turnover 35	22.6	64.3	14.7	42.9	22.7	94.6	1.1	2.4	962.2
Receivables Turnover 36	5.9	1.1	8.0	5.4	13.4	6.6	1.7	9.8	6.2
Total Liabilities to Net Worth 37	2.6	3.3	0.3	1.2	1.0	3.8	3.0	8.0	2.6
Current Assets to Working Capital 38	•	1.6	11.0	8.6	2.7	•	•	•	•
Current Liabilities to Working Capital 39	•	0.6	10.0	7.6	1.7	•	•	•	•
Working Capital to Net Sales 40	•	0.9	0.0	0.0	0.1	•	•	•	•
Inventory to Working Capital 41	•	•	0.6	0.5	0.5	•	•	•	•
Total Receipts to Cash Flow 42	3.2	2.6	1.9	4.2	2.5	2.2	1.4	2.1	5.6
Cost of Goods to Cash Flow 43	1.1	0.1	0.5	2.7	1.3	0.7	0.0	0.2	2.0
Cash Flow to Total Debt 44	0.2	0.1	1.2	0.6	1.3	0.4	0.2	0.2	0.1

Selected Financial Factors (in Percentages)

Debt Ratio 45	72.4	76.6	25.8	55.0	50.1	79.1	75.0	88.9	72.5
Return on Total Assets 46	6.7	3.9	9.1	17.8	37.7	6.4	6.3	8.2	4.0
Return on Equity Before Income Taxes 47	14.2	12.9	12.0	35.6	72.1	23.5	12.9	51.0	3.4
Return on Equity After Income Taxes 48	8.6	12.9	8.2	19.5	47.3	13.1	7.2	28.0	•
Profit Margin (Before Income Tax) 49	11.1	27.0	14.5	11.5	21.4	6.9	19.6	12.8	3.8
Profit Margin (After Income Tax) 50	6.7	27.0	9.9	6.3	14.1	3.9	11.0	7.0	•

Table II
Corporations with Net Income

PIPELINE TRANSPORTATION

MONEY AMOUNTS AND SIZE OF ASSETS IN THOUSANDS OF DOLLARS

Item Description for Accounting Period 7/03 Through 6/04	Total	Zero Assets	Under 500	500 to 1,000	1,000 to 5,000	5,000 to 10,000	10,000 to 25,000	25,000 to 50,000	50,000 to 100,000	100,000 to 250,000	250,000 to 500,000	500,000 to 2,500,000	2,500,000 and over
Number of Enterprises 1	349	•	•	•	105	14	7	10	•	•	•	•	•
Revenues ($ in Thousands)													
Net Sales 2	3301329	•	•	•	29006	113288	253034	580323	•	•	•	•	•
Interest 3	13791	•	•	•	273	170	118	965	•	•	•	•	•
Rents 4	5994	•	•	•	0	178	2	94	•	•	•	•	•
Royalties 5	0	•	•	•	0	0	0	0	•	•	•	•	•
Other Portfolio Income 6	75952	•	•	•	0	2561	21	38618	•	•	•	•	•
Other Receipts 7	219006	•	•	•	14291	153	297	2250	•	•	•	•	•
Total Receipts 8	3616072	•	•	•	43570	116350	253472	622250	•	•	•	•	•
Average Total Receipts 9	10361	•	•	•	415	8311	36210	62225	•	•	•	•	•
Operating Costs/Operating Income (%)													
Cost of Operations 10	25.8	•	•	•	•	28.6	66.5	49.9	•	•	•	•	•
Salaries and Wages 11	9.0	•	•	•	•	1.6	1.1	2.8	•	•	•	•	•
Taxes Paid 12	4.2	•	•	•	1.4	5.5	1.9	3.7	•	•	•	•	•
Interest Paid 13	7.6	•	•	•	14.9	0.3	0.5	1.0	•	•	•	•	•
Depreciation 14	14.2	•	•	•	34.5	15.0	2.6	3.1	•	•	•	•	•
Amortization and Depletion 15	0.3	•	•	•	0.0	0.1	0.0	0.0	•	•	•	•	•
Pensions and Other Deferred Comp. 16	0.2	•	•	•	•	0.1	0.0	0.2	•	•	•	•	•
Employee Benefits 17	0.5	•	•	•	•	0.3	0.0	0.7	•	•	•	•	•
Advertising 18	0.2	•	•	•	•	•	0.0	0.0	•	•	•	•	•
Other Expenses 19	25.3	•	•	•	11.6	34.7	10.3	23.8	•	•	•	•	•
Officers' Compensation 20	0.7	•	•	•	•	0.1	0.2	0.5	•	•	•	•	•
Operating Margin 21	12.0	•	•	•	37.6	13.9	16.7	14.2	•	•	•	•	•
Operating Margin Before Officers' Comp. 22	12.7	•	•	•	37.6	14.0	16.9	14.7	•	•	•	•	•

Selected Average Balance Sheet ($ in Thousands)

Net Receivables 23	1321	860	1582	2686	4925
Inventories 24	189	0	137	607	2385
Net Property, Plant and Equipment 25	16071	857	6834	9510	17981
Total Assets 26	22541	3383	9521	15687	34569
Notes and Loans Payable 27	10169	2008	685	2060	8464
All Other Liabilities 28	6511	-196	2569	5071	8860
Net Worth 29	5861	1571	6267	8556	17244

Selected Financial Ratios (Times to 1)

Current Ratio 30	1.2	18.1	1.0	1.5	1.6
Quick Ratio 31	0.8	18.1	0.8	1.1	1.2
Net Sales to Working Capital 32	23.4	0.3	.	18.8	12.5
Coverage Ratio 33	3.8	6.9	49.1	38.5	21.8
Total Asset Turnover 34	0.4	0.1	0.8	2.3	1.7
Inventory Turnover 35	12.9	.	16.9	39.6	12.2
Receivables Turnover 36	8.3	0.4	6.5	10.9	23.6
Total Liabilities to Net Worth 37	2.8	1.2	0.5	0.8	1.0
Current Assets to Working Capital 38	7.4	1.1	.	3.1	2.7
Current Liabilities to Working Capital 39	6.4	0.1	.	2.1	1.7
Working Capital to Net Sales 40	0.0	3.2	.	0.1	0.1
Inventory to Working Capital 41	0.6	.	.	0.3	0.5
Total Receipts to Cash Flow 42	2.3	1.0	2.0	3.8	2.5
Cost of Goods to Cash Flow 43	0.6	0.6	0.6	2.5	1.3
Cash Flow to Total Debt 44	0.2	0.1	1.2	1.3	1.3

Selected Financial Factors (in Percentages)

Debt Ratio 45	74.0	53.6	34.2	45.5	50.1
Return on Total Assets 46	12.2	8.4	14.4	40.0	37.7
Return on Equity Before Income Taxes 47	34.7	15.4	21.4	71.4	72.1
Return on Equity After Income Taxes 48	25.0	15.4	15.4	46.7	47.3
Profit Margin (Before Income Tax) 49	21.5	87.8	16.6	16.9	21.4
Profit Margin (After Income Tax) 50	15.5	87.8	11.9	11.1	14.1

Table I

Corporations with and without Net Income

OTHER TRANSPORTATION AND SUPPORT ACTIVITIES

MONEY AMOUNTS AND SIZE OF ASSETS IN THOUSANDS OF DOLLARS

Item Description for Accounting Period 7/03 Through 6/04		Total	Zero Assets	Under 500	500 to 1,000	1,000 to 5,000	5,000 to 10,000	10,000 to 25,000	25,000 to 50,000	50,000 to 100,000	100,000 to 250,000	250,000 to 500,000	500,000 to 2,500,000	2,500,000 and over
Number of Enterprises	1	41012	6601	29534	2282	2066	213	189	57	27	26	7	7	3
Revenues ($ in Thousands)														
Net Sales	2	155356906	3699989	25226563	10184507	10776447	4927834	6278660	3900720	2976349	6200054	2866573	9038582	69280628
Interest	3	705810	3894	3260	3708	8261	3655	6499	7431	8500	30332	18324	96900	515045
Rents	4	167107	11	171	9681	6659	2950	2717	2752	19908	25202	16777	17532	62747
Royalties	5	1856853	0	0	0	9	0	2	0	624	34972	54492	4150	1762603
Other Portfolio Income	6	478401	12572	36945	13047	25524	13798	14655	4850	17905	13252	7827	94473	223553
Other Receipts	7	979550	21499	105206	7246	45533	52780	114247	42437	29691	100721	51662	118556	289975
Total Receipts	8	159544627	3737965	25372145	10218189	10862433	5001017	6416780	3958190	3052977	6404533	3015655	9370193	72134551
Average Total Receipts	9	3890	566	859	4478	5258	23479	33951	69442	113073	246328	430808	1338599	24044850
Operating Costs/Operating Income (%)														
Cost of Operations	10	41.2	40.5	68.7	43.0	65.9	66.8	56.3	62.3	52.0	53.3	60.7	41.9	20.4
Salaries and Wages	11	17.2	22.3	7.2	5.1	11.5	9.8	12.7	13.0	16.0	18.2	15.9	18.8	24.3
Taxes Paid	12	4.2	2.6	1.5	22.2	3.1	1.8	2.8	2.7	6.2	2.6	4.1	2.3	3.6
Interest Paid	13	0.9	0.6	0.5	0.2	0.6	0.3	0.7	1.6	1.7	1.4	1.2	2.4	0.9
Depreciation	14	3.2	3.6	1.6	0.6	2.2	1.0	2.5	2.6	3.9	2.5	1.9	2.8	4.7
Amortization and Depletion	15	0.2	0.2	0.0	0.1	0.2	0.0	0.3	0.5	0.7	0.5	0.9	0.6	0.2
Pensions and Other Deferred Comp.	16	2.1	0.6	0.2	0.1	0.2	0.3	0.5	0.2	0.2	0.4	0.8	0.6	4.2
Employee Benefits	17	3.5	3.6	1.0	0.4	0.8	1.0	2.1	1.7	2.1	2.2	1.6	2.6	6.0
Advertising	18	0.4	0.2	0.2	0.2	0.2	0.2	0.3	0.3	0.3	0.1	0.1	0.2	0.7
Other Expenses	19	25.6	32.6	15.1	23.8	12.1	17.8	24.1	16.5	17.6	20.9	13.4	30.6	33.3
Officers' Compensation	20	1.2	1.1	2.9	2.4	2.7	1.4	1.6	1.1	1.0	0.7	0.6	0.5	0.2
Operating Margin	21	0.1	•	0.9	2.0	0.6	•	•	•	•	•	•	•	1.4
Operating Margin Before Officers' Comp.	22	1.3	•	3.9	4.4	3.3	1.0	•	•	•	•	•	•	1.6

Selected Average Balance Sheet ($ in Thousands)

Net Receivables 23	399	0	19	358	590	2859	4627	9463	18825	40086	64166	257125	2644614
Inventories 24	28	0	2	5	40	144	442	1050	2622	3484	2780	21125	161457
Net Property, Plant and Equipment 25	698	0	36	162	687	1313	4710	9212	22242	36574	44987	248268	6830025
Total Assets 26	1983	0	99	735	2083	6777	15457	34638	71925	156945	355038	1227881	16336639
Notes and Loans Payable 27	527	0	74	218	1554	1189	5272	13637	23112	45441	79150	410120	2815415
All Other Liabilities 28	679	0	21	320	507	3452	7051	13962	21755	59679	117000	439427	5516925
Net Worth 29	778	0	4	197	22	2136	3134	7039	27058	51825	158888	378334	8004299

Selected Financial Ratios (Times to 1)

Current Ratio 30	1.3	•	1.5	1.4	1.7	1.3	1.0	1.2	1.4	1.3	1.1	1.6	1.2
Quick Ratio 31	1.0	•	1.2	1.3	1.3	1.1	0.8	0.9	1.1	1.0	0.5	1.4	1.0
Net Sales to Working Capital 32	23.7	•	50.7	30.4	12.8	21.0	27.7	•	10.9	13.0	36.7	8.2	26.3
Coverage Ratio 33	4.3	•	4.3	11.1	3.4	4.5	0.4	•	1.7	1.4	4.3	1.3	6.9
Total Asset Turnover 34	1.9	•	8.7	6.1	2.5	3.4	2.0	2.1	1.5	1.5	1.2	1.1	1.4
Inventory Turnover 35	56.1	•	289.0	363.7	86.7	107.4	42.3	40.6	21.8	36.5	89.4	25.6	29.1
Receivables Turnover 36	10.0	•	43.4	15.2	9.0	8.9	7.5	7.2	6.7	5.8	7.1	4.4	9.6
Total Liabilities to Net Worth 37	1.5	•	25.4	2.7	94.3	2.2	3.9	3.9	1.7	2.0	1.2	2.2	1.0
Current Assets to Working Capital 38	4.5	•	2.9	3.4	2.5	4.6	7.4	•	3.3	3.9	15.5	2.6	5.5
Current Liabilities to Working Capital 39	3.5	•	1.9	2.4	1.5	3.6	6.4	•	2.3	2.9	14.5	1.6	4.5
Working Capital to Net Sales 40	0.0	•	0.0	0.0	0.1	0.0	0.0	•	0.1	0.1	0.0	0.0	0.0
Inventory to Working Capital 41	0.2	•	0.2	0.1	0.1	0.2	0.5	•	0.3	0.2	0.3	0.2	0.1
Total Receipts to Cash Flow 42	4.4	7.0	7.3	4.7	10.1	7.2	5.6	9.2	8.3	6.2	7.6	4.0	3.2
Cost of Goods to Cash Flow 43	1.8	2.8	5.1	2.0	6.6	4.8	3.2	5.8	4.3	3.3	4.6	1.7	0.7
Cash Flow to Total Debt 44	0.7	1.2	1.8	1.8	0.3	0.7	0.5	0.3	0.3	0.4	0.3	0.4	0.9

Selected Financial Factors (in Percentages)

Debt Ratio 45	60.8	•	96.2	73.2	99.0	79.7	68.5	79.7	62.4	67.0	55.2	69.2	51.0
Return on Total Assets 46	7.3	•	17.1	15.3	4.9	1.3	4.7	•	4.4	2.9	6.0	3.2	9.3
Return on Equity Before Income Taxes 47	14.3	•	347.7	52.0	326.0	•	11.7	•	4.9	2.4	10.3	2.1	16.2
Return on Equity After Income Taxes 48	8.9	•	341.7	48.6	260.5	•	8.6	•	2.9	•	5.0	•	10.2
Profit Margin (Before Income Tax) 49	2.9	•	1.5	2.3	1.4	•	1.1	•	1.2	0.5	4.0	0.6	5.6
Profit Margin (After Income Tax) 50	1.8	•	1.5	2.1	1.1	•	0.8	•	0.7	•	1.9	•	3.5

Table II
Corporations with Net Income

OTHER TRANSPORTATION AND SUPPORT ACTIVITIES

MONEY AMOUNTS AND SIZE OF ASSETS IN THOUSANDS OF DOLLARS

Item Description for Accounting Period 7/03 Through 6/04	Total	Zero Assets	Under 500	500 to 1,000	1,000 to 5,000	5,000 to 10,000	10,000 to 25,000	25,000 to 50,000	50,000 to 100,000	100,000 to 250,000	250,000 to 500,000	500,000 to 2,500,000	2,500,000 and over
Number of Enterprises 1	19744	2078	14740	1401	1149	180	119	36	18	13	•	•	•
Revenues ($ in Thousands)													
Net Sales 2	128347716	1342550	20511577	7413648	6949698	4140606	4264222	2998281	2176613	4276116	•	•	•
Interest 3	629708	180	1762	3560	7443	3047	4594	5791	7995	9083	•	•	•
Rents 4	119683	7	171	4370	3362	1105	926	2196	15927	18087	•	•	•
Royalties 5	1813197	0	0	0	0	0	0	0	624	0	•	•	•
Other Portfolio Income 6	434820	11369	35543	6076	20964	13792	13552	4770	14338	12442	•	•	•
Other Receipts 7	704237	23469	95417	6015	32082	14964	98184	32589	23028	59994	•	•	•
Total Receipts 8	132049361	1377575	20644470	7433669	7013549	4173514	4381478	3043627	2238525	4375722	•	•	•
Average Total Receipts 9	6688	663	1401	5306	6104	23186	36819	84545	124362	336594	•	•	•
Operating Costs/Operating Income (%)													
Cost of Operations 10	40.1	49.9	75.1	45.2	63.9	74.2	59.9	69.1	56.5	60.0	•	•	•
Salaries and Wages 11	17.2	12.7	5.5	3.7	11.0	9.5	12.3	10.2	12.2	11.9	•	•	•
Taxes Paid 12	4.4	2.0	1.2	27.4	3.0	1.7	3.2	2.5	6.3	2.2	•	•	•
Interest Paid 13	0.8	0.1	0.2	0.2	0.3	0.3	0.6	0.7	1.3	0.7	•	•	•
Depreciation 14	3.2	0.7	1.1	0.5	2.1	1.0	2.2	1.6	2.8	2.1	•	•	•
Amortization and Depletion 15	0.2	0.0	0.0	0.1	0.1	0.0	0.1	0.3	0.5	0.3	•	•	•
Pensions and Other Deferred Comp. 16	2.4	0.0	0.2	0.1	0.3	0.3	0.4	0.2	0.3	0.4	•	•	•
Employee Benefits 17	3.8	0.1	1.2	0.3	0.9	1.0	2.3	1.7	2.0	1.8	•	•	•
Advertising 18	0.5	0.2	0.1	0.1	0.2	0.2	0.2	0.2	0.2	0.1	•	•	•
Other Expenses 19	24.4	30.1	10.6	17.0	11.7	9.0	15.0	10.8	15.5	19.1	•	•	•
Officers' Compensation 20	1.0	2.0	2.4	2.1	2.8	1.5	1.8	0.9	0.9	0.6	•	•	•
Operating Margin 21	2.0	2.1	2.2	3.3	3.9	1.3	2.0	1.8	1.3	0.9	•	•	•
Operating Margin Before Officers' Comp. 22	3.0	4.1	4.7	5.4	6.7	2.8	3.8	2.7	2.2	1.5	•	•	•

Selected Average Balance Sheet ($ in Thousands)

Item										
Net Receivables 23	667	0	18	395	700	2881	4857	10868	20403	42433
Inventories 24	43	0	2	3	16	145	380	1021	2637	1941
Net Property, Plant and Equipment 25	1219	0	29	55	433	1375	4389	7311	17996	31887
Total Assets 26	3309	0	104	708	2091	6836	14859	36057	73354	144777
Notes and Loans Payable 27	667	0	57	169	773	1172	4152	8617	17288	34025
All Other Liabilities 28	1145	0	19	336	506	3312	5438	14061	21395	46722
Net Worth 29	1496	0	28	203	811	2353	5269	13379	34671	64031

Selected Financial Ratios (Times to 1)

Item										
Current Ratio 30	1.3	•	1.6	1.5	2.0	1.3	1.3	1.3	1.7	1.6
Quick Ratio 31	1.1	•	1.3	1.5	1.6	1.1	1.1	1.0	1.4	1.4
Net Sales to Working Capital 32	20.8	•	74.4	27.0	9.0	20.1	17.5	16.2	7.7	12.1
Coverage Ratio 33	7.4	37.4	13.4	20.2	15.4	8.3	9.5	5.6	4.3	5.8
Total Asset Turnover 34	2.0	•	13.4	7.5	2.9	3.4	2.4	2.3	1.6	2.3
Inventory Turnover 35	60.3	•	419.6	922.2	244.1	117.6	56.4	56.3	25.9	101.7
Receivables Turnover 36	10.2	•	67.0	14.4	9.3	9.2	7.5	7.7	6.8	6.8
Total Liabilities to Net Worth 37	1.2	•	2.7	2.5	1.6	1.9	1.8	1.7	1.1	1.3
Current Assets to Working Capital 38	3.9	•	2.7	2.9	2.0	4.5	4.1	4.2	2.4	2.7
Current Liabilities to Working Capital 39	2.9	•	1.7	1.9	1.0	3.5	3.1	3.2	1.4	1.7
Working Capital to Net Sales 40	0.0	•	0.0	0.0	0.1	0.0	0.1	0.1	0.1	0.1
Inventory to Working Capital 41	0.1	•	0.2	0.0	0.0	0.2	0.1	0.2	0.2	0.1
Total Receipts to Cash Flow 42	4.3	4.6	8.7	6.3	7.8	14.7	6.3	9.2	7.2	5.8
Cost of Goods to Cash Flow 43	1.7	2.3	6.6	2.8	5.0	10.9	3.8	6.4	4.1	3.5
Cash Flow to Total Debt 44	0.8	•	2.1	1.7	0.6	0.3	0.6	0.4	0.4	0.7

Selected Financial Factors (in Percentages)

Item										
Debt Ratio 45	54.8	•	72.9	71.3	61.2	65.6	64.5	62.9	52.7	55.8
Return on Total Assets 46	11.3	•	41.4	28.2	14.8	8.2	12.8	9.2	9.4	9.0
Return on Equity Before Income Taxes 47	21.7	•	141.5	93.6	35.7	20.9	32.3	20.4	15.3	16.8
Return on Equity After Income Taxes 48	15.8	•	139.9	88.3	32.5	17.5	28.8	16.2	12.9	12.0
Profit Margin (Before Income Tax) 49	5.0	4.7	2.9	3.6	4.8	2.1	4.7	3.3	4.4	3.3
Profit Margin (After Income Tax) 50	3.6	4.6	2.8	3.4	1.8	1.8	4.2	2.6	3.7	2.3

250

Table I

Corporations with and without Net Income

WAREHOUSING AND STORAGE

MONEY AMOUNTS AND SIZE OF ASSETS IN THOUSANDS OF DOLLARS

Item Description for Accounting Period 7/03 Through 6/04	Total	Zero Assets	Under 500	500 to 1,000	1,000 to 5,000	5,000 to 10,000	10,000 to 25,000	25,000 to 50,000	50,000 to 100,000	100,000 to 250,000	250,000 to 500,000	500,000 to 2,500,000	2,500,000 and over
Number of Enterprises **1**	6452	262	4042	724	1030	223	106	29	16	14	7	•	•
Revenues ($ in Thousands)													
Net Sales **2**	16055576	75359	1556426	701827	3082817	2526735	1675853	1055515	1318069	1301611	2761363	•	•
Interest **3**	65027	284	124	3386	2568	1320	2729	1318	962	16997	35340	•	•
Rents **4**	23120	0	115	2467	2257	1737	9156	1569	272	661	4888	•	•
Royalties **5**	9519	0	0	0	0	0	71	0	8139	701	608	•	•
Other Portfolio Income **6**	49797	1829	18	2855	11811	887	15032	5116	1280	6654	4316	•	•
Other Receipts **7**	395832	22623	16009	807	126919	75534	53190	35033	15830	17923	31960	•	•
Total Receipts **8**	16598871	100095	1572692	711342	3226372	2606213	1756031	1098551	1344552	1344547	2838475	•	•
Average Total Receipts **9**	2573	382	389	983	3132	11687	16566	37881	84034	96039	405496	•	•
Operating Costs/Operating Income (%)													
Cost of Operations **10**	35.4	19.4	41.1	15.3	53.5	66.7	36.4	17.0	31.4	10.1	9.3	•	•
Salaries and Wages **11**	20.7	20.6	10.3	17.7	15.9	10.5	16.2	22.1	28.6	39.9	31.4	•	•
Taxes Paid **12**	3.6	6.0	3.0	5.3	2.9	2.1	4.3	3.8	3.9	3.6	5.3	•	•
Interest Paid **13**	2.8	5.6	0.4	2.4	1.4	1.8	1.8	2.2	1.6	3.9	7.6	•	•
Depreciation **14**	5.5	7.9	1.8	4.4	5.8	3.4	4.2	4.7	4.8	7.3	9.8	•	•
Amortization and Depletion **15**	0.7	0.1	0.0	0.0	0.2	0.0	0.1	0.4	0.4	1.0	2.9	•	•
Pensions and Other Deferred Comp. **16**	0.5	0.5	0.1	0.1	0.4	0.3	1.3	0.5	0.6	0.6	0.6	•	•
Employee Benefits **17**	2.8	4.3	2.0	1.5	0.9	1.1	2.8	4.3	5.5	7.5	3.2	•	•
Advertising **18**	0.3	0.0	0.4	1.5	0.2	0.1	0.2	0.2	0.2	0.1	0.5	•	•
Other Expenses **19**	28.8	79.1	34.2	59.6	23.0	14.0	29.7	44.9	19.6	28.5	34.1	•	•
Officers' Compensation **20**	1.7	6.9	2.1	3.5	1.9	2.3	2.6	2.3	0.9	0.6	0.3	•	•
Operating Margin **21**	•	•	4.7	•	•	•	0.3	•	2.5	•	•	•	•
Operating Margin Before Officers' Comp. **22**	•	•	6.7	•	0.1	2.9	•	3.5	•	•	•	•	•

Selected Average Balance Sheet ($ in Thousands)

	•	•	•	•	•	•	•	•	•	•	•
Net Receivables 23	320	0	26	121	209	682	2349	7089	13477	17615	84351
Inventories 24	46	0	2	11	39	416	568	409	2642	414	2717
Net Property, Plant and Equipment 25	1075	0	48	230	1043	3118	6494	16804	41120	64737	295205
Total Assets 26	2614	0	139	691	2014	6824	15049	35634	71721	163750	876539
Notes and Loans Payable 27	1204	0	25	449	642	3021	6723	12888	27976	58329	522374
All Other Liabilities 28	511	0	26	300	407	966	2486	7900	11356	37051	163821
Net Worth 29	898	0	87	-59	965	2837	5840	14846	32389	68371	190344

Selected Financial Ratios (Times to 1)

	•	•	•	•	•	•	•	•	•	•	•
Current Ratio 30	1.3	•	2.1	0.8	2.5	1.5	1.5	1.2	1.5	1.5	1.0
Quick Ratio 31	1.0	•	1.9	0.5	2.0	0.8	1.0	1.0	1.1	1.1	0.7
Net Sales to Working Capital 32	14.8	•	12.9	•	8.9	15.2	8.2	16.6	11.9	7.7	•
Coverage Ratio 33	1.2	•	17.1	•	0.0	1.5	3.8	1.8	3.9	1.1	0.7
Total Asset Turnover 34	1.0	•	2.8	1.4	1.5	1.7	1.1	1.0	1.1	0.6	0.5
Inventory Turnover 35	19.0	•	65.9	13.0	40.8	18.2	10.1	15.1	9.8	22.6	13.5
Receivables Turnover 36	7.5	•	17.1	5.7	12.8	33.2	6.8	5.6	5.6	6.0	4.3
Total Liabilities to Net Worth 37	1.9	•	0.6	•	1.1	1.4	1.6	1.4	1.2	1.4	3.6
Current Assets to Working Capital 38	4.2	•	1.9	•	1.7	3.1	3.0	5.3	3.2	3.2	•
Current Liabilities to Working Capital 39	3.2	•	0.9	•	0.7	2.1	2.0	4.3	2.2	2.2	•
Working Capital to Net Sales 40	0.1	•	0.1	•	0.1	0.1	0.1	0.1	0.1	0.1	•
Inventory to Working Capital 41	0.3	•	0.1	•	0.1	0.6	0.3	0.2	0.4	0.0	•
Total Receipts to Cash Flow 42	5.5	2.1	5.6	4.0	7.6	10.2	4.4	3.1	6.1	4.8	4.9
Cost of Goods to Cash Flow 43	1.9	0.4	2.3	0.6	4.1	6.8	1.6	0.5	1.9	0.5	0.5
Cash Flow to Total Debt 44	0.3	•	1.3	0.3	0.4	0.3	0.4	0.6	0.3	0.2	0.1

Selected Financial Factors (in Percentages)

	•	•	•	•	•	•	•	•	•	•	•
Debt Ratio 45	65.6	•	37.3	108.5	52.1	58.4	61.2	58.3	54.8	58.2	78.3
Return on Total Assets 46	3.2	•	16.8	0.0	4.5	7.2	4.0	7.0		2.4	2.4
Return on Equity Before Income Taxes 47	1.6	•	25.2	164.9	•	3.7	13.7	4.3	11.5	0.3	•
Return on Equity After Income Taxes 48	0.5	•	23.8	167.4	•	2.5	12.2	2.9	8.7	•	•
Profit Margin (Before Income Tax) 49	0.6	•	5.7	•	•	0.9	5.1	1.7	4.5	0.3	•
Profit Margin (After Income Tax) 50	0.2	•	5.4	•	•	0.6	4.5	1.2	3.4	•	•

Table II
Corporations with Net Income

WAREHOUSING AND STORAGE

MONEY AMOUNTS AND SIZE OF ASSETS IN THOUSANDS OF DOLLARS

Item Description for Accounting Period 7/03 Through 6/04	Total	Zero Assets	Under 500	500 to 1000	251 to 500	501 to 1,000	1,001 to 5,000	5,001 to 10,000	10,001 to 25,000	25,001 to 50,000	50,001 to 100,000	100,001 to 250,000	250,001 and over
Number of Enterprises **1**	3522	•	2497	275	519	118	71	16	12	•	•	•	•
Revenues ($ in Thousands)													
Net Sales **2**	10221785	•	1329684	286847	1344474	2268843	1209197	596906	1196550	•	•	•	•
Interest **3**	15956	•	43	2710	1991	1318	1825	1048	962	•	•	•	•
Rents **4**	16419	•	115	1826	2257	1454	6530	1074	272	•	•	•	•
Royalties **5**	8143	•	0	0	0	0	4	0	8139	•	•	•	•
Other Portfolio Income **6**	34116	•	0	2776	2492	425	12377	4975	1268	•	•	•	•
Other Receipts **7**	257442	•	15992	102	53056	63920	46412	30135	14869	•	•	•	•
Total Receipts **8**	10553861	•	1345834	294261	1404270	2335960	1276345	634138	1222060	•	•	•	•
Average Total Receipts **9**	2997	•	539	1070	2706	19796	17977	39634	101838	•	•	•	•
Operating Costs/Operating Income (%)													
Cost of Operations **10**	36.4	•	40.5	28.1	27.9	69.1	36.5	21.5	34.3	•	•	•	•
Salaries and Wages **11**	18.4	•	10.4	15.7	18.2	9.9	16.2	21.6	27.2	•	•	•	•
Taxes Paid **12**	3.4	•	2.1	6.1	2.6	1.7	3.9	3.3	3.8	•	•	•	•
Interest Paid **13**	2.6	•	0.3	1.7	2.1	1.3	1.5	1.9	1.4	•	•	•	•
Depreciation **14**	5.2	•	1.1	3.2	5.2	3.2	3.7	4.8	4.1	•	•	•	•
Amortization and Depletion **15**	0.6	•	0.0	0.0	0.5	0.0	0.1	0.2	0.4	•	•	•	•
Pensions and Other Deferred Comp. **16**	0.4	•	0.1	0.2	0.6	0.2	0.8	0.7	0.5	•	•	•	•
Employee Benefits **17**	2.5	•	1.4	1.6	1.6	1.1	2.9	4.0	5.5	•	•	•	•
Advertising **18**	0.2	•	0.3	1.0	0.4	0.0	0.1	0.2	0.1	•	•	•	•
Other Expenses **19**	25.9	•	33.8	38.3	32.8	12.7	28.6	40.1	18.2	•	•	•	•
Officers' Compensation **20**	1.6	•	1.4	3.0	2.1	1.7	2.6	3.1	0.9	•	•	•	•
Operating Margin **21**	2.7	•	8.7	1.0	6.0	•	3.2	•	3.5	•	•	•	•
Operating Margin Before Officers' Comp. **22**	4.3	•	10.0	4.0	8.1	0.8	5.8	2.0	4.3	•	•	•	•

Selected Average Balance Sheet ($ in Thousands)

Net Receivables 23	392	•	33	123	311	1019	2446	6854	15578
Inventories 24	73	•	4	28	59	815	620	503	3308
Net Property, Plant and Equipment 25	1311	•	65	273	962	3805	6082	18515	42712
Total Assets 26	2883	153	743	1974	6895	14985	36583	74154
Notes and Loans Payable 27	1268	25	426	870	3236	6180	11778	27905
All Other Liabilities 28	433	23	326	232	1250	2434	8926	13156
Net Worth 29	1182	105	-9	873	2409	6370	15879	33094

Selected Financial Ratios (Times to 1)

Current Ratio 30	1.5	•	3.6	0.8	3.5	1.3	1.6	1.3	1.7
Quick Ratio 31	1.1	3.2	0.4	2.8	0.7	1.1	1.0	1.3
Net Sales to Working Capital 32	9.4	9.9	•	4.7	29.7	7.5	14.9	9.1
Coverage Ratio 33	3.3	30.5	3.1	6.0	2.5	6.8	3.8	4.9
Total Asset Turnover 34	1.0	3.5	1.4	1.3	2.8	1.1	1.0	1.3
Inventory Turnover 35	14.4	55.8	10.7	12.2	16.3	10.0	15.9	10.3
Receivables Turnover 36	7.0	20.2	4.6	7.3	18.9	7.3	5.1	12.8
Total Liabilities to Net Worth 37	1.4	0.4	•	1.3	1.9	1.4	1.3	1.2
Current Assets to Working Capital 38	3.0	1.4	•	1.4	4.3	2.8	4.9	2.4
Current Liabilities to Working Capital 39	2.0	0.4	•	0.4	3.3	1.8	3.9	1.4
Working Capital to Net Sales 40	0.1	0.1	•	0.2	0.0	0.1	0.1	0.1
Inventory to Working Capital 41	0.2	0.1	•	0.1	1.2	0.3	0.2	0.3
Total Receipts to Cash Flow 42	4.9	4.5	6.2	3.4	10.2	4.0	3.1	6.0
Cost of Goods to Cash Flow 43	1.8	1.8	1.8	0.9	7.1	1.4	0.7	2.1
Cash Flow to Total Debt 44	0.3	2.5	0.2	0.7	0.4	0.5	0.6	0.4

Selected Financial Factors (in Percentages)

Debt Ratio 45	59.0	•	31.0	101.2	55.8	65.1	57.5	56.6	55.4
Return on Total Assets 46	8.6	35.7	7.5	16.4	9.4	11.6	7.2	9.4
Return on Equity Before Income Taxes 47	14.7	50.1	•	30.9	16.1	23.3	12.1	16.8
Return on Equity After Income Taxes 48	13.2	48.2	•	30.1	13.4	21.2	9.8	13.1
Profit Margin (Before Income Tax) 49	6.0	9.9	3.6	10.4	2.0	8.7	5.2	5.6
Profit Margin (After Income Tax) 50	5.4	9.5	3.2	10.1	1.7	7.9	4.2	4.3

Table I

Corporations with and without Net Income

NEWSPAPER PUBLISHERS

MONEY AMOUNTS AND SIZE OF ASSETS IN THOUSANDS OF DOLLARS

Item Description for Accounting Period 7/03 Through 6/04	Total	Zero Assets	Under 500	500 to 1,000	1,000 to 5,000	5,000 to 10,000	10,000 to 25,000	25,000 to 50,000	50,000 to 100,000	100,000 to 250,000	250,000 to 500,000	500,000 to 2,500,000	2,500,000 and over
Number of Enterprises **1**	7729	735	5739	565	387	110	84	41	20	15	8	17	9
Revenues ($ in Thousands)													
Net Sales **2**	49859246	116701	2354655	668916	1922013	1411295	1656204	1277392	1217267	1956723	1828382	10029118	25420579
Interest **3**	305032	395	1179	659	1994	126	6226	2550	3696	7909	6015	101199	173084
Rents **4**	126920	39	99	0	0	1314	988	4942	3262	8719	7127	18175	82255
Royalties **5**	412462	0	0	0	0	3	9	1387	38	0	1764	92613	316648
Other Portfolio Income **6**	634030	45	11552	250	9653	535	3946	31691	51907	7488	105311	118905	292765
Other Receipts **7**	1503024	-4471	18754	-49	29070	13768	25167	45736	24941	19337	2684	456631	871459
Total Receipts **8**	52840714	112709	2386219	669776	1962730	1427041	1692540	1363698	1301111	2000176	1951283	10816641	27156790
Average Total Receipts **9**	6837	153	416	1185	5072	12973	20149	33261	65056	133345	243910	636273	3017421
Operating Costs/Operating Income (%)													
Cost of Operations **10**	24.1	22.3	32.4	34.0	38.2	43.3	24.4	32.6	31.5	26.9	16.6	16.6	23.3
Salaries and Wages **11**	24.1	18.7	23.1	21.8	15.0	23.4	25.7	25.1	22.0	24.2	26.0	27.2	23.5
Taxes Paid **12**	3.5	3.5	3.1	4.1	3.2	3.7	3.6	3.8	3.3	3.7	4.3	3.8	3.3
Interest Paid **13**	3.1	3.6	0.9	1.1	0.8	3.5	1.4	2.4	2.8	2.1	5.3	4.8	2.9
Depreciation **14**	4.7	5.1	0.9	2.7	4.5	4.6	4.0	4.5	6.2	6.6	7.2	5.4	4.6
Amortization and Depletion **15**	2.6	4.6	0.0	0.9	0.3	0.2	0.9	2.3	1.5	2.6	5.9	5.5	1.9
Pensions and Other Deferred Comp. **16**	1.5	0.5	0.6	0.9	0.1	0.6	1.1	1.5	0.8	1.5	1.6	2.5	1.4
Employee Benefits **17**	3.3	1.0	1.4	5.0	1.1	1.9	3.1	3.0	2.8	2.9	3.3	3.7	3.7
Advertising **18**	1.7	1.4	0.8	0.7	1.2	0.3	6.2	1.6	0.9	1.9	1.7	2.0	1.5
Other Expenses **19**	25.4	29.8	32.5	22.0	31.1	19.4	23.3	21.8	22.5	25.2	23.6	24.6	25.6
Officers' Compensation **20**	2.3	0.5	8.9	4.2	3.3	2.8	3.6	2.1	2.3	1.5	1.6	1.5	1.9
Operating Margin **21**	3.8	9.2	•	2.5	1.1	•	2.6	•	3.4	1.0	2.7	2.3	6.3
Operating Margin Before Officers' Comp. **22**	6.1	9.7	4.2	6.7	4.5	•	6.1	1.3	5.7	2.4	4.3	3.9	8.3

Selected Average Balance Sheet ($ in Thousands)

Net Receivables 23	1100	0	121	407	1288	2553	4196	7511	15844	25335	90658	608345
Inventories 24	82	0	12	17	101	237	489	937	2072	3721	8704	36897
Net Property, Plant and Equipment 25	2025	0	119	939	2429	4159	10316	19947	49076	91849	216031	946085
Total Assets 26	11184	0	718	2469	6944	16118	38003	69709	161949	376065	1167473	6023648
Notes and Loans Payable 27	3057	0	375	923	6860	5171	12546	25128	35667	197360	415290	1278290
All Other Liabilities 28	2580	0	57	604	2833	3636	7138	16898	36205	78223	55880	1774148
Net Worth 29	5547	-0	286	942	-2749	7312	18319	27682	90078	100483	696302	2971210

Selected Financial Ratios (Times to 1)

Current Ratio 30	0.9	•	2.1	1.2	0.3	1.7	1.6	0.9	2.2	1.2	1.2	0.8
Quick Ratio 31	0.7	•	1.9	1.1	0.3	1.3	1.3	0.7	1.7	0.9	1.0	0.6
Net Sales to Working Capital 32	•	•	9.4	34.7	•	8.4	8.2	•	5.6	23.0	21.5	•
Coverage Ratio 33	4.1	2.6	3.4	5.0	0.3	4.5	3.5	4.7	2.5	2.8	3.1	5.5
Total Asset Turnover 34	0.6	•	1.6	2.0	1.8	1.2	0.8	0.9	0.8	0.6	0.5	0.5
Inventory Turnover 35	19.0	•	33.9	108.7	55.3	20.3	20.8	20.4	16.9	10.3	11.3	17.9
Receivables Turnover 36	6.5	•	9.1	14.4	14.7	7.9	7.7	6.4	8.6	8.9	6.3	5.4
Total Liabilities to Net Worth 37	1.0	•	1.5	1.6	•	1.2	1.1	1.5	0.8	2.7	0.7	1.0
Current Assets to Working Capital 38	•	•	1.9	5.9	•	2.5	2.8	•	1.9	5.4	6.4	•
Current Liabilities to Working Capital 39	•	•	0.9	4.9	•	1.5	1.8	•	0.9	4.4	5.4	•
Working Capital to Net Sales 40	•	•	0.1	0.0	•	0.1	0.1	•	0.2	0.0	0.0	•
Inventory to Working Capital 41	•	•	0.1	0.2	•	0.1	0.1	•	0.1	0.4	0.3	•
Total Receipts to Cash Flow 42	3.2	3.5	5.2	3.6	8.3	3.9	4.1	3.9	4.0	3.7	3.2	2.8
Cost of Goods to Cash Flow 43	0.8	0.8	1.8	1.4	3.6	1.0	1.3	1.2	1.1	0.6	0.5	0.7
Cash Flow to Total Debt 44	0.4	•	0.5	0.9	0.2	0.6	0.4	0.4	0.5	0.2	0.4	0.3

Selected Financial Factors (in Percentages)

Debt Ratio 45	50.4	100.6	60.2	61.9	139.6	54.6	51.8	60.3	44.4	73.3	40.4	50.7
Return on Total Assets 46	7.5	•	6.1	8.1	1.9	7.4	6.9	11.4	4.2	9.0	7.6	7.7
Return on Equity Before Income Taxes 47	11.4	2731.4	10.9	17.0	11.6	12.7	10.2	22.5	4.6	21.4	8.6	12.7
Return on Equity After Income Taxes 48	7.6	2982.9	10.4	15.3	12.0	11.2	8.2	16.8	3.7	13.6	5.4	8.5
Profit Margin (Before Income Tax) 49	9.8	5.8	2.6	3.2	•	4.7	6.0	10.2	3.2	9.4	10.2	13.4
Profit Margin (After Income Tax) 50	6.5	2.3	2.5	2.9	•	4.1	4.8	7.6	2.5	6.0	6.3	8.9

Table II
Corporations with Net Income

NEWSPAPER PUBLISHERS

MONEY AMOUNTS AND SIZE OF ASSETS IN THOUSANDS OF DOLLARS

Item Description for Accounting Period 7/03 Through 6/04	Total	Zero Assets	Under 500	500 to 1,000	1,000 to 5,000	5,000 to 10,000	10,000 to 25,000	25,000 to 50,000	50,000 to 100,000	100,000 to 250,000	250,000 to 500,000	500,000 to 2,500,000	2,500,000 and over
Number of Enterprises **1**	3854	10	3016	442	189	53	61	30	15	10	5	•	•
Revenues ($ in Thousands)													
Net Sales **2**	39489831	92331	1150561	611205	737418	727759	1277790	940697	967452	1189627	1065538	•	•
Interest **3**	291997	395	293	34	1852	31	3649	1819	2735	5675	4904	•	•
Rents **4**	81190	39	11	0	0	20	736	4913	3160	5895	4492	•	•
Royalties **5**	395267	0	0	0	0	3	0	0	38	0	1764	•	•
Other Portfolio Income **6**	588721	45	11188	0	9429	529	3342	31194	51791	1732	105311	•	•
Other Receipts **7**	1391409	7	18170	-49	14693	13448	22066	46765	23985	12320	23	•	•
Total Receipts **8**	42238415	92817	1180223	611190	763392	741790	1307583	1025388	1049161	1215249	1182032	•	•
Average Total Receipts **9**	10960	9282	391	1383	4039	13996	21436	34180	69944	121525	236406	•	•
Operating Costs/Operating Income (%)													
Cost of Operations **10**	23.7	11.5	34.1	33.4	17.6	17.3	24.8	29.1	29.5	32.9	25.1	•	•
Salaries and Wages **11**	23.7	23.1	16.6	20.4	26.4	39.5	24.1	27.1	21.4	16.1	22.0	•	•
Taxes Paid **12**	3.5	3.6	3.5	4.2	2.7	4.1	3.6	4.0	3.4	3.7	4.9	•	•
Interest Paid **13**	3.2	0.3	1.3	1.2	1.0	0.2	0.9	1.9	2.0	2.5	3.5	•	•
Depreciation **14**	4.8	5.9	1.2	2.8	5.5	1.8	3.5	4.3	5.5	7.3	6.9	•	•
Amortization and Depletion **15**	2.5	5.4	0.0	1.0	0.4	0.2	0.5	1.9	1.4	3.2	5.0	•	•
Pensions and Other Deferred Comp. **16**	1.6	0.5	1.2	0.9	0.2	1.0	1.2	1.8	0.9	0.8	1.1	•	•
Employee Benefits **17**	3.4	0.5	1.2	5.3	1.9	2.5	3.1	3.1	2.6	1.9	1.8	•	•
Advertising **18**	1.8	1.7	0.6	0.7	0.6	0.4	7.6	1.5	0.9	0.9	1.4	•	•
Other Expenses **19**	22.7	31.2	26.4	21.8	28.5	20.5	21.3	21.5	23.2	23.5	18.7	•	•
Officers' Compensation **20**	2.2	0.6	9.4	4.2	5.5	4.5	3.5	2.2	2.6	1.4	1.5	•	•
Operating Margin **21**	6.8	15.7	4.5	4.1	9.9	8.0	6.0	1.5	6.6	5.6	8.1	•	•
Operating Margin Before Officers' Comp. **22**	9.1	16.4	13.9	8.3	15.4	12.5	9.5	3.7	9.2	7.0	9.6	•	•

Selected Average Balance Sheet ($ in Thousands)

	•	•	•	•	•	•	•	•	•	•	•
Net Receivables 23	1892	0	26	136	402	1435	2517	4312	7856	14251	23644
Inventories 24	126	0	1	14	32	153	258	453	1046	1921	3429
Net Property, Plant and Equipment 25	3440	0	36	139	1268	1337	3975	9745	19392	52609	81026
Total Assets 26	19603	92	707	2733	6249	15923	37270	69178	160368	347873	
Notes and Loans Payable 27	4849	0	33	279	1105	298	2776	10641	23638	42958	116834
All Other Liabilities 28	4082	0	62	53	327	2281	3816	8199	17496	27946	61094
Net Worth 29	10672	0	-3	376	1301	3670	9331	18430	28044	89464	169945

Selected Financial Ratios (Times to 1)

	•	•	•	•	•	•	•	•	•	•	•
Current Ratio 30	0.9	•	1.7	2.1	1.7	1.9	1.8	1.6	0.9	2.0	1.3
Quick Ratio 31	0.7	•	1.5	2.0	1.3	1.7	1.4	1.4	0.7	1.4	1.0
Net Sales to Working Capital 32	•	•	21.7	11.3	12.9	9.8	7.3	7.0	•	6.2	18.1
Coverage Ratio 33	5.4	60.5	6.3	4.5	15.0	53.7	10.8	6.4	8.4	4.1	6.4
Total Asset Turnover 34	0.5	•	4.2	2.0	1.4	2.2	1.3	0.8	0.9	0.7	0.6
Inventory Turnover 35	19.3	•	156.7	31.9	21.7	15.5	20.1	20.1	18.2	20.4	15.6
Receivables Turnover 36	6.1	•	15.6	10.7	9.8	11.5	8.2	8.0	6.3	7.4	8.5
Total Liabilities to Net Worth 37	0.8	•	•	0.9	1.1	0.7	0.7	1.0	1.5	0.8	1.0
Current Assets to Working Capital 38	•	•	2.5	1.9	2.5	2.1	2.2	2.6	•	2.0	4.7
Current Liabilities to Working Capital 39	•	•	1.5	0.9	1.5	1.1	1.2	1.6	•	1.0	3.7
Working Capital to Net Sales 40	•	•	0.0	0.1	0.1	0.1	0.1	0.1	•	0.2	0.1
Inventory to Working Capital 41	•	•	0.0	0.1	0.1	0.1	0.1	0.1	•	0.1	0.3
Total Receipts to Cash Flow 42	3.1	2.4	3.3	4.9	2.5	3.6	3.7	3.6	3.3	3.6	3.4
Cost of Goods to Cash Flow 43	0.7	0.3	1.1	1.6	0.4	0.6	0.9	1.1	1.0	1.2	0.8
Cash Flow to Total Debt 44	0.4	•	1.2	0.8	1.1	1.5	0.9	0.5	0.5	0.5	0.4

Selected Financial Factors (in Percentages)

	•	•	•	•	•	•	•	•	•	•	•
Debt Ratio 45	45.6	•	103.4	46.9	52.4	41.3	41.4	50.5	59.5	44.2	51.1
Return on Total Assets 46	8.9	•	35.0	10.3	20.5	22.0	12.1	10.4	15.9	7.6	13.8
Return on Equity Before Income Taxes 47	13.3	•	•	15.0	40.2	36.8	18.7	17.7	34.6	10.3	23.8
Return on Equity After Income Taxes 48	9.3	•	•	14.6	37.7	36.3	17.0	15.1	27.0	8.9	16.5
Profit Margin (Before Income Tax) 49	13.9	16.2	7.1	4.1	13.4	9.8	8.3	10.4	15.0	7.7	19.0
Profit Margin (After Income Tax) 50	9.7	11.8	6.5	4.0	12.6	9.7	7.6	8.9	11.7	6.7	13.1

Table I

Corporations with and without Net Income

PERIODICAL PUBLISHERS

MONEY AMOUNTS AND SIZE OF ASSETS IN THOUSANDS OF DOLLARS

Item Description for Accounting Period 7/03 Through 6/04	Total	Zero Assets	Under 500	500 to 1,000	1,000 to 5,000	5,000 to 10,000	10,000 to 25,000	25,000 to 50,000	50,000 to 100,000	100,000 to 250,000	250,000 to 500,000	500,000 to 2,500,000	2,500,000 and over
Number of Enterprises **1**	7138	24	5556	535	813	73	73	28	10	8	12	7	•
Revenues ($ in Thousands)													
Net Sales **2**	21849647	96797	2403303	452336	5782020	631116	1616178	1409135	745623	1092013	2189978	5431148	•
Interest **3**	239842	403	1016	2501	3513	1136	4517	2058	4647	3016	75012	142024	•
Rents **4**	43379	0	1176	870	7970	117	844	5184	2476	3142	12200	9400	•
Royalties **5**	263133	0	20	0	37150	1	7	466	2449	271	91515	131253	•
Other Portfolio Income **6**	165833	80	317	4	4710	2751	34007	13168	9247	3876	44959	52710	•
Other Receipts **7**	437352	5630	2284	2378	118517	4714	39920	9524	26670	79079	31014	117626	•
Total Receipts **8**	22999186	102910	2408116	458089	5953880	639835	1695473	1439535	791112	1181397	2244678	5884161	•
Average Total Receipts **9**	3222	4288	433	856	7323	8765	23226	51412	79111	147675	203723	840594	•
Operating Costs/Operating Income (%)													
Cost of Operations **10**	40.3	44.2	34.3	8.3	52.9	39.8	41.9	41.7	43.9	39.4	39.6	31.5	•
Salaries and Wages **11**	17.3	23.3	16.9	22.4	16.6	17.8	17.1	15.9	16.1	18.6	21.2	16.2	•
Taxes Paid **12**	2.2	3.1	2.1	3.3	2.1	2.5	2.6	1.8	2.0	3.4	2.6	1.8	•
Interest Paid **13**	3.9	2.5	0.1	0.9	0.6	2.4	1.7	1.6	3.3	3.2	7.9	9.4	•
Depreciation **14**	1.8	0.9	0.7	0.7	0.7	3.1	1.8	2.1	1.5	2.4	3.4	2.6	•
Amortization and Depletion **15**	2.7	2.6	0.2	2.6	1.1	2.1	1.2	1.9	1.6	2.8	5.0	5.4	•
Pensions and Other Deferred Comp. **16**	0.8	0.5	0.5	•	0.8	1.6	0.6	0.3	0.8	1.9	1.1	0.6	•
Employee Benefits **17**	1.6	2.6	1.0	1.5	1.7	0.8	1.9	1.7	1.7	2.2	2.2	1.5	•
Advertising **18**	2.1	1.4	1.5	0.4	2.3	0.9	1.5	1.6	2.2	2.9	5.9	1.1	•
Other Expenses **19**	28.0	29.8	32.5	38.1	17.4	26.5	25.8	25.4	23.0	29.8	29.9	37.7	•
Officers' Compensation **20**	3.1	0.3	7.5	10.1	3.4	3.4	3.3	2.7	1.4	3.2	2.0	0.8	•
Operating Margin **21**	•	•	2.8	11.7	0.5	•	0.7	3.3	2.4	•	•	•	•
Operating Margin Before Officers' Comp. **22**	•	•	10.3	21.8	3.8	2.4	4.0	6.0	3.9	•	•	•	•

Selected Average Balance Sheet ($ in Thousands)

Line item													
Net Receivables 23	•	115084	34538	26122	11726	5769	3028	1039	925	263	16	0	418
Inventories 24	•	23963	4063	4506	2952	1309	724	445	72	11	7	0	71
Net Property, Plant and Equipment 25	•	67052	16215	22707	6475	4471	2143	1216	249	41	7	0	217
Total Assets 26	•	2884878	359637	165202	78972	34504	15939	7604	2679	743	86	0	4534
Notes and Loans Payable 27	•	979205	131544	47346	18544	14158	4723	3770	729	163	25	0	1517
All Other Liabilities 28	•	398293	96912	72194	42657	17431	8051	1697	1919	221	29	0	1120
Net Worth 29	•	1507380	131181	45662	17772	2915	3164	2137	32	359	33	0	1896

Selected Financial Ratios (Times to 1)

Line item													
Current Ratio 30	•	0.6	1.7	1.0	1.5	1.3	1.1	1.4	0.9	1.4	1.7		1.0
Quick Ratio 31	•	0.4	1.3	0.7	0.9	0.9	0.8	1.1	0.7	1.3	1.1		0.7
Net Sales to Working Capital 32	•	•	3.2	241.6	5.8	11.9	36.7	10.0	•	7.2	13.9		•
Coverage Ratio 33	•	1.1	•	0.4	3.5	4.2	4.3	1.2	6.6	15.3	25.4		1.5
Total Asset Turnover 34	•	0.3	0.5	0.8	0.9	1.5	1.4	1.1	2.7	1.1	5.0		0.7
Inventory Turnover 35	•	10.2	17.8	11.9	11.1	16.0	12.8	7.7	52.2	6.5	21.3		17.4
Receivables Turnover 36	•	6.1	6.1	5.4	6.1	7.6	8.0	6.5	9.1	3.4	24.9		7.5
Total Liabilities to Net Worth 37	•	0.9	1.7	2.6	3.4	10.8	4.0	2.6	82.9	1.1	1.6		1.4
Current Assets to Working Capital 38	•	•	2.3	94.2	3.2	4.3	12.8	3.5	•	3.2	2.4		•
Current Liabilities to Working Capital 39	•	•	1.3	93.2	2.2	3.3	11.8	2.5	•	2.2	1.4		•
Working Capital to Net Sales 40	•	•	0.3	0.0	0.2	0.1	0.0	0.1	•	0.1	0.1		•
Inventory to Working Capital 41	•	0.1	0.1	6.8	0.2	0.3	1.2	0.4	•	0.2	0.2		•
Total Receipts to Cash Flow 42	•	2.9	7.1	4.5	3.5	3.6	3.8	4.0	5.7	2.1	3.1	3.9	7.0
Cost of Goods to Cash Flow 43	•	0.9	2.8	1.8	1.5	1.6	1.6	1.6	3.0	0.2	1.1	1.6	3.1
Cash Flow to Total Debt 44	•	0.2	0.1	0.3	0.3	0.4	0.5	0.4	0.5	1.1	2.6		0.3

Selected Financial Factors (in Percentages)

Line item													
Debt Ratio 45	•	47.7	63.5	72.4	77.5	91.6	80.1	71.9	98.8	51.7	62.1		58.2
Return on Total Assets 46	•	2.8	•	1.1	11.0	10.1	10.1	3.3	10.7	15.8	15.8		3.9
Return on Equity Before Income Taxes 47	•	0.5	•	34.8	91.1	38.9	1.7	765.6	30.6	40.0			2.9
Return on Equity After Income Taxes 48	•	•	•	23.8	83.5	36.5	•	744.0	30.5	39.9			1.7
Profit Margin (Before Income Tax) 49	•	0.9	•	8.3	5.3	5.6	0.4	3.4	13.0	3.0			1.8
Profit Margin (After Income Tax) 50	•	•	•	5.7	4.8	5.2	•	3.3	12.9	3.0			1.1

Table II

Corporations with Net Income

PERIODICAL PUBLISHERS

MONEY AMOUNTS AND SIZE OF ASSETS IN THOUSANDS OF DOLLARS

Item Description for Accounting Period 7/03 Through 6/04	Total	Zero Assets	Under 500	500 to 1,000	1,000 to 5,000	5,000 to 10,000	10,000 to 25,000	25,000 to 50,000	50,000 to 100,000	100,000 to 250,000	250,000 to 500,000	500,000 to 2,500,000	2,500,000 and over
Number of Enterprises 1	4010	3	2984	416	470	50	47	•	•	5	6	3	•
Revenues ($ in Thousands)													
Net Sales 2	13885564	69917	1442668	328937	4088943	520533	1186582	•	•	764994	888055	2947163	•
Interest 3	55289	403	876	2409	1406	1042	4271	•	•	2086	14273	22372	•
Rents 4	24584	0	1176	0	633	117	831	•	•	2771	2309	9205	•
Royalties 5	126123	0	0	0	37150	0	7	•	•	271	16319	72245	•
Other Portfolio Income 6	126434	80	0	0	188	1523	33238	•	•	3874	40875	24384	•
Other Receipts 7	292423	3141	1547	1866	117196	4595	35718	•	•	70977	15681	16669	•
Total Receipts 8	14510417	73541	1446267	333212	4245516	527810	1260647	•	•	844973	977512	3092038	•
Average Total Receipts 9	3619	24514	485	801	9033	10556	26822	•	•	168995	162919	1030679	•
Operating Costs/Operating Income (%)													
Cost of Operations 10	40.6	49.2	31.2	2.0	53.2	40.8	41.8	•	•	34.0	32.1	36.7	•
Salaries and Wages 11	16.1	19.6	16.2	19.6	16.0	14.3	15.5	•	•	17.7	24.4	13.3	•
Taxes Paid 12	2.2	2.7	1.9	2.8	2.1	2.4	2.7	•	•	3.6	3.5	1.8	•
Interest Paid 13	1.4	0.3	0.2	0.8	0.2	0.6	1.5	•	•	0.6	2.8	3.6	•
Depreciation 14	1.4	0.4	0.7	0.4	0.5	3.6	1.8	•	•	2.8	1.8	1.6	•
Amortization and Depletion 15	1.8	1.2	0.0	3.4	1.1	1.3	0.9	•	•	0.9	1.4	4.8	•
Pensions and Other Deferred Comp. 16	0.8	0.7	0.5	•	0.9	1.8	0.5	•	•	1.9	2.3	0.4	•
Employee Benefits 17	1.7	2.4	0.5	2.1	2.0	0.6	1.6	•	•	2.4	2.7	1.5	•
Advertising 18	1.7	1.9	0.5	0.3	2.7	1.1	1.2	•	•	2.9	2.4	0.6	•
Other Expenses 19	24.8	20.5	29.9	40.1	14.8	24.7	22.7	•	•	31.7	25.7	33.8	•
Officers' Compensation 20	3.2	0.3	7.8	10.9	3.7	3.4	3.4	•	•	2.8	2.0	0.6	•
Operating Margin 21	4.2	0.7	10.6	17.4	2.9	5.5	6.5	•	•	•	•	1.4	•
Operating Margin Before Officers' Comp. 22	7.4	1.0	18.4	28.4	6.6	8.9	9.8	•	•	1.5	0.9	2.0	•

Selected Average Balance Sheet ($ in Thousands)

Net Receivables 23	437	0	10	288	1194	1208	3480	•	28344	24928	103903
Inventories 24	100	0	13	1	103	551	730	•	6631	4379	45820
Net Property, Plant and Equipment 25	245	0	11	16	221	1734	2507	•	23939	9447	98346
Total Assets 26	2910	0	75	763	2720	8094	16088	•	149802	349309	1522556
Notes and Loans Payable 27	855	0	40	127	439	2563	4190	•	19190	64554	644527
All Other Liabilities 28	1265	0	37	250	2553	1819	7876	•	72360	92362	533156
Net Worth 29	791	0	-2	386	-273	3711	4022	•	58251	192393	344873

Selected Financial Ratios (Times to 1)

Current Ratio 30	1.1	•	0.9	1.2	0.8	2.4	1.2	•	1.4	1.5	0.8
Quick Ratio 31	0.8	•	0.5	1.2	0.7	2.0	0.9	•	1.0	1.1	0.4
Net Sales to Working Capital 32	30.1	•	•	12.4	•	4.7	14.9	•	9.6	2.7	•
Coverage Ratio 33	7.6	23.8	55.7	23.3	29.7	12.5	9.5	•	14.6	4.8	3.1
Total Asset Turnover 34	1.2	•	6.4	1.0	3.2	1.3	1.6	•	1.0	0.4	0.6
Inventory Turnover 35	14.1	•	11.7	15.4	45.1	7.7	14.5	•	7.8	10.9	7.9
Receivables Turnover 36	7.4	•	37.0	3.5	9.0	8.5	8.7	•	5.5	5.2	5.6
Total Liabilities to Net Worth 37	2.7	•	•	1.0	•	1.2	3.0	•	1.6	0.8	3.4
Current Assets to Working Capital 38	10.1	•	•	5.7	•	1.7	5.0	•	3.4	2.9	•
Current Liabilities to Working Capital 39	9.1	•	•	4.7	•	0.7	4.0	•	2.4	1.9	•
Working Capital to Net Sales 40	0.0	•	•	0.1	•	0.2	0.1	•	0.1	0.4	•
Inventory to Working Capital 41	0.8	•	•	0.0	•	0.2	0.4	•	0.3	0.0	•
Total Receipts to Cash Flow 42	3.3	4.2	2.6	1.8	5.4	3.3	3.3	•	2.8	3.5	2.7
Cost of Goods to Cash Flow 43	1.4	2.1	0.8	0.0	2.9	1.4	1.4	•	1.0	1.1	1.0
Cash Flow to Total Debt 44	0.5	•	2.4	1.1	0.5	0.7	0.6	•	0.6	0.3	0.3

Selected Financial Factors (in Percentages)

Debt Ratio 45	72.8	•	103.0	49.4	110.0	54.1	75.0	•	61.1	44.9	77.3
Return on Total Assets 46	12.4	•	71.0	20.3	22.4	9.6	22.2	•	9.7	5.7	7.3
Return on Equity Before Income Taxes 47	39.6	•	•	38.4	•	19.4	79.5	•	23.2	8.2	22.0
Return on Equity After Income Taxes 48	34.5	•	•	38.2	•	16.5	76.7	•	18.8	5.4	15.0
Profit Margin (Before Income Tax) 49	9.0	5.8	10.8	18.7	6.8	6.9	12.7	•	8.8	10.6	7.7
Profit Margin (After Income Tax) 50	7.9	4.3	10.8	18.6	6.6	5.9	12.2	•	7.2	7.0	5.3

Table I

Corporations with and without Net Income

BOOK PUBLISHERS

MONEY AMOUNTS AND SIZE OF ASSETS IN THOUSANDS OF DOLLARS

Item Description for Accounting Period 7/03 Through 6/04	Total	Zero Assets	Under 500	500 to 1,000	1,000 to 5,000	5,000 to 10,000	10,000 to 25,000	25,000 to 50,000	50,000 to 100,000	100,000 to 250,000	250,000 to 500,000	500,000 to 2,500,000	2,500,000 and over
Number of Enterprises **1**	5611	1417	3391	118	515	63	58	18	4	11	6	4	5
Revenues ($ in Thousands)													
Net Sales **2**	25912766	131945	244450	73741	1041300	893563	1119725	651400	371661	1359803	1070093	4143605	14811480
Interest **3**	720066	38	484	1144	533	21	577	1588	237	6814	14661	5871	688099
Rents **4**	70947	742	0	0	0	1101	1032	82	217	57	0	12145	55571
Royalties **5**	333622	0	0	0	0	2	1948	11134	1198	11684	5109	74111	228437
Other Portfolio Income **6**	801641	22	9187	0	7120	23	6554	4597	464	3015	169	6124	764366
Other Receipts **7**	695676	13096	5938	198	654	1825	10138	7158	9110	71949	18778	44873	511958
Total Receipts **8**	28534718	145843	260059	75083	1049607	896535	1139974	675959	382887	1453322	1108810	4286729	17059911
Average Total Receipts **9**	5085	103	77	636	2038	14231	19655	37553	95722	132120	184802	1071682	3411982
Operating Costs/Operating Income (%)													
Cost of Operations **10**	28.1	40.6	25.6	28.1	35.3	9.5	47.9	39.3	50.9	36.4	35.5	40.7	21.2
Salaries and Wages **11**	21.6	12.7	12.6	9.4	8.2	44.5	16.6	19.7	14.6	18.2	17.8	18.2	23.6
Taxes Paid **12**	2.8	1.3	3.1	3.1	1.3	4.4	2.4	2.3	1.5	2.0	2.1	2.0	3.3
Interest Paid **13**	6.8	0.6	0.1	3.1	2.4	0.4	1.2	1.1	0.7	3.1	13.8	5.7	8.7
Depreciation **14**	4.4	0.0	1.1	0.4	1.1	3.3	1.9	2.6	1.5	1.0	1.1	5.5	5.4
Amortization and Depletion **15**	3.3	•	•	0.0	2.2	0.2	1.4	1.7	0.9	2.1	7.8	2.0	4.0
Pensions and Other Deferred Comp. **16**	1.2	0.1	4.0	•	1.7	0.8	0.6	0.5	0.6	0.7	0.4	1.6	1.2
Employee Benefits **17**	2.4	1.0	1.4	•	3.0	4.4	1.3	1.8	1.2	2.1	1.4	3.9	2.3
Advertising **18**	2.7	30.4	0.4	4.7	0.6	1.5	3.3	3.9	5.2	2.1	2.7	2.7	2.7
Other Expenses **19**	27.6	35.0	35.7	16.0	27.6	26.7	19.8	22.6	18.2	29.3	22.5	19.7	30.9
Officers' Compensation **20**	2.2	2.3	19.7	33.1	10.7	3.9	3.7	2.8	2.0	2.5	0.8	1.6	1.1
Operating Margin **21**	•	•	•	•	8.4	0.4	•	2.0	2.8	0.3	•	•	•
Operating Margin Before Officers' Comp. **22**	•	•	16.1	32.2	19.1	4.2	3.4	4.8	4.8	2.9	•	•	•

Selected Average Balance Sheet ($ in Thousands)

Net Receivables 23	1554	0	1	73	309	2483	3595	6547	26174	24907	43796	163387	1354016
Inventories 24	547	0	11	178	373	947	3615	7664	18147	14694	17448	151493	293794
Net Property, Plant and Equipment 25	516	0	20	12	230	1821	1325	3250	9834	3764	10671	159321	334489
Total Assets 26	9425	0	54	721	1951	6905	15066	33900	84536	152340	330569	1640120	7827094
Notes and Loans Payable 27	3232	0	29	342	774	2930	3705	5536	12676	94621	164183	648419	2485631
All Other Liabilities 28	2858	0	4	46	295	2575	6302	11547	27797	63631	111738	245094	2534275
Net Worth 29	3335	0	21	333	883	1400	5059	16817	44062	-5912	54648	746607	2807188

Selected Financial Ratios (Times to 1)

Current Ratio 30	1.4	•	1.9	1.3	2.7	1.3	1.3	1.7	2.2	1.1	0.8	1.7	1.4
Quick Ratio 31	0.7	•	0.9	0.3	1.3	0.8	0.7	0.7	1.2	0.6	0.5	0.8	0.7
Net Sales to Working Capital 32	3.6	•	5.4	7.3	3.0	11.9	7.6	3.9	2.6	14.3	•	5.8	2.7
Coverage Ratio 33	2.0	•	43.1	1.3	4.8	2.7	2.2	6.4	9.6	3.3	0.8	1.0	2.3
Total Asset Turnover 34	0.5	•	1.3	0.9	1.0	2.1	1.3	1.1	1.1	0.8	0.5	0.6	0.4
Inventory Turnover 35	2.4	•	1.7	1.0	1.9	1.4	2.6	1.9	2.6	3.1	3.6	2.8	2.1
Receivables Turnover 36	3.8	•	81.1	11.3	8.8	8.2	5.4	5.1	3.9	4.9	5.5	6.3	2.9
Total Liabilities to Net Worth 37	1.8	•	1.6	1.2	1.2	3.9	2.0	1.0	0.9	•	5.0	1.2	1.8
Current Assets to Working Capital 38	3.2	•	2.1	4.8	1.6	3.9	3.9	2.4	1.8	7.7	•	2.4	3.2
Current Liabilities to Working Capital 39	2.2	•	1.1	3.8	0.6	2.9	2.9	1.4	0.8	6.7	•	1.4	2.2
Working Capital to Net Sales 40	0.3	•	0.2	0.1	0.3	0.1	0.1	0.3	0.4	0.1	•	0.2	0.4
Inventory to Working Capital 41	0.4	•	0.8	3.4	0.7	0.8	1.4	0.8	0.5	1.5	•	0.8	0.3
Total Receipts to Cash Flow 42	3.5	7.2	3.1	7.8	3.1	4.4	5.7	4.1	4.4	2.9	5.7	6.5	2.9
Cost of Goods to Cash Flow 43	1.0	2.9	0.8	2.2	1.1	0.4	2.7	1.6	2.3	1.1	2.0	2.6	0.6
Cash Flow to Total Debt 44	0.2	•	0.7	0.2	0.6	0.6	0.3	0.5	0.5	0.3	0.1	0.2	0.2

Selected Financial Factors (in Percentages)

Debt Ratio 45	64.6	•	60.8	53.9	54.8	79.7	66.4	50.4	47.9	103.9	83.5	54.5	64.1
Return on Total Assets 46	6.8	•	3.7	3.4	12.0	2.3	3.4	7.2	7.0	8.5	6.2	3.5	7.4
Return on Equity Before Income Taxes 47	9.9	•	9.2	1.6	20.9	7.2	5.5	12.3	12.0	•	•	•	11.5
Return on Equity After Income Taxes 48	6.6	•	8.6	1.1	18.7	7.2	2.8	8.8	10.4	•	•	•	7.8
Profit Margin (Before Income Tax) 49	7.1	•	2.7	0.9	9.1	0.7	1.4	5.7	5.7	7.3	•	•	10.9
Profit Margin (After Income Tax) 50	4.7	•	2.5	0.6	8.2	0.7	0.7	4.1	5.0	5.1	•	•	7.4

Table II

Corporations with Net Income

BOOK PUBLISHERS

MONEY AMOUNTS AND SIZE OF ASSETS IN THOUSANDS OF DOLLARS

Item Description for Accounting Period 7/03 Through 6/04	Total	Zero Assets	Under 500	500 to 1,000	1,000 to 5,000	5,000 to 10,000	10,000 to 25,000	25,000 to 50,000	50,000 to 100,000	100,000 to 250,000	250,000 to 500,000	500,000 to 2,500,000	2,500,000 and over
Number of Enterprises **1**	2207	250	1459	62	350	13	37	14	•	•	•	•	•
Revenues ($ in Thousands)													
Net Sales **2**	18306499	461	176655	41832	898857	101916	824413	522849	•	•	•	•	•
Interest **3**	260124	0	238	1144	520	0	446	1585	•	•	•	•	•
Rents **4**	60958	0	0	0	0	1101	832	82	•	•	•	•	•
Royalties **5**	270025	0	0	0	0	0	1479	11134	•	•	•	•	•
Other Portfolio Income **6**	776876	0	0	0	7120	23	814	4593	•	•	•	•	•
Other Receipts **7**	659500	7	68	0	538	594	6515	6393	•	•	•	•	•
Total Receipts **8**	20333982	468	176961	42976	907035	103634	834499	546636	•	•	•	•	•
Average Total Receipts **9**	9213	2	121	693	2592	7972	22554	39045	•	•	•	•	•
Operating Costs/Operating Income (%)													
Cost of Operations **10**	26.2	10.2	15.1	17.6	33.4	14.6	46.2	35.4	•	•	•	•	•
Salaries and Wages **11**	20.3	•	5.6	•	7.6	31.6	15.9	20.5	•	•	•	•	•
Taxes Paid **12**	2.9	3.9	2.9	3.2	1.4	3.7	2.2	2.5	•	•	•	•	•
Interest Paid **13**	3.8	•	•	3.2	1.2	1.5	0.8	0.8	•	•	•	•	•
Depreciation **14**	3.6	•	0.4	•	1.1	3.8	2.1	2.7	•	•	•	•	•
Amortization and Depletion **15**	3.1	•	•	•	0.1	0.1	0.6	2.1	•	•	•	•	•
Pensions and Other Deferred Comp. **16**	1.3	•	5.5	•	2.0	0.6	0.7	0.6	•	•	•	•	•
Employee Benefits **17**	2.0	•	1.6	3.7	0.6	6.8	1.3	1.7	•	•	•	•	•
Advertising **18**	2.9	•	0.2	3.4	0.5	5.5	2.8	4.3	•	•	•	•	•
Other Expenses **19**	30.4	58.8	29.2	22.1	25.4	16.1	18.0	21.4	•	•	•	•	•
Officers' Compensation **20**	2.4	•	27.3	46.5	12.2	4.3	3.5	3.1	•	•	•	•	•
Operating Margin **21**	1.0	27.1	12.3	0.4	14.5	11.5	6.1	5.0	•	•	•	•	•
Operating Margin Before Officers' Comp. **22**	3.4	27.1	39.6	46.8	26.8	15.8	9.6	8.1	•	•	•	•	•

Selected Average Balance Sheet ($ in Thousands)

Net Receivables 23	2147	0	0	34	389	319	4091	6009
Inventories 24	939	0	10	37	282	3588	4130	7610
Net Property, Plant and Equipment 25	976	0	21	0	329	1965	1639	3662
Total Assets 26	18032	0	49	652	2137	5738	15535	33799
Notes and Loans Payable 27	6733	0	12	397	680	8352	3268	4492
All Other Liabilities 28	5022	0	2	42	273	5127	5218	11872
Net Worth 29	6278	0	36	213	1184	-7741	7048	17435

Selected Financial Ratios (Times to 1)

Current Ratio 30	1.2	•	14.5	0.2	2.9	0.6	1.8	1.8
Quick Ratio 31	0.5	•	14.5	0.1	1.7	0.1	0.9	0.7
Net Sales to Working Capital 32	7.3	•	5.7	•	3.4	•	4.6	3.7
Coverage Ratio 33	4.2	•	•	2.0	14.3	9.9	10.0	13.0
Total Asset Turnover 34	0.5	•	2.5	1.0	1.2	1.4	1.4	1.1
Inventory Turnover 35	2.3	•	1.8	3.2	3.0	0.3	2.5	1.7
Receivables Turnover 36	4.8	•	116.1	27.4	9.5	3.1	5.5	5.6
Total Liabilities to Net Worth 37	1.9	•	0.4	2.1	0.8	•	1.2	0.9
Current Assets to Working Capital 38	6.6	•	1.1	•	1.5	•	2.3	2.3
Current Liabilities to Working Capital 39	5.6	•	0.1	•	0.5	•	1.3	1.3
Working Capital to Net Sales 40	0.1	•	0.2	•	0.3	•	0.2	0.3
Inventory to Working Capital 41	0.8	•	•	•	0.5	•	0.9	0.7
Total Receipts to Cash Flow 42	2.8	1.1	2.7	4.0	2.7	3.6	4.4	3.7
Cost of Goods to Cash Flow 43	0.7	0.1	0.4	0.7	0.9	0.5	2.1	1.3
Cash Flow to Total Debt 44	0.3	•	3.4	0.4	1.0	0.2	0.6	0.6

Selected Financial Factors (in Percentages)

Debt Ratio 45	65.2	•	26.7	67.3	44.6	234.9	54.6	48.4
Return on Total Assets 46	7.4	•	30.9	6.5	20.0	20.0	11.6	11.4
Return on Equity Before Income Taxes 47	16.1	•	42.1	9.8	33.5	•	23.0	20.4
Return on Equity After Income Taxes 48	11.6	•	41.3	8.3	31.1	•	20.0	16.1
Profit Margin (Before Income Tax) 49	12.2	28.6	12.5	3.1	15.4	13.1	7.3	9.5
Profit Margin (After Income Tax) 50	8.8	27.1	12.3	2.6	14.3	13.1	6.3	7.5

Table I

Corporations with and without Net Income

DATABASE, DIRECTORY, AND OTHER PUBLISHERS

MONEY AMOUNTS AND SIZE OF ASSETS IN THOUSANDS OF DOLLARS

Item Description for Accounting Period 7/03 Through 6/04	Total	Zero Assets	Under 500	500 to 1,000	1,000 to 5,000	5,000 to 10,000	10,000 to 25,000	25,000 to 50,000	50,000 to 100,000	100,000 to 250,000	250,000 to 500,000	500,000 to 2,500,000	2,500,000 and over
Number of Enterprises **1**	4435	1016	2713	502	108	22	31	16	7	8	4	3	5
Revenues ($ in Thousands)													
Net Sales **2**	27070173	63979	61848	886627	536062	432034	694172	742717	345872	930543	1613806	1406609	19355905
Interest **3**	1024659	48	1214	489	96	174	794	1010	165	3211	6545	8077	1002835
Rents **4**	100880	0	0	0	0	7	43	788	2089	0	113	0	97839
Royalties **5**	614423	0	0	0	0	114	133	147	9	9404	0	17626	586991
Other Portfolio Income **6**	348928	1305	7809	0	0	0	1032	13	516	66806	1651	69064	200729
Other Receipts **7**	558235	1574	117	9333	-2650	1627	6679	4339	10959	47346	2194	270755	205964
Total Receipts **8**	29717298	66906	70988	896449	533508	433958	702853	749014	359610	1057310	1624309	1772131	21450263
Average Total Receipts **9**	6701	66	26	1786	4940	19725	22673	46813	51373	132164	406077	590710	4290053
Operating Costs/Operating Income (%)													
Cost of Operations **10**	30.0	18.6	40.7	24.2	20.7	73.8	43.5	32.1	49.3	29.4	16.4	13.1	31.1
Salaries and Wages **11**	20.4	9.9	18.6	16.5	29.9	10.6	20.2	23.4	19.3	18.5	32.3	37.8	18.3
Taxes Paid **12**	3.2	2.5	2.4	3.0	2.9	1.8	2.5	2.6	2.4	1.9	3.9	3.1	3.3
Interest Paid **13**	9.9	0.1	0.3	0.1	0.4	0.6	0.6	1.2	1.9	1.5	1.2	13.6	12.5
Depreciation **14**	3.9	5.5	5.6	1.0	3.4	2.4	2.7	1.9	1.7	2.2	3.2	2.6	4.5
Amortization and Depletion **15**	4.7	•	7.7	0.0	0.0	0.2	0.7	0.8	3.5	3.3	3.4	5.1	5.6
Pensions and Other Deferred Comp. **16**	1.1	•	0.1	1.8	0.3	0.1	0.5	1.0	0.3	0.6	0.4	0.3	1.3
Employee Benefits **17**	1.9	0.7	0.3	0.9	0.2	1.4	1.7	2.2	3.9	2.0	2.7	3.6	1.8
Advertising **18**	2.1	0.1	0.6	0.5	0.8	2.6	2.3	4.9	2.5	3.6	3.0	3.6	1.8
Other Expenses **19**	28.4	69.0	83.5	37.1	30.0	11.5	20.8	19.4	23.5	38.4	25.5	35.2	27.9
Officers' Compensation **20**	1.7	0.6	11.6	12.2	10.8	2.8	3.7	1.7	3.0	1.2	0.5	3.6	0.8
Operating Margin **21**	•	•	•	2.6	0.7	•	0.7	8.7	•	•	7.6	•	•
Operating Margin Before Officers' Comp. **22**	•	•	•	14.8	11.5	•	4.4	10.4	8.1	•	•	•	•

Selected Average Balance Sheet ($ in Thousands)

Net Receivables **23**	1099	0	4	174	612	2192	3343	10373	14477	43316	70247	197150	614363
Inventories **24**	496	0	4	71	79	436	1452	2663	1792	4763	5787	4276	391642
Net Property, Plant and Equipment **25**	792	0	0	75	585	1510	2129	3641	8356	9731	39371	33748	571258
Total Assets **26**	11735	36	0	683	1681	7604	15086	32671	75793	192973	397930	1019954	8708123
Notes and Loans Payable **27**	6184	0	49	32	435	1767	2971	7310	25086	35954	90960	1336942	4428405
All Other Liabilities **28**	3625	0	15	417	700	4804	6546	16747	36452	69499	52495	362101	2613090
Net Worth **29**	1927	0	-29	233	546	1032	5569	8614	14255	87520	254476	-679089	1666629

Selected Financial Ratios (Times to 1)

Current Ratio **30**	1.1	·	0.5	1.7	1.7	0.7	1.1	1.7	0.7	1.6	1.2	1.0	1.1
Quick Ratio **31**	0.6	·	0.4	1.4	1.4	0.5	0.7	1.3	0.5	0.9	1.0	0.6	0.6
Net Sales to Working Capital **32**	19.4	·	·	8.2	11.4	·	43.6	5.3	·	3.4	29.4	34.0	21.8
Coverage Ratio **33**	1.3	·	·	36.3	1.6	·	4.3	8.9	·	8.2	8.2	1.4	1.2
Total Asset Turnover **34**	0.5	·	0.6	2.6	3.0	2.6	1.5	1.4	0.7	0.6	1.0	0.5	0.4
Inventory Turnover **35**	3.7	·	2.2	6.0	13.1	33.2	6.7	5.6	13.6	7.2	11.4	14.4	3.1
Receivables Turnover **36**	5.0	·	6.5	8.8	5.1	13.4	5.6	5.3	3.5	2.7	5.5	1.3	6.3
Total Liabilities to Net Worth **37**	5.1	·	·	1.9	2.1	6.4	1.7	2.8	4.3	1.2	0.6	·	4.2
Current Assets to Working Capital **38**	7.8	·	2.4	2.4	2.4	·	16.0	2.4	·	2.7	7.3	30.0	8.2
Current Liabilities to Working Capital **39**	6.8	·	1.4	1.4	1.4	·	15.0	1.4	·	1.7	6.3	29.0	7.2
Working Capital to Net Sales **40**	0.1	·	0.1	0.1	0.1	·	0.0	0.2	·	0.3	0.0	0.0	0.0
Inventory to Working Capital **41**	1.9	·	0.1	0.2	0.2	·	2.6	0.4	·	0.2	0.3	0.2	2.7
Total Receipts to Cash Flow **42**	4.5	1.6	8.4	6.6	4.4	382.7	5.1	3.9	8.8	2.5	3.5	2.7	4.9
Cost of Goods to Cash Flow **43**	1.4	0.3	3.4	1.6	0.9	282.5	2.2	1.2	4.4	0.7	0.6	0.4	1.5
Cash Flow to Total Debt **44**	0.1	0.0	0.0	0.6	1.0	0.0	0.5	0.5	0.1	0.4	0.8	0.1	0.1

Selected Financial Factors (in Percentages)

Debt Ratio **45**	83.6	·	180.2	65.9	67.5	86.4	63.1	73.6	81.2	54.6	36.1	166.6	80.9
Return on Total Assets **46**	6.5	·	·	9.9	1.8	·	3.7	15.3	·	7.5	9.5	8.7	6.4
Return on Equity Before Income Taxes **47**	8.3	·	45.1	28.1	2.1	·	7.8	51.4	·	14.5	13.1	·	4.5
Return on Equity After Income Taxes **48**	4.1	·	45.2	27.5	·	·	7.3	49.1	·	10.0	7.8	·	1.7
Profit Margin (Before Income Tax) **49**	2.6	·	3.7	0.2	·	·	1.9	9.5	·	10.9	8.3	5.4	1.9
Profit Margin (After Income Tax) **50**	1.3	·	3.6	·	·	·	1.8	9.1	·	7.5	4.9	3.1	0.7

Table II

Corporations with Net Income

DATABASE, DIRECTORY, AND OTHER PUBLISHERS

MONEY AMOUNTS AND SIZE OF ASSETS IN THOUSANDS OF DOLLARS

Item Description for Accounting Period 7/03 Through 6/04	Total	Zero Assets	Under 500	500 to 1,000	1,000 to 5,000	5,000 to 10,000	10,000 to 25,000	25,000 to 50,000	50,000 to 100,000	100,000 to 250,000	250,000 to 500,000	500,000 to 2,500,000	2,500,000 and over
Number of Enterprises 1	2508	290	1775	313	73	5	21	·	4	·	·	·	·
Revenues ($ in Thousands)													
Net Sales 2	15215685	45840	23319	781756	369595	65856	440826	·	294657	·	·	·	·
Interest 3	575717	25	191	489	53	80	502	·	151	·	·	·	·
Rents 4	45901	0	0	0	0	0	43	·	0	·	·	·	·
Royalties 5	497399	0	0	0	0	0	0	·	9	·	·	·	·
Other Portfolio Income 6	288116	0	7615	0	0	2	1030	·	516	·	·	·	·
Other Receipts 7	433238	43	116	3796	23	131	5794	·	9297	·	·	·	·
Total Receipts 8	17056056	45908	31241	786041	369671	66069	448195	·	304630	·	·	·	·
Average Total Receipts 9	6801	158	18	2511	5064	13214	21343	·	76158	·	·	·	·
Operating Costs/Operating Income (%)													
Cost of Operations 10	30.1	1.0	25.0	23.5	14.9	21.6	43.3	·	54.3	·	·	·	·
Salaries and Wages 11	20.3	7.4	12.8	17.6	30.8	19.4	18.9	·	9.9	·	·	·	·
Taxes Paid 12	2.7	0.1	2.0	2.9	3.9	2.2	2.1	·	2.8	·	·	·	·
Interest Paid 13	8.7	0.0	0.0	0.1	0.5	0.2	0.4	·	1.5	·	·	·	·
Depreciation 14	4.3	0.0	10.3	1.1	2.4	0.9	2.1	·	1.4	·	·	·	·
Amortization and Depletion 15	2.4	·	·	0.0	0.0	0.1	1.1	·	1.6	·	·	·	·
Pensions and Other Deferred Comp. 16	1.2	·	·	0.4	0.4	0.4	0.5	·	0.3	·	·	·	·
Employee Benefits 17	2.0	0.0	0.6	1.0	0.1	1.5	1.6	·	2.4	·	·	·	·
Advertising 18	1.4	0.0	1.2	0.5	1.2	11.6	2.8	·	2.6	·	·	·	·
Other Expenses 19	29.0	88.9	48.7	40.4	24.7	15.0	19.0	·	14.9	·	·	·	·
Officers' Compensation 20	1.9	0.4	0.4	8.3	15.0	1.7	4.1	·	2.9	·	·	·	·
Operating Margin 21	·	2.6	·	3.9	6.1	25.4	4.1	·	5.3	·	·	·	·
Operating Margin Before Officers' Comp. 22	·	2.6	·	12.2	21.2	27.2	8.3	·	8.2	·	·	·	·

Selected Average Balance Sheet ($ in Thousands)

Net Receivables 23	1325	0	0	270	645	1273	3042	21727
Inventories 24	357	0	6	0	48	501	1439	3278
Net Property, Plant and Equipment 25	809	0	0	109	637	211	2037	12591
Total Assets 26	9587	0	27	725	1726	7709	14841	73867
Notes and Loans Payable 27	2917	0	18	52	296	234	2244	33765
All Other Liabilities 28	4555	0	16	416	160	3967	5096	15323
Net Worth 29	2115	0	-6	257	1269	3508	7502	24780

Selected Financial Ratios (Times to 1)

Current Ratio 30	1.2	·	7.2	1.1	5.4	1.2	1.3	1.9
Quick Ratio 31	0.8	·	3.6	0.9	4.8	1.0	0.9	1.5
Net Sales to Working Capital 32	18.7	·	1.0	40.4	5.8	14.3	10.3	4.0
Coverage Ratio 33	2.0	1263.0	1099.6	38.5	14.1	167.3	15.7	6.8
Total Asset Turnover 34	0.6	·	0.5	3.4	2.9	1.7	1.4	1.0
Inventory Turnover 35	5.1	·	0.5	·	15.9	5.7	6.3	12.2
Receivables Turnover 36	5.2	·	6.3	18.5	4.7	7.1	5.2	1.4
Total Liabilities to Net Worth 37	3.5	·	·	1.8	0.4	1.2	1.0	2.0
Current Assets to Working Capital 38	7.1	·	1.2	7.7	1.2	5.3	3.9	2.1
Current Liabilities to Working Capital 39	6.1	·	0.2	6.7	0.2	4.3	2.9	1.1
Working Capital to Net Sales 40	0.1	·	1.0	0.0	0.2	0.1	0.1	0.2
Inventory to Working Capital 41	0.7	·	0.1	·	0.1	0.4	0.7	0.1
Total Receipts to Cash Flow 42	3.4	1.1	1.9	6.0	4.6	2.6	4.6	4.8
Cost of Goods to Cash Flow 43	1.0	0.0	0.5	1.4	0.7	0.6	2.0	2.6
Cash Flow to Total Debt 44	0.2	·	0.2	0.9	2.4	1.2	0.6	0.3

Selected Financial Factors (in Percentages)

Debt Ratio 45	77.9	·	123.6	64.6	26.5	54.5	49.5	66.5
Return on Total Assets 46	10.8	·	16.1	15.8	19.4	44.3	8.7	10.1
Return on Equity Before Income Taxes 47	24.0	·	·	43.5	24.5	96.7	16.1	25.8
Return on Equity After Income Taxes 48	17.2	·	·	42.7	22.8	80.8	15.5	24.8
Profit Margin (Before Income Tax) 49	8.4	2.8	33.0	4.5	6.1	25.8	5.8	8.7
Profit Margin (After Income Tax) 50	6.0	2.4	32.8	4.4	5.7	21.5	5.5	8.3

Table I

Corporations with and without Net Income

SOFTWARE PUBLISHERS

MONEY AMOUNTS AND SIZE OF ASSETS IN THOUSANDS OF DOLLARS

Item Description for Accounting Period 7/03 Through 6/04	Total	Zero Assets	Under 500	500 to 1,000	1,000 to 5,000	5,000 to 10,000	10,000 to 25,000	25,000 to 50,000	50,000 to 100,000	100,000 to 250,000	250,000 to 500,000	500,000 to 2,500,000	2,500,000 and over
Number of Enterprises 1	8427	612	5599	539	940	288	218	76	38	43	34	32	8
Revenues ($ in Thousands)													
Net Sales 2	82130121	835458	1293083	745420	2339883	3542845	2716976	2120167	2268865	3748901	5444501	14928593	42145430
Interest 3	929656	3046	4823	1886	6373	8414	15961	17503	16264	44426	78743	284227	447990
Rents 4	66414	1796	13	0	147	170	618	1633	926	6666	24326	19165	10953
Royalties 5	3107435	48888	2112	94	717	12694	52460	10423	39874	157425	170596	1146995	1465158
Other Portfolio Income 6	1085616	13880	2869	4579	11547	56455	25419	5768	17296	5823	43898	254108	643970
Other Receipts 7	8976589	14615	50643	9006	36602	8548	90967	47079	17212	139302	80301	456971	8025346
Total Receipts 8	96295831	917683	1353543	760985	2395269	3629126	2902401	2202573	2360437	4102543	5842365	17090059	52738847
Average Total Receipts 9	11427	1499	242	1412	2548	12601	13314	28981	62117	95408	171834	534064	6592356
Operating Costs/Operating Income (%)													
Cost of Operations 10	18.2	29.6	8.4	38.1	17.1	29.1	25.3	23.0	18.8	23.5	22.8	22.6	13.6
Salaries and Wages 11	36.5	44.3	35.2	40.8	46.9	39.5	45.2	39.6	37.6	34.4	38.1	43.1	32.3
Taxes Paid 12	3.1	5.1	5.8	4.0	4.4	3.7	4.2	4.1	4.1	3.2	3.3	3.0	2.6
Interest Paid 13	1.2	0.8	1.5	1.8	3.0	1.2	1.4	1.2	0.6	0.5	1.1	2.1	0.8
Depreciation 14	3.4	2.6	2.2	2.2	4.5	2.3	4.2	3.4	3.8	3.1	3.6	4.9	2.9
Amortization and Depletion 15	1.7	4.9	1.2	3.8	2.5	0.9	1.9	1.6	1.4	2.9	4.9	2.4	0.8
Pensions and Other Deferred Comp. 16	0.3	0.1	1.0	3.4	0.3	0.2	0.6	0.4	0.5	0.5	0.8	0.5	0.1
Employee Benefits 17	3.2	3.5	3.6	3.1	3.3	4.0	3.7	3.1	3.3	2.3	3.7	4.3	2.8
Advertising 18	5.2	1.5	2.3	1.7	1.6	3.0	2.1	1.7	2.2	2.4	1.9	4.1	7.3
Other Expenses 19	31.6	36.7	43.3	28.2	49.0	24.7	36.1	30.5	32.3	37.2	31.2	29.2	31.0
Officers' Compensation 20	2.3	5.4	18.3	5.6	8.0	6.1	5.7	4.7	2.4	1.9	2.3	1.5	1.1
Operating Margin 21	•	•	•	•	•	•	•	•	•	•	•	•	4.7
Operating Margin Before Officers' Comp. 22	•	•	•	•	•	•	•	•	•	•	•	•	5.7

Selected Average Balance Sheet ($ in Thousands)

Net Receivables 23	2232	0	8	248	413	1198	2864	7541	13840	31004	55173	126120	1116427
Inventories 24	147	0	5	47	46	117	156	255	519	904	1620	12662	66957
Net Property, Plant and Equipment 25	1082	0	13	48	169	462	903	2108	4837	6979	18361	80025	587790
Total Assets 26	21379	0	70	669	2347	7928	15053	34314	70538	157382	349161	1072897	14172033
Notes and Loans Payable 27	1478	0	156	387	944	894	2051	5012	4171	9369	15796	133341	503920
All Other Liabilities 28	6763	0	43	316	1131	6152	8475	15020	27437	64072	98754	315630	4186924
Net Worth 29	13138	0	-130	-34	272	882	4526	14282	38930	83941	234611	623926	9481190

Selected Financial Ratios (Times to 1)

Current Ratio 30	1.2	•	0.5	1.5	1.1	1.9	1.7	1.7	1.8	1.8	2.2	2.0	0.8
Quick Ratio 31	0.8	•	0.4	1.3	1.0	1.4	1.4	1.4	1.5	1.4	1.8	1.3	0.5
Net Sales to Working Capital 32	8.5	•	•	8.3	20.7	4.1	2.9	3.2	2.9	2.0	1.8	1.9	•
Coverage Ratio 33	11.7	•	•	•	•	•	•	•	•	•	•	•	40.0
Total Asset Turnover 34	0.5	•	3.3	2.1	1.1	1.6	0.8	0.8	0.8	0.6	0.5	0.4	0.4
Inventory Turnover 35	12.0	•	3.6	11.2	9.3	30.7	20.1	25.2	21.6	22.6	22.5	8.3	10.7
Receivables Turnover 36	4.6	•	14.8	6.8	6.7	10.1	4.8	3.9	3.4	3.1	2.9	4.1	5.1
Total Liabilities to Net Worth 37	0.6	•	•	•	7.6	8.0	2.3	1.4	0.8	0.9	0.5	0.7	0.5
Current Assets to Working Capital 38	6.3	•	•	3.0	11.1	2.1	2.4	2.5	2.2	2.2	1.8	2.0	•
Current Liabilities to Working Capital 39	5.3	•	•	2.0	10.1	1.1	1.4	1.5	1.2	1.2	0.8	1.0	•
Working Capital to Net Sales 40	0.1	•	•	0.1	0.0	0.2	0.4	0.3	0.3	0.5	0.6	0.5	•
Inventory to Working Capital 41	0.1	•	0.4	0.4	0.4	0.0	0.0	0.0	0.0	0.0	0.0	0.1	•
Total Receipts to Cash Flow 42	2.6	31.7	5.5	•	24.2	16.7	16.9	6.3	4.3	3.5	5.6	5.1	1.7
Cost of Goods to Cash Flow 43	0.5	9.4	0.5	•	4.1	4.9	4.3	1.5	0.8	0.8	1.3	1.1	0.2
Cash Flow to Total Debt 44	0.4	0.2	0.2	•	0.0	0.1	0.1	0.2	0.4	0.3	0.2	0.2	0.7

Selected Financial Factors (in Percentages)

Debt Ratio 45	38.5	•	286.2	105.0	88.4	88.9	69.9	58.4	44.8	46.7	32.8	41.8	33.1
Return on Total Assets 46	6.4	•	•	•	•	•	•	•	•	•	•	0.7	12.6
Return on Equity Before Income Taxes 47	9.4	•	32.0	1256.2	•	•	•	•	•	•	•	•	18.3
Return on Equity After Income Taxes 48	4.8	•	32.4	1279.3	•	•	•	•	•	•	•	•	12.0
Profit Margin (Before Income Tax) 49	12.7	•	•	•	•	•	•	•	•	•	•	•	32.9
Profit Margin (After Income Tax) 50	6.5	•	•	•	•	•	•	•	•	•	•	•	21.7

261

Table II
Corporations with Net Income

SOFTWARE PUBLISHERS

MONEY AMOUNTS AND SIZE OF ASSETS IN THOUSANDS OF DOLLARS

Item Description for Accounting Period 7/03 Through 6/04	Total	Zero Assets	Under 500	500 to 1,000	1,000 to 5,000	5,000 to 10,000	10,000 to 25,000	25,000 to 50,000	50,000 to 100,000	100,000 to 250,000	250,000 to 500,000	500,000 to 2,500,000	2,500,000 and over
Number of Enterprises 1	3732	11	2917	307	252	94	61	28	12	18	11	13	8
Revenues ($ in Thousands)													
Net Sales 2	60912277	398787	884398	495326	981589	906234	1242524	1011193	893438	1801032	2514273	7638054	42145430
Interest 3	599287	336	1838	441	1000	980	3722	4748	3889	27258	16398	90686	447990
Rents 4	29827	0	0	0	0	0	602	0	926	111	10294	6941	10953
Royalties 5	2664511	0	2095	0	0	3	12924	1597	29661	72479	139169	941426	1465158
Other Portfolio Income 6	993381	13864	81	4524	8791	43321	14280	2580	16841	3248	29850	212029	643970
Other Receipts 7	8694093	2488	46876	5616	23603	4183	41460	19594	6988	86176	35183	396582	8025346
Total Receipts 8	73893376	415475	935288	505907	1014983	954721	1315512	1039712	951743	1990304	2745167	9285718	52733847
Average Total Receipts 9	19800	37770	321	1648	4028	10157	21566	37133	79312	110572	249561	714286	6592356
Operating Costs/Operating Income (%)													
Cost of Operations 10	17.7	51.0	10.6	45.8	15.9	21.9	23.9	21.9	11.1	26.2	19.9	33.6	13.6
Salaries and Wages 11	31.9	15.5	25.9	20.5	13.2	29.2	31.0	30.7	37.1	30.5	35.1	33.2	32.3
Taxes Paid 12	2.8	4.7	5.1	2.0	1.7	3.0	3.3	3.7	5.0	2.7	3.1	3.1	2.6
Interest Paid 13	0.9	0.1	0.6	0.3	0.5	1.5	0.7	0.7	1.0	0.4	0.2	1.6	0.8
Depreciation 14	3.0	1.4	2.2	0.8	1.3	1.9	3.0	2.5	3.8	2.3	3.3	4.0	2.9
Amortization and Depletion 15	1.0	1.0	1.3	•	0.1	0.2	0.6	1.1	1.8	1.2	2.5	1.3	0.8
Pensions and Other Deferred Comp. 16	0.3	0.1	1.2	4.9	0.4	0.4	0.8	0.5	0.7	0.7	1.6	0.6	0.1
Employee Benefits 17	2.7	2.3	1.9	0.8	0.6	1.8	2.5	1.9	2.2	2.1	3.8	2.9	2.8
Advertising 18	6.1	0.6	3.2	0.9	1.4	1.0	1.7	1.5	1.4	1.9	2.5	5.6	7.3
Other Expenses 19	29.2	17.9	23.8	17.4	40.9	16.3	22.5	20.4	24.4	26.1	21.1	27.3	31.0
Officers' Compensation 20	1.7	1.1	15.8	3.1	5.2	9.7	4.1	3.7	3.0	1.3	1.7	1.4	1.1
Operating Margin 21	2.8	4.2	8.3	3.5	18.7	13.0	5.8	11.4	8.6	4.6	5.1	•	4.7
Operating Margin Before Officers' Comp. 22	4.5	5.3	24.2	6.6	23.9	22.8	9.9	15.1	11.6	6.0	6.8	•	5.7

Selected Average Balance Sheet ($ in Thousands)

Net Receivables 23	3447	0	14	296	309	1161	3947	8528	15071	34987	81826	109510	1116427
Inventories 24	283	0	10	90	103	147	127	193	186	374	3182	29624	55734
Net Property, Plant and Equipment 25	1779	0	11	17	134	264	1277	2947	6302	6664	33573	85713	587790
Total Assets 26	37197	0	86	639	2167	8235	15626	34821	77324	162341	343888	1085654	14172033
Notes and Loans Payable 27	1686	0	161	117	242	236	1681	6482	6682	1671	1197	97143	503920
All Other Liabilities 28	11364	0	25	288	793	7549	8110	15518	25888	83107	107150	302421	4186924
Net Worth 29	24147	0	-100	234	1132	451	5835	12821	44754	77563	235541	686090	9481190

Selected Financial Ratios (Times to 1)

Current Ratio 30	1.0	•	1.0	1.6	2.1	1.7	1.5	1.5	1.8	2.1	2.1	2.2	0.8
Quick Ratio 31	0.7	•	0.8	1.2	1.8	0.9	1.3	1.3	1.5	1.6	1.8	1.3	0.5
Net Sales to Working Capital 32	80.2	•	•	9.8	5.1	3.2	5.8	5.1	3.5	•	2.1	2.0	•
Coverage Ratio 33	30.8	68.9	25.9	23.5	47.6	13.1	17.6	20.3	16.5	36.0	80.0	6.5	40.0
Total Asset Turnover 34	0.4	•	3.5	2.5	1.8	1.2	1.3	1.0	1.0	0.6	0.7	0.5	0.4
Inventory Turnover 35	10.2	•	3.2	8.2	6.0	14.3	38.5	40.9	44.4	70.0	14.3	6.7	12.9
Receivables Turnover 36	5.0	•	19.6	10.9	9.9	6.4	6.1	5.3	3.3	3.0	2.5	4.6	9.4
Total Liabilities to Net Worth 37	0.5	•	•	1.7	0.9	17.3	1.7	1.7	0.7	1.1	0.5	0.6	0.5
Current Assets to Working Capital 38	53.0	•	•	2.8	1.9	2.4	3.1	2.9	2.3	1.9	1.9	1.9	•
Current Liabilities to Working Capital 39	52.0	•	•	1.8	0.9	1.4	2.1	1.9	1.3	0.9	0.9	0.9	•
Working Capital to Net Sales 40	0.0	•	•	0.1	0.2	0.3	0.2	0.2	0.3	0.6	0.5	0.5	•
Inventory to Working Capital 41	1.2	•	•	0.5	0.2	0.0	0.0	0.0	0.0	0.0	0.0	0.1	•
Total Receipts to Cash Flow 42	2.0	4.9	3.1	5.1	1.7	3.7	3.3	3.1	3.0	2.7	3.2	3.5	1.7
Cost of Goods to Cash Flow 43	0.4	2.5	0.3	2.3	0.3	0.8	0.8	0.7	0.3	0.7	0.6	1.2	0.2
Cash Flow to Total Debt 44	0.6	0.5	•	0.8	2.3	0.3	0.6	0.5	0.8	0.4	0.7	0.4	0.7

Selected Financial Factors (in Percentages)

Debt Ratio 45	35.1	•	216.4	63.4	47.8	94.5	62.7	63.2	42.1	52.2	31.5	36.8	33.1
Return on Total Assets 46	12.1	•	51.7	14.8	40.6	23.3	16.2	15.5	15.9	9.6	9.8	5.8	12.6
Return on Equity Before Income Taxes 47	18.0	•	•	38.8	76.1	393.5	41.0	40.1	25.8	19.6	14.1	7.8	18.3
Return on Equity After Income Taxes 48	12.3	•	•	32.9	72.2	370.7	37.1	35.3	20.9	16.7	11.4	5.9	12.0
Profit Margin (Before Income Tax) 49	26.6	8.4	14.1	5.6	22.1	18.4	11.7	14.3	15.5	15.2	14.5	9.1	32.9
Profit Margin (After Income Tax) 50	18.2	6.9	13.8	4.8	21.0	17.3	10.6	12.5	12.6	12.9	11.8	6.9	21.7

262

Table I

Corporations with and without Net Income

MOTION PICTURE AND VIDEO INDUSTRIES (EXCEPT VIDEO RENTAL)

MONEY AMOUNTS AND SIZE OF ASSETS IN THOUSANDS OF DOLLARS

Item Description for Accounting Period 7/03 Through 6/04	Total	Zero Assets	Under 500	500 to 1,000	1,000 to 5,000	5,000 to 10,000	10,000 to 25,000	25,000 to 50,000	50,000 to 100,000	100,000 to 250,000	250,000 to 500,000	500,000 to 2,500,000	2,500,000 and over
Number of Enterprises 1	23499	3178	18586	672	762	120	87	42	18	11	6	11	5
Revenues ($ in Thousands)													
Net Sales 2	63702445	283429	6330140	1506484	2160144	1408205	1062205	1511871	952621	803468	1289381	6977168	39417328
Interest 3	7358928	466	3711	597	23881	3097	4624	1858	2737	8641	19549	148197	7141569
Rents 4	276856	0	0	0	0	532	3358	982	1416	5593	1051	8785	255139
Royalties 5	1169069	45	46170	5271	0	0	629	7	259	0	3228	41961	1071499
Other Portfolio Income 6	300977	3784	11999	0	11673	244	1875	666	210	14806	4085	25916	225721
Other Receipts 7	1406996	124984	106026	11064	24657	23311	100032	29937	9403	7174	65598	154525	750283
Total Receipts 8	74215271	412708	6498046	1523416	2220355	1435389	1172723	1545321	966646	839682	1382892	7356552	48861539
Average Total Receipts 9	3158	130	350	2267	2914	11962	13480	36793	53703	76335	230482	668777	9772308
Operating Costs/Operating Income (%)													
Cost of Operations 10	36.6	27.1	48.8	15.0	52.2	39.0	29.7	44.2	26.0	44.4	34.6	28.8	36.1
Salaries and Wages 11	10.9	14.2	3.8	20.9	10.4	12.4	15.7	9.3	6.7	8.5	14.0	12.4	11.3
Taxes Paid 12	2.2	1.6	1.5	2.4	2.3	1.5	4.5	2.5	2.0	1.7	1.8	3.9	2.0
Interest Paid 13	14.0	0.7	0.3	0.7	1.4	0.7	1.6	2.5	3.1	3.7	6.1	5.7	20.9
Depreciation 14	7.0	11.8	1.1	6.9	4.8	6.7	11.4	4.9	7.4	1.8	5.2	7.1	8.2
Amortization and Depletion 15	6.9	0.8	0.2	0.2	0.9	0.5	4.1	2.5	12.1	30.7	10.2	2.2	9.1
Pensions and Other Deferred Comp. 16	0.8	0.0	1.5	1.9	0.6	0.1	0.2	0.2	0.0	0.1	0.0	0.2	0.9
Employee Benefits 17	1.0	1.7	0.6	1.3	1.0	1.3	1.1	1.5	0.4	0.5	1.1	1.1	0.9
Advertising 18	3.5	5.4	0.2	1.7	0.7	0.4	1.0	0.6	1.1	0.4	0.7	1.8	5.0
Other Expenses 19	23.9	63.5	21.8	36.5	20.9	24.9	28.2	21.3	30.1	27.4	22.4	34.7	21.5
Officers' Compensation 20	3.1	1.5	16.6	10.0	6.0	10.0	5.8	6.6	1.6	3.0	9.0	0.9	0.2
Operating Margin 21	•	•	3.5	2.4	•	2.4	•	3.9	9.3	•	•	1.2	•
Operating Margin Before Officers' Comp. 22	•	•	20.1	12.4	4.8	12.5	2.4	10.5	10.9	•	3.9	•	2.1

Selected Average Balance Sheet ($ in Thousands)

Line Item													
Net Receivables 23	642	0	8	43	196	1591	1379	4288	7611	17913	20490	46584	2660262
Inventories 24	322	0	4	90	158	316	727	1339	1211	21717	1550	31604	1307987
Net Property, Plant and Equipment 25	700	0	10	414	460	2680	3701	8709	18745	15659	61013	427534	1812063
Total Assets 26	16263	56	876	1876	7294	15075	34809	70435	161715	329609	1069318		71736581
Notes and Loans Payable 27	4951	40	502	1249	4524	5196	14916	22842	34634	109811	398027		21370015
All Other Liabilities 28	2106	26	73	451	3324	3060	12086	16196	75789	105662	191504		8717652
Net Worth 29	9206	-10	301	176	-554	6819	7807	31397	51291	114136	479787		41648914

Selected Financial Ratios (Times to 1)

Line Item													
Current Ratio 30	1.7	•	1.7	2.1	1.1	0.6	1.3	1.1	1.3	0.9	1.4	1.1	1.9
Quick Ratio 31	0.8	•	1.4	1.6	0.7	0.4	0.9	0.8	0.9	0.4	0.9	0.5	0.8
Net Sales to Working Capital 32	2.7	•	22.1	11.9	38.5	•	10.8	53.1	11.8	•	10.9	18.3	1.8
Coverage Ratio 33	1.5	27.8	22.8	5.7	2.1	7.4	5.3	3.4	4.5	•	1.4	2.1	1.4
Total Asset Turnover 34	0.2	•	6.1	2.6	1.5	1.6	0.8	1.0	0.8	0.5	0.7	0.6	0.1
Inventory Turnover 35	3.1	•	42.0	3.7	9.3	14.5	5.0	11.9	11.4	1.5	48.0	5.8	2.2
Receivables Turnover 36	4.6	•	59.8	38.7	8.6	8.0	7.5	7.8	6.1	3.1	9.0	10.6	3.3
Total Liabilities to Net Worth 37	0.8	•	1.9	9.7	•	1.2	3.5	1.2	2.2	1.9	8.1	1.2	0.7
Current Assets to Working Capital 38	2.4	•	1.9	8.5	•	4.1	20.1	4.6	•	3.3	8.1		2.1
Current Liabilities to Working Capital 39	1.4	•	0.9	11.9	7.5	3.1	19.1	3.6	•	2.3	7.1		1.1
Working Capital to Net Sales 40	0.4	•	0.0	0.0	0.0	0.1	0.1	0.0	0.1	0.1	0.1	0.1	0.6
Inventory to Working Capital 41	0.3	•	0.2	0.1	1.6	0.5	1.8	0.3	•	0.1	0.1	0.1	0.3
Total Receipts to Cash Flow 42	4.0	1.5	4.1	2.9	6.3	3.7	4.6	3.2	4.6	4.7	3.9		3.9
Cost of Goods to Cash Flow 43	1.5	0.4	2.0	0.4	3.3	1.5	2.0	0.8	1.6	1.6	1.1		1.4
Cash Flow to Total Debt 44	0.1	•	1.3	1.4	0.3	0.4	0.3	0.4	0.1	0.2	0.1	0.3	0.1

Selected Financial Factors (in Percentages)

Line Item													
Debt Ratio 45	43.4	118.3	65.7	90.6	107.6	54.8	77.6	55.4	68.3	65.4	55.1		41.9
Return on Total Assets 46	3.5	39.4	10.8	4.5	8.1	7.0	8.9	10.4	5.4	7.2			3.2
Return on Equity Before Income Taxes 47	2.0	•	26.0	25.3	•	12.6	28.3	18.1	4.2	8.6			1.5
Return on Equity After Income Taxes 48	1.5	•	25.0	23.8	•	11.8	27.5	17.1	2.8	6.1			1.1
Profit Margin (Before Income Tax) 49	6.8	17.5	3.5	1.6	4.4	7.0	6.1	10.7	2.2	6.5			7.9
Profit Margin (After Income Tax) 50	5.2	17.5	3.4	1.5	4.4	6.6	6.0	10.2	1.5	4.6			5.7

263

Table II
Corporations with Net Income

MOTION PICTURE AND VIDEO INDUSTRIES (EXCEPT VIDEO RENTAL)

MONEY AMOUNTS AND SIZE OF ASSETS IN THOUSANDS OF DOLLARS

Item Description for Accounting Period 7/03 Through 6/04	Total	Zero Assets	Under 500	500 to 1,000	1,000 to 5,000	5,000 to 10,000	10,000 to 25,000	25,000 to 50,000	50,000 to 100,000	100,000 to 250,000	250,000 to 500,000	500,000 to 2,500,000	2,500,000 and over
Number of Enterprises **1**	12968	1537	10580	223	467	•	43	18	•	4	3	•	•
Revenues ($ in Thousands)													
Net Sales **2**	56723952	101531	4684722	657939	1484080	•	805109	974219	•	133835	765699	•	•
Interest **3**	7288351	25	1527	442	1178	•	1634	720	•	6797	108	•	•
Rents **4**	273816	0	0	0	0	•	3145	0	•	4595	1051	•	•
Royalties **5**	319290	0	46170	5271	0	•	24	0	•	0	0	•	•
Other Portfolio Income **6**	294769	3784	11906	0	11412	•	1672	92	•	12058	4085	•	•
Other Receipts **7**	1280138	122027	40210	4518	26314	•	95826	19106	•	12291	63879	•	•
Total Receipts **8**	66180316	227367	4784535	668170	1522984	•	907410	994137	•	169576	834822	•	•
Average Total Receipts **9**	5103	148	452	2996	3261	•	21103	55230	•	42394	278274	•	•
Operating Costs/Operating Income (%)													
Cost of Operations **10**	36.0	44.9	47.4	10.6	43.4	•	30.8	37.2	•	19.6	36.5	•	•
Salaries and Wages **11**	10.7	3.0	3.8	5.5	12.7	•	14.8	7.3	•	7.4	10.5	•	•
Taxes Paid **12**	2.2	1.8	1.4	1.5	2.2	•	5.1	2.4	•	2.0	2.4	•	•
Interest Paid **13**	15.2	0.3	0.2	0.1	0.7	•	1.2	1.0	•	2.7	1.7	•	•
Depreciation **14**	6.0	1.8	0.7	0.1	2.9	•	10.3	5.3	•	1.0	6.3	•	•
Amortization and Depletion **15**	6.8	0.0	0.1	0.5	1.1	•	0.7	0.2	•	23.3	1.2	•	•
Pensions and Other Deferred Comp. **16**	0.8	•	1.3	1.9	0.7	•	0.2	0.2	•	•	0.1	•	•
Employee Benefits **17**	0.9	0.7	0.2	0.0	1.0	•	1.0	1.8	•	0.4	0.3	•	•
Advertising **18**	2.9	11.3	0.3	0.6	0.9	•	0.8	0.7	•	0.8	1.0	•	•
Other Expenses **19**	23.1	55.1	17.4	48.9	21.6	•	24.9	18.2	•	59.9	16.8	•	•
Officers' Compensation **20**	2.6	•	16.6	14.8	6.8	•	6.0	8.8	•	2.0	13.9	•	•
Operating Margin **21**	•	•	10.4	15.6	6.0	•	4.1	16.9	•	•	9.3	•	•
Operating Margin Before Officers' Comp. **22**	•	•	27.1	30.3	12.8	•	10.1	25.7	•	•	23.3	•	•

Selected Average Balance Sheet ($ in Thousands)

Net Receivables 23	1064	0	10	19	205	1700	6076	15824	6376
Inventories 24	401	0	3	76	27	497	637	3006	1583
Net Property, Plant and Equipment 25	1030	0	6	35	389	4472	10717	8182	103012
Total Assets 26	28707	0	61	960	1671	14394	33885	127886	338054
Notes and Loans Payable 27	8644	0	27	204	1017	3573	5658	13968	23466
All Other Liabilities 28	3577	0	11	89	339	3400	13107	74952	92801
Net Worth 29	16486	0	23	668	315	7421	15120	38966	221786

Selected Financial Ratios (Times to 1)

Current Ratio 30	1.8	•	2.5	2.6	1.6	1.6	1.2	0.7	0.6
Quick Ratio 31	0.8	•	2.1	1.7	1.2	1.1	1.1	0.3	0.4
Net Sales to Working Capital 32	2.5	•	16.4	6.4	14.7	8.0	16.5	3.7	•
Coverage Ratio 33	1.6	363.9	69.6	215.9	13.7	14.8	19.4	3.7	11.4
Total Asset Turnover 34	0.2	•	7.3	3.1	1.9	1.3	1.6	0.3	0.8
Inventory Turnover 35	3.9	•	69.0	4.1	50.2	11.6	31.6	2.2	58.9
Receivables Turnover 36	5.1	•	76.0	304.0	31.1	9.0	10.7	2.5	80.1
Total Liabilities to Net Worth 37	0.7	•	1.6	0.4	4.3	0.9	1.2	2.3	0.5
Current Assets to Working Capital 38	2.2	•	1.7	1.6	2.7	2.7	5.1	•	•
Current Liabilities to Working Capital 39	1.2	•	0.7	0.6	1.7	1.7	4.1	•	•
Working Capital to Net Sales 40	0.4	•	0.1	0.2	0.1	0.1	0.1	•	•
Inventory to Working Capital 41	0.3	•	0.2	0.2	0.1	0.2	0.2	•	•
Total Receipts to Cash Flow 42	3.7	0.6	3.8	1.5	4.4	3.0	3.1	1.8	3.0
Cost of Goods to Cash Flow 43	1.3	0.3	1.8	0.2	1.9	0.9	1.1	0.4	1.1
Cash Flow to Total Debt 44	0.1	•	3.1	6.6	0.5	0.9	0.9	0.2	0.7

Selected Financial Factors (in Percentages)

Debt Ratio 45	42.6	•	62.1	30.5	81.1	48.4	55.4	69.5	34.4
Return on Total Assets 46	3.7	•	93.3	52.8	17.7	23.4	31.9	2.7	14.7
Return on Equity Before Income Taxes 47	2.5	•	242.9	75.6	87.2	42.4	67.8	6.4	20.5
Return on Equity After Income Taxes 48	2.0	•	241.0	74.3	85.9	41.0	66.8	6.1	19.0
Profit Margin (Before Income Tax) 49	9.3	105.1	12.6	17.1	8.7	16.8	18.9	7.5	17.8
Profit Margin (After Income Tax) 50	7.5	105.1	12.5	16.8	8.5	16.2	18.7	7.2	16.5

Table I

Corporations with and without Net Income

SOUND RECORDING INDUSTRIES

MONEY AMOUNTS AND SIZE OF ASSETS IN THOUSANDS OF DOLLARS

Item Description for Accounting Period 7/03 Through 6/04	Total	Zero Assets	Under 500	500 to 1,000	1,000 to 5,000	5,000 to 10,000	10,000 to 25,000	25,000 to 50,000	50,000 to 100,000	100,000 to 250,000	250,000 to 500,000	500,000 to 2,500,000	2,500,000 and over
Number of Enterprises 1	10574	2985	7030	237	233	55	21	6	5	•	•	3	•
Revenues ($ in Thousands)													
Net Sales 2	7561592	33676	1358760	330693	33715	247888	271975	120639	160485	•	•	5003761	•
Interest 3	158171	10	56	28	207	1275	1835	250	6212	•	•	148298	•
Rents 4	6646	14	0	563	363	0	200	300	27	•	•	5179	•
Royalties 5	1002369	2510	0	0	27253	13	15551	25262	0	•	•	931780	•
Other Portfolio Income 6	167811	158	0	4	4455	48	3678	2644	1382	•	•	155441	•
Other Receipts 7	291044	2078	13904	14475	15801	904	8387	3147	-519	•	•	232869	•
Total Receipts 8	9187633	38446	1372720	345763	81794	250128	301626	152242	167587	•	•	6477328	•
Average Total Receipts 9	869	13	195	1459	351	4548	14363	25374	33517	•	•	2159109	•
Operating Costs/Operating Income (%)													
Cost of Operations 10	52.5	5.3	9.5	57.8	44.1	33.5	47.8	47.4	68.7	•	•	65.0	•
Salaries and Wages 11	15.3	6.0	10.0	5.9	11.8	4.1	14.7	11.6	7.4	•	•	18.3	•
Taxes Paid 12	3.2	0.9	1.9	1.5	5.0	0.7	2.1	1.5	0.7	•	•	4.0	•
Interest Paid 13	5.0	5.8	1.1	1.0	2.7	0.7	2.2	1.3	3.3	•	•	6.9	•
Depreciation 14	4.9	58.9	3.5	0.2	2.5	5.3	4.5	1.5	0.6	•	•	5.4	•
Amortization and Depletion 15	2.3	0.4	0.1	•	52.5	0.5	1.3	0.8	3.0	•	•	2.9	•
Pensions and Other Deferred Comp. 16	1.1	0.1	3.2	0.0	0.2	0.0	0.5	0.7	0.2	•	•	0.7	•
Employee Benefits 17	1.9	0.3	1.2	0.6	0.8	0.2	1.0	1.1	0.4	•	•	2.4	•
Advertising 18	4.6	3.1	0.7	4.3	3.3	1.0	3.1	1.2	2.3	•	•	6.1	•
Other Expenses 19	33.5	81.8	55.6	13.6	110.9	42.3	31.5	51.8	5.6	•	•	28.2	•
Officers' Compensation 20	3.1	1.5	10.4	9.6	22.6	0.6	3.7	10.7	1.9	•	•	0.6	•
Operating Margin 21	•	•	2.7	5.5	•	11.0	•	•	5.9	•	•	•	•
Operating Margin Before Officers' Comp. 22	•	•	13.2	15.1	•	11.5	•	•	7.8	•	•	•	•

Selected Average Balance Sheet ($ in Thousands)

Net Receivables 23	308	0	2	229	240	422	2859	2188	4771	•	1003229
Inventories 24	65	0	8	20	119	38	1531	2945	4087	•	174182
Net Property, Plant and Equipment 25	182	0	17	233	38	1809	2512	3598	1958	•	520215
Total Assets 26	3662	0	51	1929	636	6232	14986	33096	65241	•	12193994
Notes and Loans Payable 27	447	0	113	738	245	1760	10682	12032	18269	•	1073598
All Other Liabilities 28	1622	0	11	242	399	1378	6658	14789	19399	•	5506756
Net Worth 29	1593	0	-72	948	-9	3094	-2354	6275	27572	•	5613639

Selected Financial Ratios (Times to 1)

Current Ratio 30	0.8	•	2.3	1.1	1.5	2.7	1.1	1.0	1.1	•	0.7
Quick Ratio 31	0.4	•	1.5	0.5	1.1	0.9	0.6	0.6	0.8	•	0.4
Net Sales to Working Capital 32	•	•	10.2	3.6	7.1	2.0	13.7	33.8	15.9	•	•
Coverage Ratio 33	•	•	4.4	•	11.0	18.6	0.3	•	4.1	•	•
Total Asset Turnover 34	0.2	•	3.8	0.1	2.2	0.7	0.9	0.6	0.5	•	0.1
Inventory Turnover 35	5.7	•	2.2	3.2	6.8	39.5	4.0	3.2	5.4	•	6.2
Receivables Turnover 36	0.2	•	39.4	0.6	8.8	12.6	5.2	4.1	13.5	•	0.2
Total Liabilities to Net Worth 37	1.3	•	•	1.0	•	1.0	•	4.3	1.4	•	1.2
Current Assets to Working Capital 38	•	•	1.7	13.4	3.0	1.6	8.0	27.0	7.7	•	•
Current Liabilities to Working Capital 39	•	•	0.7	12.4	2.0	0.6	7.0	26.0	6.7	•	•
Working Capital to Net Sales 40	•	•	0.1	0.3	0.1	0.5	0.1	0.0	0.1	•	•
Inventory to Working Capital 41	•	•	0.4	0.3	0.8	0.0	1.7	3.0	2.0	•	•
Total Receipts to Cash Flow 42	4.5	4.8	2.1	1.2	4.5	1.9	4.0	2.3	7.1	•	7.7
Cost of Goods to Cash Flow 43	2.4	0.3	0.2	0.5	2.6	0.6	1.9	1.1	4.8	•	5.0
Cash Flow to Total Debt 44	0.1	•	0.8	0.1	0.5	0.7	0.2	0.3	0.1	•	0.0

Selected Financial Factors (in Percentages)

Debt Ratio 45	56.5	•	240.4	50.8	101.4	50.3	115.7	81.0	57.7	•	54.0
Return on Total Assets 46	•	•	18.3	•	24.3	9.1	0.6	•	6.7	•	•
Return on Equity Before Income Taxes 47	•	•	•	•	•	17.3	8.2	•	12.0	•	•
Return on Equity After Income Taxes 48	•	•	•	•	•	16.5	9.4	•	11.0	•	•
Profit Margin (Before Income Tax) 49	•	•	3.8	•	10.1	11.9	•	•	10.3	•	•
Profit Margin (After Income Tax) 50	•	•	3.7	•	10.1	11.3	•	•	9.5	•	•

Table II

Corporations with Net Income

SOUND RECORDING INDUSTRIES

MONEY AMOUNTS AND SIZE OF ASSETS IN THOUSANDS OF DOLLARS

Item Description for Accounting Period 7/03 Through 6/04	Total	Zero Assets	Under 500	500 to 1,000	1,000 to 5,000	5,000 to 10,000	10,000 to 25,000	25,000 to 50,000	50,000 to 100,000	100,000 to 250,000	250,000 to 500,000	500,000 to 2,500,000	2,500,000 and over
Number of Enterprises 1	4166	423	3341	183	149	•	14	•	•	•	•	•	•
Revenues ($ in Thousands)													
Net Sales 2	2992025	6481	1148495	295405	16085	•	191198	•	•	•	•	•	•
Interest 3	9432	8	56	0	183	•	1076	•	•	•	•	•	•
Rents 4	696	14	0	0	0	•	442	•	•	•	•	•	•
Royalties 5	589425	2510	0	0	17933	•	28943	•	•	•	•	•	•
Other Portfolio Income 6	9724	30	0	4	17	•	5676	•	•	•	•	•	•
Other Receipts 7	59426	111	13070	13455	15355	•	5540	•	•	•	•	•	•
Total Receipts 8	3660728	9154	1161621	308864	49573	•	232875	•	•	•	•	•	•
Average Total Receipts 9	879	22	348	1688	333	•	16634	•	•	•	•	•	•
Operating Costs/Operating Income (%)													
Cost of Operations 10	29.0	0.7	5.2	57.6	7.3	•	45.1	•	•	•	•	•	•
Salaries and Wages 11	11.6	17.1	10.3	5.1	13.2	•	17.2	•	•	•	•	•	•
Taxes Paid 12	1.7	2.1	1.9	1.4	7.2	•	2.1	•	•	•	•	•	•
Interest Paid 13	1.5	0.4	1.0	0.6	0.0	•	0.8	•	•	•	•	•	•
Depreciation 14	5.9	4.4	3.6	0.1	0.6	•	2.6	•	•	•	•	•	•
Amortization and Depletion 15	1.2	0.6	0.0	•	•	•	0.9	•	•	•	•	•	•
Pensions and Other Deferred Comp. 16	1.5	•	3.8	0.0	0.1	•	0.6	•	•	•	•	•	•
Employee Benefits 17	0.9	0.7	0.9	0.7	1.7	•	1.3	•	•	•	•	•	•
Advertising 18	2.5	•	0.2	4.5	1.9	•	2.4	•	•	•	•	•	•
Other Expenses 19	49.2	89.5	49.3	12.6	162.1	•	35.4	•	•	•	•	•	•
Officers' Compensation 20	6.5	2.4	10.9	9.7	39.1	•	5.4	•	•	•	•	•	•
Operating Margin 21	•	•	12.8	7.7	•	•	•	•	•	•	•	•	•
Operating Margin Before Officers' Comp. 22	•	•	23.8	17.3	•	•	•	•	•	•	•	•	•

Selected Average Balance Sheet ($ in Thousands)

Net Receivables 23	91	0	1	215	344	•	•	2285
Inventories 24	18	0	0	146	3	•	•	1418
Net Property, Plant and Equipment 25	75	0	26	5	1	•	•	2358
Total Assets 26	723	0	68	613	1124	•	•	16836
Notes and Loans Payable 27	255	0	35	0	723	•	•	4795
All Other Liabilities 28	248	0	14	513	166	•	•	5021
Net Worth 29	220	0	19	99	236	•	•	7020

Selected Financial Ratios (Times to 1)

Current Ratio 30	1.2	•	4.3	1.2	2.2	•	•	1.3
Quick Ratio 31	0.7	•	3.9	0.9	2.2	•	•	0.7
Net Sales to Working Capital 32	18.6	•	11.3	17.8	0.5	•	•	7.6
Coverage Ratio 33	8.3	60.9	15.0	21.2	3003.2	•	•	12.2
Total Asset Turnover 34	1.0	•	5.0	2.6	0.1	•	•	0.8
Inventory Turnover 35	11.7	•	•	6.4	2.4	•	•	4.3
Receivables Turnover 36	11.1	•	593.5	15.0	0.6	•	•	6.9
Total Liabilities to Net Worth 37	2.3	•	2.6	5.2	3.8	•	•	1.4
Current Assets to Working Capital 38	7.4	•	1.3	6.7	1.8	•	•	4.8
Current Liabilities to Working Capital 39	6.4	•	0.3	5.7	0.8	•	•	3.8
Working Capital to Net Sales 40	0.1	•	0.1	0.1	1.9	•	•	0.1
Inventory to Working Capital 41	0.5	•	•	1.6	0.0	•	•	0.9
Total Receipts to Cash Flow 42	1.8	0.9	1.8	4.2	0.4	•	•	2.7
Cost of Goods to Cash Flow 43	0.5	0.0	0.1	2.4	0.0	•	•	1.2
Cash Flow to Total Debt 44	0.8	•	3.8	0.7	0.3	•	•	0.5

Selected Financial Factors (in Percentages)

Debt Ratio 45	69.6	•	72.1	83.8	79.0	•	•	58.3
Return on Total Assets 46	12.5	•	75.3	33.8	7.2	•	•	8.2
Return on Equity Before Income Taxes 47	36.1	•	251.8	198.8	34.2	•	•	18.1
Return on Equity After Income Taxes 48	35.2	•	249.4	198.8	29.9	•	•	16.7
Profit Margin (Before Income Tax) 49	11.0	23.1	14.0	12.2	74.7	•	•	9.3
Profit Margin (After Income Tax) 50	10.8	21.5	13.9	12.2	65.2	•	•	8.6

Table I

Corporations with and without Net Income

BROADCASTING (EXCEPT INTERNET)

MONEY AMOUNTS AND SIZE OF ASSETS IN THOUSANDS OF DOLLARS

Item Description for Accounting Period 7/03 Through 6/04		Total	Zero Assets	Under 500	500 to 1,000	1,000 to 5,000	5,000 to 10,000	10,000 to 25,000	25,000 to 50,000	50,000 to 100,000	100,000 to 250,000	250,000 to 500,000	500,000 to 2,500,000	2,500,000 and over
Number of Enterprises	1	7565	1270	4685	547	658	132	118	38	28	37	10	29	11
Revenues ($ in Thousands)														
Net Sales	2	68449298	223560	801793	690294	1715057	764325	1330225	460992	778528	2839763	1653024	7742003	49491735
Interest	3	1894854	629	1985	2129	1805	2334	3158	5253	3111	93152	29215	414661	1337424
Rents	4	484991	9	540	433	2204	2086	1677	1298	2890	20308	13717	14438	425391
Royalties	5	2344617	0	0	77213	0	0	21	2	0	23	0	189340	2078017
Other Portfolio Income	6	1594327	98978	27610	0	7265	114078	48073	185087	23899	174769	74241	144611	695712
Other Receipts	7	2191180	-5031	64516	1848	48813	41858	43623	16791	23002	47704	37422	517470	1353165
Total Receipts	8	77001267	318145	896444	771917	1775144	924681	1426777	669423	831430	3175719	1807619	9022523	55381444
Average Total Receipts	9	10179	251	191	1411	2698	7005	12091	17616	29694	85830	180762	311121	5034677
Operating Costs/Operating Income (%)														
Cost of Operations	10	27.1	9.8	21.5	57.7	21.0	38.5	25.3	14.8	7.1	43.1	11.7	14.3	28.9
Salaries and Wages	11	16.1	18.7	24.4	16.6	30.9	12.3	20.4	27.5	29.2	11.7	20.7	22.5	14.1
Taxes Paid	12	3.1	16.4	4.2	2.0	4.9	2.4	3.6	5.2	3.8	2.1	3.2	4.8	2.7
Interest Paid	13	7.9	64.6	2.7	0.4	3.5	3.0	3.7	20.3	6.0	9.5	11.8	17.6	6.3
Depreciation	14	11.7	4.8	3.9	2.1	5.6	6.0	6.5	10.0	9.5	8.1	16.1	9.7	12.8
Amortization and Depletion	15	5.2	20.4	0.6	1.2	2.1	3.7	4.1	6.7	8.6	5.8	7.1	17.8	3.3
Pensions and Other Deferred Comp.	16	0.2	0.0	0.5	0.0	0.1	0.1	0.5	0.3	0.6	0.3	0.4	0.4	0.2
Employee Benefits	17	2.4	1.6	2.7	1.3	1.2	0.6	1.5	1.8	2.2	1.1	2.5	1.6	2.7
Advertising	18	2.0	0.7	1.9	0.3	1.1	4.0	2.3	1.9	2.5	1.7	3.3	2.9	1.9
Other Expenses	19	41.5	74.7	36.6	32.5	28.0	37.9	31.0	39.9	37.4	28.5	27.1	68.5	39.4
Officers' Compensation	20	1.1	6.0	6.7	3.6	4.3	6.3	3.9	4.0	3.4	1.5	1.6	1.3	0.6
Operating Margin	21	•	•	•	•	•	•	•	•	•	•	•	•	•
Operating Margin Before Officers' Comp.	22	•	1.0	•	•	1.6	•	1.1	•	•	•	•	•	•

Selected Average Balance Sheet ($ in Thousands)

Net Receivables 23	2285	0	17	143	436	858	2222	2537	5888	16267	41034	47126	1256563
Inventories 24	262	0	0	3	36	25	222	557	419	3044	1065	14236	123876
Net Property, Plant and Equipment 25	4603	0	33	132	532	1978	3226	5143	12946	25120	89203	112514	2542036
Total Assets 26	30807	0	90	576	1969	6702	15173	36445	68820	166638	361742	1372757	15949465
Notes and Loans Payable 27	9145	0	119	60	2082	5637	6247	9908	28548	61500	199019	578814	3955485
All Other Liabilities 28	8809	0	17	1012	459	2840	3275	8691	9505	49122	71338	202410	5086082
Net Worth 29	12853	0	-46	-496	-573	-1775	5651	17845	30767	56016	91386	591533	6907898

Selected Financial Ratios (Times to 1)

Current Ratio 30	1.7	•	2.0	0.2	1.5	0.8	1.7	1.7	1.2	1.1	1.5	2.3	1.8
Quick Ratio 31	1.2	•	1.8	0.2	1.2	0.7	1.3	1.3	1.0	0.8	1.3	1.4	1.3
Net Sales to Working Capital 32	4.7	•	10.7	•	10.8	•	4.8	3.0	12.0	40.1	6.3	2.2	4.7
Coverage Ratio 33	0.3	•	3.3	•	1.2	3.1	2.2	1.6	0.4	0.8	1.3	•	0.9
Total Asset Turnover 34	0.3	•	1.9	2.2	1.3	0.9	0.7	0.3	0.4	0.5	0.5	0.2	0.3
Inventory Turnover 35	9.3	•	4005.8	239.2	15.4	90.5	12.9	3.2	4.7	10.9	18.2	2.7	10.5
Receivables Turnover 36	2.6	•	8.6	6.7	6.1	7.6	5.4	4.1	4.2	4.8	3.8	4.9	2.2
Total Liabilities to Net Worth 37	1.4	•	•	•	•	•	1.7	1.0	1.2	2.0	3.0	1.3	1.3
Current Assets to Working Capital 38	2.4	•	2.0	3.1	3.1	•	2.4	2.5	5.5	19.8	2.8	1.8	2.3
Current Liabilities to Working Capital 39	1.4	•	1.0	2.1	2.1	•	1.4	1.5	4.5	18.8	1.8	0.8	1.3
Working Capital to Net Sales 40	0.2	•	0.1	•	0.1	•	0.2	0.3	0.1	0.0	0.2	0.5	0.2
Inventory to Working Capital 41	0.1	•	•	0.2	0.2	•	0.1	0.2	0.1	1.5	0.0	0.0	0.1
Total Receipts to Cash Flow 42	3.2	•	3.0	4.5	4.0	3.2	3.5	7.4	3.8	5.2	3.8	5.1	2.9
Cost of Goods to Cash Flow 43	0.9	•	0.6	2.6	0.8	1.2	0.9	1.1	0.3	2.2	0.4	0.7	0.8
Cash Flow to Total Debt 44	0.2	•	0.4	0.3	0.3	0.2	0.3	0.1	0.2	0.1	0.2	0.1	0.2

Selected Financial Factors (in Percentages)

Debt Ratio 45	58.3	•	150.9	186.1	129.1	126.5	62.8	51.0	55.3	66.4	74.7	56.9	56.7
Return on Total Assets 46	0.7	•	16.6	•	5.7	7.9	6.1	11.0	0.9	3.7	7.1	•	1.6
Return on Equity Before Income Taxes 47	•	•	•	15.1	•	•	8.9	8.6	•	6.9	•	•	•
Return on Equity After Income Taxes 48	•	•	•	17.1	•	•	5.8	6.9	•	0.7	•	•	•
Profit Margin (Before Income Tax) 49	•	•	6.1	0.8	•	6.2	4.5	12.7	•	3.8	•	3.8	•
Profit Margin (After Income Tax) 50	•	•	5.8	0.7	•	4.7	2.9	10.2	•	0.4	•	•	•

Table II
Corporations with Net Income

BROADCASTING (EXCEPT INTERNET)

MONEY AMOUNTS AND SIZE OF ASSETS IN THOUSANDS OF DOLLARS

Item Description for Accounting Period 7/03 Through 6/04	Total	Zero Assets	Under 500	500 to 1,000	1,000 to 5,000	5,000 to 10,000	10,000 to 25,000	25,000 to 50,000	50,000 to 100,000	100,000 to 250,000	250,000 to 500,000	500,000 to 2,500,000	2,500,000 and over
Number of Enterprises **1**	3790	313	2769	163	306	105	67	18	11	17	5	7	8
Revenues ($ in Thousands)													
Net Sales **2**	54288490	80509	476471	407890	1015432	691348	945225	262517	367490	802650	1008186	2412107	45818664
Interest **3**	1323472	53	118	2049	1679	2272	2131	2557	1653	53387	21495	3559	1232519
Rents **4**	467266	9	0	0	1929	2086	1375	1199	509	19768	13489	1955	424947
Royalties **5**	2319757	0	0	77213	0	0	0	2	0	0	164525	0	2078017
Other Portfolio Income **6**	1201039	98969	24405	0	2198	22866	46785	184210	14489	168388	71515	19908	547306
Other Receipts **7**	1448861	4851	69471	270	17877	39132	34726	20433	7009	26070	6558	47667	1174796
Total Receipts **8**	61048885	184391	570465	487422	1039115	757704	1030242	470918	391150	1070263	1121243	2649721	51276249
Average Total Receipts **9**	16108	589	206	2990	3396	7216	15377	26162	35559	62957	224249	378532	6409531
Operating Costs/Operating Income (%)													
Cost of Operations **10**	28.9	22.2	27.4	85.8	14.6	40.0	20.7	17.2	7.1	13.9	8.5	11.9	30.6
Salaries and Wages **11**	14.9	12.6	19.9	0.3	33.6	11.0	21.5	17.8	27.2	13.6	21.0	24.2	13.8
Taxes Paid **12**	2.9	4.5	3.2	0.5	4.5	2.2	3.6	5.2	3.7	3.3	3.2	5.8	2.7
Interest Paid **13**	5.4	3.8	2.1	*	0.6	2.9	3.3	28.7	1.5	12.9	7.6	5.1	5.4
Depreciation **14**	10.1	2.9	3.4	0.1	3.8	5.6	4.9	6.2	6.9	9.5	14.0	4.1	10.9
Amortization and Depletion **15**	3.4	5.0	*	0.0	0.0	3.0	3.1	4.6	2.8	6.7	5.6	10.1	3.1
Pensions and Other Deferred Comp. **16**	0.2	0.0	0.0	0.0	0.2	0.1	0.6	0.5	0.7	0.4	0.5	0.6	0.2
Employee Benefits **17**	2.5	0.7	2.8	0.0	1.5	0.5	1.5	1.5	1.9	0.8	2.7	1.9	2.7
Advertising **18**	2.0	0.2	1.0	0.0	0.7	4.3	2.5	1.8	2.8	2.9	4.6	2.3	2.0
Other Expenses **19**	34.9	39.7	28.5	21.7	24.4	17.5	28.6	35.5	26.9	40.9	24.8	27.2	36.3
Officers' Compensation **20**	1.0	9.1	6.5	2.5	5.2	6.6	3.2	3.7	3.6	2.4	1.9	1.6	0.6
Operating Margin **21**	*	*	5.4	*	10.8	6.3	6.2	*	14.8	*	5.7	5.1	*
Operating Margin Before Officers' Comp. **22**	*	8.3	11.9	*	16.1	12.9	9.4	*	18.4	*	7.6	6.7	*

Selected Average Balance Sheet ($ in Thousands)

Net Receivables 23	3002	22	294	534	998	2887	3050	4930	9640	58301	72034	1217205
Inventories 24	357	0	0	4	19	151	1137	255	5874	1427	262	151601
Net Property, Plant and Equipment 25	5264	11	13	433	2333	3084	3622	9633	22720	92637	66815	2230897
Total Assets 26	43245	68	643	1560	6310	15169	36310	65067	164020	356186	1444516	18174605
Notes and Loans Payable 27	8800	90	88	1340	4495	5357	9887	18457	43666	126347	369834	3438055
All Other Liabilities 28	14300	3	1812	349	2936	2253	9231	10707	31853	80071	229931	6311602
Net Worth 29	20144	-25	-1256	-129	-1121	7558	17191	35903	88501	149768	844751	8424949

Selected Financial Ratios (Times to 1)

Current Ratio 30	1.6	•	13.1	0.2	2.5	1.1	2.3	1.8	1.5	1.7	2.2	1.5
Quick Ratio 31	1.1	•	12.7	0.2	2.0	1.0	1.8	1.2	1.2	0.9	1.8	1.0
Net Sales to Working Capital 32	6.9	•	4.6	•	6.3	25.2	3.8	2.7	7.5	3.3	3.2	9.0
Coverage Ratio 33	2.2	35.1	13.2	•	22.6	6.5	5.5	3.0	15.2	3.0	3.2	1.8
Total Asset Turnover 34	0.3	•	2.5	3.9	2.1	1.0	0.9	0.4	0.5	0.3	0.6	0.3
Inventory Turnover 35	11.6	•	•	•	120.5	138.6	19.4	2.2	9.4	1.1	12.1	11.5
Receivables Turnover 36	2.7	•	10.5	8.6	6.9	8.0	5.7	5.5	5.8	3.3	6.9	2.5
Total Liabilities to Net Worth 37	1.1	•	•	•	•	•	1.0	1.1	0.8	0.9	1.4	1.2
Current Assets to Working Capital 38	2.7	•	1.1	•	1.7	12.1	1.7	2.2	3.1	2.5	1.8	3.2
Current Liabilities to Working Capital 39	1.7	•	0.1	•	0.7	11.1	0.7	1.2	2.1	1.5	0.8	2.2
Working Capital to Net Sales 40	0.1	•	0.2	•	0.2	0.0	0.3	0.4	0.1	0.3	0.2	0.1
Inventory to Working Capital 41	0.2	•	•	•	0.0	0.1	0.0	0.2	0.1	0.4	0.0	0.2
Total Receipts to Cash Flow 42	2.7	0.7	2.2	3.3	2.9	3.5	2.7	3.4	2.4	2.1	2.7	2.8
Cost of Goods to Cash Flow 43	0.8	0.2	0.6	2.9	0.4	1.4	0.6	0.6	0.2	0.3	0.2	0.8
Cash Flow to Total Debt 44	0.2	•	0.9	0.4	0.7	0.3	0.7	0.2	0.5	0.3	0.4	0.2

Selected Financial Factors (in Percentages)

Debt Ratio 45	53.4	•	136.1	295.2	108.3	117.8	50.2	52.7	44.8	46.0	58.0	53.6
Return on Total Assets 46	3.9	•	68.3	33.6	29.3	19.6	17.2	34.3	11.5	11.3	13.8	3.0
Return on Equity Before Income Taxes 47	4.6	•	•	•	•	•	28.3	48.0	19.4	14.1	22.7	2.8
Return on Equity After Income Taxes 48	3.7	•	•	•	•	•	24.2	44.3	16.9	12.2	15.1	2.2
Profit Margin (Before Income Tax) 49	6.4	128.2	25.1	8.6	13.2	15.9	15.2	56.6	20.9	26.4	16.8	4.1
Profit Margin (After Income Tax) 50	5.2	120.9	24.7	7.3	13.0	14.3	13.0	52.2	18.2	22.8	11.2	3.2

Table I

Corporations with and without Net Income

INTERNET PUBLISHING AND BROADCASTING

MONEY AMOUNTS AND SIZE OF ASSETS IN THOUSANDS OF DOLLARS

Item Description for Accounting Period 7/03 Through 6/04	Total	Zero Assets	Under 500	500 to 1,000	1,000 to 5,000	5,000 to 10,000	10,000 to 25,000	25,000 to 50,000	50,000 to 100,000	100,000 to 250,000	250,000 to 500,000	500,000 to 2,500,000	2,500,000 and over
Number of Enterprises **1**	3350	796	2401	36	53	22	19	12	8	4	•	•	•
Revenues ($ in Thousands)													
Net Sales **2**	3673355	17643	481233	85772	466387	276029	196491	299038	323159	1527604	•	•	•
Interest **3**	13429	114	206	53	344	624	591	3875	2774	4848	•	•	•
Rents **4**	7187	0	1387	0	47	0	0	521	393	4840	•	•	•
Royalties **5**	41854	0	0	2	6	32	0	946	23034	17834	•	•	•
Other Portfolio Income **6**	92307	0	0	2	3807	0	28	0	9	88460	•	•	•
Other Receipts **7**	85737	128	23	4084	2067	2471	13591	674	61385	1312	•	•	•
Total Receipts **8**	3913869	17885	482849	89913	472658	279156	210701	305054	410754	1644898	•	•	•
Average Total Receipts **9**	1168	22	201	2498	8918	12689	11090	25421	51344	411224	•	•	•
Operating Costs/Operating Income (%)													
Cost of Operations **10**	27.3	•	29.0	48.0	59.4	42.4	26.0	11.9	49.4	12.0	•	•	•
Salaries and Wages **11**	30.0	31.0	18.0	49.1	18.6	26.1	33.5	42.6	34.9	33.0	•	•	•
Taxes Paid **12**	2.8	0.2	1.6	6.9	1.8	2.5	2.8	3.1	3.2	3.3	•	•	•
Interest Paid **13**	4.5	0.3	1.5	0.3	0.6	1.4	1.8	0.9	2.1	9.1	•	•	•
Depreciation **14**	5.3	1.6	2.5	2.8	1.6	5.8	5.3	7.8	20.4	3.8	•	•	•
Amortization and Depletion **15**	4.5	21.5	•	0.1	1.3	1.1	1.7	1.8	9.7	7.2	•	•	•
Pensions and Other Deferred Comp. **16**	0.5	•	0.2	0.2	0.0	0.4	0.1	0.0	1.0	0.8	•	•	•
Employee Benefits **17**	2.2	0.2	1.7	0.4	1.3	1.9	2.9	2.2	4.3	2.3	•	•	•
Advertising **18**	1.3	3.9	1.2	1.3	0.5	3.4	7.4	1.7	2.2	0.1	•	•	•
Other Expenses **19**	38.4	66.8	31.5	14.9	19.0	27.4	26.2	49.0	125.8	30.5	•	•	•
Officers' Compensation **20**	4.1	2.6	7.1	0.8	4.2	5.8	6.6	5.1	2.2	2.9	•	•	•
Operating Margin **21**	•	•	6.0	•	•	•	•	•	•	•	•	•	•
Operating Margin Before Officers' Comp. **22**	•	•	13.2	•	•	•	•	•	•	•	•	•	•

Selected Average Balance Sheet ($ in Thousands)

Net Receivables 23	152	•	6	334	643	1315	2538	3828	14092	53172
Inventories 24	6	0	0	•	1	198	208	191	0	2375
Net Property, Plant and Equipment 25	107	0	19	111	223	800	1342	2695	2966	50027
Total Assets 26	2393	0	53	843	3695	6248	15723	40246	73158	1539549
Notes and Loans Payable 27	873	0	26	190	1717	1657	2363	3323	5664	649088
All Other Liabilities 28	585	0	9	227	1537	2364	4468	33484	22646	282497
Net Worth 29	935	0	18	425	441	2228	8891	3439	44849	607964

Selected Financial Ratios (Times to 1)

Current Ratio 30	1.4	•	3.2	3.0	1.4	1.7	1.7	0.9	1.9	1.3
Quick Ratio 31	1.0	•	2.5	2.3	1.4	1.4	1.5	0.7	1.8	0.6
Net Sales to Working Capital 32	6.6	•	9.6	4.9	13.9	5.8	2.7	•	1.9	8.0
Coverage Ratio 33	•	•	5.4	•	•	•	•	•	•	1.3
Total Asset Turnover 34	0.5	•	3.7	2.8	2.4	2.0	0.7	0.6	0.6	0.2
Inventory Turnover 35	48.3	•	231.6	•	4327.6	26.9	12.9	15.5	•	19.2
Receivables Turnover 36	•	•	•	•	•	•	•	•	•	•
Total Liabilities to Net Worth 37	1.6	•	1.9	1.0	7.4	1.8	0.8	10.7	0.6	1.5
Current Assets to Working Capital 38	3.6	•	1.5	1.5	3.5	2.5	2.4	•	2.1	4.5
Current Liabilities to Working Capital 39	2.6	•	0.5	0.5	2.5	1.5	1.4	•	1.1	3.5
Working Capital to Net Sales 40	0.2	•	0.1	0.2	0.1	0.2	0.4	•	0.5	0.1
Inventory to Working Capital 41	0.0	•	0.0	•	0.0	0.1	0.1	•	•	0.0
Total Receipts to Cash Flow 42	8.4	3.1	3.1	•	•	10.2	13.9	7.3	5.6	4.3
Cost of Goods to Cash Flow 43	2.3	•	0.9	•	6.1	5.9	1.9	•	•	0.5
Cash Flow to Total Debt 44	0.1	•	1.9	•	0.3	0.2	0.2	0.1	•	0.1

Selected Financial Factors (in Percentages)

Debt Ratio 45	60.9	•	65.5	49.6	88.1	64.3	43.4	91.5	38.7	60.5
Return on Total Assets 46	•	•	29.2	•	•	•	•	•	•	2.9
Return on Equity Before Income Taxes 47	•	•	68.9	•	•	•	•	•	•	1.6
Return on Equity After Income Taxes 48	•	•	67.4	•	•	•	•	•	•	1.4
Profit Margin (Before Income Tax) 49	•	•	6.3	•	•	•	•	•	•	2.6
Profit Margin (After Income Tax) 50	•	•	6.2	•	•	•	•	•	•	2.3

Table II

Corporations with Net Income

INTERNET PUBLISHING AND BROADCASTING

MONEY AMOUNTS AND SIZE OF ASSETS IN THOUSANDS OF DOLLARS

Item Description for Accounting Period 7/03 Through 6/04	Total	Zero Assets	Under 500	500 to 1,000	1,000 to 5,000	5,000 to 10,000	10,000 to 25,000	25,000 to 50,000	50,000 to 100,000	100,000 to 250,000	250,000 to 500,000	500,000 to 2,500,000	2,500,000 and over
Number of Enterprises **1**	1251	395	826	•	13	4	6	3	4	•	•	•	•
Revenues ($ in Thousands)													
Net Sales **2**	2581406	17643	351488	•	330842	96963	98879	146304	1539288	•	•	•	•
Interest **3**	5248	114	206	•	28	23	120	232	4525	•	•	•	•
Rents **4**	6227	0	1387	•	0	0	0	0	4840	•	•	•	•
Royalties **5**	18780	0	0	•	0	0	0	946	17834	•	•	•	•
Other Portfolio Income **6**	88509	0	0	•	46	0	3	0	88460	•	•	•	•
Other Receipts **7**	12709	0	23	•	118	253	11073	38	1204	•	•	•	•
Total Receipts **8**	2712879	17757	353104	•	331034	97239	110075	147520	1656151	•	•	•	•
Average Total Receipts **9**	2169	45	427	•	25464	24310	18346	49173	414038	•	•	•	•
Operating Costs/Operating Income (%)													
Cost of Operations **10**	23.4	•	34.4	•	75.9	26.3	15.6	5.9	11.9	•	•	•	•
Salaries and Wages **11**	25.4	31.0	19.1	•	1.6	12.1	27.9	24.4	32.6	•	•	•	•
Taxes Paid **12**	2.4	0.1	1.4	•	0.3	1.0	0.8	1.7	3.3	•	•	•	•
Interest Paid **13**	5.5	•	0.4	•	0.0	0.2	0.5	0.2	9.0	•	•	•	•
Depreciation **14**	3.3	1.6	3.2	•	0.2	2.7	4.0	5.6	3.8	•	•	•	•
Amortization and Depletion **15**	4.2	0.2	•	•	0.0	0.5	1.4	0.2	6.9	•	•	•	•
Pensions and Other Deferred Comp. **16**	0.5	•	•	•	0.0	0.5	0.0	0.0	0.8	•	•	•	•
Employee Benefits **17**	1.7	0.2	1.0	•	0.1	0.5	2.5	1.3	2.2	•	•	•	•
Advertising **18**	1.1	3.9	1.5	•	0.3	9.1	7.7	0.0	0.3	•	•	•	•
Other Expenses **19**	26.3	21.6	19.7	•	9.1	8.7	32.0	49.0	30.2	•	•	•	•
Officers' Compensation **20**	3.4	2.6	9.1	•	0.3	3.1	2.2	3.5	2.9	•	•	•	•
Operating Margin **21**	2.8	38.8	10.2	•	12.2	35.3	5.3	8.2	•	•	•	•	•
Operating Margin Before Officers' Comp. **22**	6.3	41.3	19.3	•	12.5	38.4	7.6	11.6	•	•	•	•	•

Selected Average Balance Sheet ($ in Thousands)

Net Receivables 23	286	0	4	•	177	2451	3942	6888	74442
Inventories 24	8	0	0	•	0	4	16	13	2375
Net Property, Plant and Equipment 25	193	0	25	•	102	846	861	5189	48816
Total Assets 26	4692	0	96	•	3284	6458	15868	46910	1371499
Notes and Loans Payable 27	2119	0	23	•	1656	739	1704	511	648794
All Other Liabilities 28	1005	0	22	•	361	3028	6392	24184	277912
Net Worth 29	1568	0	51	•	1268	2691	7772	22216	444792

Selected Financial Ratios (Times to 1)

Current Ratio 30	1.5	•	3.1	•	8.3	1.7	1.4	1.4	1.4
Quick Ratio 31	1.0	•	2.2	•	8.3	1.6	1.0	1.3	0.8
Net Sales to Working Capital 32	6.6	•	9.3	•	11.0	11.1	6.0	4.9	5.8
Coverage Ratio 33	2.4	•	25.1	•	1453.1	199.3	33.6	38.7	1.4
Total Asset Turnover 34	0.4	•	4.4	•	7.7	3.8	1.0	1.0	0.3
Inventory Turnover 35	58.9	•	200.5	•	•	1594.9	159.1	220.7	19.2
Receivables Turnover 36	•	•	•	•	•	•	•	•	•
Total Liabilities to Net Worth 37	2.0	•	0.9	•	1.6	1.4	1.0	1.1	2.1
Current Assets to Working Capital 38	3.1	•	1.5	•	1.1	2.4	3.8	3.3	3.4
Current Liabilities to Working Capital 39	2.1	•	0.5	•	0.1	1.4	2.8	2.3	2.4
Working Capital to Net Sales 40	0.2	•	0.1	•	0.1	0.1	0.2	0.2	0.2
Inventory to Working Capital 41	0.0	•	0.0	•	0.0	0.0	0.0	0.0	0.0
Total Receipts to Cash Flow 42	3.7	1.9	4.0	•	4.7	2.4	2.2	1.8	4.2
Cost of Goods to Cash Flow 43	0.9	•	1.4	•	3.6	0.6	0.3	0.1	0.5
Cash Flow to Total Debt 44	0.2	•	2.4	•	2.7	0.9	1.1	•	0.1

Selected Financial Factors (in Percentages)

Debt Ratio 45	66.6	•	46.8	•	61.4	58.3	51.0	52.6	67.6
Return on Total Assets 46	5.9	•	49.3	•	95.3	134.3	17.8	9.6	3.5
Return on Equity Before Income Taxes 47	10.4	•	89.0	•	246.8	320.6	35.3	19.7	3.0
Return on Equity After Income Taxes 48	9.8	•	87.3	•	232.7	297.9	34.6	19.4	2.8
Profit Margin (Before Income Tax) 49	7.9	39.4	10.7	•	12.3	35.6	16.7	9.0	3.5
Profit Margin (After Income Tax) 50	7.4	35.4	10.5	•	11.6	33.1	16.3	8.8	3.2

Table I

Corporations with and without Net Income

TELECOMMUNICATIONS

MONEY AMOUNTS AND SIZE OF ASSETS IN THOUSANDS OF DOLLARS

Item Description for Accounting Period 7/03 Through 6/04	Total	Zero Assets	Under 500	500 to 1,000	1,000 to 5,000	5,000 to 10,000	10,000 to 25,000	25,000 to 50,000	50,000 to 100,000	100,000 to 250,000	250,000 to 500,000	500,000 to 2,500,000	2,500,000 and over
Number of Enterprises **1**	18213	3323	11574	639	1484	259	411	199	115	92	31	44	41
Revenues ($ in Thousands)													
Net Sales **2**	379065407	895185	3532614	678230	7098003	2545890	5572466	4918356	6331730	9854150	6278373	20128178	311232233
Interest **3**	11714762	37345	3217	653	8292	6559	29268	28445	28897	53127	39155	421336	11058468
Rents **4**	8831242	1351	0	4549	2265	3778	7425	6464	15102	27399	11589	36684	8714637
Royalties **5**	1739203	0	0	0	1879	0	213	851	1915	24396	2638	76142	1631169
Other Portfolio Income **6**	16888355	54182	9198	0	27130	9930	66367	41838	31739	116828	9028	508022	16014093
Other Receipts **7**	12083454	83367	68312	2659	359834	35469	291497	143681	249445	127108	166882	644227	9910971
Total Receipts **8**	430322423	1071430	3613341	686091	7497403	2601626	5967236	5139635	6658828	10203008	6507665	21814589	358561571
Average Total Receipts **9**	23627	322	312	1074	5052	10045	14519	25827	57903	110902	209925	495786	8745404
Operating Costs/Operating Income (%)													
Cost of Operations **10**	24.8	33.3	41.7	33.6	60.1	54.0	49.0	47.1	47.8	41.8	43.2	45.0	20.1
Salaries and Wages **11**	13.8	16.7	18.3	28.0	11.8	14.7	13.7	10.8	12.1	15.5	15.1	13.4	13.8
Taxes Paid **12**	2.8	2.0	2.5	4.0	1.8	1.9	3.7	2.2	2.0	2.4	2.1	2.5	2.8
Interest Paid **13**	8.7	13.5	0.9	2.5	1.0	1.6	2.4	2.9	2.6	3.9	4.3	11.5	9.4
Depreciation **14**	18.6	15.3	4.1	2.3	5.1	8.1	10.9	11.3	11.4	15.4	20.6	23.3	19.3
Amortization and Depletion **15**	2.0	3.6	0.2	0.3	0.7	0.8	1.1	1.5	1.4	2.2	2.0	3.5	1.9
Pensions and Other Deferred Comp. **16**	0.9	0.0	1.8	0.3	0.1	0.3	0.3	0.2	0.2	0.5	0.9	0.4	1.1
Employee Benefits **17**	3.5	1.2	0.5	1.8	0.8	0.7	1.1	0.9	1.4	1.4	2.1	1.9	3.9
Advertising **18**	2.2	1.2	1.4	1.0	1.2	1.6	1.0	0.7	1.8	1.3	1.3	2.8	2.3
Other Expenses **19**	40.0	83.7	24.3	32.2	25.3	23.9	30.8	31.2	31.7	27.4	31.2	32.9	42.0
Officers' Compensation **20**	0.5	2.7	13.5	7.0	3.2	3.0	2.2	1.8	1.1	0.9	0.9	0.7	0.1
Operating Margin **21**	•	•	•	•	•	•	•	•	•	•	•	•	•
Operating Margin Before Officers' Comp. **22**	•	4.3	•	•	•	•	•	•	•	•	•	•	•

Selected Average Balance Sheet ($ in Thousands)

Net Receivables 23	4452	0	14	108	452	1282	2111	3849	9530	21145	54550	125471	1657799
Inventories 24	330	0	4	37	96	257	393	767	1558	2307	4702	13393	104516
Net Property, Plant and Equipment 25	18077	0	23	66	624	3279	5926	12617	29041	56409	147736	386821	7123588
Total Assets 26	68556	0	99	780	2214	7634	16107	35022	70540	151033	372181	1133363	27919379
Notes and Loans Payable 27	22249	0	100	338	1407	2786	5177	11652	25647	64016	193842	594058	8673088
All Other Liabilities 28	19610	0	124	407	1108	2308	5000	12001	19018	46699	117245	283567	7955604
Net Worth 29	26697	0	-125	35	-302	2540	5930	11369	25874	40318	61095	255738	11290688

Selected Financial Ratios (Times to 1)

Current Ratio 30	1.0	•	1.1	1.1	1.0	1.2	1.1	1.3	1.3	1.2	1.1	0.9	1.0
Quick Ratio 31	0.6	•	0.7	0.7	0.7	1.0	0.9	1.0	1.0	0.9	0.9	0.7	0.6
Net Sales to Working Capital 32	109.6	•	57.6	18.1	257.4	16.1	16.9	8.1	9.7	12.7	23.2	•	211.7
Coverage Ratio 33	0.6	•	•	•	•	•	•	•	•	•	•	•	0.9
Total Asset Turnover 34	0.3	•	3.1	1.4	2.2	1.3	0.8	0.7	0.8	0.7	0.5	0.4	0.3
Inventory Turnover 35	15.6	•	28.7	9.7	29.8	20.6	16.9	15.2	16.9	19.4	18.6	15.4	14.6
Receivables Turnover 36	4.8	•	33.2	8.2	10.4	6.2	6.8	6.1	6.6	5.5	3.9	3.7	4.7
Total Liabilities to Net Worth 37	1.6	•	21.4	•	2.0	1.7	2.1	2.7	1.7	2.7	5.1	3.4	1.5
Current Assets to Working Capital 38	63.3	•	11.6	12.0	60.2	5.3	7.8	4.0	4.1	6.1	11.8	•	127.6
Current Liabilities to Working Capital 39	62.3	•	10.6	11.0	59.2	4.3	6.8	3.0	3.1	5.1	10.8	•	126.6
Working Capital to Net Sales 40	0.0	•	0.0	0.1	0.0	0.1	0.1	0.1	0.1	0.1	0.0	•	0.0
Inventory to Working Capital 41	1.5	•	0.9	0.3	3.8	0.2	0.5	0.2	0.2	0.3	0.5	•	2.5
Total Receipts to Cash Flow 42	4.0	4.4	8.7	9.5	9.3	9.5	6.8	5.0	5.4	10.8	168.0	•	3.4
Cost of Goods to Cash Flow 43	1.0	1.5	3.6	3.2	5.6	5.1	3.3	2.3	2.6	4.5	72.6	•	0.7
Cash Flow to Total Debt 44	0.1	•	0.2	0.1	0.2	0.2	0.2	0.2	0.2	0.1	0.0	•	0.1

Selected Financial Factors (in Percentages)

Debt Ratio 45	61.1	•	226.1	95.5	113.6	66.7	63.2	67.5	63.3	73.3	83.6	77.4	59.6
Return on Total Assets 46	1.6	•	•	•	•	•	•	•	•	•	•	•	2.4
Return on Equity Before Income Taxes 47	•	•	16.8	•	86.7	•	•	•	•	•	•	•	•
Return on Equity After Income Taxes 48	•	•	16.9	•	91.3	•	•	•	•	•	•	•	•
Profit Margin (Before Income Tax) 49	•	•	•	•	•	•	•	•	•	•	•	•	•
Profit Margin (After Income Tax) 50	•	•	•	•	•	•	•	•	•	•	•	•	•

Table II
Corporations with Net Income

TELECOMMUNICATIONS

MONEY AMOUNTS AND SIZE OF ASSETS IN THOUSANDS OF DOLLARS

Item Description for Accounting Period 7/03 Through 6/04	Total	Zero Assets	Under 500	500 to 1,000	1,000 to 5,000	5,000 to 10,000	10,000 to 25,000	25,000 to 50,000	50,000 to 100,000	100,000 to 250,000	250,000 to 500,000	500,000 to 2,500,000	2,500,000 and over
Number of Enterprises **1**	6098	464	3937	468	663	106	231	105	53	40	8	10	12
Revenues ($ in Thousands)													
Net Sales **2**	197728911	222020	1831287	298869	3896083	825915	2999549	2094649	2449093	3704449	1425405	2625484	175356109
Interest **3**	6785596	2882	2506	472	4399	4646	19529	13362	15015	23004	16083	55076	6628620
Rents **4**	4975228	0	0	0	679	3625	6490	3703	13628	20118	8210	6813	4911962
Royalties **5**	1644570	0	0	0	0	0	206	851	65	23526	293	216	1619413
Other Portfolio Income **6**	15583189	54179	707	0	23170	9087	58645	35321	22746	81138	2270	165821	15130107
Other Receipts **7**	7328741	51926	57925	1852	343208	34317	216987	79055	77488	67845	84556	87338	6226242
Total Receipts **8**	234046235	331007	1892425	301193	4267539	877590	3301406	2226941	2578035	3920080	1536817	2940748	209872453
Average Total Receipts **9**	38381	713	481	644	6437	8279	14292	21209	48642	98002	192102	294075	17489371
Operating Costs/Operating Income (%)													
Cost of Operations **10**	20.3	25.0	27.1	10.2	55.4	39.5	43.8	30.1	35.4	32.0	33.8	39.2	18.0
Salaries and Wages **11**	13.5	21.0	24.6	22.6	10.8	7.5	11.8	7.4	8.6	12.3	11.9	11.7	13.7
Taxes Paid **12**	3.0	2.9	1.6	4.2	2.0	2.8	2.5	2.7	2.4	2.7	2.1	2.1	3.1
Interest Paid **13**	8.0	2.0	0.1	0.1	0.7	1.1	1.7	3.4	2.0	3.4	5.3	11.0	8.7
Depreciation **14**	16.7	8.8	1.1	2.1	5.1	9.9	8.9	12.6	12.2	12.2	13.8	11.5	17.6
Amortization and Depletion **15**	1.8	1.3	0.0	0.0	0.1	0.3	0.5	0.7	0.8	2.0	3.1	1.6	1.9
Pensions and Other Deferred Comp. **16**	1.4	•	1.1	0.1	0.1	0.5	0.4	0.3	0.3	0.7	0.5	0.7	1.5
Employee Benefits **17**	2.7	2.7	0.3	2.0	0.4	0.7	0.9	0.8	1.6	1.5	2.2	2.7	2.9
Advertising **18**	1.9	0.6	2.0	1.4	1.5	2.9	0.7	0.6	1.1	0.9	1.6	0.6	1.9
Other Expenses **19**	41.6	21.3	16.8	26.4	23.6	26.8	24.2	31.6	29.7	26.4	25.8	20.4	43.7
Officers' Compensation **20**	0.4	5.8	14.7	12.3	3.4	1.9	2.2	2.4	1.3	1.1	1.1	1.7	0.1
Operating Margin **21**	•	8.6	10.7	18.4	•	6.0	2.3	7.4	4.7	4.8	•	•	•
Operating Margin Before Officers' Comp. **22**	•	14.5	25.4	30.7	0.3	7.9	4.5	9.8	5.9	5.8	•	•	•

Selected Average Balance Sheet ($ in Thousands)

Net Receivables 23	7666	0	19	31	580	765	1925	2883	6935	17067	32738	82323	3609285
Inventories 24	262	0	4	19	124	298	371	436	2011	1538	680	9933	87708
Net Property, Plant and Equipment 25	30626	0	9	46	554	4313	6400	14097	30557	54482	101450	161986	14723915
Total Assets 26	86258	0	121	799	2423	8119	16479	34430	68694	150420	349738	1096458	40986795
Notes and Loans Payable 27	24154	0	30	25	359	1605	4030	10643	18130	43316	133693	312843	11484771
All Other Liabilities 28	29634	0	28	111	1106	1456	3295	5411	13391	37092	69930	172686	14487405
Net Worth 29	32469	0	63	662	958	5057	9153	18376	37174	70012	146114	610929	15014620

Selected Financial Ratios (Times to 1)

Current Ratio 30	1.0	•	2.8	6.6	1.4	2.6	1.8	2.1	2.0	1.6	1.3	1.6	0.9
Quick Ratio 31	0.8	•	2.7	3.9	1.0	2.1	1.4	1.6	1.5	1.2	1.2	1.4	0.8
Net Sales to Working Capital 32	1024.1	•	6.9	1.0	14.7	4.1	4.8	3.5	4.4	5.5	14.7	4.1	•
Coverage Ratio 33	1.9	29.6	235.4	145.6	9.7	12.6	8.2	5.1	5.9	4.3	2.2	1.8	1.8
Total Asset Turnover 34	0.4	•	3.9	0.8	2.4	1.0	0.8	0.6	0.7	0.6	0.5	0.2	0.4
Inventory Turnover 35	25.1	•	30.0	3.5	26.3	15.3	13.8	8.1	8.1	19.3	88.6	10.4	30.0
Receivables Turnover 36	5.6	•	41.3	16.6	10.1	5.6	7.2	6.8	6.6	5.5	4.6	3.4	5.5
Total Liabilities to Net Worth 37	1.7	•	0.9	0.2	1.5	0.6	0.8	0.9	0.8	1.1	1.4	0.8	1.7
Current Assets to Working Capital 38	425.5	•	1.5	1.2	3.3	1.6	2.2	1.9	2.0	2.7	4.9	2.7	2.7
Current Liabilities to Working Capital 39	424.5	•	0.5	0.2	2.3	1.2	1.2	0.9	1.0	1.7	3.9	1.7	1.7
Working Capital to Net Sales 40	0.0	•	0.1	1.0	0.1	0.1	0.2	0.3	0.2	0.2	0.1	0.2	•
Inventory to Working Capital 41	8.3	•	0.1	0.0	0.2	0.1	0.2	0.1	0.1	0.1	0.1	0.1	•
Total Receipts to Cash Flow 42	2.8	1.3	3.6	2.7	5.5	2.9	3.2	2.5	2.9	3.2	3.6	5.2	2.7
Cost of Goods to Cash Flow 43	0.6	0.3	1.0	0.3	3.1	1.2	1.4	0.8	1.0	1.0	1.2	2.0	0.5
Cash Flow to Total Debt 44	0.2	•	2.2	1.7	0.7	0.9	0.5	0.5	0.5	0.4	0.2	0.1	0.2

Selected Financial Factors (in Percentages)

Debt Ratio 45	62.4	•	47.6	17.1	60.5	37.7	44.5	46.6	45.9	53.5	58.2	44.3	63.4
Return on Total Assets 46	5.7	•	54.3	15.5	17.2	12.7	11.1	9.9	8.0	9.0	6.1	4.8	5.5
Return on Equity Before Income Taxes 47	7.2	•	103.2	18.5	39.0	18.8	17.5	14.8	12.3	14.9	8.1	3.8	6.5
Return on Equity After Income Taxes 48	5.6	•	102.4	18.0	35.7	14.7	14.5	12.0	8.7	12.2	6.0	3.1	5.0
Profit Margin (Before Income Tax) 49	7.2	57.7	14.0	19.2	6.4	12.2	12.3	13.7	9.9	11.2	6.6	8.9	6.7
Profit Margin (After Income Tax) 50	5.6	55.0	13.9	18.6	5.8	9.6	10.2	11.0	7.0	9.2	4.9	7.3	5.1

Table I

Corporations with and without Net Income

INTERNET SERVICE PROVIDERS, WEB PORTALS, AND D.P. SERVICES

MONEY AMOUNTS AND SIZE OF ASSETS IN THOUSANDS OF DOLLARS

Item Description for Accounting Period 7/03 Through 6/04	Total	Zero Assets	Under 500	500 to 1,000	1,000 to 5,000	5,000 to 10,000	10,000 to 25,000	25,000 to 50,000	50,000 to 100,000	100,000 to 250,000	250,000 to 500,000	500,000 to 2,500,000	2,500,000 and over
Number of Enterprises 1	13548	1810	10261	523	703	90	78	25	20	15	7	10	7
Revenues ($ in Thousands)													
Net Sales 2	73611904	795542	1605087	662483	1633154	883968	1507487	894179	1454499	1396139	1250241	6928627	54600499
Interest 3	3950457	11574	223	109	2652	2372	10396	4113	9240	17762	10764	82424	3798828
Rents 4	786686	0	159	0	77	1019	10	299	826	1891	327	12989	769087
Royalties 5	9617012	0	0	0	5080	0	708	404	896	1663	0	7500	9600762
Other Portfolio Income 6	405641	3216	13665	8	2134	14693	2046	1120	4998	37281	5723	8588	312171
Other Receipts 7	5025236	89241	63388	1857	15861	16791	30779	17682	45636	11819	49491	121731	4560959
Total Receipts 8	93396936	899573	1682522	664457	1658958	918843	1551426	917797	1516095	1466555	1316546	7161859	73642306
Average Total Receipts 9	6894	497	164	1270	2360	10209	19890	36712	75805	97770	188078	716186	10520329
Operating Costs/Operating Income (%)													
Cost of Operations 10	21.9	91.1	29.4	25.1	27.9	32.9	36.4	35.6	49.6	17.0	24.1	19.0	19.3
Salaries and Wages 11	24.3	42.1	14.2	30.4	29.8	26.6	27.9	26.5	24.6	36.3	32.7	22.0	23.7
Taxes Paid 12	2.9	5.1	2.8	4.1	4.2	3.2	2.8	2.8	3.0	9.0	3.3	2.8	2.7
Interest Paid 13	8.3	3.5	1.2	0.8	1.6	0.9	1.0	1.8	1.1	3.0	3.7	1.9	10.6
Depreciation 14	7.3	33.9	2.6	4.0	7.6	6.2	5.6	7.2	4.5	5.3	15.9	7.9	7.0
Amortization and Depletion 15	6.9	20.2	0.2	1.7	2.0	2.9	4.4	2.8	2.1	2.9	2.1	5.2	7.9
Pensions and Other Deferred Comp. 16	0.9	0.0	0.4	0.5	0.3	0.5	0.4	0.2	0.8	0.3	2.5	0.1	1.1
Employee Benefits 17	2.6	4.4	0.6	2.0	2.0	2.3	2.4	3.4	2.3	2.6	2.7	1.8	2.8
Advertising 18	5.7	2.4	1.0	0.9	5.1	0.9	2.0	2.2	4.7	0.8	0.8	5.7	6.5
Other Expenses 19	56.9	673.3	48.3	38.2	34.4	37.7	33.8	40.4	72.0	109.0	35.1	35.0	51.8
Officers' Compensation 20	1.5	1.6	11.1	15.3	6.5	3.8	3.7	1.9	2.7	1.1	1.8	0.4	0.8
Operating Margin 21	•	•	•	•	•	•	•	•	•	•	•	•	•
Operating Margin Before Officers' Comp. 22	•	•	•	•	•	•	•	•	•	•	•	•	•

Selected Average Balance Sheet ($ in Thousands)

Item													
Net Receivables 23	1895	0	6	92	306	757	3507	7119	8356	19770	17995	89195	3334571
Inventories 24	242	0	1	17	27	65	227	444	821	432	1807	4553	447003
Net Property, Plant and Equipment 25	1315	0	11	57	708	1704	2693	5240	7474	21637	91306	166862	1985015
Total Assets 26	25782	0	49	630	1771	7657	15918	32828	67623	146103	341357	1110399	46774768
Notes and Loans Payable 27	3248	0	58	508	1363	2065	3458	8045	22194	80536	99889	248175	5240802
All Other Liabilities 28	10677	0	30	435	814	2449	7000	12704	16092	43411	35777	184203	19913297
Net Worth 29	11858	0	-39	-314	-406	3143	5460	12080	29337	22155	205691	678021	21620668

Selected Financial Ratios (Times to 1)

Item													
Current Ratio 30	1.0	•	0.9	1.3	0.8	1.1	1.2	2.3	1.3	1.7	1.7	1.8	0.9
Quick Ratio 31	0.4	•	0.5	0.9	0.7	1.0	0.9	1.8	1.0	1.2	1.0	1.4	0.3
Net Sales to Working Capital 32	•	•	•	9.4	27.5	7.1	13.6	3.7	6.5	3.8	•	4.2	•
Coverage Ratio 33	•	•	•	•	•	•	•	•	•	•	•	1.7	1.1
Total Asset Turnover 34	0.2	•	3.2	2.0	1.3	1.2	1.1	1.1	0.6	0.5	1.3	0.6	0.2
Inventory Turnover 35	4.9	•	85.2	18.9	23.7	31.0	28.6	44.0	36.6	23.8	49.7	29.0	3.4
Receivables Turnover 36	2.0	•	18.0	13.9	9.0	6.1	6.3	6.1	5.1	5.9	9.3	8.8	1.6
Total Liabilities to Net Worth 37	1.2	•	•	•	1.4	1.9	1.7	1.3	5.6	0.7	•	0.6	1.2
Current Assets to Working Capital 38	•	•	•	3.9	8.1	3.8	6.3	1.8	4.5	2.4	•	2.2	2.2
Current Liabilities to Working Capital 39	•	•	•	2.9	7.1	2.8	5.3	0.8	3.5	1.4	•	1.2	1.2
Working Capital to Net Sales 40	•	•	•	0.1	0.0	0.1	0.1	0.3	0.2	0.3	•	0.2	0.2
Inventory to Working Capital 41	•	•	•	0.2	•	0.1	0.2	0.0	0.0	0.0	•	0.0	0.0
Total Receipts to Cash Flow 42	3.3	•	3.0	19.8	10.3	9.1	17.7	27.0	20.7	20.7	•	3.2	2.2
Cost of Goods to Cash Flow 43	0.7	•	0.9	5.0	2.9	3.3	6.3	13.4	5.0	5.0	•	0.6	0.4
Cash Flow to Total Debt 44	0.1	•	0.6	0.1	0.1	0.2	0.1	0.1	0.1	0.1	•	0.5	0.1

Selected Financial Factors (in Percentages)

Item													
Debt Ratio 45	54.0	•	178.8	149.8	122.9	59.0	65.7	63.2	56.6	84.8	39.7	38.9	53.8
Return on Total Assets 46	•	•	•	•	•	•	•	•	•	•	•	2.0	1.9
Return on Equity Before Income Taxes 47	•	•	28.4	91.9	112.5	•	•	•	•	•	•	1.3	0.3
Return on Equity After Income Taxes 48	29.0	•	29.0	95.0	113.4	•	•	•	•	•	•	•	0.0
Profit Margin (Before Income Tax) 49	•	•	•	•	•	•	•	•	•	•	•	1.3	0.9
Profit Margin (After Income Tax) 50	•	•	•	•	•	•	•	•	•	•	•	•	0.1

273

Table II
Corporations with Net Income

INTERNET SERVICE PROVIDERS, WEB PORTALS, AND D.P. SERVICES

MONEY AMOUNTS AND SIZE OF ASSETS IN THOUSANDS OF DOLLARS

Item Description for Accounting Period 7/03 Through 6/04	Total	Zero Assets	Under 500	500 to 1,000	1,000 to 5,000	5,000 to 10,000	10,000 to 25,000	25,000 to 50,000	50,000 to 100,000	100,000 to 250,000	250,000 to 500,000	500,000 to 2,500,000	2,500,000 and over
Number of Enterprises **1**	6462	413	5698	123	134	36	28	10	7	7	•	•	•
Revenues ($ in Thousands)													
Net Sales **2**	45920021	21574	1111283	246542	539792	654188	645361	418400	966132	1009852	•	•	•
Interest **3**	852161	98	107	0	375	600	929	747	877	9242	•	•	•
Rents **4**	364034	0	0	0	0	874	0	85	824	0	•	•	•
Royalties **5**	9181755	0	0	0	0	0	0	0	0	1663	•	•	•
Other Portfolio Income **6**	213288	2344	13663	0	784	6600	113	362	3401	33583	•	•	•
Other Receipts **7**	3777119	510	61156	99	11967	5615	10938	3508	13810	26524	•	•	•
Total Receipts **8**	60308378	24526	1186209	246641	552918	667877	657341	423102	985044	1080864	•	•	•
Average Total Receipts **9**	9333	59	208	2005	4126	18552	23476	42310	140721	154409	•	•	•
Operating Costs/Operating Income (%)													
Cost of Operations **10**	20.8	•	25.7	37.2	32.6	34.4	36.8	34.8	57.9	3.9	•	•	•
Salaries and Wages **11**	20.4	4.2	14.1	21.6	29.3	20.0	19.5	24.4	14.9	37.7	•	•	•
Taxes Paid **12**	2.9	0.2	2.9	3.8	2.7	2.5	2.4	3.1	1.8	11.6	•	•	•
Interest Paid **13**	4.5	•	0.8	0.1	1.1	0.4	0.5	2.3	0.4	2.2	•	•	•
Depreciation **14**	4.3	•	1.6	3.0	4.5	3.5	3.7	4.5	2.4	4.6	•	•	•
Amortization and Depletion **15**	8.6	•	0.1	0.9	0.5	0.5	0.4	1.7	1.4	3.9	•	•	•
Pensions and Other Deferred Comp. **16**	1.1	•	0.6	1.4	0.1	0.6	0.5	0.2	1.0	0.3	•	•	•
Employee Benefits **17**	2.2	0.2	0.2	0.0	1.7	1.7	2.6	5.0	1.2	2.4	•	•	•
Advertising **18**	7.6	4.1	0.7	0.2	0.2	0.7	3.1	2.0	0.3	1.1	•	•	•
Other Expenses **19**	50.1	47.8	37.2	16.9	15.6	26.0	19.5	18.4	8.4	32.9	•	•	•
Officers' Compensation **20**	1.3	2.6	12.3	1.1	5.8	1.9	3.9	1.0	1.7	1.2	•	•	•
Operating Margin **21**	•	40.9	3.8	13.7	5.9	7.8	7.1	2.6	8.6	•	•	•	•
Operating Margin Before Officers' Comp. **22**	•	43.5	16.2	14.8	11.7	9.7	11.0	3.6	10.4	•	•	•	•

Selected Average Balance Sheet ($ in Thousands)

Net Receivables 23	2970	0	9	190	539	927	5401	6645	10269	33783
Inventories 24	473	0	0	2	10	73	276	121	724	0
Net Property, Plant and Equipment 25	1078	0	4	50	389	1755	1915	8137	11499	13415
Total Assets 26	39876	0	56	531	2609	8256	16122	33587	72349	193208
Notes and Loans Payable 27	4061	0	33	185	455	982	1585	11793	10029	33149
All Other Liabilities 28	13343	0	25	137	835	2067	7853	16292	18833	48570
Net Worth 29	22472	0	-2	208	1320	5207	6684	5502	43487	111489

Selected Financial Ratios (Times to 1)

Current Ratio 30	0.9	•	1.0	2.5	1.4	1.5	1.6	0.9	1.7	2.8
Quick Ratio 31	0.5	•	0.7	1.5	1.4	1.2	1.4	0.7	1.5	2.5
Net Sales to Working Capital 32	•	•	1401.4	8.2	10.5	16.1	5.5	•	12.3	2.2
Coverage Ratio 33	2.7	•	14.4	122.5	8.8	26.9	20.1	2.6	31.1	3.3
Total Asset Turnover 34	0.2	•	3.5	3.8	1.5	2.2	1.4	1.2	1.9	0.7
Inventory Turnover 35	3.1	•	235.4	327.4	127.2	86.1	30.8	120.6	110.4	•
Receivables Turnover 36	2.4	•	14.8	7.9	14.9	12.3	5.1	10.5	7.3	8.5
Total Liabilities to Net Worth 37	0.8	•	1.5	1.0	0.6	1.4	5.1	0.7	0.7	
Current Assets to Working Capital 38	•	•	289.6	1.7	3.4	3.0	2.7	•	2.5	1.6
Current Liabilities to Working Capital 39	•	•	288.6	0.7	2.4	2.0	1.7	•	1.5	0.6
Working Capital to Net Sales 40	•	•	0.0	0.1	0.1	0.1	0.2	•	0.1	0.5
Inventory to Working Capital 41	•	•	0.0	0.0	0.0	0.0	0.0	•	0.0	•
Total Receipts to Cash Flow 42	1.9	1.1	2.3	4.2	4.7	3.2	4.0	5.3	5.9	3.2
Cost of Goods to Cash Flow 43	0.4	•	0.6	1.5	1.5	1.1	1.5	1.8	3.4	0.1
Cash Flow to Total Debt 44	0.2	•	1.4	1.5	0.7	1.8	0.6	0.3	0.8	0.6

Selected Financial Factors (in Percentages)

Debt Ratio 45	43.6	•	104.2	60.7	49.4	36.9	58.5	83.6	39.9	42.3
Return on Total Assets 46	2.2	•	39.7	52.2	14.6	22.6	13.5	7.6	21.1	5.5
Return on Equity Before Income Taxes 47	2.4	•	•	131.8	25.5	34.5	30.9	28.6	33.9	6.7
Return on Equity After Income Taxes 48	1.9	•	•	112.0	24.1	31.5	28.7	24.3	27.4	6.5
Profit Margin (Before Income Tax) 49	7.6	54.6	10.6	13.7	8.4	9.9	9.0	3.8	10.7	5.2
Profit Margin (After Income Tax) 50	6.0	54.6	10.4	11.7	7.9	9.0	8.3	3.2	8.6	5.1

Table I

Corporations with and without Net Income

OTHER INFORMATION SERVICES, NEWS SYNDICATES, LIBRARIES

MONEY AMOUNTS AND SIZE OF ASSETS IN THOUSANDS OF DOLLARS

Item Description for Accounting Period 7/03 Through 6/04	Total	Zero Assets	Under 500	500 to 1,000	1,000 to 5,000	5,000 to 10,000	10,000 to 25,000	25,000 to 50,000	50,000 to 100,000	100,000 to 250,000	250,000 to 500,000	500,000 to 2,500,000	2,500,000 and over
Number of Enterprises **1**	9785	2629	6320	57	528	125	61	15	15	12	8	14	•
Revenues ($ in Thousands)													
Net Sales **2**	19232190	381519	1813029	185469	943182	1311193	1135180	632722	1062517	1637573	2017762	8112043	•
Interest **3**	168857	816	967	39	3163	2759	4786	2074	2753	5248	15796	130456	•
Rents **4**	15196	0	385	0	0	1733	2044	0	0	482	77	10476	•
Royalties **5**	100394	0	0	0	0	0	14500	0	0	10079	1781	74034	•
Other Portfolio Income **6**	235894	1331	3042	0	375	832	11892	7340	20706	34617	8215	147541	•
Other Receipts **7**	496381	587	20373	1864	19091	3166	30904	46579	8982	-129625	53006	441459	•
Total Receipts **8**	20248912	384253	1837796	187372	965811	1319683	1199306	688715	1094958	1558374	2096637	8916009	•
Average Total Receipts **9**	2069	146	291	3287	1829	10557	19661	45914	72997	129864	262080	636858	•
Operating Costs/Operating Income (%)													
Cost of Operations **10**	25.9	51.0	37.5	9.1	40.2	40.9	26.1	4.2	8.9	13.3	42.0	20.8	•
Salaries and Wages **11**	24.3	9.6	14.4	32.0	25.6	25.8	27.0	30.8	30.7	31.3	18.5	25.0	•
Taxes Paid **12**	2.7	2.1	2.2	3.7	2.9	4.4	2.8	3.2	3.0	2.6	1.5	2.7	•
Interest Paid **13**	3.1	0.2	1.5	9.4	2.5	0.5	1.4	0.6	1.2	2.2	2.9	4.7	•
Depreciation **14**	3.9	3.6	1.3	2.6	10.5	2.6	5.5	4.6	5.4	3.9	5.3	3.2	•
Amortization and Depletion **15**	2.4	0.8	0.8	10.6	2.3	0.6	2.3	1.4	1.8	3.3	3.2	2.8	•
Pensions and Other Deferred Comp. **16**	0.9	0.0	1.2	0.0	0.1	0.5	0.5	1.0	0.7	1.7	2.2	0.7	•
Employee Benefits **17**	2.6	1.4	0.4	3.3	2.0	2.6	2.4	2.8	2.0	2.5	1.9	3.4	•
Advertising **18**	2.1	4.4	0.9	0.2	1.7	1.2	8.8	1.5	9.4	1.6	0.6	1.1	•
Other Expenses **19**	34.0	33.7	26.1	30.8	42.6	27.6	30.9	53.6	34.4	52.6	22.6	33.9	•
Officers' Compensation **20**	3.8	1.8	15.2	13.4	6.5	3.7	3.7	2.4	3.3	3.4	1.4	1.7	•
Operating Margin **21**	•	•	•	•	•	•	•	•	•	•	•	0.1	•
Operating Margin Before Officers' Comp. **22**	•	13.7	•	•	•	•	•	•	2.4	•	•	1.8	•

Selected Average Balance Sheet ($ in Thousands)

Net Receivables 23	469	0	14	139	242	1939	2735	2684	9616	30005	49249	215376
Inventories 24	14	0	3	4	5	33	173	56	766	392	3585	3991
Net Property, Plant and Equipment 25	195	0	6	83	322	827	2453	4294	7873	12971	28103	62984
Total Assets 26	2798	0	57	809	1752	6834	16684	35807	70488	164003	330029	1283726
Notes and Loans Payable 27	1019	0	141	1457	1479	1977	3151	3058	7756	36196	63504	476600
All Other Liabilities 28	1030	0	259	1156	560	3171	7947	13405	19971	66520	88548	370703
Net Worth 29	749	0	-344	-1804	-287	1687	5586	19344	42760	61287	177977	436423

Selected Financial Ratios (Times to 1)

Current Ratio 30	0.8	•	0.1	0.5	0.9	1.5	1.4	1.4	1.5	2.1	1.2	0.8
Quick Ratio 31	0.6	•	0.1	0.5	0.7	1.4	1.2	1.0	1.3	1.7	0.9	0.5
Net Sales to Working Capital 32	•	•	•	•	•	6.4	8.0	9.2	5.5	2.7	13.5	•
Coverage Ratio 33	1.1	0.9	•	•	•	•	5.4	2.8	•	1.6	3.5	•
Total Asset Turnover 34	0.7	•	5.1	4.0	1.0	1.5	1.1	1.2	1.0	0.8	0.8	0.5
Inventory Turnover 35	36.0	•	35.7	81.3	134.8	131.6	28.2	32.0	8.3	46.4	29.5	30.1
Receivables Turnover 36	4.9	•	20.8	•	6.3	6.7	8.3	7.0	7.5	5.8	5.2	3.3
Total Liabilities to Net Worth 37	2.7	•	•	•	3.1	2.0	0.9	1.7	0.6	1.7	0.9	1.9
Current Assets to Working Capital 38	•	•	•	•	•	2.9	3.5	3.6	3.0	1.9	5.8	•
Current Liabilities to Working Capital 39	•	•	•	•	•	1.9	2.5	2.6	2.0	0.9	4.8	•
Working Capital to Net Sales 40	•	•	•	•	•	0.2	0.1	0.1	0.2	0.4	0.1	•
Inventory to Working Capital 41	•	•	•	•	•	0.0	0.0	0.0	0.1	0.0	0.0	•
Total Receipts to Cash Flow 42	3.5	•	5.4	8.2	83.4	7.8	5.3	2.0	3.0	4.4	5.1	2.5
Cost of Goods to Cash Flow 43	0.9	•	2.8	0.7	33.6	3.2	1.4	0.3	•	0.3	2.1	0.5
Cash Flow to Total Debt 44	0.3	•	0.1	0.2	0.0	0.3	0.3	1.3	0.8	0.0	0.3	0.3

Selected Financial Factors (in Percentages)

Debt Ratio 45	73.2	•	706.2	323.0	116.4	75.3	66.5	46.0	39.3	62.6	46.1	66.0
Return on Total Assets 46	2.4	•	6.5	•	•	•	•	3.8	3.4	•	3.5	7.5
Return on Equity Before Income Taxes 47	1.0	•	0.2	25.4	214.5	5.7	•	3.6	•	2.3	•	15.7
Return on Equity After Income Taxes 48	•	•	0.3	25.5	215.2	0.8	•	2.9	•	•	•	9.5
Profit Margin (Before Income Tax) 49	0.4	•	•	•	•	2.6	2.2	1.7	•	•	1.7	11.9
Profit Margin (After Income Tax) 50	•	•	•	•	•	0.4	1.7	•	•	•	•	7.2

Table II
Corporations with Net Income

OTHER INFORMATION SERVICES, NEWS SYNDICATES, LIBRARIES

MONEY AMOUNTS AND SIZE OF ASSETS IN THOUSANDS OF DOLLARS

Item Description for Accounting Period 7/03 Through 6/04	Total	Zero Assets	Under 500	500 to 1,000	1,000 to 5,000	5,000 to 10,000	10,000 to 25,000	25,000 to 50,000	50,000 to 100,000	100,000 to 250,000	250,000 to 500,000	500,000 to 2,500,000	2,500,000 and over
Number of Enterprises **1**	3562	302	2971	36	126	69	27	5	9	4	5	9	•
Revenues ($ in Thousands)													
Net Sales **2**	13611229	341393	992488	127718	475537	1129944	763703	224911	600538	529808	1622572	6802616	•
Interest **3**	125981	547	827	0	1718	674	1352	724	648	1200	5768	112523	•
Rents **4**	12461	0	0	0	0	0	1911	0	0	0	77	10474	•
Royalties **5**	72749	0	0	0	0	0	121	0	0	0	1732	70896	•
Other Portfolio Income **6**	191230	2	3025	0	9	690	11888	244	20452	30685	5721	118516	•
Other Receipts **7**	246304	526	4097	11	17992	792	8400	42427	6601	35323	31658	98475	•
Total Receipts **8**	14259954	342468	1000437	127729	495256	1132100	787375	268306	628239	597016	1667528	7213500	•
Average Total Receipts **9**	4003	1134	337	3548	3931	16407	29162	53661	69804	149254	333506	801500	•
Operating Costs/Operating Income (%)													
Cost of Operations **10**	26.3	56.6	13.0	11.0	38.1	44.9	34.6	4.6	5.8	14.5	49.1	20.3	•
Salaries and Wages **11**	19.9	6.9	14.3	22.9	11.3	19.8	16.0	26.7	30.6	24.5	15.8	21.9	•
Taxes Paid **12**	2.7	1.1	2.5	2.5	2.3	4.1	2.3	4.6	2.9	2.1	1.3	3.0	•
Interest Paid **13**	2.2	0.3	0.1	0.8	2.7	0.2	0.8	0.5	1.4	4.2	0.4	3.5	•
Depreciation **14**	2.9	1.3	1.3	2.2	3.3	1.2	4.2	3.2	4.6	5.1	4.6	2.5	•
Amortization and Depletion **15**	1.9	0.7	0.5	8.4	0.6	0.0	0.5	1.4	2.5	4.0	1.0	2.7	•
Pensions and Other Deferred Comp. **16**	1.1	0.0	2.2	0.1	0.1	0.6	0.4	1.3	0.2	2.7	2.7	0.8	•
Employee Benefits **17**	2.3	0.8	0.6	2.7	0.7	2.4	2.2	3.6	2.0	3.0	1.5	2.9	•
Advertising **18**	1.7	4.8	1.0	0.1	0.6	1.1	6.1	1.3	9.7	1.3	0.6	1.0	•
Other Expenses **19**	27.6	18.3	24.6	20.2	30.6	18.6	19.8	28.9	32.5	41.0	16.8	31.9	•
Officers' Compensation **20**	3.6	1.3	25.0	9.9	3.0	2.4	3.3	4.3	1.9	0.3	1.3	1.7	•
Operating Margin **21**	7.7	7.9	15.0	19.2	6.5	4.8	9.8	19.6	5.9	•	4.9	7.9	•
Operating Margin Before Officers' Comp. **22**	11.3	9.2	40.0	29.1	9.5	7.2	13.1	24.0	7.9	•	6.2	9.6	•

Selected Average Balance Sheet ($ in Thousands)

Item													
Net Receivables 23	605	0	2	104	266	2918	3217	4347	11277	20408	66061	143229	•
Inventories 24	26	0	0	18	51	110	42				5704	6163	•
Net Property, Plant and Equipment 25	272	0	5	92	226	573	3365	3403	6494	11515	20448	63110	•
Total Assets 26	4553		47	868	2137	6437	15478	40682	65450	144132	343928	1313900	•
Notes and Loans Payable 27	1273	19	0	1206	360	3737	2148	7395	34219	559		442608	•
All Other Liabilities 28	1269	0	10	416	675	3019	5869	20612	19712	33745	130528	328638	•
Net Worth 29	2010	0	18	452	256	3058	5872	17923	38343	76169	212842	542654	•

Selected Financial Ratios (Times to 1)

Item													
Current Ratio 30	0.8	•	2.4	1.9	0.6	1.6	1.5	1.7	0.9	1.1	2.3	0.6	•
Quick Ratio 31	0.5	•	2.1	1.8	0.5	1.4	1.4	1.5	0.8	0.8	2.0	0.3	•
Net Sales to Working Capital 32	•	•	22.6	•	•	9.3	7.2	5.7	5.7	3.9	19.9	•	•
Coverage Ratio 33	7.2	32.0	224.1	25.3	4.9	32.9	16.7	80.8	8.7	3.4	19.9	5.7	•
Total Asset Turnover 34	0.8	•	7.1	4.1	1.8	2.5	1.8	1.1	1.0	0.9	0.9	0.6	•
Inventory Turnover 35	38.1	•	142.8	574.5	82.1	143.5	89.0	49.1	93.3	28.0	24.8		•
Receivables Turnover 36	6.7	•	75.4	47.3	6.8	7.3	12.3	5.1	7.3	6.6	4.9	5.7	•
Total Liabilities to Net Worth 37	1.3	•	1.6	0.9	7.3	1.1	1.6	1.3	0.7	0.9	0.6	1.4	•
Current Assets to Working Capital 38	•	•	1.7	2.2	•	2.4	2.7	•	2.9	1.8	8.1	•	•
Current Liabilities to Working Capital 39	•	•	0.7	1.2	•	1.4	1.7	•	1.9	0.8	7.1	•	•
Working Capital to Net Sales 40	•	•	0.0	0.1	•	0.1	0.1	•	0.2	0.3	0.1	•	•
Inventory to Working Capital 41	•	•	0.0	•	•	0.0	0.0	•	0.0	•	0.0	•	•
Total Receipts to Cash Flow 42	2.7	3.9	2.7	2.7	2.8	4.7	3.7	1.6	2.5	2.2	4.5	2.4	•
Cost of Goods to Cash Flow 43	0.7	2.2	0.4	0.3	1.1	2.1	1.3	0.1	0.1	0.3	0.5	0.5	•
Cash Flow to Total Debt 44	0.5	•	4.2	3.1	0.7	1.0	0.8	1.2	1.0	0.9	0.4		•

Selected Financial Factors (in Percentages)

Item													
Debt Ratio 45	55.8	•	61.1	48.0	88.0	52.5	62.1	55.9	41.4	47.2	38.1	58.7	•
Return on Total Assets 46	13.2	•	111.8	81.8	23.5	13.1	25.1	43.5	12.1	12.9	7.6	11.3	•
Return on Equity Before Income Taxes 47	25.7	•	285.7	151.0	156.2	26.7	62.2	97.6	18.3	17.2	11.6	22.5	•
Return on Equity After Income Taxes 48	19.2	•	280.2	150.8	153.3	24.2	55.3	81.6	16.9	17.0	8.0	14.7	•
Profit Margin (Before Income Tax) 49	13.5	8.2	15.8	19.2	10.6	5.0	12.9	38.9	10.5	9.9	7.6	16.1	•
Profit Margin (After Income Tax) 50	10.1	6.5	15.5	19.2	10.4	4.5	11.5	32.5	9.7	9.8	5.2	10.5	•

276

Table I

Corporations with and without Net Income

FINANCE AND INSURANCE

MONEY AMOUNTS AND SIZE OF ASSETS IN THOUSANDS OF DOLLARS

Item Description for Accounting Period 7/03 Through 6/04		Total	Zero Assets	Under 500	500 to 1,000	1,000 to 5,000	5,000 to 10,000	10,000 to 25,000	25,000 to 50,000	50,000 to 100,000	100,000 to 250,000	250,000 to 500,000	500,000 to 2,500,000	2,500,000 and over
Number of Enterprises	1	60072	12442	34304	3012	4265	1553	994	797	870	890	434	373	139
Revenues ($ in Thousands)														
Net Sales	2	418730668	34414919	13443115	3407286	8877670	5326693	5832156	5389110	7343375	13170436	13019956	35331648	273174304
Interest	3	218731240	21642593	241718	97272	331113	136706	380592	894702	2339773	5937231	6656351	15950410	164122780
Rents	4	1752395	97235	2647	403	15985	642	5467	5977	5869	21622	32089	220749	1343710
Royalties	5	534948	8	0	0	22	0	102	28	20658	518	2617	36675	474320
Other Portfolio Income	6	17108960	1759242	18871	967	30610	56239	79069	70361	274277	504986	642327	2368478	11303552
Other Receipts	7	180603125	10915841	13179879	3308644	8499940	5133106	5366926	4418042	4702798	6706079	5686572	16755336	95929962
Total Receipts	8	418730668	34414919	13443115	3407286	8877670	5326693	5832156	5389110	7343375	13170436	13019956	35331648	273174304
Average Total Receipts	9	6970	2766	392	1131	2082	3430	5867	6762	8441	14798	30000	94723	1965283
Operating Costs/Operating Income (%)														
Cost of Operations	10	2.4	0.2	7.4	1.2	2.7	7.3	12.3	7.7	3.0	3.8	0.6	0.4	2.2
Salaries and Wages	11	11.6	11.2	23.7	25.7	35.5	21.7	22.7	28.8	19.9	17.0	18.2	15.1	8.1
Taxes Paid	12	1.6	1.5	3.1	3.0	3.8	2.1	2.5	3.1	2.7	2.6	2.8	2.1	1.2
Interest Paid	13	35.4	44.4	1.3	2.7	4.4	15.5	8.0	11.6	16.7	21.4	24.1	22.8	42.2
Depreciation	14	3.8	1.5	1.0	0.9	1.3	1.6	1.6	2.0	2.6	3.0	2.8	3.3	4.6
Amortization and Depletion	15	0.7	0.6	0.2	0.1	0.3	0.2	0.4	0.5	0.7	1.2	1.0	1.2	0.7
Pensions and Other Deferred Comp.	16	0.6	0.5	0.6	0.1	0.4	0.3	0.4	0.6	0.6	1.0	0.9	1.2	0.5
Employee Benefits	17	1.1	1.2	1.2	1.3	1.0	0.6	1.0	1.6	1.9	1.8	2.1	1.6	0.9
Advertising	18	1.5	0.2	2.9	0.8	3.0	1.7	1.6	1.6	2.2	1.3	1.1	3.1	1.4
Other Expenses	19	25.8	40.8	41.2	47.1	32.9	47.6	35.1	27.5	28.6	28.2	27.4	34.7	20.6
Officers' Compensation	20	1.6	1.3	8.4	6.0	7.2	5.4	6.4	6.0	6.6	4.7	3.4	1.5	0.5
Operating Margin	21	13.8	•	9.0	11.1	7.5	•	7.9	9.1	14.5	14.0	15.6	13.0	17.1
Operating Margin Before Officers' Comp.	22	15.5	•	17.3	17.0	14.6	1.4	14.3	15.0	21.1	18.7	19.0	14.5	17.6

Selected Average Balance Sheet ($ in Thousands)

Item														
Net Receivables 23	13072	0	•	16	253	880	2955	6633	15485	29758	55574	90792	257751	3926668
Inventories 24	•	•	•	•	•	•	•	•	•	•	•	•	•	•
Net Property, Plant and Equipment 25	732	0	•	15	43	158	188	458	776	1409	2697	5415	13306	218055
Total Assets 26	73657	0	•	90	696	2290	6604	16156	35994	71181	157184	349688	1037165	26002343
Notes and Loans Payable 27	44327	0	•	40	233	1161	4086	6512	7953	9517	23725	54966	282042	17828494
All Other Liabilities 28	24565	0	•	-2	173	1377	3092	7606	22706	53269	113628	252872	610250	6863673
Net Worth 29	4766	0	•	53	290	-248	-574	2038	5335	8395	19830	41851	144874	1310176

Selected Financial Ratios (Times to 1)

Item														
Current Ratio 30	0.5	•	•	1.8	3.5	1.3	0.9	1.1	0.9	0.8	0.7	0.6	0.6	0.5
Quick Ratio 31	0.4	•	•	1.6	3.0	1.2	0.8	1.0	0.9	0.8	0.7	0.5	0.5	0.4
Net Sales to Working Capital 32	•	•	•	16.5	3.0	6.3	•	6.9	•	•	•	•	•	•
Coverage Ratio 33	1.4	0.9	•	7.7	5.2	2.7	0.7	2.0	1.7	1.8	1.6	1.6	1.6	1.4
Total Asset Turnover 34	0.1	•	•	4.3	1.6	0.9	0.5	0.4	0.2	0.1	0.1	0.1	0.1	0.1
Inventory Turnover 35	•	•	•	•	•	•	•	•	•	•	•	•	•	•
Receivables Turnover 36	•	•	•	•	•	•	•	•	•	•	•	•	•	•
Total Liabilities to Net Worth 37	14.5	•	•	0.7	1.4	•	•	6.9	5.7	7.5	6.9	7.4	6.2	18.8
Current Assets to Working Capital 38	•	•	•	2.3	1.4	4.4	•	12.6	•	•	•	•	•	•
Current Liabilities to Working Capital 39	•	•	•	1.3	0.4	3.4	•	11.6	•	•	•	•	•	•
Working Capital to Net Sales 40	•	•	•	0.1	0.3	0.2	•	0.1	0.2	0.1	0.1	•	•	•
Inventory to Working Capital 41	•	•	•	•	•	0.0	•	0.0	•	•	•	•	•	•
Total Receipts to Cash Flow 42	2.8	3.6	•	2.3	1.8	2.8	2.6	2.7	3.0	2.6	2.6	2.6	2.3	2.9
Cost of Goods to Cash Flow 43	0.1	0.0	•	0.2	0.0	0.1	0.2	0.3	0.2	0.1	0.1	0.0	0.0	0.1
Cash Flow to Total Debt 44	0.0	•	•	4.5	1.5	0.3	0.2	0.2	0.1	0.1	0.1	0.0	0.0	•

Selected Financial Factors (in Percentages)

Item														
Debt Ratio 45	93.5	•	•	41.6	58.4	110.8	108.7	87.4	85.2	88.2	87.4	88.0	86.0	95.0
Return on Total Assets 46	4.6	•	•	44.7	22.3	10.8	5.9	5.7	3.8	3.6	3.2	3.3	3.2	4.4
Return on Equity Before Income Taxes 47	19.5	•	•	66.6	43.3	•	24.6	22.4	10.9	13.7	9.5	10.5	8.3	24.6
Return on Equity After Income Taxes 48	13.2	•	•	64.2	41.1	•	28.9	20.4	9.2	11.3	6.7	7.4	5.4	16.6
Profit Margin (Before Income Tax) 49	13.3	•	•	9.0	11.1	7.4	•	7.8	8.6	13.6	12.7	14.7	12.7	16.4
Profit Margin (After Income Tax) 50	9.0	•	•	8.6	10.5	7.0	•	7.1	7.3	11.3	8.9	10.4	8.3	11.1

Table II
Corporations with Net Income

FINANCE AND INSURANCE

MONEY AMOUNTS AND SIZE OF ASSETS IN THOUSANDS OF DOLLARS

Item Description for Accounting Period 7/03 Through 6/04	Total	Zero Assets	Under 500	500 to 1,000	1,000 to 5,000	5,000 to 10,000	10,000 to 25,000	25,000 to 50,000	50,000 to 100,000	100,000 to 250,000	250,000 to 500,000	500,000 to 2,500,000	2,500,000 and over
Number of Enterprises **1**	35303	3611	21538	•	•	1257	755	628	714	791	395	331	125
Revenues ($ in Thousands)													
Net Sales **2**	376450270	19391224	11490463	•	•	4593924	4639632	4736814	6236508	11311394	11500421	27095065	265023219
Interest **3**	200139819	10737183	164461	•	•	107823	291633	703289	1932359	5185486	5976131	14085986	160637328
Rents **4**	1481251	- 36003	2647	•	•	452	4637	5413	4767	15592	26433	165893	1208510
Royalties **5**	512748	0	0	•	•	0	102	25	20654	511	2462	36675	452297
Other Portfolio Income **6**	15602770	1176065	18329	•	•	53753	72839	61674	254380	460166	613555	1821256	11040971
Other Receipts **7**	158713682	7441973	11305026	•	•	4431896	4270421	3966413	4024348	5649639	4881840	10985255	91684113
Total Receipts **8**	376450270	19391224	11490463	•	•	4593924	4639632	4736814	6236508	11311394	11500421	27095065	265023219
Average Total Receipts **9**	10663	5370	533	•	•	3655	6145	7543	8735	14300	29115	81858	2120186
Operating Costs/Operating Income (%)													
Cost of Operations **10**	2.5	0.3	8.5	•	•	8.0	11.3	8.5	2.4	4.4	0.4	0.4	2.3
Salaries and Wages **11**	11.4	9.5	23.6	•	•	22.4	21.8	28.5	19.7	17.2	18.7	16.8	8.1
Taxes Paid **12**	1.6	1.8	2.9	•	•	2.2	2.4	3.1	2.8	2.7	2.9	2.5	1.2
Interest Paid **13**	35.5	38.1	0.6	•	•	5.0	8.0	10.2	16.1	20.3	22.8	22.8	42.5
Depreciation **14**	3.2	1.2	0.9	•	•	1.6	1.4	1.8	2.5	2.5	2.9	3.3	3.7
Amortization and Depletion **15**	0.7	0.1	0.1	•	•	0.2	0.3	0.3	0.7	0.7	1.1	1.0	0.7
Pensions and Other Deferred Comp. **16**	0.6	0.3	0.7	•	•	0.3	0.4	0.6	0.7	1.1	0.9	1.0	0.5
Employee Benefits **17**	1.1	0.7	1.1	•	•	0.5	1.0	1.6	1.9	1.8	2.2	1.9	0.9
Advertising **18**	1.5	0.2	2.3	•	•	1.9	1.4	1.6	2.4	1.4	1.2	2.4	1.4
Other Expenses **19**	23.2	36.4	37.5	•	•	42.4	30.6	23.8	25.1	23.4	23.5	26.1	20.4
Officers' Compensation **20**	1.5	1.0	8.0	•	•	5.7	6.0	5.8	6.7	5.0	3.6	1.8	0.5
Operating Margin **21**	17.3	10.3	13.9	•	•	10.0	15.4	14.2	19.1	19.4	19.8	19.8	17.7
Operating Margin Before Officers' Comp. **22**	18.8	11.3	21.9	•	•	15.7	21.5	20.0	25.8	24.5	23.4	21.6	18.2

Selected Average Balance Sheet ($ in Thousands)											
Net Receivables 23	18890	0	13	3029	6728	15246	28883	55304	88558	224333	3767531
Inventories 24											
Net Property, Plant and Equipment 25	1004	0	17	148	385	677	1411	2654	5579	13357	191342
Total Assets 26	119076	0	96	6527	16182	35995	71177	157445	351107	1015362	27998583
Notes and Loans Payable 27	71720	0	27	3806	6364	7531	8426	19929	44376	226738	19191122
All Other Liabilities 28	39631	0	-64	1161	6625	23108	53739	117367	262792	641808	7441275
Net Worth 29	7725	0	134	1560	3193	5356	9012	20149	43939	146816	1366186

Selected Financial Ratios (Times to 1)											
Current Ratio 30	0.5	3.5		1.2	1.1	0.9	0.8	0.7	0.5	0.5	0.5
Quick Ratio 31	0.4	3.1		1.2	0.9	0.9	0.8	0.7	0.5	0.4	0.4
Net Sales to Working Capital 32		12.7		4.4	7.3						
Coverage Ratio 33	1.5	23.6	1.3	3.0	2.9	2.4	2.1	1.9	1.8	1.9	1.4
Total Asset Turnover 34	0.1	5.6		0.6	0.4	0.2	0.1	0.1	0.1	0.1	0.1
Inventory Turnover 35											
Receivables Turnover 36											
Total Liabilities to Net Worth 37	14.4			3.2	4.1	5.7	6.9	6.8	7.0	5.9	19.5
Current Assets to Working Capital 38		1.4		5.0	12.9						
Current Liabilities to Working Capital 39		0.4		4.0	11.9						
Working Capital to Net Sales 40		0.1		0.2	0.1						
Inventory to Working Capital 41				0.0	0.0						
Total Receipts to Cash Flow 42	2.7	2.5		2.2	2.1	2.3	2.4	2.6	2.5	2.3	2.8
Cost of Goods to Cash Flow 43	0.1	0.0		0.2	0.3	0.2	0.1	0.1	0.0	0.0	0.0
Cash Flow to Total Debt 44	0.0	0.0		0.3	0.2	0.1	0.1	0.0	0.0	0.0	0.0

Selected Financial Factors (in Percentages)											
Debt Ratio 45	93.5			76.1	80.3	85.1	87.3	87.2	87.5	85.5	95.1
Return on Total Assets 46	4.7	80.4		8.3	8.8	4.2	3.5	3.5	4.2	3.4	4.5
Return on Equity Before Income Taxes 47	23.0	55.4		23.1	29.5	19.4	17.6	12.9	12.5	10.9	26.4
Return on Equity After Income Taxes 48	16.4	53.9		21.2	27.8	17.3	14.9	9.8	9.2	7.7	17.9
Profit Margin (Before Income Tax) 49	16.7	13.9	10.3	9.9	15.3	13.7	18.1	18.2	18.8	19.6	17.0
Profit Margin (After Income Tax) 50	11.9	13.5	8.1	9.0	14.4	12.3	15.4	13.9	13.9	13.7	11.6

Table I

Corporations with and without Net Income

COMMERCIAL BANKING

MONEY AMOUNTS AND SIZE OF ASSETS IN THOUSANDS OF DOLLARS

Item Description for Accounting Period 7/03 Through 6/04	Total	Zero Assets	Under 500	500 to 1,000	1,000 to 5,000	5,000 to 10,000	10,000 to 25,000	25,000 to 50,000	50,000 to 100,000	100,000 to 250,000	250,000 to 500,000	500,000 to 2,500,000	2,500,000 and over
Number of Enterprises **1**	2507	279	448	12	51	69	230	371	483	388	116	50	9
Revenues ($ in Thousands)													
Net Sales **2**	45346160	31236876	84421	59267	17984	83050	225905	777801	2334663	3717655	2369402	2708389	1730747
Interest **3**	28182314	20124856	0	121	3413	12120	131969	440380	1246384	2075455	1345285	1737874	1064457
Rents **4**	289797	93469	0	0	0	19	339	1022	3489	6739	14119	33586	137015
Royalties **5**	1501	8	0	0	0	0	0	0	67	59	0	1351	17
Other Portfolio Income **6**	2316880	1673723	540	0	8	951	9113	31132	123374	142218	115056	143526	77236
Other Receipts **7**	14555668	9344820	83881	59146	14563	69960	84484	305267	961349	1493184	894942	792052	452022
Total Receipts **8**	45346160	31236876	84421	59267	17984	83050	225905	777801	2334663	3717655	2369402	2708389	1730747
Average Total Receipts **9**	18088	111960	188	4939	353	1204	982	2096	4834	9582	20426	54168	192305
Operating Costs/Operating Income (%)													
Cost of Operations **10**	0.0	•	•	•	•	•	1.2	•	•	•	•	•	•
Salaries and Wages **11**	11.9	10.7	44.4	•	5.3	4.5	17.5	13.8	12.8	14.3	15.2	16.2	14.1
Taxes Paid **12**	1.9	1.5	0.1	•	1.6	1.0	3.8	3.2	2.7	2.9	3.0	3.4	2.5
Interest Paid **13**	39.1	46.1	0.0	3.7	0.0	2.7	22.8	24.3	21.6	23.2	23.6	22.5	30.8
Depreciation **14**	2.4	1.5	2.9	•	0.8	1.0	5.3	4.4	3.3	3.3	4.5	3.9	10.0
Amortization and Depletion **15**	0.6	0.6	12.2	•	0.1	0.3	1.1	0.8	0.6	1.4	0.3	0.3	0.5
Pensions and Other Deferred Comp. **16**	0.6	0.5	•	•	•	0.0	0.8	0.8	0.7	0.7	0.8	1.0	0.8
Employee Benefits **17**	1.5	1.1	0.0	•	•	0.8	3.9	3.2	2.3	2.3	2.4	2.6	2.5
Advertising **18**	0.4	0.2	0.0	•	0.1	0.4	1.2	1.2	0.8	0.9	0.7	0.8	0.8
Other Expenses **19**	36.1	41.3	46.5	12.0	135.9	77.5	27.5	25.8	30.4	26.0	20.2	21.4	20.2
Officers' Compensation **20**	2.4	0.9	•	•	7.7	4.4	14.7	12.5	7.6	6.5	5.2	3.5	2.8
Operating Margin **21**	3.0	•	•	84.3	•	7.5	0.1	9.9	17.2	18.5	24.1	24.4	15.1
Operating Margin Before Officers' Comp. **22**	5.5	•	•	84.3	84.3	11.9	14.8	22.4	24.8	25.0	29.2	27.8	17.9

Selected Average Balance Sheet ($ in Thousands)

Line Item												
Net Receivables 23	45914	0	0	753	2307	9114	21209	40916	87271	181838	416434	1045159
Inventories 24	•	•	•	•	•	•	•	•	•	•	•	•
Net Property, Plant and Equipment 25	1355	9	0	703	95	364	701	1295	2663	5648	10197	20201
Total Assets 26	91463	25	651	2403	8302	17716	36786	70807	151019	335915	841165	4115539
Notes and Loans Payable 27	3760	0	0	0	3	79	432	1354	4818	11184	51055	319181
All Other Liabilities 28	78706	0	21903	6428	6027	18021	31427	63672	130437	290133	703269	3369258
Net Worth 29	8997	25	-21252	-4025	2272	-385	4927	5781	15764	34598	86840	427100

Selected Financial Ratios (Times to 1)

Line Item													
Current Ratio 30	0.9	•	28.7	0.0	1.7	1.7	1.1	1.0	1.0	1.0	0.9	0.9	0.8
Quick Ratio 31	0.9	•	28.7	0.0	1.7	1.7	1.1	1.0	0.9	0.9	0.9	0.8	0.7
Net Sales to Working Capital 32	•	•	12.0	0.5	0.4	0.7	1.4	•	1.7	•	•	•	•
Coverage Ratio 33	1.1	0.9	23.9	•	3.5	0.9	1.3	1.7	1.7	1.9	2.0	1.5	
Total Asset Turnover 34	0.2	•	7.4	7.6	0.1	0.1	0.1	0.1	0.1	0.1	0.1	0.0	
Inventory Turnover 35	•	•	•	•	•	•	•	•	•	•	•	•	•
Receivables Turnover 36	•	•	•	•	•	•	•	•	•	•	•	•	•
Total Liabilities to Net Worth 37	9.2	0.0	•	2.7	•	6.5	11.2	8.6	8.6	8.7	8.7	8.6	
Current Assets to Working Capital 38	•	1.0	2.3	2.5	11.9	21.7	•	•	•	•	•	•	
Current Liabilities to Working Capital 39	•	0.0	1.3	1.5	10.9	20.7	•	•	•	•	•	•	
Working Capital to Net Sales 40	•	0.1	2.1	2.7	1.4	0.7	•	•	•	•	•	•	
Inventory to Working Capital 41	•	•	•	•	•	•	•	•	•	•	•	•	•
Total Receipts to Cash Flow 42	3.3	2.6	1.0	3.8	4.3	3.1	2.5	2.7	2.4	2.4	3.4		
Cost of Goods to Cash Flow 43	0.0	•	•	•	0.1	•	•	•	•	•	•		
Cash Flow to Total Debt 44	0.1	123.3	0.2	0.1	0.0	0.0	0.0	0.0	0.0	0.0	0.0		

Selected Financial Factors (in Percentages)

Line Item												
Debt Ratio 45	90.2	2.3	3365.0	267.5	72.6	102.2	86.6	91.8	89.6	89.7	89.7	89.6
Return on Total Assets 46	8.2	•	667.5	1.4	1.1	1.8	2.5	2.5	2.7	2.7	2.9	2.1
Return on Equity Before Income Taxes 47	4.6	•	•	4.5	3.5	6.4	3.0	12.5	9.8	12.6	13.7	6.5
Return on Equity After Income Taxes 48	0.1	•	•	4.5	3.1	11.1	2.0	10.1	7.4	9.4	9.4	4.0
Profit Margin (Before Income Tax) 49	2.3	•	84.3	6.7	6.7	7.2	14.9	16.1	21.3	21.3	22.0	14.4
Profit Margin (After Income Tax) 50	0.1	•	82.6	5.8	4.7	12.1	12.2	15.9	15.9	21.3	15.1	8.8

Table II
Corporations with Net Income

COMMERCIAL BANKING

MONEY AMOUNTS AND SIZE OF ASSETS IN THOUSANDS OF DOLLARS

Item Description for Accounting Period 7/03 Through 6/04		Total	Zero Assets	Under 500	500 to 1,000	1,000 to 5,000	5,000 to 10,000	10,000 to 25,000	25,000 to 50,000	50,000 to 100,000	100,000 to 250,000	250,000 to 500,000	500,000 to 2,500,000	2,500,000 and over
Number of Enterprises	1	1579	156	•	•	•	44	163	286	391	359	•	•	•
Revenues ($ in Thousands)														
Net Sales	2	29542296	17283929	•	•	•	75060	171599	646381	1801494	3381505	•	•	•
Interest	3	16999151	9821172	•	•	•	8700	106079	356904	1006215	1923152	•	•	•
Rents	4	89680	32544	•	•	•	19	310	816	2650	6624	•	•	•
Royalties	5	1483	0	•	•	•	0	0	0	63	53	•	•	•
Other Portfolio Income	6	1741803	1140794	•	•	•	874	6010	26530	115269	135116	•	•	•
Other Receipts	7	10710179	6289419	•	•	•	65467	59200	262131	677297	1316560	•	•	•
Total Receipts	8	29542296	17283929	•	•	•	75060	171599	646381	1801494	3381505	•	•	•
Average Total Receipts	9	18709	110794	•	•	•	1706	1053	2260	4607	9419	•	•	•
Operating Costs/Operating Income (%)														
Cost of Operations	10	•	•	•	•	•	•	•	•	•	•	•	•	•
Salaries and Wages	11	11.4	9.3	•	•	•	1.9	12.9	12.2	12.4	14.2	•	•	•
Taxes Paid	12	2.3	1.8	•	•	•	0.6	3.2	3.0	2.9	3.0	•	•	•
Interest Paid	13	32.8	39.6	•	•	•	2.2	24.5	23.8	23.1	23.4	•	•	•
Depreciation	14	2.2	1.3	•	•	•	0.8	2.6	3.3	3.4	3.3	•	•	•
Amortization and Depletion	15	0.2	0.1	•	•	•	0.0	0.3	0.4	0.5	0.4	•	•	•
Pensions and Other Deferred Comp.	16	0.5	0.3	•	•	•	0.0	0.8	0.9	0.8	0.8	•	•	•
Employee Benefits	17	1.4	0.7	•	•	•	0.6	3.6	3.1	2.4	2.3	•	•	•
Advertising	18	0.5	0.2	•	•	•	0.2	0.8	1.0	0.8	0.9	•	•	•
Other Expenses	19	30.9	38.1	•	•	•	58.3	20.9	20.4	20.0	23.5	•	•	•
Officers' Compensation	20	3.0	0.9	•	•	•	3.0	14.0	11.6	8.2	6.5	•	•	•
Operating Margin	21	14.6	7.8	•	•	•	32.4	16.3	20.4	25.6	21.6	•	•	•
Operating Margin Before Officers' Comp.	22	17.6	8.7	•	•	•	35.4	30.3	32.0	33.8	28.2	•	•	•

Selected Average Balance Sheet ($ in Thousands)

Net Receivables 23	64622	·	2344	9121	21279	40744	87563
Inventories 24	·	·	·	·	·	·	·
Net Property, Plant and Equipment 25	1881	·	26	204	606	1257	2658
Total Assets 26	128577	·	8540	17864	37049	70666	151264
Notes and Loans Payable 27	5019	0	0	77	422	1347	4581
All Other Liabilities 28	110901	0	7500	15452	31945	62863	130789
Net Worth 29	12657	0	1039	2335	4682	6455	15895

Selected Financial Ratios (Times to 1)

Current Ratio 30	0.9	·	1.5	1.1	1.1	1.0	1.0
Quick Ratio 31	0.9	·	1.5	1.0	1.0	0.9	0.9
Net Sales to Working Capital 32	·	·	0.6	1.3	1.2	·	·
Coverage Ratio 33	1.4	1.2	15.2	1.6	1.7	2.0	1.8
Total Asset Turnover 34	0.1	·	0.2	0.1	0.1	0.1	0.1
Inventory Turnover 35	·	·	·	·	·	·	·
Receivables Turnover 36	·	·	·	·	·	·	·
Total Liabilities to Net Worth 37	9.2	·	7.2	6.6	6.9	9.9	8.5
Current Assets to Working Capital 38	·	·	3.1	19.6	17.5	·	·
Current Liabilities to Working Capital 39	·	·	2.1	18.6	16.5	·	·
Working Capital to Net Sales 40	·	·	1.6	0.8	0.9	·	·
Inventory to Working Capital 41	·	·	·	·	·	·	·
Total Receipts to Cash Flow 42	2.5	2.5	2.6	2.9	2.6	2.3	2.7
Cost of Goods to Cash Flow 43	·	·	·	·	·	·	·
Cash Flow to Total Debt 44	0.1	·	0.1	0.0	0.0	0.0	0.0

Selected Financial Factors (in Percentages)

Debt Ratio 45	90.2	·	87.8	86.9	87.4	90.9	89.5
Return on Total Assets 46	6.8	·	6.7	2.2	2.5	3.0	2.6
Return on Equity Before Income Taxes 47	20.1	·	51.7	6.1	8.3	16.3	11.3
Return on Equity After Income Taxes 48	15.1	·	50.1	5.0	6.9	13.6	8.7
Profit Margin (Before Income Tax) 49	13.6	7.8	31.5	13.5	17.2	22.8	19.1
Profit Margin (After Income Tax) 50	10.2	5.8	30.5	11.1	14.2	19.0	14.7

Table I
Corporations with and without Net Income

SAVINGS INSTITUTIONS AND OTHER DEPOSITORY CREDIT

MONEY AMOUNTS AND SIZE OF ASSETS IN THOUSANDS OF DOLLARS

Item Description for Accounting Period 7/03 Through 6/04	Total	Zero Assets	Under 500	500 to 1,000	1,000 to 5,000	5,000 to 10,000	10,000 to 25,000	25,000 to 50,000	50,000 to 100,000	100,000 to 250,000	250,000 to 500,000	500,000 to 2,500,000	2,500,000 and over
Number of Enterprises **1**	1925	68	442	61	22	59	65	132	217	349	236	215	60
Revenues ($ in Thousands)													
Net Sales **2**	87544818	1562554	147562	539248	96313	71085	76013	314246	932727	3472842	4944799	13325292	62062138
Interest **3**	54058546	1023056	119470	311	53478	6763	49622	228774	721621	2667680	3875408	8928996	36383367
Rents **4**	912308	3763	0	0	255	37	415	1175	1633	7641	11295	129821	756272
Royalties **5**	201	0	0	0	0	0	35	8	0	0	10	24	124
Other Portfolio Income **6**	5340158	71656	868	0	620	1853	1453	8772	36667	154243	247036	889999	3926990
Other Receipts **7**	27233605	464079	27224	538937	41960	62432	24488	75517	172806	643278	811050	3376452	20995385
Total Receipts **8**	87544818	1562554	147562	539248	96313	71085	76013	314246	932727	3472842	4944799	13325292	62062138
Average Total Receipts **9**	45478	22979	334	8840	4378	1205	1169	2381	4298	9951	20953	61978	1034369
Operating Costs/Operating Income (%)													
Cost of Operations **10**	0.5	•	•	6.5	•	•	2.3	•	0.1	0.0	0.0	0.2	0.6
Salaries and Wages **11**	16.1	18.5	0.1	3.7	22.4	20.0	17.0	16.9	13.2	16.5	15.2	15.6	16.4
Taxes Paid **12**	2.5	2.0	0.6	0.8	5.3	3.0	3.5	2.9	3.0	3.0	3.0	2.6	2.4
Interest Paid **13**	29.5	33.2	17.1	0.0	40.5	752.4	29.5	31.8	34.4	32.6	34.1	32.6	27.6
Depreciation **14**	4.1	1.2	2.2	0.4	2.4	1.6	3.4	2.4	3.1	3.9	2.9	3.6	4.5
Amortization and Depletion **15**	1.0	0.4	0.2	0.0	0.1	0.4	0.7	0.2	0.2	0.3	0.3	0.9	1.2
Pensions and Other Deferred Comp. **16**	0.9	1.8	•	0.1	1.4	0.1	1.3	1.4	1.6	1.5	1.5	1.4	0.7
Employee Benefits **17**	1.9	3.2	0.4	0.7	2.7	1.1	2.7	2.6	2.4	2.4	2.5	2.3	1.7
Advertising **18**	1.2	0.6	0.0	0.1	0.6	0.2	3.2	1.2	1.0	1.1	1.3	1.1	1.2
Other Expenses **19**	17.4	18.7	20.3	82.1	26.5	49.3	22.0	21.6	18.2	18.5	16.7	18.6	16.4
Officers' Compensation **20**	1.7	7.4	4.5	4.6	2.2	9.3	10.0	7.2	6.6	4.9	3.7	2.2	0.9
Operating Margin **21**	23.3	13.0	54.6	0.9	•	•	4.4	11.8	16.2	15.2	18.8	18.8	26.5
Operating Margin Before Officers' Comp. **22**	24.9	20.4	59.1	5.5	•	•	14.4	19.0	22.8	20.1	22.4	21.0	27.4

Selected Average Balance Sheet ($ in Thousands)

Item	1	2	3	4	5	6	7	8	9	10	11	12	13
Net Receivables **23**	40289	0	4	314	149	2869	1201	2919	6959	13410	21909	68175	848030
Inventories **24**	·	·	·	·	·	·	·	·	·	·	·	·	·
Net Property, Plant and Equipment **25**	7652	·	0	14	34	795	246	508	1258	2851	5706	12856	153670
Total Assets **26**	620953	4	20	742	2068	5554	17738	36730	73528	164165	358621	994848	13618841
Notes and Loans Payable **27**	144086	0	8	6	281	3718	1029	1624	4373	13695	29730	127766	3944001
All Other Liabilities **28**	451442	0	2429	579	162649	50089	13917	30731	59693	131579	290655	755812	9440904
Net Worth **29**	25425	0	-2417	158	-160862	-48253	2792	4375	9463	18891	38235	111270	233936

Selected Financial Ratios (Times to 1)

Item	1	2	3	4	5	6	7	8	9	10	11	12	13
Current Ratio **30**	0.3	0.0	0.0	1.0	0.0	0.1	0.4	0.4	0.3	0.3	0.3	0.2	0.2
Quick Ratio **31**	0.2	0.0	0.0	1.0	0.0	0.1	0.4	0.4	0.3	0.2	0.2	0.2	0.2
Net Sales to Working Capital **32**	·	·	·	·	·	·	·	·	·	·	·	·	·
Coverage Ratio **33**	1.8	1.4	4.2	36.6	0.9	0.0	1.1	1.3	1.4	1.4	1.5	1.6	2.0
Total Asset Turnover **34**	0.1	16.5	11.9	2.1	0.2	0.1	0.1	0.1	0.1	0.1	0.1	0.1	0.1
Inventory Turnover **35**	·	·	·	·	·	·	·	·	·	·	·	·	·
Receivables Turnover **36**	·	·	·	·	·	·	·	·	·	·	·	·	·
Total Liabilities to Net Worth **37**	23.4	·	·	3.7	·	·	5.4	7.4	6.8	7.7	8.4	7.9	57.2
Current Assets to Working Capital **38**	·	·	·	·	·	·	·	·	·	·	·	·	·
Current Liabilities to Working Capital **39**	·	·	·	·	·	·	·	·	·	·	·	·	·
Working Capital to Net Sales **40**	·	·	·	·	·	·	·	·	·	·	·	·	·
Inventory to Working Capital **41**	·	·	·	·	·	·	·	·	·	·	·	·	·
Total Receipts to Cash Flow **42**	2.7	3.5	1.4	1.2	6.4	4.2	3.4	3.2	3.2	3.0	3.0	3.0	2.6
Cost of Goods to Cash Flow **43**	0.0	·	0.1	0.1	·	0.1	0.0	0.0	0.0	0.0	0.0	0.0	0.0
Cash Flow to Total Debt **44**	0.0	0.1	·	12.4	0.0	0.0	0.0	0.0	0.0	0.0	0.0	0.0	0.0

Selected Financial Factors (in Percentages)

Item	1	2	3	4	5	6	7	8	9	10	11	12	13
Debt Ratio **45**	95.9	·	12045.5	78.8	7879.5	968.8	84.3	88.1	87.1	88.5	89.3	88.8	98.3
Return on Total Assets **46**	3.8	·	1183.4	10.9	77.1	3.3	2.2	2.8	2.9	2.8	3.0	3.2	4.1
Return on Equity Before Income Taxes **47**	41.0	·	50.0	0.1	18.4	1.7	6.0	6.9	7.5	9.8	10.1		116.3
Return on Equity After Income Taxes **48**	27.1	·	40.5	0.3	18.4	0.3	3.9	4.6	4.8	6.6	6.8		78.0
Profit Margin (Before Income Tax) **49**	22.9	12.5	0.9	54.6	18.4	4.0	11.0	15.3	14.2	17.9	18.1		26.3
Profit Margin (After Income Tax) **50**	15.2	8.0	0.7	54.6	18.4	0.6	7.3	10.2	9.1	12.1	12.3		17.6

Table II

Corporations with Net Income

SAVINGS INSTITUTIONS AND OTHER DEPOSITORY CREDIT

MONEY AMOUNTS AND SIZE OF ASSETS IN THOUSANDS OF DOLLARS

Item Description for Accounting Period 7/03 Through 6/04		Total	Zero Assets	Under 500	500 to 1,000	1,000 to 5,000	5,000 to 10,000	10,000 to 25,000	25,000 to 50,000	50,000 to 100,000	100,000 to 250,000	250,000 to 500,000	500,000 to 2,500,000	2,500,000 and over
Number of Enterprises	1	1710	19	439	61	•	•	58	111	195	322	•	•	•
Revenues ($ in Thousands)														
Net Sales	2	85430588	1103405	147334	539248	•	•	66657	258034	850269	3199059	•	•	•
Interest	3	52490403	618411	119395	311	•	•	48535	193654	669392	2488823	•	•	•
Rents	4	867388	3459	0	0	•	•	344	1109	1516	6826	•	•	•
Royalties	5	201	0	0	0	•	•	35	8	0	0	•	•	•
Other Portfolio Income	6	5177815	31728	868	0	•	•	1437	7212	32623	144532	•	•	•
Other Receipts	7	26894781	449807	27071	538937	•	•	16306	56051	146738	558878	•	•	•
Total Receipts	8	85430588	1103405	147334	539248	•	•	66657	258034	850269	3199059	•	•	•
Average Total Receipts	9	49959	58074	336	8840	•	•	1149	2325	4360	9935	•	•	•
Operating Costs/Operating Income (%)														
Cost of Operations	10	0.5	•	•	6.5	•	•	•	•	0.1	0.0	•	•	•
Salaries and Wages	11	15.9	7.3	0.1	3.7	•	•	14.9	16.2	12.9	16.1	•	•	•
Taxes Paid	12	2.5	1.2	0.6	0.8	•	•	3.6	2.9	3.0	3.1	•	•	•
Interest Paid	13	28.5	29.3	0.1	0.0	•	•	31.2	31.6	33.9	31.9	•	•	•
Depreciation	14	4.0	0.7	2.2	0.4	•	•	2.6	2.3	2.9	2.9	•	•	•
Amortization and Depletion	15	1.0	0.3	0.2	0.0	•	•	0.1	0.1	0.1	0.2	•	•	•
Pensions and Other Deferred Comp.	16	0.8	0.7	•	0.1	•	•	1.5	1.4	1.4	1.5	•	•	•
Employee Benefits	17	1.8	1.1	0.4	0.7	•	•	2.7	2.4	2.3	2.4	•	•	•
Advertising	18	1.2	0.4	0.0	0.1	•	•	1.1	1.0	1.0	1.1	•	•	•
Other Expenses	19	17.1	7.6	10.7	82.1	•	•	17.2	18.1	17.0	17.4	•	•	•
Officers' Compensation	20	1.5	1.3	4.5	4.6	•	•	9.9	7.3	6.3	5.0	•	•	•
Operating Margin	21	25.2	50.2	81.1	0.9	•	•	15.2	16.6	19.0	18.2	•	•	•
Operating Margin Before Officers' Comp.	22	26.7	51.4	85.6	5.5	•	•	25.1	23.9	25.3	23.3	•	•	•

Selected Average Balance Sheet ($ in Thousands)

Net Receivables 23	44194	0	4	314	•	937	2883	6723	13547
Inventories 24	•	•	•	•	•	•	•	•	•
Net Property, Plant and Equipment 25	8389	0	0	14	•	219	476	1233	2787
Total Assets 26	681307	0	19	742	•	17930	36725	73650	164425
Notes and Loans Payable 27	158350	0	8	6	•	814	1534	3955	13023
All Other Liabilities 28	492023	0	108	579	•	14627	30740	60264	132163
Net Worth 29	30934	0	-97	158	•	2490	4451	9430	19239

Selected Financial Ratios (Times to 1)

Current Ratio 30	0.2	•	0.9	1.0	•	0.3	0.4	0.3	0.3
Quick Ratio 31	0.2	•	0.2	1.0	•	0.3	0.4	0.3	0.3
Net Sales to Working Capital 32	•	•	•	•	•	•	•	•	•
Coverage Ratio 33	1.9	2.7	557.0	36.6	•	1.5	1.5	1.5	1.5
Total Asset Turnover 34	0.1	•	17.6	11.9	•	0.1	0.1	0.1	0.1
Inventory Turnover 35	•	•	•	•	•	•	•	•	•
Receivables Turnover 36	•	•	•	•	•	•	•	•	•
Total Liabilities to Net Worth 37	21.0	•	3.7	•	6.2	7.3	6.8	7.5	
Current Assets to Working Capital 38	•	•	•	•	•	•	•	•	•
Current Liabilities to Working Capital 39	•	•	•	•	•	•	•	•	•
Working Capital to Net Sales 40	•	•	•	•	•	•	•	•	•
Inventory to Working Capital 41	•	•	•	•	•	•	•	•	•
Total Receipts to Cash Flow 42	2.6	1.8	1.1	1.2	•	3.3	3.1	3.0	3.0
Cost of Goods to Cash Flow 43	0.0	•	•	0.1	•	•	•	0.0	0.0
Cash Flow to Total Debt 44	0.0	•	2.6	12.4	•	0.0	0.0	0.0	0.0

Selected Financial Factors (in Percentages)

Debt Ratio 45	95.5	•	607.0	78.8	•	86.1	87.9	87.2	88.3
Return on Total Assets 46	3.9	•	1432.8	10.9	•	2.9	3.0	3.1	3.0
Return on Equity Before Income Taxes 47	40.1	•	•	50.0	•	6.8	8.3	8.4	8.9
Return on Equity After Income Taxes 48	27.3	•	•	40.5	•	5.0	6.0	5.8	6.1
Profit Margin (Before Income Tax) 49	24.8	49.9	81.1	0.9	•	14.7	15.9	18.1	17.2
Profit Margin (After Income Tax) 50	16.9	43.4	81.1	0.7	•	10.9	11.4	12.5	11.7

Table I

Corporations with and without Net Income

CREDIT CARD ISSUING AND OTHER CONSUMER CREDIT

MONEY AMOUNTS AND SIZE OF ASSETS IN THOUSANDS OF DOLLARS

Item Description for Accounting Period 7/03 Through 6/04		Total	Zero Assets	Under 500	500 to 1,000	1,000 to 5,000	5,000 to 10,000	10,000 to 25,000	25,000 to 50,000	50,000 to 100,000	100,000 to 250,000	250,000 to 500,000	500,000 to 2,500,000	2,500,000 and over
Number of Enterprises	1	8053	1861	3093	739	1372	551	220	76	34	39	25	24	20
Revenues ($ in Thousands)														
Net Sales	2	89987369	149162	589610	144409	1500483	1183659	988863	583599	686965	1536300	2207592	6588462	73828265
Interest	3	29564055	29039	27668	4790	101995	71293	65371	86503	44665	495963	784009	2104972	25747785
Rents	4	266069	0	0	0	2105	372	497	538	178	268	2410	7864	251836
Royalties	5	46206	0	0	0	22	0	0	0	20592	0	2453	0	23140
Other Portfolio Income	6	4549205	1137	206	2	16947	44867	9766	5960	452	4272	1722	449146	4014730
Other Receipts	7	55561834	118986	561736	139617	1379414	1067127	913229	490598	621078	1035797	1416998	4026480	43790774
Total Receipts	8	89987369	149162	589610	144409	1500483	1183659	988863	583599	686965	1536300	2207592	6588462	73828265
Average Total Receipts	9	11174	80	191	195	1094	2148	4495	7679	20205	39392	88304	274519	3691413
Operating Costs/Operating Income (%)														
Cost of Operations	10	5.9	•	•	•	•	0.0	3.2	0.8	2.5	0.9	0.0	0.0	7.1
Salaries and Wages	11	8.6	16.4	25.2	24.7	19.2	14.5	16.6	22.6	21.0	14.8	17.7	6.5	7.5
Taxes Paid	12	1.2	2.1	2.7	3.0	2.6	2.2	2.1	2.4	2.3	2.5	2.0	0.7	1.0
Interest Paid	13	17.4	13.3	6.4	10.7	6.0	11.1	12.5	15.6	13.1	15.9	16.3	21.8	17.7
Depreciation	14	10.1	2.2	0.4	1.3	1.3	4.0	3.1	2.7	4.0	4.1	2.3	3.0	11.7
Amortization and Depletion	15	1.0	2.5	0.1	0.8	0.2	0.4	1.1	0.9	2.2	1.2	2.7	1.1	1.0
Pensions and Other Deferred Comp.	16	0.5	0.5	2.3	•	0.2	0.6	0.3	0.7	0.6	0.2	0.1	0.2	0.6
Employee Benefits	17	0.9	0.9	1.7	3.0	0.8	1.0	0.9	0.9	2.7	1.0	0.8	0.5	0.9
Advertising	18	2.6	3.8	2.4	1.2	8.0	0.8	1.6	2.1	1.2	1.7	1.6	0.9	2.7
Other Expenses	19	42.8	58.6	54.6	56.5	41.7	51.8	41.3	34.8	32.5	42.8	51.0	60.9	40.8
Officers' Compensation	20	0.9	4.3	11.9	4.5	5.5	5.8	6.2	5.7	4.6	3.2	1.1	0.3	0.5
Operating Margin	21	8.1	•	•	•	14.5	7.7	11.0	10.9	13.3	11.6	4.3	4.1	8.5
Operating Margin Before Officers' Comp.	22	9.0	•	4.1	•	20.0	13.5	17.2	16.6	17.9	14.9	5.5	4.4	9.0

Selected Average Balance Sheet ($ in Thousands)

	1	2	3	4	5	6	7	8	9	10	11	12	13
Net Receivables 23	38819	0	18	496	1368	4802	11173	24498	39464	93931	230500	744280	13735750
Inventories 24	•	•	•	•	•	•	•	•	•	•	•	•	•
Net Property, Plant and Equipment 25	2383	0	4	5	59	160	385	962	2258	1769	4454	17050	909146
Total Assets 26	72716	0	57	722	2012	6434	15199	34857	72181	149238	344421	1198850	26345855
Notes and Loans Payable 27	39112	0	80	309	1020	3965	9892	23552	43993	98505	187172	705336	13999857
All Other Liabilities 28	22332	0	21	98	428	1077	2356	4614	14326	19016	108402	245161	8391702
Net Worth 29	11272	0	-44	316	564	1392	2951	6690	13862	31717	48847	248353	3954296

Selected Financial Ratios (Times to 1)

	1	2	3	4	5	6	7	8	9	10	11	12	13
Current Ratio 30	1.9	•	1.9	3.6	2.7	2.3	2.1	1.8	2.0	2.2	1.6	1.8	1.9
Quick Ratio 31	1.8	•	1.9	3.1	2.6	2.0	2.0	1.7	1.9	1.9	1.6	1.5	1.8
Net Sales to Working Capital 32	0.5	•	10.3	0.5	1.1	0.7	0.6	0.6	0.9	0.6	0.9	0.6	0.5
Coverage Ratio 33	1.5	•	0.6	0.5	3.4	1.7	1.9	1.7	2.0	1.7	1.3	1.2	1.5
Total Asset Turnover 34	0.2	•	3.4	0.3	0.5	0.3	0.3	0.2	0.3	0.3	0.3	0.2	0.1
Inventory Turnover 35	•	•	•	•	•	•	•	•	•	•	•	•	•
Receivables Turnover 36	•	•	•	•	•	•	•	•	•	•	•	•	•
Total Liabilities to Net Worth 37	5.5	•	•	1.3	2.6	3.6	4.2	4.2	4.2	3.7	6.1	3.8	5.7
Current Assets to Working Capital 38	2.1	•	2.1	1.4	1.6	1.8	1.9	2.2	2.0	1.8	2.6	2.3	2.1
Current Liabilities to Working Capital 39	1.1	•	1.1	0.4	0.6	0.8	0.9	1.2	1.0	0.8	1.6	1.3	1.1
Working Capital to Net Sales 40	1.9	•	0.1	2.2	0.9	1.5	1.5	1.6	1.1	1.7	1.2	1.6	2.0
Inventory to Working Capital 41	0.0	•	•	•	0.0	0.0	0.0	0.0	0.0	0.0	0.0	0.0	0.0
Total Receipts to Cash Flow 42	2.1	•	2.3	2.2	2.0	1.8	2.0	2.3	2.4	2.0	2.1	1.7	2.1
Cost of Goods to Cash Flow 43	0.1	•	•	•	0.0	0.0	0.1	0.1	0.1	0.0	0.0	0.0	0.1
Cash Flow to Total Debt 44	0.1	•	0.8	0.2	0.4	0.2	0.2	0.1	0.1	0.2	0.1	0.1	0.1

Selected Financial Factors (in Percentages)

	1	2	3	4	5	6	7	8	9	10	11	12	13
Debt Ratio 45	84.5	•	177.9	56.2	72.0	78.4	80.6	80.8	80.8	78.7	85.8	79.3	85.0
Return on Total Assets 46	3.9	•	1.4	11.1	6.3	6.9	5.8	7.4	7.2	5.3	5.9	•	3.7
Return on Equity Before Income Taxes 47	8.2	33.6	•	28.2	11.8	16.8	12.4	19.4	14.4	7.8	4.4	•	8.1
Return on Equity After Income Taxes 48	5.8	35.5	•	26.8	8.9	15.6	11.1	18.1	9.9	3.6	1.8	•	5.7
Profit Margin (Before Income Tax) 49	8.2	•	•	14.5	7.7	11.0	10.8	13.3	11.6	4.3	4.0	•	8.6
Profit Margin (After Income Tax) 50	5.8	•	•	13.8	5.8	10.2	9.7	12.4	7.9	2.0	1.6	•	6.1

Table II
Corporations with Net Income

CREDIT CARD ISSUING AND OTHER CONSUMER CREDIT

MONEY AMOUNTS AND SIZE OF ASSETS IN THOUSANDS OF DOLLARS

Item Description for Accounting Period 7/03 Through 6/04	Total	Zero Assets	Under 500	500 to 1,000	1,000 to 5,000	5,000 to 10,000	10,000 to 25,000	25,000 to 50,000	50,000 to 100,000	100,000 to 250,000	250,000 to 500,000	500,000 to 2,500,000	2,500,000 and over
Number of Enterprises **1**	3992	449	1021	626	1115	443	179	59	27	30	11	18	13
Revenues ($ in Thousands)													
Net Sales **2**	77423074	132621	535813	118355	1431280	994410	841437	490805	640704	1267268	1384259	2849105	66737017
Interest **3**	25646001	18120	3228	3610	94264	70647	48367	68753	27286	285094	448099	1595259	22983273
Rents **4**	262135	0	0	0	2105	372	199	408	178	268	458	6310	251836
Royalties **5**	24182	0	0	0	22	0	0	0	20592	0	2453	0	1116
Other Portfolio Income **6**	3872918	347	204	0	16947	44773	8697	4637	286	2502	233	21886	3772406
Other Receipts **7**	47617838	114154	532381	114745	1317942	878618	784174	417007	592362	979404	933016	1225650	39728386
Total Receipts **8**	77423074	132621	535813	118355	1431280	994410	841437	490805	640704	1267268	1384259	2849105	66737017
Average Total Receipts **9**	19395	295	525	189	1284	2245	4701	8319	23730	42242	125842	158284	5133617
Operating Costs/Operating Income (%)													
Cost of Operations **10**	6.8	•	•	•	•	•	3.5	1.0	2.6	1.1	0.0	0.0	7.8
Salaries and Wages **11**	8.8	17.5	25.8	19.9	17.8	11.8	16.4	23.8	21.5	16.5	22.2	9.0	7.7
Taxes Paid **12**	1.2	2.3	2.6	2.5	2.4	2.3	2.1	2.5	2.4	2.9	2.4	1.2	1.0
Interest Paid **13**	15.6	7.2	1.9	4.9	4.8	9.8	11.8	12.4	10.8	9.3	11.2	16.1	16.4
Depreciation **14**	8.0	2.4	0.3	1.0	1.0	3.9	2.8	3.0	2.7	2.2	1.9	4.5	8.9
Amortization and Depletion **15**	0.9	2.3	0.0	•	0.1	0.3	1.2	0.2	2.3	0.2	4.2	0.5	0.9
Pensions and Other Deferred Comp. **16**	0.5	0.6	2.6	•	0.2	0.7	0.4	0.7	0.7	0.2	0.2	0.2	0.5
Employee Benefits **17**	1.0	1.0	1.9	2.8	0.8	0.9	0.9	1.0	2.9	1.1	0.6	0.6	1.0
Advertising **18**	2.9	4.2	2.7	1.5	8.2	0.8	1.6	1.7	1.2	2.0	2.2	0.7	2.9
Other Expenses **19**	42.3	50.4	42.0	46.0	38.6	48.5	33.9	27.2	32.1	37.8	33.9	47.6	42.6
Officers' Compensation **20**	0.9	4.7	12.2	1.7	4.2	6.2	6.1	6.4	4.9	3.7	1.3	0.6	0.5
Operating Margin **21**	11.0	7.5	7.9	19.7	21.8	14.7	19.4	20.1	16.0	23.0	19.9	19.0	9.8
Operating Margin Before Officers' Comp. **22**	11.9	12.2	20.2	21.4	26.0	21.0	25.5	26.5	20.8	26.8	21.2	19.7	10.3

Selected Average Balance Sheet ($ in Thousands)

Item	1	2	3	4	5	6	7	8	9	10	11	12
Net Receivables 23	62686	9	491	1503	5060	11576	25413	43385	93956	270101	698212	17146910
Inventories 24	•	•	•	•	•	•	•	•	•	•	•	•
Net Property, Plant and Equipment 25	3135	4	4	57	123	323	1025	1962	2103	5659	15429	909074
Total Assets 26	122549	97	731	2101	6174	15108	34222	69610	147905	356221	1117376	34500925
Notes and Loans Payable 27	60830	79	288	1078	3648	9633	21999	40109	92191	136003	575387	17002356
All Other Liabilities 28	41549	55	102	384	1050	2385	5064	14277	16515	120474	239384	12123835
Net Worth 29	20170	-37	341	639	1476	3090	7158	15224	39199	99744	302604	5374734

Selected Financial Ratios (Times to 1)

Item	1	2	3	4	5	6	7	8	9	10	11	12
Current Ratio 30	1.9	1.4	4.8	2.7	2.7	2.2	1.7	2.1	2.2	1.9	1.7	1.9
Quick Ratio 31	1.9	1.3	4.0	2.6	2.6	2.0	1.6	2.1	1.9	1.8	1.4	1.9
Net Sales to Working Capital 32	0.5	30.0	0.4	1.2	0.6	0.7	0.7	1.0	0.6	0.9	0.4	0.5
Coverage Ratio 33	1.7	2.0	5.2	5.0	5.5	2.5	2.6	2.6	2.5	3.5	2.8	1.6
Total Asset Turnover 34	0.2	5.4	0.3	0.6	0.4	0.3	0.2	0.3	0.3	0.4	0.1	0.1
Inventory Turnover 35	•	•	•	•	•	•	•	•	•	•	•	•
Receivables Turnover 36	•	•	•	•	•	•	•	•	•	•	•	•
Total Liabilities to Net Worth 37	5.1	3.8	1.1	2.3	3.2	3.9	3.8	3.6	2.8	2.6	2.7	5.4
Current Assets to Working Capital 38	2.1	3.8	1.3	1.6	1.6	1.8	2.4	1.9	1.8	2.2	2.3	2.1
Current Liabilities to Working Capital 39	1.1	2.8	0.3	0.6	0.6	0.8	1.4	0.9	0.8	1.2	1.3	1.1
Working Capital to Net Sales 40	1.8	0.0	2.5	0.9	1.6	1.5	1.4	1.1	1.6	1.1	2.4	1.9
Inventory to Working Capital 41	0.0	0.0	•	•	•	•	0.0	0.0	0.0	0.0	•	0.0
Total Receipts to Cash Flow 42	2.0	1.8	2.1	1.7	1.9	2.0	2.2	2.2	1.8	2.0	1.5	2.0
Cost of Goods to Cash Flow 43	0.1	•	•	•	0.1	0.0	0.0	0.1	0.0	0.0	0.0	0.2
Cash Flow to Total Debt 44	0.1	1.8	0.3	0.5	0.3	0.2	0.2	0.2	0.1	0.2	0.1	0.1

Selected Financial Factors (in Percentages)

Item	1	2	3	4	5	6	7	8	9	10	11	12
Debt Ratio 45	83.5	138.2	53.3	69.6	76.1	79.5	79.1	78.1	73.5	72.0	72.9	84.4
Return on Total Assets 46	4.2	53.2	6.4	16.2	8.9	9.7	7.9	9.1	9.2	11.0	5.0	3.9
Return on Equity Before Income Taxes 47	10.8	•	10.9	43.7	22.4	29.5	23.4	24.9	24.8	25.1	10.0	9.5
Return on Equity After Income Taxes 48	8.0	•	9.5	42.2	19.0	28.1	21.8	23.3	20.0	20.5	7.0	6.8
Profit Margin (Before Income Tax) 49	11.2	7.9	19.7	21.8	14.7	19.4	20.1	16.0	23.0	19.9	19.0	10.0
Profit Margin (After Income Tax) 50	8.3	7.4	17.2	21.0	12.5	18.5	18.8	15.0	18.6	16.2	13.4	7.2

Table I

Corporations with and without Net Income

REAL ESTATE CREDIT INCL. MORTGAGE BANKERS AND ORIGINATORS

MONEY AMOUNTS AND SIZE OF ASSETS IN THOUSANDS OF DOLLARS

Item Description for Accounting Period 7/03 Through 6/04	Total	Zero Assets	Under 500	500 to 1,000	1,000 to 5,000	5,000 to 10,000	10,000 to 25,000	25,000 to 50,000	50,000 to 100,000	100,000 to 250,000	250,000 to 500,000	500,000 to 2,500,000	2,500,000 and over
Number of Enterprises 1	18199	2985	12132	712	1305	566	237	107	57	45	23	23	6
Revenues ($ in Thousands)													
Net Sales 2	39646808	257863	5830553	1281565	3434881	2032586	2350426	2036186	1892665	1847069	1752737	3561596	13368680
Interest 3	5447109	58678	8198	1770	45514	27682	80027	63376	170610	226162	300066	991989	3473038
Rents 4	38260	0	402	0	8088	213	3771	1426	395	5115	127	9113	9610
Royalties 5	542	0	0	0	0	0	66	17	0	459	0	0	0
Other Portfolio Income 6	1458659	283	12515	1	8301	7533	51327	18591	111872	131822	258348	808673	49397
Other Receipts 7	32702238	198902	5809438	1279794	3372978	1997158	2215235	1952776	1609788	1483511	1194196	1751821	9836635
Total Receipts 8	39646808	257863	5830553	1281565	3434881	2032586	2350426	2036186	1892665	1847069	1752737	3561596	13368680
Average Total Receipts 9	2179	86	481	1800	2632	3591	9917	19030	33205	41046	76206	154852	2228113
Operating Costs/Operating Income (%)													
Cost of Operations 10	2.6	0.3	1.2	0.4	0.5	6.8	7.3	8.9	2.0	2.5	3.8	0.8	2.0
Salaries and Wages 11	27.5	31.1	23.6	32.4	45.7	26.9	25.8	39.3	31.9	27.8	28.0	26.7	22.0
Taxes Paid 12	2.9	5.8	3.4	2.8	4.4	2.0	2.5	3.6	3.1	3.0	3.6	3.4	2.2
Interest Paid 13	9.8	5.0	0.4	0.7	3.4	5.1	6.4	6.7	8.9	13.3	14.5	15.9	15.7
Depreciation 14	1.3	1.0	0.9	1.1	0.8	1.0	0.8	1.0	1.1	1.2	1.7	2.1	1.7
Amortization and Depletion 15	0.4	0.1	0.1	0.0	0.1	0.2	0.2	0.2	0.9	2.2	0.6	1.8	0.2
Pensions and Other Deferred Comp. 16	0.5	0.5	0.4	0.2	0.3	0.1	0.4	0.3	0.3	1.6	0.3	0.2	0.7
Employee Benefits 17	1.3	0.9	1.4	1.9	1.0	0.3	0.9	1.1	1.2	1.1	1.3	1.5	1.6
Advertising 18	1.9	2.8	3.3	0.8	2.7	2.6	1.6	2.2	3.3	1.8	1.0	2.5	0.9
Other Expenses 19	33.2	54.6	46.7	31.9	23.2	42.3	40.1	23.7	25.2	28.2	22.9	29.9	32.6
Officers' Compensation 20	4.5	1.9	8.4	8.5	9.0	6.0	7.4	5.0	8.5	4.9	5.0	1.7	0.4
Operating Margin 21	14.0	•	10.2	19.3	8.9	6.7	6.6	8.1	13.6	12.3	17.3	13.3	20.1
Operating Margin Before Officers' Comp. 22	18.4	•	18.6	27.8	17.9	12.7	14.0	13.1	22.1	17.3	22.3	15.0	20.5

Selected Average Balance Sheet ($ in Thousands)

Net Receivables 23	1154	0	7	52	774	1434	2403	5268	8587	29193	37099	258315	1554162
Inventories 24	•	•	•	•	•	•	•	•	•	•	•	•	•
Net Property, Plant and Equipment 25	114	0	19	79	141	164	467	909	1509	2431	3279	9608	137511
Total Assets 26	8608	102	676	2630	6447	15594	34390	66979	163344	345076	1075104	16107307
Notes and Loans Payable 27	3967	26	87	1520	4371	8521	19316	35959	101518	188730	590318	6457068
All Other Liabilities 28	3627	18	117	398	795	4380	9962	18720	44140	114247	341693	8181566
Net Worth 29	1014	58	472	712	1281	2694	5113	12301	17686	42099	143094	1468674

Selected Financial Ratios (Times to 1)

Current Ratio 30	0.4	•	2.9	3.6	1.2	0.6	0.6	0.5	0.6	0.6	0.5	0.7	0.3
Quick Ratio 31	0.4	•	2.7	3.4	1.0	0.4	0.3	0.4	0.4	0.5	0.4	0.6	0.3
Net Sales to Working Capital 32	•	•	14.2	6.0	12.7	•	•	•	•	•	•	•	•
Coverage Ratio 33	2.4	0.2	26.5	28.6	3.6	2.0	2.2	2.5	1.9	2.2	1.8	2.3
Total Asset Turnover 34	0.3	•	4.7	2.7	1.0	0.6	0.6	0.5	0.3	0.2	0.1	0.1
Inventory Turnover 35	•	•	•	•	•	•	•	•	•	•	•	•	•
Receivables Turnover 36	•	•	•	•	•	•	•	•	•	•	•	•	•
Total Liabilities to Net Worth 37	7.5	•	0.8	0.4	2.7	4.8	5.7	4.4	8.2	7.2	6.5	10.0
Current Assets to Working Capital 38	•	•	1.5	1.4	6.3	•	•	•	•	•	•	•	•
Current Liabilities to Working Capital 39	•	•	0.5	0.4	5.3	•	•	•	•	•	•	•	•
Working Capital to Net Sales 40	•	0.2	0.1	0.2	0.1	•	•	•	•	•	•	•	•
Inventory to Working Capital 41	•	•	•	•	0.0	•	•	•	•	•	•	•	•
Total Receipts to Cash Flow 42	2.6	2.3	2.0	2.1	3.5	2.2	2.6	3.5	2.8	2.7	2.7	2.5	3.0
Cost of Goods to Cash Flow 43	0.1	0.0	0.0	0.0	0.0	0.2	0.3	0.1	0.1	0.1	0.0	0.1
Cash Flow to Total Debt 44	0.1	•	5.5	4.3	0.4	0.3	0.2	0.2	0.2	0.1	0.1	0.1

Selected Financial Factors (in Percentages)

Debt Ratio 45	88.2	•	42.9	30.3	72.9	82.7	85.1	81.6	89.2	87.8	86.7	90.9
Return on Total Assets 46	6.0	•	49.9	53.1	12.3	8.3	8.2	11.2	6.3	7.0	4.2	5.0
Return on Equity Before Income Taxes 47	30.0	•	84.1	73.5	32.7	24.4	30.0	36.7	27.6	31.1	14.4	30.5
Return on Equity After Income Taxes 48	25.3	•	83.5	69.8	32.0	22.3	27.7	33.1	23.0	26.3	8.9	24.8
Profit Margin (Before Income Tax) 49	14.0	10.2	19.3	8.9	6.4	6.6	8.1	13.6	11.9	17.2	13.3	20.1
Profit Margin (After Income Tax) 50	11.8	10.1	18.3	8.6	6.0	6.1	7.4	12.2	9.9	14.5	8.2	16.3

285

Table II
Corporations with Net Income

REAL ESTATE CREDIT INCL. MORTGAGE BANKERS AND ORIGINATORS

MONEY AMOUNTS AND SIZE OF ASSETS IN THOUSANDS OF DOLLARS

Item Description for Accounting Period 7/03 Through 6/04	Total	Zero Assets	Under 500	500 to 1,000	1,000 to 5,000	5,000 to 10,000	10,000 to 25,000	25,000 to 50,000	50,000 to 100,000	100,000 to 250,000	250,000 to 500,000	500,000 to 2,500,000	2,500,000 and over
Number of Enterprises 1	11014	286	8261	678	861	545	181	83	47	34	17	16	6
Revenues ($ in Thousands)													
Net Sales 2	36346252	147405	5223459	1240778	3022475	1911007	1838770	1820168	1724527	1562850	1502583	2983550	13368680
Interest 3	4991156	58678	3401	459	37048	23117	55440	49131	137965	153650	180373	818857	3473038
Rents 4	31658	0	402	0	8088	60	3430	1296	255	864	91	7563	9610
Royalties 5	542	0	0	0	0	0	66	17	0	459	0	0	0
Other Portfolio Income 6	1422413	283	12515	1	6965	7267	50832	18530	104547	125168	258348	790562	49397
Other Receipts 7	29898483	88444	5207141	1240318	2970374	1880563	1729002	1751194	1481760	1282709	1063771	1366568	9836635
Total Receipts 8	36346252	147405	5223459	1240778	3022475	1911007	1838770	1820168	1724527	1562850	1502583	2983550	13368680
Average Total Receipts 9	3300	515	632	1830	3510	3506	10159	21930	36692	45966	88387	186472	2228113
Operating Costs/Operating Income (%)													
Cost of Operations 10	2.4	0.5	1.2	0.4	0.5	6.1	6.6	9.9	2.2	2.3	2.6	·	2.0
Salaries and Wages 11	27.4	24.7	23.4	33.5	48.9	27.5	24.6	38.1	31.7	26.5	29.3	26.2	22.0
Taxes Paid 12	2.9	8.3	3.1	2.9	4.6	2.0	2.4	3.7	2.9	2.9	4.0	3.7	2.2
Interest Paid 13	9.3	7.8	0.2	0.6	3.4	5.2	6.5	5.9	8.0	10.0	9.0	12.7	15.7
Depreciation 14	1.3	1.2	0.8	1.1	0.7	1.0	0.8	0.9	0.9	1.0	1.8	1.8	1.7
Amortization and Depletion 15	0.4	0.2	0.1	0.0	0.0	0.2	0.1	0.2	0.8	2.3	0.7	1.5	0.2
Pensions and Other Deferred Comp. 16	0.5	0.9	0.5	0.1	0.3	0.1	0.5	0.3	0.3	1.7	0.4	0.2	0.7
Employee Benefits 17	1.3	1.6	1.1	2.0	0.9	0.3	0.8	1.2	1.0	1.2	1.3	1.6	1.6
Advertising 18	1.7	1.0	2.6	0.8	1.7	2.7	1.4	2.2	3.5	2.0	0.9	2.4	0.9
Other Expenses 19	31.8	34.3	47.2	30.5	18.9	40.7	35.5	22.8	24.6	26.0	23.5	23.4	32.6
Officers' Compensation 20	4.2	3.3	7.7	8.3	8.8	6.3	6.7	5.0	8.3	5.4	5.7	2.0	0.4
Operating Margin 21	16.9	16.4	12.2	19.9	11.2	8.1	14.1	9.9	15.8	18.9	20.7	24.5	20.1
Operating Margin Before Officers' Comp. 22	21.1	19.6	19.9	28.2	20.0	14.3	20.8	14.9	24.0	24.3	26.4	26.5	20.5

Selected Average Balance Sheet ($ in Thousands)

Net Receivables 23	1584	0	5	18	1078	1420	2386	5566	10067	31074	49401	193813	1554162
Inventories 24	•	•	•	•	•	•	•	•	•	•	•	•	•
Net Property, Plant and Equipment 25	159	0	16	79	179	157	502	571	1412	1615	3981	10677	137511
Total Assets 26	12858	0	96	663	2971	6433	15531	34610	68480	162466	349079	1081559	16107307
Notes and Loans Payable 27	5535	0	15	73	1703	4027	8682	19316	35188	93357	153784	485031	6457068
All Other Liabilities 28	5738	0	8	98	517	693	3315	10538	19305	41591	142901	433342	8181566
Net Worth 29	1585	0	73	492	751	1713	3534	4757	13987	27519	52393	163186	1468674

Selected Financial Ratios (Times to 1)

Current Ratio 30	0.4	•	5.6	4.1	1.1	0.6	0.6	0.5	0.6	0.6	0.5	0.5	0.3
Quick Ratio 31	0.3	•	4.9	3.8	1.0	0.5	0.4	0.3	0.4	0.5	0.4	0.4	0.3
Net Sales to Working Capital 32	•	•	15.5	6.2	45.6	•	•	•	•	•	•	•	•
Coverage Ratio 33	2.8	3.1	63.7	33.0	4.3	2.5	3.2	2.7	3.0	2.9	3.3	2.9	2.3
Total Asset Turnover 34	0.3	•	6.6	2.8	1.2	0.5	0.7	0.6	0.5	0.3	0.3	0.2	0.1
Inventory Turnover 35	•	•	•	•	•	•	•	•	•	•	•	•	•
Receivables Turnover 36	•	•	•	•	•	•	•	•	•	•	•	•	•
Total Liabilities to Net Worth 37	7.1	•	0.3	•	3.0	2.8	3.4	6.3	3.9	4.9	5.7	5.6	10.0
Current Assets to Working Capital 38	•	•	1.2	1.3	20.2	•	•	•	•	•	•	•	•
Current Liabilities to Working Capital 39	•	•	0.2	0.3	19.2	•	•	•	•	•	•	•	•
Working Capital to Net Sales 40	•	•	0.1	0.2	0.0	•	•	•	•	•	•	•	•
Inventory to Working Capital 41	•	•	•	•	•	•	•	•	•	•	•	•	•
Total Receipts to Cash Flow 42	2.5	2.1	1.9	2.1	3.8	2.2	2.1	3.4	2.7	2.4	2.4	2.2	3.0
Cost of Goods to Cash Flow 43	0.1	0.0	0.0	0.0	0.0	0.1	0.1	0.3	0.1	0.1	0.1	0.1	0.1
Cash Flow to Total Debt 44	0.1	•	14.7	5.1	0.4	0.3	0.4	0.2	0.3	0.1	0.1	0.1	0.1

Selected Financial Factors (in Percentages)

Debt Ratio 45	87.7	•	24.0	25.8	74.7	73.4	77.2	86.3	79.6	83.1	85.0	84.9	90.9
Return on Total Assets 46	6.7	•	81.6	56.7	17.3	7.1	13.4	9.9	12.7	8.1	7.5	6.4	5.0
Return on Equity Before Income Taxes 47	35.1	•	105.7	74.1	52.4	16.0	40.5	45.4	41.3	31.4	34.8	28.0	30.5
Return on Equity After Income Taxes 48	30.2	•	104.9	70.3	51.3	15.1	38.4	42.2	37.4	27.4	29.6	21.1	24.8
Profit Margin (Before Income Tax) 49	16.9	16.4	12.2	19.9	11.2	7.8	14.1	9.8	15.8	18.8	20.7	24.5	20.1
Profit Margin (After Income Tax) 50	14.5	11.5	12.1	18.9	11.0	7.4	13.4	9.2	14.3	16.4	17.5	18.4	16.3

Table I

Corporations with and without Net Income

INTL. TRADE, SECONDARY FINANCING, OTHER NONDEPOSITORY CREDIT

MONEY AMOUNTS AND SIZE OF ASSETS IN THOUSANDS OF DOLLARS

Item Description for Accounting Period 7/03 Through 6/04	Total	Zero Assets	Under 500	500 to 1,000	1,000 to 5,000	5,000 to 10,000	10,000 to 25,000	25,000 to 50,000	50,000 to 100,000	100,000 to 250,000	250,000 to 500,000	500,000 to 2,500,000	2,500,000 and over
Number of Enterprises 1	6601	1862	3071	711	549	49	102	51	43	48	28	47	40

Revenues ($ in Thousands)

Item	Total	Zero Assets	Under 500	500 to 1,000	1,000 to 5,000	5,000 to 10,000	10,000 to 25,000	25,000 to 50,000	50,000 to 100,000	100,000 to 250,000	250,000 to 500,000	500,000 to 2,500,000	2,500,000 and over
Net Sales 2	119721937	619869	497116	584394	1097594	66506	760843	388319	366101	901836	660962	2467958	111310439
Interest 3	100160892	405512	80465	90133	95000	8297	22281	55592	105399	352357	256630	1572398	97116829
Rents 4	101246	2	0	403	1114	0	108	1388	168	1683	2448	15168	78764
Royalties 5	31753	0	0	0	0	0	0	3	0	0	154	0	31595
Other Portfolio Income 6	2694342	12438	0	157	1169	196	3116	5176	301	35674	18265	55267	2562588
Other Receipts 7	16733704	201917	416651	493701	1000311	58013	735338	326160	260233	512122	383465	825125	11520663
Total Receipts 8	119721937	619869	497116	584394	1097594	66506	760843	388319	366101	901836	660962	2467958	111310439
Average Total Receipts 9	18137	333	162	822	1999	1357	7459	7614	8514	18788	23606	52510	2782761

Operating Costs/Operating Income (%)

Item	Total	Zero Assets	Under 500	500 to 1,000	1,000 to 5,000	5,000 to 10,000	10,000 to 25,000	25,000 to 50,000	50,000 to 100,000	100,000 to 250,000	250,000 to 500,000	500,000 to 2,500,000	2,500,000 and over
Cost of Operations 10	0.4	7.8	0.0	0.0	1.5	•	27.7	3.4	9.1	5.5	•	2.5	0.0
Salaries and Wages 11	2.4	3.2	15.4	44.8	25.9	27.1	14.7	21.8	14.3	15.0	14.4	8.1	1.4
Taxes Paid 12	0.3	0.5	4.9	6.5	2.5	3.2	1.8	2.8	2.4	1.2	2.2	1.1	0.2
Interest Paid 13	70.2	54.2	10.7	10.5	8.8	28.9	6.4	12.7	19.5	19.7	31.4	38.4	73.6
Depreciation 14	0.6	0.3	2.4	1.6	2.7	1.3	1.4	2.2	1.4	1.5	2.4	4.5	0.5
Amortization and Depletion 15	0.3	0.1	0.2	0.1	0.5	0.2	0.5	1.1	0.2	0.9	0.6	0.3	0.3
Pensions and Other Deferred Comp. 16	0.4	•	0.0	0.2	1.5	0.5	0.4	1.5	0.4	0.5	0.8	0.4	0.4
Employee Benefits 17	0.2	0.7	0.0	1.1	1.8	1.8	0.9	2.2	1.4	1.0	1.3	0.8	0.2
Advertising 18	0.1	0.3	4.5	1.3	0.4	0.9	0.5	1.2	0.9	0.6	1.1	0.3	0.1
Other Expenses 19	7.8	37.9	50.1	36.8	53.6	81.3	32.3	48.8	29.3	32.7	31.7	23.8	5.7
Officers' Compensation 20	0.6	1.0	8.6	7.4	9.9	2.8	4.3	3.4	4.6	3.4	3.2	0.3	0.3
Operating Margin 21	16.8	•	3.0	•	•	•	9.2	•	16.7	18.2	10.9	19.6	17.5
Operating Margin Before Officers' Comp. 22	17.3	•	11.7	•	•	•	13.5	2.3	21.3	21.6	14.1	19.9	17.8

Selected Average Balance Sheet ($ in Thousands)

	1	2	3	4	5	6	7	8	9	10	11	12	13
Net Receivables **23**	37679	0	50	302	594	2794	8755	19147	47349	102479	216485	699871	5002713
Inventories **24**	•	•	•	•	•	•	•	•	•	•	•	•	•
Net Property, Plant and Equipment **25**	263	0	8	58	275	176	462	831	717	1519	2721	6518	23278
Total Assets **26**	330833	0	120	673	2117	7380	15950	34707	73895	156683	338094	1312957	52404717
Notes and Loans Payable **27**	297059	0	64	326	943	6604	10988	19980	47181	97965	199450	902683	47568433
All Other Liabilities **28**	19607	0	-542	51	508	1047	3761	6478	7563	17167	55589	138545	3019830
Net Worth **29**	14167	0	599	295	666	-270	1202	8248	19152	41551	83055	271730	1816454

Selected Financial Ratios (Times to 1)

	1	2	3	4	5	6	7	8	9	10	11	12	13
Current Ratio **30**	0.4	•	2.5	4.4	1.3	1.7	1.5	1.6	1.4	1.3	1.1	1.3	0.4
Quick Ratio **31**	0.3	•	1.7	3.7	1.1	1.4	1.3	1.5	1.3	1.2	1.0	1.1	0.3
Net Sales to Working Capital **32**	•	•	2.6	1.8	5.8	0.8	1.9	0.8	0.5	0.7	0.9	0.2	•
Coverage Ratio **33**	1.2	•	0.9	1.3	0.0	•	2.5	0.9	1.9	1.7	1.3	1.6	1.2
Total Asset Turnover **34**	0.1	•	1.3	1.2	0.9	0.2	0.5	0.2	0.1	0.1	0.1	0.0	0.1
Inventory Turnover **35**	•	•	•	•	•	•	•	•	•	•	•	•	•
Receivables Turnover **36**	•	•	•	•	•	•	•	•	•	•	•	•	•
Total Liabilities to Net Worth **37**	22.4	•	•	1.3	2.2	•	12.3	3.2	2.9	2.8	3.1	3.8	27.9
Current Assets to Working Capital **38**	•	•	1.7	1.3	2.4	3.0	3.4	2.6	3.4	4.3	9.6	4.0	•
Current Liabilities to Working Capital **39**	•	•	0.7	0.3	1.4	2.0	2.4	1.6	2.4	3.3	8.6	3.0	•
Working Capital to Net Sales **40**	•	•	0.4	0.5	0.2	1.2	0.5	1.3	1.9	1.4	1.1	4.8	•
Inventory to Working Capital **41**	•	•	0.0	0.0	0.0	0.0	0.0	0.0	•	0.0	0.0	0.0	0.0
Total Receipts to Cash Flow **42**	4.2	3.4	2.3	4.8	2.5	3.4	2.7	2.4	2.3	2.0	2.6	2.4	4.5
Cost of Goods to Cash Flow **43**	0.0	0.3	0.0	0.0	•	0.3	0.7	0.1	0.2	0.1	0.1	0.1	0.0
Cash Flow to Total Debt **44**	0.0	•	0.5	0.1	0.6	0.1	0.2	0.1	0.1	0.1	0.0	0.0	0.0

Selected Financial Factors (in Percentages)

	1	2	3	4	5	6	7	8	9	10	11	12	13
Debt Ratio **45**	95.7	•	•	56.1	68.5	103.7	92.5	76.2	74.1	73.5	75.4	79.3	96.5
Return on Total Assets **46**	4.7	•	•	18.5	0.3	7.4	2.5	4.2	4.1	4.2	2.9	2.4	4.8
Return on Equity Before Income Taxes **47**	20.1	•	•	0.8	242.0	•	58.2	7.4	6.5	5.9	4.2	4.3	24.9
Return on Equity After Income Taxes **48**	13.0	•	•	0.3	256.1	•	53.8	5.9	4.2	4.2	2.8	2.8	16.3
Profit Margin (Before Income Tax) **49**	15.7	•	3.0	9.4	16.7	•	14.4	10.4	16.7	14.4	10.4	22.2	16.3
Profit Margin (After Income Tax) **50**	10.1	•	8.7	13.2	9.3	•	5.1	14.4	13.2	9.3	5.1	14.4	10.6

287

Table II
Corporations with Net Income

INTL. TRADE, SECONDARY FINANCING, OTHER NONDEPOSITORY CREDIT

MONEY AMOUNTS AND SIZE OF ASSETS IN THOUSANDS OF DOLLARS

Item Description for Accounting Period 7/03 Through 6/04	Total	Zero Assets	Under 500	500 to 1,000	1,000 to 5,000	5,000 to 10,000	10,000 to 25,000	25,000 to 50,000	50,000 to 100,000	100,000 to 250,000	250,000 to 500,000	500,000 to 2,500,000	2,500,000 and over
Number of Enterprises 1	3030	1007	1240	169	339	13	71	36	25	33	23	38	36
Revenues ($ in Thousands)													
Net Sales 2	116972070	404519	374338	109332	666104	39560	594224	321225	280398	772436	450268	1983683	110975984
Interest 3	98914569	219959	38017	67582	30832	2887	9384	15590	50593	268644	229959	1135522	96845600
Rents 4	96251	0	0	0	0	0	90	1356	166	1010	2146	12719	78764
Royalties 5	31595	0	0	0	0	0	0	0	0	0	0	0	31595
Other Portfolio Income 6	2654094	2908	0	157	1100	0	2565	4387	49	16139	8932	55267	2562588
Other Receipts 7	15275561	181652	336321	41593	634172	36673	582185	299892	229590	486643	209231	780175	11457437
Total Receipts 8	116972070	404519	374338	109332	666104	39560	594224	321225	280398	772436	450268	1983683	110975984
Average Total Receipts 9	38605	402	302	647	1965	3043	8369	8923	11216	23407	19577	52202	3082666
Operating Costs/Operating Income (%)													
Cost of Operations 10	0.4	11.9	•	•	2.4	•	35.5	3.3	11.8	6.4	•	3.1	0.0
Salaries and Wages 11	2.0	3.4	12.1	7.1	27.7	19.1	12.3	23.2	13.1	15.8	8.2	9.1	1.4
Taxes Paid 12	0.3	0.7	4.4	3.6	3.4	3.8	1.6	3.1	2.6	1.3	1.5	1.2	0.2
Interest Paid 13	71.0	52.0	4.3	42.4	3.9	2.9	5.8	8.9	13.3	17.5	29.0	31.4	73.7
Depreciation 14	0.6	0.4	0.3	0.3	1.9	1.2	1.0	2.1	1.5	1.6	2.3	5.4	0.5
Amortization and Depletion 15	0.3	0.0	0.1	•	0.9	0.3	0.1	0.7	0.2	1.0	0.1	0.4	0.3
Pensions and Other Deferred Comp. 16	0.4	•	•	•	2.3	•	0.2	1.7	0.5	0.4	0.6	0.4	0.4
Employee Benefits 17	0.2	1.1	•	•	2.5	1.0	0.5	2.2	1.3	0.7	1.1	0.9	0.2
Advertising 18	0.1	0.4	5.3	0.7	0.6	1.1	0.6	1.4	1.0	0.6	0.4	0.4	0.1
Other Expenses 19	6.6	24.6	32.8	37.8	25.1	23.5	22.8	32.7	23.8	30.9	27.6	22.3	5.6
Officers' Compensation 20	0.5	1.4	10.3	5.4	13.6	2.1	3.5	3.5	4.2	3.6	3.7	0.4	0.3
Operating Margin 21	17.7	4.2	30.4	2.8	15.8	45.1	16.1	17.3	26.8	20.3	25.5	25.0	17.5
Operating Margin Before Officers' Comp. 22	18.2	5.6	40.7	8.2	29.4	47.2	19.6	20.7	30.9	23.9	29.2	25.3	17.8

Selected Average Balance Sheet ($ in Thousands)

Line Item													
Net Receivables 23	70703	0	70	310	506	4515	9366	18846	46740	107254	211478	600236	5003834
Inventories 24	•	•	•	•	•	•	•	•	•	•	•	•	•
Net Property, Plant and Equipment 25	501	0	4	12	199	296	386	571	1050	1966	1976	7691	25865
Total Assets 26	706454	0	119	637	2138	6430	16152	34175	76174	157023	336094	1216082	57669062
Notes and Loans Payable 27	635467	0	41	70	673	2199	8914	17356	43459	104787	196433	753839	52393895
All Other Liabilities 28	40995	0	-1364	18	295	388	2714	7263	8904	17289	45527	164675	3256869
Net Worth 29	29991	0	1443	548	1170	3842	4523	9556	23810	34947	94134	297568	2018298

Selected Financial Ratios (Times to 1)

Line Item													
Current Ratio 30	0.4	•	2.5	14.4	2.3	3.4	1.6	1.7	1.5	1.4	1.1	1.5	0.4
Quick Ratio 31	0.3	•	2.0	12.1	1.9	2.9	1.3	1.5	1.3	1.0	1.2	•	0.3
Net Sales to Working Capital 32	•	•	4.5	1.2	2.1	0.8	1.7	0.9	0.6	0.7	1.1	0.2	•
Coverage Ratio 33	1.2	1.1	8.0	1.1	5.1	16.6	3.8	2.9	3.0	2.1	1.8	1.9	1.2
Total Asset Turnover 34	0.1	•	2.5	1.0	0.9	0.5	0.5	0.3	0.1	0.1	0.0	0.1	0.1
Inventory Turnover 35	•	•	•	•	•	•	•	•	•	•	•	•	•
Receivables Turnover 36	•	•	•	•	•	•	•	•	•	•	•	•	•
Total Liabilities to Net Worth 37	22.6	•	•	0.2	0.8	0.7	2.6	2.6	2.2	3.5	2.6	3.1	27.6
Current Assets to Working Capital 38	•	•	1.7	1.1	1.8	1.4	2.6	2.4	3.0	3.6	13.0	2.9	•
Current Liabilities to Working Capital 39	•	•	0.7	0.1	0.8	0.4	1.6	1.4	2.0	2.6	12.0	1.9	•
Working Capital to Net Sales 40	•	•	0.2	0.9	0.5	1.3	0.6	1.2	1.7	1.4	0.9	6.0	•
Inventory to Working Capital 41	•	•	•	0.0	0.0	0.0	0.0	•	0.0	0.0	•	0.0	•
Total Receipts to Cash Flow 42	4.3	3.6	1.7	2.8	2.8	1.6	2.8	2.3	2.1	2.0	1.9	2.2	4.5
Cost of Goods to Cash Flow 43	0.0	0.4	•	0.1	0.1	•	1.0	0.1	0.2	0.1	•	0.1	0.0
Cash Flow to Total Debt 44	0.0	•	2.6	0.7	0.7	0.3	0.2	0.1	0.1	0.0	0.0	0.0	0.0

Selected Financial Factors (in Percentages)

Line Item													
Debt Ratio 45	95.8	•	13.8	45.3	40.2	72.0	72.0	68.7	77.7	72.0	75.5	•	96.5
Return on Total Assets 46	4.8	87.7	45.9	18.1	22.7	11.4	6.8	5.9	5.3	3.1	2.6	•	4.8
Return on Equity Before Income Taxes 47	21.4	6.4	3.3	26.6	35.7	29.9	16.1	12.6	12.3	4.9	4.9	•	24.9
Return on Equity After Income Taxes 48	14.0	4.7	2.7	25.3	31.9	28.2	13.1	10.4	8.3	3.3	3.2	•	16.3
Profit Margin (Before Income Tax) 49	16.6	4.2	30.4	2.8	15.8	45.1	16.1	17.2	26.8	18.4	23.7	28.2	16.3
Profit Margin (After Income Tax) 50	10.9	3.7	22.2	2.3	15.1	40.3	15.2	14.0	22.2	12.3	15.9	18.4	10.6

Table I

Corporations with and without Net Income

ACTIVITIES RELATED TO CREDIT INTERMEDIATION

MONEY AMOUNTS AND SIZE OF ASSETS IN THOUSANDS OF DOLLARS

Item Description for Accounting Period 7/03 Through 6/04		Total	Zero Assets	Under 500	500 to 1,000	1,000 to 5,000	5,000 to 10,000	10,000 to 25,000	25,000 to 50,000	50,000 to 100,000	100,000 to 250,000	250,000 to 500,000	500,000 to 2,500,000	2,500,000 and over
Number of Enterprises	1	22788	5388	15119	777	966	259	139	59	35	21	6	14	4
Revenues ($ in Thousands)														
Net Sales	2	36483576	588595	6293853	798403	2730414	1889806	1430105	1288960	1130255	1694735	1084464	6679950	10874036
Interest	3	1318324	1452	5917	148	31713	10550	31322	20077	51093	119615	94953	614182	337303
Rents	4	144715	0	2245	0	4423	0	337	428	6	174	1692	25198	110212
Royalties	5	454745	0	0	0	0	0	0	0	0	0	0	35301	419444
Other Portfolio Income	6	749713	5	4742	808	3565	840	4292	733	1612	36755	1899	21871	672593
Other Receipts	7	33816079	587138	6280949	797447	2690713	1878416	1394154	1267722	1077544	1538191	985920	5983398	9334484
Total Receipts	8	36483576	588595	6293853	798403	2730414	1889806	1430105	1288960	1130255	1694735	1084464	6679950	10874036
Average Total Receipts	9	1601	109	416	1028	2827	7297	10289	21847	32293	80702	180744	477139	2718509
Operating Costs/Operating Income (%)														
Cost of Operations	10	7.3	3.3	14.8	•	7.6	13.2	21.0	16.5	11.6	23.2	1.0	0.5	1.7
Salaries and Wages	11	20.9	18.0	24.7	18.0	36.1	21.3	27.2	29.2	20.9	15.5	26.2	18.5	15.3
Taxes Paid	12	2.9	2.1	2.9	2.4	4.0	2.2	2.8	2.6	2.3	1.6	1.9	1.8	3.9
Interest Paid	13	3.5	0.7	0.6	0.3	1.8	1.9	5.1	4.7	6.4	9.0	5.9	2.1	5.2
Depreciation	14	2.3	1.1	1.0	0.6	1.4	0.9	1.4	1.7	2.9	2.5	2.1	3.3	3.2
Amortization and Depletion	15	1.3	0.1	0.1	0.1	0.5	0.2	0.3	0.4	0.5	1.7	2.7	1.9	2.2
Pensions and Other Deferred Comp.	16	0.9	0.5	0.6	0.0	0.2	0.2	0.3	0.3	0.5	0.9	0.4	2.5	0.8
Employee Benefits	17	1.6	0.7	1.1	0.7	0.8	0.5	0.9	1.3	1.5	1.2	4.7	1.5	2.3
Advertising	18	5.3	1.7	2.5	1.1	1.8	1.6	2.2	1.1	4.8	1.9	0.6	11.3	7.4
Other Expenses	19	42.2	64.6	34.5	56.3	31.6	48.0	25.8	26.4	36.5	37.5	48.5	53.1	44.1
Officers' Compensation	20	2.9	4.9	8.2	2.4	4.8	4.3	4.5	4.1	3.2	2.0	0.6	0.8	0.4
Operating Margin	21	8.9	2.3	9.0	18.1	9.2	5.8	8.5	11.7	8.8	3.1	5.4	2.8	13.6
Operating Margin Before Officers' Comp.	22	11.8	7.2	17.1	20.5	14.1	10.1	13.0	15.8	12.0	5.0	6.0	3.6	13.9

Selected Average Balance Sheet ($ in Thousands)

Net Receivables 23	451	•	16	160	517	2572	3588	11623	21416	48768	77135	283134	342530
Inventories 24	•	•	•	•	•	•	•	•	•	•	•	•	•
Net Property, Plant and Equipment 25	123	0	17	35	228	192	811	1330	3825	5755	14239	53774	242123
Total Assets 26	3249	0	85	707	2322	6953	15575	35459	66348	157749	358341	1121672	10101442
Notes and Loans Payable 27	1227	0	41	231	1081	4414	7709	18448	31503	64479	156115	160549	4292770
All Other Liabilities 28	1494	0	15	40	602	1300	4105	10739	21649	49815	100359	693270	4889093
Net Worth 29	528	0	30	437	640	1239	3760	6271	13197	43455	101867	267853	919579

Selected Financial Ratios (Times to 1)

Current Ratio 30	0.6	•	3.4	9.2	1.6	1.1	1.0	1.0	1.0	1.4	1.0	0.8	0.3
Quick Ratio 31	0.4	•	3.2	7.7	1.4	1.0	0.7	0.9	0.9	1.2	1.0	0.7	0.1
Net Sales to Working Capital 32	•	•	11.0	2.2	5.8	17.7	51.5	144.7	•	3.2	410.3	•	•
Coverage Ratio 33	3.3	4.5	15.4	53.8	6.1	4.0	2.6	3.5	2.4	1.3	1.9	2.5	2.9
Total Asset Turnover 34	0.5	•	4.9	1.5	1.2	1.0	0.7	0.6	0.5	0.5	0.5	0.4	0.3
Inventory Turnover 35	•	•	•	•	•	•	•	•	•	•	•	•	•
Receivables Turnover 36	•	•	•	•	•	•	•	•	•	•	•	•	•
Total Liabilities to Net Worth 37	5.1	•	1.8	0.6	2.6	4.6	3.1	4.7	4.0	2.6	2.5	3.2	10.0
Current Assets to Working Capital 38	•	•	1.4	1.1	2.7	10.6	43.1	128.0	•	3.3	321.9	•	•
Current Liabilities to Working Capital 39	•	•	0.4	0.1	1.7	9.6	42.1	127.0	•	2.3	320.9	•	•
Working Capital to Net Sales 40	•	•	0.1	0.5	0.2	0.1	0.0	0.0	0.0	0.3	0.0	•	•
Inventory to Working Capital 41	•	•	•	•	0.0	0.0	0.1	0.1	0.1	0.0	1.5	•	•
Total Receipts to Cash Flow 42	2.1	1.7	2.8	1.5	2.7	2.0	3.2	2.9	2.4	2.6	2.1	1.9	1.8
Cost of Goods to Cash Flow 43	0.2	0.1	0.4	•	0.2	0.3	0.7	0.5	0.3	0.6	0.0	0.0	0.0
Cash Flow to Total Debt 44	0.3	•	2.7	2.6	0.6	0.6	0.3	0.3	0.3	0.3	0.3	0.3	0.2

Selected Financial Factors (in Percentages)

Debt Ratio 45	83.7	•	64.8	38.2	72.4	82.2	75.9	82.3	80.1	72.5	71.6	76.1	90.9
Return on Total Assets 46	5.6	•	46.7	26.8	13.4	8.1	9.0	10.1	7.4	6.1	5.7	2.2	4.1
Return on Equity Before Income Taxes 47	23.7	•	124.1	42.6	40.7	34.3	23.1	40.6	21.4	5.4	9.5	5.4	29.6
Return on Equity After Income Taxes 48	19.3	•	123.0	42.3	39.1	32.8	21.7	38.2	18.7	2.0	7.1	3.5	19.8
Profit Margin (Before Income Tax) 49	7.8	2.3	9.0	18.1	9.2	5.8	8.4	11.7	8.7	2.9	5.4	3.0	10.0
Profit Margin (After Income Tax) 50	6.4	1.9	8.9	18.0	8.8	5.6	7.9	11.0	7.7	1.1	4.0	1.9	6.7

289

Table II
Corporations with Net Income

ACTIVITIES RELATED TO CREDIT INTERMEDIATION

MONEY AMOUNTS AND SIZE OF ASSETS IN THOUSANDS OF DOLLARS

Item Description for Accounting Period 7/03 Through 6/04		Total	Zero Assets	Under 500	500 to 1,000	1,000 to 5,000	5,000 to 10,000	10,000 to 25,000	25,000 to 50,000	50,000 to 100,000	100,000 to 250,000	250,000 to 500,000	500,000 to 2,500,000	2,500,000 and over
Number of Enterprises	1	13977	1695	10577	592	686	213	102	52	28	14	6	8	4
Revenues ($ in Thousands)														
Net Sales	2	30735989	319344	5209518	726055	2419923	1573886	1126946	1200201	939117	1128275	1084464	4134225	10874036
Interest	3	1098540	843	421	134	27689	2472	23829	19257	40907	66123	94953	484608	337303
Rents	4	134139	0	2245	0	455	0	265	428	2	0	1692	18840	110212
Royalties	5	454745	0	0	0	0	0	0	0	0	0	0	35301	419444
Other Portfolio Income	6	731728	5	4742	808	1921	840	3297	380	1606	36707	1899	6932	672593
Other Receipts	7	28316837	318496	5202110	725113	2389858	1570574	1099555	1180136	896602	1025445	985920	3588544	9334484
Total Receipts	8	30735989	319344	5209518	726055	2419923	1573886	1126946	1200201	939117	1128275	1084464	4134225	10874036
Average Total Receipts	9	2199	188	493	1226	3528	7389	11048	23081	33540	80591	180744	516778	2718509
Operating Costs/Operating Income (%)														
Cost of Operations	10	7.5	2.4	17.6	•	3.8	15.8	14.4	17.4	6.3	34.8	1.0	0.4	1.7
Salaries and Wages	11	22.1	26.6	25.1	16.4	37.3	23.8	27.9	28.8	18.5	17.7	26.2	24.5	15.3
Taxes Paid	12	3.1	2.7	2.7	2.0	4.1	2.4	2.8	2.5	2.5	1.8	1.9	2.3	3.9
Interest Paid	13	3.5	0.2	0.6	0.1	1.2	1.8	4.8	4.2	5.8	7.3	5.9	2.8	5.2
Depreciation	14	2.3	0.4	1.0	0.4	1.3	1.0	1.3	1.7	3.4	2.0	2.1	3.3	3.2
Amortization and Depletion	15	1.4	0.1	0.1	0.1	0.4	0.2	0.1	0.4	0.4	1.1	2.7	3.1	2.2
Pensions and Other Deferred Comp.	16	0.7	0.1	0.7	0.0	0.2	0.2	0.3	0.3	0.6	1.4	0.4	1.6	0.8
Employee Benefits	17	1.6	•	1.0	0.7	0.6	0.5	1.0	1.2	1.7	0.9	4.7	1.8	2.3
Advertising	18	4.9	0.6	1.8	1.1	1.7	1.8	2.0	1.1	5.5	2.7	0.6	9.6	7.4
Other Expenses	19	38.0	49.6	28.4	56.1	31.8	40.3	26.4	24.5	38.9	15.5	48.5	42.9	44.1
Officers' Compensation	20	2.8	5.3	7.9	1.7	4.3	4.8	4.7	4.0	3.4	2.4	0.6	0.7	0.4
Operating Margin	21	12.1	12.2	13.0	21.2	13.2	7.4	14.2	13.8	12.7	12.5	5.4	7.2	13.6
Operating Margin Before Officers' Comp.	22	14.9	17.5	21.0	22.9	17.6	12.2	18.9	17.8	16.1	14.9	6.0	7.9	13.9

Selected Average Balance Sheet ($ in Thousands)

Net Receivables 23	526	0	14	195	455	2961	3622	10171	20267	38094	77135	290182	342530
Inventories 24	•	•	•	•	•	•	•	•	•	•	•	•	•
Net Property, Plant and Equipment 25	168	0	21	10	214	200	670	1360	4623	4652	14239	67744	242123
Total Assets 26	4600	0	96	690	2260	7061	15715	34814	65212	153385	358341	1234620	10101442
Notes and Loans Payable 27	1716	0	30	190	783	4432	8005	17548	31963	37757	156115	101139	4292770
All Other Liabilities 28	2099	0	13	31	693	1323	4066	10160	18667	60510	100359	743368	4889093
Net Worth 29	786	0	53	469	784	1306	3644	7106	14582	55118	101867	390113	919579

Selected Financial Ratios (Times to 1)

Current Ratio 30	0.5	•	3.7	15.4	1.5	1.1	1.0	1.0	0.8	1.1	1.0	0.8	0.3
Quick Ratio 31	0.4	•	3.4	14.5	1.3	1.0	0.7	0.9	0.8	0.8	1.0	0.7	0.1
Net Sales to Working Capital 32	•	•	11.2	2.5	7.7	15.4	621.9	48.8	15.2	410.3	•	•	•
Coverage Ratio 33	4.1	81.5	21.2	178.7	12.5	5.2	3.9	4.3	3.2	2.7	1.9	3.7	2.9
Total Asset Turnover 34	0.5	•	5.1	1.8	1.6	1.0	0.7	0.5	0.5	0.5	0.5	0.4	0.3
Inventory Turnover 35	•	•	•	•	•	•	•	•	•	•	•	•	•
Receivables Turnover 36	•	•	•	•	•	•	•	•	•	•	•	•	•
Total Liabilities to Net Worth 37	4.9	•	0.8	0.5	1.9	4.4	3.3	3.9	3.5	1.8	2.5	2.2	10.0
Current Assets to Working Capital 38	•	•	1.4	1.1	2.9	9.5	482.2	39.0	15.7	321.9	•	•	•
Current Liabilities to Working Capital 39	•	•	0.4	0.1	1.9	8.5	481.2	38.0	14.7	320.9	•	•	•
Working Capital to Net Sales 40	•	•	0.1	0.4	0.1	0.1	0.0	0.1	0.0	0.0	•	•	•
Inventory to Working Capital 41	•	•	•	•	0.1	0.1	0.0	0.0	0.0	1.5	0.0	•	•
Total Receipts to Cash Flow 42	2.2	1.8	2.9	1.4	2.4	2.3	2.7	2.9	3.8	2.1	2.1	2.2	1.8
Cost of Goods to Cash Flow 43	0.2	0.0	0.5	0.0	0.1	0.4	0.4	0.5	1.3	0.0	0.0	0.0	0.0
Cash Flow to Total Debt 44	0.3	•	3.9	4.0	1.0	0.6	0.3	0.3	0.2	0.3	0.0	0.3	0.2

Selected Financial Factors (in Percentages)

Debt Ratio 45	82.9	•	44.7	32.0	65.3	81.5	76.8	79.6	77.6	64.1	71.6	68.4	90.9
Return on Total Assets 46	6.9	•	69.9	38.0	22.5	9.6	13.3	12.0	9.5	10.3	5.7	4.3	4.1
Return on Equity Before Income Taxes 47	30.5	•	120.6	55.5	59.6	42.0	42.8	44.8	28.9	18.0	9.5	10.0	29.6
Return on Equity After Income Taxes 48	25.6	•	119.7	55.2	57.7	40.2	40.8	42.3	25.9	13.9	7.1	7.6	19.8
Profit Margin (Before Income Tax) 49	10.9	12.2	13.0	21.2	13.2	7.4	14.1	13.8	12.6	12.3	5.4	7.5	10.0
Profit Margin (After Income Tax) 50	9.2	11.6	12.9	21.1	12.8	7.1	13.5	13.0	11.3	9.5	4.0	5.8	6.7

Table I

Corporations with and without Net Income

INVESTMENT BANKING AND SECURITIES DEALING

MONEY AMOUNTS AND SIZE OF ASSETS IN THOUSANDS OF DOLLARS

Item Description for Accounting Period 7/03 Through 6/04	Total	Zero Assets	Under 500	500 to 1,000	1,000 to 5,000	5,000 to 10,000	10,000 to 25,000	25,000 to 50,000	50,000 to 100,000	100,000 to 250,000	250,000 to 500,000	500,000 to 2,500,000	2,500,000 and over
Number of Enterprises **1**	3437	1234	1720	112	239	21	48	13	14	10	7	5	13
Revenues ($ in Thousands)													
Net Sales **2**	82075013	316615	582329	7206	120613	199786	435722	299949	408319	73407	713558	286989	78630520
Interest **3**	45082896	90666	1588	325	4826	2809	15475	1407	3747	12686	61770	106728	44780867
Rents **4**	773489	3866	0	1403	2	0	94	31	60	0	48	4450	763534
Royalties **5**	155	14	0	0	0	0	0	0	0	0	0	0	140
Other Portfolio Income **6**	4562961	8873	20467	1916	4825	782	7367	4089	4995	5447	10308	7322	4486571
Other Receipts **7**	31655512	213196	560274	3562	110960	196195	412786	294422	399517	55274	641432	168489	28599408
Total Receipts **8**	82075013	316615	582329	7206	120613	199786	435722	299949	408319	73407	713558	286989	78630520
Average Total Receipts **9**	23880	257	339	64	505	9514	9078	23073	29166	7341	101937	57398	6048502
Operating Costs/Operating Income (%)													
Cost of Operations **10**	0.1	•	•	•	9.6	0.0	1.9	9.3	•	•	•	•	0.0
Salaries and Wages **11**	18.8	26.8	5.7	9.4	15.2	48.2	40.9	27.3	22.6	35.4	33.7	25.3	18.5
Taxes Paid **12**	1.3	1.7	1.0	9.7	1.8	2.8	3.0	1.9	2.0	3.5	2.3	1.6	1.2
Interest Paid **13**	38.6	39.5	0.0	4.1	7.1	0.3	1.2	0.6	44.6	12.4	7.6	7.0	39.8
Depreciation **14**	2.4	0.7	1.2	8.7	2.0	1.5	1.6	3.4	0.9	2.4	2.6	3.7	2.4
Amortization and Depletion **15**	0.4	0.0	0.1	0.1	0.0	0.0	1.0	0.3	0.1	0.2	0.3	0.0	0.4
Pensions and Other Deferred Comp. **16**	0.7	0.8	•	•	1.1	1.4	0.8	0.2	1.0	1.7	2.4	0.4	0.7
Employee Benefits **17**	1.1	0.6	1.8	0.0	1.9	2.6	2.8	1.0	1.9	1.4	1.1	0.5	1.1
Advertising **18**	0.3	0.1	2.1	•	0.8	0.0	0.6	0.2	0.4	0.1	0.4	0.0	0.2
Other Expenses **19**	26.2	29.2	83.2	35.3	31.9	31.0	43.5	52.5	26.6	39.8	21.6	31.5	25.6
Officers' Compensation **20**	3.2	3.9	0.1	•	10.3	17.8	7.7	3.8	17.3	17.1	3.8	1.8	3.1
Operating Margin **21**	7.0	•	4.7	32.7	18.2	12.1	2.8	•	•	•	24.1	28.3	7.0
Operating Margin Before Officers' Comp. **22**	10.2	0.6	4.8	32.7	28.5	12.1	2.8	3.3	•	3.1	27.9	30.1	10.1

Selected Average Balance Sheet ($ in Thousands)

Net Receivables 23	128450	0	4	0	18	178	3534	7146	13109	55086	56736	161091	33789874
Inventories 24	•	•	•	•	•	•	•	•	•	•	•	•	•
Net Property, Plant and Equipment 25	3567	•	5	252	89	368	393	2277	1042	611	6594	4996	927174
Total Assets 26	583368	0	104	601	1562	6277	15701	36983	63241	141649	350260	1097319	15293074
Notes and Loans Payable 27	80809	0	32	285	388	3524	1867	2625	19668	21585	110286	127303	21189460
All Other Liabilities 28	456986	0	5	5	273	3341	4928	10721	16111	73544	156060	403912	120466790
Net Worth 29	45573	0	67	311	900	-588	8906	23636	27462	46520	83914	566104	11636824

Selected Financial Ratios (Times to 1)

Current Ratio 30	0.8	•	13.9	11.7	3.6	1.1	1.9	2.1	1.1	1.3	1.0	1.1	0.8
Quick Ratio 31	0.4	•	2.3	10.8	1.4	0.4	1.4	1.4	0.7	1.0	0.5	1.1	0.4
Net Sales to Working Capital 32	•	•	5.3	0.6	0.7	23.3	2.0	2.3	6.5	0.4	•	1.3	•
Coverage Ratio 33	1.2	0.9	221.8	8.3	3.6	•	•	•	0.6	•	4.1	5.0	1.2
Total Asset Turnover 34	0.0	•	3.3	0.1	0.3	1.5	0.6	0.6	0.5	0.1	0.3	0.1	0.0
Inventory Turnover 35	•	•	•	•	•	•	•	•	•	•	•	•	•
Receivables Turnover 36	•	•	•	•	•	•	•	•	•	•	•	•	•
Total Liabilities to Net Worth 37	11.8	•	0.6	0.9	0.7	•	0.8	0.6	1.3	2.0	3.2	0.9	12.2
Current Assets to Working Capital 38	•	•	1.1	1.1	1.4	9.2	2.1	1.9	8.7	4.1	•	9.7	•
Current Liabilities to Working Capital 39	•	•	0.1	-0.1	0.4	8.2	1.1	0.9	7.7	3.1	•	8.7	•
Working Capital to Net Sales 40	•	•	0.2	1.7	1.5	0.0	0.5	0.4	0.2	2.8	•	0.8	•
Inventory to Working Capital 41	•	•	•	•	•	•	•	•	•	•	•	•	•
Total Receipts to Cash Flow 42	3.6	6.7	1.3	2.3	2.4	4.9	3.0	2.1	15.3	6.0	2.3	1.8	3.7
Cost of Goods to Cash Flow 43	0.0	•	•	0.2	0.2	0.0	0.1	0.2	•	•	•	0.0	0.0
Cash Flow to Total Debt 44	0.0	•	7.1	0.1	0.3	0.3	0.4	0.8	0.1	0.0	0.2	0.1	0.0

Selected Financial Factors (in Percentages)

Debt Ratio 45	92.2	•	35.9	48.2	42.3	109.4	43.3	36.1	56.6	67.2	76.0	48.4	92.4
Return on Total Assets 46	2.0	•	15.4	3.6	8.1	•	•	•	12.0	•	9.0	1.8	1.9
Return on Equity Before Income Taxes 47	4.8	•	23.9	6.1	10.1	92.7	•	•	•	•	28.5	2.9	4.9
Return on Equity After Income Taxes 48	3.2	•	18.6	5.4	8.3	92.7	•	•	•	•	19.9	2.0	3.3
Profit Margin (Before Income Tax) 49	9.1	4.7	29.7	18.0	•	•	•	•	•	•	23.4	28.2	9.3
Profit Margin (After Income Tax) 50	6.1	•	3.7	25.9	14.8	•	•	•	•	•	16.4	19.3	6.3

Table II
Corporations with Net Income

INVESTMENT BANKING AND SECURITIES DEALING

MONEY AMOUNTS AND SIZE OF ASSETS IN THOUSANDS OF DOLLARS

Item Description for Accounting Period 7/03 Through 6/04	Total	Zero Assets	Under 500	500 to 1,000	1,000 to 5,000	5,000 to 10,000	10,000 to 25,000	25,000 to 50,000	50,000 to 100,000	100,000 to 250,000	250,000 to 500,000	500,000 to 2,500,000	2,500,000 and over
Number of Enterprises **1**	2132	790	1065	•	97	10	25	6	10	•	4	•	10
Revenues ($ in Thousands)													
Net Sales **2**	80703634	148825	582205	•	97098	151200	320080	276231	225759	•	658425	•	77979890
Interest **3**	44575092	179	1582	•	3913	1347	4287	1190	7519	•	13672	•	44437014
Rents **4**	632102	0	0	•	2	0	94	0	60	•	48	•	630298
Royalties **5**	0	0	0	•	0	0	0	0	0	•	0	•	0
Other Portfolio Income **6**	4542999	7329	20467	•	4116	219	6494	3756	4945	•	10308	•	4478785
Other Receipts **7**	30953441	141317	560156	•	89067	149634	309205	271285	213235	•	634397	•	28433793
Total Receipts **8**	80703634	148825	582205	•	97098	151200	320080	276231	225759	•	658425	•	77979890
Average Total Receipts **9**	37853	188	547	•	1001	15120	12803	46038	22576	•	164606	•	7797989
Operating Costs/Operating Income (%)													
Cost of Operations **10**	0.1	•	•	•	11.9	0.0	•	10.1	•	•	•	•	0.0
Salaries and Wages **11**	18.8	11.4	5.6	•	3.8	52.1	30.5	27.8	35.1	•	36.5	•	18.6
Taxes Paid **12**	1.3	1.5	1.0	•	1.5	2.6	2.8	1.9	3.6	•	2.5	•	1.3
Interest Paid **13**	38.4	26.7	•	•	7.3	0.3	1.1	0.1	1.3	•	0.7	•	39.6
Depreciation **14**	2.2	0.5	1.2	•	1.9	1.3	0.9	1.2	1.0	•	2.8	•	2.2
Amortization and Depletion **15**	0.4	0.0	0.1	•	0.0	0.0	0.3	0.1	0.2	•	0.3	•	0.4
Pensions and Other Deferred Comp. **16**	0.7	1.7	•	•	0.3	0.8	1.0	0.3	1.7	•	2.6	•	0.7
Employee Benefits **17**	1.1	•	1.8	•	0.6	2.3	2.3	1.0	1.1	•	1.1	•	1.1
Advertising **18**	0.3	0.0	2.1	•	0.9	0.0	0.5	0.2	0.7	•	0.5	•	0.2
Other Expenses **19**	26.1	32.1	79.0	•	18.9	30.0	37.1	45.0	29.1	•	21.8	•	25.6
Officers' Compensation **20**	3.2	3.5	•	•	3.9	6.8	8.3	3.1	15.2	•	4.1	•	3.1
Operating Margin **21**	7.6	22.5	9.2	•	48.8	3.6	15.1	9.1	11.1	•	26.9	•	7.2
Operating Margin Before Officers' Comp. **22**	10.8	26.0	9.2	•	52.7	10.5	23.5	12.2	26.3	•	31.0	•	10.3

Selected Average Balance Sheet ($ in Thousands)

Item	1	2	3	4	5	6	7	8	9	10
Net Receivables 23	206379	0	6	31	272	3642	11238	23691	97377	43839669
Inventories 24	•	•	•	•	•	•	•	•	•	•
Net Property, Plant and Equipment 25	5710	0	8	202	306	413	1496	810	11539	1203887
Total Assets 26	927850	0	74	1937	5652	15736	38033	74731	369608	197004541
Notes and Loans Payable 27	129656	0	0	928	834	2697	340	16931	63917	27516573
All Other Liabilities 28	725939	0	8	411	3446	5017	8812	18031	161070	154472037
Net Worth 29	72255	0	66	598	1372	8022	28882	39769	144620	15015931

Selected Financial Ratios (Times to 1)

Item	1	2	3	4	5	6	7	8	9	10
Current Ratio 30	0.8	•	2.2	2.3	1.3	1.7	4.6	2.4	0.9	0.8
Quick Ratio 31	0.4	•	2.1	2.0	0.2	1.4	3.5	1.8	0.7	0.4
Net Sales to Working Capital 32	•	•	58.2	1.7	13.4	3.3	2.2	0.8	•	•
Coverage Ratio 33	1.3	•	1.8	7.6	11.7	14.6	78.9	7.9	36.4	1.2
Total Asset Turnover 34	0.0	•	7.4	0.5	2.7	0.8	1.2	0.3	0.4	0.0
Inventory Turnover 35	•	•	•	•	•	•	•	•	•	•
Receivables Turnover 36	•	•	•	•	•	•	•	•	•	•
Total Liabilities to Net Worth 37	11.8	•	0.1	2.2	3.1	1.0	0.3	0.9	1.6	12.1
Current Assets to Working Capital 38	•	•	1.8	1.8	4.0	2.5	1.3	1.7	•	•
Current Liabilities to Working Capital 39	•	•	0.8	0.8	3.0	1.5	0.3	0.7	•	•
Working Capital to Net Sales 40	•	•	0.0	0.6	0.1	0.3	0.5	1.3	•	•
Inventory to Working Capital 41	•	•	•	•	•	•	•	•	•	•
Total Receipts to Cash Flow 42	3.5	•	2.5	1.7	3.3	2.1	2.0	2.7	2.2	3.6
Cost of Goods to Cash Flow 43	0.0	•	0.2	0.0	0.0	0.2	•	0.2	•	0.0
Cash Flow to Total Debt 44	0.0	•	57.2	0.4	1.1	0.8	2.6	0.2	0.3	0.0

Selected Financial Factors (in Percentages)

Item	1	2	3	4	5	6	7	8	9	10
Debt Ratio 45	92.2	•	10.7	69.1	75.7	49.0	24.1	46.8	60.9	92.4
Return on Total Assets 46	2.0	•	67.9	28.9	10.6	12.5	10.2	3.1	12.0	1.9
Return on Equity Before Income Taxes 47	5.1	•	76.1	81.3	40.0	22.8	13.3	5.0	29.8	5.0
Return on Equity After Income Taxes 48	3.6	•	67.4	74.7	40.0	21.5	12.6	4.2	21.1	3.4
Profit Margin (Before Income Tax) 49	9.8	22.5	9.2	48.6	3.6	14.3	8.3	8.9	26.1	9.5
Profit Margin (After Income Tax) 50	6.8	20.3	8.1	44.6	3.6	13.4	7.9	7.5	18.5	6.5

Table I

Corporations with and without Net Income

SECURITIES BROKERAGE

MONEY AMOUNTS AND SIZE OF ASSETS IN THOUSANDS OF DOLLARS

Item Description for Accounting Period 7/03 Through 6/04	Total	Zero Assets	Under 500	500 to 1,000	1,000 to 5,000	5,000 to 10,000	10,000 to 25,000	25,000 to 50,000	50,000 to 100,000	100,000 to 250,000	250,000 to 500,000	500,000 to 2,500,000	2,500,000 and over
Number of Enterprises **1**	9736	2521	5680	493	671	160	84	28	23	18	11	13	33
Revenues ($ in Thousands)													
Net Sales **2**	105594380	713808	1820011	535055	2199527	1611163	1867687	863308	760174	893396	2039492	3906350	88784410
Interest **3**	31321057	1253	422	2558	7759	5396	26279	8225	6978	25880	66622	188311	30981373
Rents **4**	441149	0	1	0	0	367	279	2755	2266	256	7372	2675	425178
Royalties **5**	138133	0	0	0	0	0	2	1829	0	9194	0	0	127108
Other Portfolio Income **6**	2885106	4691	2302	330	12419	27954	10830	12574	9126	32521	23515	23265	2725581
Other Receipts **7**	71208935	707864	1817286	532167	2179349	1577446	1830297	837925	741804	825545	1941983	3692099	54525170
Total Receipts **8**	105594380	713808	1820011	535055	2199527	1611163	1867687	863308	760174	893396	2039492	3906350	88784410
Average Total Receipts **9**	10887	283	320	1085	3278	10070	22234	30832	33051	49633	185408	300488	2690437
Operating Costs/Operating Income (%)													
Cost of Operations **10**	2.1	0.2	0.0	3.3	0.6	14.1	5.6	19.5	0.6	1.2		•	1.9
Salaries and Wages **11**	23.1	30.3	25.0	34.0	24.1	25.8	30.8	29.2	35.7	37.1	48.2	25.7	21.7
Taxes Paid **12**	1.9	3.9	3.0	2.7	2.9	2.7	2.0	3.0	2.6	2.8	3.3	1.8	1.7
Interest Paid **13**	24.0	0.8	0.2	0.1	0.1	0.2	0.8	0.9	3.7	2.3	1.5	5.9	28.3
Depreciation **14**	1.7	0.9	0.8	0.9	0.4	0.9	0.8	1.4	1.7	3.5	2.0	1.9	1.8
Amortization and Depletion **15**	0.7	0.3	0.0	0.0	0.0	0.2	0.2	0.1	0.2	0.4	0.6	5.9	0.5
Pensions and Other Deferred Comp. **16**	0.6	0.7	2.5	0.3	0.4	0.1	0.4	0.9	1.2	1.3	0.4	0.2	0.6
Employee Benefits **17**	1.3	1.3	1.3	1.7	1.0	1.6	1.1	1.2	1.3	2.1	2.3	1.7	1.3
Advertising **18**	0.6	0.9	2.0	0.3	0.5	0.4	0.4	0.6	0.5	0.5	0.3	1.2	0.6
Other Expenses **19**	32.2	44.5	42.3	53.3	38.6	45.9	46.6	28.3	34.4	28.7	26.9	41.8	30.8
Officers' Compensation **20**	5.3	11.0	15.3	7.6	13.7	4.7	6.8	7.7	13.5	14.6	3.3	3.4	4.8
Operating Margin **21**	6.4	5.2	7.7	•	17.6	3.2	4.5	7.3	4.8	5.6	11.1	10.6	6.0
Operating Margin Before Officers' Comp. **22**	11.7	16.3	23.0	3.5	31.3	7.9	11.3	15.0	18.2	20.2	14.5	14.0	10.8

Selected Average Balance Sheet ($ in Thousands)

Net Receivables 23	28033	0	10	53	285	708	1939	7305	13861	39015	117226	278416	8068032
Inventories 24	•	•	•	•	•	•	•	•	•	•	•	•	•
Net Property, Plant and Equipment 25	589	•	2	22	69	335	641	1977	1937	4727	9927	15041	153495
Total Assets 26	164625	•	101	690	1867	6860	15461	34664	64745	151171	372738	1395639	47600114
Notes and Loans Payable 27	30827	0	6	29	24	285	1573	4522	8965	15717	37763	49996	9036696
All Other Liabilities 28	124699	0	15	148	719	1304	5560	13833	33788	74579	187464	1089844	36182177
Net Worth 29	9099	0	80	513	1125	5270	8327	16309	21993	60875	147512	255799	2381241

Selected Financial Ratios (Times to 1)

Current Ratio 30	1.1	•	5.3	3.3	3.9	2.4	1.8	1.6	1.3	1.2	1.1	1.0	1.1
Quick Ratio 31	0.4	•	3.6	3.1	3.2	1.4	1.2	1.2	0.9	0.8	0.9	0.6	0.4
Net Sales to Working Capital 32	1.1	•	6.0	3.1	3.3	4.7	5.1	3.5	3.4	3.2	7.1	43.2	0.9
Coverage Ratio 33	1.3	6.8	45.3	•	152.7	16.8	6.7	8.5	2.3	3.2	8.3	2.8	1.2
Total Asset Turnover 34	0.1	•	3.2	1.6	1.8	1.5	1.4	0.9	0.5	0.3	0.5	0.2	0.1
Inventory Turnover 35	•	•	•	•	•	•	•	•	•	•	•	•	•
Receivables Turnover 36	•	•	•	•	•	•	•	•	•	•	•	•	•
Total Liabilities to Net Worth 37	17.1	•	0.3	0.3	0.7	0.3	0.9	1.1	1.9	1.5	1.5	4.5	19.0
Current Assets to Working Capital 38	11.4	•	1.2	1.4	1.3	1.7	2.3	2.6	4.6	5.7	8.6	120.2	11.5
Current Liabilities to Working Capital 39	10.4	•	0.2	0.4	0.3	0.7	1.3	1.6	3.6	4.7	7.6	119.2	10.5
Working Capital to Net Sales 40	1.0	•	0.2	0.3	0.3	0.2	0.2	0.3	0.3	0.3	0.1	0.0	1.1
Inventory to Working Capital 41	0.0	•	•	•	•	•	0.0	0.0	•	0.0	0.0	0.0	0.0
Total Receipts to Cash Flow 42	3.0	2.3	2.3	2.3	1.9	2.2	2.1	3.4	2.9	3.7	3.0	2.0	3.1
Cost of Goods to Cash Flow 43	0.1	0.0	0.0	0.1	0.0	0.3	0.1	0.7	0.0	0.0	•	•	0.1
Cash Flow to Total Debt 44	0.0	6.5	2.6	2.3	2.3	2.8	1.5	0.5	0.3	0.1	0.3	0.1	0.0

Selected Financial Factors (in Percentages)

Debt Ratio 45	94.5	•	21.0	25.6	39.8	23.2	46.1	53.0	66.0	59.7	60.4	81.7	95.0
Return on Total Assets 46	2.0	•	24.9	•	31.0	4.8	7.4	7.0	4.3	2.3	6.1	3.5	1.9
Return on Equity Before Income Taxes 47	7.3	•	30.8	•	51.2	5.8	11.7	13.1	7.1	4.0	13.6	12.4	6.4
Return on Equity After Income Taxes 48	5.1	•	30.4	•	50.3	3.5	9.0	9.1	6.2	1.8	7.9	8.2	4.3
Profit Margin (Before Income Tax) 49	6.1	4.8	7.7	•	17.5	3.1	4.4	7.0	4.7	4.9	10.8	10.5	5.7
Profit Margin (After Income Tax) 50	4.2	3.6	7.6	•	17.3	1.8	3.4	4.8	4.1	2.2	6.3	7.0	3.8

Table II

Corporations with Net Income

SECURITIES BROKERAGE

MONEY AMOUNTS AND SIZE OF ASSETS IN THOUSANDS OF DOLLARS

Item Description for Accounting Period 7/03 Through 6/04	Total	Zero Assets	Under 500	500 to 1,000	1,000 to 5,000	5,000 to 10,000	10,000 to 25,000	25,000 to 50,000	50,000 to 100,000	100,000 to 250,000	250,000 to 500,000	500,000 to 2,500,000	2,500,000 and over
Number of Enterprises 1	5546	1391	2978	•	605	96	56	15	11	15	7	•	24
Revenues ($ in Thousands)													
Net Sales 2	93222561	603110	790605	•	1984637	1445195	1547522	572220	462517	880459	1663899	•	79173087
Interest 3	2679290	1181	310	•	6073	4335	22044	4604	2458	25131	49715	•	26381616
Rents 4	231146	0	0	•	0	367	30	113	2019	0	7372	•	218570
Royalties 5	73942	0	0	•	0	0	2	316	0	9194	0	•	64430
Other Portfolio Income 6	2207627	0	1918	•	2864	26564	7766	2019	538	32070	19716	•	2090667
Other Receipts 7	64030556	601929	788377	•	1975700	1413929	1517680	565168	457502	814064	1587096	•	50417804
Total Receipts 8	93222561	603110	790605	•	1984637	1445195	1547522	572220	462517	880459	1663899	•	79173087
Average Total Receipts 9	16809	434	265	•	3280	15054	27634	38148	42047	58697	237700	•	3298879
Operating Costs/Operating Income (%)													
Cost of Operations 10	2.3	0.1	0.0	•	0.4	15.8	5.8	27.2	0.2	1.2	•	•	2.0
Salaries and Wages 11	23.6	32.7	17.2	•	25.0	25.5	30.4	23.2	31.1	33.8	46.5	•	22.7
Taxes Paid 12	1.9	2.8	2.7	•	3.0	2.6	1.8	3.0	3.0	2.6	3.7	•	1.8
Interest Paid 13	22.9	0.5	0.3	•	0.1	0.1	0.7	0.5	1.7	2.1	1.5	•	26.6
Depreciation 14	1.7	0.6	0.9	•	0.4	0.8	0.6	0.8	1.9	3.5	2.0	•	1.8
Amortization and Depletion 15	0.7	0.0	0.1	•	0.0	0.1	0.1	0.0	0.1	0.1	0.4	•	0.5
Pensions and Other Deferred Comp. 16	0.6	0.8	3.3	•	0.4	0.1	0.5	0.9	0.4	1.2	0.5	•	0.6
Employee Benefits 17	1.4	1.5	2.3	•	1.0	1.7	1.0	0.7	0.8	2.1	2.1	•	1.4
Advertising 18	0.6	1.0	1.6	•	0.6	0.4	0.3	0.4	0.7	0.5	0.3	•	0.6
Other Expenses 19	30.4	38.0	21.2	•	34.6	38.8	42.1	22.1	27.1	23.1	23.5	•	29.6
Officers' Compensation 20	5.5	6.7	18.7	•	13.8	4.7	6.8	6.5	13.1	14.7	3.3	•	5.2
Operating Margin 21	8.3	15.2	31.8	•	20.6	9.4	9.9	14.6	19.9	15.0	16.3	•	7.1
Operating Margin Before Officers' Comp. 22	13.8	21.9	50.5	•	34.4	14.0	16.7	21.1	33.0	29.8	19.6	•	12.3

Selected Average Balance Sheet ($ in Thousands)

	Total	C1	C2	C3	C4	C5	C6	C7	C8	Largest
Net Receivables 23	45648	•	11	175	796	1744	8631	12248	44241	154915 • 10348882
Inventories 24	•	•	•	•	•	•	•	•	•	•
Net Property, Plant and Equipment 25	964	0	1	69	415	647	750	2924	5414	13070 • 200622
Total Assets 26	234798	•	84	1877	7166	15436	34679	62799	151786	411338 • 53210187
Notes and Loans Payable 27	49832	0	3	23	67	1342	3371	2625	18820	34835 • 11458669
All Other Liabilities 28	171717	•	13	691	1547	5646	14754	27959	79074	220332 • 39016188
Net Worth 29	13249	•	68	1163	5552	8448	16554	32215	53892	156171 • 2735330

Selected Financial Ratios (Times to 1)

	Total	C1	C2	C3	C4	C5	C6	C7	C8	C9	Largest
Current Ratio 30	1.1	•	5.1	3.6	3.0	1.8	1.8	1.4	1.2	1.3	1.1
Quick Ratio 31	0.4	•	2.7	2.9	1.7	1.2	1.3	1.2	0.9	1.0	0.4
Net Sales to Working Capital 32	1.1	•	5.1	3.5	4.8	6.0	3.0	3.8	3.6	4.2	0.9
Coverage Ratio 33	1.3	34.3	115.2	171.9	148.8	14.6	29.5	12.8	7.8	11.9	1.3
Total Asset Turnover 34	0.1	•	3.2	1.7	2.1	1.8	1.1	0.7	0.4	0.6	0.1
Inventory Turnover 35	•	•	•	•	•	•	•	•	•	•	•
Receivables Turnover 36	•	•	•	•	•	•	•	•	•	•	•
Total Liabilities to Net Worth 37	16.7	•	0.2	0.6	0.3	0.8	1.1	0.9	1.8	1.6	18.5
Current Assets to Working Capital 38	9.9	•	1.2	1.4	1.5	2.3	2.3	3.5	5.8	4.9	10.1
Current Liabilities to Working Capital 39	8.9	•	0.2	0.4	0.5	1.3	1.3	2.5	4.8	3.9	9.1
Working Capital to Net Sales 40	0.9	•	0.2	0.3	0.2	0.2	0.3	0.3	0.3	0.2	1.1
Inventory to Working Capital 41	0.0	•	•	0.0	•	0.0	•	•	•	•	•
Total Receipts to Cash Flow 42	2.9	2.1	2.1	2.0	2.3	3.1	2.0	2.3	3.2	2.9	3.1
Cost of Goods to Cash Flow 43	0.1	0.0	0.0	0.0	0.4	0.9	0.1	0.0	0.0	0.0	0.1
Cash Flow to Total Debt 44	0.0	•	7.6	2.3	4.1	2.0	0.7	0.6	0.2	0.3	0.0

Selected Financial Factors (in Percentages)

	Total	C1	C2	C3	C4	C5	C6	C7	C8	C9	Largest
Debt Ratio 45	94.4	•	19.5	38.0	22.5	45.3	52.3	48.7	64.5	62.0	94.9
Return on Total Assets 46	2.2	•	101.0	36.1	19.7	18.8	16.5	14.4	6.4	10.2	2.1
Return on Equity Before Income Taxes 47	10.1	•	124.4	58.0	25.3	31.9	33.3	25.8	15.6	24.6	8.2
Return on Equity After Income Taxes 48	7.4	•	123.4	57.1	21.6	28.0	25.8	24.5	12.7	16.1	5.7
Profit Margin (Before Income Tax) 49	8.0	15.2	31.7	20.6	9.3	9.8	14.5	19.8	14.3	16.2	6.8
Profit Margin (After Income Tax) 50	5.9	13.7	31.5	20.2	8.0	8.6	11.2	18.7	11.6	10.6	4.7

Table I

Corporations with and without Net Income

COMMODITY CONTRACTS DEALING AND BROKERAGE

MONEY AMOUNTS AND SIZE OF ASSETS IN THOUSANDS OF DOLLARS

Item Description for Accounting Period 7/03 Through 6/04	Total	Zero Assets	Under 500	500 to 1,000	1,000 to 5,000	5,000 to 10,000	10,000 to 25,000	25,000 to 50,000	50,000 to 100,000	100,000 to 250,000	250,000 to 500,000	500,000 to 2,500,000	2,500,000 and over
Number of Enterprises 1	2324	409	1679	94	51	8	33	14	14	11	3	3	4
Revenues ($ in Thousands)													
Net Sales 2	3647637	449946	259914	27049	204408	85067	468434	86947	273940	157663	142159	251760	1240349
Interest 3	271957	530	1001	0	63	26	3415	307	3134	9107	800	25814	227760
Rents 4	7571	0	129	349	0	0	4941	306	0	85	0	945	815
Royalties 5	17805	0	0	0	0	0	17805	0	0	0	0	0	0
Other Portfolio Income 6	63479	4728	621	0	6	2123	17010	403	12108	3494	72	5	22912
Other Receipts 7	3286825	444688	258163	26700	204339	82918	425263	85931	258698	144977	141287	224996	988862
Total Receipts 8	3647637	449946	259914	27049	204408	85067	468434	86947	273940	157663	142159	251760	1240349
Average Total Receipts 9	1570	1100	155	288	4008	10633	14195	6210	19567	14333	47386	83920	310087
Operating Costs/Operating Income (%)													
Cost of Operations 10	24.9	81.9	21.0	•	69.5	•	65.5	•	3.3	13.5	•	1.8	•
Salaries and Wages 11	20.0	0.3	7.1	23.0	11.8	28.7	11.9	42.7	31.5	17.1	17.5	18.3	30.5
Taxes Paid 12	1.7	0.1	2.4	15.4	0.7	3.7	1.2	6.0	1.7	2.3	3.9	1.1	1.6
Interest Paid 13	9.5	0.3	0.1	3.9	0.3	0.3	0.9	2.9	2.4	3.0	71.4	9.0	16.1
Depreciation 14	1.5	0.4	1.3	33.6	0.2	2.0	1.5	4.7	1.2	0.9	0.4	0.9	1.5
Amortization and Depletion 15	0.4	•	•	•	0.0	0.2	0.1	0.4	0.2	0.0	•	0.8	0.9
Pensions and Other Deferred Comp. 16	0.5	0.0	0.3	9.1	0.1	1.9	0.4	2.0	0.3	0.6	1.4	0.2	0.5
Employee Benefits 17	1.1	0.0	0.5	•	0.1	0.6	1.1	3.6	0.7	1.4	1.1	1.7	1.6
Advertising 18	0.2	0.0	0.3	0.0	0.0	0.1	0.4	1.3	0.5	0.6	0.1	0.2	0.1
Other Expenses 19	35.4	8.0	50.5	153.0	6.6	18.0	29.4	50.1	43.0	57.1	37.0	57.5	37.7
Officers' Compensation 20	4.7	0.1	16.6	96.2	3.8	28.1	3.1	19.5	3.0	4.4	4.7	3.7	1.1
Operating Margin 21	0.1	8.7	•	•	6.9	16.6	•	•	12.1	•	•	4.7	8.4
Operating Margin Before Officers' Comp. 22	4.8	8.8	16.3	•	10.7	44.7	•	•	15.2	3.5	8.4	8.4	9.5

Selected Average Balance Sheet ($ in Thousands)

Line Item													
Net Receivables 23	2361	0	24	8	192	35	5243	7274	23142	21780	191433	424961	686985
Inventories 24	•	•	•	•	•	•	•	•	•	•	•	•	•
Net Property, Plant and Equipment 25	105	0	8	264	11	436	658	1356	991	406	30141	3592	10385
Total Assets 26	14587	0	94	716	2270	7480	16370	32835	73889	134638	392369	1092081	6382937
Notes and Loans Payable 27	2461	0	6	215	1402	375	6630	7362	14316	7420	403238	116111	863161
All Other Liabilities 28	11139	0	12	90	165	976	7194	10593	32587	116165	268272	912958	5044318
Net Worth 29	987	0	75	411	703	6129	2546	14880	26986	11053	-279141	63012	475458

Selected Financial Ratios (Times to 1)

Line Item													
Current Ratio 30	1.2	•	3.6	0.8	0.8	3.7	1.1	1.5	1.1	1.0	0.4	0.8	1.4
Quick Ratio 31	0.6	•	3.0	0.8	0.7	2.8	0.8	1.1	0.9	0.6	0.3	0.6	0.6
Net Sales to Working Capital 32	0.9	•	3.4	•	•	2.9	11.1	1.0	7.6	•	•	•	0.2
Coverage Ratio 33	1.0	32.8	•	•	26.0	58.7	•	•	6.1	0.7	0.5	1.5	1.5
Total Asset Turnover 34	0.1	•	1.6	0.4	1.8	1.4	0.9	0.2	0.3	0.1	0.1	1.5	0.0
Inventory Turnover 35	•	•	•	•	•	•	•	•	•	•	•	•	•
Receivables Turnover 36	•	•	•	•	•	•	•	•	•	•	•	•	•
Total Liabilities to Net Worth 37	13.8	•	0.3	0.7	2.2	0.2	5.4	1.2	1.7	11.2	•	16.3	12.4
Current Assets to Working Capital 38	5.8	•	1.4	•	•	3.0	9.6	•	17.4	•	•	•	3.5
Current Liabilities to Working Capital 39	4.8	•	0.4	•	•	2.0	8.6	•	16.4	•	•	•	2.5
Working Capital to Net Sales 40	1.2	•	0.3	•	•	0.3	0.1	•	0.1	•	•	•	4.5
Inventory to Working Capital 41	0.0	•	•	•	•	•	•	•	1.4	•	•	•	•
Total Receipts to Cash Flow 42	3.1	7.5	2.2	7.6	3.1	•	•	8.9	9.9	2.0	25.8	1.6	2.3
Cost of Goods to Cash Flow 43	0.8	6.2	0.5	5.3	5.8	•	•	5.8	0.1	0.3	0.0	0.0	0.0
Cash Flow to Total Debt 44	0.0	•	3.7	0.3	2.5	0.1	•	0.1	0.0	0.1	0.0	0.0	0.0

Selected Financial Factors (in Percentages)

Line Item													
Debt Ratio 45	93.2	•	20.0	42.6	69.0	18.1	84.4	54.7	63.5	91.8	171.1	94.2	92.6
Return on Total Assets 46	1.0	•	•	12.7	•	23.9	•	3.9	0.2	•	4.7	1.0	1.2
Return on Equity Before Income Taxes 47	0.3	•	•	39.5	28.7	•	•	8.9	•	•	5.6	6.2	5.7
Return on Equity After Income Taxes 48	•	•	•	38.9	28.7	•	•	2.5	•	•	5.6	4.4	4.1
Profit Margin (Before Income Tax) 49	0.2	8.7	6.9	•	•	16.5	18.1	12.2	•	•	•	4.7	8.7
Profit Margin (After Income Tax) 50	•	6.1	6.8	•	•	16.5	16.5	•	•	•	•	3.3	6.2

Table II
Corporations with Net Income

COMMODITY CONTRACTS DEALING AND BROKERAGE

MONEY AMOUNTS AND SIZE OF ASSETS IN THOUSANDS OF DOLLARS

Item Description for Accounting Period 7/03 Through 6/04	Total	Zero Assets	Under 500	500 to 1,000	1,000 to 5,000	5,000 to 10,000	10,000 to 25,000	25,000 to 50,000	50,000 to 100,000	100,000 to 250,000	250,000 to 500,000	500,000 to 2,500,000	2,500,000 and over
Number of Enterprises 1	1389	6	1243	56	33	4	16	7	10	7	•	3	4
Revenues ($ in Thousands)													
Net Sales 2	3109377	63416	265710	22088	203165	111064	393614	119265	275295	163652	•	251760	1240349
Interest 3	267264	530	881	0	13	26	2546	307	3134	6252	•	25814	227760
Rents 4	7541	0	129	349	0	0	4911	306	0	85	•	945	815
Royalties 5	17805	0	0	0	0	0	17805	0	0	0	0	0	0
Other Portfolio Income 6	57341	4728	621	0	6	1817	14259	0	12092	903	•	5	22912
Other Receipts 7	2759426	58158	264079	21739	203146	109221	354093	118652	260069	156412	•	224996	988862
Total Receipts 8	3109377	63416	265710	22088	203165	111064	393614	119265	275295	163652	•	251760	1240349
Average Total Receipts 9	2239	10569	214	394	6157	27766	24601	17038	27530	23379	•	83920	310087
Operating Costs/Operating Income (%)													
Cost of Operations 10	16.2	•	20.6	•	70.0	•	69.2	•	3.3	13.0	•	1.8	•
Salaries and Wages 11	19.9	2.5	6.1	•	10.5	19.2	7.1	30.1	17.8	13.8	•	18.3	30.5
Taxes Paid 12	1.7	1.0	2.2	4.5	0.5	2.4	0.8	3.6	1.5	3.4	•	1.1	1.6
Interest Paid 13	7.8	1.9	0.1	4.7	0.0	0.2	0.4	1.4	1.3	7.2	•	9.0	16.1
Depreciation 14	1.6	0.2	1.0	41.1	0.2	1.4	1.6	3.4	0.9	0.7	•	0.9	1.5
Amortization and Depletion 15	0.4	•	•	•	0.0	0.0	0.0	0.3	0.2	0.0	•	0.8	0.9
Pensions and Other Deferred Comp. 16	0.5	0.1	0.3	•	0.0	0.2	0.4	1.4	0.3	1.5	•	0.2	0.5
Employee Benefits 17	1.1	0.3	0.5	•	0.1	0.2	0.7	2.6	0.6	1.2	•	1.7	1.6
Advertising 18	0.2	0.0	0.2	0.0	0.0	•	0.3	0.9	0.4	0.1	•	0.2	0.1
Other Expenses 19	32.4	9.0	43.7	25.2	4.7	10.3	12.1	28.6	39.4	35.5	•	57.5	37.7
Officers' Compensation 20	4.1	0.4	15.9	1.0	3.1	19.3	2.4	13.1	2.4	2.2	•	3.7	1.1
Operating Margin 21	14.0	84.6	9.3	23.4	10.8	46.8	5.0	14.6	32.1	21.5	•	4.7	8.4
Operating Margin Before Officers' Comp. 22	18.1	85.0	25.3	24.4	13.9	66.1	7.4	27.7	34.4	23.6	•	8.4	9.5

Selected Average Balance Sheet ($ in Thousands)

Net Receivables 23	3624	0	13	104	70	7300	9338	30910	67833	•	424961	686985
Inventories 24	•	•	•	•	•	•	•	•	•	•	•	•
Net Property, Plant and Equipment 25	162	0	443	12	727	665	2500	1123	13263	•	3592	10385
Total Assets 26	22905	116	710	1163	7362	15999	33398	77932	212232	•	1092081	6382937
Notes and Loans Payable 27	3312	3	362	14	0	3962	5716	9283	82800	•	116111	863161
All Other Liabilities 28	17548	17	71	116	706	8054	15053	42694	109449	•	912958	5044318
Net Worth 29	2044	97	277	1033	6656	3982	12629	25955	19983	•	63012	475458

Selected Financial Ratios (Times to 1)

Current Ratio 30	1.3	•	4.3	0.4	9.6	6.5	1.3	1.1	1.1	1.0	0.8	1.4
Quick Ratio 31	0.6	•	3.4	0.4	8.5	6.3	1.0	0.8	1.1	0.6	0.6	0.6
Net Sales to Working Capital 32	0.6	•	3.7	•	6.2	7.1	7.7	7.4	4.2	11.0	•	0.2
Coverage Ratio 33	2.8	44.5	128.8	6.0	4395.0	228.8	15.2	11.8	26.7	4.0	1.5	1.5
Total Asset Turnover 34	0.1	•	1.8	0.6	5.3	3.8	1.5	0.5	0.4	0.1	1.5	0.0
Inventory Turnover 35	•	•	•	•	•	•	•	•	•	•	•	•
Receivables Turnover 36	•	•	•	•	•	•	•	•	•	•	•	•
Total Liabilities to Net Worth 37	10.2	0.2	1.6	1.6	0.1	0.1	3.0	1.6	2.0	9.6	16.3	12.4
Current Assets to Working Capital 38	4.3	1.3	1.3	•	1.1	1.2	4.1	8.6	8.5	80.2	•	3.5
Current Liabilities to Working Capital 39	3.3	0.3	0.3	•	0.1	0.2	3.1	7.6	7.5	79.2	•	2.5
Working Capital to Net Sales 40	1.8	0.3	0.3	•	0.2	0.1	0.1	0.1	0.2	0.1	•	4.5
Inventory to Working Capital 41	0.0	•	•	•	•	•	•	•	•	•	•	•
Total Receipts to Cash Flow 42	2.3	1.1	2.0	2.2	6.5	1.8	6.4	2.6	1.6	1.8	1.6	2.3
Cost of Goods to Cash Flow 43	0.4	•	0.4	•	4.6	•	4.4	•	0.1	0.2	0.0	0.0
Cash Flow to Total Debt 44	0.0	5.6	•	0.4	7.3	21.9	0.3	0.3	0.3	0.1	0.0	0.0

Selected Financial Factors (in Percentages)

Debt Ratio 45	91.1	•	16.5	61.0	11.1	9.6	75.1	62.2	66.7	90.6	94.2	92.6
Return on Total Assets 46	2.1	•	17.3	15.7	57.3	177.2	8.3	8.2	11.8	3.2	1.0	1.2
Return on Equity Before Income Taxes 47	15.4	•	20.5	33.4	64.4	195.1	31.1	19.7	34.1	25.1	6.2	5.7
Return on Equity After Income Taxes 48	12.7	19.3	19.3	33.3	63.8	195.0	29.3	19.2	24.8	21.5	4.4	4.1
Profit Margin (Before Income Tax) 49	14.1	84.6	9.3	23.4	10.8	46.8	5.0	14.6	32.2	21.5	4.7	8.7
Profit Margin (After Income Tax) 50	11.6	65.9	8.8	23.4	10.7	46.7	4.7	14.2	23.4	18.4	3.3	6.2

Table I

Corporations with and without Net Income

SECURITIES & COMMODITY EXCHANGES, OTHER FINANCIAL INVESTMENT

MONEY AMOUNTS AND SIZE OF ASSETS IN THOUSANDS OF DOLLARS

Item Description for Accounting Period 7/03 Through 6/04		Total	Zero Assets	Under 500	500 to 1,000	1,000 to 5,000	5,000 to 10,000	10,000 to 25,000	25,000 to 50,000	50,000 to 100,000	100,000 to 250,000	250,000 to 500,000	500,000 to 2,500,000	2,500,000 and over
Number of Enterprises	1	31197	3603	23362	954	2158	386	402	129	67	61	21	33	21
Revenues ($ in Thousands)														
Net Sales	2	67620169	349393	7352040	761641	4446419	3310013	3736533	2064513	1142722	2965519	1848297	9158728	30484351
Interest	3	4915598	4726	14545	3758	35719	13022	32853	55782	35747	142493	55861	203267	4317826
Rents	4	59139	20	2866	0	555	599	3182	181	1883	3105	7274	11931	27543
Royalties	5	81326	0	15095	0	66	0	1145	227	2547	60571	149	1526	0
Other Portfolio Income	6	1137570	9002	17596	23501	65760	22418	89477	31477	23488	81004	26676	191530	555644
Other Receipts	7	6142536	335645	7301938	734382	4344319	3273974	3609876	1976846	1079057	2678346	1755337	8750474	25583338
Total Receipts	8	67620169	349393	7352040	761641	4446419	3310013	3736533	2064513	1142722	2965519	1848297	9158728	30484351
Average Total Receipts	9	2168	97	315	798	2060	8575	9295	16004	17056	48615	88014	277537	1451636
Operating Costs/Operating Income (%)														
Cost of Operations	10	0.7	0.4	1.0	•	1.1	0.9	4.5	3.5	3.3	1.5	0.2	0.0	0.0
Salaries and Wages	11	24.1	12.8	20.6	20.1	36.3	35.2	31.2	25.0	36.8	26.8	29.5	27.7	19.0
Taxes Paid	12	2.3	2.9	3.3	3.2	2.7	2.3	2.5	2.7	3.3	3.2	3.4	2.2	1.8
Interest Paid	13	3.8	5.4	0.3	0.7	0.8	0.7	2.0	4.0	3.3	4.8	6.1	2.9	5.8
Depreciation	14	2.4	0.7	0.9	2.1	2.1	2.7	2.0	2.2	3.6	4.4	5.9	3.8	2.1
Amortization and Depletion	15	1.2	0.4	0.1	0.3	1.1	0.0	0.4	1.8	1.0	1.7	3.4	2.7	1.0
Pensions and Other Deferred Comp.	16	1.3	1.5	2.6	3.3	1.5	1.3	0.9	1.1	2.3	0.7	1.5	2.2	0.6
Employee Benefits	17	2.5	0.1	1.8	1.9	2.4	1.4	1.4	1.4	1.3	1.3	1.8	3.6	3.0
Advertising	18	2.2	1.5	0.9	0.4	0.4	0.4	1.1	0.6	0.4	1.7	0.3	2.6	3.5
Other Expenses	19	36.6	63.8	39.1	37.3	32.5	34.4	29.3	32.1	29.1	27.8	38.0	34.2	39.4
Officers' Compensation	20	9.4	6.8	20.2	27.8	17.6	16.5	16.3	22.7	5.6	10.1	8.6	6.4	3.7
Operating Margin	21	13.4	3.6	9.3	3.0	1.4	4.1	8.5	2.9	10.0	16.0	1.3	11.5	20.0
Operating Margin Before Officers' Comp.	22	22.8	10.4	29.5	30.8	19.0	20.6	24.8	25.6	15.6	26.1	9.9	17.9	23.7

Selected Average Balance Sheet ($ in Thousands)

Item	#													
Net Receivables	23	1244	0	3	1	257	598	2189	4526	5672	16862	88334	87139	1445256
Inventories	24	•	•	•	•	•	•	•	•	•	•	•	•	•
Net Property, Plant and Equipment	25	265	0	6	154	287	986	1185	1691	3598	13161	29352	53118	136628
Total Assets	26	11098	0	71	722	2001	6819	15341	35137	69303	153256	359471	1089302	12797460
Notes and Loans Payable	27	3543	0	131	334	728	3105	5192	12303	17603	44491	117842	143607	4265812
All Other Liabilities	28	3825	0	16	102	497	1466	2729	10093	14574	25843	126496	329828	4701054
Net Worth	29	3731	0	-76	286	777	2248	7420	12741	37125	82922	115133	615867	3830595

Selected Financial Ratios (Times to 1)

Item	#													
Current Ratio	30	1.0	•	2.6	2.7	1.5	0.8	1.8	1.4	1.7	1.5	1.0	1.7	0.9
Quick Ratio	31	0.6	•	2.1	2.4	1.0	0.7	1.3	1.1	1.2	0.9	0.9	1.3	0.5
Net Sales to Working Capital	32	•	•	12.3	5.0	7.3	•	3.3	3.7	1.8	2.5	70.6	2.2	•
Coverage Ratio	33	4.5	1.6	29.7	5.1	2.6	6.7	5.2	1.8	3.9	4.3	1.2	5.1	4.4
Total Asset Turnover	34	0.2	•	4.4	1.1	1.0	1.3	0.6	0.5	0.2	0.3	0.2	0.3	0.1
Inventory Turnover	35	•	•	•	•	•	•	•	•	•	•	•	•	•
Receivables Turnover	36	•	•	•	•	•	•	•	•	•	•	•	•	•
Total Liabilities to Net Worth	37	2.0	•	1.5	1.6	2.0	1.8	1.1	1.8	0.9	0.8	2.1	0.8	2.3
Current Assets to Working Capital	38	•	1.6	1.6	3.2	•	3.5	2.3	2.5	2.5	2.9	108.6	2.5	•
Current Liabilities to Working Capital	39	0.6	•	0.6	2.2	•	2.5	1.3	1.5	1.9	•	107.6	1.5	•
Working Capital to Net Sales	40	0.1	•	0.2	0.1	•	0.3	0.3	0.4	0.5	0.4	0.0	0.4	•
Inventory to Working Capital	41	•	•	0.0	0.0	•	0.0	0.0	0.0	0.0	0.0	•	0.0	•
Total Receipts to Cash Flow	42	2.2	2.0	2.4	3.6	3.7	•	3.3	3.1	2.9	2.7	3.1	2.4	1.8
Cost of Goods to Cash Flow	43	0.0	0.0	0.0	0.0	0.0	0.0	0.1	0.1	0.1	0.0	0.0	0.0	0.0
Cash Flow to Total Debt	44	0.1	0.9	0.6	0.5	0.5	0.2	0.3	0.4	0.2	0.3	0.1	0.2	0.1

Selected Financial Factors (in Percentages)

Item	#													
Debt Ratio	45	66.4	•	206.6	60.3	61.2	67.0	51.6	63.7	46.4	45.9	68.0	43.5	70.1
Return on Total Assets	46	3.4	•	42.6	4.1	2.2	6.0	6.3	3.3	3.1	6.5	1.7	3.7	2.9
Return on Equity Before Income Taxes	47	7.8	•	•	8.2	3.4	15.5	10.5	3.9	4.4	9.2	0.8	5.3	7.5
Return on Equity After Income Taxes	48	5.2	•	•	5.4	1.4	13.7	9.2	1.7	3.7	7.6	•	2.8	4.8
Profit Margin (Before Income Tax)	49	13.4	3.4	9.3	3.0	1.3	4.1	8.3	3.1	9.5	15.8	1.0	11.8	19.9
Profit Margin (After Income Tax)	50	8.9	•	9.1	2.0	0.5	3.6	7.4	1.4	8.1	13.0	•	6.2	12.7

SECURITIES & COMMODITY EXCHANGES, OTHER FINANCIAL INVESTMENT

Table II
Corporations with Net Income

MONEY AMOUNTS AND SIZE OF ASSETS IN THOUSANDS OF DOLLARS

Item Description for Accounting Period 7/03 Through 6/04		Total	Zero Assets	Under 500	500 to 1,000	1,000 to 5,000	5,000 to 10,000	10,000 to 25,000	25,000 to 50,000	50,000 to 100,000	100,000 to 250,000	250,000 to 500,000	500,000 to 2,500,000	2,500,000 and over
Number of Enterprises	1	17423	1304	14122	531	928	156	202	63	36	34	11	21	15
Revenues ($ in Thousands)														
Net Sales	2	55851010	325278	6138492	715294	2687429	1259272	2749034	1566684	967658	2566115	1320255	6955259	28600240
Interest	3	4459145	342	7159	1627	21830	7345	14142	38592	21686	81081	54144	101090	4110108
Rents	4	52610	0	2313	0	555	93	2028	181	1883	2286	7274	10642	25355
Royalties	5	76425	0	15095	0	66	0	101	225	217	60571	149	1	0
Other Portfolio Income	6	932471	8851	17107	21765	50771	21305	73615	24640	19180	54479	23991	128440	488327
Other Receipts	7	50330359	316085	6096818	691902	2614207	1230529	2659148	1503046	924692	2367698	1234697	6715086	23976450
Total Receipts	8	55851010	325278	6138492	715294	2687429	1259272	2749034	1566684	967658	2566115	1320255	6955259	28600240
Average Total Receipts	9	3206	249	435	1347	2896	8072	13609	24868	26879	75474	120023	331203	1906683
Operating Costs/Operating Income (%)														
Cost of Operations	10	0.5	0.0	1.2	•	1.3	0.0	3.1	0.5	2.4	0.5	0.3	0.0	0.0
Salaries and Wages	11	21.2	5.3	17.5	19.6	25.4	24.7	28.8	20.2	35.5	26.9	32.8	26.4	18.2
Taxes Paid	12	2.2	2.5	3.0	3.1	2.1	2.1	2.5	2.5	3.5	3.1	4.0	2.5	1.8
Interest Paid	13	3.4	0.3	0.2	0.1	0.8	0.8	1.1	1.9	1.8	1.9	4.9	2.0	5.3
Depreciation	14	2.0	0.6	0.7	1.7	1.5	1.6	1.5	1.5	2.3	2.1	5.5	3.1	2.0
Amortization and Depletion	15	0.6	0.3	0.1	0.0	0.1	0.1	0.2	0.4	0.2	1.6	2.3	1.5	0.6
Pensions and Other Deferred Comp.	16	1.1	1.6	2.3	3.5	2.1	1.3	0.8	1.1	2.3	0.7	1.5	2.3	0.5
Employee Benefits	17	2.2	0.0	1.7	1.9	1.7	1.3	1.2	1.1	0.9	1.3	2.2	1.1	3.1
Advertising	18	2.5	0.2	0.7	0.4	0.5	0.3	0.6	0.7	0.4	1.9	0.4	2.7	3.7
Other Expenses	19	34.5	38.2	35.4	21.3	29.3	30.7	20.9	25.1	24.2	23.7	32.0	29.6	39.6
Officers' Compensation	20	8.5	6.4	21.6	28.7	19.1	18.7	18.7	23.3	5.4	8.9	1.5	5.0	3.2
Operating Margin	21	21.3	44.5	15.7	19.6	16.1	18.6	20.8	21.7	21.1	27.4	12.6	23.9	22.2
Operating Margin Before Officers' Comp.	22	29.8	50.9	37.3	48.3	35.1	37.3	39.5	45.0	26.5	36.3	14.1	28.9	25.3

Selected Average Balance Sheet ($ in Thousands)

Line Item	1	2	3	4	5	6	7	8	9	10	11	12	13
Net Receivables 23	1968	0	5	0	318	782	2834	5270	4848	17867	114224	114291	1897135
Inventories 24	•	•	•	•	•	•	•	•	•	•	•	•	•
Net Property, Plant and Equipment 25	321	0	237	253	429	1136	1813	3211	7576	47044	57025	•	176005
Total Assets 26	15734	0	80	639	2181	6967	15341	33767	71067	150291	360438	1053492	15371871
Notes and Loans Payable 27	5175	0	28	221	665	2210	4088	6610	12665	27795	187123	142769	5399093
All Other Liabilities 28	4789	0	14	75	362	1628	3071	8480	18865	32899	73463	244313	4914241
Net Worth 29	5771	0	38	343	1154	3128	8182	18677	39537	89597	99853	666410	5058537

Selected Financial Ratios (Times to 1)

Line Item	1	2	3	4	5	6	7	8	9	10	11	12	13
Current Ratio 30	0.9	•	4.1	4.4	2.4	1.4	1.9	2.0	1.5	1.7	1.2	2.1	0.8
Quick Ratio 31	0.5	•	3.5	4.4	1.9	1.1	1.4	1.5	1.0	1.0	1.2	1.7	0.4
Net Sales to Working Capital 32	•	•	10.6	4.9	4.5	11.0	3.6	3.0	3.1	2.8	4.0	1.8	•
Coverage Ratio 33	7.3	154.8	68.2	140.8	20.7	25.3	20.7	12.9	12.5	15.7	3.5	13.0	5.2
Total Asset Turnover 34	0.2	•	5.5	2.1	1.3	1.2	0.9	0.7	0.4	0.5	0.3	0.3	0.1
Inventory Turnover 35	•	•	•	•	•	•	•	•	•	•	•	•	•
Receivables Turnover 36	•	•	•	•	•	•	•	•	•	•	•	•	•
Total Liabilities to Net Worth 37	1.7	•	1.1	0.9	1.2	3.3	0.9	2.0	0.8	0.7	2.6	0.6	2.0
Current Assets to Working Capital 38	•	•	1.3	1.3	1.7	2.1	2.0	2.4	2.9	2.4	5.2	1.9	2.0
Current Liabilities to Working Capital 39	•	•	0.3	0.3	0.7	2.3	1.0	1.9	1.4	0.9	4.2	0.9	•
Working Capital to Net Sales 40	•	•	0.2	0.2	0.1	0.3	0.3	0.3	0.3	0.4	0.2	0.6	0.6
Inventory to Working Capital 41	•	•	•	•	•	•	•	•	•	0.0	0.0	0.0	•
Total Receipts to Cash Flow 42	2.0	1.3	2.2	2.8	2.6	2.5	2.8	2.3	2.4	2.2	2.6	2.0	1.7
Cost of Goods to Cash Flow 43	0.0	•	0.0	0.0	0.0	0.0	0.1	0.1	0.0	0.0	0.0	0.0	0.0
Cash Flow to Total Debt 44	0.2	•	1.6	1.1	0.8	0.7	0.4	1.0	1.4	0.6	0.2	0.4	0.1

Selected Financial Factors (in Percentages)

Line Item	1	2	3	4	5	6	7	8	9	10	11	12	13
Debt Ratio 45	63.3	•	52.4	46.3	47.1	55.1	46.7	44.7	44.4	40.4	72.3	36.7	67.1
Return on Total Assets 46	5.0	•	87.4	41.5	22.3	22.5	19.3	17.7	8.6	14.6	5.8	8.0	3.4
Return on Equity Before Income Taxes 47	11.8	•	181.0	76.8	48.1	34.5	29.6	22.9	14.3	15.0	11.7	•	8.3
Return on Equity After Income Taxes 48	8.8	•	178.5	72.6	44.9	32.3	26.6	20.3	13.1	10.5	8.1	•	5.4
Profit Margin (Before Income Tax) 49	21.2	44.2	15.8	19.5	16.0	18.6	20.7	22.2	21.0	27.2	12.5	23.6	22.1
Profit Margin (After Income Tax) 50	15.9	39.6	15.6	18.5	14.7	17.4	19.4	20.0	19.3	24.0	8.7	16.3	14.4

Table I

Corporations with and without Net Income

LIFE INSURANCE

MONEY AMOUNTS AND SIZE OF ASSETS IN THOUSANDS OF DOLLARS

Item Description for Accounting Period 7/03 Through 6/04		Total	Zero Assets	Under 500	500 to 1,000	1,000 to 5,000	5,000 to 10,000	10,000 to 25,000	25,000 to 50,000	50,000 to 100,000	100,000 to 250,000	250,000 to 500,000	500,000 to 2,500,000	2,500,000 and over
Number of Enterprises	1	1321	75	314	107	260	80	106	64	46	47	56	67	99
Revenues ($ in Thousands)														
Net Sales	2	732355050	17181772	50685	41247	248873	194508	670115	1046266	1207833	2699523	6135077	21703208	681175942
Interest	3	122738981	801298	941	1899	15619	16249	62247	95007	111842	297725	835240	3358888	117142026
Rents	4	4507571	3445	0	0	78	510	2354	2124	6361	12377	22291	57563	4400470
Royalties	5	8233	0	0	0	0	0	0	0	2575	371	195	56	5036
Other Portfolio Income	6	14929254	1708267	57	399	3015	2196	23276	17524	19491	39774	71596	313202	12730456
Other Receipts	7	590171011	14668762	49687	38949	230161	175553	582238	931611	1067564	2349276	5205755	17973499	546897954
Total Receipts	8	732355050	17181772	50685	41247	248873	194508	670115	1046266	1207833	2699523	6135077	21703208	681175942
Average Total Receipts	9	554394	229090	161	385	957	2431	6322	16348	26257	57437	109555	323928	6880565
Operating Costs/Operating Income (%)														
Cost of Operations	10	45.8	67.2	26.3	26.7	35.1	22.9	42.9	48.2	39.1	46.9	43.2	39.8	45.5
Salaries and Wages	11	2.0	0.1	•	•	•	•	0.1	0.0	1.3	0.6	0.4	0.2	2.2
Taxes Paid	12	0.8	0.2	0.8	0.8	0.7	0.8	1.6	1.0	1.4	1.9	1.6	1.0	0.8
Interest Paid	13	1.5	0.0	0.4	0.0	0.1	0.7	0.2	0.1	0.3	0.3	0.6	0.3	1.6
Depreciation	14	0.4	0.0	0.0	0.0	0.2	0.2	0.4	0.4	0.5	0.4	0.3	0.3	0.4
Amortization and Depletion	15	1.1	0.1	0.5	0.7	1.0	0.9	2.2	1.1	2.3	2.7	2.4	1.6	1.1
Pensions and Other Deferred Comp.	16	0.4	0.0	•	•	0.6	0.2	0.5	0.4	1.2	0.9	0.5	0.5	0.4
Employee Benefits	17	0.3	0.0	•	•	0.2	0.0	0.2	0.2	0.7	0.2	0.2	0.1	0.3
Advertising	18	0.2	0.0	0.1	0.1	0.1	0.1	0.2	0.4	0.1	0.3	0.3	0.7	0.2
Other Expenses	19	45.1	31.1	70.1	49.3	57.6	57.7	38.2	39.7	46.1	38.6	47.2	53.0	45.2
Officers' Compensation	20	0.1	•	•	•	•	0.2	0.3	0.1	0.1	0.1	0.1	0.1	0.1
Operating Margin	21	2.3	1.2	1.9	22.4	4.5	16.1	13.2	8.4	7.0	7.1	3.1	2.3	2.3
Operating Margin Before Officers' Comp.	22	2.4	1.2	1.9	22.4	4.5	16.3	13.5	8.5	7.1	7.1	3.2	2.4	2.4

Selected Average Balance Sheet ($ in Thousands)

Item	1	2	3	4	5	6	7	8	9	10	11	12	13
Net Receivables 23	22742	0	6	37	195	242	717	581	613	1136	3136	10221	292025
Inventories 24	•	•	•	•	•	•	•	•	•	•	•	•	•
Net Property, Plant and Equipment 25	11830	0	0	0	10	43	142	222	852	1123	2446	5532	151435
Total Assets 26	2908589	0	185	764	2483	6937	16458	37292	69734	163490	364051	1179766	37640925
Notes and Loans Payable 27	45309	0	0	0	0	0	27	76	181	1521	3253	2425	600208
All Other Liabilities 28	2534999	0	212	424	1261	5580	10849	26210	48165	129835	296270	982368	32871639
Net Worth 29	328282	0	-27	340	1222	1357	5583	11006	21388	32133	64528	194973	4169079

Selected Financial Ratios (Times to 1)

Item	1	2	3	4	5	6	7	8	9	10	11	12	13
Current Ratio 30	1.1	•	0.5	6.0	5.8	5.1	2.2	1.7	2.0	2.3	1.8	1.7	1.1
Quick Ratio 31	0.8	•	0.4	4.3	4.6	3.4	1.7	1.4	1.3	1.8	1.4	1.1	0.8
Net Sales to Working Capital 32	9.9	•	0.8	0.8	0.7	0.9	1.5	2.9	1.8	1.7	1.8	2.3	11.9
Coverage Ratio 33	2.4	549.5	5.5	772.0	63.0	23.0	65.7	72.6	21.8	24.9	5.9	9.5	2.3
Total Asset Turnover 34	0.2	0.9	0.5	0.5	0.4	0.4	0.4	0.4	0.4	0.4	0.3	0.3	0.2
Inventory Turnover 35	•	•	•	•	•	•	•	•	•	•	•	•	•
Receivables Turnover 36	•	•	•	•	•	•	•	•	•	•	•	•	•
Total Liabilities to Net Worth 37	7.9	•	1.2	1.2	1.0	4.1	1.9	2.4	2.3	4.1	4.6	5.1	8.0
Current Assets to Working Capital 38	8.3	•	1.2	1.2	1.2	1.2	1.9	2.3	2.0	1.8	2.2	2.4	10.1
Current Liabilities to Working Capital 39	7.3	•	0.2	0.2	0.2	0.2	0.9	1.3	1.0	0.8	1.2	1.4	9.1
Working Capital to Net Sales 40	0.1	•	1.2	1.2	1.4	1.1	0.7	0.3	0.5	0.6	0.5	0.4	0.1
Inventory to Working Capital 41	0.0	•	•	•	•	•	•	•	0.0	0.0	0.0	0.0	0.0
Total Receipts to Cash Flow 42	2.2	3.1	1.4	1.4	1.6	1.4	1.4	2.1	2.0	2.3	2.1	1.8	2.2
Cost of Goods to Cash Flow 43	1.0	2.1	0.4	0.4	0.6	0.3	0.9	1.0	0.8	1.1	0.9	0.7	1.0
Cash Flow to Total Debt 44	0.1	•	0.5	0.7	0.5	0.3	0.3	0.3	0.3	0.2	0.2	0.2	0.1

Selected Financial Factors (in Percentages)

Item	1	2	3	4	5	6	7	8	9	10	11	12
Debt Ratio 45	88.7	114.5	55.5	50.8	80.4	66.1	70.5	69.3	80.3	82.3	83.5	88.9
Return on Total Assets 46	0.7	•	2.0	1.8	5.9	5.2	3.7	2.8	2.6	1.1	0.7	0.7
Return on Equity Before Income Taxes 47	3.6	•	25.4	3.6	28.9	15.0	12.5	8.6	12.6	5.3	3.8	3.5
Return on Equity After Income Taxes 48	1.7	•	23.5	1.5	21.8	11.3	9.7	5.8	8.1	3.2	0.8	1.6
Profit Margin (Before Income Tax) 49	2.1	1.2	22.4	4.5	16.1	13.2	8.4	7.0	7.0	3.1	2.3	2.1
Profit Margin (After Income Tax) 50	1.0	0.9	20.8	1.9	12.1	10.0	6.5	4.8	4.6	1.9	0.5	1.0

Table II
Corporations with Net Income

LIFE INSURANCE

MONEY AMOUNTS AND SIZE OF ASSETS IN THOUSANDS OF DOLLARS

Item Description for Accounting Period 7/03 Through 6/04	Total	Zero Assets	Under 500	500 to 1,000	1,000 to 5,000	5,000 to 10,000	10,000 to 25,000	25,000 to 50,000	50,000 to 100,000	100,000 to 250,000	250,000 to 500,000	500,000 to 2,500,000	2,500,000 and over
Number of Enterprises **1**	989	50	209	86	202	68	80	52	34	32	41	51	84
Revenues ($ in Thousands)													
Net Sales **2**	578144547	17164237	28389	34695	168077	144623	524015	862803	933552	2050321	4838018	14766961	536628857
Interest **3**	97870590	797202	729	1688	12225	14828	47657	79904	88836	206399	632387	2478965	93509769
Rents **4**	3904434	3445	0	0	27	505	1232	1919	2544	8422	18848	27233	3840259
Royalties **5**	2790	0	0	0	0	0	0	0	0	29	195	56	2509
Other Portfolio Income **6**	10540042	1708267	54	398	2357	1976	18895	14175	9971	27689	64683	193179	8498397
Other Receipts **7**	465826691	14655323	27606	32609	153468	127314	456231	766805	832201	1807782	4121905	12067528	430777923
Total Receipts **8**	578144547	17164237	28389	34695	168077	144623	524015	862803	933552	2050321	4838018	14766961	536628857
Average Total Receipts **9**	584575	343285	136	403	832	2127	6550	16592	27457	64073	118000	289548	6388439
Operating Costs/Operating Income (%)													
Cost of Operations **10**	43.8	67.2	24.3	27.9	30.9	20.0	41.8	52.2	40.1	45.7	42.2	40.7	43.1
Salaries and Wages **11**	1.8	0.1	•	•	•	•	0.2	0.0	1.0	0.5	0.3	0.3	1.9
Taxes Paid **12**	0.8	0.2	1.0	0.7	0.8	1.0	1.4	0.9	1.4	1.7	1.5	1.4	0.8
Interest Paid **13**	1.3	0.0	0.0	0.0	0.1	1.0	0.1	0.1	0.4	0.2	0.2	0.2	1.4
Depreciation **14**	0.4	0.0	0.0	0.0	0.2	0.2	0.3	0.4	0.4	0.4	0.3	0.4	0.4
Amortization and Depletion **15**	1.0	0.1	0.6	0.8	0.9	0.9	1.5	1.0	2.3	2.4	2.2	2.1	1.0
Pensions and Other Deferred Comp. **16**	0.4	0.0	•	•	0.9	0.3	0.4	0.4	1.4	0.6	0.5	0.7	0.4
Employee Benefits **17**	0.3	0.0	•	•	0.2	0.1	0.2	0.2	0.8	0.2	0.2	0.2	0.3
Advertising **18**	0.2	0.0	•	0.0	0.0	0.1	0.1	0.1	0.1	0.2	0.2	0.9	0.2
Other Expenses **19**	45.3	31.1	47.9	40.5	40.1	51.6	33.4	31.4	41.0	36.8	46.6	44.4	45.8
Officers' Compensation **20**	0.1	•	•	•	•	0.3	0.3	0.1	0.1	0.1	0.1	0.1	0.1
Operating Margin **21**	4.6	1.2	26.1	30.0	26.0	24.6	20.1	13.2	11.1	11.1	5.7	8.7	4.5
Operating Margin Before Officers' Comp. **22**	4.7	1.2	26.1	30.0	26.0	24.9	20.5	13.3	11.2	11.1	5.8	8.8	4.6

Selected Average Balance Sheet ($ in Thousands)

Line Item												
Net Receivables 23	22191	0	47	182	285	902	668	583	915	3157	5345	253894
Inventories 24	•	•	•	•	•	•	•	•	•	•	•	•
Net Property, Plant and Equipment 25	11434	0	0	2	34	73	268	561	904	2617	6081	128812
Total Assets 26	3003861	195	766	2496	6995	16208	37468	68745	161590	375226	1165208	34688559
Notes and Loans Payable 27	46586	0	0	0	0	36	90	205	1215	796	2534	545933
All Other Liabilities 28	2604810	154	440	1170	4494	9988	25433	44524	125068	308728	935849	29851445
Net Worth 29	382465	41	326	1326	2501	6185	11945	24016	35308	65701	226825	4291181

Selected Financial Ratios (Times to 1)

Line Item												
Current Ratio 30	1.4	0.4	5.4	7.3	6.9	3.1	1.9	2.1	2.7	2.1	1.7	1.4
Quick Ratio 31	1.0	0.3	3.8	5.6	4.4	2.3	1.4	1.6	2.1	1.7	1.1	1.0
Net Sales to Working Capital 32	4.1	•	0.9	0.6	0.7	1.3	2.8	1.8	1.6	1.6	2.3	4.1
Coverage Ratio 33	4.5	555.8	823.0	869.4	242.6	25.9	158.3	126.7	31.3	50.7	25.2	37.3
Total Asset Turnover 34	0.2	0.7	0.5	0.3	0.3	0.4	0.4	0.4	0.4	0.3	0.2	0.2
Inventory Turnover 35	•	•	•	•	•	•	•	•	•	•	•	•
Receivables Turnover 36	•	•	•	•	•	•	•	•	•	•	•	•
Total Liabilities to Net Worth 37	6.9	3.8	1.4	0.9	1.8	1.6	2.1	1.9	3.6	4.7	4.1	7.1
Current Assets to Working Capital 38	3.3	•	1.2	1.2	1.2	1.5	2.1	1.9	1.6	1.9	2.4	3.4
Current Liabilities to Working Capital 39	2.3	•	0.2	0.2	0.2	0.5	1.1	0.9	0.6	0.9	1.4	2.4
Working Capital to Net Sales 40	0.2	•	1.2	1.6	1.4	0.8	0.4	0.6	0.6	0.6	0.4	0.2
Inventory to Working Capital 41	0.0	•	•	•	•	•	•	•	0.0	0.0	0.0	0.0
Total Receipts to Cash Flow 42	2.1	3.1	1.4	1.5	1.3	2.0	2.3	2.0	2.2	2.0	1.9	2.0
Cost of Goods to Cash Flow 43	0.9	2.1	0.4	0.5	0.3	0.8	1.2	0.8	1.0	0.8	0.8	0.9
Cash Flow to Total Debt 44	0.1	•	0.6	0.5	0.4	0.3	0.3	0.3	0.2	0.2	0.2	0.1

Selected Financial Factors (in Percentages)

Line Item												
Debt Ratio 45	87.4	79.0	57.4	46.9	64.2	61.8	68.1	65.1	78.1	82.5	80.5	87.6
Return on Total Assets 46	1.1	18.2	15.8	8.7	7.8	8.2	5.9	4.6	4.5	1.9	2.2	1.1
Return on Equity Before Income Taxes 47	6.9	86.4	37.2	16.3	20.9	21.3	18.3	12.7	20.0	10.2	11.0	6.6
Return on Equity After Income Taxes 48	4.7	83.4	34.7	13.9	16.4	17.0	15.1	9.4	14.1	7.4	7.6	4.5
Profit Margin (Before Income Tax) 49	4.5	26.1	30.0	26.0	24.6	20.1	13.2	11.1	11.0	5.7	8.6	4.4
Profit Margin (After Income Tax) 50	3.1	25.2	28.1	22.1	19.2	16.0	10.9	8.2	7.8	4.1	5.9	3.0

Table I

Corporations with and without Net Income

LIFE INSURANCE, STOCK COMPANIES (FORM 1120L)

MONEY AMOUNTS AND SIZE OF ASSETS IN THOUSANDS OF DOLLARS

Item Description for Accounting Period 7/03 Through 6/04	Total	Zero Assets	Under 500	500 to 1,000	1,000 to 5,000	5,000 to 10,000	10,000 to 25,000	25,000 to 50,000	50,000 to 100,000	100,000 to 250,000	250,000 to 500,000	500,000 to 2,500,000	2,500,000 and over
Number of Enterprises 1	1255	72	306	104	252	77	106	56	46	39	48	56	91
Revenues ($ in Thousands)													
Net Sales 2	645262456	17181680	49387	41228	244545	190772	670115	957993	1207833	2353462	5385852	18847006	598132582
Interest 3	104852056	801291	868	1895	14658	15792	62247	78462	111842	240985	669692	2760293	10009032
Rents 4	3608566	3445	0	0	27	510	2354	2090	6361	10640	16874	43058	3523207
Royalties 5	5631	0	0	0	0	0	0	0	2575	29	0	0	3027
Other Portfolio Income 6	13133059	1708267	57	399	2695	2182	23276	15843	19491	31532	52971	254862	11021486
Other Receipts 7	523663144	14668677	48462	38934	227165	172288	582238	861598	1067564	2070276	4646315	15788793	483490830
Total Receipts 8	645262456	17181680	49387	41228	244545	190772	670115	957993	1207833	2353462	5385852	18847006	598132582
Average Total Receipts 9	514153	238634	161	396	970	2478	6322	17107	26257	60345	112205	336554	6572886
Operating Costs/Operating Income (%)													
Cost of Operations 10	46.5	67.2	26.9	26.7	35.2	22.7	42.9	47.7	39.1	47.3	43.0	39.3	46.2
Salaries and Wages 11	2.2	0.1	•	•	•	•	0.1	0.0	1.3	0.7	0.5	0.2	2.3
Taxes Paid 12	0.9	0.2	0.8	0.8	0.7	0.8	1.6	0.9	1.4	1.8	1.6	1.0	0.9
Interest Paid 13	1.6	0.0	0.2	0.0	0.1	0.7	0.2	0.1	0.3	0.3	0.7	0.2	1.7
Depreciation 14	0.4	0.0	0.0	0.0	0.2	0.2	0.4	0.3	0.5	0.4	0.3	0.3	0.4
Amortization and Depletion 15	1.0	0.1	0.5	0.7	0.9	0.9	2.2	0.9	2.3	2.8	2.2	1.5	1.0
Pensions and Other Deferred Comp. 16	0.4	0.0	•	•	0.6	0.3	0.5	0.4	1.2	0.6	0.5	0.5	0.4
Employee Benefits 17	0.3	0.0	•	•	0.1	0.1	0.2	0.1	0.7	0.2	0.2	0.1	0.3
Advertising 18	0.2	0.0	•	0.1	0.1	0.1	0.2	0.4	0.1	0.4	0.3	0.7	0.2
Other Expenses 19	44.4	31.1	69.4	49.2	57.3	57.8	38.2	40.5	46.1	37.3	48.0	53.9	44.4
Officers' Compensation 20	0.1	•	•	•	•	0.2	0.3	0.1	0.1	0.1	0.0	0.1	0.1
Operating Margin 21	2.2	1.2	2.2	22.6	4.9	16.3	13.2	8.6	7.0	8.0	2.9	2.2	2.1
Operating Margin Before Officers' Comp. 22	2.3	1.2	2.2	22.6	4.9	16.5	13.5	8.7	7.1	8.0	2.9	2.2	2.2

Selected Average Balance Sheet ($ in Thousands)

Net Receivables 23	22375	0	6	39	201	252	717	659	613	1131	3437	11911	296562
Inventories 24	•	•	•	•	•	•	•	•	•	•	•	•	•
Net Property, Plant and Equipment 25	11224	•	0	0	8	45	142	229	852	1113	2386	5519	148863
Total Assets 26	2703255	•	184	763	2475	7009	16458	36666	69734	163505	360865	1181906	36202150
Notes and Loans Payable 27	44857	•	0	0	0	0	27	87	181	1833	3795	2892	613892
All Other Liabilities 28	2346540	•	211	431	1252	5627	10849	25066	48165	124174	288845	971028	31496657
Net Worth 29	311858	•	-27	332	1224	1381	5583	11512	21388	37498	68225	207986	4091602

Selected Financial Ratios (Times to 1)

Current Ratio 30	1.2	•	0.5	6.0	6.1	4.9	2.2	1.9	2.0	3.0	1.7	1.8	1.1
Quick Ratio 31	0.8	•	0.4	4.3	4.8	3.3	1.7	1.4	1.3	2.3	1.2	1.1	0.7
Net Sales to Working Capital 32	8.9	•	0.8	0.7	0.9	1.5	2.7	1.8	1.4	2.2	2.2	•	10.3
Coverage Ratio 33	2.3	14.3	549.6	775.9	66.8	22.7	65.7	68.0	21.8	26.5	5.0	10.0	2.2
Total Asset Turnover 34	0.2	•	0.9	0.5	0.4	0.4	0.4	0.5	0.4	0.4	0.3	0.3	0.2
Inventory Turnover 35	•	•	•	•	•	•	•	•	•	•	•	•	•
Receivables Turnover 36	•	•	•	•	•	•	•	•	•	•	•	•	•
Total Liabilities to Net Worth 37	7.7	•	1.3	1.0	1.9	4.1	1.9	2.2	2.3	3.4	4.3	4.7	7.8
Current Assets to Working Capital 38	7.3	•	1.2	1.2	1.9	1.3	2.2	2.0	1.5	2.5	2.3	•	8.6
Current Liabilities to Working Capital 39	6.3	•	0.2	0.2	0.9	0.3	1.2	1.0	0.5	1.5	1.3	•	7.6
Working Capital to Net Sales 40	0.1	•	1.2	1.4	0.7	1.1	0.4	0.5	0.7	0.5	0.5	•	0.1
Inventory to Working Capital 41	0.0	•	•	0.0	•	•	•	0.0	0.0	0.0	0.0	0.0	0.0
Total Receipts to Cash Flow 42	2.2	•	3.1	1.4	1.6	2.1	1.4	2.1	2.0	2.3	2.0	1.8	2.2
Cost of Goods to Cash Flow 43	1.0	•	2.1	0.4	0.6	0.9	0.3	1.0	0.8	1.1	0.9	0.7	1.0
Cash Flow to Total Debt 44	0.1	•	0.7	0.5	0.3	0.3	0.3	0.3	0.2	0.2	0.2	•	0.1

Selected Financial Factors (in Percentages)

Debt Ratio 45	88.5	•	114.9	56.5	50.6	80.3	66.1	68.6	69.3	77.1	81.1	82.4	88.7
Return on Total Assets 46	0.7	•	2.0	11.7	1.9	6.0	5.2	4.1	2.8	3.0	1.1	0.7	0.7
Return on Equity Before Income Taxes 47	3.3	•	•	26.9	3.9	29.2	15.0	12.7	8.6	12.8	4.7	3.4	3.2
Return on Equity After Income Taxes 48	1.4	•	•	24.9	1.7	21.9	11.3	9.8	5.8	8.2	2.7	0.3	1.3
Profit Margin (Before Income Tax) 49	2.0	•	2.2	22.6	4.9	16.3	13.2	8.6	7.0	7.9	2.8	2.1	2.0
Profit Margin (After Income Tax) 50	0.9	•	1.6	20.9	2.2	12.2	10.0	6.6	4.8	5.1	1.6	0.2	0.8

Table II

Corporations with Net Income

LIFE INSURANCE, STOCK COMPANIES (FORM 1120L)

MONEY AMOUNTS AND SIZE OF ASSETS IN THOUSANDS OF DOLLARS

Item Description for Accounting Period 7/03 Through 6/04	Total	Zero Assets	Under 500	500 to 1000	251 to 500	501 to 1,000	1,001 to 5,000	5,001 to 10,000	10,001 to 25,000	25,001 to 50,000	50,001 to 100,000	100,001 to 250,000	250,001 and over
Number of Enterprises 1	949	50	207	86	202	65	80	44	34	29	•	•	•
Revenues ($ in Thousands)													
Net Sales 2	493029133	17164237	28348	34695	168077	140887	524015	774530	933552	1983623	•	•	•
Interest 3	80436835	797202	729	1688	12225	14370	47657	63359	88836	184284	•	•	•
Rents 4	3034159	3445	0	0	27	505	1232	1885	2544	7456	•	•	•
Royalties 5	529	0	0	0	0	0	0	0	0	29	•	•	•
Other Portfolio Income 6	8766817	1708267	54	398	2357	1963	18895	12492	9971	27383	•	•	•
Other Receipts 7	400790793	14655323	27565	32609	153468	124049	456231	696794	832201	1764471	•	•	•
Total Receipts 8	493029133	17164237	28348	34695	168077	140887	524015	774530	933552	1983623	•	•	•
Average Total Receipts 9	519525	343285	137	403	832	2167	6550	17603	27457	68401	•	•	•
Operating Costs/Operating Income (%)													
Cost of Operations 10	44.3	67.2	24.3	27.9	30.9	19.7	41.8	52.0	40.1	46.2	•	•	•
Salaries and Wages 11	1.9	0.1	•	•	•	•	0.2	0.0	1.0	0.5	•	•	•
Taxes Paid 12	0.9	0.2	1.0	0.7	0.8	1.0	1.4	0.8	1.4	1.7	•	•	•
Interest Paid 13	1.4	0.0	0.0	0.0	0.1	1.0	0.1	0.1	0.4	0.2	•	•	•
Depreciation 14	0.4	0.0	0.0	0.0	0.2	0.2	0.3	0.2	0.4	0.4	•	•	•
Amortization and Depletion 15	1.0	0.1	0.6	0.8	0.9	0.9	1.5	0.8	2.3	2.4	•	•	•
Pensions and Other Deferred Comp. 16	0.4	0.0	•	•	0.9	0.3	0.4	0.4	1.4	0.6	•	•	•
Employee Benefits 17	0.3	0.0	•	•	0.2	0.1	0.2	0.1	0.8	0.2	•	•	•
Advertising 18	0.2	0.0	•	0.0	0.0	0.1	0.1	0.1	0.1	0.2	•	•	•
Other Expenses 19	44.3	31.1	47.9	40.5	40.1	51.5	33.4	31.4	41.0	36.3	•	•	•
Officers' Compensation 20	0.1	•	•	•	•	0.3	0.3	0.1	0.1	0.1	•	•	•
Operating Margin 21	4.8	1.2	26.1	30.0	26.0	25.0	20.1	13.9	11.1	11.1	•	•	•
Operating Margin Before Officers' Comp. 22	4.9	1.2	26.1	30.0	26.0	25.3	20.5	14.1	11.2	11.2	•	•	•

Selected Average Balance Sheet ($ in Thousands)

Net Receivables 23	21073	0	9	47	182	298	902	783	583	1006
Inventories 24	.	.	.	.	.	.	.	.	.	.
Net Property, Plant and Equipment 25	10616	0	0	0	2	35	73	286	561	957
Total Assets 26	2702388	0	192	766	2496	7083	16208	36703	68745	164688
Notes and Loans Payable 27	44802	0	0	0	0	0	36	107	205	1340
All Other Liabilities 28	2302682	0	151	440	1170	4500	9988	23836	44524	123504
Net Worth 29	354904	0	41	326	1326	2583	6185	12760	24016	39844

Selected Financial Ratios (Times to 1)

Current Ratio 30	1.6	.	0.4	5.4	7.3	6.6	3.1	2.1	2.1	3.0
Quick Ratio 31	1.1	.	0.3	3.8	5.6	4.1	2.3	1.6	1.6	2.2
Net Sales to Working Capital 32	3.4	.	.	0.9	0.6	0.7	1.3	2.5	1.8	1.6
Coverage Ratio 33	4.4	555.8	822.0	869.4	242.6	25.6	158.3	120.5	31.3	51.6
Total Asset Turnover 34	0.2	.	0.7	0.5	0.3	0.3	0.4	0.5	0.4	0.4
Inventory Turnover 35	.	.	.	.	.	.	.	.	.	.
Receivables Turnover 36	.	.	.	.	.	.	.	.	.	.
Total Liabilities to Net Worth 37	6.6	.	3.6	1.4	0.9	1.7	1.6	1.9	1.9	3.1
Current Assets to Working Capital 38	2.7	.	.	1.2	1.2	1.2	1.5	1.9	1.9	1.5
Current Liabilities to Working Capital 39	1.7	.	.	0.2	0.2	0.2	0.5	0.9	0.9	0.5
Working Capital to Net Sales 40	0.3	.	.	1.2	1.6	1.4	0.8	0.4	0.6	0.6
Inventory to Working Capital 41	0.0	.	.	.	.	.	.	.	.	0.0
Total Receipts to Cash Flow 42	2.1	3.1	1.4	1.4	1.5	1.3	2.0	2.3	2.0	2.2
Cost of Goods to Cash Flow 43	0.9	2.1	0.3	0.4	0.5	0.3	0.8	1.2	0.8	1.0
Cash Flow to Total Debt 44	0.1	.	0.7	0.6	0.5	0.4	0.3	0.3	0.3	0.3

Selected Financial Factors (in Percentages)

Debt Ratio 45	86.9	.	78.5	57.4	46.9	63.5	61.8	65.2	65.1	75.8
Return on Total Assets 46	1.2	.	18.6	15.8	8.7	8.0	8.2	6.7	4.6	4.7
Return on Equity Before Income Taxes 47	6.9	.	86.3	37.2	16.3	21.0	21.3	19.2	12.7	19.0
Return on Equity After Income Taxes 48	4.7	.	83.3	34.7	13.9	16.4	17.0	15.8	9.4	13.2
Profit Margin (Before Income Tax) 49	4.7	1.2	26.1	30.0	26.0	25.0	20.1	13.9	11.1	11.0
Profit Margin (After Income Tax) 50	3.2	0.9	25.2	28.1	22.1	19.5	16.0	11.5	8.2	7.7

Table I

Corporations with and without Net Income

LIFE INSURANCE, MUTUAL COMPANIES (FORM 1120L)

MONEY AMOUNTS AND SIZE OF ASSETS IN THOUSANDS OF DOLLARS

Item Description for Accounting Period 7/03 Through 6/04	Total	Zero Assets	Under 500	500 to 1,000	1,000 to 5,000	5,000 to 10,000	10,000 to 25,000	25,000 to 50,000	50,000 to 100,000	100,000 to 250,000	250,000 to 500,000	500,000 to 2,500,000	2,500,000 and over
Number of Enterprises 1	65	3	8	3	8	3	•	8	•	7	8	11	8

Revenues ($ in Thousands)

Item	Total	Zero Assets	Under 500	500 to 1,000	1,000 to 5,000	5,000 to 10,000	10,000 to 25,000	25,000 to 50,000	50,000 to 100,000	100,000 to 250,000	250,000 to 500,000	500,000 to 2,500,000	2,500,000 and over
Net Sales 2	87092594	92	1297	20	4328	3736	•	88273	•	346061	749225	2856202	83043361
Interest 3	17786925	8	72	4	961	458	•	16545	•	56740	165548	598594	17047994
Rents 4	899005	0	0	0	50	0	•	34	•	1737	5417	14505	877262
Royalties 5	2602	0	0	0	0	0	•	0	•	341	195	56	2010
Other Portfolio Income 6	1796195	0	0	0	321	13	•	1683	•	8241	18628	58340	1708970
Other Receipts 7	66507867	84	1225	16	2996	3265	•	70011	•	279002	559437	2184707	63407125
Total Receipts 8	87092594	92	1297	20	4328	3736	•	88273	•	346061	749225	2856202	83043361
Average Total Receipts 9	1339886	31	162	7	541	1245	•	11034	•	49437	93653	259655	10380420

Operating Costs/Operating Income (%)

Item	Total	Zero Assets	Under 500	500 to 1,000	1,000 to 5,000	5,000 to 10,000	10,000 to 25,000	25,000 to 50,000	50,000 to 100,000	100,000 to 250,000	250,000 to 500,000	500,000 to 2,500,000	2,500,000 and over
Cost of Operations 10	41.2	119.6	4.3	•	28.7	31.7	•	53.9	•	44.0	44.7	43.2	41.1
Salaries and Wages 11	0.9	•	•	•	•	•	•	•	•	•	0.2	0.0	0.9
Taxes Paid 12	0.8	1.1	0.2	5.0	3.9	0.6	•	2.1	•	2.5	2.1	1.4	0.7
Interest Paid 13	0.8	•	10.0	•	•	•	•	0.0	•	0.2	0.1	0.5	0.8
Depreciation 14	0.4	•	•	•	0.3	•	•	1.7	•	0.4	0.3	0.5	0.4
Amortization and Depletion 15	1.5	•	0.5	•	3.3	1.4	•	2.5	•	1.7	3.8	2.2	1.4
Pensions and Other Deferred Comp. 16	0.3	•	•	•	0.2	•	•	0.6	•	2.9	1.2	1.0	0.3
Employee Benefits 17	0.1	•	•	•	1.1	•	•	0.9	•	0.2	0.6	0.2	0.1
Advertising 18	0.2	•	•	•	0.2	•	•	0.1	•	0.1	0.1	0.3	0.2
Other Expenses 19	50.4	16.3	94.0	330.0	76.9	56.2	•	31.6	•	47.1	41.5	47.2	50.6
Officers' Compensation 20	0.2	•	•	•	•	•	•	•	•	•	0.3	•	0.2
Operating Margin 21	3.2	•	•	•	10.1	•	•	6.5	•	0.9	5.1	3.5	3.1
Operating Margin Before Officers' Comp. 22	3.4	•	•	•	10.1	•	•	6.5	•	0.9	5.5	3.5	3.4

Selected Average Balance Sheet ($ in Thousands)

Net Receivables 23	30174	•	0	0	0	0	36	•	1324	1329	1619	240416
Inventories 24	•	•	•	•	•	•	•	•	•	•	•	•
Net Property, Plant and Equipment 25	23704	•	0	218	•	51	169	•	1339	2808	5599	180698
Total Assets 26	6917857	•	0	788	2711	5089	41678	•	186761	383167	1168870	54006994
Notes and Loans Payable 27	54722	•	0	0	0	0	0	•	0	0	47	444550
All Other Liabilities 28	6212695	•	0	218	169	1552	34216	•	179925	340817	1040103	48512068
Net Worth 29	650440	•	0	0	619	1160	7461	•	6836	42350	128720	5050375

Selected Financial Ratios (Times to 1)

Current Ratio 30	1.0	•	2.4	107.9	•	1.0	•	•	0.8	4.2	1.3	1.0
Quick Ratio 31	0.8	•	•	0.7	89.8	0.8	•	•	0.6	3.5	1.1	0.8
Net Sales to Working Capital 32	68.3	•	26.5	0.5	2.7	0.3	59.4	•	•	0.8	3.5	•
Coverage Ratio 33	4.8	•	0.1	•	•	2868.0	6.1	•	48.9	8.0	4.7	•
Total Asset Turnover 34	0.2	•	0.7	0.0	0.2	0.2	0.3	•	0.3	0.2	0.2	0.2
Inventory Turnover 35	•	•	•	•	•	•	•	•	•	•	•	•
Receivables Turnover 36	•	•	•	•	•	•	•	•	•	•	•	•
Total Liabilities to Net Worth 37	9.6	•	0.3	6.0	•	4.6	•	•	26.3	8.0	8.1	9.7
Current Assets to Working Capital 38	69.9	•	•	1.7	3.7	1.0	46.6	•	•	1.3	4.0	•
Current Liabilities to Working Capital 39	68.9	•	•	0.7	2.7	•	45.6	•	•	0.3	3.0	•
Working Capital to Net Sales 40	0.0	•	•	1.9	0.4	0.0	0.0	•	•	1.2	0.3	•
Inventory to Working Capital 41	•	•	•	•	•	•	•	•	•	•	•	•
Total Receipts to Cash Flow 42	1.9	•	1.2	1.8	1.1	2.8	•	•	2.2	2.4	2.0	1.9
Cost of Goods to Cash Flow 43	0.8	•	0.1	0.5	0.5	1.5	•	•	1.0	1.1	0.9	0.8
Cash Flow to Total Debt 44	0.1	•	0.6	0.2	0.0	0.1	•	•	0.1	0.1	0.1	0.1

Selected Financial Factors (in Percentages)

Debt Ratio 45	90.6	•	100.0	21.5	57.2	85.7	82.1	•	96.3	88.9	89.0	90.6
Return on Total Assets 46	0.8	•	0.7	•	•	2.5	1.7	•	0.3	1.3	0.9	0.7
Return on Equity Before Income Taxes 47	6.4	•	•	•	17.3	9.6	6.5	•	11.2	7.1	6.3	•
Return on Equity After Income Taxes 48	4.3	•	•	•	16.1	8.0	5.3	•	8.2	4.4	4.2	•
Profit Margin (Before Income Tax) 49	3.1	•	•	•	10.1	6.5	0.9	•	5.1	3.5	3.1	•
Profit Margin (After Income Tax) 50	2.1	•	•	•	9.4	5.4	0.7	•	3.7	2.2	2.1	•

Table II
Corporations with Net Income

LIFE INSURANCE, MUTUAL COMPANIES (FORM 1120L)

MONEY AMOUNTS AND SIZE OF ASSETS IN THOUSANDS OF DOLLARS

Item Description for Accounting Period 7/03 Through 6/04		Total	Zero Assets	Under 500	500 to 1,000	1,000 to 5,000	5,000 to 10,000	10,000 to 25,000	25,000 to 50,000	50,000 to 100,000	100,000 to 250,000	250,000 to 500,000	500,000 to 2,500,000	2,500,000 and over
Number of Enterprises	1	40	·	3	·	·	3	·	8	·	3	·	·	·
Revenues ($ in Thousands)														
Net Sales	2	85115414	·	41	·	·	3736	·	88273	·	66697	·	·	·
Interest	3	17433755	·	0	·	·	458	·	16545	·	22115	·	·	·
Rents	4	870275	·	0	·	·	0	·	34	·	965	·	·	·
Royalties	5	2261	·	0	·	·	0	·	0	·	0	·	·	·
Other Portfolio Income	6	1773226	·	0	·	·	13	·	1683	·	306	·	·	·
Other Receipts	7	65035897	·	41	·	·	3265	·	70011	·	43311	·	·	·
Total Receipts	8	85115414	·	41	·	·	3736	·	88273	·	66697	·	·	·
Average Total Receipts	9	2127885	·	14	·	·	1245	·	11034	·	22232	·	·	·
Operating Costs/Operating Income (%)														
Cost of Operations	10	40.6	·	19.5	·	·	31.7	·	53.9	·	32.2	·	·	·
Salaries and Wages	11	0.9	·	·	·	·	·	·	·	·	·	·	·	·
Taxes Paid	12	0.7	·	2.4	·	·	0.6	·	2.1	·	2.0	·	·	·
Interest Paid	13	0.8	·	·	·	·	·	·	0.0	·	0.3	·	·	·
Depreciation	14	0.4	·	·	·	·	·	·	1.7	·	0.7	·	·	·
Amortization and Depletion	15	1.5	·	·	·	·	1.4	·	2.5	·	2.9	·	·	·
Pensions and Other Deferred Comp.	16	0.3	·	·	·	·	·	·	0.6	·	0.5	·	·	·
Employee Benefits	17	0.1	·	·	·	·	·	·	0.9	·	0.1	·	·	·
Advertising	18	0.2	·	·	·	·	·	·	0.1	·	0.1	·	·	·
Other Expenses	19	50.9	·	51.2	·	·	56.2	·	31.6	·	51.3	·	·	·
Officers' Compensation	20	0.2	·	·	·	·	·	·	·	·	·	·	·	·
Operating Margin	21	3.3	·	24.4	·	·	10.1	·	6.5	·	9.9	·	·	·
Operating Margin Before Officers' Comp.	22	3.5	·	24.4	·	·	10.1	·	6.5	·	9.9	·	·	·

Selected Average Balance Sheet ($ in Thousands)

Item					
Net Receivables 23	48721		0	36	34
Inventories 24					
Net Property, Plant and Equipment 25	30837	0	0	169	382
Total Assets 26	10898065	317	5089	41678	131644
Notes and Loans Payable 27	88923	0	0	0	0
All Other Liabilities 28	9772789	317	4361	34216	140183
Net Worth 29	1036353	0	727	7461	-8539

Selected Financial Ratios (Times to 1)

Item					
Current Ratio 30	1.0		1.0	107.9	1.2
Quick Ratio 31	0.8		0.8	89.8	1.0
Net Sales to Working Capital 32			0.3	59.4	4.1
Coverage Ratio 33	5.0			2868.0	32.5
Total Asset Turnover 34	0.2	0.0	0.2	0.3	0.2
Inventory Turnover 35					
Receivables Turnover 36					
Total Liabilities to Net Worth 37	9.5			6.0	4.6
Current Assets to Working Capital 38			1.0	46.6	7.5
Current Liabilities to Working Capital 39			0.0	45.6	6.5
Working Capital to Net Sales 40			2.9	0.0	0.2
Inventory to Working Capital 41					
Total Receipts to Cash Flow 42	1.9	2.2	1.5	2.8	1.7
Cost of Goods to Cash Flow 43	0.8	0.4	0.5	1.5	0.5
Cash Flow to Total Debt 44	0.1	0.0	0.2	0.1	0.1

Selected Financial Factors (in Percentages)

Item					
Debt Ratio 45	90.5	100.0	85.7	82.1	106.5
Return on Total Assets 46	0.8	1.1		2.5	1.7
Return on Equity Before Income Taxes 47	6.6			17.3	9.6
Return on Equity After Income Taxes 48	4.5			16.1	8.0
Profit Margin (Before Income Tax) 49	3.2	24.4	10.1	6.5	9.9
Profit Margin (After Income Tax) 50	2.2	22.0	9.4	5.4	9.3

Table I

Corporations with and without Net Income

MUTUAL PROPERTY AND CASUALTY COMPANIES (FORM 1120-PC)

MONEY AMOUNTS AND SIZE OF ASSETS IN THOUSANDS OF DOLLARS

Item Description for Accounting Period 7/03 Through 6/04	Total	Zero Assets	Under 500	500 to 1,000	1,000 to 5,000	5,000 to 10,000	10,000 to 25,000	25,000 to 50,000	50,000 to 100,000	100,000 to 250,000	250,000 to 500,000	500,000 to 2,500,000	2,500,000 and over
Number of Enterprises **1**	1495	•	117	•	551	149	190	94	68	85	37	62	23
Revenues ($ in Thousands)													
Net Sales **2**	207382733	•	2835	•	504046	521300	2057351	1534356	2334542	8585953	7878135	37907036	145991231
Interest **3**	12650509	•	779	•	31555	25949	89353	89894	135717	376272	305689	1623900	9969011
Rents **4**	512587	•	0	•	1159	874	3012	2418	2468	17889	14394	75463	394831
Royalties **5**	291	•	0	•	0	0	24	0	0	0	0	266	1
Other Portfolio Income **6**	5494343	•	76	•	6048	7716	51226	32485	66572	195674	125308	752853	4255909
Other Receipts **7**	188725003	•	1980	•	465284	486761	1913736	1409559	2129785	7996118	7432744	35454554	131371479
Total Receipts **8**	207382733	•	2835	•	504046	521300	2057351	1534356	2334542	8585953	7878135	37907036	145991231
Average Total Receipts **9**	138718	•	24	•	915	3499	10828	16323	34332	101011	212923	611404	6347445
Operating Costs/Operating Income (%)													
Cost of Operations **10**	61.0	•	95.5	•	50.6	59.3	65.1	57.9	58.8	61.5	64.9	63.7	60.1
Salaries and Wages **11**	11.3	•	•	•	13.4	9.6	14.0	12.2	16.3	16.0	15.2	14.9	9.7
Taxes Paid **12**	2.8	•	1.7	•	5.9	2.9	2.6	3.2	2.7	2.8	2.1	2.5	3.0
Interest Paid **13**	0.5	•	0.0	•	0.3	0.0	0.2	0.3	0.1	0.2	0.1	0.3	0.6
Depreciation **14**	1.1	•	•	•	0.6	0.3	0.4	0.6	0.9	1.0	0.9	0.9	1.1
Amortization and Depletion **15**	0.2	•	•	•	0.0	0.0	0.1	0.1	0.1	0.1	0.1	0.1	0.3
Pensions and Other Deferred Comp. **16**	0.4	•	•	•	0.1	0.1	0.2	0.4	0.2	0.2	0.9	0.7	0.3
Employee Benefits **17**	1.8	•	•	•	0.9	0.5	0.5	1.3	1.5	1.6	1.6	1.7	1.9
Advertising **18**	0.3	•	•	•	0.3	0.1	0.2	0.2	0.2	0.3	0.1	0.3	0.3
Other Expenses **19**	13.9	•	73.4	•	22.9	20.1	23.2	20.9	16.3	10.6	9.5	10.2	15.0
Officers' Compensation **20**	0.2	•	•	•	1.9	0.6	0.6	1.3	0.8	0.6	0.5	0.4	0.1
Operating Margin **21**	6.5	•	•	•	3.1	6.3	•	1.7	2.2	5.2	4.0	4.4	7.5
Operating Margin Before Officers' Comp. **22**	6.7	•	•	•	5.0	6.9	•	3.0	3.0	5.7	4.5	4.8	7.6

Selected Average Balance Sheet ($ in Thousands)

	1	2	3	4	5	6	7	8	9	10	11
Net Receivables 23	24611	•	101	374	1377	3057	7090	17422	33337	100644	1160588
Inventories 24	•	•	•	•	•	•	•	•	•	•	•
Net Property, Plant and Equipment 25	5335	•	58	56	232	367	906	3958	6804	17647	265652
Total Assets 26	313818	•	2346	7337	16310	35915	70564	166716	331706	1095385	15697178
Notes and Loans Payable 27	8021	•	10	29	87	141	156	1256	1993	5989	494897
All Other Liabilities 28	198757	•	1045	4270	13782	24139	48110	105704	214960	694836	9898988
Net Worth 29	107040	•	1290	3039	2442	11635	22299	59755	114753	394560	5303293

Selected Financial Ratios (Times to 1)

	1	2	3	4	5	6	7	8	9	10	11
Current Ratio 30	0.9	•	1.7	1.2	0.9	0.9	0.9	0.9	1.0	0.9	0.9
Quick Ratio 31	0.8	•	1.5	1.1	0.8	0.7	0.8	0.8	0.9	0.7	0.8
Net Sales to Working Capital 32	•	•	1.3	3.7	•	•	•	•	•	•	•
Coverage Ratio 33	12.0	•	10.5	301.1	•	4.7	14.4	27.6	32.5	14.8	11.4
Total Asset Turnover 34	0.4	•	0.4	0.5	0.7	0.5	0.5	0.6	0.6	0.6	0.4
Inventory Turnover 35	•	•	•	•	•	•	•	•	•	•	•
Receivables Turnover 36	•	•	•	•	•	•	•	•	•	•	•
Total Liabilities to Net Worth 37	1.9	3.2	0.8	1.4	5.7	2.1	2.2	1.8	1.9	1.8	2.0
Current Assets to Working Capital 38	•	•	2.3	5.4	•	•	•	•	•	•	•
Current Liabilities to Working Capital 39	•	•	1.3	4.4	•	•	•	•	•	•	•
Working Capital to Net Sales 40	•	•	0.8	0.3	•	•	•	•	•	•	•
Inventory to Working Capital 41	•	•	•	•	•	•	•	•	•	•	•
Total Receipts to Cash Flow 42	5.4	37.8	3.9	3.9	4.9	6.1	7.3	8.3	7.3	7.8	4.9
Cost of Goods to Cash Flow 43	3.3	36.1	2.0	2.3	2.8	3.6	4.5	5.4	4.8	5.0	2.9
Cash Flow to Total Debt 44	0.1	0.0	0.2	0.2	0.1	0.1	0.1	0.1	0.1	0.1	0.1

Selected Financial Factors (in Percentages)

	1	2	3	4	5	6	7	8	9	10	11
Debt Ratio 45	65.9	76.3	45.0	58.6	85.0	67.6	68.4	64.2	65.4	64.0	66.2
Return on Total Assets 46	2.7	•	1.1	2.7	•	0.6	0.8	2.9	2.2	2.2	2.9
Return on Equity Before Income Taxes 47	7.1	•	1.8	6.4	•	1.5	2.2	7.8	6.1	5.7	7.7
Return on Equity After Income Taxes 48	4.8	•	0.7	4.2	•	•	•	2.5	4.8	3.4	5.5
Profit Margin (Before Income Tax) 49	5.5	•	2.5	5.6	•	1.1	1.4	4.6	3.3	3.7	6.5
Profit Margin (After Income Tax) 50	3.7	•	1.0	3.7	•	•	•	2.8	1.4	2.2	4.6

Table II
Corporations with Net Income

MUTUAL PROPERTY AND CASUALTY COMPANIES (FORM 1120-PC)

MONEY AMOUNTS AND SIZE OF ASSETS IN THOUSANDS OF DOLLARS

Item Description for Accounting Period 7/03 Through 6/04	Total	Zero Assets	Under 500	500 to 1,000	1,000 to 5,000	5,000 to 10,000	10,000 to 25,000	25,000 to 50,000	50,000 to 100,000	100,000 to 250,000	250,000 to 500,000	500,000 to 2,500,000	2,500,000 and over
Number of Enterprises **1**	1006	•	21	117	363	107	126	57	45	69	•	46	•
Revenues ($ in Thousands)													
Net Sales **2**	181845522	•	163	62288	323933	340420	1312662	1031243	1582906	7105599	•	29376453	•
Interest **3**	11568934	•	118	1942	22170	18628	45250	51962	86985	309063	•	1110208	•
Rents **4**	492322	•	0	80	956	648	2662	2035	2399	13970	•	65333	•
Royalties **5**	267	•	0	0	0	0	0	0	0	0	•	266	•
Other Portfolio Income **6**	4996307	•	0	140	4075	5204	18678	16992	48527	152365	•	495811	•
Other Receipts **7**	16487692	•	45	60126	296732	315940	1246072	960254	1444995	6630201	•	27704835	•
Total Receipts **8**	181845522	•	163	62288	323933	340420	1312662	1031243	1582906	7105599	•	29376453	•
Average Total Receipts **9**	180761	•	8	532	892	3181	10418	18092	35176	102980	•	638619	•
Operating Costs/Operating Income (%)													
Cost of Operations **10**	59.4	•	•	52.8	44.6	51.4	53.1	53.9	50.3	58.7	•	61.8	•
Salaries and Wages **11**	11.5	•	•	12.3	12.4	11.3	17.4	12.9	19.9	16.7	•	15.6	•
Taxes Paid **12**	2.9	•	•	4.4	2.6	1.8	2.2	3.2	2.9	2.7	•	2.5	•
Interest Paid **13**	0.5	•	•	0.3	0.0	0.0	0.2	0.3	0.1	0.2	•	0.2	•
Depreciation **14**	1.1	•	•	0.3	0.6	0.4	0.5	0.5	1.0	0.8	•	1.0	•
Amortization and Depletion **15**	0.3	•	•	•	0.0	0.0	0.1	0.1	0.1	0.1	•	0.1	•
Pensions and Other Deferred Comp. **16**	0.4	•	•	•	0.1	0.0	0.2	0.3	0.2	0.3	•	0.7	•
Employee Benefits **17**	1.9	•	•	0.6	1.0	0.6	0.6	1.2	1.7	1.4	•	1.8	•
Advertising **18**	0.3	•	•	0.3	0.4	0.1	0.3	0.2	0.3	0.3	•	0.3	•
Other Expenses **19**	13.5	•	38.0	14.7	23.2	18.7	15.8	16.9	13.2	11.0	•	9.1	•
Officers' Compensation **20**	0.2	•	•	1.9	2.0	0.9	0.7	1.3	0.8	0.6	•	0.3	•
Operating Margin **21**	8.1	•	62.6	12.5	12.9	14.6	8.9	9.3	9.4	7.3	•	6.6	•
Operating Margin Before Officers' Comp. **22**	8.3	•	62.6	14.3	14.9	15.5	9.7	10.5	10.2	7.9	•	6.9	•

Selected Average Balance Sheet ($ in Thousands)

Item	•	•	•	•	•	•	•	•	•	•
Net Receivables 23	32145	0	28	73	294	1494	3673	6750	18601	85141
Inventories 24	•	•	•	•	•	•	•	•	•	•
Net Property, Plant and Equipment 25	7401	0	20	62	66	292	432	1263	4035	21322
Total Assets 26	425311	135	723	2356	7304	16580	36635	70556	166877	1059509
Notes and Loans Payable 27	11426	0	41	5	40	85	17	233	1509	6751
All Other Liabilities 28	265097	76	522	905	3726	10674	23356	42987	107374	635352
Net Worth 29	148788	59	160	1446	3538	5821	13262	27337	57994	417406

Selected Financial Ratios (Times to 1)

Item	•	•	•	•	•	•	•	•	•	•
Current Ratio 30	0.9	22.2	1.0	1.8	1.4	1.1	1.0	1.0	0.9	0.9
Quick Ratio 31	0.8	22.2	0.9	1.7	1.2	1.0	0.9	0.8	0.8	0.7
Net Sales to Working Capital 32	•	0.1	•	1.4	2.4	9.2	59.2	•	•	•
Coverage Ratio 33	14.5	•	46.4	797.8	488.0	52.5	25.8	139.7	•	31.0
Total Asset Turnover 34	0.4	0.1	0.7	0.4	0.6	0.5	0.6	0.5	0.6	0.6
Inventory Turnover 35	•	•	•	•	•	•	•	•	•	•
Receivables Turnover 36	•	•	•	•	•	•	•	•	•	•
Total Liabilities to Net Worth 37	1.9	1.3	3.5	0.6	1.1	1.8	1.8	1.6	1.9	1.5
Current Assets to Working Capital 38	1.0	•	•	2.2	3.7	9.4	72.1	•	•	•
Current Liabilities to Working Capital 39	0.0	•	•	1.2	2.7	8.4	71.1	•	•	•
Working Capital to Net Sales 40	16.7	•	•	0.7	0.4	0.1	0.0	•	•	•
Inventory to Working Capital 41	•	•	•	•	•	0.0	•	•	•	•
Total Receipts to Cash Flow 42	5.1	1.0	3.7	2.8	3.1	4.2	4.0	4.9	6.1	7.2
Cost of Goods to Cash Flow 43	3.0	•	2.0	1.3	1.6	2.2	2.2	2.5	3.6	4.4
Cash Flow to Total Debt 44	0.1	0.1	0.3	0.3	0.3	0.2	0.2	0.2	0.2	0.1

Selected Financial Factors (in Percentages)

Item	•	•	•	•	•	•	•	•	•	•
Debt Ratio 45	65.0	56.5	77.9	38.6	51.6	64.9	63.8	61.3	65.2	60.6
Return on Total Assets 46	3.2	3.6	9.4	4.7	6.1	5.3	4.4	4.2	4.2	3.7
Return on Equity Before Income Taxes 47	8.6	8.2	41.5	7.6	12.5	14.8	11.6	10.8	11.9	9.1
Return on Equity After Income Taxes 48	6.3	7.3	39.9	6.2	9.8	11.4	8.6	7.6	8.0	6.3
Profit Margin (Before Income Tax) 49	7.1	62.0	12.5	12.3	13.9	8.3	8.5	8.4	6.7	6.0
Profit Margin (After Income Tax) 50	5.2	55.2	12.0	10.9	10.0	6.4	5.9	6.3	4.5	4.1

Table I
Corporations with and without Net Income

STOCK PROPERTY AND CASUALTY COMPANIES (FORM 1120-PC)

MONEY AMOUNTS AND SIZE OF ASSETS IN THOUSANDS OF DOLLARS

Item Description for Accounting Period 7/03 Through 6/04	Total	Zero Assets	Under 500	500 to 1,000	1,000 to 5,000	5,000 to 10,000	10,000 to 25,000	25,000 to 50,000	50,000 to 100,000	100,000 to 250,000	250,000 to 500,000	500,000 to 2,500,000	2,500,000 and over
Number of Enterprises 1	3032	•	866	•	653	238	236	148	97	119	39	98	70
Revenues ($ in Thousands)													
Net Sales 2	553825304	•	82319	•	575190	909202	3277381	4701715	7043348	14483693	6831132	85111088	428921280
Interest 3	34558985	•	2190	•	28724	38881	70610	97436	136380	419895	288701	2599117	30746479
Rents 4	1017073	•	0	•	866	160	2323	3037	6382	9718	13136	79759	901185
Royalties 5	583699	•	0	•	10128	0	0	563	0	1929	0	69137	501942
Other Portfolio Income 6	14620995	•	535	•	4740	8855	20555	32538	47003	165454	169550	1164531	12987530
Other Receipts 7	503044552	•	79594	•	530732	861306	3183893	4568141	6853583	13886697	6359745	81198544	383784144
Total Receipts 8	553825304	•	82319	•	575190	909202	3277381	4701715	7043348	14483693	6831132	85111088	428921280
Average Total Receipts 9	182660	•	95	•	881	3820	13887	31768	72612	121712	175157	868480	6127447
Operating Costs/Operating Income (%)													
Cost of Operations 10	54.7	•	63.0	•	49.7	55.5	59.5	66.4	69.9	63.9	56.7	66.8	51.6
Salaries and Wages 11	12.9	•	9.7	•	30.9	19.3	14.1	12.2	12.6	12.1	15.5	13.3	12.8
Taxes Paid 12	2.1	•	1.1	•	0.4	2.6	2.2	2.1	2.0	2.3	2.7	1.8	2.2
Interest Paid 13	2.5	•	0.3	•	0.1	0.2	0.2	0.3	0.1	0.3	0.3	0.6	3.1
Depreciation 14	1.1	•	0.0	•	0.0	0.3	0.4	0.6	0.5	0.6	0.8	0.8	1.3
Amortization and Depletion 15	0.3	•	0.3	•	0.1	0.4	0.1	0.1	0.1	0.1	0.3	0.2	0.3
Pensions and Other Deferred Comp. 16	0.5	•	0.0	•	•	0.0	0.1	0.1	0.1	0.2	0.2	0.4	0.6
Employee Benefits 17	0.8	•	•	•	0.9	0.6	0.5	0.9	0.5	1.0	1.3	0.8	0.8
Advertising 18	0.4	•	•	•	0.0	0.5	0.2	0.3	0.3	0.5	0.2	0.4	0.4
Other Expenses 19	18.4	•	31.6	•	25.5	13.4	19.2	13.5	10.3	14.7	15.0	11.6	20.1
Officers' Compensation 20	0.5	•	1.0	•	0.1	1.4	0.9	0.8	0.5	0.5	0.6	0.5	0.4
Operating Margin 21	5.7	•	•	•	•	5.7	2.6	2.7	3.2	3.9	6.2	2.7	6.5
Operating Margin Before Officers' Comp. 22	6.2	•	•	•	•	7.1	3.5	3.5	3.7	4.4	6.8	3.2	7.0

Selected Average Balance Sheet ($ in Thousands)

Net Receivables 23	42457	•	2	•	42	402	1622	3113	7035	•	14549	29318	109194	1621253
Inventories 24	•	•	•	•	•	•	•	•	•	•	•	•	•	•
Net Property, Plant and Equipment 25	14446	•	0	•	9	56	166	514	934	•	2813	7103	22196	582681
Total Assets 26	580687	•	177	•	2391	7358	16395	35576	70396	•	154995	340764	1164694	22786632
Notes and Loans Payable 27	53102	•	12	•	51	84	539	1405	1584	•	7178	8177	68622	2179162
All Other Liabilities 28	329627	•	209	•	2604	4829	12062	28302	50604	•	104130	217007	728882	12739832
Net Worth 29	197959	•	-43	•	-264	2446	3794	5869	18208	•	43687	115581	367190	7867638

Selected Financial Ratios (Times to 1)

Current Ratio 30	0.8	•	0.7	•	1.0	1.0	0.9	0.9	1.0	•	0.9	0.9	0.9	0.8
Quick Ratio 31	0.7	•	0.6	•	0.5	0.8	0.8	0.7	0.9	•	0.8	0.7	0.8	0.7
Net Sales to Working Capital 32	•	•	•	•	18.8	•	•	•	37.8	•	•	•	•	3.0
Coverage Ratio 33	3.1	•	27.8	•	12.4	8.5	27.7	15.2	19.8	•	5.0	•	•	3.0
Total Asset Turnover 34	0.3	•	0.5	•	0.5	0.9	0.8	1.0	0.5	•	0.8	0.5	0.7	0.3
Inventory Turnover 35	•	•	•	•	•	•	•	•	•	•	•	•	•	•
Receivables Turnover 36	•	•	•	•	•	•	•	•	•	•	•	•	•	•
Total Liabilities to Net Worth 37	1.9	•	2.0	•	3.3	5.1	2.9	2.5	1.9	•	2.2	•	•	1.9
Current Assets to Working Capital 38	•	•	•	•	24.1	•	•	•	24.3	•	•	•	•	•
Current Liabilities to Working Capital 39	•	•	•	•	23.1	•	•	•	23.3	•	•	•	•	•
Working Capital to Net Sales 40	•	•	•	•	0.1	•	•	•	0.0	•	•	•	•	•
Inventory to Working Capital 41	•	•	•	•	0.1	•	•	•	0.0	•	•	•	•	•
Total Receipts to Cash Flow 42	4.5	•	5.9	•	5.8	4.8	6.6	8.0	5.8	•	5.4	•	7.8	4.1
Cost of Goods to Cash Flow 43	2.5	•	2.6	•	3.2	2.9	4.4	5.6	3.7	•	3.1	•	5.2	2.1
Cash Flow to Total Debt 44	0.1	•	0.1	•	0.1	0.2	0.2	0.2	0.2	•	0.1	•	0.1	0.1

Selected Financial Factors (in Percentages)

Debt Ratio 45	65.9	•	124.3	•	111.1	66.8	76.9	83.5	74.1	•	71.8	66.1	68.5	65.5
Return on Total Assets 46	2.4	•	3.0	•	3.0	2.4	2.3	2.4	3.1	•	3.0	3.1	2.1	2.4
Return on Equity Before Income Taxes 47	4.8	•	15.9	•	26.4	8.7	8.9	12.9	11.5	•	10.0	8.6	5.3	4.7
Return on Equity After Income Taxes 48	2.9	•	18.7	•	33.9	3.3	3.6	3.5	5.4	•	5.1	5.7	1.7	2.9
Profit Margin (Before Income Tax) 49	5.2	•	•	•	5.5	2.4	2.9	3.6	5.5	•	5.7	5.7	2.2	6.0
Profit Margin (After Income Tax) 50	3.1	•	2.1	•	1.4	1.0	0.6	•	•	•	1.8	3.7	0.7	3.8

Table II
Corporations with Net Income

STOCK PROPERTY AND CASUALTY COMPANIES (FORM 1120-PC)

MONEY AMOUNTS AND SIZE OF ASSETS IN THOUSANDS OF DOLLARS

Item Description for Accounting Period 7/03 Through 6/04		Total	Zero Assets	Under 500	500 to 1,000	1,000 to 5,000	5,000 to 10,000	10,000 to 25,000	25,000 to 50,000	50,000 to 100,000	100,000 to 250,000	250,000 to 500,000	500,000 to 2,500,000	2,500,000 and over
Number of Enterprises	1	2301	69	599	363	510	169	156	117	70	92	28	75	53
Revenues ($ in Thousands)														
Net Sales	2	487262678	1301334	21626	58752	479282	719623	2634609	3816185	5043662	12987050	6104096	69805738	384290720
Interest	3	28435366	19910	1664	3668	24219	28360	46968	77011	102465	332125	197849	1877073	25724054
Rents	4	871456	0	0	0	455	160	1480	2826	1300	7867	12145	43820	801403
Royalties	5	49443	0	0	0	0	0	0	5	0	1929	0	37037	10472
Other Portfolio Income	6	12901245	17786	256	343	4463	7046	14481	26972	37389	141072	135619	950002	11565817
Other Receipts	7	445005168	1263638	19706	54741	450145	684057	2571680	3709371	4902508	12504057	5758483	66897806	346188974
Total Receipts	8	487262678	1301334	21626	58752	479282	719623	2634609	3816185	5043662	12987050	6104096	69805738	384290720
Average Total Receipts	9	211761	18860	36	162	940	4258	16889	32617	72052	141164	218003	930743	7250768
Operating Costs/Operating Income (%)														
Cost of Operations	10	53.7	75.7	32.7	52.6	15.0	48.5	55.8	64.8	66.4	63.3	56.0	63.9	51.1
Salaries and Wages	11	12.7	6.1	9.7	5.1	34.1	20.1	13.0	11.8	13.5	11.3	15.5	13.2	12.6
Taxes Paid	12	2.0	0.9	0.8	0.2	0.4	2.8	2.2	2.0	2.3	2.2	2.6	1.8	2.0
Interest Paid	13	2.5	0.0	0.1	0.0	0.0	0.1	0.2	0.2	0.1	0.2	0.2	0.5	3.1
Depreciation	14	1.2	0.6	•	•	0.0	0.2	0.4	0.5	0.5	0.6	0.8	0.8	1.3
Amortization and Depletion	15	0.3	0.2	0.8	0.0	0.0	0.3	0.1	0.1	0.1	0.1	0.3	0.2	0.3
Pensions and Other Deferred Comp.	16	0.5	0.0	0.0	•	•	0.0	0.1	0.1	0.1	0.2	0.2	0.4	0.6
Employee Benefits	17	0.8	0.7	•	•	1.0	0.4	0.5	0.9	0.6	0.9	1.3	0.8	0.8
Advertising	18	0.4	0.3	•	•	0.0	0.6	0.2	0.4	0.4	0.5	0.2	0.5	0.4
Other Expenses	19	17.8	8.5	12.3	1.7	24.8	10.4	18.8	10.2	7.9	13.7	13.4	12.2	19.2
Officers' Compensation	20	0.4	0.8	•	•	1.7	•	0.8	0.8	0.6	0.4	0.5	0.5	0.4
Operating Margin	21	7.8	6.2	43.5	40.3	24.7	14.8	8.0	8.2	7.6	6.6	8.8	5.4	8.2
Operating Margin Before Officers' Comp.	22	8.2	7.0	43.5	40.3	24.7	16.5	8.8	9.0	8.2	7.0	9.3	5.9	8.6

Selected Average Balance Sheet ($ in Thousands)

Net Receivables 23	49024	0	2	20	25	328	1731	3465	7929	15864	34123	112787	1898551
Inventories 24	•	•	•	•	•	•	•	•	•	•	•	•	•
Net Property, Plant and Equipment 25	17686	0	0	0	75	156	531	708	3280	8832	20332	•	725860
Total Assets 26	643509	•	704	2354	7427	16824	35454	70543	161105	343895	1178524	•	25534773
Notes and Loans Payable 27	59104	0	25	8	105	409	1189	1394	6896	10053	63689	•	2452357
All Other Liabilities 28	360083	158	608	2131	4205	10609	23479	45002	99153	210160	684798	•	1418476
Net Worth 29	224322	23	72	215	3117	5806	10787	24147	55057	123682	430038	•	8883941

Selected Financial Ratios (Times to 1)

Current Ratio 30	0.8	•	1.0	0.8	1.3	1.2	1.1	1.1	1.0	1.0	0.9	1.0	0.8
Quick Ratio 31	0.7	•	0.9	0.6	1.0	1.0	0.9	1.0	0.9	0.9	0.8	0.8	0.6
Net Sales to Working Capital 32	•	•	•	4.2	9.1	20.3	12.2	66.2	27.9	34.5	11.7	•	3.5
Coverage Ratio 33	3.9	302.4	•	4724.8	7853.1	496.5	145.5	44.6	73.5	•	•	•	•
Total Asset Turnover 34	0.3	0.2	•	0.2	0.6	1.0	0.9	1.0	0.9	0.6	0.8	0.8	0.3
Inventory Turnover 35	•	•	•	•	•	•	•	•	•	•	•	•	•
Receivables Turnover 36	•	•	•	•	•	•	•	•	•	•	•	•	•
Total Liabilities to Net Worth 37	1.9	6.8	8.8	9.9	1.4	1.9	2.3	1.9	1.9	1.8	1.7	•	1.9
Current Assets to Working Capital 38	•	•	•	4.8	6.2	14.5	8.3	43.5	•	•	•	•	•
Current Liabilities to Working Capital 39	•	•	•	3.8	5.2	13.5	7.3	42.5	•	•	•	•	•
Working Capital to Net Sales 40	•	•	•	0.2	0.1	0.0	0.0	0.0	0.0	0.0	0.0	0.0	0.0
Inventory to Working Capital 41	•	7.5	•	•	0.0	0.0	0.0	0.0	0.0	0.0	0.0	0.0	0.0
Total Receipts to Cash Flow 42	4.2	7.5	2.4	2.0	4.2	5.7	3.9	6.8	5.3	5.1	6.2	•	3.9
Cost of Goods to Cash Flow 43	2.3	5.7	1.3	0.3	2.2	3.7	2.2	4.5	3.3	2.8	4.0	•	2.0
Cash Flow to Total Debt 44	0.1	•	0.1	0.2	0.2	0.4	0.2	0.2	0.3	0.2	0.2	•	0.1

Selected Financial Factors (in Percentages)

Debt Ratio 45	65.1	•	87.1	89.8	90.9	58.0	65.5	69.6	65.8	65.8	64.0	63.5	65.2
Return on Total Assets 46	3.2	•	8.7	9.2	9.8	8.4	8.1	7.4	7.5	5.7	5.4	4.3	3.0
Return on Equity Before Income Taxes 47	6.9	•	67.5	90.8	107.3	20.0	22.7	23.8	21.5	16.1	14.5	10.7	6.3
Return on Equity After Income Taxes 48	4.6	•	60.0	87.1	95.6	14.1	17.4	17.3	15.2	11.1	10.7	6.8	4.2
Profit Margin (Before Income Tax) 49	7.3	5.5	43.5	40.2	24.6	14.6	7.8	7.9	7.2	6.3	8.2	4.9	7.7
Profit Margin (After Income Tax) 50	4.9	4.4	38.7	38.6	21.9	10.3	5.7	6.0	5.1	4.3	6.1	3.1	5.2

Table I

Corporations with and without Net Income

INSURANCE AGENCIES AND BROKERAGES

MONEY AMOUNTS AND SIZE OF ASSETS IN THOUSANDS OF DOLLARS

Item Description for Accounting Period 7/03 Through 6/04	Total	Zero Assets	Under 500	500 to 1,000	1,000 to 5,000	5,000 to 10,000	10,000 to 25,000	25,000 to 50,000	50,000 to 100,000	100,000 to 250,000	250,000 to 500,000	500,000 to 2,500,000	2,500,000 and over
Number of Enterprises 1	81674	11649	60882	3947	4315	456	272	77	31	22	8	9	5
Revenues ($ in Thousands)													
Net Sales 2	90885446	1900144	19930325	4346205	12736104	3400374	4531359	2572025	2317928	2536577	935109	4174499	31504796
Interest 3	544950	1658	20338	10588	22307	15881	15937	12111	13869	16343	8279	73776	333863
Rents 4	73237	417	18452	3001	17490	13166	5594	1568	216	572	4712	143	7906
Royalties 5	8277	0	0	8079	0	46	15	109	0	0	0	0	28
Other Portfolio Income 6	597082	31219	55598	4402	12234	12081	6890	5243	11537	5394	38784	97694	316005
Other Receipts 7	89661900	1866850	19835937	4320135	12684073	3359200	4502923	2552994	2292306	2514268	883334	4002886	30846994
Total Receipts 8	90885446	1900144	19930325	4346205	12736104	3400374	4531359	2572025	2317928	2536577	935109	4174499	31504796
Average Total Receipts 9	1113	163	327	1101	2952	7457	16659	33403	74772	115299	116889	463833	6300959
Operating Costs/Operating Income (%)													
Cost of Operations 10	26.1	6.9	13.1	9.0	10.9	17.0	17.0	17.3	23.0	5.7	6.2	1.1	52.7
Salaries and Wages 11	22.7	23.8	23.5	23.5	25.0	26.5	30.2	25.9	28.1	34.1	34.6	29.6	16.8
Taxes Paid 12	2.5	2.2	2.8	3.0	2.9	3.0	2.9	2.3	2.0	2.4	3.2	3.5	1.8
Interest Paid 13	1.2	0.3	0.6	1.6	0.8	0.8	1.0	0.7	0.6	0.5	3.5	2.0	1.9
Depreciation 14	1.4	1.0	1.3	1.1	2.2	2.0	1.6	1.6	1.2	1.5	1.8	1.9	0.9
Amortization and Depletion 15	0.9	0.0	0.4	1.0	0.9	1.0	0.7	0.6	2.1	0.7	1.5	3.2	0.8
Pensions and Other Deferred Comp. 16	1.3	1.4	1.5	1.8	1.7	1.0	1.1	1.0	0.9	0.5	0.8	0.9	1.2
Employee Benefits 17	1.6	2.3	1.2	2.1	1.7	1.2	2.2	1.8	1.1	2.0	2.7	2.9	1.6
Advertising 18	0.8	2.5	1.5	1.3	0.9	0.6	1.1	0.6	0.5	0.3	0.7	0.4	0.2
Other Expenses 19	23.2	39.3	26.5	27.5	24.0	25.1	28.6	34.9	29.0	43.4	28.5	33.4	13.7
Officers' Compensation 20	9.5	5.9	14.3	19.5	16.2	12.2	8.4	7.5	4.3	3.9	8.2	6.1	4.0
Operating Margin 21	8.8	14.5	13.1	8.7	12.8	9.6	5.4	5.6	7.3	5.2	8.3	15.1	4.4
Operating Margin Before Officers' Comp. 22	18.3	20.4	27.5	28.2	29.0	21.7	13.7	13.2	11.5	9.1	16.5	21.2	8.4

Selected Average Balance Sheet ($ in Thousands)

Net Receivables 23	271	0	5	122	376	1343	4328	10716	17647	37688	83058	217815	2630753
Inventories 24	•	•	•	•	•	•	•	•	•	•	•	•	•
Net Property, Plant and Equipment 25	59	0	14	86	196	549	849	2535	3712	5576	7922	51167	269465
Total Assets 26	1241	0	83	713	2000	6520	15118	35480	64442	140385	312308	1108584	11492480
Notes and Loans Payable 27	199	0	34	197	493	1275	2532	4769	6683	11710	67288	199639	1370034
All Other Liabilities 28	576	0	24	300	1034	3788	9867	22908	38513	105090	188016	431227	4966838
Net Worth 29	466	0	25	216	472	1457	2718	7803	19245	23585	57005	477717	5155608

Selected Financial Ratios (Times to 1)

Current Ratio 30	1.0	•	1.2	1.3	1.2	1.1	1.1	1.1	1.0	0.8	0.9	1.0	1.0
Quick Ratio 31	0.9	•	1.1	1.2	1.1	1.0	0.9	1.0	1.0	0.7	0.8	0.8	0.8
Net Sales to Working Capital 32	77.3	•	51.5	12.0	14.0	9.9	27.8	18.4	17.9	•	•	•	•
Coverage Ratio 33	8.5	51.7	24.2	6.5	16.2	13.4	6.3	8.8	13.0	11.6	2.6	9.0	4.0
Total Asset Turnover 34	0.9	•	4.0	1.5	1.5	1.1	1.1	0.9	1.2	0.8	0.4	0.4	0.5
Inventory Turnover 35	•	•	•	•	•	•	•	•	•	•	•	•	•
Receivables Turnover 36	•	•	•	•	•	•	•	•	•	•	•	•	•
Total Liabilities to Net Worth 37	1.7	2.3	2.3	3.2	4.6	3.5	4.6	3.5	2.3	5.0	4.5	1.3	1.2
Current Assets to Working Capital 38	37.2	5.7	4.2	6.3	17.8	6.0	13.4	10.1	•	•	•	•	•
Current Liabilities to Working Capital 39	36.2	4.7	3.2	5.3	16.8	5.0	12.4	9.1	•	•	•	•	•
Working Capital to Net Sales 40	0.0	0.0	0.1	0.1	0.1	0.0	0.0	0.0	0.1	0.1	•	•	•
Inventory to Working Capital 41	0.2	•	0.1	0.0	0.0	0.0	0.0	0.0	0.0	•	•	•	•
Total Receipts to Cash Flow 42	3.6	2.2	2.9	3.3	3.1	3.4	3.3	2.7	2.9	2.2	3.2	2.3	6.6
Cost of Goods to Cash Flow 43	0.9	0.2	0.4	0.3	0.3	0.6	0.6	0.5	0.7	0.1	0.2	0.0	3.5
Cash Flow to Total Debt 44	0.4	2.0	0.7	0.6	0.4	0.4	0.5	0.5	0.6	0.4	0.1	0.3	0.2

Selected Financial Factors (in Percentages)

Debt Ratio 45	62.4	•	69.7	69.8	76.4	77.7	82.0	78.0	70.1	83.2	81.7	56.9	55.1
Return on Total Assets 46	9.4	•	54.2	15.9	20.1	11.8	7.0	5.9	9.1	4.6	3.3	7.3	4.2
Return on Equity Before Income Taxes 47	22.1	•	171.1	44.4	79.8	48.8	32.7	23.9	28.1	24.8	11.0	15.2	7.0
Return on Equity After Income Taxes 48	18.8	•	168.7	42.2	76.7	42.6	27.5	18.0	22.2	17.8	7.3	10.0	4.3
Profit Margin (Before Income Tax) 49	9.2	14.5	13.1	8.7	12.8	9.5	5.3	5.6	7.2	5.1	5.4	15.6	5.7
Profit Margin (After Income Tax) 50	7.9	13.7	13.0	8.3	12.3	8.3	4.5	4.2	5.7	3.6	3.6	10.3	3.5

Table II

Corporations with Net Income

INSURANCE AGENCIES AND BROKERAGES

MONEY AMOUNTS AND SIZE OF ASSETS IN THOUSANDS OF DOLLARS

Item Description for Accounting Period 7/03 Through 6/04	Total	Zero Assets	Under 500	500 to 1,000	1,000 to 5,000	5,000 to 10,000	10,000 to 25,000	25,000 to 50,000	50,000 to 100,000	100,000 to 250,000	250,000 to 500,000	500,000 to 2,500,000	2,500,000 and over
Number of Enterprises 1	64591	7719	48623	3697	3825	375	226	63	27	19	•	•	•
Revenues ($ in Thousands)													
Net Sales 2	64646486	1090378	16976594	4222041	11237802	2565968	3869746	2128877	2086744	2354107	•	•	•
Interest 3	433280	1626	18260	9419	19783	14897	11942	10874	13513	11741	•	•	•
Rents 4	46448	417	7332	3001	5185	10906	4683	1376	216	572	•	•	•
Royalties 5	8277	0	0	8079	0	46	15	109	0	0	•	•	•
Other Portfolio Income 6	553141	31140	54705	2665	9775	10872	5954	5064	11278	3504	•	•	•
Other Receipts 7	63605340	1057195	16896297	4198877	11203059	2529247	3847152	2111454	2061737	2338290	•	•	•
Total Receipts 8	64646486	1090378	16976594	4222041	11237802	2565968	3869746	2128877	2086744	2354107	•	•	•
Average Total Receipts 9	1001	141	349	1142	2938	6843	17123	33792	77287	123900	•	•	•
Operating Costs/Operating Income (%)													
Cost of Operations 10	10.3	1.6	9.6	9.2	11.5	5.7	18.3	20.8	22.3	4.1	•	•	•
Salaries and Wages 11	27.2	21.4	24.8	23.5	24.9	28.3	30.2	25.1	28.7	32.1	•	•	•
Taxes Paid 12	3.0	2.1	2.8	3.0	2.9	3.3	2.8	2.3	2.0	2.3	•	•	•
Interest Paid 13	1.4	0.2	0.6	1.6	0.7	1.0	0.6	0.6	0.5	0.4	•	•	•
Depreciation 14	1.4	0.4	1.2	1.1	1.1	1.7	1.6	1.4	1.1	1.4	•	•	•
Amortization and Depletion 15	0.9	0.0	0.4	1.0	0.6	0.3	0.4	0.6	1.8	0.7	•	•	•
Pensions and Other Deferred Comp. 16	1.7	0.2	1.6	1.8	1.8	1.2	1.2	1.0	1.0	0.3	•	•	•
Employee Benefits 17	1.9	2.2	1.2	2.1	1.8	1.3	2.0	1.7	1.1	1.9	•	•	•
Advertising 18	1.0	2.4	1.7	1.3	0.9	0.5	1.0	0.5	0.5	0.3	•	•	•
Other Expenses 19	25.9	32.5	25.0	26.8	22.3	26.8	23.1	29.8	27.3	44.5	•	•	•
Officers' Compensation 20	11.6	6.6	14.6	19.5	16.0	15.2	9.0	8.0	4.3	3.8	•	•	•
Operating Margin 21	13.7	30.3	16.5	9.2	15.5	14.6	9.8	8.1	9.3	8.3	•	•	•
Operating Margin Before Officers' Comp. 22	25.3	36.9	31.1	28.7	31.5	29.8	18.8	16.1	13.7	12.1	•	•	•

Selected Average Balance Sheet ($ in Thousands)

Net Receivables 23	258	0	5	122	348	1043	4250	10785	19456	41112
Inventories 24	•	•	•	•	•	•	•	•	•	•
Net Property, Plant and Equipment 25	61	0	15	91	117	486	882	2423	3880	5649
Total Assets 26	1336	0	90	717	1923	6579	15027	35260	64127	142241
Notes and Loans Payable 27	215	0	35	190	353	892	2303	4637	6471	10089
All Other Liabilities 28	571	0	23	303	1039	3958	9665	23519	39193	100871
Net Worth 29	550	0	32	224	531	1729	3059	7104	18462	31281

Selected Financial Ratios (Times to 1)

Current Ratio 30	1.1	•	1.3	1.3	1.2	1.2	1.1	1.1	1.2	0.9
Quick Ratio 31	0.9	•	1.1	1.1	1.1	1.0	0.9	1.0	1.1	0.8
Net Sales to Working Capital 32	19.3	•	43.4	12.7	13.5	8.1	33.5	18.9	10.7	•
Coverage Ratio 33	11.1	122.7	28.5	6.9	22.0	15.6	16.3	14.2	18.4	20.5
Total Asset Turnover 34	0.7	•	3.9	1.6	1.5	1.0	1.1	1.0	1.2	0.9
Inventory Turnover 35	•	•	•	•	•	•	•	•	•	•
Receivables Turnover 36	•	•	•	•	•	•	•	•	•	•
Total Liabilities to Net Worth 37	1.4	•	1.8	2.2	2.6	2.8	3.9	4.0	2.5	3.5
Current Assets to Working Capital 38	10.6	•	4.8	4.4	6.0	5.5	20.9	13.9	6.5	•
Current Liabilities to Working Capital 39	9.6	•	3.8	3.4	5.0	4.5	19.9	12.9	5.5	•
Working Capital to Net Sales 40	0.1	•	0.0	0.1	0.1	0.1	0.0	0.1	0.1	•
Inventory to Working Capital 41	0.0	•	•	•	•	•	0.0	0.0	0.0	•
Total Receipts to Cash Flow 42	2.8	1.9	2.7	3.3	2.9	2.7	3.4	2.9	2.9	2.0
Cost of Goods to Cash Flow 43	0.3	0.0	0.3	0.3	0.3	0.2	0.6	0.6	0.6	0.1
Cash Flow to Total Debt 44	0.4	•	2.2	0.7	0.7	0.5	0.4	0.4	0.6	0.6

Selected Financial Factors (in Percentages)

Debt Ratio 45	58.8	•	64.7	68.8	72.4	73.7	79.6	79.9	71.2	78.0
Return on Total Assets 46	11.8	•	66.1	17.2	24.7	16.2	11.8	8.3	11.9	7.5
Return on Equity Before Income Taxes 47	26.1	•	180.7	47.0	85.5	57.8	54.5	38.1	39.0	32.4
Return on Equity After Income Taxes 48	22.6	•	178.3	44.7	82.4	51.4	49.0	30.2	32.0	26.2
Profit Margin (Before Income Tax) 49	14.3	30.3	16.5	9.2	15.5	14.6	9.7	8.0	9.3	8.2
Profit Margin (After Income Tax) 50	12.4	28.9	16.3	8.8	14.9	13.0	8.7	6.3	7.6	6.6

Table I

Corporations with and without Net Income

OTHER INSURANCE RELATED ACTIVITIES

MONEY AMOUNTS AND SIZE OF ASSETS IN THOUSANDS OF DOLLARS

Item Description for Accounting Period 7/03 Through 6/04	Total	Zero Assets	Under 500	500 to 1,000	1,000 to 5,000	5,000 to 10,000	10,000 to 25,000	25,000 to 50,000	50,000 to 100,000	100,000 to 250,000	250,000 to 500,000	500,000 to 2,500,000	2,500,000 and over
Number of Enterprises **1**	14553	2047	10934	505	697	148	102	48	28	25	9	6	3
Revenues ($ in Thousands)													
Net Sales **2**	42954343	496359	3373771	1384232	2585360	2411881	2295019	2228032	2587510	4800960	2451793	2886621	15452806
Interest **3**	796513	1297	5132	2222	9721	6437	13779	35885	24111	48195	41816	42024	565893
Rents **4**	98881	0	5488	4539	7333	575	1188	86	7641	9632	0	1737	60663
Royalties **5**	37363	0	0	0	0	0	0	0	0	9508	27853	2	0
Other Portfolio Income **6**	283886	6085	2350	135	1736	9221	3260	22739	2557	6056	47350	80241	102158
Other Receipts **7**	41737700	488977	3360801	1377336	2566570	2395648	2276792	2169322	2553201	4727569	2334774	2762617	1474092
Total Receipts **8**	42954343	496359	3373771	1384232	2585360	2411881	2295019	2228032	2587510	4800960	2451793	2886621	15452806
Average Total Receipts **9**	2952	242	309	2741	3709	16296	22500	46417	92411	192038	272421	481104	5150935
Operating Costs/Operating Income (%)													
Cost of Operations **10**	36.9	0.9	8.2	19.9	7.6	4.0	19.5	32.4	5.6	41.0	47.2	18.8	64.9
Salaries and Wages **11**	16.3	12.1	34.6	22.9	28.4	14.6	25.5	15.5	12.1	17.7	19.8	22.7	7.4
Taxes Paid **12**	1.9	1.1	4.1	2.8	3.8	1.5	2.3	1.3	1.6	1.9	2.3	1.7	1.2
Interest Paid **13**	1.2	1.2	0.4	1.9	1.1	0.3	0.8	0.5	0.5	1.3	0.5	3.2	1.4
Depreciation **14**	1.2	0.4	1.1	1.3	2.3	0.8	1.4	1.1	1.0	1.6	1.2	2.4	0.8
Amortization and Depletion **15**	0.6	0.3	0.0	0.4	0.4	0.2	0.3	0.5	1.1	0.7	1.1	2.7	0.3
Pensions and Other Deferred Comp. **16**	0.5	0.1	2.4	0.3	0.6	0.2	0.7	0.3	0.4	0.1	0.5	0.5	0.4
Employee Benefits **17**	2.3	0.3	2.5	0.9	2.8	0.8	2.3	12.3	1.7	2.1	1.7	3.4	1.3
Advertising **18**	0.4	0.5	0.8	0.7	0.8	0.4	0.7	0.4	0.2	0.3	0.2	0.7	0.2
Other Expenses **19**	29.1	79.8	30.5	48.4	37.1	71.7	40.1	29.5	74.3	28.3	15.7	24.1	11.6
Officers' Compensation **20**	2.3	2.3	10.7	4.1	9.0	1.1	3.4	2.7	0.7	1.8	0.8	0.8	0.1
Operating Margin **21**	7.2	1.0	4.7	•	6.1	4.5	2.9	3.5	0.8	3.2	8.9	19.0	10.4
Operating Margin Before Officers' Comp. **22**	9.5	3.3	15.4	0.5	15.1	5.5	6.3	6.3	1.5	5.1	9.7	19.8	10.6

Selected Average Balance Sheet ($ in Thousands)

Net Receivables 23	314	0	6	171	751	1106	3659	6975	13580	16995	116601	104968	181716
Inventories 24	•	•	•	•	•	•	•	•	•	•	•	•	•
Net Property, Plant and Equipment 25	134	0	12	334	303	405	1007	1597	4177	10869	9767	48782	142257
Total Assets 26	3305	0	58	873	2681	7570	15507	35497	72918	162375	373553	1079183	8268366
Notes and Loans Payable 27	587	0	31	1397	460	2786	2611	5149	8844	23256	48856	242402	1176039
All Other Liabilities 28	1331	0	13	249	1908	3779	9448	22807	38601	113606	214970	199699	2702964
Net Worth 29	1386	0	14	-774	313	1006	3448	7541	25473	25513	109727	637082	4389364

Selected Financial Ratios (Times to 1)

Current Ratio 30	1.2	•	2.1	1.9	1.7	1.1	1.3	1.1	1.4	0.8	1.3	1.1	1.2
Quick Ratio 31	0.9	•	1.9	1.4	1.3	1.0	0.9	0.9	1.1	0.6	0.8	0.9	0.9
Net Sales to Working Capital 32	18.8	•	15.3	12.0	4.4	40.5	9.6	20.4	9.5	•	4.9	23.1	32.6
Coverage Ratio 33	7.1	1.8	11.7	•	6.6	15.4	4.3	8.8	2.6	3.8	18.3	6.9	8.6
Total Asset Turnover 34	0.9	•	5.3	3.1	1.4	2.2	1.5	1.3	1.3	1.2	0.7	0.4	0.6
Inventory Turnover 35	•	•	•	•	•	•	•	•	•	•	•	•	•
Receivables Turnover 36	•	•	•	•	•	•	•	•	•	•	•	•	•
Total Liabilities to Net Worth 37	1.4	•	3.0	•	7.6	6.5	3.5	3.7	1.9	5.4	2.4	0.7	0.9
Current Assets to Working Capital 38	6.2	•	1.9	2.2	2.4	10.2	4.7	9.4	3.9	•	4.2	8.5	7.5
Current Liabilities to Working Capital 39	5.2	•	0.9	1.2	1.4	9.2	3.7	8.4	2.9	•	3.2	7.5	6.5
Working Capital to Net Sales 40	0.1	•	0.1	0.1	0.2	0.0	0.1	0.0	0.1	0.0	0.2	0.0	0.0
Inventory to Working Capital 41	0.0	•	•	0.0	0.0	0.0	0.0	0.0	0.0	0.0	0.0	0.0	0.0
Total Receipts to Cash Flow 42	3.0	1.4	3.5	2.4	2.7	1.4	2.5	3.3	1.4	3.4	4.9	2.5	4.8
Cost of Goods to Cash Flow 43	1.1	0.0	0.3	0.5	0.2	0.1	0.5	1.1	0.1	1.4	2.3	0.5	3.1
Cash Flow to Total Debt 44	0.5	•	2.0	0.7	0.6	1.8	0.7	0.5	1.4	0.4	0.2	0.4	0.3

Selected Financial Factors (in Percentages)

Debt Ratio 45	58.0	•	75.2	188.7	88.3	86.7	77.8	78.8	65.1	84.3	70.6	41.0	46.9
Return on Total Assets 46	7.4	•	27.4	•	9.9	10.2	5.3	5.4	1.7	5.8	6.8	9.8	7.3
Return on Equity Before Income Taxes 47	15.3	•	101.3	12.8	71.6	72.0	18.4	22.7	3.0	27.0	22.0	14.2	12.2
Return on Equity After Income Taxes 48	10.4	•	98.0	13.3	69.8	65.5	13.0	19.6	•	16.1	13.2	10.0	7.8
Profit Margin (Before Income Tax) 49	7.2	1.0	4.7	•	6.0	4.4	2.8	3.7	0.8	3.6	8.9	18.8	10.4
Profit Margin (After Income Tax) 50	4.9	0.1	4.6	•	5.9	4.0	2.0	3.2	•	2.1	5.3	13.2	6.7

Table II
Corporations with Net Income

OTHER INSURANCE RELATED ACTIVITIES

MONEY AMOUNTS AND SIZE OF ASSETS IN THOUSANDS OF DOLLARS

Item Description for Accounting Period 7/03 Through 6/04	Total	Zero Assets	Under 500	500 to 1,000	1,000 to 5,000	5,000 to 10,000	10,000 to 25,000	25,000 to 50,000	50,000 to 100,000	100,000 to 250,000	250,000 to 500,000	500,000 to 2,500,000	2,500,000 and over
Number of Enterprises **1**	8238	•	6560	252	428	109	63	26	18	13	•	•	•
Revenues ($ in Thousands)													
Net Sales **2**	35751699	•	2490998	821778	2235928	958862	1386778	1226601	2313447	3541025	•	•	•
Interest **3**	644985	•	3492	2204	8661	2859	10981	28791	9605	11093	•	•	•
Rents **4**	94029	•	5488	4539	3866	361	296	8	7641	9430	•	•	•
Royalties **5**	37363	•	0	0	0	0	0	0	0	9508	•	•	•
Other Portfolio Income **6**	262716	•	2340	135	1521	9190	2472	4417	2003	4844	•	•	•
Other Receipts **7**	3712606	•	2479678	814900	2221880	946452	1373029	1193385	2294198	3506150	•	•	•
Total Receipts **8**	35751699	•	2490998	821778	2235928	958862	1386778	1226601	2313447	3541025	•	•	•
Average Total Receipts **9**	4340	•	380	3261	5224	8797	22012	47177	128525	272387	•	•	•
Operating Costs/Operating Income (%)													
Cost of Operations **10**	39.7	•	2.7	•	8.7	10.0	25.4	25.9	6.3	35.9	•	•	•
Salaries and Wages **11**	16.1	•	41.3	21.9	27.1	30.0	23.9	18.4	8.5	17.0	•	•	•
Taxes Paid **12**	1.8	•	3.4	2.4	3.5	3.6	2.4	1.3	1.3	1.8	•	•	•
Interest Paid **13**	0.8	•	0.4	0.0	0.6	0.4	0.7	0.8	0.4	0.7	•	•	•
Depreciation **14**	1.2	•	1.2	0.9	2.1	1.2	1.2	1.3	0.6	1.5	•	•	•
Amortization and Depletion **15**	0.6	•	0.0	0.0	0.2	0.2	0.3	0.7	0.6	0.5	•	•	•
Pensions and Other Deferred Comp. **16**	0.4	•	0.8	0.5	0.5	0.3	0.6	0.4	0.3	0.1	•	•	•
Employee Benefits **17**	2.4	•	2.3	0.1	2.6	1.2	2.3	21.5	1.0	2.0	•	•	•
Advertising **18**	0.4	•	1.1	0.4	0.6	0.8	0.4	0.6	0.2	0.4	•	•	•
Other Expenses **19**	24.0	•	24.6	66.7	35.1	36.1	28.9	16.8	74.5	31.6	•	•	•
Officers' Compensation **20**	2.1	•	12.2	4.7	7.4	2.5	4.9	1.1	0.5	1.7	•	•	•
Operating Margin **21**	10.6	•	9.9	2.5	11.5	13.7	9.1	11.3	5.6	6.9	•	•	•
Operating Margin Before Officers' Comp. **22**	12.7	•	22.1	7.2	18.9	16.2	13.9	12.4	6.2	8.6	•	•	•

Selected Average Balance Sheet ($ in Thousands)

Net Receivables 23	443	·	8	290	835	725	3378	7340	15745	25454
Inventories 24	·	·	·	·	·	·	·	·	·	·
Net Property, Plant and Equipment 25	180	·	13	133	391	285	800	1435	3794	15836
Total Assets 26	4282	·	75	889	3109	7627	15433	36095	75049	162651
Notes and Loans Payable 27	681	·	17	5	568	3159	2686	6364	12125	26731
All Other Liabilities 28	1726	·	14	338	2002	2994	7242	17353	33607	68635
Net Worth 29	1874	·	45	546	539	1474	5505	12377	29317	67285

Selected Financial Ratios (Times to 1)

Current Ratio 30	1.4	·	3.1	2.4	2.9	1.2	1.7	1.3	1.5	1.2
Quick Ratio 31	1.1	·	2.8	1.6	2.3	1.1	1.3	1.0	1.2	1.0
Net Sales to Working Capital 32	12.3	·	10.8	7.5	3.3	18.7	5.0	9.6	8.1	22.0
Coverage Ratio 33	13.6	·	27.4	141.2	18.7	33.0	14.5	15.8	13.7	12.0
Total Asset Turnover 34	1.0	·	5.1	3.7	1.7	1.2	1.4	1.3	1.7	1.7
Inventory Turnover 35	·	·	·	·	·	·	·	·	·	·
Receivables Turnover 36	·	·	·	·	·	·	·	·	·	·
Total Liabilities to Net Worth 37	1.3	·	0.7	0.6	4.8	4.2	1.8	1.9	1.6	1.4
Current Assets to Working Capital 38	3.8	·	1.5	1.7	1.5	7.1	2.5	4.5	3.0	5.6
Current Liabilities to Working Capital 39	2.8	·	0.5	0.7	0.5	6.1	1.5	3.5	2.0	4.6
Working Capital to Net Sales 40	0.1	·	0.1	0.1	0.3	0.1	0.2	0.1	0.1	0.0
Inventory to Working Capital 41	0.0	·	·	·	0.0	·	0.0	0.0	0.0	0.5
Total Receipts to Cash Flow 42	3.1	·	3.5	1.5	2.4	2.2	2.8	3.8	1.3	2.8
Cost of Goods to Cash Flow 43	1.2	·	0.1	·	0.2	0.2	0.7	1.0	0.1	1.0
Cash Flow to Total Debt 44	0.6	·	3.6	6.4	0.8	0.6	0.8	0.5	2.2	1.0

Selected Financial Factors (in Percentages)

Debt Ratio 45	56.2	·	40.4	38.6	82.7	80.7	64.3	65.7	60.9	58.6
Return on Total Assets 46	11.6	·	52.0	9.2	20.3	16.3	13.8	16.2	10.4	13.5
Return on Equity Before Income Taxes 47	24.6	·	84.0	14.9	111.0	81.7	36.0	44.3	24.6	30.0
Return on Equity After Income Taxes 48	18.3	·	82.2	13.3	109.3	75.7	30.5	40.8	18.9	22.1
Profit Margin (Before Income Tax) 49	10.6	·	9.9	2.5	11.5	13.7	9.0	11.6	5.6	7.4
Profit Margin (After Income Tax) 50	7.9	·	9.7	2.2	11.3	12.7	7.6	10.7	4.3	5.5

Table I

Corporations with and without Net Income

OPEN-END INVESTMENT FUNDS (FORM 1120-RIC)

MONEY AMOUNTS AND SIZE OF ASSETS IN THOUSANDS OF DOLLARS

Item Description for Accounting Period 7/03 Through 6/04	Total	Zero Assets	Under 500	500 to 1,000	1,000 to 5,000	5,000 to 10,000	10,000 to 25,000	25,000 to 50,000	50,000 to 100,000	100,000 to 250,000	250,000 to 500,000	500,000 to 2,500,000	2,500,000 and over
Number of Enterprises 1	10979	678	60	60	438	379	860	1037	1357	2069	1437	1985	617

Revenues ($ in Thousands)

	Total	Zero Assets	Under 500	500 to 1,000	1,000 to 5,000	5,000 to 10,000	10,000 to 25,000	25,000 to 50,000	50,000 to 100,000	100,000 to 250,000	250,000 to 500,000	500,000 to 2,500,000	2,500,000 and over
Net Sales 2	187143695	879528	798	3244	35200	77051	383714	1041522	3040324	10078776	13663650	54555284	103384604
Interest 3	87299721	366219	532	1881	8376	29782	115757	331520	1019822	3573147	5442423	24239679	52170582
Rents 4	0	0	0	0	0	0	0	0	0	0	0	0	0
Royalties 5	0	0	0	0	0	0	0	0	0	0	0	0	0
Other Portfolio Income 6	35519695	172889	196	672	9319	20987	135266	362402	1163270	3623068	4546029	13947499	11538095
Other Receipts 7	64324279	340420	70	691	17505	26282	132691	347600	857232	2882561	3675198	16368106	39675927
Total Receipts 8	187143695	879528	798	3244	35200	77051	383714	1041522	3040324	10078776	13663650	54555284	103384604
Average Total Receipts 9	17046	1297	13	54	80	203	446	1004	2240	4871	9508	27484	167560

Operating Costs/Operating Income (%)

	Total	Zero Assets	Under 500	500 to 1,000	1,000 to 5,000	5,000 to 10,000	10,000 to 25,000	25,000 to 50,000	50,000 to 100,000	100,000 to 250,000	250,000 to 500,000	500,000 to 2,500,000	2,500,000 and over
Cost of Operations 10	•	•	•	•	•	•	•	•	•	•	•	•	•
Salaries and Wages 11	0.0	0.0	•	0.5	0.4	0.1	0.3	0.2	0.2	0.1	0.0	0.1	0.0
Taxes Paid 12	0.2	0.6	•	0.2	1.5	0.6	0.4	0.6	0.4	0.4	0.2	0.2	0.1
Interest Paid 13	0.2	0.2	•	•	6.3	0.0	0.6	0.7	0.5	0.4	0.3	0.3	0.1
Depreciation 14	0.0	•	•	•	•	•	0.0	0.0	0.0	0.0	0.0	0.0	0.0
Amortization and Depletion 15	0.0	0.1	•	0.4	0.7	0.3	0.1	0.1	0.0	0.0	0.1	0.0	0.0
Pensions and Other Deferred Comp. 16	•	•	•	•	•	•	•	•	•	•	•	•	•
Employee Benefits 17	•	•	•	•	•	•	•	•	•	•	•	•	•
Advertising 18	0.0	•	•	•	•	•	0.0	0.0	0.0	0.0	0.0	0.0	0.0
Other Expenses 19	26.4	50.3	21.2	22.9	45.7	36.8	37.7	31.8	26.0	26.2	26.4	26.0	26.4
Officers' Compensation 20	0.0	•	•	•	•	•	0.0	0.2	0.0	0.0	0.0	0.0	0.0
Operating Margin 21	73.1	48.8	78.8	76.1	45.4	62.1	60.8	66.6	72.8	72.9	73.0	73.4	73.4
Operating Margin Before Officers' Comp. 22	73.2	48.8	78.8	76.1	45.4	62.1	60.8	66.8	72.8	72.9	73.0	73.5	73.4

Selected Average Balance Sheet ($ in Thousands)

Net Receivables 23	10599	0	0	13	77	83	337	600	1039	2951	5414	16085	110467
Inventories 24	·	·	·	·	·	·	·	·	·	·	·	·	·
Net Property, Plant and Equipment 25	2	·	0	0	0	0	0	0	4	0	0	8	3
Total Assets 26	757781	0	252	674	2876	7155	17249	37202	73110	165702	357000	1075254	8383796
Notes and Loans Payable 27	612	0	0	0	0	0	59	94	265	352	617	1412	2903
All Other Liabilities 28	34079	8	4	8	82	130	554	1527	2876	8011	20127	68937	301070
Net Worth 29	723091	0	245	670	2746	7073	16637	35580	69970	157339	336256	1004905	8079824

Selected Financial Ratios (Times to 1)

Current Ratio 30	3.8	·	13.2	86.4	4.0	7.9	2.8	4.2	5.1	4.9	4.0	3.3	4.0
Quick Ratio 31	3.5	·	8.1	86.2	3.3	7.0	2.3	3.9	4.8	4.5	3.7	3.0	3.7
Net Sales to Working Capital 32	0.2	·	0.1	0.1	0.3	0.4	0.2	0.2	0.2	0.2	0.2	0.2	0.2
Coverage Ratio 33	299.6	282.0	·	·	8.2	37155.0	77.5	69.4	87.6	110.4	174.8	180.5	679.1
Total Asset Turnover 34	0.0	·	0.1	0.1	0.0	0.0	0.0	0.0	0.0	0.0	0.0	0.0	0.0
Inventory Turnover 35	·	·	·	·	·	·	·	·	·	·	·	·	·
Receivables Turnover 36	·	·	·	·	·	·	·	·	·	·	·	·	·
Total Liabilities to Net Worth 37	0.0	·	0.0	0.0	0.0	0.0	0.0	0.0	0.0	0.1	0.1	0.1	0.0
Current Assets to Working Capital 38	1.4	·	1.1	1.0	1.6	1.1	1.3	1.3	1.2	1.3	1.3	1.4	1.3
Current Liabilities to Working Capital 39	0.4	·	0.1	0.0	0.6	0.1	0.3	0.3	0.2	0.3	0.3	0.4	0.3
Working Capital to Net Sales 40	5.5	·	6.9	7.1	2.9	2.7	4.4	4.8	5.4	6.4	6.3	5.7	5.3
Inventory to Working Capital 41	·	1.2	·	·	·	·	·	·	·	·	·	·	·
Total Receipts to Cash Flow 42	1.1	1.2	1.3	1.3	1.5	1.2	1.3	1.2	1.1	1.1	1.1	1.1	1.0
Cost of Goods to Cash Flow 43	·	·	·	·	·	·	·	·	·	·	·	·	·
Cash Flow to Total Debt 44	0.5	·	1.3	9.5	0.4	2.1	0.6	0.5	0.6	0.5	0.4	0.4	0.5

Selected Financial Factors (in Percentages)

Debt Ratio 45	4.6	·	3.0	0.7	4.5	1.1	3.5	4.4	4.3	5.0	5.8	6.5	3.6
Return on Total Assets 46	1.3	·	4.2	6.1	1.4	1.4	1.2	1.3	1.4	1.4	1.2	1.4	1.3
Return on Equity Before Income Taxes 47	1.4	·	4.3	6.1	1.3	1.4	1.3	1.3	1.5	1.4	1.3	1.5	1.4
Return on Equity After Income Taxes 48	1.4	·	4.3	6.1	1.3	1.4	1.3	1.3	1.5	1.4	1.3	1.5	1.4
Profit Margin (Before Income Tax) 49	59.8	42.2	78.8	76.1	45.4	48.2	47.1	46.5	45.8	46.1	46.4	54.4	66.5
Profit Margin (After Income Tax) 50	59.7	42.2	78.8	76.0	45.4	48.2	47.1	46.5	45.7	46.1	46.4	54.1	66.5

Table II
Corporations with Net Income

OPEN-END INVESTMENT FUNDS (FORM 1120-RIC)

MONEY AMOUNTS AND SIZE OF ASSETS IN THOUSANDS OF DOLLARS

Item Description for Accounting Period 7/03 Through 6/04		Total	Zero Assets	Under 500	500 to 1,000	1,000 to 5,000	5,000 to 10,000	10,000 to 25,000	25,000 to 50,000	50,000 to 100,000	100,000 to 250,000	250,000 to 500,000	500,000 to 2,500,000	2,500,000 and over
Number of Enterprises	1	8091	425	53	53	325	258	559	707	969	1526	1096	1593	527
Revenues ($ in Thousands)														
Net Sales	2	173457945	707048	792	3243	29051	67754	327451	882093	2559484	8775209	12377371	50302575	97425872
Interest	3	86823363	358784	532	1879	7696	28976	110225	323180	994675	3521102	5375677	24085467	52015168
Rents	4	0	0	0	0	0	0	0	0	0	0	0	0	0
Royalties	5	0	0	0	0	0	0	0	0	0	0	0	0	0
Other Portfolio Income	6	27477164	138239	196	672	9255	15713	106336	258615	831248	2755065	3446751	11613512	8301564
Other Receipts	7	59157418	210025	64	692	12100	23065	110890	300298	733561	2499042	3554943	14603596	37109140
Total Receipts	8	173457945	707048	792	3243	29051	67754	327451	882093	2559484	8775209	12377371	50302575	97425872
Average Total Receipts	9	21438	1664	15	61	89	263	586	1248	2641	5750	11293	31577	184869
Operating Costs/Operating Income (%)														
Cost of Operations	10	•	•	•	•	•	•	•	•	•	•	•	•	•
Salaries and Wages	11	0.0	0.0	•	0.5	0.2	0.1	0.1	0.1	0.2	0.1	0.1	0.1	0.0
Taxes Paid	12	0.1	0.3	•	0.2	1.2	0.6	0.3	0.5	0.3	0.3	0.2	0.1	0.1
Interest Paid	13	0.2	0.2	•	•	0.0	0.1	0.1	0.3	0.3	0.5	0.3	0.3	0.1
Depreciation	14	0.0	•	•	•	•	•	•	0.0	0.0	0.0	0.0	0.0	0.0
Amortization and Depletion	15	0.0	0.1	•	0.4	0.7	0.2	0.1	0.1	0.1	0.0	0.0	0.0	0.0
Pensions and Other Deferred Comp.	16	•	•	•	•	•	•	•	•	•	•	•	•	•
Employee Benefits	17	•	•	•	•	•	•	•	•	•	•	•	•	•
Advertising	18	0.0	•	•	•	•	•	•	0.0	0.0	•	0.0	0.0	0.0
Other Expenses	19	22.5	29.2	20.6	22.8	31.4	25.4	26.3	22.9	20.4	20.5	21.1	21.2	23.5
Officers' Compensation	20	0.0	•	•	•	0.0	0.0	•	0.1	0.0	0.0	0.0	0.0	0.0
Operating Margin	21	77.1	70.2	79.4	76.1	66.4	73.7	73.0	76.0	78.7	78.7	78.3	78.3	76.2
Operating Margin Before Officers' Comp.	22	77.1	70.2	79.4	76.1	66.4	73.7	73.1	76.1	78.7	78.3	78.3	78.4	76.2

Line Item													
Net Receivables 23	12717	0	0	12	81	50	371	613	973	3055	5902	17744	117413
Inventories 24	•	•	•	•	•	•	•	•	•	•	•	•	•
Net Property, Plant and Equipment 25	1	0	0	0	0	0	5	0	0	0	0	1	3
Total Assets 26	875777	0	286	661	2921	7406	17179	37322	73022	167023	359445	1082842	8733320
Notes and Loans Payable 27	738	0	0	0	0	0	36	61	233	470	738	1580	3112
All Other Liabilities 28	38711	0	9	5	95	72	475	1411	2779	7735	20933	71370	305059
Net Worth 29	836329	0	277	656	2825	7334	16668	35851	70010	158819	337774	1009892	8425149

Line Item													
Current Ratio 30	3.7	•	13.2	70.5	4.0	6.4	3.7	4.0	4.7	5.0	3.7	3.3	3.9
Quick Ratio 31	3.5	•	8.1	70.4	3.6	5.2	3.2	3.6	4.3	4.7	3.4	3.1	3.7
Net Sales to Working Capital 32	0.2	•	0.1	0.2	0.3	0.7	0.3	0.3	0.3	0.2	0.2	0.2	0.2
Coverage Ratio 33	364.2	382.9	•	2757.9	481.8	•	200.4	189.8	124.0	206.1	239.3	•	695.8
Total Asset Turnover 34	0.0	0.1	•	0.1	0.0	0.0	0.0	0.0	0.0	0.0	0.0	0.0	0.0
Inventory Turnover 35	•	•	•	•	•	•	•	•	•	•	•	•	•
Receivables Turnover 36	•	•	•	•	•	•	•	•	•	•	•	•	•
Total Liabilities to Net Worth 37	0.0	•	0.0	0.0	0.0	0.0	0.0	0.0	0.1	0.1	0.1	0.1	0.0
Current Assets to Working Capital 38	1.4	1.1	1.0	1.3	1.4	1.2	1.3	1.3	1.2	1.2	1.4	1.4	1.3
Current Liabilities to Working Capital 39	0.4	0.1	0.0	0.3	0.4	0.2	0.3	0.3	0.2	0.2	0.4	0.4	0.3
Working Capital to Net Sales 40	4.9	6.9	5.4	3.2	3.0	1.5	3.4	4.0	5.5	5.0	5.2	•	4.8
Inventory to Working Capital 41	•	•	•	•	•	•	•	•	•	•	•	•	•
Total Receipts to Cash Flow 42	1.1	1.2	1.3	1.3	1.5	1.2	1.2	1.2	1.1	1.1	1.1	1.1	1.0
Cost of Goods to Cash Flow 43	•	•	•	•	•	•	•	•	•	•	•	•	•
Cash Flow to Total Debt 44	0.5	•	1.3	10.1	0.6	3.0	0.8	0.7	0.6	0.6	0.5	0.4	0.6

Line Item													
Debt Ratio 45	4.5	•	3.0	0.7	3.3	1.0	3.0	3.9	4.1	4.9	6.0	6.7	3.5
Return on Total Assets 46	1.7	•	4.2	7.1	2.0	2.3	2.2	2.1	2.2	2.0	1.8	1.8	1.5
Return on Equity Before Income Taxes 47	1.7	•	4.3	7.1	2.1	2.4	2.2	2.2	2.2	2.1	1.9	1.9	1.6
Return on Equity After Income Taxes 48	1.7	•	4.3	7.1	2.1	2.4	2.2	2.2	2.1	2.1	1.9	1.9	1.6
Profit Margin (Before Income Tax) 49	67.3	66.9	79.4	76.1	66.4	65.7	65.8	63.9	59.6	57.8	57.7	62.3	72.2
Profit Margin (After Income Tax) 50	67.2	66.9	79.4	76.0	66.4	65.7	65.8	63.9	59.5	57.8	57.7	62.0	72.2

Table I

Corporations with and without Net Income

REAL ESTATE INVESTMENT TRUSTS (FORM 1120-REIT)

MONEY AMOUNTS AND SIZE OF ASSETS IN THOUSANDS OF DOLLARS

Item Description for Accounting Period 7/03 Through 6/04	Total	Zero Assets	Under 500	500 to 1,000	1,000 to 5,000	5,000 to 10,000	10,000 to 25,000	25,000 to 50,000	50,000 to 100,000	100,000 to 250,000	250,000 to 500,000	500,000 to 2,500,000	2,500,000 and over
Number of Enterprises **1**	1059	113	53	•	37	30	74	85	100	146	115	213	92

Revenues ($ in Thousands)

Item Description for Accounting Period 7/03 Through 6/04	Total	Zero Assets	Under 500	500 to 1,000	1,000 to 5,000	5,000 to 10,000	10,000 to 25,000	25,000 to 50,000	50,000 to 100,000	100,000 to 250,000	250,000 to 500,000	500,000 to 2,500,000	2,500,000 and over
Net Sales **2**	68914016	3815709	23541	•	24977	40517	254281	594597	1128641	2631501	3967493	20090960	36341799
Interest **3**	24432083	774850	123	•	237	2676	25746	135223	388663	640365	1110950	6969932	14383318
Rents **4**	30118335	456899	14701	•	8532	31916	132833	340949	526782	1284210	2128342	9477601	15715569
Royalties **5**	0	0	0	•	0	0	0	0	0	0	0	0	0
Other Portfolio Income **6**	6490963	2288211	8875	•	2381	190	88307	92078	145824	374305	373859	808558	2308372
Other Receipts **7**	7872635	295749	-158	•	13827	5735	7395	26347	67372	332621	354342	2834869	3934540
Total Receipts **8**	68914016	3815709	23541	•	24977	40517	254281	594597	1128641	2631501	3967493	20090960	36341799
Average Total Receipts **9**	65075	33767	444	•	675	1351	3436	6995	11286	18024	34500	94324	395020

Operating Costs/Operating Income (%)

Item Description for Accounting Period 7/03 Through 6/04	Total	Zero Assets	Under 500	500 to 1,000	1,000 to 5,000	5,000 to 10,000	10,000 to 25,000	25,000 to 50,000	50,000 to 100,000	100,000 to 250,000	250,000 to 500,000	500,000 to 2,500,000	2,500,000 and over
Cost of Operations **10**	•	•	•	•	•	•	•	•	•	•	•	•	•
Salaries and Wages **11**	1.7	0.4	•	•	•	1.4	0.7	0.6	1.1	1.2	1.5	1.9	1.8
Taxes Paid **12**	2.8	0.1	0.7	•	0.2	2.0	2.8	1.9	3.6	2.5	3.6	3.4	2.6
Interest Paid **13**	9.7	1.2	0.2	•	2.0	22.6	4.5	9.9	25.2	10.4	8.7	11.4	9.2
Depreciation **14**	7.3	0.1	13.2	•	5.7	2.6	6.3	4.0	8.0	5.7	8.1	8.2	7.6
Amortization and Depletion **15**	0.7	0.0	0.2	•	0.4	0.4	2.5	1.4	1.4	0.6	0.7	0.9	0.7
Pensions and Other Deferred Comp. **16**	•	•	•	•	•	•	•	•	•	•	•	•	•
Employee Benefits **17**	•	•	•	•	•	•	•	•	•	•	•	•	•
Advertising **18**	0.2	0.0	0.2	•	0.1	0.3	0.1	0.1	0.2	0.2	0.2	0.4	0.2
Other Expenses **19**	17.3	29.1	51.1	•	101.6	44.0	26.2	38.4	26.5	30.2	21.6	15.4	14.9
Officers' Compensation **20**	0.4	•	0.8	•	•	0.2	0.1	0.2	0.2	0.3	0.3	0.5	0.4
Operating Margin **21**	60.0	69.1	33.6	•	•	26.8	56.5	43.5	33.7	48.9	55.3	57.9	62.6
Operating Margin Before Officers' Comp. **22**	60.4	69.1	34.3	•	•	26.8	56.7	43.6	34.0	49.2	55.7	58.4	63.1

Selected Average Balance Sheet ($ in Thousands)

Item											
Net Receivables 23	36831	0	162	96	352	2193	1784	11280	13341	65934	232382
Inventories 24	·	·	·	·	·	·	·	·	·	·	·
Net Property, Plant and Equipment 25	182120	39	47	1096	3488	9597	19317	36009	94382	283004	1232952
Total Assets 26	862748	154	2663	7787	16680	37147	71478	163488	352474	1177316	6376064
Notes and Loans Payable 27	149654	53	849	4489	3654	7548	15690	33066	51304	201817	1109989
All Other Liabilities 28	87618	1	63	837	-2425	767	2551	5886	14718	86687	778296
Net Worth 29	625476	100	1751	2461	15451	28831	53236	124537	286452	888813	4487779

Selected Financial Ratios (Times to 1)

Item											
Current Ratio 30	1.2	·	15.7	0.6	3.3	2.6	1.6	3.6	4.5	2.1	0.9
Quick Ratio 31	1.1	·	13.0	0.6	2.1	2.3	1.4	3.1	3.9	1.8	0.8
Net Sales to Working Capital 32	3.7	·	30.1	2.2	1.6	2.5	4.3	1.0	1.0	1.1	·
Coverage Ratio 33	7.2	58.2	193.7	2.2	13.4	5.4	2.3	5.7	7.4	6.1	7.8
Total Asset Turnover 34	0.1	·	2.9	0.3	0.2	0.2	0.2	0.1	0.1	0.1	0.1
Inventory Turnover 35	·	·	·	·	·	·	·	·	·	·	·
Receivables Turnover 36	·	·	·	·	·	·	·	·	·	·	·
Total Liabilities to Net Worth 37	0.4	·	0.5	2.2	0.1	0.3	0.3	0.3	0.2	0.3	0.4
Current Assets to Working Capital 38	5.6	·	1.1	1.1	1.4	1.6	2.6	1.4	1.3	1.9	·
Current Liabilities to Working Capital 39	4.6	·	0.1	0.4	0.4	0.6	1.6	0.4	0.3	0.9	·
Working Capital to Net Sales 40	0.3	·	0.5	0.6	0.6	0.4	0.2	1.0	1.0	0.9	·
Inventory to Working Capital 41	·	·	·	·	·	·	·	·	·	·	·
Total Receipts to Cash Flow 42	1.6	3.4	6.9	1.5	2.3	1.8	2.3	1.6	1.7	1.5	1.5
Cost of Goods to Cash Flow 43	·	·	·	·	·	·	·	·	·	·	·
Cash Flow to Total Debt 44	0.2	3.8	0.1	0.2	1.2	0.5	0.3	0.3	0.3	0.2	0.1

Selected Financial Factors (in Percentages)

Item											
Debt Ratio 45	27.5	35.1	34.3	68.4	7.4	22.4	25.5	23.8	18.7	24.5	29.6
Return on Total Assets 46	5.2	97.4	·	8.6	12.5	10.1	9.3	6.5	6.3	5.6	4.4
Return on Equity Before Income Taxes 47	6.2	149.3	14.7	14.7	12.5	10.6	7.1	7.1	6.7	6.1	5.5
Return on Equity After Income Taxes 48	6.2	149.0	14.7	14.7	12.4	10.5	7.1	7.1	6.7	6.1	5.5
Profit Margin (Before Income Tax) 49	59.6	69.1	33.6	26.8	56.1	43.5	33.7	48.7	55.3	57.9	62.0
Profit Margin (After Income Tax) 50	59.6	69.1	33.5	26.8	56.0	43.5	33.7	48.7	55.3	57.9	62.0

Table II
Corporations with Net Income

REAL ESTATE INVESTMENT TRUSTS (FORM 1120-REIT)

MONEY AMOUNTS AND SIZE OF ASSETS IN THOUSANDS OF DOLLARS

Item Description for Accounting Period 7/03 Through 6/04	Total	Zero Assets	Under 500	500 to 1,000	1,000 to 5,000	5,000 to 10,000	10,000 to 25,000	25,000 to 50,000	50,000 to 100,000	100,000 to 250,000	250,000 to 500,000	500,000 to 2,500,000	2,500,000 and over
Number of Enterprises 1	903	95	40	•	23	20	55	61	83	122	108	204	92
Revenues ($ in Thousands)													
Net Sales 2	67273139	3606079	23347	•	10189	41487	242127	501253	922655	2308291	3701020	19574892	36341799
Interest 3	24158561	676778	118	•	126	2592	24947	131633	335771	620044	1104467	6878768	14383318
Rents 4	28817511	347940	14514	•	2305	31916	119378	250633	376289	1043654	1877442	9037871	15715569
Royalties 5	0	0	0	•	0	0	0	0	0	0	0	0	0
Other Portfolio Income 6	6462447	2288211	8875	•	2381	190	86112	91837	144674	359187	373859	798746	2308372
Other Receipts 7	7834620	293150	-160	•	5377	6789	11690	27150	65921	285406	345252	2859507	3934540
Total Receipts 8	67273139	3606079	23347	•	10189	41487	242127	501253	922655	2308291	3701020	19574892	36341799
Average Total Receipts 9	74500	37959	584	•	443	2074	4402	8217	11116	18920	34269	95955	395020
Operating Costs/Operating Income (%)													
Cost of Operations 10	•	•	•	•	•	•	•	•	•	•	•	•	•
Salaries and Wages 11	1.6	0.5	•	•	•	1.4	0.6	0.4	1.1	0.7	1.2	1.7	1.8
Taxes Paid 12	2.7	0.1	0.4	•	0.5	2.0	2.2	1.0	3.3	1.8	3.4	3.3	2.6
Interest Paid 13	9.2	0.7	0.1	•	4.9	22.1	4.2	4.3	21.1	7.4	8.1	10.9	9.2
Depreciation 14	7.1	0.0	13.2	•	0.2	2.5	5.6	2.8	5.7	4.0	7.8	7.7	7.6
Amortization and Depletion 15	0.7	0.0	0.2	•	0.1	0.4	2.2	1.1	1.0	0.5	0.7	0.9	0.7
Pensions and Other Deferred Comp. 16	•	•	•	•	•	•	•	•	•	•	•	•	•
Employee Benefits 17	•	•	•	•	•	•	•	•	•	•	•	•	•
Advertising 18	0.2	0.0	0.2	•	•	0.1	0.3	0.0	0.2	0.1	0.1	0.4	0.2
Other Expenses 19	15.1	13.1	47.6	•	4.9	38.8	19.6	28.1	16.2	26.2	18.1	13.5	14.9
Officers' Compensation 20	0.4	•	0.8	•	•	•	0.2	0.1	0.3	0.4	0.4	0.5	0.4
Operating Margin 21	63.0	85.7	37.4	•	89.5	32.7	65.2	62.2	51.2	59.0	60.2	61.0	62.6
Operating Margin Before Officers' Comp. 22	63.4	85.7	38.2	•	89.5	32.7	65.4	62.3	51.5	59.3	60.6	61.5	63.1

Selected Average Balance Sheet ($ in Thousands)

Net Receivables 23	43051	0	0	261	144	416	2949	2084	13364	14100	68420	232382
Inventories 24	·	·	·	·	·	·	·	·	·	·	·	·
Net Property, Plant and Equipment 25	205645	0	27	76	1644	3495	7229	18502	28083	87892	280112	1232952
Total Assets 26	992451	27	160	2308	7510	16900	37009	70876	162651	353769	1187527	6376064
Notes and Loans Payable 27	165946	0	66	273	6734	4204	4093	14705	23526	44937	187069	1109989
All Other Liabilities 28	101935	0	1	99	1255	-3378	669	2658	6534	14335	88216	778296
Net Worth 29	724569	0	93	1936	-478	16074	32247	53513	132591	294496	912242	4487779

Selected Financial Ratios (Times to 1)

Current Ratio 30	1.2	·	11.9	19.8	0.6	3.4	5.4	1.7	4.6	4.4	2.1	0.9
Quick Ratio 31	1.1	·	11.6	16.3	0.6	2.1	4.7	1.4	3.9	3.8	1.8	0.8
Net Sales to Working Capital 32	3.8	·	30.2	0.9	·	1.7	1.8	3.4	0.9	1.0	1.1	·
Coverage Ratio 33	7.8	127.7	302.2	19.4	2.5	16.7	15.4	3.4	9.0	8.5	6.6	7.8
Total Asset Turnover 34	0.1	·	3.6	0.2	0.3	0.2	0.2	0.1	0.1	0.1	0.1	0.1
Inventory Turnover 35	·	·	·	·	·	·	·	·	·	·	·	·
Receivables Turnover 36	·	·	·	·	·	·	·	·	·	·	·	·
Total Liabilities to Net Worth 37	0.4	·	0.7	0.2	0.1	0.1	0.3	0.2	0.2	0.3	0.3	0.4
Current Assets to Working Capital 38	5.8	·	1.1	1.1	·	1.4	1.2	2.4	2.0	1.3	1.6	1.9
Current Liabilities to Working Capital 39	4.8	·	0.1	0.1	·	0.4	0.1	0.2	1.4	0.3	0.3	0.9
Working Capital to Net Sales 40	0.3	·	0.0	1.1	·	0.6	0.5	0.3	1.1	1.0	0.9	0.9
Inventory to Working Capital 41	·	·	·	·	·	·	·	·	·	·	·	·
Total Receipts to Cash Flow 42	1.5	2.8	2.2	1.4	1.5	2.2	1.5	2.0	1.5	1.6	1.5	1.5
Cost of Goods to Cash Flow 43	·	·	·	·	·	·	·	·	·	·	·	·
Cash Flow to Total Debt 44	0.2	·	4.0	0.8	0.2	2.5	1.1	0.3	0.4	0.4	0.2	0.1

Selected Financial Factors (in Percentages)

Debt Ratio 45	27.0	·	41.8	16.1	106.4	4.9	12.9	24.5	18.5	16.8	23.2	29.6
Return on Total Assets 46	5.4	·	136.7	18.1	15.1	18.1	14.8	11.3	7.7	6.6	5.8	4.4
Return on Equity Before Income Taxes 47	6.4	·	234.1	20.5	·	17.9	15.9	10.6	8.4	7.0	6.4	5.5
Return on Equity After Income Taxes 48	6.4	·	233.6	20.4	·	17.8	15.8	10.6	8.4	7.0	6.4	5.5
Profit Margin (Before Income Tax) 49	62.6	85.7	37.4	89.5	32.7	65.2	62.2	51.2	58.8	60.2	61.0	62.0
Profit Margin (After Income Tax) 50	62.6	85.7	37.3	89.3	32.7	65.1	62.1	51.2	58.8	60.2	61.0	62.0

Table I

Corporations with and without Net Income

OTHER FINANCIAL VEHICLES

MONEY AMOUNTS AND SIZE OF ASSETS IN THOUSANDS OF DOLLARS

Item Description for Accounting Period 7/03 Through 6/04		Total	Zero Assets	Under 500	500 to 1,000	1,000 to 5,000	5,000 to 10,000	10,000 to 25,000	25,000 to 50,000	50,000 to 100,000	100,000 to 250,000	250,000 to 500,000	500,000 to 2,500,000	2,500,000 and over
Number of Enterprises	1	13869	3789	7184	1115	1147	190	111	58	29	43	48	104	50
Revenues ($ in Thousands)														
Net Sales	2	13678460	666894	318420	383635	317047	122601	387454	201861	127574	491145	703251	3494597	6461982
Interest	3	9890628	534484	22724	66841	14030	7228	32890	36720	55422	225014	645567	2983511	5266197
Rents	4	79762	370	0	0	3332	1170	800	1334	5591	67086	81	0	0
Royalties	5	326	0	0	0	0	166	116	44	0	0	0	0	0
Other Portfolio Income	6	877895	77786	78803	3487	53635	8514	34134	18858	21244	23264	8911	285320	263937
Other Receipts	7	2829849	56254	216893	313307	246050	105523	319514	144905	45317	175781	48692	225766	931848
Total Receipts	8	13678460	666894	318420	383635	317047	122601	387454	201861	127574	491145	703251	3494597	6461982
Average Total Receipts	9	986	177	44	344	276	645	3491	3480	4399	11422	14651	33602	129240
Operating Costs/Operating Income (%)														
Cost of Operations	10	0.3	•	2.0	1.8	0.0	4.3	3.8	0.7	5.6	•	0.0	0.0	•
Salaries and Wages	11	1.8	1.9	15.2	1.5	24.7	16.6	12.9	12.0	3.3	0.0	0.0	0.0	0.0
Taxes Paid	12	0.6	0.4	4.2	4.6	4.3	3.4	1.7	1.6	2.0	1.6	0.3	0.0	0.0
Interest Paid	13	45.4	39.0	9.8	13.6	3.5	4.4	13.0	22.2	15.2	53.5	51.1	45.2	54.6
Depreciation	14	1.1	0.1	0.8	3.6	1.1	1.8	1.3	0.7	0.8	25.5	0.0	0.0	0.0
Amortization and Depletion	15	0.2	0.2	0.2	0.1	0.8	4.8	1.0	5.3	0.4	0.5	0.4	0.0	0.0
Pensions and Other Deferred Comp.	16	0.2	•	•	1.8	6.4	1.7	0.2	0.2	0.1	•	•	•	0.0
Employee Benefits	17	2.2	0.0	2.6	3.2	3.4	2.9	0.8	0.2	0.2	0.0	0.0	0.0	4.1
Advertising	18	0.1	0.6	0.5	0.0	0.1	0.0	0.6	0.5	0.1	0.0	•	•	•
Other Expenses	19	18.1	25.3	61.8	34.4	53.3	65.6	59.7	37.2	56.8	9.1	22.2	9.8	12.6
Officers' Compensation	20	2.0	0.6	8.2	35.3	12.3	28.0	5.1	2.3	3.4	•	0.0	0.0	0.0
Operating Margin	21	27.9	31.8	2.9	0.0	•	•	0.1	17.3	12.2	9.7	26.2	44.7	28.6
Operating Margin Before Officers' Comp.	22	29.9	32.4	2.9	35.4	2.2	•	5.2	19.5	15.6	9.7	26.2	44.7	28.6

Selected Average Balance Sheet ($ in Thousands)

Item														
Net Receivables 23	5773	•	4	23	198	23	290	1309	2480	12373	34513	27427	238192	1030180
Inventories 24	•	•	•	•	•	•	•	•	•	•	•	•	•	•
Net Property, Plant and Equipment 25	22	•	0	3	33	15	25	417	558	1873	1370	795	2	0
Total Assets 26	33826		65	676	1828	7222	15108	33314	74641	174539	353951	1078191		6440781
Notes and Loans Payable 27	20554		28	226	623	3968	4907	12933	16350	99348	165009	536060		4268600
All Other Liabilities 28	3458		13	134	481	513	2215	2676	19595	39687	49619	100205		631716
Net Worth 29	9814		24	317	724	2741	7986	17704	38697	35504	139323	441925		1540465

Selected Financial Ratios (Times to 1)

Item												
Current Ratio 30	0.5	1.6	4.5	2.0	3.2	2.6	3.2	1.3	1.1	0.7	0.5	
Quick Ratio 31	0.5	1.4	2.7	1.8	1.7	1.9	2.4	1.2	0.9	0.7	0.4	
Net Sales to Working Capital 32	•	4.3	1.5	0.8	0.2	0.6	0.2	0.9	3.8	•	1.5	
Coverage Ratio 33	1.6	0.5	0.9	•	1.0	1.7	1.8	1.2	1.5	2.0	1.5	
Total Asset Turnover 34	0.0	0.7	0.5	0.2	0.1	0.1	0.1	0.1	0.0	0.0	0.0	
Inventory Turnover 35	•	•	•	•	•	•	•	•	•	•	•	
Receivables Turnover 36	•	•	•	•	•	•	•	•	•	•		
Total Liabilities to Net Worth 37	2.4	1.7	1.1	1.5	1.6	0.9	0.9	3.9	1.5	1.4	3.2	
Current Assets to Working Capital 38	•	2.8	1.3	2.0	1.5	1.6	1.4	4.3	19.1			
Current Liabilities to Working Capital 39	•	1.8	0.3	1.0	0.5	0.6	0.4	3.3	18.1			
Working Capital to Net Sales 40	•	0.2	0.7	1.3	4.1	1.7	5.3	1.1	0.3			
Inventory to Working Capital 41	•	•	0.0	0.0	0.0	0.0	0.0	•				
Total Receipts to Cash Flow 42	2.3	4.2	3.1	3.6	4.3	2.2	1.6	5.7	2.1	1.9	2.5	
Cost of Goods to Cash Flow 43	0.0	0.1	0.1	0.0	0.2	0.0	0.1	0.1	0.0	0.0	0.0	
Cash Flow to Total Debt 44	0.0	0.3	0.3	0.1	0.0	0.1	0.1	0.0	0.0	0.0	0.0	

Selected Financial Factors (in Percentages)

Item												
Debt Ratio 45	71.0	63.2	53.1	60.4	62.0	47.1	46.9	48.2	79.7	60.6	59.0	76.1
Return on Total Assets 46	2.1	3.0	6.5	•	•	3.0	4.0	1.6	4.3	3.2	2.8	1.7
Return on Equity Before Income Taxes 47	2.8	•	•	•		3.1	1.3		2.8	3.4	2.5	
Return on Equity After Income Taxes 48	1.7	•	•	•	•	2.0	0.5	0.4	1.3	2.3	1.6	
Profit Margin (Before Income Tax) 49	28.2	31.3	•	•	•	15.7	11.8	12.4	26.2	44.3	29.5	
Profit Margin (After Income Tax) 50	17.2	15.2	•	•	•	10.0	4.2	1.2	12.4	29.9	18.8	

Table II
Corporations with Net Income

OTHER FINANCIAL VEHICLES

MONEY AMOUNTS AND SIZE OF ASSETS IN THOUSANDS OF DOLLARS

Item Description for Accounting Period 7/03 Through 6/04		Total	Zero Assets	Under 500	500 to 1,000	1,000 to 5,000	5,000 to 10,000	10,000 to 25,000	25,000 to 50,000	50,000 to 100,000	100,000 to 250,000	250,000 to 500,000	500,000 to 2,500,000	2,500,000 and over
Number of Enterprises	1	5867	1445	3191	535	423	50	45	23	15	15	23	73	29
Revenues ($ in Thousands)														
Net Sales	2	9344932	486763	337147	360264	261139	120849	173910	131636	88267	226612	404386	2596617	4157341
Interest	3	6097668	320332	5115	52244	5940	1996	5583	17701	26342	44459	338297	2148758	3130901
Rents	4	29823	127	0	0	1894	0	370	30	5591	21731	81	0	0
Royalties	5	44	0	0	0	0	0	0	44	0	0	0	0	0
Other Portfolio Income	6	791809	73515	78803	118	51414	8492	33332	15560	20791	22015	8911	269260	209596
Other Receipts	7	2425588	92789	253229	307902	201891	110361	134625	98301	35543	138407	57097	178599	816844
Total Receipts	8	9344932	486763	337147	360264	261139	120849	173910	131636	88267	226612	404386	2596617	4157341
Average Total Receipts	9	1593	337	106	673	617	2417	3865	5723	5884	15107	17582	35570	143357
Operating Costs/Operating Income (%)														
Cost of Operations	10	0.1	•	1.2	•	•	•	•	•	0.5	•	•	•	•
Salaries and Wages	11	1.5	0.9	4.9	0.5	17.4	13.8	16.0	17.1	3.1	•	•	0.0	0.0
Taxes Paid	12	0.7	0.3	2.8	2.7	3.9	2.3	2.4	2.1	2.5	3.6	0.0	0.5	0.0
Interest Paid	13	29.1	17.2	4.8	14.4	0.9	1.3	5.0	10.4	9.5	24.0	23.3	30.7	38.2
Depreciation	14	0.4	0.0	0.3	3.7	0.9	1.3	1.0	0.8	1.1	5.4	0.0	0.0	0.0
Amortization and Depletion	15	0.0	0.0	0.2	0.0	0.0	0.0	1.0	0.2	0.1	0.0	0.0	•	•
Pensions and Other Deferred Comp.	16	0.1	•	•	1.9	1.7	0.0	0.1	0.3	0.1	0.0	0.0	•	•
Employee Benefits	17	3.0	•	1.8	0.1	0.3	3.1	0.4	1.0	0.2	0.3	•	•	6.4
Advertising	18	0.0	0.1	0.4	•	0.1	0.0	0.0	0.9	0.6	0.1	•	•	•
Other Expenses	19	9.9	7.4	31.6	24.8	22.0	9.7	31.8	16.1	15.4	1.9	5.2	4.4	9.4
Officers' Compensation	20	2.5	0.0	7.7	37.1	8.3	28.1	6.4	2.6	4.4	•	•	0.0	0.0
Operating Margin	21	52.7	74.1	44.4	14.7	43.2	41.4	34.4	49.7	63.0	65.0	71.4	64.4	45.9
Operating Margin Before Officers' Comp.	22	55.2	74.1	52.1	51.8	69.4	51.5	40.8	52.3	67.4	65.0	71.4	64.4	45.9

Selected Average Balance Sheet ($ in Thousands)

Item													
Net Receivables 23	8642	0	2	44	528	148	1565	2614	20006	41561	15570	250384	1060320
Inventories 24	•	•	•	•	•	•	•	•	•	•	•	•	•
Net Property, Plant and Equipment 25	38	0	6	65	22	66	141	174	3394	3844	1659	0	1
Total Assets 26	49042	0	70	713	1785	5875	14525	34430	72701	170834	370260	1045853	6762528
Notes and Loans Payable 27	21763	0	17	265	105	1830	5194	12597	8266	52497	94089	373620	3326744
All Other Liabilities 28	5910	0	11	59	823	746	2057	2254	10963	38815	3737	69868	970457
Net Worth 29	21370	0	42	389	857	3298	7273	19579	53472	79522	272434	602366	2465327

Selected Financial Ratios (Times to 1)

Item													
Current Ratio 30	0.8	•	2.0	6.8	1.3	6.3	1.6	1.9	3.4	3.8	1.6	1.2	0.7
Quick Ratio 31	0.7	•	1.9	3.8	1.1	6.1	1.0	1.5	2.8	2.9	1.1	1.1	0.6
Net Sales to Working Capital 32	•	•	6.9	1.6	3.5	1.1	2.1	1.5	0.2	0.4	1.0	0.6	•
Coverage Ratio 33	2.9	5.3	10.3	2.0	47.6	7.8	32.0	5.8	7.6	3.9	4.1	3.1	2.3
Total Asset Turnover 34	0.0	•	1.5	0.9	0.3	0.4	0.3	0.2	0.2	0.1	0.0	0.0	0.0
Inventory Turnover 35	•	•	•	•	•	•	•	•	•	•	•	•	•
Receivables Turnover 36	•	•	•	•	•	•	•	•	•	•	•	•	•
Total Liabilities to Net Worth 37	1.3	•	0.7	0.8	1.1	0.8	1.0	0.8	0.4	1.1	0.4	0.7	1.7
Current Assets to Working Capital 38	•	•	2.0	1.2	4.7	1.2	2.7	2.2	1.4	1.4	2.6	5.4	•
Current Liabilities to Working Capital 39	•	•	1.0	0.2	3.7	0.2	1.7	1.2	0.4	0.4	1.6	4.4	•
Working Capital to Net Sales 40	•	•	0.1	0.6	0.3	0.9	0.5	0.7	4.8	2.9	1.0	1.8	0.0
Inventory to Working Capital 41	•	•	•	•	•	•	•	•	•	•	•	•	•
Total Receipts to Cash Flow 42	1.7	1.5	2.6	2.1	2.0	2.3	2.0	1.9	1.4	1.6	1.3	1.5	1.8
Cost of Goods to Cash Flow 43	0.0	•	0.0	0.0	0.0	0.0	0.0	0.0	0.0	0.0	0.0	0.0	0.0
Cash Flow to Total Debt 44	0.0	•	1.8	0.8	0.3	0.4	0.2	0.2	0.2	0.1	0.1	0.0	0.0

Selected Financial Factors (in Percentages)

Item													
Debt Ratio 45	56.4	•	40.0	45.4	52.0	43.9	49.9	43.1	26.4	53.5	26.4	42.4	63.5
Return on Total Assets 46	2.7	•	74.4	27.6	15.0	17.5	10.4	10.0	5.9	8.4	4.5	3.2	1.8
Return on Equity Before Income Taxes 47	4.0	•	112.0	25.5	30.7	30.3	18.1	14.5	6.9	13.5	4.6	3.8	2.8
Return on Equity After Income Taxes 48	2.8	•	104.2	25.4	27.7	26.9	16.5	11.9	5.8	8.8	3.1	2.7	1.9
Profit Margin (Before Income Tax) 49	54.0	•	74.1	44.4	14.7	42.6	41.3	49.5	63.0	70.9	71.4	64.4	48.5
Profit Margin (After Income Tax) 50	38.0	•	52.0	41.3	14.7	38.4	36.7	40.8	52.5	46.6	47.5	45.4	32.0

Table I

Corporations with and without Net Income

LESSORS OF BUILDINGS

MONEY AMOUNTS AND SIZE OF ASSETS IN THOUSANDS OF DOLLARS

Item Description for Accounting Period 7/03 Through 6/04	Total	Zero Assets	Under 500	500 to 1,000	1,000 to 5,000	5,000 to 10,000	10,000 to 25,000	25,000 to 50,000	50,000 to 100,000	100,000 to 250,000	250,000 to 500,000	500,000 to 2,500,000	2,500,000 and over
Number of Enterprises **1**	213641	18064	121067	34371	33667	3966	1759	456	163	94	24	6	4
Revenues ($ in Thousands)													
Net Sales **2**	33078750	1791197	4134664	3157798	7644307	3299267	3662408	2082014	1900569	1856303	1705427	553633	1291164
Interest **3**	618889	18134	40882	42961	86515	57858	58543	42078	47675	32975	54334	57221	79713
Rents **4**	151393	15838	47852	11711	32833	9775	16995	6791	1464	1720	522	5893	0
Royalties **5**	28052	1	11512	0	11398	2088	1091	920	132	0	458	0	452
Other Portfolio Income **6**	2317797	571882	241281	97811	339504	153481	251399	113658	208281	114955	123491	11303	90749
Other Receipts **7**	29962619	1185342	3793137	3005315	7174057	3076065	3334380	1918567	1643017	1706653	1526622	479216	1120250
Total Receipts **8**	33078750	1791197	4134664	3157798	7644307	3299267	3662408	2082014	1900569	1856303	1705427	553633	1291164
Average Total Receipts **9**	155	99	34	92	227	832	2082	4566	11660	19748	71059	92272	322791
Operating Costs/Operating Income (%)													
Cost of Operations **10**	11.8	1.2	10.4	15.8	11.6	3.2	12.7	8.8	18.3	22.1	21.3	10.9	10.3
Salaries and Wages **11**	9.7	3.9	5.3	7.3	11.8	13.1	11.6	12.4	8.1	8.8	9.2	13.7	9.7
Taxes Paid **12**	11.6	8.9	10.5	11.3	14.1	16.8	13.4	12.6	8.0	6.9	7.1	3.5	5.5
Interest Paid **13**	12.9	14.5	7.7	10.2	12.0	14.6	15.1	14.7	12.0	15.5	9.8	32.6	18.4
Depreciation **14**	10.1	10.1	6.6	8.8	10.2	11.5	12.4	12.7	11.1	10.0	7.3	22.9	6.4
Amortization and Depletion **15**	0.7	1.8	0.2	0.7	0.5	0.5	0.8	0.7	0.7	1.3	0.7	0.3	0.3
Pensions and Other Deferred Comp. **16**	0.4	0.0	0.5	0.1	0.5	0.5	0.3	0.4	0.3	0.2	0.4	0.1	0.1
Employee Benefits **17**	1.2	0.4	1.1	0.8	1.2	1.8	1.4	1.5	1.3	0.9	1.2	0.0	0.2
Advertising **18**	0.5	0.3	0.3	1.1	0.3	0.5	0.3	0.4	0.4	0.7	1.2	0.3	0.5
Other Expenses **19**	33.5	41.8	45.5	36.3	31.1	31.7	34.5	33.9	28.2	28.1	31.5	21.3	16.1
Officers' Compensation **20**	4.0	0.8	7.5	7.5	4.8	3.9	2.2	2.4	1.6	1.6	1.3	0.4	4.3
Operating Margin **21**	3.7	16.1	4.3	0.2	1.8	1.8	•	•	10.1	3.9	9.1	•	28.2
Operating Margin Before Officers' Comp. **22**	7.7	16.9	11.8	7.6	6.6	5.6	•	2.0	11.7	5.4	10.4	•	32.5

Selected Average Balance Sheet ($ in Thousands)

Item												
Net Receivables 23	37	3	21	59	150	381	1276	2654	7774	12006	100058	220027
Inventories 24	•	•	•	•	•	•	•	•	•	•	•	•
Net Property, Plant and Equipment 25	738	133	521	1464	4784	10279	22510	39355	78865	176569	365735	1704882
Total Assets 26	1111	181	705	2055	6833	15059	34027	65339	150132	344025	744694	3875154
Notes and Loans Payable 27	688	121	480	1378	4459	9712	19568	36203	81921	148756	513853	1373179
All Other Liabilities 28	92	10	36	144	550	1094	2489	6554	21985	35098	128656	571369
Net Worth 29	332	50	189	533	1824	4253	11971	22582	46226	160171	102185	1930606

Selected Financial Ratios (Times to 1)

Item												
Current Ratio 30	1.9	2.5	2.1	1.8	1.5	1.8	1.8	1.7	1.6	1.5	1.6	3.0
Quick Ratio 31	1.3	2.0	1.7	1.4	1.1	1.2	1.3	1.2	1.2	1.1	1.4	0.9
Net Sales to Working Capital 32	1.9	2.4	1.7	1.7	2.7	2.1	2.0	2.7	1.9	4.3	1.9	0.5
Coverage Ratio 33	1.3	1.6	1.0	1.1	1.1	0.7	1.0	1.7	1.2	1.9	0.8	2.5
Total Asset Turnover 34	0.1	0.2	0.1	0.1	0.1	0.1	0.1	0.2	0.1	0.2	0.1	0.1
Inventory Turnover 35	•	•	•	•	•	•	•	•	•	•	•	•
Receivables Turnover 36	•	•	•	•	•	•	•	•	•	•	•	•
Total Liabilities to Net Worth 37	2.3	2.6	2.7	2.9	2.7	2.5	1.9	1.9	2.2	1.1	6.3	1.0
Current Assets to Working Capital 38	2.1	1.7	1.9	2.2	3.0	2.3	2.3	2.5	2.5	2.9	2.7	1.5
Current Liabilities to Working Capital 39	1.1	0.7	0.9	1.2	2.0	1.3	1.3	1.5	1.5	1.9	1.7	0.5
Working Capital to Net Sales 40	0.5	0.4	0.6	0.6	0.4	0.5	0.5	0.4	0.5	0.2	0.5	1.9
Inventory to Working Capital 41	0.0	•	•	0.0	0.0	0.0	0.0	0.1	0.1	0.1	•	0.0
Total Receipts to Cash Flow 42	4.4	3.4	4.7	4.6	4.7	5.4	4.6	4.0	4.8	3.6	14.7	3.0
Cost of Goods to Cash Flow 43	0.5	0.4	0.7	0.5	0.2	0.7	0.4	0.7	1.1	0.8	1.6	0.3
Cash Flow to Total Debt 44	0.0	0.1	0.0	0.0	0.0	0.0	0.0	0.1	0.0	0.1	0.0	0.1

Selected Financial Factors (in Percentages)

Item												
Debt Ratio 45	70.1	72.3	73.2	74.1	73.3	71.8	64.8	65.4	69.2	53.4	86.3	50.2
Return on Total Assets 46	2.3	2.3	1.3	1.5	2.0	1.4	1.9	3.7	2.5	3.9	3.3	3.9
Return on Equity Before Income Taxes 47	1.6	2.9	0.0	0.7	0.7	•	•	4.4	1.6	4.0	•	4.7
Return on Equity After Income Taxes 48	0.3	1.7	•	•	•	•	•	2.8	0.6	2.7	•	3.2
Profit Margin (Before Income Tax) 49	3.5	4.3	0.1	1.6	1.6	•	•	8.6	3.6	9.0	•	28.2
Profit Margin (After Income Tax) 50	0.7	2.5	•	•	•	•	•	5.5	1.4	6.2	•	19.0

Table II

Corporations with Net Income

LESSORS OF BUILDINGS

MONEY AMOUNTS AND SIZE OF ASSETS IN THOUSANDS OF DOLLARS

Item Description for Accounting Period 7/03 Through 6/04	Total	Zero Assets	Under 500	500 to 1,000	1,000 to 5,000	5,000 to 10,000	10,000 to 25,000	25,000 to 50,000	50,000 to 100,000	100,000 to 250,000	250,000 to 500,000	500,000 to 2,500,000	2,500,000 and over
Number of Enterprises **1**	46445	4317	25571	6898	7701	1107	535	171	82	44	16	•	4
Revenues ($ in Thousands)													
Net Sales **2**	20521791	1193203	2963428	2089903	4395786	1738352	1730732	1208318	1285045	1210763	1415098	•	1291164
Interest **3**	395510	9238	34038	30773	57952	28349	30830	26572	31616	23715	42714	•	79713
Rents **4**	68606	12402	18674	2734	15972	1326	9385	5694	710	1186	522	•	0
Royalties **5**	19951	1	3551	0	11326	2088	1078	905	93	0	458	•	452
Other Portfolio Income **6**	1953178	443944	232295	91144	324333	128083	207683	87262	149665	85502	112516	•	90749
Other Receipts **7**	18084546	727618	2674870	1965252	3986203	1578506	1481756	1087885	1102961	1100360	1258888	•	1120250
Total Receipts **8**	20521791	1193203	2963428	2089903	4395786	1738352	1730732	1208318	1285045	1210763	1415098	•	1291164
Average Total Receipts **9**	442	276	116	303	571	1570	3235	7066	15671	27517	88444	•	322791
Operating Costs/Operating Income (%)													
Cost of Operations **10**	15.3	0.6	13.7	19.5	18.4	4.9	13.3	11.3	16.9	31.9	22.3	•	10.3
Salaries and Wages **11**	7.3	1.5	2.5	7.9	10.9	9.1	6.7	9.2	6.2	6.0	7.1	•	9.7
Taxes Paid **12**	7.8	9.0	7.3	7.1	8.6	10.5	8.8	9.1	7.0	5.1	6.9	•	5.5
Interest Paid **13**	9.1	13.0	4.9	5.8	7.0	10.0	12.2	10.3	10.1	11.0	8.4	•	18.4
Depreciation **14**	7.6	9.0	4.4	5.9	7.0	9.0	9.1	9.4	9.8	7.9	11.3	•	6.4
Amortization and Depletion **15**	0.5	1.0	0.1	0.2	0.4	0.4	0.5	0.6	0.6	1.0	0.7	•	0.3
Pensions and Other Deferred Comp. **16**	0.3	0.0	0.5	0.1	0.4	0.7	0.2	0.5	0.3	0.1	0.1	•	0.1
Employee Benefits **17**	0.8	0.1	1.1	0.9	0.7	0.8	0.6	1.1	1.3	0.6	0.7	•	0.2
Advertising **18**	0.5	0.2	0.2	1.2	0.4	0.8	0.3	0.4	0.4	0.6	1.4	•	0.5
Other Expenses **19**	24.4	19.9	35.9	25.7	22.3	25.1	22.9	26.9	21.6	18.2	22.2	•	16.1
Officers' Compensation **20**	4.6	0.1	8.6	8.8	5.0	5.0	2.8	2.7	1.7	1.2	1.3	•	4.3
Operating Margin **21**	21.9	45.5	20.9	16.9	18.8	23.7	22.8	18.3	24.2	16.3	17.6	•	28.2
Operating Margin Before Officers' Comp. **22**	26.5	45.6	29.5	25.7	23.9	28.7	25.5	21.0	25.9	17.5	18.9	•	32.5

Selected Average Balance Sheet ($ in Thousands)

Item												
Net Receivables 23	64	0	4	25	63	155	485	1457	3071	4843	13029	220027
Inventories 24	•	•	•	•	•	•	•	•	•	•	•	•
Net Property, Plant and Equipment 25	972	0	106	491	1220	4285	9388	21042	38052	82826	168319	1704882
Total Assets 26	1710	0	169	734	2009	6700	15360	34879	67141	148728	339856	3875154
Notes and Loans Payable 27	824	0	118	412	1018	2897	8558	17739	33656	74581	138111	1373179
All Other Liabilities 28	166	0	13	42	188	437	1082	2822	6126	17324	34546	571369
Net Worth 29	720	0	38	279	803	3365	5721	14319	27359	56823	167199	1930606

Selected Financial Ratios (Times to 1)

Item												
Current Ratio 30	2.3	•	3.6	2.8	2.1	2.3	2.0	2.0	2.4	1.6	1.4	3.0
Quick Ratio 31	1.5	•	3.1	2.4	1.6	1.9	1.4	1.5	1.6	1.2	1.0	0.9
Net Sales to Working Capital 32	2.3	•	4.1	3.4	2.5	2.5	2.3	2.4	2.3	3.0	6.4	0.5
Coverage Ratio 33	3.4	4.5	5.2	3.9	3.3	2.9	2.8	2.8	3.2	2.5	3.1	2.5
Total Asset Turnover 34	0.3	•	0.7	0.4	0.3	0.2	0.2	0.2	0.2	0.2	0.3	0.1
Inventory Turnover 35	•	•	•	•	•	•	•	•	•	•	•	•
Receivables Turnover 36	•	•	•	•	•	•	•	•	•	•	•	•
Total Liabilities to Net Worth 37	1.4	•	3.5	1.6	1.5	1.0	1.7	1.4	1.5	1.6	1.0	1.0
Current Assets to Working Capital 38	1.8	•	1.4	1.6	1.9	1.8	2.0	2.0	1.7	2.6	3.3	1.5
Current Liabilities to Working Capital 39	0.8	•	0.4	0.6	0.9	0.8	1.0	1.0	0.7	1.6	2.3	0.5
Working Capital to Net Sales 40	0.4	•	0.2	0.3	0.4	0.4	0.4	0.4	0.4	0.3	0.2	1.9
Inventory to Working Capital 41	0.0	•	•	0.0	0.0	0.0	0.0	0.0	0.1	0.3	0.2	0.0
Total Receipts to Cash Flow 42	3.2	3.3	2.7	3.5	3.4	2.8	3.2	3.1	3.0	4.0	3.7	3.0
Cost of Goods to Cash Flow 43	0.5	0.0	0.4	0.7	0.6	0.1	0.4	0.4	0.5	1.3	0.8	0.3
Cash Flow to Total Debt 44	0.1	•	0.3	0.2	0.1	0.2	0.1	0.1	0.1	0.1	0.1	0.1

Selected Financial Factors (in Percentages)

Item												
Debt Ratio 45	57.9	•	77.6	62.0	60.0	49.8	62.8	58.9	59.3	61.8	50.8	50.2
Return on Total Assets 46	7.9	•	17.7	9.3	7.3	7.9	7.3	5.8	7.5	5.0	6.7	3.9
Return on Equity Before Income Taxes 47	13.3	•	64.2	18.2	13.2	11.0	12.7	8.9	12.6	7.8	9.3	4.7
Return on Equity After Income Taxes 48	10.6	•	57.9	16.4	11.3	7.9	9.7	6.6	10.0	6.1	7.5	3.2
Profit Margin (Before Income Tax) 49	21.6	45.5	20.9	16.8	18.6	23.5	22.5	18.1	22.1	16.1	17.5	28.2
Profit Margin (After Income Tax) 50	17.3	33.8	18.9	15.1	15.9	17.0	17.2	13.4	17.5	12.6	14.1	19.0

Table I
Corporations with and without Net Income

LESSORS OF MINIWAREHOUSES, SELF-STORAGE, OTHER REAL ESTATE

MONEY AMOUNTS AND SIZE OF ASSETS IN THOUSANDS OF DOLLARS

Item Description for Accounting Period 7/03 Through 6/04	Total	Zero Assets	Under 500	500 to 1,000	1,000 to 5,000	5,000 to 10,000	10,000 to 25,000	25,000 to 50,000	50,000 to 100,000	100,000 to 250,000	250,000 to 500,000	500,000 to 2,500,000	2,500,000 and over
Number of Enterprises **1**	57388	8746	33148	8033	6049	787	413	115	52	24	12	10	•
Revenues ($ in Thousands)													
Net Sales **2**	9530151	496813	1382227	1036539	1647678	541351	1123179	468798	325110	427133	364743	1716580	•
Interest **3**	364342	6071	13748	18861	41126	22627	23792	14569	20052	13973	67125	122396	•
Rents **4**	67705	339	2132	1203	5024	18055	3299	43	1385	1152	9672	25400	•
Royalties **5**	65981	21368	8	10257	13864	4812	7491	0	8180	0	0	0	•
Other Portfolio Income **6**	1170442	267474	77724	52112	143015	49381	60681	40002	44978	104345	39269	291465	•
Other Receipts **7**	7861681	201561	1288615	954106	1444649	446476	1027916	414184	250515	307663	248677	1277319	•
Total Receipts **8**	9530151	496813	1382227	1036539	1647678	541351	1123179	468798	325110	427133	364743	1716580	•
Average Total Receipts **9**	166	57	42	129	272	688	2720	4077	6252	17797	30395	171658	•
Operating Costs/Operating Income (%)													
Cost of Operations **10**	4.9	0.0	2.1	2.5	3.6	3.9	8.8	2.7	7.4	2.6	1.8	10.2	•
Salaries and Wages **11**	10.2	3.1	13.8	11.4	9.6	13.0	11.3	13.1	9.7	8.9	11.1	6.9	•
Taxes Paid **12**	6.7	8.7	7.9	5.9	7.7	7.3	5.2	8.1	6.0	5.7	3.6	6.2	•
Interest Paid **13**	14.5	10.1	5.1	4.9	13.0	17.7	9.7	14.1	20.6	18.5	19.0	29.8	•
Depreciation **14**	8.4	5.6	4.6	5.3	8.3	10.3	7.0	10.6	14.0	8.5	6.3	13.4	•
Amortization and Depletion **15**	0.9	0.2	0.9	0.3	0.5	0.7	0.8	0.9	1.0	1.0	0.2	1.9	•
Pensions and Other Deferred Comp. **16**	1.6	0.3	1.4	10.4	0.2	1.4	0.4	0.4	0.2	0.6	0.1	0.1	•
Employee Benefits **17**	1.3	0.5	1.4	0.2	2.6	0.9	1.2	1.2	1.4	0.8	0.9	1.1	•
Advertising **18**	0.9	0.1	0.7	1.9	1.5	0.5	0.8	1.4	0.8	0.2	0.3	0.6	•
Other Expenses **19**	38.1	46.9	38.9	32.7	42.2	30.2	48.4	39.9	36.2	29.1	54.6	28.7	•
Officers' Compensation **20**	6.8	1.8	15.4	10.8	6.2	10.6	4.1	7.0	3.7	3.0	4.5	2.1	•
Operating Margin **21**	5.8	22.6	7.9	13.8	4.6	3.4	2.3	0.6	•	21.3	•	•	•
Operating Margin Before Officers' Comp. **22**	12.6	24.4	23.3	24.6	10.8	14.0	6.4	7.6	2.7	24.3	2.1	1.1	•

Selected Average Balance Sheet ($ in Thousands)

Net Receivables 23	47	0	7	17	38	348	678	1970	4028	15820	32262	35598
Inventories 24	•	•	•	•	•	•	•	•	•	•	•	•
Net Property, Plant and Equipment 25	505	0	96	438	1155	3309	7075	14888	25629	58757	51446	469682
Total Assets 26	1022	0	152	689	2012	7468	14999	33287	68269	153125	320736	894674
Notes and Loans Payable 27	559	0	70	444	1310	4546	8354	16698	29023	72513	118236	466753
All Other Liabilities 28	120	0	18	46	156	953	1756	5033	12387	9905	68519	121067
Net Worth 29	343	0	64	199	545	1969	4889	11556	26859	70707	133981	306854

Selected Financial Ratios (Times to 1)

Current Ratio 30	2.1	•	1.6	1.9	2.2	2.2	1.6	1.7	1.7	4.0	2.3	2.7
Quick Ratio 31	1.3	•	1.2	1.2	1.4	1.4	1.0	1.2	1.4	3.3	1.1	1.2
Net Sales to Working Capital 32	1.5	•	4.2	1.8	1.4	0.8	2.3	1.3	1.0	0.8	0.5	1.5
Coverage Ratio 33	1.4	3.2	2.5	3.8	1.3	1.2	1.2	1.0	0.9	2.1	0.9	1.0
Total Asset Turnover 34	0.2	•	0.3	0.2	0.1	0.1	0.2	0.1	0.1	0.1	0.1	0.2
Inventory Turnover 35	•	•	•	•	•	•	•	•	•	•	•	•
Receivables Turnover 36	•	•	•	•	•	•	•	•	•	•	•	•
Total Liabilities to Net Worth 37	2.0	•	1.4	2.5	2.7	2.8	2.1	1.9	1.5	1.2	1.4	1.9
Current Assets to Working Capital 38	1.9	•	2.8	2.1	1.8	1.8	2.6	2.3	2.4	1.3	1.8	1.6
Current Liabilities to Working Capital 39	0.9	•	1.8	1.1	0.8	0.8	1.6	1.3	1.4	0.3	0.8	0.6
Working Capital to Net Sales 40	0.7	•	0.2	0.5	0.7	1.3	0.4	0.8	1.0	1.3	1.9	0.7
Inventory to Working Capital 41	0.0	•	0.0	•	0.0	0.0	0.0	0.0	0.0	0.0	0.0	0.0
Total Receipts to Cash Flow 42	3.9	12.7	3.1	3.2	3.1	4.6	2.5	4.7	5.7	3.8	3.2	12.3
Cost of Goods to Cash Flow 43	0.2	0.0	0.1	0.1	0.1	0.2	0.2	0.1	0.4	0.1	0.1	1.3
Cash Flow to Total Debt 44	0.1	•	0.2	0.1	0.1	0.0	0.1	0.0	0.0	0.1	0.1	0.0

Selected Financial Factors (in Percentages)

Debt Ratio 45	66.5	•	58.0	71.1	72.9	73.6	67.4	65.3	60.7	53.8	58.2	65.7
Return on Total Assets 46	3.3	•	3.5	3.5	2.4	1.9	2.1	1.7	1.8	4.4	1.7	5.5
Return on Equity Before Income Taxes 47	2.7	•	5.0	9.0	2.2	1.0	1.1	•	4.9	•	•	•
Return on Equity After Income Taxes 48	0.9	•	4.0	8.0	•	•	0.1	•	4.1	•	•	•
Profit Margin (Before Income Tax) 49	5.5	22.5	7.6	13.8	4.4	2.8	2.0	•	19.6	•	•	•
Profit Margin (After Income Tax) 50	1.9	10.7	6.2	12.4	•	0.2	0.2	•	16.4	•	•	•

LESSORS OF MINIWAREHOUSES, SELF-STORAGE, OTHER REAL ESTATE

Table II
Corporations with Net Income

MONEY AMOUNTS AND SIZE OF ASSETS IN THOUSANDS OF DOLLARS

Item Description for Accounting Period 7/03 Through 6/04	Total	Zero Assets	Under 500	500 to 1,000	1,000 to 5,000	5,000 to 10,000	10,000 to 25,000	25,000 to 50,000	50,000 to 100,000	100,000 to 250,000	250,000 to 500,000	500,000 to 2,500,000	2,500,000 and over
Number of Enterprises 1	19136	2249	11369	2797	2217	260	146	•	•	15	6	•	•
Revenues ($ in Thousands)													
Net Sales 2	6399737	453107	1082537	616151	1379946	352838	784414	•	•	359178	269249	•	•
Interest 3	188981	4956	12198	8528	29928	12401	16967	•	•	6028	17028	•	•
Rents 4	62785	273	1377	1155	4188	17947	3241	•	•	1152	9489	•	•
Royalties 5	63666	21368	8	9323	13864	4812	6110	•	•	0	0	•	•
Other Portfolio Income 6	1050730	266170	68353	41810	136429	44523	45105	•	•	98281	38840	•	•
Other Receipts 7	5035575	160340	1000601	555335	1195537	273155	712991	•	•	253717	203892	•	•
Total Receipts 8	6399737	453107	1082537	616151	1379946	352838	784414	•	•	359178	269249	•	•
Average Total Receipts 9	334	201	95	220	622	1357	5373	•	•	23945	44875	•	•
Operating Costs/Operating Income (%)													
Cost of Operations 10	1.3	0.1	1.1	1.0	0.9	4.4	2.1	•	•	3.1	•	•	•
Salaries and Wages 11	7.5	1.8	10.5	6.9	9.3	10.4	5.6	•	•	9.9	9.1	•	•
Taxes Paid 12	6.4	7.8	6.8	6.4	5.5	6.8	4.7	•	•	5.0	4.0	•	•
Interest Paid 13	8.6	6.2	4.6	5.0	7.1	11.5	6.8	•	•	13.1	21.1	•	•
Depreciation 14	5.6	2.6	4.1	5.5	5.0	7.1	4.7	•	•	7.9	6.8	•	•
Amortization and Depletion 15	0.4	0.1	0.0	0.4	0.3	0.5	0.6	•	•	0.8	0.2	•	•
Pensions and Other Deferred Comp. 16	0.5	0.4	1.7	0.1	0.1	1.1	0.3	•	•	0.7	•	•	•
Employee Benefits 17	1.2	0.6	1.0	0.3	3.1	0.3	0.7	•	•	0.9	0.9	•	•
Advertising 18	0.8	0.1	0.5	2.9	1.3	0.3	0.3	•	•	0.2	0.4	•	•
Other Expenses 19	31.4	23.9	28.5	36.2	33.3	22.2	52.8	•	•	25.5	33.1	•	•
Officers' Compensation 20	5.2	0.8	13.6	2.1	5.9	3.3	3.1	•	•	3.4	5.9	•	•
Operating Margin 21	31.1	55.8	27.6	33.2	28.3	32.1	18.3	•	•	29.5	18.4	•	•
Operating Margin Before Officers' Comp. 22	36.3	56.5	41.2	35.3	34.2	35.4	21.4	•	•	32.9	24.3	•	•

Selected Average Balance Sheet ($ in Thousands)

Net Receivables 23	73	·	19	11	76	407	712	·	7021	28371
Inventories 24	·	·	·	·	·	·	·	·	·	·
Net Property, Plant and Equipment 25	566	0	96	422	1046	3496	6717	·	69500	90789
Total Assets 26	1231	·	159	679	1997	7239	14851	·	156370	307496
Notes and Loans Payable 27	524	0	66	338	1121	4271	7304	·	63992	120758
All Other Liabilities 28	133	0	22	22	182	504	1665	·	12690	45859
Net Worth 29	575	0	71	319	694	2464	5882	·	79688	140878

Selected Financial Ratios (Times to 1)

Current Ratio 30	2.4	·	1.8	5.3	2.9	5.3	1.8	·	2.3	1.1
Quick Ratio 31	1.5	·	1.6	3.4	2.3	2.2	1.2	·	1.6	0.5
Net Sales to Working Capital 32	1.8	·	5.4	1.8	1.9	0.7	3.2	·	2.1	6.7
Coverage Ratio 33	4.6	10.0	6.9	7.6	5.0	3.7	3.7	·	3.1	1.9
Total Asset Turnover 34	0.3	·	0.6	0.3	0.3	0.2	0.4	·	0.2	0.1
Inventory Turnover 35	·	·	·	·	·	·	·	·	·	·
Receivables Turnover 36	·	·	·	·	·	·	·	·	·	·
Total Liabilities to Net Worth 37	1.1	·	1.2	1.1	1.9	1.9	1.5	·	1.0	1.2
Current Assets to Working Capital 38	1.7	·	2.3	1.2	1.5	1.2	2.2	·	1.8	12.6
Current Liabilities to Working Capital 39	0.7	·	1.3	0.2	0.5	0.2	1.2	·	0.8	11.6
Working Capital to Net Sales 40	0.6	·	0.2	0.5	0.5	1.4	0.3	·	0.5	0.1
Inventory to Working Capital 41	0.0	·	·	0.0	0.0	0.0	0.0	·	0.0	·
Total Receipts to Cash Flow 42	2.4	5.0	2.4	2.2	2.1	2.4	1.6	·	3.6	3.1
Cost of Goods to Cash Flow 43	0.0	0.0	0.0	0.0	0.0	0.1	0.0	·	0.1	0.0
Cash Flow to Total Debt 44	0.2	·	0.5	0.3	0.2	0.1	0.4	·	0.1	0.1

Selected Financial Factors (in Percentages)

Debt Ratio 45	53.3	·	55.3	53.0	65.3	66.0	60.4	·	49.0	54.2
Return on Total Assets 46	10.7	·	19.2	12.4	11.0	8.1	9.0	·	6.2	5.8
Return on Equity Before Income Taxes 47	17.9	·	36.8	22.9	25.3	17.3	16.6	·	8.3	5.9
Return on Equity After Income Taxes 48	14.9	·	34.3	21.2	20.4	13.6	14.3	·	7.1	4.7
Profit Margin (Before Income Tax) 49	30.8	55.8	27.4	33.2	28.1	31.5	18.1	·	27.5	18.4
Profit Margin (After Income Tax) 50	25.5	42.8	25.5	30.7	22.8	24.6	15.6	·	23.7	14.7

Table I
Corporations with and without Net Income

OFFICES OF REAL ESTATE AGENTS AND BROKERS

MONEY AMOUNTS AND SIZE OF ASSETS IN THOUSANDS OF DOLLARS

Item Description for Accounting Period 7/03 Through 6/04	Total	Zero Assets	Under 500	500 to 1,000	1,000 to 5,000	5,000 to 10,000	10,000 to 25,000	25,000 to 50,000	50,000 to 100,000	100,000 to 250,000	250,000 to 500,000	500,000 to 2,500,000	2,500,000 and over
Number of Enterprises **1**	89568	10826	73654	2812	1905	245	86	18	8	7	·	6	·
Revenues ($ in Thousands)													
Net Sales **2**	52268599	948750	30845383	4301212	6972083	937275	1870550	970759	793497	1046859	·	3582230	·
Interest **3**	120569	5058	12651	9142	28376	3388	7383	3593	3961	7116	·	39901	·
Rents **4**	301142	6305	18194	11055	61436	12182	20598	1989	605	15897	·	152882	·
Royalties **5**	7402	0	3043	0	49	0	0	0	0	0	·	4310	·
Other Portfolio Income **6**	326514	13955	12659	18565	123067	15315	4644	13351	929	3232	·	120796	·
Other Receipts **7**	51512972	923432	30798836	4262450	6759155	906390	1837925	951826	788002	1020614	·	3264341	·
Total Receipts **8**	52268599	948750	30845383	4301212	6972083	937275	1870550	970759	793497	1046859	·	3582230	·
Average Total Receipts **9**	584	88	419	1530	3660	3826	21751	53931	99187	149551	·	597038	·
Operating Costs/Operating Income (%)													
Cost of Operations **10**	19.5	12.3	17.3	31.8	10.3	47.2	35.8	23.6	48.2	49.9	·	10.9	·
Salaries and Wages **11**	24.8	13.9	23.0	16.0	32.3	14.9	28.5	18.8	9.4	11.4	·	48.7	·
Taxes Paid **12**	1.7	1.7	1.5	1.6	1.5	2.0	2.0	1.9	1.5	1.7	·	4.4	·
Interest Paid **13**	0.8	0.5	0.3	0.7	1.2	3.0	1.2	1.0	1.3	1.8	·	3.8	·
Depreciation **14**	1.2	1.0	1.0	0.8	1.1	3.3	1.7	1.8	1.7	2.4	·	2.2	·
Amortization and Depletion **15**	0.2	0.1	0.1	0.2	0.1	0.1	0.2	0.1	0.4	0.2	·	1.0	·
Pensions and Other Deferred Comp. **16**	1.1	1.1	1.6	0.8	0.5	0.3	0.2	0.4	0.1	0.6	·	0.1	·
Employee Benefits **17**	0.7	0.8	0.7	0.3	0.9	0.4	0.6	0.8	0.8	0.7	·	1.4	·
Advertising **18**	3.0	3.2	3.4	3.7	2.1	1.5	2.9	3.7	2.1	1.6	·	0.8	·
Other Expenses **19**	30.3	46.9	31.0	30.3	37.8	15.6	18.6	31.1	21.9	11.8	·	22.1	·
Officers' Compensation **20**	8.7	6.3	11.6	5.9	5.5	2.7	2.5	6.9	2.6	4.8	·	1.7	·
Operating Margin **21**	8.0	12.1	8.7	7.8	6.6	9.0	5.9	10.0	10.0	13.2	·	2.8	·
Operating Margin Before Officers' Comp. **22**	16.7	18.5	20.2	13.7	12.1	11.7	8.3	16.9	12.6	18.0	·	4.5	·

Selected Average Balance Sheet ($ in Thousands)

	1	2	3	4	5	6	7	8	9	10
Net Receivables 23	26	3	38	140	565	1788	4520	3401	7806	213309
Inventories 24	·	0	·	·	·	·	·	·	·	·
Net Property, Plant and Equipment 25	70	24	174	393	3320	4361	8368	12831	45075	245597
Total Assets 26	282	74	699	1988	7136	14706	37920	64055	182831	1424999
Notes and Loans Payable 27	107	35	215	1155	3525	6767	16044	26140	31523	339963
All Other Liabilities 28	88	18	134	550	915	3344	7034	12684	38590	681703
Net Worth 29	86	20	350	283	2695	4595	14842	25231	112718	403333

Selected Financial Ratios (Times to 1)

	1	2	3	4	5	6	7	8	9	10
Current Ratio 30	1.4	·	1.7	1.6	1.2	1.2	1.4	1.5	2.0	1.0
Quick Ratio 31	1.0	·	1.0	1.1	0.5	0.7	0.7	0.9	1.5	0.8
Net Sales to Working Capital 32	19.9	29.0	11.6	13.2	10.2	16.4	8.9	14.0	3.5	1.8
Coverage Ratio 33	10.5	28.6	23.8	12.0	6.5	4.0	5.7	11.0	8.7	8.3
Total Asset Turnover 34	2.1	·	5.7	2.2	1.8	0.5	1.5	1.4	1.5	0.8
Inventory Turnover 35	·	·	·	·	·	·	·	·	·	·
Receivables Turnover 36	·	·	·	·	·	·	·	·	·	·
Total Liabilities to Net Worth 37	2.3	2.7	1.0	2.8	1.6	2.2	1.6	1.5	0.6	2.5
Current Assets to Working Capital 38	3.7	2.4	2.4	2.8	6.5	5.0	3.3	3.1	2.0	·
Current Liabilities to Working Capital 39	2.7	1.4	1.4	1.8	5.5	4.0	2.3	2.1	1.0	·
Working Capital to Net Sales 40	0.1	0.0	0.1	0.1	0.1	0.1	0.1	0.1	0.3	·
Inventory to Working Capital 41	0.0	·	0.0	·	0.0	0.0	0.0	0.0	·	·
Total Receipts to Cash Flow 42	3.0	2.8	3.0	2.5	4.9	5.2	2.9	3.6	4.9	4.8
Cost of Goods to Cash Flow 43	0.6	0.5	0.9	0.3	2.3	1.9	0.7	1.7	2.5	0.5
Cash Flow to Total Debt 44	1.0	2.7	1.5	0.9	0.2	0.4	0.8	0.7	0.4	0.1

Selected Financial Factors (in Percentages)

	1	2	3	4	5	6	7	8	9	10
Debt Ratio 45	69.4	73.0	49.9	85.8	62.2	68.8	60.9	60.6	38.3	71.7
Return on Total Assets 46	18.4	50.9	18.6	14.4	6.4	10.5	15.6	17.5	12.3	2.8
Return on Equity Before Income Taxes 47	54.3	181.7	34.1	85.9	12.6	27.9	36.3	39.2	17.5	4.3
Return on Equity After Income Taxes 48	52.3	180.3	33.3	83.3	11.1	26.0	32.1	37.1	13.9	2.6
Profit Margin (Before Income Tax) 49	8.0	12.1	8.7	7.8	6.6	8.9	5.9	10.0	13.2	2.9
Profit Margin (After Income Tax) 50	7.7	11.5	8.6	7.6	6.4	7.9	5.5	8.8	10.5	1.7

323

Table II
Corporations with Net Income

OFFICES OF REAL ESTATE AGENTS AND BROKERS

MONEY AMOUNTS AND SIZE OF ASSETS IN THOUSANDS OF DOLLARS

Item Description for Accounting Period 7/03 Through 6/04	Total	Zero Assets	Under 500	500 to 1,000	1,000 to 5,000	5,000 to 10,000	10,000 to 25,000	25,000 to 50,000	50,000 to 100,000	100,000 to 250,000	250,000 to 500,000	500,000 to 2,500,000	2,500,000 and over
Number of Enterprises 1	61871	5941	52560	2038	1121	115	66	•	•	4	•	•	•
Revenues ($ in Thousands)													
Net Sales 2	42559616	623952	24366854	3915622	6417246	505129	1768202	•	•	1017904	•	•	•
Interest 3	88583	96	5981	7461	22110	2695	5129	•	•	4000	•	•	•
Rents 4	206905	0	8926	1254	36652	999	12306	•	•	0	•	•	•
Royalties 5	7402	0	3043	0	49	0	0			0			
Other Portfolio Income 6	292078	13761	11031	10747	115565	10624	3620	•	•	3193	•	•	•
Other Receipts 7	41964648	610095	24337873	3896160	6242870	490811	1747147	•	•	1010711	•	•	•
Total Receipts 8	42559616	623952	24366854	3915622	6417246	505129	1768202	•	•	1017904	•	•	•
Average Total Receipts 9	688	105	464	1921	5725	4392	26791	•	•	254476	•	•	•
Operating Costs/Operating Income (%)													
Cost of Operations 10	21.6	4.1	20.4	30.0	10.7	30.8	37.0	•	•	51.4	•	•	•
Salaries and Wages 11	21.3	10.5	18.4	16.0	33.1	14.3	29.2	•	•	11.6	•	•	•
Taxes Paid 12	1.6	2.0	1.4	1.5	1.4	1.9	1.9	•	•	1.3	•	•	•
Interest Paid 13	0.5	0.1	0.2	0.4	0.7	1.2	0.9	•	•	1.3	•	•	•
Depreciation 14	1.0	1.2	0.8	0.8	1.0	1.2	1.3	•	•	1.9	•	•	•
Amortization and Depletion 15	0.2	0.1	0.1	0.2	0.2	0.1	0.2	•	•	0.2	•	•	•
Pensions and Other Deferred Comp. 16	1.2	1.7	1.7	0.9	0.2	0.5	0.2	•	•	0.6	•	•	•
Employee Benefits 17	0.7	0.5	0.6	0.2	0.8	0.4	0.5	•	•	0.7	•	•	•
Advertising 18	2.7	1.8	3.0	3.7	2.1	1.9	3.0	•	•	1.7	•	•	•
Other Expenses 19	28.8	42.6	29.1	30.2	35.5	18.6	16.3	•	•	10.8	•	•	•
Officers' Compensation 20	8.6	6.4	11.6	6.1	5.2	2.1	2.4	•	•	4.8	•	•	•
Operating Margin 21	11.8	29.1	12.7	9.9	8.9	26.9	7.1	•	•	13.9	•	•	•
Operating Margin Before Officers' Comp. 22	20.4	35.5	24.3	16.1	14.1	29.0	9.5	•	•	18.7	•	•	•

Selected Average Balance Sheet ($ in Thousands)

Net Receivables 23	24	0	1	37	134	1123	1782	·	12832
Inventories 24	·	·	·	·	·	·	·	·	·
Net Property, Plant and Equipment 25	59	0	18	165	376	808	3410	·	15146
Total Assets 26	252	0	67	686	2102	6681	14459	·	180394
Notes and Loans Payable 27	80	0	19	186	954	1287	5693	·	14947
All Other Liabilities 28	74	0	17	145	648	1021	3886	·	65862
Net Worth 29	97	0	31	354	500	4373	4880	·	99585

Selected Financial Ratios (Times to 1)

Current Ratio 30	1.3	·	2.0	1.7	1.4	4.4	1.3	·	1.5
Quick Ratio 31	1.0	·	1.8	0.9	0.9	2.4	0.7	·	0.8
Net Sales to Working Capital 32	25.1	·	25.7	12.9	24.4	1.8	17.7	·	10.0
Coverage Ratio 33	23.4	402.5	61.7	24.2	13.0	23.2	8.7	·	11.9
Total Asset Turnover 34	2.7	·	6.9	2.8	2.7	0.7	1.9	·	1.4
Inventory Turnover 35	·	·	·	·	·	·	·	·	·
Receivables Turnover 36	·	·	·	·	·	·	·	·	·
Total Liabilities to Net Worth 37	1.6	·	1.2	0.9	3.2	0.5	2.0	·	0.8
Current Assets to Working Capital 38	3.9	·	2.0	2.4	3.6	1.3	4.8	·	3.2
Current Liabilities to Working Capital 39	2.9	·	1.0	1.4	2.6	0.3	3.8	·	2.2
Working Capital to Net Sales 40	0.0	·	0.0	0.1	0.0	0.6	0.1	·	0.1
Inventory to Working Capital 41	0.0	·	·	·	·	0.0	0.0	·	·
Total Receipts to Cash Flow 42	2.8	1.5	2.7	2.8	2.5	2.4	5.5	·	4.9
Cost of Goods to Cash Flow 43	0.6	0.1	0.5	0.8	0.3	0.8	2.0	·	2.5
Cash Flow to Total Debt 44	1.6	·	4.8	2.1	1.4	0.8	0.5	·	0.6

Selected Financial Factors (in Percentages)

Debt Ratio 45	61.3	·	54.4	48.3	76.2	34.5	66.3	·	44.8
Return on Total Assets 46	33.6	·	89.6	29.1	26.2	18.4	14.9	·	21.4
Return on Equity Before Income Taxes 47	83.2	·	193.3	53.9	101.7	26.9	38.9	·	35.5
Return on Equity After Income Taxes 48	80.8	·	192.0	52.8	99.2	24.9	36.7	·	28.3
Profit Margin (Before Income Tax) 49	11.8	29.0	12.7	9.9	8.9	26.7	7.1	·	13.9
Profit Margin (After Income Tax) 50	11.4	28.1	12.7	9.7	8.7	24.8	6.7	·	11.1

Table I

Corporations with and without Net Income

OTHER REAL ESTATE ACTIVITIES

MONEY AMOUNTS AND SIZE OF ASSETS IN THOUSANDS OF DOLLARS

Item Description for Accounting Period 7/03 Through 6/04	Total	Zero Assets	Under 500	500 to 1,000	1,000 to 5,000	5,000 to 10,000	10,000 to 25,000	25,000 to 50,000	50,000 to 100,000	100,000 to 250,000	250,000 to 500,000	500,000 to 2,500,000	2,500,000 and over
Number of Enterprises **1**	164427	23599	120765	7059	10489	1275	822	240	126	40	8	3	•
Revenues ($ in Thousands)													
Net Sales **2**	48564318	2068297	21077402	2156006	7731772	2975224	3788482	1859315	3227694	1572432	443817	1663877	•
Interest **3**	1187281	29009	561190	57654	96008	27541	68668	54194	47095	45060	37364	163501	•
Rents **4**	1411582	46877	231406	89050	300125	144387	216931	145394	151800	70948	9236	5428	•
Royalties **5**	45506	6610	1418	0	24325	3567	348	0	9227	10	0	0	
Other Portfolio Income **6**	1677967	285585	184430	144141	263991	156384	156024	86309	89020	128064	6736	177283	•
Other Receipts **7**	44241982	1700216	20098958	1865161	7047323	2643345	3346511	1573418	2930552	1328350	390481	1317665	•
Total Receipts **8**	48564318	2068297	21077402	2156006	7731772	2975224	3788482	1859315	3227694	1572432	443817	1663877	•
Average Total Receipts **9**	295	88	175	305	737	2334	4609	7747	25617	39311	55477	554626	•
Operating Costs/Operating Income (%)													
Cost of Operations **10**	11.2	27.7	6.1	3.5	17.4	12.8	19.7	19.3	7.8	14.4	27.3	4.4	•
Salaries and Wages **11**	22.5	6.4	24.0	22.7	23.0	17.1	21.6	21.4	24.0	22.1	20.4	32.6	•
Taxes Paid **12**	3.5	4.1	3.2	4.8	4.1	3.3	4.0	4.3	2.2	5.3	4.6	0.6	•
Interest Paid **13**	4.2	3.7	3.2	4.4	4.4	3.4	6.0	7.2	4.8	5.0	10.3	7.1	•
Depreciation **14**	2.4	3.9	1.5	5.8	2.4	2.3	3.0	4.7	3.0	3.9	7.1	1.1	•
Amortization and Depletion **15**	0.3	0.9	0.1	0.1	0.2	0.2	0.4	0.9	0.4	0.6	1.4	0.8	•
Pensions and Other Deferred Comp. **16**	0.7	0.0	0.9	2.4	0.6	0.3	0.4	0.9	0.2	0.8	0.2	0.5	•
Employee Benefits **17**	1.8	0.3	1.8	2.7	1.7	1.1	1.2	1.1	3.0	1.5	1.2	4.0	•
Advertising **18**	1.0	2.0	1.1	0.4	0.2	0.4	1.1	1.2	2.2	1.8	2.8	0.1	•
Other Expenses **19**	38.4	46.1	39.9	36.6	34.8	49.4	31.9	30.6	50.2	26.1	29.6	24.6	•
Officers' Compensation **20**	7.3	2.7	10.3	13.9	5.8	4.4	4.6	4.2	2.9	3.8	1.6	1.3	•
Operating Margin **21**	6.6	2.3	7.9	2.7	5.4	5.4	5.9	3.7	•	14.8	•	22.9	•
Operating Margin Before Officers' Comp. **22**	13.9	5.0	18.2	16.6	11.2	9.9	10.6	7.9	2.1	18.6	•	24.3	•

Selected Average Balance Sheet ($ in Thousands)

	1	2	3	4	5	6	7	8	9	10	11	12
Net Receivables 23	43	0	5	52	113	565	1192	2429	6067	7821	13826	490444
Inventories 24	•	•	•	•	•	•	•	•	•	•	•	•
Net Property, Plant and Equipment 25	143	0	23	207	612	1991	4327	10444	19106	30473	40231	101599
Total Assets 26	518	0	86	692	2001	6264	15121	34885	71055	144295	339856	906765
Notes and Loans Payable 27	251	0	64	396	1048	3379	7280	14852	29344	40824	49514	89884
All Other Liabilities 28	111	0	20	132	274	815	2783	9520	16204	44647	207509	295408
Net Worth 29	157	0	3	164	679	2070	5057	10513	25506	58824	82832	521473

Selected Financial Ratios (Times to 1)

	1	2	3	4	5	6	7	8	9	10	11	12
Current Ratio 30	1.9	•	2.1	2.0	2.7	2.0	1.7	1.5	1.3	1.4	1.0	2.1
Quick Ratio 31	1.2	•	1.6	1.2	1.6	1.1	1.0	0.9	0.8	0.8	0.7	1.9
Net Sales to Working Capital 32	3.4	•	7.5	2.1	1.7	2.6	2.2	2.1	6.7	2.7	24.3	1.7
Coverage Ratio 33	2.5	1.6	3.5	1.6	2.2	2.5	2.0	1.5	0.8	4.0	0.4	4.2
Total Asset Turnover 34	0.6	•	2.0	0.4	0.4	0.4	0.3	0.2	0.4	0.3	0.2	0.6
Inventory Turnover 35	•	•	•	•	•	•	•	•	•	•	•	•
Receivables Turnover 36	•	•	•	•	•	•	•	•	•	•	•	•
Total Liabilities to Net Worth 37	2.3	27.9	3.2	1.9	2.0	2.0	2.3	1.8	1.5	3.1		0.7
Current Assets to Working Capital 38	2.2	1.9	2.0	1.6	2.0	2.0	3.0	4.8	3.6	40.1		1.9
Current Liabilities to Working Capital 39	1.2	0.9	1.0	0.6	1.0	1.4	2.0	3.8	2.6	39.1		0.9
Working Capital to Net Sales 40	0.3	•	0.1	0.6	0.4	0.5	0.5	0.1	0.4	0.0	0.0	0.6
Inventory to Working Capital 41	0.0	•	•	0.0	0.0	0.0	0.0	0.1	0.0	2.2	0.0	0.2
Total Receipts to Cash Flow 42	3.1	3.4	2.8	3.7	3.5	3.9	3.5	4.2	3.0	3.4	5.4	2.2
Cost of Goods to Cash Flow 43	0.3	0.9	0.2	0.1	0.6	0.5	0.7	0.8	0.2	0.5	1.5	0.1
Cash Flow to Total Debt 44	0.3	0.7	0.7	0.2	0.2	0.1	0.1	0.1	0.2	0.1	0.0	0.7

Selected Financial Factors (in Percentages)

	1	2	3	4	5	6	7	8	9	10	11	12
Debt Ratio 45	69.8	96.5	76.3	66.1	67.0	66.6	69.9	64.1	59.2	75.6		42.5
Return on Total Assets 46	6.1	•	3.1	3.6	3.1	3.6	2.4	1.4	5.4	0.6		18.4
Return on Equity Before Income Taxes 47	12.3	22.5	5.0	5.8	5.6	5.3	2.5	6.7	9.8	•		24.4
Return on Equity After Income Taxes 48	10.1	461.8	2.4	4.8	4.2	3.7	1.3	•	8.0	•		16.0
Profit Margin (Before Income Tax) 49	6.5	443.7	2.7	5.4	5.0	5.8	3.4	•	14.7	•		22.9
Profit Margin (After Income Tax) 50	5.3	7.9	1.3	4.5	3.7	4.1	1.8	•	11.9	•		15.1

Table II
Corporations with Net Income

OTHER REAL ESTATE ACTIVITIES

MONEY AMOUNTS AND SIZE OF ASSETS IN THOUSANDS OF DOLLARS

Item Description for Accounting Period 7/03 Through 6/04	Total	Zero Assets	Under 500	500 to 1,000	1,000 to 5,000	5,000 to 10,000	10,000 to 25,000	25,000 to 50,000	50,000 to 100,000	100,000 to 250,000	250,000 to 500,000	500,000 to 2,500,000	2,500,000 and over
Number of Enterprises **1**	71936	7407	55463	3574	4444	456	386	119	55	24	4	3	•
Revenues ($ in Thousands)													
Net Sales **2**	35219350	1633707	15261389	1533716	6278788	2512160	2472377	1210126	1121508	1302141	229561	1663877	•
Interest **3**	1019950	18339	541112	55947	71651	17408	36805	34368	24356	32022	24442	163501	•
Rents **4**	799789	21673	112944	57332	139616	105531	121943	103190	107379	23947	806	5428	•
Royalties **5**	39784	3038	1418	0	24262	1864	227	0	8974	0	0	0	•
Other Portfolio Income **6**	1480412	267153	165305	143311	212715	134456	116113	77962	76854	105111	4153	177283	•
Other Receipts **7**	31879415	1323504	14440610	1277126	5830544	2252901	2197289	994606	903945	1141061	200160	1317665	•
Total Receipts **8**	35219350	1633707	15261389	1533716	6278788	2512160	2472377	1210126	1121508	1302141	229561	1663877	•
Average Total Receipts **9**	490	221	275	429	1413	5509	6405	10169	20391	54256	57390	554626	•
Operating Costs/Operating Income (%)													
Cost of Operations **10**	10.9	16.8	6.6	2.8	19.3	14.2	16.2	8.0	3.0	17.2	43.2	4.4	•
Salaries and Wages **11**	20.5	4.4	21.2	15.2	21.3	14.7	22.2	19.6	31.3	19.1	15.5	32.6	•
Taxes Paid **12**	2.9	1.9	2.6	3.8	3.8	2.4	3.8	4.1	4.2	3.0	3.7	0.6	•
Interest Paid **13**	3.8	1.0	3.9	3.4	3.2	2.2	3.8	4.9	5.9	4.7	10.3	7.1	•
Depreciation **14**	1.6	2.4	1.0	1.6	1.8	1.4	2.1	3.5	3.5	2.3	2.5	1.1	•
Amortization and Depletion **15**	0.2	0.7	0.1	0.1	0.2	0.2	0.2	0.5	0.5	0.7	0.1	0.8	•
Pensions and Other Deferred Comp. **16**	0.5	0.0	0.5	2.2	0.6	0.1	0.4	0.3	0.3	0.9	0.3	0.5	•
Employee Benefits **17**	1.3	0.3	1.2	1.8	1.1	0.7	1.1	1.3	1.6	1.5	0.2	4.0	•
Advertising **18**	0.9	0.7	1.1	0.3	0.2	0.3	1.2	1.3	2.7	2.0	0.3	0.1	•
Other Expenses **19**	32.0	38.0	35.9	29.2	27.6	44.2	22.0	29.1	24.7	21.2	13.4	24.6	•
Officers' Compensation **20**	6.4	1.8	7.9	13.5	6.0	3.9	5.3	4.3	5.8	4.0	1.8	1.3	•
Operating Margin **21**	19.0	31.9	18.0	26.1	14.9	15.8	21.6	23.0	16.6	23.3	8.8	22.9	•
Operating Margin Before Officers' Comp. **22**	25.4	33.7	25.9	39.6	20.9	19.7	26.9	27.3	22.4	27.3	10.6	24.3	•

Selected Average Balance Sheet ($ in Thousands)

	•	•	•	•	•	•	•	•	•	•	•	•
Net Receivables 23	59	0	·	37	122	982	1463	2419	4083	10758	7895	490444
Inventories 24	·	·	·	·	·	·	·	·	·	·	·	·
Net Property, Plant and Equipment 25	124	0	13	138	564	1565	3419	8813	21846	24024	2456	101599
Total Assets 26	571	0	88	694	2061	6459	15165	35223	70731	142512	393412	906765
Notes and Loans Payable 27	206	0	35	262	883	1804	6272	12909	27978	47449	70286	89884
All Other Liabilities 28	133	0	18	126	340	1323	3044	7667	15984	46310	249687	295408
Net Worth 29	233	0	35	306	839	3332	5848	14647	26769	48753	73438	521473

Selected Financial Ratios (Times to 1)

	•	•	•	•	•	•	•	•	•	•	•	•
Current Ratio 30	1.9	·	2.9	2.3	2.6	2.1	1.8	1.6	1.3	1.4	0.8	2.1
Quick Ratio 31	1.3	·	2.3	1.4	1.7	1.4	1.1	1.0	0.7	0.8	0.5	1.9
Net Sales to Working Capital 32	4.2	·	8.0	2.2	3.0	4.0	2.3	2.1	4.8	3.2	·	1.7
Coverage Ratio 33	6.0	32.8	5.7	8.7	5.6	8.1	6.7	5.6	3.8	5.9	1.8	4.2
Total Asset Turnover 34	0.9	·	3.1	0.6	0.7	0.9	0.4	0.3	0.3	0.4	0.1	0.6
Inventory Turnover 35	·	·	·	·	·	·	·	·	·	·	·	·
Receivables Turnover 36	·	·	·	·	·	·	·	·	·	·	·	·
Total Liabilities to Net Worth 37	1.5	·	1.5	1.3	1.5	0.9	1.6	1.4	1.6	1.9	4.4	0.7
Current Assets to Working Capital 38	2.1	·	1.5	1.7	1.6	1.9	2.2	2.7	4.1	3.7	·	1.9
Current Liabilities to Working Capital 39	1.1	·	0.5	0.7	0.6	0.9	1.2	1.7	3.1	2.7	·	0.9
Working Capital to Net Sales 40	0.2	·	0.1	0.5	0.3	0.3	0.4	0.5	0.2	0.3	0.1	0.6
Inventory to Working Capital 41	0.0	·	·	0.0	0.0	0.0	0.0	0.0	0.1	0.0	·	0.2
Total Receipts to Cash Flow 42	2.6	1.9	2.4	2.3	3.0	3.5	2.7	2.6	3.5	3.0	5.7	2.2
Cost of Goods to Cash Flow 43	0.3	0.3	0.2	0.1	0.6	0.5	0.4	0.2	0.1	0.5	2.5	0.1
Cash Flow to Total Debt 44	0.6	·	2.2	0.5	0.4	0.5	0.3	0.2	0.1	0.2	0.0	0.7

Selected Financial Factors (in Percentages)

	•	•	•	•	•	•	•	•	•	•	•	•
Debt Ratio 45	59.2	·	60.7	56.0	59.3	48.4	61.4	58.4	62.2	65.8	81.3	42.5
Return on Total Assets 46	19.5	·	68.5	18.3	12.4	15.1	10.7	8.0	6.5	10.6	2.8	18.4
Return on Equity Before Income Taxes 47	39.9	·	143.3	36.7	25.1	25.7	23.6	15.7	12.6	25.8	6.7	24.4
Return on Equity After Income Taxes 48	36.5	·	139.9	33.9	23.2	23.2	20.8	14.0	10.8	22.1	4.6	16.0
Profit Margin (Before Income Tax) 49	19.0	31.9	18.0	26.1	15.5	14.9	21.5	22.6	16.5	23.2	8.6	22.9
Profit Margin (After Income Tax) 50	17.4	27.4	17.6	24.1	14.0	13.8	19.0	20.2	14.1	19.9	5.9	15.1

Table I
Corporations with and without Net Income

AUTOMOTIVE EQUIPMENT RENTAL AND LEASING

MONEY AMOUNTS AND SIZE OF ASSETS IN THOUSANDS OF DOLLARS

Item Description for Accounting Period 7/03 Through 6/04	Total	Zero Assets	Under 500	500 to 1,000	1,000 to 5,000	5,000 to 10,000	10,000 to 25,000	25,000 to 50,000	50,000 to 100,000	100,000 to 250,000	250,000 to 500,000	500,000 to 2,500,000	2,500,000 and over
Number of Enterprises **1**	9257	1034	5876	785	1234	98	139	48	18	12	3	4	5
Revenues ($ in Thousands)													
Net Sales **2**	40677510	108174	517232	363818	2596258	462905	1911427	1015899	744252	4062987	403911	3525651	24964996
Interest **3**	909332	0	2085	415	509	2684	3590	1852	3251	12428	1047	15841	865630
Rents **4**	258786	0	0	299	2149	174	2082	2384	478	9014	923	517	240765
Royalties **5**	16147	343	0	0	0	0	0	0	0	1068	1268	0	13468
Other Portfolio Income **6**	1322855	3324	27870	12403	154031	41378	172617	159120	65656	199615	35875	48159	402806
Other Receipts **7**	38170390	104507	487277	350701	2439569	418669	1733138	852543	674867	3840862	364798	3461134	23442327
Total Receipts **8**	40677510	108174	517232	363818	2596258	462905	1911427	1015899	744252	4062987	403911	3525651	24964996
Average Total Receipts **9**	4394	105	88	463	2104	4724	13751	21165	41347	338582	134637	881413	4992999
Operating Costs/Operating Income (%)													
Cost of Operations **10**	38.6	40.8	7.2	39.7	16.9	20.1	36.7	21.5	32.8	30.8	1.6	30.6	45.9
Salaries and Wages **11**	10.2	1.8	10.0	10.0	13.2	8.5	8.4	7.9	8.4	9.0	12.1	4.8	11.2
Taxes Paid **12**	2.3	0.8	3.0	1.9	4.7	2.8	1.9	2.4	2.3	1.7	1.3	0.6	2.4
Interest Paid **13**	5.4	1.8	4.2	3.9	3.3	6.2	5.0	5.8	5.3	5.8	2.6	3.8	5.9
Depreciation **14**	23.1	17.0	29.2	11.8	27.7	30.9	32.5	42.9	32.0	22.7	84.4	61.9	14.4
Amortization and Depletion **15**	0.2	0.0	1.1	0.0	0.3	0.1	0.1	0.1	0.3	0.7	0.4	0.3	0.1
Pensions and Other Deferred Comp. **16**	0.5	0.0	0.1	•	0.1	0.1	0.1	0.2	0.1	0.7	0.1	0.1	0.7
Employee Benefits **17**	1.2	0.1	1.8	0.1	0.6	0.7	0.6	0.8	0.6	0.7	0.9	0.6	1.4
Advertising **18**	0.8	0.8	0.6	3.5	2.3	1.0	0.9	0.6	0.7	1.4	0.2	0.3	0.6
Other Expenses **19**	21.8	27.5	48.1	14.7	33.5	28.7	12.7	14.1	19.9	31.2	15.8	3.5	22.1
Officers' Compensation **20**	0.7	16.1	6.7	4.9	2.6	1.1	1.6	1.4	1.7	0.5	0.5	0.3	0.3
Operating Margin **21**	•	•	•	9.5	•	•	•	2.3	•	•	•	•	•
Operating Margin Before Officers' Comp. **22**	•	9.4	•	14.4	•	1.0	•	3.7	•	•	•	•	•

Selected Average Balance Sheet ($ in Thousands)

Item													
Net Receivables 23	382	0	12	31	211	209	1535	4389	6255	31310	18706	115464	345795
Inventories 24	•	•	•	•	•	•	•	•	•	•	•	•	•
Net Property, Plant and Equipment 25	3149	0	55	241	1636	4167	9822	21854	46459	81433	221359	868046	3569475
Total Assets 26	4777	0	112	745	2136	7439	15572	34865	72428	151412	335736	1410510	5201569
Notes and Loans Payable 27	2522	0	91	246	1319	4933	10773	25067	47154	103580	475511	1165002	1925114
All Other Liabilities 28	1397	0	6	79	175	1872	1445	4047	12312	59081	39512	152821	2075630
Net Worth 29	859	0	15	421	642	633	3354	5751	12962	-11248	-179287	92687	1200825

Selected Financial Ratios (Times to 1)

Item													
Current Ratio 30	0.5	•	1.9	4.5	1.2	0.7	0.8	0.7	1.2	0.6	1.1	0.3	0.4
Quick Ratio 31	0.3	•	1.5	3.3	1.0	0.5	0.5	0.6	0.8	0.3	0.5	0.2	0.3
Net Sales to Working Capital 32	•	•	5.3	2.0	23.9	•	•	14.9	•	•	7.0	•	•
Coverage Ratio 33	0.1	•	•	3.4	•	1.0	1.4	0.2	0.2	0.1	•	•	0.2
Total Asset Turnover 34	0.9	•	0.8	0.6	1.0	0.6	0.9	0.6	0.6	2.2	0.4	0.6	1.0
Inventory Turnover 35	•	•	•	•	•	•	•	•	•	•	•	•	•
Receivables Turnover 36	•	•	•	•	•	•	•	•	•	•	•	•	•
Total Liabilities to Net Worth 37	4.6	•	6.4	0.8	2.3	10.7	3.6	5.1	4.6	•	•	14.2	3.3
Current Assets to Working Capital 38	•	•	2.1	1.3	5.1	•	•	5.3	•	•	8.5	•	•
Current Liabilities to Working Capital 39	•	•	1.1	0.3	4.1	•	•	4.3	•	•	7.5	•	•
Working Capital to Net Sales 40	•	•	0.2	0.5	0.0	•	•	0.1	•	•	0.1	•	•
Inventory to Working Capital 41	•	•	0.2	0.1	0.3	•	•	0.9	•	•	0.0	•	•
Total Receipts to Cash Flow 42	11.4	10.9	5.7	5.7	21.5	6.6	13.2	9.2	16.3	5.2	•	10.6	•
Cost of Goods to Cash Flow 43	4.4	4.5	0.4	2.3	3.6	1.3	4.8	2.0	5.4	1.6	•	4.9	•
Cash Flow to Total Debt 44	0.1	•	0.2	0.2	0.1	0.1	0.1	0.1	0.0	0.4	0.1	0.1	0.1

Selected Financial Factors (in Percentages)

Item													
Debt Ratio 45	82.0	•	86.5	43.6	70.0	91.5	78.5	83.5	82.1	107.4	153.4	93.4	76.9
Return on Total Assets 46	0.6	•	•	8.3	4.0	3.9	•	4.9	0.7	1.6	•	0.9	•
Return on Equity Before Income Taxes 47	•	•	10.5	•	•	•	•	8.5	•	152.2	14.8	•	•
Return on Equity After Income Taxes 48	•	•	9.5	•	•	•	•	4.4	•	152.9	14.8	•	•
Profit Margin (Before Income Tax) 49	•	•	9.5	•	•	•	•	2.3	•	•	•	•	•
Profit Margin (After Income Tax) 50	•	•	8.6	•	•	•	•	1.2	•	•	•	•	•

Table II

Corporations with Net Income

AUTOMOTIVE EQUIPMENT RENTAL AND LEASING

MONEY AMOUNTS AND SIZE OF ASSETS IN THOUSANDS OF DOLLARS

Item Description for Accounting Period 7/03 Through 6/04	Total	Zero Assets	Under 500	500 to 1,000	1,000 to 5,000	5,000 to 10,000	10,000 to 25,000	25,000 to 50,000	50,000 to 100,000	100,000 to 250,000	250,000 to 500,000	500,000 to 2,500,000	2,500,000 and over
Number of Enterprises 1	3896	•	1920	756	454	28	67	16	•	6	•	•	•
Revenues ($ in Thousands)													
Net Sales 2	13272530	•	212964	362264	1235257	158432	1268382	413545	•	840016	•	•	•
Interest 3	401659	•	251	415	317	2455	1757	1286	•	10414	•	•	•
Rents 4	93712	•	0	299	489	174	2072	2377	•	9001	•	•	•
Royalties 5	1611	•	0	0	0	0	0	0	•	1268	•	•	•
Other Portfolio Income 6	537818	•	27870	12403	107252	17173	105151	100789	•	30335	•	•	•
Other Receipts 7	12237730	•	184843	349147	1127199	138630	1159402	309093	•	788998	•	•	•
Total Receipts 8	13272530	•	212964	362264	1235257	158432	1268382	413545	•	840016	•	•	•
Average Total Receipts 9	3407	•	111	479	2721	5658	18931	25847	•	140003	•	•	•
Operating Costs/Operating Income (%)													
Cost of Operations 10	20.3	•	15.2	39.8	15.2	20.2	41.0	25.7	•	10.3	•	•	•
Salaries and Wages 11	10.8	•	3.1	10.1	7.7	9.8	7.9	7.1	•	14.8	•	•	•
Taxes Paid 12	3.1	•	1.9	1.9	3.0	2.3	1.5	2.6	•	2.7	•	•	•
Interest Paid 13	5.4	•	5.8	3.9	3.4	1.4	4.8	5.4	•	2.6	•	•	•
Depreciation 14	16.9	•	37.8	11.6	30.9	15.6	26.5	22.5	•	6.1	•	•	•
Amortization and Depletion 15	0.2	•	0.0	0.0	0.6	0.0	0.1	0.1	•	0.2	•	•	•
Pensions and Other Deferred Comp. 16	1.2	•	•	•	0.1	0.0	0.2	0.1	•	3.0	•	•	•
Employee Benefits 17	1.6	•	1.1	0.1	0.4	1.0	0.6	1.2	•	2.8	•	•	•
Advertising 18	0.7	•	0.9	3.5	0.8	0.4	0.9	0.4	•	0.1	•	•	•
Other Expenses 19	35.5	•	20.9	14.5	30.4	24.8	11.1	10.9	•	53.8	•	•	•
Officers' Compensation 20	1.0	•	2.3	4.9	2.5	1.5	1.5	1.3	•	0.7	•	•	•
Operating Margin 21	3.5	•	11.1	9.6	5.0	22.8	3.9	22.9	•	3.0	•	•	•
Operating Margin Before Officers' Comp. 22	4.5	•	13.4	14.4	7.6	24.3	5.3	24.2	•	3.6	•	•	•

Selected Average Balance Sheet ($ in Thousands)

Net Receivables 23	369	•	26	28	106	347	1849	5969	54051
Inventories 24	•	•	•	•	•	•	•	•	•
Net Property, Plant and Equipment 25	1754	•	83	232	1944	1750	8512	17206	47821
Total Assets 26	3758	•	161	736	2406	7273	15544	35695	183435
Notes and Loans Payable 27	1972	•	141	256	1411	2993	9634	19417	236243
All Other Liabilities 28	1042	•	11	25	303	625	1747	6412	37746
Net Worth 29	744	•	9	455	692	3655	4163	9866	-90554

Selected Financial Ratios (Times to 1)

Current Ratio 30	0.8	•	2.1	4.4	1.3	2.2	0.8	1.0	2.6
Quick Ratio 31	0.5	•	1.7	3.2	0.7	1.6	0.5	0.8	1.7
Net Sales to Working Capital 32	•	•	2.7	2.0	25.5	2.7	•	•	1.7
Coverage Ratio 33	1.7	•	2.9	3.4	2.5	17.2	1.8	5.3	2.1
Total Asset Turnover 34	0.9	•	0.7	0.7	1.1	0.8	1.2	0.7	0.8
Inventory Turnover 35	•	•	•	•	•	•	•	•	•
Receivables Turnover 36	•	•	•	•	•	•	•	•	•
Total Liabilities to Net Worth 37	4.1	•	17.5	0.6	2.5	1.0	2.7	2.6	•
Current Assets to Working Capital 38	•	•	1.9	1.3	3.9	1.8	•	•	1.6
Current Liabilities to Working Capital 39	•	•	0.9	0.3	2.9	0.8	•	•	0.6
Working Capital to Net Sales 40	•	•	0.4	0.5	0.0	0.4	•	•	0.6
Inventory to Working Capital 41	•	•	0.3	0.1	0.6	0.2	•	•	0.0
Total Receipts to Cash Flow 42	4.5	•	3.3	5.7	8.8	3.1	8.9	3.3	2.8
Cost of Goods to Cash Flow 43	0.9	•	0.5	2.3	1.3	0.6	3.7	0.8	0.3
Cash Flow to Total Debt 44	0.3	•	0.2	0.3	0.2	0.5	0.2	0.3	0.2

Selected Financial Factors (in Percentages)

Debt Ratio 45	80.2	•	94.6	38.1	71.2	49.7	73.2	72.4	149.4
Return on Total Assets 46	8.0	•	11.6	8.8	9.5	18.8	10.6	20.4	4.3
Return on Equity Before Income Taxes 47	16.1	•	141.3	10.1	19.8	35.3	17.5	59.9	•
Return on Equity After Income Taxes 48	14.6	•	136.0	9.1	18.3	27.6	17.2	52.6	•
Profit Margin (Before Income Tax) 49	3.5	•	11.1	9.6	5.0	22.8	3.9	22.9	3.0
Profit Margin (After Income Tax) 50	3.2	•	10.7	8.6	4.7	17.8	3.8	20.1	2.9

Table I

Corporations with and without Net Income

OTHER CONSUMER GOODS AND GENERAL RENTAL CENTERS

MONEY AMOUNTS AND SIZE OF ASSETS IN THOUSANDS OF DOLLARS

Item Description for Accounting Period 7/03 Through 6/04	Total	Zero Assets	Under 500	500 to 1,000	1,000 to 5,000	5,000 to 10,000	10,000 to 25,000	25,000 to 50,000	50,000 to 100,000	100,000 to 250,000	250,000 to 500,000	500,000 to 2,500,000	2,500,000 and over
Number of Enterprises **1**	12496	1046	10080	932	274	99	35	11	11	3	5	•	•
Revenues ($ in Thousands)													
Net Sales **2**	11865069	42766	3097538	1419772	653163	931543	617675	334950	531821	623651	3612190	•	•
Interest **3**	9548	48	316	1066	1348	1175	1388	478	1588	54	2088	•	•
Rents **4**	11590	0	5557	0	5	280	4341	0	0	1045	364	•	•
Royalties **5**	2848	0	0	0	0	2848	0	0	0	0	0	•	•
Other Portfolio Income **6**	69774	14	5176	8951	2657	281	7043	3560	4147	241	37704	•	•
Other Receipts **7**	11771309	42704	3086489	1409755	649153	926959	604903	330912	526086	622311	3572034	•	•
Total Receipts **8**	11865069	42766	3097538	1419772	653163	931543	617675	334950	531821	623651	3612190	•	•
Average Total Receipts **9**	950	41	307	1523	2384	9410	17648	30450	48347	207884	722438	•	•
Operating Costs/Operating Income (%)													
Cost of Operations **10**	25.0	48.5	21.8	22.9	33.9	19.2	42.3	37.1	10.2	17.1	27.7	•	•
Salaries and Wages **11**	20.9	10.7	21.1	24.0	19.3	26.1	14.7	16.7	18.6	24.6	19.8	•	•
Taxes Paid **12**	3.5	5.5	3.7	3.6	3.9	3.0	3.0	2.7	2.2	3.4	3.8	•	•
Interest Paid **13**	2.0	0.0	1.0	1.5	5.1	1.4	2.1	2.5	4.0	1.0	2.5	•	•
Depreciation **14**	10.4	5.5	9.5	8.2	5.0	10.9	12.3	14.1	22.9	11.7	10.1	•	•
Amortization and Depletion **15**	3.5	0.0	0.1	0.2	3.6	0.1	0.8	0.4	1.7	9.9	8.4	•	•
Pensions and Other Deferred Comp. **16**	0.2	0.1	0.1	0.2	0.3	0.5	0.3	0.5	0.0	0.2	0.1	•	•
Employee Benefits **17**	1.2	1.0	1.0	1.0	0.5	2.4	1.6	1.3	1.4	0.8	1.1	•	•
Advertising **18**	2.5	0.3	2.4	2.1	0.9	2.6	1.8	2.1	12.1	3.7	1.6	•	•
Other Expenses **19**	27.5	31.5	32.2	26.8	19.0	27.3	19.4	26.9	30.1	24.8	27.0	•	•
Officers' Compensation **20**	3.3	•	5.7	5.4	4.5	3.5	2.2	2.6	1.2	2.3	0.7	•	•
Operating Margin **21**	0.0	•	1.4	3.9	3.8	3.1	•	•	•	0.6	•	•	•
Operating Margin Before Officers' Comp. **22**	3.3	•	7.1	9.4	8.3	6.5	1.8	•	•	2.9	•	•	•

Selected Average Balance Sheet ($ in Thousands)

Net Receivables 23	45	0	7	59	113	999	2600	3998	5566	7048	18316
Inventories 24	•	•	•	•	•	•	•	•	•	•	•
Net Property, Plant and Equipment 25	338	0	74	532	1167	3016	6779	12900	32615	74975	278813
Total Assets 26	660	0	125	787	2488	5838	15131	32968	67786	178025	562951
Notes and Loans Payable 27	361	0	96	820	1561	2903	6353	29995	43947	40756	181882
All Other Liabilities 28	128	0	13	48	240	776	3924	5680	11795	51653	160991
Net Worth 29	170	0	17	-81	687	2159	4854	-2707	12044	85617	220078

Selected Financial Ratios (Times to 1)

Current Ratio 30	1.1	•	2.1	1.6	2.6	1.6	1.2	0.6	0.8	1.2	0.8
Quick Ratio 31	0.6	•	1.3	1.0	1.2	0.7	0.8	0.4	0.5	0.9	0.3
Net Sales to Working Capital 32	48.9	•	14.5	17.2	5.7	10.2	16.6	•	•	22.8	•
Coverage Ratio 33	1.0	•	2.4	3.6	1.8	3.2	0.8	•	•	1.6	•
Total Asset Turnover 34	1.4	•	2.5	1.9	1.0	1.6	1.2	0.9	0.7	1.2	1.3
Inventory Turnover 35	•	•	•	•	•	•	•	•	•	•	•
Receivables Turnover 36	•	•	•	•	•	•	•	•	•	•	•
Total Liabilities to Net Worth 37	2.9	•	6.4	2.6	2.6	1.7	2.1	•	4.6	1.1	1.6
Current Assets to Working Capital 38	9.9	•	1.9	2.7	1.6	2.8	5.1	•	•	7.3	•
Current Liabilities to Working Capital 39	8.9	•	0.9	1.7	0.6	1.8	4.1	•	•	6.3	•
Working Capital to Net Sales 40	0.0	•	0.1	0.1	0.2	0.1	0.1	•	•	0.0	•
Inventory to Working Capital 41	2.5	•	0.5	0.4	0.8	0.7	1.0	•	•	0.9	•
Total Receipts to Cash Flow 42	6.7	5.0	5.3	4.8	6.7	7.6	7.8	7.0	9.7	5.5	9.8
Cost of Goods to Cash Flow 43	1.7	2.4	1.1	1.1	2.3	1.5	3.3	2.6	1.0	0.9	2.7
Cash Flow to Total Debt 44	0.3	•	0.5	0.4	0.2	0.3	0.2	0.1	0.1	0.4	0.2

Selected Financial Factors (in Percentages)

Debt Ratio 45	74.2	•	86.5	110.3	72.4	63.0	67.9	108.2	82.2	51.9	60.9
Return on Total Assets 46	2.9	•	5.6	10.5	8.5	7.2	2.0	•	•	1.9	•
Return on Equity Before Income Taxes 47	0.2	•	24.1	13.2	13.2	13.4	78.6	•	•	1.4	•
Return on Equity After Income Taxes 48	•	•	22.1	•	9.0	13.2	78.6	•	•	•	•
Profit Margin (Before Income Tax) 49	0.0	•	1.3	3.9	3.8	3.1	•	•	•	0.6	•
Profit Margin (After Income Tax) 50	•	•	1.2	3.8	2.6	3.0	•	•	•	•	•

OTHER CONSUMER GOODS AND GENERAL RENTAL CENTERS

Table II
Corporations with Net Income

MONEY AMOUNTS AND SIZE OF ASSETS IN THOUSANDS OF DOLLARS

Item Description for Accounting Period 7/03 Through 6/04	Total	Zero Assets	Under 500	500 to 1,000	1,000 to 5,000	5,000 to 10,000	10,000 to 25,000	25,000 to 50,000	50,000 to 100,000	100,000 to 250,000	250,000 to 500,000	500,000 to 2,500,000	2,500,000 and over
Number of Enterprises 1	6497	•	5637	•	197	•	18	6	•	3	•	•	•
Revenues ($ in Thousands)													
Net Sales 2	6950524	•	2346403	•	410012	•	324856	274624	•	1624932	•	•	•
Interest 3	2234	•	272	•	142	•	247	255	•	268	•	•	•
Rents 4	11447	•	5557	•	0	•	4226	0	•	1385	•	•	•
Royalties 5	2848	•	0	•	0	•	0	0	•	0	•	•	•
Other Portfolio Income 6	15323	•	1832	•	1621	•	2139	187	•	334	•	•	•
Other Receipts 7	6918672	•	2338742	•	408249	•	318244	274182	•	1622945	•	•	•
Total Receipts 8	6950524	•	2346403	•	410012	•	324856	274624	•	1624932	•	•	•
Average Total Receipts 9	1070	•	416	•	2081	•	18048	45771	•	541644	•	•	•
Operating Costs/Operating Income (%)													
Cost of Operations 10	25.4	•	23.8	•	30.9	•	38.8	17.8	•	27.5	•	•	•
Salaries and Wages 11	19.3	•	17.3	•	14.7	•	13.9	17.1	•	20.7	•	•	•
Taxes Paid 12	3.4	•	3.4	•	4.1	•	3.0	2.6	•	3.4	•	•	•
Interest Paid 13	1.4	•	1.0	•	7.2	•	2.2	1.6	•	0.6	•	•	•
Depreciation 14	9.9	•	7.3	•	6.1	•	13.9	11.6	•	13.6	•	•	•
Amortization and Depletion 15	1.5	•	0.1	•	5.0	•	0.2	0.6	•	4.6	•	•	•
Pensions and Other Deferred Comp. 16	0.2	•	0.2	•	0.5	•	0.3	0.1	•	0.1	•	•	•
Employee Benefits 17	1.1	•	1.0	•	0.8	•	1.8	1.1	•	0.8	•	•	•
Advertising 18	2.9	•	2.4	•	1.2	•	2.0	22.0	•	1.3	•	•	•
Other Expenses 19	25.1	•	30.6	•	13.5	•	18.1	17.1	•	23.5	•	•	•
Officers' Compensation 20	4.4	•	6.2	•	6.3	•	1.8	1.9	•	1.3	•	•	•
Operating Margin 21	5.3	•	6.7	•	9.8	•	4.0	6.4	•	2.7	•	•	•
Operating Margin Before Officers' Comp. 22	9.7	•	12.9	•	16.1	•	5.8	8.3	•	4.0	•	•	•

Selected Average Balance Sheet ($ in Thousands)

	1	2	3	4	5	6
Net Receivables 23	49	11	147	2286	7443	11958
Inventories 24						
Net Property, Plant and Equipment 25	346	64	1463	7525	18380	276952
Total Assets 26	608	129	2629	15650	41574	403494
Notes and Loans Payable 27	248	63	1818	6956	15702	51142
All Other Liabilities 28	110	17	202	3374	9164	120793
Net Worth 29	251	49	609	5321	16708	231559

Selected Financial Ratios (Times to 1)

	1	2	3	4	5	6
Current Ratio 30	1.4	2.1	2.4	1.6	2.4	0.4
Quick Ratio 31	0.9	1.5	1.9	1.0	1.6	0.3
Net Sales to Working Capital 32	20.5	14.0	6.9	7.9	3.9	5.3
Coverage Ratio 33	4.6	7.9	2.4	2.8	5.0	1.3
Total Asset Turnover 34	1.8	3.2	0.8	1.2	1.1	
Inventory Turnover 35						
Receivables Turnover 36						
Total Liabilities to Net Worth 37	1.4	1.6	3.3	1.9	1.5	0.7
Current Assets to Working Capital 38	3.5	1.9	1.7	2.6	1.7	
Current Liabilities to Working Capital 39	2.5	0.9	0.7	1.6	0.7	
Working Capital to Net Sales 40	0.0	0.1	0.1	0.1	0.3	
Inventory to Working Capital 41	0.8	0.5	0.2	0.5	0.5	0.5
Total Receipts to Cash Flow 42	5.0	4.1	5.8	6.6	5.1	6.7
Cost of Goods to Cash Flow 43	1.3	1.0	1.8	2.6	0.9	1.8
Cash Flow to Total Debt 44	0.6	1.3	0.2	0.3	0.4	0.5

Selected Financial Factors (in Percentages)

	1	2	3	4	5	6
Debt Ratio 45	58.8	61.7	76.8	66.0	59.8	42.6
Return on Total Assets 46	11.8	24.5	13.4	7.1	8.8	4.4
Return on Equity Before Income Taxes 47	22.4	55.8	33.3	13.4	17.5	6.2
Return on Equity After Income Taxes 48	20.6	54.6	26.8	13.1	17.3	4.1
Profit Margin (Before Income Tax) 49	5.2	6.6	9.8	4.0	6.4	2.7
Profit Margin (After Income Tax) 50	4.8	6.5	7.8	3.9	6.3	1.7

COMMERCIAL AND INDUSTRIAL MACHINERY AND EQUIPMENT RENTAL

Table I
Corporations with and without Net Income

MONEY AMOUNTS AND SIZE OF ASSETS IN THOUSANDS OF DOLLARS

Item Description for Accounting Period 7/03 Through 6/04	Total	Zero Assets	Under 500	500 to 1,000	1,000 to 5,000	5,000 to 10,000	10,000 to 25,000	25,000 to 50,000	50,000 to 100,000	100,000 to 250,000	250,000 to 500,000	500,000 to 2,500,000	2,500,000 and over
Number of Enterprises **1**	29147	3288	19605	2309	2936	526	249	108	44	37	15	20	10
Revenues ($ in Thousands)													
Net Sales **2**	3631823	498290	2741751	1741779	4335483	2832578	2512650	2445014	1151656	3170704	1255851	3681774	9951295
Interest **3**	984570	6656	5408	3627	20081	2785	11689	21714	50227	126484	72057	315114	348727
Rents **4**	52460	42	6029	161	677	5616	1186	2698	29499	171	2473	3638	270
Royalties **5**	52626	0	0	0	60	0	1193	211	0	4972	0	0	46190
Other Portfolio Income **6**	1448088	40399	121307	13264	100884	26231	93939	111809	49818	113388	19278	208959	548815
Other Receipts **7**	33781079	451193	2609007	1724727	4213781	2797946	2404643	2308582	1022112	2925689	1162043	3154063	9007293
Total Receipts **8**	3631823	498290	2741751	1741779	4335483	2832578	2512650	2445014	1151656	3170704	1255851	3681774	9951295
Average Total Receipts **9**	1246	152	140	754	1477	5385	10091	22639	26174	85695	83723	184089	995130
Operating Costs/Operating Income (%)													
Cost of Operations **10**	23.8	35.4	15.3	17.3	37.8	37.1	36.7	33.1	35.1	29.4	5.8	11.7	14.9
Salaries and Wages **11**	11.6	10.8	15.2	15.4	11.3	10.7	10.6	8.4	10.0	11.8	11.1	11.6	11.6
Taxes Paid **12**	2.2	2.6	3.9	2.6	2.6	4.0	2.4	1.6	1.9	1.7	1.5	1.4	1.7
Interest Paid **13**	8.4	7.6	2.7	3.3	4.2	3.0	4.5	4.1	9.2	7.2	10.7	12.8	14.8
Depreciation **14**	26.9	20.6	16.6	21.5	19.5	19.7	23.0	24.3	26.0	25.6	69.0	29.3	32.3
Amortization and Depletion **15**	0.7	0.5	0.1	0.0	0.1	0.3	0.2	0.2	0.6	0.9	0.4	1.0	1.5
Pensions and Other Deferred Comp. **16**	0.3	0.1	0.1	0.5	0.4	0.7	0.4	0.2	0.2	0.3	0.3	0.2	0.3
Employee Benefits **17**	1.6	0.4	1.4	1.2	1.0	0.9	1.2	0.7	2.4	1.2	1.5	2.1	2.5
Advertising **18**	0.5	0.5	1.6	0.8	0.3	0.8	0.4	0.4	0.4	0.3	1.1	0.4	0.3
Other Expenses **19**	25.2	21.0	34.0	28.8	24.9	20.9	19.9	26.9	15.9	25.6	23.3	31.7	23.6
Officers' Compensation **20**	2.5	1.0	9.3	5.4	3.7	4.6	2.5	1.8	1.4	1.6	1.3	1.0	0.5
Operating Margin **21**	•	•	3.2	•	•	•	•	•	•	•	•	•	•
Operating Margin Before Officers' Comp. **22**	•	0.5	9.2	8.6	•	1.7	0.7	•	•	•	•	•	•

Selected Average Balance Sheet ($ in Thousands)

Net Receivables 23	580	0	20	51	393	559	2077	4740	11104	18319	72251	197527	772863
Inventories 24	•	•	•	•	•	•	•	•	•	•	•	•	•
Net Property, Plant and Equipment 25	1250	0	67	434	844	4454	7639	14797	26884	66438	130201	189178	1641163
Total Assets 26	3332	0	132	696	2065	6855	14929	34477	71148	160363	313492	936592	4330892
Notes and Loans Payable 27	1639	0	79	698	1122	4883	8449	18387	38752	104258	163492	372662	1917098
All Other Liabilities 28	835	0	10	53	353	761	2293	6776	14170	36824	73091	233805	1351421
Net Worth 29	859	0	43	-56	591	1211	4186	9315	18226	19281	76909	330125	1062373

Selected Financial Ratios (Times to 1)

Current Ratio 30	1.6	•	2.2	2.0	1.7	1.4	1.1	1.5	1.5	1.1	1.3	1.8	1.6
Quick Ratio 31	1.1	•	1.9	1.5	1.0	0.9	0.7	0.9	1.1	0.7	1.1	1.4	1.2
Net Sales to Working Capital 32	3.4	•	5.3	8.1	3.9	10.3	18.0	6.4	3.5	20.6	3.4	1.4	2.2
Coverage Ratio 33	0.6	0.9	1.0	2.0	•	0.1	0.6	0.6	0.6	0.3	•	1.1	0.7
Total Asset Turnover 34	0.4	•	1.1	1.1	0.7	0.8	0.7	0.7	0.4	0.5	0.3	0.2	0.2
Inventory Turnover 35	•	•	•	•	•	•	•	•	•	•	•	•	•
Receivables Turnover 36	•	•	•	•	•	•	•	•	•	•	•	•	•
Total Liabilities to Net Worth 37	2.9	•	2.1	2.5	2.6	4.7	2.6	2.7	2.9	7.3	3.1	1.8	3.1
Current Assets to Working Capital 38	2.8	•	1.9	2.4	2.4	3.3	8.2	3.1	3.0	11.4	4.2	2.3	2.6
Current Liabilities to Working Capital 39	1.8	•	0.9	1.4	1.0	2.3	7.2	2.1	2.0	10.4	3.2	1.3	1.6
Working Capital to Net Sales 40	0.3	•	0.2	0.3	0.1	0.1	0.1	0.2	0.3	0.0	0.3	0.7	0.5
Inventory to Working Capital 41	0.2	•	0.1	0.4	0.2	0.1	1.4	0.5	0.3	1.5	0.2	0.1	0.1
Total Receipts to Cash Flow 42	11.1	12.0	4.4	5.0	12.0	13.4	13.1	11.1	13.5	12.0	•	7.6	16.2
Cost of Goods to Cash Flow 43	2.6	4.2	0.7	0.9	4.5	5.0	4.8	3.7	4.7	3.5	•	0.9	2.4
Cash Flow to Total Debt 44	0.0	•	0.4	0.2	0.1	0.1	0.1	0.1	0.0	0.1	•	0.0	0.0

Selected Financial Factors (in Percentages)

Debt Ratio 45	74.2	•	67.6	108.1	71.4	82.3	72.0	73.0	74.4	88.0	75.5	64.8	75.5
Return on Total Assets 46	1.9	•	2.8	7.0	•	0.1	1.8	1.7	2.2	1.0	•	2.7	2.5
Return on Equity Before Income Taxes 47	•	•	•	•	•	•	•	•	•	•	•	•	0.6
Return on Equity After Income Taxes 48	•	•	•	•	•	•	•	•	•	•	•	•	•
Profit Margin (Before Income Tax) 49	•	•	•	3.2	•	•	•	•	•	•	•	•	1.0
Profit Margin (After Income Tax) 50	•	•	•	2.9	•	•	•	•	•	•	•	•	•

COMMERCIAL AND INDUSTRIAL MACHINERY AND EQUIPMENT RENTAL

Table II
Corporations with Net Income

MONEY AMOUNTS AND SIZE OF ASSETS IN THOUSANDS OF DOLLARS

Item Description for Accounting Period 7/03 Through 6/04	Total	Zero Assets	Under 500	500 to 1,000	1,000 to 5,000	5,000 to 10,000	10,000 to 25,000	25,000 to 50,000	50,000 to 100,000	100,000 to 250,000	250,000 to 500,000	500,000 to 2,500,000	2,500,000 and over
Number of Enterprises 1	9649	837	5979	1292	1198	118	121	50	•	18	4	•	5
Revenues ($ in Thousands)													
Net Sales 2	18694251	155797	1321574	1143072	2752304	764890	1581561	1463404	•	1499972	296876	•	5229795
Interest 3	545691	2144	2128	3477	10225	1279	9452	15087	•	69823	664	•	224119
Rents 4	21984	42	6028	161	247	5531	801	2488	•	162	2227	•	270
Royalties 5	47750	0	0	0	60	0	1154	211	•	134	0	•	46190
Other Portfolio Income 6	1057585	22561	115865	4739	59751	18326	55842	90447	•	62109	19277	•	391665
Other Receipts 7	17021241	131050	1197553	1134695	2682021	739754	1514312	1355171	•	1367744	274708	•	4567551
Total Receipts 8	18694251	155797	1321574	1143072	2752304	764890	1581561	1463404	•	1499972	296876	•	5229795
Average Total Receipts 9	1937	186	221	885	2297	6482	13071	29268	•	83332	74219	•	1045959
Operating Costs/Operating Income (%)													
Cost of Operations 10	23.7	0.4	16.1	20.6	37.3	30.2	36.3	33.4	•	28.9	4.0	•	15.3
Salaries and Wages 11	9.7	4.1	8.6	9.4	12.2	9.3	10.1	5.6	•	9.7	9.3	•	8.7
Taxes Paid 12	2.1	3.5	3.0	2.8	2.7	3.7	2.5	1.5	•	1.6	2.7	•	1.9
Interest Paid 13	7.4	10.7	2.1	3.6	2.4	3.4	3.1	2.7	•	5.0	1.1	•	14.4
Depreciation 14	21.5	21.6	15.9	19.8	13.7	18.6	17.0	16.9	•	22.0	54.4	•	29.9
Amortization and Depletion 15	0.4	1.0	0.0	0.2	0.2	0.1	0.1	0.1	•	1.3	0.9	•	0.6
Pensions and Other Deferred Comp. 16	0.4	0.0	0.1	0.8	0.5	0.2	0.5	0.2	•	0.4	0.1	•	0.4
Employee Benefits 17	1.3	0.1	1.8	1.3	0.8	0.6	1.0	0.5	•	0.9	1.5	•	1.5
Advertising 18	0.5	0.3	1.3	1.0	0.3	0.2	0.4	0.5	•	0.5	0.6	•	0.4
Other Expenses 19	21.3	16.6	23.9	21.8	17.9	22.1	18.5	28.7	•	20.2	9.9	•	19.4
Officers' Compensation 20	2.3	0.1	5.9	7.0	3.9	2.8	2.6	1.4	•	2.5	0.9	•	0.3
Operating Margin 21	9.5	41.5	21.4	11.8	8.1	8.6	8.0	8.6	•	7.0	14.6	•	7.3
Operating Margin Before Officers' Comp. 22	11.8	41.6	27.3	18.8	12.0	11.4	10.5	10.0	•	9.5	15.5	•	7.6

Selected Average Balance Sheet ($ in Thousands)

Net Receivables 23	1260	0	23	59	464	1286	2432	4493	13787	144150	•	1421464
Inventories 24	•	•	•	•	•	•	•	•	•	•	•	•
Net Property, Plant and Equipment 25	1529	0	77	450	815	3891	6513	13015	62829	70291	•	1427841
Total Assets 26	4395	155	763	2247	7142	14932	34502	•	165885	310734	•	3547882
Notes and Loans Payable 27	2010	62	741	852	3268	6981	17094	•	57749	16561	•	2017135
All Other Liabilities 28	915	13	51	251	1102	2244	5384	•	44610	78235	•	795756
Net Worth 29	1470	80	-29	1144	2772	5707	12024	•	63526	215938	•	734991

Selected Financial Ratios (Times to 1)

Current Ratio 30	2.3	1.8	2.4	2.2	1.8	1.5	1.8	•	1.5	4.3	•	2.9
Quick Ratio 31	1.9	1.5	2.0	1.4	1.3	0.9	0.9	•	1.1	4.0	•	2.7
Net Sales to Working Capital 32	2.0	8.2	6.3	3.4	4.6	6.9	5.7	•	5.2	0.6	•	1.0
Coverage Ratio 33	2.4	11.4	4.3	4.3	3.5	3.6	4.4	•	2.5	14.2	•	1.5
Total Asset Turnover 34	0.4	4.9	1.4	1.0	1.0	0.9	0.8	•	0.5	0.2	•	0.3
Inventory Turnover 35	•	•	•	•	•	•	•	•	•	•	•	•
Receivables Turnover 36	•	•	•	•	•	•	•	•	•	•	•	•
Total Liabilities to Net Worth 37	2.0	0.9	1.0	1.0	1.6	1.6	1.9	•	1.6	0.4	•	3.8
Current Assets to Working Capital 38	1.8	2.2	1.7	1.8	2.2	3.1	2.3	•	3.0	1.3	•	1.5
Current Liabilities to Working Capital 39	0.8	1.2	0.7	0.8	1.2	2.1	1.3	•	2.0	0.3	•	0.5
Working Capital to Net Sales 40	0.5	0.1	0.2	0.3	0.2	0.1	0.2	•	0.2	1.8	•	1.0
Inventory to Working Capital 41	0.1	0.1	0.1	0.4	0.1	0.6	0.5	•	0.4	0.1	•	0.0
Total Receipts to Cash Flow 42	5.2	2.1	3.7	5.6	5.2	6.3	6.6	•	6.5	4.4	•	6.3
Cost of Goods to Cash Flow 43	1.2	0.0	0.8	2.1	1.6	2.3	2.2	•	1.9	0.2	•	1.0
Cash Flow to Total Debt 44	0.1	1.1	0.3	0.4	0.3	0.2	0.2	•	0.1	0.2	•	0.1

Selected Financial Factors (in Percentages)

Debt Ratio 45	66.6	48.4	103.8	49.1	61.2	61.8	65.1	•	61.7	30.5	•	79.3
Return on Total Assets 46	7.8	33.5	17.9	10.8	10.9	9.7	10.1	•	6.1	3.7	•	6.4
Return on Equity Before Income Taxes 47	13.7	59.1	16.2	20.1	18.2	22.3	•	•	9.5	5.0	•	10.4
Return on Equity After Income Taxes 48	11.9	57.7	15.2	17.0	16.7	19.7	•	•	8.1	3.3	•	8.2
Profit Margin (Before Income Tax) 49	10.4	41.5	21.4	11.8	8.1	8.6	8.0	9.2	7.3	14.5	•	7.3
Profit Margin (After Income Tax) 50	9.1	35.0	20.9	11.3	7.6	7.3	7.3	8.1	6.2	9.5	•	5.7

REAL ESTATE AND RENTAL AND LEASING
533110

LESSORS OF NONFINAN. INTANGIBLE ASSETS (EX. COPYRIGHTED WORKS)

Table I
Corporations with and without Net Income

MONEY AMOUNTS AND SIZE OF ASSETS IN THOUSANDS OF DOLLARS

Item Description for Accounting Period 7/03 Through 6/04	Total	Zero Assets	Under 500	500 to 1,000	1,000 to 5,000	5,000 to 10,000	10,000 to 25,000	25,000 to 50,000	50,000 to 100,000	100,000 to 250,000	250,000 to 500,000	500,000 to 2,500,000	2,500,000 and over
Number of Enterprises 1	1475	267	1106	53	18	4	11	3	7	3	3	•	•
Revenues ($ in Thousands)													
Net Sales 2	987990	14266	52912	3434	77441	12434	193450	19202	186667	233008	195178	•	•
Interest 3	19057	207	1	0	1468	360	748	0	1081	2164	13029	•	•
Rents 4	715	193	0	182	11	251	79	0	0	0	0	•	•
Royalties 5	382693	3666	23099	586	3296	5863	73755	5601	37203	99627	129996	•	•
Other Portfolio Income 6	12935	6740	0	0	1689	31	9	0	384	4082	0	•	•
Other Receipts 7	572590	3460	29812	2666	70977	5929	118859	13601	147999	127135	52153	•	•
Total Receipts 8	987990	14266	52912	3434	77441	12434	193450	19202	186667	233008	195178	•	•
Average Total Receipts 9	670	53	48	65	4302	3108	17586	6401	26667	77669	65059	•	•
Operating Costs/Operating Income (%)													
Cost of Operations 10	8.5	1.8	40.4	•	1.9	0.6	15.3	•	11.1	4.6	•	•	•
Salaries and Wages 11	13.6	3.1	14.3	4.2	33.1	14.6	9.7	20.3	11.8	16.8	7.9	•	•
Taxes Paid 12	3.5	17.7	2.9	10.1	3.4	7.4	5.8	5.2	1.1	3.3	2.4	•	•
Interest Paid 13	2.7	14.4	0.0	0.0	0.0	0.5	1.7	10.5	4.1	0.1	5.7	•	•
Depreciation 14	3.3	0.9	0.0	•	0.7	2.4	2.1	1.0	0.7	4.6	8.1	•	•
Amortization and Depletion 15	4.1	0.3	0.3	2.6	1.6	14.5	1.1	9.8	11.5	4.4	0.6	•	•
Pensions and Other Deferred Comp. 16	0.1	•	0.0	•	•	0.6	0.2	•	•	0.1	0.3	•	•
Employee Benefits 17	1.3	0.4	•	•	1.8	1.9	0.7	•	1.5	2.2	0.9	•	•
Advertising 18	1.6	1.5	0.2	•	1.6	5.4	3.0	2.0	3.4	0.3	0.0	•	•
Other Expenses 19	31.3	10.6	9.2	14.5	25.4	35.6	39.0	22.0	19.1	62.4	9.3	•	•
Officers' Compensation 20	7.4	3.3	27.9	29.1	29.1	5.7	4.3	2.6	2.1	4.0	6.7	•	•
Operating Margin 21	22.4	45.9	4.8	68.6	1.4	10.8	17.0	26.5	33.6	•	58.1	•	•
Operating Margin Before Officers' Comp. 22	29.9	49.2	32.6	68.6	30.5	16.6	21.3	29.1	35.7	1.4	64.8	•	•

Selected Average Balance Sheet ($ in Thousands)

Net Receivables 23	104	•	0	6	0	2120	36	2536	317	2876	14338	5447
Inventories 24	•	•	•	•	•	•	•	•	•	•	•	•
Net Property, Plant and Equipment 25	256	•	0	0	489	155	942	2375	1052	1052	14746	88247
Total Assets 26	1996	60	0	651	3416	6752	17490	39762	67048	181580	476499	
Notes and Loans Payable 27	311	13	0	0	86	1534	4498	3391	27607	13719	47209	
All Other Liabilities 28	367	31	0	4	1006	529	3147	9500	11295	33970	80823	
Net Worth 29	1319	16	0	647	2323	4689	9845	26871	28146	133891	348466	

Selected Financial Ratios (Times to 1)

Current Ratio 30	1.9	•	1.9	29.4	2.8	2.8	2.0	2.0	0.7	2.0	2.0	1.0
Quick Ratio 31	1.3	•	1.8	29.4	2.4	1.8	1.6	1.6	0.6	1.7	0.7	1.0
Net Sales to Working Capital 32	4.3	•	1.7	0.6	2.2	2.3	4.6	8.9	•	2.5	159.6	
Coverage Ratio 33	9.3	4.2	420.8	•	33.6	21.1	11.0	9.1	3.5	•	11.2	
Total Asset Turnover 34	0.3	•	0.8	0.1	1.3	0.5	1.0	0.4	0.2	0.4	0.4	0.1
Inventory Turnover 35	•	•	•	•	•	•	•	•	•	•	•	•
Receivables Turnover 36	•	•	•	•	•	•	•	•	•	•	•	•
Total Liabilities to Net Worth 37	0.5	•	2.7	0.0	0.5	0.4	0.8	0.5	0.4	1.4	0.4	
Current Assets to Working Capital 38	2.1	•	2.1	1.0	1.6	1.6	2.0	2.0	2.0	2.0	22.9	
Current Liabilities to Working Capital 39	1.1	•	1.1	0.0	0.6	0.6	1.0	1.0	1.0	1.0	21.9	
Working Capital to Net Sales 40	0.2	•	0.6	1.6	0.4	0.4	0.2	0.1	0.4	0.0	0.0	
Inventory to Working Capital 41	0.0	•	0.0	•	0.0	0.0	0.0	0.2	0.0	0.2	0.2	
Total Receipts to Cash Flow 42	2.0	6.9	7.5	1.2	4.8	2.3	1.9	1.9	2.1	1.8	1.5	
Cost of Goods to Cash Flow 43	0.2	0.1	3.0	•	0.1	0.0	0.3	0.2	•	0.1		
Cash Flow to Total Debt 44	0.5	•	0.1	14.3	0.8	0.6	1.2	0.4	0.2	0.9	0.3	

Selected Financial Factors (in Percentages)

Debt Ratio 45	33.9	•	72.8	0.6	32.0	30.5	43.7	58.0	32.4	43.7	26.3	26.9
Return on Total Assets 46	8.4	•	3.8	6.8	1.8	5.2	6.0	14.9	18.7	6.0	•	8.7
Return on Equity Before Income Taxes 47	11.4	•	14.0	6.9	2.6	7.2	6.3	31.6	30.3	•	•	10.9
Return on Equity After Income Taxes 48	8.7	•	13.5	5.8	2.6	•	5.2	29.9	25.6	•	•	7.1
Profit Margin (Before Income Tax) 49	22.4	45.9	68.6	1.4	10.8	26.5	17.0	33.4	•	•	•	58.1
Profit Margin (After Income Tax) 50	17.1	38.7	58.3	1.4	14.3	21.6	31.5	•	•	•	•	37.8

LESSORS OF NONFINAN. INTANGIBLE ASSETS (EX. COPYRIGHTED WORKS)

Table II
Corporations with Net Income

MONEY AMOUNTS AND SIZE OF ASSETS IN THOUSANDS OF DOLLARS

Item Description for Accounting Period 7/03 Through 6/04	Total	Zero Assets	Under 500	500 to 1,000	1,000 to 5,000	5,000 to 10,000	10,000 to 25,000	25,000 to 50,000	50,000 to 100,000	100,000 to 250,000	250,000 to 500,000	500,000 to 2,500,000	2,500,000 and over
Number of Enterprises 1	441	17	349	•	•	•	11	•	•	•	3	•	•
Revenues ($ in Thousands)													
Net Sales 2	778983	12083	45000	•	•	•	212176	•	•	•	195178	•	•
Interest 3	16041	207	0	•	•	•	302	•	•	•	13029	•	•
Rents 4	704	193	0	•	•	•	79	•	•	•	0	•	•
Royalties 5	279165	3666	23099	•	•	•	79355	•	•	•	12996	•	•
Other Portfolio Income 6	7166	6740	0	•	•	•	0	•	•	•	0	•	•
Other Receipts 7	475907	1277	21901	•	•	•	132440	•	•	•	52153	•	•
Total Receipts 8	778983	12083	45000	•	•	•	212176	•	•	•	195178	•	•
Average Total Receipts 9	1766	711	129	•	•	•	19289	•	•	•	65059	•	•
Operating Costs/Operating Income (%)													
Cost of Operations 10	8.2	2.1	34.5	•	•	•	13.9	•	•	•	•	•	•
Salaries and Wages 11	12.0	3.7	16.3	•	•	•	10.7	•	•	•	7.9	•	•
Taxes Paid 12	3.7	2.4	2.8	•	•	•	5.7	•	•	•	2.4	•	•
Interest Paid 13	3.3	17.0	•	•	•	•	2.5	•	•	•	5.7	•	•
Depreciation 14	3.5	1.1	•	•	•	•	2.0	•	•	•	8.1	•	•
Amortization and Depletion 15	3.7	0.4	•	•	•	•	1.9	•	•	•	0.6	•	•
Pensions and Other Deferred Comp. 16	0.2	•	•	•	•	•	0.2	•	•	•	0.3	•	•
Employee Benefits 17	1.2	0.5	•	•	•	•	0.7	•	•	•	0.9	•	•
Advertising 18	1.6	1.8	0.1	•	•	•	3.0	•	•	•	0.0	•	•
Other Expenses 19	23.9	12.5	6.6	•	•	•	37.3	•	•	•	9.3	•	•
Officers' Compensation 20	6.0	3.9	32.7	•	•	•	4.2	•	•	•	6.7	•	•
Operating Margin 21	32.6	54.6	7.0	•	•	•	17.9	•	•	•	58.1	•	•
Operating Margin Before Officers' Comp. 22	38.6	58.5	39.6	•	•	•	22.1	•	•	•	64.8	•	•

Selected Average Balance Sheet ($ in Thousands)

Item					
Net Receivables 23	236	0	18	2467	5447
Inventories 24					
Net Property, Plant and Equipment 25	754	0	0	2144	88247
Total Assets 26	5105	0	158	22013	476499
Notes and Loans Payable 27	804	0	0	4535	47209
All Other Liabilities 28	907	0	93	5733	80823
Net Worth 29	3394	0	65	11745	348466

Selected Financial Ratios (Times to 1)

Item				
Current Ratio 30	1.9	1.7	1.7	1.0
Quick Ratio 31	1.2	1.7	1.4	1.0
Net Sales to Working Capital 32	4.3	2.0	5.9	159.6
Coverage Ratio 33	10.9	4.2	8.2	11.2
Total Asset Turnover 34	0.3	0.8	0.9	0.1
Inventory Turnover 35				
Receivables Turnover 36				
Total Liabilities to Net Worth 37	0.5	1.4	0.9	0.4
Current Assets to Working Capital 38	2.1	2.4	2.4	22.9
Current Liabilities to Working Capital 39	1.1	1.4	1.4	21.9
Working Capital to Net Sales 40	0.2	0.5	0.2	0.0
Inventory to Working Capital 41	0.0		0.1	0.2
Total Receipts to Cash Flow 42	1.8	5.8	1.9	1.5
Cost of Goods to Cash Flow 43	0.2	0.1	0.3	0.3
Cash Flow to Total Debt 44	0.6	0.2	1.0	0.3

Selected Financial Factors (in Percentages)

Item				
Debt Ratio 45	33.5	59.2	46.6	26.9
Return on Total Assets 46	12.4	5.7	17.8	8.7
Return on Equity Before Income Taxes 47	17.0	13.9	29.4	10.9
Return on Equity After Income Taxes 48	13.5	13.6	24.7	7.1
Profit Margin (Before Income Tax) 49	32.6	54.6	17.9	58.1
Profit Margin (After Income Tax) 50	25.9	46.0	15.0	37.8

LEGAL SERVICES

Table I

Corporations with and without Net Income

MONEY AMOUNTS AND SIZE OF ASSETS IN THOUSANDS OF DOLLARS

Item Description for Accounting Period 7/03 Through 6/04	Total	Zero Assets	Under 500	500 to 1,000	1,000 to 5,000	5,000 to 10,000	10,000 to 25,000	25,000 to 50,000	50,000 to 100,000	100,000 to 250,000	250,000 to 500,000	500,000 to 2,500,000	2,500,000 and over
Number of Enterprises **1**	96784	12949	78759	3052	1733	162	92	26	7	3	•	•	•
Revenues ($ in Thousands)													
Net Sales **2**	72344842	1402217	43339484	7872130	8764183	3994726	3853049	2080892	611617	426546			
Interest **3**	49411	1573	23526	7731	6311	2042	2943	1201	1286	2797			
Rents **4**	68804	0	32420	23345	5128	3867	2195	1791	0	56			
Royalties **5**	6713	0	801	5880	0	0	5	27	0	0			
Other Portfolio Income **6**	97447	6172	29708	50521	3400	919	1096	2798	443	2391			
Other Receipts **7**	3228268	69739	1089656	506434	574386	618098	150191	165434	26024	28307			
Total Receipts **8**	75795485	1479701	44515595	8466041	9353408	4619652	4009479	2252143	639370	460097			
Average Total Receipts **9**	783	114	565	2774	5397	28516	43581	86621	91339	153366			
Operating Costs/Operating Income (%)													
Cost of Operations **10**	6.2	5.5	8.6	1.3	2.8	1.7	3.7	0.8	4.3	16.7			
Salaries and Wages **11**	29.1	16.3	23.1	28.7	31.4	62.4	49.5	52.2	43.8	14.3			
Taxes Paid **12**	3.4	3.6	3.4	3.5	3.4	4.0	3.4	3.3	3.1	1.8			
Interest Paid **13**	0.4	0.6	0.3	0.5	0.4	0.6	0.4	0.5	1.1	0.5			
Depreciation **14**	1.2	0.9	1.0	1.2	1.3	1.6	1.7	2.2	1.7	1.9			
Amortization and Depletion **15**	0.0	0.0	0.0	0.0	0.0	0.0	0.1	0.2	0.4	1.8			
Pensions and Other Deferred Comp. **16**	2.2	2.3	1.9	1.6	3.0	3.8	2.4	2.8	0.5	0.4			
Employee Benefits **17**	1.8	0.7	1.6	2.3	1.7	2.5	2.4	2.1	2.6	1.4			
Advertising **18**	1.6	3.1	1.6	2.5	1.5	0.6	0.7	0.4	1.8	1.1			
Other Expenses **19**	26.8	51.7	27.8	27.6	19.2	21.5	24.5	26.7	30.0	48.9			
Officers' Compensation **20**	24.1	16.4	24.2	29.2	35.8	12.9	10.8	13.7	3.7	1.0			
Operating Margin **21**	3.3	•	6.4	1.5	•	•	0.5	•	7.2	10.2			
Operating Margin Before Officers' Comp. **22**	27.3	15.3	30.6	30.7	35.4	1.2	11.3	8.8	10.8	11.2			

Selected Average Balance Sheet ($ in Thousands)

Net Receivables 23	9	0	3	24	124	301	1018	4774	7016	19797
Inventories 24	1	0	0	11	11	74	120	11	0	0
Net Property, Plant and Equipment 25	28	0	16	87	219	1890	2751	5856	4001	7286
Total Assets 26	156	0	70	711	1783	7238	14951	32136	73813	149344
Notes and Loans Payable 27	56	0	35	230	393	2531	4297	8489	19595	26568
All Other Liabilities 28	72	0	31	352	906	2937	6627	14219	30323	75037
Net Worth 29	28	0	4	130	485	1770	4027	9429	23895	47739

Selected Financial Ratios (Times to 1)

Current Ratio 30	1.1	•	1.0	1.1	1.2	1.0	1.2	1.3	1.4	1.0
Quick Ratio 31	0.7	•	0.6	0.8	0.7	0.5	0.7	0.9	0.8	0.8
Net Sales to Working Capital 32	83.5	•	52.8	19.2	•	21.8	17.0	8.0	•	•
Coverage Ratio 33	21.0	8.1	26.9	21.0	16.6	8.0	11.2	7.3	12.5	36.5
Total Asset Turnover 34	4.8	•	7.9	3.6	2.8	3.4	2.8	2.5	1.2	1.0
Inventory Turnover 35	86.5	•	403.0	2708.6	12.5	5.7	12.9	55.7	•	•
Receivables Turnover 36	70.7	•	168.7	98.4	27.9	85.7	40.5	16.5	8.2	14.4
Total Liabilities to Net Worth 37	4.5	•	17.6	4.5	2.7	3.1	2.7	2.4	2.1	2.1
Current Assets to Working Capital 38	10.4	•	•	9.8	5.0	•	5.0	3.9	3.8	•
Current Liabilities to Working Capital 39	9.4	•	•	8.8	4.0	•	4.0	2.9	2.8	•
Working Capital to Net Sales 40	0.0	•	0.0	0.0	0.1	•	0.0	0.1	0.1	•
Inventory to Working Capital 41	0.1	•	•	0.0	0.1	0.0	0.0	•	•	•
Total Receipts to Cash Flow 42	3.5	2.2	3.3	3.3	5.0	5.4	4.4	4.7	2.7	1.5
Cost of Goods to Cash Flow 43	0.2	0.1	0.3	0.0	0.1	0.1	0.2	0.0	0.1	0.3
Cash Flow to Total Debt 44	1.7	•	2.5	1.3	0.8	0.8	0.9	0.8	0.6	0.9

Selected Financial Factors (in Percentages)

Debt Ratio 45	81.8	•	94.6	81.8	72.8	75.5	73.1	70.7	67.6	68.0
Return on Total Assets 46	40.2	•	73.9	34.3	19.0	15.3	13.9	9.7	15.5	17.2
Return on Equity Before Income Taxes 47	210.9	•	1322.2	179.5	65.6	54.8	47.1	28.5	44.0	52.4
Return on Equity After Income Taxes 48	206.5	•	1309.4	176.4	64.4	49.2	43.6	23.0	38.9	45.5
Profit Margin (Before Income Tax) 49	8.0	4.4	9.0	9.0	6.3	3.9	4.5	3.4	12.0	17.6
Profit Margin (After Income Tax) 50	7.8	4.3	8.9	8.9	6.2	3.5	4.2	2.7	10.6	15.3

Table II
Corporations with Net Income

LEGAL SERVICES

MONEY AMOUNTS AND SIZE OF ASSETS IN THOUSANDS OF DOLLARS

Item Description for Accounting Period 7/03 Through 6/04	Total	Zero Assets	Under 500	500 to 1,000	1,000 to 5,000	5,000 to 10,000	10,000 to 25,000	25,000 to 50,000	50,000 to 100,000	100,000 to 250,000	250,000 to 500,000	500,000 to 2,500,000	2,500,000 and over
Number of Enterprises **1**	66172	6666	56053	2375	871	101	72	•	•	3	•	•	•
Revenues ($ in Thousands)													
Net Sales **2**	56145140	830704	34178996	6850893	4142238	3657266	3417212	•	•	426546	•	•	•
Interest **3**	31889	1507	15546	4175	1813	1539	2336	•	•	2797	•	•	•
Rents **4**	40118	0	15454	17772	1575	1405	2064	•	•	56	•	•	•
Royalties **5**	5912	0	0	5880	0	0	4	•	•	0	•	•	•
Other Portfolio Income **6**	71081	3852	8026	50264	1447	850	1014	•	•	2391	•	•	•
Other Receipts **7**	1996148	69402	935774	499389	108107	43842	121025	•	•	28307	•	•	•
Total Receipts **8**	58290288	905465	35153796	7428373	4255180	3704902	3543655	•	•	460097	•	•	•
Average Total Receipts **9**	881	136	627	3128	4885	36682	49217	•	•	153366	•	•	•
Operating Costs/Operating Income (%)													
Cost of Operations **10**	6.5	1.3	9.1	1.0	3.8	1.8	4.1	•	•	16.7	•	•	•
Salaries and Wages **11**	28.1	17.2	21.6	29.0	30.4	52.0	50.1	•	•	14.3	•	•	•
Taxes Paid **12**	3.3	3.8	3.3	3.5	3.3	3.6	3.3	•	•	1.8	•	•	•
Interest Paid **13**	0.4	0.6	0.3	0.4	0.5	0.3	0.4	•	•	0.5	•	•	•
Depreciation **14**	1.1	1.0	0.9	1.0	1.4	1.7	1.6	•	•	1.9	•	•	•
Amortization and Depletion **15**	0.0	0.0	0.0	0.1	0.1	0.0	0.1	•	•	1.8	•	•	•
Pensions and Other Deferred Comp. **16**	2.1	3.6	2.0	1.8	2.2	2.8	2.4	•	•	0.4	•	•	•
Employee Benefits **17**	1.6	0.9	1.3	2.5	1.6	1.9	2.4	•	•	1.4	•	•	•
Advertising **18**	1.6	3.3	1.7	2.0	2.3	0.6	0.7	•	•	1.1	•	•	•
Other Expenses **19**	26.5	38.2	27.4	27.8	19.3	21.3	23.6	•	•	48.9	•	•	•
Officers' Compensation **20**	21.0	18.7	22.5	28.8	23.0	10.3	9.5	•	•	1.0	•	•	•
Operating Margin **21**	7.7	11.4	9.9	2.1	12.1	3.6	1.8	•	•	10.2	•	•	•
Operating Margin Before Officers' Comp. **22**	28.7	30.1	32.4	30.9	35.1	13.9	11.3	•	•	11.2	•	•	•

Selected Average Balance Sheet ($ in Thousands)

	1	2	3	4	5	6	7	8	9
Net Receivables 23	11	0	3	10	208	421	1126	•	19797
Inventories 24	1	0	0	0	22	118	153	•	0
Net Property, Plant and Equipment 25	30	0	17	73	244	2793	2849	•	7286
Total Assets 26	167	0	78	721	1574	7715	15403	•	149344
Notes and Loans Payable 27	51	0	30	182	360	2988	3745	•	26568
All Other Liabilities 28	74	0	34	402	648	2364	6972	•	75037
Net Worth 29	41	0	14	137	567	2363	4686	•	47739

Selected Financial Ratios (Times to 1)

	1	2	3	4	5	6	7	8	9
Current Ratio 30	1.2	•	1.2	1.1	1.4	1.2	1.3	•	1.0
Quick Ratio 31	0.8	•	0.8	0.7	1.0	0.7	0.7	•	0.8
Net Sales to Working Capital 32	52.3	•	94.9	74.1	16.7	50.2	21.4	•	36.5
Coverage Ratio 33	31.3	34.1	38.5	27.0	29.7	16.0	16.3	•	
Total Asset Turnover 34	5.1	•	7.8	4.0	3.0	4.7	3.1	•	1.0
Inventory Turnover 35	71.6	•	356.7	•	8.2	5.7	12.9	•	
Receivables Turnover 36	65.8	•	170.7	142.2	15.1	84.3	39.4	•	14.4
Total Liabilities to Net Worth 37	3.0	•	4.5	4.3	1.8	2.3	2.3	•	2.1
Current Assets to Working Capital 38	6.1	•	6.7	13.5	3.5	5.2	4.5	•	
Current Liabilities to Working Capital 39	5.1	•	5.7	12.5	2.5	4.2	3.5	•	
Working Capital to Net Sales 40	0.0	•	0.0	0.0	0.1	0.0	0.0	•	
Inventory to Working Capital 41	0.1	•	0.0	•	0.1	0.2	0.0	•	
Total Receipts to Cash Flow 42	3.2	2.0	3.0	3.2	3.5	5.2	4.4	•	1.5
Cost of Goods to Cash Flow 43	0.2	0.0	0.3	0.0	0.1	0.1	0.2	•	0.3
Cash Flow to Total Debt 44	2.1	•	3.2	1.5	1.4	1.3	1.0	•	0.9

Selected Financial Factors (in Percentages)

	1	2	3	4	5	6	7	8	9
Debt Ratio 45	75.3	•	81.9	81.1	64.0	69.4	69.6	•	68.0
Return on Total Assets 46	60.3	•	101.9	44.0	46.3	24.6	18.0	•	17.2
Return on Equity Before Income Taxes 47	235.7	•	547.4	223.5	124.3	75.4	55.5	•	52.4
Return on Equity After Income Taxes 48	231.3	•	542.7	219.8	122.3	68.7	51.6	•	45.5
Profit Margin (Before Income Tax) 49	11.5	20.4	12.7	10.6	14.8	4.9	5.5	•	17.6
Profit Margin (After Income Tax) 50	11.3	20.2	12.6	10.4	14.6	4.5	5.1	•	15.3

336

Table I

Corporations with and without Net Income

ACCOUNTING, TAX PREPARATION, BOOKKEEPING, AND PAYROLL SERVICES

MONEY AMOUNTS AND SIZE OF ASSETS IN THOUSANDS OF DOLLARS

Item Description for Accounting Period 7/03 Through 6/04	Total	Zero Assets	Under 500	500 to 1,000	1,000 to 5,000	5,000 to 10,000	10,000 to 25,000	25,000 to 50,000	50,000 to 100,000	100,000 to 250,000	250,000 to 500,000	500,000 to 2,500,000	2,500,000 and over
Number of Enterprises 1	61619	10011	50498	362	652	38	31	19	5	•	3	•	•
Revenues ($ in Thousands)													
Net Sales 2	26767738	779106	15911017	953139	2553120	353295	294466	1988239	266738	•	3668618	•	•
Interest 3	462661	160	11137	5280	3223	325	1343	4552	5313	•	431329	•	•
Rents 4	24949	0	1762	7863	1299	36	0	0	1681	•	12308	•	•
Royalties 5	479097	51	0	11	0	39	0	6419	0	•	472576	•	•
Other Portfolio Income 6	109149	2184	27050	0	10068	2488	2240	10363	1527	•	53229	•	•
Other Receipts 7	1206701	10137	81810	5776	14437	125	32509	19089	8611	•	1034206	•	•
Total Receipts 8	29050295	791638	16032776	972069	2582147	356308	330558	2028662	283870	•	5672266	•	•
Average Total Receipts 9	471	79	317	2685	3960	9377	10663	106772	56774	•	1890755	•	•
Operating Costs/Operating Income (%)													
Cost of Operations 10	19.5	0.3	16.2	4.6	31.8	30.8	43.2	74.8	1.0	•	1.1	•	•
Salaries and Wages 11	26.9	20.7	24.4	44.8	25.4	32.5	26.6	11.0	49.5	•	42.2	•	•
Taxes Paid 12	5.0	4.2	4.9	4.2	5.4	4.2	3.2	4.6	3.0	•	5.7	•	•
Interest Paid 13	1.7	0.7	0.5	1.5	0.6	0.9	0.8	0.3	3.6	•	9.2	•	•
Depreciation 14	1.3	1.6	1.1	2.9	1.0	2.0	1.7	0.4	4.0	•	2.3	•	•
Amortization and Depletion 15	0.8	0.1	0.3	0.1	0.5	0.3	0.5	0.1	1.3	•	4.0	•	•
Pensions and Other Deferred Comp. 16	1.3	0.3	1.4	2.9	0.8	1.2	0.9	0.6	0.0	•	1.4	•	•
Employee Benefits 17	2.1	1.5	1.9	4.5	1.6	1.9	1.2	4.0	2.1	•	1.8	•	•
Advertising 18	1.0	1.7	0.6	0.9	0.4	1.4	0.7	0.5	1.0	•	3.3	•	•
Other Expenses 19	27.1	43.4	23.3	23.5	17.3	23.7	18.8	4.0	30.9	•	61.2	•	•
Officers' Compensation 20	13.9	18.9	19.6	11.0	10.5	5.5	3.2	0.8	0.9	•	1.0	•	•
Operating Margin 21	•	6.5	5.8	•	4.7	•	•	•	2.6	•	•	•	•
Operating Margin Before Officers' Comp. 22	13.3	25.4	25.5	10.1	15.2	1.0	2.3	•	3.4	•	•	•	•

Selected Average Balance Sheet ($ in Thousands)

Net Receivables 23	63	0	5	78	319	1215	3279	7340	15184	996463
Inventories 24	3	0	0	1	1	47	13	1696	463	24618
Net Property, Plant and Equipment 25	20	0	11	161	241	440	343	1757	7997	114391
Total Assets 26	320	0	50	598	1901	7825	15417	34888	81857	4630530
Notes and Loans Payable 27	156	0	27	711	564	2369	1828	6739	17305	2423441
All Other Liabilities 28	136	0	16	204	843	5348	15724	26380	38186	1848741
Net Worth 29	28	0	7	-317	494	108	-2136	1769	26367	358347

Selected Financial Ratios (Times to 1)

Current Ratio 30	0.9	•	1.0	0.5	0.6	1.2	0.8	0.9	1.1	1.0
Quick Ratio 31	0.8	•	0.9	0.5	0.5	0.5	0.6	0.6	0.7	0.9
Net Sales to Working Capital 32	•	•	•	•	•	14.2	•	•	17.7	20.8
Coverage Ratio 33	5.5	12.5	15.3	1.8	11.0	•	16.0	4.7	3.5	3.3
Total Asset Turnover 34	1.4	•	6.3	4.4	2.1	1.2	0.6	3.0	0.7	0.3
Inventory Turnover 35	25.2	•	168.1	175.6	1081.5	60.8	326.7	46.1	1.2	0.5
Receivables Turnover 36	9.2	•	56.1	19.1	13.9	5.4	2.7	17.2	2.7	2.5
Total Liabilities to Net Worth 37	10.3	•	6.1	•	2.8	71.4	•	18.7	2.1	11.9
Current Assets to Working Capital 38	•	•	•	•	•	7.4	•	•	13.9	25.8
Current Liabilities to Working Capital 39	•	•	•	•	•	6.4	•	•	12.9	24.8
Working Capital to Net Sales 40	•	•	•	•	•	0.1	•	•	0.1	0.0
Inventory to Working Capital 41	•	•	•	•	•	•	•	•	0.3	0.4
Total Receipts to Cash Flow 42	3.5	2.4	4.2	5.7	5.6	7.6	3.7	28.3	3.1	1.3
Cost of Goods to Cash Flow 43	0.7	0.0	0.7	0.3	1.8	2.4	1.6	21.2	0.0	0.0
Cash Flow to Total Debt 44	0.4	•	1.7	0.5	0.5	0.2	0.1	0.1	0.3	0.2

Selected Financial Factors (in Percentages)

Debt Ratio 45	91.2	•	85.9	152.9	74.0	98.6	113.9	94.9	67.8	92.3
Return on Total Assets 46	13.1	•	44.7	11.6	13.1	•	7.5	4.1	8.2	8.1
Return on Equity Before Income Taxes 47	122.0	•	296.0	•	45.9	•	64.3	•	18.3	73.1
Return on Equity After Income Taxes 48	103.2	•	291.2	•	44.1	•	52.0	•	12.3	46.8
Profit Margin (Before Income Tax) 49	7.9	8.1	6.6	1.2	5.8	•	11.4	1.1	9.0	21.4
Profit Margin (After Income Tax) 50	6.7	7.8	6.5	1.0	5.6	•	9.8	0.9	6.1	13.7

ACCOUNTING, TAX PREPARATION, BOOKKEEPING, AND PAYROLL SERVICES

Table II
Corporations with Net Income

MONEY AMOUNTS AND SIZE OF ASSETS IN THOUSANDS OF DOLLARS

Item Description for Accounting Period 7/03 Through 6/04	Total	Zero Assets	Under 500	500 to 1,000	1,000 to 5,000	5,000 to 10,000	10,000 to 25,000	25,000 to 50,000	50,000 to 100,000	100,000 to 250,000	250,000 to 500,000	500,000 to 2,500,000	2,500,000 and over
Number of Enterprises **1**	42859	6622	35421	287	471	16	23	13	•	•	•	•	•
Revenues ($ in Thousands)													
Net Sales **2**	19891523	469350	11427767	890896	1274559	126406	288264	1713809	•	•	•	•	•
Interest **3**	453689	0	8121	4778	332	55	1007	2754	•	•	•	•	•
Rents **4**	24619	0	1496	7863	1236	36	0	0	•	•	•	•	•
Royalties **5**	479045	0	0	11	0	39	0	6419	•	•	•	•	•
Other Portfolio Income **6**	89130	2168	15601	0	2063	2488	2240	9814	•	•	•	•	•
Other Receipts **7**	1143216	10539	26084	5620	9907	107	32363	19090	•	•	•	•	•
Total Receipts **8**	22081222	482057	11479069	909168	1288097	129131	323874	1751886	•	•	•	•	•
Average Total Receipts **9**	515	73	324	3168	2735	8071	14081	134760	•	•	•	•	•
Operating Costs/Operating Income (%)													
Cost of Operations **10**	11.1	0.2	4.5	0.0	0.5	31.7	43.7	86.6	•	•	•	•	•
Salaries and Wages **11**	29.0	11.1	26.7	46.1	38.5	27.8	25.5	3.3	•	•	•	•	•
Taxes Paid **12**	4.4	4.4	4.1	4.5	3.3	1.9	2.9	4.3	•	•	•	•	•
Interest Paid **13**	2.2	0.5	0.5	1.2	0.7	0.1	0.7	0.3	•	•	•	•	•
Depreciation **14**	1.4	2.2	1.1	3.0	1.4	1.8	1.6	0.3	•	•	•	•	•
Amortization and Depletion **15**	0.9	0.1	0.3	0.1	0.1	0.0	0.4	0.1	•	•	•	•	•
Pensions and Other Deferred Comp. **16**	1.4	0.4	1.6	3.0	1.0	1.1	0.9	0.1	•	•	•	•	•
Employee Benefits **17**	1.9	0.7	2.1	4.2	0.8	1.7	1.2	1.4	•	•	•	•	•
Advertising **18**	1.2	0.9	0.7	0.9	0.6	0.4	0.7	0.5	•	•	•	•	•
Other Expenses **19**	29.3	37.1	25.0	23.1	24.2	15.7	17.2	2.3	•	•	•	•	•
Officers' Compensation **20**	15.6	26.2	23.0	11.4	15.4	3.0	2.7	0.8	•	•	•	•	•
Operating Margin **21**	1.6	16.3	10.5	2.4	13.5	14.8	2.4	0.0	•	•	•	•	•
Operating Margin Before Officers' Comp. **22**	17.2	42.4	33.5	13.8	28.9	17.8	5.2	0.8	•	•	•	•	•

Selected Average Balance Sheet ($ in Thousands)

Net Receivables 23	80	0	7	1	163	999	3519	6853
Inventories 24	4	0	0	0	0		13	2581
Net Property, Plant and Equipment 25	23	0	12	199	280	289	433	1854
Total Assets 26	416	0	56	598	1859	8561	15779	34788
Notes and Loans Payable 27	206	0	26	756	380	38	2164	8058
All Other Liabilities 28	159	0	12	247	822	6883	9358	21555
Net Worth 29	52	0	18	-406	657	1639	4257	5175

Selected Financial Ratios (Times to 1)

Current Ratio 30	1.0	•	1.2	0.3	1.0	1.2	1.5	0.9
Quick Ratio 31	0.9	•	1.1	0.3	0.9	0.3	0.9	0.6
Net Sales to Working Capital 32	107.1	•	79.4	•	1061.2	7.1	3.1	•
Coverage Ratio 33	6.7	37.8	21.3	4.7	21.2	201.5	21.5	9.6
Total Asset Turnover 34	1.1	•	5.8	5.2	1.5	0.9	0.8	3.8
Inventory Turnover 35	11.7	•	262.7	0.8	273.1	3206.4	415.5	44.2
Receivables Turnover 36	7.8	•	54.2	45.1	13.6	3.9	4.1	38.5
Total Liabilities to Net Worth 37	7.0	•	2.1	•	1.8	4.2	2.7	5.7
Current Assets to Working Capital 38	33.6	•	5.7	•	232.7	7.1	2.9	•
Current Liabilities to Working Capital 39	32.6	•	4.7	•	231.7	6.1	1.9	•
Working Capital to Net Sales 40	0.0	•	0.0	0.0	0.0	0.0	0.1	0.3
Inventory to Working Capital 41	0.6	•	0.0	0.0	0.0	•	0.0	•
Total Receipts to Cash Flow 42	2.8	2.1	3.4	4.7	3.1	3.6	3.5	28.1
Cost of Goods to Cash Flow 43	0.3	0.0	0.2	0.0	0.0	1.2	1.5	24.3
Cash Flow to Total Debt 44	0.5	•	2.5	0.7	0.7	0.3	0.3	0.2

Selected Financial Factors (in Percentages)

Debt Ratio 45	87.5	•	67.5	167.8	64.6	80.9	73.0	85.1
Return on Total Assets 46	16.5	•	66.2	29.4	22.2	15.7	12.3	9.6
Return on Equity Before Income Taxes 47	112.3	•	194.5	•	59.8	81.8	43.4	57.8
Return on Equity After Income Taxes 48	97.7	•	191.8	•	57.9	79.7	38.6	51.7
Profit Margin (Before Income Tax) 49	12.6	19.0	11.0	4.5	14.5	17.0	14.7	2.3
Profit Margin (After Income Tax) 50	10.9	18.5	10.8	4.3	14.1	16.5	13.1	2.0

Table I

Corporations with and without Net Income

ARCHITECTURAL, ENGINEERING, AND RELATED SERVICES

MONEY AMOUNTS AND SIZE OF ASSETS IN THOUSANDS OF DOLLARS

Item Description for Accounting Period 7/03 Through 6/04	Total	Zero Assets	Under 500	500 to 1,000	1,000 to 5,000	5,000 to 10,000	10,000 to 25,000	25,000 to 50,000	50,000 to 100,000	100,000 to 250,000	250,000 to 500,000	500,000 to 2,500,000	2,500,000 and over
Number of Enterprises **1**	93343	9651	77073	3178	3223	397	233	76	47	37	12	11	4
Revenues ($ in Thousands)													
Net Sales **2**	146525525	1614196	52228735	7801865	21247030	6831597	7578435	5291956	5143786	9160493	4521683	11286434	13819314
Interest **3**	257897	14728	23892	4418	12067	7790	7652	4868	5067	23006	32751	81736	39921
Rents **4**	170628	9	2251	0	8690	10984	3364	3166	14701	5852	14927	12648	94037
Royalties **5**	121033	0	0	0	713	6024	713	17	329	11651	696	332	100559
Other Portfolio Income **6**	325463	50854	56726	3708	18549	3625	9638	3916	40537	55468	14323	19280	48842
Other Receipts **7**	1394815	53851	74054	106357	245484	46862	70817	38384	42050	37926	21737	324091	333200
Total Receipts **8**	148795361	1733638	52385658	7916348	21532533	6906882	7670619	5342307	5246470	9294396	4606117	11724521	14435873
Average Total Receipts **9**	1584	180	680	2491	6681	17398	32921	70294	111627	251200	383843	1065866	3608968
Operating Costs/Operating Income (%)													
Cost of Operations **10**	39.0	25.2	23.7	25.2	35.2	38.7	40.6	51.4	42.4	47.0	72.6	60.0	71.9
Salaries and Wages **11**	20.2	17.1	21.7	30.1	23.8	25.2	22.2	15.5	21.5	18.4	9.2	9.6	15.2
Taxes Paid **12**	3.1	3.7	3.5	3.7	3.5	3.6	3.8	3.0	2.5	2.6	1.4	3.1	1.3
Interest Paid **13**	0.7	0.9	0.3	0.7	0.7	0.4	0.7	0.7	0.7	0.8	2.4	1.3	1.4
Depreciation **14**	1.9	3.6	1.4	2.4	2.6	1.8	2.3	1.6	2.2	2.2	2.6	1.9	1.7
Amortization and Depletion **15**	0.2	0.1	0.0	0.3	0.1	0.2	0.2	0.4	0.3	0.5	1.1	0.4	0.4
Pensions and Other Deferred Comp. **16**	1.1	0.4	1.2	1.4	1.5	1.1	1.3	1.0	0.9	1.0	0.3	1.0	0.3
Employee Benefits **17**	2.3	1.1	1.8	1.2	2.7	3.2	2.6	2.4	2.2	2.7	1.9	2.4	3.6
Advertising **18**	0.3	0.4	0.4	0.3	0.3	0.3	0.3	0.3	0.3	0.3	0.1	0.2	0.1
Other Expenses **19**	21.7	37.4	26.4	26.1	20.4	18.6	20.2	19.9	23.6	20.7	13.4	19.2	8.8
Officers' Compensation **20**	8.2	12.0	15.6	8.2	7.1	5.7	4.3	2.7	2.1	1.9	0.9	2.2	0.4
Operating Margin **21**	1.2	•	3.7	0.5	2.0	1.3	1.4	1.2	1.3	1.9	•	•	•
Operating Margin Before Officers' Comp. **22**	9.4	10.1	19.4	8.7	9.1	6.9	5.7	3.9	3.4	3.8	•	0.9	•

Selected Average Balance Sheet ($ in Thousands)

Net Receivables 23	168	803	154	10	6095	2648	13585	24960	41134	95426	241642	489125
Inventories 24	20	59	22	1	598	226	1855	1987	5386	8896	17342	157246
Net Property, Plant and Equipment 25	91	490	164	28	2647	1023	4368	9073	16615	45223	49396	211750
Total Assets 26	631	2189	684	78	15083	6805	34593	66955	146645	359753	884513	3154351
Notes and Loans Payable 27	189	806	264	48	3836	1974	6747	12491	40720	137515	178356	678624
All Other Liabilities 28	240	611	150	28	6169	2836	16851	28791	49813	116331	362802	1385162
Net Worth 29	203	771	270	2	5078	1996	10994	25673	56112	105906	343355	1090565

Selected Financial Ratios (Times to 1)

Current Ratio 30	1.4	•	1.8	1.1	1.5	1.4	1.4	1.4	1.6	1.4	1.5	1.0
Quick Ratio 31	1.0	•	1.5	0.9	1.2	1.0	1.1	1.1	1.2	1.1	1.0	0.5
Net Sales to Working Capital 32	17.0	•	13.4	366.6	9.2	12.2	9.3	9.3	8.5	7.5	7.0	136.3
Coverage Ratio 33	5.0	7.2	3.9	12.8	4.7	6.7	4.2	5.6	5.0	•	3.0	2.0
Total Asset Turnover 34	2.5	•	3.6	8.7	2.2	2.5	2.0	1.6	1.7	1.0	1.2	1.1
Inventory Turnover 35	29.9	•	28.6	203.2	22.1	29.4	19.3	23.4	21.6	30.8	35.5	15.8
Receivables Turnover 36	8.8	•	15.5	81.2	5.4	6.3	4.4	4.7	5.3	5.0	3.0	6.8
Total Liabilities to Net Worth 37	2.1	•	1.5	32.9	2.0	2.4	2.1	1.6	1.6	2.4	1.6	1.9
Current Assets to Working Capital 38	3.6	•	2.2	20.5	3.0	3.5	3.3	3.6	2.7	3.4	2.9	42.8
Current Liabilities to Working Capital 39	2.6	•	1.2	19.5	2.0	2.5	2.3	2.6	1.7	2.4	1.9	41.8
Working Capital to Net Sales 40	0.1	•	0.1	0.0	0.1	0.1	0.1	0.1	0.1	0.1	0.1	0.0
Inventory to Working Capital 41	0.2	•	0.1	0.5	0.2	0.1	0.2	0.2	0.2	0.3	0.1	6.5
Total Receipts to Cash Flow 42	5.0	3.1	4.3	3.8	5.4	6.0	5.6	4.6	5.1	17.3	5.5	17.5
Cost of Goods to Cash Flow 43	1.9	0.8	1.1	0.9	2.2	2.3	2.9	1.9	2.4	12.5	3.3	12.6
Cash Flow to Total Debt 44	0.7	•	1.4	2.3	0.6	0.6	0.5	0.6	0.5	0.1	0.3	0.1

Selected Financial Factors (in Percentages)

Debt Ratio 45	67.9	•	64.8	97.0	66.3	70.7	68.2	61.7	61.7	70.6	61.2	65.4
Return on Total Assets 46	9.1	•	12.3	38.2	7.2	7.0	5.6	6.6	7.2	•	4.6	3.0
Return on Equity Before Income Taxes 47	22.7	•	28.6	1192.1	16.8	20.3	13.5	14.1	15.1	•	7.9	4.2
Return on Equity After Income Taxes 48	19.5	•	26.3	1172.4	13.3	16.5	11.1	9.3	11.1	•	5.0	2.3
Profit Margin (Before Income Tax) 49	2.9	5.5	3.3	4.0	2.6	2.4	2.1	3.3	3.4	•	2.7	1.3
Profit Margin (After Income Tax) 50	2.5	3.1	3.1	4.0	2.1	1.9	1.7	2.2	2.5	•	1.7	0.7

Table II

Corporations with Net Income

ARCHITECTURAL, ENGINEERING, AND RELATED SERVICES

MONEY AMOUNTS AND SIZE OF ASSETS IN THOUSANDS OF DOLLARS

Item Description for Accounting Period 7/03 Through 6/04	Total	Zero Assets	Under 500	500 to 1,000	1,000 to 5,000	5,000 to 10,000	10,000 to 25,000	25,000 to 50,000	50,000 to 100,000	100,000 to 250,000	250,000 to 500,000	500,000 to 2,500,000	2,500,000 and over
Number of Enterprises **1**	56831	5232	46612	2067	2352	286	163	•	32	25	5	•	•
Revenues ($ in Thousands)													
Net Sales **2**	110369516	1078163	38568111	6551313	16481016	5147001	6002176	•	3936141	6803470	1829438	•	•
Interest **3**	187360	13591	11928	3722	6637	4533	4210	•	4090	16742	18766	•	•
Rents **4**	137180	1	1816	0	2174	9306	1684	•	10668	5721	8634	•	•
Royalties **5**	113518	0	0	0	0	6024	26	•	100	11549	696	•	•
Other Portfolio Income **6**	225479	50693	52656	1923	16754	3122	5275	•	12049	52343	1594	•	•
Other Receipts **7**	1099417	62177	29133	87264	171584	18691	54661	•	23709	33250	21547	•	•
Total Receipts **8**	112132470	1204625	38663644	6644222	16678165	5188677	6068032	•	3986757	6923075	1880675	•	•
Average Total Receipts **9**	1973	230	829	3214	7091	18142	37227	•	124586	276923	376135	•	•
Operating Costs/Operating Income (%)													
Cost of Operations **10**	37.9	20.9	25.0	23.4	33.9	40.4	39.8	•	40.2	47.9	63.2	•	•
Salaries and Wages **11**	20.4	16.8	21.2	30.4	24.2	22.5	22.0	•	21.7	17.3	11.0	•	•
Taxes Paid **12**	3.1	3.5	3.2	3.5	3.6	3.7	3.8	•	2.7	2.6	1.5	•	•
Interest Paid **13**	0.5	0.3	0.3	0.4	0.5	0.3	0.4	•	0.4	0.8	1.8	•	•
Depreciation **14**	1.6	3.7	1.3	1.7	2.3	1.7	1.9	•	1.6	2.3	2.2	•	•
Amortization and Depletion **15**	0.1	0.1	0.0	0.1	0.0	0.1	0.1	•	0.2	0.3	1.1	•	•
Pensions and Other Deferred Comp. **16**	1.2	0.3	1.3	1.6	1.5	1.2	1.4	•	1.1	0.9	0.4	•	•
Employee Benefits **17**	2.5	0.6	1.9	1.2	2.9	3.3	2.6	•	2.2	2.7	2.1	•	•
Advertising **18**	0.3	0.3	0.4	0.3	0.4	0.4	0.3	•	0.2	0.3	0.3	•	•
Other Expenses **19**	20.5	39.9	23.8	25.4	19.5	16.7	19.1	•	22.8	19.0	16.3	•	•
Officers' Compensation **20**	7.5	6.5	14.1	8.2	6.8	4.9	4.3	•	2.2	2.0	1.0	•	•
Operating Margin **21**	4.3	7.1	7.6	3.7	4.5	4.8	4.2	•	4.7	3.8	•	•	•
Operating Margin Before Officers' Comp. **22**	11.8	13.6	21.6	12.0	11.3	9.8	8.5	•	6.9	5.8	0.2	•	•

Selected Average Balance Sheet ($ in Thousands)

Net Receivables 23	194	0	7	186	883	2804	6720	•	25083	41326	120778	•
Inventories 24	23	0	1	22	68	223	458	•	2089	4696	4786	•
Net Property, Plant and Equipment 25	97	0	30	135	440	964	2631	•	8096	18361	26655	•
Total Assets 26	673	0	83	705	2136	6739	15388	•	65749	153105	349454	•
Notes and Loans Payable 27	155	0	40	156	534	1590	3296	•	10885	34142	86507	•
All Other Liabilities 28	249	0	20	175	633	2633	6021	•	27390	52291	143896	•
Net Worth 29	269	0	22	375	969	2516	6071	•	27474	66672	119052	•

Selected Financial Ratios (Times to 1)

Current Ratio 30	1.6	•	1.5	2.1	2.0	1.7	1.7	•	1.6	1.6	2.2	•
Quick Ratio 31	1.2	•	1.3	1.8	1.7	1.2	1.3	•	1.2	1.2	1.8	•
Net Sales to Working Capital 32	13.5	•	61.1	13.6	9.8	8.3	8.5	•	7.3	9.1	3.3	•
Coverage Ratio 33	12.2	56.5	28.7	15.3	13.3	21.8	12.9	•	15.7	7.9	2.1	•
Total Asset Turnover 34	2.9		10.0	4.5	3.3	2.7	2.4	•	1.9	1.8	1.0	•
Inventory Turnover 35	31.7	•	330.5	33.8	35.2	32.6	32.0	•	23.7	27.8	48.3	•
Receivables Turnover 36	9.0	•	108.6	17.4	9.1	12.8	5.7	•	5.1	5.3	4.1	•
Total Liabilities to Net Worth 37	1.5	•	2.7	0.9	1.2	1.7	1.5	•	1.4	1.3	1.9	•
Current Assets to Working Capital 38	2.7	•	3.1	1.9	2.0	2.5	2.5	•	2.7	2.7	1.8	•
Current Liabilities to Working Capital 39	1.7	•	2.1	0.9	1.0	1.5	1.5	•	1.7	1.7	0.8	•
Working Capital to Net Sales 40	0.1	•	0.0	0.1	0.1	0.1	0.1	•	0.1	0.1	0.3	•
Inventory to Working Capital 41	0.2	•	0.0	0.1	0.1	0.1	0.1	•	0.2	0.2	0.1	•
Total Receipts to Cash Flow 42	4.5	2.1	3.7	3.9	4.7	5.4	4.9	•	4.0	5.0	6.4	•
Cost of Goods to Cash Flow 43	1.7	0.4	0.9	0.9	1.6	2.2	2.0	•	1.6	2.4	4.1	•
Cash Flow to Total Debt 44	1.1	•	3.7	2.5	1.3	0.8	0.8	•	0.8	0.6	0.2	•

Selected Financial Factors (in Percentages)

Debt Ratio 45	60.0	•	73.2	46.9	54.6	62.7	60.5	•	58.2	56.5	65.9	•
Return on Total Assets 46	18.9	•	80.6	24.7	20.2	15.8	13.7	•	12.0	11.3	4.1	•
Return on Equity Before Income Taxes 47	43.3	•	290.1	43.5	41.1	40.4	32.1	•	26.9	22.7	6.4	•
Return on Equity After Income Taxes 48	39.4	•	286.7	40.6	38.6	36.3	27.9	•	20.2	17.8	4.3	•
Profit Margin (Before Income Tax) 49	6.0	18.9	7.8	5.1	5.7	5.7	5.3	•	6.0	5.6	2.1	•
Profit Margin (After Income Tax) 50	5.5	15.2	7.7	4.8	5.3	5.1	4.6	•	4.5	4.4	1.4	•

Table I

Corporations with and without Net Income

SPECIALIZED DESIGN SERVICES

MONEY AMOUNTS AND SIZE OF ASSETS IN THOUSANDS OF DOLLARS

Item Description for Accounting Period 7/03 Through 6/04	Total	Zero Assets	Under 500	500 to 1,000	1,000 to 5,000	5,000 to 10,000	10,000 to 25,000	25,000 to 50,000	50,000 to 100,000	100,000 to 250,000	250,000 to 500,000	500,000 to 2,500,000	2,500,000 and over
Number of Enterprises 1	40804	5133	33987	901	681	73	15	8	5	•	•	•	•
Revenues ($ in Thousands)													
Net Sales 2	16736925	358158	9704733	1463724	2675251	702001	264358	255268	1313432	•	•	•	•
Interest 3	22936	0	2543	646	796	286	402	1597	16666	•	•	•	•
Rents 4	1216	0	0	0	494	0	0	625	97	•	•	•	•
Royalties 5	15603	0	0	0	0	0	0	14512	1091	•	•	•	•
Other Portfolio Income 6	29541	71	16942	66	8835	184	2190	189	1062	•	•	•	•
Other Receipts 7	142209	183	74315	23265	25307	278	4726	6816	7320	•	•	•	•
Total Receipts 8	16948430	358412	9798533	1487701	2710683	702749	271676	279007	1339668	•	•	•	•
Average Total Receipts 9	415	70	288	1651	3980	9627	18112	34876	267934	•	•	•	•
Operating Costs/Operating Income (%)													
Cost of Operations 10	46.6	28.6	41.5	61.8	64.6	66.4	49.0	60.2	21.9	•	•	•	•
Salaries and Wages 11	14.2	2.1	11.5	7.0	13.3	14.2	24.5	21.2	43.9	•	•	•	•
Taxes Paid 12	2.7	1.9	2.8	1.6	2.4	2.2	3.4	2.4	4.4	•	•	•	•
Interest Paid 13	0.6	0.4	0.7	0.2	0.2	0.3	0.5	0.3	1.9	•	•	•	•
Depreciation 14	1.8	2.5	1.3	0.5	1.4	1.3	3.4	4.8	6.6	•	•	•	•
Amortization and Depletion 15	0.1	0.2	0.1	0.0	0.0	0.1	0.0	1.6	0.2	•	•	•	•
Pensions and Other Deferred Comp. 16	1.0	0.7	1.0	1.5	1.3	0.2	0.4	0.0	0.5	•	•	•	•
Employee Benefits 17	1.4	2.5	1.2	0.9	1.1	0.8	0.9	2.1	4.6	•	•	•	•
Advertising 18	0.7	0.2	0.6	1.2	1.0	0.1	0.4	1.0	0.9	•	•	•	•
Other Expenses 19	21.2	41.3	25.5	12.0	15.0	10.4	7.1	21.4	16.0	•	•	•	•
Officers' Compensation 20	8.0	16.3	9.7	8.5	5.5	2.9	3.8	5.7	1.3	•	•	•	•
Operating Margin 21	1.7	3.5	4.2	4.7	•	1.2	6.6	•	•	•	•	•	•
Operating Margin Before Officers' Comp. 22	9.7	19.8	13.9	13.2	4.1	10.4	•	•	•	•	•	•	•

Selected Average Balance Sheet ($ in Thousands)

Line Item										
Net Receivables 23	35	0	13	126	550	1498	2965	11184	•	50285
Inventories 24	15	0	4	165	327	671	1384	738	•	9798
Net Property, Plant and Equipment 25	29	0	14	130	130	922	2114	4658	•	73672
Total Assets 26	158	0	57	598	1852	6512	13497	40321	•	337793
Notes and Loans Payable 27	44	0	31	137	463	649	3276	4017	•	33172
All Other Liabilities 28	64	0	20	241	1167	5650	3732	9793	•	73041
Net Worth 29	50	0	6	220	223	214	6489	26511	•	231579

Selected Financial Ratios (Times to 1)

Line Item										
Current Ratio 30	1.5	•	1.4	1.5	1.3	0.8	1.3	2.0	2.6	2.6
Quick Ratio 31	1.1	•	1.2	0.8	0.8	0.6	•	1.5	2.0	1.9
Net Sales to Working Capital 32	12.5	•	28.4	11.0	12.0	•	•	4.8	2.4	2.3
Coverage Ratio 33	5.7	10.2	8.5	27.4	4.9	19.0	•	1.1		
Total Asset Turnover 34	2.6	•	5.0	2.7	2.1	1.5	1.3	0.8	0.8	
Inventory Turnover 35	12.6	•	33.0	6.1	7.8	9.5	6.2	26.1	5.9	
Receivables Turnover 36	12.7	•	25.0	13.7	7.0	6.2	5.5	3.2	6.6	
Total Liabilities to Net Worth 37	2.1	•	7.9	1.7	7.3	29.5	1.1	0.5	0.5	
Current Assets to Working Capital 38	3.1	•	3.6	3.0	4.6	•	2.0	1.6	1.6	
Current Liabilities to Working Capital 39	2.1	•	2.6	2.0	3.6	•	1.0	0.6	0.6	
Working Capital to Net Sales 40	0.1	•	0.0	0.1	0.1	•	0.2	0.4	0.4	
Inventory to Working Capital 41	0.5	•	0.3	1.1	1.3	•	0.2	0.1	0.1	
Total Receipts to Cash Flow 42	5.3	4.1	3.9	6.4	17.6	12.5	8.0	27.9	11.4	
Cost of Goods to Cash Flow 43	2.5	1.2	1.6	4.0	11.4	8.3	3.9	16.8	2.5	
Cash Flow to Total Debt 44	0.7	•	1.4	0.7	0.1	0.1	0.3	0.1	0.2	

Selected Financial Factors (in Percentages)

Line Item									
Debt Ratio 45	68.1	•	88.8	63.3	88.0	96.7	51.9	34.3	31.4
Return on Total Assets 46	9.4	•	29.2	17.9	•	2.4	13.3	1.6	
Return on Equity Before Income Taxes 47	24.3	•	229.5	46.9	•	57.5	26.3	0.2	
Return on Equity After Income Taxes 48	22.8	•	225.5	46.3	49.8	21.9	•		
Profit Margin (Before Income Tax) 49	3.0	3.5	5.2	6.3	•	1.3	9.7	•	0.2
Profit Margin (After Income Tax) 50	2.8	3.5	5.1	6.3	1.1	8.1	•	0.2	

341

Table II

Corporations with Net Income

SPECIALIZED DESIGN SERVICES

MONEY AMOUNTS AND SIZE OF ASSETS IN THOUSANDS OF DOLLARS

Item Description for Accounting Period 7/03 Through 6/04	Total	Zero Assets	Under 500	500 to 1,000	1,000 to 5,000	5,000 to 10,000	10,000 to 25,000	25,000 to 50,000	50,000 to 100,000	100,000 to 250,000	250,000 to 500,000	500,000 to 2,500,000	2,500,000 and over
Number of Enterprises 1	23743	1993	20621	735	342	33	•	3	•	•	•	•	•
Revenues ($ in Thousands)													
Net Sales 2	11354316	314354	6531689	1163088	1604706	373284	•	142047	•	•	•	•	•
Interest 3	3332	0	1972	71	431	286	•	92	•	•	•	•	•
Rents 4	643	0	0	0	17	0	•	625	•	•	•	•	•
Royalties 5	9651	0	0	0	0	0	•	9651	•	•	•	•	•
Other Portfolio Income 6	25489	0	16941	1	7619	0	•	159	•	•	•	•	•
Other Receipts 7	111109	0	59509	23264	19926	268	•	83	•	•	•	•	•
Total Receipts 8	11504540	314354	6610111	1186424	1632699	373838	•	152657	•	•	•	•	•
Average Total Receipts 9	485	158	321	1614	4774	11328	•	50886	•	•	•	•	•
Operating Costs/Operating Income (%)													
Cost of Operations 10	42.1	26.3	37.1	62.2	63.7	68.1	•	42.0	•	•	•	•	•
Salaries and Wages 11	13.0	•	12.0	7.2	11.1	7.8	•	15.7	•	•	•	•	•
Taxes Paid 12	2.4	0.6	2.4	1.4	2.4	2.0	•	3.0	•	•	•	•	•
Interest Paid 13	0.4	0.3	0.5	0.3	0.1	0.4	•	0.3	•	•	•	•	•
Depreciation 14	1.3	2.7	1.1	0.5	1.2	1.2	•	2.8	•	•	•	•	•
Amortization and Depletion 15	0.1	•	0.1	0.0	0.0	0.2	•	0.8	•	•	•	•	•
Pensions and Other Deferred Comp. 16	0.5	0.8	0.2	0.9	1.5	0.4	•	0.0	•	•	•	•	•
Employee Benefits 17	1.5	•	1.2	0.8	1.4	1.4	•	1.1	•	•	•	•	•
Advertising 18	0.5	•	0.4	1.4	0.7	0.0	•	0.3	•	•	•	•	•
Other Expenses 19	22.4	40.1	24.8	13.3	12.6	9.5	•	28.2	•	•	•	•	•
Officers' Compensation 20	7.7	17.3	9.8	5.8	3.8	5.3	•	4.2	•	•	•	•	•
Operating Margin 21	8.0	11.9	10.3	6.2	1.3	3.6	•	1.5	•	•	•	•	•
Operating Margin Before Officers' Comp. 22	15.7	29.2	20.1	12.0	5.1	8.9	•	5.7	•	•	•	•	•

Selected Average Balance Sheet ($ in Thousands)

Net Receivables 23	38	0	15	105	721	1598	23891
Inventories 24	16	0	2	187	287	475	759
Net Property, Plant and Equipment 25	26	0	12	148	155	768	4668
Total Assets 26	150	0	58	590	2029	5486	41929
Notes and Loans Payable 27	40	0	24	161	339	1179	2969
All Other Liabilities 28	54	0	12	232	1317	3472	13503
Net Worth 29	56	0	22	197	373	834	25457

Selected Financial Ratios (Times to 1)

Current Ratio 30	1.7	•	2.0	1.4	1.4	1.1	2.2
Quick Ratio 31	1.2	•	1.9	0.7	1.0	0.5	2.1
Net Sales to Working Capital 32	11.9	•	16.4	12.6	10.0	30.9	2.8
Coverage Ratio 33	22.1	48.2	25.4	32.3	24.2	9.6	28.1
Total Asset Turnover 34	3.2	•	5.5	2.7	2.3	2.1	1.1
Inventory Turnover 35	12.7	•	51.6	5.3	10.4	16.2	26.2
Receivables Turnover 36	13.4	•	23.6	16.8	6.7	14.2	4.0
Total Liabilities to Net Worth 37	1.7	•	1.7	2.0	4.4	5.6	0.6
Current Assets to Working Capital 38	2.5	•	2.0	3.3	3.7	11.5	1.8
Current Liabilities to Working Capital 39	1.5	•	1.0	2.3	2.7	10.5	0.8
Working Capital to Net Sales 40	0.1	•	0.1	0.1	0.1	0.0	0.4
Inventory to Working Capital 41	0.3	•	0.1	1.4	0.7	1.3	0.0
Total Receipts to Cash Flow 42	3.8	3.2	3.2	5.4	8.5	12.3	3.2
Cost of Goods to Cash Flow 43	1.6	0.9	1.2	3.4	5.4	8.4	1.3
Cash Flow to Total Debt 44	1.3	•	2.7	0.7	0.3	0.2	0.9

Selected Financial Factors (in Percentages)

Debt Ratio 45	62.6	•	62.7	66.6	81.6	84.8	39.3
Return on Total Assets 46	31.1	•	65.6	22.6	7.4	8.6	10.5
Return on Equity Before Income Taxes 47	79.4	•	168.7	65.7	38.5	50.8	16.6
Return on Equity After Income Taxes 48	77.2	•	166.8	64.9	35.0	46.5	14.7
Profit Margin (Before Income Tax) 49	9.3	11.9	11.5	8.2	3.1	3.7	9.0
Profit Margin (After Income Tax) 50	9.0	11.9	11.4	8.1	2.8	3.4	7.9

Table I

Corporations with and without Net Income

COMPUTER SYSTEMS DESIGN AND RELATED SERVICES

MONEY AMOUNTS AND SIZE OF ASSETS IN THOUSANDS OF DOLLARS

Item Description for Accounting Period 7/03 Through 6/04	Total	Zero Assets	Under 500	500 to 1,000	1,000 to 5,000	5,000 to 10,000	10,000 to 25,000	25,000 to 50,000	50,000 to 100,000	100,000 to 250,000	250,000 to 500,000	500,000 to 2,500,000	2,500,000 and over
Number of Enterprises **1**	105232	22129	76345	2479	2938	665	348	135	81	62	26	19	5
Revenues ($ in Thousands)													
Net Sales **2**	123953125	3660100	23117666	6954041	18143340	6473038	7515625	5466928	5487060	7214811	6280082	11833306	21807129
Interest **3**	844289	1801	5831	4564	24110	24530	23738	21439	29532	72365	48545	148714	439120
Rents **4**	157232	54	15552	0	787	2479	1857	1407	5302	6233	15845	38907	68809
Royalties **5**	1712525	30604	4527	1117	8848	6812	6177	14270	13245	20096	138820	748192	719817
Other Portfolio Income **6**	1165947	33806	59762	75605	67946	171994	33473	20865	32210	115770	26105	291657	236755
Other Receipts **7**	1514644	59095	97250	44819	189346	200100	122382	65070	81205	379421	184626	95769	-4441
Total Receipts **8**	129347762	3785460	23300588	7080146	18434377	6878953	7703252	5589979	5648554	7808696	6694023	13156545	23267189
Average Total Receipts **9**	1229	171	305	2856	6274	10344	22136	41407	69735	125947	257462	692450	4653438
Operating Costs/Operating Income (%)													
Cost of Operations **10**	31.3	16.6	25.5	35.2	41.8	34.2	45.7	37.9	41.7	36.4	39.3	37.0	13.1
Salaries and Wages **11**	28.2	38.2	23.5	30.2	25.2	34.2	28.4	29.1	29.4	30.1	29.4	28.9	29.6
Taxes Paid **12**	4.1	4.3	3.4	3.7	3.6	4.1	3.4	3.2	2.9	3.5	2.9	4.4	6.5
Interest Paid **13**	1.4	0.5	0.6	0.9	0.6	1.4	1.1	1.2	1.1	2.3	2.4	1.6	2.7
Depreciation **14**	2.8	2.0	1.4	1.6	1.4	3.4	3.4	3.1	3.3	3.2	5.2	3.2	4.3
Amortization and Depletion **15**	1.6	0.9	0.2	0.4	0.8	1.9	1.4	1.1	2.1	2.5	2.6	2.4	3.2
Pensions and Other Deferred Comp. **16**	0.9	1.2	1.2	1.0	0.8	1.0	0.5	0.5	0.4	0.5	0.7	0.9	1.0
Employee Benefits **17**	2.5	1.1	1.7	2.1	2.3	3.6	2.6	3.0	2.4	2.8	2.9	4.2	2.4
Advertising **18**	0.6	0.7	0.6	0.6	0.7	1.0	1.1	0.7	0.7	0.6	0.7	0.5	0.3
Other Expenses **19**	27.4	34.8	24.8	22.9	20.0	24.9	25.7	23.5	22.1	24.9	21.6	36.2	38.0
Officers' Compensation **20**	5.9	7.1	16.1	8.7	7.0	6.1	3.3	2.7	2.0	2.2	1.4	0.7	0.9
Operating Margin **21**	•	•	1.0	•	•	•	•	•	•	•	•	•	•
Operating Margin Before Officers' Comp. **22**	•	•	17.1	2.8	•	•	•	•	•	•	•	•	•

Selected Average Balance Sheet ($ in Thousands)

Net Receivables 23	268	9	215	741	1390	4263	9363	15635	21786	74529	183801	2628214
Inventories 24	14	2	49	58	161	392	586	1216	2275	2751	7095	48965
Net Property, Plant and Equipment 25	84	10	82	209	652	1476	2437	7118	8944	28209	97442	445988
Total Assets 26	1020	51	706	2327	7133	15574	34666	69982	154061	346141	1020152	7282176
Notes and Loans Payable 27	245	44	337	749	1510	3226	5866	12656	33779	76921	172414	1621981
All Other Liabilities 28	356	22	372	1309	2845	6775	14207	22753	43166	133103	280752	2303759
Net Worth 29	419	-14	-3	269	2778	5573	14592	34573	77116	136117	566986	3356435

Selected Financial Ratios (Times to 1)

Current Ratio 30	1.4	0.9	1.3	1.5	1.6	1.6	1.5	1.8	1.5	1.7	2.0	1.2
Quick Ratio 31	1.2	0.8	1.1	1.3	1.3	1.3	1.3	1.4	1.2	1.3	1.7	1.1
Net Sales to Working Capital 32	7.3	•	22.2	12.2	5.5	5.4	5.4	3.7	4.7	3.6	2.5	9.3
Coverage Ratio 33	•	4.0	•	•	•	•	•	•	0.8	•	•	3.0
Total Asset Turnover 34	1.2	5.9	4.0	2.7	1.4	1.4	1.2	1.0	0.8	0.7	0.6	0.6
Inventory Turnover 35	26.3	34.5	20.0	44.4	20.7	25.1	26.2	23.2	18.6	34.5	32.4	11.6
Receivables Turnover 36	4.3	35.8	12.5	8.8	6.6	4.9	4.2	4.8	5.0	3.6	3.4	1.6
Total Liabilities to Net Worth 37	1.4	•	7.6	1.6	1.8	1.4	1.0	1.0	1.0	1.5	0.8	1.2
Current Assets to Working Capital 38	3.3	•	4.1	3.1	2.7	2.7	2.9	2.2	2.9	2.5	2.0	6.9
Current Liabilities to Working Capital 39	2.3	•	3.1	2.1	1.7	1.7	1.9	1.2	1.9	1.5	1.0	5.9
Working Capital to Net Sales 40	0.1	•	0.0	0.1	0.2	0.2	0.2	0.3	0.2	0.3	0.4	0.1
Inventory to Working Capital 41	0.1	•	0.4	0.1	0.1	0.1	0.1	0.1	0.1	0.1	0.0	0.1
Total Receipts to Cash Flow 42	5.0	3.9	8.0	7.1	12.5	14.1	6.3	8.4	5.4	6.7	4.8	2.6
Cost of Goods to Cash Flow 43	1.6	0.6	2.8	3.0	4.3	6.4	2.4	3.5	2.0	2.6	1.8	0.3
Cash Flow to Total Debt 44	0.4	1.0	0.5	0.4	0.2	0.2	0.3	0.2	0.3	0.2	0.3	0.4

Selected Financial Factors (in Percentages)

Debt Ratio 45	58.9	127.5	100.5	88.4	61.1	64.2	57.9	50.6	49.9	60.7	44.4	53.9
Return on Total Assets 46	•	14.3	•	•	•	•	•	•	1.5	•	•	4.8
Return on Equity Before Income Taxes 47	•	•	4536.0	•	•	•	•	•	•	•	•	7.0
Return on Equity After Income Taxes 48	•	•	4720.6	•	•	•	•	•	•	•	•	4.8
Profit Margin (Before Income Tax) 49	•	1.8	•	•	•	•	•	•	•	•	•	5.4
Profit Margin (After Income Tax) 50	•	1.7	•	•	•	•	•	•	•	•	•	3.7

Table II

Corporations with Net Income

COMPUTER SYSTEMS DESIGN AND RELATED SERVICES

MONEY AMOUNTS AND SIZE OF ASSETS IN THOUSANDS OF DOLLARS

Item Description for Accounting Period 7/03 Through 6/04	Total	Zero Assets	Under 500	500 to 1,000	1,000 to 5,000	5,000 to 10,000	10,000 to 25,000	25,000 to 50,000	50,000 to 100,000	100,000 to 250,000	250,000 to 500,000	500,000 to 2,500,000	2,500,000 and over
Number of Enterprises 1	58087	9453	44729	1632	1642	346	141	58	32	30	12	•	•
Revenues ($ in Thousands)													
Net Sales 2	89314915	2832850	16042111	5730320	13861074	4750396	4703800	3321840	2738444	4153882	3817703	•	•
Interest 3	566883	282	3499	1759	7934	1956	5733	13128	6301	24757	25518	•	•
Rents 4	133103	27	6533	0	500	1038	1434	898	2046	3859	11517	•	•
Royalties 5	909951	0	4527	0	4910	45	5741	3259	503	15731	138729	•	•
Other Portfolio Income 6	832551	25859	58051	69069	45729	90792	23977	15531	31310	99827	12415	•	•
Other Receipts 7	649891	42501	74693	19785	128469	98928	33998	38343	20515	71094	95036	•	•
Total Receipts 8	92407294	2901519	16189414	5820933	14048616	4943155	4774683	3392999	2799119	4369150	4100918	•	•
Average Total Receipts 9	1591	307	362	3567	8556	14287	33863	58500	87472	145638	341743	•	•
Operating Costs/Operating Income (%)													
Cost of Operations 10	31.3	13.8	29.5	35.3	45.6	37.6	48.5	37.5	36.4	42.3	43.1	•	•
Salaries and Wages 11	23.4	35.9	14.6	27.0	18.5	24.6	19.2	25.0	27.5	21.5	24.3	•	•
Taxes Paid 12	4.1	4.3	3.1	3.3	3.4	3.4	2.8	2.7	3.1	2.7	2.9	•	•
Interest Paid 13	1.2	0.2	0.5	0.3	0.2	0.6	0.4	0.9	0.7	2.4	2.4	•	•
Depreciation 14	2.3	0.6	1.0	1.2	0.8	2.1	1.8	2.0	2.1	2.7	5.2	•	•
Amortization and Depletion 15	1.2	0.1	0.0	0.0	0.1	0.9	0.3	0.7	0.4	2.4	2.1	•	•
Pensions and Other Deferred Comp. 16	0.9	0.6	1.2	1.0	0.9	1.2	0.6	0.6	0.5	0.4	0.6	•	•
Employee Benefits 17	2.2	0.7	1.6	1.5	1.9	3.0	2.1	2.6	2.2	2.5	2.9	•	•
Advertising 18	0.4	0.5	0.4	0.4	0.5	0.6	0.7	0.5	0.5	0.5	0.4	•	•
Other Expenses 19	23.3	26.2	21.6	18.9	15.1	15.4	13.7	19.8	16.5	17.7	17.7	•	•
Officers' Compensation 20	5.5	5.5	16.5	7.6	5.9	4.9	2.9	2.3	1.9	2.0	1.1	•	•
Operating Margin 21	4.2	11.6	9.9	3.3	7.2	5.8	6.9	5.3	8.1	2.0	2.8	•	•
Operating Margin Before Officers' Comp. 22	9.7	17.0	26.4	11.0	13.0	10.6	9.8	7.6	10.0	4.8	•	•	•

Selected Average Balance Sheet ($ in Thousands)

Net Receivables 23	368	0	8	237	935	1522	5714	12157	18018	22353	103678
Inventories 24	15	0	2	45	68	215	408	825	1410	1633	3809
Net Property, Plant and Equipment 25	90	0	9	70	176	555	1380	2149	4707	9515	36732
Total Assets 26	1198	0	55	707	2305	7208	15673	35053	70791	154641	361120
Notes and Loans Payable 27	255	0	25	136	515	1283	2394	5999	11295	35424	56703
All Other Liabilities 28	396	0	18	275	1328	2203	7020	15616	25346	42988	104283
Net Worth 29	546	0	12	295	461	3722	6259	13438	34149	76229	200133

Selected Financial Ratios (Times to 1)

Current Ratio 30	1.4	•	1.6	1.9	1.7	1.6	1.6	1.5	1.8	1.3	2.2
Quick Ratio 31	1.2	•	1.4	1.7	1.4	1.4	1.3	1.3	1.4	1.0	1.8
Net Sales to Working Capital 32	9.0	•	23.7	13.1	11.8	8.1	7.8	7.3	4.2	8.6	3.1
Coverage Ratio 33	7.6	82.9	23.1	19.0	38.6	18.5	23.1	8.8	16.1	4.6	3.0
Total Asset Turnover 34	1.3	•	6.5	5.0	3.7	1.9	2.1	1.6	1.2	0.9	0.9
Inventory Turnover 35	32.4	•	45.6	27.6	56.5	24.0	39.7	26.1	22.1	35.8	36.0
Receivables Turnover 36	4.8	•	43.9	15.7	9.8	18.0	6.0	4.9	5.1	7.7	3.7
Total Liabilities to Net Worth 37	1.2	•	3.7	1.4	4.0	0.9	1.5	1.6	1.1	1.0	0.8
Current Assets to Working Capital 38	3.6	•	2.6	2.1	2.5	2.7	2.7	3.1	2.2	4.2	1.8
Current Liabilities to Working Capital 39	2.6	•	1.6	1.1	1.5	1.7	1.7	2.1	1.2	3.2	0.8
Working Capital to Net Sales 40	0.1	•	0.0	0.1	0.1	0.1	0.1	0.1	0.2	0.1	0.3
Inventory to Working Capital 41	0.1	•	0.2	0.2	0.1	0.1	0.1	0.1	0.1	0.2	0.1
Total Receipts to Cash Flow 42	3.7	2.6	3.5	5.1	4.7	5.0	5.2	4.2	4.4	4.9	5.1
Cost of Goods to Cash Flow 43	1.2	0.4	1.0	1.8	2.2	1.9	1.6	1.6	1.6	2.1	2.2
Cash Flow to Total Debt 44	0.6	•	2.4	1.7	1.0	0.8	0.7	0.6	0.5	0.4	0.4

Selected Financial Factors (in Percentages)

Debt Ratio 45	54.4	•	78.7	58.2	80.0	48.4	60.1	61.7	51.8	50.7	44.6
Return on Total Assets 46	11.7	•	74.0	25.8	32.0	19.8	18.7	13.7	13.4	9.8	6.4
Return on Equity Before Income Taxes 47	22.3	•	331.7	58.4	155.7	36.3	44.8	31.7	26.0	15.6	7.7
Return on Equity After Income Taxes 48	19.7	•	326.5	55.2	148.0	33.4	39.7	27.5	22.5	12.4	5.9
Profit Margin (Before Income Tax) 49	7.9	14.0	10.9	4.9	8.5	9.8	8.4	7.4	10.4	8.6	4.8
Profit Margin (After Income Tax) 50	7.0	12.6	10.7	4.6	8.1	9.1	7.4	6.5	9.0	6.8	3.7

Table I

Corporations with and without Net Income

MANAGEMENT, SCIENTIFIC, AND TECHNICAL CONSULTING SERVICES

MONEY AMOUNTS AND SIZE OF ASSETS IN THOUSANDS OF DOLLARS

Item Description for Accounting Period 7/03 Through 6/04		Total	Zero Assets	Under 500	500 to 1,000	1,000 to 5,000	5,000 to 10,000	10,000 to 25,000	25,000 to 50,000	50,000 to 100,000	100,000 to 250,000	250,000 to 500,000	500,000 to 2,500,000	2,500,000 and over
Number of Enterprises	1	211748	36740	165430	4695	3550	642	401	136	67	41	21	24	•
Revenues ($ in Thousands)														
Net Sales	2	150598819	2487142	59867982	15560437	13728345	5662651	8876836	5050743	5571646	6833118	5352719	21607200	•
Interest	3	687203	6103	41852	36052	26573	13874	23995	26465	19702	50927	66519	375141	•
Rents	4	87897	288	287	3162	1310	126	4253	5349	14590	8912	1241	48379	•
Royalties	5	594234	6833	3114	1	21405	42	15041	3299	134234	27436	25721	357107	•
Other Portfolio Income	6	616623	41146	102913	34253	17959	36988	138076	13874	31485	22286	20482	157160	•
Other Receipts	7	3450342	-84071	1253102	197259	553240	171125	285883	77634	101793	69920	305183	519278	•
Total Receipts	8	156035118	2457441	61269250	15831164	14348832	5884806	9344084	5177364	5873450	7012599	5771865	23064265	•
Average Total Receipts	9	737	67	370	3372	4042	9166	23302	38069	87663	171039	274851	961011	•
Operating Costs/Operating Income (%)														
Cost of Operations	10	25.8	16.0	17.6	60.9	31.3	24.1	34.9	30.1	31.9	33.9	19.2	14.2	•
Salaries and Wages	11	25.7	17.7	20.5	18.1	32.8	25.2	24.4	29.6	27.5	29.5	32.0	38.7	•
Taxes Paid	12	3.0	3.0	3.1	1.2	3.5	4.0	2.9	2.9	3.8	2.6	3.5	3.3	•
Interest Paid	13	0.9	1.6	0.3	0.7	0.8	0.7	1.2	1.1	1.0	1.7	2.3	1.9	•
Depreciation	14	1.7	2.5	1.1	0.7	1.5	1.9	2.2	2.6	2.4	2.0	2.4	2.9	•
Amortization and Depletion	15	0.4	0.3	0.1	0.1	0.1	0.2	0.5	0.7	0.6	1.1	1.4	0.9	•
Pensions and Other Deferred Comp.	16	1.6	3.3	1.6	0.6	0.8	1.2	0.9	1.2	1.2	1.9	0.6	3.3	•
Employee Benefits	17	1.9	1.7	1.7	0.8	2.4	2.2	2.2	3.0	3.3	1.7	1.2	2.6	•
Advertising	18	0.7	1.0	0.7	0.6	0.5	0.4	0.4	1.0	0.4	0.5	0.5	1.1	•
Other Expenses	19	31.5	41.4	36.2	11.0	21.1	23.1	29.3	26.3	35.8	26.8	28.0	44.1	•
Officers' Compensation	20	8.1	13.2	13.7	3.6	6.5	14.5	3.6	3.2	2.6	1.1	9.3	1.0	•
Operating Margin	21	•	•	3.4	1.6	•	2.5	•	•	•	•	•	•	•
Operating Margin Before Officers' Comp.	22	6.9	11.5	17.2	5.2	5.2	17.0	1.0	1.5	•	•	8.8	•	•

Selected Average Balance Sheet ($ in Thousands)

Net Receivables 23	89	6	157	651	1640	3870	8013	19626	37794	81756	266653 •
Inventories 24	6	1	24	61	23	248	677	577	3320	1001	11523 •
Net Property, Plant and Equipment 25	43	10	122	257	715	1940	4123	10270	15998	20740	101529 •
Total Assets 26	430	52	741	2139	6982	15151	34850	71233	163716	382670	1516593 •
Notes and Loans Payable 27	137	43	305	833	1889	5154	11466	29201	29089	121761	286182 •
All Other Liabilities 28	143	16	218	558	2571	4860	11356	25565	51622	101948	563643 •
Net Worth 29	150	-7	218	748	2522	5137	12028	16467	83005	158961	666768 •

Selected Financial Ratios (Times to 1)

Current Ratio 30	1.3	1.3	1.8	2.1	1.6	1.5	1.3	1.4	1.5	1.3	1.0 •
Quick Ratio 31	1.0	1.1	1.5	1.6	1.2	1.1	0.9	1.2	1.2	1.1	0.8 •
Net Sales to Working Capital 32	15.5	45.0	18.9	5.3	8.9	11.0	7.5	6.1	6.8	•	•
Coverage Ratio 33	3.7	22.0	5.6	5.0	3.2	1.8	•	0.9	4.2	•	•
Total Asset Turnover 34	1.7	6.9	4.5	1.8	1.5	1.1	1.2	1.0	1.0	0.7	0.6 •
Inventory Turnover 35	31.9	50.1	85.3	19.9	91.1	31.1	16.5	46.0	17.0	48.9	11.1 •
Receivables Turnover 36	7.8	53.8	29.7	6.2	6.2	5.8	4.6	5.2	4.1	2.9	3.9 •
Total Liabilities to Net Worth 37	1.9	•	2.4	1.9	1.8	1.9	3.3	3.3	1.0	1.4	1.3 •
Current Assets to Working Capital 38	4.3	3.9	2.3	1.9	2.7	4.9	3.3	2.9	3.3	4.2	•
Current Liabilities to Working Capital 39	3.3	2.9	1.3	0.9	1.7	3.9	2.3	1.9	2.3	3.2	•
Working Capital to Net Sales 40	0.1	0.0	0.1	0.2	0.2	0.1	0.1	0.1	0.2	0.1	•
Inventory to Working Capital 41	0.1	0.2	0.2	0.1	0.0	0.1	0.1	0.2	0.1	0.0	•
Total Receipts to Cash Flow 42	3.3	3.2	2.6	7.8	4.7	3.9	4.6	4.0	4.3	3.3	3.2 •
Cost of Goods to Cash Flow 43	0.9	0.5	4.7	1.5	0.9	1.3	1.4	1.3	1.5	0.6	0.4 •
Cash Flow to Total Debt 44	0.8	2.3	0.8	0.6	0.5	0.6	0.4	0.4	0.5	0.3	0.3 •

Selected Financial Factors (in Percentages)

Debt Ratio 45	65.1	112.6	70.6	65.0	63.9	66.1	65.5	76.9	49.3	58.5	56.0 •
Return on Total Assets 46	5.4	41.8	17.7	7.3	8.8	5.7	2.1	•	1.5	6.4	•
Return on Equity Before Income Taxes 47	11.3	•	49.3	16.7	22.2	11.6	2.7	•	•	11.7	•
Return on Equity After Income Taxes 48	8.4	•	48.0	14.8	19.2	9.0	1.1	•	•	7.6	•
Profit Margin (Before Income Tax) 49	2.4	5.8	3.2	3.2	6.4	2.7	0.9	•	•	7.3	•
Profit Margin (After Income Tax) 50	1.8	5.7	3.2	2.9	5.5	2.1	0.4	•	•	4.7	•

Table II
Corporations with Net Income

MANAGEMENT, SCIENTIFIC, AND TECHNICAL CONSULTING SERVICES

MONEY AMOUNTS AND SIZE OF ASSETS IN THOUSANDS OF DOLLARS

Item Description for Accounting Period 7/03 Through 6/04	Total	Zero Assets	Under 500	500 to 1,000	1,000 to 5,000	5,000 to 10,000	10,000 to 25,000	25,000 to 50,000	50,000 to 100,000	100,000 to 250,000	250,000 to 500,000	500,000 to 2,500,000	2,500,000 and over
Number of Enterprises 1	117982	13779	97944	3257	2231	373	235	78	34	24	10	16	•
Revenues ($ in Thousands)													
Net Sales 2	99898336	1620958	32479434	13579136	9517859	4136260	6261981	4025685	4196922	4114338	4049415	15916348	•
Interest 3	384406	3761	32535	13454	18028	4437	10191	15114	13151	28014	14128	231592	•
Rents 4	44219	206	287	3018	732	0	2580	4689	11106	373	1241	19988	•
Royalties 5	423306	0	1539	0	9634	42	3980	173	131477	4399	25709	246352	•
Other Portfolio Income 6	456171	24571	79615	16271	11091	36043	119265	9745	29282	19268	8956	102067	•
Other Receipts 7	3158577	33997	1157063	170696	526139	173702	209372	55655	73883	68698	284341	405029	•
Total Receipts 8	104365015	1683493	33750473	13782575	10083483	4350484	6607369	4111061	4455821	4235090	4383790	16921376	•
Average Total Receipts 9	885	122	345	4232	4520	11663	28116	52706	131054	176462	438379	1057586	•
Operating Costs/Operating Income (%)													
Cost of Operations 10	29.6	16.0	21.4	62.2	34.7	29.4	34.0	30.0	34.0	46.9	23.8	11.1	•
Salaries and Wages 11	22.7	17.0	16.2	17.6	21.4	21.1	22.8	29.2	24.8	18.0	27.3	39.9	•
Taxes Paid 12	2.9	2.9	3.4	0.9	2.8	4.3	2.8	2.8	3.9	1.7	3.5	3.2	•
Interest Paid 13	0.6	1.4	0.3	0.4	0.5	0.3	0.8	0.7	0.8	1.0	0.5	1.5	•
Depreciation 14	1.5	2.5	1.1	0.5	1.4	1.7	1.7	1.7	1.5	1.2	2.4	2.8	•
Amortization and Depletion 15	0.3	0.1	0.1	0.1	0.0	0.1	0.3	0.5	0.4	1.5	1.1	0.9	•
Pensions and Other Deferred Comp. 16	1.4	1.1	1.7	0.4	0.9	1.1	0.8	1.2	1.0	0.1	0.7	2.7	•
Employee Benefits 17	1.7	0.9	1.2	0.8	1.9	2.3	2.1	3.0	3.5	0.8	1.1	2.7	•
Advertising 18	0.7	1.0	0.9	0.5	0.6	0.3	0.4	1.0	0.3	0.2	0.4	0.7	•
Other Expenses 19	24.2	24.4	26.3	9.0	22.5	19.2	27.2	23.0	24.0	25.5	22.0	34.3	•
Officers' Compensation 20	8.2	12.2	16.3	3.4	7.7	10.6	3.4	3.0	2.0	1.0	11.8	0.8	•
Operating Margin 21	6.2	20.7	11.1	4.1	5.5	9.6	3.8	4.0	3.7	2.1	5.4	•	•
Operating Margin Before Officers' Comp. 22	14.4	32.9	27.4	7.6	13.2	20.2	7.2	7.0	5.7	3.1	17.2	0.3	•

Selected Average Balance Sheet ($ in Thousands)

Item													
Net Receivables 23	110	0	8	150	749	2340	4362	9509	25962	49993	79765	288285	•
Inventories 24	8	0	2	21	74	13	294	672	389	3918	557	19416	•
Net Property, Plant and Equipment 25	46	0	10	136	209	629	1667	3889	9087	11494	24922	107218	•
Total Assets 26	410	0	59	744	2305	6836	15013	35441	72983	161217	386130	996403	•
Notes and Loans Payable 27	99	0	31	247	457	1109	3348	8480	14205	27721	50572	205600	•
All Other Liabilities 28	124	0	14	171	612	2383	4737	12873	28471	54356	86999	328299	•
Net Worth 29	186	0	14	326	1236	3343	6928	14088	30307	79141	248558	462504	•

Selected Financial Ratios (Times to 1)

Item												
Current Ratio 30	1.6	•	2.1	2.4	2.4	1.8	1.7	1.3	1.5	1.6	1.5	1.3
Quick Ratio 31	1.3	•	1.7	2.0	1.9	1.6	1.3	1.0	1.4	1.4	1.4	1.0
Net Sales to Working Capital 32	9.8	•	17.2	16.5	4.5	5.4	7.6	11.2	8.5	5.2	7.2	10.1
Coverage Ratio 33	17.8	19.1	50.4	16.3	23.7	48.4	12.5	9.5	13.4	6.2	27.1	5.2
Total Asset Turnover 34	2.1	•	5.6	5.6	1.9	1.6	1.8	1.5	1.7	1.1	1.0	1.0
Inventory Turnover 35	33.0	•	40.2	123.5	20.0	255.7	30.9	23.0	108.1	20.5	172.9	5.7
Receivables Turnover 36	7.2	•	42.0	37.3	6.5	9.5	6.6	5.6	5.9	4.9	3.9	6.9
Total Liabilities to Net Worth 37	1.2	•	3.2	1.3	0.9	1.0	1.2	1.5	1.4	1.0	0.6	1.2
Current Assets to Working Capital 38	2.6	•	1.9	1.7	1.7	2.3	2.5	4.0	2.8	2.6	2.9	4.6
Current Liabilities to Working Capital 39	1.6	•	0.9	0.7	0.7	1.3	1.5	3.0	1.8	1.6	1.9	3.6
Working Capital to Net Sales 40	0.1	•	0.1	0.1	0.2	0.2	0.1	0.1	0.1	0.2	0.1	0.1
Inventory to Working Capital 41	0.1	•	0.1	0.1	0.1	0.0	0.1	0.1	0.0	0.1	0.0	0.2
Total Receipts to Cash Flow 42	3.2	2.2	2.7	7.4	3.2	3.4	3.1	4.1	3.4	3.5	3.2	2.8
Cost of Goods to Cash Flow 43	1.0	0.3	0.6	4.6	1.1	1.0	1.0	1.2	1.2	1.6	0.8	0.3
Cash Flow to Total Debt 44	1.2	•	2.7	1.3	1.3	0.9	1.1	0.6	0.8	0.6	0.9	0.7

Selected Financial Factors (in Percentages)

Item												
Debt Ratio 45	54.5	•	76.3	56.1	46.4	51.1	53.9	60.2	58.5	50.9	35.6	53.6
Return on Total Assets 46	23.5	•	86.0	33.6	22.2	24.5	17.9	9.9	18.1	6.5	14.7	7.6
Return on Equity Before Income Taxes 47	48.8	•	356.6	71.8	39.7	49.0	35.8	22.3	40.3	11.1	22.0	13.2
Return on Equity After Income Taxes 48	44.7	•	352.0	70.6	37.8	45.2	32.4	19.9	30.4	8.0	16.5	8.7
Profit Margin (Before Income Tax) 49	10.7	24.5	15.0	5.6	11.5	14.8	9.3	6.1	9.9	5.1	13.5	6.1
Profit Margin (After Income Tax) 50	9.8	23.9	14.8	5.5	11.0	13.6	8.4	5.4	7.5	3.7	10.1	4.1

Table I

Corporations with and without Net Income

SCIENTIFIC RESEARCH AND DEVELOPMENT SERVICES

MONEY AMOUNTS AND SIZE OF ASSETS IN THOUSANDS OF DOLLARS

Item Description for Accounting Period 7/03 Through 6/04		Total	Zero Assets	Under 500	500 to 1,000	1,000 to 5,000	5,000 to 10,000	10,000 to 25,000	25,000 to 50,000	50,000 to 100,000	100,000 to 250,000	250,000 to 500,000	500,000 to 2,500,000	2,500,000 and over
Number of Enterprises	1	11285	729	6891	1835	1050	275	243	108	64	48	21	18	3
Revenues ($ in Thousands)														
Net Sales	2	30272076	751964	2723557	1666680	1787494	1005963	1917184	1357103	1717463	2353577	1037649	3621641	10031800
Interest	3	594581	56625	735	2999	9327	13444	27361	30909	32966	73774	75332	180067	91043
Rents	4	36441	0	0	3055	490	22	1093	1699	667	885	122	18921	9487
Royalties	5	1749734	415288	1099	42356	1111	22148	26204	18658	81203	33544	408309	141977	557837
Other Portfolio Income	6	316831	13586	1554	15349	21122	11358	18074	19750	31449	34798	21405	105380	23007
Other Receipts	7	1916157	153050	153683	25914	181872	78936	59635	128482	86490	222630	69581	719973	35910
Total Receipts	8	34885820	1390513	2880628	1756353	2001416	1131871	2049551	1556601	1950238	2719208	1612398	4787959	11049084
Average Total Receipts	9	3091	1907	418	957	1906	4116	8434	14413	30472	56650	76781	265998	3683028
Operating Costs/Operating Income (%)														
Cost of Operations	10	38.7	7.3	7.9	22.6	34.2	27.3	37.8	39.1	45.8	11.3	25.1	36.4	60.9
Salaries and Wages	11	28.7	63.7	33.5	25.4	39.9	42.9	37.5	40.4	31.7	42.0	53.5	29.9	12.5
Taxes Paid	12	4.1	5.7	3.9	4.5	6.1	5.2	6.2	5.7	5.1	4.1	6.6	4.3	2.4
Interest Paid	13	3.0	9.9	0.7	2.6	4.0	7.2	2.4	3.1	2.4	3.6	9.0	5.3	1.3
Depreciation	14	5.0	11.5	2.1	3.3	5.6	8.9	6.5	8.9	6.2	9.7	11.5	5.5	2.2
Amortization and Depletion	15	2.2	2.9	0.2	1.2	2.4	3.4	3.6	2.6	4.0	3.5	6.0	3.4	1.1
Pensions and Other Deferred Comp.	16	1.6	1.4	2.5	3.1	1.5	0.6	1.4	1.5	2.3	2.1	0.6	1.0	1.3
Employee Benefits	17	2.9	3.5	1.4	2.1	4.1	4.8	4.5	5.1	4.9	4.7	7.1	4.4	0.8
Advertising	18	0.8	0.8	3.0	0.4	1.3	1.2	0.8	1.0	1.3	0.7	0.7	0.9	0.1
Other Expenses	19	46.3	79.8	45.9	33.8	59.8	74.0	57.3	63.5	54.7	65.7	137.5	49.5	20.6
Officers' Compensation	20	5.5	3.8	11.9	20.0	10.9	12.5	7.9	8.2	6.1	4.6	5.1	2.9	0.3
Operating Margin	21	•	•	•	•	•	•	•	•	•	•	•	•	•
Operating Margin Before Officers' Comp.	22	•	0.9	•	•	•	•	•	•	•	•	•	•	•

Selected Average Balance Sheet ($ in Thousands)

Net Receivables 23	761	0	106	471	620	1733	2949	6085	13131	20110	101863	1215920
Inventories 24	109	0	4	135	147	366	499	1228	2623	5885	10225	253728
Net Property, Plant and Equipment 25	699	15	81	313	1023	2018	4373	8163	23738	47970	72308	694890
Total Assets 26	6037	90	710	2380	6671	15866	36106	71002	149864	327164	852703	6721728
Notes and Loans Payable 27	1434	0	400	778	2169	2468	4953	13050	23424	92858	315533	950457
All Other Liabilities 28	1414	45	172	894	2978	3318	7653	12705	29512	72109	158371	1783840
Net Worth 29	3189	-22	139	708	1523	10081	23500	45247	96928	162197	378799	3987430

Selected Financial Ratios (Times to 1)

Current Ratio 30	2.5	•	2.0	1.8	1.1	3.4	3.1	2.9	3.2	2.6	3.6	2.1
Quick Ratio 31	1.7	•	1.4	1.5	1.0	2.7	2.5	2.2	1.8	1.8	1.9	1.5
Net Sales to Working Capital 32	1.4	178.0	4.2	2.5	6.0	1.0	0.8	1.0	0.9	0.5	0.6	2.4
Coverage Ratio 33	•	0.5	•	•	•	•	•	•	•	•	•	3.6
Total Asset Turnover 34	0.4	•	1.3	0.7	0.5	0.3	0.3	0.4	0.3	0.2	0.2	0.5
Inventory Turnover 35	9.5	69.7	51.7	4.3	6.8	8.1	9.8	10.0	2.1	2.1	7.2	8.3
Receivables Turnover 36	4.3	32.2	12.0	3.7	6.0	4.6	4.3	5.6	4.3	2.0	1.6	5.7
Total Liabilities to Net Worth 37	0.9	•	4.1	2.4	3.4	0.6	0.5	0.6	0.5	1.0	1.3	0.7
Current Assets to Working Capital 38	1.6	21.6	2.0	2.3	7.7	1.4	1.5	1.5	1.4	1.6	1.4	1.9
Current Liabilities to Working Capital 39	0.6	20.6	1.0	1.3	6.7	0.4	0.5	0.5	0.4	0.6	0.4	0.9
Working Capital to Net Sales 40	0.7	0.0	0.2	0.4	0.2	1.0	1.3	1.0	1.1	1.9	1.6	0.4
Inventory to Working Capital 41	0.1	0.1	0.0	0.2	0.3	0.0	0.0	0.1	0.1	0.0	0.0	0.2
Total Receipts to Cash Flow 42	6.6	1.5	3.2	7.9	•	•	•	•	5.3	10.0	3.2	4.8
Cost of Goods to Cash Flow 43	2.6	0.1	1.8	•	•	•	•	•	0.6	2.5	1.2	2.9
Cash Flow to Total Debt 44	0.1	1.1	0.2	•	•	•	•	•	0.2	0.0	0.1	0.3

Selected Financial Factors (in Percentages)

Debt Ratio 45	47.2	124.2	80.5	70.2	77.2	36.5	34.9	36.3	35.3	50.4	55.6	40.7
Return on Total Assets 46	•	•	•	•	•	•	•	•	•	•	•	2.4
Return on Equity Before Income Taxes 47	•	130.6	•	•	•	•	•	•	•	•	•	2.9
Return on Equity After Income Taxes 48	•	130.7	•	•	•	•	•	•	•	•	•	2.4
Profit Margin (Before Income Tax) 49	•	•	•	•	•	•	•	•	•	•	•	3.4
Profit Margin (After Income Tax) 50	•	•	•	•	•	•	•	•	•	•	•	2.7

Table II
Corporations with Net Income

PROFESSIONAL, SCIENTIFIC, AND TECHNICAL SERVICES
541700

SCIENTIFIC RESEARCH AND DEVELOPMENT SERVICES

MONEY AMOUNTS AND SIZE OF ASSETS IN THOUSANDS OF DOLLARS

Item Description for Accounting Period 7/03 Through 6/04	Total	Zero Assets	Under 500	500 to 1,000	1,000 to 5,000	5,000 to 10,000	10,000 to 25,000	25,000 to 50,000	50,000 to 100,000	100,000 to 250,000	250,000 to 500,000	500,000 to 2,500,000	2,500,000 and over
Number of Enterprises **1**	4516	134	3344	658	189	80	52	20	12	11	4	11	·
Revenues ($ in Thousands)													
Net Sales **2**	22853395	686165	2340179	1285312	1015252	658975	1069211	853128	997601	1258350	380750	12308473	·
Interest **3**	189730	54796	7	2058	667	2285	2734	2587	3571	11039	2076	107910	·
Rents **4**	29377	0	0	3011	0	0	65	620	129	0	0	25552	·
Royalties **5**	1257526	411104	0	42337	0	17535	19330	354	68138	21216	732	676779	·
Other Portfolio Income **6**	95952	13572	895	14920	1679	11164	14368	9084	6339	2240	0	21692	·
Other Receipts **7**	1223080	155541	114107	1294	101766	53522	24889	46421	17787	163580	1300	542872	·
Total Receipts **8**	25649060	1321178	2455188	1348932	1119364	743481	1130597	912194	1093565	1456425	384858	13683278	·
Average Total Receipts **9**	5680	9860	734	2050	5923	9294	21742	45610	91130	132402	96214	1243934	·
Operating Costs/Operating Income (%)													
Cost of Operations **10**	40.8	6.2	6.8	13.6	26.2	23.6	39.1	44.7	58.2	8.7	43.3	55.9	·
Salaries and Wages **11**	19.2	55.6	28.9	24.7	25.5	22.2	18.8	14.5	14.7	32.4	24.7	13.3	·
Taxes Paid **12**	3.0	5.5	3.4	3.1	5.2	2.9	3.8	3.1	3.0	2.9	1.8	2.6	·
Interest Paid **13**	1.5	10.3	0.0	0.7	0.0	0.1	0.5	1.6	0.8	1.3	1.7	1.7	·
Depreciation **14**	3.0	11.1	1.1	2.2	3.2	3.7	2.7	2.5	2.4	6.0	4.1	2.7	·
Amortization and Depletion **15**	0.7	2.6	0.0	0.0	0.0	1.1	0.3	0.4	0.6	1.1	0.3	0.8	·
Pensions and Other Deferred Comp. **16**	1.6	1.5	2.8	3.2	1.5	0.6	1.6	1.3	3.5	1.5	0.9	1.2	·
Employee Benefits **17**	1.7	2.7	0.8	1.3	3.3	2.4	3.0	2.1	3.0	3.7	3.5	1.3	·
Advertising **18**	0.7	0.8	3.4	0.2	1.7	0.7	0.3	0.4	0.2	0.3	0.5	0.3	·
Other Expenses **19**	26.5	69.7	31.9	21.7	21.7	36.9	21.0	18.3	13.5	47.3	12.3	23.8	·
Officers' Compensation **20**	3.5	3.0	9.7	17.1	3.6	6.7	3.8	2.6	2.8	3.7	2.0	0.8	·
Operating Margin **21**	·	·	11.3	12.0	8.1	·	5.1	8.5	·	·	4.7	·	·
Operating Margin Before Officers' Comp. **22**	1.2	·	21.0	29.2	11.7	5.7	8.9	11.1	0.1	·	6.7	·	·

Selected Average Balance Sheet ($ in Thousands)

													•
Net Receivables 23	1317	0	14	170	925	1280	3828	8168	17941	16625	40411	417421	•
Inventories 24	160	0	0	9	477	69	583	987	1902	4911	5642	44074	•
Net Property, Plant and Equipment 25	801	0	13	124	378	854	2280	4507	11738	34007	33056	226775	•
Total Assets 26	7222	0	107	772	3202	6526	15214	34394	71356	152133	294968	2312159	•
Notes and Loans Payable 27	1501	0	6	180	22	370	2525	4626	10712	20563	18569	541343	•
All Other Liabilities 28	1841	0	20	57	697	1593	3925	8712	23015	38861	105726	585923	•
Net Worth 29	3880	0	81	535	2484	4562	8765	21056	37629	92710	170672	1184894	•

Selected Financial Ratios (Times to 1)

													•
Current Ratio 30	2.2	•	3.1	9.1	4.1	2.5	2.3	2.8	1.9	2.2	2.1	2.1	•
Quick Ratio 31	1.5	•	2.5	8.9	3.0	2.3	1.9	2.2	1.5	1.3	1.6	1.3	•
Net Sales to Working Capital 32	2.8	•	15.9	4.2	2.6	3.1	3.7	2.9	4.9	2.6	1.4	2.2	•
Coverage Ratio 33	7.8	3.3	1365.3	24.0	439.3	78.7	24.7	10.8	9.2	6.2	5.1	5.1	•
Total Asset Turnover 34	0.7	•	6.6	2.5	1.7	1.3	1.4	1.2	1.2	0.8	0.3	0.5	•
Inventory Turnover 35	12.9	•	•	30.8	2.9	28.2	13.8	19.3	25.4	2.0	7.3	14.2	•
Receivables Turnover 36	4.4	•	49.2	17.7	3.7	6.9	4.7	4.4	6.7	3.0	4.7	3.4	•
Total Liabilities to Net Worth 37	0.9	•	0.3	0.4	0.3	0.4	0.7	0.6	0.9	0.6	0.7	1.0	•
Current Assets to Working Capital 38	1.8	•	1.5	1.1	1.3	1.7	1.8	1.6	2.2	1.8	1.9	1.9	•
Current Liabilities to Working Capital 39	0.8	•	0.5	0.1	0.3	0.7	0.8	0.6	1.2	0.8	0.9	0.9	•
Working Capital to Net Sales 40	0.4	•	0.1	0.2	0.4	0.3	0.3	0.3	0.2	0.4	0.7	0.5	•
Inventory to Working Capital 41	0.1	•	•	0.0	0.2	0.0	0.1	0.1	0.2	0.2	0.1	0.1	•
Total Receipts to Cash Flow 42	3.1	1.2	2.4	3.0	2.9	2.4	3.6	3.4	5.9	2.1	7.7	3.6	•
Cost of Goods to Cash Flow 43	1.3	0.1	0.2	0.4	0.8	0.6	1.4	1.5	3.4	0.2	3.3	2.0	•
Cash Flow to Total Debt 44	0.5	•	11.4	2.8	2.5	1.7	0.9	0.9	0.4	0.9	0.1	0.3	•

Selected Financial Factors (in Percentages)

													•
Debt Ratio 45	46.3	•	24.4	30.7	22.4	30.1	42.4	38.8	47.3	39.1	42.1	48.8	•
Return on Total Assets 46	8.0	•	106.4	44.8	30.7	14.9	15.2	21.0	9.0	6.2	2.9	4.1	•
Return on Equity Before Income Taxes 47	13.1	•	140.8	62.0	39.5	21.0	25.4	31.2	15.3	8.5	4.0	6.4	•
Return on Equity After Income Taxes 48	11.5	•	140.7	57.4	38.0	19.1	21.7	28.2	13.4	6.8	2.8	5.4	•
Profit Margin (Before Income Tax) 49	10.0	23.8	16.2	17.0	18.3	11.6	10.8	15.4	6.9	6.9	7.2	6.8	•
Profit Margin (After Income Tax) 50	8.8	17.4	16.2	15.7	17.6	10.6	9.3	13.9	6.1	5.5	4.9	5.7	•

Table I

Corporations with and without Net Income

ADVERTISING AND RELATED SERVICES

MONEY AMOUNTS AND SIZE OF ASSETS IN THOUSANDS OF DOLLARS

Item Description for Accounting Period 7/03 Through 6/04		Total	Zero Assets	Under 500	500 to 1,000	1,000 to 5,000	5,000 to 10,000	10,000 to 25,000	25,000 to 50,000	50,000 to 100,000	100,000 to 250,000	250,000 to 500,000	500,000 to 2,500,000	2,500,000 and over
Number of Enterprises	1	44751	3053	37540	2250	1472	161	158	53	24	20	7	6	8
Revenues ($ in Thousands)														
Net Sales	2	61696224	609011	13157927	3816813	8100674	3056876	5309469	2574282	1915551	2974211	2346810	4119497	13715102
Interest	3	809655	410	2428	4787	5556	4171	3629	5787	6639	6419	27868	100065	641895
Rents	4	60979	397	2840	2660	988	0	587	12	293	172	177	587	52266
Royalties	5	147525	0	0	0	0	0	23579	25515	19	8333	13908	2520	73651
Other Portfolio Income	6	465209	445	11478	3173	1285	34856	10628	368	45127	16885	3180	1821	335959
Other Receipts	7	1850330	109539	261951	146484	89680	390747	244989	56574	5494	50488	19777	25348	449264
Total Receipts	8	65029922	719802	13436624	3973917	8198183	3486650	5592881	2662538	1973123	3056508	2411720	4249838	15268137
Average Total Receipts	9	1453	236	358	1766	5569	21656	35398	50237	82213	152825	344531	708306	1908517
Operating Costs/Operating Income (%)														
Cost of Operations	10	33.6	19.6	31.0	36.0	46.9	62.2	50.9	47.7	42.3	59.6	29.9	46.4	2.4
Salaries and Wages	11	20.5	17.6	7.9	27.2	14.3	8.8	12.6	18.0	17.6	20.0	19.6	22.3	40.6
Taxes Paid	12	2.5	2.5	2.0	3.7	2.0	1.1	1.5	1.8	2.0	1.8	1.9	2.6	4.2
Interest Paid	13	3.3	1.9	0.5	0.5	0.9	0.2	0.5	0.8	1.5	0.9	2.3	5.8	10.8
Depreciation	14	2.1	1.4	1.1	1.7	2.0	0.7	1.6	1.8	2.0	1.9	3.8	3.4	3.0
Amortization and Depletion	15	1.3	0.4	0.1	0.1	0.3	0.5	0.3	1.1	1.1	2.2	0.6	2.0	3.8
Pensions and Other Deferred Comp.	16	0.9	0.7	1.3	1.2	0.5	0.3	0.5	0.4	0.7	0.3	0.3	0.3	1.5
Employee Benefits	17	1.2	1.5	0.5	1.9	0.9	0.5	0.9	1.2	1.2	0.9	3.2	1.7	1.8
Advertising	18	5.1	32.2	5.6	2.6	4.9	15.8	15.6	6.2	2.5	0.4	0.7	2.6	0.2
Other Expenses	19	28.1	36.0	40.3	19.3	20.2	15.2	14.6	21.7	24.0	13.2	35.1	21.4	37.0
Officers' Compensation	20	5.0	7.4	10.2	10.2	4.9	3.6	2.8	2.5	1.8	2.1	0.9	0.7	3.3
Operating Margin	21	•	•	•	•	2.1	•	•	•	3.2	•	1.6	•	•
Operating Margin Before Officers' Comp.	22	1.5	9.7	•	5.8	7.1	•	1.0	•	5.0	•	2.4	•	•

Selected Average Balance Sheet ($ in Thousands)

Net Receivables 23	529	0	13	150	668	1718	5691	12474	17248	30941	83673	237727	2122958
Inventories 24	25	0	2	22	128	325	461	1091	601	285	6971	8628	61676
Net Property, Plant and Equipment 25	140	0	17	138	505	421	2269	4051	7053	8183	51627	107336	326443
Total Assets 26	2224	0	64	656	2322	6617	15355	34258	66283	163695	325395	1171396	9097940
Notes and Loans Payable 27	422	0	43	158	987	860	3070	10851	13848	28997	92056	243513	1405278
All Other Liabilities 28	1073	0	24	143	1216	6289	9730	15167	32259	60586	123622	549923	4437867
Net Worth 29	729	0	-3	356	119	-532	2554	8240	20177	74112	109717	377960	3254795

Selected Financial Ratios (Times to 1)

Current Ratio 30	0.9	•	1.1	2.2	1.1	1.0	1.1	1.1	1.1	1.4	1.4	0.9	0.8
Quick Ratio 31	0.7	•	0.9	1.8	0.9	0.8	0.9	0.9	0.9	1.1	0.9	0.7	0.7
Net Sales to Working Capital 32	•	•	102.1	8.1	31.4	174.9	38.2	14.6	17.9	6.4	7.6	•	•
Coverage Ratio 33	1.6	•	4.3	0.4	4.6	21.5	8.7	1.0	5.1	0.3	2.9	•	1.4
Total Asset Turnover 34	0.6	•	5.5	2.6	2.4	2.9	1.4	1.2	1.2	0.9	1.0	0.6	0.2
Inventory Turnover 35	18.8	•	62.3	28.1	20.1	36.4	37.1	21.3	56.2	311.3	14.4	36.9	0.7
Receivables Turnover 36	2.7	•	30.5	8.1	7.4	6.7	6.0	3.9	4.9	4.4	4.4	2.3	0.9
Total Liabilities to Net Worth 37	2.0	•	0.8	18.5	5.0	3.2	2.3	•	1.2	2.0	•	2.1	1.8
Current Assets to Working Capital 38	•	•	11.2	1.8	8.6	52.5	12.3	7.8	8.0	3.3	3.8	•	•
Current Liabilities to Working Capital 39	•	•	10.2	0.8	7.6	51.5	11.3	6.8	7.0	2.3	2.8	•	•
Working Capital to Net Sales 40	•	•	0.0	0.1	0.0	0.0	0.0	0.1	0.1	0.2	0.1	•	•
Inventory to Working Capital 41	•	•	0.5	0.1	1.1	4.6	0.5	0.4	0.1	0.0	0.2	•	•
Total Receipts to Cash Flow 42	4.1	•	2.7	7.7	5.1	6.3	6.5	5.6	4.2	10.5	2.7	10.2	3.2
Cost of Goods to Cash Flow 43	1.4	•	0.8	2.8	3.3	3.9	2.4	2.7	1.8	6.2	0.8	4.7	0.1
Cash Flow to Total Debt 44	0.2	•	2.0	0.7	0.5	0.4	0.4	0.3	0.4	0.2	0.1	0.1	0.1

Selected Financial Factors (in Percentages)

Debt Ratio 45	67.2	•	105.3	45.8	94.9	108.0	83.4	75.9	69.6	54.7	66.3	67.7	64.2
Return on Total Assets 46	3.4	•	11.4	0.6	10.1	15.2	8.7	1.2	9.3	0.3	•	6.9	2.8
Return on Equity Before Income Taxes 47	4.0	•	•	•	153.5	46.1	•	24.5	•	•	•	13.3	2.2
Return on Equity After Income Taxes 48	2.9	•	•	•	149.2	42.9	•	23.9	•	•	•	5.9	1.2
Profit Margin (Before Income Tax) 49	2.1	•	1.6	3.3	3.3	5.0	3.5	6.2	6.0	•	•	4.3	4.1
Profit Margin (After Income Tax) 50	1.5	•	1.5	3.2	4.7	3.3	3.3	6.0	6.0	•	•	1.9	2.2

Table II

Corporations with Net Income

ADVERTISING AND RELATED SERVICES

MONEY AMOUNTS AND SIZE OF ASSETS IN THOUSANDS OF DOLLARS

Item Description for Accounting Period 7/03 Through 6/04	Total	Zero Assets	Under 500	500 to 1,000	1,000 to 5,000	5,000 to 10,000	10,000 to 25,000	25,000 to 50,000	50,000 to 100,000	100,000 to 250,000	250,000 to 500,000	500,000 to 2,500,000	2,500,000 and over
Number of Enterprises **1**	23694	973	20363	1236	844	109	•	25	13	10	7	•	•
Revenues ($ in Thousands)													
Net Sales **2**	43815298	309501	7332576	2030578	6528921	2616821	•	1317211	1419749	2302675	3351045	•	•
Interest **3**	683574	265	1468	3025	3100	1432	•	1534	2090	4498	25950	•	•
Rents **4**	55951	0	1474	1910	472	0	•	12	0	93	81	•	•
Royalties **5**	143795	0	0	0	0	0	•	24463	0	8333	13806	•	•
Other Portfolio Income **6**	404295	445	5986	2993	1230	23935	•	98	32704	16885	279	•	•
Other Receipts **7**	928109	82234	18832	139171	54887	12008	•	23011	2667	46402	23238	•	•
Total Receipts **8**	46031022	392445	7360336	2177677	6588610	2654196	•	1366329	1457210	2378886	3414399	•	•
Average Total Receipts **9**	1943	403	361	1762	7806	24350	•	54653	112093	237889	487771	•	•
Operating Costs/Operating Income (%)													
Cost of Operations **10**	34.5	19.0	43.5	19.0	45.6	69.8	•	55.4	39.4	69.3	37.3	•	•
Salaries and Wages **11**	22.0	23.7	7.3	37.4	11.6	7.0	•	17.1	17.5	14.6	18.0	•	•
Taxes Paid **12**	2.6	3.1	2.4	4.6	1.6	0.9	•	1.8	1.8	1.4	1.8	•	•
Interest Paid **13**	3.1	0.2	0.4	0.3	0.5	0.2	•	0.3	0.7	0.3	1.1	•	•
Depreciation **14**	1.6	1.7	0.9	1.9	1.6	0.4	•	1.3	1.6	1.5	2.7	•	•
Amortization and Depletion **15**	0.9	0.1	0.1	0.0	0.3	0.0	•	0.2	0.6	0.1	1.0	•	•
Pensions and Other Deferred Comp. **16**	0.9	1.3	0.8	1.9	0.6	0.3	•	0.4	0.9	0.3	0.4	•	•
Employee Benefits **17**	1.2	1.0	0.5	2.0	0.8	0.4	•	1.1	1.1	0.6	2.3	•	•
Advertising **18**	2.9	20.9	2.2	3.9	5.9	1.2	•	2.0	2.9	0.1	3.1	•	•
Other Expenses **19**	23.3	34.1	21.0	20.6	19.3	8.7	•	16.0	23.3	9.3	27.9	•	•
Officers' Compensation **20**	5.0	13.8	12.0	9.6	4.6	3.1	•	3.0	2.1	1.6	1.0	•	•
Operating Margin **21**	2.0	•	8.9	•	7.7	7.8	•	1.3	8.0	0.9	3.4	•	•
Operating Margin Before Officers' Comp. **22**	7.0	•	20.9	8.3	12.3	10.9	•	4.4	10.1	2.5	4.4	•	•

Selected Average Balance Sheet ($ in Thousands)

Net Receivables 23	896	0	15	182	810	1725	16032	20197	43470	175961
Inventories 24	27	0	2	19	90	114	1303	259	25	2734
Net Property, Plant and Equipment 25	130	0	13	141	410	385	4271	5198	11808	53367
Total Assets 26	3401	0	67	684	2558	6339	35564	64883	155110	567520
Notes and Loans Payable 27	407	0	35	47	561	931	3284	11546	11174	43585
All Other Liabilities 28	1783	0	27	136	1115	4061	21607	36658	82761	330384
Net Worth 29	1211	0	4	501	881	1347	10673	16679	61175	193552

Selected Financial Ratios (Times to 1)

Current Ratio 30	0.9	•	1.1	2.6	1.4	1.3	1.3	1.1	1.3	0.9
Quick Ratio 31	0.7	•	1.0	2.5	1.2	1.2	1.2	0.9	1.1	0.7
Net Sales to Working Capital 32	•	•	87.0	6.7	16.0	17.8	7.7	22.3	9.5	•
Coverage Ratio 33	3.4	36.8	25.6	21.2	19.4	60.1	17.8	15.3	17.4	5.9
Total Asset Turnover 34	0.5	•	5.4	2.4	3.0	3.8	1.5	1.7	1.5	0.8
Inventory Turnover 35	24.0	•	81.0	16.7	39.1	147.4	22.4	166.2	6374.6	65.4
Receivables Turnover 36	2.3	•	31.1	7.7	9.6	10.3	3.3	5.9	5.4	2.7
Total Liabilities to Net Worth 37	1.8	•	14.0	0.4	1.9	3.7	2.3	2.9	1.5	1.9
Current Assets to Working Capital 38	•	•	10.5	1.6	3.6	4.1	3.9	9.1	4.0	•
Current Liabilities to Working Capital 39	•	•	9.5	0.6	2.6	3.1	2.9	8.1	3.0	•
Working Capital to Net Sales 40	•	•	0.0	0.1	0.1	0.1	0.1	0.0	0.1	•
Inventory to Working Capital 41	•	•	0.6	0.0	0.3	0.1	0.2	0.1	0.0	•
Total Receipts to Cash Flow 42	3.9	2.7	3.9	4.7	4.1	7.0	5.8	3.4	8.7	3.4
Cost of Goods to Cash Flow 43	1.4	0.5	1.7	0.9	1.9	4.9	3.2	1.4	6.0	1.3
Cash Flow to Total Debt 44	0.2	•	1.5	1.9	1.1	0.7	0.4	0.7	0.3	0.4

Selected Financial Factors (in Percentages)

Debt Ratio 45	64.4	•	93.3	26.7	65.5	78.8	70.0	74.3	60.6	65.9
Return on Total Assets 46	5.7	•	52.0	15.1	27.4	35.5	8.0	19.2	6.6	5.4
Return on Equity Before Income Taxes 47	11.4	•	749.9	19.6	75.4	164.5	25.0	69.7	15.7	13.1
Return on Equity After Income Taxes 48	10.0	•	743.3	18.7	74.4	157.7	22.8	68.3	13.7	8.9
Profit Margin (Before Income Tax) 49	7.4	7.8	9.3	6.0	8.6	9.2	5.1	10.6	4.2	5.3
Profit Margin (After Income Tax) 50	6.6	6.7	9.2	5.7	8.5	8.8	4.6	10.4	3.7	3.6

Table I
Corporations with and without Net Income

OTHER PROFESSIONAL, SCIENTIFIC, AND TECHNICAL SERVICES

MONEY AMOUNTS AND SIZE OF ASSETS IN THOUSANDS OF DOLLARS

Item Description for Accounting Period 7/03 Through 6/04	Total	Zero Assets	Under 500	500 to 1,000	1,000 to 5,000	5,000 to 10,000	10,000 to 25,000	25,000 to 50,000	50,000 to 100,000	100,000 to 250,000	250,000 to 500,000	500,000 to 2,500,000	2,500,000 and over
Number of Enterprises 1	93921	11189	76774	3417	1955	216	213	77	33	33	7	6	•
Revenues ($ in Thousands)													
Net Sales 2	62713641	2750544	26727794	4683461	6220576	2707883	5830601	3315676	2378170	4750351	1089392	2259194	•
Interest 3	161044	28614	9504	3797	10891	8107	11185	11752	8263	37885	8224	22823	•
Rents 4	16920	166	3050	231	2360	1339	2690	3155	1072	2355	108	394	•
Royalties 5	136215	1117	37549	0	817	561	1804	6592	8659	64145	118	14852	•
Other Portfolio Income 6	205779	11564	33418	7661	17566	60688	14432	15946	17753	24676	945	1131	•
Other Receipts 7	1296520	105721	337919	43041	122519	92627	184657	30557	26968	262738	6331	83441	•
Total Receipts 8	64530119	2897726	27149234	4738191	6374729	2871205	6045369	3383678	2440885	5142150	1105118	2381835	•
Average Total Receipts 9	687	259	354	1387	3261	13293	28382	43944	73966	155823	157874	396972	•
Operating Costs/Operating Income (%)													
Cost of Operations 10	28.0	18.0	20.0	35.9	37.6	32.0	45.1	25.7	41.1	38.3	23.9	11.9	•
Salaries and Wages 11	22.9	29.3	23.2	15.4	19.9	22.3	18.5	19.9	27.9	28.5	19.3	35.4	•
Taxes Paid 12	3.4	3.1	3.5	5.1	3.0	2.4	2.7	2.4	3.9	3.1	1.7	4.8	•
Interest Paid 13	1.1	0.9	0.7	0.8	1.2	1.1	0.9	1.4	2.5	2.6	2.4	2.7	•
Depreciation 14	2.3	2.1	1.9	2.4	2.7	2.7	2.0	2.9	3.3	3.2	2.2	3.4	•
Amortization and Depletion 15	0.7	0.3	0.3	0.4	0.7	0.4	0.7	1.5	1.2	1.7	3.6	1.8	•
Pensions and Other Deferred Comp. 16	1.2	0.3	1.3	0.8	0.8	0.4	0.5	0.6	0.6	2.7	0.2	3.2	•
Employee Benefits 17	2.1	1.2	1.2	1.8	1.1	1.4	6.8	2.0	2.4	3.5	1.0	2.8	•
Advertising 18	0.8	0.8	0.8	0.4	1.0	0.3	0.7	0.6	0.5	1.6	0.3	1.2	•
Other Expenses 19	30.1	42.7	32.0	20.6	24.7	40.6	22.3	47.0	20.4	22.0	46.4	30.4	•
Officers' Compensation 20	7.8	3.8	11.0	18.1	7.7	7.0	2.1	2.5	1.3	2.0	0.9	1.5	•
Operating Margin 21	•	•	4.1	•	•	•	•	•	•	•	•	1.0	•
Operating Margin Before Officers' Comp. 22	7.4	1.2	15.0	16.4	7.1	•	•	•	•	•	•	2.5	•

Selected Average Balance Sheet ($ in Thousands)

Net Receivables 23	71	0	7	142	648	2013	3587	8040	13368	28107	54723	138629 •
Inventories 24	10	0	3	25	45	212	415	395	1698	2391	31442	2460 •
Net Property, Plant and Equipment 25	65	0	24	141	598	849	2067	4821	10073	17940	23956	91740 •
Total Assets 26	439	0	84	702	2423	7017	15086	34976	69537	166914	339721	1680193 •
Notes and Loans Payable 27	174	0	55	677	914	2201	4135	8846	21988	35170	169388	487280 •
All Other Liabilities 28	143	0	20	162	867	3177	6771	15190	20641	63760	91388	480188 •
Net Worth 29	122	0	8	-136	642	1639	4181	10940	26907	67985	78946	712725 •

Selected Financial Ratios (Times to 1)

Current Ratio 30	1.3	•	1.5	2.3	1.5	1.2	1.3	1.3	1.3	1.2	1.7	0.8 •
Quick Ratio 31	1.0	•	1.2	1.8	1.2	1.0	1.0	1.1	1.0	0.9	0.9	0.5 •
Net Sales to Working Capital 32	15.0	•	29.4	6.5	6.9	13.1	13.0	10.5	9.8	12.5	2.3	• •
Coverage Ratio 33	3.1	4.0	9.2	0.4	2.6	•	2.6	•	0.0	0.7	0.8	3.5 •
Total Asset Turnover 34	1.5	•	4.2	2.0	1.3	1.8	1.8	1.2	1.0	0.9	0.5	0.2 •
Inventory Turnover 35	18.6	•	22.7	19.9	26.5	18.9	29.7	28.1	17.5	23.1	1.2	18.2 •
Receivables Turnover 36	9.6	•	57.8	10.7	4.6	5.5	7.3	4.9	4.6	5.3	3.5	3.9 •
Total Liabilities to Net Worth 37	2.6	•	9.2	•	2.8	3.3	2.6	2.2	1.6	1.5	3.3	1.4 •
Current Assets to Working Capital 38	4.1	•	3.1	1.8	2.9	5.3	4.3	4.3	4.0	5.6	2.5	• •
Current Liabilities to Working Capital 39	3.1	•	2.1	0.8	1.9	4.3	3.3	3.3	3.0	4.6	1.5	• •
Working Capital to Net Sales 40	0.1	•	0.0	0.2	0.1	0.1	0.1	0.1	0.1	0.1	0.4	• •
Inventory to Working Capital 41	0.2	•	0.2	0.2	0.3	0.2	0.1	0.1	0.2	0.1	•	• •
Total Receipts to Cash Flow 42	3.7	2.5	3.3	6.5	3.4	4.5	4.9	2.6	7.7	5.8	2.3	3.0 •
Cost of Goods to Cash Flow 43	1.0	0.5	0.7	2.3	1.1	1.7	2.2	0.7	3.2	2.2	0.6	0.4 •
Cash Flow to Total Debt 44	0.6	•	1.4	0.3	0.7	0.7	0.5	0.7	0.2	0.2	0.3	0.1 •

Selected Financial Factors (in Percentages)

Debt Ratio 45	72.2	•	90.2	119.4	73.5	76.6	72.3	68.7	61.3	59.3	76.8	57.6 •
Return on Total Assets 46	5.5	•	26.3	0.6	4.1	•	4.3	•	0.1	1.6	0.9	2.1 •
Return on Equity Before Income Taxes 47	13.5	•	240.0	5.0	9.5	•	9.6	•	•	•	•	3.6 •
Return on Equity After Income Taxes 48	11.6	•	236.5	6.0	6.9	•	6.5	•	•	•	•	3.2 •
Profit Margin (Before Income Tax) 49	2.5	2.8	5.6	•	1.9	•	1.5	•	•	•	•	6.8 •
Profit Margin (After Income Tax) 50	2.1	2.3	5.6	•	1.4	•	1.0	•	•	•	•	6.1 •

Table II
Corporations with Net Income

OTHER PROFESSIONAL, SCIENTIFIC, AND TECHNICAL SERVICES

MONEY AMOUNTS AND SIZE OF ASSETS IN THOUSANDS OF DOLLARS

Item Description for Accounting Period 7/03 Through 6/04		Total	Zero Assets	Under 500	500 to 1000	251 to 500	501 to 1,000	1,001 to 5,000	5,001 to 10,000	10,001 to 25,000	25,001 to 50,000	50,001 to 100,000	100,001 to 250,000	250,001 and over
Number of Enterprises	1	50985	2708	44686	2007	1299	96	116	35	14	18	3	3	·
Revenues ($ in Thousands)														
Net Sales	2	41263306	850965	19258576	3353348	4855164	1651099	3257269	1406478	938300	3262257	452911	1976940	·
Interest	3	49375	2988	3336	3536	7302	3370	5339	6664	645	7955	820	7419	·
Rents	4	11801	94	2588	0	2234	3	2545	2989	0	954	0	394	·
Royalties	5	106139	0	35161	0	0	0	1782	454	0	54108	0	14633	·
Other Portfolio Income	6	173046	10324	31443	4153	15154	56625	12825	9343	12445	20568	158	10	·
Other Receipts	7	925497	112961	253596	35162	130048	64412	138293	28736	13116	95093	2046	52034	·
Total Receipts	8	42529164	977332	19584700	3396199	5009902	1775509	3418053	1454664	964506	3440935	455935	2051430	·
Average Total Receipts	9	834	361	438	1692	3857	18495	29466	41562	68893	191163	151978	683810	·
Operating Costs/Operating Income (%)														
Cost of Operations	10	28.3	34.5	18.6	38.4	37.8	35.8	43.8	22.7	42.1	46.9	31.8	13.2	·
Salaries and Wages	11	21.1	19.4	22.7	11.8	18.5	13.4	19.1	26.9	26.5	19.5	21.4	33.7	·
Taxes Paid	12	3.4	3.2	3.4	5.6	2.9	2.0	2.5	3.3	3.5	2.5	1.7	5.1	·
Interest Paid	13	0.9	0.9	0.6	0.7	1.1	0.3	0.6	1.1	1.1	2.1	1.7	1.7	·
Depreciation	14	1.7	1.3	1.4	1.0	2.0	1.0	1.6	2.9	2.1	2.9	1.2	3.1	·
Amortization and Depletion	15	0.5	0.3	0.2	0.4	0.5	0.1	0.4	0.7	0.8	0.9	6.3	1.4	·
Pensions and Other Deferred Comp.	16	1.1	0.8	1.0	1.1	0.9	0.5	0.6	1.3	1.0	1.0	0.3	3.3	·
Employee Benefits	17	1.4	1.8	1.0	1.6	0.9	0.9	1.7	2.6	2.1	2.1	1.4	2.8	·
Advertising	18	0.7	0.7	0.6	0.2	0.9	0.2	0.9	0.4	0.4	0.8	0.5	1.3	·
Other Expenses	19	25.0	21.4	28.8	12.1	19.9	37.7	23.8	30.5	14.5	19.0	22.9	27.2	·
Officers' Compensation	20	8.7	3.5	11.1	21.8	7.1	6.4	2.3	4.0	1.5	2.0	0.6	1.2	·
Operating Margin	21	7.4	12.1	10.5	5.3	7.6	1.7	2.7	3.6	4.4	0.2	7.7	6.2	·
Operating Margin Before Officers' Comp.	22	16.1	15.7	21.6	27.1	14.7	8.0	4.9	7.6	6.0	2.2	8.3	7.4	·

Selected Average Balance Sheet ($ in Thousands)

Net Receivables 23	63	0	5	169	573	2185	3840	9575	13468	30245	28669	35908	•
Inventories 24	9	0	3	36	47	248	385	350	2568	2606	10389	5209	•
Net Property, Plant and Equipment 25	68	0	28	106	565	355	1764	4477	7705	22631	20324	110255	•
Total Assets 26	412	0	87	704	2315	7517	14820	34803	68866	163568	281575	1423673	•
Notes and Loans Payable 27	146	0	45	288	1103	723	3148	7577	12541	37709	190028	429161	•
All Other Liabilities 28	104	0	17	111	760	3520	6028	11599	15009	57641	46288	161736	•
Net Worth 29	162	0	25	306	451	3274	5644	15628	41317	68218	45259	832776	•

Selected Financial Ratios (Times to 1)

Current Ratio 30	1.7	•	1.7	3.4	1.6	1.4	1.5	1.5	2.0	1.4	2.8	1.6	•
Quick Ratio 31	1.3	•	1.5	2.5	1.3	1.0	1.2	1.2	1.3	1.0	1.0	0.6	•
Net Sales to Working Capital 32	10.9	•	27.2	4.8	8.6	10.7	9.0	6.8	4.3	8.3	2.2	7.4	•
Coverage Ratio 33	12.4	31.8	20.4	10.2	10.5	29.9	12.8	7.5	7.9	3.9	3.0	7.1	•
Total Asset Turnover 34	2.0	•	5.0	2.4	1.6	2.3	1.9	1.2	1.0	1.1	0.5	0.5	•
Inventory Turnover 35	24.7	•	24.0	18.0	30.1	24.8	31.9	26.0	11.0	32.6	4.6	16.7	•
Receivables Turnover 36	11.4	•	70.8	12.2	5.5	5.4	6.8	4.0	4.2	12.0	10.5	36.7	•
Total Liabilities to Net Worth 37	1.5	•	2.5	1.3	4.1	1.3	1.6	1.2	0.7	1.4	5.2	0.7	•
Current Assets to Working Capital 38	2.5	•	2.4	1.4	2.7	3.4	3.1	3.1	2.0	3.5	1.6	2.6	•
Current Liabilities to Working Capital 39	1.5	•	1.4	0.4	1.7	2.4	2.1	2.1	1.0	2.5	0.6	1.6	•
Working Capital to Net Sales 40	0.1	•	0.0	0.2	0.1	0.1	0.1	0.1	0.2	0.1	0.5	0.1	•
Inventory to Working Capital 41	0.1	•	0.1	0.2	0.1	0.2	0.2	0.0	0.0	0.1	0.1	0.1	•
Total Receipts to Cash Flow 42	3.3	2.2	2.9	6.6	3.7	2.4	3.6	3.0	6.3	4.6	3.4	2.9	•
Cost of Goods to Cash Flow 43	0.9	0.8	0.5	2.5	1.4	0.9	1.6	0.7	2.6	2.2	1.1	0.4	•
Cash Flow to Total Debt 44	1.0	2.4	0.6	0.6	0.5	1.7	0.9	0.7	0.4	0.4	0.2	0.4	•

Selected Financial Factors (in Percentages)

Debt Ratio 45	60.6	•	71.5	56.6	80.5	56.4	61.9	55.1	40.0	58.3	83.9	41.5	•
Return on Total Assets 46	22.4	•	63.5	17.2	19.2	21.7	15.6	9.4	8.4	9.0	6.7	5.5	•
Return on Equity Before Income Taxes 47	52.3	•	212.1	35.9	89.1	48.3	37.8	18.1	12.2	16.0	27.9	8.1	•
Return on Equity After Income Taxes 48	49.7	•	210.1	35.2	83.7	40.8	33.6	14.1	10.5	13.3	19.5	7.5	•
Profit Margin (Before Income Tax) 49	10.5	27.0	12.2	6.6	10.7	9.2	7.6	7.0	7.5	6.0	8.4	10.2	•
Profit Margin (After Income Tax) 50	10.0	25.3	12.1	6.4	10.1	7.8	6.7	5.5	6.5	5.0	5.8	9.5	•

Table I
Corporations with and without Net Income

OFFICES OF BANK HOLDING COMPANIES

MONEY AMOUNTS AND SIZE OF ASSETS IN THOUSANDS OF DOLLARS

Item Description for Accounting Period 7/03 Through 6/04	Total	Zero Assets	Under 500	500 to 1,000	1,000 to 5,000	5,000 to 10,000	10,000 to 25,000	25,000 to 50,000	50,000 to 100,000	100,000 to 250,000	250,000 to 500,000	500,000 to 2,500,000	2,500,000 and over
Number of Enterprises **1**	5501	80	395	99	45	31	276	656	1156	1478	662	475	147
Revenues ($ in Thousands)													
Net Sales **2**	188900892	384812	41	124	1160	10364	80311	357431	1460786	3463604	2962536	6714564	173465160
Interest **3**	334625412	2385389	462	0	6635	7370	151670	661937	2651723	8116168	8639902	19012335	292991824
Rents **4**	31209854	19448	0	0	69	0	490	2593	13636	39684	54079	302852	30777005
Royalties **5**	378582	0	0	0	0	0	3	73	135	174	20341	202	357654
Other Portfolio Income **6**	30800071	264324	18096	54	13836	2181	12212	78658	250087	722781	798243	1790317	26849283
Other Receipts **7**	73185941	47342	58	-63254	-1041	2806	78883	389696	891836	2316011	1864103	3812843	63846652
Total Receipts **8**	659100752	3101315	18657	-63076	20659	22721	323569	1490388	5268203	14658422	14339204	31633113	588287578
Average Total Receipts **9**	119815	38766	47	-637	459	733	1172	2272	4557	9918	21660	66596	4001956
Operating Costs/Operating Income (%)													
Cost of Operations **10**	4.9	•	•	•	•	•	•	•	0.2	1.5	0.0	0.4	5.3
Salaries and Wages **11**	51.6	82.3	295.1	423.4	406.8	14.3	53.1	52.2	50.2	62.3	81.4	79.8	49.7
Taxes Paid **12**	6.9	11.3	1700.0	47.6	58.1	2.9	12.1	12.7	10.9	12.4	14.9	13.6	6.3
Interest Paid **13**	82.1	591.6	456.1	774.2	200.6	21.5	91.8	106.9	92.8	108.2	122.8	109.1	78.6
Depreciation **14**	22.8	6.4	48.8	58.1	26.1	3.1	14.0	14.1	14.1	16.2	19.9	19.9	23.2
Amortization and Depletion **15**	5.4	2.1	2.4	18.5	5.9	0.1	6.9	2.2	1.4	1.7	2.0	2.9	5.7
Pensions and Other Deferred Comp. **16**	4.5	9.2	•	•	1.1	0.5	4.4	3.8	3.9	4.1	5.2	5.5	4.5
Employee Benefits **17**	7.4	8.8	53.7	294.4	41.2	1.8	13.7	12.5	9.8	10.7	11.2	10.1	7.1
Advertising **18**	4.2	2.1	19.5	14.5	86.7	0.2	3.7	4.2	3.7	4.2	5.0	6.1	4.1
Other Expenses **19**	107.1	204.5	690.2	5044.4	945.9	74.4	98.6	97.2	76.4	85.8	98.2	103.9	107.9
Officers' Compensation **20**	4.9	11.2	•	•	108.5	16.3	61.9	47.2	34.0	29.4	24.8	18.7	3.1
Operating Margin **21**	•	•	•	•	•	•	•	•	•	•	•	•	•
Operating Margin Before Officers' Comp. **22**	•	•	•	•	•	•	•	•	•	•	•	•	•

Selected Average Balance Sheet ($ in Thousands)

Net Receivables 23	723278	0	0	765	1707	9917	21352	43897	95969	206438	548409		22933978
Inventories 24	17	0	0	0	30		604	1476	3224	6607	18321		528
Net Property, Plant and Equipment 25	17423	0	0	54	262								515801
Total Assets 26	1772168	597	2228	7070	18877	37506	72925	158895	344927	1006333			59135948
Notes and Loans Payable 27	281820	0	1071	77	110	425	947	3121	7270	19075	79954		10098507
All Other Liabilities 28	1298283	0	2	277	3915	14921	31878	62171	135624	292385	835525		42543767
Net Worth 29	192065	46	-477	1874	3044	3531	4682	7633	16001	33466	90854		6493674

Selected Financial Ratios (Times to 1)

Current Ratio 30	0.8	•	0.6	4.0	5.8	1.5	1.1	1.0	1.0	1.0	1.0	0.9	0.8
Quick Ratio 31	0.7	•	0.5	4.0	5.7	0.8	1.0	1.0	1.0	1.0	0.9	0.9	0.7
Net Sales to Working Capital 32	•	•	•	0.2	0.2	0.9	1.5	•	•	•	•	•	•
Coverage Ratio 33	1.6	0.8	93.6	•	0.3	1.4	1.5	1.6	1.7	1.7	1.7	1.8	1.5
Total Asset Turnover 34	0.0	0.0	0.0	0.0	0.0	0.0	0.0	0.0	0.0	0.0	0.0	0.0	0.0
Inventory Turnover 35	98.7	•	•	•	•	•	0.4	25.5	0.2	21.4			117.8
Receivables Turnover 36	0.0	•	•	0.2	0.0	0.0	0.0	0.0	0.0	0.0	0.0	0.0	0.1
Total Liabilities to Net Worth 37	8.2	•	•	0.1	0.2	1.3	4.3	7.0	8.6	8.9	9.3	10.1	8.1
Current Assets to Working Capital 38	•	•	•	1.3	3.2	14.0	53.0	74.8	•	•	•	•	•
Current Liabilities to Working Capital 39	•	•	•	0.3	0.2	13.0	52.0	73.8	•	•	•	•	•
Working Capital to Net Sales 40	•	•	4.4	65.7	4.6	4.0	1.1	0.7	•	•	•	•	•
Inventory to Working Capital 41	•	•	•	•	0.0	0.0	0.0	0.0	0.0	0.0	0.0	0.0	0.0
Total Receipts to Cash Flow 42	0.7	2.2	•	0.2	0.8	0.8	0.7	0.6	0.6	0.5	0.5	0.5	0.7
Cost of Goods to Cash Flow 43	0.0	0.0	•	•	0.0	0.0	0.0	0.0	0.0	0.0	0.0	0.0	0.0
Cash Flow to Total Debt 44	0.0	•	16.0	0.4	0.1	0.0	0.0	0.0	0.0	0.0	0.0	0.0	0.0

Selected Financial Factors (in Percentages)

Debt Ratio 45	89.2	•	5.6	179.9	15.9	56.9	81.3	87.5	89.5	89.9	90.3	91.0	89.0
Return on Total Assets 46	2.5	•	90.2	•	0.8	4.9	1.9	2.3	2.5	2.7	2.7	2.8	2.4
Return on Equity Before Income Taxes 47	8.1	•	94.5	151.3	9.1	2.7	5.9	8.5	10.6	11.1	13.9		7.8
Return on Equity After Income Taxes 48	5.4	•	88.1	151.3	5.4	2.0	4.8	6.7	8.1	8.0	9.7		5.1
Profit Margin (Before Income Tax) 49	45.5	•	42241.5		83.1	32.6	50.9	51.4	72.4	82.7	89.2		43.0
Profit Margin (After Income Tax) 50	30.1	•	39353.7	•	49.3	24.3	41.6	40.4	55.0	59.9	62.3		28.1

Table II

Corporations with Net Income

OFFICES OF BANK HOLDING COMPANIES

MONEY AMOUNTS AND SIZE OF ASSETS IN THOUSANDS OF DOLLARS

Item Description for Accounting Period 7/03 Through 6/04	Total	Zero Assets	Under 500	500 to 1,000	1,000 to 5,000	5,000 to 10,000	10,000 to 25,000	25,000 to 50,000	50,000 to 100,000	100,000 to 250,000	250,000 to 500,000	500,000 to 2,500,000	2,500,000 and over
Number of Enterprises **1**	4542	42	11	•	•	21	224	560	1034	1409	640	462	139
Revenues ($ in Thousands)													
Net Sales **2**	184346640	50893	896	•	•	10276	68817	318448	1347394	3321638	2901145	6604945	169722187
Interest **3**	324574199	337020	1426	•	•	5903	127467	562680	2370232	7720981	8281415	18584363	286582713
Rents **4**	29782963	665	67	•	•	0	372	2233	11888	34263	51568	283380	29398528
Royalties **5**	377954	0	0	•	•	0	3	71	105	174	202	•	357058
Other Portfolio Income **6**	29680727	33860	20639	•	•	1477	10576	68950	230563	679431	745217	1764754	26125262
Other Receipts **7**	71614767	41911	134	•	•	1095	63588	353622	858396	2234600	1800465	3660534	62600419
Total Receipts **8**	640377250	464349	23162	•	•	18751	270823	1306004	4818578	13991087	13800151	30898178	574786167
Average Total Receipts **9**	140990	11056	2106	•	•	893	1209	2332	4660	9930	21563	66879	4135152
Operating Costs/Operating Income (%)													
Cost of Operations **10**	5.0	•	•	•	•	•	•	•	0.2	1.6	0.0	0.4	5.4
Salaries and Wages **11**	51.5	163.4	30.5	•	•	6.9	41.7	49.2	47.5	61.1	79.2	79.1	49.8
Taxes Paid **12**	6.9	28.9	89.4	•	•	2.4	10.8	12.4	10.7	12.4	14.4	13.5	6.3
Interest Paid **13**	80.7	259.8	68.0	•	•	18.9	92.8	103.6	90.8	106.7	119.9	106.9	78.3
Depreciation **14**	22.1	24.6	19.4	•	•	3.1	9.9	12.7	13.4	15.8	18.2	19.4	22.5
Amortization and Depletion **15**	5.3	5.1	0.3	•	•	0.1	6.9	1.5	1.2	1.6	1.9	2.8	5.6
Pensions and Other Deferred Comp. **16**	4.4	20.8	0.4	•	•	0.5	3.5	3.9	4.0	4.2	5.1	5.5	4.4
Employee Benefits **17**	7.4	22.8	7.4	•	•	1.6	12.7	12.1	9.5	10.6	10.9	9.9	7.2
Advertising **18**	4.2	7.5	1.9	•	•	0.1	3.2	4.0	3.5	4.2	4.9	6.1	4.1
Other Expenses **19**	106.0	189.8	248.5	•	•	12.8	84.9	79.5	70.3	82.0	93.1	101.3	107.2
Officers' Compensation **20**	4.5	34.8	20.0	•	•	16.5	54.9	44.9	33.5	29.2	24.0	18.6	2.8
Operating Margin **21**	•	•	•	•	•	37.0	•	•	•	•	•	•	•
Operating Margin Before Officers' Comp. **22**	•	•	•	•	•	53.5	•	•	•	•	•	•	•

Selected Average Balance Sheet ($ in Thousands)

Net Receivables 23	852380	0	342	•	2382	10456	21530	44380	96050	207674	553207	23649939
Inventories 24	19	0	0	.	0	0	0	1	1	7	3	552
Net Property, Plant and Equipment 25	20484	0	92	.	45	197	561	1429	3195	6585	18243	532770
Total Assets 26	2094015	0	604	.	6613	19215	37571	73237	159059	344785	1007659	61147380
Notes and Loans Payable 27	333133	0	88	.	148	435	869	2593	7217	18895	76237	10448478
All Other Liabilities 28	1536987	0	85	.	4704	15619	32139	62623	135691	292496	839876	44088035
Net Worth 29	223895	0	431	•	1761	3161	4563	8021	16151	33394	91545	6610867

Selected Financial Ratios (Times to 1)

Current Ratio 30	0.8	•	2.4	•	1.3	1.1	1.0	1.0	1.0	1.0	0.9	0.8
Quick Ratio 31	0.7	•	2.3	•	0.7	1.0	1.0	1.0	1.0	0.9	0.9	0.7
Net Sales to Working Capital 32	•	•	0.4	•	0.4	0.3	0.7	1.1	•	•	•	•
Coverage Ratio 33	1.6	1.5	31.8	•	7.3	1.7	1.7	1.7	1.7	1.7	1.9	1.6
Total Asset Turnover 34	0.0	•	0.1	•	0.1	0.0	0.0	0.0	0.0	0.0	0.0	0.0
Inventory Turnover 35	107.9	•	•	•	•	•	6.0	25.5	0.2	22.0	118.8	
Receivables Turnover 36	0.1	•	0.5	•	0.4	0.0	0.0	0.0	0.0	0.0	0.0	0.1
Total Liabilities to Net Worth 37	8.4	•	0.4	•	2.8	5.1	7.2	8.1	8.8	9.3	10.0	8.2
Current Assets to Working Capital 38	•	•	1.7	•	4.8	14.1	38.3	55.3	•	•	•	•
Current Liabilities to Working Capital 39	•	•	0.7	•	3.8	13.1	37.3	54.3	•	•	•	•
Working Capital to Net Sales 40	•	•	2.8	•	2.6	3.9	1.5	0.9	•	•	•	•
Inventory to Working Capital 41	•	•	•	•	•	0.0	0.0	0.0	0.0	0.0	0.0	0.0
Total Receipts to Cash Flow 42	0.7	0.3	0.0	•	0.8	0.7	0.6	0.7	0.6	0.5	0.5	0.7
Cost of Goods to Cash Flow 43	0.0	0.0	0.0	•	•	0.0	0.0	0.0	0.0	0.0	0.0	0.0
Cash Flow to Total Debt 44	0.0	0.0	10.0	•	0.1	0.0	0.0	0.0	0.0	0.0	0.0	0.0

Selected Financial Factors (in Percentages)

Debt Ratio 45	89.3	•	28.6	•	73.4	83.6	87.9	89.0	89.8	90.3	90.9	89.2
Return on Total Assets 46	2.5	•	291.8	•	10.2	2.5	2.7	2.7	2.7	2.7	2.8	2.5
Return on Equity Before Income Taxes 47	8.7	•	395.8	•	32.9	6.1	9.1	9.9	11.3	12.0	14.4	8.2
Return on Equity After Income Taxes 48	5.8	•	369.3	•	23.5	5.1	7.8	8.0	8.6	8.8	10.2	5.4
Profit Margin (Before Income Tax) 49	47.8	131.3	2095.0	•	118.5	62.4	73.1	61.2	77.3	88.4	92.3	44.5
Profit Margin (After Income Tax) 50	31.9	88.6	1954.8	•	84.4	52.9	62.7	49.3	59.2	65.1	65.0	29.3

Table I

Corporations with and without Net Income

OFFICES OF OTHER HOLDING COMPANIES

MONEY AMOUNTS AND SIZE OF ASSETS IN THOUSANDS OF DOLLARS

Item Description for Accounting Period 7/03 Through 6/04	Total	Zero Assets	Under 500	500 to 1,000	1,000 to 5,000	5,000 to 10,000	10,000 to 25,000	25,000 to 50,000	50,000 to 100,000	100,000 to 250,000	250,000 to 500,000	500,000 to 2,500,000	2,500,000 and over
Number of Enterprises 1	41386	6450	25190	2897	4187	915	841	358	199	161	72	94	21
Revenues ($ in Thousands)													
Net Sales 2	1325095	148267	12331	1493	102828	73926	73383	64909	125704	151788	77229	343584	149653
Interest 3	5053696	102288	50808	30070	172407	99578	66689	102838	179179	211738	509529	1443796	2084775
Rents 4	522456	2524	2459	2607	22134	22610	12960	19605	28166	23270	13897	123240	248983
Royalties 5	319532	171	239	0	3262	2156	14529	1351	12885	8740	102780	164409	9009
Other Portfolio Income 6	5216698	382910	151513	156633	280689	132088	219843	225722	206116	274897	384744	413221	2388325
Other Receipts 7	5544137	-176493	282019	56167	557351	273367	580736	345213	328133	467835	159857	2214488	455465
Total Receipts 8	17981614	459667	499369	246970	1138671	603725	968140	759638	880183	1138268	1248036	4702738	5336210
Average Total Receipts 9	434	71	20	85	272	660	1151	2122	4423	7070	17334	50029	254105
Operating Costs/Operating Income (%)													
Cost of Operations 10	22.2	1.3	1.2	•	47.3	12.6	35.4	2.8	11.9	57.1	4.2	24.5	11.3
Salaries and Wages 11	78.2	60.3	258.0	169.3	56.8	44.7	62.6	65.0	70.4	71.3	307.3	41.2	104.9
Taxes Paid 12	28.8	17.9	497.1	255.7	20.6	28.3	44.1	32.7	16.6	22.6	48.1	24.9	11.0
Interest Paid 13	249.0	150.8	296.8	488.5	131.1	69.6	116.5	171.4	143.3	115.0	447.0	263.1	698.0
Depreciation 14	15.7	4.8	42.6	231.3	8.0	9.6	16.5	43.7	22.7	18.0	43.0	11.0	6.1
Amortization and Depletion 15	19.0	12.3	33.9	369.5	8.4	4.6	11.4	16.4	16.0	13.6	15.2	36.5	10.0
Pensions and Other Deferred Comp. 16	6.0	0.0	42.7	1.9	6.4	1.8	3.9	7.1	0.9	16.7	33.3	1.7	0.4
Employee Benefits 17	12.9	0.3	60.1	171.3	4.4	5.6	5.6	5.6	18.3	3.9	7.8	26.7	12.0
Advertising 18	0.8	0.1	•	1.0	0.6	0.4	3.8	2.8	0.1	1.0	0.9	0.8	0.0
Other Expenses 19	413.7	544.6	2267.7	10970.7	480.8	447.2	382.5	586.0	300.2	494.3	253.2	309.8	239.0
Officers' Compensation 20	24.4	1.9	153.9	202.9	32.1	62.9	45.3	38.6	11.2	22.6	30.8	24.5	3.2
Operating Margin 21	•	•	•	•	•	•	•	•	•	•	•	•	•
Operating Margin Before Officers' Comp. 22	•	•	•	•	•	•	•	•	•	•	•	•	•

Selected Average Balance Sheet ($ in Thousands)

Net Receivables 23	534	0	3	51	117	291	580	1812	4391	9289	24422	112470	250361
Inventories 24	2	0	0	0	0	30	19	23	54	89	111	89	288
Net Property, Plant and Equipment 25	87	0	4	48	102	334	375	1406	1682	2905	3016	7556	3019
Total Assets 26	8366	0	130	723	2245	7096	15629	35234	70609	158395	359192	1050699	6429512
Notes and Loans Payable 27	1136	0	44	84	642	1238	2962	8866	20044	24187	53060	116443	644781
All Other Liabilities 28	1067	0	8	1	214	697	1814	2833	5890	19698	53604	170075	747482
Net Worth 29	6162	0	77	638	1389	5162	10853	23535	44675	114510	252528	764181	5037249

Selected Financial Ratios (Times to 1)

Current Ratio 30	1.8	•	5.8	3.0	4.0	1.8	1.9	2.5	2.2	2.5	2.6	1.8	1.4
Quick Ratio 31	1.3	•	4.4	1.9	2.6	1.2	1.3	1.7	1.7	1.9	1.5	1.4	1.1
Net Sales to Working Capital 32	0.0	•	0.0	0.0	0.1	0.1	0.1	0.0	0.1	0.1	0.0	0.0	0.0
Coverage Ratio 33	3.3	•	1.8	8.1	3.4	2.5	5.9	1.9	1.6	0.4	2.3	3.5	5.3
Total Asset Turnover 34	0.0	•	0.0	0.0	0.0	0.0	0.0	0.0	0.0	0.0	0.0	0.0	0.0
Inventory Turnover 35	2.9	•	•	•	52.4	0.3	1.6	0.2	1.4	6.0	0.4	10.0	2.8
Receivables Turnover 36	0.1	•	0.2	0.0	0.2	0.2	0.1	0.1	0.2	0.1	0.1	0.0	0.0
Total Liabilities to Net Worth 37	0.4	•	0.7	0.1	0.6	0.4	0.4	0.5	0.6	0.4	0.4	0.4	0.3
Current Assets to Working Capital 38	2.2	•	1.2	1.5	1.3	2.3	2.1	1.6	1.8	1.7	1.6	2.3	3.5
Current Liabilities to Working Capital 39	1.2	•	0.2	0.5	0.3	1.3	1.1	0.6	0.8	0.7	0.6	1.3	2.5
Working Capital to Net Sales 40	22.0	•	80.5	271.0	17.8	8.4	17.2	28.2	11.6	16.2	45.5	25.6	40.3
Inventory to Working Capital 41	0.0	•	•	•	0.0	0.0	0.0	0.0	0.0	0.0	0.0	0.0	•
Total Receipts to Cash Flow 42	0.1	•	0.1	0.0	0.2	0.2	0.1	0.2	0.3	0.4	0.2	0.1	0.0
Cost of Goods to Cash Flow 43	0.0	•	0.0	•	0.1	0.0	0.0	0.0	0.0	0.2	0.0	0.0	0.0
Cash Flow to Total Debt 44	0.1	•	0.2	0.4	0.2	0.2	0.2	0.1	0.1	0.1	0.0	0.1	0.1

Selected Financial Factors (in Percentages)

Debt Ratio 45	26.3	•	40.4	11.7	38.1	27.3	30.6	33.2	36.7	27.7	29.7	27.3	21.7
Return on Total Assets 46	3.1	•	2.0	2.8	4.8	2.0	3.9	1.7	2.0	0.3	3.0	3.2	4.1
Return on Equity Before Income Taxes 47	2.9	•	1.4	2.8	5.5	1.6	4.6	1.3	1.2	•	2.4	3.1	4.2
Return on Equity After Income Taxes 48	1.8	•	0.8	1.8	4.4	0.9	3.8	0.4	0.2	•	1.1	2.3	2.8
Profit Margin (Before Income Tax) 49	562.8	•	224.3	3447.6	312.2	105.4	574.6	162.6	85.6	•	573.5	654.6	2972.8
Profit Margin (After Income Tax) 50	337.8	•	127.0	2222.6	250.1	58.7	469.1	53.2	10.7	•	249.5	485.5	1990.2

Table II

Corporations with Net Income

OFFICES OF OTHER HOLDING COMPANIES

MONEY AMOUNTS AND SIZE OF ASSETS IN THOUSANDS OF DOLLARS

Item Description for Accounting Period 7/03 Through 6/04	Total	Zero Assets	Under 500	500 to 1,000	1,000 to 5,000	5,000 to 10,000	10,000 to 25,000	25,000 to 50,000	50,000 to 100,000	100,000 to 250,000	250,000 to 500,000	500,000 to 2,500,000	2,500,000 and over
Number of Enterprises **1**	14245	1663	8234	1356	1907	280	372	150	80	81	43	64	15
Revenues ($ in Thousands)													
Net Sales **2**	458383	4829	11209	0	65176	20080	66282	50678	39122	11277	40249	108808	40673
Interest **3**	3447162	69960	16105	23623	152005	25751	40249	58895	100110	130133	383514	1174533	1272284
Rents **4**	424169	1940	608	2607	12343	1212	8494	13845	13687	13482	13837	93711	248403
Royalties **5**	237249	5	214	0	2926	204	14468	1126	3628	7323	33939	164408	9009
Other Portfolio Income **6**	4607445	325934	110892	148160	181175	118310	191483	192592	170373	231114	380597	340382	2216434
Other Receipts **7**	6154576	245838	332889	116775	633315	253710	654860	367738	358829	466847	195445	1937767	590562
Total Receipts **8**	15328984	648506	471917	291165	1046940	419267	975836	684874	685749	860176	1047581	3819609	4377365
Average Total Receipts **9**	1076	390	57	215	549	1497	2623	4566	8572	10619	24362	59681	291824
Operating Costs/Operating Income (%)													
Cost of Operations **10**	21.2	•	•	•	34.1	•	38.2	2.0	33.8	49.9	8.1	8.7	41.7
Salaries and Wages **11**	46.4	18.0	254.9	•	20.8	41.4	54.4	25.4	29.4	180.7	43.4	56.7	0.3
Taxes Paid **12**	54.8	335.8	492.0	•	18.7	45.2	29.4	29.7	25.9	146.2	74.5	59.3	1.1
Interest Paid **13**	303.5	616.5	105.7	•	148.3	88.2	49.3	80.6	111.0	524.3	472.5	553.5	649.5
Depreciation **14**	17.1	68.7	11.4	•	4.1	7.7	12.9	15.5	14.9	46.5	43.7	21.1	0.4
Amortization and Depletion **15**	37.5	28.1	5.9	•	12.1	1.0	7.8	4.8	32.1	124.3	19.9	109.5	0.4
Pensions and Other Deferred Comp. **16**	2.8	•	•	•	2.6	3.9	2.2	7.1	2.9	8.2	2.7	1.8	•
Employee Benefits **17**	23.7	0.1	25.7	•	0.7	3.7	4.2	2.3	32.6	19.2	3.7	77.2	•
Advertising **18**	0.5	0.3	•	•	0.2	0.2	0.7	0.1	0.3	1.4	0.1	1.4	•
Other Expenses **19**	271.6	629.8	623.9	•	181.4	221.4	109.0	240.1	218.8	914.3	234.6	316.9	144.8
Officers' Compensation **20**	34.9	5.4	140.3	•	31.5	39.3	24.9	27.0	28.5	155.0	16.4	43.2	•
Operating Margin **21**	•	•	•	•	•	•	•	•	•	•	•	•	•
Operating Margin Before Officers' Comp. **22**	•	•	•	•	•	•	•	•	•	•	•	•	•

Selected Average Balance Sheet ($ in Thousands)

Net Receivables 23	1089	0	5	23	30	816	763	2215	5858	11871	20624	125020	281127
Inventories 24	4	0	0	0	0	1	21	50	124	139	167	135	404
Net Property, Plant and Equipment 25	99	0	0	34	87	66	162	1480	1708	2237	3183	6890	41
Total Assets 26	15483	0	176	674	2206	7152	15780	35509	73695	160437	360213	1056854	6585035
Notes and Loans Payable 27	1452	0	55	47	289	958	2082	6808	11497	22176	54623	117400	331542
All Other Liabilities 28	1574	0	6	-97	166	492	1410	3175	6173	11456	67728	159362	434659
Net Worth 29	12458	0	115	724	1752	5702	12287	25526	56024	126805	237862	780092	5818834

Selected Financial Ratios (Times to 1)

Current Ratio 30	2.4	•	21.8	4.4	6.1	1.8	3.1	2.9	2.8	3.3	2.3	2.2	2.4
Quick Ratio 31	2.0	•	16.3	2.3	3.2	1.6	2.1	1.9	2.0	2.3	1.1	1.7	2.4
Net Sales to Working Capital 32	0.0	•	0.0	•	0.1	0.1	0.1	0.1	0.1	0.0	0.0	0.0	0.0
Coverage Ratio 33	10.2	22.9	25.0	72.3	8.8	19.0	24.3	12.4	12.1	12.0	5.2	5.4	19.1
Total Asset Turnover 34	0.0	•	0.0	•	0.0	0.0	0.0	0.0	0.0	0.0	0.0	0.0	0.0
Inventory Turnover 35	1.8	•	•	•	14.6	•	3.2	0.1	1.3	0.5	0.5	1.1	2.8
Receivables Turnover 36	0.0	•	0.6	•	2.3	0.1	0.2	0.2	0.1	0.0	0.0	0.0	0.0
Total Liabilities to Net Worth 37	0.2	•	0.5	•	0.3	0.3	0.3	0.4	0.3	0.3	0.5	0.4	0.1
Current Assets to Working Capital 38	1.7	•	1.0	1.3	1.2	2.2	1.5	1.5	1.6	1.4	1.8	1.8	1.7
Current Liabilities to Working Capital 39	0.7	•	0.0	0.3	0.2	1.2	0.5	0.5	0.6	0.4	0.8	0.8	0.7
Working Capital to Net Sales 40	55.5	•	40.7	•	13.2	15.2	12.6	18.0	18.0	124.7	52.6	78.3	222.3
Inventory to Working Capital 41	0.0	•	•	•	0.0	•	0.0	0.0	0.0	0.0	0.0	0.0	•
Total Receipts to Cash Flow 42	0.0	0.0	0.0	•	0.1	0.1	0.1	0.1	0.0	0.0	0.0	0.0	0.0
Cost of Goods to Cash Flow 43	0.0	•	•	•	0.0	•	0.0	0.0	0.0	0.0	0.0	0.0	0.0
Cash Flow to Total Debt 44	0.3	•	0.6	•	0.9	0.7	0.6	0.3	0.4	0.2	0.1	0.1	0.4

Selected Financial Factors (in Percentages)

Debt Ratio 45	19.5	•	34.3	•	20.6	20.3	22.1	28.1	24.0	21.0	34.0	26.2	11.6
Return on Total Assets 46	6.4	•	20.4	19.8	20.3	16.8	13.5	9.5	8.9	5.4	6.4	4.8	5.1
Return on Equity Before Income Taxes 47	7.2	•	29.9	18.1	22.7	19.9	16.7	12.2	10.8	6.3	7.8	5.3	5.5
Return on Equity After Income Taxes 48	5.5	•	28.6	16.3	20.8	18.0	15.0	10.3	8.8	5.0	5.3	4.1	3.8
Profit Margin (Before Income Tax) 49	2787.4	13493.0	2533.6	•	1163.4	1584.0	1148.7	919.2	1236.4	5742.1	1973.8	2430.8	11774.9
Profit Margin (After Income Tax) 50	2139.6	9986.2	2426.5	•	1065.5	1434.7	1032.2	779.5	1010.2	4514.6	1352.9	1896.9	8159.6

ADMINISTRATIVE AND SUPPORT AND WASTE MANAGEMENT AND REMEDIATION SERVICES
561300

EMPLOYMENT SERVICES

Table I

Corporations with and without Net Income

MONEY AMOUNTS AND SIZE OF ASSETS IN THOUSANDS OF DOLLARS

Item Description for Accounting Period 7/03 Through 6/04	Total	Zero Assets	Under 500	500 to 1,000	1,000 to 5,000	5,000 to 10,000	10,000 to 25,000	25,000 to 50,000	50,000 to 100,000	100,000 to 250,000	250,000 to 500,000	500,000 to 2,500,000	2,500,000 and over
Number of Enterprises **1**	24475	2180	20321	576	1133	114	67	30	20	16	7	11	•
Revenues ($ in Thousands)													
Net Sales **2**	105018812	1497434	21310990	2002795	17320396	3313535	8091595	5818249	5671015	4870435	14893557	20228811	•
Interest **3**	198072	109	3698	999	5359	653	2561	4687	4231	6951	24937	143886	•
Rents **4**	3125	0	0	0	294	0	1118	297	457	0	0	959	•
Royalties **5**	160861	0	0	0	0	0	0	0	11127	13015	617	136102	•
Other Portfolio Income **6**	122696	1071	651	52	10305	26435	3900	9148	14519	388	1416	54812	•
Other Receipts **7**	907751	203718	50615	5194	28171	1083	27990	3996	22043	18069	10095	536780	•
Total Receipts **8**	106411317	1702332	21365954	2009040	17364525	3341706	8127164	5836377	5723392	4908858	14930622	21101350	•
Average Total Receipts **9**	4348	781	1051	3488	15326	29313	121301	194546	286170	306804	2132946	1918305	•
Operating Costs/Operating Income (%)													
Cost of Operations **10**	61.6	99.2	49.4	71.4	69.4	75.9	64.0	51.1	76.7	50.0	58.5	64.7	•
Salaries and Wages **11**	18.5	8.6	28.6	10.4	7.7	5.5	21.3	30.0	8.3	28.3	24.5	12.6	•
Taxes Paid **12**	5.3	0.1	3.9	6.3	5.9	6.3	5.7	6.5	6.0	3.7	4.1	6.9	•
Interest Paid **13**	0.6	0.3	0.3	0.4	0.2	0.3	0.2	0.5	0.7	0.8	0.4	1.5	•
Depreciation **14**	0.5	0.1	0.3	0.3	0.2	0.4	0.3	0.4	0.5	0.6	0.4	1.0	•
Amortization and Depletion **15**	0.4	0.0	0.0	•	0.0	0.2	0.1	0.4	0.5	1.0	0.3	1.0	•
Pensions and Other Deferred Comp. **16**	0.3	0.0	0.7	0.0	0.0	0.0	0.1	0.0	0.2	0.2	0.1	0.2	•
Employee Benefits **17**	2.6	0.0	1.7	2.9	4.0	2.0	3.1	3.3	2.7	3.0	2.8	1.9	•
Advertising **18**	0.4	0.1	0.6	0.5	0.3	0.1	0.2	0.3	0.3	0.4	0.2	0.6	•
Other Expenses **19**	8.9	6.7	9.2	8.6	9.2	5.6	4.6	7.7	5.2	12.4	7.7	12.2	•
Officers' Compensation **20**	1.6	7.9	4.7	0.6	1.6	2.6	0.4	0.5	0.3	0.6	0.2	0.3	•
Operating Margin **21**	•	•	0.4	•	1.1	0.9	0.1	•	•	•	0.9	•	•
Operating Margin Before Officers' Comp. **22**	1.0	•	5.1	•	2.7	3.6	0.5	•	•	•	1.1	•	•

Selected Average Balance Sheet ($ in Thousands)

	•	•	•	•	•	•	•	•	•	•	•
Net Receivables 23	296	20	238	789	2140	5771	11438	21316	44666	149686	241677
Inventories 24	2	0	0	1	4	83	264	30	127	1991	1997
Net Property, Plant and Equipment 25	66	11	52	107	314	1516	1967	4215	7052	26347	59700
Total Assets 26	1131	83	662	1916	6113	15966	33089	71425	146157	410323	1276883
Notes and Loans Payable 27	328	58	399	669	2417	4422	10853	22135	43739	65231	307420
All Other Liabilities 28	400	31	99	858	1799	8497	14153	32252	44594	182214	391365
Net Worth 29	402	-6	164	390	1897	3047	8083	17038	57824	162878	578098

Selected Financial Ratios (Times to 1)

	•	•	•	•	•	•	•	•	•	•	•
Current Ratio 30	1.3	1.0	3.3	1.3	1.3	1.4	1.2	1.3	1.8	1.4	1.3
Quick Ratio 31	1.1	0.8	2.9	1.2	0.9	1.1	1.0	1.0	1.6	1.0	1.0
Net Sales to Working Capital 32	33.2	841.0	8.6	59.3	24.6	37.7	66.1	31.8	9.4	25.0	22.9
Coverage Ratio 33	2.3	2.9	•	9.2	6.4	3.5	0.5	0.4	0.8	3.8	2.1
Total Asset Turnover 34	3.8	12.7	5.3	8.0	4.8	7.6	5.9	4.0	2.1	5.2	1.4
Inventory Turnover 35	1210.9	438281.8	•	12477.9	5777.6	928.1	375.6	7368.6	1195.7	624.9	595.8
Receivables Turnover 36	14.1	48.5	7.9	21.1	13.9	22.4	18.5	13.9	6.8	15.1	7.0
Total Liabilities to Net Worth 37	1.8	•	3.0	3.9	2.2	3.1	3.1	3.2	1.5	1.5	1.2
Current Assets to Working Capital 38	4.1	42.9	1.4	4.9	3.9	3.4	6.4	4.2	2.2	3.3	4.9
Current Liabilities to Working Capital 39	3.1	41.9	0.4	3.9	2.9	2.4	5.4	3.2	1.2	2.3	3.9
Working Capital to Net Sales 40	0.0	0.0	0.1	0.0	0.0	0.0	0.0	0.0	0.1	0.0	0.0
Inventory to Working Capital 41	0.0	0.0	0.0	0.0	•	0.0	0.1	0.0	0.0	0.0	0.0
Total Receipts to Cash Flow 42	12.3	12.4	15.9	10.5	14.9	22.9	15.5	27.5	9.8	13.6	8.5
Cost of Goods to Cash Flow 43	7.6	6.1	11.3	7.3	11.3	14.7	7.9	21.1	4.9	7.9	5.5
Cash Flow to Total Debt 44	0.5	1.0	0.4	1.0	0.5	0.4	0.5	0.2	0.4	0.6	0.3

Selected Financial Factors (in Percentages)

	•	•	•	•	•	•	•	•	•	•	•
Debt Ratio 45	64.4	106.9	75.2	79.6	69.0	80.9	75.6	76.1	60.4	60.3	54.7
Return on Total Assets 46	5.1	13.0	•	12.4	10.1	5.6	1.7	1.1	1.3	7.7	4.7
Return on Equity Before Income Taxes 47	8.0	•	•	54.3	27.5	20.8	•	•	•	14.3	5.4
Return on Equity After Income Taxes 48	4.9	•	•	53.8	27.5	18.0	•	•	•	11.6	1.8
Profit Margin (Before Income Tax) 49	0.8	0.7	•	1.4	1.8	0.5	0.0	•	•	1.1	1.7
Profit Margin (After Income Tax) 50	0.5	0.6	1.4	1.4	1.8	0.5	0.0	•	•	0.9	0.6

Table II
Corporations with Net Income

EMPLOYMENT SERVICES

MONEY AMOUNTS AND SIZE OF ASSETS IN THOUSANDS OF DOLLARS

Item Description for Accounting Period 7/03 Through 6/04	Total	Zero Assets	Under 500	500 to 1,000	1,000 to 5,000	5,000 to 10,000	10,000 to 25,000	25,000 to 50,000	50,000 to 100,000	100,000 to 250,000	250,000 to 500,000	500,000 to 2,500,000	2,500,000 and over
Number of Enterprises 1	11923	795	9873	348	768	•	42	15	8	•	•	•	5
Revenues ($ in Thousands)													
Net Sales 2	61128787	2921	9072222	1610274	14779884	•	645493	4248171	2666385	•	•	•	9640032
Interest 3	138986	0	3023	552	832	•	1940	1655	405	•	•	•	116198
Rents 4	2371	0	0	0	0	•	1118	290	3	•	•	•	959
Royalties 5	135065	0	0	0	0	•	0	0	459	•	•	•	122594
Other Portfolio Income 6	92881	615	203	52	10245	•	3349	3149	4706	•	•	•	42769
Other Receipts 7	585183	4436	5306	5112	24526	•	19554	15472	11517	•	•	•	487657
Total Receipts 8	62083273	7972	9080754	1615990	14815487	•	6671454	4268737	2683475	•	•	•	10410209
Average Total Receipts 9	5207	10	920	4644	19291	•	158844	284582	335434	•	•	•	2082042
Operating Costs/Operating Income (%)													
Cost of Operations 10	56.5	7.8	24.0	66.2	70.7	•	68.1	41.9	78.6	•	•	•	55.6
Salaries and Wages 11	21.0	8.1	42.2	12.6	6.6	•	18.4	37.3	8.9	•	•	•	17.2
Taxes Paid 12	5.4	2.7	5.6	7.8	5.7	•	5.5	7.0	4.9	•	•	•	6.3
Interest Paid 13	0.5	•	0.4	0.5	0.1	•	0.1	0.2	0.4	•	•	•	1.5
Depreciation 14	0.4	0.4	0.4	0.2	0.2	•	0.2	0.3	0.3	•	•	•	1.0
Amortization and Depletion 15	0.2	1.8	0.1	•	0.0	•	0.0	0.1	0.5	•	•	•	0.3
Pensions and Other Deferred Comp. 16	0.2	•	0.6	0.0	0.2	•	0.1	0.0	0.3	•	•	•	0.2
Employee Benefits 17	2.6	1.8	2.4	3.5	3.8	•	3.2	3.3	2.0	•	•	•	1.9
Advertising 18	0.4	2.2	0.8	0.3	0.3	•	0.2	0.2	0.2	•	•	•	0.7
Other Expenses 19	9.3	80.7	11.0	6.6	8.8	•	3.3	8.1	3.5	•	•	•	16.3
Officers' Compensation 20	1.8	•	7.1	0.8	1.6	•	0.3	0.4	0.2	•	•	•	0.4
Operating Margin 21	1.6	•	5.3	1.5	2.0	•	0.7	1.1	0.1	•	•	•	•
Operating Margin Before Officers' Comp. 22	3.4	•	12.5	2.2	3.5	•	1.1	1.6	0.4	•	•	•	•

Selected Average Balance Sheet ($ in Thousands)

Net Receivables 23	346	0	17	249	758	•	5509	11574	19503	•	395609
Inventories 24	2	0	0	0	•	28	295	40	•	4393	
Net Property, Plant and Equipment 25	73	0	11	41	92	•	1880	2164	5166	•	57069
Total Assets 26	1325	0	91	729	1784	•	16223	34236	68497	•	1657719
Notes and Loans Payable 27	256	0	57	236	359	•	3216	8347	14545	•	185673
All Other Liabilities 28	428	0	20	157	775	•	8127	18834	39553	•	489922
Net Worth 29	640	0	14	336	650	•	4881	7055	14399	•	982125

Selected Financial Ratios (Times to 1)

Current Ratio 30	1.5	•	1.3	2.2	1.5	•	1.4	1.1	1.5	•	1.4
Quick Ratio 31	1.2	•	1.1	1.9	1.4	•	1.0	0.9	0.9	•	1.2
Net Sales to Working Capital 32	24.8	•	70.4	13.1	46.6	•	46.4	111.6	24.9	•	11.2
Coverage Ratio 33	7.4	•	14.7	4.4	25.1	•	17.9	8.6	2.7	•	5.5
Total Asset Turnover 34	3.9	•	10.0	6.3	10.8	•	9.8	8.3	4.9	•	1.2
Inventory Turnover 35	1202.8	•	90766.4	•	44858.9	•	3825.7	402.2	6563.0	•	244.1
Receivables Turnover 36	15.4	•	33.8	10.8	27.4	•	31.4	25.0	21.4	•	5.8
Total Liabilities to Net Worth 37	1.1	•	5.5	1.2	1.7	•	2.3	3.9	3.8	•	0.7
Current Assets to Working Capital 38	3.2	•	4.3	1.8	3.1	•	3.4	8.7	2.9	•	3.7
Current Liabilities to Working Capital 39	2.2	•	3.3	0.8	2.1	•	2.4	7.7	1.9	•	2.7
Working Capital to Net Sales 40	0.0	•	0.0	0.1	0.0	•	0.0	0.0	0.0	•	0.1
Inventory to Working Capital 41	0.0	•	0.0	•	0.0	•	0.0	0.2	0.0	•	0.0
Total Receipts to Cash Flow 42	9.1	0.4	7.2	13.7	9.9	•	25.7	11.2	27.9	•	4.8
Cost of Goods to Cash Flow 43	5.2	0.0	1.7	9.1	7.0	•	17.5	4.7	21.9	•	2.7
Cash Flow to Total Debt 44	0.8	•	1.6	0.9	1.7	•	0.5	0.9	0.2	•	0.6

Selected Financial Factors (in Percentages)

Debt Ratio 45	51.7	•	84.7	54.0	63.6	•	69.9	79.4	79.0	•	40.8
Return on Total Assets 46	14.5	•	58.5	14.9	24.9	•	11.6	15.0	5.7	•	9.6
Return on Equity Before Income Taxes 47	25.9	•	356.0	25.1	65.5	•	36.5	64.2	17.2	•	13.3
Return on Equity After Income Taxes 48	21.9	•	349.8	24.7	65.1	•	33.7	57.3	13.2	•	8.7
Profit Margin (Before Income Tax) 49	3.2	167.2	5.4	1.8	2.2	•	1.1	1.6	0.7	•	6.8
Profit Margin (After Income Tax) 50	2.7	167.2	5.3	1.8	2.2	•	1.0	1.4	0.6	•	4.4

Table I

Corporations with and without Net Income

TRAVEL ARRANGEMENT AND RESERVATION SERVICES

MONEY AMOUNTS AND SIZE OF ASSETS IN THOUSANDS OF DOLLARS

Item Description for Accounting Period 7/03 Through 6/04	Total	Zero Assets	Under 500	500 to 1,000	1,000 to 5,000	5,000 to 10,000	10,000 to 25,000	25,000 to 50,000	50,000 to 100,000	100,000 to 250,000	250,000 to 500,000	500,000 to 2,500,000	2,500,000 and over
Number of Enterprises **1**	27256	3889	22497	172	508	60	55	24	22	14	8	7	•
Revenues ($ in Thousands)													
Net Sales **2**	40738034	1315759	17355687	484836	2390558	1102919	2325224	1431236	2054477	1570251	2332589	8374498	•
Interest **3**	221079	409	2294	392	2167	1210	4158	2040	4384	5738	45060	153226	•
Rents **4**	33260	0	221	0	240	2695	549	553	3054	3376	1945	20625	•
Royalties **5**	36325	0	0	0	0	72	570	0	7695	25847	0	2141	•
Other Portfolio Income **6**	137576	7325	16378	7	458	1283	2015	25400	10152	16343	6198	52021	•
Other Receipts **7**	1120057	5252	87006	376	80277	16587	130795	44108	75213	117290	311010	252142	•
Total Receipts **8**	42286331	1328745	17461586	485611	2473700	1124766	2463311	1503337	2154975	1738845	2696802	8854653	•
Average Total Receipts **9**	1551	342	776	2823	4869	18746	44787	62639	97953	124203	337100	1264950	•
Operating Costs/Operating Income (%)													
Cost of Operations **10**	61.6	62.5	75.7	66.1	36.2	80.2	64.1	71.2	57.9	53.0	57.2	38.1	•
Salaries and Wages **11**	13.1	13.7	5.3	6.5	31.4	7.6	14.0	12.1	16.5	20.0	20.7	20.6	•
Taxes Paid **12**	1.5	1.9	1.0	1.0	3.4	1.5	1.7	1.4	2.1	2.3	1.9	1.7	•
Interest Paid **13**	0.6	0.2	0.3	0.3	0.5	0.1	0.3	0.4	0.6	0.9	3.3	0.6	•
Depreciation **14**	1.2	0.5	0.6	0.9	1.4	1.2	1.0	1.4	2.1	2.2	1.7	2.1	•
Amortization and Depletion **15**	0.5	1.0	0.1	0.0	0.1	0.2	0.2	0.2	0.8	0.7	1.1	1.2	•
Pensions and Other Deferred Comp. **16**	0.3	0.0	0.2	0.0	0.3	0.1	0.3	0.3	0.9	0.4	0.5	0.5	•
Employee Benefits **17**	1.1	1.2	0.3	0.1	2.3	0.6	1.3	0.8	2.3	2.0	2.9	1.4	•
Advertising **18**	2.3	2.5	1.1	0.0	1.4	0.4	1.2	2.1	2.1	3.9	2.3	5.6	•
Other Expenses **19**	18.5	16.3	12.4	14.0	23.7	7.1	19.1	15.0	18.5	21.3	22.5	30.3	•
Officers' Compensation **20**	3.2	2.1	3.5	9.6	5.8	2.7	1.5	0.8	1.3	0.8	0.8	4.3	•
Operating Margin **21**	•	•	•	1.3	•	•	•	•	•	•	•	•	•
Operating Margin Before Officers' Comp. **22**	•	0.1	3.1	10.9	0.9	•	•	•	•	•	•	•	•

Selected Average Balance Sheet ($ in Thousands)

Line Item													
Net Receivables 23	141	0	8	0	462	1117	3480	7230	5866	16546	29269	344764	•
Inventories 24	4	0	1	0	3	40	127	508	515	495	1092	5079	•
Net Property, Plant and Equipment 25	96	0	15	49	276	1218	1723	3522	11597	26017	36063	140633	•
Total Assets 26	1619	0	70	718	2183	5806	16144	36804	68541	166660	359075	4640505	•
Notes and Loans Payable 27	204	0	51	18	350	1785	1961	5498	13401	23266	161126	283183	•
All Other Liabilities 28	600	0	29	420	1445	2588	10961	20641	33956	74869	104512	1573452	•
Net Worth 29	814	0	-10	281	389	1434	3222	10665	21184	68525	93437	2783869	•

Selected Financial Ratios (Times to 1)

Line Item													
Current Ratio 30	1.1	•	1.5	1.0	0.9	1.1	0.9	1.5	1.1	0.9	1.2	0.7	1.2
Quick Ratio 31	0.7	•	1.4	0.2	0.7	0.8	0.7	1.1	0.7	0.7	0.8	0.5	0.7
Net Sales to Working Capital 32	58.0	•	58.4	808.1	•	36.3	•	14.8	•	•	10.6	•	12.3
Coverage Ratio 33	1.0	•	1.8	5.7	5.9	•	•	3.4	0.5	1.4	4.2	1.2	0.2
Total Asset Turnover 34	0.9	•	11.0	3.9	2.2	1.6	2.6	3.2	1.4	•	0.7	0.8	0.3
Inventory Turnover 35	247.7	•	838.0	•	593.1	83.6	214.2	365.8	105.1	•	119.9	152.7	89.8
Receivables Turnover 36	10.5	•	92.9	24.9	10.4	9.4	11.7	7.6	15.1	•	6.8	5.6	3.9
Total Liabilities to Net Worth 37	1.0	•	•	1.6	4.6	2.5	4.0	3.1	2.2	•	1.4	2.8	0.7
Current Assets to Working Capital 38	14.8	•	2.9	119.7	•	12.4	•	2.9	•	•	7.1	•	7.4
Current Liabilities to Working Capital 39	13.8	•	1.9	118.7	•	11.4	•	1.9	•	•	6.1	•	6.4
Working Capital to Net Sales 40	0.0	•	0.0	0.0	•	0.0	•	0.1	•	•	0.1	•	0.1
Inventory to Working Capital 41	0.2	•	0.1	•	•	0.3	•	0.1	•	•	0.1	•	0.1
Total Receipts to Cash Flow 42	6.4	8.3	9.6	7.3	6.3	8.1	5.4	16.3	6.7	5.4	4.9	5.2	3.7
Cost of Goods to Cash Flow 43	3.9	5.2	7.3	4.8	2.3	5.8	3.5	13.1	3.9	2.6	2.9	1.4	•
Cash Flow to Total Debt 44	0.3	•	1.0	0.9	0.4	0.3	0.6	0.3	0.3	0.2	0.2	0.2	0.2

Selected Financial Factors (in Percentages)

Line Item													
Debt Ratio 45	49.7	•	114.6	60.9	82.2	75.3	80.0	71.0	69.1	58.9	74.0	•	40.0
Return on Total Assets 46	0.5	•	5.7	6.9	4.1	0.8	•	0.4	•	0.4	2.5	3.2	0.0
Return on Equity Before Income Taxes 47	•	•	•	14.6	•	17.1	2.3	•	•	•	4.6	1.8	•
Return on Equity After Income Taxes 48	•	•	•	10.3	•	10.2	•	•	•	•	3.3	1.3	•
Profit Margin (Before Income Tax) 49	•	0.2	1.5	1.3	0.2	•	•	•	•	2.8	•	0.6	•
Profit Margin (After Income Tax) 50	•	0.2	1.0	0.8	•	•	•	•	•	2.0	•	0.4	•

Table II
Corporations with Net Income

TRAVEL ARRANGEMENT AND RESERVATION SERVICES

MONEY AMOUNTS AND SIZE OF ASSETS IN THOUSANDS OF DOLLARS

Item Description for Accounting Period 7/03 Through 6/04		Total	Zero Assets	Under 500	500 to 1,000	1,000 to 5,000	5,000 to 10,000	10,000 to 25,000	25,000 to 50,000	50,000 to 100,000	100,000 to 250,000	250,000 to 500,000	500,000 to 2,500,000	2,500,000 and over
Number of Enterprises	1	14219	418	13432	57	189	•	39	13	13	9	•	•	•
Revenues ($ in Thousands)														
Net Sales	2	22837498	694175	12030621	211379	954282	•	1559802	744178	1054471	1208579	•	•	•
Interest	3	64758	351	1728	151	1359	•	3541	1785	3218	4352	•	•	•
Rents	4	12093	0	47	0	0	•	549	228	2787	2984	•	•	•
Royalties	5	34112	0	0	0	0	•	570	0	7695	25847	•	•	•
Other Portfolio Income	6	84299	7325	15842	7	409	•	1858	22325	7384	13588	•	•	•
Other Receipts	7	763993	198	73996	24	62862	•	125545	11938	72221	87493	•	•	•
Total Receipts	8	23796753	702049	12122234	211561	1018912	•	1691865	780454	1147776	1342843	•	•	•
Average Total Receipts	9	1674	1680	902	3712	5391	•	43381	60035	88290	149205	•	•	•
Operating Costs/Operating Income (%)														
Cost of Operations	10	58.8	69.2	72.7	72.7	0.7	•	54.1	62.2	50.7	49.5	•	•	•
Salaries and Wages	11	11.8	6.4	5.2	6.2	49.2	•	17.0	12.9	15.0	20.6	•	•	•
Taxes Paid	12	1.6	1.2	1.0	0.7	5.2	•	1.9	1.7	2.3	2.4	•	•	•
Interest Paid	13	0.5	0.1	0.1	0.6	0.1	•	0.2	0.4	0.7	0.5	•	•	•
Depreciation	14	1.1	0.5	0.5	0.3	1.9	•	1.2	1.0	2.6	1.1	•	•	•
Amortization and Depletion	15	0.3	1.8	0.1	•	0.0	•	0.2	0.1	0.4	0.4	•	•	•
Pensions and Other Deferred Comp.	16	0.4	0.0	0.2	0.0	0.4	•	0.5	0.3	1.4	0.4	•	•	•
Employee Benefits	17	1.1	0.3	0.3	0.3	3.6	•	1.5	0.9	3.2	2.0	•	•	•
Advertising	18	1.9	3.6	1.1	0.0	1.5	•	1.1	2.3	1.9	4.0	•	•	•
Other Expenses	19	20.2	10.7	13.3	9.5	34.3	•	25.5	18.7	24.4	21.9	•	•	•
Officers' Compensation	20	2.6	0.6	3.6	0.4	6.4	•	1.9	1.1	1.4	0.7	•	•	•
Operating Margin	21	•	5.8	2.0	9.3	•	•	•	•	•	•	•	•	•
Operating Margin Before Officers' Comp.	22	2.4	6.3	5.5	9.6	3.0	•	•	•	•	•	•	•	•

Selected Average Balance Sheet ($ in Thousands)

Net Receivables 23	88	0	7	0	350	•	3770	9046	4602	20332
Inventories 24	4	0	2	0	111	•	726	362	164	
Net Property, Plant and Equipment 25	87	0	14	11	281	•	2011	3939	12515	19203
Total Assets 26	841	0	78	724	2328	•	16555	37762	69246	161346
Notes and Loans Payable 27	221	0	29	25	106	•	1900	3299	10228	14553
All Other Liabilities 28	333	0	24	508	1792	•	11647	18117	33228	88992
Net Worth 29	287	0	25	191	430	•	3007	16346	25790	57800

Selected Financial Ratios (Times to 1)

Current Ratio 30	1.2	•	2.2	1.4	1.0	•	0.9	1.3	1.0	1.1
Quick Ratio 31	0.7	•	1.9	0.1	0.9	•	0.7	1.1	0.8	0.8
Net Sales to Working Capital 32	25.6	•	36.3	18.3	•	•	11.2	315.2	14.1	
Coverage Ratio 33	9.6	115.9	23.8	16.7	32.8	•	14.9	10.1	7.1	13.7
Total Asset Turnover 34	1.9	•	11.5	5.1	2.2	•	2.4	1.5	1.2	0.8
Inventory Turnover 35	253.4	•	401.2	31.7	•	•	195.1	49.0	113.6	406.4
Receivables Turnover 36	10.1	•	113.4	11.0	11.5	•	11.1	6.6	35.3	6.4
Total Liabilities to Net Worth 37	1.9	•	2.2	2.8	4.4	•	4.5	1.3	1.7	1.8
Current Assets to Working Capital 38	5.6	•	1.8	3.5	•	•	4.1	109.8	9.0	
Current Liabilities to Working Capital 39	4.6	•	0.8	2.5	•	•	3.1	108.8	8.0	
Working Capital to Net Sales 40	0.0	•	0.0	0.1	•	•	0.1	0.0	0.1	
Inventory to Working Capital 41	0.1	•	0.1	•	•	•	0.2	1.4	0.0	
Total Receipts to Cash Flow 42	4.6	6.2	7.1	5.7	3.3	•	3.7	5.0	3.9	4.1
Cost of Goods to Cash Flow 43	2.7	4.3	5.2	4.1	0.0	•	2.0	3.1	2.0	2.0
Cash Flow to Total Debt 44	0.6	•	2.4	1.2	0.8	•	0.8	0.5	0.5	0.3

Selected Financial Factors (in Percentages)

Debt Ratio 45	65.8	•	68.4	73.7	81.5	•	81.8	56.7	62.8	64.2
Return on Total Assets 46	8.5	•	32.8	51.0	7.6	•	8.6	5.4	5.9	6.1
Return on Equity Before Income Taxes 47	22.2	•	99.6	182.2	39.7	•	44.3	11.2	13.6	15.9
Return on Equity After Income Taxes 48	19.3	•	99.3	163.1	37.5	•	33.8	8.5	10.7	13.4
Profit Margin (Before Income Tax) 49	4.0	6.6	2.7	9.4	3.4	•	3.3	3.2	4.3	6.8
Profit Margin (After Income Tax) 50	3.4	4.9	2.7	8.4	3.2	•	2.5	2.4	3.4	5.8

Table I
Corporations with and without Net Income

OTHER ADMINISTRATIVE AND SUPPORT SERVICES

MONEY AMOUNTS AND SIZE OF ASSETS IN THOUSANDS OF DOLLARS

Item Description for Accounting Period 7/03 Through 6/04	Total	Zero Assets	Under 500	500 to 1,000	1,000 to 5,000	5,000 to 10,000	10,000 to 25,000	25,000 to 50,000	50,000 to 100,000	100,000 to 250,000	250,000 to 500,000	500,000 to 2,500,000	2,500,000 and over
Number of Enterprises 1	179069	26355	140838	5899	5140	324	276	98	52	39	21	23	4
Revenues ($ in Thousands)													
Net Sales 2	165987983	2520911	49621519	15682131	26934292	4721597	9144204	5022212	5417003	5867172	5949605	18931348	16175989
Interest 3	1380996	6972	11849	10139	23165	6367	11994	15185	20036	33243	93001	186411	962634
Rents 4	497881	214	3296	9478	2037	977	4562	15512	205	2892	11093	7557	440056
Royalties 5	1223725	9394	0	0	8013	0	1999	6853	11848	9866	0	133250	1042502
Other Portfolio Income 6	1063699	25942	109086	32887	20969	29674	22591	24920	2791	9817	56583	213549	514885
Other Receipts 7	6733881	114561	1617606	30873	169772	115266	450594	212914	178901	494485	164538	477870	2706508
Total Receipts 8	176888165	2677994	51363356	15765508	27155248	4873881	9635944	5297596	5630784	6417475	6274820	19949985	21842574
Average Total Receipts 9	988	102	365	2673	5284	15043	34913	54057	108284	164551	298801	867391	5460644
Operating Costs/Operating Income (%)													
Cost of Operations 10	36.6	13.1	33.9	41.8	52.2	49.1	48.1	49.0	43.9	26.5	29.6	27.4	17.8
Salaries and Wages 11	21.5	26.3	20.5	17.9	15.4	18.4	23.6	19.8	19.8	35.7	29.0	30.1	19.8
Taxes Paid 12	4.1	3.8	3.5	3.5	3.3	4.2	3.6	3.3	3.2	3.8	3.9	4.6	8.7
Interest Paid 13	2.0	2.0	0.7	0.6	0.9	0.7	1.1	1.9	1.8	3.1	3.3	2.7	8.8
Depreciation 14	3.2	3.3	3.0	2.4	2.7	2.0	2.1	2.5	2.1	3.2	3.0	3.0	7.3
Amortization and Depletion 15	1.2	1.3	0.1	0.1	0.1	0.2	0.4	0.7	0.9	1.6	1.7	1.8	7.2
Pensions and Other Deferred Comp. 16	0.5	0.6	0.3	0.2	0.3	0.6	0.5	0.5	0.2	0.5	1.1	1.1	0.5
Employee Benefits 17	1.9	1.8	1.0	1.9	1.5	1.4	3.1	2.5	2.0	2.9	3.6	2.7	2.5
Advertising 18	1.2	2.0	1.2	0.7	0.8	0.2	0.6	1.8	0.2	0.7	1.7	0.8	3.6
Other Expenses 19	26.2	42.7	25.9	21.4	16.2	20.0	18.3	20.3	27.9	31.2	26.2	24.1	53.8
Officers' Compensation 20	4.2	8.3	7.9	5.3	4.2	3.7	1.8	1.6	1.4	1.3	1.4	0.9	0.1
Operating Margin 21	•	•	2.1	4.2	2.2	•	•	•	•	•	•	0.8	•
Operating Margin Before Officers' Comp. 22	1.7	3.1	10.0	9.4	6.4	3.1	•	•	•	•	•	1.7	•

Selected Average Balance Sheet ($ in Thousands)

						1987							
Net Receivables 23	97	0	8	131	522	168	4336	9079	17017	27953	55998	133193	951861
Inventories 24	11	0	2	36	73	168	497	1221	2313	3273	6670	90922	
Net Property, Plant and Equipment 25	105	0	25	216	447	1166	2688	5292	9701	23280	41539	135495	1138726
Total Assets 26	739	0	70	697	1899	6734	15703	34365	69922	144248	331958	965389	15087066
Notes and Loans Payable 27	287	0	45	291	803	2355	6266	15715	23829	62229	124888	257914	5740291
All Other Liabilities 28	238	0	16	154	725	2311	5970	12021	22814	53473	109066	190689	5575527
Net Worth 29	214	0	9	252	371	2068	3467	6629	23279	28546	98004	516785	3771248

Selected Financial Ratios (Times to 1)

						1987							
Current Ratio 30	1.0	•	1.3	1.4	1.3	1.3	1.2	1.3	1.1	1.4	1.3	2.0	0.5
Quick Ratio 31	0.7	•	1.0	1.1	1.0	1.0	0.9	1.0	0.8	1.0	0.8	1.4	0.3
Net Sales to Working Capital 32	1233.5	•	60.4	23.1	21.4	15.8	19.9	10.7	37.8	7.6	8.7	5.5	•
Coverage Ratio 33	3.0	1.5	9.6	8.5	4.4	4.7	2.9	1.8	1.4	0.6	1.7	3.3	1.6
Total Asset Turnover 34	1.3	•	5.0	3.8	2.8	2.2	2.1	1.5	1.5	1.0	0.9	0.9	0.3
Inventory Turnover 35	30.6	•	72.4	30.8	37.5	42.6	32.0	20.6	19.8	10.7	25.6	33.8	7.9
Receivables Turnover 36	9.5	•	42.4	19.2	10.8	6.1	7.8	5.3	5.9	5.5	5.0	6.2	4.2
Total Liabilities to Net Worth 37	2.5	•	6.9	1.8	4.1	2.3	3.5	4.2	2.0	4.1	2.4	0.9	3.0
Current Assets to Working Capital 38	296.5	•	4.9	3.3	4.8	4.6	5.2	3.9	11.6	3.3	4.0	2.0	•
Current Liabilities to Working Capital 39	295.5	•	3.9	2.3	3.8	3.6	4.2	2.9	10.6	2.3	3.0	1.0	•
Working Capital to Net Sales 40	0.0	•	0.0	0.0	0.0	0.1	0.1	0.1	0.0	0.1	0.1	0.2	•
Inventory to Working Capital 41	16.5	•	0.3	0.3	0.3	0.0	0.3	0.2	0.8	0.2	0.1	0.0	•
Total Receipts to Cash Flow 42	4.0	2.8	3.7	4.5	6.4	5.4	5.9	5.5	3.9	4.0	4.4	4.3	2.0
Cost of Goods to Cash Flow 43	1.5	0.4	1.3	1.9	3.3	2.6	2.8	2.7	1.7	1.1	1.3	1.2	0.4
Cash Flow to Total Debt 44	0.4	•	1.5	1.3	0.5	0.6	0.5	0.3	0.6	0.3	0.3	0.4	0.2

Selected Financial Factors (in Percentages)

						1987							
Debt Ratio 45	71.1	•	87.3	63.8	80.5	69.3	77.9	80.7	66.7	80.2	70.5	46.5	75.0
Return on Total Assets 46	7.7	•	31.6	20.3	10.8	7.4	6.8	5.2	3.6	1.9	4.8	7.6	3.7
Return on Equity Before Income Taxes 47	17.8	•	222.5	49.5	42.9	19.0	20.2	11.9	2.9	6.7	9.9	5.2	
Return on Equity After Income Taxes 48	15.9	•	219.7	47.9	40.7	14.7	16.3	8.8	0.8	3.9	6.9	4.9	
Profit Margin (Before Income Tax) 49	4.1	1.0	5.6	4.7	3.0	2.7	2.1	1.5	0.6	2.3	6.2	4.9	
Profit Margin (After Income Tax) 50	3.7	0.6	5.5	4.5	2.9	2.1	1.7	1.1	0.2	1.3	4.3	4.6	

Table II
Corporations with Net Income

OTHER ADMINISTRATIVE AND SUPPORT SERVICES

MONEY AMOUNTS AND SIZE OF ASSETS IN THOUSANDS OF DOLLARS

Item Description for Accounting Period 7/03 Through 6/04	Total	Zero Assets	Under 500	500 to 1,000	1,000 to 5,000	5,000 to 10,000	10,000 to 25,000	25,000 to 50,000	50,000 to 100,000	100,000 to 250,000	250,000 to 500,000	500,000 to 2,500,000	2,500,000 and over
Number of Enterprises **1**	116847	10884	97370	4461	3544	267	174	60	28	21	•	19	•
Revenues ($ in Thousands)													
Net Sales **2**	128955393	1085850	36464198	13779773	21699425	3952532	6346339	3805048	3281552	3718588	•	17976763	•
Interest **3**	1191248	970	10083	8721	8533	3990	5357	5949	8354	10570	•	181095	•
Rents **4**	483169	205	2087	2970	865	977	3810	13413	70	681	•	7557	•
Royalties **5**	1201986	0	0	0	7991	0	0	6516	11612	4793	•	133250	•
Other Portfolio Income **6**	1022289	21818	100886	29526	12534	28134	16933	22254	1886	8041	•	213415	•
Other Receipts **7**	4694520	104231	812735	4923	123076	112138	213488	161704	143671	262801	•	466358	•
Total Receipts **8**	137548605	1213074	37389989	13825913	21852424	4097771	6585927	4014884	3447145	4005474	•	1898438	•
Average Total Receipts **9**	1177	111	384	3099	6166	15347	37850	66915	123112	190737	•	998865	•
Operating Costs/Operating Income (%)													
Cost of Operations **10**	35.8	16.6	33.2	40.9	51.5	48.1	45.6	49.1	51.0	28.5	•	28.7	•
Salaries and Wages **11**	20.6	12.7	17.5	17.6	15.3	19.1	22.0	19.7	16.1	34.0	•	29.3	•
Taxes Paid **12**	4.3	2.0	3.3	3.5	3.2	4.4	3.5	3.2	2.9	4.6	•	4.6	•
Interest Paid **13**	1.8	1.1	0.6	0.6	0.5	0.4	0.5	1.1	1.4	2.7	•	2.5	•
Depreciation **14**	2.9	3.6	2.6	2.1	2.2	1.7	1.9	2.1	2.0	2.9	•	3.0	•
Amortization and Depletion **15**	1.0	0.6	0.1	0.1	0.1	0.0	0.3	0.5	0.7	1.1	•	1.5	•
Pensions and Other Deferred Comp. **16**	0.5	0.2	0.3	0.2	0.3	0.6	0.4	0.5	0.2	0.8	•	1.0	•
Employee Benefits **17**	1.9	1.4	1.0	2.0	1.3	1.5	2.5	2.4	1.7	3.3	•	2.7	•
Advertising **18**	1.3	2.5	1.2	0.6	0.8	0.2	0.7	1.1	0.3	0.8	•	0.8	•
Other Expenses **19**	25.1	37.8	24.9	21.1	14.6	18.4	17.7	18.9	21.0	24.5	•	23.8	•
Officers' Compensation **20**	4.1	7.9	8.1	5.3	4.2	3.9	1.8	1.6	1.7	1.0	•	0.9	•
Operating Margin **21**	0.8	13.7	7.3	6.0	5.9	1.6	3.2	•	0.9	•	•	1.3	•
Operating Margin Before Officers' Comp. **22**	4.9	21.6	15.4	11.3	10.1	5.4	5.0	1.3	2.6	•	•	2.2	•

Selected Average Balance Sheet ($ in Thousands)

Net Receivables 23	115	0	9	123	493	2147	4222	10381	17986	22533	154087	•
Inventories 24	13	0	2	43	67	178	549	1567	3681	6515	7001	•
Net Property, Plant and Equipment 25	105	0	24	192	441	943	2787	4285	11804	27853	153178	•
Total Assets 26	912	0	72	705	1965	6652	15396	34417	66505	145885	1033680	•
Notes and Loans Payable 27	344	0	36	283	638	1821	4253	11470	19699	55931	258034	•
All Other Liabilities 28	270	0	17	144	646	2514	4873	13109	26932	38750	223581	•
Net Worth 29	298	0	20	278	681	2317	6270	9838	19874	51205	552065	•

Selected Financial Ratios (Times to 1)

Current Ratio 30	1.0	•	1.5	1.5	1.3	1.3	1.4	1.3	1.0	1.5	1.8	•
Quick Ratio 31	0.7	•	1.3	1.1	1.0	1.0	1.1	1.0	0.7	1.1	1.2	•
Net Sales to Working Capital 32	•	•	35.0	23.5	20.3	13.7	14.4	14.2	600.8	8.4	6.9	•
Coverage Ratio 33	5.2	24.1	18.4	11.5	13.9	13.4	14.3	5.7	5.2	2.3	3.8	•
Total Asset Turnover 34	1.2	•	5.2	4.4	3.1	2.2	2.4	1.8	1.8	1.2	0.9	•
Inventory Turnover 35	29.5	•	69.6	29.5	47.0	40.0	30.3	19.9	16.2	7.7	38.8	•
Receivables Turnover 36	10.3	•	43.5	25.6	12.6	7.1	8.4	5.8	13.0	7.1	12.3	•
Total Liabilities to Net Worth 37	2.1	•	2.7	1.5	1.9	1.9	1.5	2.5	2.3	1.8	0.9	•
Current Assets to Working Capital 38	•	•	3.0	3.2	3.9	4.3	3.4	4.6	170.3	3.1	2.3	•
Current Liabilities to Working Capital 39	•	•	2.0	2.2	2.9	3.3	2.4	3.6	169.3	2.1	1.3	•
Working Capital to Net Sales 40	•	•	0.0	0.0	0.0	0.0	0.1	0.1	0.0	0.1	0.1	•
Inventory to Working Capital 41	•	•	0.2	0.3	0.2	0.0	0.2	0.3	18.9	0.4	0.1	•
Total Receipts to Cash Flow 42	3.7	1.8	3.3	4.3	5.5	5.1	4.7	4.7	4.1	4.2	4.2	•
Cost of Goods to Cash Flow 43	1.3	0.3	1.1	1.7	2.9	2.5	2.2	2.3	2.1	1.2	1.2	•
Cash Flow to Total Debt 44	0.5	•	2.1	1.7	0.9	0.7	0.8	0.6	0.6	0.4	0.5	•

Selected Financial Factors (in Percentages)

Debt Ratio 45	67.3	•	72.9	60.5	65.3	65.2	59.3	71.4	70.1	64.9	46.6	•
Return on Total Assets 46	11.2	•	53.8	30.3	22.3	12.6	17.8	11.7	13.1	7.6	8.6	•
Return on Equity Before Income Taxes 47	27.8	•	187.8	70.1	59.7	33.4	40.7	33.6	35.3	12.3	11.9	•
Return on Equity After Income Taxes 48	25.7	•	186.0	68.2	58.0	28.8	37.2	30.3	30.7	9.3	8.4	•
Profit Margin (Before Income Tax) 49	7.5	25.4	9.8	6.3	6.6	5.2	7.0	5.2	6.0	3.6	6.9	•
Profit Margin (After Income Tax) 50	7.0	24.6	9.7	6.1	6.5	4.5	6.4	4.7	5.2	2.7	4.9	•

WASTE MANAGEMENT AND REMEDIATION SERVICES

Table I

Corporations with and without Net Income

MONEY AMOUNTS AND SIZE OF ASSETS IN THOUSANDS OF DOLLARS

Item Description for Accounting Period 7/03 Through 6/04	Total	Zero Assets	Under 500	500 to 1,000	1,000 to 5,000	5,000 to 10,000	10,000 to 25,000	25,000 to 50,000	50,000 to 100,000	100,000 to 250,000	250,000 to 500,000	500,000 to 2,500,000	2,500,000 and over
Number of Enterprises 1	12104	1690	7288	1143	1570	194	123	46	20	12	4	9	4
Revenues ($ in Thousands)													
Net Sales 2	48146136	618375	4317565	2375589	6802626	2005665	2598729	1680308	1437512	1655931	1154019	5319604	18180213
Interest 3	280536	4529	772	932	10375	669	5092	1661	8744	14715	4065	80396	148587
Rents 4	142553	0	914	484	2249	422	2203	2288	0	687	37	6242	127025
Royalties 5	25493	0	0	0	0	0	0	0	54	360	0	12624	12455
Other Portfolio Income 6	617029	262605	63643	680	7415	3725	11003	13944	9416	2439	21843	23489	196829
Other Receipts 7	3142956	2034859	1173	2138	31964	21868	22582	20819	28002	19525	5104	187286	767634
Total Receipts 8	52354703	2920368	4384067	2379823	6854629	2032349	2639609	1719020	1483728	1693657	1185068	5629641	19432743
Average Total Receipts 9	4325	1728	602	2082	4366	10476	21460	37370	74186	141138	296267	625516	4858186
Operating Costs/Operating Income (%)													
Cost of Operations 10	42.3	9.8	40.3	16.1	49.8	50.3	51.0	42.6	52.2	15.3	35.6	40.7	44.9
Salaries and Wages 11	13.6	24.3	9.0	9.3	8.4	12.9	10.5	12.5	8.9	33.1	16.2	18.2	14.6
Taxes Paid 12	3.8	2.9	2.5	1.9	3.2	4.9	2.8	3.0	2.6	4.2	4.2	5.0	4.4
Interest Paid 13	4.8	5.0	0.9	1.1	1.6	1.3	1.7	2.6	2.0	3.3	4.0	7.7	7.8
Depreciation 14	8.4	8.8	5.6	3.2	5.8	3.3	5.5	7.4	4.5	6.1	8.6	8.6	12.3
Amortization and Depletion 15	1.5	0.3	0.1	0.2	0.1	0.6	0.5	1.2	1.2	1.7	0.9	3.4	2.4
Pensions and Other Deferred Comp. 16	0.4	0.0	0.1	0.2	0.4	0.2	0.5	0.7	0.3	0.6	1.9	0.7	0.2
Employee Benefits 17	1.9	3.0	1.0	1.5	1.5	1.4	2.6	3.1	1.6	4.6	3.4	3.1	1.6
Advertising 18	0.4	0.9	1.2	0.4	0.4	0.5	0.4	0.4	0.1	0.3	0.1	0.3	0.2
Other Expenses 19	30.8	407.5	30.3	59.8	21.0	23.2	21.7	28.4	22.1	33.1	22.5	36.1	19.9
Officers' Compensation 20	1.7	6.4	4.8	3.9	3.7	2.5	2.2	2.9	1.8	0.4	0.8	0.4	0.0
Operating Margin 21	•	•	4.3	2.3	4.0	•	0.6	•	2.8	•	1.9	•	•
Operating Margin Before Officers' Comp. 22	•	•	9.1	6.3	7.7	1.4	2.8	•	4.6	•	2.7	•	•

Selected Average Balance Sheet ($ in Thousands)

Net Receivables 23	516	0	7	177	569	1301	3475	5777	11611	18440	43138	90687	678480
Inventories 24	50	0	0	4	111	90	255	468	237	1301	2371	23246	28941
Net Property, Plant and Equipment 25	2080	0	67	271	869	2508	5474	11749	16312	41141	137848	370417	4152162
Total Assets 26	5831	0	109	748	2043	6235	15573	35553	72957	139712	360104	1234923	11317143
Notes and Loans Payable 27	3162	0	86	415	1095	2277	7089	16542	22596	46546	151179	1020906	5643476
All Other Liabilities 28	1794	0	28	159	557	2960	4986	10775	29684	55787	126872	300058	3574360
Net Worth 29	875	0	-5	175	391	998	3499	8235	20677	37378	82054	-86041	2099306

Selected Financial Ratios (Times to 1)

Current Ratio 30	0.8	·	0.7	1.8	1.4	0.9	1.2	1.2	1.2	0.9	1.4	0.6	0.7
Quick Ratio 31	0.6	·	0.5	1.2	1.1	0.7	0.9	0.9	0.9	0.8	0.9	0.4	0.5
Net Sales to Working Capital 32	·	·	·	11.5	16.6	·	17.3	18.6	16.1	9.7	·	·	0.8
Coverage Ratio 33	0.8	1.7	7.4	3.3	3.9	1.2	2.3	0.0	3.9	2.1	2.1	·	0.8
Total Asset Turnover 34	0.7	·	5.4	2.8	2.1	1.0	1.4	1.0	1.0	1.0	0.8	0.5	0.4
Inventory Turnover 35	33.4	·	336.4	81.2	19.5	58.1	42.3	33.2	158.1	16.3	43.3	10.3	70.5
Receivables Turnover 36	7.8	·	67.2	14.5	9.2	8.9	7.0	6.9	7.0	6.9	4.6	7.0	6.3
Total Liabilities to Net Worth 37	5.7	·	·	3.3	4.2	5.2	3.5	3.3	2.5	2.7	3.4	·	4.4
Current Assets to Working Capital 38	·	·	·	2.3	3.7	·	5.6	6.2	6.0	·	3.5	·	·
Current Liabilities to Working Capital 39	·	·	·	1.3	2.7	·	4.6	5.2	5.0	·	2.5	·	·
Working Capital to Net Sales 40	·	·	·	0.1	0.1	0.1	0.1	0.1	0.1	·	0.1	·	·
Inventory to Working Capital 41	·	·	·	0.0	0.6	·	0.2	0.3	0.1	·	0.0	·	·
Total Receipts to Cash Flow 42	4.4	0.3	3.3	1.8	5.6	5.2	5.3	4.9	4.1	3.6	4.8	12.4	8.2
Cost of Goods to Cash Flow 43	1.9	0.0	1.3	0.3	2.8	2.6	2.7	2.1	2.1	0.6	1.7	5.0	3.7
Cash Flow to Total Debt 44	0.2	·	1.6	2.0	0.5	0.4	0.3	0.3	0.3	0.4	0.2	0.0	0.1

Selected Financial Factors (in Percentages)

Debt Ratio 45	85.0	·	104.6	76.6	80.8	84.0	77.5	76.8	71.7	73.2	77.2	107.0	81.5
Return on Total Assets 46	2.7	·	36.5	10.1	13.5	2.5	5.3	0.1	7.9	2.8	6.9	·	2.6
Return on Equity Before Income Taxes 47	·	·	·	30.1	52.4	2.7	13.3	·	20.8	·	16.0	·	·
Return on Equity After Income Taxes 48	·	·	·	28.9	49.8	·	10.0	·	20.1	·	11.4	·	·
Profit Margin (Before Income Tax) 49	·	3.4	5.8	2.5	4.7	0.3	2.2	·	6.0	·	4.6	·	·
Profit Margin (After Income Tax) 50	·	3.3	5.8	2.4	4.5	·	1.7	·	5.8	·	3.2	·	·

ADMINISTRATIVE AND SUPPORT AND WASTE MANAGEMENT AND REMEDIATION SERVICES

WASTE MANAGEMENT AND REMEDIATION SERVICES
562000

Table II
Corporations with Net Income

MONEY AMOUNTS AND SIZE OF ASSETS IN THOUSANDS OF DOLLARS

Item Description for Accounting Period 7/03 Through 6/04	Total	Zero Assets	Under 500	500 to 1,000	1,000 to 5,000	5,000 to 10,000	10,000 to 25,000	25,000 to 50,000	50,000 to 100,000	100,000 to 250,000	250,000 to 500,000	500,000 to 2,500,000	2,500,000 and over
Number of Enterprises 1	8338	1248	4820	641	1404	105	80	18	10	5	4	3	•
Revenues ($ in Thousands)													
Net Sales 2	28012581	337730	2529871	1798891	5884753	802270	1867618	819298	1010336	1143827	1154019	10663969	•
Interest 3	113920	0	514	874	9554	280	2678	482	172	175	4065	95127	•
Rents 4	19020	0	757	484	2249	139	2172	112	0	23	37	13046	•
Royalties 5	13666	0	0	0	0	0	0	0	0	0	0	13666	•
Other Portfolio Income 6	63765	19466	5	624	5991	1579	5941	1437	257	73	21843	6550	•
Other Receipts 7	756929	11654	871	2103	41085	16718	20205	12956	22187	861	5104	623182	•
Total Receipts 8	28979881	368850	2532018	1802976	5943632	820986	1898614	834285	1032952	1144959	1185068	11415540	•
Average Total Receipts 9	3476	296	525	2813	4233	7819	23733	46349	103295	228992	296267	3805180	•
Operating Costs/Operating Income (%)													
Cost of Operations 10	32.9	6.6	25.3	11.2	50.8	27.3	45.7	48.7	47.3	14.2	35.6	26.7	•
Salaries and Wages 11	16.1	21.9	9.6	5.9	8.1	20.8	10.8	8.4	9.8	41.5	16.2	22.7	•
Taxes Paid 12	4.6	2.3	3.2	1.5	3.2	2.3	2.8	3.0	2.3	4.6	4.2	7.1	•
Interest Paid 13	2.7	1.1	0.9	0.3	1.7	1.7	1.3	1.0	1.3	2.1	4.0	4.7	•
Depreciation 14	8.1	7.4	3.2	2.8	6.2	2.7	5.3	5.5	4.0	3.5	8.6	13.2	•
Amortization and Depletion 15	1.1	0.0	0.1	0.0	0.1	0.0	0.3	0.7	0.8	1.4	0.9	2.3	•
Pensions and Other Deferred Comp. 16	0.4	0.1	0.2	0.3	0.4	0.2	0.5	0.5	0.3	0.6	1.9	0.2	•
Employee Benefits 17	2.1	2.8	0.9	0.9	1.7	0.9	2.7	3.1	1.7	5.8	3.4	2.1	•
Advertising 18	0.5	0.6	1.6	0.4	0.5	1.1	0.4	0.2	0.1	0.2	0.1	0.3	•
Other Expenses 19	27.0	39.1	34.0	68.5	17.9	35.5	22.8	19.9	20.4	23.5	22.5	25.1	•
Officers' Compensation 20	2.1	11.7	5.7	2.6	4.0	2.1	2.2	2.1	1.8	0.5	0.8	0.1	•
Operating Margin 21	2.5	6.5	15.1	5.5	5.4	5.6	5.3	6.9	10.2	2.1	1.9	•	•
Operating Margin Before Officers' Comp. 22	4.6	18.2	20.9	8.1	9.5	7.6	7.5	9.0	12.0	2.6	2.7	•	•

Selected Average Balance Sheet ($ in Thousands)

Item													
Net Receivables 23	404	0	9	169	518	894	3427	7947	15505	29001	43138	501003	•
Inventories 24	39	0	0	13	122	85	282	681	401	2937	1222	22532	•
Net Property, Plant and Equipment 25	1608	0	40	343	901	2994	5875	11260	18599	49101	137848	3254649	•
Total Assets 26	4278	0	82	720	2022	6043	15562	36059	76951	118669	360104	8879286	•
Notes and Loans Payable 27	1978	0	41	305	1052	2783	6109	10876	20678	58787	151179	4179055	•
All Other Liabilities 28	1343	0	13	152	446	1843	4148	10332	30438	31489	126872	2911107	•
Net Worth 29	957	0	28	263	523	1417	5305	14851	25835	28393	82054	1789123	•

Selected Financial Ratios (Times to 1)

Item													
Current Ratio 30	0.9	•	1.6	2.0	1.6	2.0	1.3	1.6	0.9	1.0	1.4	0.6	•
Quick Ratio 31	0.6	•	1.5	1.9	1.2	1.6	1.0	1.4	0.7	0.9	0.9	0.4	•
Net Sales to Working Capital 32	•	•	60.4	15.5	11.9	7.4	13.8	8.2	•	•	9.7	•	•
Coverage Ratio 33	3.2	•	17.3	17.7	4.8	5.8	6.4	10.0	10.7	2.1	2.1	1.5	•
Total Asset Turnover 34	0.8	15.0	6.4	3.9	2.1	1.3	1.5	1.3	1.3	1.9	0.8	0.4	•
Inventory Turnover 35	28.6	•	145.0	24.0	17.5	24.6	37.9	32.6	119.2	11.0	84.1	42.1	•
Receivables Turnover 36	8.1	•	67.8	20.5	9.7	7.3	8.0	6.6	13.0	6.3	7.8	14.2	•
Total Liabilities to Net Worth 37	3.5	•	1.9	1.7	2.9	3.3	1.9	1.4	2.0	3.2	3.4	4.0	•
Current Assets to Working Capital 38	•	•	2.7	2.0	2.7	2.0	4.0	2.7	•	•	3.5	•	•
Current Liabilities to Working Capital 39	•	•	1.7	1.0	1.7	1.0	3.0	1.7	•	•	2.5	•	•
Working Capital to Net Sales 40	•	•	0.0	0.1	0.1	0.1	0.1	0.1	•	•	0.1	•	•
Inventory to Working Capital 41	•	•	0.1	0.5	0.5	0.1	0.2	0.2	•	•	0.0	•	•
Total Receipts to Cash Flow 42	3.8	2.0	2.4	1.5	5.7	2.6	4.1	4.1	3.4	4.7	4.8	4.9	•
Cost of Goods to Cash Flow 43	1.2	0.1	0.6	0.2	2.9	0.7	1.9	2.0	1.6	0.7	1.7	1.3	•
Cash Flow to Total Debt 44	0.3	•	4.1	4.1	0.5	0.6	0.6	0.5	0.6	0.5	0.2	0.1	•

Selected Financial Factors (in Percentages)

Item													
Debt Ratio 45	77.6	•	65.4	63.5	74.1	76.6	65.9	58.8	66.4	76.1	77.2	79.9	•
Return on Total Assets 46	6.8	•	103.1	23.5	16.9	12.1	12.3	12.2	18.0	8.4	6.9	2.9	•
Return on Equity Before Income Taxes 47	20.7	•	280.5	60.6	51.6	42.7	30.6	26.6	48.5	18.0	16.0	5.0	•
Return on Equity After Income Taxes 48	18.7	•	279.6	59.2	49.5	37.6	27.3	24.7	47.4	14.8	11.4	3.3	•
Profit Margin (Before Income Tax) 49	5.9	15.4	15.2	5.7	6.4	7.9	6.9	8.7	12.4	2.2	4.6	2.5	•
Profit Margin (After Income Tax) 50	5.3	15.4	15.2	5.5	6.2	7.0	6.2	8.1	12.1	1.8	3.2	1.6	•

Table I

Corporations with and without Net Income

EDUCATIONAL SERVICES

MONEY AMOUNTS AND SIZE OF ASSETS IN THOUSANDS OF DOLLARS

Item Description for Accounting Period 7/03 Through 6/04	Total	Zero Assets	Under 500	500 to 1,000	1,000 to 5,000	5,000 to 10,000	10,000 to 25,000	25,000 to 50,000	50,000 to 100,000	100,000 to 250,000	250,000 to 500,000	500,000 to 2,500,000	2,500,000 and over
Number of Enterprises **1**	44059	7717	34469	715	871	137	72	28	23	14	7	6	•
Revenues ($ in Thousands)													
Net Sales **2**	29746218	629300	8176824	1073387	4775904	1606689	1561405	1101882	2263969	1813775	2578920	4164162	•
Interest **3**	86397	193	2816	3210	5207	1311	2947	1940	4080	19395	11524	33774	•
Rents **4**	22404	155	552	3	1328	1230	693	621	4938	6332	1520	5031	•
Royalties **5**	244781	0	0	0	65907	14	687	220	961	1931	73416	101645	•
Other Portfolio Income **6**	148341	10429	2149	21	5720	2570	1161	1219	10782	38618	1382	74290	•
Other Receipts **7**	436138	3301	54953	4775	27912	19632	39851	11628	47071	21595	26577	178844	•
Total Receipts **8**	30684279	643378	8237294	1081396	4881978	1631446	1606744	1117510	2331801	1901646	2693339	4557746	•
Average Total Receipts **9**	696	83	239	1512	5605	11908	22316	39911	101383	135832	384763	759624	•
Operating Costs/Operating Income (%)													
Cost of Operations **10**	16.5	25.7	8.7	27.9	15.7	36.4	17.0	18.1	31.8	31.2	18.3	4.0	•
Salaries and Wages **11**	29.5	26.8	26.0	18.9	34.7	24.8	31.4	29.1	27.2	21.6	30.8	38.6	•
Taxes Paid **12**	3.5	3.9	3.9	2.8	4.1	3.4	3.5	3.5	2.7	2.9	3.9	2.9	•
Interest Paid **13**	1.1	1.4	0.8	0.4	0.4	1.1	1.8	1.1	1.2	1.7	2.0	1.2	•
Depreciation **14**	3.1	2.3	1.8	6.6	1.8	3.5	3.0	3.3	3.3	3.7	4.5	4.9	•
Amortization and Depletion **15**	0.7	0.2	0.3	0.4	0.1	0.6	0.6	0.8	0.9	1.8	1.5	1.1	•
Pensions and Other Deferred Comp. **16**	0.7	0.3	1.2	0.7	0.4	0.3	0.7	0.3	0.2	0.3	0.8	0.4	•
Employee Benefits **17**	2.2	0.8	2.0	2.1	2.8	0.8	2.0	2.3	1.5	2.1	3.6	2.7	•
Advertising **18**	4.6	2.5	3.5	4.6	1.5	2.5	4.5	8.6	4.1	3.7	7.6	9.2	•
Other Expenses **19**	30.2	31.4	36.3	28.5	30.4	23.1	30.2	28.0	24.9	21.0	26.5	30.7	•
Officers' Compensation **20**	6.3	4.0	15.0	5.1	4.8	2.3	3.4	1.3	2.4	1.2	2.0	2.6	•
Operating Margin **21**	1.8	0.7	0.7	2.1	3.4	1.3	2.0	3.5	•	8.9	•	1.7	•
Operating Margin Before Officers' Comp. **22**	8.1	4.7	15.7	7.2	8.1	3.6	5.4	4.8	2.2	10.1	0.4	4.3	•

Selected Average Balance Sheet ($ in Thousands)

Net Receivables 23	94	9	38	847	1462	3166	5401	18571	27766	48531	225220	•
Inventories 24	6	2	5	35	255	283	1118	615	2092	1378	3095	•
Net Property, Plant and Equipment 25	103	21	371	540	1585	4001	6195	19366	38673	70312	149762	•
Total Assets 26	453	71	658	2247	7131	15145	33194	72347	143923	390735	941595	•
Notes and Loans Payable 27	141	57	302	573	2787	5264	6799	21611	34252	102376	148095	•
All Other Liabilities 28	147	22	176	1436	2481	5474	11107	26790	40976	115530	212352	•
Net Worth 29	165	-8	181	238	1863	4408	15287	23946	68694	172829	581148	•

Selected Financial Ratios (Times to 1)

Current Ratio 30	1.3	•	1.2	1.2	1.0	1.4	1.3	1.5	1.4	1.7	1.5	1.3
Quick Ratio 31	1.1	•	1.1	1.1	0.9	1.2	1.2	1.2	1.2	1.3	1.2	1.2
Net Sales to Working Capital 32	13.9	49.3	43.7	120.7	9.6	10.8	6.4	10.1	4.9	9.3		7.5
Coverage Ratio 33	5.7	3.1	8.2	16.5	3.7	3.7	5.4	3.4	9.0	2.4		10.0
Total Asset Turnover 34	1.5	•	3.3	2.3	1.6	1.4	1.2	1.4	0.9	0.9		0.7
Inventory Turnover 35	20.0	13.6	78.7	24.6	16.8	13.0	6.4	50.9	19.4	48.8		9.1
Receivables Turnover 36	8.1	31.6	21.6	7.2	8.5	7.2	6.3	5.4	5.1	5.8		4.7
Total Liabilities to Net Worth 37	1.7	•	2.6	8.5	2.4	1.2	2.0	1.1	1.3			0.6
Current Assets to Working Capital 38	4.4	6.2	6.8	33.0	3.3	2.9	3.7	3.7	2.5	3.1		4.8
Current Liabilities to Working Capital 39	3.4	5.2	5.8	32.0	2.3	1.9	2.7	2.1	1.5			3.8
Working Capital to Net Sales 40	0.1	0.0	0.0	0.0	0.1	0.2	0.1	0.2	0.2	0.1		0.1
Inventory to Working Capital 41	0.1	0.4	0.3	0.9	0.2	0.1	0.2	0.1	0.1			0.0
Total Receipts to Cash Flow 42	3.7	3.3	4.5	3.5	5.3	3.7	4.2	4.6	3.7	4.8		3.1
Cost of Goods to Cash Flow 43	0.6	0.3	1.3	0.5	1.9	0.6	0.8	1.5	1.1	0.9		0.1
Cash Flow to Total Debt 44	0.6	0.9	0.7	0.8	0.4	0.5	0.4	0.4	0.5	0.4		0.6

Selected Financial Factors (in Percentages)

Debt Ratio 45	63.6	•	111.4	72.5	89.4	73.9	70.9	53.9	66.9	52.3	55.8	38.3
Return on Total Assets 46	8.9	•	7.4	7.4	14.6	6.4	9.5	7.0	5.8	13.8	4.7	9.0
Return on Equity Before Income Taxes 47	20.1	•	•	23.8	129.4	18.0	23.9	12.5	12.3	25.7	6.3	13.1
Return on Equity After Income Taxes 48	15.4	•	•	22.6	126.4	12.4	20.2	11.0	8.3	19.8	3.0	8.2
Profit Margin (Before Income Tax) 49	4.9	2.9	1.4	2.9	5.6	2.9	4.9	4.8	3.0	13.6	2.9	10.9
Profit Margin (After Income Tax) 50	3.8	2.7	1.3	2.7	5.5	2.0	4.1	4.3	2.0	10.5	1.4	6.9

Table II

Corporations with Net Income

EDUCATIONAL SERVICES

MONEY AMOUNTS AND SIZE OF ASSETS IN THOUSANDS OF DOLLARS

Item Description for Accounting Period 7/03 Through 6/04		Total	Zero Assets	Under 500	500 to 1,000	1,000 to 5,000	5,000 to 10,000	10,000 to 25,000	25,000 to 50,000	50,000 to 100,000	100,000 to 250,000	250,000 to 500,000	500,000 to 2,500,000	2,500,000 and over
Number of Enterprises	1	21688	3444	16965	419	675	78	49	19	15	•	•	•	•
Revenues ($ in Thousands)														
Net Sales	2	22557510	438740	5451323	757322	3448727	763827	1234215	1003128	1704233	•	•	•	•
Interest	3	53973	158	672	6	4605	1096	2162	1401	3487	•	•	•	•
Rents	4	18330	155	552	0	1328	1155	196	621	4866	•	•	•	•
Royalties	5	199459	0	0	0	65342	14	75	220	0	•	•	•	•
Other Portfolio Income	6	145923	10425	1215	0	5506	2228	335	1219	10770	•	•	•	•
Other Receipts	7	321781	3009	21221	222	26326	9168	36170	5061	23530	•	•	•	•
Total Receipts	8	23296976	452487	5474983	757550	3551834	777488	1273153	1011650	1746886	•	•	•	•
Average Total Receipts	9	1074	131	323	1808	5262	9968	25983	53245	116459	•	•	•	•
Operating Costs/Operating Income (%)														
Cost of Operations	10	16.7	12.7	11.8	26.4	20.3	18.1	16.2	17.5	36.4	•	•	•	•
Salaries and Wages	11	26.7	27.8	20.0	10.5	28.4	29.6	29.3	27.2	23.5	•	•	•	•
Taxes Paid	12	3.2	4.2	3.3	1.8	3.9	3.8	3.2	3.5	2.3	•	•	•	•
Interest Paid	13	0.6	1.0	0.5	0.2	0.3	0.8	0.6	0.7	1.0	•	•	•	•
Depreciation	14	2.8	1.8	1.3	2.8	2.0	2.3	2.4	3.1	2.8	•	•	•	•
Amortization and Depletion	15	0.5	0.0	0.0	0.5	0.0	0.6	0.4	0.7	0.6	•	•	•	•
Pensions and Other Deferred Comp.	16	0.7	0.1	1.5	0.0	0.6	0.6	0.6	0.3	0.2	•	•	•	•
Employee Benefits	17	2.1	0.8	1.8	0.5	1.6	1.4	1.6	2.3	1.2	•	•	•	•
Advertising	18	5.1	3.0	3.3	6.0	2.0	3.0	5.0	9.3	2.7	•	•	•	•
Other Expenses	19	27.9	31.7	32.2	27.5	26.1	24.5	30.1	27.4	23.4	•	•	•	•
Officers' Compensation	20	6.4	4.9	16.4	5.1	6.2	2.2	3.5	1.3	2.0	•	•	•	•
Operating Margin	21	7.2	11.9	7.9	18.5	8.5	13.2	7.1	6.6	3.8	•	•	•	•
Operating Margin Before Officers' Comp.	22	13.6	16.8	24.3	23.6	14.7	15.4	10.5	8.0	5.8	•	•	•	•

Selected Average Balance Sheet ($ in Thousands)

Net Receivables 23	115	0	5	17	729	1679	3298	5177	20577
Inventories 24	9	0	2	16	38	301	246	1354	671
Net Property, Plant and Equipment 25	153	0	23	388	595	1343	3514	7776	15210
Total Assets 26	691	0	83	716	2171	7110	15043	32633	69943
Notes and Loans Payable 27	138	0	30	189	307	1735	3465	6528	20505
All Other Liabilities 28	185	0	26	77	807	2688	5526	12866	26605
Net Worth 29	368	0	27	450	1057	2687	6051	13239	22833

Selected Financial Ratios (Times to 1)

Current Ratio 30	1.5	•	1.2	3.1	1.7	1.7	1.4	1.3	1.6
Quick Ratio 31	1.3	•	1.0	2.8	1.6	1.5	1.1	0.9	1.4
Net Sales to Working Capital 32	9.5	•	53.7	11.3	8.6	4.9	9.9	10.9	7.4
Coverage Ratio 33	17.2	15.3	18.0	80.0	37.4	19.8	17.4	11.6	7.6
Total Asset Turnover 34	1.5	•	3.9	2.5	2.4	1.4	1.7	1.6	1.6
Inventory Turnover 35	20.2	•	15.6	29.8	27.4	5.9	16.6	6.8	61.5
Receivables Turnover 36	9.9	•	48.0	19.8	6.8	5.8	7.7	8.8	5.6
Total Liabilities to Net Worth 37	0.9	•	2.1	0.6	1.1	1.6	1.5	1.5	2.1
Current Assets to Working Capital 38	2.9	•	5.9	1.5	2.4	2.5	3.3	4.0	2.7
Current Liabilities to Working Capital 39	1.9	•	4.9	0.5	1.4	1.5	2.3	3.0	1.7
Working Capital to Net Sales 40	0.1	•	0.0	0.1	0.1	0.2	0.1	0.1	0.1
Inventory to Working Capital 41	0.1	•	0.5	0.1	0.1	0.1	0.1	0.3	0.0
Total Receipts to Cash Flow 42	3.3	3.2	2.9	2.5	3.3	3.0	3.0	3.8	4.1
Cost of Goods to Cash Flow 43	0.5	0.4	0.3	0.7	0.7	0.5	0.5	0.7	1.5
Cash Flow to Total Debt 44	1.0	•	2.0	2.7	1.4	0.7	0.9	0.7	0.6

Selected Financial Factors (in Percentages)

Debt Ratio 45	46.8	•	67.3	37.2	51.3	62.2	59.8	59.4	67.4
Return on Total Assets 46	16.7	•	34.1	47.4	27.8	21.8	18.2	13.2	12.2
Return on Equity Before Income Taxes 47	29.5	•	98.6	74.6	55.6	54.7	42.6	29.6	32.6
Return on Equity After Income Taxes 48	25.2	•	96.2	74.6	54.7	47.8	38.5	27.1	26.2
Profit Margin (Before Income Tax) 49	10.4	15.0	8.4	18.6	11.5	15.0	10.2	7.4	6.5
Profit Margin (After Income Tax) 50	8.9	14.8	8.2	18.6	11.3	13.1	9.3	6.8	5.3

Table I

Corporations with and without Net Income

OFFICES OF PHYSICIANS

MONEY AMOUNTS AND SIZE OF ASSETS IN THOUSANDS OF DOLLARS

Item Description for Accounting Period 7/03 Through 6/04	Total	Zero Assets	Under 500	500 to 1,000	1,000 to 5,000	5,000 to 10,000	10,000 to 25,000	25,000 to 50,000	50,000 to 100,000	100,000 to 250,000	250,000 to 500,000	500,000 to 2,500,000	2,500,000 and over
Number of Enterprises **1**	137716	13676	118517	3309	1821	212	118	41	12	6	•	•	3
Revenues ($ in Thousands)													
Net Sales **2**	190363448	2283663	115754786	21196749	23274278	7114225	5075307	3751496	1356199	1632973	•	8923772	•
Interest **3**	106761	577	33817	4880	11300	5055	7341	2815	5411	5510	•	30056	•
Rents **4**	171072	107	50171	46855	7854	3941	12258	7692	4353	865	•	36974	•
Royalties **5**	1489	0	0	0	0	1489	0	0	0	0	•	0	•
Other Portfolio Income **6**	264733	2784	101707	33595	5401	18257	12440	1482	19188	3103	•	66776	•
Other Receipts **7**	4149333	39460	1638678	313590	529712	341004	193407	83695	32151	465041	•	512597	•
Total Receipts **8**	195056836	2326591	117579159	21595669	23828545	7483971	5300753	3847180	1417302	2107492	•	9570175	•
Average Total Receipts **9**	1416	170	992	6526	13085	35302	44922	93834	118108	351249	•	3190058	•
Operating Costs/Operating Income (%)													
Cost of Operations **10**	3.9	0.6	3.4	6.4	1.9	8.7	8.0	11.9	10.6	9.6	•	0.0	•
Salaries and Wages **11**	27.2	14.2	24.3	25.6	32.6	35.6	35.7	39.4	43.1	35.2	•	36.2	•
Taxes Paid **12**	3.1	3.4	3.2	3.0	3.0	2.4	2.4	2.4	3.4	2.1	•	4.0	•
Interest Paid **13**	0.4	0.5	0.2	0.3	0.3	0.4	0.6	0.8	0.3	1.6	•	2.5	•
Depreciation **14**	1.3	1.4	1.1	1.6	1.7	1.6	1.9	1.7	2.4	2.3	•	1.3	•
Amortization and Depletion **15**	0.1	0.2	0.0	0.0	0.0	0.2	0.2	0.2	0.1	0.8	•	0.8	•
Pensions and Other Deferred Comp. **16**	3.5	1.3	3.8	3.2	3.4	2.2	1.8	2.2	1.9	1.2	•	2.8	•
Employee Benefits **17**	2.1	1.2	2.0	1.7	2.1	2.3	3.1	2.9	5.3	3.2	•	4.0	•
Advertising **18**	0.6	0.3	0.6	0.3	0.7	0.4	0.2	0.2	1.1	0.7	•	0.0	•
Other Expenses **19**	32.5	49.1	28.7	31.8	31.7	44.1	46.0	38.6	35.1	68.4	•	54.2	•
Officers' Compensation **20**	24.4	27.2	29.9	25.1	22.2	6.8	2.9	1.1	0.8	0.3	•	0.1	•
Operating Margin **21**	1.0	0.6	2.8	1.0	0.2	•	•	•	•	•	•	•	•
Operating Margin Before Officers' Comp. **22**	25.4	27.8	32.6	26.1	22.4	2.2	0.0	•	•	•	•	•	•

Selected Average Balance Sheet ($ in Thousands)

Item											
Net Receivables **23**	29	0	2	56	255	2382	3514	8018	11340	27252	492386
Inventories **24**	1	0	0	15	62	179	170	765	902		0
Net Property, Plant and Equipment **25**	57		27	245	680	2092	4174	10714	25186	29490	241449
Total Assets **26**	221		82	695	1859	6835	14922	33584	73636	164009	2894931
Notes and Loans Payable **27**	104		48	366	1112	4076	5597	13246	14992	35042	1000313
All Other Liabilities **28**	83		31	300	712	2525	6791	17338	39332	66125	867747
Net Worth **29**	34		3	28	35	234	2534	3000	19312	62842	1026870

Selected Financial Ratios (Times to 1)

Item											
Current Ratio **30**	1.0		0.9	1.0	1.4	1.0	0.8	1.4	1.4		2.0
Quick Ratio **31**	0.9		0.8	0.9	0.7	1.3	0.8	0.7	1.1	1.2	1.7
Net Sales to Working Capital **32**	326.2				29.8			12.3	16.9		8.3
Coverage Ratio **33**	9.6	5.8	11.8	8.6	2.8	3.6	2.5	2.1	3.2		1.5
Total Asset Turnover **34**	6.2		12.0	9.2	6.9	4.9	2.9	2.7	1.5	1.7	1.0
Inventory Turnover **35**	62.0		116.8	725.1	15.9	46.5	19.3	64.1	15.6	28.8	
Receivables Turnover **36**	44.6		620.8	113.4	41.1	14.9	11.3	11.6	11.5	11.3	12.1
Total Liabilities to Net Worth **37**	5.6		28.0	23.6	52.2	28.2	4.9	10.2	2.8	1.6	1.8
Current Assets to Working Capital **38**	21.2				3.7			3.5	3.6		2.0
Current Liabilities to Working Capital **39**	20.2				2.7			2.5	2.6		1.0
Working Capital to Net Sales **40**	0.0				0.0			0.1	0.1		0.1
Inventory to Working Capital **41**	0.2				0.1			0.1	0.1		
Total Receipts to Cash Flow **42**	3.2		3.5	3.4	2.6	2.4	2.7	3.4	1.5		2.0
Cost of Goods to Cash Flow **43**	0.1		0.2	0.1	0.2	0.2	0.3	0.4	0.1		0.0
Cash Flow to Total Debt **44**	2.3		2.8	2.1	2.0	1.5	1.1	0.6	1.8		0.8

Selected Financial Factors (in Percentages)

Item											
Debt Ratio **45**	84.7		96.6	95.9	98.1	96.6	83.0	91.1	73.8	61.7	64.5
Return on Total Assets **46**	24.3		54.7	29.3	20.1	5.1	6.4	5.1	1.1	8.7	3.9
Return on Equity Before Income Taxes **47**	142.6		1504.2	660.5	946.2	94.9	27.4	34.6	2.1	15.5	3.5
Return on Equity After Income Taxes **48**	136.9		1480.8	648.5	912.2	57.2	21.0	21.2	0.0	8.8	1.3
Profit Margin (Before Income Tax) **49**	3.5	2.4	4.3	2.9	2.6	0.7	1.6	1.1	0.4	3.6	1.2
Profit Margin (After Income Tax) **50**	3.3	2.3	4.3	2.9	2.5	0.4	1.2	0.7	0.0	2.0	0.5

Table II

Corporations with Net Income

OFFICES OF PHYSICIANS

MONEY AMOUNTS AND SIZE OF ASSETS IN THOUSANDS OF DOLLARS

Item Description for Accounting Period 7/03 Through 6/04	Total	Zero Assets	Under 500	500 to 1,000	1,000 to 5,000	5,000 to 10,000	10,000 to 25,000	25,000 to 50,000	50,000 to 100,000	100,000 to 250,000	250,000 to 500,000	500,000 to 2,500,000	2,500,000 and over
Number of Enterprises **1**	82428	5789	73294	2136	989	118	64	25	7	6	•	•	•
Revenues ($ in Thousands)													
Net Sales **2**	109400007	851559	65461140	11044070	14405755	4526759	3316702	2508373	958274	6327377	•	•	•
Interest **3**	50338	127	11569	2934	6623	3098	4703	2658	4595	14031	•	•	•
Rents **4**	47579	104	10239	7340	6446	3748	7402	6620	4180	1500	•	•	•
Royalties **5**	0	0	0	0	0	0	0	0	0	0			
Other Portfolio Income **6**	149357	2784	94561	541	1959	5942	9007	1148	19188	14226	•	•	•
Other Receipts **7**	2672144	769	1094385	177095	250778	325885	106594	36138	17302	663197	•	•	•
Total Receipts **8**	112319425	855343	66671894	11231980	14671561	4865432	3444408	2554937	1003539	7020331	•	•	•
Average Total Receipts **9**	1363	148	910	5258	14835	41232	53819	102197	143363	1170055	•	•	•
Operating Costs/Operating Income (%)													
Cost of Operations **10**	2.9	1.6	2.1	4.6	2.1	1.9	9.1	15.5	13.0	0.7	•	•	•
Salaries and Wages **11**	26.1	9.4	21.4	26.7	31.6	40.9	29.1	35.5	38.5	45.0	•	•	•
Taxes Paid **12**	3.1	4.3	3.1	3.2	2.9	2.4	2.2	2.4	3.6	4.3	•	•	•
Interest Paid **13**	0.3	1.0	0.3	0.3	0.2	0.2	0.5	0.4	0.4	0.5	•	•	•
Depreciation **14**	1.1	1.3	1.0	1.8	1.3	1.0	1.5	1.2	2.4	0.4	•	•	•
Amortization and Depletion **15**	0.1	0.4	0.0	0.0	0.0	0.0	0.2	0.2	0.0	0.2	•	•	•
Pensions and Other Deferred Comp. **16**	3.5	2.6	3.7	3.3	3.6	1.7	1.5	2.8	1.7	4.2	•	•	•
Employee Benefits **17**	1.9	1.1	1.5	2.0	1.6	2.6	2.4	2.6	4.3	4.9	•	•	•
Advertising **18**	0.4	0.1	0.5	0.3	0.4	0.4	0.2	0.2	1.4	0.0	•	•	•
Other Expenses **19**	30.6	28.7	27.0	25.3	32.5	49.8	50.1	37.2	34.6	46.1	•	•	•
Officers' Compensation **20**	24.8	32.2	31.8	27.3	19.4	2.7	2.9	1.0	0.8	0.2	•	•	•
Operating Margin **21**	5.2	17.2	7.4	5.2	4.4	•	0.3	1.0	•	•	•	•	•
Operating Margin Before Officers' Comp. **22**	30.0	49.4	39.2	32.5	23.7	•	3.2	2.0	0.1	•	•	•	•

Selected Average Balance Sheet ($ in Thousands)

	·	·	·	·	·	·	·	·	·	·
Net Receivables 23	19	0	31	180	1940	3967	8606	10103	66924	
Inventories 24	1	0	0	20	84	229	95	262	556	
Net Property, Plant and Equipment 25	45	0	24	228	575	1488	3890	7775	24408	21688
Total Assets 26	185	0	85	677	1828	6830	15236	33308	72054	444616
Notes and Loans Payable 27	67	0	42	336	682	1517	4808	8947	17529	32558
All Other Liabilities 28	73	0	26	186	610	3429	6910	15855	24155	279099
Net Worth 29	46	0	17	155	536	1884	3518	8506	30369	132958

Selected Financial Ratios (Times to 1)

	·	·	·	·	·	·	·	·	·	·
Current Ratio 30	1.2	·	1.1	1.3	1.0	1.5	1.1	1.1	1.5	1.2
Quick Ratio 31	1.0	·	1.0	1.2	0.8	1.4	0.9	0.9	1.3	1.2
Net Sales to Working Capital 32	113.6	·	262.0	60.4	·	23.0	51.7	90.5	11.7	32.8
Coverage Ratio 33	25.9	18.2	30.9	25.0	30.2	24.7	9.3	7.6	10.2	9.7
Total Asset Turnover 34	7.2	·	10.5	7.6	8.0	5.6	3.4	3.0	1.9	2.4
Inventory Turnover 35	45.9	·	74.2	545.0	15.3	8.7	20.6	162.8	67.8	12.8
Receivables Turnover 36	74.6	·	550.7	131.7	58.9	24.8	26.1	13.0	19.0	31.5
Total Liabilities to Net Worth 37	3.1	·	4.0	3.4	2.4	2.6	3.3	2.9	1.4	2.3
Current Assets to Working Capital 38	7.6	·	11.9	4.0	·	2.9	8.4	16.2	3.0	5.1
Current Liabilities to Working Capital 39	6.6	·	10.9	3.0	·	1.9	7.4	15.2	2.0	4.1
Working Capital to Net Sales 40	0.0	·	0.0	0.0	·	0.0	0.0	0.0	0.1	0.0
Inventory to Working Capital 41	0.1	·	0.1	0.0	·	0.1	0.2	0.1	0.0	0.0
Total Receipts to Cash Flow 42	3.0	2.4	3.2	3.7	2.9	2.1	2.0	2.7	3.1	2.2
Cost of Goods to Cash Flow 43	0.1	0.0	0.1	0.2	0.1	0.0	0.2	0.4	0.4	0.0
Cash Flow to Total Debt 44	3.2	·	4.1	2.7	3.9	3.7	2.2	1.5	1.1	1.6

Selected Financial Factors (in Percentages)

	·	·	·	·	·	·	·	·	·	·
Debt Ratio 45	75.3	·	80.1	77.1	70.7	72.4	76.9	74.5	57.9	70.1
Return on Total Assets 46	58.3	·	100.4	54.9	51.2	22.1	15.9	9.8	8.3	11.2
Return on Equity Before Income Taxes 47	227.0	·	489.1	230.7	168.8	76.7	61.6	33.5	17.7	33.5
Return on Equity After Income Taxes 48	220.0	·	482.8	227.3	164.8	68.3	53.2	25.7	15.4	21.8
Profit Margin (Before Income Tax) 49	7.8	17.6	9.3	6.9	6.2	3.8	4.2	2.8	3.9	4.2
Profit Margin (After Income Tax) 50	7.6	17.3	9.2	6.8	6.1	3.4	3.6	2.2	3.4	2.7

Table I

Corporations with and without Net Income

OFFICES OF DENTISTS

MONEY AMOUNTS AND SIZE OF ASSETS IN THOUSANDS OF DOLLARS

Item Description for Accounting Period 7/03 Through 6/04	Total	Zero Assets	Under 500	500 to 1,000	1,000 to 5,000	5,000 to 10,000	10,000 to 25,000	25,000 to 50,000	50,000 to 100,000	100,000 to 250,000	250,000 to 500,000	500,000 to 2,500,000	2,500,000 and over
Number of Enterprises **1**	62347	3876	54780	3386	288	•	10	4	•	4	•	•	•
Revenues ($ in Thousands)													
Net Sales **2**	53448676	1596791	36148206	5561615	8816169	•	377407	439434	•	509054	•	•	•
Interest **3**	17729	1338	15498	377	99	•	196	4	•	216	•	•	•
Rents **4**	7780	0	7378	0	0	•	0	0	•	402	•	•	•
Royalties **5**	0	0	0	0	0	•	0	0	•	0	•	•	•
Other Portfolio Income **6**	138131	31076	86387	20351	1	•	172	46	•	97	•	•	•
Other Receipts **7**	567463	9481	502502	19791	4823	•	1148	16737	•	12984	•	•	•
Total Receipts **8**	54179779	1638686	36759971	5602134	8821092	•	378923	456221	•	522753	•	•	•
Average Total Receipts **9**	869	423	671	1654	30629	•	37892	114055	•	130688	•	•	•
Operating Costs/Operating Income (%)													
Cost of Operations **10**	4.9	6.9	5.5	7.1	0.2	•	10.1	5.4	•	12.6	•	•	•
Salaries and Wages **11**	23.9	15.8	22.9	27.0	25.4	•	25.7	38.3	•	46.1	•	•	•
Taxes Paid **12**	3.4	2.6	3.7	3.7	1.7	•	2.8	2.8	•	4.3	•	•	•
Interest Paid **13**	0.8	0.1	0.8	1.8	0.1	•	0.8	2.0	•	4.7	•	•	•
Depreciation **14**	2.0	0.3	2.5	2.6	0.1	•	2.2	2.3	•	3.1	•	•	•
Amortization and Depletion **15**	0.3	0.4	0.2	0.8	0.0	•	0.5	1.1	•	4.5	•	•	•
Pensions and Other Deferred Comp. **16**	2.1	1.3	2.6	2.1	0.1	•	3.2	0.0	•	0.3	•	•	•
Employee Benefits **17**	1.1	0.5	1.2	1.2	0.9	•	1.4	1.0	•	2.8	•	•	•
Advertising **18**	0.9	0.5	1.1	0.9	0.1	•	0.9	4.0	•	1.6	•	•	•
Other Expenses **19**	38.9	59.7	32.9	24.6	69.0	•	48.1	41.0	•	26.6	•	•	•
Officers' Compensation **20**	16.9	10.5	21.5	17.3	1.2	•	1.3	0.3	•	0.7	•	•	•
Operating Margin **21**	4.8	1.4	5.0	11.1	1.2	•	2.9	1.9	•	•	•	•	•
Operating Margin Before Officers' Comp. **22**	21.7	11.9	26.6	28.4	2.4	•	4.2	2.2	•	•	•	•	•

Selected Average Balance Sheet ($ in Thousands)

Net Receivables 23	6	0	3	7	52	•	3618	22216	•	11564
Inventories 24	1	0	0	0	3	•	24	812	•	2039
Net Property, Plant and Equipment 25	59	0	51	203	282	•	2475	9618	•	17506
Total Assets 26	164	0	121	665	1648	•	14542	48087	•	128740
Notes and Loans Payable 27	102	0	78	475	203	•	2864	30456	•	70423
All Other Liabilities 28	26	0	19	65	741	•	5140	7467	•	13984
Net Worth 29	35	0	24	126	704	•	6538	10164	•	44333

Selected Financial Ratios (Times to 1)

Current Ratio 30	1.2	•	1.2	0.9	1.7	•	1.2	1.3	•	0.4
Quick Ratio 31	1.0	•	1.1	0.8	0.8	•	1.1	1.2	•	0.3
Net Sales to Working Capital 32	135.1	•	100.7	•	56.4	•	37.4	18.3	•	
Coverage Ratio 33	8.7	32.7	9.6	7.7	21.5	•	5.1	3.8	•	0.1
Total Asset Turnover 34	5.2	•	5.5	2.5	18.6	•	2.6	2.3	•	1.0
Inventory Turnover 35	78.8	•	94.8	•	22.6	•	160.2	7.2	•	7.9
Receivables Turnover 36	144.9	•	207.2	192.8	846.2	•	12.2	5.1	•	13.3
Total Liabilities to Net Worth 37	3.6	•	4.1	4.3	1.3	•	1.2	3.7	•	1.9
Current Assets to Working Capital 38	7.4	•	5.2	•	2.4	•	6.5	4.3	•	
Current Liabilities to Working Capital 39	6.4	•	4.2	•	1.4	•	5.5	3.3	•	
Working Capital to Net Sales 40	0.0	•	0.0	•	0.0	•	0.0	0.1	•	0.1
Inventory to Working Capital 41	0.1	•	0.1	•	0.0	•	0.0	0.1	•	
Total Receipts to Cash Flow 42	2.6	1.8	3.1	3.2	1.4	•	2.1	2.5	•	7.2
Cost of Goods to Cash Flow 43	0.1	0.1	0.2	0.2	0.0	•	0.2	0.1	•	0.9
Cash Flow to Total Debt 44	2.6	•	2.2	0.9	22.7	•	2.3	1.2	•	0.2

Selected Financial Factors (in Percentages)

Debt Ratio 45	78.4	•	80.6	81.1	57.3	•	55.0	78.9	•	65.6
Return on Total Assets 46	36.3	•	41.0	33.5	24.9	•	10.8	17.7	•	0.3
Return on Equity Before Income Taxes 47	149.2	•	188.9	154.0	55.7	•	19.2	61.9	•	
Return on Equity After Income Taxes 48	147.9	•	187.3	153.7	55.3	•	15.6	61.6	•	
Profit Margin (Before Income Tax) 49	6.1	4.1	6.7	11.8	1.3	•	3.3	5.7	•	
Profit Margin (After Income Tax) 50	6.1	4.0	6.7	11.8	1.3	•	2.7	5.7	•	

Table II

Corporations with Net Income

OFFICES OF DENTISTS

MONEY AMOUNTS AND SIZE OF ASSETS IN THOUSANDS OF DOLLARS

Item Description for Accounting Period 7/03 Through 6/04	Total	Zero Assets	Under 500	500 to 1,000	1,000 to 5,000	5,000 to 10,000	10,000 to 25,000	25,000 to 50,000	50,000 to 100,000	100,000 to 250,000	250,000 to 500,000	500,000 to 2,500,000	2,500,000 and over
Number of Enterprises 1	43177	3117	37094	2768	187	•	7	4	•	•	•	•	•
Revenues ($ in Thousands)													
Net Sales 2	32484591	1244531	24857108	4745819	839648	•	260085	537401	•	•	•	•	•
Interest 3	11455	1130	9824	204	99	•	193	5	•	•	•	•	•
Rents 4	4197	0	3795	0	0	•	0	402	•	•	•	•	•
Royalties 5	0	0	0	0	0	•	0	0	•	•	•	•	•
Other Portfolio Income 6	85051	31076	33424	20345	1	•	158	46	•	•	•	•	•
Other Receipts 7	277853	9480	244329	17100	4822	•	1148	973	•	•	•	•	•
Total Receipts 8	32863147	1286217	25148480	4783468	844570	•	261584	538827	•	•	•	•	•
Average Total Receipts 9	761	413	678	1728	4516	•	37369	134707	•	•	•	•	•
Operating Costs/Operating Income (%)													
Cost of Operations 10	6.6	8.2	6.2	8.3	2.3	•	14.7	7.7	•	•	•	•	•
Salaries and Wages 11	23.0	19.7	22.1	24.6	34.7	•	20.7	39.5	•	•	•	•	•
Taxes Paid 12	3.7	2.9	3.7	3.9	3.5	•	3.0	3.3	•	•	•	•	•
Interest Paid 13	0.9	0.2	0.8	1.6	0.7	•	0.8	1.7	•	•	•	•	•
Depreciation 14	2.2	0.2	2.2	2.3	1.2	•	2.2	3.0	•	•	•	•	•
Amortization and Depletion 15	0.3	0.2	0.2	0.7	0.2	•	0.6	1.0	•	•	•	•	•
Pensions and Other Deferred Comp. 16	2.1	0.7	2.3	2.1	0.6	•	0.2	0.0	•	•	•	•	•
Employee Benefits 17	1.0	0.2	1.1	1.1	1.0	•	0.2	1.5	•	•	•	•	•
Advertising 18	1.1	0.2	1.2	0.8	1.1	•	0.9	3.1	•	•	•	•	•
Other Expenses 19	31.6	55.9	31.9	22.8	29.8	•	47.8	33.3	•	•	•	•	•
Officers' Compensation 20	17.5	7.9	18.6	18.0	12.1	•	1.5	0.2	•	•	•	•	•
Operating Margin 21	10.1	3.9	9.7	13.7	12.9	•	6.1	5.7	•	•	•	•	•
Operating Margin Before Officers' Comp. 22	27.6	11.8	28.3	31.7	25.0	•	7.5	5.9	•	•	•	•	•

Selected Average Balance Sheet ($ in Thousands)

Net Receivables 23	6	0	3	8	80	•	2806	21148
Inventories 24	1	0	1	0	3	•	58	1074
Net Property, Plant and Equipment 25	61	0	52	196	434	•	2563	16144
Total Assets 26	171	0	131	669	1474	•	15292	71858
Notes and Loans Payable 27	97	0	76	425	313	•	3244	27383
All Other Liabilities 28	23	0	18	68	77	•	4320	17796
Net Worth 29	51	0	37	175	1084	•	7728	26678

Selected Financial Ratios (Times to 1)

Current Ratio 30	1.5	•	1.4	1.4	9.8	•	1.4	1.4
Quick Ratio 31	1.3	•	1.2	1.3	9.6	•	1.3	1.2
Net Sales to Working Capital 32	45.4	•	61.7	41.6	5.4	•	19.9	18.0
Coverage Ratio 33	13.2	45.4	14.2	10.0	21.5	•	8.9	4.6
Total Asset Turnover 34	4.4	•	5.1	2.6	3.0	•	2.4	1.9
Inventory Turnover 35	83.3	•	76.0	•	30.0	•	94.1	9.7
Receivables Turnover 36	123.2	•	202.4	166.2	112.8	•	26.5	6.6
Total Liabilities to Net Worth 37	2.3	•	2.6	2.8	0.4	•	1.0	1.7
Current Assets to Working Capital 38	3.1	•	3.6	3.5	1.1	•	3.6	3.5
Current Liabilities to Working Capital 39	2.1	•	2.6	2.5	0.1	•	2.6	2.5
Working Capital to Net Sales 40	0.0	•	0.0	0.0	0.2	•	0.1	0.1
Inventory to Working Capital 41	0.1	•	0.1	•	0.0	•	0.0	0.2
Total Receipts to Cash Flow 42	2.7	1.8	2.8	3.1	2.5	•	1.9	3.2
Cost of Goods to Cash Flow 43	0.2	0.1	0.2	0.3	0.1	•	0.3	0.2
Cash Flow to Total Debt 44	2.3	•	2.6	1.1	4.5	•	2.5	0.9

Selected Financial Factors (in Percentages)

Debt Ratio 45	70.0	•	72.0	73.8	26.4	•	49.5	62.9
Return on Total Assets 46	53.4	•	59.8	41.4	43.0	•	18.1	14.3
Return on Equity Before Income Taxes 47	164.8	•	198.3	142.0	55.7	•	31.9	30.0
Return on Equity After Income Taxes 48	163.5	•	196.8	141.7	55.3	•	27.5	27.7
Profit Margin (Before Income Tax) 49	11.2	7.3	10.9	14.5	13.4	•	6.6	6.0
Profit Margin (After Income Tax) 50	11.1	7.2	10.8	14.5	13.4	•	5.7	5.5

Table I

Corporations with and without Net Income

OFFICES OF OTHER HEALTH PRACTITIONERS

MONEY AMOUNTS AND SIZE OF ASSETS IN THOUSANDS OF DOLLARS

Item Description for Accounting Period 7/03 Through 6/04		Total	Zero Assets	Under 500	500 to 1,000	1,000 to 5,000	5,000 to 10,000	10,000 to 25,000	25,000 to 50,000	50,000 to 100,000	100,000 to 250,000	250,000 to 500,000	500,000 to 2,500,000	2,500,000 and over
Number of Enterprises	1	81020	11212	67797	1452	414	64	40	17	13	11	•	•	•
Revenues ($ in Thousands)														
Net Sales	2	37549880	931129	20641966	1930138	3312739	2700882	1222807	1401161	864628	4544430	•	•	•
Interest	3	64842	599	2765	1199	2277	2716	2227	5294	5248	42517	•	•	•
Rents	4	18012	0	455	0	3353	60	2269	3287	3471	5116	•	•	•
Royalties	5	164	0	164	0	0	0	0	0	0	0			
Other Portfolio Income	6	103185	37386	18563	7882	9031	8083	11920	1274	2447	6603	•	•	•
Other Receipts	7	818828	37766	131601	21110	23739	84851	70022	19995	320524	109216	•	•	•
Total Receipts	8	38554911	1006880	20795514	1960329	3351139	2796592	1309245	1431011	1196318	4707882	•	•	•
Average Total Receipts	9	476	90	307	1350	8095	43697	32731	84177	92024	427989	•	•	•
Operating Costs/Operating Income (%)														
Cost of Operations	10	14.6	2.7	10.7	16.9	2.0	71.7	32.6	13.5	11.8	4.6	•	•	•
Salaries and Wages	11	23.7	12.8	22.3	19.1	40.0	10.9	23.4	16.8	31.6	30.5	•	•	•
Taxes Paid	12	3.1	3.4	3.6	4.7	2.4	1.9	1.9	1.9	3.2	1.7	•	•	•
Interest Paid	13	0.7	0.7	0.5	0.7	0.6	0.0	0.9	0.7	2.7	2.0	•	•	•
Depreciation	14	1.6	1.0	1.8	2.0	1.4	0.7	1.3	0.9	3.0	1.5	•	•	•
Amortization and Depletion	15	0.3	0.0	0.2	0.4	0.0	0.0	0.3	0.3	1.1	0.8	•	•	•
Pensions and Other Deferred Comp.	16	1.1	1.5	1.3	1.6	1.3	0.1	1.8	0.5	0.2	0.0	•	•	•
Employee Benefits	17	3.3	0.7	1.3	1.3	3.1	0.5	3.1	4.9	3.5	15.5	•	•	•
Advertising	18	1.7	2.5	2.4	3.2	0.6	0.4	0.2	0.2	1.0	0.3	•	•	•
Other Expenses	19	34.5	46.9	30.5	23.2	45.0	13.9	39.4	61.1	75.5	42.6	•	•	•
Officers' Compensation	20	10.7	17.7	16.6	13.4	3.6	0.8	1.4	0.4	2.1	0.2	•	•	•
Operating Margin	21	4.8	10.1	8.9	13.6	•	•	•	•	•	0.2	•	•	•
Operating Margin Before Officers' Comp.	22	15.5	27.8	25.5	27.0	3.6	•	•	•	•	0.5	•	•	•

Selected Average Balance Sheet ($ in Thousands)

Net Receivables 23	21	0	5	132	460	822	5009	8304	10985	40097
Inventories 24	3	0	2	18		216	225	576	472	635
Net Property, Plant and Equipment 25	28	0	16	145	444	1646	2581	4731	12611	30043
Total Assets 26	130	0	57	630	1883	6693	15434	35066	66485	222805
Notes and Loans Payable 27	52	0	28	268	933	432	4169	11453	30414	69141
All Other Liabilities 28	38	0	11	79	672	4596	4016	11016	22806	85575
Net Worth 29	40	0	17	283	279	1665	7248	12596	13264	68088

Selected Financial Ratios (Times to 1)

Current Ratio 30	1.6	•	1.9	2.4	1.5	1.0	1.4	1.2	1.3	1.3
Quick Ratio 31	1.3	•	1.7	2.3	1.1	0.8	1.1	0.9	0.9	1.0
Net Sales to Working Capital 32	19.4	•	21.8	6.3	19.7	4307.6	11.5	33.3	11.9	15.5
Coverage Ratio 33	11.1	26.9	20.8	23.9	2.9	79.7	1.8	2.3	2.0	2.9
Total Asset Turnover 34	3.6	•	5.4	2.1	4.2	6.3	2.0	2.4	1.0	1.9
Inventory Turnover 35	26.7	•	16.8	12.5	78.9	139.8	44.3	19.4	16.6	30.1
Receivables Turnover 36	21.5	•	57.4	11.9	14.8	26.1	6.3	10.7	5.9	10.7
Total Liabilities to Net Worth 37	2.3	•	2.3	1.2	5.8	3.0	1.1	1.8	4.0	2.3
Current Assets to Working Capital 38	2.8	•	2.1	1.7	3.1	480.1	3.7	6.6	4.7	3.9
Current Liabilities to Working Capital 39	1.8	•	1.1	0.7	2.1	479.1	2.7	5.6	3.7	2.9
Working Capital to Net Sales 40	0.1	•	0.0	0.2	0.1	0.0	0.1	0.0	0.1	0.1
Inventory to Working Capital 41	0.1	•	0.1	0.1	0.0	4.6	0.1	0.3	0.1	0.0
Total Receipts to Cash Flow 42	2.8	1.9	3.2	3.0	2.4	7.1	2.7	1.7	1.4	2.2
Cost of Goods to Cash Flow 43	0.4	0.1	0.3	0.5	0.0	5.1	0.9	0.2	0.2	0.1
Cash Flow to Total Debt 44	1.8	•	2.4	1.3	2.1	1.2	1.4	2.2	0.9	1.2

Selected Financial Factors (in Percentages)

Debt Ratio 45	69.4	•	69.9	55.1	85.2	75.1	53.0	64.1	80.0	69.4
Return on Total Assets 46	29.2	•	54.5	33.3	7.1	17.3	3.1	3.9	5.4	10.9
Return on Equity Before Income Taxes 47	86.6	•	172.2	71.1	31.5	68.5	3.0	6.2	13.5	23.2
Return on Equity After Income Taxes 48	83.9	•	170.6	70.3	30.6	60.9	0.8	3.0	9.7	18.3
Profit Margin (Before Income Tax) 49	7.4	18.3	9.7	15.1	1.1	2.7	0.7	0.9	2.7	3.8
Profit Margin (After Income Tax) 50	7.2	18.2	9.6	15.0	1.1	2.4	0.2	0.5	1.9	3.0

Table II

Corporations with Net Income

OFFICES OF OTHER HEALTH PRACTITIONERS

MONEY AMOUNTS AND SIZE OF ASSETS IN THOUSANDS OF DOLLARS

Item Description for Accounting Period 7/03 Through 6/04		Total	Zero Assets	Under 500	500 to 1,000	1,000 to 5,000	5,000 to 10,000	10,000 to 25,000	25,000 to 50,000	50,000 to 100,000	100,000 to 250,000	250,000 to 500,000	500,000 to 2,500,000	2,500,000 and over
Number of Enterprises	1	57846	6692	49640	1146	266	•	20	9	10	•	•	•	•
Revenues ($ in Thousands)														
Net Sales	2	25654354	770397	14390908	1598967	1291203	•	749418	553015	489707	•	•	•	•
Interest	3	44214	598	643	399	1853	•	1900	2385	4369	•	•	•	•
Rents	4	4777	0	51	0	3190	•	265	0	1259	•	•	•	•
Royalties	5	164	0	164	0	0	•	0	0	0	•	•	•	•
Other Portfolio Income	6	91125	37385	13519	7880	8965	•	10508	1239	2447	•	•	•	•
Other Receipts	7	640679	37716	72394	8938	6751	•	54056	22416	316577	•	•	•	•
Total Receipts	8	26435313	846096	14477679	1616184	1311962	•	816147	579055	814359	•	•	•	•
Average Total Receipts	9	457	126	292	1410	4932	•	40807	64339	81436	•	•	•	•
Operating Costs/Operating Income (%)														
Cost of Operations	10	16.3	2.6	9.1	16.0	5.0	•	41.0	10.3	11.8	•	•	•	•
Salaries and Wages	11	19.5	12.6	18.5	16.6	30.9	•	15.7	18.8	32.7	•	•	•	•
Taxes Paid	12	2.9	3.3	3.2	5.0	2.3	•	1.6	2.6	3.1	•	•	•	•
Interest Paid	13	0.7	0.8	0.4	0.6	0.9	•	0.6	1.0	1.9	•	•	•	•
Depreciation	14	1.4	0.9	1.5	1.7	1.5	•	1.2	0.7	3.6	•	•	•	•
Amortization and Depletion	15	0.3	•	0.2	0.5	0.0	•	0.1	0.5	1.3	•	•	•	•
Pensions and Other Deferred Comp.	16	1.0	1.8	1.2	1.8	3.2	•	0.0	0.4	0.1	•	•	•	•
Employee Benefits	17	3.6	0.6	1.0	1.5	0.3	•	2.5	9.8	4.6	•	•	•	•
Advertising	18	1.9	2.0	2.7	3.2	1.3	•	0.3	0.2	0.5	•	•	•	•
Other Expenses	19	31.5	39.6	30.9	20.2	42.0	•	38.6	54.6	99.7	•	•	•	•
Officers' Compensation	20	10.4	19.9	15.1	15.0	4.5	•	1.3	0.8	0.6	•	•	•	•
Operating Margin	21	10.4	15.9	16.2	17.8	8.3	•	•	•	•	•	•	•	•
Operating Margin Before Officers' Comp.	22	20.8	35.9	31.4	32.8	12.8	•	•	•	1.1	•	•	•	•

Selected Average Balance Sheet ($ in Thousands)

Net Receivables 23	17	0	4	159	170	•	5064	3598	8114
Inventories 24	2	0	2	3	3	•	205	51	473
Net Property, Plant and Equipment 25	26	0	15	142	427	•	2879	4718	13961
Total Assets 26	127	0	56	617	1690	•	16660	34593	64354
Notes and Loans Payable 27	41	0	20	235	621	•	2434	10102	18092
All Other Liabilities 28	36	0	9	93	693	•	3017	10356	23269
Net Worth 29	50	0	27	290	376	•	11208	14134	22993

Selected Financial Ratios (Times to 1)

Current Ratio 30	1.7	•	2.7	2.0	1.4	•	1.3	0.8	1.0
Quick Ratio 31	1.4	•	2.5	1.9	0.9	•	1.1	0.7	0.7
Net Sales to Working Capital 32	16.7	•	16.1	8.1	15.4	•	14.7	•	342.2
Coverage Ratio 33	20.3	33.7	41.8	31.1	12.1	•	10.2	6.1	4.3
Total Asset Turnover 34	3.5	•	5.1	2.3	2.9	•	2.2	1.8	0.8
Inventory Turnover 35	37.7	•	13.7	64.1	72.1	•	75.0	124.6	12.2
Receivables Turnover 36	26.1	•	58.6	11.6	57.1	•	6.4	17.2	5.7
Total Liabilities to Net Worth 37	1.5	•	1.1	1.1	3.5	•	0.5	1.4	1.8
Current Assets to Working Capital 38	2.5	•	1.6	2.0	3.3	•	4.3	•	157.4
Current Liabilities to Working Capital 39	1.5	•	0.6	1.0	2.3	•	3.3	•	156.4
Working Capital to Net Sales 40	0.1	•	0.1	0.1	0.1	•	0.1	•	0.0
Inventory to Working Capital 41	0.1	•	0.1	0.0	0.0	•	0.1	•	3.9
Total Receipts to Cash Flow 42	2.6	1.8	2.6	2.9	2.0	•	2.4	1.7	1.0
Cost of Goods to Cash Flow 43	0.4	0.0	0.2	0.5	0.1	•	1.0	0.2	0.1
Cash Flow to Total Debt 44	2.2	•	3.8	1.5	1.8	•	2.9	1.7	1.2

Selected Financial Factors (in Percentages)

Debt Ratio 45	60.4	•	52.8	53.1	77.8	•	32.7	59.1	64.3
Return on Total Assets 46	49.1	•	88.6	44.1	31.2	•	14.6	10.6	6.3
Return on Equity Before Income Taxes 47	118.0	•	183.2	91.0	128.5	•	19.6	21.8	13.6
Return on Equity After Income Taxes 48	115.0	•	181.9	90.1	127.4	•	16.7	16.4	10.7
Profit Margin (Before Income Tax) 49	13.4	25.7	16.8	18.9	9.9	•	5.9	5.0	6.4
Profit Margin (After Income Tax) 50	13.1	25.7	16.7	18.7	9.9	•	5.0	3.8	5.0

Table I

Corporations with and without Net Income

OUTPATIENT CARE CENTERS

MONEY AMOUNTS AND SIZE OF ASSETS IN THOUSANDS OF DOLLARS

Item Description for Accounting Period 7/03 Through 6/04	Total	Zero Assets	Under 500	500 to 1,000	1,000 to 5,000	5,000 to 10,000	10,000 to 25,000	25,000 to 50,000	50,000 to 100,000	100,000 to 250,000	250,000 to 500,000	500,000 to 2,500,000	2,500,000 and over
Number of Enterprises **1**	6128	822	4712	122	357	35	40	12	6	8	6	9	•
Revenues ($ in Thousands)													
Net Sales **2**	39792904	470671	3646340	201596	4146088	427789	1515425	534338	890572	2957772	1568742	23433570	•
Interest **3**	130077	1047	238	40	2149	2927	4831	788	6284	1821	16128	93823	•
Rents **4**	11636	0	0	0	106	0	285	163	1569	3	622	8889	•
Royalties **5**	286678	0	0	0	0	0	0	0	0	0	0	286678	•
Other Portfolio Income **6**	46204	0	5	2	14	415	1471	351	236	2110	2704	38895	•
Other Receipts **7**	671030	7661	27701	435	104601	9140	23989	56789	4776	17222	84898	333821	•
Total Receipts **8**	40938529	479379	3674284	202073	4252958	440271	1546001	592429	903437	2978928	1673094	24195676	•
Average Total Receipts **9**	6681	583	780	1656	11913	12579	38650	49369	150573	372366	278849	2688408	•
Operating Costs/Operating Income (%)													
Cost of Operations **10**	44.1	56.1	21.6	32.1	7.1	38.5	36.3	3.1	3.2	24.6	49.2	59.3	•
Salaries and Wages **11**	15.7	1.6	16.9	12.8	32.5	32.3	13.2	40.0	14.6	21.6	17.6	11.3	•
Taxes Paid **12**	2.3	0.4	3.2	2.6	2.7	2.0	1.3	3.0	2.3	1.9	1.1	2.2	•
Interest Paid **13**	1.8	0.7	0.6	2.1	0.5	1.5	0.8	1.7	1.6	1.5	2.9	2.3	•
Depreciation **14**	1.7	0.2	1.4	4.9	1.1	1.1	1.0	2.8	1.0	1.9	2.8	1.8	•
Amortization and Depletion **15**	0.9	•	0.0	0.6	0.0	0.2	0.3	0.8	1.4	0.6	3.0	1.1	•
Pensions and Other Deferred Comp. **16**	0.5	•	0.3	0.2	1.7	0.1	0.3	0.2	0.5	0.0	0.2	0.4	•
Employee Benefits **17**	3.0	•	2.1	1.8	2.6	2.4	6.4	30.1	1.0	2.1	1.1	2.7	•
Advertising **18**	0.4	0.4	0.8	0.1	0.2	0.8	0.3	0.5	0.3	0.8	0.4	0.3	•
Other Expenses **19**	26.2	50.8	30.5	32.2	47.6	21.2	38.5	33.7	74.4	40.8	20.2	17.0	•
Officers' Compensation **20**	1.5	1.8	9.5	3.1	1.4	0.9	0.9	1.0	0.5	0.4	0.9	0.5	•
Operating Margin **21**	2.1	•	13.2	7.5	2.7	•	0.7	•	•	3.7	0.5	1.1	•
Operating Margin Before Officers' Comp. **22**	3.6	•	22.7	10.6	4.1	1.6	1.6	•	•	4.2	1.4	1.6	•

Selected Average Balance Sheet ($ in Thousands)

												•
Net Receivables 23	505	0	0		810	1367	2694	7345	10230	19945	36544	234210
Inventories 24	60	0	2		68	23	298	588	201	1426	4168	30589
Net Property, Plant and Equipment 25	501	0	65	650	342	792	3579	5616	12368	31472	28654	203159
Total Assets 26	5166	0	132	727	2661	5958	16319	33481	69371	161803	302168	2800759
Notes and Loans Payable 27	2003	0	106	398	670	2542	5686	6704	21132	34960	84552	1130383
All Other Liabilities 28	1363	0	15	763	1301	2588	6367	19620	24790	53151	61994	688707
Net Worth 29	1800	0	11	-433	690	829	4266	7158	23449	73692	155621	981669

Selected Financial Ratios (Times to 1)

												•
Current Ratio 30	1.3	•	1.0	1.2	1.2	1.8	1.2	1.6	2.4	1.3		
Quick Ratio 31	1.0	•	0.9	0.7	1.0	1.6	1.1	1.5	1.7	0.9		
Net Sales to Working Capital 32	19.6	•	•	18.8	32.7	7.1	28.3	11.5	4.0	17.4		
Coverage Ratio 33	3.7	•	26.3	11.7	2.3	4.2	1.3	4.0	3.5	2.9		
Total Asset Turnover 34	1.3	•	5.9	4.4	2.1	2.3	1.3	2.3	0.9	0.9		
Inventory Turnover 35	48.0	•	87.7	12.2	207.9	46.1	2.3	63.8	30.9	50.4		
Receivables Turnover 36	13.0	•	233.1	14.8	19.0	5.7	12.9	6.4	16.5	11.6	10.9	
Total Liabilities to Net Worth 37	1.9	•	10.7	•	2.9	6.2	2.8	3.7	2.0	1.2	0.9	1.9
Current Assets to Working Capital 38	4.7	•	•	•	•	5.9	6.9	2.3	5.2	2.6	1.7	4.9
Current Liabilities to Working Capital 39	3.7	•	•	•	•	4.9	5.9	1.3	4.2	1.6	0.7	3.9
Working Capital to Net Sales 40	0.1	•	•	•	0.1	0.0	0.0	0.1	0.0	0.1	0.3	0.1
Inventory to Working Capital 41	0.2	•	•	•	0.0	0.0	0.2	0.1	0.0	0.0	0.1	0.2
Total Receipts to Cash Flow 42	3.6	2.6	2.6	2.9	2.0	5.0	2.6	4.5	1.4	2.3	4.1	5.4
Cost of Goods to Cash Flow 43	1.6	1.4	0.6	0.9	0.1	1.9	0.9	0.1	0.0	0.6	2.0	3.2
Cash Flow to Total Debt 44	0.5	•	2.4	0.5	3.0	0.5	1.2	0.4	2.3	1.8	0.4	0.3

Selected Financial Factors (in Percentages)

												•
Debt Ratio 45	65.2	•	91.5	159.6	74.1	86.1	73.9	78.6	66.2	54.5	64.9	
Return on Total Assets 46	8.5	•	84.9	22.5	25.1	7.1	8.3	•	4.5	13.5	8.7	6.1
Return on Equity Before Income Taxes 47	17.8	•	958.8	88.3	29.0	24.2	3.1	22.2	12.0	11.4		
Return on Equity After Income Taxes 48	13.9	•	947.1	85.3	28.6	20.2	•	17.0	6.8	7.7		
Profit Margin (Before Income Tax) 49	4.9	•	13.9	7.8	5.2	2.0	2.7	0.5	4.4	7.2	4.3	
Profit Margin (After Income Tax) 50	3.8	•	13.8	7.8	5.1	1.9	2.3	•	3.4	4.1	2.9	

Table II
Corporations with Net Income

OUTPATIENT CARE CENTERS

MONEY AMOUNTS AND SIZE OF ASSETS IN THOUSANDS OF DOLLARS

Item Description for Accounting Period 7/03 Through 6/04	Total	Zero Assets	Under 500	500 to 1,000	1,000 to 5,000	5,000 to 10,000	10,000 to 25,000	25,000 to 50,000	50,000 to 100,000	100,000 to 250,000	250,000 to 500,000	500,000 to 2,500,000	2,500,000 and over
Number of Enterprises 1	3182	396	2388	37	289	•	24	6	•	•	3	•	9
Revenues ($ in Thousands)													
Net Sales 2	34142337	181461	2672581	144116	2034649	•	833756	704297	•	•	1077343	•	23433570
Interest 3	107093	1035	227	0	435	•	2035	1034	•	•	4542	•	93823
Rents 4	9310	0	0	0	106	•	283	30	•	•	0	•	8889
Royalties 5	286678	0	0	0	0	•	0	0	•	•	0	•	286678
Other Portfolio Income 6	43164	0	5	2	14	•	1081	7	•	•	635	•	38895
Other Receipts 7	607346	7533	26294	56	102132	•	17802	36559	•	•	67125	•	333821
Total Receipts 8	35195928	190029	2699107	144174	2137336	•	854957	741927	•	•	1149645	•	24195676
Average Total Receipts 9	11061	480	1130	3897	7396	•	35623	123654	•	•	383215	•	2688408
Operating Costs/Operating Income (%)													
Cost of Operations 10	49.2	•	24.1	19.3	14.4	•	46.8	0.6	•	•	61.5	•	59.3
Salaries and Wages 11	13.4	4.2	11.1	17.3	31.8	•	9.1	13.1	•	•	12.9	•	11.3
Taxes Paid 12	2.2	1.0	2.9	1.3	3.5	•	1.2	2.2	•	•	1.0	•	2.2
Interest Paid 13	1.7	1.3	0.1	3.0	0.5	•	0.7	0.3	•	•	0.3	•	2.3
Depreciation 14	1.6	0.4	0.8	3.8	1.7	•	1.1	0.7	•	•	1.9	•	1.8
Amortization and Depletion 15	0.9	•	0.0	0.8	0.0	•	0.4	0.5	•	•	1.6	•	1.1
Pensions and Other Deferred Comp. 16	0.3	•	0.2	0.0	0.1	•	0.1	0.1	•	•	0.1	•	0.4
Employee Benefits 17	2.8	•	0.8	1.6	3.1	•	3.8	21.4	•	•	0.1	•	2.7
Advertising 18	0.4	0.2	0.9	0.0	0.4	•	0.4	0.2	•	•	0.3	•	0.3
Other Expenses 19	22.5	89.8	28.5	35.8	36.0	•	30.5	61.0	•	•	13.1	•	17.0
Officers' Compensation 20	1.3	4.6	9.2	1.0	1.7	•	1.0	0.5	•	•	1.0	•	0.5
Operating Margin 21	3.7	•	21.5	16.1	6.7	•	4.9	•	•	•	6.2	•	1.1
Operating Margin Before Officers' Comp. 22	5.0	3.0	30.7	17.0	8.3	•	5.9	•	•	•	7.2	•	1.6

Selected Average Balance Sheet ($ in Thousands)

Item									
Net Receivables 23	858	0	1	0	865	1777	8457	32796	234210
Inventories 24	92	0	3	0	83	83	177	2373	31021
Net Property, Plant and Equipment 25	717	0	17	740	361	4050	1961	30544	203159
Total Assets 26	9092	0	112	884	2694	15822	43044	301888	2800759
Notes and Loans Payable 27	3380	0	41	1228	375	4422	5194	16824	1130383
All Other Liabilities 28	2295	0	4	24	900	6271	17567	66795	688707
Net Worth 29	3417	0	66	-368	1419	5128	20283	218269	981669

Selected Financial Ratios (Times to 1)

Item									
Current Ratio 30	1.3		5.8	0.1	1.2	1.3	1.6	2.9	1.3
Quick Ratio 31	1.0		5.2	0.1	1.1	1.1	1.5	2.1	0.9
Net Sales to Working Capital 32	15.4		21.6		25.9	22.0	12.0	3.5	17.4
Coverage Ratio 33	4.9	3.4	170.7	6.4	22.6	11.4	18.9	42.1	2.9
Total Asset Turnover 34	1.2		10.0	4.4	2.6	2.2	2.7	1.2	0.9
Inventory Turnover 35	57.3		81.5		12.2	195.2	4.0	93.1	49.7
Receivables Turnover 36	13.6		299.3	10.6	11.3	17.2	11.7	21.9	22.2
Total Liabilities to Net Worth 37	1.7		0.7		0.9	2.1	1.1	0.4	1.9
Current Assets to Working Capital 38	3.9		1.2		5.2	4.7	2.6	1.5	4.9
Current Liabilities to Working Capital 39	2.9		0.2		4.2	3.7	1.6	0.5	3.9
Working Capital to Net Sales 40	0.1		0.0		0.0	0.0	0.1	0.3	0.1
Inventory to Working Capital 41	0.1		0.1	0.3	0.0	0.1	0.0	0.0	0.2
Total Receipts to Cash Flow 42	3.8	1.1	2.2	2.1	2.3	2.8	1.6	4.2	5.4
Cost of Goods to Cash Flow 43	1.9		0.5	0.4	0.3	1.3	0.0	2.6	3.2
Cash Flow to Total Debt 44	0.5		11.2	1.5	2.4	1.2	3.3	1.0	0.3

Selected Financial Factors (in Percentages)

Item									
Debt Ratio 45	62.4		40.6	141.7	47.3	67.6	52.9	27.7	64.9
Return on Total Assets 46	9.9		227.0	84.0	32.1	17.9	13.9	15.8	6.1
Return on Equity Before Income Taxes 47	21.0		380.2		58.2	50.3	27.9	21.3	11.4
Return on Equity After Income Taxes 48	17.0		376.2		56.4	44.7	18.9	13.9	7.7
Profit Margin (Before Income Tax) 49	6.7	3.1	22.5	16.1	11.7	7.4	4.8	12.9	4.3
Profit Margin (After Income Tax) 50	5.4	2.8	22.3	16.1	11.4	6.6	3.3	8.4	2.9

Table I

Corporations with and without Net Income

MISC. HEALTH CARE AND SOCIAL ASSISTANCE

MONEY AMOUNTS AND SIZE OF ASSETS IN THOUSANDS OF DOLLARS

Item Description for Accounting Period 7/03 Through 6/04		Total	Zero Assets	Under 500	500 to 1,000	1,000 to 5,000	5,000 to 10,000	10,000 to 25,000	25,000 to 50,000	50,000 to 100,000	100,000 to 250,000	250,000 to 500,000	500,000 to 2,500,000	2,500,000 and over
Number of Enterprises	1	50015	6849	38600	2171	1985	151	110	62	33	30	10	13	•
Revenues ($ in Thousands)														
Net Sales	2	71928478	2002743	20726707	4346706	8917514	3382041	3319286	3054406	3463054	5409064	2609870	14697085	•
Interest	3	183949	720	2152	540	3563	2984	4231	14606	10754	50442	39941	54017	•
Rents	4	21635	85	10	0	4068	466	1781	3148	9004	2423	0	651	•
Royalties	5	73805	0	992	0	0	288	0	4215	26131	9241	18240	14699	•
Other Portfolio Income	6	216371	26969	15691	593	3200	46670	12461	5629	36835	8657	6363	53303	•
Other Receipts	7	1311952	16121	233664	71675	183572	310605	47761	96820	58446	37824	115323	140140	•
Total Receipts	8	73736190	2046638	20979216	4419514	9111917	3743054	3385520	3178824	3604224	5517651	2789737	14959895	•
Average Total Receipts	9	1474	299	544	2036	4590	24788	30777	51271	109219	183922	278974	1150761	•
Operating Costs/Operating Income (%)														
Cost of Operations	10	19.5	9.2	12.2	11.2	22.4	49.5	30.7	24.8	20.9	23.3	14.6	20.4	•
Salaries and Wages	11	30.1	25.8	32.3	39.7	29.9	19.7	29.8	32.5	30.2	30.0	41.1	24.9	•
Taxes Paid	12	3.7	3.1	4.4	4.2	4.1	2.0	3.5	4.1	4.0	3.6	3.2	2.9	•
Interest Paid	13	1.9	0.7	0.7	0.8	1.6	1.1	1.4	1.5	2.1	2.6	4.1	3.8	•
Depreciation	14	3.2	0.9	1.7	2.4	3.3	1.4	3.0	3.0	3.5	4.2	2.9	6.2	•
Amortization and Depletion	15	0.8	0.6	0.1	0.2	0.5	0.2	0.5	0.9	1.1	1.4	1.8	1.9	•
Pensions and Other Deferred Comp.	16	0.4	1.3	0.5	0.3	0.5	0.4	0.4	0.4	0.4	0.3	0.1	0.0	•
Employee Benefits	17	2.7	1.0	1.0	2.1	1.8	1.9	2.8	2.8	8.4	3.1	2.7	4.4	•
Advertising	18	0.6	0.7	0.7	0.8	0.5	0.3	0.5	0.6	0.7	0.5	0.3	0.6	•
Other Expenses	19	32.2	62.3	33.6	31.8	30.0	33.3	26.2	35.8	29.8	32.6	42.1	26.7	•
Officers' Compensation	20	4.7	6.4	9.6	4.3	6.5	1.5	2.3	1.8	2.0	1.3	0.8	1.2	•
Operating Margin	21	0.2	•	3.2	2.2	•	•	•	•	•	•	•	6.8	•
Operating Margin Before Officers' Comp.	22	4.9	•	12.8	6.5	5.5	•	1.2	•	•	•	•	8.0	•

Selected Average Balance Sheet ($ in Thousands)

Net Receivables 23	163	0	5	198	469	2325	4433	8139	15133	29313	48793	260692	•
Inventories 24	17	0	2	16	68	96	486	564	1570	3027	8273	21393	•
Net Property, Plant and Equipment 25	191	0	44	272	680	931	3632	6826	15067	32543	35767	239811	•
Total Assets 26	893	0	87	748	2077	6485	15508	35309	69155	164939	330115	1551192	•
Notes and Loans Payable 27	367	0	69	333	1168	1708	5942	9782	27017	40640	150068	579283	•
All Other Liabilities 28	259	0	17	163	623	4057	4813	10583	20474	47786	77622	461426	•
Net Worth 29	268	0	1	253	285	720	4753	14943	21664	76513	102424	510484	•

Selected Financial Ratios (Times to 1)

Current Ratio 30	1.4	•	0.8	1.4	1.0	0.9	1.4	1.5	1.2	1.6	2.2	1.7	•
Quick Ratio 31	1.0	•	0.6	1.2	0.7	0.8	1.1	1.2	0.9	1.3	1.2	1.0	•
Net Sales to Working Capital 32	13.5	•	•	17.8	118.2	•	14.5	8.0	18.4	7.4	2.9	5.0	•
Coverage Ratio 33	2.4	•	7.4	5.6	1.7	0.4	1.6	•	1.6	0.7	•	3.3	•
Total Asset Turnover 34	1.6	•	6.2	2.7	2.2	3.5	1.9	1.4	1.5	1.1	0.8	0.7	•
Inventory Turnover 35	16.3	•	29.6	14.1	14.8	115.1	19.1	21.7	13.9	13.9	4.6	10.8	•
Receivables Turnover 36	9.1	•	119.3	13.1	9.2	7.2	6.2	6.6	6.2	6.4	4.7	4.9	•
Total Liabilities to Net Worth 37	2.3	•	83.3	2.0	6.3	8.0	2.3	1.4	2.2	1.2	2.2	2.0	•
Current Assets to Working Capital 38	3.4	•	•	3.6	25.6	•	3.8	3.0	5.3	2.6	1.8	2.4	•
Current Liabilities to Working Capital 39	2.4	•	•	2.6	24.6	•	2.8	2.0	4.3	1.6	0.8	1.4	•
Working Capital to Net Sales 40	0.1	•	•	0.1	0.0	•	0.1	0.1	0.1	0.1	0.3	0.2	•
Inventory to Working Capital 41	0.2	•	•	0.2	1.5	•	0.2	0.1	0.3	0.1	0.1	0.1	•
Total Receipts to Cash Flow 42	3.5	2.5	3.2	4.7	4.0	3.5	4.4	3.9	4.4	3.6	3.4	3.3	•
Cost of Goods to Cash Flow 43	0.7	0.2	0.4	0.5	0.9	1.7	1.4	1.0	0.9	0.8	0.5	0.7	•
Cash Flow to Total Debt 44	0.7	•	1.9	0.9	0.6	1.1	0.6	0.6	0.5	0.6	0.3	0.3	•

Selected Financial Factors (in Percentages)

Debt Ratio 45	70.0	•	98.8	66.2	86.3	88.9	69.4	57.7	68.7	53.6	69.0	67.1	•
Return on Total Assets 46	7.4	•	31.4	12.6	5.8	1.5	4.3	•	4.9	2.0	•	9.0	•
Return on Equity Before Income Taxes 47	14.5	•	2285.9	30.7	17.4	•	5.4	•	5.6	•	•	19.0	•
Return on Equity After Income Taxes 48	9.9	•	2229.9	29.4	13.3	•	0.7	•	0.7	•	•	12.4	•
Profit Margin (Before Income Tax) 49	2.7	•	4.4	3.9	1.1	•	0.9	•	1.2	•	•	8.6	•
Profit Margin (After Income Tax) 50	1.8	•	4.3	3.7	0.8	•	0.1	•	0.1	•	•	5.6	•

375

Table II
Corporations with Net Income

MISC. HEALTH CARE AND SOCIAL ASSISTANCE

MONEY AMOUNTS AND SIZE OF ASSETS IN THOUSANDS OF DOLLARS

Item Description for Accounting Period 7/03 Through 6/04	Total	Zero Assets	Under 500	500 to 1,000	1,000 to 5,000	5,000 to 10,000	10,000 to 25,000	25,000 to 50,000	50,000 to 100,000	100,000 to 250,000	250,000 to 500,000	500,000 to 2,500,000	2,500,000 and over
Number of Enterprises **1**	28542	2948	22607	1645	1138	61	65	32	16	15	6	9	•
Revenues ($ in Thousands)													
Net Sales **2**	50882759	386313	15129258	3269814	7020684	883349	2211189	1910475	1528448	3436495	2502613	12604119	•
Interest **3**	91938	55	897	392	2542	1411	2691	4075	1807	13642	24069	40358	•
Rents **4**	13656	0	10	0	3931	337	1781	716	5968	874	0	39	•
Royalties **5**	39485	0	0	0	0	0	0	1617	0	6211	17716	13941	•
Other Portfolio Income **6**	169106	22011	15072	486	2962	46393	12125	3660	7409	4309	5781	48896	•
Other Receipts **7**	838077	5415	92315	67921	170154	183568	33992	22832	49776	14821	70519	126767	•
Total Receipts **8**	52035021	413794	15237552	3338613	7200273	1115058	2261778	1943375	1593408	3476352	2620698	12834120	•
Average Total Receipts **9**	1823	140	674	2030	6327	18280	34797	60730	99588	231757	436783	1426013	•
Operating Costs/Operating Income (%)													
Cost of Operations **10**	18.2	10.4	13.8	13.7	21.7	28.8	32.8	14.6	9.5	18.1	14.4	22.2	•
Salaries and Wages **11**	29.7	29.2	31.9	31.6	29.3	39.5	29.1	36.2	26.4	32.1	37.7	23.4	•
Taxes Paid **12**	3.6	3.5	4.3	3.6	3.9	3.3	3.7	4.1	3.2	3.6	2.9	2.7	•
Interest Paid **13**	1.6	0.8	0.6	0.9	1.4	1.9	1.0	1.3	1.0	1.0	3.5	3.0	•
Depreciation **14**	2.9	2.3	1.3	2.9	2.7	2.5	2.1	2.5	4.4	1.9	2.4	5.5	•
Amortization and Depletion **15**	0.7	0.6	0.1	0.1	0.4	0.2	0.3	0.5	0.7	1.0	1.2	1.5	•
Pensions and Other Deferred Comp. **16**	0.3	0.2	0.5	0.3	0.4	0.4	0.5	0.6	0.8	0.4	0.1	0.0	•
Employee Benefits **17**	3.0	1.5	0.9	1.9	1.7	5.1	2.7	2.4	16.5	3.0	2.5	4.9	•
Advertising **18**	0.6	0.5	0.6	0.6	0.5	0.8	0.4	0.8	0.3	0.4	0.2	0.6	•
Other Expenses **19**	29.2	45.1	29.2	33.5	28.9	30.0	20.7	32.0	29.3	33.0	38.3	25.8	•
Officers' Compensation **20**	4.4	2.3	8.7	4.7	5.8	2.6	1.7	1.3	3.2	1.3	0.5	1.4	•
Operating Margin **21**	5.8	3.7	8.1	6.2	3.4	•	4.9	3.7	4.7	4.0	•	8.9	•
Operating Margin Before Officers' Comp. **22**	10.2	6.0	16.7	10.8	9.3	•	6.6	5.0	7.9	5.3	•	10.3	•

Selected Average Balance Sheet ($ in Thousands)

Line Item													
Net Receivables 23	215	0	5	149	615	2961	4767	9507	14252	32317	74452	347117	•
Inventories 24	22	0	2	16	96	162	612	594	1435	2889	8249	25085	•
Net Property, Plant and Equipment 25	222	0	48	293	678	1143	3024	6608	17568	23083	44955	290983	•
Total Assets 26	1083	0	97	737	2402	6505	14851	33084	63689	159233	350920	1873206	•
Notes and Loans Payable 27	399	0	55	317	1085	1355	5141	9647	20385	36065	189462	627306	•
All Other Liabilities 28	320	0	19	100	887	2886	4666	9702	16310	51465	76998	584664	•
Net Worth 29	364	0	22	319	430	2264	5044	13735	26994	71704	84460	661236	•

Selected Financial Ratios (Times to 1)

Line Item													
Current Ratio 30	1.4	0.9	2.0	1.1	1.6	1.6	1.6	1.6	1.3	1.5	1.5	1.6	•
Quick Ratio 31	1.0	0.7	1.6	0.7	1.4	1.3	1.2	1.2	1.1	1.2	1.2	0.9	•
Net Sales to Working Capital 32	13.1	•	10.4	91.5	7.4	10.6	9.7	12.3	11.7	9.7	5.3		•
Coverage Ratio 33	6.1	15.3	14.8	10.3	5.3	6.7	8.1	5.3	9.9	6.0	1.3	4.6	•
Total Asset Turnover 34	1.6	•	6.9	2.7	2.6	2.2	2.3	1.8	1.5	1.4	1.2	0.7	•
Inventory Turnover 35	15.0	•	39.4	17.1	13.9	25.7	18.2	14.7	6.4	14.3	7.3	12.4	•
Receivables Turnover 36	8.9	•	123.7	14.1	11.0	3.3	14.3	7.0	6.6	7.0	6.4	8.1	•
Total Liabilities to Net Worth 37	2.0	3.3	1.3	4.6	1.9	1.9	1.4	1.4	1.2	3.2	1.8		•
Current Assets to Working Capital 38	3.3	•	2.0	19.3	2.5	2.6	2.8	3.9	3.2	3.2	2.6	1.8	•
Current Liabilities to Working Capital 39	2.3	•	1.0	18.3	1.5	1.6	1.8	2.9	2.2	2.2	1.6		•
Working Capital to Net Sales 40	0.1	•	0.1	0.0	0.1	0.1	0.1	0.1	0.1	0.1	0.1	0.2	•
Inventory to Working Capital 41	0.2	•	0.1	1.4	0.1	0.1	0.2	0.1	0.1	0.1	0.2	0.1	•
Total Receipts to Cash Flow 42	3.2	2.1	4.1	3.5	3.3	3.3	4.2	3.1	3.0	2.9	2.9	3.2	•
Cost of Goods to Cash Flow 43	0.6	0.2	0.6	0.8	0.9	0.9	1.4	0.4	0.3	0.5	0.4	0.7	•
Cash Flow to Total Debt 44	0.8	•	2.9	0.9	1.0	1.0	0.8	1.0	0.9	0.9	0.5	0.4	•

Selected Financial Factors (in Percentages)

Line Item													
Debt Ratio 45	66.4	•	76.7	56.6	82.1	65.2	66.0	58.5	57.6	55.0	75.9	64.7	•
Return on Total Assets 46	15.9	•	65.2	24.7	18.9	28.9	18.8	12.0	15.1	8.9	5.6	10.3	•
Return on Equity Before Income Taxes 47	39.6	•	261.3	51.4	85.9	70.8	48.4	23.4	32.0	16.5	6.0	22.8	•
Return on Equity After Income Taxes 48	33.6	•	256.9	50.1	81.2	68.8	40.9	19.8	23.9	12.2	4.1	15.4	•
Profit Margin (Before Income Tax) 49	8.1	10.8	8.8	8.3	6.0	11.1	7.2	5.4	9.0	5.2	1.2	10.8	•
Profit Margin (After Income Tax) 50	6.9	10.4	8.6	8.1	5.7	10.8	6.1	4.6	6.7	3.8	0.8	7.3	•

Table I
Corporations with and without Net Income

HOSPITALS, NURSING, AND RESIDENTIAL CARE FACILITIES

MONEY AMOUNTS AND SIZE OF ASSETS IN THOUSANDS OF DOLLARS

Item Description for Accounting Period 7/03 Through 6/04	Total	Zero Assets	Under 500	500 to 1,000	1,000 to 5,000	5,000 to 10,000	10,000 to 25,000	25,000 to 50,000	50,000 to 100,000	100,000 to 250,000	250,000 to 500,000	500,000 to 2,500,000	2,500,000 and over
Number of Enterprises 1	17376	1957	11702	938	2126	281	198	70	40	33	6	18	6
Revenues ($ in Thousands)													
Net Sales 2	95326125	1104611	6000557	2474611	6809049	3020912	4704469	2992191	3374983	5931220	2408960	23373877	33130685
Interest 3	767475	26951	11	618	867	1129	8180	8312	14591	20786	20537	297688	367805
Rents 4	372549	80	0	0	271	2032	15210	13998	3333	35568	5957	57885	238214
Royalties 5	451	0	0	0	0	0	450	0	0	0	0	2	0
Other Portfolio Income 6	1121873	30953	19	0	11069	4492	9784	22570	57027	25931	11620	527982	420427
Other Receipts 7	3028742	77568	4712	1691	102288	36071	97964	47803	71511	164803	25410	529269	1869651
Total Receipts 8	100617215	1240163	6005299	2476920	6923544	3064636	4836057	3084874	3521445	6178308	2472484	24786703	36026782
Average Total Receipts 9	5791	634	513	2641	3257	10906	24425	44070	88036	187221	412081	1377039	6004464
Operating Costs/Operating Income (%)													
Cost of Operations 10	11.9	0.3	6.1	3.0	6.4	3.8	12.8	5.2	9.9	10.0	5.7	19.7	11.7
Salaries and Wages 11	41.9	35.0	35.6	39.0	45.1	37.1	36.9	45.1	42.4	45.6	48.1	37.6	45.6
Taxes Paid 12	5.5	5.8	6.2	5.1	7.0	5.7	5.8	5.7	5.1	5.7	6.7	5.1	5.2
Interest Paid 13	3.2	6.6	1.6	1.7	2.3	3.2	2.2	2.8	3.2	3.1	3.4	3.0	4.0
Depreciation 14	3.7	3.3	1.4	2.0	2.4	2.7	2.0	2.8	2.7	3.0	3.2	3.4	5.5
Amortization and Depletion 15	0.7	3.3	0.2	0.1	0.2	0.2	0.2	0.2	0.5	0.9	1.4	1.2	0.6
Pensions and Other Deferred Comp. 16	0.4	0.1	0.3	0.1	0.1	0.8	0.3	0.4	0.3	0.2	0.1	0.1	0.9
Employee Benefits 17	4.7	3.7	2.9	2.5	3.3	2.3	4.4	4.0	4.3	4.9	10.2	4.6	5.6
Advertising 18	0.3	0.4	0.5	0.3	0.5	0.3	0.3	0.3	0.3	0.2	0.2	0.3	0.2
Other Expenses 19	30.1	57.3	38.8	42.7	33.3	41.4	35.8	36.8	31.8	30.4	29.3	28.8	24.4
Officers' Compensation 20	0.9	2.7	5.6	1.9	1.4	1.5	1.0	0.9	1.0	0.5	0.3	0.5	0.1
Operating Margin 21	•	•	0.9	1.7	•	0.9	•	•	•	•	•	•	•
Operating Margin Before Officers' Comp. 22	•	•	6.5	3.6	2.4	•	•	•	•	•	•	•	•

Selected Average Balance Sheet ($ in Thousands)

Net Receivables 23	701	0	19	174	316	1053	3180	5563	12010	25854	50745	159813	881569
Inventories 24	15	0	0	1	6	22	96	115	414	975	3458	4557	9519
Net Property, Plant and Equipment 25	2085	0	66	437	1143	4565	6436	16040	29023	76371	202263	474536	2583756
Total Assets 26	5885	0	117	703	2046	7131	15141	34453	70137	153155	356791	1145685	9642470
Notes and Loans Payable 27	2569	0	187	770	1490	5706	9283	19482	37147	108947	160821	541394	2995843
All Other Liabilities 28	1598	0	37	400	477	2093	4935	10827	22883	43161	134943	358209	2336008
Net Worth 29	1718	0	-107	-467	79	-669	923	4144	10107	1048	61027	246082	4310619

Selected Financial Ratios (Times to 1)

Current Ratio 30	1.1	•	0.8	0.9	0.8	0.7	1.1	1.1	0.9	1.0	1.2	1.3	1.3
Quick Ratio 31	0.9	•	0.6	0.8	0.7	0.6	0.9	0.8	0.7	0.8	1.1	1.1	0.9
Net Sales to Working Capital 32	35.1	•	•	•	•	•	38.7	60.8	•	92.4	25.1	19.1	18.4
Coverage Ratio 33	1.7	0.0	1.6	2.1	0.8	1.7	1.5	0.6	1.9	0.9	•	1.6	2.2
Total Asset Turnover 34	0.9	•	4.4	3.8	1.6	1.5	1.6	1.2	1.2	1.2	1.1	1.1	0.6
Inventory Turnover 35	44.4	•	656.4	131.3	37.0	18.4	31.7	19.4	20.2	18.4	6.6	56.2	68.0
Receivables Turnover 36	7.8	•	39.4	14.3	8.2	8.9	7.8	7.5	6.5	7.5	4.8	8.8	6.3
Total Liabilities to Net Worth 37	2.4	•	•	•	25.0	•	15.4	7.3	5.9	145.2	4.8	3.7	1.2
Current Assets to Working Capital 38	8.0	•	•	•	•	•	9.4	16.9	•	25.8	5.4	4.4	4.9
Current Liabilities to Working Capital 39	7.0	•	•	•	•	•	8.4	15.9	•	24.8	4.4	3.4	3.9
Working Capital to Net Sales 40	0.0	•	•	•	•	•	0.0	0.0	•	0.0	0.0	0.1	0.1
Inventory to Working Capital 41	0.1	•	•	•	•	•	0.2	0.2	•	0.6	0.1	0.1	0.0
Total Receipts to Cash Flow 42	3.9	3.3	4.2	3.1	4.0	2.6	3.3	3.5	3.6	4.4	7.6	4.1	4.1
Cost of Goods to Cash Flow 43	0.5	0.0	0.3	0.1	0.3	0.1	0.4	0.2	0.4	0.4	0.4	0.8	0.5
Cash Flow to Total Debt 44	0.3	•	0.5	0.7	0.4	0.5	0.5	0.4	0.4	0.3	0.2	0.4	0.3

Selected Financial Factors (in Percentages)

Debt Ratio 45	70.8	•	191.9	166.5	96.2	109.4	93.9	88.0	85.6	99.3	82.9	78.5	55.3
Return on Total Assets 46	5.0	•	11.3	13.4	2.9	8.4	5.2	2.0	7.2	3.2	•	5.4	5.0
Return on Equity Before Income Taxes 47	6.8	•	•	•	•	•	29.8	23.8	•	•	•	9.2	6.1
Return on Equity After Income Taxes 48	4.4	•	•	•	23.6	•	•	•	14.7	•	•	6.4	4.4
Profit Margin (Before Income Tax) 49	2.1	•	1.0	1.8	•	2.4	1.2	•	2.8	•	•	1.7	4.8
Profit Margin (After Income Tax) 50	1.4	•	1.0	1.8	•	2.2	0.9	•	1.8	•	•	1.2	3.4

Table II

Corporations with Net Income

HOSPITALS, NURSING, AND RESIDENTIAL CARE FACILITIES

MONEY AMOUNTS AND SIZE OF ASSETS IN THOUSANDS OF DOLLARS

Item Description for Accounting Period 7/03 Through 6/04		Total	Zero Assets	Under 500	500 to 1,000	1,000 to 5,000	5,000 to 10,000	10,000 to 25,000	25,000 to 50,000	50,000 to 100,000	100,000 to 250,000	250,000 to 500,000	500,000 to 2,500,000	2,500,000 and over
Number of Enterprises	1	8981	856	6402	389	977	147	118	35	24	16	•	11	6
Revenues ($ in Thousands)														
Net Sales	2	65414630	610399	2641730	1392911	3219326	1813356	3156898	1768581	2683137	3066500	•	11931109	33130685
Interest	3	559387	26823	5	532	610	1100	4555	3656	1900	10415	•	141986	367805
Rents	4	306821	0	0	0	236	68	2381	9925	2523	18069	•	35405	238214
Royalties	5	0	0	0	0	0	0	0	0	0	0		0	0
Other Portfolio Income	6	1037527	30932	19	0	8288	3966	5339	15277	54561	20585	•	478133	420427
Other Receipts	7	2538596	76932	738	992	44075	33867	80261	29897	49907	103156	•	249118	1869651
Total Receipts	8	69856961	745086	2642492	1394435	3272535	1852357	3249434	1827336	2792028	3218725	•	12835751	36026782
Average Total Receipts	9	7778	870	413	3585	3350	12601	27538	52210	116334	201170	•	1166886	6004464
Operating Costs/Operating Income (%)														
Cost of Operations	10	13.1	0.6	5.3	3.5	3.4	3.8	15.1	6.3	10.8	7.4	•	26.8	11.7
Salaries and Wages	11	40.2	31.2	29.4	35.9	44.4	47.6	35.0	43.1	43.1	41.7	•	26.0	45.6
Taxes Paid	12	5.3	5.3	4.8	3.8	7.2	6.2	5.7	5.4	5.4	6.5	•	5.0	5.2
Interest Paid	13	3.2	6.3	0.9	1.0	1.5	2.6	1.6	1.8	1.4	3.2	•	3.3	4.0
Depreciation	14	4.2	2.3	1.1	1.0	1.7	2.8	1.8	2.3	2.1	3.4	•	4.1	5.5
Amortization and Depletion	15	0.7	2.2	0.0	0.1	0.1	0.1	0.2	0.2	0.2	0.6	•	1.6	0.6
Pensions and Other Deferred Comp.	16	0.5	0.0	0.6	0.1	0.1	1.2	0.3	0.4	0.3	0.1	•	0.0	0.9
Employee Benefits	17	4.8	1.7	1.2	2.3	3.0	3.1	4.3	4.1	4.1	4.6	•	4.8	5.6
Advertising	18	0.3	0.1	0.2	0.2	0.6	0.4	0.4	0.3	0.2	0.4	•	0.4	0.2
Other Expenses	19	28.2	51.4	37.2	42.8	30.9	25.9	32.7	33.4	29.4	31.3	•	30.3	24.4
Officers' Compensation	20	0.9	2.4	9.4	2.6	1.6	2.1	1.0	1.0	1.0	0.8	•	0.7	0.1
Operating Margin	21	•	•	9.8	6.7	5.6	4.1	1.7	1.7	2.1	0.2	•	•	•
Operating Margin Before Officers' Comp.	22	•	•	19.2	9.3	7.1	6.3	2.8	2.7	3.0	0.9	•	•	•

Selected Average Balance Sheet ($ in Thousands)

	1	2	3	4	5	6	7	8	9	10	11	12	13
Net Receivables 23	971	0	5	178	189	791	3035	6305	13461	27664	•	153061	881569
Inventories 24	16	0	0	15	4	121	149	486	1239	2032	•		10680
Net Property, Plant and Equipment 25	2889	0	42	378	848	5308	6158	15649	25897	91305	•	459859	2583756
Total Assets 26	9039	0	89	705	1717	7431	14825	34425	69315	179697	•	1110764	9642470
Notes and Loans Payable 27	3481	0	67	890	1072	5620	7394	17299	29366	105140	•	615583	2995843
All Other Liabilities 28	2318	0	15	246	319	1422	4869	7443	23739	49346	•	354014	2336008
Net Worth 29	3241	0	7	-430	326	390	2562	9683	16210	25211	•	141166	4310619

Selected Financial Ratios (Times to 1)

	1	2	3	4	5	6	7	8	9	10	11	12	13
Current Ratio 30	1.3	•	1.3	0.9	1.7	0.9	1.2	1.4	1.1	1.5	•	1.2	1.3
Quick Ratio 31	0.9	•	0.6	0.7	1.3	0.8	0.9	1.1	0.8	1.2	•	1.0	0.9
Net Sales to Working Capital 32	21.2	•	67.2	•	15.2	•	29.6	14.7	37.6	9.4	•	27.0	18.4
Coverage Ratio 33	2.7	4.0	11.8	8.0	5.9	3.4	3.9	3.7	5.5	2.6	•	2.4	2.2
Total Asset Turnover 34	0.8	•	4.6	5.1	1.9	1.7	1.8	1.5	1.6	1.1	•	1.0	0.6
Inventory Turnover 35	59.9	•	250.8	8839.8	28.7	30.9	33.5	21.4	24.8	11.4	•	142.9	60.6
Receivables Turnover 36	7.4	•	149.1	16.6	8.3	11.9	8.5	7.9	7.0	6.5	•	7.9	12.5
Total Liabilities to Net Worth 37	1.8	•	11.7	•	4.3	18.0	4.8	2.6	3.3	6.1	•	6.9	1.2
Current Assets to Working Capital 38	5.0	•	4.6	•	2.5	•	6.5	3.6	9.4	3.0	•	6.3	4.9
Current Liabilities to Working Capital 39	4.0	•	3.6	•	1.5	•	5.5	2.6	8.4	2.0	•	5.3	3.9
Working Capital to Net Sales 40	0.0	•	0.0	•	0.1	•	0.0	0.1	0.0	0.1	•	0.0	0.1
Inventory to Working Capital 41	0.1	•	0.0	•	0.0	•	0.1	0.1	0.2	0.1	•	0.1	0.0
Total Receipts to Cash Flow 42	3.7	1.7	3.0	2.9	3.3	4.0	3.2	3.1	3.6	3.3	•	3.6	4.1
Cost of Goods to Cash Flow 43	0.5	0.0	0.2	0.1	0.2	0.2	0.5	0.2	0.4	0.2	•	1.0	0.5
Cash Flow to Total Debt 44	0.3	•	1.7	1.1	0.7	0.4	0.7	0.7	0.6	0.4	•	0.3	0.3

Selected Financial Factors (in Percentages)

	1	2	3	4	5	6	7	8	9	10	11	12	13
Debt Ratio 45	64.2	•	92.1	161.0	81.0	94.8	82.7	71.9	76.6	86.0	•	87.3	55.3
Return on Total Assets 46	6.9	•	49.6	39.7	16.6	14.8	11.3	10.0	12.1	8.8	•	7.6	5.0
Return on Equity Before Income Taxes 47	12.0	•	577.7	•	72.9	199.1	48.8	25.8	42.2	38.4	•	34.6	6.1
Return on Equity After Income Taxes 48	9.6	•	575.8	•	71.3	190.1	45.0	22.7	32.8	28.7	•	26.6	4.4
Profit Margin (Before Income Tax) 49	5.3	18.6	9.8	6.9	7.2	6.3	4.7	4.9	6.1	5.0	•	4.5	4.8
Profit Margin (After Income Tax) 50	4.3	16.9	9.8	6.7	6.0	4.4	4.3	4.4	4.8	3.8	•	3.5	3.4

Table I

Corporations with and without Net Income

OTHER ARTS, ENTERTAINMENT, AND RECREATION

MONEY AMOUNTS AND SIZE OF ASSETS IN THOUSANDS OF DOLLARS

Item Description for Accounting Period 7/03 Through 6/04	Total	Zero Assets	Under 500	500 to 1,000	1,000 to 5,000	5,000 to 10,000	10,000 to 25,000	25,000 to 50,000	50,000 to 100,000	100,000 to 250,000	250,000 to 500,000	500,000 to 2,500,000	2,500,000 and over
Number of Enterprises **1**	57648	7765	47073	1500	1042	74	97	38	19	28	6	6	•
Revenues ($ in Thousands)													
Net Sales **2**	29072306	451777	8783879	2602106	4687217	1082325	1612365	1098273	848001	3741836	1749609	2414919	
Interest **3**	88341	233	3744	440	2495	643	7455	3351	3387	32437	15817	18339	
Rents **4**	88191	3549	4167	2465	986	248	3014	1238	3426	24401	91	44604	
Royalties **5**	82045	842	164	0	11145	5068	14149	0	104	22306	24067	4201	
Other Portfolio Income **6**	154002	45721	4508	5322	3434	10439	23158	23842	4256	19432	5835	8059	
Other Receipts **7**	1802006	-58204	327219	14948	148460	14490	107430	180610	190885	859805	20361	-4003	
Total Receipts **8**	31286891	443918	9123681	2625281	4853737	1113213	1767571	1307314	1050059	4700217	1815780	2486119	
Average Total Receipts **9**	543	57	194	1750	4658	15043	18222	34403	55266	167865	302630	414353	
Operating Costs/Operating Income (%)													
Cost of Operations **10**	17.3	6.4	10.7	26.5	12.1	10.0	35.3	19.9	3.2	26.3	26.8	17.5	
Salaries and Wages **11**	17.6	4.5	11.9	17.4	10.8	12.0	13.5	40.8	57.3	33.8	11.7	14.5	
Taxes Paid **12**	3.0	3.5	3.1	1.9	2.0	1.8	3.1	3.8	4.9	4.0	2.8	3.2	
Interest Paid **13**	1.4	1.3	0.6	0.7	0.2	0.5	1.1	2.0	2.6	2.6	1.9	5.2	
Depreciation **14**	4.2	12.6	2.3	4.2	3.2	1.1	5.7	5.2	3.5	4.1	5.0	11.0	
Amortization and Depletion **15**	1.0	0.0	0.3	0.1	0.0	0.1	2.0	1.0	2.1	3.7	0.6	2.3	
Pensions and Other Deferred Comp. **16**	1.8	0.1	2.8	3.2	1.0	0.1	0.4	0.8	1.2	2.0	0.9	0.7	
Employee Benefits **17**	1.0	0.7	0.7	0.3	0.3	0.1	1.1	1.3	2.2	2.4	1.5	1.7	
Advertising **18**	1.7	1.9	1.2	2.8	0.9	0.8	2.3	1.8	2.3	1.8	2.1	3.3	
Other Expenses **19**	36.5	77.6	40.4	30.0	21.8	58.5	34.0	41.4	34.8	36.0	45.3	34.6	
Officers' Compensation **20**	17.6	10.0	27.1	7.3	41.9	9.2	8.2	4.7	8.2	3.4	1.7	1.5	
Operating Margin **21**	•	•	•	5.6	5.8	5.7	•	•	•	•	•	4.5	
Operating Margin Before Officers' Comp. **22**	14.6	•	26.0	12.9	47.7	14.9	1.4	•	•	1.3	•	6.0	

Selected Average Balance Sheet ($ in Thousands)

Net Receivables 23	32	0	2	46	160	1754	3028	2962	9154	16153	27213	32753
Inventories 24	8	0	3	25	127	44	276	421	718	1814	539	4162
Net Property, Plant and Equipment 25	129	0	9	233	629	1665	4249	7774	14951	38825	153635	477006
Total Assets 26	389	0	50	634	2105	6829	15767	34579	69943	150837	372448	968010
Notes and Loans Payable 27	187	0	49	231	2066	3149	6591	9347	31371	53236	78016	368301
All Other Liabilities 28	129	0	19	123	368	2786	4713	13780	35636	54574	173312	260783
Net Worth 29	72	0	-18	281	-329	895	4463	11451	2936	43027	121120	338926

Selected Financial Ratios (Times to 1)

Current Ratio 30	1.2	•	1.5	1.7	2.2	1.4	1.7	1.4	1.1	1.1	0.9	0.7
Quick Ratio 31	0.9	•	1.1	1.4	1.6	1.2	1.2	1.0	0.9	0.7	0.8	0.6
Net Sales to Working Capital 32	18.3	•	16.0	15.0	7.6	13.1	5.5	7.5	17.5	32.4	•	2.5
Coverage Ratio 33	4.3	•	5.8	10.6	60.3	17.4	3.6	•	1.6	3.1	2.7	2.5
Total Asset Turnover 34	1.3	•	3.8	2.7	2.1	2.1	1.1	0.8	0.6	0.9	0.8	0.4
Inventory Turnover 35	10.6	•	5.7	18.2	4.3	33.6	21.3	13.7	2.0	19.4	144.9	16.9
Receivables Turnover 36	16.0	•	117.2	51.5	33.5	11.2	5.4	6.6	4.2	8.1	10.9	14.6
Total Liabilities to Net Worth 37	4.4	•	1.3	•	6.6	3.4	2.5	2.0	22.8	2.5	2.1	1.9
Current Assets to Working Capital 38	5.2	•	2.9	2.5	1.9	3.4	2.5	3.5	8.9	12.4	•	•
Current Liabilities to Working Capital 39	4.2	•	1.9	1.5	0.9	2.4	1.5	2.5	7.9	11.4	•	•
Working Capital to Net Sales 40	0.1	•	0.1	0.1	0.1	0.1	0.2	0.1	0.1	0.0	•	•
Inventory to Working Capital 41	0.3	•	0.3	0.3	0.0	0.0	0.1	0.1	0.1	0.2	•	•
Total Receipts to Cash Flow 42	2.7	2.4	2.6	3.3	3.4	1.5	3.0	3.1	3.3	2.7	2.2	2.7
Cost of Goods to Cash Flow 43	0.5	0.2	0.3	0.9	0.4	0.2	1.1	0.6	0.7	0.6	0.5	0.5
Cash Flow to Total Debt 44	0.6	•	1.1	0.5	1.5	1.6	0.5	0.4	0.2	0.5	0.5	0.2

Selected Financial Factors (in Percentages)

Debt Ratio 45	81.4	•	136.7	55.7	115.6	86.9	71.7	66.9	95.8	71.5	67.5	65.0
Return on Total Assets 46	7.7	•	12.9	19.6	20.3	19.4	4.1	2.7	7.2	•	4.2	5.3
Return on Equity Before Income Taxes 47	31.6	•	40.1	•	139.2	10.5	23.8	•	•	17.1	8.1	8.9
Return on Equity After Income Taxes 48	27.5	•	39.8	•	131.9	9.4	19.0	•	•	13.1	3.4	6.8
Profit Margin (Before Income Tax) 49	4.5	2.8	6.5	9.3	8.5	2.8	1.6	•	•	5.5	3.4	7.5
Profit Margin (After Income Tax) 50	3.9	2.7	6.4	9.3	8.1	2.5	1.3	•	•	4.2	1.4	5.7

Table II
Corporations with Net Income

OTHER ARTS, ENTERTAINMENT, AND RECREATION

MONEY AMOUNTS AND SIZE OF ASSETS IN THOUSANDS OF DOLLARS

Item Description for Accounting Period 7/03 Through 6/04	Total	Zero Assets	Under 500	500 to 1,000	1,000 to 5,000	5,000 to 10,000	10,000 to 25,000	25,000 to 50,000	50,000 to 100,000	100,000 to 250,000	250,000 to 500,000	500,000 to 2,500,000	2,500,000 and over
Number of Enterprises 1	27251	3598	22025	798	689	35	52	17	11	17	•	•	•
Revenues ($ in Thousands)													
Net Sales 2	21006993	342407	5453906	1884592	3967282	1040301	1206316	639220	662673	2407377	•	•	•
Interest 3	63110	223	1206	251	1772	452	1914	1333	2324	21172	•	•	•
Rents 4	60764	0	1090	1935	423	0	2940	825	3426	24401	•	•	•
Royalties 5	56876	0	164	0	0	5068	1136	0	0	22241	•	•	•
Other Portfolio Income 6	104621	40734	1905	2751	1425	9812	17784	5269	922	16229	•	•	•
Other Receipts 7	1332188	13400	261310	16782	148205	17343	93960	96367	102975	569904	•	•	•
Total Receipts 8	22624552	396764	5719581	1906311	4119107	1072976	1324050	743014	772320	3061324	•	•	•
Average Total Receipts 9	830	110	260	2389	5978	30656	25462	43707	70211	180078	•	•	•
Operating Costs/Operating Income (%)													
Cost of Operations 10	14.1	8.2	7.7	19.1	9.0	9.2	36.2	28.2	3.9	23.9	•	•	•
Salaries and Wages 11	16.5	0.3	12.3	20.3	10.7	11.7	12.4	24.4	47.2	33.1	•	•	•
Taxes Paid 12	2.8	3.3	3.2	2.1	1.8	1.6	2.9	2.8	5.1	3.6	•	•	•
Interest Paid 13	1.1	0.2	0.3	0.2	0.1	0.1	0.6	1.9	1.4	2.5	•	•	•
Depreciation 14	3.3	4.8	1.4	2.9	2.2	0.5	2.3	2.8	2.7	4.3	•	•	•
Amortization and Depletion 15	0.9	0.0	0.0	0.0	0.0	0.0	2.5	0.6	0.3	3.5	•	•	•
Pensions and Other Deferred Comp. 16	1.7	•	2.8	3.5	1.2	0.1	0.4	0.6	1.2	1.5	•	•	•
Employee Benefits 17	0.9	•	0.5	0.4	0.3	0.1	1.1	1.1	2.1	2.7	•	•	•
Advertising 18	1.4	2.1	0.7	3.1	0.4	0.7	1.7	1.4	2.1	1.4	•	•	•
Other Expenses 19	32.0	60.6	35.1	26.9	13.2	57.8	23.6	20.3	29.8	36.5	•	•	•
Officers' Compensation 20	19.1	2.0	27.1	8.5	48.9	9.3	9.9	4.1	10.4	2.6	•	•	•
Operating Margin 21	6.1	18.6	8.7	12.9	12.1	8.8	6.3	11.8	•	•	•	•	•
Operating Margin Before Officers' Comp. 22	25.2	20.6	35.9	21.4	61.0	18.1	16.2	15.9	4.2	•	•	•	•

Selected Average Balance Sheet ($ in Thousands)

Net Receivables 23	37	0	2	7	186	1383	1952	3661	13958	8628
Inventories 24	5	0	1	31	6	46	223	596	870	1006
Net Property, Plant and Equipment 25	171	0	10	256	375	660	4549	4533	15523	40671
Total Assets 26	523	0	47	683	1950	6641	15398	32848	71386	152719
Notes and Loans Payable 27	174	0	38	253	181	673	4159	5982	30359	45276
All Other Liabilities 28	156	0	17	43	260	3349	4376	8391	27895	49610
Net Worth 29	192	0	-8	388	1509	2620	6864	18475	13132	57833

Selected Financial Ratios (Times to 1)

Current Ratio 30	1.4	•	2.3	3.7	4.6	1.3	1.4	2.1	1.3	1.3
Quick Ratio 31	1.1	•	1.8	3.0	4.3	1.2	1.0	1.8	1.1	0.6
Net Sales to Working Capital 32	13.1	•	13.1	9.0	6.7	27.0	11.7	4.5	7.2	13.1
Coverage Ratio 33	13.1	213.5	49.9	71.1	131.2	164.9	26.3	15.8	8.4	5.6
Total Asset Turnover 34	1.5	•	5.3	3.5	3.0	4.5	1.5	1.1	0.8	0.9
Inventory Turnover 35	22.8	•	17.5	14.7	93.1	59.7	37.7	17.8	2.7	33.7
Receivables Turnover 36	21.4	•	160.5	126.0	62.0	33.5	13.6	8.2	5.2	11.3
Total Liabilities to Net Worth 37	1.7	•	0.8	1.4	1.3	1.5	1.2	0.8	4.4	1.6
Current Assets to Working Capital 38	3.4	•	1.8	1.4	1.3	4.4	3.3	1.9	4.0	4.6
Current Liabilities to Working Capital 39	2.4	•	0.8	0.4	0.3	3.4	2.3	0.9	3.0	3.6
Working Capital to Net Sales 40	0.1	•	0.1	0.1	0.1	0.0	0.1	0.2	0.1	0.1
Inventory to Working Capital 41	0.1	•	0.0	0.1	0.0	0.0	0.1	0.1	0.1	0.1
Total Receipts to Cash Flow 42	2.4	1.2	2.2	2.8	3.6	1.5	2.7	2.3	2.8	2.3
Cost of Goods to Cash Flow 43	0.3	0.1	0.2	0.5	0.3	0.1	1.0	0.6	0.1	0.5
Cash Flow to Total Debt 44	1.0	•	2.0	2.9	3.6	5.0	1.0	1.2	0.4	0.7

Selected Financial Factors (in Percentages)

Debt Ratio 45	63.2	•	117.4	43.3	22.6	60.6	55.4	43.8	81.6	62.1
Return on Total Assets 46	22.0	•	73.9	49.2	47.3	53.8	25.0	34.3	9.9	12.8
Return on Equity Before Income Taxes 47	55.3	•	•	85.5	60.7	135.5	54.0	57.0	47.5	27.7
Return on Equity After Income Taxes 48	52.0	•	•	85.2	60.6	130.2	52.6	52.3	45.7	22.7
Profit Margin (Before Income Tax) 49	13.8	34.4	13.6	14.0	15.9	11.9	16.0	28.0	10.4	11.3
Profit Margin (After Income Tax) 50	13.0	31.7	13.5	14.0	15.9	11.5	15.6	25.7	10.0	9.3

Table I

Corporations with and without Net Income

AMUSEMENT, GAMBLING, AND RECREATION INDUSTRIES

MONEY AMOUNTS AND SIZE OF ASSETS IN THOUSANDS OF DOLLARS

Item Description for Accounting Period 7/03 Through 6/04	Total	Zero Assets	Under 500	500 to 1,000	1,000 to 5,000	5,000 to 10,000	10,000 to 25,000	25,000 to 50,000	50,000 to 100,000	100,000 to 250,000	250,000 to 500,000	500,000 to 2,500,000	2,500,000 and over
Number of Enterprises **1**	52471	6611	37070	3709	4137	468	302	107	25	24	5	13	•
Revenues ($ in Thousands)													
Net Sales **2**	40805321	900851	8485505	3653038	7664138	2768018	2701341	1804032	1004663	1998015	1044702	8781019	•
Interest **3**	655400	10268	4827	3693	10789	3276	7616	6030	3114	11333	10767	583687	•
Rents **4**	124462	1464	7406	3569	13943	19583	9659	9794	7094	6642	6820	38489	•
Royalties **5**	71365	0	0	0	5406	778	2817	44	260	5923	377	55760	•
Other Portfolio Income **6**	326573	31225	106204	8695	45414	2130	35266	34804	2410	4579	3881	51966	•
Other Receipts **7**	3585070	3080	141243	691909	338822	197363	207730	147720	272422	175252	62848	1346678	•
Total Receipts **8**	45568191	946888	8745185	4360904	8078512	2991148	2964429	2002424	1289963	2201744	1129395	10857599	•
Average Total Receipts **9**	868	143	236	1176	1953	6391	9816	18714	51599	91739	225879	835200	•
Operating Costs/Operating Income (%)													
Cost of Operations **10**	22.1	51.8	19.4	25.6	25.4	24.2	33.4	20.2	20.9	24.0	5.6	15.1	•
Salaries and Wages **11**	23.1	31.3	18.9	16.5	21.1	26.5	22.8	27.4	34.1	23.8	29.9	26.7	•
Taxes Paid **12**	7.3	10.8	5.3	5.4	6.7	5.6	6.2	7.5	14.5	9.2	7.3	9.7	•
Interest Paid **13**	5.8	4.0	1.8	2.0	3.9	3.3	3.8	3.3	2.8	6.5	9.5	14.9	•
Depreciation **14**	8.5	3.3	6.0	7.8	7.7	8.7	8.7	11.1	8.0	10.9	11.2	10.7	•
Amortization and Depletion **15**	0.7	1.5	0.4	0.6	0.4	0.2	0.8	0.5	0.9	1.2	1.7	1.4	•
Pensions and Other Deferred Comp. **16**	0.3	•	0.2	0.5	0.2	0.9	0.3	0.4	0.5	0.3	0.4	0.2	•
Employee Benefits **17**	1.7	0.4	0.4	1.0	1.6	1.8	2.1	1.9	2.0	2.0	1.5	3.3	•
Advertising **18**	2.9	1.4	2.7	2.6	1.8	4.0	2.4	2.8	5.8	3.1	3.8	3.5	•
Other Expenses **19**	36.1	21.0	41.9	42.9	33.0	26.0	27.7	32.4	32.6	30.2	35.1	40.4	•
Officers' Compensation **20**	3.4	2.9	7.6	5.4	3.1	2.6	1.9	1.4	1.3	1.1	3.8	0.7	•
Operating Margin **21**	•	•	•	•	•	•	•	•	•	•	•	•	•
Operating Margin Before Officers' Comp. **22**	•	•	3.0	•	•	•	•	•	•	•	•	•	•

Selected Average Balance Sheet ($ in Thousands)

Net Receivables 23	80	0	1	25	110	656	780	1632	2313	7634	5053	202181	•
Inventories 24	25	0	6	20	64	412	363	498	623	2612	6079	20866	•
Net Property, Plant and Equipment 25	559	0	58	480	1322	5081	9124	22863	44009	78972	239492	627308	•
Total Assets 26	1081	0	101	714	2098	7424	15204	35694	70162	148222	365710	1742107	•
Notes and Loans Payable 27	606	0	108	348	1399	3952	6851	14054	26380	64662	215565	922295	•
All Other Liabilities 28	214	0	25	65	275	1565	2617	6354	14131	35995	62590	401414	•
Net Worth 29	261	-32	301	423	1906	5736	15285	29651	47566	87555	418399		•

Selected Financial Ratios (Times to 1)

Current Ratio 30	1.2	•	1.1	1.6	1.2	0.9	1.2	0.8	0.6	1.2	0.3	1.5	•
Quick Ratio 31	0.9	•	0.7	1.2	0.8	0.7	0.7	0.6	0.5	1.0	0.1	1.2	•
Net Sales to Working Capital 32	20.6	•	100.9	14.1	22.7	•	20.5	•	•	15.0	•	4.5	•
Coverage Ratio 33	1.0	•	0.1	5.5	1.1	2.2	0.9	1.7	2.8	0.7	0.8	0.8	•
Total Asset Turnover 34	0.7	•	2.3	1.4	0.9	0.8	0.6	0.5	0.6	0.6	0.6	0.4	•
Inventory Turnover 35	6.9	•	7.3	12.4	7.3	3.5	8.2	6.8	13.4	7.6	1.9	4.9	•
Receivables Turnover 36	10.5	•	86.5	28.6	16.9	9.9	12.7	10.9	17.2	10.5	19.1	3.9	•
Total Liabilities to Net Worth 37	3.1	•	•	1.4	4.0	2.9	1.7	1.3	1.4	2.1	3.2	3.2	•
Current Assets to Working Capital 38	6.5	•	13.9	2.6	5.7	•	7.6	•	•	5.2	•	2.8	•
Current Liabilities to Working Capital 39	5.5	•	12.9	1.6	4.7	•	6.6	•	•	4.2	•	1.8	•
Working Capital to Net Sales 40	0.0	•	0.0	0.1	0.0	•	0.0	•	•	0.1	•	0.2	•
Inventory to Working Capital 41	0.6	•	2.3	0.2	0.7	•	1.0	•	•	0.4	•	0.2	•
Total Receipts to Cash Flow 42	4.2	•	4.2	2.6	4.7	4.4	5.4	3.8	3.4	4.9	4.4	4.1	•
Cost of Goods to Cash Flow 43	0.9	•	0.8	0.7	1.2	1.1	1.8	0.8	0.7	1.2	0.2	0.6	•
Cash Flow to Total Debt 44	0.2	•	0.4	0.9	0.2	0.2	0.2	0.2	0.3	0.2	0.2	0.1	•

Selected Financial Factors (in Percentages)

Debt Ratio 45	75.9	•	132.0	57.8	79.8	74.3	62.3	57.2	57.7	67.9	76.1	76.0	•
Return on Total Assets 46	4.0	•	0.4	15.5	3.9	5.8	2.0	2.6	4.5	2.6	4.4	4.6	•
Return on Equity Before Income Taxes 47	•	•	11.2	30.0	2.3	12.4	•	2.4	6.8	•	•	•	•
Return on Equity After Income Taxes 48	•	•	12.4	29.8	1.8	12.1	•	1.4	6.3	•	•	•	•
Profit Margin (Before Income Tax) 49	•	•	•	9.2	0.5	4.0	•	2.2	5.1	•	•	•	•
Profit Margin (After Income Tax) 50	•	•	•	9.1	0.4	3.9	•	1.3	4.6	•	•	•	•

Table II
Corporations with Net Income

AMUSEMENT, GAMBLING, AND RECREATION INDUSTRIES

MONEY AMOUNTS AND SIZE OF ASSETS IN THOUSANDS OF DOLLARS

Item Description for Accounting Period 7/03 Through 6/04	Total	Zero Assets	Under 500	500 to 1,000	1,000 to 5,000	5,000 to 10,000	10,000 to 25,000	25,000 to 50,000	50,000 to 100,000	100,000 to 250,000	250,000 to 500,000	500,000 to 2,500,000	2,500,000 and over
Number of Enterprises **1**	22786	1989	16044	2117	2321	136	110	40	13	10	·	·	6
Revenues ($ in Thousands)													
Net Sales **2**	22459992	190216	4651902	2707755	4784746	1757691	1511769	983230	606928	1036677	·	·	4229078
Interest **3**	240904	365	3197	2830	5199	1531	2426	4116	2790	2861	·	·	215589
Rents **4**	69168	192	4	2030	11257	14475	3207	6204	6697	7153	·	·	17949
Royalties **5**	64570	0	0	0	5289	0	2629	1	260	4649	·	·	51743
Other Portfolio Income **6**	260036	31210	96668	957	43420	2020	28759	30871	2408	2880	·	·	20842
Other Receipts **7**	1906931	1614	80821	677431	205760	96149	123222	91516	250365	59423	·	·	320630
Total Receipts **8**	25001601	223597	4832592	3391003	5055671	1871866	1672012	1115938	869448	1113643	·	·	4855831
Average Total Receipts **9**	1097	112	301	1602	2178	13764	15200	27898	66881	111364	·	·	809305
Operating Costs/Operating Income (%)													
Cost of Operations **10**	24.8	28.4	22.4	29.8	25.1	22.5	37.4	13.6	28.0	28.4	·	·	21.4
Salaries and Wages **11**	19.2	16.1	14.7	16.6	20.4	25.3	19.8	27.7	37.5	16.9	·	·	17.6
Taxes Paid **12**	7.4	11.2	5.0	5.8	5.5	5.8	6.2	8.8	13.2	9.7	·	·	12.4
Interest Paid **13**	3.8	3.1	0.9	1.0	3.5	1.1	2.1	2.0	1.5	3.4	·	·	11.6
Depreciation **14**	6.7	3.0	2.8	6.6	6.6	6.6	5.5	7.3	6.6	8.5	·	·	11.2
Amortization and Depletion **15**	0.5	0.0	0.5	0.2	0.3	0.1	0.3	0.6	0.1	0.6	·	·	1.3
Pensions and Other Deferred Comp. **16**	0.4	·	0.2	0.6	0.2	0.9	0.3	0.5	0.8	0.4	·	·	0.2
Employee Benefits **17**	1.4	0.5	0.3	0.8	1.4	1.8	1.8	2.1	1.5	2.2	·	·	2.6
Advertising **18**	2.4	1.3	2.6	2.2	1.7	4.3	2.0	3.6	7.1	1.9	·	·	1.5
Other Expenses **19**	30.1	28.6	34.7	39.7	28.6	24.1	21.9	26.2	29.7	22.0	·	·	28.9
Officers' Compensation **20**	3.9	13.4	8.8	6.3	2.8	1.3	2.1	1.6	1.3	1.3	·	·	0.8
Operating Margin **21**	·	·	7.0	·	3.8	6.3	0.6	6.0	·	4.7	·	·	·
Operating Margin Before Officers' Comp. **22**	3.4	7.8	15.8	·	6.6	7.6	2.7	7.6	6.1	6.1	·	·	·

Selected Average Balance Sheet ($ in Thousands)

Net Receivables 23	94	0	2	19	79	210	1009	2448	3433	10133	•	252561	•
Inventories 24	35	0	8	28	75	1230	385	411	508	2354	•	23868	•
Net Property, Plant and Equipment 25	470	0	37	454	1171	5875	7294	21506	35064	72242	•	464005	•
Total Assets 26	1096	0	91	778	2009	7677	15007	36195	70802	143918	•	1784046	•
Notes and Loans Payable 27	519	0	50	253	1193	2436	5378	9980	17383	37826	•	962928	•
All Other Liabilities 28	176	0	13	82	240	1751	2732	6233	15744	31635	•	291514	•
Net Worth 29	402	0	27	443	576	3491	6897	19982	37675	74458	•	529605	•

Selected Financial Ratios (Times to 1)

Current Ratio 30	1.4	•	1.7	1.8	1.4	0.5	1.5	1.5	0.7	1.8	•	1.5	•
Quick Ratio 31	1.0	•	1.2	1.4	0.8	0.4	1.0	1.2	0.6	1.3	•	1.1	•
Net Sales to Working Capital 32	11.1	•	17.1	11.4	13.9	•	10.0	8.3	•	8.3	•	4.3	•
Coverage Ratio 33	3.9	4.9	13.2	16.8	3.7	13.0	6.4	10.9	11.5	4.6	•	1.5	•
Total Asset Turnover 34	0.9	•	3.2	1.6	1.0	1.7	0.9	0.7	0.7	0.7	•	0.4	•
Inventory Turnover 35	7.1	•	8.6	13.7	6.9	2.4	13.3	8.2	25.7	12.5	•	6.3	•
Receivables Turnover 36	11.7	•	184.7	52.3	52.5	33.4	16.4	10.3	18.2	12.4	•	3.6	•
Total Liabilities to Net Worth 37	1.7	•	2.4	0.8	2.5	1.2	1.2	0.8	0.9	0.9	•	2.4	•
Current Assets to Working Capital 38	3.4	•	2.4	2.2	3.7	•	3.1	3.0	•	2.3	•	3.1	•
Current Liabilities to Working Capital 39	2.4	•	1.4	1.2	2.7	•	2.1	2.0	•	1.3	•	2.1	•
Working Capital to Net Sales 40	0.1	•	0.1	0.1	0.1	•	0.1	0.1	•	0.1	•	0.2	•
Inventory to Working Capital 41	0.3	•	0.4	0.2	0.5	•	0.3	0.1	•	0.2	•	0.2	•
Total Receipts to Cash Flow 42	3.3	3.1	3.2	2.4	3.6	3.4	4.0	2.7	2.4	3.3	•	3.9	•
Cost of Goods to Cash Flow 43	0.8	0.9	0.7	0.7	0.9	0.8	1.5	0.4	0.7	0.9	•	0.8	•
Cash Flow to Total Debt 44	0.4	•	1.4	1.6	0.4	0.9	0.4	0.6	0.6	0.4	•	0.1	•

Selected Financial Factors (in Percentages)

Debt Ratio 45	63.4	•	70.4	43.1	71.3	54.5	54.0	44.8	46.8	48.3	•	70.3	•
Return on Total Assets 46	13.2	•	37.7	27.2	13.3	23.2	12.1	14.6	11.6	11.2	•	6.7	•
Return on Equity Before Income Taxes 47	26.7	•	117.5	44.9	33.9	47.1	22.2	24.0	19.8	16.9	•	7.2	•
Return on Equity After Income Taxes 48	25.3	•	114.2	44.6	33.4	46.6	21.3	21.9	19.0	13.1	•	5.8	•
Profit Margin (Before Income Tax) 49	10.9	12.0	10.9	15.5	9.5	12.7	11.1	19.5	16.0	12.2	•	5.4	•
Profit Margin (After Income Tax) 50	10.3	12.0	10.6	15.4	9.3	12.6	10.7	17.8	15.3	9.4	•	4.4	•

Table I

Corporations with and without Net Income

ACCOMMODATION

MONEY AMOUNTS AND SIZE OF ASSETS IN THOUSANDS OF DOLLARS

Item Description for Accounting Period 7/03 Through 6/04		Total	Zero Assets	Under 500	500 to 1,000	1,000 to 5,000	5,000 to 10,000	10,000 to 25,000	25,000 to 50,000	50,000 to 100,000	100,000 to 250,000	250,000 to 500,000	500,000 to 2,500,000	2,500,000 and over
Number of Enterprises	1	35808	3069	20720	2909	7858	617	348	114	61	43	31	23	14
Revenues ($ in Thousands)														
Net Sales	2	106543539	1433937	4365802	1219293	7426682	2317735	3197590	2716306	2502884	7111477	3878785	15566263	54803784
Interest	3	1991618	38699	4492	2305	15586	3640	14712	16965	24679	32756	117782	233909	1486094
Rents	4	814967	7852	1333	1331	8744	3620	14776	3589	13616	37995	14981	102345	604787
Royalties	5	1321788	87928	0	0	0	0	277	0	5	1987	151917	24434	1055239
Other Portfolio Income	6	715110	21149	23710	30380	53196	16195	21796	31587	20902	88871	21590	64868	320867
Other Receipts	7	7038310	287915	77779	62721	192648	170296	193566	148497	134965	256663	146947	627737	4738575
Total Receipts	8	118425332	1877480	4473116	1316030	7696856	2511486	3442717	2916944	2697051	7532749	4332002	16619556	63009346
Average Total Receipts	9	3307	612	216	452	979	4070	9893	25587	44214	175180	139742	722589	4500668
Operating Costs/Operating Income (%)														
Cost of Operations	10	41.9	9.5	21.6	3.9	16.1	30.1	21.9	20.3	25.8	46.7	24.0	42.9	52.5
Salaries and Wages	11	18.2	30.7	16.3	19.8	17.2	17.5	19.7	19.3	21.3	11.5	17.8	15.2	19.7
Taxes Paid	12	6.2	12.7	6.6	9.1	7.3	6.0	5.7	5.6	5.7	3.5	5.7	10.0	5.1
Interest Paid	13	6.2	6.5	2.1	6.8	10.2	6.9	5.6	4.9	5.3	3.6	5.5	6.1	6.5
Depreciation	14	5.5	7.5	4.6	9.3	9.1	7.7	8.0	6.4	8.3	4.4	8.1	6.1	4.2
Amortization and Depletion	15	0.6	1.5	0.2	0.9	0.8	0.8	0.4	0.6	0.5	0.9	0.8	0.8	0.5
Pensions and Other Deferred Comp.	16	0.4	1.0	0.2	•	0.1	0.0	0.2	0.2	0.2	0.2	0.8	0.2	0.6
Employee Benefits	17	2.0	2.1	0.5	0.3	0.9	1.6	2.0	2.9	2.0	1.3	2.5	1.6	2.5
Advertising	18	2.4	4.6	1.7	3.1	2.6	2.0	3.2	2.8	2.6	1.8	4.6	1.9	2.3
Other Expenses	19	26.8	56.8	45.8	55.0	36.4	34.4	43.9	47.5	40.1	34.6	43.9	20.8	19.0
Officers' Compensation	20	1.0	1.6	4.2	1.7	3.2	2.0	1.2	0.9	0.9	0.6	1.2	0.4	0.6
Operating Margin	21	•	•	•	•	•	•	•	•	•	•	•	•	•
Operating Margin Before Officers' Comp.	22	•	•	0.4	•	•	•	•	•	•	•	•	•	•

Selected Average Balance Sheet ($ in Thousands)

Net Receivables 23	201	0	7	26	30	283	926	1290	3852	8771	45490	29951	242962
Inventories 24	68	0	2	8	13	37	177	269	778	1940	4962	16056	106317
Net Property, Plant and Equipment 25	2377	0	96	541	1653	4874	9515	22825	42658	96164	153564	603825	2446970
Total Assets 26	5313	0	140	718	2198	6462	15022	35135	68057	163975	336546	1170739	7584451
Notes and Loans Payable 27	2614	0	103	809	1955	4522	9996	23750	36302	82383	144545	514413	3049155
All Other Liabilities 28	1037	0	18	55	154	488	2262	5106	9413	37904	76338	193459	1763241
Net Worth 29	1662	0	19	-147	89	1452	2764	6279	22342	43687	115662	462867	2772056

Selected Financial Ratios (Times to 1)

Current Ratio 30	1.1	•	1.0	0.7	1.1	1.4	1.1	0.9	1.3	0.9	1.4	1.5	1.0
Quick Ratio 31	0.7	•	0.8	0.6	0.6	1.0	0.8	0.6	0.6	0.6	0.9	0.9	0.6
Net Sales to Working Capital 32	44.7	•	203.4	•	43.3	14.5	33.1	•	10.3	•	4.4	10.6	•
Coverage Ratio 33	1.0	0.4	0.4	0.7	1.0	0.9	0.2	0.2	0.1	0.1	0.4	1.1	1.3
Total Asset Turnover 34	0.6	•	1.5	0.6	0.4	0.6	0.6	0.7	0.6	1.0	0.4	0.6	0.5
Inventory Turnover 35	18.4	•	22.0	2.1	11.4	30.5	11.4	18.0	13.6	39.8	6.0	18.1	19.3
Receivables Turnover 36	14.3	•	40.7	17.5	25.7	15.4	10.4	21.5	10.3	15.0	4.1	18.3	14.0
Total Liabilities to Net Worth 37	2.2	•	6.6	•	23.8	3.4	4.4	4.6	2.0	2.8	1.9	1.5	1.7
Current Assets to Working Capital 38	10.5	•	26.2	•	11.3	3.6	10.5	•	4.7	•	3.6	2.8	•
Current Liabilities to Working Capital 39	9.5	•	25.2	•	10.3	2.6	9.5	•	3.7	•	2.6	1.8	•
Working Capital to Net Sales 40	0.0	•	0.0	•	0.0	0.1	0.0	•	0.1	•	0.2	0.1	•
Inventory to Working Capital 41	1.1	•	2.0	•	0.6	0.2	0.6	•	0.2	•	0.3	0.4	•
Total Receipts to Cash Flow 42	5.3	2.4	3.7	2.8	3.7	4.4	4.1	3.9	4.5	7.7	4.4	5.9	6.2
Cost of Goods to Cash Flow 43	2.2	0.2	0.8	0.1	0.6	1.3	0.9	0.8	1.2	3.6	1.1	2.5	3.2
Cash Flow to Total Debt 44	0.2	•	0.5	0.2	0.1	0.2	0.2	0.2	0.2	0.2	0.1	0.2	0.1

Selected Financial Factors (in Percentages)

Debt Ratio 45	68.7	•	86.8	120.5	96.0	77.5	81.6	82.1	67.2	73.4	65.6	60.5	63.5
Return on Total Assets 46	3.5	•	1.1	2.8	4.2	3.6	0.9	0.7	0.3	0.4	0.9	3.9	4.2
Return on Equity Before Income Taxes 47	0.3	•	•	5.7	•	•	•	•	•	•	•	1.1	2.4
Return on Equity After Income Taxes 48	•	•	7.3	•	•	•	•	•	•	•	•	0.1	1.4
Profit Margin (Before Income Tax) 49	0.2	•	•	•	•	•	•	•	•	•	•	0.7	1.7
Profit Margin (After Income Tax) 50	•	•	•	•	•	•	•	•	•	•	•	0.1	1.0

383

Table II
Corporations with Net Income

ACCOMMODATION

Money Amounts and Size of Assets in Thousands of Dollars

Item Description for Accounting Period 7/03 Through 6/04		Total	Zero Assets	Under 500	500 to 1,000	1,000 to 5,000	5,000 to 10,000	10,000 to 25,000	25,000 to 50,000	50,000 to 100,000	100,000 to 250,000	250,000 to 500,000	500,000 to 2,500,000	2,500,000 and over
Number of Enterprises	1	16470	743	9772	1353	4067	255	166	47	18	14	14	•	•
Revenues ($ in Thousands)														
Net Sales	2	77418618	1194128	2980470	735685	4472695	790477	1467758	910043	773069	1636675	1822872	•	•
Interest	3	1574095	36224	4188	984	12223	3426	4451	8942	6334	10932	83956	•	•
Rents	4	531681	3403	1333	832	6813	3019	6812	2007	6374	14339	5809	•	•
Royalties	5	1271404	85865	0	0	0	0	0	0	5	0	151917	•	•
Other Portfolio Income	6	536645	17734	21850	30100	45771	11013	15388	27475	7248	27637	17074	•	•
Other Receipts	7	4676175	175905	71064	57335	142351	121691	80463	34304	23922	85831	122190	•	•
Total Receipts	8	86008618	1513259	3078905	824936	4679853	929626	1574872	982771	816952	1775414	2203818	•	•
Average Total Receipts	9	5222	2037	315	610	1151	3646	9487	20910	45386	126815	157416	•	•
Operating Costs/Operating Income (%)														
Cost of Operations	10	48.5	10.1	19.4	4.4	18.1	30.0	18.0	16.0	20.9	24.3	15.0	•	•
Salaries and Wages	11	16.5	30.6	16.0	17.3	14.4	18.2	21.7	27.1	24.1	19.7	24.8	•	•
Taxes Paid	12	5.6	13.5	4.9	7.9	6.7	7.8	6.2	7.1	6.3	5.6	6.1	•	•
Interest Paid	13	5.4	6.4	0.9	5.3	8.3	7.5	5.1	6.6	2.5	4.6	5.9	•	•
Depreciation	14	4.3	7.7	2.9	6.9	7.5	9.9	8.3	7.5	8.7	7.9	8.1	•	•
Amortization and Depletion	15	0.4	1.5	0.2	0.0	0.6	0.3	0.3	0.3	0.3	0.7	1.2	•	•
Pensions and Other Deferred Comp.	16	0.5	1.2	0.2	•	0.1	0.1	0.2	0.2	0.3	0.7	1.1	•	•
Employee Benefits	17	2.0	2.0	0.6	0.2	1.0	2.0	2.3	3.6	2.6	2.2	2.8	•	•
Advertising	18	2.2	4.8	1.5	2.4	1.7	1.2	2.9	2.7	2.0	3.3	3.4	•	•
Other Expenses	19	20.3	37.8	41.7	52.3	30.7	28.2	31.6	27.6	28.3	30.6	38.3	•	•
Officers' Compensation	20	0.9	1.5	5.0	2.0	4.2	2.0	1.6	1.5	0.8	1.4	1.4	•	•
Operating Margin	21	•	6.5	6.5	1.2	6.7	•	1.9	•	3.1	•	•	•	•
Operating Margin Before Officers' Comp.	22	•	•	11.5	3.2	10.9	•	3.5	1.3	4.0	0.6	•	•	•

Selected Average Balance Sheet ($ in Thousands)

	1	2	3	4	5	6	7	8	9	10	11
Net Receivables 23	262	0	4	53	31	76	857	827	4706	7729	60504
Inventories 24	122	0	1	9	13	37	192	318	779	2333	9509
Net Property, Plant and Equipment 25	2878	0	78	495	1561	4810	9614	22928	44596	101317	133890
Total Assets 26	7559	0	149	765	2146	6572	15097	34418	71070	171877	323734
Notes and Loans Payable 27	3297	0	91	658	1566	3740	8843	21268	20241	62673	146311
All Other Liabilities 28	1556	0	11	68	150	356	1426	2592	13214	32376	66853
Net Worth 29	2706	0	48	39	429	2475	4828	10559	37616	76828	110570

Selected Financial Ratios (Times to 1)

	1	2	3	4	5	6	7	8	9	10	11
Current Ratio 30	1.1	•	3.3	0.9	2.2	0.8	1.7	1.2	1.8	1.7	1.5
Quick Ratio 31	0.7	•	2.4	0.7	1.4	0.6	1.3	0.8	1.4	1.3	1.2
Net Sales to Working Capital 32	48.2	•	11.8	•	7.4	•	6.7	27.4	6.2	6.8	3.4
Coverage Ratio 33	1.8	2.5	11.5	3.5	2.4	2.4	2.8	2.2	4.5	2.7	3.2
Total Asset Turnover 34	0.6	•	2.0	0.7	0.5	0.5	0.6	0.6	0.6	0.7	0.4
Inventory Turnover 35	18.8	•	52.1	2.7	14.9	25.2	8.3	9.7	11.5	12.2	2.1
Receivables Turnover 36	20.3	•	81.5	11.3	30.2	21.4	10.5	17.8	9.7	14.8	3.6
Total Liabilities to Net Worth 37	1.8	•	2.1	18.6	4.0	1.7	2.1	2.3	0.9	1.2	1.9
Current Assets to Working Capital 38	8.9	•	1.4	•	1.8	•	2.3	7.0	2.3	2.4	2.8
Current Liabilities to Working Capital 39	7.9	•	0.4	•	0.8	•	1.3	6.0	1.3	1.4	1.8
Working Capital to Net Sales 40	0.0	•	0.1	•	0.1	•	0.1	0.0	0.2	0.1	0.3
Inventory to Working Capital 41	1.4	•	0.1	•	0.1	•	0.1	0.2	0.1	0.1	0.4
Total Receipts to Cash Flow 42	5.0	2.5	2.8	2.3	2.9	3.0	3.1	3.4	3.1	3.3	2.5
Cost of Goods to Cash Flow 43	2.4	0.3	0.5	0.1	0.5	0.9	0.6	0.5	0.6	0.8	0.4
Cash Flow to Total Debt 44	0.2	•	1.1	0.3	0.2	0.3	0.3	0.2	0.4	0.4	0.2

Selected Financial Factors (in Percentages)

	1	2	3	4	5	6	7	8	9	10	11
Debt Ratio 45	64.2	•	68.2	94.9	80.0	62.3	68.0	69.3	47.1	55.3	65.8
Return on Total Assets 46	6.2	•	21.9	13.2	10.0	8.5	8.4	8.1	6.8	8.3	7.5
Return on Equity Before Income Taxes 47	7.8	•	62.7	186.0	29.0	13.1	16.8	14.3	10.1	11.6	15.1
Return on Equity After Income Taxes 48	6.3	•	61.3	172.9	28.1	12.3	15.6	13.2	8.7	8.2	11.8
Profit Margin (Before Income Tax) 49	4.5	9.7	9.8	13.3	11.3	10.5	9.2	7.8	8.8	7.6	12.8
Profit Margin (After Income Tax) 50	3.6	7.0	9.6	12.4	11.0	9.8	8.5	7.2	7.6	5.4	10.0

Table I

Corporations with and without Net Income

FOOD SERVICES AND DRINKING PLACES

MONEY AMOUNTS AND SIZE OF ASSETS IN THOUSANDS OF DOLLARS

Item Description for Accounting Period 7/03 Through 6/04	Total	Zero Assets	Under 500	500 to 1,000	1,000 to 5,000	5,000 to 10,000	10,000 to 25,000	25,000 to 50,000	50,000 to 100,000	100,000 to 250,000	250,000 to 500,000	500,000 to 2,500,000	2,500,000 and over
Number of Enterprises **1**	242914	25702	195370	12567	7989	666	369	100	51	45	20	22	12
Revenues ($ in Thousands)													
Net Sales **2**	275815088	3217430	89984851	24751038	34912890	8155750	10456573	6157522	6710115	11467074	9374063	20540841	50086941
Interest **3**	1314746	4231	15250	8821	7999	8479	9628	5323	25067	20287	42618	238820	928223
Rents **4**	505007	1595	23073	5923	11662	11260	8944	15918	12612	40775	78453	178385	116409
Royalties **5**	3795996	3	99	25778	3958	1478	39229	56716	19427	187943	507579	626580	2327206
Other Portfolio Income **6**	836464	128356	123875	92910	63653	26673	16890	10526	2515	58006	25172	73542	214346
Other Receipts **7**	6415031	72202	572409	266462	556163	241800	237133	97022	46271	226946	260480	973801	2864340
Total Receipts **8**	288682332	3423817	90719557	25150932	35556325	8445440	10768397	6343027	6816007	12001031	10288365	22631969	56537465
Average Total Receipts **9**	1188	133	464	2001	4451	12681	29183	63430	133647	266690	514418	1028726	4711455
Operating Costs/Operating Income (%)													
Cost of Operations **10**	41.4	48.5	41.9	41.0	40.6	39.9	43.7	43.8	40.5	40.1	39.2	41.1	41.1
Salaries and Wages **11**	19.9	11.5	18.0	19.5	19.1	20.9	19.4	18.6	18.4	21.4	24.8	22.3	22.8
Taxes Paid **12**	4.1	4.5	4.4	4.2	3.8	4.0	3.7	3.9	3.7	3.7	4.4	3.9	3.7
Interest Paid **13**	1.9	1.8	0.6	1.2	1.2	1.8	2.0	2.2	2.5	2.5	3.1	3.5	3.8
Depreciation **14**	3.4	3.0	2.0	2.8	3.3	3.0	3.6	3.7	3.4	4.6	4.3	6.3	4.7
Amortization and Depletion **15**	0.5	0.5	0.2	0.3	0.5	0.8	0.7	0.6	0.6	0.7	0.9	0.4	1.2
Pensions and Other Deferred Comp. **16**	0.2	0.0	0.1	0.1	0.0	0.4	0.1	0.2	0.2	0.1	0.3	0.2	0.7
Employee Benefits **17**	1.3	0.3	0.5	0.8	1.0	1.3	1.3	1.4	1.4	1.5	1.8	2.1	2.6
Advertising **18**	2.7	2.3	1.8	3.4	3.3	3.9	3.5	2.5	2.3	3.2	3.3	3.3	2.5
Other Expenses **19**	24.4	36.3	25.2	24.7	23.9	23.4	22.8	24.7	28.5	24.2	23.8	23.1	23.1
Officers' Compensation **20**	2.4	4.9	4.6	2.8	2.2	2.4	1.3	1.2	0.9	0.7	0.6	0.5	0.4
Operating Margin **21**	•	•	0.7	•	1.1	•	•	•	•	•	•	•	•
Operating Margin Before Officers' Comp. **22**	0.3	•	5.3	1.9	3.2	0.6	•	•	•	•	•	•	•

Selected Average Balance Sheet ($ in Thousands)

Net Receivables 23	38	0	5	21	88	292	805	1973	4014	7308	16458	45810	385991
Inventories 24	20	0	7	29	56	353	368	1008	1753	4874	11660	23990	105444
Net Property, Plant and Equipment 25	287	0	52	387	1027	3186	8127	19656	36787	89654	170858	435103	1716121
Total Assets 26	688	0	106	676	1900	6815	15287	34647	67043	157270	350276	835074	6109042
Notes and Loans Payable 27	298	0	77	478	1134	4185	8956	17896.	37663	65022	169063	276174	1665954
All Other Liabilities 28	170	0	21	123	432	1373	3412	5756	18673	40126	85398	207658	1692905
Net Worth 29	221	0	8	75	335	1257	2919	10995	10707	52123	95815	351243	2750182

Selected Financial Ratios (Times to 1)

Current Ratio 30	1.0	•	1.3	0.9	1.0	0.8	0.8	0.8	0.6	0.8	0.8	1.1	0.9
Quick Ratio 31	0.6	•	0.8	0.6	0.7	0.3	0.5	0.5	0.4	0.6	0.4	0.6	0.7
Net Sales to Working Capital 32	•	•	62.7	•	201.4	•	•	•	•	•	•	57.4	•
Coverage Ratio 33	2.4	•	3.6	1.6	3.4	1.9	1.4	1.1	0.7	1.7	2.1	2.0	2.7
Total Asset Turnover 34	1.6	•	4.4	2.9	2.3	1.8	1.9	1.8	2.0	1.6	1.3	1.1	0.7
Inventory Turnover 35	23.2	•	28.9	28.3	31.6	13.8	33.7	26.7	30.4	21.0	15.7	16.0	16.3
Receivables Turnover 36	28.0	•	102.2	78.6	50.7	44.0	38.2	29.9	37.0	36.3	17.9	19.0	9.6
Total Liabilities to Net Worth 37	2.1	•	12.8	8.0	4.7	4.4	4.2	2.2	5.3	2.0	2.7	1.4	1.2
Current Assets to Working Capital 38	•	•	4.5	•	22.6	•	•	•	•	•	•	11.1	•
Current Liabilities to Working Capital 39	•	•	3.5	•	21.6	•	•	•	•	•	•	10.1	•
Working Capital to Net Sales 40	•	•	0.0	•	0.0	•	•	•	•	•	•	0.0	•
Inventory to Working Capital 41	•	•	0.9	•	2.9	•	•	•	•	•	•	1.3	•
Total Receipts to Cash Flow 42	5.5	9.0	5.8	6.3	5.6	5.9	6.4	6.0	5.3	5.8	4.8	5.6	4.6
Cost of Goods to Cash Flow 43	2.3	4.4	2.4	2.6	2.3	2.4	2.8	2.6	2.1	2.3	1.9	2.3	1.9
Cash Flow to Total Debt 44	0.4	0.0	0.8	0.5	0.5	0.4	0.4	0.4	0.4	0.4	0.4	0.3	0.3

Selected Financial Factors (in Percentages)

Debt Ratio 45	67.9	•	92.7	88.9	82.4	81.6	80.9	68.3	84.0	66.9	72.6	57.9	55.0
Return on Total Assets 46	7.3	•	9.4	5.5	9.3	6.2	5.4	4.4	3.3	7.2	8.5	7.8	7.0
Return on Equity Before Income Taxes 47	13.0	•	93.3	19.1	37.4	16.4	8.7	1.4	•	9.2	16.1	9.2	9.7
Return on Equity After Income Taxes 48	9.6	•	90.3	16.7	36.1	15.5	7.1	0.2	•	5.6	10.0	5.5	6.2
Profit Margin (Before Income Tax) 49	2.5	•	1.6	0.7	2.9	1.7	0.9	0.2	•	1.9	3.3	3.5	6.4
Profit Margin (After Income Tax) 50	1.9	•	1.5	0.6	2.8	1.6	0.7	0.0	•	1.2	2.0	2.1	4.1

385

Table II

Corporations with Net Income

FOOD SERVICES AND DRINKING PLACES

MONEY AMOUNTS AND SIZE OF ASSETS IN THOUSANDS OF DOLLARS

Item Description for Accounting Period 7/03 Through 6/04	Total	Zero Assets	Under 500	500 to 1,000	1,000 to 5,000	5,000 to 10,000	10,000 to 25,000	25,000 to 50,000	50,000 to 100,000	100,000 to 250,000	250,000 to 500,000	500,000 to 2,500,000	2,500,000 and over
Number of Enterprises 1	118773	10547	95583	6735	5077	433	236	60	29	30	16	•	•
Revenues ($ in Thousands)													
Net Sales 2	198516204	1438476	57261676	16267905	22696668	6049892	6936124	3811458	4000282	7953294	7710910		
Interest 3	1152371	2697	13019	4875	6158	8292	6338	4339	1495	15299	41225		
Rents 4	354598	0	17695	1706	9849	10962	6141	10705	8046	37324	44036		
Royalties 5	3473892	0	99	73	3958	93	32753	25833	5280	178328	497046		
Other Portfolio Income 6	695331	102638	109137	51632	39859	20376	13470	7817	1540	56001	18982		
Other Receipts 7	5688901	65397	430890	107602	327047	218076	188287	66725	33927	223649	243890		
Total Receipts 8	209881297	1609208	57832516	16433793	23083539	6307691	7183113	3926877	4050570	8463895	8556089		
Average Total Receipts 9	1767	153	605	2440	4547	14567	30437	65448	139675	282130	534756		
Operating Costs/Operating Income (%)													
Cost of Operations 10	41.3	38.1	41.8	38.6	41.5	41.0	43.5	42.4	36.0	44.2	40.7		
Salaries and Wages 11	19.5	13.1	16.9	19.5	16.4	19.6	19.3	19.6	19.1	18.0	25.6		
Taxes Paid 12	3.9	5.0	4.1	4.1	3.5	4.1	3.6	3.7	3.6	3.6	4.4		
Interest Paid 13	1.8	0.8	0.5	0.8	1.0	1.4	1.6	1.7	1.3	1.8	2.9		
Depreciation 14	3.3	1.9	1.5	2.0	2.7	2.2	3.2	3.4	3.3	4.7	4.6		
Amortization and Depletion 15	0.5	0.2	0.2	0.2	0.3	0.9	0.5	0.5	0.4	0.5	0.7		
Pensions and Other Deferred Comp. 16	0.3	0.0	0.1	0.2	0.1	0.5	0.1	0.2	0.2	0.2	0.3		
Employee Benefits 17	1.3	0.3	0.5	0.7	1.1	1.5	1.3	1.4	1.1	1.3	1.7		
Advertising 18	2.7	3.2	1.8	4.0	3.3	3.5	3.4	2.7	2.1	3.0	3.8		
Other Expenses 19	23.0	30.4	22.6	24.1	22.5	23.5	21.2	22.7	31.3	23.3	20.9		
Officers' Compensation 20	2.2	5.4	4.5	2.4	2.6	1.6	1.4	1.3	0.8	0.9	0.6		
Operating Margin 21	0.3	1.6	5.6	3.6	5.0	0.2	0.8	0.5	0.9	•	•		
Operating Margin Before Officers' Comp. 22	2.4	7.0	10.1	6.0	7.6	1.7	2.3	1.8	1.7	•	•		

Selected Average Balance Sheet ($ in Thousands)

	1	2	3	4	5	6	7	8	9	10	11
Net Receivables 23	64	0	7	31	112	355	799	2431	5242	8479	10412
Inventories 24	32	0	8	34	61	408	379	1229	1522	5526	12773
Net Property, Plant and Equipment 25	431	0	54	335	917	2715	7815	18888	37560	93738	182155
Total Assets 26	1096	0	124	673	1897	6657	15117	34458	67206	163625	359549
Notes and Loans Payable 27	383	0	65	353	870	3350	7567	15556	31691	58795	158927
All Other Liabilities 28	267	0	20	107	441	1351	3235	7477	17678	41703	86348
Net Worth 29	446	0	39	213	586	1955	4315	11424	17837	63126	114275

Selected Financial Ratios (Times to 1)

	1	2	3	4	5	6	7	8	9	10	11
Current Ratio 30	1.1	•	1.8	1.4	1.3	0.9	0.9	0.9	0.8	1.0	0.8
Quick Ratio 31	0.7	•	1.2	1.0	1.0	0.5	0.6	0.6	0.5	0.6	0.4
Net Sales to Working Capital 32	115.9	•	28.8	45.8	34.7	•	•	•	•	•	•
Coverage Ratio 33	4.4	17.1	13.0	6.7	7.9	4.2	3.0	2.7	3.9	2.6	
Total Asset Turnover 34	1.5	•	4.8	3.6	2.4	2.1	1.8	2.1	1.6	1.3	
Inventory Turnover 35	21.7	•	31.1	27.1	30.5	14.1	33.7	21.9	32.6	21.2	15.3
Receivables Turnover 36	23.8	•	102.1	78.2	46.8	40.9	38.3	25.1	33.2	30.5	22.9
Total Liabilities to Net Worth 37	1.5	•	2.2	2.2	2.2	2.4	2.5	2.0	2.8	1.6	2.1
Current Assets to Working Capital 38	15.2	•	2.2	3.7	4.4	•	•	•	•	•	•
Current Liabilities to Working Capital 39	14.2	•	1.2	2.7	3.4	•	•	•	•	•	•
Working Capital to Net Sales 40	0.0	•	0.0	0.0	0.0	•	•	•	•	•	•
Inventory to Working Capital 41	2.1	•	0.4	0.5	0.5	•	•	•	•	•	•
Total Receipts to Cash Flow 42	4.8	3.4	4.9	5.2	4.7	5.2	5.3	4.0	5.0	5.1	
Cost of Goods to Cash Flow 43	2.0	1.3	2.1	2.0	2.0	2.1	2.2	1.4	2.2	2.1	
Cash Flow to Total Debt 44	0.5	•	1.4	1.0	0.7	0.6	0.5	0.7	0.5	0.4	

Selected Financial Factors (in Percentages)

	1	2	3	4	5	6	7	8	9	10	11
Debt Ratio 45	59.3	•	68.5	68.3	69.1	70.6	71.5	66.8	73.5	61.4	68.2
Return on Total Assets 46	12.0	•	34.4	19.4	18.1	12.2	11.6	9.6	6.9	11.1	10.2
Return on Equity Before Income Taxes 47	22.6	•	101.0	52.2	51.2	31.6	29.8	19.3	16.3	21.2	19.6
Return on Equity After Income Taxes 48	19.2	•	99.8	50.6	50.0	30.7	28.2	17.4	13.8	16.8	13.2
Profit Margin (Before Income Tax) 49	6.0	13.4	6.6	4.6	6.7	4.4	4.4	3.5	2.1	5.1	4.6
Profit Margin (After Income Tax) 50	5.1	13.1	6.5	4.5	6.6	4.3	4.1	3.1	1.8	4.0	3.1

Table I
Corporations with and without Net Income

AUTOMOTIVE REPAIR AND MAINTENANCE

MONEY AMOUNTS AND SIZE OF ASSETS IN THOUSANDS OF DOLLARS

Item Description for Accounting Period 7/03 Through 6/04	Total	Zero Assets	Under 500	500 to 1,000	1,000 to 5,000	5,000 to 10,000	10,000 to 25,000	25,000 to 50,000	50,000 to 100,000	100,000 to 250,000	250,000 to 500,000	500,000 to 2,500,000	2,500,000 and over
Number of Enterprises **1**	103209	8960	87531	4633	1885	134	45	6	12	•	3	•	•
Revenues ($ in Thousands)													
Net Sales **2**	59359623	1177485	36496727	7862834	8261026	1747099	1192309	257586	1265225	•	1099332	•	•
Interest **3**	27132	785	10520	5675	6885	371	726	1154	399	•	615	•	•
Rents **4**	33669	351	13606	2954	10784	3115	1694	374	256	•	536	•	•
Royalties **5**	30327	0	0	0	0	0	8522	0	20339	•	1466	•	•
Other Portfolio Income **6**	212039	43209	147271	721	6828	9614	1484	2702	204	•	6	•	•
Other Receipts **7**	245502	49044	97866	22297	37404	12895	11279	3104	4001	•	7614	•	•
Total Receipts **8**	59908292	1270874	36765990	7894481	8322927	1773094	1216014	264920	1290424	•	1109569	•	•
Average Total Receipts **9**	580	142	420	1704	4415	13232	27023	44153	107535	•	369856	•	•
Operating Costs/Operating Income (%)													
Cost of Operations **10**	50.3	55.0	47.3	55.8	55.6	52.5	53.6	44.1	47.3	•	62.6	•	•
Salaries and Wages **11**	12.5	8.2	12.2	11.3	14.8	13.1	13.1	11.3	18.8	•	6.5	•	•
Taxes Paid **12**	3.5	3.1	3.6	3.7	3.3	3.8	3.8	2.7	3.7	•	1.5	•	•
Interest Paid **13**	1.1	0.5	0.9	1.7	1.1	1.6	1.3	2.1	3.9	•	3.4	•	•
Depreciation **14**	2.2	3.4	2.0	2.2	2.5	2.4	3.3	3.4	3.7	•	5.1	•	•
Amortization and Depletion **15**	0.3	0.1	0.2	0.1	0.2	0.6	0.4	1.0	2.7	•	1.4	•	•
Pensions and Other Deferred Comp. **16**	0.1	0.0	0.1	0.1	0.1	0.2	0.3	0.1	0.1	•	0.5	•	•
Employee Benefits **17**	1.2	0.1	1.1	1.7	1.0	0.6	1.6	1.8	1.4	•	1.7	•	•
Advertising **18**	1.7	3.1	1.6	1.8	1.4	3.4	2.4	3.0	2.1	•	1.6	•	•
Other Expenses **19**	19.8	29.3	21.8	17.2	13.8	16.5	18.9	31.2	18.6	•	12.4	•	•
Officers' Compensation **20**	6.3	4.1	7.8	4.2	4.8	2.3	2.5	0.7	0.7	•	0.7	•	•
Operating Margin **21**	1.0	•	1.4	0.1	1.4	3.0	•	•	•	•	2.5	•	•
Operating Margin Before Officers' Comp. **22**	7.2	•	9.2	4.3	6.3	5.3	1.3	•	•	•	3.2	•	•

Selected Average Balance Sheet ($ in Thousands)

Net Receivables 23	18	0	9	88	189	1034	1630	4589	3636	13064
Inventories 24	20	0	11	67	270	654	1428	1872	3875	39800
Net Property, Plant and Equipment 25	79	0	40	346	747	3753	6467	6533	27968	134034
Total Assets 26	187	0	98	710	1815	7342	14808	31775	90778	357018
Notes and Loans Payable 27	109	0	63	451	834	3888	5912	14263	51285	181387
All Other Liabilities 28	40	0	24	117	292	1754	3797	8670	19580	78521
Net Worth 29	38	0	11	142	689	1700	5100	8842	19912	97109

Selected Financial Ratios (Times to 1)

Current Ratio 30	1.4	•	1.3	1.7	1.8	1.0	1.2	1.1	1.0	1.2
Quick Ratio 31	0.9	•	0.9	1.2	1.0	0.7	0.7	0.6	0.5	0.3
Net Sales to Working Capital 32	30.1	•	49.5	15.7	12.9	•	25.4	33.8	389.7	32.4
Coverage Ratio 33	2.7	3.1	3.5	1.3	2.9	3.8	1.6	1.8	0.7	2.0
Total Asset Turnover 34	3.1	•	4.3	2.4	2.4	1.8	1.8	1.4	1.2	1.0
Inventory Turnover 35	14.1	•	18.0	14.1	9.0	10.5	10.0	10.1	12.9	5.8
Receivables Turnover 36	30.8	•	44.7	22.8	18.0	16.5	15.2	10.2	35.4	56.1
Total Liabilities to Net Worth 37	3.9	•	8.0	4.0	1.6	3.3	1.9	2.6	3.6	2.7
Current Assets to Working Capital 38	3.6	•	4.5	2.4	2.2	•	5.2	7.9	53.4	6.5
Current Liabilities to Working Capital 39	2.6	•	3.5	1.4	1.2	•	4.2	6.9	52.4	5.5
Working Capital to Net Sales 40	0.0	•	0.0	0.1	0.1	•	0.0	0.0	0.0	0.0
Inventory to Working Capital 41	1.0	•	1.2	0.5	0.8	•	1.7	1.3	13.7	3.5
Total Receipts to Cash Flow 42	6.7	6.1	6.1	8.1	8.6	6.7	8.4	4.4	9.0	8.5
Cost of Goods to Cash Flow 43	3.4	3.4	2.9	4.5	4.8	3.5	4.5	1.9	4.3	5.3
Cash Flow to Total Debt 44	0.6	•	0.8	0.4	0.5	0.3	0.3	0.4	0.2	0.2

Selected Financial Factors (in Percentages)

Debt Ratio 45	79.6	•	88.9	80.0	62.1	76.8	65.6	72.2	78.1	72.8
Return on Total Assets 46	9.4	•	12.8	5.2	7.9	10.9	3.9	4.9	3.3	7.1
Return on Equity Before Income Taxes 47	28.7	•	82.8	6.1	13.8	34.6	4.2	7.6	•	13.0
Return on Equity After Income Taxes 48	26.9	•	79.3	5.0	13.2	34.0	3.8	5.9	•	8.3
Profit Margin (Before Income Tax) 49	1.9	1.0	2.2	0.5	2.2	4.5	1.6	1.6	•	3.4
Profit Margin (After Income Tax) 50	1.8	0.4	2.1	0.4	2.1	4.4	0.7	1.2	•	2.2

Table II

Corporations with Net Income

AUTOMOTIVE REPAIR AND MAINTENANCE

MONEY AMOUNTS AND SIZE OF ASSETS IN THOUSANDS OF DOLLARS

Item Description for Accounting Period 7/03 Through 6/04	Total	Zero Assets	Under 500	500 to 1,000	1,000 to 5,000	5,000 to 10,000	10,000 to 25,000	25,000 to 50,000	50,000 to 100,000	100,000 to 250,000	250,000 to 500,000	500,000 to 2,500,000	2,500,000 and over
Number of Enterprises 1	53439	3135	46365	2400	1422	83	24	6	•	3	•	•	•

Revenues ($ in Thousands)

Item Description for Accounting Period 7/03 Through 6/04	Total	Zero Assets	Under 500	500 to 1,000	1,000 to 5,000	5,000 to 10,000	10,000 to 25,000	25,000 to 50,000	50,000 to 100,000	100,000 to 250,000	250,000 to 500,000	500,000 to 2,500,000	2,500,000 and over
Net Sales 2	37348357	732557	22548296	3771631	7210578	1517681	699670	184662	•	683281	•	•	•
Interest 3	18900	785	8129	3713	4670	335	120	767	•	382	•	•	•
Rents 4	12709	0	4566	2954	4537	91	118	53	•	391	•	•	•
Royalties 5	20455	0	0	0	0	0	0	18989	•	1466	•	•	•
Other Portfolio Income 6	182154	37224	125986	451	5611	9614	772	2490	•	6	•	•	•
Other Receipts 7	196656	48606	78148	10287	30875	14489	3047	4855	•	6347	•	•	•
Total Receipts 8	37779231	819172	22765125	3789036	7256271	1542210	703727	211816	•	691873	•	•	•
Average Total Receipts 9	707	261	491	1579	5103	18581	29322	35303	•	230624	•	•	•

Operating Costs/Operating Income (%)

Item Description for Accounting Period 7/03 Through 6/04	Total	Zero Assets	Under 500	500 to 1,000	1,000 to 5,000	5,000 to 10,000	10,000 to 25,000	25,000 to 50,000	50,000 to 100,000	100,000 to 250,000	250,000 to 500,000	500,000 to 2,500,000	2,500,000 and over
Cost of Operations 10	48.5	52.1	45.0	50.7	55.9	52.2	57.0	36.3	•	52.9	•	•	•
Salaries and Wages 11	12.3	7.4	11.7	13.1	14.6	13.6	10.2	16.5	•	6.3	•	•	•
Taxes Paid 12	3.4	3.4	3.4	3.5	3.3	3.6	2.5	1.5	•	3.1	•	•	•
Interest Paid 13	0.9	0.2	0.7	1.5	1.0	1.2	0.9	2.7	•	5.3	•	•	•
Depreciation 14	1.9	2.9	1.6	2.2	2.3	1.3	2.8	3.4	•	4.5	•	•	•
Amortization and Depletion 15	0.2	0.1	0.2	0.1	0.2	0.6	0.3	2.5	•	1.3	•	•	•
Pensions and Other Deferred Comp. 16	0.1	0.0	0.2	0.1	0.1	0.1	0.3	0.2	•	0.1	•	•	•
Employee Benefits 17	1.0	0.0	1.0	1.8	1.0	0.7	1.0	0.8	•	1.0	•	•	•
Advertising 18	1.6	1.2	1.6	0.9	1.3	3.6	2.2	3.4	•	1.7	•	•	•
Other Expenses 19	19.0	28.1	21.7	14.5	12.9	16.8	13.8	34.8	•	15.0	•	•	•
Officers' Compensation 20	6.4	3.2	7.6	6.3	4.8	0.9	3.1	0.7	•	1.3	•	•	•
Operating Margin 21	4.7	1.5	5.3	5.3	2.6	5.4	6.0	•	•	7.4	•	•	•
Operating Margin Before Officers' Comp. 22	11.1	4.7	13.0	11.6	7.4	6.3	9.1	8.8	•	8.8	•	•	•

Selected Average Balance Sheet ($ in Thousands)

	1	2	3	4	5	6	7	8	9
Net Receivables 23	23	0	11	104	192	1466	1798	3231	8601
Inventories 24	23	0	11	89	226	1186	1311	1325	26857
Net Property, Plant and Equipment 25	79	0	35	289	791	2722	6549	5434	126338
Total Assets 26	214	0	105	700	1885	7978	14466	42332	308788
Notes and Loans Payable 27	100	0	50	367	821	3215	4808	6527	179945
All Other Liabilities 28	44	0	25	91	304	2300	4109	23326	50482
Net Worth 29	70	0	31	241	760	2463	5549	12480	78361

Selected Financial Ratios (Times to 1)

	1	2	3	4	5	6	7	8	9
Current Ratio 30	1.6	•	1.5	2.0	1.9	1.6	1.2	1.1	1.2
Quick Ratio 31	1.1	•	1.1	1.5	1.1	1.0	0.8	0.6	0.3
Net Sales to Working Capital 32	21.3	•	33.2	10.7	13.1	12.6	28.4	39.2	31.0
Coverage Ratio 33	7.2	79.0	10.1	4.7	4.2	6.7	8.7	•	5.5
Total Asset Turnover 34	3.3	•	4.6	2.2	2.7	2.3	2.0	•	0.7
Inventory Turnover 35	14.5	•	20.0	9.0	12.5	8.1	12.7	8.4	4.5
Receivables Turnover 36	31.1	•	46.1	14.8	25.8	24.9	15.3	19.1	53.0
Total Liabilities to Net Worth 37	2.1	•	2.4	1.9	1.5	2.2	1.6	2.4	2.9
Current Assets to Working Capital 38	2.7	•	3.1	2.0	2.1	2.8	5.2	11.9	6.6
Current Liabilities to Working Capital 39	1.7	•	2.1	1.0	1.1	1.8	4.2	10.9	5.6
Working Capital to Net Sales 40	0.0	•	0.0	0.1	0.1	0.1	0.0	0.0	0.0
Inventory to Working Capital 41	0.7	•	0.6	0.3	0.7	0.8	1.6	1.7	3.7
Total Receipts to Cash Flow 42	5.5	3.9	4.8	6.6	8.4	5.8	6.6	2.6	6.2
Cost of Goods to Cash Flow 43	2.6	2.0	2.2	3.3	4.7	3.0	3.8	1.0	3.3
Cash Flow to Total Debt 44	0.9	•	1.4	0.5	0.5	0.6	0.5	0.4	0.2

Selected Financial Factors (in Percentages)

	1	2	3	4	5	6	7	8	9
Debt Ratio 45	67.3	•	70.8	65.6	59.7	69.1	61.6	70.5	74.6
Return on Total Assets 46	22.3	•	32.2	16.3	11.3	18.9	15.0	10.6	10.4
Return on Equity Before Income Taxes 47	58.8	•	99.2	37.3	21.4	52.2	34.6	29.5	25.5
Return on Equity After Income Taxes 48	56.9	•	96.9	36.1	20.7	51.5	33.8	28.2	19.6
Profit Margin (Before Income Tax) 49	5.9	13.3	6.3	5.7	3.2	7.0	6.6	12.0	8.8
Profit Margin (After Income Tax) 50	5.7	12.4	6.1	5.5	3.1	6.9	6.4	11.4	6.7

Table I

Corporations with and without Net Income

OTHER REPAIR AND MAINTENANCE

MONEY AMOUNTS AND SIZE OF ASSETS IN THOUSANDS OF DOLLARS

Item Description for Accounting Period 7/03 Through 6/04	Total	Zero Assets	Under 500	500 to 1,000	1,000 to 5,000	5,000 to 10,000	10,000 to 25,000	25,000 to 50,000	50,000 to 100,000	100,000 to 250,000	250,000 to 500,000	500,000 to 2,500,000	2,500,000 and over
Number of Enterprises **1**	55521	6278	45633	1547	1884	98	52	17	7	6	·	·	·
Revenues ($ in Thousands)													
Net Sales **2**	29409413	502537	12443243	3188787	6879899	1448638	1495586	864096	855870	1730758	·	·	·
Interest **3**	24622	1708	3305	1159	5277	864	1647	461	15	10187	·	·	·
Rents **4**	5239	0	1204	2022	1371	365	271	0	6	0	·	·	·
Royalties **5**	12248	7974	0	0	0	424	20	19	349	3462	·	·	·
Other Portfolio Income **6**	87754	0	49502	2143	23117	1359	5541	2020	91	3980	·	·	·
Other Receipts **7**	200833	74	18316	2824	63238	18141	14690	10053	1628	71869	·	·	·
Total Receipts **8**	29740109	512293	12515570	3196935	6972902	1469791	1517755	876649	857959	1820256	·	·	·
Average Total Receipts **9**	536	82	274	2067	3701	14998	29188	51568	122566	303376	·	·	·
Operating Costs/Operating Income (%)													
Cost of Operations **10**	49.3	48.4	41.9	33.4	55.1	58.2	67.7	64.3	72.4	66.0	·	·	·
Salaries and Wages **11**	13.9	10.2	12.7	29.2	12.8	12.1	8.6	11.2	7.1	11.3	·	·	·
Taxes Paid **12**	3.1	2.3	3.3	3.6	2.9	2.9	2.8	2.2	5.0	2.6	·	·	·
Interest Paid **13**	1.0	0.6	0.6	0.8	1.3	0.9	0.8	1.2	3.5	1.9	·	·	·
Depreciation **14**	2.4	2.6	2.5	1.6	2.6	2.8	3.0	2.5	1.4	1.5	·	·	·
Amortization and Depletion **15**	0.2	0.3	0.1	0.2	0.4	0.1	0.1	0.3	0.9	1.0	·	·	·
Pensions and Other Deferred Comp. **16**	0.2	0.1	0.2	0.2	0.2	0.7	0.5	0.3	0.1	0.1	·	·	·
Employee Benefits **17**	2.2	1.1	1.1	7.7	1.3	2.7	3.1	2.1	1.8	3.3	·	·	·
Advertising **18**	0.7	1.0	0.7	0.2	1.2	0.5	0.4	0.5	0.2	0.2	·	·	·
Other Expenses **19**	19.1	37.0	24.2	17.2	16.3	13.7	9.5	13.7	9.3	12.9	·	·	·
Officers' Compensation **20**	6.0	4.7	9.3	4.0	4.7	4.7	2.3	1.3	0.8	0.5	·	·	·
Operating Margin **21**	1.8	·	3.5	2.1	1.2	0.6	1.4	0.6	·	·	·	·	·
Operating Margin Before Officers' Comp. **22**	7.8	·	12.8	6.1	5.9	5.4	3.6	1.9	·	·	·	·	·

Selected Average Balance Sheet ($ in Thousands)

Net Receivables 23	49	0	10	168	493	2527	4302	9849	25187	47390
Inventories 24	37	0	12	85	334	2039	3767	7018	10687	17211
Net Property, Plant and Equipment 25	40	0	20	141	284	1288	3560	4276	10367	20534
Total Assets 26	197	0	62	686	1716	6875	15036	33755	67679	217416
Notes and Loans Payable 27	87	0	35	295	723	2848	3951	13722	32127	73190
All Other Liabilities 28	59	0	13	198	473	2578	4255	11057	35058	93288
Net Worth 29	52	0	14	192	520	1449	6829	8975	494	50938

Selected Financial Ratios (Times to 1)

Current Ratio 30	1.7	•	2.0	1.6	1.7	1.5	1.8	1.8	1.1	1.4
Quick Ratio 31	1.0	•	1.2	1.1	1.0	0.8	1.0	0.9	0.7	0.8
Net Sales to Working Capital 32	10.8	•	15.0	12.4	7.9	9.3	6.6	4.8	34.7	9.3
Coverage Ratio 33	4.0	•	8.4	4.1	2.9	3.3	4.6	2.7	0.4	3.1
Total Asset Turnover 34	2.7	•	4.4	3.0	2.1	2.2	1.9	1.5	1.8	1.3
Inventory Turnover 35	7.0	•	9.7	8.1	6.0	4.2	5.2	4.7	8.3	11.1
Receivables Turnover 36	9.7	•	28.6	11.4	8.3	6.3	5.9	5.8	5.5	6.6
Total Liabilities to Net Worth 37	2.8	•	3.5	2.6	2.3	3.7	1.2	2.8	136.0	3.3
Current Assets to Working Capital 38	2.5	•	2.0	2.6	2.5	3.1	2.3	2.3	11.5	3.8
Current Liabilities to Working Capital 39	1.5	•	1.0	1.6	1.5	2.1	1.3	1.3	10.5	2.8
Working Capital to Net Sales 40	0.1	•	0.1	0.1	0.1	0.1	0.2	0.2	0.0	0.1
Inventory to Working Capital 41	0.8	•	0.7	0.6	0.8	1.1	0.8	0.7	2.8	0.5
Total Receipts to Cash Flow 42	5.6	5.1	4.4	5.8	6.8	8.5	10.9	8.5	23.0	6.9
Cost of Goods to Cash Flow 43	2.8	2.5	1.8	1.9	3.7	4.9	7.4	5.5	16.7	4.5
Cash Flow to Total Debt 44	0.6	•	1.3	0.7	0.4	0.3	0.3	0.2	0.1	0.3

Selected Financial Factors (in Percentages)

Debt Ratio 45	73.8	•	77.8	72.0	69.7	78.9	54.6	73.4	99.3	76.6
Return on Total Assets 46	10.5	•	20.4	9.4	8.3	6.5	7.0	4.8	2.3	7.6
Return on Equity Before Income Taxes 47	30.2	•	81.0	25.2	18.0	21.4	12.0	11.5	•	21.8
Return on Equity After Income Taxes 48	27.4	•	79.3	24.6	16.4	16.9	9.5	10.4	•	12.1
Profit Margin (Before Income Tax) 49	2.9	•	4.1	2.4	2.6	2.1	2.8	2.0	•	3.8
Profit Margin (After Income Tax) 50	2.7	•	4.0	2.3	2.3	1.7	2.2	1.8	•	2.1

Table II

Corporations with Net Income

OTHER REPAIR AND MAINTENANCE

MONEY AMOUNTS AND SIZE OF ASSETS IN THOUSANDS OF DOLLARS

Item Description for Accounting Period 7/03 Through 6/04	Total	Zero Assets	Under 500	500 to 1,000	1,000 to 5,000	5,000 to 10,000	10,000 to 25,000	25,000 to 50,000	50,000 to 100,000	100,000 to 250,000	250,000 to 500,000	500,000 to 2,500,000	2,500,000 and over
Number of Enterprises 1	31982	3338	26430	886	1202	67	40	12	3	3	•	•	•
Revenues ($ in Thousands)													
Net Sales 2	20130412	259835	8609384	2506283	4496412	1025021	1196845	712510	294213	1029909	•	•	•
Interest 3	17271	60	2012	267	4532	324	1136	200	2	8736	•	•	•
Rents 4	4094	0	221	2022	1371	321	157	0	2	0	•	•	•
Royalties 5	4255	0	0	0	0	424	20	0	349	3462	•	•	•
Other Portfolio Income 6	72366	0	37182	1886	21896	1231	5504	837	62	3766	•	•	•
Other Receipts 7	146471	-6	5723	2074	35695	17290	8620	5378	940	70762	•	•	•
Total Receipts 8	20374869	259889	8654522	2512532	4559906	1044611	1212282	718925	295568	1116635	•	•	•
Average Total Receipts 9	637	78	327	2836	3794	15591	30307	59910	98523	372212	•	•	•
Operating Costs/Operating Income (%)													
Cost of Operations 10	46.5	36.8	38.7	24.3	59.0	54.0	66.3	62.4	63.0	67.6	•	•	•
Salaries and Wages 11	14.8	9.3	13.7	34.5	9.8	14.2	7.9	12.0	8.1	12.1	•	•	•
Taxes Paid 12	2.8	2.8	2.6	3.9	2.7	2.9	2.8	2.2	6.6	1.9	•	•	•
Interest Paid 13	0.7	0.3	0.5	0.7	1.0	1.0	0.6	0.9	1.9	1.2	•	•	•
Depreciation 14	2.2	0.8	2.3	1.4	2.4	3.2	2.1	2.6	2.6	1.6	•	•	•
Amortization and Depletion 15	0.1	0.4	0.0	0.2	0.3	0.2	0.1	0.3	0.0	0.2	•	•	•
Pensions and Other Deferred Comp. 16	0.2	0.2	0.1	0.2	0.3	0.5	0.5	0.2	0.3	0.0	•	•	•
Employee Benefits 17	2.3	0.8	0.7	9.2	1.0	2.7	3.7	2.2	1.5	2.7	•	•	•
Advertising 18	0.7	1.1	0.7	0.2	1.4	0.6	0.4	0.3	0.4	0.3	•	•	•
Other Expenses 19	17.5	34.8	22.9	17.0	12.7	14.2	9.1	11.8	8.8	10.6	•	•	•
Officers' Compensation 20	5.6	4.4	8.6	3.9	4.0	4.2	2.5	1.4	1.8	0.5	•	•	•
Operating Margin 21	6.4	8.3	9.1	4.5	5.4	2.4	3.9	3.6	5.0	1.2	•	•	•
Operating Margin Before Officers' Comp. 22	12.0	12.8	17.8	8.4	9.4	6.6	6.4	5.0	6.8	1.8	•	•	•

Selected Average Balance Sheet ($ in Thousands)

Net Receivables 23	55	0	10	233	498	2377	4352	10657	19388	54192
Inventories 24	38	0	10	61	371	2300	3417	8110	8897	19594
Net Property, Plant and Equipment 25	42	0	18	150	280	1404	2841	5265	13620	31329
Total Assets 26	214	0	63	685	1734	7031	14393	34456	73182	267980
Notes and Loans Payable 27	69	0	24	316	571	2780	3217	12280	17715	31949
All Other Liabilities 28	63	0	14	157	437	2542	4005	11776	24143	139056
Net Worth 29	82	0	25	212	725	1709	7171	10400	31324	96974

Selected Financial Ratios (Times to 1)

Current Ratio 30	1.9	•	2.1	2.2	2.1	1.7	2.1	1.6	1.4	1.3
Quick Ratio 31	1.2	•	1.5	1.5	1.2	0.9	1.2	0.9	0.8	0.6
Net Sales to Working Capital 32	9.4	•	15.5	10.7	5.9	8.0	5.8	6.3	9.8	9.1
Coverage Ratio 33	11.4	32.0	20.3	8.2	7.9	5.1	9.1	6.0	3.9	9.0
Total Asset Turnover 34	2.9	•	5.2	4.1	2.2	2.2	2.1	1.7	1.3	1.3
Inventory Turnover 35	7.6	•	13.3	11.3	6.0	3.6	5.8	4.6	6.9	11.8
Receivables Turnover 36	11.5	•	33.5	11.4	8.2	6.2	6.7	11.1	10.1	12.7
Total Liabilities to Net Worth 37	1.6	•	1.5	2.2	1.4	3.1	1.0	2.3	1.3	1.8
Current Assets to Working Capital 38	2.1	•	1.9	1.8	1.9	2.5	1.9	2.6	3.8	4.4
Current Liabilities to Working Capital 39	1.1	•	0.9	0.8	0.9	1.5	0.9	1.6	2.8	3.4
Working Capital to Net Sales 40	0.1	•	0.1	0.1	0.2	0.1	0.2	0.2	0.1	0.1
Inventory to Working Capital 41	0.6	•	0.5	0.2	0.6	1.0	0.7	0.9	0.9	0.5
Total Receipts to Cash Flow 42	4.6	2.9	3.5	5.0	6.2	7.0	8.6	7.5	9.1	5.3
Cost of Goods to Cash Flow 43	2.2	1.1	1.4	1.2	3.7	3.8	5.7	4.7	5.7	3.6
Cash Flow to Total Debt 44	1.0	2.4	1.2	1.2	0.6	0.4	0.5	0.3	0.3	0.4

Selected Financial Factors (in Percentages)

Debt Ratio 45	61.6	•	60.5	69.1	58.2	75.7	50.2	69.8	57.2	63.8
Return on Total Assets 46	24.5	•	52.5	22.2	16.7	11.6	12.2	9.4	9.8	13.8
Return on Equity Before Income Taxes 47	58.1	•	126.3	63.0	34.9	38.2	21.8	25.9	17.1	33.8
Return on Equity After Income Taxes 48	55.1	•	124.7	62.0	33.1	32.6	18.7	24.6	11.3	23.6
Profit Margin (Before Income Tax) 49	7.6	8.4	9.7	4.7	6.8	4.3	5.2	4.5	5.5	9.5
Profit Margin (After Income Tax) 50	7.2	8.4	9.5	4.6	6.4	3.6	4.5	4.3	3.6	6.7

Table I

Corporations with and without Net Income

PERSONAL AND LAUNDRY SERVICES

MONEY AMOUNTS AND SIZE OF ASSETS IN THOUSANDS OF DOLLARS

Item Description for Accounting Period 7/03 Through 6/04	Total	Zero Assets	Under 500	500 to 1,000	1,000 to 5,000	5,000 to 10,000	10,000 to 25,000	25,000 to 50,000	50,000 to 100,000	100,000 to 250,000	250,000 to 500,000	500,000 to 2,500,000	2,500,000 and over
Number of Enterprises 1	134955	19785	106006	4795	3834	330	115	34	22	12	5	12	4
Revenues ($ in Thousands)													
Net Sales 2	67404455	1641196	26818893	4865025	10049688	3367668	1733838	1426985	1538293	2048114	1538240	5892607	6483910
Interest 3	342607	564	13113	10701	19571	5079	5289	6749	9468	6335	27722	144877	93141
Rents 4	79214	0	8695	2259	5722	474	3365	1483	3263	6210	1871	31213	14658
Royalties 5	169324	0	11313	0	0	0	48	10404	1609	17183	0	25118	103648
Other Portfolio Income 6	718675	17251	117094	28914	54090	62208	8136	3824	7273	12393	8778	309757	88957
Other Receipts 7	1158074	17422	231618	50604	274063	42354	53221	43835	108754	66504	22265	208327	39105
Total Receipts 8	69872349	1676433	27200726	4957503	10403134	3477783	1803897	1493280	1668660	2156739	1598876	6611899	6823419
Average Total Receipts 9	518	85	257	1034	2713	10539	15686	43920	75848	179728	319775	550992	1705855
Operating Costs/Operating Income (%)													
Cost of Operations 10	29.7	18.7	24.1	26.7	32.5	48.4	36.2	27.4	38.5	21.2	27.3	37.1	37.0
Salaries and Wages 11	20.9	17.7	20.7	25.4	24.1	11.3	20.0	21.9	20.2	19.1	29.7	18.4	19.9
Taxes Paid 12	3.9	3.0	3.8	4.7	4.3	3.8	3.6	3.2	3.4	2.3	3.7	3.8	4.5
Interest Paid 13	2.3	2.5	1.1	1.9	2.0	1.5	2.5	2.2	2.2	3.7	2.0	5.8	4.4
Depreciation 14	4.0	4.7	3.0	5.6	4.4	7.6	4.9	2.8	4.3	3.8	4.8	3.9	4.4
Amortization and Depletion 15	0.8	1.1	0.5	0.4	0.5	0.5	0.7	0.9	0.6	1.5	0.8	2.5	1.2
Pensions and Other Deferred Comp. 16	0.4	0.2	0.2	0.6	0.5	0.2	0.6	0.5	0.5	0.2	0.6	0.4	0.7
Employee Benefits 17	1.5	1.2	0.9	1.7	1.7	1.4	2.4	2.4	6.8	1.0	3.6	2.0	1.0
Advertising 18	2.0	2.0	2.3	2.5	1.5	2.1	1.1	2.4	1.6	5.6	0.7	1.4	1.4
Other Expenses 19	30.2	43.7	33.5	26.7	25.9	21.1	25.9	36.5	26.4	47.1	25.9	30.9	22.5
Officers' Compensation 20	5.3	8.2	8.3	8.5	4.6	3.0	3.6	2.1	2.0	0.9	0.4	0.5	0.5
Operating Margin 21	•	•	1.5	•	•	•	•	•	•	•	0.3	•	2.5
Operating Margin Before Officers' Comp. 22	4.3	5.2	9.8	3.9	2.5	2.2	2.3	•	•	•	0.8	•	3.1

Selected Average Balance Sheet ($ in Thousands)

Net Receivables 23	57	0	5	66	221	899	2058	4048	8706	16183	64667	210899	538142
Inventories 24	16	0	3	26	56	203	832	2033	3654	8333	9804	50597	117658
Net Property, Plant and Equipment 25	130	0	33	336	859	2731	4994	9570	24493	29049	102322	154351	1035657
Total Assets 26	406	0	78	710	1863	6757	14973	35276	67669	143602	378661	957984	3545602
Notes and Loans Payable 27	164	0	57	441	1019	3007	6186	14324	21920	87798	55631	216426	856315
All Other Liabilities 28	122	0	13	77	423	1339	4675	14594	18015	36028	163380	406786	1255664
Net Worth 29	120	0	8	192	421	2411	4112	6358	27734	19777	159650	334772	1433623

Selected Financial Ratios (Times to 1)

Current Ratio 30	1.6	•	1.5	2.1	1.3	1.7	1.4	1.4	2.1	0.9	1.8	1.3	2.7
Quick Ratio 31	1.1	•	1.1	1.6	1.0	1.3	0.9	1.0	1.2	0.6	1.1	1.1	1.7
Net Sales to Working Capital 32	10.7	•	30.1	9.4	17.3	10.0	8.7	10.9	5.9	•	5.3	6.3	2.9
Coverage Ratio 33	2.3	0.6	3.6	•	1.7	2.6	2.1	2.0	1.9	0.7	3.3	2.4	2.8
Total Asset Turnover 34	1.2	•	3.3	1.4	1.4	1.5	1.0	1.2	1.0	1.2	0.8	0.5	0.5
Inventory Turnover 35	9.2	•	22.0	10.4	15.2	24.3	6.6	5.7	7.4	4.3	8.6	3.6	5.1
Receivables Turnover 36	9.5	•	57.2	14.6	12.6	12.8	7.4	9.3	7.3	11.6	5.7	3.7	2.5
Total Liabilities to Net Worth 37	2.4	•	8.8	2.7	3.4	1.8	2.6	4.5	1.4	6.3	1.4	1.9	1.5
Current Assets to Working Capital 38	2.6	•	2.8	1.9	4.0	2.4	3.4	3.6	1.9	•	2.3	3.9	1.6
Current Liabilities to Working Capital 39	1.6	•	1.8	0.9	3.0	1.4	2.4	2.6	0.9	•	1.3	2.9	0.6
Working Capital to Net Sales 40	0.1	•	0.0	0.1	0.1	0.1	0.1	0.1	0.2	•	0.2	0.2	0.3
Inventory to Working Capital 41	0.4	•	0.3	0.2	0.4	0.2	0.4	0.5	0.3	•	0.2	0.5	0.3
Total Receipts to Cash Flow 42	4.5	3.4	4.2	6.6	5.5	5.8	5.2	2.9	5.3	3.5	3.7	3.9	4.4
Cost of Goods to Cash Flow 43	1.3	0.6	1.0	1.8	1.8	2.8	1.9	0.8	2.0	0.7	1.0	1.4	1.6
Cash Flow to Total Debt 44	0.4	•	0.9	0.3	0.3	0.4	0.3	0.5	0.3	0.4	0.4	0.2	0.2

Selected Financial Factors (in Percentages)

Debt Ratio 45	70.3	•	89.8	73.0	77.4	64.3	72.5	82.0	59.0	86.2	57.8	65.1	59.6
Return on Total Assets 46	6.4	•	13.2	•	4.7	6.0	5.2	5.2	4.3	3.0	5.5	7.2	5.6
Return on Equity Before Income Taxes 47	12.3	•	93.6	•	8.2	10.3	9.9	14.5	5.0	•	9.0	12.0	9.0
Return on Equity After Income Taxes 48	9.4	•	91.4	•	7.0	9.6	8.3	10.1	4.0	•	7.1	6.7	6.0
Profit Margin (Before Income Tax) 49	3.0	•	2.9	•	1.3	2.4	2.7	2.2	2.0	•	4.7	8.2	7.9
Profit Margin (After Income Tax) 50	2.3	•	2.9	•	1.1	2.3	2.3	1.5	1.6	•	3.7	4.6	5.3

Table II
Corporations with Net Income

PERSONAL AND LAUNDRY SERVICES

MONEY AMOUNTS AND SIZE OF ASSETS IN THOUSANDS OF DOLLARS

Item Description for Accounting Period 7/03 Through 6/04		Total	Zero Assets	Under 500	500 to 1,000	1,000 to 5,000	5,000 to 10,000	10,000 to 25,000	25,000 to 50,000	50,000 to 100,000	100,000 to 250,000	250,000 to 500,000	500,000 to 2,500,000	2,500,000 and over
Number of Enterprises	1	72112	10045	56931	2617	2173	209	76	21	•	•	5	6	4
Revenues ($ in Thousands)														
Net Sales	2	48392612	1162432	17472009	2657590	7790593	2247095	1391468	979936	•	•	1538240	3782902	6483910
Interest	3	260472	480	11618	8748	13857	2949	3266	3916	•	•	27722	81909	93141
Rents	4	57149	0	5	1510	3448	243	2810	803	•	•	1871	24523	14658
Royalties	5	169039	0	11313	0	0	0	38	10404	•	•	0	25118	103648
Other Portfolio Income	6	621134	12401	67986	15738	41399	60975	7429	502	•	•	8778	305299	88957
Other Receipts	7	743482	21237	200208	33855	40907	39032	47346	39407	•	•	22265	125521	39105
Total Receipts	8	50243888	1196550	17763139	2717441	7890204	2350294	1452357	1034968	•	•	1598876	4345272	6823419
Average Total Receipts	9	697	119	312	1038	3631	11245	19110	49284	•	•	319775	724212	1705855
Operating Costs/Operating Income (%)														
Cost of Operations	10	29.3	19.0	20.8	24.9	34.7	44.6	37.0	31.6	•	•	27.3	37.1	37.0
Salaries and Wages	11	20.8	17.1	21.5	24.7	22.6	10.4	19.5	17.6	•	•	29.7	19.9	19.9
Taxes Paid	12	3.8	3.1	3.6	4.6	4.1	4.2	3.4	2.5	•	•	3.7	4.4	4.5
Interest Paid	13	1.8	0.7	0.9	1.1	1.3	0.9	1.7	1.5	•	•	2.0	3.5	4.4
Depreciation	14	3.2	2.8	2.2	4.0	2.4	6.9	4.5	2.8	•	•	4.8	2.9	4.4
Amortization and Depletion	15	0.7	0.2	0.4	0.4	0.6	0.5	0.5	0.2	•	•	0.8	2.4	1.2
Pensions and Other Deferred Comp.	16	0.4	0.3	0.2	0.9	0.5	0.3	0.7	0.5	•	•	0.6	0.6	0.7
Employee Benefits	17	1.5	1.0	1.1	1.5	1.8	0.7	2.5	1.4	•	•	3.6	1.7	1.0
Advertising	18	1.9	1.8	2.2	1.2	1.2	1.4	1.1	3.2	•	•	0.7	1.7	1.4
Other Expenses	19	27.6	39.0	30.6	22.5	23.2	24.7	23.7	36.2	•	•	25.9	27.3	22.5
Officers' Compensation	20	4.9	6.5	7.9	10.3	4.9	2.8	3.7	2.3	•	•	0.4	0.6	0.5
Operating Margin	21	4.1	8.6	8.5	3.9	2.8	2.6	1.6	0.2	•	•	0.3	•	2.5
Operating Margin Before Officers' Comp.	22	8.9	15.0	16.4	14.2	7.7	5.4	5.3	2.6	•	•	0.8	•	3.1

Selected Average Balance Sheet ($ in Thousands)

Net Receivables 23	76	0	6	66	211	852	2252	3403	•	64667	225213	538142
Inventories 24	21	0	3	26	65	125	944	2162	•	9669	68230	174622
Net Property, Plant and Equipment 25	158	0	34	317	650	2599	5024	9023	•	102322	139149	1035657
Total Assets 26	523	0	82	714	1881	6544	15036	34800	•	378661	930301	3545602
Notes and Loans Payable 27	160	0	40	218	818	1867	4685	10444	•	55631	243205	856315
All Other Liabilities 28	151	0	10	68	464	1254	5323	11914	•	163380	297772	1255664
Net Worth 29	212	0	32	429	600	3423	5028	12442	•	159650	389324	1433623

Selected Financial Ratios (Times to 1)

Current Ratio 30	1.7	•	2.1	2.7	1.6	1.8	1.4	1.4	•	1.8	1.1	2.7
Quick Ratio 31	1.2	•	1.5	2.2	1.2	1.4	1.0	1.0	•	1.1	0.9	1.7
Net Sales to Working Capital 32	9.4	•	19.2	6.9	13.4	10.5	9.7	11.9	•	5.3	32.5	2.9
Coverage Ratio 33	5.6	17.5	12.4	6.5	4.0	8.6	4.4	4.8	•	3.3	5.8	2.8
Total Asset Turnover 34	1.3	•	3.7	1.4	1.9	1.6	1.2	1.3	•	0.8	0.7	0.5
Inventory Turnover 35	9.5	•	18.9	9.8	19.1	38.5	7.2	6.8	•	8.7	3.4	3.4
Receivables Turnover 36	12.6	•	55.1	12.1	16.7	15.2	9.0	12.7	•	9.5	4.0	6.0
Total Liabilities to Net Worth 37	1.5	•	1.6	0.7	2.1	0.9	2.0	1.8	•	1.4	1.4	1.5
Current Assets to Working Capital 38	2.3	•	1.9	1.6	2.6	2.2	3.3	3.8	•	2.3	16.0	1.6
Current Liabilities to Working Capital 39	1.3	•	0.9	0.6	1.6	1.2	2.3	2.8	•	1.3	15.0	0.6
Working Capital to Net Sales 40	0.1	•	0.1	0.1	0.1	0.1	0.1	0.1	•	0.2	0.0	0.3
Inventory to Working Capital 41	0.3	•	0.2	0.2	0.2	0.2	0.4	0.6	•	0.2	1.6	0.3
Total Receipts to Cash Flow 42	3.8	2.5	3.4	4.9	5.3	4.0	4.7	2.6	•	3.7	3.7	4.4
Cost of Goods to Cash Flow 43	1.1	0.5	0.7	1.2	1.8	1.8	1.8	0.8	•	1.0	1.4	1.6
Cash Flow to Total Debt 44	0.6	•	1.8	0.7	0.5	0.9	0.4	0.8	•	0.4	0.3	0.2

Selected Financial Factors (in Percentages)

Debt Ratio 45	59.5	•	61.1	40.0	68.1	47.7	66.6	64.2	•	57.8	58.2	59.6
Return on Total Assets 46	12.9	•	41.3	10.1	9.9	13.3	9.4	9.9	•	5.5	13.7	5.6
Return on Equity Before Income Taxes 47	26.1	•	97.6	14.3	23.4	22.5	21.8	22.0	•	9.0	27.1	9.0
Return on Equity After Income Taxes 48	23.0	•	96.6	13.9	21.9	21.7	19.9	18.4	•	7.1	18.1	6.0
Profit Margin (Before Income Tax) 49	8.2	11.5	10.2	6.0	3.9	7.2	6.0	5.9	•	4.7	16.8	7.9
Profit Margin (After Income Tax) 50	7.2	11.2	10.1	5.9	3.7	6.9	5.5	4.9	•	3.7	11.2	5.3

Table I
Corporations with and without Net Income

RELIGIOUS, GRANTMAKING, CIVIC AND PROFESSIONAL ORGANIZATIONS

MONEY AMOUNTS AND SIZE OF ASSETS IN THOUSANDS OF DOLLARS

Item Description for Accounting Period 7/03 Through 6/04	Total	Zero Assets	Under 500	500 to 1,000	1,000 to 5,000	5,000 to 10,000	10,000 to 25,000	25,000 to 50,000	50,000 to 100,000	100,000 to 250,000	250,000 to 500,000	500,000 to 2,500,000	2,500,000 and over
Number of Enterprises **1**	35650	3017	28727	2128	1608	86	64	9	5	6	•	•	•
Revenues ($ in Thousands)													
Net Sales **2**	8803237	300563	2568591	993848	2093421	186690	753752	233305	201375	1471692	•	•	•
Interest **3**	120709	146	29626	16164	38049	5278	3481	802	920	26242	•	•	•
Rents **4**	34770	0	7999	7293	2448	8998	1594	55	0	6383	•	•	•
Royalties **5**	6372	0	0	0	0	983	5389	0	0	0	•	•	•
Other Portfolio Income **6**	59630	0	737	21777	9332	27	19000	4825	70	3861	•	•	•
Other Receipts **7**	2187471	1603	374179	121959	529506	87330	101518	7808	21811	941760	•	•	•
Total Receipts **8**	11212189	302312	2981132	1161041	2672756	289306	884734	246795	224176	2449938	•	•	•
Average Total Receipts **9**	315	100	104	546	1662	3364	13824	27422	44835	408323	•	•	•
Operating Costs/Operating Income (%)													
Cost of Operations **10**	29.1	17.0	8.4	25.0	24.6	9.8	53.6	37.9	0.8	69.0	•	•	•
Salaries and Wages **11**	14.9	7.4	11.6	12.6	17.7	33.4	14.2	15.4	24.4	16.2	•	•	•
Taxes Paid **12**	2.5	2.0	2.7	1.8	2.9	5.8	2.7	1.8	1.5	1.7	•	•	•
Interest Paid **13**	0.6	1.2	0.3	0.6	0.7	3.6	1.2	0.2	0.6	0.1	•	•	•
Depreciation **14**	2.3	0.3	1.2	1.6	2.5	11.6	3.8	5.0	7.5	1.5	•	•	•
Amortization and Depletion **15**	0.2	0.0	0.0	0.0	0.1	0.3	0.2	0.1	1.4	0.6	•	•	•
Pensions and Other Deferred Comp. **16**	0.4	•	0.3	0.3	0.1	0.3	0.4	0.6	1.0	0.8	•	•	•
Employee Benefits **17**	2.2	•	1.1	1.1	1.9	5.7	8.2	1.3	1.9	2.4	•	•	•
Advertising **18**	0.8	0.5	0.5	0.0	0.4	0.7	0.3	1.1	0.4	2.6	•	•	•
Other Expenses **19**	72.3	68.0	88.1	70.4	74.2	83.4	31.2	37.4	70.0	69.4	•	•	•
Officers' Compensation **20**	1.6	•	3.9	1.1	0.4	0.2	0.8	0.9	2.0	0.7	•	•	•
Operating Margin **21**	•	3.6	•	•	•	•	•	•	•	•	•	•	•
Operating Margin Before Officers' Comp. **22**	•	3.6	•	•	•	•	•	•	•	•	•	•	•

Selected Average Balance Sheet ($ in Thousands)

Net Receivables 23	25	0	3	33	145	111	1561	2082	5007	55436
Inventories 24	1	0	0	1	11	80	99	192	118	1869
Net Property, Plant and Equipment 25	85	0	9	93	694	3926	8998	20566	33221	35429
Total Assets 26	306	86	694	694	2071	6779	14842	34811	68388	241550
Notes and Loans Payable 27	29	0	7	141	134	999	2145	1696	4866	8147
All Other Liabilities 28	84	0	17	145	437	707	3374	9879	14094	176574
Net Worth 29	193	0	62	408	1500	5073	9323	23236	49428	56829

Selected Financial Ratios (Times to 1)

Current Ratio 30	2.4	•	4.8	2.3	3.4	3.2	1.7	1.3	5.5	0.9
Quick Ratio 31	2.2	•	4.5	2.2	2.9	2.8	1.4	1.0	3.4	0.7
Net Sales to Working Capital 32	2.3	•	1.5	1.6	1.6	1.4	6.9	14.0	3.0	12.9
Coverage Ratio 33	2.2	4.4	•	4.3	4.1	1.0	1.6	17.2	0.6	12.9
Total Asset Turnover 34	0.8	•	1.0	0.7	0.6	0.3	0.8	0.7	0.6	1.0
Inventory Turnover 35	51.2	•	73.0	84.3	29.6	2.7	64.0	51.0	2.9	90.6
Receivables Turnover 36	10.2	•	22.8	12.7	10.0	9.1	7.4	14.9	2.9	5.8
Total Liabilities to Net Worth 37	0.6	•	0.4	0.7	0.4	0.3	0.6	0.5	0.4	3.3
Current Assets to Working Capital 38	1.7	•	1.3	1.8	1.4	1.5	2.5	4.1	1.2	•
Current Liabilities to Working Capital 39	0.7	•	0.3	0.8	0.4	0.5	1.5	3.1	0.2	•
Working Capital to Net Sales 40	0.4	•	0.7	0.6	0.6	0.7	0.1	0.1	0.3	•
Inventory to Working Capital 41	0.0	•	0.0	0.0	0.0	0.0	0.1	0.1	0.0	•
Total Receipts to Cash Flow 42	1.7	1.6	1.6	1.8	1.5	1.7	3.9	2.6	1.5	1.5
Cost of Goods to Cash Flow 43	0.5	0.3	0.1	0.4	0.4	0.2	2.1	1.0	0.0	1.0
Cash Flow to Total Debt 44	1.3	•	2.4	0.9	1.5	0.7	0.5	0.9	1.4	0.9

Selected Financial Factors (in Percentages)

Debt Ratio 45	36.9	•	28.0	41.2	27.6	25.2	37.2	33.2	27.7	76.5
Return on Total Assets 46	1.0	•	•	1.9	1.8	1.2	1.4	3.1	0.2	1.4
Return on Equity Before Income Taxes 47	0.9	•	•	2.4	1.9	0.0	0.8	4.4	•	5.7
Return on Equity After Income Taxes 48	0.2	•	•	1.4	1.2	•	0.2	2.6	•	4.5
Profit Margin (Before Income Tax) 49	0.7	4.1	•	2.1	2.1	0.1	0.7	3.9	•	1.3
Profit Margin (After Income Tax) 50	0.2	3.8	•	1.3	1.4	•	0.1	2.3	•	1.0

Table II

Corporations with Net Income

RELIGIOUS, GRANTMAKING, CIVIC AND PROFESSIONAL ORGANIZATIONS

MONEY AMOUNTS AND SIZE OF ASSETS IN THOUSANDS OF DOLLARS

Item Description for Accounting Period 7/03 Through 6/04	Total	Zero Assets	Under 500	500 to 1,000	1,000 to 5,000	5,000 to 10,000	10,000 to 25,000	25,000 to 50,000	50,000 to 100,000	100,000 to 250,000	250,000 to 500,000	500,000 to 2,500,000	2,500,000 and over
Number of Enterprises **1**	18819	1710	14229	1560	1251	24	33	5	•	•	•	•	•
Revenues ($ in Thousands)													
Net Sales **2**	5161291	175475	1358013	733088	1262244	65085	406114	205175	•	•	•	•	•
Interest **3**	101927	85	20873	14792	35315	1469	1889	665	•	•	•	•	•
Rents **4**	19378	0	3320	6284	2291	0	1099	0	•	•	•	•	•
Royalties **5**	5389	0	0	0	0	0	5389	0	•	•	•	•	•
Other Portfolio Income **6**	41718	0	737	21446	9251	27	2042	4284	•	•	•	•	•
Other Receipts **7**	1706073	493	157607	115939	436990	1079	57415	3566	•	•	•	•	•
Total Receipts **8**	7035776	176053	1540550	891549	1746091	67660	473948	213690	•	•	•	•	•
Average Total Receipts **9**	374	103	108	572	1396	2819	14362	42738	•	•	•	•	•
Operating Costs/Operating Income (%)													
Cost of Operations **10**	24.5	5.0	8.1	33.8	23.5	13.3	41.0	41.2	•	•	•	•	•
Salaries and Wages **11**	17.3	8.4	11.9	7.6	23.7	28.2	13.4	11.5	•	•	•	•	•
Taxes Paid **12**	2.7	0.8	3.2	1.1	3.4	6.0	3.0	1.4	•	•	•	•	•
Interest Paid **13**	0.5	0.5	0.3	0.3	0.5	6.7	0.6	0.1	•	•	•	•	•
Depreciation **14**	2.3	0.5	1.7	1.4	2.7	10.9	2.9	3.0	•	•	•	•	•
Amortization and Depletion **15**	0.3	•	0.0	0.0	0.1	0.0	0.1	0.1	•	•	•	•	•
Pensions and Other Deferred Comp. **16**	0.5	•	0.3	0.1	0.1	0.5	0.8	0.6	•	•	•	•	•
Employee Benefits **17**	2.8	•	1.3	0.7	2.2	2.9	13.9	1.2	•	•	•	•	•
Advertising **18**	1.1	0.0	0.4	0.0	0.7	1.3	0.4	1.2	•	•	•	•	•
Other Expenses **19**	78.5	74.6	80.2	70.6	75.1	22.7	36.1	37.2	•	•	•	•	•
Officers' Compensation **20**	0.9	•	1.0	0.8	0.7	0.7	1.3	0.9	•	•	•	•	•
Operating Margin **21**	•	10.2	•	•	•	6.7	•	1.5	•	•	•	•	•
Operating Margin Before Officers' Comp. **22**	•	10.2	•	•	•	7.4	•	2.5	•	•	•	•	•

Selected Average Balance Sheet ($ in Thousands)

Net Receivables 23	30	0	4	24	102	285	2038	3423
Inventories 24	2	0	0	2	11	89	86	50
Net Property, Plant and Equipment 25	81	0	10	47	517	5328	7533	12008
Total Assets 26	402	0	113	700	1993	7757	15241	34815
Notes and Loans Payable 27	30	0	7	146	71	2302	1365	1108
All Other Liabilities 28	123	0	23	121	432	871	4015	15157
Net Worth 29	249	0	83	432	1489	4583	9862	18550

Selected Financial Ratios (Times to 1)

Current Ratio 30	2.5	•	5.4	2.4	3.9	2.0	2.0	1.3
Quick Ratio 31	2.2	•	5.1	2.3	3.4	1.8	1.7	1.0
Net Sales to Working Capital 32	1.8	•	1.2	1.4	1.2	3.0	4.3	17.3
Coverage Ratio 33	11.6	21.1	16.0	15.8	11.7	2.6	7.1	57.1
Total Asset Turnover 34	0.7	•	0.8	0.7	0.5	0.3	0.8	1.2
Inventory Turnover 35	37.9	•	36.3	92.5	21.8	4.1	58.7	337.7
Receivables Turnover 36	10.4	•	25.1	16.0	9.9	19.1	5.8	16.3
Total Liabilities to Net Worth 37	0.6	•	0.4	0.6	0.3	0.7	0.5	0.9
Current Assets to Working Capital 38	1.7	•	1.2	1.7	1.3	2.0	2.0	5.0
Current Liabilities to Working Capital 39	0.7	•	0.2	0.7	0.3	1.0	1.0	4.0
Working Capital to Net Sales 40	0.5	•	0.8	0.7	0.9	0.3	0.2	0.1
Inventory to Working Capital 41	0.0	•	0.0	0.0	0.0	0.1	0.0	0.0
Total Receipts to Cash Flow 42	1.4	1.3	1.5	1.7	1.5	3.6	2.8	2.5
Cost of Goods to Cash Flow 43	0.3	0.1	0.1	0.6	0.3	0.5	1.2	1.0
Cash Flow to Total Debt 44	1.3	•	2.2	1.1	1.4	0.2	0.8	1.0

Selected Financial Factors (in Percentages)

Debt Ratio 45	38.0	•	26.2	38.3	25.3	40.9	35.3	46.7
Return on Total Assets 46	3.6	•	4.6	3.5	3.1	6.1	3.2	6.5
Return on Equity Before Income Taxes 47	5.3	•	5.8	5.4	3.8	6.3	4.2	12.0
Return on Equity After Income Taxes 48	4.4	•	5.2	4.1	3.0	5.4	3.0	7.9
Profit Margin (Before Income Tax) 49	4.8	10.5	5.0	4.9	5.6	10.7	3.3	5.4
Profit Margin (After Income Tax) 50	4.0	10.0	4.6	3.8	4.5	9.2	2.4	3.6

Index

Index

E

Educational services, 365, 366
Electric power generation, transmission, and
distribution, 17, 18
Electrical contractors, 31, 32
Electrical equipment, appliance, and component
manufacturing, 147-152
Electrical equipment, 149, 150
Electrical goods, 175, 176
Electrical lighting equipment and household
appliance, 147, 148
Electronics and appliance stores, 209, 210
Employment services, 357, 358
Engine, turbine, and power transmission
equipment, 133, 134

F

Fabricated metal product manufacturing,
111-122
Farm product raw material, 191, 192
Finance and insurance, 277-318
Food and beverage stores, 219, 220
Food, beverage, and liquor stores, 219-236
Food manufacturing, 37-50
Food services and drinking places, 385, 386
Forestry and logging, 3, 4
Forging and stamping, 111, 112
Foundries, 109, 110
Fruit and vegetable preserving and specialty
food, 41, 42
Furniture and home furnishing stores, 207, 208
Furniture and related product manufacturing,
161, 162
Furniture, sports, toys, jewelry, other durable
goods, 181, 182

G

Gasoline stations, 225, 226
General merchandise stores, 231, 232
Glass and glass product manufacturing, 101, 102
Grocery and related product, 189, 190

H

Hardware, plumbing, heating equipment, and
supplies, 177, 178
Hardware stores, 213, 214
Health and personal care stores, 223, 224
Health care and social assistance, 367-378
Heavy and civil engineering construction, 27, 28
Home centers; paint and wallpaper stores,
211, 212
Hospitals, nursing and residential care facilities,
377, 378

I

Industrial machinery 125, 126
Information, 253-276
Insurance agencies and brokerages, 309, 310
Insurance carriers and related activities, 299-312
Intl. trade, secondary financing, other
nondepository credit, 287, 288
Internet publishing and broadcasting, 269, 270
Internet service providers, Web portals, and D.P.
services, 273, 274
Investment banking and securities dealing,
291, 292
Iron, steel mills, and steel product, 105, 106

L

Land subdivision, 29, 30
Lawn and garden equipment and supplies
stores, 217, 218
Leather and allied product manufacturing,
69, 70
Legal services, 335, 336
Lessors of buildings, 319, 320
Lessors of miniwarehouses, self-storage, other
real estate, 321, 322
Lessors of nonfinan. intangible assets
(ex. Copyrighted works), 333, 334
Life insurance, 299, 300
Life insurance, mutual companies (Form 1120L),
302, 303
Life insurance, stock companies (Form 1120L),
301, 302
Lumber and other construction materials
wholesalers, 169, 170

M

Machinery, equipment, and supplies, 179, 180
Machinery manufacturing, 123-136
Management of companies (holding companies),
353-356
Management, scientific, and technical consulting
services, 345, 346
Manufacturing, 37-166
Meat and seafood processing, 45, 46
Medical equipment and supplies, 163, 164
Metal and mineral (except petroleum), 173, 174
Metal ore mining, 11, 12
Metalworking machinery, 131, 132
Mining, 7-16
Misc. health care and social assistance, 375, 376
Miscellaneous manufacturing, 163-166
Miscellaneous nondurable goods, 199, 200
Miscellaneous store retailers, 233, 234
Motion picture and sound recording industries,
263-266

Motion picture and video industries (except video rental), 263, 264
Motor vehicle and motor vehicle parts and supplies, 167, 168
Motor vehicle and parts manufacturing, 153, 154
Motor vehicle dealers and parts dealers, 203-206
Mutual property and casualty companies (Form 1120-PC), 305, 306

N

Natural gas distribution, 19, 20
Navigational, measuring, electromedical, and control instruments, 145, 146
New and used car dealers, 203, 204
Newspaper publishers, 253, 254
Nondepository credit intermediation, 283-290
Nonferrous metal production and processing, 107, 108
Nonmetallic mineral mining and quarrying, 13, 14
Nonmetallic mineral product manufacturing, 99-104
Nonstore retailers, 235, 236

O

Offices of bank holding companies, 353, 354
Offices of dentists, 369, 370
Offices of other bank holding companies, 355, 356
Offices of other health practitioners, 371, 372
Offices of physicians, 367, 368
Offices of real estate agents and brokers, 323, 324
Oil and gas extraction, 7, 8
Open-end investment funds (Form 1120-RIC), 313, 314
Other administrative and support services, 361, 362
Other arts, entertainment, and recreation, 379, 380
Other building material dealers, 215, 216
Other consumer goods and general rental centers, 329, 330
Other electrical equipment and component manufacturing, 151, 152
Other fabricated metal product, 121, 122
Other financial vehicles, 317, 318
Other financial vehicles and other investment companies, 313-318
Other food, 49, 50
Other general purpose machinery, 135, 136
Other information services, news syndicates, libraries, 275, 276
Other insurance related activities, 311, 312
Other miscellaneous manufacturing, 165, 166

Other motor vehicle and parts dealers, 205, 206
Other professional, scientific, and technical services, 351, 352
Other real estate activities, 325, 326
Other repair and maintenance, 389, 390
Other services, 387-394
Other special trade contractors, 35, 36
Other transportation and support activities, 249, 250
Other transportation equipment and railroad rolling stock manufacturing, 159, 160
Outpatient care centers, 373, 374

P

Paint, coating, and adhesive, 89, 90
Paper and paper product, 183, 184
Paper manufacturing, 73-76
Periodical publishers, 255, 256
Personal and laundry services, 391, 392
Petroleum and coal products manufacturing, 79-82
Petroleum and petroleum products, 195, 196
Petroleum refineries (including integrated), 79, 80
Pharmaceutical and medicine, 87, 88
Pipeline transportation, 247, 248
Plastics and rubber product manufacturing, 95-98
Plastics product, 95, 96
Plumbing, heating, and air conditioning contractors, 33, 34
Primary metal manufacturing, 105-110
Printing and related support activities, 77, 78
Professional and commercial equipment and supplies 171, 172
Professional, scientific, and technical services, 335-352
Publishing industries, 253-262
Pulp, paper, and paperboard mills, 73, 74

R

Rail transportation, 239, 240
Real estate, 319-326
Real estate and rental leasing, 319-334
Real estate credit Incl. Mortgage Bankers and Originators, 285, 286
Real estate investment trusts (Form 1120-REIT), 315, 316
Religious, grantmaking, civic, professional organizations, 393, 394
Rental and leasing services, 327-334
Repair and maintenance, 387-388
Resin, synthetic rubber, and fibers and filaments, 85, 86